CELTIC
CULTURE
A HISTORICAL
ENCYCLOPEDIA

CELTIC CULTURE

A HISTORICAL ENCYCLOPEDIA

Volume II

Celto–F

John T. Koch, Editor

Marion Löffler, Managing Editor

Marian Beech Hughes, Assistant Editor

Glenys Howells, Assistant Editor

Anne Holley, Bibliographer

Petra S. Hellmuth, Contributing Editor (Ireland and Scotland)
Thomas Owen Clancy, Contributing Editor (Scotland)
Antone Minard, Editorial Assistant

ABC◉CLIO

SANTA BARBARA, CALIFORNIA ◆ DENVER, COLORADO ◆ OXFORD, ENGLAND

Copyright © 2006 by ABC-CLIO

Cataloging-in-Publication Data is available from the Library of Congress
ISBN: 1–85109–440–7   1–85109–445–8 (e-book)

10 09 08 07 06 05   10 9 8 7 6 5 4 3 2 1

This book is also available on the World Wide Web as an ebook.
Visit abc-clio.com for details.

ABC-CLIO, Inc.
130 Cremona Drive, P.O. Box 1911
Santa Barbara, California 93116–1911

This book is printed on acid-free paper ∞.
Manufactured in the United States of America

CONTENTS
Volume II: Celtomania–Fulup, Marc'harid

C

Celtomania

Enthusiasm and admiration for Celtic civilizations and languages reached new heights in 19th-century France. We may trace the beginnings of the modern discipline of CELTIC STUDIES, and indeed the origins of the cultural movements and devolved administrations of today's Celtic regions, to this time of extraordinary activity. Commonly referred to as the Celtic revival, this activity is inseparable from the fashion for all things Celtic that swept through Europe with ROMANTICISM. Against a backdrop of Chateaubriand's druidic adventures in *Les Martyrs* (1809), and Walter SCOTT's Romantic Celtophilia, not to mention the pan-European Ossianic cult (see OISÍN), diffused and remodulated by Goethe's *Werther* (1774), linguists and historians were investigating the history and development of Celtic literature, language and civilization in unprecedented detail. The work of historians such as Comte de Boulainvilliers, Guizot, the Thierry brothers, Henri Martin, and Michelet did much to popularize the idea that the Gauls were the true ancestors of the French (see GAUL), whereas the Franks were the ancestors of the aristocracy overthrown in the Revolution of 1789. During Romanticism attention turned from 'Gaulois' to 'Celtic', and thus to Brittany (BREIZH), thanks to the popular equation of the modern Breton with the ancient Celt.

'Celtomanie' was a retrospective and pejorative label, and its coining around 1838 shows to what extent this fashion and enthusiasm had also given rise to a certain Celtoscepticism or Celtophobia. Evidence of this is clear in the short history of the Académie celtique,
which was formed under Napoleon with the purpose of elevating the study of France's own distant past to the position of a new classics. Founded by Éloi Johanneau, Jacques Cambry, and Michel-Ange de Mangourit, the Académie held its inaugural séance on 30 March 1805, only to be completely revamped and given the rather safer title Societé royale des Antiquaires de France in 1814. The preface to the *Mémoires* of the new society explains that it wished to be more scientific than its predecessor, and claims that much of the recent glorification of the Celts, and the Bretons, had been misguided, if not blindly pro-Celtic wishful thinking. Keen to distance itself from claims such as that by La Tour d'Auvergne that Celtic was the original human language (1792), and that of Johanneau, the Académie's most outspoken member, that nearly all the peoples were descendants of the Celts (1807), the new society is extra cautious, going as far as to suggest that 'bas-breton' might not even be the language of the Celts. Later on Raynouard even declared BRETON to be a dialect born in the 15th century.

The climate of suspicion that followed, but also overlapped with the fashion for Celtic themes, explains why both positive and negative clichés of Brittany are found at the same date in 19th-century French culture: for instance, Balzac's overwhelmingly negative portrayal in *Les Chouans* (1828, 1834), and Brizeux's idyllic Brittany in *Marie* (1831). This climate also explains why the portraits of Brittany that were most successful in their day are insipid, since 'difference' was only tolerated by mainstream French culture if it was unthreatening, apolitical, and preferably restricted to the level of the picturesque. The main reason for this intolerance was the political threat posed by the counter-Revolutionary forces of *chouannerie*, but accompanied by a generous helping of French nationalist pride. Many would argue that the same is true today, and that Celtoscepticism, as well as Celtomania, is alive and well.

FURTHER READING
BREIZH; BRETON; CELTIC STUDIES; GAUL; OISÍN; ROMANTICISM; SCOTT; Belmont, *Aux sources de l'ethnologie française*; Brown, *Celticism*; Dietler, *American Anthropologist* 96.584–605; D. Ellis Evans, ZCP 49/50.1–27; Guiomar, *Le bretonisme*; Sims-Williams, CMCS 36.1–35; Tanguy, *Aux origines du nationalisme breton*; Viallaneix & Ehrard, *Nos ancêtres les Gaulois*; Heather Williams, *French Studies* 57.395–410.

Heather Williams

Cerdd dafod (literally 'tongue craft') is the Welsh term for the composing of poetry in strict metres. When poetry is studied as a cross-cultural and international phenomenon, this traditional system of poetic ornamentation in the WELSH language is remarkable for its use of intensive phonetic correspondences; there are comparable features in early Irish and Classical Modern Irish systems of versification (see IRISH LITERATURE; METRICS), which gives warrant to the idea that this is associated with the outgrowth of a Celtic cultural inheritance. Within the corpus of attested WELSH POETRY, the principles of *cerdd dafod* can be traced back to the poetry of ANEIRIN and TALIESIN, the 6th-century poets (see also CYNFEIRDD), and presumably behind that to a preliterate, non-extant oral tradition with Celtic antecedents, having absorbed a debated degree of Latin influence.

The basic discipline of *cerdd dafod* is the mastery of CYNGHANEDD, which consists of a strict and skilful alliterative system of consonants echoing within a line of poetry and internal rhyming. The two methods—consonant repetition and internal rhyme—can be used together within a line.

EINION OFFEIRIAD (*fl. c.* 1320–*c.* 1349) is credited with the authorship of the earliest book on the topic to survive; it lists twenty-four canonical metres, used for the composition of poems in *cerdd dafod*. In the EISTEDDFOD held at Carmarthen (CAERFYRDDIN) *c.* 1450, DAFYDD AB EDMWND replaced two of these metres with two highly complicated ones which he himself had devised, and these were subsequently accepted as the traditional twenty-four metres. Some of these

metres were not often used by the poets, and the schematic figure of 'two dozen' may have been filled out with metres intended mainly for didactic purposes.

At the beginning of the 20th century, the Celtic linguist, poet, and literary critic Sir John MORRIS-JONES classified the *cynganeddion* ('patterns of *cynghanedd*'), studied the traditional strict metres, and published his findings in a book, *Cerdd Dafod* (1925), which he wrote in Welsh and which remains the definitive work on the subject. This volume takes a strongly historical view of the subject and is thus largely responsible for the powerful vision of a seamless tradition persisting from the era of the Cynfeirdd, through the medieval Poets of the Princes (partly synonymous with the GOGYNFEIRDD) and Poets of the Nobility (roughly corresponding to the CYWYDDWYR), to the strict-metre competitions of the *eisteddfodau* of today (see EISTEDDFOD GENEDLAETHOL CYMRU).

At the end of the 20th century a renaissance occurred in *cerdd dafod*, especially in the verse form known as the ENGLYN, one of the few of the twenty-four metres still in common use. Alan LLWYD, poet and critic, was the main inspiration behind this trend.

FURTHER READING
ANEIRIN; AWDL; CAERFYRDDIN; CYNFEIRDD; CYNGHANEDD; CYWYDD; CYWYDDWYR; DAFYDD AB EDMWND; EINION OFFEIRIAD; EISTEDDFOD; EISTEDDFOD GENEDLAETHOL CYMRU; ENGLYN; FIVE POETS; GOGYNFEIRDD; IRISH LITERATURE; LLWYD; METRICS; MORRIS-JONES; TALIESIN; WELSH; WELSH POETRY; Ap Dafydd, *Clywed Cynghanedd*; Llwyd, *Trafod Cerdd Dafod y Dydd*; Morris-Jones, *Cerdd Dafod*.

Dafydd Islwyn

Cerdic of Wessex (†534) figures as the founder of the powerful Anglo-Saxon kingdom and their dynasty, the Cerdicingas. The fact that his name is BRYTHONIC (cf. Old Welsh CERETIC and CERTIC < *Caraticos* and/or ROMANO-BRITISH *Coroticus*) raises important questions for the poorly understood process of the post-Roman Anglicization of south-eastern Britain, often termed, possibly misleadingly, the ANGLO-SAXON 'CONQUEST'. In the Anglo-Saxon Chronicle, Cerdic is the key figure in seven entries (paraphrased as follows):

495 Cerdic and his son Cynric came to BRITAIN with five ships, landed at 'Cerdic's shore', and fought the

Welsh; 508 Cerdic and Cynric killed a British king Natanleod and 5000 of his men, conquering the land up 'Cerdic's ford' (Charford); 514 the West Saxons Stuf and Wihtgar landed at 'Cerdic's ford' and put the BRITONS to flight; 519 Cerdic and Cynric succeeded to the kingdom of the West Saxons and fought the Britons at 'Cerdic's ford'; 527 Cerdic and Cynric fought the Britons at 'Cerdic's wood'; 530 Cerdic and Cynric conquered the Isle of Wight and killed a few men at 'Wihtgar's stronghold'; 534 Cerdic died and was succeeded by Cynric who gave the Isle of Wight to Stuf and Wihtgar.

One possibility would be that Cerdic arose from a sub-Roman dynasty which eventually adopted the language and culture of their Saxon *foederati* (barbarian mercenaries), a theory consistent with the fact that Cerdic's successors, Ceawlin (†593) and CÆDUALLA (†689), also had Brythonic names. Two features of the Anglo-Saxon Chronicle entries suggest that the landings and battles are not necessarily historical: (1) the structure provided by the explanation of place-names and (2) repetitions, in which Wessex and Wight are each founded twice and battles of the same description are fought at 'Cerdic's ford'. As to the names, the first element of *Wiht-gar* is the old Celtic name of Wight (*$*Wi\chi t\bar{a}$) and therefore unlikely to have been the name of a Saxon chieftain at all, which raises the possibility that the Brythonic man's name Cerdic, which occurs in a number of place-names in south-east Wessex, was similarly used as the kernel of a foundation legend. Furthermore, Wight and the parts of Hampshire to which the Cerdic entries relate seem to have been settled by Jutes rather than Saxons; the entries may thus be an attempt retrospectively to rewrite history following the takeover by the West Saxons. This possibility raises the question whether the historical Cerdic was a sub-Roman magnate in the area of Portsmouth and Winchester or had in fact been connected with the earlier Saxon communities on the upper Thames.

St PATRICK's Coroticus and Ceredig son of CUNEDDA would both have been approximate contemporaries of Cerdic of Wessex, as would Ceredig (Old Welsh Ceretic), GWRTHEYRN's interpreter in HISTORIA BRITTONUM, but the name is common and the identity of any two of these figures is accordingly doubtful.

PRIMARY SOURCE
TRANS. Swanton, *Anglo-Saxon Chronicle* 14–17.

FURTHER READING
ANGLO-SAXON 'CONQUEST'; BRITAIN; BRITONS; BRYTHONIC; CÆDUALLA; CERETIC; CERTIC; CUNEDDA; GWRTHEYRN; HISTORIA BRITTONUM; PATRICK; ROMANO-BRITISH; Coates, *Nomina* 13.1–11; Dumville, *Peritia* 4.21–66; Myres, *English Settlements* 145–8, 150–5, 161–4, 225; Parsons, CMCS 33.1–8; Ann Williams et al., *Biographical Dictionary of Dark Age Britain* 78; Yorke, *Origins of the Anglo-Saxon Kingdoms* 84–96.

JTK

Ceredigion is a county in Wales (CYMRU) with about 74,941 inhabitants, 61.2% of whom are WELSH speakers according to the 2001 Census. It is located between the estuaries of the Dyfi in the north and the Teifi in the south. Between 1974 and 1993, what is now Ceredigion was part of the larger county of DYFED. Before 1974, a county broadly coterminous with post-1993 Ceredigion was called Sir ABERTEIFI in Welsh and Cardiganshire in English. Ceredigion is still sometimes called Cardiganshire in English, although officially it is Ceredigion in both languages.

Ceredigion continues the name of a post-Roman Welsh kingdom (Old Welsh *Cereticiaun* 'the lands of Ceredig'), said to have been founded in the 6th century and named after CERETIC son of CUNEDDA, the semi-legendary founder of GWYNEDD. The foundation of this kingdom on part of what had been the territory of the pre-Roman tribe of the ORDOVICES forms part of the story of the migration of Cunedda from GODODDIN to Wales, and the expulsion of Irish settlers from north and west Wales, whose historical presence is manifested by bilingual inscribed stones with Latinized BRYTHONIC versions of personal names alongside GOIDELIC versions in the OGAM script. Versions of the story of the migration of Cunedda occur in HISTORIA BRITTONUM and the Old Welsh GENEALOGIES.

Ceredigion contains several important early Christian sites, which show the county's significance in the religious conversion (or perhaps reconversion) of the 6th century (see CHRISTIANITY). Such early foundations include Llanddewi-brefi and LLANBADARN FAWR, near ABERYSTWYTH. The transformation of the *clas* (enclosed monastic site of a distinctively 'Celtic' type) of Llanbadarn Fawr into a Benedictine monastery in the 10th/11th centuries, the foundation of the

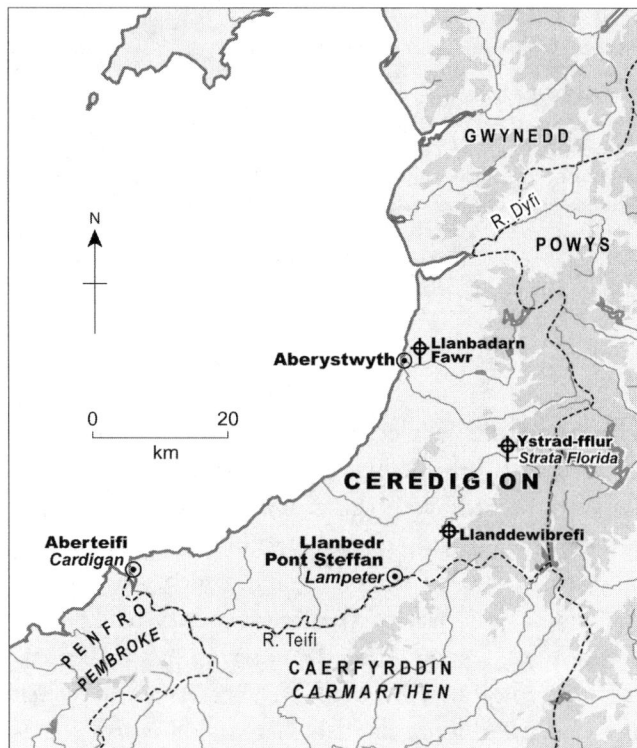

improvement led to the foundation of major educational and national institutions. Two universities—at Lampeter (Llanbedr Pont Steffan) and Aberystwyth—were established in 1827 and 1872 respectively, and by Royal Charter in 1907 the National Library of Wales (LLYFRGELL GENEDLAETHOL CYMRU), a superb neoclassical building which overlooks Aberystwyth, was founded. These major institutions became critically important components of the socio-economic life of Ceredigion and continue to contribute richly to the cultural well-being of Wales.

FURTHER READING
ABERTEIFI; ABERYSTWYTH; AGRICULTURE; BRYTHONIC; CERETIC; CHRISTIANITY; CISTERCIAN ABBEYS IN WALES; CUNEDDA; CYMRU; DAFYDD AP GWILYM; DYFED; GENEALOGIES; GODODDIN; GOIDELIC; GWYNEDD; HISTORIA BRITTONUM; LEGENDARY HISTORY; LLANBADARN FAWR; LLYFRGELL GENEDLAETHOL CYMRU; LLYWELYN AP GRUFFUDD; MONASTICISM; OGAM; ORDOVICES; WELSH; YSTRAD-FFLUR; J. L. Davies & Kirby, *From the Earliest Times to the Coming of the Normans*; Jenkins & Jones, *Cardiganshire in Modern Times*; Ieuan Gwynedd Jones, *Aberystwyth 1277–1977*; Lloyd, *Story of Ceredigion (400–1277)*.

PEB, Geraint H. Jenkins

Cistercian monastery of Strata Florida (YSTRAD-FFLUR; see also CISTERCIAN ABBEYS IN WALES), as well as the foundation of the castles and towns of Aberystwyth and Cardigan in the 12th/13th centuries, were milestones in the development of the medieval kingdom and the county. Ceredigion changed its ruling dynasty frequently from the 10th to the 13th centuries until it finally became part of the Principality of Wales, established after the defeat of LLYWELYN AP GRUFFUDD by Edward I in 1282. Ystrad-fflur is often cited as an important centre for the composition and copying of medieval Welsh literature, and Ceredigion was also the birthplace of DAFYDD AP GWILYM (c. 1315–c. 1350), widely regarded as the greatest of all Welsh-language poets.

From the early modern period onwards, farming, fishing, and the rearing and selling of sheep and cattle became the mainstay of the economy (see AGRICULTURE), though the lead mines also proved profitable ventures until the 1870s and a host of shipyards sprang up in tiny coastal towns. The coming of the railways in the mid-Victorian period injected new life into attractive tourist resorts such as Aberystwyth and Cardigan, and both greater wealth and a thirst for

Ceretic/Ceredig ap Cunedda (*fl.* ?5th–early 6th century) figures in Welsh tradition as the namesake and founder of CEREDIGION (Old Welsh *Cereticiaun*). He is first named as such in the Old Welsh GENEALOGIES in BL MS Harley 3859, though unnamed sons of 'Cuneda(g)' reconquering wide tracts of north and west Wales (CYMRU) figure importantly in HISTORIA BRITTONUM (see CUNEDDA). As to historical identification, there is a Ceretic known from contemporary 5th-century records to have fought successfully against the Irish, namely the Coroticus excommunicated by St PATRICK. But the Irish scholars who assembled the Book of ARMAGH in the first decade of the 9th century identified Coroticus with another 5th-century Ceretic, king of Dumbarton (i.e., *Coirthech rex Aloo*; see YSTRAD CLUD). In light of the story of the migration from north Britain of Cunedda and his sons, it is not inconceivable that the ruler of Dumbarton and founder of Ceredigion were one and the same (as proposed by Tolstoy), despite their treatment as distinct in the genealogies, whose reliability is doubtful this far back; however, the name *Ceredig* was common in the early post-Roman period (cf. CERDIC; CERTIC).

In the Old Welsh genealogies, Ceredig ap Cunedda figures as the ancestor of the historical dynasty of early medieval Ceredigion; this dynasty also included SEISYLL AP CLYDOG, Seisyll's son Arthien (Old Welsh Arthgen, ANNALES CAMBRIAE †807) and great-great-grandson Gwgon (Guocaun, *Annales Cambriae* †871). *Progenies Keredic* (The descendants of Ceredig) is a genealogical tract, probably dating from the 11th century or earlier; in it, Ceredig figures as the grandfather of DEWI SANT, of Gwynllyw (founder of the kingdom of Gwynllŵg), and of St Dogmael. There, he is also the father of a SAMSON, though not explicitly the saint of that name. In the genealogies of saints compiled in the Middle Welsh period, Ceredig is prominent, and a number of these tracts mention his wife, Meleri ferch BRYCHAN. It is possible that two originally separate Old Celtic names, **Caraticos* 'beloved' and *Coroticus*, have converged as *Ceredig* (see Parsons, CMCS 33.1–8), but it also may be that the Welsh name derives exclusively from *Coroticus* or even from **Caraticos* (in other words, Patrick's *Coroticus* could be an attempt to spell the name after the vowels of its first two syllables had become the central round vowels /ə/ or /ö/).

FURTHER READING
ANNALES CAMBRIAE; ARMAGH, BOOK OF; BRYCHAN; CERDIC; CEREDIGION; CERTIC; CUNEDDA; CYMRU; DEWI SANT; GENEALOGIES; HISTORIA BRITTONUM; PATRICK; SAMSON; SEISYLL AP CLYDOG; YSTRAD CLUD; Bartrum, *Welsh Classical Dictionary* 124; Parsons, CMCS 33.1–8; Tolstoy, *Irish Ecclesiastical Record* 97.137–47.

JTK

Cerne Abbas is a parish just north of Dorchester, in Dorset, England, where a human figure has been cut into the chalk hillside. The figure, generally referred to as a giant, is the outline of an ithyphallic man carrying a club in his right hand. Parallel lines are drawn at the ribs, and there is a line at the waist. Castleden, 'using a resistivity meter to locate filled and grassed-over trenches', reconstructed a corrected outline with minor modifications (including a navel and a shorter phallus) and 'lost' features, including a cloak and severed head on the giant's left side (Darvill et al., *Cerne Giant* 44; see also HEAD CULT).

A local legend relates that the figure is an outline drawn around the body of an actual giant after he was killed. The figure is associated with fertility beliefs; for example, a woman who sleeps on the giant will bear many children, and sexual intercourse on the giant (or specifically on the giant's phallus) is believed to cure infertility. There is no documentation of these beliefs before the Victorian era, though, of course, they may be older.

Antiquarian interest in the giant has focused on his identification with a Saxon deity whose various names all begin with *Hel-*. Gotselin's Life of Saint AUGUSTINE, written *c.* 1091, mentions Helia. Walter of Coventry (*fl.* 1290) wrote of the worship of the god Helith, and

The Cerne Abbas Giant

William Camden referred to the Saxon god Heil or Hegle in his *Britannia* (1637). An editor of Camden's text in 1789 linked this figure with the Cerne giant. The antiquarian William Stukeley (1687–1765) stated that the figure was called Helis locally, and he was also the first to identify the figure as the Roman HERCULES, an explanation still favoured by some scholars. Whatever the Old English name of the figure, it is unlikely to be Saxon in origin.

John Sydenham suggested that the figure was Celtic in 1842, identifying it as Baal, his spelling of Bel/ Belinus (see BELENOS; BELTAINE), although there is no iconographic support for his argument. Stuart Piggott linked the forms Heil/ Helith/Helis with Hercules, often depicted naked and with a club. The rediscovered features bolster the identification, although it remains unclear whether the giant is meant to be the Roman Hercules or a deity that the local Celtic people, the Durotriges, identified with him (see INTERPRETATIO ROMANA). Castleden notes that belted, naked warriors occur in other Iron Age ART throughout Europe, usually identified by the Romans with Mars. These iconographic considerations would date the figure to the period of the Roman occupation of BRITAIN. The earliest published account of the giant, however, was not printed until 1763, in the *Royal Magazine*, with another account and illustration printed in *The Gentleman's Magazine* in 1764, both anonymously; the lack of medieval references to the figure has made many scholars inclined to believe that the figure is not much older than the 18th century.

FURTHER READING
ART; AUGUSTINE; BELENOS; BELTAINE; BRITAIN; HEAD CULT; HERCULES; INTERPRETATIO ROMANA; Bergamar, *Discovering Hill Figures*; Castleden, *Cerne Giant*; Darvill et al., *Cerne Giant*; Piggott, *Ancient Britons and the Antiquarian Imagination*.

AM

Detail of the Gundestrup cauldron

Cernunnos was a Gaulish god whose distinctive representative features are thought to include antlers or horns on his head, multiple TORCS (neck-rings), accompanying stags and sometimes ram-horned snakes. These patterns of representations, which recur fairly consistently and are easily recognized, have been understood by modern writers as reflecting 'the lord of the animals'. Although in general use today for a complex of related artistic motifs, the name *Cernunnos* occurs only once, and some modern scholars have misleadingly implied that this name was in wide currency amongst the ancient Celts. In addition to the above-mentioned attributes, the distinctive iconography of 'Cernunnos' depicts the god sitting cross-legged. The most famous example of this is on the GUNDESTRUP CAULDRON, which has been interpreted variously as a 'Buddha position' (Maier), i.e. the lotus position, and even 'levitating on one toe', although both terms are inaccurate and unfortunately imply a connection with south and east Asian iconographic traditions and religious practices. The most important representation of the god is on the monument of the Nautae Parisiaci ('the sailors of the Parisi' [a Gaulish tribe]). The accompanying inscription is the single instance where Cernunnos is named as such. Other important images of gods with a similar iconography are the rock carving of Val Camonica and the Gundestrup cauldron. There are antlered goddesses at Clermont-Ferrand and Besançon, and the antlered god is also known from Britain on the relief from the ROMANO-BRITISH town of Corinium (modern Cirencester) and appears on one coin from Petersfield, Hampshire (see COINAGE).

The etymology is usually traced to INDO-EUROPEAN *$k'er-n-$ 'horn', although disputed by Maier (*Dictionary of Celtic Religion and Culture* 69). The epithet *cernach* (angular; victorious; bearing a prominent growth) of CONALL CERNACH of the Irish ULSTER CYCLE may derive from the same root, and it has been suggested that Conall Cernach and Cernunnos are ultimately the same figure.

FURTHER READING
COINAGE; CONALL CERNACH; GUNDESTRUP CAULDRON; INDO-EUROPEAN; ROMANO-BRITISH; TORC; ULSTER CYCLE; Anati, *Camonica Valley*; Bober, *American Journal of Archaeology* 55.13–51; Boon, *Seaby Coin and Medal Bulletin* 37.769.276–82; CIL 13, no. 3026; Maier, *Dictionary of Celtic Religion and Culture*; Thévenot, *Divinités et sanctuaires de la Gaule* 144–53; Vertet, *Bulletin de la Société nationale des antiquaires de France* 1985.163–75.

PEB

Certic/Ceredig ap Gwallawg was the last

ruler of the northern BRYTHONIC kingdom of Elmet/
ELFED, the district east of the southern Pennines
around the modern English city of Leeds and west of
York (Welsh Caerefrog). The expulsion of Certic *rex
Elmet* by the Anglo-Saxon king EADWINE of Northumbria is noted in HISTORIA BRITTONUM (§63). As
to the date of Certic's 'expulsion', Eadwine ruled from
617 to 633/4, and this might be the same event as, or
immediately preceded, the death of 'Ceretic' noted in
ANNALES CAMBRIAE in 616. This Certic is probably
the same *rex Brettonum Cerdic* who was involved in
murderous Northumbrian political intrigues 614×620,
according to BEDA (*Historia Ecclesiastica* 4.23). A 'Keredic
ap Gvallavc' occurs in one version of the Welsh Triad
of the Lovers' Horses (Bromwich, TYP no. 41; see
further TYP 308; Rowland, *Early Welsh Saga Poetry* 100–
1; Gruffydd, SC 28.69–75). Brythonic *Certic* in its more
usual unsyncopated form *Ceretic* was a common name.
Not so his father's name, GWALLAWG; there is only
one in Bartrum, *Early Welsh Genealogical Tracts*, although
the variant *Gualluc* does occur in the Llandaf charters.
It is thus likely that the Gvallavc of the TRIADS is one
and the same as the descendant of COEL HEN of this
name, who ruled Elmet (according to a poem in LLYFR
TALIESIN) and is known from *Historia Brittonum* §63
and the Old Welsh GENEALOGIES of BL MS Harley
3859. This identification is made more likely by the
fact that the triad's Gvallavc had a son with the same
name as the man who succeeded Gwallawg as ruler of
Elmet. In fact, Gwallawg and Certic are the only two
rulers of Elmet known to us. Gwallawg is mentioned
in MOLIANT CADWALLON in connection with past and
anticipated fighting at the Yorkshire places—*tir Elued*
(Elmet's land), CATRAETH, and Caerefrog. It therefore seems that Eadwine's conquest of Elmet and
expulsion of Certic son of Gwallawg had figured as
key provocations leading to CADWALLON's invasion of
Northumbria and overthrow of Eadwine in 633–5. On
the name CERTIC see CERETIC; CERDIC.

FURTHER READING
ANNALES CAMBRIAE; BEDA; BRYTHONIC; CADWALLON;
CATRAETH; CERDIC; CERETIC; CERTIC; COEL HEN; EADWINE;
ELFED; GENEALOGIES; GWALLAWG; HISTORIA BRITTONUM;
LLYFR TALIESIN; MOLIANT CADWALLON; TRIADS; Bartrum,
EWGT; Bartrum, *Welsh Classical Dictionary* 124; Bromwich, TYP
308; Gruffydd, SC 28.63–79; Rowland, *Early Welsh Saga Poetry*.

JTK

Chadwick, H. M. and Nora K. were pioneers

of interdisciplinary study. Both were educated at
Cambridge, where Hector Munroe Chadwick (1870–
1947) read the Classical Tripos, became a Fellow of
Clare College and, in 1912, Elrington and Bosworth
Professor of Anglo-Saxon, a post he held until his
retirement in 1941. Nora Kershaw Chadwick (1891–
1972), whom he married in 1922, read the Medieval
and Modern Languages Tripos, held various Associate
Fellowships and Lectureships at Cambridge, and was
awarded numerous honorary doctorates from universities in the CELTIC COUNTRIES.

H. M. Chadwick combined his expertise in Anglo-
Saxon studies with that in other European cultures,
crossing boundaries of both cultures and disciplines.
The work of Nora K. Chadwick, who had been one
of his students, is likewise based on those principles.
Their magnum opus, *The Growth of Literature*, is one of
the masterpieces of 20th-century comparative study
and provided one of the most compelling models for
the study of the early Celtic literatures for scholars
working in the mid-20th century.

Their contribution, especially that of Nora Chadwick, to our knowledge about the Celtic world near
the horizon of history, at what can be described as the
'dark ages' or the 'heroic age', is imposing. Best known
for her popular and repeatedly reprinted volumes *The
Celts* and *The Druids*, her many other works on Celtic
culture and literature and the early Celtic church are
also still relevant to modern scholars. Her method
included comparing archaeology and literature, allowing
both types of evidence to inform each other and add
to our knowledge of the period under review, a syn-
thesis integral to the classics, but exceptional in CELTIC
STUDIES. She also published widely on Slavonic,
especially Russian, topics.

The idea of a cross-cultural literary stage of development under the heading of the heroic age (see HEROIC
ETHOS) loomed large in *The Growth of Literature* and
other works of the Chadwicks. This provided a
framework in which another great Cambridge Celticist,
Kenneth JACKSON, and his generation regularly applied
insights derived from the Homeric epics or the Anglo-
Saxon *Beowulf* to early WELSH POETRY or the ULSTER
CYCLE. Although subsequent Celtic scholarship has
naturally tended to move on to other approaches and
interests, the Chadwickian vision remains a powerful

influence, often serving as a required starting point for current discussions. The concept of the 'early cultures of north-west Europe'—still strongly associated with the Department of Anglo-Saxon, Norse and Celtic at Cambridge—is widely viewed as the intellectual legacy of the Chadwicks and remains a touchstone in Celtic studies at the beginning of the 21st century.

SELECTIONS OF MAIN WORKS

H. M. CHADWICK
Origin of the English Nation (1907); *Heroic Age* (1912); *Nationalities of Europe and the Growth of National Ideologies* (1945); *Early Scotland* (1949).

NORA K. CHADWICK
Early Irish Reader (1927); *Poetry and Prophecy* (1942); *Poetry and Letters in Early Christian Gaul* (1955); *Age of the Saints in the Early Celtic Church* (1961); *Celtic Britain* (1963); *Druids* (1966); *Early Brittany* (1969); *Celts* (1971).
(with Dillon) *Celtic Realms* (1967).
(ed.) *Studies in Early British History* (1954); *Studies in the Early British Church* (1958); *Celt and Saxon* (1963).

H. M. CHADWICK & NORA K. CHADWICK
Growth of Literature (1932–40).

FURTHER READING
CELTIC COUNTRIES; CELTIC STUDIES; HEROIC ETHOS; JACKSON; ULSTER CYCLE; WELSH POETRY; De Navarro, PBA 33.307–30; Fox & Dickins, *Early Cultures of North-West Europe*; Jackson, PBA 58.537–49; Lapidge, *Interpreters of Early Medieval Britain*.
BIBLIOGRAPHY OF PUBLISHED WORKS. National Library of Scotland, *List of the Published Writings of Hector Munro Chadwick and of his wife Nora Kershaw Chadwick*.

MBL

Chamalières [1] sanctuary

In 1968 construction works in the department of Puy-de-Dôme led to the discovery of the most important series of wooden votive figures (see RITUAL) known up to the present day in France (1500 sculptures, 8500 fragments). Most of the objects can be dated to the second half century of the Roman occupation of GAUL, that is, *c.* AD 1–*c.* 50. Doubtlessly originally placed around pools from which water sprang (see WATERY DEPOSITIONS), they lay crammed together and tangled in a layer of peat which was up to 50 cm wide. These sculptures represent parts of the body (arms, legs, &c.), often roughly designed, and also busts and entire bodies (full-length figures, male and female, dressed) and stylized horses. The style is more of a GALLO-ROMAN type than that of the votive figures found in the springs of the Seine (SAINT-GERMAIN-

SOURCE-SEINE). They are displayed in the Musée Bargoin at Clermont-Ferrand.

Also discovered at the site were remains of pitchers and cups, some Roman coins, numerous small knobs, and a leaden tablet engraved with a magical inscription written in GAULISH (see CHAMALIÈRES [2]; INSCRIPTIONS). No elaborate architectural setting for the site has been discovered, except for a stone enclosure of the principal basin. In the middle of the 1st century AD the site, which was probably situated within the tribal CIVITAS of the ARVERNI, was abandoned after only a few decades of use.

FURTHER READING
ARVERNI; CHAMALIÈRES [2]; CIVITAS; GALLO-ROMAN; GAUL; GAULISH; INSCRIPTIONS; RITUAL; SAINT-GERMAIN-SOURCE-SEINE; WATERY DEPOSITIONS; Coulon, *Les Gallo-Romains* 2.80, 126, 128, 169; Romeuf, *Gallia* 44.65–89.

M. Lévery

Chamalières [2] inscription

Discovered in 1971 at the major GALLO-ROMAN sanctuary described in the preceding article, this inscription in the GAULISH language is written in Roman cursive script, similar to that of many of the ROMANO-BRITISH curse tablets from BATH, on a small lead tablet, roughly 6 × 4 cm. Like the thousands of wooden sculptures from the same sanctuary, the Chamalières inscription probably dates from the first half of the 1st century AD.

Although there is by now increasing agreement among the experts as to the reading and what many words, phrases, and even whole sentences must mean, several interpretations of the function and overall meaning of the text have been advanced (see INSCRIPTIONS IN THE CELTIC WORLD [1] §3). The text is of special importance for several reasons. Along with those from LARZAC and Chateaubleau, it is one of the longest surviving Gaulish texts. It contains much Gaulish religious vocabulary and provides invaluable insight into pagan Celtic ideas about magic and religion. It illuminates the history of the CELTIC LANGUAGES, with numerous points of comparison in its vocabulary, grammar, and syntax to the better attested medieval and modern INSULAR CELTIC languages.

The verb of the first sentence is *uediiu-mi* 'I beseech, pray'; cf. Old Irish *guidiu*, Welsh *gweddïaf*. It then

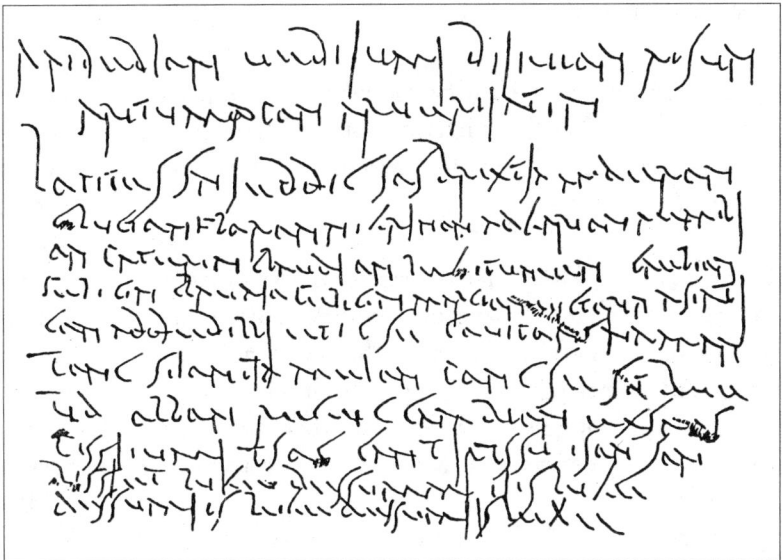

invokes *Mapon Aruerniiatin*, probably meaning '[the god] MAPONOS of the ARVERNI tribe'. The third line includes the phrase *briχtia anderon* 'by a magical spell of underworld beings' (see BRICTA). There follows a list of men's names, one of whom is called *adgarion* 'invoker', presumably the individual charged with communicating with the supernatural. Between lines 7 and 8 is the phrase *toncnaman tonsciiontio*, which has been compared with the formulaic oaths, Old Irish *tongu do dia toinges mo thuath* 'I swear to the god by whom my tribe swears' (common with several variations in the ULSTER CYCLE) and Welsh *tynghaf tynghet* 'I swear a destiny' (CULHWCH AC OLWEN 50; see Koch, ÉC 29.249–61). In lines 9 and 10, we find the short sentences *regu-c cambion* 'and I straighten what is crooked' (cf. Old Irish *camm* 'crooked' = Old Welsh and Old Cornish *cam*) and *eχsops pissiiumi* '[though] blind I shall see' (cf. Old Irish *ad·cíu* 'I see'); these could be either entreaties for medical miracles from the gods or religious allegories. The text culminates with the repeated formula: *Luge dessu-mmi-iis; Luge dessu-mi-is; Luge dessu-mi-is; Luχe*, probably invoking the chief god LUGUS, 'By Lugus I prepare them (set them right), by Lugus I prepare them; by Lugus I prepare them, by Lugus' (Schmidt, BBCS 29.262–3; Koch, BBCS 32.37).

FURTHER READING

ARVERNI; BATH; BRICTA; CELTIC LANGUAGES; CULHWCH AC OLWEN; GALLO-ROMAN; GAULISH; INSCRIPTIONS; INSULAR CELTIC; LARZAC; LUGUS; MAPONOS; ROMANO-BRITISH; ULSTER CYCLE; Fleuriot, ÉC 15.173–90; Henry, ÉC 21.141–50; Koch, BBCS 32.1–37; Koch, ÉC 29.249–61; Koch & Carey, *Celtic Heroic Age* 1–3; Lambert, BBCS 34.10–7; Lambert, ÉC 16.141–69; Lambert, *La langue gauloise* 150–9; Lejeune & Marichal, ÉC 15.151–71; Meid, *Anzeiger der philosophisch-historischen Klasse der österreichischen Akademie der Wissenschaften* 123.36–55; Meid, *Zur Lesung un Deutung gallischer Inschriften* 27–31, 37–8; Schmidt, BBCS 29.256–68.

JTK

Champion's portion is a term that refers to a practice found in heroic societies in which a great, or the greatest, hero receives a choice portion (usually a cut of meat) at a public FEAST as a token of his honour. In early IRISH LITERATURE the display and competitive determining of hierarchical status are widespread themes, and the champion's portion figures as a frequently occurring sub-type. In the first recension of TÁIN BÓ CUAILNGE ('The Cattle Raid of Cooley') and FLED BRICRENN ('Bricriu's Feast'), the term for the champion's portion is *curadmír* (specifically localized in the chief assembly site of ULAID as *curathmír Emna Macha* 'the champion's portion of EMAIN MACHAE'). In other Irish texts the variant *mír curad* occurs, *mír* meaning 'portion' and *curad* being the genitive of *caur, cor* 'hero' (although the latter resembles Welsh *cawr* 'giant' and the GALATIAN king's name Καουαρος *Cavaros*, the etymological connection is uncertain).

The concept is by no means confined to Celtic cultures, as was already recognized in the GREEK AND ROMAN ACCOUNTS of the ancient Gauls; thus, DIODORUS SICULUS, working from the lost history of POSIDONIUS, wrote (*Historical Library* §28):

While dining [the Gauls] are served by adolescents, both male and female. Nearby are blazing hearths and CAULDRONS with spits of meat. They honour the brave warriors with the choicest portion, just as Homer says that the chieftains honoured Ajax when he returned having defeated Hector in single combat [*Iliad* 7.320–1].

In a passage quoted in the article on ATHENAEUS (another Greek author who drew on the Celtic ethnography of Posidonius), he wrote that in former times two Gaulish heroes might claim the honour of the choicest piece of meat at a feast and that they would then and there engage in a duel to the death to decide the matter.

The conjunction of these two themes—violent contention at feasts and the champion's portion—is similarly the pivot for the narrative of two of the best-known sagas of the early Irish ULSTER CYCLE of tales, *Fled Bricrenn* and SCÉLA MUCCE MEIC DÁ THÓ. In 'Bricriu's Feast', the supreme hero CÚ CHULAINN repeatedly proves himself worthy of the *curadmír*. In the 'Story of Mac Dá Thó's Pig', although the term *curad-mír* is curiously not used, CONALL CERNACH triumphs at the climax, earning the right to carve a wonderful pig at the centre of the feasting hall, Cú Chulainn being absent from that tale.

Some modern scholars have written as though the champion's portion and associated descriptions of heroic contention at feasts belonged to the reality of early Celtic life. However, the Posidonian evidence, alongside that of the Irish sagas and HOMER, raises the question whether we are dealing essentially with a literary theme which has little or no basis in fact or an actual social practice that once existed in warrior-aristocratic societies. Although Posidonius represents the champion's portion as a reality, it is clear from the account of Athenaeus that Posidonius did not claim to have witnessed the practice nor even that it was still current in his day, but rather that he relied on oral accounts of what had been done in ancient times. Therefore, we seem to have traditions of the deeds of legendary heroes—possibly reflecting actual social institutions, but possibly not—in all instances, and the comparison with Ajax suggests that the Greeks understood this.

In Welsh tradition the theme of a special cut of meat for the greatest hero does not survive prominently, but the more general idea of conferring and displaying status at feasts is well developed. For example, in the saga ENGLYNION the idea that luxurious drink was the privilege accorded the leader is found in the proverbial *penn gwr pan gwin a 6yly* 'it is the chief of men who deserves a cup of wine' (Ifor Williams, *Canu Llywarch Hen* 1.48c). In the GODODDIN, in the line *aryant am-y·ue6, eur dylyi* '[there was] silver around his mead, it was gold that he deserved' (A64.798), the theme is extended to imply a ranking of precious-metal vessels given to ranked heroes. This is similarly developed explicitly in *Fled Bricrenn* (§§60–2) in an extended episode in which Loegaire Buadach, then Conall Cernach, then Cú Chulainn are offered draughts of WINE within an ascending scale of precious-metal vessels as tokens of their heroism. As in the Posidonian accounts and the Irish sagas, a seat of honour is given to the most important man. Thus, a variant of the proverb above occurs in a stray ENGLYN in the *Gododdin*, *penn gwyr tal being a 6yly* 'it is the chief of men who deserves the end of the bench' (A44.537).

PRIMARY SOURCE
DIODORUS SICULUS, *Historical Library* §28.
FURTHER READING
ATHENAEUS; CAULDRONS; CONALL CERNACH; CÚ CHULAINN; EMAIN MACHAE; ENGLYN; ENGLYNION; FEAST; FLED BRICRENN; GALATIAN; GODODDIN; GREEK AND ROMAN ACCOUNTS; HOMER; IRISH LITERATURE; POSIDONIUS; SCÉLA MUCCE MEIC DÁ THÓ; TÁIN BÓ CUAILNGE; ULAID; ULSTER CYCLE; WINE; Aitchison, *Journal of Medieval History* 13.87–116; Enright, *Lady with a Mead Cup*; Henderson, *Fled Bricrend / The Feast of Bricriu*; Jackson, *Oldest Irish Tradition*; Koch, *Ulidia* 229–37; O'Brien, *Irish Sagas* 67–78; O'Leary, *Éigse* 20.115–27; Ó Riain, *Fled Bricrenn: Reassessments*; Tierney, PRIA C 60.189–275; Ifor Williams, *Canu Llywarch Hen*.

JTK

chariot and wagon

The chariot, or more generally the high-status wheeled vehicle, is considered to be one of the characteristic features of Celtic aristocratic display. First appearing as a four-wheeled wagon in HALLSTATT aristocratic tombs, it is largely replaced by the two-wheeled chariot at the beginning of the LA TÈNE period.

§1. ARCHAEOLOGICAL SOURCES
The earliest wheeled vehicles that can be more or less certainly assigned to ancient peoples known to have spoken CELTIC LANGUAGES are the four-wheeled examples found in Hallstatt period burials in central

Europe (for example, HOCHDORF; see VEHICLE BURIALS), often interpreted as ceremonial and funeral procession vehicles (see RITUAL). They are replaced at the end of the Hallstatt period or at the very beginning of the La Tène period by lighter, faster and more versatile two-wheeled chariots. In fact, the transition from the four-wheeled wagon to the two-wheeled chariot may be viewed as an important diagnostic or corollary of the Hallstatt–La Tène transition. Another important change that occurred at roughly this time was a technological improvement in the production of the iron-tyred wheels, from an earlier nailed-on cold iron rim to the more efficient and secure shrinking of a hot iron rim onto the single felloe of the wooden wheel.

Early chariots appeared in great numbers in burials in central Germany, Belgium, and the Champagne region of France from about 500/450 BC onwards, and later also in East Yorkshire, England, in the area of the ARRAS culture. More isolated finds, both from burials and from other contexts such as WATERY DEPOSITIONS (for example, LLYN CERRIG BACH) are known across Celtic Europe. These chariots have often been interpreted as battle-chariots (Furger-Gunti, *Zeitschrift für schweizerische Archäologie und Kunstgeschichte* 50.213–22; see also WARFARE). Their greatest technological advantage was the flexible spring suspension on which the chariot platform was mounted. The chariots were approximately 4–4.5 m in length, had an overall width of around 1.6–2.0 m, and an average wheel-gauge of around 1.35–1.45 m. The spoked wheels had iron tyres with an average diameter of approximately 0.95 m. They were usually drawn by two yoked horses (Karl & Stifter, *Pferd und Wagen in der Eisenzeit* 152–76).

§2. ICONOGRAPHIC SOURCES

Soon after their first appearance in burial contexts, wagons and chariots also appear in the iconographic record. In the early period, four-wheeled wagons and some two-wheeled chariots appeared on decorated sheet metal, especially on situlae (wine buckets), and also, for example, on the bronze κλινη *klinē* (couch) in the Hochdorf burial. In the La Tène period from the mid-3rd century BC, chariots frequently appear on COINAGE and on burial monuments from CISALPINE GAUL (Frey, *Die Situla von Kuffarn*). The inscribed stone from Briona in northern Italy combined a Gaulish text in the alphabet of Lugano (see SCRIPTS) with a relief

sculpture of four spoked wheels. Finally, chariots appear on HIGH CROSSES, such as one at Ahenny, Co. Tipperary, Ireland (Contae Thiobraid Árainn, ÉIRE; see Harbison, *High Crosses of Ireland* 11).

§3. HISTORICAL SOURCES

Chariots are also mentioned in the historical sources, and records for the use of chariots by Continental Celts can be found in many places, for example, Appian (*Roman History* 4.12), ATHENAEUS (*Deipnosophistae* 4.37), LIVY (*Ab Urbe Condita* 10.28.9) and STRABO (*Geography* 4.2.3). The most concise summary of chariot use by the ancient Gauls is given by DIODORUS SICULUS who wrote: 'In both journeys and battles the Gauls use two-horse chariots which carry both the warrior and charioteer' (*Historical Library* 5.29.1; trans. Koch & Carey, *Celtic Heroic Age* 12). CAESAR records the use of chariots in Britain (*De Bello Gallico* 4.33.1–3), as well as the existence of ROADS on which they are driven (*De Bello Gallico* 5.19.2). Chariots are also mentioned in various types of sources from early medieval Ireland (ÉRIU), for example, in the ANNALS of Ulster for the year AD 811, in the Life of COLUM CILLE (*Vita Columbae* 2.43), and in legal material such as *Bretha Crólige* (Laws of sick maintenance).

§4. LINGUISTIC SOURCES

Terms for chariots and their parts in the ancient Celtic languages are known mainly from Celtic loanwords in Latin and from place-names. Those for wheeled vehicles of probably Celtic origin known from classical sources are *benna* (cf. Welsh *ben*/*men*), *carpentum* (cf. Old Irish *carpat*), *carruca*, *carrus*, *cisium*, *colisatum*, *couinnus* (cf. Welsh *cywain* 'convey'), *epir(h)edium* (cf. Welsh *ebrwydd* 'swift, speedy'), *essedum*, *petorritum*, *pilentum*, *raeda* (Billy, *Thesaurus Linguae Gallicae* 184). *Carrus* survives in French *char* 'chariot', Spanish *carro* 'cart' ('car' in American Spanish), and English *car*. *Carbantia*, *Carbantorāte*, *Karbantorigon* (cf. Welsh *Nantcarfan*) *Carrodūnum*, *Manduessedum* or *Rotomagus* can be found in the place-name record. The most important terms in classical sources seem to have been *carpentum* for the Gaulish chariot and *essedum* (variant *asseda*) for the Belgic and southern British chariot (see BELGAE). Much more about chariot terminology can be learned from the various early medieval Irish sources, especially in TÁIN BÓ CUAILNGE, in which numerous terms can

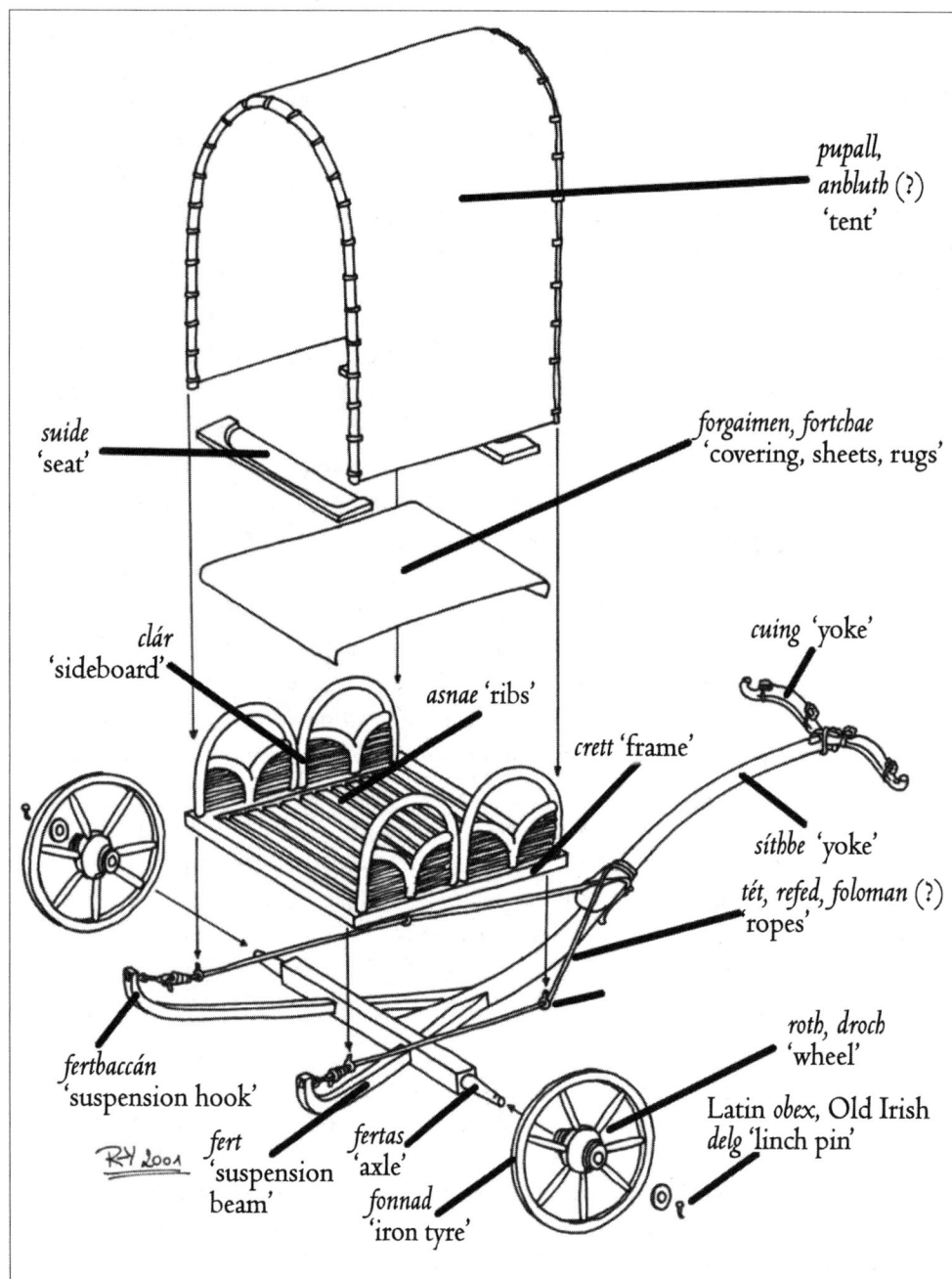

pupall, anbluth (?) 'tent'

suide 'seat'

forgaimen, fortchae 'covering, sheets, rugs'

The chariot (carpat) and its parts as described in early Irish literature

clár 'sideboard'

asnae 'ribs'

crett 'frame'

cuing 'yoke'

síthbe 'yoke'

tét, refed, foloman (?) 'ropes'

fertbaccán 'suspension hook'

roth, droch 'wheel'

Latin *obex*, Old Irish *delg* 'linch pin'

RY 2001

fert 'suspension beam'

fertas 'axle'

fonnad 'iron tyre'

be found. If this Irish textual evidence is put together with archaeological material almost entirely from outside Ireland, it allows fairly precise reconstructions of Celtic chariots (see illustration; Karl & Stifter, *Pferd und Wagen in der Eisenzeit* 152–76).

§5. FUNCTIONS

The wheeled vehicles discussed above were used for multiple purposes, with the possible exception of the early four-wheeled Hallstatt wagons, which were perhaps limited to funerary contexts. The lightweight, fast, and easily manoeuvrable two-wheeled chariots of Iron Age Celtic Europe and early medieval Ireland were primarily used as vehicles for personal transport or for going to war. In war, however, the warrior stepped off the platform to fight on foot in close combat. Chariots were also used as sport vehicles and as death biers and, in some parts of the Celtic world, even as funerary gifts.

Chariots are one of the few things that seem to be relatively characteristic for Celtic peoples from very early in Celtic history to as late as the early medieval period in Ireland. They were relatively similar in function and technology for most of this time, from the latest Hallstatt period, during their widespread use in the La Tène period, to well after the Christianization of Ireland, and thus allow valuable insights into an aspect of cultural continuity over a very long time and across a large area.

CLASSICAL SOURCES
Appian, *Roman History* 4.12; ATHENAEUS, *Deipnosophistae* 4.37; CAESAR, *De Bello Gallico*; DIODORUS SICULUS, *Historical Library*; LIVY, *Ab Urbe Condita*; STRABO, *Geography*.

FURTHER READING
ADOMNÁN; ANNALS; ARRAS CULTURE; BELGAE; CELTIC LANGUAGES; CISALPINE GAUL; COINAGE; COLUM CILLE; ÉIRE; ÉRIU; HALLSTATT; HIGH CROSSES; HOCHDORF; LA TÈNE; LLYN CERRIG BACH; RITUAL; ROADS; SCRIPTS; TÁIN BÓ CUAILNGE; VEHICLE BURIALS; WARFARE; WATERY DEPOSITIONS; Barth et al., *Vierrädrige Wagen der Hallstattzeit*; Billy, *Thesaurus Linguae Gallicae*; Binchy, *Ériu* 12.1–77; Egg, *Hallstattzeitliche Wagen*; Egg & Pare, *Das keltische Jahrtausend* 209–18; Endert, *Die Wagenbestattungen der späten Hallstattzeit*; Fox, *Find of the Early Iron Age from Llyn Cerrig Bach, Anglesey*; Frey, *Die Situla von Kuffarn*; Lucke, *Die Situla in Providence (Rhode Island)*; Frey, *Germania* 46.317–20; Furger-Gunti, *Zeitschrift für schweizerische Archäologie und Kunstgeschichte* 50.213–22; Harbison, *High Crosses of Ireland*; Karl & Stifter, *Pferd und Wagen in der Eisenzeit* 152–76; Koch & Carey, *Celtic Heroic Age* 12; Metzler, *Archäologisches Korrespondenzblatt* 16.161–77; Pare, *Wagons and Wagon-graves of the Early Iron Age in Central Europe*; Piggott, *Earliest Wheeled Transport*; Piggott, *Wagon, Chariot and Carriage*; Stead, *Arras Culture*; Stead, *New Light on the Parisi* 1–6; Stifter, 'Irish Chariot'; Vosteen, *Urgeschichtliche Wagen in Mitteleuropa*.

RK

charter tradition, medieval Celtic

The charter-writing tradition of Celtic areas in the early Middle Ages is overwhelmingly a Latin tradition, although a few translations and equivalents exist in the vernacular languages (see CELTIC COUNTRIES). The charters deal, for the most part, with the transfer of property rights, including the manumission or freeing of slaves (see SLAVERY; BODMIN MANUMISSIONS), in western BRITAIN, Wales (CYMRU), Scotland (ALBA), Ireland (ÉRIU), and Brittany (BREIZH); they relate to transactions which took place, or were supposed to have taken place, between the 6th and the 12th centuries. The form of charter used in these areas is distinctive, and is almost the only charter-form to have been used there before the Norman Conquest; most of the exceptions were from eastern Brittany (on which see BRETON LITERATURE). In addition to the surviving complete or fragmentary charters, there are many echoes of the language of this charter tradition in narrative

and other texts from Celtic areas. The existence of these echoes emphasizes that a distinctive mode of writing was employed when recording the transfer of property rights, revealed in the characteristic words and phrases used in writing about these transactions.

§1. SUBSTANCE

The Latin charter form from Celtic areas characteristically includes disposition, witness list, and sanction, and invariably uses the third person and past historic tenses. While many charters also include preambles, narrations, and boundary clauses, they lack formal protocol, i.e., initial invocation, formal title and address, and final dating clause and subscriptions. This distinguishes them from the western European charter tradition of a comparable date, as manifest in England and on the European continent, as does the use of retrospective tenses rather than first person present. These texts were intended to be narrative records of the occasions at which transactions were performed.

Here is an example, written into the 'LICHFIELD GOSPELS' when they were at Llandeilo Fawr (south Wales) in the 9th century, concerning a local transaction (J. Gwenogvryn Evans & Rhŷs, *Book of Llan Dâv* xlvi, with a slightly emended reading):

Notification: *Necesse est scribere literas quod*

Disposition: *quatuor filii Bledri . . . dederunt libertatem Bleidiud filio Sulgen et semini suo in sempiternum pro pretio atque hoc est confirmatio quod dedit pro libertate eius quatuor libras et octo uncias.*

Witness list: *Coram idoneis his testibus, de laicis Riguollaun filius Coffro, Guen . . . Guoluic filius . . . Merchguinn filius Salus, Arthan filius Cimulch, Iudri filius Iudnerth. De clericis vero Nobis episcopus Teiliau, Saturnguid sacerdos Teiliau, Dubrino et Cuhelin filii episcopi, Saturnbiu cam ibiau, et Sulgen scholasticus qui hec fideliter scripsit.*

Sanction: *Qui custodierit hoc decretum libertatis Bleidiud et prolis eius sit benedictus; qui autem non custodierit sit maledictus a deo et a Teiliau in cuius evangelio scriptum est et dicat omnis populus fiat fiat.*

And, for comparison, a second example, from the 'Cartulary of LANDEVENNEG', written at Landevenneg

(Landévennec) in western Brittany in the 11th century, concerning an early 11th-century transaction (La Borderie, *Cartulaire de l'Abbaye de Landévennec* no. 46):

Notification: *Haec cartula custodit quod*

Disposition: *Budic, nobilis comes, tradidit sancto Uuingualoeo de sua propria hereditate vicarium unum, Edern nomine, pro sui redemptione suorumque omnium utrorumque sexuum, in sepulturam suam, totum omnino, sicut ipso vivente tenuerat.*

Sanction: *Sic affirmavit dicens: Quisquis hoc custodiendo servaverit Dominus custodiat eum ab omni malo; custodiat animam tuam Dominus. Amen. Si quis vero temere frangere aut minuere voluerit, de libro viventium et cum justis non scribatur. Sit pars ejus cum Dathan et Abiron, quos terra deglutivit, nec non cum Juda et Pilato, qui Dominum crucifixerunt.*

Witness list: *Hujus donationis testes sunt plures: Alan dux Britanniae, qui obitui ejus affuit, testis; Benedictus episcopus, filius istius Budic, testis; Cadnou abba Sancti Uuingualoei, testis; Euharn vicecomes, testis; Saluten, testis; Riuuelen, testis; Blinliuguet, testis; Catguallon, testis; Moruuethen, testis.*

By identifying complete charter texts we can see that characteristic formulae were often used, for example, gifts made *sine censu* 'without property' or *usque in diem iudicii* 'till Judgement Day'; none of these formulae were exclusive to Celtic areas, although they were relatively more common there than elsewhere. Characteristic words are more distinctive, and tend to be found within, but not across, all Celtic areas; these include, for example, use of the verb *immolare* for 'to give' (ordinarily 'to offer, to sacrifice'), the noun *graphium* for 'charter', and the pattern *custodire . . . benedicere, frangere . . . maledicere* ('to keep . . . to be blessed, to break . . . to be cursed') in sanctions. Most of the small number of vernacular examples come from Ireland and Scotland, although there are a few passages in WELSH. The GAELIC examples occur late in the period (in 11th- and 12th-century texts) and include formulae which are clearly translations of the Latin tradition, e.g., Middle Irish *co bráth/go bràd* and Old Welsh *bit/hit braut* 'until Judgement (Day)' for *usque in diem iudicii* and the Middle Irish nouns *bennacht . . . mallacht* 'blessing . . . curse' for *benedicetur . . . maledicetur* 'will be blessed . . . will be

cursed'. For further examples, see §3 below.

The corpus of charters consists of over 200 complete texts, at least 100 incomplete texts and a handful of formulae inscribed on stone (Broun, *Charters of Gaelic Scotland and Ireland in the Early and Central Middle Ages*; Wendy Davies, *Francia* 17.69–90; Wendy Davies, *Ireland in Early Mediaeval Europe* 258–80; Wendy Davies, *Landévennec et le monachisme breton dans le haut Moyen Âge* 85–95; La Borderie, *Bulletin de la Société archéologique du Finistère* 24.96–113; Lemoine, *Chronique de Landévennec* 1995.58–62); Mac Niocaill, *Book of Kells*; Poppe, *Celtica* 18.35–52; Pryce, CMCS 25.25.15–34). Many are written into gospel or liturgical books; some are written into cartularies (and were sometimes edited in the process); a few are recorded in formal extents and surveys; and a few are appended to saints' *Vitae*. The complete examples include 25 from Brittany, 14 from south-west England (including some in Old English), 169 from Wales (of which three include some Old Welsh), two from Scotland (one in Middle IRISH) and six from Ireland (all in Middle Irish). Three of the stones are from Wales, and another comes from Ireland; the reference to the *cirografum* on a slab in the floor of a north Devon church, probably from the late 12th century, may well be a reference to another (Thomas, *And Shall These Mute Stones Speak?* 177; Wendy Davies, *Literacy in Medieval Celtic Societies* 104). The fragments come from the same areas, although there are far fewer from Wales and rather more from Ireland (both in Latin and Old Irish). Recognizable charter language in narrative and other texts adds at least 40 further examples, from Wales, Ireland, Brittany, Scotland, and south-west England, in order of frequency.

§2. CONTEXT

The earliest of the indisputable and uncontroversial material is Irish, and belongs to the 8th century; the earliest indisputably Welsh material is of the 9th century, although a very good case can be made for the production of 7th- and 8th-century exemplars, and possibly some of the later 6th. Material from central and western Brittany is notable in the late 9th century: from Vannes (GWENED), Saint-Malo (Sant-Maloù), Saint-Pol-de-Léon (Kastell-Paol), and Landevenneg.

The bulk of the material is of a 9th- to 10th-century date, as befits a period of growing concern with the security of ecclesiastical property. The latest known south-western English examples are from the years 1042–66, Breton 1085–1112, Welsh 1132–51, Irish from 1133, and Scottish from the later 12th century, after 1131/2. This recording tradition originated in a variety of ways. The detailed record of witness names has parallels in late Roman and very early medieval contexts elsewhere in Europe, where insistence on the formal registration of transactions occasioned the development of elaborate public procedures. Witnesses were subsequently subject to recall in cases of disputed ownership. Registration procedures of this kind were clearly known in the Celtic West in the early Middle Ages since, for example, the early 8th-century collection of Irish canons reiterates earlier patristic and synodal prescriptions that a sale should be confirmed by witnesses, writing, and sureties. The language of imperial rescripts (replies from the emperor to his subjects) and Continental formularies is echoed in charter formulae from southern Wales and Brittany. The context of this Celtic material is exclusively ecclesiastical: all the transactions recorded involved the Christian church in some way. Precise parallels for the charter tradition's characteristic language tend to come from explicitly religious contexts such as papal letters. The common features in the Irish and British material indicate the 5th–7th centuries as the period of origin, when British missionaries were working in Ireland before the ecclesiastical traditions of the areas diverged.

The practice of making this kind of record is likely to have developed in episcopal circles in the 5th century in Britain when the bishops met in synods and drew upon the language of the early Church Fathers for their texts. We must imagine the bishops of the late Roman period securing endowments and registering them with their city councils, as required by the state; the language and form of the resulting records continued to influence ways of recording transactions in the Celtic West. The tradition is therefore the fossilized practice of the increasingly isolated bishops of western Britain in the mid-5th century, a practice which was carried to Brittany with the migrants (see BRETON MIGRATIONS), and to Ireland with the early missions. Thereafter, the form tended to be retained while the formulae varied— perhaps reinforced in Ireland by knowledge of the work of the papal scriptorium (manuscript-production centre) in the 6th and early 7th centuries.

§3. USES

There can be no doubt that some people in Celtic areas considered a written record to be valid proof of ownership, and we have evidence that records were occasionally used in cases of dispute. There is an Irish heptad (meaningful group of seven items) of *c.* 700, in which 'old writing' (in fact, 'godly old writing') is listed alongside valid witnesses, immovable stones, *rath*-sureties (a way in which third parties could guarantee a contract), and a bequest, as viable proofs of ownership (Stacey, *Lawyers and Laymen* 221). From Saint-Pol-de-Léon in Brittany come references, in the later 9th century, to the belief that people should be notified of transactions in writing. In Welsh material of the 9th–11th centuries a stock phrase occurs that invokes the same respect for the written record: *in sempiterno graphio* (this transaction is recorded 'in an eternal writing'). By implication, writing the record made the recorded action permanent: writing was a way of making things last.

It is of considerable interest that a special word for writing about property, in effect for 'charter-writing', seems to have been used in BRYTHONIC areas in the early Middle Ages. The medieval Latin word (*chiro*)*graphum* 'deed; charter-party' was borrowed into the Welsh language by the 10th century in the word *grefiat*; it occurs in Latin on a stone monument from Merthyr Mawr (*in grefium in proprium usq*[*ue*] *in diem iudici*[*i*] '[this was done] in writing into ownership until Judgement Day', perhaps meaning something like 'permanent ownership was registered') and on the Devon stone noted above (Nash-Williams, *Early Christian Monuments of Wales* no. 240). In early 10th-century charters from the bishopric of Vannes, the word became the Latin verb *graffiare*, 'to register a change of ownership' (Cartulary of REDON nos. 275, 276, 278). We have here a distinctive usage in Brythonic areas in the 9th–11th centuries which underlines the importance of the idea of writing as permanent 'proof': it was a type of guarantee, to add to the personal sureties (third-party guarantees) that were those societies' main enforcing mechanisms. Writing as proof of ownership could occur in other media, as on the stones already cited. The Irish heptad mentioned above refers to immovable stones (see also OGAM), symbols of permanence. At Blair Athol in Perthshire, Scotland, there is a stone called *Clach na h-Ìobairt* 'the stone of the offering', where *ìobairt* 'offering' is the Gaelic equivalent of Latin *immolavit* 'he or she sacrificed' (Watson, *History of the Celtic Place-Names of Scotland* 254, 310). The 8th-century Kilnasaggart stone in Co. Armagh (ARD MHACHA) also records a grant of the place (*in loc*) to the Apostle Peter, as 7th-/9th- and 11th-century Welsh stones found at Llanllŷr (CEREDIGION) and Ogmore, Glamorgan (Ogwr, MORGANNWG) also record grants (Wendy Davies, *Ireland in Early Mediaeval Europe* 259, 261; Nash-Williams, *Early Christian Monuments of Wales* nos. 124, 255; Thomas, *And Shall These Mute Stones Speak?* 100). Since people perceived writing as a mechanism for achieving permanence of possession, charters were also written into gospel books and hagiographic texts (Wendy Davies, *Ireland in Early Mediaeval Europe* 271–4; Jenkins, *Vom mittelalterlichen Recht zur neuzeitlichen Rechtswissenschaft* 79–86).

By the 9th century ecclesiastical charter writing was an aspect of property management: it helped the owner to know what rights he had in landed property and from whom he might expect income. This concern was certainly evident early on in Wales and Brittany, and in Scotland at least by the 12th century (Broun, *Charters of Gaelic Scotland and Ireland in the Early and Central Middle Ages* 34–5).

Ecclesiastical charter writing could also make claims to establish proprietary rights. Records could be massaged to support an existing position, or claim a new one, by endorsements on the original or expansion when recopying. This happened all over Celtic areas, and beyond. The first twenty or so charters of the Landevenneg Cartulary were put together in the mid- to late 10th century to demonstrate the absorption of small monasteries and churches by the larger monastic community of Landevenneg. At this level, charter writing was about securing public recognition of property rights, whether legitimately or not.

In Ireland, by contrast, charter writing does not seem to have been a major protective technique used in the 9th to 11th centuries. The notion that the written record had value as proof of ownership was obviously influential in the Armagh sphere by the late 7th century, and it may be evident in material collected at 8th-century Lorrha (Ó Riain, *Éigse* 23.117 n.50). The influence of charter writing can be seen in other traditions, especially those of central southern Ireland, in Latin hagiographic material from Kinnitty (Ceann Ettaig), Lismore (Liosmór) and Clonfertmulloe (Cluain

Fearte Molua) (Plummer, *Vitae Sanctorum Hiberniae* 1.195, 196, 2.66, 89, 92, 222), and in texts such as the 7th-/8th-century *Cáin Éimíne* from Monasterevin, Co. Offaly, whose 'legal core' is in essence a vernacular derivation from a Latin charter model (Poppe, *Celtica* 18.42–4; Poppe, *Celtica* 21.592). It is therefore likely that some charter writing took place at some centres in Ireland through the 9th–11th centuries, and that the charter tradition influenced the formulation of written property claims both in Latin and the vernacular. However, charter writing was clearly not taken up in Ireland in the way that it was in other Celtic areas and there are alternative influences on some of the 11th-century Middle Irish charters (Herbert, *Book of Kells*). The Irish habit of citing the names of guarantors rather than of witnesses indicates a significantly different approach to the transfer of property rights as well as a substantial variation in the form of the record (Poppe, *Celtica* 21.588–92; Ní Dhonnchadha, *Peritia* 1.178–215).

There is much to suggest that Scottish practice reflected the Irish: the distinctive 'Celtic' charter language occurs in the Abernethy material in Paris, Bibliothèque Nationale, Latin MS 4126, clearly implying a knowledge of the Latin tradition in Scotland before the 11th century (Anderson, *Kings and Kingship in Early Scotland* 247). The survival of 10th- and 11th-century charters in 12th-century copies indicates the use of charter writing before the impact of the new wave of religious foundations in the 12th century (Broun, *Charters of Gaelic Scotland and Ireland in the Early and Central Middle Ages* 26). Charters I–V from DEER, in particular, although preserved in Gaelic, are strongly reminiscent of 'Celtic' charter language; those from Loch Leven much less so (Jackson, *Gaelic Notes in the 'Book of Deer'* 30–2; cf. Lawrie, *Early Scottish Charters prior to AD 1153* no. 14).

Charter writing was about property rights—and was one of the techniques used by churches in the central Middle Ages to maintain and extend them. The language chosen for these records was often decidedly archaic: old formulations could be repeated for centuries.

PRIMARY SOURCES
J. Gwenogvryn Evans & Rhŷs, *Book of Llan Dâv* xlvi; La Borderie, *Cartulaire de l'abbaye de Landévennec* no. 46.

FURTHER READING
ALBA; ARD MHACHA; BODMIN MANUMISSIONS; BREIZH; BRETON

LITERATURE; BRETON MIGRATIONS; BRITAIN; BRYTHONIC; CELTIC COUNTRIES; CEREDIGION; CYMRU; DEER; ÉRIU; GAELIC; GWENED; IRISH; KELLS; LANDEVENNEG; LICHFIELD GOSPELS; LLANDAF; MORGANNWG; OGAM; REDON; SLAVERY; WELSH; Anderson, *Kings and Kingship in Early Scotland*; Broun, *Charters of Gaelic Scotland and Ireland in the Early and Central Middle Ages*; Wendy Davies, *Francia* 17.69–90; Wendy Davies, *Ireland in Early Mediaeval Europe* 258–80; Wendy Davies, *Landévennec et le monachisme breton dans le haut Moyen Âge* 85–95; Wendy Davies, *Literacy in Medieval Celtic Societies* 99–112; Herbert, *Book of Kells* 60–77; Herbert, *Iona, Kells, and Derry*; Jackson, *Gaelic Notes in the Book of Deer*; Jackson, LHEB; Jenkins, *Vom mittelalterlichen Recht zur neuzeitlichen Rechtswissenschaft* 75–88; Jenkins & Owen, CMCS 5.37–66, 7.91–120; La Borderie, *Bulletin de la Société archéologique du Finistère* 24.96–113; Lawrie, *Early Scottish Charters prior to AD 1153*; Lemoine, *Chronique de Landévennec* 1995.58–62; Mac Niocaill, *Book of Kells* 153–65; Mac Niocaill, *Notitiae as Leabhar Cheanannais* 1033–1161; Nash-Williams, *Early Christian Monuments of Wales*; Ní Dhonnchadha, *Peritia* 1.178–215; Ó Riain, *Éigse* 23.107–30; Padel, *Cornish Studies* 6.20–7; Plummer, *Vitae Sanctorum Hiberniae*; Poppe, *Celtica* 18.35–52; Poppe, *Celtica* 21.588–92; Pryce, CMCS 25.15–54; Sharpe, *Scriptorium* 36.3–28; Stacey, *Lawyers and Laymen* 210–33; Thomas, *And Shall These Mute Stones Speak?*

Wendy Davies

Yn **Cheshaght Ghailckagh (The Manx Society**) was founded in 1899 in Douglas (Doolish), the capital of the Isle of Man (ELLAN VANNIN), 'for the preservation of MANX as a living language' and for the study and publication of existing Manx Gaelic literature and the cultivation of a modern literature (see MANX LITERATURE). The Society members were not native Manx speakers, but were concerned about the decline of the language from 12,350 recorded speakers in 1871 to 2382 in 1911. They were well-known and respected figures; the first President was Arthur William MOORE, MHK (Member of the House of Keys), Speaker of the House of Keys, and members included Deemster Gill, Canon Savage, Dr J. Clague, and J. C. Crellin, MHK. Dedicated scholars Sophia MORRISON, Edmund Goodwin, and William Cubbon were members of its first committee.

From the foundation of the Society there were members who favoured a literary approach, and the publication of books remained one of the cornerstones of the Society's work throughout the 20th century. Many of these works were designed to help teachers and students, from Goodwin's *Lessoonyn ayns Chengey ny Mayrey Ellan Vannin* (1901) to *Learn Manx* on CD-ROM (2001) (see DICTIONARIES AND GRAMMARS).

The Society has provided many fine teachers of the language, from J. J. Kneen's short-lived venture teaching Manx to children in Ballamodha School, with permission from the Malew Board of Education in 1905, and paid by Yn Cheshaght Ghailckagh, to the creation of posts by the Isle of Man Department of Education in 1992 for a Manx Language Officer, Dr T. B. Stowell, and two peripatetic teachers of Manx. The first Manx-medium school unit was formed in 2001 (see EDUCATION). Many members of Yn Cheshaght Ghailckagh, some of whom learned Manx from the last of the native speakers, have also willingly given their time and talents to teach adults and children on a voluntary basis.

Some members of the Society believed that the best way of preserving the language was by collecting examples of speech and song (others were interested too in music and dance) from those native speakers whom they knew (see MANX MUSIC). As he visited his patients, Dr Clague also collected folklore, sayings, and tunes (see FOLK-TALES). Sir John RHŷS from Oxford encouraged Sophia Morrison to collect, particularly from the west of the island. In 1905 Yn Cheshaght Ghailckagh bought an 'Edison' phonograph and the first recordings of the language were made 'in order that the accent and pronunciation of the words in the Manx may be fully preserved for future generations'. During the early 1950s the Society, following the Irish Folklore Commission's recordings of Manx in 1948 and earlier recordings by Professor Marstrander of Oslo University in the 1930s, made a series of recordings of the last native speakers.

For many years the Society had no home, until in 1986 Thie ny Gaelgey (House of the Manx language), formerly St Jude's School, was opened by Mona DOUGLAS. Now, Yn Cheshaght Ghailckagh works with the Isle of Man Government to promote the Manx language. From a nadir of two native speakers and a handful of learners in 1961, the future of the language looks much brighter with 2.2% of the population in 2001 claiming to speak Manx, thanks to recent educational initiatives (see also LANGUAGE [REVIVAL]).

RELATED ARTICLES
DICTIONARIES AND GRAMMARS; DOUGLAS; EDUCATION; ELLAN VANNIN; FOLK-TALES; LANGUAGE (REVIVAL); MANX; MANX LITERATURE; MANX MUSIC; MOORE; MORRISON; RHŷS.

Fiona McArdle

Chrétien de Troyes, the most influential author of French romances, was a court poet, active between about 1170 and 1190, but little is now known about his life. The term *roman* (romance) had first been applied to the *romans d'antiquité*, French adaptations of classical stories, but it was Chrétien's works which firmly established the new genre and helped to develop ARTHURIAN traditions on the Continent. Although he was undoubtedly influenced by classical and scholastic texts, it has sometimes been argued that his Arthurian romances were influenced by tales originally in WELSH or other CELTIC LANGUAGES, though GEOFFREY OF MONMOUTH'S HISTORIA REGUM BRITANNIAE, translated into Norman French by Wace in 1155, seems to be a more likely source for much of the raw material. The relationship between three of his romances and their Middle Welsh counterparts, the Three Romances, has been the subject of heated debate since the 19th century, the so-called *Mabinogionfrage*. Today many Welsh scholars tend to agree that *Yvain* or *Le Chevalier au Lion*, *Erec et Enide* and *Le Conte du Graal* or *Le Roman de Perceval*, predate the three corresponding Welsh romances—OWAIN *neu Iarlles y Ffynnon*, GERAINT *fab Erbin* and PEREDUR *fab Efrawg*, and that the latter have been, to a greater or lesser extent, influenced by Chrétien's romances, or possibly by different French versions of the same stories (see TAIR RHAMANT for further discussion of the relationship). Chrétien's other verse romances, written in octosyllabic rhyming couplets, comprise *Lancelot* or *Le Chevalier de la Charrette*, which explores the theme of the eponymous knight's adulterous love for Guenevere, and *Cligès*, which combines Arthurian and classical elements and owes not a little to the TRISTAN AND ISOLT legend which was circulating in French by the mid-12th century. Another romance, *Guillaume d'Angleterre*, is attributed to him by some scholars. He also left two lyric poems and a French adaptation of the tale of Philomena from Ovid's *Metamorphoses*, now only surviving in a 13th-century version.

The narrative base (*matière*) of Chrétien's romances provides a vehicle for debating ideas and problems of courtly and chivalric behaviour, that *sen*, as he called it, which gives his work a strong intellectual dimension. The fanciful Arthurian context also provided a usefully distanced context in which to provide subtle commentary on contemporary life and politics, without the poet risking the displeasure of his patrons, Marie de Champagne and Philippe d'Alsace, count of Flanders. His romances, which were initially probably read aloud to an audience, seem to have met with immediate success. After Chrétien's death, perhaps *c.* 1190, other writers provided *Continuations* of his *Perceval*, which he had left unfinished, and his influence and popularity continued unabated. Later French GRAIL romances, now composed in the newly fashionable medium of prose, assume familiarity with his work, whilst in other western European countries not only *Perceval* but also his *Erec*, *Yvain* and *Lancelot* were adapted into other languages or provided the ultimate source for new texts about these knights.

There are many editions of the romances of Chrétien de Troyes, based on different texts, methodologies, &c., and countless critical works. Those selected below are recent. The bibliography by Douglas Kelly (1st ed. 1976, Supplement 1, 2002) is indispensable.

PRIMARY SOURCES
EDITIONS. Busby, *Chrétien de Troyes*; Gregory & Luttrell, *Cligés*; Holden, *Guillaume d'Angleterre*.
ED. & TRANS. Cormier, *Three Ovidian Tales of Love*; Fritz, *Erec et Enide*; Hult, *Le chevalier au lion*; Méla, *Le chevalier de la charrette*.

RELATED ARTICLES
ARTHURIAN; CELTIC LANGUAGES; GEOFFREY OF MONMOUTH; GERAINT; GRAIL; HISTORIA REGUM BRITANNIAE; OWAIN AB URIEN; PEREDUR; TAIR RHAMANT; TRISTAN AND ISOLT; WELSH.
BIBLIOGRAPHY. Kelly, *Chrétien de Troyes: An Analytic Bibliography*; Kelly et al., *Chrétien de Troyes: An Analytic Bibliography, Supplement 1*.

Ceridwen Lloyd-Morgan

Christianity in the Celtic countries [1] Ireland

§1. ORIGINS

According to legend, the arrival of Christianity in Ireland (ÉRIU) was sudden, decisive, and dramatic: PATRICK the Bishop returned to Ireland at Easter 432 and baptized the nation (*gens*), transforming it from being a pagan people into a Christian one. This picture, essentially the dramatic creation of Muirchú's *Vita Patricii* (late 7th century), for all its theological sophistication in presenting an analysis of conversion and its subtle message of the ideal of Christian unity/harmony for an island riven by warfare between petty kings, is valueless as history. When Christians first reached Ireland is unknown, but there were Christian communities in BRITAIN by the late 2nd century; therefore any time after that is possible. The first Irish contacts were most likely through traders, and later through slaves brought from Britain (see SLAVERY). From this early period we have one enigmatic piece of evidence: the question of the original home of PELAGIUS (c. 350–c. 425), who in Rome became a famous spiritual guide and subsequently a heretic. Pelagius is usually said to have come from Roman Britain. However, JEROME, a contemporary who is unusually precise with geographical information, held he belonged to the Irish people (*Scotticae gentis*). If so, then Pelagius is our evidence for a vibrant church in the 4th century.

§2. THE 5TH CENTURY

We know that by the 430s there were sizeable communities of Christians in Ireland. It is quite likely that these were composed mainly of slaves captured from Britain, or their descendants. From elsewhere in the Roman world we know that communities of Christians continued to concern themselves with the spiritual welfare of their brethren who had been taken into slavery, for example, by supplying them with clergy and, most probably, the British church continued to care about Christians in Ireland. These Christian communities in Ireland were sufficiently numerous for there to be a need for a bishop to minister to them and, indeed, for this need to be given a hearing in far-off Rome. Prosper of Aquitaine (c. 390–c. 463) records that in 431 Pope Celestine sent them (those in Ireland 'who believed in Christ') a bishop named PALLADIUS. This Palladius is not mentioned in any other insular source until the late 7th century when Muirchú found it necessary to 'write him out' of the history of the conversion of Ireland in order for Patrick to become the sole patron and evangelist. In all probability he spent the rest of his life in Ireland working among slaves, traders, and whatever few Irish he was able to convert. We have only one other piece of information about Irish Christians from this time, and again Prosper is the source. In his *De gratia Dei et libero arbitrio contra Collatorem* (written in 434), he tells us that Celestine had sent a bishop to the British Church to free it from 'Pelagianism'—Prosper's pet-hate—and

that he had ordained a bishop for the Irish so that 'the barbarian island might be made Christian'. These passages, taken with other references to missionary work beyond the imperial frontiers, point to a Roman mission to Ireland which was still working there 20 years later in the 450s when Leo the Great was concerned with the state of the Christians in Ireland.

Our most important sources for the 5th century are the two documents written by Patrick. His *Confessio* justifies his mission as a bishop in Ireland—he came from Britain—against Christian critics either in Ireland or Britain; while his 'Letter to the Soldiers of Coroticus' is a sentence of excommunication of Christians (he calls them 'apostates') involved in the slave trade who were taking Irish converts to Christianity into slavery. Patrick's dates are uncertain (the traditional dates are simply a later accommodation to Prosper's Chronicle), but a period down to the later 5th century would fit the situation he describes in GAUL where Romans were ransoming Christians from the still pagan Franks. There are no contemporary references to Patrick's mission, and Patrick makes no mention of anyone working in Ireland before him. But, equally, Patrick does not present himself as the sole missionary, merely as the one who has travelled where no one has already preached Christianity. Patrick's own perception is that he is the harbinger of Christ's Second Coming, rather than that he is the 'apostle of the Irish', and we must assume that he was but one among many bishops and missionaries working in Ireland in the 5th century. Quite probably, Patrick was an erratic among that group because of his apocalypticism, a feature of his ministry that would explain both why he was criticized by other bishops (presumably working nearby) and the shape taken by his *Confessio*.

§3. THE EARLY CHRISTIAN PERIOD

The assumption that there were many missionaries working in Ireland over a long period—the whole of the 5th century—receives support from the fact that by the mid-6th century, when the silence of our sources begins to end, we find a well-organized Christianity with important monastic foundations, well-known teachers such as Comgall at BEANN CHAR (Bangor), a church that is able to see itself as equal to those on the Continent and which is at one with the learning of Latin Christianity at the time as demonstrated by

COLUMBANUS, and with the confidence to examine new approaches to pressing western problems in pastoral praxis, as witness the penitentials.

From the 7th century we have much better evidence, and through contemporary ANNALS we have accurate dates. MONASTERIES grew to become the great centres of learning and economic life, and we see Christianity emerging as the intellectual form of the society. For, while the Church took over several native features into its law, its canon law was taken over into secular law and became its pattern as a written corpus (see LAW TEXTS). We also see Ireland emerging as one more region within Latin Christendom, with travel in both directions by monks, teachers, and administrators. By the later 7th century Ireland had a vibrant theological community whose works were having an impact on the rest of the Latin Church. The best examples are in the area of law: e.g., CÁIN ADOMNÁIN (697), an attempt to limit the effects of warfare, shows the Church seeking to influence society. Likewise, the first systematic canonical collection (COLLECTIO CANONUM HIBERNENSIS) was compiled in Ireland and was soon copied and imitated abroad—its new directions affected all subsequent western canon law. It is against this background that we should view the Irish clerics active in Charlemagne's kingdoms, and later writers such as ERIUGENA.

§4. ISSUES OF PERCEPTION

In historical writing about Irish Christianity in the early medieval period there has been a tendency for several centuries to note as many discrepancies as possible between Ireland and the Latin West, and then to assert that this was a distinctive 'Celtic Christianity' or a 'Celtic Church'. This approach, while it may suit particular modern religious agenda, is flawed as a way of understanding the past on three counts. First, it assumes that there were monolithic institutions in the past: one 'Roman', the other 'Celtic', whereas we should note that there was a spectrum of rites, practices, and favoured approaches across western Europe and that these patterns were continually shifting. Thus, we can observe two very different monastic ideals, both well-rooted in Ireland, in conflict at the end of the 8th century: one championed by the ascetic reform movement, the Céili Dé (Fellows of God), the other by the author of the NAVIGATIO SANCTI BRENDANI;

but, rather than a clash between a 'Celtic MONASTICISM' and some imagined 'normative' monasticism, we have two *Irish* local theologies, both relating closely with contemporary monastic disputes elsewhere in the Latin West. Interest in the notion of 'Celtic idiosyncrasies' easily occludes serious comparisons with Britain and the Continent. Second, at no point did Irish Christians perceive themselves as religiously separate *as Christians* from others in the West. At the beginning of the 7th century Columbanus had a notion of Europe as a Christian unity reaching right out to the Ocean, while at the end of that century ADOMNÁN imagined the cult of COLUM CILLE reaching from the Ocean right across Europe to Rome. And while it is clear that they recognized their cultural separation from Christians elsewhere in that they prepared lists of 'their saints', meaning those born in Ireland, they were equally conscious that they expressed that cultural distinctiveness in Latin which was the bond of their Christian solidarity as one *gens christiana* among those nations which made up the *gens sancta Dei*—Muirchú's *Vita Patricii* is the classic extant expression of this complex sense of being one as Christians, yet distinct as a culture. This sense of being one ethnic group within the unity of Latin Christianity is seen in the number of *peregrini* (see PEREGRINATIO) who went to the Continent and settled there as monks or teachers; while fully seen as being from a part of the Latin Church, they distinguished themselves with the appellation *Scottus*. Third, in what survives of early Irish learning (liturgy would be an even better indicator, but only fragmentary evidence has survived) we find a Latin culture that drew from, and contributed to, the wider Latin culture of the Western Church.

It is this issue of difference within a mosaic, in contrast to a monolith, that has fired the debate about the 'miracle' or 'myth' of a flowering of Christian culture in Ireland in this period. Thus, there were those who saw only a golden age of 'an island of saints and scholars', while others see disorganization and erratic items being built into a myth. This debate rages on between those who claim that there are a great many distinctive Irish writings in Latin, and those who, because they cannot find such distinctiveness, claim that there are almost none. In all these cases, the debate rages since its foundation relies on a false opposition of 'Christian Ireland' vs. 'Christian elsewhere'; we can only appreciate Irish Christian culture—both what is distinctive and what is not—when we locate the early Christian period in Ireland within a pattern of such different Christian cultures at the period, especially that mosaic that forms the 'Latin West' at the time.

If one feature of the study of Christianity in Ireland has been a desire to see a religion radically different from Christianity elsewhere, another long-standing desire—going back at least to John Toland's *History of the Druids* (1726)—has been to find 'pagan' elements mixed with Christianity either 'persisting in spite of Christian attempts at suppressing them' or 'contaminating the purity of Christianity' (depending on the perspective of the author). While it is undoubtedly the case that a religion takes on a different appearance with every new cultural situation it encounters, and such is true of Christianity in Ireland, the perspective of those who can easily uncover 'the pagan elements' in early Irish Christianity is distorted by two religious assumptions whose origins lie in the theological disputes of the late-medieval/Reformation period. The first is the illusion that historically there was a 'pure' or 'genuine' Christianity—as opposed to the confessional belief that one's version of Christianity is the true one—or that one can identify 'the Christian' from every other cultural/religious element in society; and conversely that every society's 'Christianity' which does not conform to this pure Christian essence is a syncretism. The second assumption is that, prior to the 16th century, proponents of Christianity saw themselves in relationship to other religions in an absolutist manner, i.e., if Christianity is the true religion, then everything else is false, and anything that belongs to such a system of falsehood must be kept radically separate from Christianity. In this view there is no basis for any truck between 'Christians' and 'pagans' (assuming both to be well-defined systems) and any failure to maintain strict segregation results in a syncretism whereby Christianity is traduced, with the implication that later Christians have to jettison contaminations, while later supporters of 'paganism' imagine they have simply to pick those elements they judge not to be Christian property.

In the first millennium Christianity showed itself remarkably flexible in adapting to various environments and taking on local colour (acculturation), and in this it was far more successful than its parent Judaism

in that it abandoned notions of ethnic distinctiveness linked to dietary laws or circumcision, and equally it avoided being presented as exotic where other expanding religions of the period (e.g., Mithraism) failed. Therefore, any attempt to isolate a 'pure' Christian essence as distinct from the various Christian cultures—i.e., societies in which Christianity has established itself—is doomed to failure except as a confessional undertaking. Thus, when Christianity came to Ireland it came in its late antique Latin dress, and it was this that took on new local hues as it encountered a society that was non-urban, did not have a Roman imperial background nor legal system, and where Latin was not the prestige language. Once there, the agenda of the proponents of Christianity would have been to see how the native religion could be used as a 'preparation for the gospel' in the manner in which this is found in Acts 17. However, Christianity also showed from its outset a concern that it would not import elements from other religious systems which it considered 'superstitious', although what constituted 'SUPERSTITIONS' varied with time and place, and therefore there was an on-going fear of assimilation. Remembering that assimilation is not the same as acculturation means that any attempt to identify any particular aspect of their Christian system or practice is a very delicate matter. This theoretical difficulty is further compounded in the case of Ireland in that (1) we have no record of resistance to Christianity which would show us directly the nature of the other religion's content; (2) by Muirchú's time there was no longer any living memory of what the pre-Christian Irish believed—while the *Vita Patricii* is regularly ransacked by those seeking information of 'DRUIDS', what they find is Muirchú's use of Daniel 1–4 for his pagan *magi* in lieu of memory; (3) there is a frequently met use of the term *lex naturae* (law of nature) to indicate the acceptability of some Irish custom, but by this stage it is indistinguishable from Christian custom; and (4) using Continental parallels—usually from much earlier—carries with it many difficulties of method. The result is that, far from being easily uncovered, reconstructing the pre-Christian religion of Ireland is a most difficult but important academic task, and the absence of such understanding is our single greatest limitation in understanding early Irish Christianity.

§5. THE 12TH CENTURY

Between the 9th and later 11th century Christianity in Ireland seemed to be in a period without major developments. The monasteries continued to be great religious centres (even if they lamented the depredations of the Vikings), and there was still a literary and artistic culture, along with the occasional significant writer. However, developments on the Continent seemed to bypass Ireland, especially the new, more codified, monasticism that can be traced to Benedict of Aniane (c. 750–821)—this resulted in Benedictinism and led to later monastic 'reforms' such as those of Cluny and, later still, the Cistercians. Later, developments of new models of church/secular relations linked to the name of Pope Gregory VII (c. 1021–85), 'the Gregorian reforms', seemed to leave Ireland lagging behind. However, in the 12th century in Ireland we see a situation where a key running theme in church activities was the desire for 'reforms' so that the Irish Church had the same structures as those elsewhere. This is best seen in the various synods, most importantly Ráith Bressail (1111) and KELLS (Ceanannas Mór, 1152), which established dioceses and provinces in Ireland and sought to give the same shape to Irish structures as those found elsewhere. Linked to this process are the names of the powerful bishops of the period such as CELLACH, Mael Maedóc, and Lorcan Ua Tuathail (St Laurence O'Toole). This period also saw the introduction of several new orders which brought contemporary ideals of religious life from the Continent and which left its mark in many ways in religious writings produced in Irish from the 12th century until the Reformation. The two most important groups were the Cistercians, who arrived in the mid-12th century (see CISTERCIAN ABBEYS IN IRELAND), and the Franciscans, who arrived in the 13th century. However, the vision of an Irish Church, which closely resembled the Church on the Continent that inspired the 'reformers', did not come about because of the arrival of the Anglo-Normans (ostensibly, according to the papal bull *Laudabiliter*, as agents of church reform). This resulted in the growth of two distinct churches: one in the Norman controlled areas, the other in the Gaelic areas, and this situation continued until the 17th century.

§6. THE PERIOD OF REFORMATION AND COUNTER-REFORMATION

The 16th-century revolution within Latin Christianity affected the two churches in Ireland (ÉIRE) differently. The English Reformation directly altered the organization of the *ecclesia inter Anglos* while hardly touching that *inter Hibernos*. However, by 1612—with the execution in Dublin (BAILE ÁTHA CLIATH) of Bishop Conor O'Devaney, who had been with the last of the Gaelic rulers defeated less than a decade earlier, yet was mourned by Dubliners—it was clear that religious and political divisions would not simply follow the old medieval divisions, and that from then on there would be an increasingly close identification of non-English with Catholic. This resulted in the last great flowering of religious writing in Latin, and more importantly in IRISH, in Ireland. On the one hand, there was a desire to translate materials into Irish to advance the Protestant cause, e.g., William Bedell (1571–1642) insisted that clerical graduates of Trinity College Dublin should be able to minister to Irish people in their native language, and oversaw the translation of the Old Testament into Irish (see BIBLE). On the other hand, there was also a desire to provide material which would introduce Counter-Reformation Catholicism into Ireland and equally to provide it with material to rebut the Protestant advance. This resulted not only in many catechisms and religious manuals being translated into Irish, but also in many new devotional works being written in Irish. In this process the rôle of the Irish Franciscans has a unique place, for it was their desire to preserve the Catholicism of Ireland and to strengthen it by new works in Irish that placed them at the forefront of the attempts in the 17th century to preserve as much as possible of the inheritance of early Irish history, e.g., the work of the Franciscan John Colgan (Seán MAC COLGÁIN, 1592–1658) on Irish HAGIOGRAPHY.

PRIMARY SOURCES

CÁIN ADOMNÁIN; COLLECTIO CANONUM HIBERNENSIS; NAVIGATIO SANCTI BRENDANI; Bieler, *Patrician Texts in the Book of Armagh*; Carey, *King of Mysteries*; McNally, *Scriptores Hiberniae Minores 1*; Plummer, *Vitae Sanctorum Hibernia*.

FURTHER READING

ADOMNÁN; ANNALS; BAILE ÁTHA CLIATH; BEANN CHAR; BIBLE; BRITAIN; CELLACH; CHRISTIANITY, CELTIC; CISTERCIAN ABBEYS IN IRELAND; COLUM CILLE; COLUMBANUS; DRUIDS; ÉIRE; ÉRIU; ERIUGENA; GAUL; HAGIOGRAPHY; IRISH; JEROME; KELLS; LAW TEXTS; MAC COLGÁIN; MONASTERIES; MONAS-

TICISM; PALLADIUS; PATRICK; PELAGIUS; PEREGRINATIO; SLAV-
ERY; SUPERSTITIONS; Carey, *Single Ray of the Sun*; Charles-
Edwards, *Early Christian Ireland*; Dumville et al., *Saint Patrick
A.D. 493–1993*; Herbert, *Iona, Kells, and Derry*; Herren, *Jean
Scot écrivain*, 265–86; Hughes, *Church in Early Irish Society*;
Hughes, *Early Christian Ireland*; Kenney, *Sources for the Early
History of Ireland*; Lennon, *Lord of Dublin in the Age of Reforma-
tion*; McNamara, *Apocrypha in the Irish Church*; Millett, *New
History of Ireland* 3.561–86; Ó Cuív, *New History of Ireland* 3.509–
45; O'Loughlin, *Celtic Theology*; O'Meara, *Eriugena*; Watt,
Church in Medieval Ireland.

Thomas O'Loughlin

Christianity in the Celtic countries [2a] Scotland before 1100

Early medieval Scotland (ALBA) was home to a range of distinct peoples, only some of whom were Celtic-speaking. The Christianization of the BRYTHONIC peoples living in close proximity and contact with northern Roman BRITAIN seems to have begun shortly before the end of direct Roman rule in Britain in AD 409/410 (perhaps somewhat earlier in the north). This process has attracted little comment from scholars, as has the Christianization of the Gaels of the Atlantic seaboard, but the Christianization of the PICTS has been the subject of lively ongoing debate. A traditional focus upon proselytizing saints such as NINIAN or COLUM CILLE has given way recently to the growing realization that such individuals did not play the key rôles formerly ascribed to them, and that the Christianization of northern Britain was a longer-drawn-out and more complex process than such saint-focused models have allowed.

Historical, place-name, and archaeological evidence come together to suggest that Christianity was already firmly established among the GAELIC and Pictish peoples by the time that Colum Cille came into contact with them (563–97). His monastery on Iona (EILEAN Ì) was the most influential force in northern ecclesiastical culture until the 8th century, when key kingdoms such as Gaelic DÁL RIATA and Pictish Fortrinn came into their own as thoroughly Christianized societies. Colum Cille himself seems to have been influential in the politics of Dál Riata and Brythonic Alt Clut (Dumbarton; see YSTRAD CLUD), as well as a monastic founder and influence among the Picts. Ionan daughter houses were the dominant ecclesiastical and Christianizing influence in northern England until 664

(see EASTER CONTROVERSY), and the monastery retained a degree of influence in Northumbria thereafter. Surviving sources from this period from Iona are uncharacteristically plentiful, and scholars have probably not exercised enough caution in assessing their understandably Iona-centred perspectives. The monastery's influence in 7th-century Pictland has probably been exaggerated as a result, but it is significant that by the end of the century it was possible for the Columban *familia* to credit itself with the Christianization of the northern Pictish zone and the founder as the father of Pictish monasticism.

Even with its formal interests in Pictland curtailed by royal decree in 717, Iona remained prominent, its influence with regard to monastic practices, ecclesiastical sculpture and art, historiography, theology, and law transcending even the insular Celtic zone, before repeated attacks on the community by Scandinavian raiders forced a reorganization of the Columban *familia* in the 9th century. Surviving contemporary evidence allows few insights, however, into the range of devotional behaviour that took place at other centres in Celtic-speaking northern Britain or in the areas affiliated with them. Scholars have long turned to the evidence of names and the retrospective writings of later periods in the hope of filling in some of these gaps, but such methods remain controversial. It is therefore difficult to move much beyond listing a few important clerics and ecclesiastical centres of northern Britain during what might be called the 'Age of Iona'. The extent to which the problematic concepts of a 'Celtic Church' or 'Celtic Christianity' may be employed to shed light upon such things as ecclesiastical organization and devotional activities among the different Celtic-speaking peoples of northern Britain is not clear. The monumental ecclesiastical sculpture of the Picts is perhaps the main body of evidence for devotional activity in northern Britain during this period, and more work is needed in this regard.

In those regions of Scotland that became occupied by Scandinavians in the Viking Age, it is difficult to ascertain the extent to which Christianity had been established beforehand or, where it had done so, the extent to which the religion endured thereafter. Meanwhile, the Gaelicization of the Pictish peoples during the course of the 9th and subsequent centuries seems to have included an ecclesiastical element. Some kind of formal realignment from Pictish to Gaelic practices took place early in the 10th century, but the details of this adjustment are quite obscure. Certainly, the severe form of Gaelic MONASTICISM practised by the Céili Dé took firm root in the Gaelicized kingdom of Alba, and prominent Pictish ecclesiastical centres such as Meigle, Portmahomack, and Abernethy seem to have declined as others such as Dunkeld (Dùn Chailleann) and, particularly, St Andrews (Cennrìmonad) grew to greater prominence. The impression of moral turpitude and decline in canonicity in the Church of 10th- and 11th-century Alba created by 12th-century reformist commentators is exaggerated, but few scholars would argue that it was entirely without foundation.

PRIMARY SOURCES

BEDA, *Historia Ecclesiastica*; Allen & Anderson, *Early Christian Monuments of Scotland*; Alan O. Anderson, *Early Sources of Scottish History AD 500 to 1286*; Alan O. Anderson & Marjorie O. Anderson, *Adomnan's Life of Columba*; Clancy & Márkus, *Iona*; Forbes, *Lives of S. Ninian and S. Kentigern*; Macquarrie, *Innes Review* 44.122–52 (Life of St Serf); Macquarrie, *Innes Review* 47.95–109 (Foundation Legend of Laurencekirk); Strecker, *Monumenta Germaniae Historica: Poetae Latini Aevi Carolini* 4.943–61.

FURTHER READING

ADOMNÁN; ALBA; BRITAIN; BRYNAICH; BRYTHONIC; CHRISTIANITY, CELTIC; COLUM CILLE; DÁL RIATA; EASTER CONTROVERSY; EILEAN Ì; GAELIC; MONASTICISM; NINIAN; PICTS; YSTRAD CLUD; Bannerman, *Innes Review* 44.14–47; Broun, *Innes Review* 42.143–50; Broun & Clancy, *Spes Scotorum*; Clancy, *Innes Review* 52.1–28; Crawford, *Conversion and Christianity in the North Sea World*; Crawford, *Scotland in Dark Age Britain*; Driscoll, *Social Identity in Early Medieval Britain* 233–52; Duncan, *Scotland*; Foster, *Picts, Gaels and Scots*; Foster, *St Andrews Sarcophagus*; Herbert, *Iona, Kells, and Derry*; Hughes, *Celtic Britain in the Early Middle Ages*; Kirby, *Innes Review* 24.6–25; Macquarrie, *Saints of Scotland*; Smith, *Church Archaeology* 19–37; Smyth, *Warlords and Holy Men*; Taylor, *Innes Review* 51.109–28. Taylor, *Records of the Scottish Church History Society* 28.1–22; Thomas, *Christianity in Britain 300–700* 93–121; Thomas, *Early Christian Archaeology of North Britain*.

James E. Fraser

Christianity in the Celtic countries [2b] Scotland c. 1100–c. 1560

Traditionally, the 12th century has been regarded as a period of change for the Scottish church. The realm was certainly brought more fully into the mainstream of western Christendom: new monastic orders made an appearance in Scotland (see MONASTICISM), with the Tironensians being introduced to Selkirk (Sailcirc) as early as 1113, from where they later moved to Kelso; a system of territorial dioceses was established, with archdeaconries, deaneries of Christianity, parishes, and cathedral chapters evolving across much of Scotland; closer links with the papacy were forged. These developments were paralleled in the secular sphere, and owe much to the influx of settlers of English or northern French origin under the encouragement of King David I (1124–53) and his successors. However, the changes must not be exaggerated. There is evidence that the diocesan system was based on ancient provinces dating from Pictish times (see PICTS), although in eastern Scotland territorial coherence was compromised by the necessity to preserve distant property rights attached to ancient churches such as Dunkeld (Dùn Chailleann); bishops with Celtic names in David I's reign point to a line of native prelates, and the diocese of Caithness (Gallaibh) was probably the only new foundation by David. Irish MONASTERIES, including houses of the ascetic reform movement, the Céili Dé, were almost certainly less decadent and secularized than the reformers suggested: some ancient foundations, as at Brechin (Breichinn), became cathedral chapters; others, like Inchaffray and Monymusk, slowly evolved into houses of Augustinian canons; Iona (not without resistance) became a Benedictine abbey (see EILEAN Ì). The changes were essentially organizational rather than spiritual.

Little is known about religious observance in medieval Scotland (ALBA); as elsewhere, there was doubtless an attachment to ancient holy sites and semi-mythical saints (see HAGIOGRAPHY), and SUPERSTITIONS, some drawing on a pagan past. Most parish churches were small, and priests usually ill-educated; there was no university in Scotland until 1410, and only the privileged few could afford to study abroad. In the 12th and 13th centuries papal legates endeavoured to standardize canonical practice to make it like that elsewhere in Europe, but there are few indications of serious deviations from orthodox doctrine, even in the 15th century when Lollard ideas were circulating in England. Some 13th-century statutes, made in the wake of the Fourth Lateran Council, survive, but evidence from the later Middle Ages suggests that many beneficed clerics were not ordained to the priesthood, and ignored the requirement for celibacy; in GAELIC-speaking areas clerical dynasties can be traced, with churches passing from father to son. These irregularities probably had little effect on pastoral work; more freely criticized were exactions of mortuaries and offerings on the part of underpaid pensionary vicars who struggled to survive on increasingly inadequate stipends due to the annexation of most parochial revenues to cathedrals, monasteries, and colleges.

The Scottish bishops, except the Bishop of WHITHORN, were freed from the metropolitan jurisdiction of York by the papal bull *Cum universi* towards the end of the 12th century. Papal involvement in Scotland, however, became increasingly important, although the initiative almost always originated locally: grants and agreements were confirmed, dispensations granted, taxes imposed, lawsuits determined by judges delegate or at the papal curia, benefices throughout the realm filled by papal provision.

The Reformation came late to Scotland. King James V (1513–42) perceived the material benefits of remaining loyal to Rome, and enacted legislation against Lutheran heresies. There was little desire for the dissolution of monasteries, since kings and magnates could use papal provisions to bestow religious houses on their children and connections, often at a young age. The reckless sale of indulgences found in parts of Europe was not paralleled in Scotland. Although there had been a growing interest in the cult of native saints such as NINIAN at Whithorn and Duthac at Tain (Baile Dubhthaich), marked by the publication of the ABERDEEN BREVIARY shortly after 1500, evidence for widespread religious change is elusive until the late 1550s, and even then it was connected with fears that the marriage of Queen Mary (1542–67) to the French dauphin might involve Scotland in undesirable Continental entanglements. Even after the formal breach with Rome in 1560, much of rural Scotland remained doctrinally conservative, and the reformers struggled to find sufficient ministers or adequate endowment for the new Protestant Church.

FURTHER READING
ABERDEEN BREVIARY; ALBA; EILEAN Ì; GAELIC; HAGIOGRAPHY; MONASTERIES; MONASTICISM; NINIAN; PICTS; SUPERSTITIONS; WHITHORN; Bannerman, *Innes Review* 48.27–44; Barrell, *Innes Review* 46.116–38; Barrell, *Medieval Scotland*; Barrell, *Papacy, Scotland and Northern England 1342–1378*; Barrow, *Kingdom of the Scots*; Cowan, *Medieval Church in Scotland*; Cowan, *Parishes of Medieval Scotland*; Cowan, *Scottish Reformation*; Cowan & Easson, *Medieval Religious Houses, Scotland*; Dilworth, *Innes Review* 37.51– 72; Dilworth, *Scottish Monasteries in the Late Middle Ages*; Donaldson, *Scottish Church History* 11–24; Dowden, *Bishops of Scotland*; Duncan, *Scotland*; Ferguson, *Medieval Papal Representatives in Scotland*; Grant, *Independence and Nationhood: Scotland*; MacGregor, *Church in the Highlands* 1–36; Sanderson, *Ayrshire and the Reformation*; Sanderson, *Scottish Historical Review* 52.117– 36; Steer & Bannerman, *Late Medieval Monumental Sculpture in the West Highlands*; Stringer, *Alba* 127–65; Veitch, *Records of the Scottish Church History Society* 29.1–22; Watt, *Biographical Dictionary of Scottish Graduates to AD 1410*; Watt, *Fasti Ecclesiae Scoticanae Medii Aevi ad annum 1638*; Watt, *Medieval Church Councils in Scotland*; Watt, *Scotland and Europe 1200–1850* 1–18; Watt & Shead, *Heads of Religious Houses in Scotland from Twelfth to Sixteenth Centuries*; Yeoman, *Pilgrimage in Medieval Scotland*.

Andrew D. M. Barrell

Christianity in the Celtic countries [2c] Scotland after 1560

In contrast to Wales (CYMRU), the Reformation in Scotland and subsequent developments affecting the Christian churches there have taken place at a period when the majority of the population and the main cultural institutions were already English and/or Scots speaking.

The Reformation in Scotland (ALBA) began as a rebellion against the state and it struck an anti-Erastian note (i.e. opposing the subordination of the church to secular authority) that has resonated to the present. From its origin in 1560, the reformed Church of Scotland was conciliar in government and hostile to state control, unlike the Church of England. Through the influence of John Knox (1505–72), who had had personal experience of John Calvin's Geneva, the Church of Scotland was Calvinistic, but its presbyterian structure was not fully established until 1592 (Burleigh, *Church History of Scotland* 142ff.). It was later undermined by King James VI (James I of England) who, in 1612, managed to secure parliamentary sanction for a mixed Episcopalian-cum-Presbyterian system. Presbyterian resentment was hard to overcome, however, and under Charles I growing discontent led in 1637 to a revolt against a new Anglican-style Prayer Book. A year later, the National Covenant against the King's policies was signed in Edinburgh (DÙN ÈIDEANN), and shortly after the Covenanters seized power and swept away not only the bishops but also royal control of parliament. Reform of the state as well as the church was essential to the movement (Stevenson, *Covenanters*). The political theories of George Buchanan, the great 16th-century humanist and associate of Knox, strongly influenced the Presbyterians, who rejected the claims of divine right kingship (McFarlane, *Buchanan* 392–415).

In 1641 Charles I was forced to accept the new Scottish constitution in church and state, but a year after the outbreak of the Civil War in England the Covenanters, fearful of a royal victory, allied with the Parliamentarians under the Solemn League and Covenant. This gave rise to the Westminster Assembly of 1643, which produced its famous Confession of Faith and Catechisms. These were markedly Calvinist, and in later opinion hyper-Calvinist. They were accepted by the Church of Scotland and have been retained to this day, though now much criticized (*Westminster Confession of Faith*; Heron, *Westminster Confession in the Church Today*). The breach between the Covenanters and the English Independents came at the end of the First Civil War over the execution of Charles I in 1649, and this quarrel led ultimately to the Cromwellian conquest of Scotland and its incorporation into the Commonwealth.

After the Restoration of the Monarchy in 1660, however, Episcopacy was restored in Scotland, the Westminster standards were dropped, and jettisoned also were the constitutional reforms that had been accepted by the Crown in 1641. But the repressive Restoration regime failed to overcome Presbyterian resentment and this became apparent at the Revolution of 1688. The Scottish Revolution Settlement under William and Mary rejected the Episcopalian regime in 1689, and a year later Presbyterianism and Westminster Standards were reinstated, but without reference to the Covenants.

At the UNION of England and Scotland in 1707 Presbyterian Church government in Scotland was guaranteed; but in 1712 the seeds of future strife were sown by the Act of Parliament restoring lay patronage in Scotland, an Act designed to cause trouble and notably successful in doing so until its repeal in 1874. Successive schisms arose over lay patronage, for example, the First Secession headed by the Revd Ebenezer Erskine in 1733, which later repeatedly split (MacEwen, *Erskines*). Then, in 1761, disputes over presentations led to the founding of the Relief Church. All the dissenting Presbyterian Churches, however, clung to the standards of the Church of Scotland and its Reformation principles, and some (Cameronians and Seceders) to the Covenants. They were, however, opposed not only to lay patronage but also to the attitudes of the Moderate Party, which from 1752 controlled the General Assemblies of the established Church. The Moderates struck a *modus vivendi* with the state, equated enthusiasm in religion with fanaticism, and contributed to the Enlightenment (Clark, *Scotland in the Age of Improvement* 200–24). But, to their evangelical opponents, they seemed to preach enlightened philosophy rather than the gospel. The problem for the Moderates came to be that the evangelical tradition in the Church of Scotland itself, let alone among the Presbyterian dissenters, did not die out but was reinvigorated by the 'Awakening' of the late 18th century.

In 1834, after years of struggle, the Evangelical Party gained control of the General Assembly of the Church of Scotland and passed the Veto Act which empowered congregations to reject unwelcome presentations made by patrons. The resulting bitter 'Ten Years' Conflict' ended with the intervention of the civil courts and the defeat of the non-intrusionists led by the Revd Thomas Chalmers (Brown, *Thomas Chalmers and the Godly Commonwealth in Scotland* 282–349). This crisis brought on the Disruption in 1843 and the setting up of the Free Church of Scotland, a serious blow to the established church (Henderson, *Heritage*). The Disruption was the last and greatest rift in Scottish Presbyterianism and from then on the trend was towards reunion (McCrie, *Church of Scoltand*). Thus, in 1847, the United Secession Church and the Relief Church joined to form the United Presbyterian Church.

Then, towards the end of the 19th century, the churches were alarmed by the onward march of science and its ally, rationalism (Ferguson, *Scottish Christianity in the Modern World* 53–89). In 1882, for example, a noted Presbyterian Church historian, John Cunningham, lamented the spread of atheism in Scotland (Cunningham, *Church History of Scotland* 2.549). The rise of theological liberalism, which refuted the literal acceptance of Scripture, was opposed by traditional Calvinists (Cheyne, *Transforming of the Kirk*). On this issue, in 1893, the rigidly Calvinist Free Presbyterians broke away from the Free Church. But, overall, reunion was still the prevailing trend, and in 1900 the United Presbyterian Church merged with the Free Church to form the United Free Church, a majority of which, in

1929, rejoined the Church of Scotland whose spiritual independence was fully recognized in Acts of Parliament of 1921 and 1925 (Burleigh, *Church History of Scotland* Part 4, Chapter 6; Sjölinder, *Presbyterian Reunion in Scotland 1907–1921*). Evidently, the stance of the dissenters had not been in vain. Remnants of the old dissenting denominations, however, refused to unite and have continued as separate, though now dwindling, churches, chiefly the Free Presbyterians (1893), the Free Church (1900), and the United Free Church (1929). It should be noted, however, that in spite of its divisive history Scottish Presbyterianism has long had links with other reformed churches, not only in the British Isles and Europe but also in the USA, Canada, Australia, New Zealand, South Africa, and Malawi (Cowan, *Influence of the Scottish Church in Christendom*; Moffat, *Presbyterian Churches*).

Other denominations exist in present-day Scotland, two of which have had chequered histories since the Reformation. Roman Catholicism survived, but was steadily worn down. By the mid-18th century the old faith was mainly confined to a few areas in the HIGHLANDS and Western Isles. Here, all the competing churches found difficulties owing to remoteness, rugged terrain, and not least a culture clash. With inadequate resources, they all needed to provide a GAELIC-speaking ministry and were hampered by the absence of Christian literature in SCOTTISH GAELIC. The lack of a Gaelic BIBLE long troubled the Protestants and, in spite of prolonged efforts, little was achieved until 1690 when Robert Kirk, minister of Aberfoyle, published his rendering of the Irish Bible into Gaelic and in Roman type. This led, in the course of the 18th century, to the triumph of Presbyterianism in the Highlands (MacInnes, *Evangelical Movement in the Highlands of Scotland 1688 to 1800*).

How weak the Roman Catholic Church had become in 18th-century Scotland plainly emerges from the Revd Alexander Webster's work on the population of Scotland in 1755. Based on the returns made to him by his fellow Church of Scotland ministers most shires recorded very low numbers of Roman Catholics, and some Lowland shires made nil returns (Kyd, *Scottish Population Statistics*). Support for the Jacobite cause had worsened the situation of the Roman Catholics since 1688 (see JACOBITE REBELLIONS). In the institutional sense, the Roman Catholic Church in Scotland scarcely existed, being little more than an impoverished mission feebly directed from Rome. Catholic Emancipation in 1829 improved the position, while immigration from Ireland (ÉIRE), particularly after the catastrophic FAMINE Years of 1845–50, greatly increased the number of Roman Catholics in Scotland. This was especially the case in the industrializing Lowland counties where there was a demand for labour (see LOWLANDS). The Roman Catholic Episcopal hierarchy was restored in 1878 in spite of some opposition, and since then the Roman Catholic Church's adherents have flourished and now constitute the second largest Christian denomination in Scotland (Anson, *Underground Catholicism in Scotland 1622–1878*).

The third largest communion in Scotland today, the Episcopalians, actually derive from the 17th century when bishops governed the Church of Scotland from 1610 to 1638 and again from 1661 to 1689. After the reintroduction of Presbyterian government in 1690 many people in Scotland still adhered to Episcopacy, but their support for the exiled Stewarts in the rebellions of 1715 and 1745 led to persecution, and their numbers steadily diminished. From the early 19th century, however, when their loyalty was no longer in question, the Episcopal Church in Scotland, formed in 1804 by a union of nonjurors (who refused to recognize the Revolution Settlement) and the Qualified Episcopalians (who did), has prospered. It is in full communion with the Church of England, but is autonomous with its own constitution headed by a Primus and with its own Prayer Book (Goldie, *Short History of the Episcopal Church in Scotland*).

Baptists and Congregationalists appeared in Scotland in the second half of the 18th century, but like the Methodists their main institutional development came in the 19th century. More recently Pentecostal Churches, Brethren, and Salvation Army, with some Mormons, are also represented.

The outstanding fact, however, is that the main Christian influence in Scotland from the Reformation to the present has been Presbyterian, and this has had a marked impact on education and general culture. But, today, Christianity in Scotland is no longer the potent force that it was. Secular trends have led to falling church attendances and to church closures, and in varying degrees these developments have affected all denominations (Highet, *Scottish Churches*). A more recent writer on the subject strikes a sharper note and concludes that 'organized religion appears at present to be on the path towards the margins of social significance' (Brown, *Social History of Religion in Scotland since 1730* 256). But the ways of providence are proverbially inscrutable, and it may be that the present perceived threat to Christianity will do more for Christian unity than decades of ecumenical talks have done.

FURTHER READING
ALBA; BIBLE; CYMRU; DÙN ÈIDEANN; ÉIRE; FAMINE; GAELIC; HIGHLANDS; JACOBITE REBELLIONS; LOWLANDS; SCOTTISH GAELIC; UNION; Anson, *Underground Catholicism in Scotland 1622–1878*; Brown, *Social History of Religion in Scotland since 1730*; Brown, *Thomas Chalmers and the Godly Commonwealth in Scotland* 282–349; Burleigh, *Church History of Scotland*; Cheyne, *Transforming of the Kirk*; Clark, *Scotland in the Age of Improvement* 200–24; Cowan, *Influence of the Scottish Church in Christendom*; Cunningham, *Church History of Scotland*; Ferguson, *Scottish Christianity in the Modern World* 53–89; Goldie, *Short History of the Episcopal Church in Scotland*; Henderson, *Heritage*; Heron, *Westminster Confession in the Church Today*; Highet, *Scottish Churches*; Kyd, *Scottish Population Statistics*; McCrie, *Church of Scotland*; MacEwen, *Erskines*; McFarlane, *Buchanan*; MacInnes, *Evangelical Movement in the Highlands of Scotland 1688 to 1800*; Moffat, *Presbyterian Churches*; Sjölinder, *Presbyterian Reunion in Scotland 1907–1921*; Stevenson, *Covenanters*.

William Ferguson

Christianity in the Celtic countries [3] Isle of Man

§1. OVERVIEW

The date at which the Isle of Man (ELLAN VANNIN) became Christian and the origin of the missionaries who arrived on the island are both uncertain. While the dominant tradition is of conversion by a Patrician mission from Ireland (ÉRIU)—there are four quite standard OGAM inscriptions—other strands of linguistic evidence link the earliest church on the island with Wales (CYMRU), north-west England, and Galloway (Gall Ghàidhil). It is possible that Christianity arrived from Britain during the Roman period and that the later medieval interpretations of this earliest phase merely reflect the dominant tradition that emerged from a complex of Irish, Welsh, and Northumbrian influences. The multiple dedications of churches to PATRICK, Columba (COLUM CILLE), Cuthbert, and NINIAN seem to reflect this diversity of influence—the island has no patron saint.

Despite the problem of absolute chronology, the wealth of cross slabs, INSCRIPTIONS, and chapel sites that date on typological grounds from between AD 600 and 800 suggests a strong and vigorous religious life during this period. One major monastery at Maughold, another at Peel and possibly a third, dedicated to Leoc, near modern Ballasalla provided literate, educated foci that were in regular contact with religious communities around the Irish Sea.

The arrival and eventual acquisition of the island by the Vikings may have brought a brief period of paganism, but the persistence of the local population—evidenced by personal names in runic inscriptions—suggests that Christianity probably survived in some form throughout the Viking Age. The Vikings used existing cemeteries, such as the one at Balladoole, from the start and within a generation were burying their dead in Manx-style coffins and marking their graves with Christianized forms of contemporary Scandinavian art styles.

With the creation of the Norse KINGDOM OF MAN and the Isles, Peel Castle became the focal point for both secular and religious authority on the island. An 11th-century church and Irish round tower, which now dominate St Patrick's Isle off the town of Peel, appear to have been preceded by a structure close in form to a 9th-century Irish cathedral, suggesting that the existing monastic community was used as a major seat of an early 'itinerant' bishop.

The 12th century saw a raft of reforms, many of them introduced by Ólafr I, who, having been educated in the court of Henry II in England, returned to the island to reign for 40 years. The King brought in the Savignacs from Furness to found Rushen Abbey in 1134. At the time of his death in 1153 the Pope was in the process of reorganizing the northern European dioceses on 'modern' lines, leading to the creation of a diocese usually dubbed *sodorensis*—of the southern isles, that is, the Scottish Western Isles and Man (see SODOR; HIGHLANDS)—within the province of Nidaros (modern Trondheim). The new diocesesan organization directly reflected the power politics of the region at the time.

The other major reform was the creation of parishes, originally 16 in all. The earliest Synodal Ordinances (*c.* 1230) show that these were already in place, but that adequate provision still had to be made to accommodate resident parish priests.

In the early 13th century a new cathedral was built by Bishop Simon on St Patrick's Isle, and the bishop became a significant landowner and secular baron of the island. With the sale of the Isle of Man and the Western Isles to the Scots by the Treaty of Perth in 1266 Scottish kings appointed the bishops until 1374, by which time English control of the island had become more secure. The diocese became divided and Man on its own came within the province of York. In addition to the bishop, the Abbot of Rushen and Prioress of Douglas were significant landowners and barons in their own right and, together with the bishop, in a period of political instability, provided a major source of civil and well as religious authority. In the late 14th century the Order of Friars Minor were invited to establish a house on the island, with land provided at Bymaken in Arbory.

At the Dissolution, Edward, sixth earl of Derby and 'king' of Man, dissolved the monasteries on the island and eventually paid the proceeds to Henry VIII's exchequer in London. During the latter part of the 16th century the Reformation came to Man, and the Manx exchanged services in one foreign language, Latin, for another, English. There is no evidence of any recusancy, as occurred in the Earl's Lancashire estates. In 1611 Bishop Phillips began the process of rectifying this situation with a Manx translation of the Prayer Book—the earliest document to survive in the language (see MANX LITERATURE [2]). Although parts of the New Testament were translated later in the century, not until the late 18th century was the whole Bible made available in MANX.

The English Civil Wars came to Man and forced a short break in ecclesiastical authority, although the Church courts seem to have operated more or less normally throughout the period. During the latter part of the 17th century there is evidence for a degree of persecution of the Quakers who had established themselves on the island, especially in the north-eastern parish of Maughold. By the end of the century, however, presentation at the Church courts, the principal means of controlling religious deviancy, had ceased. In other words, the Manx were content to allow the Quakers to worship according to their own beliefs.

The 18th century is dominated by the work of two Anglican bishops—Wilson (r. 1698–1755) and Hildesley (r. 1755–72), and by the arrival of Methodism in 1758—John Wesley himself visiting in 1777 and 1781. The bishops did much for the Manx people. In addition to completing the translation of the Bible in 1775, they interested themselves in educational reform, poor relief and the development of an educated clergy. Bishop Wilson, who displayed great personal generosity, was a man of saintly life, and is still greatly revered today.

Methodism was very successful on the island. It seems to have appealed to the many independent small farmers who had received virtual freehold of their farms as early as the 1500s. In a Methodist context they could become readers and preachers, and enjoy a significant rôle in religious life denied them by the more formal and 'educated' Anglican establishment. Although Methodism coexisted with the established church for a number of decades, with many individuals attending both 'churches', by the middle of the 19th century they had become major competitors for the souls and minds of the Manx.

Small numbers of Roman Catholics arrived in the island during the 18th and 19th centuries, and with emancipation became firmly established there.

Christianity is still a major influence in Manx life. Church attendance has declined less than in neighbouring Britain, and relations between the major traditions are good. Despite a still active 'High-Church' presence deriving from the Oxford Movement, the Anglican church is mainly 'Low Church' and Protestant values still extend far beyond the walls of the churches, evidenced by the size and longevity of Manx temperance movements, for example. Even today there is a strongly dissenting tone (i.e. in opposition to the Anglican Church) to many of the debates in the House of Keys. The bishop, the one surviving medieval baron, still retains a seat and a vote in the Legislative Council, the upper house of the Manx parliament, TYNWALD. The churches themselves, often working ecumenically, remain significant players in education, welfare and social life.

FURTHER READING
COLUM CILLE; CYMRU; ELLAN VANNIN; ÉRIU; HIGH CROSSES; HIGHLANDS; INSCRIPTIONS; KINGDOM OF MAN; MANX; MANX LITERATURE [2]; NINIAN; OGAM; PATRICK; SODOR; TYNWALD; Belchem, *New History of the Isle of Man 5*; Beuermann, *Man amongst Kings and Bishops*; Cubbon, *Early Church in Western Britain and Ireland* 257–82; Davey et al., *New History of the Isle of Man 2*; Davey, *New History of the Isle of Man 3*; Freke, *Excavations on St Patrick's Isle, Peel, Isle of Man 1982–88*;

Kermode, *Manx Crosses*; Moore, *History of the Isle of Man*; Woolf, *New History of the Isle of Man 3*.

§2. HIGH MEDIEVAL MONASTICISM

By the middle of the 13th century, with the consecration of St German's Cathedral in Peel, the Norse kings of Man (ELLAN VANNIN) had brought the island into the mainstream of contemporary western Christianity (Broderick, *Cronica Regum Mannie et Insularum /Chronicles of the Kings of Man and the Isles*). The bishop of SODOR and Man ceased to be peripatetic and had a permanent seat on St Patrick's Isle, Peel (Harrison, *Account of the Diocese of Sodor and Man and St German's Cathedral*). The present parish structure had been created, together with resident priests and an elaborate tithe system, all based on coherent episcopal policy and authority. An essential element in these developments was the introduction of the reformed orders into the Island.

In 1134 Ólafr I (1113–53) donated land 'in Russin' for the foundation of a daughter house to the Savignac Abbey of Furness. In 1176 Ólafr's son Godred II (1153–87) was married to Fionnula, a daughter to Mac Lochlann, son of Muircheartach, king of Ireland (ÉRIU), by Sylvanus, abbot of Rievaulx, to whom he granted land in the north of the island at Myroscough to build a monastery. By the end of the 13th century the whole estate had been taken over by Rushen Abbey (Broderick, *Cronica Regum Mannie et Insularum/ Chronicles of the Kings of Man and the Isles* fo. 40r).

At some point during his reign, Godred's son Reginald I (1187–1228) founded a Cistercian nunnery at Douglas.

The Norse kings' interest in the expansion of monastic influence was not restricted to the endowment of monasteries located on the island. Grants of Manx lands and vicarages were made to a number of houses, of different orders, which were located at sites around the northern Irish Sea. St Bees (Benedictine—Cumbria; Wilson, *Register of the Priory of St Bees*), WHITHORN (Premonstratensian—Galloway; Talbot, *Priory of Whithern*), BEANN CHAR (Ireland) and Sabal (Augustinian—Co. Down; Broderick, *Bulletin of the Ulster Place-name Society* 2nd series 4.24–6), and Furness itself were all endowed to a greater or lesser extent. St Bees was also given favourable trading rights. Thus, by the mid-13th century the monastic orders owned a significant proportion of Manx farmland, and tithe income from at least half of the parishes. Other neighbouring abbeys such as Holm Cultram (Cistercian—Cumbria; Granger & Collingwood, *Register and Records of Holm Cultram*) and the important Benedictine abbey of St Werburghs, Chester (CAER; Tait, *Chartulary or Register of the Abbey of St Werburgh, Chester*) were given economic advantages on the island and in its waters (Davey, *New History of the Isle of Man 3*).

The other major landholder on the island, apart from the Lord himself, was the Bishop of the Isles who, because the power of election had been given to the monks of Furness, was often a Cistercian himself or a man with strong monastic affiliations.

The history of medieval MONASTICISM on Man is completed by the foundation of the Friary of Bemaken (Ballabeg; Barratt, *Journal of the Manx Museum* 6.80.209–13) for the Dublin-based order of Friars Minor by William de Montacute in 1367. Although the dissolution of Rushen Abbey, Douglas Priory, and Bemaken Friary took place in June 1540, their lands continued to be administered as separate entities until 1911.

The influence of the monasteries, especially Rushen, on the development of Manx social, economic, and cultural life was profound. Not only did the Abbey bring from the Continent new agricultural and industrial ideas to Man, but also, during periods of marginalization and uncertainty, especially following the Treaty of Perth in 1266, maintained its links with Furness and represented a vital element of stability and political continuity.

PRIMARY SOURCES
Broderick, *Cronica Regum Mannie et Insularum / Chronicles of the Kings of Man and the Isles*.

FURTHER READING
BEANN CHAR; CAER; ELLAN VANNIN; ÉRIU; MONASTICISM; SODOR; WHITHORN; Barratt, *Journal of the Manx Museum* 6.209–13; Broderick, *Bulletin of the Ulster Place-name Society* 2nd series 4.24–6; Castle Rushen Papers, *Journal of the Manx Museum* 2.21; Cheney, CMCS 7.63; Granger & Collingwood, *Register and Records of Holm Cultram*; Harrison, *Account of the Diocese of Sodor and Man and St German's Cathedral*; Tait, *Chartulary*; Talbot, *Priory of Whithern*; Wilson, *Register of the Priory of St Bees*.

P. J. **Davey**

Christianity in the Celtic countries [4] Wales

Christianity first came to what is now Wales (CYMRU) during the Roman occupation. The Christian martyrs Aaron and Julian of CAERLLION, mentioned by GILDAS, probably died in the persecution of Emperor Diocletian (AD 303–5). Having survived the collapse of Roman rule in Britain (AD 409/10), Christianity underwent a period of consolidation and expansion during the late 5th and 6th centuries, at which point it becomes meaningful to refer to the WELSH language and nation first emerging into history as distinct entities, and there began what has become known as the 'Age of the Saints'. This was a period during which men such as Cybi and DEINIOL in the north, and TEILO and David (DEWI SANT) in the south, prepared a foundation upon which the Church would develop into the future. Under their guidance Welsh Christianity developed apace and was strong enough to safeguard its autonomy even after the arrival of the Roman mission of AUGUSTINE of Canterbury in Britain in 597. It was not until 768 that it came into conformity with the practices of Augustine's successors in England by accepting the Roman calculation of the date for Easter (see EASTER CONTROVERSY), but the influence of the Welsh saints had by then left an indelible mark on the Welsh mind and culture, as evidenced by the innumerable *llannau* (churches, churchyards) which bear their names.

Following the Norman Conquest, the Welsh Church, which even after the 8th century had still enjoyed a considerable measure of independence, was deprived of its status as a 'national' Church, a development which caused considerable resentment among native Christians, both lay and clerical. The Normans believed that a centralized Church would help strengthen their hold on the land, and therefore sought to subject the Church throughout Britain to the rule of the Archbishop of Canterbury. In their desire to remain self-governing, the Welsh held out until 1108 when Urban, the first Norman bishop of Llandaf, swore allegiance to the English see. By the mid-12th century, the other Welsh bishops had also capitulated, and where previously the Welsh had looked directly to Rome, they now came under the authority of Canterbury and thus, indirectly, the authority of the English Crown.

Uniformity now became the order of the day and, as territorial parishes were established, the traditional *clas* of the old Welsh church disappeared. Continental monastic orders were introduced and, although the Benedictines proved unpopular since they were too closely associated with the conquerors, the Cistercians were regarded with greater favour and able, as a result, to erect houses away from towns and garrisons at locations such as Strata Florida (YSTRAD-FFLUR), Aberconwy, Margam, Neath, and Whitland (see CISTERCIAN ABBEYS IN WALES; MONASTICISM).

The subjugation of Wales by outside influences and authorities continued. By 1283, Edward I of England had finally secured a military conquest, while the Pope, by intervening in ecclesiastical appointments, ensured that the number of native Welshmen appointed to Welsh livings and offices after 1323 declined. As bubonic plague spread throughout Europe in 1347–8, and between 30% and 40% of the population succumbed, the Roman Catholic Church, though having by now become a major power in European politics, could do little to comfort the people. At the same time, the standard of discipline, learning, and even morality among the clergy was rapidly deteriorating.

The frustration and resentment that these factors caused did not find expression in Wales until 1400, when a revolt occurred under the leadership of OWAIN GLYNDŴR. He insisted that the Welsh people had a right not only to political self-determination but also to ecclesiastical autonomy, and that a specifically Welsh archbishop should be enthroned at St David's (Tyddewi). By 1413, however, the rebellion was over and the vision but a memory. The church limped on and, although a partial spiritual renewal occurred during the second half of the 15th century, this was not sufficient to counter the effects of years of decline, or to generate men of suitable calibre to secure the radical reformation that was by then needed.

As in England, it was politics rather than theology which first instituted change as Henry VIII attempted to secure for himself a male heir. Wales's loyalty to him as a descendant of a Welsh dynasty (see TUDUR), coupled with the widespread spiritual lethargy and the disillusionment that was so characteristic of the period, ensured that there was little opposition to his reorganization of the Church and his abolition of the monastic orders. By 1540, all 47 of the Welsh religious houses had been dissolved. However, the political imperatives which had initially provided the motivation for change were soon replaced by the renewing forces of Protestant theology, and it was not long before the emphases found on the Continent were also to be seen in Wales: a new vitality, a deeper spirituality, a recognition of the need for evangelization and an acceptance of the Scriptures as the ultimate authority in both faith and conduct were all in evidence among leading churchmen. It was they who, eager to ensure that the Welsh accepted the principles of the REFORMATION, gained the authorities' permission to translate both the Book of Common Prayer and the BIBLE into Welsh. The New Testament and the Prayer Book, both translated mainly by William SALESBURY and Richard Davies, bishop of St David's, were published in 1567, followed in 1588 by William MORGAN's monumental translation of the whole of the Bible, an achievement which has been rightly described by many as one of the most momentous events in Welsh history.

The 1567 New Testament was presented to the nation with a preface, written by Bishop Richard Davies, in which he sought to promote the new Anglican way by describing it as a return to the practices and beliefs of the native Celtic Church (see CHRISTIANITY, CELTIC). He claimed that the gospel had been brought to Wales by the preaching of Joseph of Arimathea, and that the Celtic Church had preserved an early and pure tradition of Christian witness and preaching until the arrival of Augustine at Canterbury in 597. It was Augustine who had corrupted this Church with the errors of Rome and, according to Bishop Davies, the Reformation had now purged the Celtic Church and returned it to its former purity.

Although some had hoped that Mary's accession in 1553 would restore Roman Catholicism to Wales, the same general lukewarmness that had greeted her father's changes now blighted her attempts to reverse the reforming process. Protestantism had not yet established itself in the minds of the common people as the only valid expression of the Christian faith, and for that reason they showed little reaction to Mary's policies and to the return to the 'old faith'. In fact, there were only three Protestant martyrs in Wales during Mary's reign: Robert Ferrar, the former bishop of St David's, William Nichol of Haverfordwest (Hwlffordd), and Rawlins White, a fisherman from Cardiff (CAERDYDD).

Among the positive repercussions of William Morgan's translation of the Bible were the preservation of the Welsh language and the Welsh way of life. Morgan's feat contributed towards a rediscovery of a national and religious identity, and this was reinforced by Welsh Puritans who not only believed that the religious settlement of Elizabeth I had been insufficiently radical, but also that more should have been done to enlighten the people as to the true meaning of the gospel. These were the pioneers of the dissenting and nonconforming congregations which were soon to appear, and among them was John Penry (1563–93), a young Welshman who bemoaned the apparent lack of concern among the bishops over the spiritual condition of his compatriots. His protests, together with his association with a group of clandestine and illegal nonconformists, branded Penry a traitor, and he was executed at London during the spring of 1593, aged 29.

It was towards the middle of the 17th century that nonconformist churches were established in Wales. Under the leadership of William Wroth, William Erbury, Walter Cradock, Vavasor Powell, Morgan Llwyd, and John Miles, Puritanism achieved a tenuous foothold that allowed the gathering of Congregationalist, Baptist, Presbyterian, and Quaker congregations. Although some EMIGRATION occurred, especially among the Quakers, following the restoration of 1660, many of the other Churches succeeded in maintaining their witness despite sometimes savage persecution. When religious tolerance was partly achieved through the 1689 Toleration Act, the Dissenters entered a period of inertia as they enjoyed the peace that had eluded them for so long, and this was to last well into the 18th century.

The Methodist Revival began in Wales during the spring of 1735, when Howell Harris (1714–73), a young Anglican from Breconshire (sir Frycheiniog), underwent a conversion experience. Though much was done to prepare the way for an awakening by the CIRCULATING SCHOOLS of Griffith Jones (1684–1761), the educationalist from Llanddowror, it was the preaching of men like Harris, Daniel Rowland (1713–90) of Llangeitho and Howell Davies of Pembrokeshire (sir Benfro) that ignited the spirits of the converts. The hymns, poetry and prose of William WILLIAMS of Pantycelyn then provided them with a means of expressing their newly-found faith. The revival gained its following among ordinary Welsh people by means of the *seiat* or 'society meeting' in which converts met regularly to pray and to learn about the new life into which they had been reborn. These were organized in every part of the country. In 1742, the leaders, doctrinally all Calvinists, formed an Association, which assumed control of the Calvinistic Methodist movement throughout Wales. They remained loyal to the Anglican Church, though conscious of its shortcomings, and it was not until 1811, long after the first generation had died, that the movement seceded to form the Calvinistic Methodist Connexion, later the Presbyterian Church of Wales. Despite their departure, there still remained a large group of evangelicals within the established Church, which demonstrated the strength, extent and influence of the revival.

Although the Dissenters had initially failed to assimilate the spirit of Methodism, long before the end of the 18th century they had not only been strongly influenced by it, but they had also gained hugely from it. As their numbers grew, and as the Calvinistic and by then Wesleyan Methodists seceded and joined their ranks, under the leadership of men such as Thomas Charles (1755–1814) of Bala, Thomas Jones (1756–1820) of Denbigh (Dinbych), John Elias (1774–1841), Christmas Evans (1776–1838) and William Williams (1781–1840) of Wern, a large and multifarious body of Nonconformists had emerged which by 1851 had exceeded the number of Welsh Anglicans. This led not only to a new vitality in Welsh culture, but also to a desire to see the Church of England disestablished. Following a prolonged campaign, this was finally achieved in 1920.

The religious history of Wales during the 19th and early 20th centuries was characterized by sporadic revivals. These were varied in the extent of their influence and in their duration, some being short and local and others national and lasting for several months. Among the better known are the revivals of 1859 and 1904–5, both of which secured thousands of new members for the Nonconformist Churches. However, the 1904–5 Revival was the last revival to take place on a national scale, and since that time Welsh Christianity has been in decline. Changes in working practices, the rise of the Labour Movement with its often quasi-religious message of social improvement, greater leisure opportunities and a wide range of other factors, all contributed towards the working-class rejection of traditional religious forms. Two World Wars also affected attitudes: soldiers returning from the trenches of the Great War had little time for a religion which had seemingly given its wholesale support to the conflict, while the dawn of the atomic age at Hiroshima and Nagasaki horrified a later generation. Against this background, the rise of liberal theology, with its belief in the fundamental goodness and unity of creation and the inevitable progress of history towards perfection, appeared inconsistent with the experiences of many. The claims of Christianity suddenly rang hollow. Having been relegated to the shadows of public life in Wales for generations, the Roman Catholic Church re-emerged during the 20th century to take its place alongside the other Christian traditions. The Anglican tradition also flourished briefly during the 1950s and 1960s as Nonconformity continued to decline. In an attempt to turn the tide, an ecumenical movement appeared among the Nonconformist denominations, and called on the various strands of the dissenting tradition to merge into a single national Church. A process of consultation was embarked upon in the 1990s and a draft plan submitted to the churches. This was rejected by the Congregationalists (Annibynwyr) in 2001. With many new non-denominational, charismatic and Pentecostal churches thriving, mainly as English-language communities, the traditional denominations continue to decline, but are now seeking new ways of co-operating as Welsh Christianity faces an uncertain future.

The elevation of a Welsh-speaking Welshman Rowan Williams as Augustine's successor as Archbishop of Canterbury in 2002 was accompanied by an immediate swell of national pride in Wales as well as controversy in the British press over the popular perceptions of pre-Christian associations of the modern DRUIDS of GORSEDD BEIRDD YNYS PRYDAIN, of which Dr Williams is one. However, it is as yet too early to judge whether this historically evocative milestone will prove a turning point for Christianity in Wales in the 21st century.

FURTHER READING
AUGUSTINE; BIBLE; CAERDYDD; CAERLLION; CHRISTIANITY, CELTIC; CIRCULATING SCHOOLS; CISTERCIAN ABBEYS IN WALES; CYMRU; DEINIOL; DEWI SANT; DRUIDS; EASTER CONTROVERSY; EMIGRATION; GILDAS; GORSEDD BEIRDD YNYS PRYDAIN; MONASTICISM; MORGAN; OWAIN GLYNDŴR; REFORMATION; SALESBURY; TEILO; TUDUR; WELSH; WILLIAMS; YSTRAD-FFLUR; Bowen, *Saints, Seaways and Settlements*; Bowen, *Settlements of the Celtic Saints in Wales*; E. T. Davies, *Religion and Society in the Nineteenth Century*; Oliver Davies, *Celtic Christianity*

in Early Medieval Wales; Jenkins, Foundations of Modern Wales 1642–1780; Jenkins, Literature, Religion and Society in Wales 1660–1730; R. Tudur Jones, Great Reformation; Morgan, Span of the Cross; Victory, Celtic Church in Wales; Walker, History of the Church in Wales; Glanmor Williams, Welsh Church from Conquest to Reformation.

Geraint Tudur

Christianity in the Celtic countries [5] Brittany

§1. LATE ANTIQUITY AND THE MIDDLE AGES

Introduction

The migration of people to Brittany (BREIZH) in late antiquity and the early Middle Ages is the defining event in the early history of the country. Our view of the date, nature, and motivation of this event has changed greatly in recent years, and is still a matter of debate; it is clear, however, that the rôle played by Christianity in this migration is of central importance. The subsequent development of the Breton churches, under the Normans and Angevins in particular, shows that Brittany was increasingly drawn, politically and ecclesiastically, into a wider European world, although some features, such as its abundance of saints, gave the Breton Church a noticeably 'Celtic' appearance (see CHRISTIANITY, CELTIC).

Roman Armorica and the coming of Christianity

In the Roman period, the portion of ARMORICA which was roughly equivalent to the later extent of Brittany came under the jurisdiction of the Roman province of Lugdunensis III, presided over by the metropolitan of Tours. By the 5th century Christianity must have been relatively well established there, as it was in other peripheral regions of GAUL. Two reputedly 3rd-century Nantes martyrs, St Donatien and St Rogatien, are attested in 5th- and 6th-century sources. Other areas of Brittany show fragmentary and isolated evidence of Christianity prior to the 6th century, in particular the regional centres of Rennes (ROAZHON), Vannes (GWENED), Alet, Quimper (KEMPER), and Carhaix (KARAEZ). The diocesan structure is more difficult to identify, but Breton bishops attended provincial councils in the 5th century. Nantes (NAONED), Rennes, and Vannes (itself the site of a council c. 463) are the diocesan seats mentioned by name (Clercq, Concilia Galliae A. 511–A. 695 13), but other sees are implied. The council of Tours of 567 (Clercq, Concilia Galliae A. 511–A. 695 179) asserted the authority of Tours over the 'Romans' and 'Bretons'; since Rennes, Nantes, and Vannes already acknowledged the authority of Tours, this decree may be assumed to refer to Christians further afield.

The Breton migrations

One of the most vexed questions, however, is the extent to which the Christianity of the Brythonic emigrants of the 4th to the 7th centuries might have set them apart (either self-consciously or not) from the Armoricans, and the effect this may or may not have had on the development of Brittany as a distinctive social and political entity (see BRETON MIGRATIONS). At the very least, the migration included significant numbers of clergy, and coincided with an increasing, especially rural, Christianization of Armorica/Brittany.

Notwithstanding the reasonable objections to the unexamined use of the term 'Celtic' with respect to medieval Christianity, it is fair to say that in many ways early medieval Christianity in Brittany seems to have resembled that of other Celtic regions. The promulgations of the 5th-century Council of Vannes (Munier, Concilia Galliae A. 314–A. 505 150–6) seem to describe monastic practices similar to those found in other Celtic regions (see Fleuriot, Les origines de la Bretagne 232–3). An early 6th-century letter (Duchesne, Revue de Bretagne et de Vendée 57.5–21) from several bishops, among them the bishop of Rennes and the metropolitan of Tours, to the peripatetic Breton priests Louocatus and Catihernus identifies what could be seen as distinctively 'Celtic' practices—the moving from house to house and the distribution of the sacrament in two kinds, with women (conhospitae) administering the chalice to the congregation while the priests administered the host themselves. Wrdisten, the 9th-century author of a Life of St Guénolé (Old Breton UUINUUALOE), the founder of the abbey of LANDEVENNEG, includes a diploma from the Carolingian emperor Louis the Pious which criticizes the monks' customs and tonsure as 'Irish' (2.12–13, see Smedt, Analecta Bollandiana 7.226–7). The diploma can be seen as evidence of Louis's attempt to regularize the diverse customs which occurred not just in Brittany or even other Celtic regions, but throughout western Europe—though the description of the monks' habits as 'Irish' is not necessarily to be taken literally.

Another way in which the Christianity of medieval Brittany is visibly similar to that of other 'Celtic' regions is in the cults of its saints. Brittany is very well provided with saints, some common to other Brythonic or even Celtic areas, many common to Cornwall (Kernow) and Brittany alone, and many unique to Brittany. Some of these saints are the subjects of written Lives (see HAGIOGRAPHY); many more are known chiefly or only from church dedications and place-names.

Saints and place-names

The toponymy of the Celtic regions, including Brittany, shows a notably higher proportion of place-names (especially, but not solely, those of parishes), which are religious in origin than is found in non-Celtic regions. This, Oliver Padel has argued, must show a drastic impact of Christianity on settlement habits in a number of ways particular to the Celtic regions (*Local Saints and Local Churches in the Early Medieval West* 304–6). The majority of these place-names consist of an ecclesiastical place-name element together with a personal name, the latter often obscure. These personal names are understood to be those of 'saints', some of whom, as noted above, are provided with Lives and other markers of hagiographical respectability (for example, mentions in martyrologies).

In particular, the Breton place-name evidence shows a close relationship with that of Cornwall. This similarity of the place-name elements is mainly due to a shared language, with terms being used in a similar way on both sides of the Channel (Wales [Cymru], as the other BRYTHONIC-language area, shows many similarities as well). The saints known from place-names (as indeed those known from Lives and other sources) also show the same pattern of connection: a few are common to Wales, Cornwall and Brittany, many more are common to Cornwall and Brittany, and many are unique to one area.

Brittany, however, has a particularly distinctive toponymic usage, which is directly relevant to the question of the nature of early Breton Christianity and the significance of the migration from Britain at its formative period. This is the place-name element *plou,* which has no real equivalent in Cornwall or in other Brythonic (or GOIDELIC, for that matter) speaking areas. The element is derived from the Latin *plēbs* (accusative *plēb-em*), and is cognate with the Welsh word *plwyf* and the Cornish word *plu;* its broad meaning is 'parish'. Our earliest detailed documentary evidence, in the form of the 9th-century Cartulary of REDON, shows the term *plebs* indicating a distinctive civil and social community and its territory, with what seems to be a deliberately organized provision of pastoral care. Although this evidence is confined to the area around Redon, we can broadly assume that this was generally the significance of the *plebs,* and that the place-name element *plou* denotes a similar unit. By the 15th century, the French word for 'parish' was borrowed into Breton, presumably because the *plebs*-derivatives had acquired this entirely separate meaning. This situation is distinctly Breton—although it has been suggested that a precocious development of a parochial structure might be a distinctly Celtic trait, the civil function of such a body is unique to Brittany. (There is a map of the distribution of place-names in *plou-* attested before 1200 with the article BRETON MIGRATIONS.)

Medieval and modern historiography treats the names associated with the place-name element *plou* as those of 'saints'—itself a notably elastic concept, especially in an age long before official canonization. It is reasonable to suggest that the place-names and traditions of sainthood both reflect local commemoration, which is perhaps not easily classifiable as religious or secular. The involvement, official or otherwise, of ecclesiastical institutions rather than individuals, and the amount of deliberate organization involved, are very much topics of debate. The difficulty remains, as Wendy Davies has noted, that the apparent coincidence between the migration of Bretons from Britain, the installation of Christianity, and the development of communities with place-names in *plou* has perhaps created a misleading causal relationship between these events (ÉC 20.177–97; Astill & Davies, *Breton Landscape* III, 114–15).

Lives of saints, especially those written a relatively long time after the events they narrate, are very difficult to use as historical sources. These Lives notoriously rely on *topoi,* which give an impression of uniformity. Apart from the Life of St SAMSON of Dol (discussed below), none of the Lives of the Breton saints show significant knowledge of their subjects. Several Lives date from the 9th century, many more from the 11th century, and the rest were composed in the 12th century or later, culminating in a flurry of 'scholarly' activity in the 17th century which saw the invention of several more Lives. The Lives of the Breton saints overwhelmingly describe a period of conversion and foundation of churches from around the 5th to the 7th century. Many show their subjects travelling between one or more of the Celtic regions and meeting other Breton, Brythonic, or Celtic saints. Some show particular affinities with other Lives of Celtic saints in the formulaic events (*topoi*) that they employ, which strongly suggests that the Lives of saints from other Celtic regions were a significant source of hagiographic models.

The first Life of St Samson of Dol, the earliest Life of a Brythonic saint, tells of a saint and his companions coming to Brittany, in this case from south Wales via Cornwall. The Life is long and detailed, and seems to be full of useful information about the religious (including pre-Christian), social, and political life of the 6th century, when its subject almost certainly lived. St Samson is thought to be the signatory to the council of Paris of *c.* 562 (Clercq, *Concilia Galliae A. 511–A. 695* 2–10). His Life seems to have been written in Brittany, by a monk of the house the saint founded at Dol. It claims to have oral and written information (both derived from sources, some named, close to the saint himself) about the saint's activities on both sides of the Channel, as well as personal experience of the sites it discusses. The truth of these claims is highly debated, as is the date of the Life—it was written sometime between the early 7th century and the mid-9th century—but opinion is divided as to when exactly between these points. The portion of the Life concerned with the saint's life in Wales and Cornwall, by far the longest portion of the text, shows the saint as a reluctant participant in coenobitic MONASTICISM, and in pursuit of an increasingly eremitical life. The Breton section presents the saint much less as a monastic founder and much more as a diplomat: it describes the founding of two religious houses, Dol and Pental, but climaxes with an account of the saint's intervention with a Frankish emperor on behalf of two princes of DOMNONIA. The Frankish emperor seems to be a conflation of several historical figures, and the almost complete obscurity of Domnonia's early history renders the two princes unverifiable.

The 9th century and the Carolingian Renaissance

By the 9th century Brittany was well within the Frankish orbit, although direct political control was more theoretical than real, especially in the west of the peninsula. The Carolingian emperor, Louis the Pious, singled out NOMINOE as his representative, *missus imperatoris*, in Brittany. As we have seen above, the Emperor attempted, with some success, to regularize some ecclesiastical practices. In religious affairs, Nominoe is most notably associated with the attempt to establish a Breton archbishopric, independent of the metropolitan seat of Tours. The defining event of this struggle was the so-called 'synod' of *Coitlouh* (identification uncertain) of 849, at which Nominoe deposed the five existing Breton bishops under obscure circumstances (see Hartmann, *Monumenta Germaniae Historica, Concilia* 3.185–93), effectively putting the Breton dioceses outside Carolingian (and papal) control. One of Nominoe's successors, SALOMON, presided over an attempt to persuade Pope Nicholas I that St Samson of Dol had founded a Breton archbishopric not historically subject to Tours. The quest for archiepiscopal status for Dol was to continue until the 12th century: in 1076 Gregory VII sent the *pallium* to Dol, but in 1199 the matter was decisively settled by Innocent III in favour of Tours.

The 9th century was a period of visible activity in Breton churches. Lives of saints (with the exception of that of St Samson of Dol, discussed above), as well as manuscripts, date from this period onwards. While learned culture clearly looked to the Continent, the influence of other Celtic regions is clearly visible, in particular in the evidence of manuscripts: British and Irish texts were copied in Brittany, in a mainly insular version of the Carolingian script, and glossed at times in several CELTIC LANGUAGES. Hagiography, as noted above, also shows the Bretons looking more across the Channel than to the rest of the Continent for literary borrowings.

The 9th century also saw the beginning of Viking raids which were to devastate Brittany's political and ecclesiastical structures. Breton historiography represents the Viking raids as initiating what looks like the migration in reverse: political and ecclesiastical rulers fled with their treasures and relics to Britain and to France, leaving Brittany empty and devastated. This, it is clear, is overly dramatic. Nevertheless, some political rulers and clerics (carrying relics) clearly did take refuge elsewhere: to ÆTHELSTAN's involvement in the plight of these rulers and clerics, for example, we owe renewed interest in Breton saints shown by churches in the south-west of England. The literary and political Breton renaissance of the 11th century is also clearly part of a larger recovery from the effects of the Vikings on the part of local political and religious leaders. Moreover, as part of the larger European monastic revival, religious houses were founded or refounded, including many that attracted both men and women (sometimes, as in the case of Robert of Arbrissel, to considerable scandal). New orders, such as the Cistercians, gained in popularity, at times under specifically Norman aegis, and Breton monasticism came to resemble, and to be in contact with, that of the larger European world in both spiritual and economic terms.

Angevin Brittany

In Brittany, as elsewhere in his dominions, the Angevin King Henry II was effective in centralizing, rationalizing, and establishing control over the Church. Henry took an active interest in Breton ecclesiastical politics (for example, he supported Dol against Tours in the struggle for the *pallium*, with some success, albeit temporary). His efforts hastened and strengthened the adoption of the Gregorian reforms throughout Brittany. Dynastic control of bishoprics waned, although that by priests seems to have continued. With the death of Richard I, the Breton duchy (as it was by then constituted) became a direct fief of the Capetian crown and, ultimately, was absorbed politically into France.

PRIMARY SOURCES
Clercq, *Concilia Galliae A. 511–A. 695*; Duchesne, *Revue de Bretagne et de Vendée* 57.5–21; Hartmann, *Monumenta Germaniae Historica, Concilia* 3.185–93; Munier, *Concilia Galliae A. 314–A. 505*; Smedt, *Analecta Bollandiana* 7.167–264.

FURTHER READING
ÆTHELSTAN; ARMORICA; BREIZH; BRETON; BRETON MIGRATIONS; BRYTHONIC; CELTIC LANGUAGES; CHRISTIANITY, CELTIC; CYMRU; DOMNONIA; GAUL; GAULISH; GOIDELIC; GWENED; HAGIOGRAPHY; KARAEZ; KERNOW; LANDEVENNEG; MONASTICISM; NAONED; NOMINOE; REDON; ROAZHON; SALOMON; SAMSON; UUINUUALOE; Astill & Davies, *Breton Landscape*; Bernier, *Les chrétientés bretonnes continentales depuis les origines jusqu'au IXème siècle*; Brett, CMCS 18.1–25; Chédeville & Guillotel, *La Bretagne des saints et des rois, Ve–Xe siècle*; Chédeville & Tonnerre, *La Bretagne féodale XIe–XIIIe siècle*; Wendy Davies, ÉC 20.177–97; Wendy Davies, *Small Worlds*; Duine, *Mémento des sources hagiographiques de l'histoire de Bretagne*; Fleuriot, *Annales de Bretagne* 78.601–60; Fleuriot, *Les origines de la Bretagne*; Galliou & Jones, *Bretons*; Giot et al., *British Settlement of Brittany*; Guillotel, *Mémoires de la Société d'histoire et d'archéologie de Bretagne* 59.269–315; Irien, *Landévennec et le monachisme breton dans le haut Moyen Âge* 167–88; Jankulak, *Celtic Hagiography and Saints' Cults* 271–84; Largillière, *Les saints et l'organisation chrétienne primitive dans l'Armorique bretonne*; Le Duc, *Celtic Connections* 1.133–51; Loth, *Les noms de saints bretons*; Padel, *Local Saints and Local Churches in the Early Medieval West* 303–60; Price, *Vikings in Brittany*; Smith, *Speculum* 65.309–43; Smith, *Studies in Church History* 22.53–63; Tanguy, *Actes du 107e congrès national des sociétés savantes* 2.323–40; Tanguy, *Annales de Bretagne* 87.429–62; Tanguy, *Bulletin de la Société archéologique du Finistère* 109.121–55; Tanguy, *Bulletin de la Société archéologique du Finistère* 113.93–116; Tanguy, *Bulletin de la Société archéologique du Finistère* 115.117–42; Tanguy, *Dictionnaire des noms de communes, trèves et paroisses des Côtes-d'Armor*; Tanguy, *Dictionnaire des noms de communes trèves et paroisses du Finistère*; Tanguy, *Histoire de la paroisse* 9–32; Tanguy, *Ar Men* 5.18–29; Tanguy, *Saint Ronan et la Troménie* 109–22.

Karen Jankulak

§2. PROTESTANTISM IN BRITTANY

Protestantism has never been the religion of the majority in Brittany (BREIZH), and it is unlikely that there were more than about 5000 adherents at any given time during the 17th to the 19th century. The vast majority of the population remained Roman Catholic. Nonetheless, Breton Protestants have had a cultural significance, particularly in the shaping of Modern BRETON LITERATURE and standard literary forms of the BRETON language in the 19th and 20th centuries.

The Breton Huguenots

From the 1530s Protestantism gained ground among élite social groups in Brittany: cultivated craftsmen, printers, magistrates, mariners and soldiers. Protestant Breton seamen may have influenced John Knox, one of the founders of Scottish Calvinist Presbyterianism, when he was a galley slave at the Breton port city of Nantes (NAONED). The great families of the Breton nobility were attracted by Calvinism and at the denomination's peak in Brittany (1565) about a quarter of the upper class were followers. Particularly prominent were the leading aristocratic families, including Rohan, Rieux, Laval, Montjean, Maure, Goulaine, La Chapelle, Gouyon, and Montbourcher. However, there is little evidence that they attempted to impose their religion on their vassals or serfs, who remained firmly Catholic throughout this period. For more than a century, this first wave of Breton Protestantism was tolerated because of the social status of its adherents. It remained confined to cities and castles, mainly in

BREIZH-UHEL (that is, French-speaking eastern Brittany), for example, Vitré, Nantes, Rennes (ROAZHON), Blain, and Sion, while the Breton-speaking countryside in the west remained untouched. The early Protestants evangelized in French and most of the population of BREIZH-IZEL (western Brittany) understood only Breton. Attempts to preach in Breton in Morlaix (MONTROULEZ) and Pontivy (Pontivi) were crushed by persecution during the St Bartholomew's Day Massacre, which began on 24 August 1572 and continued into the autumn. Nonetheless, the Huguenots (French Protestants) represented an important part of the scientific and literary achievements of the French-speaking élite, among them writer and magistrate Noël du Fail (c. 1520–91), mathematician François Viète (1540–1603), and Roch Le Baillif (doctor, astrologer, alchemist, and advisor to King Henri IV of France). Henri IV had granted freedom of worship and some civil rights to Protestants with the Edict of Nantes in 1598, and most of these noblemen remained professed Protestants until the Edict was revoked by Louis XIV in 1685. This first phase of Protestantism came to an end with this revocation of religious freedom, and many Protestants fled to Britain, Ireland (ÉIRE), and the Netherlands. Protestantism was not to flourish again until after 1815, when a second wave of activity was launched, this time focused on the Breton-speaking rural west.

From tolerance to recovery (1787–1850)

When Napoleon Bonaparte pronounced freedom of worship in 1802, Protestantism was largely confined to foreigners living in France. In Brittany, this meant chiefly businessmen from Switzerland, Germany, and Britain, who lived in Nantes. Congregations were established in a few other large towns such as Brest, Rennes, and Lorient (An Oriant). The presence of English fishermen, businessmen, and tourists led to the building of Anglican churches on the Breton coastal 'Riviera', in Dinard (Dinarzh), Saint-Servan, and Dinan. Chaplains accompanied the numerous Scottish technicians in Saint-Nazaire (Sant-Nazer) and Landerneau (Landerne).

Nineteenth-century Breton Protestantism expanded most rapidly in the west of Brittany. In Brest, the British consul, Anthony Perrier, a member of the Anglo-Irish ASCENDANCY and a figure of the Enlightenment, gathered around him a small congregation in the 1820s. These comprised largely the British wives of those French officers who had been prisoners of war in Britain during the Napoleonic wars. The Protestant minister Achille Le Fourdrey established himself in Brest in spring 1832, and the community of Protestants there was officially recognized by the French government in 1833.

The arrival of Welsh missionaries marked a major new direction in Protestant proselytizing in Brittany. With communications re-established after the end of the Napoleonic wars, the Protestant churches of Wales were able to begin a project which was of concern to them: to spread their reformed creed among the Bretons, whom modern comparative linguistics had recently rediscovered as their 'cousins' (see PAN-CELTICISM). In 1818 the Welsh periodical *Goleuad Gwynedd* (The light of GWYNEDD) published a contribution lamenting the 900,000 Breton speakers in France who languished under the 'iron yoke of Catholicism'. In April 1819 the Anglican minister and linguist Thomas PRICE (also known as 'Carnhuanawc') noted the fact that the Bretons did not possess a complete translation of the BIBLE, and brought it to the attention of the Committee of the British and Foreign Bible Society. Price then began to collect money in order to finance the work of translating the Bible into Breton. His collaborator, the Revd David Jones, met Jean-François Le Gonidec, one of the founding members of L'Academie Celtique in Paris, who had already published an authoritative Breton dictionary and grammar (see DICTIONARIES AND GRAMMAR [5]). Le Gonidec finished the translation of the Bible in 1835, although only the New Testament was published. His highly literary use of language represents a major milestone in the revival of a high-culture written style in Modern Breton. In 1835, the Revd John Jenkins settled in Morlaix, with funding from the Baptist missionary society and at the suggestion of the minister of Brest. Seven years later, the Methodist James Williams came to south Finistère (Penn-ar-Bed) and took charge of the Protestants of Quimper and Lorient. Together, they revised Le Gonidec's translation of the Bible and published multiple small works in Breton. Using colloquial Breton speech, they succeeded in reaching the rural population, mainly with the aid of itinerant pedlars. Literacy in Breton was key to their efforts, and thus the first book written in Breton by John Jenkins (1807–72) was a primer, *An A B K* ('A B C' in the Breton alphabet).

After 1870: a strong Protestant proselytism

The foundation of the Third Republic in 1870, during the Franco-Prussian War, opened a new era in Breton Protestantism, which was by then more readily accepted. The half-century between 1875 and 1925 marked the peak of Protestant missionary activity. The Methodist charity in Quimper, restarted by the minister William Jenkyn Jones with the aid of his brother Evan and the Breton evangelist Le Groignec, created lasting congregations in Douarnenez and in the ports of the Bro-Vigoudenn (Bigouden country) in south-west Brittany, at Pont-L'Abbé (Pont-'n-Abad), Lesconil (Leskonil), Léchiagat, and Pennmarc'h. The impact on the population of fishermen of the region was remarkable. The Baptist mission in Morlaix multiplied its daughter foundations on the north coast, in Plougasnou (Plouganoù)/Roscoff (Rosko), and diffused into the inland region of Argoad. A school was built at Guilly in Poullaouen as well as chapels in Lannéanou, at Kerelcun in La Feuillée (Ar Fouilhez) and at Huelgoat (An Uhelgoad). The successor and son of John Jenkins, Alfred-Llywelyn Jenkins, carried out this work, together with the missionaries Collobert and David. The Baptist mission in Trémel (Tremael) also became a major centre; its influence peaked around 1900, owing much to the personality of its charismatic minister G. Le Coat, who was assisted by his nephew, Georges Somerville.

A new wave of Protestant evangelism in the early 20th century multiplied the number of places of worship on this part of the north coast of Brittany. The Quaker Charles Terell founded a meeting house at Paimpol (Pempoull) in 1906, which was later taken over by the Welsh Baptist minister Caradoc Jones.

In 1905, with the approval of the Reformed Church in Rennes, the Protestants of Saint Brieuc (Sant-Brieg) employed a Methodist minister, Jean Scarabin. Scarabin organized a major missionary drive in the *département* of Côtes-d'Armor (formerly Côtes du Nord, Aodoù-an-Arvor), and particularly on the coast in the region of Perros-Guirec (Perroz-Gireg). By the 1920s the Methodist mission of Côtes-d'Armor employed three ministers and evangelists, who had noteworthy results in Lannion (Lannuon) and Perros-Guirec.

The Calvinist churches of the major towns received the support of a major French Protestant organization, the 'Mission Populaire' in Paris, which financed the installation of meeting places in the workers' quarters of the cities of Nantes, Rennes, Brest, Lorient, and Saint-Nazaire (Sant-Nazer).

The Protestants denounced the cultural backwardness of the province, starting with the weak local production of newspapers and writings in Breton. They considered this void to be an indictment of Catholicism for having failed in its rôle as a cultural and educational institution.

In the course of the 19th century the general progress of EDUCATION permitted a growing output of Protestant works in the Breton language. From 1830 to 1930 several million pamphlets, *gwerzioù* (BALLADS) and gospels, more than 100,000 New Testaments and as many issues of the *Almanach mad ar Vretoned* (The Bretons' good almanack), 20,000 Bibles and numerous polemical works came off the presses. The most productive centre for Protestant publications in Breton at this period was Trémel. The Baptist minister Le Coat and his brother-in-law François Le Quéré were admirably equipped to express Protestant ideas in their native TREGER dialect (see BRETON DIALECTS), adapting the message to rural Breton sensibilities. Their poems and songs on broadsides mocked the Catholic clergy and became bestsellers (see BRETON BROADSIDES). In Breizh-Izel, broadside pedlars were the spearhead of Protestant proselytism. From the middle of the 19th century there were ten or more of them continuously travelling the Breton countryside, going from market to market selling their popular publications. Those who were not singers themselves worked together with singers, and their evangelical *gwerzioù* sometimes inspired spontaneous gatherings in market places.

The written controversy between Catholics and Protestants, which mainly occurred between 1830 and 1920, shows a great variety, ranging from theological dispute to songs. The debate found expression in books, magazines, newspapers, and broadside sheets. After 1914, Protestant publications in Breton declined steeply. The Breton Bible, a legacy of 19th-century Protestantism, was adopted by the Catholic Church in the later 20th century and endures as the one great monument of Protestant literary activity in Brittany.

The second characteristic of Protestant strategy in Brittany between 1832 and 1914 was its constant association with anticlerical, republican, reputedly Freemason, and socialist movements. Under the Second Empire (1852–70) in particular, the Protestants formed a lasting alliance with the *Bleus* ('Blues', supporters of a republican constitution for France) who, as secularists, were also viewed with hostility by the Catholic clergy. Tradition and family solidarity weighed so heavily that it was virtually impossible to achieve conversions in social settings where the parish priest was a presence. The ministers thus focused their efforts primarily on places that were physically remote from Catholic churches. Almost all of the rural and coastal Protestant foundations in Breizh-Izel belong to an 'anti-establishment diagonal' running from Trégor in the north via Poher to the Bro-Vigoudenn in the south. Failing in their goal to convert entire parishes, ministers enjoyed their main success in villages distant from parish churches, i.e., rural communities at the edge of the forest in Guilly or in the clearance of the heath in Kerelcun, and recent settlements of fishermen at Léchiagat, Guilvinec (Gelveneg), Diben, and Plougasnou. These isolated communities tended naturally to form a sense of solidarity, in which the Catholic superintendent, as an outsider, came to be distrusted.

FURTHER READING
ASCENDANCY; BALLADS; BIBLE; BREIZH; BREIZH-IZEL; BREIZH-UHEL; BRETON; BRETON BROADSIDES; BRETON DIALECTS; BRETON LITERATURE; DICTIONARIES AND GRAMMAR [5]; EDUCATION; ÉIRE; GWYNEDD; MONTROULEZ; NAONED; PAN-CELTICISM; PRICE; ROAZHON; TREGER; Carluer, *Protestants et Bretons*; Dewi M. Jones, *Études sur la Bretagne et les pays celtiques* 167–86; Rihet, *Mémoire de maîtrise*.

Jean-Yves Carluer, Erwan Rihet

Christianity in the Celtic countries [6] Cornwall

Christianity may have reached Cornwall (KERNOW) during the ROMANO-BRITISH period, and was probably a significant force by the 5th century when Christian Latin INSCRIPTIONS begin to survive on tall 'pillar' stones commemorating local aristocracy. The author of the earliest Life of St SAMSON, written in Brittany (BREIZH) between the early 7th and mid 9th centuries, believed that this Welsh saint crossed Cornwall in the mid 6th century—calling at a monastery at Docco (St Kew), confirming the baptisms of local people, and founding another monastery at an unspecified site. ALDHELM, the Anglo-Saxon bishop of Sherborne, visited Cornwall in about 700 and wrote a letter to Gerontius (Gerent), the king of the region, urging him and his clergy to adopt the Roman CALENDAR (see EASTER CONTROVERSY; GERAINT FAB ERBIN). During the 9th century, Cornwall and its Church came under the control of the kings of Wessex. King Ecgberht of Wessex (†839) granted estates to the bishops of Sherborne, and a Cornish bishop named Kenstec, based at Dinuurrin (possibly Bodmin), acknowledged the authority of the Archbishop of Canterbury.

By the time that Cornwall became a county of England in the 10th century, the early monasteries had evolved into minsters staffed by canons, priests, or clerks. Fifteen minsters are recorded in the Domesday Survey of 1086, all of which were also parish churches. There were many smaller religious sites by the 10th century that had acquired or would acquire graveyards, church buildings, and parishes. These eventually numbered about 155, giving a total of about 170 parishes in the county by 1291. Cornish churches were usually named after Brythonic men or women, who came to be regarded as saints and patrons of the churches. Over 100 churches had a unique saint, while another 62 commemorated saints from other Brythonic lands, chiefly from Brittany with a few from Wales (CYMRU). Some other churches eventually adopted international and English patron saints. A series of bishops based at Bodmin and St Germans ruled Cornwall until 1050, when the diocese was merged into that of Exeter in Devon.

During the 12th century, following the Norman Conquest, the minsters declined in number. New religious houses were founded, and there was a great rebuilding of parish churches, often on cruciform plans. MONASTICISM did not make great gains in Cornwall, however, although much property there was granted to monasteries outside the county. Inside it, three minsters were converted into Augustinian priories at Bodmin, St Germans and Launceston, and some small Benedictine, Cluniac, and Augustinian cells were established, dependent on larger houses elsewhere. Two communities of friars settled at Bodmin and Truro in the 13th century, but other major religious orders never entered Cornwall and there were no nuns. Medieval Christianity flourished chiefly in the parish churches and in the collegiate church of Glasney at Penryn, founded in 1265 as a kind of surrogate cathedral (see GLASNEY COLLEGE). Many parish churches were rebuilt in the 15th and early 16th centuries, housing numerous cults of international saints supported by groups of parishioners. Hundreds of additional chapels were founded in gentry houses and outlying communities, or to promote saint cults, and pilgrimage took place, notably to St Michael's Mount. Religious drama became popular, and plays on Biblical and hagiographical topics survive in the CORNISH language, linked with Camborne, Kea, and possibly Glasney (see BEUNANS KE; BEUNANS MERIASEK; CORNISH LITERATURE; ORDINALIA).

The Reformation of the 1530s and 1540s closed the religious houses, abolished images and pilgrimage, and replaced Latin worship by English. This caused discontent, culminating in the so-called Prayer-Book Rebellion of 1549, during which protesters from Cornwall and Devon besieged Exeter, before being routed by royal troops. Under Queen Elizabeth I (1558–1603), Cornwall became nominally Protestant, although the contemporary Cornish writers Richard Carew and Nicholas Roscarrock state that saints' days continued to be celebrated and holy wells visited for cures or divination. In the 17th century there was strong political support in Cornwall for Charles I, and consequently for the Church of England or 'Anglican Church'. Protestant nonconformists (such as Baptists and Presbyterians) had little impact in the county during this period.

The Anglican dominance was challenged by the rise of Methodism at the end of the 18th century. This began as an evangelical movement within the Church of England and then, from the 1780s, seceded to form not one but several different Methodist denominations. At the national English census of attendance at worship in 1851, Methodists and other nonconformists in Cornwall greatly outnumbered Anglicans. Later, there was also a modest growth of Roman Catholicism. The Church of England revived in the second half of the 19th century. Religious movements (High-Church 'Tractarianism' and Low-Church evangelicalism) instilled fresh vigour into clergy and their congregations, there was much church building and restoration, and a bishop and diocese were re-established in 1877, centred at Truro. The building of Truro Cathedral (1880–1910) gave Anglicans a major building and powerful symbol.

Cornwall's economy declined in the 20th century due to the extinction of mining, the principal industry, leaving the county poor by British standards. This was partly offset by tourism and by immigration (especially of retired people). A parallel decline took place in

the Christian churches in terms of church attendance, economic resources, and vocations to be clergy, while interest in 'new age' ideas led to a growth of spirituality that was not necessarily Christian. The decline was most spectacular among the Methodists, despite the reunion of nearly all their denominations in 1932. They lost their superiority of numbers, and a great many of their chapels were closed. The Church of England, while also suffering losses, benefited from the immigration and managed to maintain virtually all its ancient places of worship, while the Catholic Church made further moderate gains of churches and worshippers. All the Christian churches experienced positive developments in terms of new liturgies, ecumenical links between the denominations, and the opening of church government and ministry to wider categories of people. Collectively, they remain a strong force in EDUCATION, charity and welfare, and in social life (especially in the countryside).

FURTHER READING
ALDHELM; BEUNANS KE; BEUNANS MERIASEK; BREIZH; CALENDAR; CORNISH; CORNISH LITERATURE; CYMRU; EDUCATION; EASTER CONTROVERSY; GERAINT FAB ERBIN; GLASNEY COLLEGE; INSCRIPTIONS; KERNOW; MONASTICISM; ORDINALIA; ROMANO-BRITISH; SAMSON; Brown, *Catholic Revival in Cornish Anglicanism 1833–1906*; Brown, *Century for Cornwall*; Cook, *Diocese of Exeter in 1821, vol. 1: Cornwall*; Deacon et al., *Cornwall at the Crossroads*; Isaac, *History of Evangelical Christianity in Cornwall*; Kain & Ravenhill, *Historical Atlas of South-West England*; Mattingly, *Journal of the Royal Institution of Cornwall*, new ser. 10.290–329; Olson & Padel, CMCS 12.33–71; Olson, *Early Monasteries in Cornwall*; Orme, *English Church Dedications*; Orme, *Nicholas Roscarrock's Lives of the Saints: Cornwall and Devon*; Orme, *Saints of Cornwall*; Orme, *Unity and Variety*; Pearse, *Wesleys in Cornwall*; Pevsner, *Buildings of England: Cornwall*; Rowse, *Tudor Cornwall*; Shaw, *Bible Christians 1815–1907*; Shaw, *History of Cornish Methodism*; Thomas & Mattingly, *History of Christianity in Cornwall AD 500–2000*.

Nicholas Orme

Christianity, Celtic

'Celtic Christianity' is a phrase used, with varying degrees of specificity, to designate a complex of features held to have been common to the Celtic-speaking countries in the early Middle Ages. Doubts concerning the term's usefulness have repeatedly been expressed, however, and the majority of scholars consider it to be problematic. There are three ways in which 'Celtic Christianity' has been conceived: (1) as a separate institution or denomination within Christianity, a 'Celtic Church' which can be contrasted with the Roman Church or the Orthodox Churches of the East; (2) as a body of distinctive beliefs and practices; and (3) as a more impalpable assemblage of attitudes and values. The article concludes with a brief look at some of the motivations that have lain behind the positing of 'Celtic Christianity' as a distinct phenomenon.

§1. 'THE CELTIC CHURCH'

The view that at one time there existed a 'Celtic Church', uniting the Celtic-speaking peoples with one another and dividing them from the rest of Christendom, has often been asserted, even by scholars as eminent as Heinrich ZIMMER (*Celtic Church in Britain and Ireland*), but it no longer has a place within serious scholarly discourse. There is no persuasive evidence which can be advanced in support of such a model. Thus, when COLUMBANUS, in a letter to a synod in Merovingian Frankia in the late 6th century, defends his own usage as being that of 'all the churches of the entire West' (*omnes . . . ecclesiae totius Occidentis*), he is speaking not of a monolithic institution but of a multitude of communities (Walker, *Sancti Columbani Opera* 16–17). Again, it is misleading to portray the debate concerning the date of Easter at Whitby in 664 as one which pitted 'Celts' against 'Romans' (see EASTER CONTROVERSY). Those on the losing side were arguing not on behalf of a 'Celtic Church', but specifically of the traditions of the monastery of Iona (EILEAN Ì), whose foundation of LINDISFARNE exercised a dominant rôle in the spread of Christianity in northern England. All the councils and ecclesiastical enactments of the early period were more or less local—even the sweeping adoption in 697 of the CÁIN ADOMNÁIN ('ADOMNÁN's Law'), a law protecting non-combatants, did not extend beyond the Gaelic and Pictish spheres.

To these considerations should be added the frequent assertions of harmony with Rome in early sources: Columbanus's indignant denial that any of the Irish has ever been a schismatic (Walker, *Sancti Columbani Opera* 38–9). The early *Vita prima Brigitae* relates St BRIGIT's insistence that the *ordo et universa regula* ('order and universal rule') of Rome, without any modification, be instituted at Kildare (Cill Dara) (Colgan, *Trias Thaumaturga* 539). The deference of the see of Armagh (ARD MHACHA) to Rome was prescribed in the (evidently 7th-century) *Liber Angeli* (Bieler, *Patrician Texts*

188–91). In 6th-century BRITAIN, GILDAS wrote of clerics 'sailing across seas and traversing wide lands' in search of ordination (Winterbottom, *Gildas* 54, 120). *Kanones Wallici*, a collection of early Breton Latin laws, sometimes regarded as canon law, cite the authority of the 'books of the Romans' (Bieler, *Irish Penitentials* 136–7; see BRETON LITERATURE §2).

PRIMARY SOURCES
Bieler, *Irish Penitentials* 136–7; Bieler, *Patrician Texts* 188–91; Colgan, *Trias Thaumaturga* 539; Walker, *Sancti Columbani Opera* 16–17; Winterbottom, *Gildas* 54, 120.

FURTHER READING
Wendy Davies, *Early Church in Wales* 12–21; Sharpe, *Irland und Europa* 58–72; Zimmer, *Celtic Church in Britain and Ireland*.

§2. 'CELTIC' PRACTICES AND BELIEFS

Even given all of the above, it can certainly be maintained that the churches of the Celtic-speaking countries had much in common with one another. There are good historical reasons for this. Ireland (ÉRIU) derived its Christian faith primarily from Britain (see PATRICK; UINNIAU), and its churches remained under strong British influence during the 6th century. Ireland in turn was responsible for the evangelization of much of Scotland (ALBA). Brittany (BREIZH) was settled from Cornwall (KERNOW) and Wales (CYMRU), and retained a vivid sense of the British background of its early saints; at a later date, Irish manuscripts found their way to Breton monasteries. As a result of such connections, the same or similar usages can be found in various parts of the medieval Celtic world, but it should be stressed that such correspondences have nothing to do with 'Celticity' as such. Resemblances that are as close, or closer, can be found in non-Celtic lands which were subject to Gaelic influence (notably in Northumbria, see BRYNAICH). Furthermore, few or none of these 'Celtic' features can be shown to have been present at any given time throughout the Celtic area.

From the 6th century onward, a divergent Easter reckoning has been the 'Celtic' trait which has attracted the most attention (see EASTER CONTROVERSY). While various systems prevailed elsewhere, among which the 19-year cycle of Victorius of Aquitaine came to predominate, the 84-year cycle attributed to Anatolius was favoured by the Britons, Gaels, and PICTS. The correct date for the celebration of one of the most important Christian feasts, in which the cosmos is attuned to the Christian theme of the triumph of light and life over darkness, and the rival claims of unity of observance versus cherished tradition, were clearly issues of real importance, but they need to be placed in context. There is no question of the 84-year cycle being a 'Celtic' invention: it seems to have been introduced into Britain and Ireland as part of the spread of the cult of St Martin of Tours. Different regions went over to mainstream usage at different times, spanning the interval from *c.* 630 (southern Ireland) to 768 (north Wales). Certainly in Ireland, and probably elsewhere, other systems were known, although they seem to have been little practised. The attempt by adherents of the Victorian cycle to give the controversy a doctrinal dimension, by claiming that their opponents subscribed to the Quartodeciman heresy (whereby Easter was to be celebrated on the 14th day of the moon), rested on a misunderstanding.

The claim that Irish and British clerics used an irregular tonsure is rendered more colourful by the fact that some of its critics associated this tonsure with the wizard Simon Magus: there may be some connection here with traditions that the DRUIDS as well had a tonsure of their own. Here too, however, practice within the Celtic areas (and indeed beyond) was by no means uniform: thus the early (6th-century?) Irish tract *Synodus episcoporum* (The synod of the bishops) penalizes clerics who do not cut their hair 'after the Roman custom' (*more Romano*; Bieler, *Irish Penitentials* 54–5), and criticism of the British tonsure is attributed to Gildas (Wasserschleben, *Die irische Kanonensammlung* 242).

While there is considerable evidence for divergent Irish and (to an even greater degree) British practice in matters of liturgy, baptism, and ecclesiastical administration, the usages in question seem only to have characterized specific regions, and not necessarily to have been uniformly present there. Only the Britons were accused of practising a heterodox baptism; traces of an archaic liturgy in Wales find no counterpart in the eclectic, but largely Gallican, worship attested from Ireland; and the superiority of abbots to bishops appears to have been limited to some parts of the Gaelic sphere of influence. Those whose worship contrasted with Roman norms in Ireland were called simply 'Irish' (*Hibernenses*; see also COLLECTIO CANONUM HIBERNENSIS): there was no sense that they felt an allegiance to anything broader than local custom. Other practices which became current, such as marriage on

the part of the higher clergy and hereditary proprietorship of churches, were characteristic of unreformed usage throughout Christendom. The only peculiarly 'Celtic' thing about them is that the reform movement championed by Pope Gregory VII reached the CELTIC COUNTRIES later than it did other parts of Europe. With respect to theological doctrine, none of the various imputations of heresy directed at groups in medieval Ireland or Britain appear to have had any substance.

Seen against this background, features which were genuinely common to Brythonic and Gaelic Christians can be investigated and appreciated, without being seen as a pretext for painting an excessively homogeneous picture of the religious culture of the islands. There is much here which is worthy of consideration: the pervasive influence of Britain on Ireland in matters of religious vocabulary, monastic life, and scribal and penitential practice; the extension of the cults of saints from one Celtic area to another; and comparable approaches to Biblical scholarship and pastoral care. Again, however, it must be borne in mind that several of these features have parallels in contemporary England.

PRIMARY SOURCES
Bieler, *Irish Penitentials* 54–5; Wasserschleben, *Die irische Kanonensammlung* 242.

FURTHER READING
Blair & Sharpe, *Pastoral Care before the Parish* 1–10; Charles-Edwards, *Early Christian Ireland* 391–415; Hughes, CMCS 1.1–20; James, *Peritia* 3.85–98; Stevenson, *Liturgy and Ritual of the Celtic Church* liii–xxii.

§3. 'CELTIC' ATTITUDES AND VALUES
These are the most difficult aspects of 'Celtic Christianity' to define—perhaps designedly so, since it could be argued that they have arisen largely in an attempt to salvage some valid application for the label in the wake of damaging scholarly criticism of the conceptions discussed above. If the term 'Celtic Christianity' is used to designate something as diffuse as a type of spiritual flavour, assessments of its presence, absence and character will almost inevitably be subjective. Such subjective assessments abound, and are primarily indicative of modern preoccupations and desires: a point which is taken up again in the concluding section. In the paragraphs which follow, there is an assessment of a few of the elements which have most frequently been held to characterize a 'Celtic Christian' mentality.

If there is more to 'Celtic Christianity' than the important—but by no means exclusively Celtic—common features mentioned at the end of the preceding section, then what could be its basis? Unless we succumb to racial stereotypes, there would seem to be only one possible answer to this question: that the pre-Christian cultures which the new religion encountered in the various Celtic countries resembled one another in significant ways, reflecting a shared inheritance; and that this substratum had a formative influence on the nascent churches. Such a view has led Oliver Davies, for example, to speak of 'spiritual forms which are more generally common to the Celtic peoples as a whole and whose origins lie in the interaction of original Celtic primal or tribal religion with the young Christianity' (*Celtic Christianity in Early Medieval Wales* 5).

This scenario is not without its appeal, but cannot readily be supported by the evidence. Thus there seems to have been no uniformly 'Celtic' attitude towards the old religion. In Ireland, clerical condemnation of paganism existed side by side with a keen curiosity concerning the native past, and with attempts to accommodate aspects of non-Christian belief within a Christian framework. But there are no persuasive indications of a corresponding mentality in Wales, where monastic scriptoria (centres for producing manuscripts) do not seem to have thrown themselves into the task of copying vernacular sagas, and where much of the earliest surviving evidence for native legend (allusively present in the 'mythological' poems in LLYFR TALIESIN) occurs in a context which is outspokenly anti-clerical.

One of the features most frequently claimed for a 'Celtic Christian' mentality is a sense of the natural world as God's handiwork, leading to a spirituality which contemplates and celebrates the creation. It is indeed the case that such an attitude is reflected in much Irish devotional poetry (see NATURE POETRY), and also in the cosmological interest evident in some theological writings; and it is certainly striking that some early WELSH POETRY (notably the longer of the two sequences of ENGLYNION in the JUVENCUS manuscript) is closely comparable to what we find in Ireland. Such correspondences are worthy of further study, but they cannot be used to characterize 'Celtic Christianity' as a whole; other, and more disparaging, attitudes to the material world can, for instance, also be found in Irish

writings. Nor is a 'Celtic' enthusiasm for nature necessarily to be seen as a relic of paganism: the terms in which it is expressed are clearly indebted to such patristic writers as St Augustine of Hippo (†430), and there is no reason not to see much of its inspiration as deriving from the same source.

FURTHER READING
Carey, *Single Ray of the Sun* 1–38; Oliver Davies, *Celtic Christianity in Early Medieval Wales* 5; O'Loughlin, *Celtic Theology* 1–24; Smyth, *Understanding the Universe*.

§4. MOTIVATIONS FOR POSITING 'CELTIC CHRISTIANITY'

A forerunner of the modern idea of a 'Celtic Church' can be found as far back as the 13th century, when the claim that Joseph of Arimathaea founded the church of Glastonbury seemed to give British Christianity an antiquity greater than that of Rome; in his *Discourse on the Religion Anciently Professed by the Irish and the British* (1623), James Ussher (1581–1656) postulated such a church as a predecessor for the Protestant Church of Ireland. A whole series of subsequent writings arguing for the existence of a 'Celtic Church' have had the same sectarian agenda. During the 19th century such a concept of a 'Celtic Church' gained widespread support, for it fitted the 'diverse branches' theory favoured by Anglican 'High Churchmen', and could account for variations in practice, found in many texts, from what was seen as a monolithic 'Roman system'.

A vision of 'Celtic Christianity' which was not so determined by denominational politics was promulgated by the Breton scholar Ernest Renan (see PAN-CELTICISM), in an essay published in 1854. Renan, estranged from his Roman Catholic roots, held that 'to the Celts . . . Christianity did not come from Rome; they had their native clergy, their own peculiar usages, their faith at first hand.' Furthermore,

The Church did not feel herself bound to be hard on the caprices of religious imagination, but gave fair scope to the instincts of the people, and from this liberty there resulted a cult perhaps the most mythological and the most analogous to the mysteries of antiquity to be found in the annals of Christianity.

Allowing for the nuances of individual expression, Renan's conception has survived virtually unmodified down to the present day, and doubtless has a long future still before it: the progress of scholarship has, however, rendered it increasingly unacceptable to most specialists. For others, such a conception of 'Celtic Christianity' offers an alternative to aspects of actual Christian practice and belief with which they have become disenchanted, and draws added strength from deeply entrenched romantic ideas concerning the 'Celtic character' more generally.

FURTHER READING
Meek, *Quest for Celtic Christianity* esp. 38–59; O'Loughlin, *Irish Theological Quarterly* 67.153–68.

RELATED ARTICLES
ADOMNÁN; ALBA; ARD MHACHA; BREIZH; BRETON LITERATURE; BRIGIT; BRITAIN; BRYNAICH; CÁIN ADOMNÁIN; CELTIC COUNTRIES; COLLECTIO CANONUM HIBERNENSIS; COLUMBANUS; CYMRU; DRUIDS; EASTER CONTROVERSY; EILEAN Ì; ENGLYNION; ÉRIU; GILDAS; JUVENCUS; KERNOW; LINDISFARNE; LLYFR TALIESIN; NATURE POETRY; PAN-CELTICISM; PATRICK; PICTS; UINNIAU; WELSH POETRY; ZIMMER.

John Carey (with Thomas O'Loughlin)

Chronicle of the Kings of Alba

survives in the Poppleton Manuscript, written 1357×1364. Compiled from contemporary eastern Scottish annals (perhaps from Dunkeld/Dùn Chailleann), king-lists and other, possibly later, material by 1202×1214, it covers the period from 843 to 971×995, giving evidence regarding the supposed demise of the PICTS (see LEGENDARY HISTORY; SCOTTISH KING-LISTS), Scandinavian attacks and the emergence of the kingdom of ALBA.

PRIMARY SOURCE
MS. Paris, Bibliothèque Nationale, Latin 4126 (Poppleton).

FURTHER READING
ALBA; LEGENDARY HISTORY; PICTS; SCOTTISH GAELIC; SCOTTISH KING-LISTS; Marjorie O. Anderson, *Kings and Kingship in Early Scotland*; Broun, *Innes Review* 48.112–24 (also in Broun & Clancy, *Spes Scotorum, Hope of Scots*); Cowan, *Innes Review* 32.3–21; Dumville, *Kings, Clerics, and Chronicles in Scotland 500–1297* 73–86; Hudson, *Scottish Gaelic Studies* 18.57–73; Hudson, *Scottish Historical Review* 77.129–61.

Nicholas Evans

Yn Chruinnaght (Inter-Celtic Festival)

is held annually in Ramsey (Rumsaa), in the Isle of Man (ELLAN VANNIN). The title Yn Chruinnaght means 'the gathering' in MANX Gaelic. Based on a Manx arts festival established in the 1920s, it was revived by folklorist and folk-song and folk-dance collector Mona Douglas (1898–1987) in 1978 and continues to the present day. The original Cruinnaght Vanninagh Ashoonagh (Manx national gathering), a one-day event first held in 1924, provided the blueprint for the revival 53 years later. It was organized by the Manx Society (Yn CHESHAGHT GHAILCKAGH) and the World Manx Association, and was inspired by the life and work of the Manx poet, the Revd T. E. Brown (1830–97). Based on competitions, it thrived until the outbreak of the Second World War when it fell into abeyance. The 1970s saw a cultural resurgence in the Isle of Man, and in 1977 Mona Douglas and a team of co-workers decided to revive the festival. They organized a three-day event called Feailley Vanninagh Rhumsaa (Ramsey Manx festival), which featured a re-enactment of a traditional Manx wedding, complete with dancing and music. This was the precursor of the five-day event held the following year called Yn Chruinnaght.

The new Yn Chruinnaght was to place Manx culture on an equal footing with its Celtic counterparts and today it is officially recognized as the Manx national festival, comparable to the National Eisteddfod of Wales (EISTEDDFOD GENEDLAETHOL CYMRU), the Mòd (see COMUNN GAIDHEALACH) in Scotland (ALBA), and the Oireachtas (FEISEANNA) of Ireland (ÉIRE). In the foreword to the 1978 programme, Mona Douglas noted the difference between the new festival and the old: '. . . it places far greater emphasis upon the Manx Gaelic language and the traditional arts as pursued today in both education and public events. [This] has been made possible . . . through the almost incredible interest in the Manx language and culture.'

In recent years, Yn Chruinnaght has spanned a fortnight, beginning with a week of Manx dance, MANX MUSIC and MANX LITERATURE competitions, and an arts and crafts exhibition. The second week is an inter-Celtic event, with visitors from Scotland, Ireland, Wales (CYMRU), Cornwall (KERNOW), and Brittany (BREIZH) taking part. It comprises concerts and céilidhs, a parade, outdoor displays, music sessions and workshops, all in a variety of venues.

As it continues to evolve, Yn Chruinnaght provides a platform for up-and-coming talent in the fields of music and dance, and also serves as an indicator of the status of traditional Manx culture in the modern world.

PRIMARY SOURCES
Yn Chruinnaght Inter-Celtic Festival Programmes, 1981–2001.

FURTHER READING
ALBA; BREIZH; CHESHAGHT GHAILCKAGH; COMUNN GAIDHEAL-
ACH; CYMRU; DOUGLAS; EDUCATION; ÉIRE; EISTEDDFOD
GENEDLAETHOL CYMRU; ELLAN VANNIN; FEISEANNA;
KERNOW; LANGUAGE (REVIVAL); MANX; MANX LITERATURE;
MANX MUSIC; Bazin, *Mona Douglas*; Bazin, *Much Inclin'd to Music*;
Bazin, *Our Living Heritage*; Broderick, *Carn* 108.22; Broderick,
Die Deutsche Keltologie und ihre Berliner Gelehrten bis 1945 195–
209; Dean, *Isle of Man Weekly Times* (6 Sept. 1977); Douglas,
Keltica 1.57–60; Douglas, *Manx Folk-song, Folk Dance, Folklore*;
Douglas, *Manx Life* (March/Apr. 1978) 30–3; Jerry, *For a Celtic
Future* 289–95; Jerry, *Manx Life* (Sept. 1993) 38–41; MacArdle,
Inheritance 2.26–9; Sawyers, *Complete Guide to Celtic Music*;
Speers, *Béaloideas* 64/5.225–78; Stowell & Ó Bréasláin, *Short
History of the Manx Language*.
WEBSITES. www.ceolas.org; www.ynchruinnaght.org

Chloë Woolley

Chwedlau Odo (Odo's stories) is the name given to
a Middle Welsh translation of parts of the Latin
Narraciones (or *Parabole*) *Sancti Odonis* by the English
churchman Odo of Cheriton (†1247). The earliest and
best text is found in Llanstephan MS 4, *c.* 1400. Odo's
internationally popular work comprised over a hundred moralizing tales illustrating various virtues and
vices of both clerics and the laity. They are acted out
generally by animals and derive from a number of
sources, especially Aesop's Fables, the *Roman de Renart*,
and various bestiaries, although there may be an original element as well. Twenty-four of Odo's tales were
selected, somewhat haphazardly, but were well rendered
by the anonymous translator.

PRIMARY SOURCES
MS. Aberystwyth, NLW, Llanstephan 4.
EDITION. Ifor Williams, *Chwedlau Odo*.

RELATED ARTICLE
WELSH PROSE LITERATURE.

R. Iestyn Daniel

Chwedleu Seith Doethon Rufein ('Tales of the
Seven Sages of Rome') is a Middle Welsh independ-
ent retelling by Llywelyn Offeiriad (Llywelyn the
Priest) of the international popular tale 'The Seven
Sages of Rome'. The earliest extant text occurs in Jesus
College MS III (LLYFR COCH HERGEST), *c.* 1400, but
the date of composition could be considerably earlier.

The story has been traced to eastern prototypes, beginning with Indian versions over 2000 years old, followed by Persian and Arabic versions of the 8th century AD. A western Latin version set in Rome survives
from the later 12th century, *Dolopathos, sive De rege et
septem sapientibus* (Dolopathos, or concerning the king
and the seven sages). The story is structured as a series
of brief narratives told by the Emperor of Rome's
wife, which she uses in an attempt to convince her
husband to kill his son, her stepson. The seven sages
wish to save the young man and ultimately succeed, as
it becomes clear that the Emperor's wife is maliciously
conniving for her stepson's inheritance. Llywelyn's retelling is masterly and, interestingly, shows the influence in parts of some of the native Welsh tales, particularly those which share such key themes with
Chwedlau Saith Ddoethion Rhufain (the Modern Welsh
spelling of the title), such as the malicious and grasping
stepmother in CULHWCH AC OLWEN and the majesty
of the Roman Empire in *Breuddwyd* MACSEN WLEDIG.

PRIMARY SOURCES
MS. Oxford, Jesus College III (LLYFR COCH HERGEST).
EDITION. Lewis, *Chwedleu Seith Doethon Rufein*.

RELATED ARTICLES
CULHWCH AC OLWEN; MACSEN WLEDIG; WELSH PROSE LIT-
ERATURE.

R. Iestyn Daniel

Chysauster, around 5 km (3 miles) north of
Penzance, is one of the typical late IRON AGE and
Roman period settlements in Cornwall (KERNOW). It
has produced the best-preserved examples of the characteristic type of building found in the westernmost
regions of Cornwall—the courtyard house, which has
a number of relatively small rooms or cells partially
set into the thickness of the outer wall, located around
a central open area. The site was probably occupied as
early as the 1st century BC, but witnessed its greatest
activity during the ROMANO-BRITISH period, in the
2nd and 3rd centuries AD. The site also has a fogou (an
underground passage), a common feature in contemporary settlements in Cornwall.

FURTHER READING
IRON AGE; ROMANO-BRITISH; KERNOW; Cunliffe, *Facing the Ocean*;
Pearce, *Archaeology of South West Britain*; Weatherhill, *Belerion*.

RK

Cimbri and Teutones were tribes of the later European IRON AGE. Located in the North Sea area, east of the RHINE, they were Germanic in a geographical sense and were often assumed to be Germanic linguistically as well, but this is less certain. The name *Teutones* is most probably Celtic (see also TUATH; TEUTATES). They are also significant in CELTIC STUDIES because their movements disrupted core Celtic-speaking areas in central and western Europe, and catalyzed early contacts between the Romans and Celtic groups in and beyond the Alps. Furthermore, the story of the Cimbri and Teutones may help to explain several striking parallels between the Celtic world and ancient Denmark, including the presence of LA TÈNE style artefacts, for example, the GUNDESTRUP CAULDRON, in Denmark.

Together with a tribe called the Ambrones, the Cimbri and the Teutones migrated in the 2nd century BC from present-day Himmerland (which preserves the name of the Cimbri) and Thy, in present-day Denmark, by way of the river Elbe, arriving in NORICUM in 120 BC, where they defeated a Roman army. In 114 BC the Cimbri and Teutones were driven by the powerful Celtic group known as the BOII from what is now Hungary. They moved south into the BALKANS, where they came into conflict with the Celtic groups the SCORDISCI and the TAURISCI. They then advanced westward to enter the territory of the HELVETII in the ALPINE region. Around 110 BC they entered the valley of the RHÔNE, where they defeated the Roman general M. Iunius Silanus. In 105 BC, they moved south and won a major victory at Arausio, now Orange, France. They next moved on to Spain, but were repelled by the Celtiberians (see CELTIBERIA). The Teutones were then decimated in the battle of Aquae Sextiae, now Aix-en-Provence, in 103 BC against the Romans under Gaius Marius. Passing on into northern Italy across the Brenner pass, the Cimbri met a similar fate in the battle of VERCELLI in 102 BC, fighting the Romans led by Q. Lutatius Catulus and Lucius Cornelius Sulla. An inscription from Miltenberg on the Main indicates that a group called *Toutones*, the same name in a clearly Celtic spelling, lived there in Roman times (Dessau, *Inscriptiones Latinae Selectae* 9377).

Some early modern writers incorrectly identified the name *Cimbri* with *Cymry*, the Welsh name for the Welsh people (see CYMRU), but the preform for *Cymry* is ancient Celtic **Combrogī*.

PRIMARY SOURCES
CAESAR, *De Bello Gallico* 1.33, 1.40, 2.4, 2.29, 7.77; TACITUS, *Germania*.
EDITION. Dessau, *Inscriptiones Latinae Selectae* 9377.

FURTHER READING
ALPINE; BALKANS; BOII; CELTIBERIA; CELTIC STUDIES; CYMRU; GUNDESTRUP CAULDRON; HELVETII; IRON AGE; LA TÈNE; NORICUM; RHINE; RHÔNE; SCORDISCI; TAURISCI; TEUTATES; TUATH; VERCELLI; Cunliffe, *Celtic World* 140–1; *Oxford Classical Dictionary* s.v. Cimbri, Teutones; Schukin, *Rome and the Barbarians in Central and Eastern Europe*.

PEB, JTK

Cín Dromma Snechtai ('The Book of Druim Snechta') is a famous early Irish manuscript, now lost. Since the word *cín* is explained in the ancient glossaries as a 'stave of five sheets of vellum', this was probably smaller than other similar Irish manuscripts. Druim Snechta (Drumsnaght, Co. Monaghan/Contae Mhuineacháin) was probably the site of a monastery. The *Cín Dromma Snechtai* is cited as a source by some of the most important extant Irish manuscripts from the 11th and 12th centuries, among them LEBOR NA HUIDRE ('The Book of the Dun Cow'), LEBOR LAIGNECH ('The Book of Leinster'), LEABHAR BHAILE AN MHÓTA ('The Book of Ballymote'), LEABHAR MÓR LEACÁIN ('The Great Book of Lecan'), and Egerton 88. However, the codex was probably lost before the 17th century since Geoffrey Keating (Seathrún CÉITINN), who used many other manuscripts to collect material for his work on the (partially legendary) history of Ireland, *Foras Feasa ar Éirinn* (1633/4), does not seem to have had access to it.

On the basis of the scribal annotations in other manuscripts mentioned above, the approximate contents of the lost manuscript have been determined. The codex seems to have mainly contained tales on supernatural characters, along with some of the earliest references to FIANNAÍOCHT, as well as GENEALOGIES and LEGENDARY HISTORY. The comparative compactness of the manuscript suggested by its name is also reflected by these texts, both prose and poetry, which tend to be concisely worded and often short, with a large proportion of texts with prominent verse speeches, among them IMMRAM BRAIN ('The Voyage of Bran'), *Echtra Conlai* (Conla's adventure), TOGAIL BRUIDNE DA DERGA ('The Destruction of Da Derga's Hostel'), TOCHMARC ÉTAÍNE ('The Wooing of Étaín'), *Verba*

Scáthaige (The words of Scáthach), and *Forfes Fer Fálchae* (The siege of the men of Fálchae).

Those texts for which is has been possible to demonstrate that they were copied from the *Cín Dromma Snechtai* stand out in the manuscripts in which they are preserved, since linguistically they tend to be significantly more archaic than other texts found in these manuscripts; in other words, they generally belong to the Old IRISH rather than the Middle Irish linguistic horizon. The exact date of the writing of the *Cín Dromma Snechtai* is the subject of ongoing debate, however. Initially, scholars proposed the 8th century as the likely date of writing (Thurneysen, *Die irische Helden- und Königsage bis zum siebzehnten Jahrhundert* 15–18; Pokorny ZCP 9.185), although the first half of the 9th century has also been suggested (Thurneysen ZCP 20.218). More recently, a late 9th- or even 10th-century date was put forward (Mac Mathuna, *Immram Brain* 421–69), but this has been disputed by other scholars (Breatnach, *Celtica* 20.191 and Carey, *Ériu* 46.72).

FURTHER READING

CÉITINN; FIANNAÍOCHT; GENEALOGIES; IMMRAM BRAIN; IRISH; LEABHAR BHAILE AN MHÓTA; LEABHAR MÓR LEACÁIN; LEBOR LAIGNECH; LEBOR NA H-UIDRE; LEGENDARY HISTORY; TOCHMARC ÉTAÍNE; TOGAIL BRUIDNE DA DERGA; Breatnach, *Celtica* 20.177–92; Carey, *Éigse* 19.36–43; Carey, *Ériu* 46.71–92; Gwynn, ZCP 10.217–19; Hamel, ZCP 10.100; Hull, ZCP 24.131–2; Mac Cana, *Heroic Process* 75–99; Mac Mathúna, *Immram Brain* 421–69; Murphy, *Ériu* 16.145–51; Ó Cathasaigh, *Ériu* 41.103–14; Ó Concheanainn, CMCS 16.1–40; O'Curry, *Lectures on the Manuscript Materials of Ancient Irish History*; Ó Dubhthaigh, *Clogher Rec* 6.71–104; Pokorny, ZCP 9.184–6; Thurneysen, *Die irische Helden- und Königsage bis zum siebzehnten Jahrhundert*; Thurneysen, ZCP 10.391–5; Thurneysen, ZCP 20.213–27; Thurneysen, *Zu irischen Handschriften und Litteraturdenkmälern* 2.23–30; Zimmer, *Zeitschrift für vergleichende Sprachforschung auf dem Gebiete der Indogermanischen Sprachen* 28.683–5.

PSH

Cinaed mac Ailpín, also known as Kenneth I of Scotland (ALBA), was king of the SCOTS (840–58) and also of the PICTS (*rex Pictorum*, 847–58). He was not the first king in Scotland to rule both, but he did succeed in founding a dynasty that established lasting GAELIC influence over the Picts and gave Scotland its line of medieval kings.

His father, AILPÍN MAC ECHACH, is not well documented, and his family may have belonged to a remote branch of the nobility of DÁL RIATA. Cinaed

mac Ailpín began his rise to power with the assistance of Norse allies in AD 836. The marriage of his daughter to King Ólafr the White of Dublin (BAILE ÁTHA CLIATH) established ties with the Scandinavians, and he took advantage of a Viking massacre of Dál Riata in 839 to seize their kingship in 840. Only after having overcome the last Pictish king Drust in 847 did he become ruler of both Picts and Scots. At the same time he managed to take possession of part of the relics of St COLUM CILLE. Cinaed died in Fothar Tabaicht, i.e. Forteviot, in modern Perthshire, in 858 and was buried in Iona (EILEAN Ì). The name *Cinaed*, common amongst the early kings of Scotland, is probably Celtic. It is the source for the English name, *Kenneth*. The second element reflects the Celtic word **aidhu-* 'fire' (= OIr. *áed* 'fire, eye' [neuter *-u-/-i-*stem], also the common Old Irish man's name *Áed* (see AED FIND; AED SLÁINE), genitive *Áedo*, diminutive AEDÁN, and the Gaulish tribal name AEDUI, all from the INDO-EUROPEAN root **h2eidh-* 'to burn'). The father's name *Ailpín* occurred also among the Picts, and is probably the cognate of the Early Welsh man's name *Elphin* or *Elffin*, attested in both CUMBRIC and WELSH.

FURTHER READING

AED FIND; AED SLAINE; AEDÁN; AEDUI; AILPÍN MAC ECHACH; ALBA; BAILE ÁTHA CLIATH; COLUM CILLE; CUMBRIC; DÁL RIATA; EILEAN Ì; GAELIC; INDO-EUROPEAN; PICTS; SCOTS; WELSH; Marjorie O. Anderson, *Kings and Kingship in Early Scotland* 196–200; Duncan, *Scotland* 56–9; Skene, *Celtic Scotland* 1.308–24; Smyth, *Warlords and Holy Men* 176–85.

PEB

Cinaed mac Duib, known as Kenneth III, was king of Scotland (*rí Alban*) during the period 997–1005. He seems to have reigned together with his son Giric and was slain by MAEL COLUIM MAC CINAEDA (Malcolm II) in 1005 at Monzievaird, Perthshire. This murder triggered a feud that led to the assassination of Mael Coluim's grandson DÚNCHAD MAC CRINÁIN (Duncan I) by MAC BETHAD (Macbeth) in 1040.

On the Celticity of the name *Cinaed*, see CINAED MAC AILPÍN. The father's name is probably in origin the same word as Old Irish *dub*, Welsh and Breton *du* 'black, dark'.

FURTHER READING

ALBA; CINAED MAC AILPÍN; DÚNCHAD MAC CRINÁIN; MAC BETHAD; MAEL COLUIM MAC CINAEDA; Alan O. Anderson, *Early*

Sources of Scottish History AD 500 to 1286 1.518-24; Smyth, *Warlords and Holy Men* 225.

PEB

Cinaed mac Mael Choluim

Cinaed mac Mael Choluim, known as Kenneth II, king of Scotland (*rí Alban*), ruled during the years 971–95. He was the son of MAEL COLUIM MAC DOMNAILL (Malcolm I of Scotland). At the beginning of his reign, he plundered the north of England and in 973 he was recognized as overlord of Strathclyde (YSTRAD CLUD), CUMBRIA, and LOTHIAN, thus validating a significant territorial advance for the kingdom of Scotland (ALBA) beyond its core territories in what had been DÁL RIATA and the lands of the PICTS. Cinaed changed the system of succession in the Scottish dynasty of CINAED MAC AILPÍN in order to secure the throne for his son MAEL COLUIM (Malcolm II). This effort to dominate the succession sparked a conflict with his brother DUB and the descendants of Illulb (Indulf). In 977 Cinaed mac Mael Choluim slew his direct rival Amlaíb mac Illuilb (Ólafr son of Indulf). Cinaed's long reign ended in 995 when CUSANTÍN MAC CUILÉN (the future Constantine III, king of Scotland) successfully conspired against him, and slew him at Fettercairn, in modern Kincardineshire. Cinaed is buried at Iona (EILEAN Ì).

On the Celticity of the name *Cinaed*, see CINAED MAC AILPÍN. On his father's name, see MAEL COLUIM MAC DOMNAILL.

FURTHER READING
ALBA; CINAED MAC AILPÍN; CUMBRIA; CUSANTÍN MAC CUILÉN; DÁL RIATA; DUB; EILEAN Ì; LOTHIAN; MAEL COLUIM MAC CINAEDA; MAEL COLUIM MAC DOMNAILL; PICTS; YSTRAD CLUD; Alan O. Anderson, *Early Sources of Scottish History AD 500-1286* 1.511–16; Smyth, *Warlords and Holy Men: Scotland AD 80–1000* 224–8, 232–3.

PEB

circulating schools and Sunday schools, Welsh

The system of circulating schools which existed in Wales (CYMRU) between 1731 and 1779 has been called 'perhaps the most remarkable experiment in mass-religious education undertaken anywhere in Britain or its colonial possessions in the 18th century' (Glanmor Williams et al., *Pioneers of Welsh Education* 11). Its work was continued by the Welsh Sunday schools from the end of the 18th century (see also BIBLE). Both were essential for the successful development of Welsh-medium EDUCATION in the second half of the 20th century.

As in Scotland (ALBA), the Society for the Promotion of Christian Knowledge (SPCK) had attempted to establish charity schools in a number of towns in Wales from the end of the 17th century. Since most of them used English as the medium of instruction, they enjoyed only limited success. The situation was transformed when Griffith Jones (1684–1761), rector of Llanddowror, founded schools 'to teach all the ignorant People . . . to read the Word of God in their Mother Tongue' (Griffith Jones, *Welch Piety* 20). Unlike the SPCK, Jones concentrated his efforts on rural areas, and recommended using WELSH as a medium of instruction. His teachers would work in a community for three to six months, teaching children and adults alike, and move on when the reading habit in the Welsh language had been achieved. Jones's annual reports, published under the title *The Welch Piety*, show that 3750 circulating schools, attended by at least 167,853 people, were held between 1737 and 1761 (Griffith Jones, *Welch Piety* 45). After his death, Madam Bevan (1698–1779) continued his work, and under her auspices a further 3,325 schools with 153,835 pupils were held (Jenkins, *Foundations of Modern Wales, 1642–1780* 377).

When the system of circulating schools finally disintegrated, Thomas Charles of Bala (1755–1814), the famous Methodist preacher, introduced a different pattern. His Welsh Sunday schools developed into all-encompassing, powerful educational institutions. Unlike their English counterparts, developed by Robert Raikes from 1785, they did not restrict themselves to imparting basic religious knowledge to children. They provided a system of 'further education' in the Welsh language for children and adults alike. While the former learnt to read Welsh and acquired a basic religious education, the latter would read and analyse complex religious texts and hold formal discussions on secular issues. At a time when what little secular education was available was strictly in English, the 18th-century Welsh circulating schools and the 19th- and 20th-century Welsh Sunday schools ensured that Welsh children (and adults) learnt to read their native language and were enabled to discuss not only scriptural matters but also complex topics in their native language. There is no doubt that this contributed greatly to the strength of the Welsh language and its literature in the 20th century.

PRIMARY SOURCE
Griffith Jones, *Welch Piety*.

FURTHER READING
ALBA; BIBLE; CYMRU; EDUCATION; WELSH; Clement, *S.P.C.K. and Wales 1699–1740*; B. L. Davies, THSC 1988.133–51; David Evans, *Sunday Schools of Wales*; Griffith, *Nationality in the Sunday School Movement*; Jenkins, *Foundations of Modern Wales 1642–1780*; Löffler, *Englisch und Kymrisch in Wales*; Shankland, THSC 1904/5.74–216; White, *The Welsh Language Before the Industrial Revolution* 317–41; Glanmor Williams et al., *Pioneers of Welsh Education*.

MBL

Cisalpine Gaul

Cisalpine Gaul, Latin *Gallia Cisalpina*, literally 'Gaul on this side of the Alps', was the term the Romans used for the area that is roughly northern Italy today, stretching from the ALPINE passes in the north and west to the Apennines in the south-west, including the fertile plains along the river Po to the shores of the Adriatic Sea in the east, with the lands of the Raeti and Veneti to the north-east. Having been dominated by the Etruscans before the rise of the Gauls, it became the primary zone of contact between Romans and Celts for much of the 4th, 3rd and 2nd centuries BC, and the first Celtic area in Europe to come under Roman control.

§1. THE ARRIVAL OF CELTS IN ITALY

How, and especially when, Celts arrived in northern Italy is far from clear, and it was probably a complex and prolonged process consisting of several different factors. For the evidence of the Greek and Roman authors, see the entry on the Celts in ITALY. INSCRIPTIONS in the LEPONTIC language, written in the northern Italic alphabet of 'Lugano', have been found in the area of the GOLASECCA CULTURE, with the earliest dating from the 6th century BC. Identified as one of the CELTIC LANGUAGES, Lepontic thus proves the presence of significant numbers of speakers of Celtic in parts of the Cisalpina. However, the region occupied by the Golasecca culture is limited to a very restricted area around lake Como, a territory later occupied by the Insubres (coinciding with LIVY's account that the first Celtic settlers under their leader BELOVESUS settled in the Insubres territory). Therefore, the situation in this region may not apply to the other areas of the Cisalpina, where large-scale transalpine influences only seem to appear in the Early LA TÈNE period, roughly in the late 5th and 4th centuries BC. Strong HALLSTATT influences on the Golasecca culture, on the other hand, are evident from the 7th century BC, which might indicate an even earlier Celtic presence in northern Italy than at the date given in Livy's account (*I Leponti: Symposium Locarno 2000*; De Marinis, *Celts* 93–102). As such, a single massive Celtic migration into the Cisalpina is far from likely; rather, numerous small migrations and continuous acculturation processes, most of them in the area north of the river Po, throughout at least the 6th and 5th centuries BC seem to have played a rôle in the Celticization of northern Italy, perhaps finalized by a larger migration in the early 4th century BC, which brought most of the former Etruscan areas south of the Po under Celtic control (J. H. C. Williams, *Beyond the Rubicon*).

§2. EXPANSION AND CONSOLIDATION

Whether there was a Celtic mass migration into northern Italy or not, by the end of the 5th century BC most of the Gallia Cisalpina north of the Po was subject to significant 'Celtic' influences. La Tène material culture first appears in this period, mostly in form of decorated belt-hooks which also appear in numbers north of the Alps, with their highest concentration in north-eastern France and the Rhineland (Frey, *Celti ed Etruschi nell'Italia centro-settentrionale da V Secolo a.C. alla Romanizzazione* 9–22; Frey, *Celts* 144–6; De Marinis, *Italia, omnium Terrarum Alumna* 159–259). It is only during and towards the end of the first half of the 4th century BC that large amounts of La Tène material culture appear in cemeteries south of the river Po, in the territories associated with the BOII and SENONES (Grassi, *I Celti in Italia* 65–101). Even though these areas, especially around the Etruscan town of Felsina, had previously had considerable contacts with areas north and north-east of the Alps during much of the 6th and 5th centuries BC, it is only around this time that significant numbers of flat inhumation burials containing typical La Tène metalwork and weaponry appear in cemeteries such as those near Marzabotto and Bologna, the Etruscan town Felsina being renamed/replaced by Celtic BONONIA, the

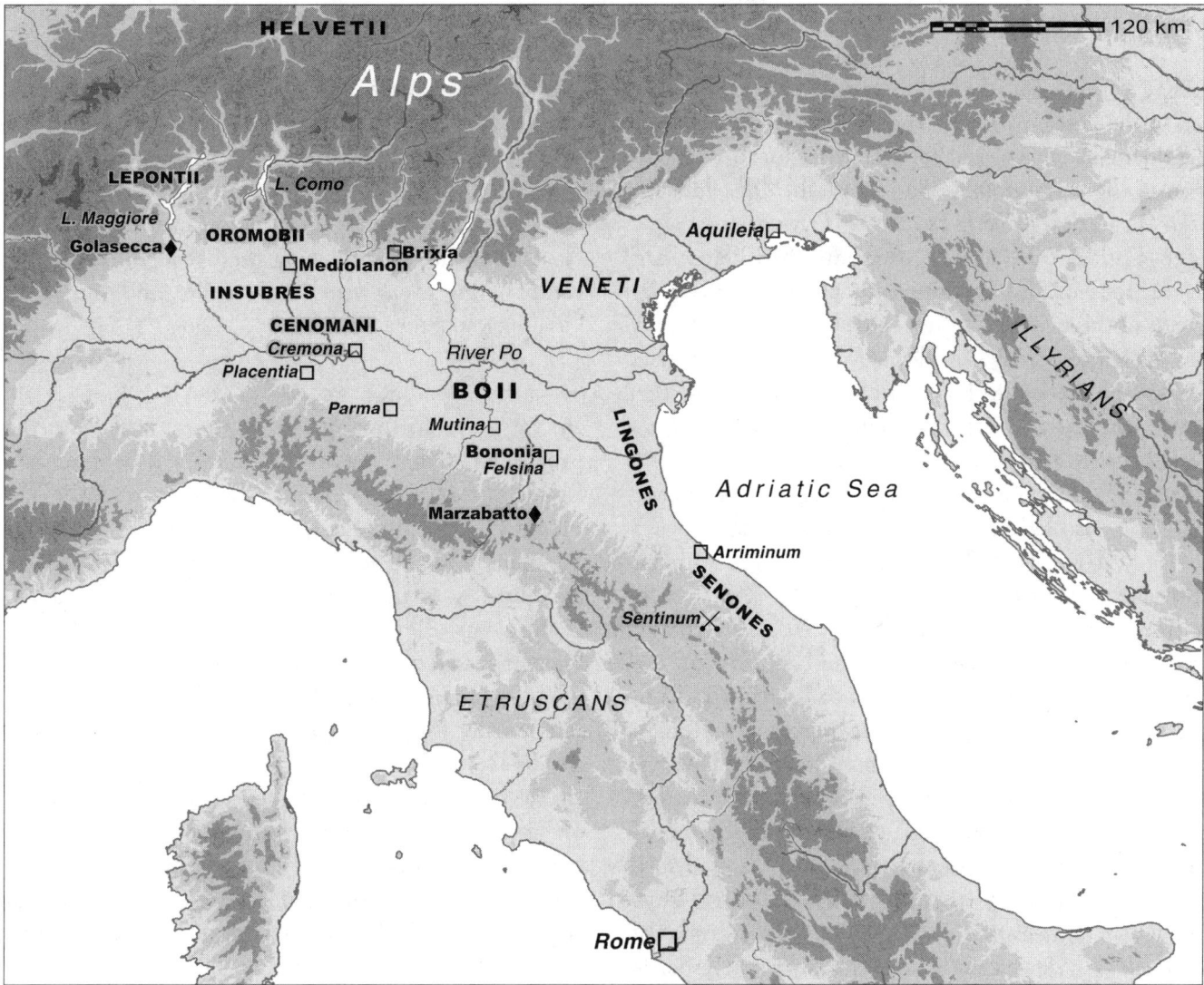

HELVETII

Alps

120 km

LEPONTII

L. Como

L. Maggiore

Golasecca ◆

OROMOBII

□Brixia

□Mediolanon

INSUBRES

Aquileia□

VENETI

CENOMANI

Cremona□

River Po

Placentia□

BOII

Parma□

LINGONES

ILLYRIANS

Mutina□

Bononia□
Felsina

Adriatic Sea

Marzabatto ◆

□*Arriminum*

SENONES

Sentinum✕

ETRUSCANS

Rome□

Cisalpine Gaul

central location of the Cisalpine Boii (J. H. C. Williams, *Beyond the Rubicon*).

For the capture of Rome by the Celts *c.* 387 BC, see the entries on BRENNOS OF THE SENONES and ROME.

By the middle of the 4th century BC most of the Cisalpina seems to have become 'Gaulish', with strong La Tène influences obvious in the material culture, and a historical source considered generally to be of late 4th-century BC date, the *Periplous* of Pseudo-Scylax (Müller 1855: 15–96; Peretti 1979: 198–218), also mentioning Κελτοί *Keltoi* as inhabitants of the shores of the northern Adriatic. Although fortunes in military conflicts with the growing Roman power were shifting, odds seem to have remained roughly even between the Cisalpine Gauls and the Romans throughout much of the second half of the 4th century BC. Settlement

patterns during this period became considerably more dispersed, which might fit in with the reference by Cato (*Origines* 2, 13) to the 112 *tribus* (communities) that made up the Boii in northern Italy, or the *vici* (villages) of the Cenomani mentioned by Livy (*Ab Urbe Condita* 32.30.6), which centred around local élites, and which, in turn, formed larger communities of kinship or clientship, or were allied with one another (J. H. C. Williams, *Beyond the Rubicon*).

§3. THE GAULISH CISALPINA IN DECLINE

During the 3rd century BC the Gaulish Cisalpina slowly declined. In the early 3rd century BC considerable numbers of imported Italian goods are found in Celtic burials in the Cisalpina; this has been interpreted as archaeological evidence for the alliances between

Italian peoples and the Celts against the Romans that led to the participation of the Senones in the battle of Sentinum in 295 BC, and the Boian–Etruscan cooperation in the years around 280 BC (Vitali, *Atti e Memorie della Deputazione di Storia Patria per le Provincie di Romagna* 35.30–5). However, fewer settlements than before can be identified, and the amount of prestige material goods in the archaeological record slowly declined. This has been interpreted as evidence for an economic crisis either due to, or leading to, a reduction of north–south long-distance trade, although other reasons have also been considered (J. H. C. Williams, *Beyond the Rubicon*). During this period, the growing military power of Rome also led to a series of military setbacks and losses of territory. Following the battle of Sentinum, the Senones were quickly subjected under Roman rule, with two colonies founded—Sena Gallica in 280 BC and Arriminum in 268 BC—in the territory of the Senones. The Boii also were subject to Roman attacks in the years around 280 BC, but no permanent Roman presence was established at that time. Otherwise, however, Cisalpina seems to have changed little in this period, although there is some evidence for the beginning of urbanization in MEDIOLANON and Brixia (Ceresa Mori, *Settlement and Economy in Italy 1500 BC–AD 1500* 465–76; Arslan, *Archeologia e storia a Milano e nella Lombardia Orientale* 59–73), which may as much have been a response to growing Roman pressure as a local process.

§4. THE ROMAN CONQUEST OF THE CISALPINA

The Roman conquest of the Po valley itself began when Roman armies crossed the Apennines into the territory of the Boii in 225 BC, following the defeat of a Celtic force, probably consisting of Celtic groups from both sides of the Alps, at Telamon earlier the same year. In a swift series of campaigns against the Cisalpine Gauls, culminating in the defeat of the Insubres at the battle of Clastidium in 222 BC and the capturing of Mediolanon. By 220 BC the Romans had reached the Alps for the first time; they moved onwards into Illyria in 219, and by 218 had founded, close to one another, two colonies in the central Po valley—at Cremona, north of the river, and at Placentia to the south. What seemed to be a firm grip, however, slipped in the following years, when Hannibal crossed the Alps during the Second Punic War (218–201 BC), and successfully recruited Celts for his armies. As a result,

Roman armies were again facing the Cisalpine Gauls all over Italy, and these may have made up almost half of Hannibal's army in the battle of Cannae (J. H. C. Williams, *Beyond the Rubicon*). As such, it is hardly surprising that Rome again turned against the Cisalpine Gauls immediately following the defeat of Hannibal, campaigning every year between 201 and 190 BC in Cisalpina to gain control over the area.

§5. ROMAN CELTS

In the years following the conquest, the Romans proceeded with a massive colonization programme. Roads (most notably the Via Aemilia and the Via Flamina) were built, colonies founded, in 189 BC at Bononia, in 183 BC at Parma and Mutina, and in 181 BC at Aquilea; in 173 BC unoccupied land in Cisalpina and Liguria was allotted to Roman citizens and Latins. Further colonizing programmes, although less concentrated, continued throughout most of the 2nd century BC. It is during this period that La Tène material slowly disappeared. This may as much be the result of a change in burial practices as anything else, with evidence of burials also disappearing during the 2nd century BC in much of the area north of the Alps, from Switzerland to Hungary (an area that had close stylistic and cultural connections with the Cisalpina in the late 4th and 3rd centuries BC). It is likely that a substantial Celtic population continued to occupy much of the Cisalpina in the same dispersed pattern in this period as had characterized the previous two centuries, with Roman settlers taking up previously unoccupied land, thereby quickly integrating the local population into their own communities. It was only in 89 BC that the inhabitants of the Cisalpina south of the Po became Roman citizens, whether of Celtic or other origin, although even the descendants of former Celtic communities seem to have been so thoroughly Latinized by that time as to be no longer distinguishable, at least as a group. In contrast, the Cenomani and Insubres in the northern half of the Padana are still mentioned by historians at that time. It was only in 42 BC that the inhabitants north of the Po were given Roman citizenship, and the province integrated into Italy (J. H. C. Williams, *Beyond the Rubicon*).

PRIMARY SOURCES
Cato, *Origines* 2, 13; LIVY, *Ab Urbe Condita* 5.33–50, 32.30.6; Pseudo-Scylax, *Periplous*.

FURTHER READING
ALPINE; BELOVESUS; BOII; BONONIA; BRENNOS OF THE SENONES; CELTIC LANGUAGES; GOLASECCA CULTURE; HALLSTATT; INSCRIPTIONS; ITALY; LA TÈNE; LEPONTIC; MEDIOLANON; ROME; SENONES; Arslan, *Archeologia e storia a Milano e nella Lombardia Orientale* 59–73; Ceresa Mori, *Settlement and Economy in Italy 1500 BC–AD 1500* 465–76; De Marinis, *Celts* 93–102; De Marinis, *Italia, omnium Terrarum Alumna* 159–259; Frey, *Celti ed Etruschi nell'Italia centro-settentrionale da V Secolo a.C. alla Romanizzazione* 9–22; Frey, *Celts* 127–45; Grassi, *I Celti in Italia*; Lejeune, *Lepontica*; Tomaschitz, *Die Wanderungen der Kelten in der antiken literarischen Überlieferung*; Vitali, *Atti e Memorie della Deputazione di Storia Patria per le Provincie di Romagna* 35.9–35; J. H. C. Williams, *Beyond the Rubicon*.

RK

Cistercian abbeys in Ireland

By the time of the death of St Bernard of Clairvaux (1090–1153), who initiated the movement within Benedictinism for a more austere monastic life which became 'the Cistercians', there were already ten such MONASTERIES in Ireland (ÉRIU). While his movement spread rapidly throughout the western church, one of its most spectacular areas of growth was in Ireland, where 36 monasteries (not counting cells and small settlements) were founded before 1272 and where they became a major force in society, religiously and economically. Although no new monastery was founded after 1272 (until Mount Melleray, 1832), they remained an important force in both English (until 1540) and Gaelic Ireland (until its disappearance).

While there had been a foundation from Savigny at Erenagh in 1127 (suppressed in 1177), the arrival of the Cistercians is usually dated to the journey of Mael Maedóc (Malachy) to visit Innocent II in 1139, when he stayed with Bernard while travelling in both directions. He was so impressed that he left four of his party to train in Clairvaux and later sent others to join them. Then, in 1142, these Irish Cistercians, along with others, arrived to found Mellifont (Co. Louth/ Contae Lú), which would become the mother-house of 23 other monasteries. It was the abbot of one of these houses (Congan of Inislounaght, founded 1148) who requested Bernard to write the *vita* of Mael Maedóc, who had died in Clairvaux, 2 November 1148.

By 1169 there were twelve monasteries, and the arrival of the Anglo-Normans brought a new pattern of foundations in the territories they acquired. For instance, John de Courcy and his wife founded Inch

Mellifont Abbey, Co. Louth

(1180) and Grey (1193), while William Marshal founded Tintern *minor* (1200) and Graiguenmanagh (1204). These Anglo-Norman sponsored monasteries, ten in total, brought monks from English or Welsh houses (see CISTERCIAN ABBEYS IN WALES), and there was a clear racial divide with the Irish houses, which looked to Mellifont. The clash between the groupings amounted to a monastic civil war, and it was only in 1228 that some order was brought to the situation; yet the divide (which is seen in every aspect of church life: the *ecclesia inter Anglos; inter Hibernos*) continued until the Reformation.

A combination of reasons can be suggested to explain the amazing popularity of Cistercianism in Ireland. The most significant factor is the absence of Benedictinism there. Since none of the new religious movements arising from the 9th century onwards had touched Ireland directly, the Cistercians marked a new way of life which was quite unlike anything found in Ireland, but which was in tune with the spirituality and theology of the Latin church at the time. Second, they arrived as part of the 12th-century revolution within the Irish church and were seen as a spearhead of that movement which was clearing out the dead wood of the past (see CHRISTIANITY)—nowhere else could they proclaim so loudly the rhetoric of 'reform' and 'renewal'. In a Church undergoing major organizational change, their claim to be the *novi milites Christi* (new

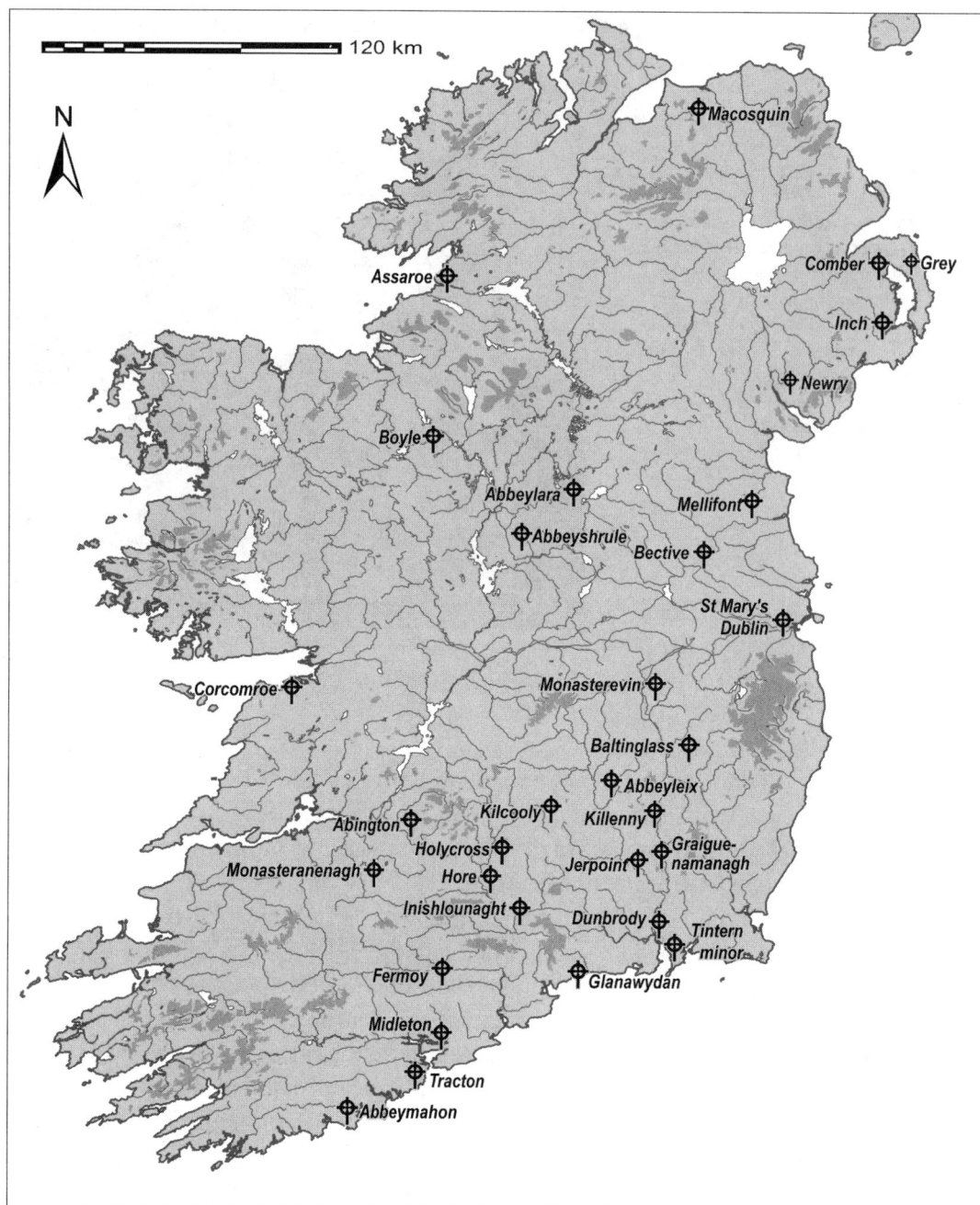

soldiers of Christ) has an obvious attraction. This can be seen in the fact that by 1170 it had 100 monks, 300 lay brothers, and yet had founded six other houses in the previous 28 years. Third, Cistercian spirituality was spread by Irish monks to Irish monks; it was not perceived as an import, and its interest in a strict asceticism allowed it to present itself as the authentic successor to the Irish MONASTICISM of an earlier 'golden age'. And, fourth, given the rural nature of 12th-century Ireland where there was little deforestation and much land that could be reclaimed, there was plenty of economic scope for their monasteries to expand.

The Cistercians brought with them a new spirituality which became embedded in Irish spirituality in the later Middle Ages, but they also brought a new scale of architecture and, as elsewhere, a revolution in agricultural methods and organization. Their production methods affected the supply of cattle, horses and wool, while their arrangement of lands into farms ('granges'), each with its own buildings to house the lay brothers who worked there, had a lasting effect on the Irish landscape (see AGRICULTURE).

In this list of monasteries, the mother-house is Mellifont (either directly or indirectly, e.g., Mellifont founded Baltinglass, which founded Jerpoint, which founded Kilcooly) unless stated otherwise; houses founded by the Anglo-Normans from England and Wales are marked *:

Erenagh, 1127, from Savigny—suppressed 1177
St Mary's Dublin, 1139, from Savigny—
    Savigniac foundations were *de facto* Cistercian
Mellifont, 1142
Bective, 1147
Baltinglass, 1148
Boyle, 1148
Monasteranenagh, 1148
Inishlounaght, 1148
Kilbeggan, 1150
Newry, 1153
Odorney, 1154
Jerpoint, 1160
Killenny, 1162—suppressed 1227
Fermoy, 1170
Glanawydan, 1171—suppressed 1228
Abbeymahon, 1172
Monasterevin, 1178
Assaroe, 1178
Midleton, 1180
Holycross, 1180
Inch*, 1180, from Furness
Dunbrody*, 1182, from St Mary's Dublin
Abbeyleix, 1148
Kilcooly, 1184
Abbeyknockmoy, 1190
Grey*, 1193, from Holm Cultram
Corcomroe, 1194
Comber*, 1199, from Whitland
Tintern minor*, 1200, from Tintern
Abbeyshrule, 1200
Graiguenamanagh*, 1204, from Stanley
Abington*, 1205, from Furness
Abbeylara*, 1214, from St Mary's Dublin
Macosquin*, 1218, from Morimond
Tracton*, 1224, from Whitland
Hore, 1272.

FURTHER READING
AGRICULTURE; CHRISTIANITY; CISTERCIAN ABBEYS IN WALES; ÉRIU; MONASTERIES; MONASTICISM; Norton & Park, *Cistercian Art and Architecture in the British Isles* (esp. 117–38, 394–401); Stalley, *Cistercian Monasteries of Ireland*.

Thomas O'Loughlin

Cistercian abbeys in Wales

The foundation in 1098 of the abbey of Cîteaux marked the beginning of a monastic order, following strictly the Rule of St Benedict, which was to have a profound impact upon the cultural, religious, economic, and architectural history of western Europe and beyond. The order traces its origins to Robert of Molesme (†1110) who, dissatisfied with the established conventual life of his day, left his abbey with a group of like-minded brothers and settled at Cîteaux near Dijon, France. Although it is unlikely that Robert's original vision had encompassed the foundation of a new order, the increasing number of those who sought to join the community led to rapid expansion and the establishment of daughter-houses colonized initially from Cîteaux. This was especially true under the order's 'second founder', the Englishman St Stephen Harding, and the towering figure of St Bernard of Clairvaux.

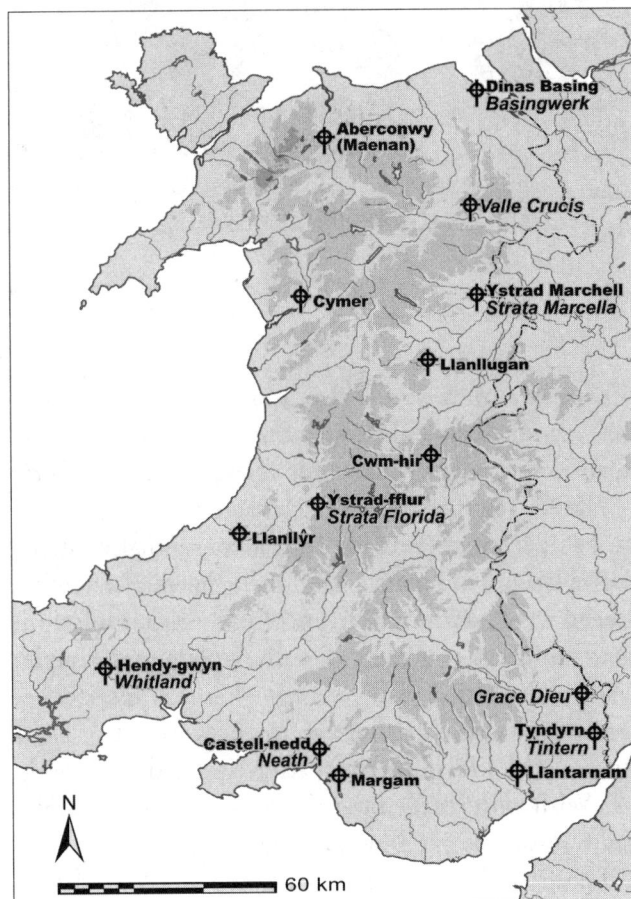

Valle Crucis Abbey, Denbighshire. South transept / Charter House from the south

By the time of Bernard's death in 1153 there were well over 300 Cistercian abbeys in Europe and the pace of expansion scarcely slackened for at least another century.

The Cistercian order was characterized by its centralized authority, coupled with a conventual contemplative life noted for its austerity. In general, Cistercian abbeys were sited away from centres of population, their buildings—at least initially—plain and simple. Wales (CYMRU), with its rugged, rural landscape, proved particularly attractive to the Cistercians, and their way of life, in its turn, attractive to those among the Welsh who recalled the rigorous, eremetic (hermit) tradition of the pre-Norman Church.

The first English Cistercian house was Waverley in Surrey, colonized from L'Aumone, a daughter of Citeaux, in 1128. It was the same abbey of L'Aumone which three years later established the first of the Welsh Cistercian houses at Tintern (Tyndyrn). Over the next century no fewer than eleven Cistercian abbeys were founded in Wales, a number which rises to thirteen when the two Savignac houses at Neath (Castell-nedd) and Basingwerk (DINAS BASING, incorporated into the Cistercian order in 1147) are included, and fifteen when the two nunneries at Llanllŷr (CEREDIGION) and Llanllugan (POWYS) are counted.

Cistercian MONASTICISM appealed particularly to the native princes of north and west Wales, and the majority of the abbeys were established in these regions.

From Clairveaux came the 'family' of Whitland (Hendy-gwyn; colonized 1140), which included Abbey Cwm-hir (original foundation 1143), Strata Florida (YSTRAD-FFLUR, 1164) and Strata Marcella (YSTRAD MARCHELL, 1170). These in their turn established colonies, Cymer (1198, from Cwm-hir), Llantarnam alias Caerleon (1179), and Aberconwy (1186), both from Strata Florida, and Valle Crucis (1201, from Strata Marcella). The two nunneries can also be included in this 'family'; Llanllugan was founded c. 1200 by Maredudd ap Rhotpert, lord of Cydewain, and came under the supervision of Strata Marcella, and Llanllŷr (c. 1180) was founded by the Lord Rhys (RHYS AP GRUFFUDD), and supervised by Strata Florida.

The Cistercian abbeys of the Whitland 'family' were notably sympathetic to the aspirations of the Welsh princes, and closely identified themselves with the language, literature, and culture of Wales, and seem to have figured importantly in the production and copying of manuscripts in the WELSH language. The lists of known abbots of these communities include names which are overwhelmingly Welsh, in marked contrast to the traceable succession in those houses founded on the initiative of Anglo-Norman patrons.

The second 'family' of Welsh Cistercian abbeys is much smaller and more loosely defined. It comprises Tintern (1131), founded from L'Aumone, Margam (1147, from Clairveaux), and Grace Dieu (1226, from Dore), as well as the two Savignac houses of Neath (1130) and Basingwerk (1131). Significantly, none of these houses themselves established colonies in Wales. Tintern's two 'daughters' were in England (Kingswood, 1139) and Ireland (Tintern Minor, 1200), and only Basingwerk in Flintshire (sir y Fflint), after a stuttering start, was to be closely identified with Welsh traditions. These distinct familial relationships were closely paralleled in Ireland (ÉIRE), but nonetheless they should not be overemphasized. The Cistercian order was international, but subject to a central control from Citeaux: 'The system of affiliation and visitation between all houses transcended political and national boundaries. They all belonged to an international order of immense strength' (Robinson, *Cistercians in Europe* 5, 10).

It was this affiliation, combined with the Cistercian emphasis upon austere simplicity, which can today be appreciated in the surviving buildings of the Welsh abbeys. Decline in the strength and economy of the communities before the dissolution of the monasteries in the 1530s, combined with neglect and depredation of the ruins thereafter until a reawakening of interest in them in the 18th and 19th centuries, has taken a heavy toll. Nothing, for example, remains above ground of Strata Marcella (whose church, if completed, would have rivalled St David's cathedral for length; see DEWI SANT), Grace Dieu, or the nunnery at Llanllŷr. The original Aberconwy abbey is now the parish church and little, if anything, remains above ground of its successor at Maenan. Llanllugan nunnery also survives as a parish church, and Llantarnam is represented by a house built on the site, though this is now once again (since 1946) home to a religious community. Whitland, the mother-house of the Welsh 'family' is little more than foundations, and Abbey Cwm-hir a few shattered walls. Only the substantial remains at Margam, Valle Crucis, Cymer, Strata Florida, Neath, Basingwerk and, supremely, Tintern now stand as reminders of the great contribution the Cistercians made to the life of Wales.

The Cistercians and their patrons aspired to build on a grand scale, but it is still an open question as to how many of the churches of their Welsh abbeys were ever completed as envisaged. Certainly Cymer does not seem to have advanced beyond the nave, and it is more than likely that Abbey Cwm-hir and Strata Marcella, both extremely ambitious undertakings, were never finished. In compensation, the 12th-century nave of Margam Abbey, still in use as a parish church, and the notable ruins at Tintern are among the finest Cistercian survivals in northern Europe. The Cistercian abbeys were also the burial place of many significant figures in Welsh religious and political history. The DEHEUBARTH dynasty of the Lord Rhys was buried at Strata Florida, the princes of Powys at Valle Crucis, and LLYWELYN AP GRUFFUDD, prince of Wales (†1282), at Abbey Cwm-hir.

FURTHER READING
CEREDIGION; CISTERCIAN ABBEYS IN IRELAND; CYMRU; DEHEUBARTH; DEWI SANT; DINAS BASING; ÉIRE; LLYWELYN AP GRUFFUDD; MONASTICISM; POWYS; RHYS AP GRUFFUDD; WELSH; YSTRAD MARCHELL; YSTRAD-FFLUR; Cowley, *Monastic Order in South Wales 1066–1349*; O'Sullivan, *Cistercian Settlements in Wales and Monmouthshire*; Robinson, *Cistercian Abbeys of Britain*; Robinson, *Cistercians in Europe 1098–1998*; D. H. Williams, *Welsh Cistercians*; D. H. Williams, *Welsh Cistercians: Aspects of their Economic History*; D. H. Williams, *White Monks in Gwent and the Border*.

John Morgan-Guy

Iron helmet from Ciumeşti with bronze crest representing a bird of prey with flexible wings

Ciumeşti

Between 1962 and 1965 a flat cemetery of the LA TÈNE culture of the IRON AGE was excavated at Ciumeşti in north-west Romania (see DACIANS). The graves lie on a sand-dune and were disturbed by modern buildings. Thirty-four graves were excavated, among which there were 21 simple cremations in pits, seven inhumations and six cremations buried in urns. Where this could be determined, the shape of the funerary pits was rectangular in the case of the inhumation graves and oval for the cremation graves; their depth varied from 0.60 to 2.20 m below the ground surface. The number and type of finds in the graves differed from one to another: the grave inventories were determined, in part at least, by the sex and the social position of the deceased.

Among the grave goods were bronze and iron objects: personal ornaments including bracelets, anklets, fibulae (brooches), girdle chains, belt hooks, buckles, and buttons; weapons comprising SWORDS, sword chains, spearheads, daggers, and a shield boss; and also tools and utensils including knives, razors, bones, and a dipper for pouring hot metal. The pottery is mainly wheel-made, of the type found in Celtic-speaking La Tène zones further west, but there were also local hand-made vessels. The burials were often accompanied by animal SACRIFICE, especially of pigs, whose bones were also found in the graves. The burials at the Ciumeşti cemetery began at the end of the 4th century BC, and it remained in use for about two centuries. Many similar cemeteries were also excavated in the Transylvania region of Romania, the most important being those in Piscolt (Satu Mare county) and Fântânele (Bistrita-Nasaud county), both with more than 100 graves.

A spectacular warrior chieftain grave, probably a cremation burial, was found accidentally in the perimeter of the Ciumeşti cemetery in 1961. This grave contained, in a more or less delicate state of preservation, an iron helmet with a bronze crest, a pair of griffins made of bronze, a spearhead, and a chain-mail shirt on which there was fixed a bronze rosette with a coat ornament. The helmet, on top of which is fixed a bird of prey with outstretched wings made of sheet bronze, is especially important since, for the time being, it is a unique item among Celtic finds, and one of the best known and most often reproduced pieces of Celtic ART. One of the scenes displayed on the inside of the GUNDESTRUP CAULDRON provides a good parallel to the Ciumeşti bird helmet. The early literatures of Wales (CYMRU) and Ireland (ÉRIU) also provide evidence for the significance of the bird of prey as the constant figure of heroic carnage on the battlefield, for example, in the GODODDIN, or as a manifestation of the war-goddess, as in TÁIN BÓ CUAILNGE and other tales of the ULSTER CYCLE. The date of manufacture of the Ciumeşti helmet has been established as the 4th century BC, but its deposition in its last owner's grave happened some generations later, in the 3rd century BC. The griffins found in the grave might come from a Hellenistic Greek source, perhaps as loot taken during the foray made by the Celts into the BALKANS in 279–8 BC (see BRENNOS OF THE PRAUSI).

A Celtic settlement was identified about 500 m to the south-west of the Ciumeşti cemetery, where eight sunken floor rectangular dwellings have been excavated. The roofs of these buildings, which had two slopes, were made of reed, and the fireplaces were placed in the centre of the main room. In these dwellings were found jewellery, tools, and fragments of Celtic wheel-made pottery, as well as local handmade pottery.

FURTHER READING
ART; BALKANS; BRENNOS OF THE PRAUSI; CYMRU; DACIANS;
ÉRIU; GODODDIN; GUNDESTRUP CAULDRON; IRON AGE; LA
TÈNE; SACRIFICE; SWORDS; TÁIN BÓ CUAILNGE; ULSTER
CYCLE; Crişan, *Materiale dacice din necropola şi aşezarea de la
Ciumeşti*; Crişan, *Marmatia* 2.54–93; Rusu & Bandula, *Mormântul
unei cacăpetenit celtice de la Crişan*; Zirra, *Un cimitir celtic în
Nord-vestul României*.

Lucian Vaida

Civitalba is the site of an important group of
Etrusco-Roman terracotta sculptural adornments for
a temple. They include depictions of Celtic warriors,
and were most probably part of a sanctuary commemorating the Roman conquest of CISALPINE GAUL.
For CELTIC STUDIES, the Civitalba sculptures are
important both as direct evidence for the appearance
of Celts and Celtic accoutrements in the later pre-
Roman IRON AGE and also as evidence for establishing
an ethnographic stereotype of the Celt in the artistic
canon of the rival civilization of Rome. In particular,
Civitalba shows early Roman artists adapting images
and themes of WARFARE between Hellenistic Greeks
and the eastern Celts to reflect events in ITALY, viewed
with a conscious parallelism.

The Civitalba group was discovered in 1896 on high
ground 6 km north-east of the ancient *municipium* at
Sentinum (Sassoferrato, in the province of Ancona),
close to a pottery oven. No further evidence of religious architecture has been found on the site. However,
the form of the terracotta pieces shows that they must
have once decorated a small temple built at the beginning of the 2nd century BC, at the time of the victories
of the Roman Republic over the Celts and its
occupation of the Po valley.

The closed pediment includes figures from classical
mythology about 65 cm in height, almost completely
in the round. The statues are part of a Dionysian
procession made up of Maenads, Satyrs, Amours, and
Winds, arranged around two central figures which are
now lost. This group most probably represents the
marriage of Dionysus and Arianna.

The frieze, much of which is also missing, is made
up of several terracotta slabs (about 45 cm in height),
hewn before baking and fixed together afterwards with
predetermined joints. The scene shows the sacking of
a temple interrupted by the intervention of female
deities (Artemis firing her arrows and Latona hurling
a torch can be identified). The destruction is being
carried out by the Gauls, easily recognized by their

*Terracotta frieze from Civitalba
depicting Gaulish / Galatian
plunderers in flight*

weaponry (elongated SHIELDS with a central boss and wide belts for their SWORDS), LA TÈNE style TORCS, full moustaches, and stiff tufted hairstyles as described in the ethnographic tradition of POSIDONIUS. The Celts are depicted in flight and laden with their booty (mostly votive offerings to the sanctuary). One group of figures consists of a Gaulish chief in a two-wheeled CHARIOT drawn by horses and flanked by two fleeing Gauls on foot. Another group depicts a Gaul supporting the body of his dead comrade and standing alongside Artemis and another Gaul dressed in a *sagos* (tunic) made of animal skin and carrying a stolen vase.

The iconography of the frieze, the *Galatomachia* (battle of the Gauls/Galatians), is found widely in Greece and Asia Minor (see GALATIA) and is generally associated with the historical event of the sacking of the sanctuary at Delphi by the Galatians in 279/278 BC. At Civitalba, however, the theme has probably been adapted for local significance, alluding to the raids that were carried out by the Cisalpine Celtic SENONES in the region during the 4th and the 3rd centuries BC (see also BRENNOS OF SENONES). Stylistically, the drapery clothing the strong tension of the figures reflects the influence of scenes of Galatian warriors at PERGAMON and was subsequently widely copied in Italy, for example, on urns from Chiusi, Volterra, and Perugia.

FURTHER READING
BRENNOS OF THE SENONES; CELTIC STUDIES; CHARIOT; CISALPINE GAUL; GALATIA; GAUL; IRON AGE; ITALY; LA TÈNE; PERGAMON; POSIDONIUS; SENONES; SHIELD; SWORDS; TORC; WARFARE; Höckmann, *Jahrbuch des Deutschen Archäologischen Instituts* 106.199–230; Landolfi, *Ostraka, Rivista di antichità* 3.1.73–93; Laurenzi, *Bollettino d'Arte* 7.259–79; Pairault-Massa, *I Galli e l'Italia* 197–203; Sassatelli, *Les Celtes en Italie* 112.56–63; Verzar, *I Galli e l'Italia* 196–7; Zuffa, *Scritti in onore di A. Calderoni e E. Paribeni* 267–88.

Luca Tori

Civitas (*cīvitās*, pl. *cīvitātes*) is a Latin word and governmental term with several meanings: 'the condition of (Roman) citizenship, the community of Roman citizens, the state, a city state'. It is the source of English *city* and is often translated as 'city'. When applied to the Celtic world in ancient Latin literature, 'city' is hardly ever a good translation. For example, when CAESAR refers to the AEDUI of GAUL or the TRINOVANTES of BRITAIN as *civitates*, he did not mean a Mediterranean-style city state or a proto-urban stronghold that functioned as their centre of assembly and chief seat of their rulers; for the latter his term was OPPIDUM. It is likely that the native word corresponding to Caesar's *civitas* was Gallo-Brittonic *toutā*; cf. Old Irish TUATH. 'Tribe' would not be a perfect translation, but is less misleading than 'state', 'city', or 'nation'.

Following the Roman conquests of Celtic peoples on the Continent and in Britain, most communities were organized as *civitates* at a sub-provincial level. These units now resembled the cities of Italy and Greece in that they generally had a Romanized market town as their *caput* (capital, centre) at the hub of the local network of Roman ROADS. For the most part, these ROMANO-CELTIC *civitates* continued the old pre-Roman tribes, for example, the ARVERNI, Atrebates (in Gaul and Britain), Bellovaci, Rēmi, BRIGANTES, CATUVELLAUNI, Demetae, and many others. In a few cases, new *civitates* seem to have been created by the Romans to reward allies with territory, for example, the Rēgni or Rēgnēnses created for the philo-Roman British ruler COGIDUBNUS, or perhaps sometimes to break up unwieldy or anti-Roman tribes, as may have led to the creation of a new *civitas* given the generic name BELGAE in south central Britain. By the later Roman period each of the *civitates* had a 'town council' (*curia* or *ordo*), made up of roughly 100 *decuriones*, well-to-do local Roman citizens; St PATRICK's father, Calpurnius, had been a ROMANO-BRITISH *decurio*. Most of Britain's *civitas* capitals received imposing defensive walls in the 3rd or 4th century. After the Roman period, individual *civitates*—themselves continuing pre-Roman tribes—sometimes survived to become independent kingdoms within roughly the same boundaries, for example, DYFED from the old *civitas Demetorum*, DUMNONIA in what is now south-west England, the Anglo-Saxon kingdom of Kent, and in ARMORICA the early medieval kingdom known alternatively as Bro-Uueroc or GWENED continued the *civitas Venetorum*. The transition process from Romanized *civitas* to Dark Age kingdom is murky, but we should consider the account of Zosimus, the 5th-century Byzantine historian, of the end of Roman rule in AD 409:

. . . the barbarians from beyond the RHINE overran everything at will and reduced the inhabitants of the British Island and of the peoples in Gaul to the necessity of rebelling from the Roman Empire and of living by themselves, no longer obeying the Romans' laws. The BRITONS, therefore, taking up arms and fighting on their own behalf, freed the cities from the barbarians . . . and the whole of Armorica and other provinces of Gaul, imitating the Britons, freed themselves in the same way, expelling Roman officials and establishing a sovereign constitution on their own authority. (Zosimus 6.5.2f.; trans. Thompson, *Britannia* 8.306)

The revolt in Britain may have involved *bacaudae* or peasant rebels as was the case in Armorica, but this is not certain. In AD 410, the Emperor Honorius wrote to Britain's *civitates* telling them to see to their own defence. They were probably the highest level of Romanized structure still functioning following the expulsion of the governors. Historians have often seen the letter of Honorius as the formal end of Roman Britain. In GILDAS's account of this period and the ANGLO-SAXON 'CONQUEST' of the 5th century, *civitates* is used to mean the fortified Roman towns—according to him there were 28 (*De Excidio Britanniae* §3)—and also the chief institutional centres of the Christian British *cives* 'citizens'. Somewhat inconsistently, he portrays these towns as undergoing both abandonment and horrific destruction at the hands of barbarian invaders (*De Excidio Britanniae* §§19, 26). HISTORIA BRITTONUM (§66) supplies the list of 28 *civitates*, each of which has a name beginning with Old Welsh *Cair* (*caer* 'fortified town').

In WELSH, Latin *civitas* survives as *ciwed*, which can mean 'rabble', but there are traces of the older meaning. The GODODDIN (A.23.261) refers once to the enemy as *Lloegrwys giwet*, 'the *civitas* of Lowland Britain, England'. The reference may be specifically to the fortified Roman town of CATRAETH. In MARWNAD CUNEDDA, there appears to be a Welsh word derived from *civitates* which refers to two Roman fortified towns immediately south of HADRIAN'S WALL that were facing destruction from the north. LE YAUDET, the name of a Roman and early medieval fortified town in northern Brittany (BREIZH), derives from *civitat-em*, the Latin oblique form of *civitas*.

FURTHER READING
AEDUI; ANGLO-SAXON 'CONQUEST'; ARMORICA; ARVERNI;

BELGAE; BREIZH; BRIGANTES; BRITAIN; BRITONS; CAESAR; CATRAETH; CATUVELLAUNI; COGIDUBNUS; DUMNONIA; DYFED; GAUL; GILDAS; GODODDIN; GWENED; HADRIAN'S WALL; HISTORIA BRITTONUM; LE YAUDET; MARWNAD CUNEDDA; OPPIDUM; PATRICK; RHINE; ROADS; ROMANO-BRITISH; ROMANO-CELTIC; TRINOVANTES; TUATH; WELSH; Bartholomew, *Britannia* 13.261–70; Dark, *Civitas to Kingdom*; Higham, *Rome, Britain and the Anglo-Saxons*; Higham, *English Conquest*; Michael E. Jones, *End of Roman Britain*; Lapidge & Dumville, *Gildas*; Miller, *Britannia* 6.141–5; Thompson, *Antiquity* 30.163–7; Thompson, *Britannia* 8.303–18; Thompson, *Britannia* 10.203–26; Thompson, *Classical Quarterly* 76 [new ser. 32] 445–62.

JTK

An **Claidheamh Soluis** (The sword of light) was a bilingual newspaper established by CONRADH NA GAEILGE (The Gaelic League) as its official organ in March 1899. Its first editor was Eoin MACNEILL (1867–1945). In August 1900 the League assumed control of the weekly bilingual paper *Fáinne an Lae* (Daybreak), when its publisher, Brian Ó Dubhghaill (Bernard Doyle), became bankrupt, and the two papers were merged as *An Claidheamh Soluis agus Fáinne an Lae*. The main medium for Gaelic League propaganda, the paper also made an important contribution to the revival of IRISH LITERATURE, particularly during the editorship of Pádraig MAC PIARAIS, from 1903 to 1909, when it published original literary works, reviews, literary criticism and instructive articles. It is a major source for the study of developing Irish cultural and political NATIONALISM in the early 20th century. In its later history the paper appeared under various names: *Fáinne an Lae agus an Claidheamh Soluis* (1918), *Misneach* (Courage; November 1919–July 1922), then again *Fáinne an Lae agus an Claidheamh Soluis*, and finally *An Claidheamh Soluis agus Fáinne an Lae* (July 1926–May 1932), after which it was discontinued.

FURTHER READING
CONRADH NA GAEILGE; IRISH LITERATURE; MACNEILL; MAC PIARAIS; NATIONALISM; Edwards, *Patrick Pearse*; Martin & Byrne, *Scholar Revolutionary*; Nic Pháidín, *Fáinne an Lae agus an Aithbheochan (1898–1900)*; O'Leary, *Prose Literature of the Gaelic Revival 1881–1921*; Ó Súilleabháin, *An Piarsach agus Conradh na Gaeilge*; Tierney, *Eoin MacNeill*.

Pádraigín Riggs

clan

As a form of social organization, clans were, and are, found in many parts of the world. The English word 'clan', by now a common term in the field of social anthropology, is a loan from GAELIC (see below), and this social institution thus has a particular association with the Celtic cultures that flourished in north-west Europe during the medieval period, most especially in the Scottish HIGHLANDS and Islands. Although popularly linked to kin-based societies, the Highland clans of Scotland (ALBA) were an institution that came into being as kin-based societies were breaking down. The extended kin-groups, or lineages, which lay at the heart of such kin-based societies (e.g., the Welsh *gwely* or Irish *fine*) had a tendency to grow from shallow or minimal lineages, extended across three or four generations, to deep maximal lineages that extended across as many as ten generations or more. Clans developed out of the latter. They differed from maximal lineages in that whereas maximal lineages were still bonded by kinship (e.g., the *cenedl* of Wales/CYMRU or the *gens* of early Ireland/ÉRIU), clans were as much about assumed or putative kin-ties as about real ones. All clans were named after an ancestor-founder. Over time, as the family of this ancestor-founder expanded, it divided into branches or septs (called *sliochd* in the Scottish Highlands), each ranked according to when it became distinguished from the main stem of the family. The genealogical ties that bound the various branches together provided clans with their functioning ties of kin. As long as these real, albeit extended, ties were the only ties involved, then the various branches are more accurately seen as constituting a maximal lineage. Once a maximal lineage absorbed non-kin as members, it became a clan. This absorption of non-kin usually occurred when a deep lineage controlled more land than it could occupy using men from within its own ranks. Their absorption of non-kindred groups was either by formal alliance, such as with the bonds of friendship used in the Scottish Highlands, or by individuals simply adopting the name of a clan. All clans had a chief (a *ceann-cinnidh* in the Scottish Highlands) who was usually a senior member of the family around which the clan had grown, but not necessarily the living person who was genealogic-ally closest to the ancestor-founder of the clan. In

large clans, a lesser chief would have led each of the various branches.

Clans in this sense were widely developed in the Highlands and Islands of Scotland and in parts of Ireland, but were not a prominent feature of native Welsh society. They emerged under specific conditions, usually in politically volatile or unstable areas that lay beyond the bounds of early state systems. In the Scottish Highlands, for instance, clans emerged during the 13th and 14th centuries in those parts, invariably the more rugged parts, which the Scottish Crown regularly threatened but could not subdue. Energized by chiefly ambition, clans provided an eruptive form of socio-political order that filled the resultant vacuum, but the endemic rivalry amongst them meant that they were never a stable form of socio-political order. Chiefs competed with one another in a number of ways. Many maintained bloody feuds with other clans that lasted for decades—feuds that were usually focused on who should occupy land around the edge of a clan's territory. Chiefs also strove to establish the most favourable marriage alliances. Like a successful feud, a marriage was an occasion for an extravagant and hugely symbolic FEAST that could last for days, its extravagance of consumption making a powerful statement in a society in which most people lived on the edge of subsistence. Supporting these different forms of display was the chiefly control of land. In practice, chiefs held all clan land, with the leading cadet branches of the clan controlling different districts on behalf of the chief and being identified through those districts (e.g., Macdonalds of Glencoe).

Among clans in both the Scottish Highlands and Ireland, there was a persistent tradition that chiefs only held the *duthchas* of clan land, that is, they held it in trust for the clan. This may have been how they first asserted their individual control over clan land at the expense of the lineage, but by the time clans become visible in early documentary sources, clan chiefs had asserted their absolute control over clan land, with many obtaining a Crown charter for it.

The term 'clan' is borrowed from SCOTTISH GAELIC and IRISH *clann*, Old Irish *cland*. This GOIDELIC word's original and more primary meaning is 'children' or 'descendants'. Old Irish *cland* reflects Primitive Irish **qlanda*, a borrowing from BRYTHONIC or British Latin *planta*, meaning 'children' (as does Welsh *plant* still), showing a special insular semantic development of Classical Latin *planta* 'sprout, shoot' (see also P-CELTIC; Q-CELTIC).

FURTHER READING
ALBA; BRYTHONIC; CYMRU; ÉRIU; FEAST; GAELIC; GOIDELIC; HIGHLANDS; IRISH; P-CELTIC; Q-CELTIC; SCOTTISH GAELIC; Charles-Edwards, *Early Irish and Welsh Kinship*; Dodgshon, *Celtic Chiefdom, Celtic State* 99–109; Dodgshon, *Scottish Society 1500–1800* 169–98; Gibson, *Celtic Chiefdom, Celtic State* 116–28; Macpherson, *Scottish Studies* 10.1–42; Nicholls, *Gaelic and Gaelicised Ireland in the Middle Ages*; Patterson, *Celtic Chiefdom, Celtic State* 129–36.

Robert A. Dodgshon

Clann MacMhuirich

Clann MacMhuirich, the MacMhuirich family of hereditary BARDS and other learned professionals, maintained a prominent rôle in GAELIC learning, and especially Classical Gaelic poetry, in Scotland (ALBA) from the time of their progenitor, Muireadhach Albanach Ó DÁLAIGH (*fl.* 1200–30), down to the 18th century. Part of the prominence of the Clann MacMhuirich undoubtedly derived from their relationship with the Clann Domhnaill Lords of the Isles (see LORDSHIP OF THE ISLES), to whom they seem frequently to have been court poets, as well as occasional lawyers and physicians. The prominence of this relationship is especially clear in the 15th century. Lachlann Mór MacMhuirich seems to have composed the battle-incitement poem before the battle of Harlaw in 1411 (Thomson, *Celtic Studies* 147–69), and one *Lacclannus mcmuredhaich archipoeta*, possibly a descendant, witnessed a charter of Aonghas of Islay, son of the last Clann Domhnaill Lord of the Isles. Poems on the murder of Aonghas composed by one or possibly two MacMhuirich poets are preserved in the Book of the DEAN OF LISMORE (Watson, *Scottish Verse from the Book of the Dean of Lismore* 82–9, 96–9). Following the downfall of the Lordship, patronage of the family seems to have shifted to the Clann Raghnaill (Clanranald), and the earliest of their poets was probably Niall Mór MacMhuirich (*c.* 1550–*c.* 1613), author of the superb and intimately enticing love lyric, *Soraidh slán don oidhch' a-reir* (Farewell forever to last night; O'Rahilly, *Dánta Grádha* 51–2). It is a MacMhuirich *seanchaidh* (tradition-bearer/genealogist) who gave the Clann Domhnaill their most coherent Gaelic narrative history, in the Books of CLANRANALD. Cathal MacMhuirich (*fl.* 1625)

and Niall MacMhuirich (*c.* 1637–1726) continued the tradition into the period of the JACOBITE REBELLIONS, by which time the family appear to be firmly linked to the Clanranald family (Thomson, *Bards and Makars*). The last Scottish practitioner of Classical Gaelic poetry, Domhnall MacMhuirich, was a tenant on Clanranald lands in South Uist in the 18th century, and his descendants were both book-learned and tradition-bearers.

PRIMARY SOURCES
ED. & TRANS. O'Rahilly, *Dánta Grádha*; Thomson, *Celtic Studies: Essays in Memory of Angus Matheson* 92–8; Watson, *Scottish Verse from the Book of the Dean of Lismore*.

FURTHER READING
ALBA; BARD; CLANRANALD; DEAN OF LISMORE; GAELIC; JACOBITE REBELLIONS; LORDSHIP OF THE ISLES; Ó DÁLAIGH; SCOTTISH GAELIC POETRY; Black, *Trans. Gaelic Society of Inverness* 50.327–66; Gillies, *Companion to Gaelic Scotland* 42; Gillies, *Scottish Gaelic Studies* 20.1–66; Thomson, *Bards and Makars* 221–46; Thomson, *Companion to Gaelic Scotland* 185–7; Thomson, *Trans. Gaelic Society of Inverness* 43.276–304; Thomson, *Trans. Gaelic Society of Inverness* 49.9–25; Thomson, *Scottish Studies* 12.57–78.

Thomas Owen Clancy

Clanranald, the Books of

Clanranald, the Books of, are two paper manuscripts of the late 17th/early 18th century. They are best known on account of the GAELIC history of the MacDonalds, whose text they both contain. The so-called Red Book was written by Niall MacMhuirich of South Uist (Uibhist mu Dheas), hereditary poet-historian to Clanranald (see CLANN MACMHUIRICH). Niall was the author of the History in its present form, and the Red Book also contains related historical and poetical materials collected by him, as well as a few items in a later hand than his. The manuscript may have been one of those removed by James MACPHERSON to London at the time of the Ossianic controversy. The so-called Black Book is a more miscellaneous compilation, containing a mass of historical, literary and other material with a clear Antrim provenance. Its version of the MacDonald history was written by one of the Beaton learned family, who would seem to have been attached to the family of the Earls of Antrim. His version of Niall's History shows adaptation of various sorts, including the insertion of details likely to be of interest to an Antrim audience.

The Clanranald History is a valuable document, both as a source with a Highland perspective on Highland history and as an example of a Scottish family history written in SCOTTISH GAELIC. Its account begins in the 'dream time' of the coming of the Sons of MÍL ESPÁINE to Ireland (ÉRIU), in order to establish the credentials of the Clan Donald within the framework of the pan-Gaelic literary LEGENDARY HISTORY. This account is based closely on the doctrines of the professional poets. The next section deals with the rise of the House of Somerled and the LORDSHIP OF THE ISLES, and draws on a lost chronicle source or sources, including one with an Iona (EILEAN Ì) orientation. Following the forfeiture of the Lordship of the Isles in 1493, the narrative focuses on the doings of the Clanranald branch, although the affairs of the Southern Clan Donald are still dealt with when they have bearing on the fortunes of Clanranald. The quality of the History changes dramatically when the 1640s are reached: it becomes increasingly detailed as it describes the Highland campaigns of Montrose and Alasdair Mac Colla Ciotaich, using eye-witnesses as sources for details of battles, but also drawing on the literary genre of the *caithréim* or 'martial exploits'. The narrative reverts to chronicle mode and a Hebridean focus for its last section, which includes the period up to the death of Charles II in 1689 (*sic*).

In addition to its historical value, the Clanranald History is interesting because of its experimental quality. It was completed at a time when the traditional world-view and historical conventions of the Gaelic poets and historians were being challenged by post-Renaissance historiographical ideals and by external interpretations of Highland history. MacMhuirich's account shows signs of an awareness of these tensions, and of the desire to counter the anti-Highland bias that he found in Lowland writers. The History is also notable in literary terms, not least for the way in which MacMhuirich wove bardic elegies for MacDonald chiefs into his narrative framework.

FURTHER READING
ALBA; CLANN MACMHUIRICH; EILEAN Ì; ÉRIU; GAELIC; HIGHLANDS; LEGENDARY HISTORY; LORDSHIP OF THE ISLES; LOWLANDS; MAC-PHERSON; MÍL ESPÁINE; SCOTTISH GAELIC; SCOTTISH GAELIC POETRY; Black, *Clan Donald Magazine* 8.43–51; Cameron, *Reliquiae Celticae* 2.138–309; Gillies, *Origins and Revivals* 315–40.

William Gillies

Clawdd Offa (**Offa's Dyke**) is a linear earthwork built in the late 8th century at the direction of the Anglo-Saxon king Offa of Mercia (r. 757–96) to separate his territory from that of independent Welsh rulers to the west. ASSER wrote about a century later in his Life of ALFRED THE GREAT of 'the king called Offa who ordered the great wall between Wales (*Britannia*) and Mercia from sea to sea'. Running near the line of the present border of England and Wales (CYMRU), it remains visible over many long stretches as a bank with a defensive ditch on its west, sometimes still quite steep. Its original course has been projected to fill gaps between a northern terminus near Prestatyn and a southern one west of the lower Wye (afon Gwy) near Chepstow (Cas-gwent). Thus spanning a distance of some 190 km or 120 miles 'as the crow flies', it is the longest linear defence in BRITAIN and on a scale comparable to that of HADRIAN'S WALL.

Earlier modern writers on British history have tended to emphasize the battles of Dyrham (Anglo-Saxon Chronicle 577) and Chester (CAER *c.* 615) as the military events that defined Wales as a compact and isolated cultural and linguistic territory, cutting it off first from DUMNONIA and then from the Britons of the north (see HEN OGLEDD). However, neither of these events is likely to have resulted in permanent occupation up to the western seas or the advance of more than a fluid and porous Anglo-Saxon cultural and linguistic frontier. In the period *c.* 630–55, CADWALLON and CADAFAEL of GWYNEDD and other 'kings of the Britons' (HISTORIA BRITTONUM §65) are known to have had a close military alliance with Offa's ancestor, PENDA. But the situation had clearly changed by the later 8th century, and we find four battles between Mercia and Welsh kingdoms in ANNALES CAMBRIAE in the period 760–96. The fact that a WELSH language, showing linguistic features distinct from the cognate Old BRETON and Old CORNISH, does not emerge until *c.* AD 800, also means that the building of the Dyke is a useful milestone at which point it becomes unproblematical to speak of Wales, the Welsh people, and the Welsh language meaning much what they do today.

The Middle English *Offa dich* occurs as the name of portions of the earthwork. The Welsh *Clawdd Offa* is first attested in earlier Middle Welsh. Today, the phrase *tu hwnt i Glawdd Offa* 'beyond Offa's Dyke', meaning 'England', is very common in everyday speech as well as in literature.

showed that Wat's Dyke was probably built to define the sub-Roman polity continuing the ROMANO-BRITISH *territorium* of the legionary fortress of Dēva (modern Chester) and/or the CIVITAS of the Cornovii against the lands dominated by Gwynedd in the west. The long east–west linear earthwork in south-west England known as the Wansdyke also appears to be a work of 5th- or 6th-century Britons. These dates for Wat's Dyke imply that Offa's project was in fact a revival of the frontier policies and strategic ideas of his sub-Roman predecessors. In this instance, the ANGLO-SAXON 'CONQUEST' is intelligible as the English take-over of a 'going concern' rather than the destruction and replacement of existing patterns.

FURTHER READING
ALFRED THE GREAT; ANGLO-SAXON 'CONQUEST'; ANNALES CAMBRIAE; ASSER; BRETON; BRITAIN; CADAFAEL; CADWALLON; CAER; CIVITAS; CORNISH; CYMRU; DUMNONIA; GWYNEDD; HADRIAN'S WALL; HEN OGLEDD; HISTORIA BRITTONUM; PENDA; ROMANO-BRITISH; WELSH; Fox, *Offa's Dyke*; Nurse, *History Today* 49.8.3–4; Wormald, *Anglo-Saxons* 120–1.

JTK

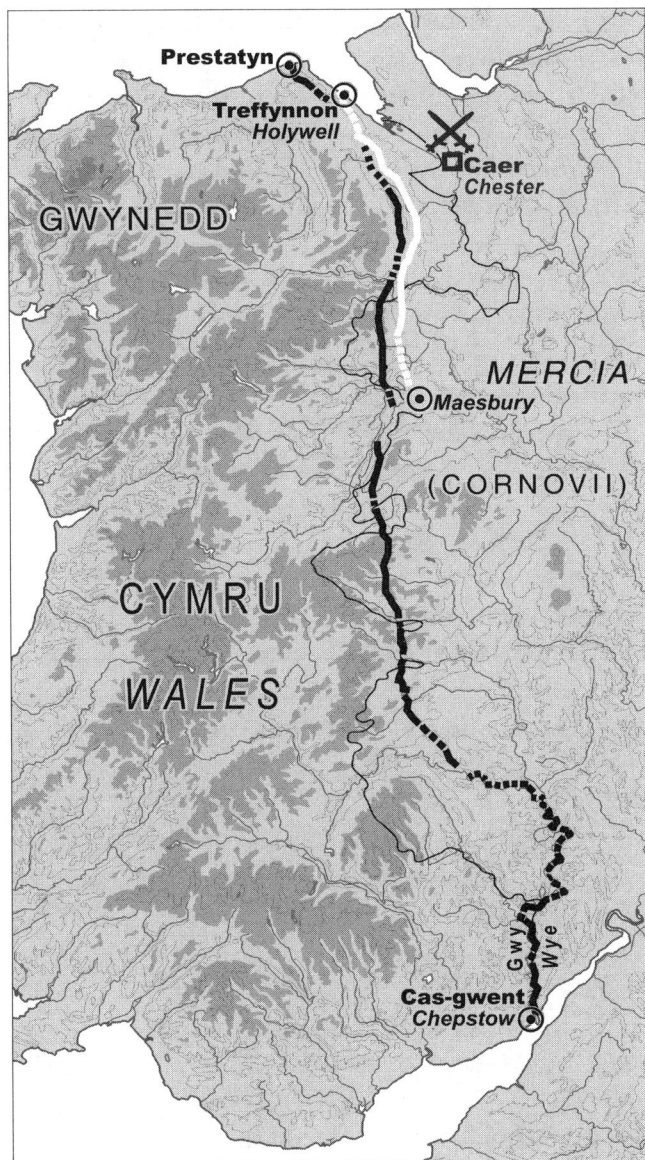

Offa's Dyke (in black) and Wat's Dyke (in white) and the modern border of England and Wales (thin black line), projected courses of the dykes are shown as broken lines

A similar ditch-and-bank structure, also defending the east from the west, known as Clawdd Wad or Wat's Dyke runs parallel to Offa's Dyke a few miles to the east between the river Morda near Maesbury in Shropshire (swydd Amwythig) and Holywell (Treffynnon) on the Dee estuary, thus about 55 km or 35 miles. It had been thought that Wat's Dyke was an earlier Mercian frontier work, perhaps built specifically by Offa's predecessor Æthelbald (r. 716–57). But radiocarbon dates centring on AD 446 obtained in the 1990s

'**Clearances**' are generally understood to be the eviction, often forced, of parts of the population of the HIGHLANDS and Islands of Scotland (ALBA) between the 1780s and the 1850s to make way for sheep and, later, deer runs (although similar events are also known from the 18th-century LOWLANDS). The wholesale eviction of communities contributed greatly to the destruction of the ancient CLAN system and the decline of the SCOTTISH GAELIC language. The subject has been called 'one of the sorest, most painful themes in Scottish history' (Richards, *Highland Clearances* 3).

From about 1760 landowners began to introduce sheep to their estates in order to maximize income derived from the land and thus 'improve' it. For winter grazing the glens and straths were required, and this is where, typically, the Highland settlements and fields were located. The communities that lived there were driven out and scattered—either to be resettled on marginal land or forced to emigrate in order to survive. Resettlement was most often on poor coastal crofts, where fishing and kelping (collecting seaweed which would be processed to make fertilizer) became the main means of making a living. Most of those evicted, however, were forced to emigrate. It is estimated that between 1762 and 1886, the first and the last clearances, about 100,000 Highlanders emigrated to Scottish towns, to Canada, the USA, and Australia.

It is now acknowledged that, as in ÉIRE, agriculture in the Highlands might not have been capable of supporting the growing population throughout the 19th century (see FAMINE), and therefore the emigration of a proportion of the population was unavoidable. However, the brutality and harshness with which many Highland clearances were conducted have left bitter memories to this day. Often, people were hardly given time to gather their belongings before they were forced to leave. During the Sutherland clearings, conducted by estate manager James Loch between 1807 and 1821, almost half the population of Sutherland (Caitibh) was driven out: their homes were scorched immediately so that they could not return, with at least one aged inhabitant dying inside. The surrounding hill-grazing was burnt so that the cattle would be denied food. The soldiers used during evictions in Ross-shire severely beat helpless women and children. Although the atrocities committed were reported in newspapers and recorded in poems, letters, and in the evidence given to the Royal Commission on the Crofters and Cottars of Scotland in 1883 (see LAND AGITATION), the perpetrators were seldom brought to justice.

FURTHER READING
ALBA; CLAN; ÉIRE; FAMINE; HIGHLANDS; LAND AGITATION; LOWLANDS; SCOTTISH GAELIC; Bumsted, *People's Clearance*; Craig, *On the Crofter's Trail*; Devine, *Transformation of Rural Scotland*; Forbes, *Sutherland Clearances 1806–1820*; Meek, *Tuath is Tighearna/Tenants and Landlords*; Prebble, *Highland Clearances*; Richards, *History of the Highland Clearances*; Richards, *Highland Clearances*; Withers, *Urban Highlanders*.

MBL

Clemency is a district of Luxembourg and the site of an important aristocratic burial attributable to the Celtic BELGAE of the region during the final generation or so of the pre-Roman IRON AGE. The tomb of

Drawing of the plank-lined chamber and contents of the aristocratic burial at Clemency

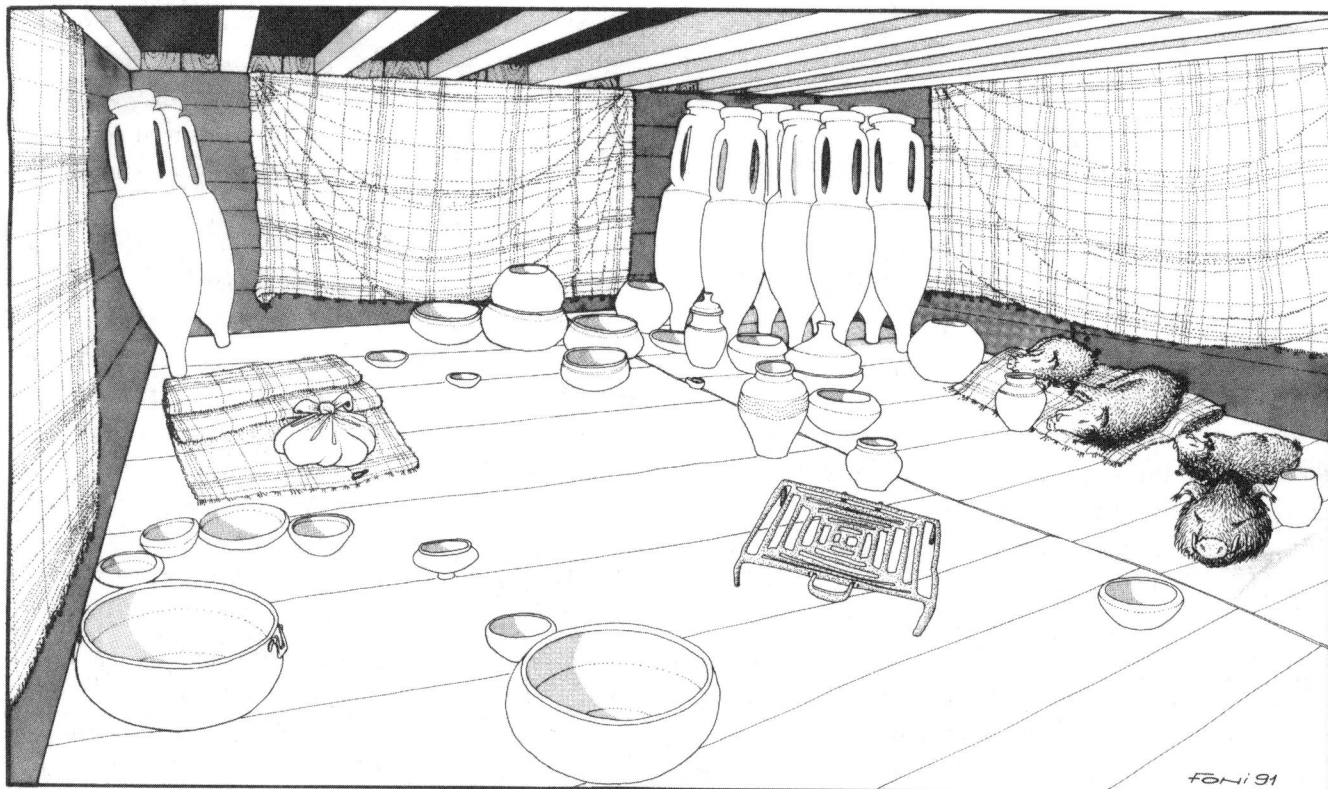

Clemency was discovered in 1987, 5 km north of the OPPIDUM of TITELBERG. It was built around 70 BC, in an isolated location on a plateau overlooking the Chiers valley. The enormous burial chamber, which had oaken timbers, was located in a ditch measuring 4.30 m × 4.20 m. The panels of the chamber walls, made of double planks, had been cut to size at the site and then lowered into the burial pit. The remains of a male cremation, probably wrapped in a shroud covered by a bear's skin, had been deposited on a floor made of large beams.

In spite of the intrusion of grave robbers even within the pre-Roman Gaulish period, the deposits and offerings bear testimony to the wealth and the important position of the deceased in the local social hierarchy. At least ten WINE amphorae (large ceramic vessels) had been deposited in the tomb. Other objects recovered included a bronze basin produced in an Italian workshop, an iron grill, a Campanian clay lamp, and over 30 Gaulish vases from the workshops of the Titelberg. Four piglets had been deposited, whole or butchered, in the southern part of the chamber; only the teeth have been preserved in the acidic soil conditions.

Through the ceiling of the burial chamber is the chimney of an iron furnace, emphasizing the connection between the deceased and the exploitation of iron ore in the region. The tomb was covered by a mound set within a deepened enclosure of 37 m per side (see also VIERECKSCHANZEN). The information gained from the environment of the tomb of Clemency is of particular interest for our knowledge of the complex burial rites of the Gaulish aristocracy. After death, the mortal remains were probably exposed on a wooden structure, as the five post-holes discovered north of the funeral enclosure seem to suggest. For the subsequent interment, the human remains were put on a pyre of oak wood. The cremation of the corpse was accompanied by a great banquet, in which one would presume the relatives of the deceased nobleman took part. In Clemency, the contents of at least 20 wine amphorae—containing more than 400 litres of wine from Falerno—played a rôle either in the FEAST or in the ceremonies around the pyre. Before the extinction of the flames, the amphorae and other pottery were broken by the audience and thrown into the embers. Then, the remains of the last meal shared with the dead man were intentionally broken into very small fragments. After the burial chamber had been closed, a mound was erected—a landmark in memory of the illustrious dead.

In the immediate neighbourhood of the tomb of Clemency excavations have revealed 29 small circular pits and a relatively important pyre. These pits contained the remains of cremated horses, cows, and pigs. The evidence of these bone fragments proves that rites of SACRIFICE were repeated over a long period on the site of the burial.

FURTHER READING
BELGAE; FEAST; IRON AGE; OPPIDUM; SACRIFICE; TITELBERG; TOMBS; VIERECKSCHANZEN; WINE; Metzler et al., *Clemency et les tombes de l'aristocratie en Gaule Belgique.*

Jeannot Metzler

Clì, the Gaelic development organization, was founded in 1984. The name is at once meaningful in itself (*clì* is Gaelic for 'vigour') and an acronym for Comann an Luchd-Ionnsachaidh (The learners' society). The organization originally focused on providing resources and support for GAELIC learners of different kinds, especially adults; more recently it has broadened its perspective to address the needs of 'non-traditional speakers', including those who learned Gaelic to fluency as adults or as a result of Gaelic-medium EDUCATION. This change of focus (which involved dropping the name Comann an Luchd-Ionnsachaidh, so that Clì no longer 'stands for' any particular meaning) has proved somewhat controversial. From its headquarters in Inverness (Inbhir Nis), Clì compiles databases and provides information on Gaelic learning opportunities and resources, organizes weekend courses throughout Scotland (ALBA), and promotes the learning and awareness of Gaelic at a national level among both decision-makers and the wider public. Since 1994 it has published the quarterly bilingual journal *Cothrom*, which includes a broad range of material at different linguistic levels, including columns, poetry, political analysis and book and music reviews.

RELATED ARTICLES
ALBA; EDUCATION; GAELIC; SCOTTISH GAELIC.
WEBSITE. www.cli.org.uk
CONTACT DETAILS. Clì, North Tower, The Castle, Inverness, Scotland, IV22 3EE; cli@ali.org.uk

Wilson McLeod

Cocidius was a Celtic deity worshipped in the northern part of Roman BRITAIN, most notably by Roman soldiers near HADRIAN'S WALL. Of about 20 INSCRIPTIONS dedicated to him, five equate him with Mars, one (RIB no. 1578) and possibly a second (RIB no. 1207) with Silvanus, the Roman god of the woods (see INTERPRETATIO ROMANA), one with the Celtic deity Toutatis (see TEUTATES), where he is also given the Celtic epithet *Riocalatis* 'of hard kings' (RIB no. 1017), and one with the otherwise unknown Celtic deity, Vernostonus. Cocidius in his function as a woodland deity is expressed on an altar (RIB no. 1207), where he is depicted as a hunter accompanied by a dog and a stag. His function as a war god is documented on two silver votive plaques where he is depicted as a warrior carrying a spear and a shield. The name is not certainly Celtic; however, the ending *-idius* possibly represents an ancient form of the adjectival suffix which appears as Old Irish *-de* and Welsh *-aidd*, in which case the name could correspond to the Modern Welsh adjective *cochaidd* 'reddish, ruddy', alternatively *cochedd* 'redness'; cf. *Da Derga* in early Irish tradition, generally explained by scholars as 'red god' (see TOGAIL BRUIDNE DA DERGA).

PRIMARY SOURCES
RIB nos. 602, 933, 1017, 1102, 1207, 1578, 2015, 2024.

FURTHER READING
BRITAIN; HADRIAN'S WALL; INSCRIPTIONS; INTERPRETATIO ROMANA; TOGAIL BRUIDNE DA DERGA; TEUTATES; Ross, *Pagan Celtic Britain*; Vries, *La religion des Celtes* 29, 64.

PEB, JTK

Coel Hen Godebog (Old Welsh Coil Hen Guotepauc) figures in Welsh GENEALOGIES as the ancestor of many of the early medieval north British rulers known collectively as *Gwŷr y Gogledd* (Men of the North; see HEN OGLEDD). These include URIEN and his dynasty—the CYNFERCHING, GWALLAWG of ELFED, and the brothers Guurci and Peretur whose deaths are noted at 580 in ANNALES CAMBRIAE. Coel's great-grandson Dunawd (Old Welsh Dunaut) may be the namesake of the *regio Dunutinga* mentioned by Eddius Stephanus in his Life of Wilfrid, but Dunawd is not a rare name. These dynasties are known collectively as the Coeling (descendants of Coel). Coel

generally occurs in the pedigrees four to five generations prior to descendants who are known from historical events in the later 6th century, placing him notionally in the earlier 5th century and his birth in the later 4th. But, since he and his sons and grandsons are otherwise unknown, we cannot confirm that early portions of the Coeling genealogies have a sound historical basis. In HISTORIA BRITTONUM §63, an alliance of four kings, including the Coeling Urien and Gwallawg, and the possibly Coeling Morgan (Old Welsh Morcant), is said to have besieged the Angles at LINDISFARNE. Therefore, the Coeling genealogical doctrine—whatever its factual basis—was in line with the political realities of the later 6th century. In the Middle Welsh pedigrees known as *Bonedd Gwŷr y Gogledd* (Lineage of the Men of the North), we find additional branches of Coeling, not present in the Old Welsh genealogies, accounting for the famous heroes Llywarch Hen, Clydno Eidyn, and Gwenddolau, which suggests that the process of growth and elaboration continued within the literary period.

In AWDL A.15 of the GODODDIN, the Coeling are presented as the enemies of the Gododdin heroes:

> It is concerning CATRAETH's variegated and ruddy
> [land] that it is told—
> the followers fell; long were the lamentations for
>   them,
> the immortalised men; [but] it was not as
>   immortals that they fought for territory
> against the descendants of Godebawg, the rightful
>   faction:
> long biers bore off blood-stained bodies.
> It was the fate of the condemned—certain doom . . .

Similarly, the Coeling are portrayed as the enemies responsible for the death of CUNEDDA in MARWNAD CUNEDDA, and he, too, was a hero from the district of Manaw in Gododdin, according to *Historia Brittonum* §62.

Welsh *coel* as a common noun means 'belief or omen' and is cognate with Old English *hæl* 'lucky omen'. Old Irish *cél* 'auspicious' is a loanword from BRYTHONIC. There is a second Welsh word which is a variant of *cofl* 'bundle'. The idea that the district of Kyle (older Cuil, Cyil) in south-west Scotland (ALBA) preserves Coel's name is doubtful on two counts: for a Brythonic territory to simply have a man's name without a prefix (*Tir, Bro, Gwlad*) or a suffix (*-ing, -iawn, -ydd, -(i)awg*) is uncommon; and the CYNWYDION of Dumbarton (see YSTRAD CLUD) seem to have been the chief dynasty of this area, not the Coeling. *Hen* is the regular Welsh word for 'old', cognate with Old Irish *sen* and Gaulish *seno-*; in genealogies, *Hen* often refers to an important ancestor figure. *Godebog* means 'protective'; cf. the 6th-century king Voteporīx who is commemorated on a bilingual stone from near Carmarthen (CAERFYRDDIN).

PRIMARY SOURCE
TRANS. Koch & Carey, *Celtic Heroic Age* 338.

FURTHER READING
ALBA; ANNALES CAMBRIAE; AWDL; BRYTHONIC; CAERFYRDDIN; CATRAETH; CUNEDDA; CYNFERCHING; CYNWYDION; ELFED; GENEALOGIES; GODODDIN; GWALLAWG; HEN OGLEDD; HISTORIA BRITTONUM; LINDISFARNE; MARWNAD CUNEDDA; URIEN; YSTRAD CLUD; Bartrum, EWGT; Bartrum, *Welsh Classical Dictionary* 136; Bromwich, TYP 238–9; Miller, BBCS 26.255–80.

JTK

Cogidubnus, Claudius Tiberius (var. Cogidumnus)

was a pro-Roman British king who ruled the client kingdom, later CIVITAS, of the Rēgni or Rēgnēnses, in what is now Sussex, during the mid- and later 1st century AD. In AGRICOLA 14, TACITUS, writing *c.* AD 98, states that *civitates* were given into the rule of Cogidumnus during the governorships of Aulus Plautius (AD 43–7) and Ostorius Scapula (AD 47–52) and that Cogidumnus had remained a faithful friend of Rome until his own time, thus implying a long reign. He is mentioned in a monumental dedicatory inscription (RIB no. 91) discovered at Chichester (NOVIOMAGOS), capital of the Rēgni, in which he is called *Legatus Augusti in Britannia* (the Emperor's representative in Britain). This exalted imperial status for a native ruler has few parallels; King Herod in the Middle East held comparable status.

An enormous Roman palace built at Fishbourne near Chichester in two stages in the mid- and later 1st century AD was probably Cogidubnus's residence. It covered roughly 100 metres square and contained elaborate mosaics and vast formal gardens within its internal quadrangle. The Rēgni were the one *civitas* in Roman Britain with a Latin name, which seems to signify 'people of the kingdom [of Cogidubnus]'. This tribe was created at the time of the Roman conquest from part of the traditional country of the Atrebates, who had lost ground during the period before the

invasion under the pressure from the anti-Roman CATUVELLAUNI.

The ancestry of Cogidubnus is uncertain, although he most probably descended from the dynasty of the Atrebates (of Britain and originally also of GAUL), who can be traced back to Commios who served as CAESAR's representative to Cassivellaunos in 54 BC; Commios later fell out with Caesar and abandoned Gaul in 50 BC, after which he ruled the British Atrebates for roughly another 30 years. His sons (Tincommios, Eppillos, and Virica) pursued philo-Roman policies in the decades before the Claudian invasion of AD 43, and all three had spent periods in exile among the Romans. Cogidubnus had no successor, the usual practice being for client kings to be a transitional arrangement with their authority passing to the emperor at death. *Cogidubnus/-dumnus* is a Romanized Celtic name, the last element signifying 'deep' and 'the world'. His Roman names, Claudius and Tiberius, were those of recent emperors who had probably shown favour to him and his family.

PRIMARY SOURCES
RIB no. 91; TACITUS, AGRICOLA.

FURTHER READING
CAESAR; CATUVELLAUNI; CIVITAS; GAUL; INSCRIPTIONS; NOVIOMAGOS; Bartrum, *Welsh Classical Dictionary* 137; Bean, *Coinage of the Atrebates and Regni*; Cunliffe, *Fishbourne*; Cunliffe, *Regni*.

JTK

Cóiced (pl. cóiceda)

was the term used for 'province' in early Ireland (ÉRIU). It literally means 'a fifth' (also Old Irish *cóiced*), and medieval Ireland had five provinces: ULAID (Ulster), CONNACHT, MUMU (Munster), LAIGIN (Leinster), and MIDE (Meath). In the modern reckoning of Ireland's traditional provinces—along with several lesser changes—most of what used to be Meath figures as northern Leinster. The Modern Irish form is *cúige*. The word *cóiced* occurs in 8th-century LAW TEXTS (e.g., *Miadslechta*) and in epic literature—furnishing the ULSTER CYCLE with the political background of a pentarchy, ruled by provincial kings of theoretically equal status, including CONCHOBAR of Ulaid and Ailill of Connacht. This arrangement, accepted as historical by MACNEILL in *Celtic Ireland*, assumes that the overkingdoms of Ulaid, Laigin, Connacht, Mumu and Mide all co-existed in antiquity—

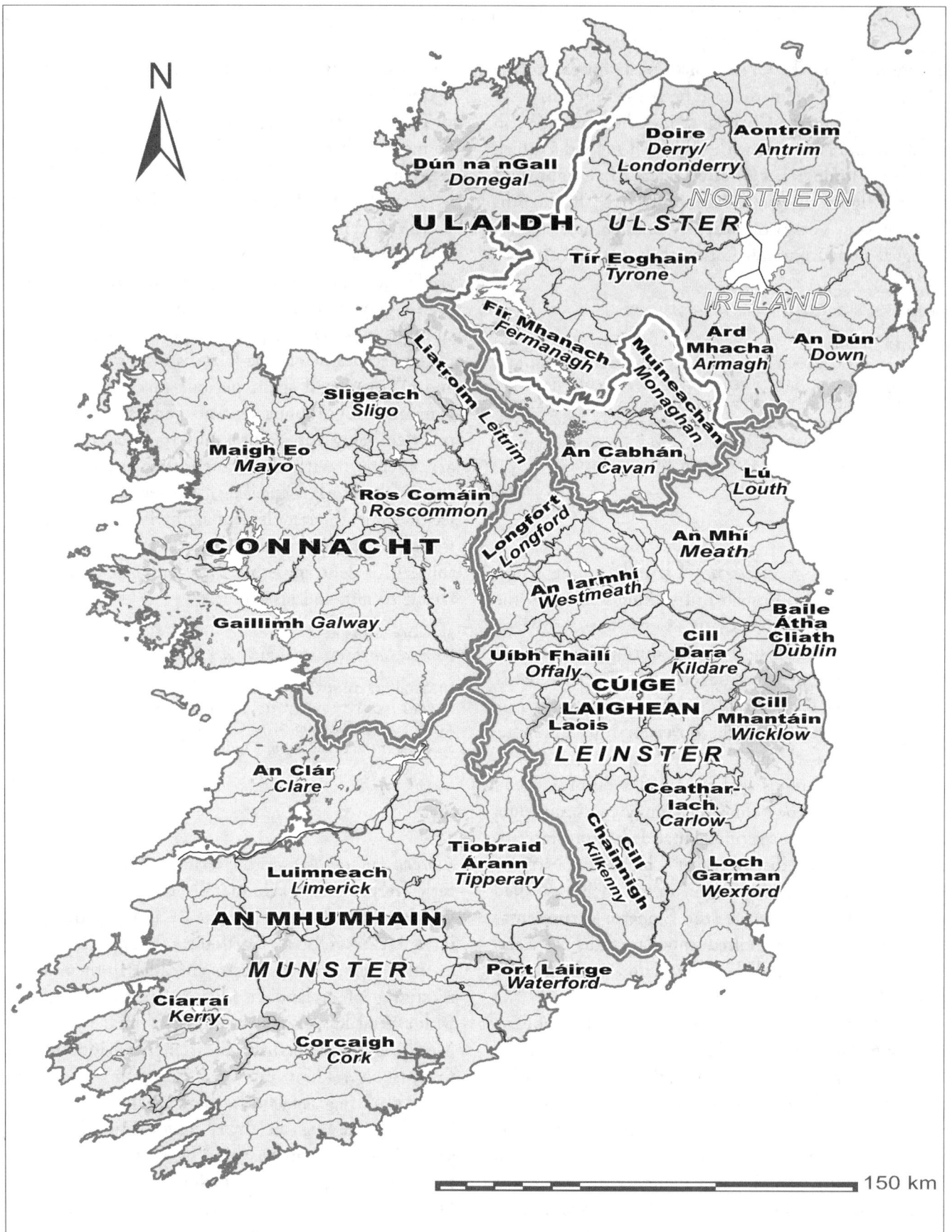

N

Dún na nGall
Donegal

Doire
Derry/
Londonderry

Aontroim
Antrim

ULAIDH *ULSTER*

NORTHERN

Tír Eoghain
Tyrone

IRELAND

Fir Mhanach
Fermanagh

Muineachán
Monaghan

Ard
Mhacha
Armagh

An Dún
Down

Liatroim Leitrim

Sligeach
Sligo

An Cabhán
Cavan

Lú
Louth

Maigh Eo
Mayo

Ros Comáin
Roscommon

Longfort
Longford

An Mhí
Meath

CONNACHT

An Iarmhí
Westmeath

Baile
Átha
Cliath
Dublin

Gaillimh *Galway*

Uíbh Fhailí
Offaly

Cill
Dara
Kildare

CÚIGE

LAIGHEAN
Laois

Cill
Mhantáin
Wicklow

LEINSTER

An Clár
Clare

Ceathar-
lach
Carlow

Tiobraid
Árann
Tipperary

Cill
Chainnigh
Kilkenny

Loch
Garman
Wexford

Luimneach
Limerick

AN MHUMHAIN

MUNSTER

Port Láirge
Waterford

Ciarraí
Kerry

Corcaigh
Cork

150 km

Major territorial divisions of contemporary Ireland: 32 counties, four traditional provinces, and the Northern Ireland border

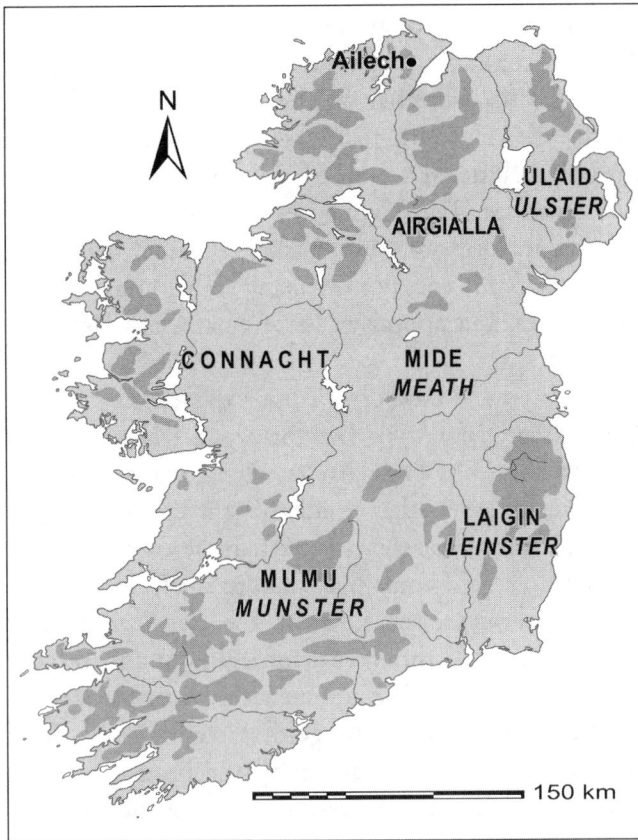

The 'heptarchy': major divisions of early Ireland as reflected in 'Lebor na Cert'

ULSTER CYCLE; Binchy, *Celtic and Anglo-Saxon Kingship* 15, 32, 44–5; Binchy, *Corpus Iuris Hibernici* 2.583.7–12; Byrne, *Irish Kings and High-kings* 42, 45–7, 58–9, 175; Charles-Edwards, *Early Christian Ireland* 423–4; Mac Airt & Mac Niocaill, *Annals of Ulster (to A.D. 1131)*; MacNeill, *Celtic Ireland* 8, 12, 74; O'Rahilly, *Early Irish History and Mythology* 172ff; O'Rahilly, *Táin Bó Cúailnge, Recension 1*; Rees, Alwyn D. & Brinley Rees, *Celtic Heritage*.

Ailbhe MacShamhráin

which probably oversimplifies historical reality. Although Mide clearly constituted an overkingship by the 7th century, its earlier status is uncertain; and even if Ulaid was by then contracting, certain overkings— for example, Fergus mac Aedáin (†692)—are described in the ANNALS of Ulster as *rex in Chóicid* (king of the Fifth—of Ulster). *Rí chóicid*, equivalent to *rí ruirech* of earlier law tracts, represents the highest order of KINGSHIP—'overking' of several mesne kings, each the lord of several local kings. Classical Irish polity was seemingly closer to the heptarchy (the five provinces plus the realms of Ailech and Airgialla) reflected in the 12th-century LEBOR NA CERT ('The Book of Rights'), where *cóiced* (presumably separated from any fractional meaning such as 'quarters' of a city), means 'province'. By this time, however, provincial readjustments had already changed Ireland's regional political structure.

FURTHER READING
ANNALS; CONCHOBAR; CONNACHT; ÉIRE; ÉRIU; KINGSHIP; LAIGIN; LAW TEXTS; LEBOR NA CERT; MACNEILL; MIDE; MUMU; ULAID;

coinage, Celtic

Celtic coinage first emerged in the late 4th to the early 3rd century BC (Middle LA TÈNE period). Several Celtic tribes had connections with the Greeks through trade and as providers of mercenaries (see WARFARE) for various campaigns (Rankin, *Celts and the Classical World*), and the earliest Celtic coins copied Greek designs. These coins did not attempt to follow the various weight and metal purity standards of the Greek world, and they usually remained in the regions in which they were issued. Thus, it is not immediately clear to what extent the appearance of coinage among Iron Age Celts signals the transition to a true cash economy on the Mediterranean model; it could have been a continuation of earlier patterns of exchange of prestigious gifts between chieftains and followers. Of course, it is possible that the socio-economic function of Celtic coinage developed over time and varied from place to place.

§1. THE FIRST GENERATION OF CELTIC COINS
Three broad geographical zones are recognized for the Celtic prototypes (Allen, *Coins of the Ancient Celts*):

(1) An eastern silver belt followed the DANUBE from the Black Sea to the southern valley of the upper Elbe. The zone extended to the south of the Sava and to the north of the upper Theiss (Tisza), although there was a gap in the middle Theiss. Most of these coins derived from the Macedonian silver coins of Philip II (359–336 BC) and his successors, ALEXANDER THE GREAT (336–323) and Philip III (323–317). A later type, issued after the Roman conquest of Macedonia in 146 BC and found at the easternmost end of this zone, copied the tetradrachms (four-drachma coins) of Thasos in Thrace. Although all the coins of this zone are commonly called Celtic, some could easily belong to other so-called barbarian cultures.

Obverse of a gold coin from one of the first issues of the Parisii in Gaul, 2nd/1st century BC, showing human head with ornamental hair style, ultimately derived from Greek images

(2) Several southern silver groups copied the coins of three Greek cities: MASSALIA in GAUL, and Emporiai and Rhoda in Iberia. Another group copied Roman Republican *quinarii* (a *quinarius* is half a *denarius*). The Massalia imitations were found north of the Po in ITALY, and Emporian types were found in an area between the Dordogne and the Liger (Loire) rivers, and in an area from the west to the south-east of the Garonne. The Rhoda type was found between the two Emporian groups. Roman derivations were found all along the left bank of the RHÔNE, and extended, at their widest point, into Switzerland. Celtiberian coins, some inscribed with names in the CELTIBERIAN language were produced in eastern Spain from the 3rd to earlier 1st century BC—some with legends in the Celtiberian script and others with Greek letters (see SCRIPTS).

(3) The northern gold belt began to the east of the middle and upper Elbe, curved south-west to the border of Hesse and Thuringia, and then north-east to the mouth of the RHINE. The southern edge ran from the Danube, south-west of the upper Elbe to Switzerland, curving north-west to a point on the Rhône south of the sources of the Meuse and the Seine (see SEQUANA),

and then westward to around La Rochelle on the French Atlantic coast. This zone included England from the south of the Humber to the mouth of the Severn (Hafren), and south to Dorset. The eastern part of the gold belt derived some of the issues from the stater of Alexander III of Macedon, but the prototype of the vast majority of regions is the stater of his father, Philip II. Some coins in Germany are without classical prototypes, and appear to be original Celtic designs.

§2. A GRAECO/CELTIC SYNTHESIS

After struggling with the foreign art form of the Greeks, the Celts began to assert their own styles on the coins. It seems that to identify the disc of metal as a coin, it was often essential to retain the Greek subjects. Since Greek gold coins were paid to the Celts for their military services, the form of the Celts' gold coins harkened back to these types, providing status to those who received them. The dominant design of the western gold belt was that of the gold stater of Philip II of Macedon, the obverse depicting the head of Apollo with short hair, and the reverse, a two-horse CHARIOT at full gallop. This coin was so popular that the Greeks continued to issue it after the death of Philip.

Two different styles began to assert themselves and draw away from classicism: Belgic (see BELGAE) and Armorican (see ARMORICA). The Belgic style in the north began a series of abstractions of the design. These were of a high artistic quality at first, and the earliest coins of the Parisii, a tribe close to the Belgic region, produced what is often considered to be the most beautiful Celtic coin of all. The style grew more abstract over time, and on the last coins of the British Durotriges appeared as little more than dots and dashes.

In north-west Gaul, the Armorican style evolved, reaching its peak at the time of the Gallic Wars (see CAESAR). It borrowed, and developed, some design elements from the earlier Celtic ART of the Rhine (Hooker, *Celtic Improvisations*), some of these themselves derived from Greek prototypes in metal and pottery—the vine scroll and especially the split palmette. The Armorican style is also rich in symbolism, with many subsidiary devices to the main themes.

Distinct styles also developed in the east, and styles associated with the Alpine Norici (see NORICUM) and, even further to the east, the Boii of the Hungarian plains are also highly characteristic (Göbl *Münzprägung und Geldverkehr der Kelten in Österreich*; Göbl, *Ostkeltischer Typenatlas*).

§3. ROME AND THE END OF CELTIC COINAGE

The conquest of Gaul did not bring about an immediate end to Celtic coinage. Legends on coins became more common, and are known both in GAULISH and Latin (Allen, *Coins of the Ancient Celts*). The larger wartime coins of Armorica gave way to numbers of very small coins, increasingly debased in value (Gruel & Taccoen, *Celtic Coinage* 165–188).

In Britain, gold continued to be used until the Claudian conquest, although this gold was often heavily debased. The British TRINOVANTES, benefiting from increased Roman trade, issued coins in gold, silver, and bronze, with the smaller denominations bearing many Roman-derived designs (Van Arsdell, *Celtic Coinage of Britain*). Large numbers of one series of bronze coins have been found at Harlow Roman temple (see FANUM), apparently freshly minted and possibly for this specific use (France & Gobel, *Romano-British Temple at Harlow, Essex*). The largest hoard of British silver coins of the Atrebates also came from a religious site: Wanborough temple in Surrey (Haselgrove, *Iron Age Coinage in South-East England*). British coins in the peripheral areas maintained Celtic styles until the end of Celtic coinage.

The Celtic Coin Index at the Institute of Archaeology, Oxford, has detailed records and photographs of more than 30,000 coins, and much of this data is freely available on the World Wide Web.

§4. THE LINGUISTIC TESTIMONY OF CELTIC COINAGE

Since they are mostly of pre-Roman date, not mediated to us by Greek or Roman authors and copyists, and closely locatable and datable, the evidence of the coin legends is of great value for the early CELTIC LANGUAGES. This evidence is mostly limited to isolated personal, place, and tribal names, and titles, all often abbreviated. No complete sentences are known to appear on Celtic coinage. Forms of interest include: LITAVICOS 'ruler of the land' (see LITAVIS), perhaps a title from central Gaul; the Gaulish title VERGO-BRETO[S] 'ruling magistrate' on the coins of the Lexovii, whose coinage also provides the form ARCANTODAN[, which may signify 'moneyer' (for

Gaulish *arganto-* 'silver, money'); coins inscribed with the name of Caesar's great opponent VERCINGETORIX; the name or title NEMET['of special (sacred) privilege' on a coin from the Danube region (see NEMETON); the Celtiberian kings' names BITOYIOC *Bituios*, BITOYKOC *Bitukos*, PIΓANTIKOC *Rigantikos* which contain the Celtic elements 'king' **rigo-* and 'world' **bitu-*); the title RIX and RICON (both meaning 'king') on coins of the British CATUVELLAUNI; CAMV[LO-DVNON] 'Colchester', VER[VLAMION] 'St Albans', and CALLEV[A] 'Silchester' as 'mint marks' in Britain; king TASCIOVAN[OS] (*c.* 20 BC–*c.* AD 10) of the British Catuvellauni, known to us only through his dynasty's coin legends and his subsequent appearance, as Old Welsh *Teuhuant*, in Welsh GENEALOGIES.

FURTHER READING
ALEXANDER THE GREAT; ARMORICA; ART; BELGAE; BOII; CAESAR; CALLEVA; CATUVELLAUNI; CELTIBERIAN; CELTIC LANGUAGES; CHARIOT; DANUBE; FANUM; GAUL; GAULISH; GENEALOGIES; IBERIAN PENINSULA; ITALY; LATÈNE; LITAVIS; MASSALIA; NEMETON; NORICUM; RHINE; RHÔNE; SCRIPTS; SEQUANA; TRINOVANTES; VERCINGETORĪX; VERULAMION; WARFARE; Allen, *Coins of the Ancient Celts*; France & Gobel, *Romano-British Temple at Harlow, Essex*; Göbl, *Münzprägung und Geldverkehr der Kelten in Österreich*; Göbl, *Ostkeltischer Typenatlas*; Gruel & Taccoen, *Celtic Coinage* 165–88; Haselgrove, *Iron Age Coinage in South-East England*; Hooker, *Celtic Improvisations*; Rankin, *Celts and the Classical World*; Van Arsdell, *Celtic Coinage of Britain*.
WEBSITE. www.writer2001.com/cciwriter2001

John Hooker

Coligny calendar

In 1897, 153 fragments of a large bronze calendar, now at the Musée de la civilisation gallo-romaine in Lyon, were discovered near Coligny (Ain, Burgundy, France). Two fragments of another calendar, known as Villards d'Héria, had been recovered nearby in the *département* of Jura nearly a century earlier, although they were not sufficient to allow a reconstruction. The fragments of the Coligny calendar represent nearly half the original calendar, and show that, although it is similar in form to other inscribed public calendars of the Mediterranean world, it is a lunar calendar where most classical examples are solar.

The calendar of Coligny covers a five-year span, including twelve lunar months of 29 or 30 days and two intercalary months inserted over the five-year period to keep the lunar calendar in line with the solar calendar. This still results in a solar year that is too

Detail from the bronze calendar from Coligny, Ain, France. Late 1st century BC

long on average (367 days), so that adjustments would have been necessary periodically. Each of the days has a small peg hole into which a marker could be inserted to note the date. The calendar contains many GAULISH words and numbers, written in the Roman script. Many of these are abbreviations of uncertain meaning.

Both the year and the months are divided into two halves. The first half of the month is 15 days long, and is followed by the word ATENOUX. This has traditionally been interpreted as 'returning night', although -nox would be expected rather than -noux. The month names, as attested, are SAMONI, DUMANN-, RIUROS, ANAGANTIO-, OGRONN-, CUTIOS, GIAMONI, SIMIUISONNA, EQUOS, ELEMBIU, EDRINI-, and

CANTLOS. They are preceded on the calendar by M or MID, presumably the Gaulish word for month (cf. Old Irish *mí*, Welsh *mis*). Month names are followed by the abbreviations MAT and ANM, usually expanded to *matus* and *anmatus* and understood as 'auspicious' and 'inauspicious', respectively.

The translations of several of these month names are secure: SAMONI is cognate with Old Irish SAMAIN, and contains the root for 'summer' (Old Irish *samrad*, Old Breton and Old Welsh *ham*). GIAMONI, six months later, contains the word for 'winter'; again, compare Old Irish *gemred*, Old Welsh *gaem*. Although the meaning is secure, the starting-point of the calendar is not. SAMONI is usually identified with Irish *Samhain* 'November' as the starting-point of the year, but other plausible theories have been advanced (see McCluskey, ÉC 27.169 for a discussion). The other month names are more difficult to explain, with the exception of EQUOS 'horse' (cf. Old Irish *ech* 'horse', Welsh *ebol* 'colt'), a month-name also attested in some Greek dialects (Calabrian *Híppios*, Aetolian and Thessalonian *Hippodrómios*). RIUROS may contain the word for frost or extreme cold—Old Irish *réud*, Welsh *rhew*, Breton *rev*. CANTLOS resembles the preform of the Old Irish verbal noun 'to sing' *cétal*; cf., Early Welsh *cathl*. OGRONN- may be related to Old Irish *úar*, Welsh *oer* 'cold'. For a discussion of the other names, see Delamarre, *Dictionnaire de la langue gauloise*. Four quarter days are also marked on the calendar: 4 CANTLOS, 2 RIUROS, 4 CUTIOS, and 2 EQUOS. If SAMONI is indeed November, these days would be the autumn equinox, winter solstice, spring equinox, and summer solstice. There is no indication as to whether these days were celebrated or merely marked in order to calibrate the calendar with the solar year. One possible festival is mentioned, however: TRINOX SAMONI SINDIU 'this/ today [is the] three-night Samhain', presumably marking a festival that lasted for three days (for 'night' meaning '24-hour period', see CALENDAR §2). There is some indication that the period around the winter solstice was celebrated, at least in some areas; 18 December is marked as the feast of EPONA on the fragments of another ancient calendar from Guidizzolo, near Mantua. Bernard Sergent has attempted to relate this to the MARI LWYD and similar traditions, which occur around Christmas and the winter solstice in Wales (CYMRU), Cornwall (KERNOW), and Brittany (BREIZH).

FURTHER READING
BREIZH; CALENDAR; CYMRU; EPONA; GAULISH; KERNOW; MARI LWYD; SAMAIN; Delamarre, *Dictionnaire de la langue gauloise*; Duval & Pinault, *Recueil des Inscriptions Gauloises* 3; Lyle, ÉC 30.285–9; McCluskey, ÉC 27.163–74; Parisot, ÉC 29.343–54; Sergent, *Ollodagos* 3.4.203–36.

AM

Collectio Canonum Hibernensis (The Irish collection of canons) is a reference book of church law. It contains decrees on all aspects of Christian living, arranged according to subject, rather than chronologically. The *Collectio* makes much use of extracts from earlier works, and the compilers cited the Bible, both Old and New Testaments. They also used the writings of the fathers of the Church, such as Gregory the Great, JEROME and ISIDORE of Seville, as well as penitential literature and collections of canons which derived from the decrees of both the western and eastern churches, such as the *Statuta Ecclesiae Antiqua* and the *Collectio Dionysiana*. It has been suggested that the *Collectio* was originally based on a *florilegium* (collection) of extracts in circulation in Ireland (ÉRIU). Some of the *Collectio* has links with Old Irish vernacular law-codes (see LAW TEXTS), particularly with the secular law collection, BRETHA NEMED, composed in Munster (MUMU). For example, the *Collectio* compilers made ingenious use of Latin terms to correspond to the carefully defined types of suretyship (that is, a third party pledging to guarantee a contract) in native Irish law. The *Collectio* contains decrees promulgated by the two factions of the Irish Church who were known as *Romani* (Romans) and *Hibernenses* (Irish), according to whether their dating of Easter conformed to Roman or Irish practice (see EASTER CONTROVERSY). Since the *Collectio* contains materials from both sides, it is perhaps the product of a compromise between them. There is little evidence for the enforcement of the decrees since hardly any penalties are stipulated.

The *Collectio*, which was edited by Hermann Wasserschleben at the end of the 19th century, survives in manuscripts copied on the European continent, particularly in Brittany (BREIZH), and no manuscript of the text survives from Ireland. It is preserved in manuscripts in two recensions: A, the shorter, in 65 books, in which the latest author mentioned is Theodore of Canterbury (†690), and B, in 68 or 69 books, in which the latest author mentioned is ADOMNÁN (†704) of Iona (EILEAN Ì). The colophon (roughly 'end note') copied into the Paris manuscript, Bibliothèque Nationale, Latin 12021, gives the names of two compilers: CÚ CHUIMNE of Iona (†747) and Ruben of Dair-Inis (†725). They are described as *scribae*, that is, learned in scriptural law.

The reforming spirit, comprehensiveness and practical arrangement of the *Collectio* ensured its considerable influence on the European continent from the 8th century onwards. It dealt with subjects such as the administration of justice, the organization of the family, contracts, as well as matters that were not usually treated in canon law collections, such as the veneration due to martyrs and relics. In the late 8th and 9th centuries the *Collectio* spread, especially in areas with long Celtic traditions such as St Gallen, Switzerland, or where texts containing edicts from Rome were scantily reproduced. There was also an insular tradition of copying and excerpting passages from the *Collectio*, as may be seen from the Welsh and Anglo-Saxon evidence. The text was read by St Boniface, Archbishop Odo of Canterbury, Bishop Arbeo of Freising, SEDULIUS SCOTTUS, Wulfstan, and possibly the Carolingian Empress Judith. One theory suggests that there was a link between the decrees of the *Collectio* on KINGSHIP and the rituals of the succession of kingship, particularly the inauguration ritual, and that this was the inspiration for the anointing of Pippin in Francia. It has been conjectured that this was drawn up under the influence of Adomnán of Iona and a faction in the Irish Church which wished to alter the nature of these rituals in this period (see Enright, *Iona, Tara, and Soissons*). The book of marriage decrees in the *Collectio* also influenced later European conciliar texts.

PRIMARY SOURCES
MSS. For a list of manuscripts, see Mordek, *Kirchenrecht und Reform im Frankenreich* 257–9.
EDITION. Wasserschleben, *Die irische Kanonensammlung*.

FURTHER READING
ADOMNÁN; BREIZH; BRETHA NEMED; CÚ CHUIMNE; EASTER CONTROVERSY; EILEAN Ì; ÉRIU; ISIDORE; JEROME; KINGSHIP; LAW TEXTS; MUMU; SEDULIUS SCOTTUS; Bradshaw, *Early Collection of Canons known as the Hibernensis*; Charles-Edwards, *Early Mediaeval Gaelic Lawyer*; Charles-Edwards, *Peritia* 12.209–37; Luned Mair Davies, *Irland und Europa im früheren Mittelalter* 17–41; Luned Mair Davies, *Peritia* 11.207–49; Dumville, *Councils and Synods of the Gaelic Early and Central Middle Ages*; Dumville, *Irlande et Bretagne* 85–95; Enright, *Iona, Tara and Soissons*; Hughes,

Church in Early Irish Society (esp. Chapter 12); Mordek, Kirchenrecht und Reform im Frankenreich 257–9; O'Loughlin, Peritia 11.188–206; Reynolds, Carolingian Essays 99–135; Sheehy, Ireland and Christendom 277–83; Sheehy, Die Iren und Europa im früheren Mittelalter 1.525–35; Sheehy, Proc. 3rd International Congress of Medieval Canon Law 31–42; Thurneysen, ZCP 6.1–5.

Luned Mair Davies

Collen, St,

is patron of Llangollen, Denbighshire, in north-east Wales (CYMRU). His feast-day was 21 May, and his tomb and probable shrine lay at the parish church in a westward annexe now demolished, known in 1749 as 'the Old Church'. A 16th-century Life identified Collen's mother as Irish, and described a miraculous lily of Collen, whose gender was by then uncertain, at Worcester. Collen's name, meaning 'hazel', occurs also in Capel Collen, Rhiwabon (Denbighshire/sir Ddinbych); Castell Collen Farm, Llanfihangel Helygen (Radnorshire/sir Faesyfed); Trallwm Gollen, Welshpool (Montgomeryshire/sir Drefaldwyn); two Collen brooks, tributaries respectively of the Tywi at Llanegwad (Carmarthenshire/sir Gaerfyrddin) and the Trowi near Llanarth (CEREDIGION); St Colan (Cornwall/KERNOW); and Langolen near Briec (Brittany/BREIZH).

RELATED ARTICLES
BREIZH; CEREDIGION; CYMRU; KERNOW.

Graham Jones

Collins, Michael

(1890–1922) was one of the most charismatic, though controversial, leaders of the Irish War of Independence and one of the most powerful men in the new Irish Free State (Saorstát na hÉireann). His talent for conspiracy—freeing political prisoners from English gaols and evading capture as the 'most wanted man in Ireland'—and his assassination in the Irish Civil War made him one of the more romantic figures in 20th-century Irish history (see IRISH INDEPENDENCE MOVEMENT).

Born in 1890 near Clonakilty, Co. Cork (Cloich na Coillte, Contae Chorcaí), Collins emigrated to London in 1906 to work in the British Civil Service. It was there that he learned IRISH at a branch of CONRADH NA GAEILGE and joined the secret Irish Republican Brotherhood (IRB; see IRISH REPUBLICAN ARMY). He returned to Ireland (ÉIRE) in 1914 when threatened with conscription into the British army. For his relatively minor rôle in the Easter Rising he was interned until December 1916. Following his release, he became one of the key figures in the campaign for Irish independence, using his network of connections in the Irish Volunteers and the IRB. By 1917 he was a member of the Sinn Féin executive (see NATIONALISM) and Director of Organization of the Irish Volunteers. These posts enabled him to extend his secret intelligence network and further IRB aims in both organizations. Following the arrest of most nationalist Irish leaders in 1918, Collins took control of the revolutionary movement. He became President of the IRB and ensured that the radical wing of Sinn Féin won an overwhelming victory at the general election of 1918. Having organized the escape of Éamonn DE VALERA from Lincoln gaol in February 1919, he led the Irish War of Independence, which began on 21 January 1919, as Director of Military Organization, acting as Minister of Finance on behalf of the Dáil Éireann, the new Irish parliament, at the same time. When the British government under LLOYD GEORGE offered a truce and negotiations, Collins became a key, though very reluctant, member of the second Irish Treaty Delegation and, on 6 December 1921, he co-signed the compromise that granted Ireland dominion status. This ultimately led to the Irish Civil War and his own premature death (see Ó GRÍOFA). Substantial opposition to the treaty in the Dáil led to the choosing of Collins as Chairman of the Provisional Government, but the bitter differences of opinion between pro-treaty and anti-treaty forces meant that by June 1922 there was civil war. Collins, as Commander-in-Chief of the pro-treaty National Army, decided to lead from the front. Convinced that he would not be killed in his own country and therefore driving an open touring car, he was assassinated during his election campaign near Béal na mBláth, Co. Cork, on 22 August 1922. His death, which robbed the country of an outstanding political personality, illuminates the tragedy of civil war in the newly liberated Ireland.

FURTHER READING
CONRADH NA GAEILGE; DE VALERA; ÉIRE; IRISH; IRISH INDEPENDENCE MOVEMENT; IRISH REPUBLICAN ARMY; LLOYD GEORGE; NATIONALISM; Ó GRÍOFA; Boyce, Ireland 1828–1923; Brown, Ireland; Coogan, Michael Collins; Costello, Michael Collins in his Own Words; Forester, Michael

Collins; Kehoe, *History Makers of 20th Century Ireland*; MacDowell, *Michael Collins and the Irish Republican Brotherhood*; Mackay, *Michael Collins*; Ó Broin, *Michael Collins*; O'Connor, *Big Fellow*; O'Connor, *Troubles*; Twohig, *Dark Secret of Béalnabláth*; Younger, *State of Disunion*.

MBL

Colmán mac Lénéni

Colmán mac Lénéni (†14 November 604) was a high-ranking Irish poet or *file* (see BARDIC ORDER). He is important as one of the earliest GAELIC poets who can be securely dated and located. The fragments of poems attributed to him which survive in the Irish bardic metrical tracts give us a valuable insight into the poet's craft at an early date, and also reveal a literary form which is already highly developed and thoroughly Christianized.

Colmán was the founder and (probably) the abbot of the monastery of Cluain Uama (Cloyne) in Munster (MUMU). He was a so-called 'ex-layman' (*aithlaec*), indicating a mid-life change of career. He seems to have been influenced to take up a religious calling by St Brenainn (Brandanus) of Clonfert (Cluain Ferta) in CONNACHT. According to traditions related by later texts, he abandoned poetry or poetic composition after becoming a monk, but in fact the surviving poems themselves contradict this idea, showing that he continued to compose Irish poetry up to his death.

The seven surviving fragments of Colmán's poetry have been discussed by THURNEYSEN (ZCP 19.193–205). More recently, Liam Breatnach has re-examined Early Irish METRICS, especially the *roscada* (unrhymed alliterative verses) and Colmán's verses, attempting to place them within the known types of early Irish poetry (*Metrik und Medienwechsel / Metrics and Media* 197–205). Stylistically, Colmán's poems stand between 'classical Old Irish syllabic poetry' and the *roscada*. They show a regular number of syllables per line with consonance, and frequently with end rhymes. The lines are linked together by alliteration. Two examples follow, which are printed showing alliteration and rhyme; syllable count and rhyme scheme are summarized in parentheses:

Dūn maic **Dāim** / *doë ōs* **roi** (3¹a + 4¹a)
ronn tart / *tacht* **coi**. (2¹b + 2¹a)

The fortress of Dāim's son, a rampart above a field, a [putting on the] chain of thirst, a strangling of moans.

Ni·fordiuchtror / *for duain indlis* (4³ + 5²a)
iar cotlud / *chāin bindris.* (3² + 3²a)
briathar Chorgais / *cen anach ndichmaircc* (4²a + 5²b)
deog nepmaircc / *rath rīgmaicc.* (3²b+3²b)

Not with an inauthentic song do I awake after sleep of sweet dreams [DIL74, 102];
[it is] a word [fitting] for Lent without anything forbidden, a drink . . . the grace of the royal son [i.e., Christ].

The syllable count is quite regular, and there is also a consistent pattern of stresses.

The highly compressed or 'telegraphic' style of these excerpts shows Colmán's mastery of metaphor. The first extract appears to have been part of a praise poem to a chieftain whose generosity quenched the thirst of his guests and stilled their sorrow. The second example shows how Irish vernacular poetry was already thoroughly adapted to a Christian milieu by *c.* AD 600. Colmán makes the point that his versecraft is even fitting for Lent, the period of penance and cleansing before Easter and a time of intense asceticism in Irish MONASTERIES in the early Middle Ages.

Colmán lived early within the Old IRISH period (*c.* 600–900); therefore his language is rather archaic, and many words are unclear or difficult to identify. He used words which had become obsolete in the subsequent centuries: for example, *ser* 'star' (perhaps a loanword from Welsh), *adand* 'rushlight', *crapscuil* '?twilight' (from Latin *crepusculum*). However, the texts have not survived in a spelling that reflects 6th- or 7th-century pronunciation, but were updated in copying. For example, the vowels already show the characteristics of the later language; thus, 7th-century *ē* has become 8th-century or later *ia*, *ō* has become *ua*. Nonetheless, Thurneysen claimed that Colmán's language could be placed without much difficulty within the expected historical timeframe, that is, at the end of the 6th century.

PRIMARY SOURCE
EDITION. Thurneysen, ZCP 19.193–205.

FURTHER READING
BARDIC ORDER; CHRISTIANITY; CONNACHT; GAELIC; IRISH; IRISH LITERATURE; METRICS; MONASTERIES; MUMU; THURNEYSEN; Breatnach, *Metrik und Medienwechsel / Metrics and Media* 197–205; Murphy, *Early Irish Metrics*; Thurneysen, ZCP 19.193–205.

PEB

Colum Cille, St (or Colmcille, Latin Columba, *c.* 521/9 to June 597), a descendant of NIALL NOÍGIALLACH (Niall of the Nine Hostages), progenitor of the Uí Néill, was the founder and the first abbot of Iona (EILEAN Ì). Apart from this, we have few details of the life of this important figure in the development of Irish CHRISTIANITY. Our knowledge derives, almost entirely, from the *Vita Columbae* by ADOMNÁN which, although based on solid traditions and earlier written accounts, was written almost a century after Colum Cille's death, and portrays him as an ideal monk and Christian. He remains one of the most popular saints of Irish and Scottish tradition. Many common stories, such as that he had to flee Ireland (ÉRIU) having made a pirate copy of a book, are much later inventions—and this specific tale, in the context of early medieval book production, is absurd!

Since Adomnán's *Vita* is episodic and without a chronological frame (although Colum Cille's death is at its end), much of our information comes from this statement: 'From his youth he devoted himself to growing in the Christian life, with God's help studying wisdom and keeping his body chaste . . . [and] he spent thirty-four years as an island soldier of Christ' (Second Preface). We know that he studied with Finnian of Clonard (see UINNIAU), and then founded several monasteries in Ireland before setting out in 563 for Iona, which became the centre for a large *familia* of MONASTERIES in Ireland and BRITAIN—it was a link-point between the Irish on both sides of the sea, and also between Ireland and Britain. Being on Iona made him 'a pilgrim for Christ' and allowed him to engage in missionary work among the PICTS. He established many contacts both with other monasteries (e.g. BEANN CHAR/Bangor) and with rulers such as the Pictish king, BRUIDE MAC MAELCON.

Many aspects of insular monastic spirituality (e.g., the rôle of islands) can be traced to the inspiration of Colum Cille, and he may have inspired others (e.g., COLUMBANUS) to combine the notions of monastic exile with missionary work (see PEREGRINATIO). Traditionally, several Latin hymns (e.g., the *Altus prosator*) have been attributed to Colum Cille, and his authorship cannot be excluded; Adomnán presents him as both a scholar and a scribe. A manuscript of the Psalms, known as the CATHACH, probably dating from the 7th century but possibly the late 6th, is traditionally regarded as Colum Cille's pen work. Legend, reaching back almost to his lifetime (the Old Irish elegy known as *Amrae Coluimb Chille* [Poem for Colum Cille], on which see DALLÁN FORGAILL), revered him as a patron of the poets.

PRIMARY SOURCES
ED. & TRANS. Alan O. Anderson & Marjorie O. Anderson, *Adomnán's Life of Columba*; Clancy & Márkus, *Iona* (*Altus Prosator, Amrae Choluimb Chille*).
TRANS. Sharpe, *Life of St Columba / Adomnán of Iona*.

FURTHER READING
ADOMNÁN; BEANN CHAR; BRITAIN; BRUIDE MAC MAELCON; CATHACH; CHRISTIANITY; COLUMBANUS; DALLÁN FORGAILL; EILEAN Ì; ÉRIU; MONASTICISM; MONASTERIES; NIALL NOÍGIALLACH; PEREGRINATIO; PICTS; UÍ NÉILL; UINNIAU; Herbert, *Iona, Kells, and Derry*.

Thomas O'Loughlin

Columbanus, St (mid-6th century–23 November 615) was born in Leinster (LAIGIN) and, according to Jonas of Bobbio who wrote his *Vita Columbani* in the 640s, he studied with Sinell, and later with Comgall at BEANN CHAR (Bangor). In Ireland (ÉRIU) until *c.* 590–1, Columbanus left for the Continent on a PEREGRINATIO. It is there that the exploits for which he is remembered took place, and it was there also, presumably, that he wrote. He is the most famous of the medieval Irish *peregrini* (international missionaries), and it is upon his life that the notion of 'the Irish re-converting Europe' is chiefly based. However, he is perhaps more significant as the first Irish person who has left a sizeable body of writings, and whose worldview we can therefore glimpse. These, in a polished Latin, indicate that he was a skilled theologian, well acquainted with the theological currents of his time. The extent of his *œuvre* is debated, but a consensus has emerged that 20 works, of the 34 attributed to him, are genuine, while six others may be 'Columbanus-plus-accretions'.

He arrived in the Vosges *c.* 591 and established several monasteries (e.g., Luxeuil) and convents there. In 603 Columbanus came into conflict with the local bishops over their authority, and appealed directly to Pope Gregory the Great. In this letter he defended the insular reckoning of Easter with an unapologetic intellectual self-confidence (see EASTER CONTROVERSY), and reveals a perception of Europe as a Christian cultural unit, in which Irish, BRITONS, and Gallo-Romans were equals as members of a common body, the Church. Later, having been expelled from Frankia over his refusal to bless King Theuderic's illegitimate sons, Columbanus with other monks, including Gall, travelled in what is now eastern France and Switzerland. Eventually, he quarrelled with Gall, who left him and became a hermit. Finally, c. 612, Columbanus arrived at Bobbio, near Piacenza in northern Italy, and established a monastery which became an important centre of learning. His ideas about monastic discipline remained widely influential until the 9th century (see MONASTICISM).

The name *Columbanus* is Latin, but was borrowed into IRISH at an early date with the Brythonic pronunciation *Colomman*, to give the Old Irish name *Colman / Colmán*, already common among men born in the 6th century.

PRIMARY SOURCE
ED. & TRANS. Walker, *Sancti Columbani Opera*.

FURTHER READING
BEANN CHAR; BRITONS; CHRISTIANITY; EASTER CONTROVERSY; ÉRIU; IRISH; LAIGIN; MONASTICISM; PEREGRINATIO; Lapidge, *Columbanus*.

Thomas O'Loughlin

Comgán mac Da Cherda

Comgán mac Da Cherda (†641/5) is mentioned in the Irish ANNALS (Annals of Tigernach 641, Annals of Inisfallen 645) and GENEALOGIES (O'Brien, *Corpus Genealogiarum Hiberniae* 1.399), thus suggesting that he was a historical person, brother of Bran Find son of Mael Ochtraig, a king of the Dési of Munster (MUMU), present-day Co. Waterford (Contae Phort Láirge). His reputation, however, is based on his literary rôle as a holy fool. According to one tale (O'Keeffe, *Ériu* 34–41), he was transformed into a fool (*óinmit*) after sleeping with the wife of his father's druid. His folly was essentially of an inspired, religious kind, and his closest companion in the literature is St CUMMÍNE FOTA. A late medieval text, *Imtheachta na nOinmhideadh* (Journeys of the fools) recounts their bizarre adventures. As with other fools and madmen in IRISH LITERATURE, various pieces of poetry are attributed to him (see WILD MAN). He makes several cameo appearances in well-known sagas (e.g., *Liadain and Cuirithir*), where he acts as a go-between or discoverer of characters' identities. The form of his epithet (traditionally meaning 'son of two arts': i.e., sense and

folly) is highly unstable (Ó Coileáin, *Ériu* 25.105 n.73).

PRIMARY SOURCES
MSS. *Imtheachta na nOinmhideadh*: Dublin, Royal Irish Academy, B. iv. 1, fos. 149a–178a (acephalous), 23 C 19, fos. 49–157 (summary), Stowe D. iv. 1, fos. 26–35.
ED. & TRANS. Meyer, *Comrac Liadaine ocus Cuirithir*; O'Keeffe, *Ériu* 5.18–44 (*Mac Dá Cherda* and *Cummaine Foda*); O'Nolan, PRIA 30 C 261–82 (*Mór of Munster and the Tragic Fate of Cuanu son of Cailchine*).

FURTHER READING
ANNALS; CUMMÍNE FOTA; DRUIDS; GENEALOGIES; IRISH LITERATURE; MUMU; WILD MAN; Clancy, *Ériu* 44.105–24; Clancy, 'Saint and Fool'; Harrison, *Irish Trickster*; O'Brien, *Corpus Genealogiarum Hiberniae*; Ó Coileáin, *Ériu* 25.88–125; Ó Riain, *Éigse* 14.179–206; Welsford, *Fool* 76–127.

Thomas Owen Clancy

Comhar

Comhar (Co-operation) is a monthly magazine founded in Dublin (BAILE ÁTHA CLIATH) in 1942 by An Comhchaidreamh, an organization of IRISH-speaking university graduates. Its aim was to provide a platform where Irish speakers, particularly graduates, could discuss current events and questions of national importance, and also to provide a literary platform, especially for new writers. Its contents include contributions from all the major literary figures writing in Irish since its foundation in 1942, as well as reviews, literary articles and features on a wide range of political, cultural, social and economic issues. Prominent contributors include poets: Máirtín Ó DIREÁIN, Seán Ó RÍORDÁIN, Máire MHAC AN TSAOI, Cathal Ó SEARCAIGH, Nuala Ní DHOMHNAILL, Séamus Ó Céileachair, Seán Ó TUAMA, Liam Ó MUIRTHILE, Michael DAVITT, Seán Mac Fheorais; novelists and short-story writers: Donncha Ó CÉILEACHAIR, Séamus Ó Néill, Dónall Mac Amhlaigh, Séamas Mac Annaidh, Pádraig Ó CÍOBHÁIN, Seán Mac Mathúna, Eoghan Ó TUAIRISC, Breandán Ó hEithir, Liam Mac Cóil, Máirtín Ó CADHAIN. Since 1974, the magazine has been produced by Comhar Teoranta.

FURTHER READING
BAILE ÁTHA CLIATH; DAVITT; IRISH; IRISH LITERATURE; MHAC AN TSAOI; NÍ DHOMHNAILL; Ó CADHAIN; Ó CÉILEACHAIR; Ó CÍOBHÁIN; Ó DIREÁIN; Ó MUIRTHILE; Ó RÍORDÁIN; Ó SEARCAIGH; Ó TUAIRISC; Ó TUAMA; Ní Chinnéide, *Léachtaí Cholm Cille* 28.74–92.
INDEX. De Grás, *Comhar: Innéacs 50 Bliain*.
WEBSITE. www.comhar-iris.ie
CONTACT DETAILS. Comhar, 5 Rae Mhuirfean, Baile Átha Cliath 2.

Pádraigín Riggs

Common Celtic is a historical linguistic term which is used in this Encyclopedia for the oldest form of prehistoric Celtic speech differentiated from the other INDO-EUROPEAN dialects. Common Celtic is thus essentially synonymous in our usage with PROTO-CELTIC. Under either name we are considering an un-attested proto-language, the speech of an original formative Celtic linguistic, living in a sufficiently compact area to maintain a language not varying with regional dialects. As an unattested language, the forms of Common Celtic are linguistic reconstructions to be cited with stars, thus Common Celtic *wiros 'man, husband, hero'. There is, however, a difference in focus between Common Celtic and Proto-Celtic. The former emphasizes this stage as the theoretical common ancestor of all the attested CELTIC LANGUAGES and implies that a given reconstruction has been reached primarily through the method of 'intra-Celtic' com-parison. The latter figures more as the theoretical 'missing link' between reconstructed Indo-European and attested Celtic forms. There can be some further subtle differences of meaning between Common Celtic and Proto-Celtic; for example, it is theoretically quite possible that by the point when Celtic had differenti-ated from Indo-European it still retained old features that were subsequently lost or changed in the same way in all the attested Celtic languages and thus must be reconstructed as Common Celtic. As one case in point, all the Celtic languages lose Indo-European *p* in most positions; therefore this is a Common Celtic feature. But traces of it still survive (perhaps in some positions as *h*, elsewhere as *w* or *w^b*) in the ROMANO-CELTIC place-name HERCYNIA SILVA and in UVAMO- 'highest' on the LEPONTIC inscription from Prestino. Thus, though Old Irish *athair* 'father' and Gaulish *atir* have lost Indo-European *p-*, we can reconstruct *φatir* to show the likelihood that a weakened initial conson-ant had been present in the Celtic proto-language. For innovations occurring in most or all of the attested Celtic languages, but likely to be an innovation shared by them after the initial separation of dialects and spreading out from the inferred compact geographi-cal homeland, such features may be termed 'pan-Celtic' rather than Common Celtic. Thus, lenition, the sys-tematic weakening of consonants between vowels and in some other positions—a characteristic feature of the medieval and modern Celtic languages, but indi-cated only in traces in the Continental Celtic languages (all of which died out in ancient times)—is sometimes called a 'pan-Celtic phenomenon', thus implying that it might have spread between the Celtic languages after Common Celtic had already broken up.

FURTHER READING
CELTIC LANGUAGES; HERCYNIA SILVA; INDO-EUROPEAN; LEPONTIC; PROTO-CELTIC; ROMANO-CELTIC; Jackson, LHEB 3.

JTK

The **Computus Fragment** is an Old Welsh com-mentary, written on one side of a single leaf of vellum dating from AD 850×910. It concerns a detail in the table (the *pagina regularis*) in BEDA's scientific works. The subject is a specific point concerning the CALENDAR and the calculation of the date of Easter (see EASTER CONTROVERSY). The text is clearly fragmentary and opens mid-sentence as follows:

> . . . *guidaur. Is·mod cephitor did hanaud. In ir·tritid urd,
> .i. in·trited retec retit loyr guor-hir seraul circhl, ir·ir tri
> VI[II] aur, is did ciman ha·c[e(ph)]i o-r bissei pan diconetent
> ir [tri] oith·aur hinnith . . .*

> . . . alphabet. It is how one gets a day from it. In the third row, that is, in the third course that the moon runs over the circuit of stars, from the three eight-hour [segments], it is a whole day that you will get from the remainder when those three eight-hour [segments] have been put together . . .

The Computus Fragment is a uniquely valuable source of linguistic information for aspects of the vocabu-lary, syntax, and morphology of the WELSH language at an early date, and also reflects the level of learning in early medieval Wales (CYMRU) and the adaptability of written Welsh as a medium for technical subjects first described in Latin texts. Some of the same points and a shared BRYTHONIC scientific vocabulary occur also in the mixed Old Breton and Old Welsh glosses in the Breton manuscript Angers 477, written in AD 897 (see BRETON EARLY MEDIEVAL MANUSCRIPTS).

PRIMARY SOURCES
MS. Cambridge, University Library, Add. 4543.
ED. & TRANS. Ifor Williams, BBCS 3.245–72.

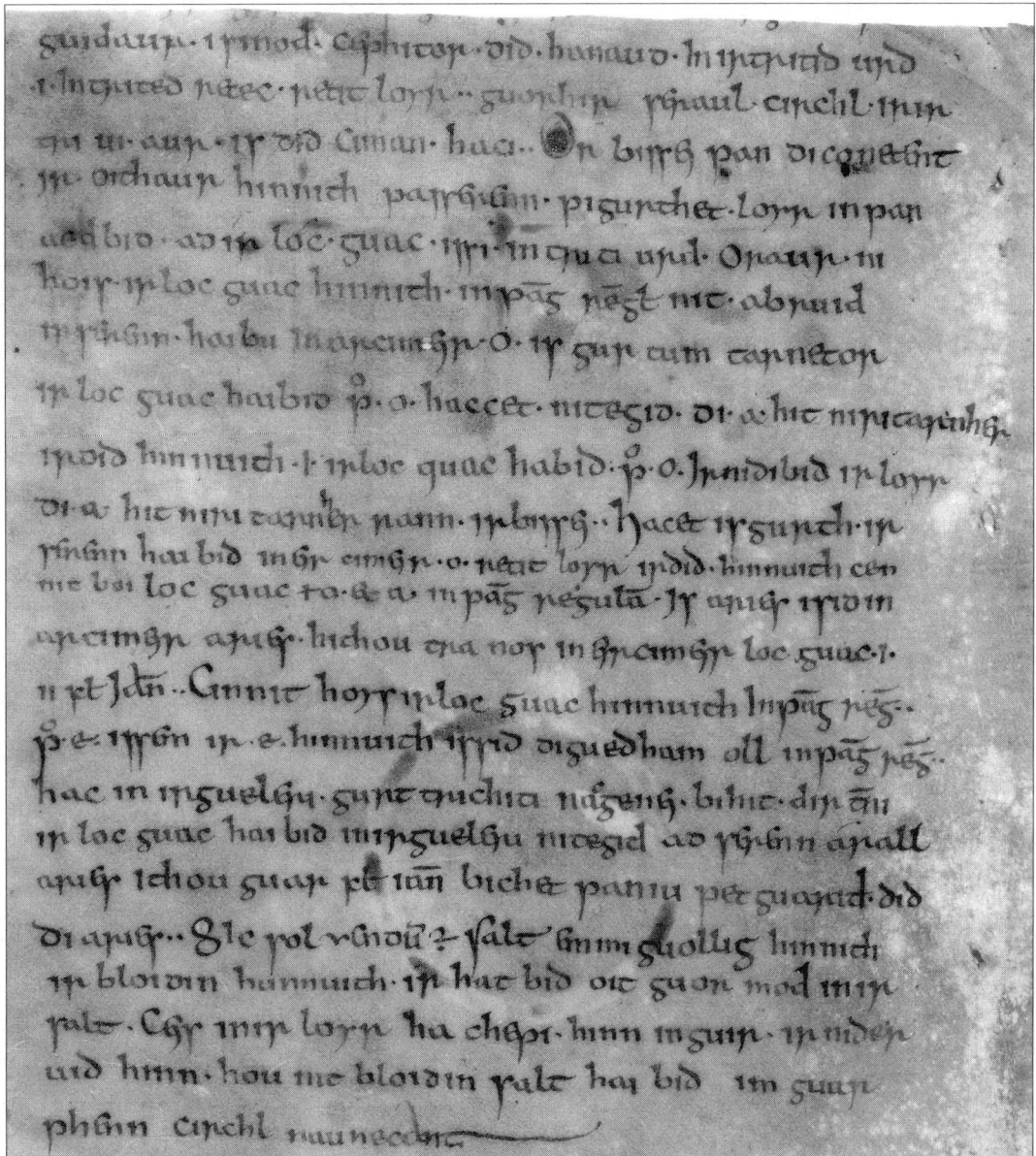

The Old Welsh Computus Fragment

FURTHER READING
BEDA; BRETON; BRETON EARLY MEDIEVAL MANUSCRIPTS; BRYTHONIC; CALENDAR; CYMRU; EASTER CONTROVERSY; WELSH; Armstrong, *Proc. Harvard Celtic Colloquium* 2.187–273.

JTK

An **Comunn Gaidhealach and Mòd**

An Comunn Gaidhealach (The Highland Association), founded in Oban (An t-Òban) in 1891, was for many years the only organization dedicated to promoting SCOTTISH GAELIC and its culture in Scotland (ALBA). The Mòd, An Comunn's annual festival of Gaelic music and arts, originally inspired by the Welsh EISTEDDFOD, remains the best-known manifestation of Gaelic culture in Scotland.

§1. AN COMUNN GAIDHEALACH

An Comunn Gaidhealach was founded with the mission of, *inter alia*, 'promot[ing] the cultivation of Gaelic Literature and Music and Home Industries in the Highlands' and 'encourag[ing] the teaching of Gaelic in Highland Schools'. From the beginning, the society was explicitly non-political in its orientation and dominated by the middle classes and the Highland gentry, many of whom knew no Gaelic.

Developing the Mòd quickly became the main priority for An Comunn and the organization never became a mass language revival movement in the manner of CONRADH NA GAEILGE, founded in Ireland (ÉIRE) just two years later. Branches were formed in various parts of the HIGHLANDS and Islands, but these often concerned themselves primarily with organizing local Mòdan, which have been running since 1905.

Although An Comunn has been involved in a range of cultural and policy initiatives, especially with regard to Gaelic EDUCATION, the organization has long been criticized because of its explicitly non-political stance, and has indeed been held in disregard by many Gaelic activists. Following the creation of a range of new Gaelic organizations with more explicit functions (Comunn na Gàidhlig, the national Gaelic development agency; Comhairle nan Sgoiltean Àraich, the Gaelic Pre-School Council; Pròiseact nan Ealan, the Gaelic Arts Agency, for example), the exact rôle of An Comunn has become rather less clear, and to many it is simply known for organizing the Mòd and little more.

§2. THE MÒD

The Mòd, An Comunn's annual cultural gathering, was explicitly patterned on the eisteddfod. The first Mòd was held in Oban in 1892 and the event has been held continuously ever since, usually moving to a different location each year. Competitions involve individual and choral Gaelic singing, Gaelic poetic composition, Gaelic speech performance and so on.

The Mòd itself has long been criticized by commentators who take the view that it promotes a fossilized and inauthentic version of Gaelic culture. For much of the 20th century, Mòd judges and performers preferred the artificial 'drawing-room' style of singing associated with Marjorie Kennedy-Fraser's Edwardian rearrangements of traditional songs. This charge is rather less valid than it once was, with singing in the traditional style (seann-nòs) much more valued today. On the other hand, the Mòd remains centred on the competitions of Gaelic choirs, even though such choirs were unknown in traditional Gaelic communities.

Other charges relate to the perceived stuffiness and dated quality of the Mòd, which creates an image, for some, of Gaelic as old-fashioned, 'twee' and unappealing. Indeed, to some hostile commentators outside the Gaelic community, the Mòd is known as the 'Whisky Olympics'. Gaelic activists, meanwhile, are concerned about the long-standing dominance of the English

language at the Mòd. Despite these shortcomings, the Mòd retains a flagship status and is recognized throughout Scotland as a manifestation of Gaelic culture.

FURTHER READING
ALBA; CONRADH NA GAEILGE; EDUCATION; ÉIRE; EISTEDD-FOD; EISTEDDFOD GENEDLAETHOL CYMRU; HIGHLANDS; SCOTTISH GAELIC; SEAN-NÓS; Thompson, History of An Comunn Gaidhealach.

Wilson McLeod

Conall Cernach is one of the leading figures in the early Irish Ulster Cycle of tales, set in the prehistoric legendary era. A detailed overview of Conall in the context of the sagas is given in the article on the ULSTER CYCLE in this Encyclopedia. Specific aspects of his character, as expressed in various texts, are also treated in other entries, as noted below. Second only to the superhero Cú CHULAINN in martial prowess, the status of Conall Cernach is made explicit in two well-known tales, the plots of which revolve around contention for the CHAMPION'S PORTION as the focus of heroic competition at FEASTS, namely FLED BRICRENN ('Bricriu's Feast') and SCÉLA MUCCE MEIC DÁ THÓ ('The Story of Mac Dá Thó's Pig'). In the latter, Conall displays his supremacy by taking the heads of enemies as trophies (see also HEAD CULT). Conall's close friendship with Cú Chulainn is apparent in his rôle as Cú Chulainn's comrade and avenger in the death tale of the latter, BREISLECH MÓR MAIGE MUIRTHEIMNI (The great rout of Mag Muirtheimne). Conall's father is AMAIRGEN MAC AITHIRNI, the poet of the ULAID. In some tales, his wife is Findchoem, daughter of CATHBAD, the DRUID of the Ulaid. Though primarily an Ulster Cycle figure, it is noteworthy that Conall also appears as the unyielding stalwart of the doomed King Conaire Mór in TOGAIL BRUIDNE DA DERGA ('The Destruction of Da Derga's Hostel'), a saga of the KINGS' CYCLES (see also IRISH LITERATURE [1] §6); 'crossover' of this sort is unusual and raises the question in which body of tradition Conall's character first developed, as does the remarkable absence of Cú Chulainn from the hierarchy of heroes in Scéla Mucce Meic Dá Thó, where Conall excels. As an essential warrior and tribal hero, Conall's character conforms to the code of conduct and value system discussed in the entry HEROIC ETHOS. The Irish name Conall is very common and is cognate with the Welsh man's name *Cynwal*, both deriving from Old Celtic *Cunovalos*, which means something like 'Hound wielder'. It is noteworthy that the first element of the name is a form of the same word, meaning 'dog, hound, wolf', as occurs in the names of many heroes, most significantly *Cú Chulainn*. The epithet *Cernach* contains the common adjectival suffix (Celtic *-āko-*) and could mean 'prominent, having a prominence' or 'horned'; a connection to the horned god CERNUNNOS has been suggested.

RELATED ARTICLES
AMAIRGEN MAC AITHIRNI; BREISLECH MÓR MAIGE MUIRTHEIMNI; CATHBAD; CERNUNNOS; CHAMPION'S PORTION; CÚ CHULAINN; DRUIDS; FEAST; FLED BRICRENN; HEAD CULT; HEROIC ETHOS; IRISH LITERATURE; KINGS' CYCLES; SCÉLA MUCCE MEIC DÁ THÓ; TOGAIL BRUIDNE DA DERGA; ULAID; ULSTER CYCLE.

JTK

Conan Meriadoc figures as a hero and founder in Breton LEGENDARY HISTORY and is given an important rôle in the scheme of ancient British history in the HISTORIA REGUM BRITANNIAE (*c.* 1139) of GEOFFREY OF MONMOUTH. The extent and substance of the Conan Meriadoc tradition before Geoffrey is unclear, and Conan's historical status as leader of the earliest BRETON MIGRATIONS in the 4th century is now considered very doubtful.

§1. CONANUS MERIADOCUS IN THE LIFE OF GOUEZNOU
Vita Sancti Uuohednouii (see UUOHEDNOU) is a Breton Latin text, of which only the prologue survives, recopied in a manuscript of the historian Pierre Le Baud (†1505). According to this prologue itself, it was written in 1019. It gives an account of the origins of Brittany (BREIZH), citing an earlier history:

We read in the *Ystoria Britannica* that the BRITONS, under the command of Brutus and Corineus, subjugated *Albidia* [see ALBION], which they renamed 'Britannia', together with its adjacent islands by virtue of their martial valour. Seeing their numbers grow and their realm prosper, Conan Meriadoc—a warlike man and an orthodox Christian—crossed the sea to the Armorican gulf of GAUL with a multitudinous and infinite number of Britons, their number having then grown to greater than one small coun-

try could contain. His first seat was on the River Guilidon within the limits of Plebis Columbae [Plougoulm], in the place which is still called *Castrum Meriadoci*. He with his Britons conquered the whole land, from sea to sea and as far as the CIVITAS of the Andegavi, with all of Bro NAONED and Bro ROAZHON [*cum omni territorio Nannetensi et Redonico* '. . . all the country of Nantes and Rennes'] by means of praiseworthy heroism. He killed all the indigenous men, who still were pagan. (Koch & Carey, *Celtic Heroic Age* 405)

Fleuriot and Le Duc have searched for fragments of this pre-Geoffrey *Ystoria Britannica* in the notes of Pierre Le Baud under the title LIVRE DES FAITS D'ARTHUR (see also ARTHURIAN LITERATURE [4]). These notes amount to 173 Latin verses extracted from a narrative relating to Maximus (MACSEN WLEDIG) and Conan Meriadoc. The book was dedicated to Arthur III, duke of Brittany 1303–12. Nevertheless, Fleuriot argued that it was 'in the poetic metres of a more ancient text', and thus could have represented one of the sources used by Geoffrey and would reinforce Geoffrey's claim to have been inspired by a *liber vetustissimus* (very ancient book). However, the date range for the *Livre des faits d'Arthur* (954–1012) depends on that of the Life of Goueznou, itself disputed. Le Duc and other scholars accept the 1019 date of the author, the priest Guillaume, who dedicates his work to the bishop Eudo. Guillotel, on the other hand, argues for a date in the second half of the 12th century for a bishop Eudo or Yvo of LEON, and we may also consider identifying the author with a Guillaume le Breton (†*c.* 1225), a canon from Leon working at the court of the French king, Philippe Auguste (r. 1180–1223). Therefore, the Life of Goueznou and its traditions of Conan Meriadoc in Brittany might post-date Geoffrey.

§2. CONANUS MERIADOCUS IN
HISTORIA REGUM BRITANNIAE
The usurpation of Magnus Maximus (AD 383–8), which provides the frame for Geoffrey's pseudo-historical tale of Conan, is a thoroughly attested historical event. Maximus, a Romano-British general of Spanish origin, led a revolt against the western Emperor Gratian in 383. He crossed the English Channel with his force of soldiers from Roman Britain and ruled Britain, Spain,

Gaul, and parts of North Africa, making Trier his imperial capital. The rule of Maximus is discussed further in the article on MACSEN WLEDIG. Already in the 6th century GILDAS, in his *De Excidio Britanniae* (On the destruction of Britain), reproached Maximus for having deprived Britain of its military resources and 'of a vast number of its youth who had accompanied this usurper . . . and who never returned home'.

Incorporating these facts, which can be verified from reliable sources, Geoffrey's account adds the following details: the Brythonic troops had 'Conanus Meriadocus' as their leader; Maximus named Conan king of AR-MORICA, which he conquered by violence after seizing Rennes and having massacred all the men in the region; 30,000 soldiers and 100,000 'civilians' (*plebani*) came from Britain to Conan's land to make 'another Britain' of Armorica (*Distribuit eos per universas armorici regni nationes fecitque alteram Britanniam*). Following the death of Maximus in Rome, 'those of his men who could escape came to their compatriots in Armorica, which was already called the other Britain'. However, Geoffrey does not report the tradition (found in the Breton chronicles of the later Middle Ages) that Breton immigrants had taken native wives as spouses and had cut their tongues out so that they could not transmit their own language to their descendants, in a form of cultural genocide.

§3. 'KENAN' IN THE LIFE OF ST GURTHIERN

This *Vita* was compiled in the Kemperle Cartulary (Cartulaire de Quimperlé) between 1118 and 1127 by the monk Gurheden, and begins with a genealogy of the saint, presented as the distant descendant of BELI MAWR, son of Outham Senis (Outham the Old). The latter character corresponds to Eudaf Hen in *Breu-ddwyd Macsen* and Octavius in *Historia Regum Britanniae*. Beli, a legendary ancestor figure, well known in Welsh tradition, is given the brother 'Kenan', which is a Middle Welsh spelling (modern *Cynan*) corresponding to Breton *Conan*. This text thus shows that Conan was known in Breton legendary history some years before Geoffrey's book. Gurheden also gives the name of the source of this information: Iuthael, son of Aidan. Although Iuthael is a name known in both Brittany and Wales (CYMRU), *Aidan* is a Gaelic name known in Wales (see AEDÁN MAC GABRÁIN), but unknown in early Brittany, according to Tanguy. Furthermore, since

many details of St Gurthiern's genealogy can be found again in the Welsh genealogy of St CADOC, the figure of 'Kenan' is probably a Welsh import.

§4. MERIADOC

The *Castrum Meriadoci* from the Life of Goueznou and *Castellum Meriadoci* in the *Livre des faits d'Arthur* should be compared with a reference by Marie de France (*c.* 1170) to a 'strong and brave castle' held by 'a knight whose name was Meriadu' in the *Lai de Guigemar* (lines 691–2; see BRETON LAYS). The Guigemar of this lay was son of the 'Lord of Leon', and his name, Breton *Guyomarc'h*, occurs in the house of the viscount of Leon (north-west Brittany). In the parish of Plou-gasnou, also in Leon, a place called Traon Meriadec (Meriadoc's valley) was recorded by the 15th century. In 1480 two feuding parties of this parish, named Hector and Arthur, still had the surname Meriadec.

§5. CONAN MERIADOC AND ST MERIADEC IN LATER DYNASTIC LEGENDS

Around 1500 Pierre le Baud stated, 'the writer of the *Livre des faits d'Arthur* calls the viscounts of Leon *Conanigènes*, which means that they descend from the line of Conan'. In the 15th century the House of Rohan sponsored the cult of St Meriadec as a tutelary saint of the family. The Life of Meriadec, bishop of Vannes (GWENED) survives in fragments. It confirms that:

> the blessed Meriadoc was from the race of the Bretons, descending in direct line from the family of King Conan the Magnificent. His natural father was minister of the duke of Lesser Britain, accord-ing to the chronicles. The viscount of Rohan was taken as his father. But one finds in antiquity that this viscount of Rohan and his successors, exclu-sively among the Bretons, descend in a direct line from the aforementioned Conan.

The Chapel of Stival, dedicated to St Meriadec and built in the second half of the 15th century near the castle which Jean II rebuilt in Pontivy, is decorated with frescoes showing the career of this patron saint. The caption of the first scene tells of 'St Meriadec, son of the Duke of Brittany, descended from the line of King Conan and closely related to the viscount of Rohan.'

This legend implied that the noble houses of Brittany

had chronological precedence over the French monarchy. Thus, the historian Alain Bouchart († post-1514) wrote of Brittany's 'eleven ruling kings, each one succeeding the other, between 386 and 690, [beginning] much earlier than the baptism of the Frankish king Clovis' (c. 466–511).

The legend of Conan Meriadoc fell into disuse after the ACTE D'UNION between Brittany and France in 1532. However, it regained a political dimension at the end of the 17th century when the Rohans claimed the status of 'foreign princes' at the court of Louis XIV in Versailles; this status was not recognized except for lineages of royal descent. The Duke of Saint-Simon ironically states in his *Mémoires*: 'they had forged a fanciful descent from a Conan Meriadoc who never existed, pretending that he had been king of Brittany in legendary times'.

The first volume of the *Histoire ecclésiastique et civile de Bretagne*, published in 1750, made an effort to re-establish Conan Meriadoc's historical status. This was followed by numerous other works from the beginning of the 19th century, but the research of the historian Arthur de la Borderie (†1901) finally exposed the medieval legend. Even so, some still see in it a distant recollection of the first Breton migration to Armorica. Fleuriot concluded that, among the chiefs of the Britons who had followed Maximus to the Continent, it was not improbable that one of them was called Conan (or rather Celtic *Kuna(g)nos* 'Little hound' at that date), but added cautiously, 'could one ever prove this?'

PRIMARY SOURCE
GEOFFREY OF MONMOUTH, HISTORIA REGUM BRITANNIAE.

FURTHER READING
ACTE D'UNION; AEDÁN MAC GABRÁIN; ALBION; ARMORICA; ARTHURIAN LITERATURE [4]; BELI MAWR; BREIZH; BRETON LAYS; BRETON MIGRATIONS; BRITONS; CADOC; CIVITAS; CYMRU; GAUL; GEOFFREY OF MONMOUTH; GILDAS; GWENED; HISTORIA REGUM BRITANNIAE; LEGENDARY HISTORY; LEON; LIVRE DES FAITS D'ARTHUR; MACSEN WLEDIG; NAONED; ROAZHON; UUOHEDNOU; Balcou & Le Gallo, *Histoire littéraire et culturelle de la Bretagne* 1; Bourgès, *Kreiz* 14.125–36; Cassard, *Annales de Bretagne et des Pays de l'Ouest* 90.415–27; Chédeville & Guillotel, *La Bretagne des saints et des rois, Ve–Xe siècle*; Fleuriot, *Les origines de la Bretagne*; Le Duc, *Annales de Bretagne* 79.819–35; Minnis, *Medieval Theory of Authorship*; Nassiet, *Noblesses de Bretagne du Moyen Age à nos jours* 103–28; Rio, *Mythes fondateurs de la Bretagne*; Short, *Speculum* 69.323–43; Tanguy, *ÉC* 26.159–85.

Bernard Merdrignac

Conan, Jean (1765–1834) was born in Gwengamp. As a child he went to work at Beauport Abbey (Kerity-Paimpol), where he learned to read and write both BRETON and French. He spent some time as a fisherman in Newfoundland (where he was saved by local people after a shipwreck), and on his return home he was sent to defend the borders of the new French Republic, where he opposed the Chouans (Royalists), and took part in several famous battles (Fleurus, Hondschotte, Wattignies) in Belgium, France, and Germany.

Of the many copyists or transcribers of the literature of popular theatre in Breton since the late Middle Ages, Conan was remarkably productive. Seldom studied, only a dozen out of a total of around 150 works written by him have been published. In the 19th century his works were collected by LUZEL and Le Braz, who later deposited them in public libraries in Rennes (ROAZHON) and Paris.

The manuscript of his best-known work— *Avanturio ar citoian Jean Conan a Voengamp* (The adventures of citizen Jean Conan from Gwengamp)—was recently discovered in a private house, and has since been published. These 'adventures' are narrated in 7054 lines of Tregereg (Tregorrois) Breton (see BRETON DIALECTS), and draw on the traditional dramatic material to which Conan had long devoted himself.

PRIMARY SOURCES
ED. & TRANS. Conan, *Avanturio ar citoien Jean Conan a Voengamb / Les aventures du citoyen Jean Conan de Guingamp*.
TRANS. Conan, *Les aventures extraordinaires du citoyen Conan*.

FURTHER READING
BRETON; BRETON DIALECTS; BRETON LITERATURE; LUZEL; ROAZHON; Combot, *Jean Conan: aventurier et écrivain breton*.

Francis Favereau

Conchobar mac Nessa, legendary king of ULAID in the pre-Christian period, is covered most fully in this Encyclopedia in the context of the ULSTER CYCLE. He also figures in several other entries noted in this summary. In current scholarship, the king and the episodes surrounding him are generally not considered to have a historical basis (see IRISH LITERATURE [1] §5). Portrayed at length in the sagas as essentially a great, beautiful, and, for the most part, good king, his attributes have often been considered by modern writers as evidence for the archetypal Celtic king (see KINGSHIP). Nonetheless, Conchobar is not an ideal king, a state of affairs intelligible for both literary and ideological reasons. Since the warrior Cú Chulainn, as supreme hero, is the central figure of the Ulster Cycle overall, Conchobar as his nominal superior is necessarily regarded unfavourably by comparison, much as Agamemnon *vis-à-vis* Achilles in the *Iliad*. The literary necessity of warfare imperilling the kingdom of Ulaid as a backdrop for the great deeds of Cú Chulainn in TÁIN BÓ CUAILNGE implies that the king must first have failed in some sense to allow the warrior the rôle of saviour of his people. Furthermore, within the scheme of early Irish LEGENDARY HISTORY, the idealized polity of ÉRIU (ancient Ireland) had a single high-king at Tara (TEAMHAIR), such as Conaire Mór in TOGAIL BRUIDNE DA DERGA ('The Destruction of Da Derga's Hostel') or CORMAC MAC AIRT. As the king of a warring province (CÓICED), Conchobar was thus inherently less than ideal. In the tale LONGAS MAC NUISLENN ('The Exile of the Sons of Uisliu') his character appears overtly negative in the socially destructive love triangle produced by his taking the young and beautiful DERDRIU against her will, leading to FERGUS MAC ROÍCH and other Ulster heroes going over to the tribe's enemies, MEDB and Ailill of CONNACHT, at a critical stage. It is noteworthy that the heroic FINN MAC CUMAILL is depicted as an ambivalent character in the similar tragic love story, TÓRUIGHEACHT DHIARMADA AGUS GHRÁINNE ('The Pursuit of Diarmaid and Gráinne'). Remarkably, Nes is not a patronym, but the name of Conchobar's mother. It is Nes, daughter of Eochaid Sálbuide, who connives that Conchobar replace Fergus as king. In his conception tale (*Compert Conchobuir*), Nes is an amazonian woman warrior; though forced to marry CATHBAD, in the complex scenario of the later version of the tale it is not Cathbad himself who is the king's father, though he does importantly foresee his future status and that his birth coincides with that of Jesus. The death of Conchobar is likewise simultaneous with the crucifixion in *Aided Conchobair* (The violent death of Conchobar).

PRIMARY SOURCE
TRANS. Koch & Carey, *Celtic Heroic Age* 59–64 (*Compert Conchobuir*).

RELATED ARTICLES
CATHBAD; CÓICED; CONNACHT; CORMAC MAC AIRT; CÚ CHULAINN; DERDRIU; ÉRIU; FERGUS MAC ROÍCH; FIANNAÍOCHT; FINN MAC CUMAILL; IRISH LITERATURE; KINGSHIP; LEGENDARY HISTORY; LONGAS MAC N-UISLENN; MEDB; TÁIN BÓ CUAILNGE; TEAMHAIR; TOGAIL BRUIDNE DA DERGA; TÓRUIGHEACHT DHIARMADA AGUS GHRÁINNE; ULAID; ULSTER CYCLE.

JTK

Conn Cétchathach

Conn Cétchathach (Conn of the hundred battles) is a legendary Irish king who, according to the medieval Irish scholars who shaped LEGENDARY HISTORY, would have lived around the 2nd century AD. He was reckoned by the genealogists to be the ancestor of several leading dynasties of early medieval Ireland, including the pre-eminent UÍ NÉILL. Within early medieval Irish doctrines of dynastic legitimacy, one often encounters the idea that the descendants of Conn were destined to monopolize the prestigious kingship of Tara (TEAMHAIR), which came to be identified with the emerging concept of a high-kingship of Ireland (ÉRIU).

Conn's name was used to explain the names of major territorial divisions and population groups. Thus, *Leth Cuinn* 'Conn's half' means the northern half of Ireland. CONNACHT, the name of Ireland's traditional northwestern province, is often understood in traditional literature to mean the 'province of Conn'. CONNACHTA of *Dál Cuinn* can mean either 'the people of Connacht' in a territorial sense, or 'the people of Conn' in a dynastic and genealogical sense, or both. According to the legend, his sons were Conlae (whose story is told in *Echtrae Chonlai*, The adventure of Conlae) and Art (*Echtrae Airt maic Chuinn*, The adventure of Art son of Conn), who himself fathered CORMAC MAC AIRT, the idealized legendary king of Tara (*Echtra Chorbmaic Uí Chuinn*, The adventure of Cormac grandson of Conn).

An Old Irish text entitled *Baile Chuinn Chétchathaig* (The ecstatic vision of Conn Cétchathach) lists the kings of Tara from Cormac to Fínshnechta Fledach, who ruled AD 675–95. Intended as a prophecy issued by the clairvoyant dynastic founder Conn concerning his unborn progeny, the extent of the list probably indicates that the text originated as a piece of late 7th-century political propaganda. Possibly Fínshnechta was only the *rígdamna* or heir apparent at the time, hence a date somewhat before 675 is possible (see Murphy, *Ériu* 16.145–56). There is a 9th- or 10th-century reworking of this text, *Baile in Scáil* (The phantom's ecstasy), in which it is the god LUG—in the company of a libation serving female personification of the sovereignty of Ériu (see SOVEREIGNTY MYTH)—who foretells the succession at Tara to Conn (Thurneysen, ZCP 20.213–27). The king-list contained in this text represents the official doctrine of descent from Conn as promoted by the Uí Néill propagandists *c.* 900.

Possibly of Old Irish date is *Airne Fíngein*, a tale concerning the birth of Conn. In it, one of the wonders foreshadowing his future greatness and allegorical significance for Ireland and the kingship of Tara is the magical appearance of five roads (probably to be taken as symbolizing the traditional five provinces of Ireland; see COÍCED) converging on Tara. There is a Middle Irish death-tale, *Aided Chuinn*, which tells of Conn's killing during preparations for the *Feis Temro* (FEAST of Teamhair) at the hands of a king of Ulster (ULAID) named Tipraite Máil.

The name *Conn* is of uncertain origin. There is an uncommon Old Irish word *cond* meaning 'intellect' or 'mind', but the name Conn and its derivatives seem to have -*nn* rather than -*nd*. Alternatively, it is not impossible that the name is based on a popular analogy applied to *Leth Cuinn* and *Dál Cuinn*, which had originally meant 'Half of the chief (*cenn*)' and 'Tribe of the chief' rather than 'Half/tribe of Conn'; Old Irish *cenn* 'head, chief' derives from Celtic **kʷennom*, genitive **kʷenni*, and *cuinn* should have been its original Old Irish genitive form. In other words, that the legendary founder and his name may have been extracted analogically from earlier, misunderstood groups and territorial labels. At any rate, as he appears in the extant literature, Conn is more significant as a namesake, founder, ancestor, and granter of authority to historical rulers than as a hero or ideal ruler in his own right.

PRIMARY SOURCES
EDITION. Vendryès, *Airne Fíngein*.
ED. & TRANS. Bergin, ZCP 8.274–7 (*Aided Chuinn*); Murphy, *Ériu* 16.145–56 (*Baile Chuinn Chétchathaig*).

FURTHER READING
COÍCED; CONNACHT; CONNACHTA; CORMAC MAC AIRT; ÉRIU; FEAST; LEGENDARY HISTORY; LUG; SOVEREIGNTY MYTH; TEAMHAIR; UÍ NÉILL; ULAID; Byrne, *Irish Kings and High-Kings*; Ó Cathasaigh, *Heroic Biography of Cormac mac Airt*.

JTK, Peter Smith, PEB

Connacht is the most north-westerly of the traditional provinces of Ireland (ÉIRE), and extends westwards from the river Shannon (Sionna) to the Atlantic. Counties Galway, Mayo, Sligo, Leitrim, and Roscommon (GAILLIMH, Maigh Eo, Sligeach, Liatroim, Ros Comáin) are within its modern borders. During the early medieval period, however, the province was more extensive, and incorporated the northern part of the Burren (Co. Clare/Contae an Chláir) and possibly parts of south Donegal (Contae Dhún na nGall) around the Erne estuary. The name *Connacht* (Anglicized *Connaught*) was derived from that of the population group name CONNACHTA. The name Ναγναται *Nagnatai* is listed in Connacht in the *Geography* of PTOLEMY of Alexandria (*c.* AD 150, but employing earlier sources). *Nagnāta* may be a Celtic name, meaning 'unknown', thus signifying a population centre of which Ptolemy's source for Ireland was ignorant. Connacht was divided between its fertile regions in the east, south and north-west and the rugged mountainous western region known as Iar-Chonnacht. The fertile areas were densely populated and many can be identified by the occurrence of the place-name element *mag* 'plain'. These plains include Mag nAidne, Móen-mag (around south Co. Galway), Mag nAirtig, Mag Luirg (north Roscommon) and most significantly Mag nAí (central and south Roscommon), the heartland of medieval Connacht. The royal ceremonial complex of the province, CRÚACHU (Rathcroghan, Co. Roscommon), is located in the centre of Mag nAí. Any king who wished to hold the provincial kingship had to dominate this part of Connacht to realize his goal.

RELATED ARTICLES
CONNACHTA; CRÚACHU; ÉIRE; GAILLIMH; PTOLEMY.

Edel Bhreathnach

Connachta is the name for a group of Irish dynasties descended from and called after the legendary king of Tara (TEAMHAIR), CONN CÉTCHATHACH 'Conn of the hundred battles'. Their territory lay primarily to the west of the Shannon (Sionna) with its royal focal point at CRÚACHU (Rathcroghan, Co. Roscommon/Ros Comáin). The relationship between the Connachta and Uí Néill kings up to the late 7th century, and their possible identity, is crucial for a meaningful un-

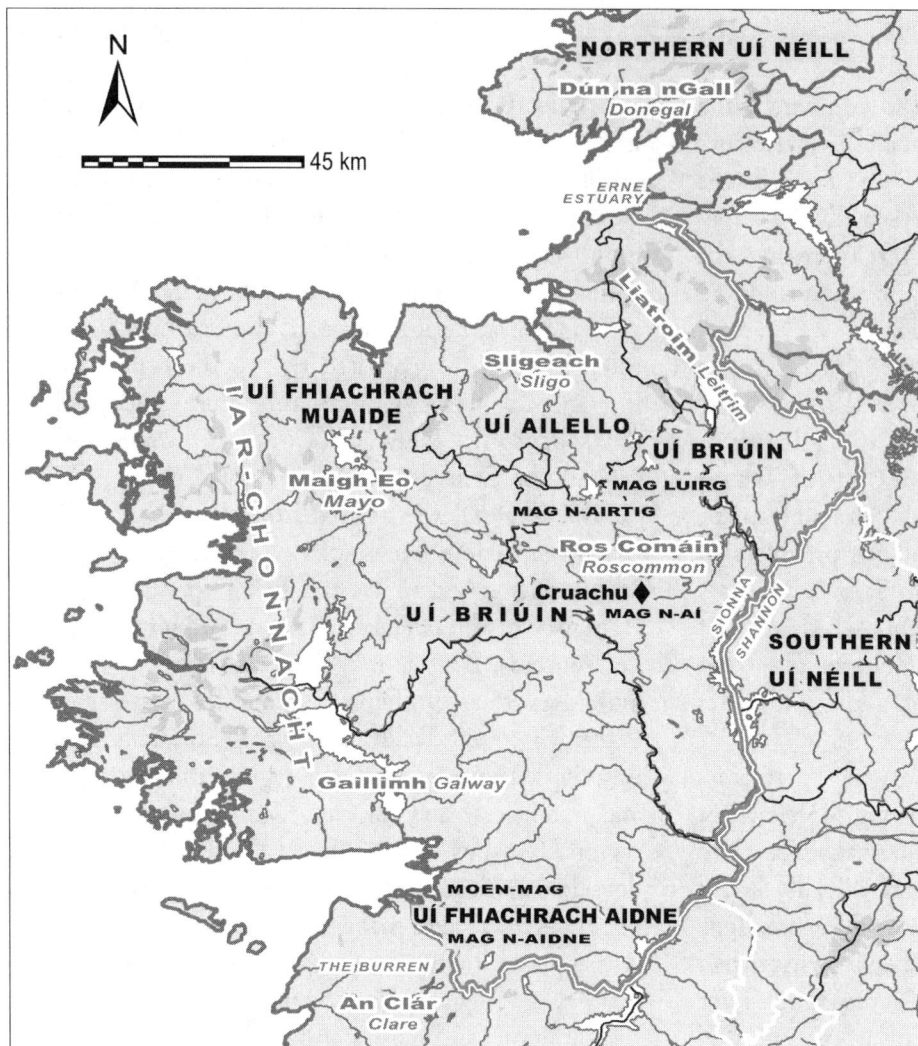

Connacht and the Connachta; pre-modern groups and place-names in black; contemporary boundary of the traditional province shown as white line on grey

derstanding of 'Connachta' and of the origins of the Uí Néill dynasties. It has been suggested that the Uí Néill originally belonged to the Connachta, but that they expanded their territories into the midlands and northwards from the 5th to the 7th centuries, and by the late 7th century had lost their identity as Connachta and appear distinct. Another term current in early IRISH LITERATURE and partially synonymous with the lands of the Connachta and Uí Néill is *Leth Cuinn*, meaning 'the half of Conn [Cétchathach]' and referring to the northern half of Ireland (ÉRIU). The term the 'Three Connachta' referred to the three dominant dynasties of the Connachta—the Uí Briúin, the Uí Ailello, and the Uí Fhiachrach, which were further divided into different branches, Uí Fhiachrach Aidne of south Galway (GAILLIMH) and Uí Fhiachrach Muaide and Muirisce of north Mayo. An alternative name given to the Connachta was Fir Ól nÉcmacht, 'the men of the unintoxicating drinks'.

FURTHER READING
CONN CÉTCHATHACH; CRÚACHU; ÉRIU; GAILLIMH; IRISH LITERATURE; TEAMHAIR; UÍ NÉILL; Charles-Edwards, *Early Christian Ireland* 36–54, 508–12; Charles-Edwards, *Early Irish and Welsh Kinship* 159–65; Ó Muraíle, *Seanchas* 161–77; Sproule, *Ériu* 35.31–7.

Edel Bhreathnach

Conradh na Gaeilge (the Gaelic League) was founded in Dublin (BAILE ÁTHA CLIATH) in 1893. Founder members included David Comyn (Daithí Ó Coimín), Eoin MACNEILL and Douglas Hyde (Dúbhghlas DE HÍDE). Its aims were: (1) the preservation of IRISH as the national language of Ireland (ÉIRE) and the extension of its use as a spoken tongue, and (2) the study and publication of existing Gaelic literature and the cultivation of a modern literature in the Irish language (see IRISH LITERATURE).

The organization established language classes which, by 1904, numbered almost 600 throughout Ireland as well as in Britain, with learners drawn from all socio-economic classes. The textbook used was *Simple Lessons in Irish* by Fr Eugene O'Growney (An tAthair Eoghan Ó Gramhnaigh). At first the teachers were untrained, but language-teaching methods employed in other countries—for example, the Gouin and Berlitz methods—were adopted early on, and in 1904 Munster College (Coláiste na Mumhan), the first of six training colleges for Gaelic League teachers, was established in Ballingeary, in the West Cork GAELTACHT.

In 1897 the League established the annual Oireachtas competition (see FEISEANNA), based on the Welsh EISTEDDFOD. The first Oireachtas was held in Dublin in 1898 in conjunction with the Feis Ceoil, an annual Irish musical festival. Initially, the competitions included categories in folklore, dramatic sketches and recitations. Literary categories were subsequently introduced and innovative writing was encouraged. Pádraic Ó CONAIRE, one of the early prize-winners, together with Patrick Pearse (Pádraig MAC PIARAIS), were instrumental in establishing the short story as a successful literary form in Modern Irish. Many Oireachtas prize-winners had their work published by the League's own publishing company, Clódhanna Teoranta, which was founded in 1908.

Pamphlets and newspapers played an important propaganda rôle in the work of the organization from the beginning. In 1894 the League took over *Irisleabhar na Gaedhilge* (the Gaelic journal), founded in 1882 by the Gaelic Union; in 1899 it established its own weekly paper, *An CLAIDHEAMH SOLUIS* (The sword of light) and in 1900 it assumed control of *Fáinne an Lae* (The ring of the day) and merged the two papers.

The achievements of the Gaelic League in securing the recognition of Irish within the EDUCATION system were significant. Having led successful campaigns to ensure that the language was taught in primary schools within normal school hours and that Irish was introduced as a teaching medium in Gaeltacht schools, it then campaigned to have Irish recognized as an examination subject by the Board of Intermediate Education. This aim was achieved with the passing of the Education Act of 1900. When the National University was established in 1908 the League became involved in the highly controversial campaign to make Irish an essential subject for matriculation. In 1910 the National University Senate made the language compulsory for matriculation as from 1913.

Primarily a cultural organization, albeit a radical one, the League became increasingly political and, as a result, Douglas Hyde, who had been president since its foundation, resigned in 1915. The 1916 Easter Rising (see IRISH INDEPENDENCE MOVEMENT), most of the leaders of which were Gaelic Leaguers, followed by the War of Independence and the Civil War, all contributed to a drop in membership from which the organization never recovered.

Although the cultural revolution advocated by its founders may not have fully succeeded, the Gaelic League achieved a great deal. Its policies regarding Irish in the education system were adopted by the independent State, founded in 1922. The Oireachtas, discontinued during some of the more turbulent years, was revived in 1939. It contributed significantly to the resurgence of Irish writing which took place during the following decades and remains a major annual Irish literary event.

The present-day headquarters of the Gaelic League are at 6 Sráid Fhearchair, Baile Átha Cliath 2.

FURTHER READING
BAILE ÁTHA CLIATH; CLAIDHEAMH SOLUIS; DE H-ÍDE; EDUCATION; ÉIRE; EISTEDDFOD; EISTEDDFOD GENEDLAETHOL CYMRU; FEISEANNA; GAELTACHT; IRISH; IRISH INDEPENDENCE MOVEMENT; IRISH LITERATURE; MAC PIARAIS; MACNEILL; Ó CONAIRE; Hyde, *Mise agus an Connradh*; Mac Aonghusa, *Ar Son na Gaeilge*; Ní Mhuiríosa, *Réamhchonraitheoirí*; Ó Conluain & Ó Céileachair, *An Duinníneach*; Ó Cuív, *The Making of 1916* 1–27; Ó Fearaíl, *Story of Conradh na Gaeilge*; O'Growney, *Simple Lessons in Irish*; Ó hAilín, *View of the Irish Language* 91–100; O'Leary, *Prose Literature of the Gaelic Revival 1881–1921*; Ó Lúing, *Studies* 62.123–38; Ó Riordáin, *Conradh na Gaeilge i gCorcaigh 1894–1910*; Ó Súilleabháin, *Cath na Gaeilge sa Chóras Oideachais 1893–1911*; Ó Súilleabháin, *Conradh na Gaeilge i Londain 1894–1917*; Ó Súilleabháin, *Scéal an Oireachtais 1897–1924*; Ó Tuama, *Gaelic League Idea*; Tierney, *Eoin MacNeill*; Tierney, *Studies* 52.337–47.

Pádraigín Riggs

Constantine, St (of Govan)

The only incontrovertible fact about this saint is the dedication to him of the parish church of GOVAN Old. The 6th-century burials and 9th-/10th-century sculpture at this church testify to its antiquity, but there is more uncertainty about its saint. He is probably commemorated in other churches in southern Scotland

(ALBA): in Kintyre, in Ayrshire, and in Galloway. To his cult may be attributed the popularity of this Roman name among royal families in northern BRITAIN in the 7th–10th centuries. There was clearly a series of legends about one or more saintly Constantines in the insular world, all of which employ 'the natural triple context—Roman, christian, and royal—of the use of the name' (Dumville, *Scottish Gaelic Studies* 19.234–5). The first saint and emperor Constantine—who was elevated to purple at the legionary fortress of York in 306—probably lies behind some of his associations; Constantine of Govan's feast day (11 March) is convincingly close to that of the 4th-century sainted emperor (10 March). However, the name was being suggestively re-used in Britain as early as 407–11, the reign of the would-be emperor Constantine III, and there are local cults of royal saints Constantine in Brittany (BREIZH), Cornwall (KERNOW) (with feast-days on 9 March), and Ireland (ÉIRE). The lections in the ABERDEEN BREVIARY ingeniously congeal all these legends, making him son of a Cornish king, husband of the daughter of the king of Brittany, a monastic miller in Ireland, disciple of Columba (COLUM CILLE) and KENTIGERN, preacher in Galloway, and martyr in Kintyre.

PRIMARY SOURCE
ED. & TRANS. Macquarrie, *Annual Report of the Society of Friends of Govan Old* 5.25–32.

FURTHER READING
ABERDEEN BREVIARY; ALBA; BREIZH; BRITAIN; COLUM CILLE; ÉIRE; GOVAN; KENTIGERN; KERNOW; Dumville, *Scottish Gaelic Studies* 19.234–40; Forbes, *Kalendars of Scottish Saints* 311–14; Macquarrie, *Records of the Scottish Church History Society* 24.1–16.

Thomas Owen Clancy

Continental Celtic

§1. INTRODUCTION

'Continental Celtic' refers to the Celtic languages spoken on the European continent during antiquity. Prior to the Roman and Germanic expansions, they were spoken throughout western and central Europe into the IBERIAN PENINSULA (with the exception of the Mediterranean coast) in the south-west, across northern ITALY and throughout the ALPINE region south-east into the BALKANS, and even into Asia Minor; they were

also spoken in eastern Europe, though it is difficult to know to what extent and precisely where. Though the attestation of Continental Celtic is fragmentary, the record is significant enough for us to have learnt a great deal about its segmental phonology (system of sounds) and morphology (how words changed form to show grammatical relations) in the regions where it is more copiously documented, and even some facts about its syntax. Since Continental Celtic inscribed texts are attested from *c.* 575 BC in northern Italy to the 3rd or 4th century AD in TRANSALPINE GAUL, it has become increasingly important for the historical study of the CELTIC LANGUAGES in particular, and the INDO-EUROPEAN languages in general.

§2. THE LANGUAGES

In the Iberian Peninsula the principal Celtic linguistic testimony comes from Hispano-Celtic (also known as CELTIBERIAN), which was spoken in the northern *meseta* of present-day Spain. There are other linguistic remains scattered around the peninsula which resemble attested forms of Celtic, but their attestation is highly fragmentary (see GALICIA). Untermann argues that LUSITANIAN, a language spoken in the central area of present-day Portugal, which is known from only a few inscriptions, is a Celtic sister to Celtiberian (*Veleia* 2/3.57–76), but other scholars believe that any Celtic elements in Lusitanian were introduced via contact (e.g. Tovar, *Actas del III Coloquio* 231). Untermann (*Hispano-Gallo-Brittonica* 244–59) has also tentatively suggested that Tartessian, a language spoken in the south-western corner of the peninsula, near Cadiz, may contain Celtic elements.

In northern Italy there are traditionally said to have been two discrete Celtic languages spoken: LEPONTIC, which was concentrated in the northern Italian lake district, and Cisalpine GAULISH. Eska, however, argues that they were not separate languages, but variants of a single language he would call 'Cisalpine Celtic', whose differences reflect the distinct times and places at which they are attested (*Proc. Berkeley Linguistic Society* 24.2–11).

In present-day France and Belgium various dialects of Transalpine Celtic were spoken. These are usually called Gaulish, but the use of this blanket term risks the misleading implication that a single uniform vari-

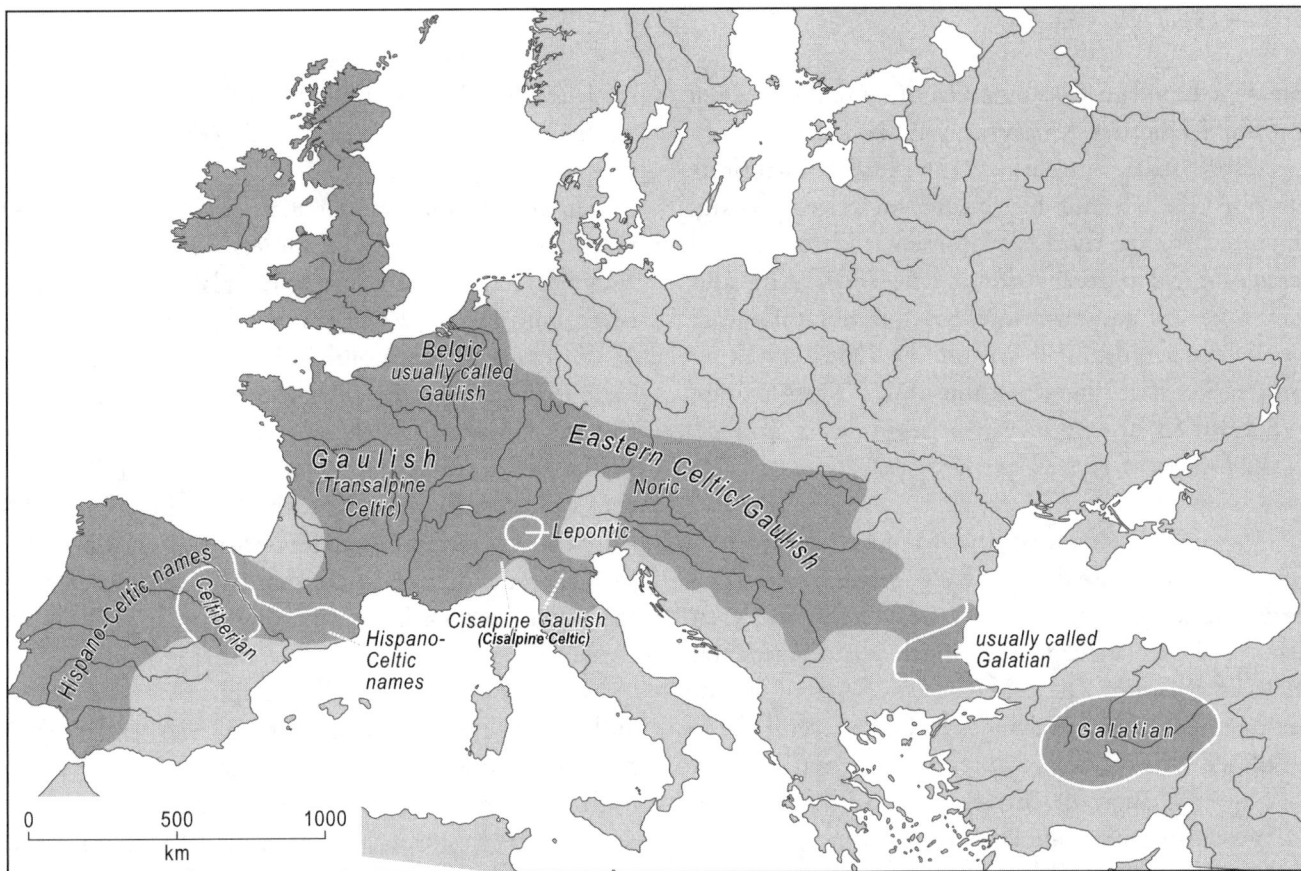

Celtic-speaking regions of the ancient world (shown in darker grey) and the Continental Celtic languages

ety of Celtic was spoken throughout Transalpine Gaul.

There are also fragments of Continental Celtic languages attested in the BALKANS, where it is sometimes called 'Noric' (see NORICUM), and in the central portion of present-day Turkey, where it is known as GALATIAN. Most of this eastern Celtic material appears very similar to Gaulish/Transalpine Celtic.

§3. LINGUISTIC AFFILIATIONS

Traditionally, the interrelationships of the Celtic language family were based upon a single criterion, the treatment of the Indo-European phoneme $*/k^w/$, it being either continued unchanged or fully labialized to $/p/$, but this isogloss is seen as less important by most Celtic scholars today (see CELTIC LANGUAGES §5). Some scholars also attached special importance to the way in which the various Celtic languages reflected the Indo-European syllabic nasals $/ṃ, ṇ/$ as *am, an* or *en, em* in order to distinguish separate branches for Celtiberian, Lepontic, GALLO-BRITTONIC, and GOIDELIC (e.g. Lejeune, *Bulletin . . . de l'Académie Royale*

de Belgique 64.119–20). However, it is now known that the proto-Indo-European syllabic nasals became *am, an* in PROTO-CELTIC, the variation across and within the individual Celtic languages being secondary developments. These facts, plus the considerable variation seen in the linguistic features of the Continental Celtic languages in particular, have caused some scholars to lose hope that Proto-Celtic can be reconstructed at all. A variety of views on the structure of the Celtic language family, therefore, is now found in contemporary scholarship:

(1) Some continue to employ the criteria listed above and separate Goidelic, Celtiberian, Lepontic, BRYTHONIC, and Gaulish from Proto-Celtic in that order (e.g. Schmidt, ZCP 41.164).

(2) Others maintain that there is a cleavage between Continental Celtic and INSULAR CELTIC (e.g. McCone, *Religión, lengua y cultura* 483–94). Among these, there is general agreement that Celtiberian separated from Proto-Celtic first, but it remains unresolved whether the Celtic of Transalpine Gaul was a different language

from that found in Cisalpine Gaul (e.g. Uhlich, *Akten des Zweiten Deutschen Keltologen-Symposiums* 2.277–304).

(3) Still others emphasize the close connections between Gaulish and Brythonic, an affinity easily accounted for on the basis of known historical and archaeological patterns during the IRON AGE and Roman period and therefore possibly not reflecting any dialect arrangement within the Celtic-speaking world earlier than the expansion of LA TÈNE culture from Gaul to Britain in waves beginning *c.* 400 BC (Koch, *Bretagne et pays celtiques* 471–95).

§4. LINGUISTIC FEATURES

Phonology. The representation of the sounds of the Continental Celtic languages is not straightforward, even within a single language area, much less Continental Celtic as a group. The evidence testifies to the fact that a number of sound changes had only recently been completed (hence, archaic orthography may not reveal a given change) or, in fact, were still in progress. One must also bear in mind that the indigenous SCRIPTS employed to engrave Celtiberian and Cisalpine Celtic inscriptions, and even the Greek script employed to engrave some Transalpine Celtic inscriptions (and the meagre records of Galatian which are embedded in Greek texts), may mask as much as they reveal of the actual sound patterns of these languages.

The vowel systems of the Continental Celtic languages preserve the late Indo-European five vowel system /i e a o u/ with a short–long opposition for /i e a u/; inherited /ē/ > Celtic /ī/, but may be vestigially preserved unchanged in a few tokens in Celtiberian; Celtic /ē/ continues the Indo-European diphthong /ej/ elsewhere; IE /ō/ is continued as Celtic /ū/ in final syllables and as /ā/ elsewhere. However, we find that a new /o/ arises in later Transalpine Celtic (including British and Goidelic) from the simplification of the diphthong /ow/. In Cisalpine Celtic, inherited VN.T (that is, vowel+nasal+stop consonant) sequences regularly developed into Ṽ.T (nasalized vowel+stop consonant) (see LEPONTIC). This development is attested sporadically elsewhere in Continental Celtic and, indeed, in many of the ancient languages of the Mediterranean area. All six of the Indo-European diphthongs /aj ej oj aw ew ow/ are preserved in the earliest attested records of Continental Celtic, but even in these inscriptions there is some

evidence for the simplification of /ej/ > /ē/. Later we find /aj/ > /ī/, /oj/ > /i/, /ew/ > /ow/, and /ow/ > /ō/.

The consonantal systems show similar variation. The stop consonants (which completely arrest the breath flow) have three places, namely, bilabial (articulation using both lips—/b/), coronal (the tip of the tongue at the front of the mouth—/t, d/), and dorsal (the surface of the tongue closing the breath flow on the top of the mouth—/k, g/), the last of which also occurs with a secondary bilabial articulation (/kʷ, gʷ/), thus yielding a four-way opposition. An inherited Indo-European voiceless–voiced opposition is continued, that is, the stop consonants may be articulated with the vocal chords still or vibrating, which gives us the three opposed sets above—/t d, k g, k gʷ/.

Proto-IE /p/ is generally completely lost in initial and intervocalic positions (see PROTO-CELTIC §2). However, Indo-European seems to occur as /w/ in both positions in the forms *uvamoKozis* /uwamo-/ and *uvlTiauioPos* /wultiawobos/ in an early Cisalpine Celtic inscription from Prestino (S–65) (Eska, *Münchener Studien zur Sprachwissenschaft* 58.63–80). The latter form has been particularly difficult to analyse, but possibly continues Indo-European *plth₂wih₂-* 'the broad earth' and is cognate with the Transalpine Celtic *Letavia*, Old Welsh *Litau*, Middle Irish *Letha* 'Brittany', and probably also the British tribal name *Corieltauvi* (Koch, *Emania* 9.17–27).

Both of the labial-velars /kʷ, gʷ/ are attested in Celtiberian and are probably attested in earliest Cisalpine Celtic (though the Lugano script makes it difficult to be certain), but, by and large, they appear to be absent in Transalpine Celtic, in which /kʷ/ > /p/ (save in some religious terms, which are a notoriously conservative semantic category in many languages) and Proto-Celtic /gʷ/ > /w/ in British and Gaulish (Koch, *Hispano-Gallo-Brittonica* 79–95). All the Continental Celtic languages possess the nasals /m n/, presumably with allophonic [ŋ] before /k/, /g/, /kʷ/, and /gʷ/; in later Cisalpine Celtic and with the exception of a few vestiges in Transalpine Celtic, final /m/ > /n/. The liquids /l r/, the glides /j w/, and the sibilant /s/ are also found in all of the languages. In later Transalpine Celtic and Galatian, /w/ tends to be lost between vowels. The sibilant /s/ is also affected in this position. It is sometimes lost in later Transalpine Celtic; in Celtiberian, it is usually represented by the characters conventially transcribed by scholars as *s* in this position (where it is likely to have been pronounced /z/), as opposed to the characters transcribed as *s'* (probably pronounced /s/; see SCRIPTS). Cisalpine and Transalpine Celtic also possess a phoneme known as the *tau gallicum* which immediately continues /ts/ < /st/ (see also D. Ellis Evans, *Gaulish Personal Names* 410–20; Eska, SC 32.115–27).

§5. MORPHOLOGY

The nouns, adjectives, and pronouns of the Continental Celtic languages possess a much richer case system than is found in INSULAR CELTIC. There is evidence for all eight Indo-European cases—nominative, accusative, genitive, dative, locative, instrumental, ablative, vocative—though not in all numbers and declensions and not in all the Continental Celtic languages. The familiar three genders—masculine, feminine, neuter—are well documented, and there is some evidence for the dual number in addition to the singular and plural. Each of the languages has undergone some remodelling in their respective systems of nominal case endings. In Celtiberian, there is some evidence for the introduction of a feminine nominative singular -*ī*, genitive -*īnos*, on the model of the -*ū*, -*ūnos* paradigm, and genitive singular in -*o* in the o-stems has emerged on the analogy of the genitive masculine pronoun (Eska, *Hispano-Gallo-Brittonica* 41–2; Prosdocimi, *Studi Etruschi* 57.139–77). In earliest attested Cisalpine Celtic, the Indo-European o-stem genitive singular in **-osjo* is continued as -*oiso* (Eska, *Hispano-Gallo-Brittonica* 42, Eska & Wallace, *Incontri Linguistici* 24.140–1), but it gives way to familiar Celtic -*ī* later. Early Cisalpine Celtic also shows the replacement of inherited consonant stem dative singular -*ej* by instrumental singular -*i* in progress (Eska & Wallace, *Indogermanische Forschungen* 106.230–42), a change that is completed by the first appearance of Transalpine Celtic.

It is in Transalpine Celtic that we find the largest number of innovations; for example, the adoption of some *i*-stem endings by the *ā*-stem declension (Lejeune, ÉC 22.88–93) and the merging of the dative and instrumental singular in the o-stem declension and of the dative and instrumental plural in all declensions.

In the verbal system, there is good evidence for the present, preterite, and future tenses, all in a variety of inherited formations. Both Cisalpine and Transalpine Celtic have also created a new *t*-preterite, in which an inherited perfect verbal ending is affixed to the inherited third person singular imperfect form of the verb. Verbal forms are attested in all six person/number (singular and plural) combinations, and in the indicative, subjunctive, and imperative moods, though not in all languages.

§6. SYNTAX

Owing to the fragmentary preservation of the Continental Celtic languages, the picture we have of syntax is far less complete than that of phonology or morphology. In Celtiberian, we find that the basic, unmarked order of the clause is consistently subject–object–verb. All of the core constituents of the clause must occur before the verb. Additional material, however—for example, adverbial phrases—could occur after the verb. This is the loose type of subject–object–verb configuration reconstructed for late proto-Indo-European. In earliest-attested Cisalpine Celtic, subject–object–verb appears still to be the unmarked configuration of the clause, but it had become possible for a core constituent, a noun phrase, to occur after the verb. This was, seemingly, the first step towards the unmarked configuration shifting to subject–verb–object as is found in later Cisalpine Celtic. (Interesting examples of later Cisalpine Celtic word order are found in the bilingual inscriptions of TODI and VERCELLI, in which the verb, as in later Insular Celtic, but unlike that in Latin parallel texts, shuns clause-final position.) In the much more copiously attested Transalpine Celtic, subject–verb–object remains the unmarked configuration (though archaic subject–object–verb configuration appears to have been possible in formal or ritualistic texts of a high register). An important syntactic innovation is observable in Transalpine Celtic (sometimes called 'Vendryes's Restriction'). This pattern required that an enclitic pronoun, i.e. an unstressed pronoun linked phonetically to the previous stressed word, had to be adjacent to that verb when functioning as the object of the verb. Since Celtic languages have a strong tendency to place these unstressed object pronouns in second position in the clause, the result was that the verb tended to move forward in the clause to be adjacent to its object. Thus, the appearance of Vendryes's Restriction as an emerging trend in GAUL on both sides of the Alps, provides an important insight into the prehistoric background leading to the preponderance of verb-initial orders in Medieval and Modern Irish and Modern Welsh, one of the most striking features of the Celtic languages today.

PRIMARY SOURCES

CELTIBERIAN. Lejeune, *Celtiberica*; Untermann, *Monumenta Linguarum Hispanicarum* 1 (coin legends) & 4.349–722 (inscriptions); Untermann & Wodtko, *Monumenta Linguarum Hispanicarum* 5 (a dictionary of most forms in *Monumenta Linguarum Hispanicarum* 1 & 4).

CISALPINE CELTIC. Solinas, *Studi Etruschi* 60.311–408 (primarily epigraphic); Tibiletti Bruno, *I Celti d'Italia* 157–207; Whatmough, *Prae-Italic Dialects* 2.65–206.

CISALPINE GAULISH. Lejeune, RIG 2/1.1–54.

GALATIAN. Freeman, *Galatian Language*; Weisgerber, *Natalicium Johannes Geffcken zum 70. Geburtstag* 151–75.

LEPONTIC. Lejeune, *Lepontica*; Motta, *I leponti tra mito e realtà* 2.181–222.

TRANSALPINE CELTIC. Colbert de Beaulieu & Fischer, RIG 4 (coin legends); Delamarre, *Dictionnaire de la langue gauloise*; Duval & Pinault, RIG 3 (calendars); Lambert, RIG 2/2 (inscriptions engraved in Roman cursive); Lejeune, *ÉC* 25.79–106, 27.175–7, 30.181–9, 31.99–113 (inscriptions engraved in Greek characters); Lejeune, RIG 1 (inscriptions engraved in Hellenic characters), 2/1.55–194 (inscriptions engraved in Roman capitals); Lejeune & Lambert, *ÉC* 32.131–7 (inscriptions engraved in Hellenic characters); Marichal, *Les graffites de La Graufesenque* (graffiti from La Graufesenque).

FURTHER READING

GENERAL. ALPINE; BALKANS; BRYTHONIC; CELTIBERIAN; CELTIC LANGUAGES; GALATIAN; GALICIA; GALLO-BRITTONIC; GAUL; GAULISH; GOIDELIC; IBERIAN PENINSULA; INDO-EUROPEAN; INSCRIPTIONS; INSULAR CELTIC; IRON AGE; ITALY; LA TÈNE; LEPONTIC; LUSITANIAN; NORICUM; PROTO-CELTIC; SCRIPTS; TODI; TRANSALPINE GAUL; VERCELLI; Eska, *Cambridge Encyclopedia of the World's Ancient Languages*; Eska, *Hispano-Gallo-Brittonica* 33–46; Eska & Evans, *Celtic Languages* 26–63; Eska & Wallace, *Incontri Linguistici* 24.137–57; D. Ellis Evans, PBA 65.497–538; D. Ellis Evans, *Proc. Sixth International Congress of Celtic Studies* 19–54; Koch, *Bretagne et pays celtiques* 471–95; Koch, *Emania* 9.17–27; Koch, *Hispano-Gallo-Brittonica* 79–95; Lejeune, *Bulletin de la Classe des lettres et de sciences morales et politiques. L'Académie royale de Belgique* 64.108–21; McCone, *Religión, lengua y cultura* 483–94; Prosdocimi, *Studi Etruschi* 57.139–77; Schmidt, BBCS 28.189–205; Schmidt, *Le lingue indoeuropee di frammentaria attestazione* 65–90.

CELTIBERIAN. Gorrochategui, *Anuario del Seminario de Filología Vasca* 14.3–31; Gorrochategui, *Los celtas* 409–29; Gorrochategui, *Emérita* 62.297–324; Hoz, *Los celtas* 357–407; Jordán Colera, *Introducción al celtibérico*; Tovar, *Actas del III Coloquio* 227–53; Untermann, *Hispano-Gallo-Brittonica* 244–59; Untermann, *Veleia* 2/3.57–76; Villar, ZCP 49/50.898–949.

CISALPINE CELTIC. Eska, *Münchener Studien zur Sprachwissenschaft* 58.63–80; Eska, *Proc. Berkeley Linguistic Society* 24.2–11; Eska & Wallace, *Indogermanische Forschungen* 106.230–42; Motta, *ÉC* 29.311–18; Schmidt, KZ 94.172–97.

GALATIAN. Schmidt, *Forschungen in Galatien* 15–28.

TRANSALPINE CELTIC/GAULISH. Eska, *Historische Sprach-forschung* 103.81–91; Eska, *Münchener Studien zur Sprachwissenschaft* 55.7–39; Eska, SC 28.39–62 (Vendryes's Restriction); Eska, SC 32.115–27; D. Ellis Evans, *Gaulish Personal Names* 410–20; Lambert, *La langue gauloise*; Lejeune, *ÉC* 22.88–93; Meid, *Die grösseren altkeltischen Sprachdenkmäler* 257–65; Schmidt, ZCP 41.159–79; Uhlich, *Akten des Zweiten Deutschen Keltologen-Symposiums* 2.277–304.

Joseph Eska

The **Coraniaid** (Middle Welsh *Corryanyeit, Korannyeit, Coranyeit, Coranneit, Coranyeyt*) were a race of sinister otherworldly magicians who figure as one of the three national *gormesoedd* (foreign oppressions, invasions) in the Middle Welsh mythological prose tale, CYFRANC LLUDD A LLEFELYS. Like the magician MATH FAB MATHONWY in the Fourth Branch of the MABINOGI, the Coraniaid had great power through being able to hear any utterance that met the wind. The Coraniaid continued to be known in later Welsh folk tradition; for example, Ann GRIFFITHS refers to them in one of her hymns *c.* 1800: *Caiff Hotentots, Goraniaid dua' eu lliw, / Farbaraidd lu, eu dwyn i deulu Duw* 'Hottentots, blackest of Coraniaid, a barbarous host, will be taken into God's family'. The sense seems to be 'outlandish heathens'. Several explanations for the name have been suggested, including a likely connection with Welsh *cor(r)* 'dwarf', and a linguistically tricky equivalence with Breton *Korriganed* 'the FAIRIES'. Etymologies once proposed, but since rejected, include a common derivation with the Old Irish names for the PICTS (CRUITHIN), a tribal group of north-east Ireland—a derivation which is linguistically impossible—or with the British tribal name *Coritanni*, but this name is now read *Corieltau(v)i*. Koch compares Old Irish *corrguinecht* 'magic, wizardry', *corrguinech* 'magician, sorcerer': apparently a compound of *corr* 'crane' and *guin* 'the act of slaying, wounding'. There are other magical associations with cranes in early IRISH LITERATURE, but the particulars of the practice of *corrguinecht* are not certain.

FURTHER READING

CRUITHIN; CYFRANC LLUDD A LLEFELYS; FAIRIES; GRIFFITHS; IRISH LITERATURE; MABINOGI; MATH FAB MATHONWY; PICTS; Bromwich, TYP 86; Koch, *Journal of Celtic Linguistics* 1.101–18; Brynley F. Roberts, *Cyfranc Lludd a Llefelys* xxxii–xxxiii.

JTK

Corc of Caisel (Conall Corc, Corc mac Luigdech) is the apical figure, although not the eponym, of the dominant Éoganacht dynastic families in the Irish province of Munster (Mumu). Date-guessing would place him in the 4th or early 5th century, but his significance derives from the genealogical and literary complex gathered around him. Traditionally, he is the 'founder' of Caisel Muman (Cashel), the prominent rock which became the royal centre of the Éoganacht kingship in the early Middle Ages. It has been thought significant that its name derives from the Latin *castellum*, and that from its earliest traditions the Éoganacht kingship appears to be Christian. Caisel is said to have been revealed by angels, and one 9th- or early 10th-century version of Corc of Caisel's finding of Caisel (*Senchas Fagbála Caisil* 'The Tradition of the Finding of Cashel') incorporates what is patently a royal, perhaps inauguration, liturgy for the Munster kings. Corc's story-cycle involves a wicked witch as foster-mother, a satirist mother, and a journey into Alba (Scotland, Britain), where he is rescued and befriended by a local poet, Gruibne *éces*; a near-disastrous union with the daughter of the Scottish king follows. Already in the early Middle Ages, this indicates that Pictish families (those of Mag Gerginn, modern Angus and the Mearns) were claiming descent from Conall Corc. Versions of these traditions were adapted around 1200 in poems by Muireadhach Albanach Ó Dálaigh for patrons in the Scottish lordship of the Lennox.

PRIMARY SOURCES
ED. & TRANS. Clancy et al., *Triumph Tree* 258–62; Dillon, *Ériu* 16.61–73; Hull, PMLA 56.937–50, 62.887–909; Hull, ZCP 27.64–74; McKenna, *Aithdioghluim Dána* 1.173–4, 2.102–3; Meyer, *Anecdota from Irish Manuscripts* 3.57–63; Ó Cuív, *Celtic Studies* 92–8.

FURTHER READING
ALBA; CAISEL MUMAN; ÉOGANACHT; MUMU; Ó DÁLAIGH; Byrne, *Irish Kings and High-Kings* 165–201, esp. 184–94.

Thomas Owen Clancy

Corcaigh (**Cork**) is a city and county in the southern province of Munster (An Mumhain, Old Irish Mumu) in the Irish Republic (Éire). The city of Cork is situated on the river Lee, near the south coast of the country and is the second largest city in the Republic. Irish is still spoken in two areas of west Cork— Ballyvourney (Baile Bhuirne) and Ballingeary (Béal Átha an Ghaortha), both near Macroom (Maigh Chromtha).

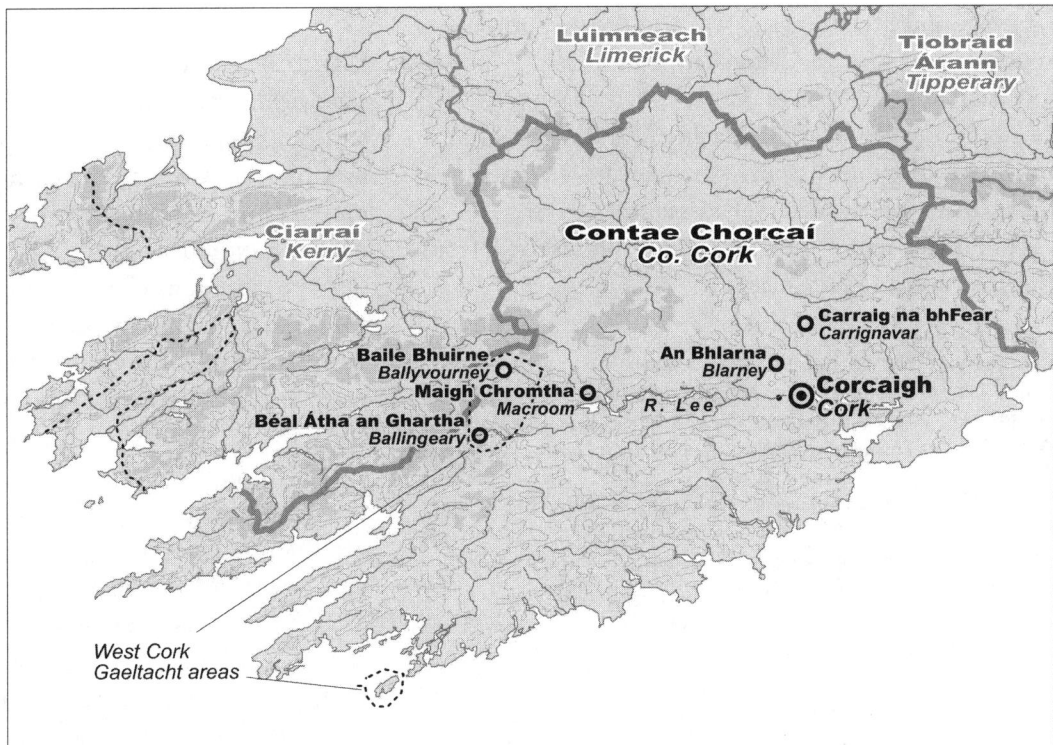

West Cork Gaeltacht areas

The city and county have produced many famous scholars, politicians, and writers, among them Dáibhí Ó Bruadair (?1625–98), Tadhg Ó Donnchadha (1874–1949), Daniel Corkery (1878–1964), Frank O'Connor (1903–66), Seán Ó Ríordáin (1916–77), and Donncha Ó Céileachair (1918–60). Originally a 7th-century monastic settlement near the present-day cathedral named after Cork's patron saint, Finbarr, and subsequently a Viking town, Cork became an important educational centre during the Middle Ages. The scribal activities of members of the famous Ó Longáin family from Carrignavar (Carraig na bhFear), Co. Cork, from the late 18th to the late 19th century were a very valuable contribution to our knowledge of Irish literary tradition. Cork played a central rôle during the nationalist resistance of the early 20th century and the city suffered much devastation during the ensuing struggle for independence (see IRISH INDEPENDENCE MOVEMENT). Cork city is home to one of the Colleges of the National University of Ireland, originally founded as Queen's College in 1849, now University College Cork (or National University of Ireland, Cork/Coláiste na hOllscoile, Corcaigh). The university has produced many important Irish writers and scholars, including Seán O'Faolain (1900–91), Nuala Ní Dhomhnaill (1952–), and Seán Ó Tuama (1926–). It offers degree courses in Irish language and literature, and was also the first university to award a degree in Celtic Civilization.

About 8 km north of Cork city is Blarney Castle (c. 1446), in the village of Blarney (An Bhlarna), home to the world-famous stone, which allegedly confers the 'gift of the gab' to whoever kisses it.

The place-name *Corcaigh* is probably derived from the Irish word *corcach* 'marsh'.

FURTHER READING
CORKERY; ÉIRE; IRISH; IRISH INDEPENDENCE MOVEMENT; IRISH LITERATURE; MUMU; NÍ DHOMHNAILL; Ó BRUADAIR; Ó CÉILEACHAIR; O'CONNOR; Ó DONNCHADHA; O'FAOLAIN; Ó RÍORDÁIN; Ó TUAMA; Hart, *I.R.A. and its Enemies*; Hewlett, *Blarney Stone*; Kelly, *Grand Tour of Cork*; Nic Craith, *Malartú Teanga*; Ó Conchúir, *Scríobhaithe Chorcaí 1700–1850*; O'Flanagan & Buttimer, *Cork*; Ó Murchú, *Cathair Chorcaí roimh an gorta Cork*; Ó Riain, *Making of a Saint*; Ó Ríordáin, *Conradh na Gaeilge i gCorcaigh 1894–1910*.

PSH

Corkery, Daniel (1878–1964) was an Irish fiction-writer, playwright, historian, and politician who championed GAELIC and rural literature in Ireland (ÉIRE). First a schoolteacher and civil servant, Corkery was professor of English at University College Cork from 1931 to 1947 and a member of Seanad Éireann (Irish Senate) from 1951 to 1954. He is best known for his short stories, set in southern Ireland, and his literary historical works, particularly *The Hidden Ireland* (1924), which shifted scholarly attention from ANGLO-IRISH LITERATURE of the 19th century to Gaelic. Now seen by some as excessively nationalistic (see NATIONALISM), Corkery nevertheless helped rehabilitate Irish-language literature and paved the way for its revival in the 20th century. He also greatly influenced writers in English, particularly Frank O'CONNOR.

SELECTION OF MAIN WORKS
Hidden Ireland (1924); *Fortunes of the Irish Language* (1954).
COLLECTIONS OF SHORT STORIES. *Munster Twilight* (1916); *Hounds of Banba* (1920); *Stormy Hills* (1929); *Earth Out of Earth* (1939).

FURTHER READING
ANGLO-IRISH LITERATURE; CORCAIGH; ÉIRE; GAELIC; IRISH LITERATURE; NATIONALISM; O'CONNOR; Delaney, *Critical Ireland* 41–8; Gonzalez, *Irish University Review* 14.191–201; Maume, '*Life that is Exile*'; Saul, *Daniel Corkery*.

Brian Ó Broin

Cormac mac Airt was a prehistoric Irish king renowned in the Middle Ages for his unwavering truth and Solomonic wisdom. He was often called Cormac ua Cuinn or 'Cormac the grandson of Conn' after his more famous progenitor CONN CÉTCHATHACH (Conn of the hundred battles). Although his historicity is open to question, Cormac is said to have lived in the 3rd century AD, but by the time his exploits came to be written down in the early Christian period he had already become a creature of legend. As such, he played a major rôle in IRISH LITERATURE, both in FIANNAÍOCHT and in the KINGS' CYCLES of tales. Included in this latter category are some 15 texts in Old and Middle Irish that have been grouped by modern scholars into 'The Cycle of Cormac mac Airt' (Dillon, *Cycles of the Kings* 15–29). These sagas, poems, and anecdotes chronicle the major events in his life from his conception on the night before the battle of Mag Mucrama to his death in the otherworldly house at Clettech. The most famous episode in this cycle centres on his first journey to Tara (TEAMHAIR), where he pronounced a *fírbreth* (true judgement) that at once revealed the falsity of the reigning king, Lugaid Mac Con, and established his own fitness to rule. It was this intimate connection with *fír flathemon* (ruler's truth) that set Cormac apart from other kings as the ideal sovereign of Irish tradition (cf. AUDACHT MORAINN; WISDOM LITERATURE). Other sources depict Cormac as a lawgiver and as a fount of gnomic wisdom, which he dispensed to his eldest son and successor Cairpre Lifechar (Ó Cathasaigh, *Heroic Biography of Cormac mac Airt* 60, 86). Cormac was also credited with the building of a number of magnificent structures on the Hill of Tara, including a massive stronghold that is described in rather fanciful terms in the metrical DINDSHENCHAS (Gwynn, *Metrical Dindshenchas* 1.28ff.). However, unlike his grandfather, the victor in a hundred battles, Cormac is not portrayed as a great warrior (Ó Cathasaigh, *Heroic Biography of Cormac mac Airt* 91). Whatever victories he enjoyed during his reign stemmed not from his prowess at arms but from his steadfast preservation of truth.

FURTHER READING
AUDACHT MORAINN; CONN CÉTCHATHACH; DINDSHENCHAS; FIANNAÍOCHT; IRISH LITERATURE; KINGS' CYCLES; TEAMHAIR; WISDOM LITERATURE; Dillon, *Cycles of the Kings*; Gwynn, *Metrical Dindshenchas*; Ó Cathasaigh, *Heroic Biography of Cormac mac Airt*; O' Daly, *Cath Maige Mucrama*.

Dan Wiley

Cormac ua Cuilennáin/Cormac mac Cuileannáin

(†908), bishop and king of CAISEL MUMAN from 902 to 908, when he was killed at the battle of Belach Mugna, belonged to one of the lesser branches of the ÉOGANACHT dynasties. The fullest version of his biography is to be found in the 17th-century compilation, the ANNALS of the Four Masters. He was brought up by the sage, Snedgus of Dísert Díarmada, who died in 890. In 902 he assumed the kingship of Caisel in place of Cenngégán. Five years later he and Flaithbertach led a Munster (MUMU) force against Flann mac Maelsechlainn, king of Ireland (ÉRIU), at Mag Léna (Offaly/Co. Uíbh Fhailí). After defeating him, they marched on into southern Meath (MIDE) and also defeated the Connachtmen and brought home hostages from the UÍ NÉILL. The

victories brought no lasting peace. In 908 Flann with Cerball, king of LAIGIN, and Cathal, king of CONNACHT, brought a great army against Cormac at Belach Mugna (Ballymoon, Co. Kildare/Contae Chill Dara). The Annals record the doom-laden prophecies accompanying Cormac, and his death is described in detail (Radner, *Fragmentary Annals* 153–9). In the coda of the annal entry he is described as 'a scholar in Irish and in Latin, the wholly pious and pure chief bishop, miraculous in chastity and prayer, a sage in government, in all wisdom, knowledge and science, a sage of poetry and learning, chief of charity and every virtue; a wise man in teaching, high king of two provinces of all Munster in his time . . .' (Radner, *Fragmentary Annals* 159).

A wide range of works have been attributed to him. They include LEBOR NA CERT ('The Book of Rights'), SANAS CHORMAIC ('Cormac's Glossary'), the manuscript compilation known as SALTAIR CHAISIL ('The Psalter of Cashel'), and numerous poems and tales. However, recent scholarship has tended towards the view that many of these attributions should be treated with scepticism (see Dillon, *Celtica* 4.239–49; Ó Riain, *Éigse* 33.107–30). Many of the poems and tales attributed to him await re-evaluation: it seems that there was a tendency to attribute works to him in order to enhance their status and that of the manuscript in which they were contained. In contrast to the prevailing trend, Breatnach has recently attributed the *Amra Senáin*, a poem in praise of St Senán, to Cormac on the basis of the historical associations in the poem and the language and vocabulary also attested in *Sanas Chormaic* ('Cormac's Glossary').

PRIMARY SOURCES
Breatnach, *Sages, Saints and Storytellers* 7–31; Byrne, *Irish Kings and High-Kings*; Meyer, *Sanas Cormaic*; O'Donovan, *Annála Ríoghachta Éireann*; Radner, *Fragmentary Annals of Ireland*.

FURTHER READING
ANNALS; CAISEL MUMAN; CONNACHT; ÉOGANACHT; ÉRIU; LAIGIN; LEBOR NA CERT; MIDE; MUMU; SALTAIR CHAISIL; SANAS CHORMAIC; UÍ NÉILL; Dillon, *Celtica* 4.239–49; Ó Riain, *Éigse* 23.107–30; Russell, CMCS 15.1–30.

Paul Russell

Cormac ua Liatháin

(Latin *Cormac[c]us nepos Lēthani*) was an Irish ascetic in the later 6th century, a contemporary and follower of St COLUM CILLE/ Columba (†597). He is of special interest as a voyager

saint whose historical exploits anticipate the more fantastic adventures of St Brendan in Navigatio
Sancti Brendani, as well as the vernacular Irish
voyage literature or immrama, such as Immram
Brain. Cormac is mentioned in three sections of
Adomnán's *Vita Columbae* (Life of Colum Cille). Chapter 1.6 relates that he made three unsuccessful attempts
to find an island hermitage on the ocean, and as he went
out a fourth time from Eirros Domn (in Connacht)
Colum Cille prophesied that he would fail once again
since his companion was a monk who did not have his
abbot's permission. In Chapter 2.42, we are told that
Cormac and his sailors made a northern voyage. Colum
Cille sought to ensure their safety by asking Brudeus
king of the Picts (Bruide mac Maelcon) to use his
authority over the sub-king of the Orcades (Orkneys),
whose kingdom possibly also included the Shetlands, to
guarantee that the voyagers would not be harmed if they
landed on the islands. They were then blown off course
by 14 days of winds from the south and experienced
terrifying sea creatures on all sides. Though they were
far away, Colum Cille and his monks were aware of
all this and prayed for the wind to reverse; it did and
Cormac returned gratefully. In Chapter 3.17, Cormac
is one of four 'holy founders of monasteries' who set
out to find Colum Cille and locate him on the island
of Hinba. There they asked him to perform the
eucharist, and as he did so a fiery light appeared above
him and rose like a column. In the Old Irish Martyrology of Oengus Céile Dé, Cormac's feast day is 21
June and he is associated with the important Columban
foundation at *Dermag a Mide* (Durrow in Meath). In a
strange little tale that follows, Cormac cuts off Colum
Cille's finger in a squabble over relics, and Colum Cille
responds by prophesying that *coin* (dogs, wolves) would
devour Cormac, a prophecy which was fulfilled, we
are told, though we are spared the details. It also tells
us that it was this Cormac against whom the sea rose
in fulfilment of Colum Cille's word, apparently an
allusion to *Vita Columbae* 1.6.

PRIMARY SOURCES
ED. & TRANS. Alan O. Anderson & Marjorie O. Anderson,
Adomnán's Life of Columba; Stokes, *Félire Óengusso Céli Dé / The
Martyrology of Oengus the Culdee*.
TRANS. Sharpe, *Life of St Columba / Adomnán of Iona*.

FURTHER READING
ADOMNÁN; BRENDAN; BRUIDE MAC MAELCON; COLUM CILLE;
CONNACHT; IMMRAM BRAIN; IMMRAMA; NAVIGATIO SANCTI

BRENDANI; OENGUS CÉILE DÉ; PICTS; VOYAGE LITERATURE;
Herbert, *Iona, Kells, and Derry*; Ann Williams et al., *Biographical Dictionary of Dark Age Britain* 90.

JTK

The **Cornish language**, like Breton, can be
explained as having developed from a common
ancestor, namely the south-western dialect of
Brythonic. This means that, within the Brythonic
subfamily of the Celtic languages, it is rather more
closely related to Breton than to Welsh. Cornish may
be usefully divided into four historical phases of
development. (1) Old Cornish denotes the phase
between about 800 and 1250, when the language was
first emerging from its parent south-west Brythonic.
Some scholars, following Jackson (LHEB), refer to a
'Primitive Cornish' period at *c.* 550–*c.* 800, but this
usage is potentially misleading because of the dearth
of evidence that Cornish and Breton were separate
dialects at this early period, or even that Welsh was by
then very distinct from a more general Brythonic.
(2) Middle Cornish refers to the phase of the language
between *c.* 1250 and *c.* 1550. (3) Late Cornish is the label
most often given to the phase from *c.* 1550 to the period
of decline in the 19th century, while (4) Revived
Cornish is applied to the language between the mid-
19th century and the present time.

The most characteristic feature of Old Cornish was
the hard endings to consonants (specifically the dental
stops /-d -t/), which later softened in the Middle
Cornish phase to *s*-like sounds (sibilants); the final
-*nt* became -*ns*, e.g. the Old Cornish masculine name
Gerent < British *Gerontios* (cf. Welsh *Geraint*) became
Middle Cornish *Gerens*, and *d* became /z/, perhaps
by way of /ð/ (the English *th* in brea*the*), e.g., in
Cornish *bys* /bɪz/ < Celtic *bitu-* 'world', contrasting
with Welsh *byd* and Breton *bed*, or Middle Breton *Meriadec*
vs. Cornish *Meriasek*. Cornish during the Tudor
(Tudur) period had many characteristics of the
Middle Cornish phase, but also contained characteristics of the Late period, making texts from this
time of crucial interest. Cornish reached its highest
development as a literary language in the 15th and 16th
centuries, as can be seen by the surviving literature,
such as the Ordinalia, Beunans Ke (The Life of St
Ke or Kea), Beunans Meriasek ('The Life of St

Meriasek'), and GWREANS AN BYS (*The Creacion of the Worlde*).

In the early Middle Ages, south-west Brythonic as it developed into Old Cornish was spoken in parts of present-day west Devon and Cornwall (KERNOW). By around 1100, Cornish was spoken from the river Tamar to Land's End. At that time, perhaps around 20,000 of Cornwall's estimated population of 21,000 may have spoken the language. By the Middle Cornish phase, around 30,000 of Cornwall's 50,000 inhabitants spoke Cornish, but by 1500 the language had retreated to Bodmin and the west.

Its decline may be attributed to several historical events, among them the Wars of the Roses, during which many old Cornish families disappeared, the discovery of America (many Cornish people travelled west) and the An Gof Rebellion of 1497, the RENAISSANCE of learning (which spread English into Cornwall), the Reformation—which meant that the age-old intercourse between Cornwall and Brittany (BREIZH) ceased to function within the framework of a common church, and the English Civil Wars. Cornish was spoken as late as 1595 in St Ewe, near Mevagissey, while monoglot Cornish speakers were found in Feock, near Truro, in 1640.

Though the language was still spoken in some easterly pockets, by 1700 it had become largely confined to Penwith and the Lizard in the extreme west of the peninsula. Thomas Tonkin noticed that a rapid decline occurred between 1700 and 1735. Despite the efforts of many scholars, the language was virtually unused by the turn of the 19th century, but fragments and pieces continued to be retained and collected, while earlier manuscripts were studied. There is also a possible mislaid manuscript, which might have contained sermons preached in Cornish by the Revd Joseph Sherwood in west Cornwall in 1680.

The language was revived by a number of scholars, including Henry JENNER and Robert Morton NANCE during the late 19th and early 20th centuries. Nance's suggested system of Unified Cornish has since been re-evaluated, and Revived Cornish has undergone an internal review, prompting, perhaps temporarily, the prevalence of different kinds of 'Cornishes'. The language underwent a large literary revival during the 20th century (see CORNISH LITERATURE) and there are now numerous authors and poets writing in the language, as well as Cornish-language films and developing MASS MEDIA. A useful reader in all phases of the Cornish language before the Revival has been edited by Kent and Saunders.

PRIMARY SOURCES
Gendall, *New Practical Dictionary of Modern Cornish*; Jago, *Ancient Language and the Dialect of Cornwall*; Jenner, *Handbook of the Cornish Language*; Norris, *Ancient Cornish Drama*; Robert Williams, *Lexicon Cornu-Britannicum*.

FURTHER READING
BEUNANS KE; BEUNANS MERIASEK; BREIZH; BRETON; BRYTHONIC; CELTIC LANGUAGES; CORNISH LITERATURE; GWREANS AN BYS; JACKSON; JENNER; KERNOW; MASS MEDIA; NANCE; ORDINALIA; RENAISSANCE; TUDUR; WELSH; George, *Celtic Languages* 410–68; George, *Pronunciation and Spelling of Revived Cornish*; Holmes, *Cornish Studies* 2nd ser. 11.270–90; Jackson, LHEB; Kent & Saunders, *Looking at the Mermaid*; Price, *Languages of Britain*; Spriggs, *Cornish Studies* 2nd ser. 11.228–69; Weatherhill, *Cornish Place Names and Language*; N. J. A. Williams, *Cornish Today*.

Alan M. Kent

Cornish literature [1] medieval

The fact that medieval Cornish literature has often been dismissed by scholars in the field of Celtic studies as 'not Celtic enough' has done much disservice to writing from Cornwall (KERNOW). While the medieval literature lacks the mythical or heroic elements of IRISH LITERATURE or WELSH PROSE LITERATURE and WELSH POETRY (see also HEROIC ETHOS), the territory's tradition is clearly more closely bound up with drama, community, and festival. The character of Cornwall's literary continuum is greatly affected by the fact that it was the first of the CELTIC COUNTRIES to be 'accommodated' into the English state.

§1. LITERATURE OF THE OLD CORNISH PERIOD
In the early medieval period, the earliest evidence of Old Cornish consists of several glosses from the 10th century, written on Smaragdus's Commentary on the classical grammarian Donatus, on the Book of Tobit found in the manuscript Oxoniensis Posterior (see GLOSSES), and in the manumissions found on the Bodmin Gospels, which record the freeing of 122 slaves, of whom 98 were Cornish, and many had native Cornish names (see BODMIN MANUMISSIONS). Evidence during this phase also indicates considerable, but now lost, ARTHURIAN material, as well as implying Cornish origins for the love story of TRISTAN AND ISOLT.

The longest surviving piece of early medieval Cornish, however, is the OLD CORNISH VOCABULARY (*c.* 1100), which provides a long list of Latin words and their Cornish equivalents. It demonstrates the vitality of Cornish as a literary language and classifies everything from the biblical creator to animals and inanimate objects. This is followed *c.* 1150 by JOHN OF CORNWALL's Latin *Prophetia Merlini* ('The Prophecy of Merlin'; see also MYRDDIN), which expresses contemporary political and religious views in the guise of an ancient prophecy. The extant text, in Latin, is believed to have been derived from a Cornish source, and the BRYTHONIC glosses indicate this.

§2. LITERATURE OF THE MIDDLE CORNISH PERIOD
The next text in the continuum is commonly known as the Charter Endorsement. It consists of 41 lines of Cornish from *c.* 1400, written on the back of a land charter from St Stephen-in-Brannel dated 1340. The text's theme is marriage, and it offers the couple advice on how to proceed:

> *an bar ma ze pons tamar*
> *my ad pes worty byz fa*
> *ag ol se voz by a wra*
>
> On this side of the Tamar bridge
> I pray thee be good to her
> And all thy pleasure she will do.

Opinion regarding the text is varied: some scholars believe it is a fragment of a longer work, while others believe it to be a wedding speech.

The most significant trend during this phase, however, is the development of Cornish-language, community-based, liturgical and biblical drama, with a resolutely Cornish treatment, of which the trilogy known as the ORDINALIA is one of the few surviving examples. Most parishes had their own play, sometimes based on saints' lives, synthesizing the contemporary with the ancient; for example, in the Passion, Christ's torturers travel to Market Jew (Marazion) in west Cornwall to obtain nails from a smith.

Broadly at the same time there emerged the elaborate and much underrated epic poem, *Pascon Agan Arluth* or 'The Poem of Mount Calvary', which has many similarities to the Passion play of the *Ordinalia*. Its quatrains are based on the canonical gospels with various apocryphal editions, though unlike the *Ordinalia* or

BEUNANS MERIASEK, it bears no explicit Cornish references. The oldest surviving copy was found at Sancreed in Penwith. The poem's quatrains are used to great effect at the moment of the crucifixion:

> *Newngo devethys an prys may tho agas theweth*
> *Yn erna y fe dorgis ha dris ol an bys ef eth*
> *Tewolgow bras a ve guris an houll a gollas y feth*
> *Hay moy merthus me agris ys a rena ve yn weathe*
>
> Twas not come the time, but twas near his end,
> In that hour there was an earthquake, over all ye
>   world it was
> Darkness great was made ye sunn left his face
> And more wonders I believe then there were also.

The post-medieval and Tudor phase, however, curtailed much of this literary activity, and several other texts, that are known to have existed, have not survived. Nevertheless, Cornwall's medieval literature shows that a distinctly dynamic theatrical culture operated in the west of the British Isles.

Such a culture is exemplified and proven by the recent rediscovery in 2002 of a new Middle Cornish saint's play (contained in a mid-16th-century manuscript) based on the life of St Kea (see BEUNANS KE). Kea is a saint venerated in Cornwall, Brittany (BREIZH), and Wales (CYMRU). A *vita* of Kea from Brittany survives in a French translation. The play is likely to have been intended for performance at a site near Kea in the Truro area called 'Playing Place'. The discovery of this play, which includes some Arthurian material, markedly increases the canon of Cornish literature.

PRIMARY SOURCES
MSS. *Donatus Glosses.* Paris, Bibliothèque Nationale, Latin 13029; Oxford, Bodleian Library 574 (14 S. C. 2026 (3)).
Tobit Glosses. Oxford, Bodleian Library 572 (*Oxoniensis Posterior*).
Bodmin Gospels, St. Petroc's Gospel. London, BL Add. 9381.
Prophetia Merlini. Vatican, Biblioteca Apostolica Vaticana, Codex Ottobonianus, Latin 1474.
Vocabularium Cornicum. London, BL, Cotton Vespasian A. xiv.
GWREANS AN BYS. Oxford, Bodleian Library 791.
Pascon agan Arluth. London, BL, Harley 1782.
FURTHER READING
ARTHUR; ARTHURIAN; BEUNANS KE; BEUNANS MERIASEK; BODMIN MANUMISSIONS; BREIZH; BRYTHONIC; CELTIC COUNTRIES; CORNISH; CYMRU; GLOSSES; HEROIC ETHOS; IRISH LITERATURE; JOHN OF CORNWALL; KERNOW; MYRDDIN; OLD CORNISH VOCABULARY; ORDINALIA; TRISTAN AND ISOLT; WELSH POETRY; WELSH PROSE LITERATURE; Kent, *Literature of Cornwall*; Kent & Saunders, *Looking at the Mermaid*; Murdoch, *Cornish Literature*; Toorians, *Middle Cornish Charter Endorsement*.

                                   Alan M. Kent

Cornish literature [2] post-medieval

To Cornish scholars, this phase of Cornish literature is perhaps best referred to as the Tudor period. It contains within it four core texts which, although they have the characteristics of medieval or Middle CORNISH, also have many of the linguistic earmarks of what would emerge as Late Cornish. This makes this post-medieval literature of immense interest to those concerned with the revival of Cornish. Politically, many of these texts came in the aftermath of the so-called An Gof (The smith) Rebellion of 1497 and the 1549 Prayer-Book Rebellion, both of which were mounted against the effects of the Reformation and Tudor centralism (see TUDOR).

The main texts are the two-day-long saints' plays BEUNANS KE (c. 1500) BEUNANS MERIASEK (1504); the TREGEAR HOMILIES (c. 1558), which consist of thirteen homilies, twelve of which were translated from the work of Bishop Bonner by John Tregear (*henna ew tha leverall in agan eyth ny* 'that is to say in our own language'), and GWREANS AN BYS (*The Creacion of the Worlde*, 1611), the first day of a longer Helston-based cycle, probably written in the mid-16th century and detailing biblical events from the Creation to the Flood.

Other interesting texts of the period include various accounts of performances of Cornish drama at various locations from the river Tamar in the east to St Just in the west, showing how widespread the theatrical continuum was in Cornwall (KERNOW). References in Launceston to the king and queen of Gall in lost texts indicate the presence of secular drama. The *Green Book of St Columb Major* (1589–95) contains a reference to a Robin Hood drama performed there, while interestingly the hagiographer Nicholas Roscarrock (c. 1548–1634) draws attention to an 'olde Cornish Rhyme' on the life of St Columb, now lost (see HAGIOGRAPHY).

Oliver Oldwanton's drama, *The Image of Idleness* (c. 1565–70), contains three Cornish characters—a Cornish priest named John Polmarghe (who is from Penborgh—a stage GLASNEY COLLEGE), Maister Jewgur, and Syr Ogier Penkyles; the playwright uses the Cornish language in the line *Marsoye thees duan Guisca ancorne Rog hatre arta* ('If there is thee grief to wear the horn, give it home again'). The 1632 English play *The Northern Lasse* by Richard Brome also contains a garbled line of Cornish: *Pedn bras vidne whee bis creegas* ('Fat [or big] head, will you be hanged?').

One of the most fascinating surviving texts is *The Fyrst Boke of the Introduction of Knowledge* by the English poet Andrew Boorde, which includes a satire (c. 1547) on the English speech of various parts of Britain, including Cornwall, and also some phrases of remarkably good Cornish—one of the few secular pieces from this phase. Though aligning himself with English culture, Richard Carew's *Survey of Cornwall* (1602) makes valuable observations on Cornish language and literature, as well as providing a description of a performance of one of the mystery plays.

Also surviving from this phase—though hardly literature—is a curious explanation by a Cornish speaker, probably Richard Pentrey, witnessed by one Don Antonio Ortes during a visit of the king and queen of Spain to the English College for training priests in Valladolid in 1600, and a marriage banns certificate (1636) written by William Drake, rector of St Just-in-Penwith.

PRIMARY SOURCES
MSS. BEUNANS KE. Aberystwyth, NLW 23849.
BEUNANS MERIASEK. Aberystwyth, NLW, Peniarth 105.
GWREANS AN BYS. Oxford, Bodleian Library 219.
TREGEAR HOMILIES. London, BL Add. 46397 (The Tregear Manuscript).
EDITIONS. Halliday, *Richard Carew of Antony*; Kent & Saunders, *Looking at the Mermaid*.

FURTHER READING
CORNISH; GLASNEY COLLEGE; HAGIOGRAPHY; KERNOW; TUDOR; Kent, *Literature of Cornwall*; Murdoch, *Cornish Literature*; Parker, *Cornwall Marches On / Keskerdh Kernow*; Rowse, *Tudor Cornwall*; Sturt, *Revolt in the West*.

Alan M. Kent

Cornish literature [3] 17th and 18th centuries

The Reformation is regarded as the main factor responsible for shutting down large-scale CORNISH literary production, for destroying many extant texts, and for changing the Cornish people's perception of themselves. The Reformation also destroyed the age-old link between the Cornish and the Bretons. With Cornwall (KERNOW) denied a Prayer Book and BIBLE, subject to the advance of English, and Cornish regarded as unrefined by the literary classes, post-Reformation literature began to be written by middle-class intellectuals of the age who realized that the language was in danger of dying, while at the same time Cornish language and literature came to be 'ennobled', as scholars looked for the last vestiges of written work (see also REFORMATION).

Relatively early (c. 1667) within this group of post-Reformation Cornish texts there is a reference to one Richard Angwyn, a fluent writer, but this period of writing was vigorously initiated by William Scawen who, in 1680, described the causes of the decay of Cornish speech. John Keigwin (1641–c. 1720) of Mousehole translated a number of texts, and additional collectors and writers, such as the Newlyn-based Nicholas Boson (c. 1624–1703), his son John (1665–c. 1720), and his cousin Thomas, William Gwavas (1676–1741) of Paul, Henry Usticke and John Tonkin, both of St Just (Lanuste), William Rowe of Sancreed, Oliver Pender of Mousehole, James Jenkin of Penzance (Pen Sans), and Thomas Tonkin of St Agnes (Bryanek), also continued the tradition of writing in Cornish. They were encouraged in their work by the Celtic scholar Edward LHUYD, who arrived in Cornwall in 1700. Unlike the religious verse writers of Middle Cornish, these writers dealt with a greater variety of form, structure, and subject matter.

John Boson wrote a poem on the process of pilchard curing, and another poem offering advice to Cornishmen leaving for London's sexual hazards; James Jenkin wrote *Poems of Advice* on marriage and homemaking; Gwavas recorded proverbs and sayings and wrote short, pithy poetry (ranging from riddles to accounts of lazy weavers). Thomas Tonkin collected songs and verse in Cornish—most famously a translation of the folk song 'Where are you going, my pretty maid?' (*Pela era why moaz, moz, fettow teag?*)—while Nicholas Boson crafted a children's story, in an admixture of English and Cornish, entitled *The Dutchesee of Cornwall's Progresse to see the Land's End and Visit the Mount*. Perhaps the best-known work from this period is the folk tale *John of Chyhanor*, a retelling of the international story of the servant's good counsels, written sometime between 1660 and 1700. Boson's other major work on the state of the language was *Nebbaz Gerriau dro tho Cornoack* (A few words about Cornish), but this was completed in English. Lhuyd recorded the following prophetic ENGLYN from a parish clerk at St Just:

An Lavor gôth ewe lavar gwîr.
Na vedn nevra doas vâs a tavaz re hir;
Bes dên heb tavaz a gollas e dir.

The old saying is a true saying.
Never will come good from a tongue too long;
But man without a tongue shall lose his land.

From the same source we also have a fantastical Williamite celebratory British song, expressing similar sentiments to those found in the writings of John Tonkin, while in 1710 Gwavas wrote a letter seemingly to Cornish speakers in America. Numerous other scraps and fragments exist, not to mention some biblical translations. It is likely that more Cornish material existed, but that it was destroyed during the English Civil Wars, and during raids on Restormel Castle at Lostwithiel, a long-standing centre of the STANNARY PARLIAMENT. However, by the middle of the 18th century, literary production in Cornish had more or less reached a standstill.

PRIMARY SOURCES
MS. London, BL Add. 28554; Truro, Maker Manuscript.
TEXT. Scawen, *Observations on an Ancient Manuscript . . . With an Account of the Language, Manners and Customs of the People of Cornwall.*

FURTHER READING
BIBLE; CORNISH; ENGLYN; KERNOW; LHUYD; REFORMATION; STANNARY PARLIAMENT; Gilbert, *Parochial History of Cornwall*; Kent, *Literature of Cornwall*; Kent & Saunders, *Looking at the Mermaid*; Lhuyd, *Archaeologia Britannica 1*; Padel, *Cornish Writings of the Bosun Family*; Pool, *Death of Cornish.*

Alan M. Kent

Cornish literature [4] 19th and 20th centuries

Fragments of the CORNISH language in Cornwall (KERNOW) persisted into the 18th century, and the German Georg Sauerwein wrote two poems in Cornish in 1865. The so-called *Cranken Rhyme* was also offered by John Davey near Penzance in 1891. Early in the 20th century, at the start of the revival, Henry JENNER and Robert Morton NANCE composed much explicitly revivalist verse, such as *Can Wlascar Agan Mamvro* (Patriotic song of our motherland) and *Nyns yu Marow Maghtern Arthur* (King Arthur is not dead) respectively, though the often medieval thematic concerns soon progressed to the decline of industrialization and the place of the language in the modern world.

Other important early writers in Revived Cornish include L. R. C. Duncombe-Jewell (b. 1866), R. St V. Allin-Collins (b. 1878) and E. G. R. Hooper (1906–1998). Probably the finest poets of the early part of the century were Edward Chirgwin (1892–1960), who was famous for diversifying the themes of modern writing in Cornish, and A. S. D. Smith (1883–1950), whose epic poem *Trystan hag Isolt* (1951; see also TRISTAN AND ISOLT) remains one of the revival's finest works.

One of the problems regarding the Cornish literature of this period is that there were many linguistic hobbyists who were content to write in Cornish, but who were disassociated from the territory. Much of the initial literature was circulated in limited magazines, and the assessment of the achievement of these poets is only just beginning to be realized. Allied to this, scholars are now beginning to reassess much of the achievement of literature in Cornwall, and this should lead to a wider appreciation.

Although the writing has been male-dominated, some successful female writers can be named, notably Katharine Lee Jenner, Phoebe Proctor (b. 1912), Helena Charles (1911–1997), Myrna Combellack, and especially Peggy Pollard (1903–1996), who wrote the agnostic play *Beunans Alysaryn* (1941) in the style of the earlier Cornish mystery dramas.

The novel has proved a more difficult form to develop in Cornwall; this is due to the relatively small number of speakers, though this is changing. The first full-length novel to be published in Cornish was Melville Bennetto's *An Gurun Wosek a Geltya* (The bloody crown of the Celtic countries; 1984). This was followed by Michael Palmer's *Jory* (1989) and *Dyroans* (1998).

Influential Cornish-language writers of the late 20th century include Richard Jenkin (1925–2002) and Richard Gendall (1924–)—two of the finest Cornish-language poets of their generation, the dramatist Donald R. Rawe (1930–), Anthony Snell (1938–), and N. J. A Williams (1942–), though Anglo-Cornish authors such as Arthur Quiller Couch (1863–1944), Charles Causley, A. L. Rowse, Jack Clemo, and D. M. Thomas have all intersected with aspects of the revival, and the continuum in Cornwall must be considered with this in mind.

Three emergent writers of the century are Tim Saunders (1952–), Nick Darke, and Alan M. Kent, all of whom have made critical assessments of the limited subject matter of the revival and advanced the literary continuum substantially. Saunders writes in Cornish, while Darke and Kent, though writing in Cornu-English, draw on much of the literary continuum of Cornish.

PRIMARY SOURCES
NOVELS. Bennetto, *An Gurun Wosek A Geltya*; Palmer, *Dyvroans*; Palmer, *Jory*.
PLAY. Pollard, *Beunans Alysaryn*.
POETRY. Saunders, *Wheel*; Smith, *Tristan and Isolt in Cornish Verse*.

FURTHER READING
CORNISH; JENNER; KERNOW; LANGUAGE (REVIVAL); NANCE; TRISTAN AND ISOLT; Kent, *Voices from West Barbary*.

Amy Hale

Courtly love, or *amour courtois*, is a theme in medieval European poetry that reached its first peak in Provence (south-eastern France). The Provençal court poets, the so-called troubadours ('finders, composers') were in their prime from the second half of the 11th century. The earliest known poet was Prince Guillaume IX of Aquitaine (1071–1127), grandfather of Eleanor of Aquitaine. The forms and subject matter of the troubadours' poetry were enthusiastically imitated all over western Europe. In northern France, these poets were called *trouvères*, the northern French cognate of troubadour. In Germany they were called *Minnesänger* (after a now obsolete Middle High German word *minne* 'love', which had a slightly more elevated meaning than its everyday synonym, Middle High German *liebe* 'love').

The chief theme expressed in poetry of this kind was that of unfulfilled love for an unattainable person, sublimated into poetic expression. Usually, this took the form of the poet's admiration for his patroness, i.e. his patron's wife, a married woman. This sublimated love is called *fins amors* in Provençal or *hohe Minne* in Middle High German, in contrast to vulgar physical love. The repertoire of the poets was not confined to love poetry, but also contained political poems, SATIRE, praise poetry, NATURE POETRY, etc.

Writers of the MATTER OF BRITAIN, such as CHRÉTIEN DE TROYES, used the ethic of courtly love to a great extent in their works (see also WELSH LITERATURE AND FRENCH), and this, in turn, influenced ARTHURIAN literature in English, German, and a number of other traditions.

The origin of poetry about courtly love is highly disputed; many authors suggest an Arabic origin (from the so-called '*Udhrī* love-poetry), which had been transmitted to Europe either via Spain or at the time of the crusades. An origin for the courtly love theme in Islamic civilization is favoured by Boase, but disputed by most other writers on the subject.

Other scholars consider the possibility of a local Provençal origin, incorporating elements from one or more sources, such as a cult of the Virgin Mary and the idealized treatment of women within the code of chivalry, and/or a spontaneous creative response to the class and sexual tensions inherent in the western European feudal society of the high Middle Ages. The society created by medieval arranged marriages resulted in many noble households with husbands a generation or more older than their wives, many of whom sought comfort in real or imagined adulterous relationships, such as those idealized by the troubadours. Recently, a continental Celtic origin has been suggested for the theme of courtly love, based on a myth of the Gaulish 'horse goddess', EPONA, preserved in the form of folkloric traditions.

With the marriage of Eleanor of Aquitaine and King Henry II Plantagenet of England in 1152, the literary fashion of courtly love was brought to BRITAIN. At the time many *trouvères* and troubadours were knights fighting on behalf of the king of England (e.g. Bertrand de Born or Savaric de Mauleon, governor of Bristol).

Courtly love came to Wales (CYMRU) during the course of the Anglo-Norman Marcher Lords' campaign to conquer south Wales. From the 12th century on, its traces have been detected in the work of the GOGYNFEIRDD, principally in the poems of HYWEL AB OWAIN GWYNEDD and CYNDDELW Brydydd Mawr. Some scholars, most prominently J. E. Caerwyn WILLIAMS, have disputed this interpretation. In the works of the 12th- and 13th-century *Gogynfeirdd*, the troubadour influence was in any event slight. Only after the downfall of the last independent Welsh prince in 1282 (see LLYWELYN AP GRUFFUDD) and the rise of the poets serving the post-conquest nobility (largely synonymous with the CYWYDDWYR) in the 14th century can a strong influence be seen, especially in the works of the greatest poet of later medieval Wales, DAFYDD AP GWILYM.

Poetry on courtly love must have come to Ireland (ÉRIU) in the wake of the Norman conquest in 1152.

The DÁNTA GRÁDHA, a class of 'love poems' sharing numerous motifs with the Provençal material, appear comparatively late. Most of them have been dated by Tomás Ó RATHILE to the end of the Classical Modern period (see IRISH LITERATURE), i.e. the 16th and 17th centuries. However, earlier works are likely to have existed, but unfortunately have not survived.

FURTHER READING
ARTHURIAN; BRITAIN; CHRÉTIEN DE TROYES; CYMRU; CYNDDELW; CYWYDDWYR; DAFYDD AP GWILYM; DÁNTA GRÁDHA; EPONA; ÉRIU; GOGYNFEIRDD; HYWEL AB OWAIN GWYNEDD; IRISH LITERATURE; LLYWELYN AP GRUFFUDD; MATTER OF BRITAIN; NATURE POETRY; Ó RATHILE; SATIRE; WELSH LITERATURE AND FRENCH; WILLIAMS; Benozzo, *Le letterature romanze del Medioevo* 259–80; Benozzo, *Medioevo Romanzo* 21.69–87; Bezzola, *Les origines et la formation de la littérature courtoise en Occident (500–1200)* 1; Boase, *Origin and Meaning of Courtly Love*; Bramley, *Gwaith Llywelyn Fardd I* 101–88; Chaytor, *Troubadours and England*; Nerys A. Jones & Parry Owen, *Gwaith Cynddelw Brydydd Mawr* 2; Mac Craith, *Lorg na hiasachta ar na Dánta Grá*; Ó Rathile, *Dánta Grádha*; Ó Tuama, *An Grá i bhFilíocht na nUaisle*; J. E. Caerwyn Williams, *Court Poet in Medieval Wales.*

PEB

Coventina

Coventina was a deity who was worshipped in the Roman period. A sanctuary devoted to her was found in 1876 near the fort of Brocolita (modern Carrawburgh, Northumberland) on HADRIAN'S WALL. Instead of the central sanctuary or *cella* which would be expected in a Roman temple, an enclosure containing a well was found on the site. This is unusual, but a similar structure, with a spring and a sacred grove in the enclosure, has been found at the oracle of Apollo at Didyma in Asia Minor (near Yenihisar, Turkey). Numerous votive figures and gifts were found in the well, and also about 13,000 coins. Fourteen INSCRIPTIONS bear the name of Coventina. The troops stationed at Brocolita were Batavians from the area now called the Netherlands, and several individuals who are named in the inscriptions hailed from near the RHINE. The goddess was generally depicted as a water nymph and is called *nimpha* in one inscription (RIB no. 1527). There are also dedications to the *Matres* (see also MATRONAE) and other goddesses at the site. Traces of the cult of Coventina have also been found in GAUL, at Narbonne, and in north-west Spain (GALICIA). The spellings *Couuentina*, *Conuentina*, *Couintina*, and *Couetina* also occur. A Celtic etymology is possible, perhaps connected to the common GALLO-BRITTONIC place-name element *venta*. Alternatively, derivation from Latin *conventio* 'assembling, meeting' is possible.

INSCRIPTIONS
Collingwood & Wright, RIB 1 nos. 1522–36.

FURTHER READING
GALICIA; GALLO-BRITTONIC; GAUL; HADRIAN'S WALL; INSCRIPTIONS; MATRONAE; RHINE; WATERY DEPOSITIONS; Allason-Jones & McKay, *Coventina's Well*; Green, *Gods of the Celts*; Ross, *Pagan Celtic Britain*.

PEB

The **Cowethas Kelto-Kernuak** (Celtic-Cornish Society) was founded in 1901 by L. C. Duncombe-Jewell for 'the study and preservation of the Celtic Remains in the Duchy of Cornwall'. It was the first Cornish society formed explicitly to promote Cornwall (KERNOW) as a Celtic nation (see CELTIC COUNTRIES), and Duncombe-Jewell's primary goal was to have Cornwall recognized by the Celtic Association as a Celtic nation. The main aims of the society, published in *Celtia: The Journal of the Pan-Celtic Association* (see PAN-CELTICISM) and in Cornish newspapers, were to preserve ancient monuments, to continue national customs such as wrestling and HURLING, to revive the CORNISH language as a spoken tongue, especially the teaching of Cornish to schoolmasters, to revive the Cornish mystery plays (see CORNISH LITERATURE) and to 're-establish' the Cornish GORSETH of the Bards at Boscawen Un.

Effectively, this was the first solid articulation of the aims of the Celtic revival in Cornwall, and set an ideological precedent for a pre-modern, pre-industrial vision of Celtic Cornwall. The organization attracted many prominent members of Cornish society, especially writers and antiquaries: among the council members were Thurstan Peter, J. B. Cornish, and the Anglo-Cornish poet Arthur Quiller Couch. However, the association was largely inactive and failed to have any real impact among the Cornish people themselves. It did not have a newsletter or journal or meetings, and much of its activity was conducted in the pages of *Celtia*. Nevertheless, Duncombe-Jewell was a prominent member of the Pan-Celtic Association and raised the international profile of Cornwall. By 1903, however, the society had ceased to be operational, and Henry JENNER took over as spokesperson for the Celtic-

Cornish revival, with Duncombe-Jewell abandoning his involvement. In many ways, the Cowethas Kelto-Kernuak was a precursor to much Celtic activism in Cornwall, including the Federation of Old Cornish Societies, the Cornish Gorseth, and Tyr ha Tavas (Land and Language).

PRIMARY SOURCE
The history of the organization may best be followed through contemporary articles in the journal *Celtia*.

FURTHER READING
CELTIC COUNTRIES; CORNISH; CORNISH LITERATURE; GORSETH; HURLING; JENNER; KERNOW; LANGUAGE (REVIVAL); PAN-CELTICISM; Hale, *Cornish Studies* 2nd series 5.100–11; Den Toll (Miners), *Gorseth Kernow*; Saunders, *Wheel*.

Amy Hale

Cras 'Murcens'

The OPPIDUM of Murcens was situated on the edge of the Causse de Granmat, 15 km east of Cahors, in the Lot region of France. A limestone cliff ensured its defence to the south and east; the other sides, fortified by a rampart, were more easily accessible, especially the northern side, where an isthmus linked the settlement to the plateau. The site covers a surface of 50 ha (around 125 acres). Here, in 1868, E. Castagné discovered a rampart made of horizontal beams embedded in a regular stone facing; the middle part of the wall was filled with loose stones. The width of the construction exceeds 10 m in some places, and the wall is preserved to a height of 4 m. At the intersection of most of the beams, a piece of square iron, 1 cm thick and 30 cm long, secures the connection.

Castagné immediately recalled the *murus gallicus* (Gaulish wall) described by CAESAR for Avaricum (*De Bello Gallico* 7.23), and brought this identification, which had been previously suggested by Jollois in 1843, to the attention of other scholars. Caesar, however, does not mention the iron spikes which are the recurring and original characteristic of this architecture of the Gaulish *oppida* (see GAUL) of the final LA TÈNE period. The site was newly excavated in the 1980s, when the architecture of the rampart was clarified and traces of the La Tène D settlement (2nd to earlier 1st century BC) located. Artefacts found on the site included numerous rotating millstones and imported amphorae (large ceramic wine vessels) from Italy, both emphasizing the importance of the site as an economic centre. No trace of early Gallo-Roman occupation could be identified. The identification of Murcens with the hill-fort whose name was recorded as *Uxellodūnon* 'the high fort', already rejected by Castagné, has been abandoned.

RELATED ARTICLES
CAESAR; GAUL; LA TÈNE; OPPIDUM.

Olivier Buchsenschutz

critical and theoretical perspectives on the study of literatures in the Celtic languages

§1. INTRODUCTION

CELTIC STUDIES began in the second half of the 19th century, primarily as a linguistic discipline concerned with the Celtic family of languages (see CELTIC LANGUAGES). It has since developed into an inter-disciplinary field which includes history, textual criticism, archaeology, anthropology, folklore, and many other disciplines alongside language.

From the beginning, Celtic studies derived its authenticity as an academic discipline by basing its methodologies on those of the classics. Greek and Roman classics has been a subject accorded special status and prestige in universities in the Western world as an ancient and demanding field of study. The three areas of interest taken over from the classics were philology (in the sense of the traditional, largely historical, study of language), literary criticism, and a specific editorial method developed for the teaching of Greek and Latin texts in schools and universities. Discovering who the 'Celts' were, as distinct from the 'Anglo-Saxons' of England or the 'Greeks and Romans' of the ancient world, was an additional part of the Celtic studies project from the beginning, one which drew, and is still drawing, on the social science disciplines of anthropology, archaeology, and ethnography.

§2. PHILOLOGY

The study of philology was perhaps the most significant building block of Celtic studies during its evolution as an academic discipline in the second half of the 19th century. As comparative historical linguistics developed during the 19th and early 20th centuries, Celtic, along with the Greek, Italic, Germanic, and Slavic families of languages, received particular atten-

tion from European scholars (see also INDO-EUROPEAN). Rudolf THURNEYSEN (1857–1940) made a significant contribution to the study of Old IRISH, identifying it as the earliest form of any of the Celtic languages which could be more or less fully retrieved from surviving texts, and producing the standard grammar in 1909 (translated from German to English in 1946).

In Wales (CYMRU), John RHŶS published his *Lectures on Welsh Philology* in 1877, the year he became the first Professor of Celtic at Oxford (Welsh Rhydychen), while his former student, John MORRIS-JONES, Professor of Welsh at BANGOR from 1895, produced the first comprehensive grammar of the WELSH language, *A Welsh Grammar, Historical and Comparative*, in 1913. It was also a Welsh scholar, Henry LEWIS, who produced handbooks of Middle CORNISH (1923) and Middle BRETON (1922).

Philology, like later varieties of linguistics, was positioned as a 'science' of language, involving a terminology and a set of methodologies apparently based on 'objective' scientific principles. The scholarly emphasis on language therefore authenticated Celtic as a legitimate field of study, like classics or Anglo-Saxon, and one that carried the guarantee of antiquity. Historical linguistics provided evidence not only for the ancient lineage of Celtic, which compared favourably with the similarly ancient Greek, Italic, and Germanic language families, but also for dating early texts in Irish and Welsh, many of which were pushed back in time as far as possible in order to provide Celtic literatures with a 'golden age' comparable to those of England and the classical world.

With the rise of linguistics as an academic discipline, along with other social sciences in the late 1950s and 1960s, historical linguistics, including philology, fell out of fashion, but continued to inform the study of the Celtic languages. Following the examples of Kenneth JACKSON and of Jackson's student Eric Hamp, the prolific American philologist active in the second half of the century, Calvert Watkins, Patrick Sims-Williams, John T. Koch, and others, have helped to sustain historical linguistics as a necessary tool of research into the history of the Celtic-speaking peoples.

§3. EDITORIAL METHODOLOGY

The first generation of editors of Celtic-language texts came from the antiquarian movement of the 18th century, assisted by newly-formed cultural bodies pursuing nationalist agendas. In Ireland (Éire), the Royal Irish Academy (ACADAMH RÍOGA NA HÉIREANN) was founded in 1785, and began collecting Irish-language manuscripts for its library, where many of the most significant manuscripts are still kept. In Wales, antiquarians such as William Owen Pughe, Owen Jones, and Iolo Morganwg (Edward WILLIAMS) made early Welsh texts available to a reading public through works such as their *Myvyrian Archaiology of Wales* (1801–7) (see also GORSEDD BEIRDD YNYS PRYDAIN).

With the spread of university colleges in both Ireland and Wales from the mid-19th century, and with the support of institutions such as the Irish Texts Society (CUMANN NA SCRÍBHEANN N-GAEDHILGE; 1898), the Board of Celtic Studies (1919) of the University of Wales (see BULLETIN), and the Dublin Institute for Advanced Studies (INSTITIÚID ARD-LÉINN; 1940), a second wave of academy-trained editors began to produce scholarly texts for their students. Their methodology, derived from classics, was primarily linguistic and philological: the texts were read not so much as evidence for a literary culture, but as evidence for the historical development of the language. In the standard format of introduction, text, notes, and glossary, the introduction gave prominence to manuscript history, linguistic features, and orthography, while the copious notes, often occupying far more space than the text itself, dealt almost exclusively with issues of grammar, philology and variant readings. Produced within the academy, the main function of these editions was to provide teaching texts with which to train scholars, who therefore inherited a particular format and style of editing, and a particular notion of the 'canon' of Celtic texts, which has survived through successive generations of scholars to the present day.

The theoretical basis of second-generation editing was the assumption that an 'original' text, as composed by a single author, was retrievable from a careful study of the manuscript record, relying on features such as orthography, philology, and linguistic forms, and that the task of the editor was to reconstruct the 'original' text, and its date of composition, from a scientific study of the empirical evidence. Relying on their considerable linguistic knowledge, scholars emended 'corrupt' readings and selected the 'best' reading from a number of manuscript copies to produce seamless texts, which, in fact, had never appeared in any manuscript, but were polished reconstructions made by skilful editors. These were claimed to be as close as possible to the 'original' text.

With the emergence of a third generation of editors in the context of post-1960 critical and oral-transmission theory, the existing editorial model has been modified, but its central aim of retrieving 'original' texts has not wavered. Most crucially, perhaps, the advent of computer technology has revolutionized the actual mechanics of editorial work for third-generation scholars, making large editorial projects feasible for the first time. Whereas the focus of second-generation texts was on the rôle of the editor as both expert and teacher, the focus of third-generation texts is on the reader, as consumer and interpreter. Edited texts have become 'user-friendly'. Already, on-line texts are appearing, where readers can download and interactively edit their own text, producing customized versions of individual texts which offer a genuinely radical challenge to the traditional concept of the single 'original' text.

§4. LITERARY CRITICISM

Approaches to literary criticism in Celtic studies have been largely borrowed from the empirical traditions of English, particularly those of literary history and genre studies. A significant function of literary history is to define the canon of recognized texts, and early histories of Celtic literature were responsible for a canon which has survived relatively unchanged to the present day. Literary histories of Ireland, prompted by the 'Irish revival' (see LANGUAGE [REVIVAL]), began appearing from the turn of the 19th and 20th centuries with Douglas Hyde's *A Literary History of Ireland* (1899; see DE H-ÍDE), while early historians of Welsh literature, such as T. Gwynn JONES and Saunders LEWIS, gave prominence to the medieval texts which continue to dominate Welsh studies in the academy.

A major impetus for the generic approach in Celtic literary studies was the magisterial work of Hector M. and Nora CHADWICK, *The Growth of Literature* (1932), which traced the development of similar generic types in classical, Celtic, Norse, and Anglo-Saxon literatures. IRISH LITERATURE had been classified into 'cycles' as long ago as 1861 by Eugene O'CURRY, and the work of the Chadwicks encouraged the division of Celtic-language texts into categories already identified in the privileged canons of classical and Germanic literatures.

Ideologically, genre studies are based on the idea that texts can be interpreted in isolation from any external social or cultural context. In this sense, a genre is viewed as an identifiable universal type of literary work. Generic criteria tend to be exclusively textual—content, style, length, format, and so on—and establishing the criteria depends on pre-existing assumptions of what a particular genre ought to contain. Interpreting texts as part of an established genre, rather than as cultural products, enables critics to expound value judgements as to how 'successfully' a text performs within the definition of its genre, and therefore to rank texts as more or less successful versions of the genre. For example, the Welsh ARTHURIAN romances (see GERAINT; OWAIN; PEREDUR) are often read as the poor relations of the CHRÉTIEN DE TROYES masterpieces.

Another influential approach to literary criticism in Celtic studies has been the search for sources and analogues to explain the provenance and development of individual texts. Borrowed from the study of classical and Middle English literatures, where paths of borrowing and influence tend to be more clearly visible, this approach uses empirical data, especially the collection of themes and motifs, to posit relationships between texts and a preceding tradition, either oral or literary or both. Most of the critical work on the major canonical texts of Celtic literature has been, and continues to be, based on this approach.

The underlying assumption or subtext of such studies is, once again, the search for, and privileging of, what is imagined to be the oldest and therefore 'original' stratum of a text—the older its roots, the more 'authentic' the text. This premise has been a particularly important issue in Celtic studies, whose credibility as a discipline depended to some extent on its antiquity relative to literature in England.

The search for King ARTHUR as a historical figure in post-Roman BRITAIN, and the identification of Welsh sources and analogues for much of the later Arthurian tradition have been major strategies in authenticating early Welsh literature as a site of legitimate scholarly relevance. Similarly, the 'nativist' approach to early Irish literature, which has been characterized as assuming oral composition in some dim pagan past, asserts the antiquity of the literature and the 'purity' of its pre-Christian Celticity.

The 'sources and analogues' approach also rests on the liberal-empiricist theory of the single gifted author, a knowable individual whose path through his sources, whether consciously chosen or not, can be seamlessly retraced by the observant and well-read critic, as if the creation of a literary text had been a simple linear process rather than a complex web of interlocking texts, authors and audiences from different times and places.

The analysis of individual texts from the Celtic canon became more common from the 1960s onwards. It drew on the methodologies privileged by English literature, particularly those of Leavisite criticism (named from Francis R. Leavis [1895–1987]) and New Criticism, both of which flourished between 1940 and 1960 and share some common ideas. Both are based on a process model of communication which assumes that every text has a single 'right' meaning, put into it by its single (uniquely gifted) author, and that the critic's task is to retrieve this intended meaning directly from the text. In its focus on individual authors (whether known or 'lost'), valued for their skills in compiling and reworking older material, this model of communication produces a literary criticism which ignores or minimizes issues related to cultural production and theories of transmission or signification.

Leavisite criticism, which focused on the novel in English, made relatively little impression in the field of Celtic studies, where long narratives tended to be read in terms of their sources and analogues rather than as moral statements about social values, the basis of Leavis's definition of 'great literature'. However, the Leavisite approach did supply a new way for some Celtic scholars to think and write. This discourse of literary evaluation enabled, for example, Kenneth Jackson in his *Studies in Early Celtic Nature Poetry* (1935) to include lyrical assertions of authorial skill.

New Criticism, emerging as a direct response to the modernist aesthetic in literary texts, privileged form over content, high culture over popular culture, the obscure over the transparent, validating newness of expression within a deeply conservative political ideology. The central concern of New Criticism was with the text itself and the ways in which literary form and language created particular 'effects'. The text was almost totally decontextualized (viewed outside its social and historical context); the process of signification (establishing meaning within its social setting) was completely sidestepped.

In its concern with poetry and form, New Criticism became the obvious tool for examining the collections of poetry which Celtic scholars were editing in increasing numbers, starting with T. F. O'Rahilly's DÁNTA GRÁDHA in 1926 (see Ó RATHILE). PARRY's authoritative edition of his canon of the poems of DAFYDD AP GWILYM in 1952 released an apparently coherent body of lyric poems composed by a single known author whose works could be closely examined using the then dominant New Critical approach. A flurry of articles followed in Welsh journals, examining individual poems, isolating images, conceits, rhetorical devices, semantic ambiguities and all the other 'effects' for which modernist poets were accorded special critical prestige, thereby endorsing the concept of the single gifted author whose responsibility for his work was distinct and separable from its social and political context.

Throughout the heat and dust of the 'theory wars' of the 1970s and 1980s, Celtic studies (like many other medieval disciplines) remained largely aloof, explicitly asserting that its concerns were primarily empirical and therefore atheoretical, while implicitly skipping over the theoretical implications of such a position. A notable exception was in the area of structuralism and its related techniques that could claim to be based on the empirical observation of particular elements which, organized into a pattern or structure, would reveal the text's 'real' meaning. Since Vladimir Propp, the Russian formalist author of the influential *Morphology of the Folktale* (1928), developed his narrative model specifically in relation to fairy stories and wonder tales, his work has had particular relevance for the study of Celtic narratives. The structuralist concept of the 'hero tale' as a universal type, expounded most famously by Joseph Campbell in his *Hero with a Thousand Faces* (1949), has been successfully exploited by a number of Celtic scholars, particularly in relation to Irish heroes, e.g. in Tómas Ó Cathasaigh's *The Heroic Biography of* CORMAC MAC AIRT (1977). These works have largely been superseded, however, as it came to be realized that the theories relied on vague, non-culture-specific universals and did not necessarily fit a given cultural context.

As in most empirical research, however, the aims and objectives of the researcher will tend to determine the structural features which are recognized and selected as being in some way significant. Through undertaking such a selective process, the researcher in effect creates his or her own secondary 'meta-text' which then becomes the object of interpretation, as W. J. Gruffydd did in his reconstruction of a 'PRYDERI saga' for the medieval Welsh prose wondertales, the MABINOGI. In many ways, then, structuralism represented no real break from the liberal-empiricism of earlier scholarship, and, in fact, worked to support the modernist aesthetic, concentrating on form and technique.

The liberal-empiricist project—to reveal the single 'right' meaning of a text and to attribute it to the single author—received its first serious critique from post-structuralist theory in the 1980s and 1990s. Post-structuralism challenges the concept of singularity and coherence in either text or author and draws attention instead to signifying practices, ways that meanings are made, both within the language of texts and in their social and political contexts. Initiatives such as Helen Fulton's *Dafydd ap Gwilym and the European Context* (1989), a contextual study of medieval WELSH POETRY based on Marxist literary criticism, and Michelle O Riordan's *The Gaelic Mind and the Collapse of the Gaelic World* (1990), an explicitly post-structuralist interpretation of the Irish 'bardic mentality', have attempted to go beyond the limits of empiricism.

Despite its relatively conservative critical tradition, the discipline of Celtic studies was at the forefront of historicist interpretation, anticipating by many decades the critical movement known as New Historicism which developed in English literary studies as recently as the 1980s. New Historicism, consciously opposed to the ahistorical text-based approach of structuralism, addresses the historical contexts in which texts are produced and consumed. Largely unaffected by the strictly text-based methodologies of New Criticism or structuralism, Celtic scholars have long drawn on the apparently empirical evidence of history and archaeology to explain the origins and meanings of Celtic-language texts.

Early studies in Ireland include *Side-Lights on the Táin Age and Other Studies* (1917) by M. E. Dobbs, *The Oldest Irish Tradition: A Window on the Iron Age* (1964) by Kenneth Jackson, and James Carney's *Studies in Irish Literature and History* (1955), while numerous articles on the historical background of literary texts in the major journals for Irish studies, ÉRIU and ÉIGSE, attest to the continuity of this approach right up to the present day. In Wales, historicist interpretation has been dominated by the debate surrounding the 'real' historical context of the GODODDIN, a debate initiated by John Morris-Jones, J. Gwenogvryn EVANS, and Ifor WILLIAMS in the first half of the 20th century and continued by Kenneth Jackson and John T. Koch in the second half.

Feminist studies, which have proved popular in Celtic studies since the 1970s, can be regarded as a sub-genre of New Historicism, since they mainly depend on constructing the historical position of women in order to argue for their significance in particular texts. Attempting to retrieve the reality of women's lives or how women were perceived in early Celtic-speaking societies is itself fraught with difficulties, mainly lack of evidence, which has led to some flawed studies. Journal-length articles on various heroines of Irish or Welsh narratives help to make the texts more accessible to modern readers, but run the risk of imposing modern concepts of gender politics on texts which have a different kind of logic and function. Much feminist research is also under-theorized and draws its assumptions, methodology, and objectives from a liberal-empiricist ideology, focusing on the interplay of individual characters in the social world of the text and naively attempting to match this to an actual reality.

§5. CONSTRUCTING 'THE CELTS'

With the rise of political and linguistic NATIONALISM in the Celtic-speaking countries from the 1960s onwards, scholars began to re-examine the assumptions and stereotypes of 'Celticity' which had been laid down by Ernest Renan, Matthew Arnold, and other 19th-century writers. In the context of imperialism and ROMANTICISM, these glamorized views of 'the Celts' as a coherent race or tribe whose enhanced sense of magic and the natural world made them distinctively different from the sober industrialized Germanic peoples of England worked to position 'the Celts' as charmingly primitive and exotic 'others'.

Welsh and Irish scholars of the early 20th century largely accepted this view of themselves. Anglo-Irish writers, such as W. B. YEATS, relied heavily on the romantic translations of early Irish myth and saga produced by antiquarians (see ANGLO-IRISH LITERATURE), and the first literary histories of Ireland and Wales provided the evidence of unfamiliar literary practices to support the imperial consensus that the Celts were the colonial 'other', an alien 'race', congenitally different from their colonizers. This imperial viewpoint has been maintained up to the present time in much of the 'New Age' writing about the Celts,

where constructions of an ancient Celtic SPIRITUALITY are grounded in a 'druidic' past invented in the 18th century. The tendency in this has been to ignore recent re-examination of the ancient and medieval literary descriptions of DRUIDS.

The impetus for change came mainly from British archaeologists who, in the 1970s, began to challenge the view that there had been a coherent people called the 'Celts' who spoke a language called 'Celtic'. Using archaeological, linguistic and historical evidence, contemporary scholars have deconstructed Matthew Arnold's view of Celticity and exposed the constructedness of the modern notion of 'Celticity' itself in any of its forms.

The pioneer in this field has been P. Sims-Williams, whose 1986 article, 'The Visionary Celt: The Construction of an Ethnic Preconception', contained a detailed critique of the Arnoldian view and its cultural and imperial basis (CMCS 11.71–96). Since then, further work in both archaeology and textual criticism, the latter drawing particularly on post-colonial theory, has continued the work of redefining the Celtic-speaking peoples into groups identifiable by language, location, and cultural practice.

§6. CELTIC LITERARY CRITICISM NOW

At the beginning of the 21st century, Celtic studies continue to embrace more or less the same repertoire of critical approaches that they deployed at the beginning of the 20th century. As the century progressed, Celtic studies moved from an initial dependence on the methodologies of classics to include those of English medieval scholarship, literature, and folkloristics. During the latter half of the century, other influences, notably comparative literature (introduced largely by the increasing numbers of American scholars entering the discipline) and some of the '-isms' from modern English literary studies, especially New Criticism, structuralism, and feminism, produced a wider range of research. At the same time, the historicist approach has been sustained throughout the century as the perennial favourite across the discipline, pointing to the close link between history, text, and language, which is the hallmark of Celtic studies.

PRIMARY SOURCES
Campbell, *Hero with a Thousand Faces*; Carney, *Studies in Irish Literature and History*; H. M. & Nora K. Chadwick, *Growth of Literature 1*; Dobbs, *Side-Lights on the Táin Age and Other Studies*; Gruffydd, *Folklore and Myth in the Mabinogion*; Hyde, *Literary*

History of Ireland; Jackson, *Gododdin*; Jackson, *Oldest Irish Tradition*; Jackson, *Studies in Early Celtic Nature Poetry*; Koch, *Gododdin of Aneirin*; Lewis, *Llawlyfr Llydaweg Canol*; Lewis, *Llawlyfr Cernyweg Canol*; Morris-Jones, *Welsh Grammar*; Ó Cathasaigh, *Heroic Biography of Cormac mac Airt*; O'Curry, *Lectures on the Manuscript Materials of Ancient Irish History*; O'Rahilly, *Dánta Grádha*; Parry, *Gwaith Dafydd ap Gwilym*; Propp, *Morphology of the Folktale*; Pughe et al., *Myvyrian Archaiology of Wales*; Rhŷs, *Lectures on Welsh Philology*; Thurneysen, *Grammar of Old Irish*; Ifor Williams, *Canu Aneirin*.

FURTHER READING
ACADAMH RÍOGA NA HÉIREANN; ANGLO-IRISH LITERATURE; ARTHUR; ARTHURIAN; BANGOR; BRETON; BRITAIN; BULLETIN; CELTIC COUNTRIES; CELTIC LANGUAGES; CELTIC STUDIES; CELTICISM; CHADWICK; CHRÉTIEN DE TROYES; CORMAC MAC AIRT; CORNISH; CUMANN NA SCRÍBHEANN N-GAEDHILGE; CYMRU; DAFYDD AP GWILYM; DÁNTA GRÁDHA; DE H-ÍDE; DRUIDS; ÉIGSE; ÉRIU; EVANS; GERAINT; GODODDIN; GORSEDD BEIRDD YNYS PRYDAIN; INDO-EUROPEAN; INSTITIÚID ARD-LÉINN; IRISH; IRISH LITERATURE; JACKSON; JONES; LANGUAGE (REVIVAL); LEWIS, HENRY; LEWIS, SAUNDERS; MABINOGI; MORRIS-JONES; NATIONALISM; NATIVISM; O'CURRY; Ó RATHILE; OWAIN AB URIEN; PARRY; PEREDUR; PRYDERI; RHŶS; ROMANTICISM; SPIRITUALITY; THURNEYSEN; WELSH; WELSH POETRY; WELSH PROSE LITERATURE; WILLIAMS, EDWARD; WILLIAMS, IFOR; YEATS; Bell, *F. R. Leavis*; Bennett, *Formalism and Marxism*; Bromwich, *Matthew Arnold and Celtic Literature*; Canadé Sautman, *Telling Tales*; Chapman, *Celts*; Collier & Geyer-Ryan, *Literary Theory Today*; Cox & Reynolds, *New Historical Literary Study* 3–68; Duff, *Modern Genre Theory*; Easthope, *British Post-Structuralism Since 1968*; Ellis, *Celtic Dawn*; Fulton, *Bulletin of the Bibliographical Society of Australia and New Zealand* 19.2.67–78; Fulton, *Dafydd ap Gwilym and the European Context*; Hawkes, *Structuralism and Semiotics*; Humm, *Reader's Guide to Contemporary Feminist Literary Criticism*; Jefferson & Robey, *Modern Literary Theory*; Novack, *Empiricism and its Evolution*; Ó Riordan, *Gaelic Mind and the Collapse of the Gaelic World*; Palmer, *Rise of English Studies*; Samson, *F. R. Leavis*; Selden et al., *Reader's Guide to Contemporary Literary Theory*; Sims-Williams, *CMCS* 11.71–96; Sims-Williams, *CMCS* 36.1–35.

Helen Fulton

Crosán (pl. *crosáin*), commonly translated 'buffoon' (DIL 550, 50), is a designation in Old, Middle, and Early Modern IRISH texts applied to a figure whose entertainment both offends and delights. The term is a derivative of Irish *cros* (cross) and entered the language from Latin *crux* (cross), the central symbol of the Christian faith (see Kelly, *Guide to Early Irish Law* 64 n.201; Vendryès, *Lexique étymologique de l'irlandais ancien* C 246–7; Ó Fiannachta, *CMCS* 19.92–4). With the added diminutive suffix *-án* (little cross), a secondary meaning 'buffoon' or 'jester' (glossed *scurrae* and *praeco*) developed for reasons that are unclear. The same semantic development took place in WELSH, where the common word for a 'jester' in the law

texts is *croesan* (< W *croes* cross). J. H. Todd's assertion that the *crosáin* were 'cross-bearers in religious processions' who sang 'satirical poems against those who had incurred Church censure' (*Leabhar Breathnach Annso Sis / Irish Version of Historia Britonum of Nennius* 182 n.j) lacks textual support; however, the *crosáin* may have had some rôle in religious festivals. The extant sources offer hints, but no conclusive evidence.

The earliest reference to the *crosán* occurs in the Old Irish legal tract BRETHA NEMED *Toísech* (*c.* AD 750) and is repeated in a late Old Irish compilation of gnomic material (*Trecheng Breth Féne*) edited under the title, 'The TRIADS of Ireland'. The triad is characteristically brief and elusive, but suggests the poses of a ribald jester: *Tri neimhtighedur crosán: righi óile, righi theighi, righi bronn* 'Three things which confer status on a *crosán*: distending his cheek, distending his bag, distending his belly' (Binchy, *Corpus Iuris Hibernici* 6.2220.2 = Triads §116). Here *tíag* 'bag' (DIL 164, 13) may refer to the inflated bladder brandished by the jester or to his testicles, perhaps exaggerated in a comic performance (Kelly, *Guide to Early Irish Law* 65 n.203). The *crosán* does not figure among the lower grades of poets and entertainers named in other early Irish tracts on status, such as the *fuirsire* (jester), *clesamnach* (juggler), or *braigetóir* (farter) named in *Uraicecht Becc* (Kelly, *Guide to Early Irish Law* 64), or the *oblaire*, a 'buffoon without skill' (*fuirseoir gan dán*), who memorizes disparaging verses (Breatnach, *Uraicecht na Ríar* 113 §20). Nevertheless, he may have shared some of their comic attributes. The Welsh law tract *Llyfr Iorwerth* (13th century) offers a later, but similarly mocking, portrait of the *croesan* (jester) who, when presented with a horse by the chief groom, ties the end of the horse's halter to its testicles as he departs from the court of the king (Wiliam, *Llyfr Iorwerth* 9 §11.12).

Other references in Irish legal sources are more puzzling. A late gloss in the tract *Bretha Étgid* states that legal compensation is due for 'shaving the locks of the *crosáin*, the [monastic] students (*na scolóc*), and the shorn maidens (*na ningen mael*)', a grouping which may indicate affiliation with the lower stratum of a monastic community (Binchy, *Corpus Iuris Hibernici* 1.304.11–12). The lexicon of legal terms compiled by Dubhaltach MAC FHIRBHISIGH (1660) identified *crosán* as a skill associated with the *forcetlaid*, the third of seven grades of teachers in an Irish monastic school, and Eugene O'CURRY (1840), who arranged Mac Fhirbhisigh's lexicon alphabetically in Trinity College MS 1401 and supplied words from the context and other sources where necessary, translates *crosán* simply as 'criticism' (*Lectures on the Manuscript Materials of Ancient Irish History* 494–5).

Crosán is a derogatory designation in two satiric epigrams from an Irish metrical tract (Tract 3, *c.* 1060), edited by Rudolf THURNEYSEN and included in Kuno MEYER's collection of verse epigrams, *Bruchstücke der älteren Lyrik Irlands*:

> Méthmac Muiredaig, mesce chírmaire,
>   crossán líath ic linn
> screpall ar f[h]eóil n-aige, ónmit ar eoch mall,
>   breccar claime i cinn.
> (Meyer, *Bruchstücke der älteren Lyrik Irlands* 30 §66 = Thurneysen, *Irische Texte* 3/1.84 §71)

A decadent son of Muiredach, the drunkenness of a comb-maker; a grey-haired, ale-drinking *crosán*; a scruple for ox meat; a fool on a slow horse; leprous spots on [his] head.

A second epigram from the same tract juxtaposes the 'wandering thieving *crosán*' (*crosán machaire ic merle*) with the *drúth . . . cen intliucht* (witless fool) and *sacard senóir ac súathad* (old priest engaged in kneading) (Meyer, *Bruchstücke der älteren Lyrik Irlands* 37 §88 = Thurneysen, *Irische Texte* 3/1.85 §83). The portraits recall the *clerici vagantes* or goliards, an amorphous class of wandering minstrels in medieval Europe who, as Helen Waddell has noted, thrived on the fringes of the Christian church and are repeatedly rebuked in church canons. Irish clerical scholars are among those chastised as *deceptores, gyrovagi, cursores* (deceivers, wanderers, and stragglers) (Waddell, *Wandering Scholars* 51), and Irish canons rebuke the 'cleric singing amid feasts' (Wasserschleben, *Die irische Kanonensammlung* 34). The ribald hero of the medieval Irish tale *Aislinge Meic Con Glinne* (The dream of Mac Con Glinne), who composes satirical verses and performs, *cáintecht 7 bragitóracht 7 duana la filidecht do gabáil* 'satire and farting and singing songs with poetry' (Jackson, *Aislinge Meic Con Glinne* 18), offers a vivid literary representation of such a figure.

The performance of a band of *crosáin* is described in the Middle Irish anecdote *Senadh Saighri* (Meyer, ZCP 12.290–1), where 'nine shaggy pitch black *crossain*' cavort at the burial of Donnchadh Reamhar, king of Ossary (†976). Their *duan agus oirfideadh* (verse and minstrelsy) praises music, fair women, and liberality towards poets, and the verses they recite are composed in the syllabic metre *snéadhbhairdne* ($8^2 4^2 8^2 4^2$). Two stanzas illustrate the spirit of the chant and its distinguishing metrical features: required alliteration in lines c/d, end rhyme (lines b/d), internal rhyme (lines c/d), and consonance* between lines c and lines b/d (that is, syllables showing phonetically similar consonants and the same vowel quantity):

> Muinter Donnchaid móir mheic Cealdaigh 8^2
> coinde **úabhair**,* 4^2
> cliara **binne** **bí**d ac glaedhaigh,* 8^2
> **sinne** ar **slúagaibh**.* 4^2
>
> Slúaig ac milradh mhuighe lána 8^2
> tighe n-**óla**,* 4^2
> óccmhná finna, **flaithi** **fiala**,* 8^2
> **maithi** **móra**.* 4^2

The people of Donnchadh Mór son of Ceallach— a proud meeting; sweet bands who are calling out; we are on hostings.

Hosts hunting full plains; alehouses, fair young women, honourable princes, great nobles.

Clerics expel the band by sprinkling them with holy water and reciting the Mass; however, two poets present at the assembly memorize the chant. One of them, *in crosán Find búa Cinga* (the *crosán* Finn Ó Cuinn), may be the poet referred to as 'Moyle Issa called Crossan ffyn a King', who composed verse in a metre 'which is called Crossanaght' (Murphy, *Annals of Clonmacnoise* AD 1137). The historical details of the tale are inconsistent, as Brian Ó Cuív has noted (PBA 49.246–7); nevertheless, the tale seems to reflect the emergence of a stylistic innovation in bardic verse known as *crosántacht* (<*crosán*), compositions which mix entertaining prose anecdotes into traditional syllabic verse (see below). The appearance of *crosán* as a personal name may indicate, as Proinsias Mac Cana has argued (*Ériu* 25.138 n.47), a gradual upward movement of lower entertainers like the *crosáin* into the ranks of the learned class. For example, an English document (1601) refers to Patrick Crosbie, Mac-Y-Crossane (son of the *crosán*), whose father had been a 'rhymer' to the O'Moore's of Co. Laois.

The comic antics and ambiguous status of the *crosán* are a theme in other Middle Irish texts. The three *crossáin* who entertain in the house of the hero FINN MAC CUMAILL are called *Cles* (Trick), *Cinnmear* (Head-mad), and *Cuitmhedh* (Mockery) (MacNeill & Murphy, *Duanaire Finn* 1.27.25). In a poem which parodies the customary distribution of meat to guests at a FEAST according to social status, the *crosán* is served the 'rump' (*crochet*)—a portion traditionally awarded to one of noble status—and the 'fools' receive the 'kidneys' (O'Sullivan, *Celtic Studies* 121). Giolla Brighde Mac Con Midhe (†1272) names the *crosán* among those who occupied the monastic guesthouse and insisted on largesse at the expense of the poor:

A chuid don chrosán i gcéadóir,
a gcuid do mhaoraibh na mionn;
cuid an bhochta ar dáil is duiligh—
cáir gorta i gcuilidh dá chionn.
(Williams, *Poems of Giolle Brighde Mac Con Midhe* 242.27)

First let the *crosán* have his portion, let the stewards of relics have their share; it is difficult to dole out the portion of the poor man—there should be short-age in the storehouse because of him.

Several religious texts portray the *crosán* as a dis-reputable figure, though the attitude ranges from fierce condemnation to distant amusement. 'The Fifteen Tokens of Doomsday' envisioned the final damnation of *na druithi 7 na cainti 7 na crosanaigh* 'the harlots and the satirists and the buffoons' (Stokes, RC 28.318 §30); the arrival of the *crossáin* is ominously predicted in the *Book of Fenagh*; and the grouping *croessan a phuttein* (buffoon and harlot) in the Welsh *Buched Dewi* (Life of St David) is similarly derogatory (D. Simon Evans, *Buched Dewi* 20). The attitude in other Irish texts is more forgiving. The 'openly sinful' *crosán* named in the Life of Brenainn is the last to enter the saint's vessel but the first to win heaven, and is honoured as a 'wonderful martyr'. Similarly, in the late medieval tale *Immram Curaig Ua Corra* (The voyage of the Uí Corra), one member of a band of *crosáin*, called a *fuirseoir* (jester), joins a group of pilgrims seeking salvation. He promises to provide 'entertainment of the mind and spirit'

(*airgairdiugud menman 7 aicenta*) that will not lessen their piety, and when he dies on the journey the pilgrims lament the loss of his delightful *airfitiud* (minstrelsy).

The *crosán* is associated with a style of composition known as *crosántacht* (see Meyer, *Senadh Saighri* above). The earliest example (*c.* 1560) occurs in J. Carney's *Poems on the Butlers*, and samples continue through the 17th and 18th centuries. Only a few later poems refer specifically to the *crosán*. The speaker of a *crosántacht* attributed to Tadhg Dall Ó HUIGINN announces that he is 'O'Caroll's *crosán*'; Tadhg Mac Dáire Mac Bruaideadha names the *crosán* among the poets who frequent the house of Maol Mordha Mac Suibhne (†1518); and a prose text composed for the same chieftain (Walsh, *Leabhar Chlainne Suibhne* 6 §5) reprimands the patron for bestowing gifts to the *crosáin* at the expense of more noble poets.

The 17th-century Irish poet Dáibhí Ó BRUADAIR provides the latest, but arguably the most vivid, por-trait of the *crosán*. Ó Bruadair assumes the comic mask of a *crosán* in the wedding *crosántacht*, *Cuirfead cluain ar chrobhaing ghealGhall*, and brings comic voices rooted in the medieval tradition to a wedding feast celebrated in 1674:

Do chiu oidhche i mbrugh Í Bhreasail
lucht um losaid;
seoltar mé mar chrosán chugaibh,
cosán cobhsaidh.
(Mac Erlean, *Duanaire Dháibhidh Uí Bhruadair* 2.56.15)

I see one night, in the dwelling of Ó Breasail, people gathered about a table; I am sent off like a *crosán* to you; firm my path.

Various strands of the tradition intersect in Ó Bruadair's poem. The poet was probably familiar with the medieval tale *Seanadh Saighre*, through the version included in the 17th-century history of Ireland by Geoffrey Keating (Seathrún CÉITINN, *Foras Feasa ar Éirinn* 3.217–21). Popular performances of mock priests at wakes and masked 'strawboys' at weddings may also have influenced the performance. Ó Bruadair exchanges the mask of a *crosán* with that of a *sagart súgach* (merry priest), who enacts a bawdy marriage, leads the couple to bed, and blesses the union. Ó Bruadair's comic pose joins the medieval to the modern: the bawdy priest and *crosán* of the poem are reminiscent of the *sacard* (priest) and *crosán* juxtaposed in the Middle Irish epigram cited above. Ó Bruadair's unified performance of verse, nonsense rhymes, and ribaldry gives coherence to the fragmented allusions to the *crosán* and reflects what seems to be a strain of licence within the Christian culture of medieval Ireland (ÉIRE), which continued for centuries in the oral, popular culture.

PRIMARY SOURCES
MS. Dublin, Trinity College 1401 (H. 5. 30) (National Library of Ireland, Microfilm A 187, Widener Library, Harvard University).
EDITIONS. Binchy, *Corpus Iuris Hibernici* 1, 6; D. Simon Evans, *Buched Dewi*; Hamel, *Immrama* 101–2; Meyer, ZCP 12.290–1 (*Senadh Saighri*); Thurneysen, *Irische Texte* 3/1.81 §60, 84 §71; Wiliam, *Llyfr Iorwerth*.
ED. & TRANS. Breatnach, *Uraicecht na Ríar*; Harrison, *Éigse* 20.136–48; Hennessy & Kelly, *Book of Fenagh in Irish and English* 302; Keating, *Foras Feasa ar Éirinn*; Knott, *Bardic Poems of Tadhg Dall Ó hUiginn (1550–1591)*; Mac Erlean, *Duanaire Dháibhidh Uí Bhruadair* 2.48–96; MacNeill & Murphy, *Duanaire Finn* 1.27.25; Meyer, *Abhandlungen der Preussischen Akademie der Wissenschaften Jahrgang* 7.30 §66, 37 §88; Meyer, *Triads of Ireland* 13, 2–43 §116; Murphy, *Annals of Clonmacnoise* 196; O'Sullivan, *Celtic Studies* 118–23; Stokes, RC 28, 318 §30; Stokes, *Lives of the Saints* 111–12; Todd & Herbert, *Leabhar Breathnach annso sis*; Walsh, *Leabhar Chlainne Suibhne*; N. J. A. Williams, *Poems of Giolla Brighde Mac Con Midhe* 242–3.
TRANS. Jenkins, *Law of Hywel Dda* 18.

FURTHER READING
BARDIC ORDER; BRETHA NEMED; CÉITINN; ÉIRE; FEAST; FINN MAC CUMAILL; IRISH; IRISH LITERATURE; LAW TEXTS; MAC FHIRBHISIGH; MEYER; Ó BRUADAIR; O'CURRY; Ó H-UIGINN; SATIRE; THURNEYSEN; TRIADS; WELSH; Carney, *Poems on the Butlers* 1–8; Harrison, *An Chrosántacht*; Harrison, *Irish Trickster*; Jackson, *Aislinge Meic Con Glinne*; Kelly, *Guide to Early Irish Law*; Mac Cana, *Cymru a'r Cymry 2000* 19–39; Mac Cana, *Ériu* 25.126–46; MacNeill & Murphy, *Duanaire Finn* 3.23–4; Ó Corráin et al., *Peritia* 3.407–8; Ó Cuív, PBA 49.233–62; Ó Fiannachta, CMCS 19.92–4; O'Curry, *Lectures on the Manuscript Materials of Ancient Irish History*; Patterson, SC 16/17.73–103; Vendryès, *Lexique étymologique de l'irlandais ancien*; Waddell, *Wandering Scholars*; Wasserschleben, *Die irische Kanonensammlung*.

Margo Griffin-Wilson

Crúachu/Crúachain/Rathcroghan

The earthworks at Rathcroghan, near Tulsk, Co. Roscommon, Ireland (Tuilsce, Contae Ros Comáin, ÉIRE) are identified with Crúachu or Crúachain, the legendary seat of the kings of CONNACHT and as the court of Queen MEDB and King Ailill, one of the principal sites related in the ULSTER CYCLE of tales.

It is listed as the site of one of the three principal plains, feasts, fairs, households, and cemeteries of ancient Ireland (ÉRIU; see also TRIADS). This latter association is emphasized in the literature, which relates both its use as the burial ground for the kings of the CONNACHTA and also its OTHERWORLD associations centred on the otherworldly mound, SÍD Crúachan. For this reason, it has been suggested that the site ultimately derives its name from *crúach* 'mound, hill', i.e. from its alleged 50 burial mounds.

The site itself is a somewhat ill-defined precinct of over 50 monuments occupying some 800 hectares (about 1900 acres). The complex centres on Rathcroghan Mound, the most spectacular monument of the precinct. Approximately 85 m in diameter at its base and rising about 6 m high, the top of the mound is roughly flat. Geophysical prospection has indicated that the mound covers three circular timber-built structures of imposing size (diameters of 80 m, 35 m and 20 m), and a series of additional structures has been discerned near the surface of the mound.

Another prominent feature is Dáithí's Mound, an embanked mound around 40 m across, with a pillar stone mounted on its top, allegedly the burial place of Ireland's last pagan king. Although no burials were discovered during its excavation, material from the surrounding ditch indicated a date somewhere between the first centuries BC and AD.

The name of Relignaree (Reilig na Rígh, burial ground of the kings) retains the association of the royal cemetery, but in fact would appear to be a large earth and stone banked enclosure that measures approximately 100 m across and contained a smaller circular structure of around 48 m across. An even larger enclosure is that of Rathnadarve (Rath na dTarbh, ring-fort of the bulls), which measures 110 m in diameter.

In addition to numerous other burial mounds and ENCLOSURES are the Mucklaghs, a paired system of linear earthworks which run for a distance of between 100 m and 200 m; they are formed by upcast earthen banks some 2–3 m high and are presumed to represent a ceremonial function.

Oweyngat, the 'cave of the cats', is a natural limestone cave fronted by a souterrain (stone-lined underground structure) over which is inscribed in OGAM script VRAICCI MAQI MEDVVI 'of Fraích son of Medb', thus

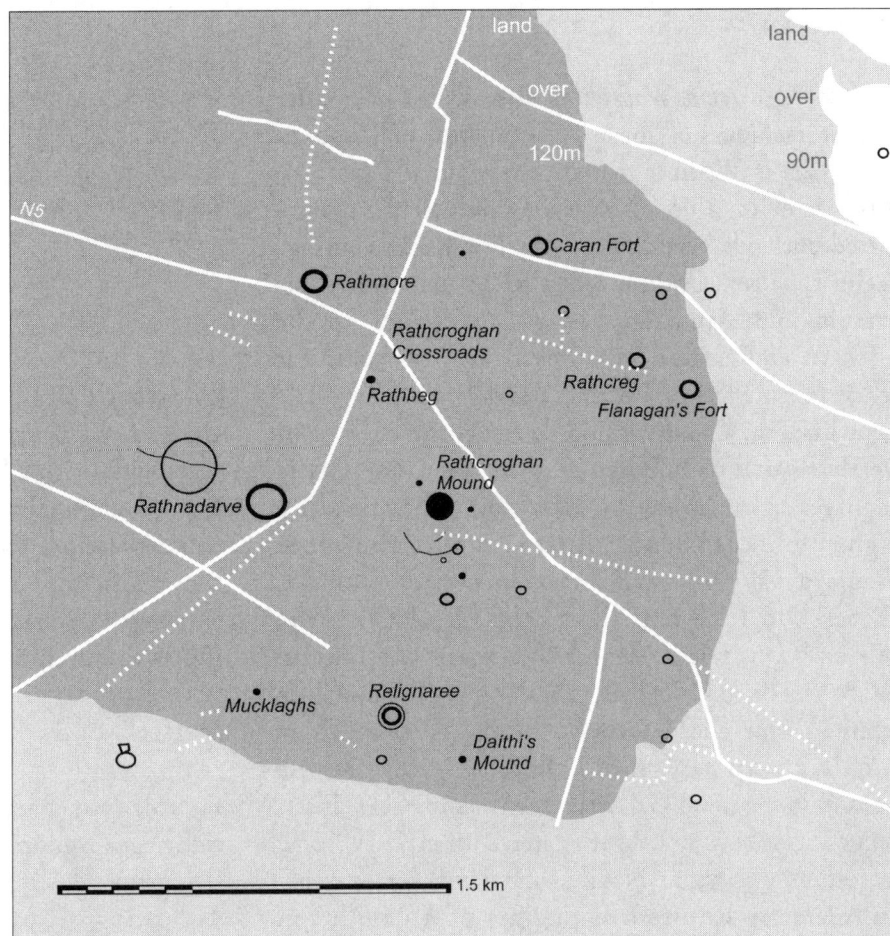

Principal features of the Rathcroghan complex: mounds shown as solid circles; ring enclosures shown as open circles; modern roads in white; dashed white lines show trackways or linear earthworks

suggesting links to prominent characters in the early Irish heroic sagas (see IRISH LITERATURE; ULSTER CYCLE). The cave is popularly seen as an entrance into the Otherworld.

The striking parallels seen between the other 'royal' sites of EMAIN MACHAE and DÚN AILINNE are not quite so obvious at Rathcroghan, although the remote sensing evidence from Rathcroghan Mound, if proven by excavation, could reveal greater architectural similarities. The Mucklaghs might find a parallel with the 'banqueting hall' at Tara (TEAMHAIR), while there are traces of mounds, a ubiquitous feature at Rathcroghan, at Emain Machae, and an impressive series of mounds and enclosures, comparable to those at Rathcroghan, are seen at Tara.

FURTHER READING
CONNACHT; CONNACHTA; DÚN AILINNE; ÉIRE; EMAIN MACHAE; ENCLOSURES; ÉRIU; FEAST; IRISH LITERATURE; MEDB; OGAM; OTHERWORLD; SÍD; TEAMHAIR; TRIADS; ULSTER CYCLE; Herity, *Rathcroghan and Carnfree*; Waddell, *Emania* 5.5–18; Waddell, *Journal of Irish Archaeology* 1.21–46; Waddell & Barton, *Archaeology Ireland* 9.38–41.

J. P. Mallory

Cruithin/Cruithni are Old Irish group names referring to the PICTS in north Britain and also to a tribal group, probably of British origin, who resided in north and east ULAID (Ulster) in the early medieval period. In the PICTISH KING-LIST, *Cruithne filius Cinge pater Pictorum* 'Pict son of Cing father of the Picts' figures as the legendary founder and namesake of the Pictish people. In historical times, the most important kingdom of the Irish Cruithin was Dál nAraidi in what is now the south of Aontroim (Co. Antrim). Congal Claen (also known as Congal Caech) was a Cruithnean king of Dál nAraidi who rose to the status of Ulaid's overking in AD 627. He is also listed as a king of TEAMHAIR (Tara), and thus came to be reckoned as an ancient *ard-rí* or 'high-king' of Ireland (ÉRIU) by later historians. Congal was killed in the battle of MAG ROTH in 637.

The name *Cruithin* corresponds to Welsh *Prydyn* 'the Picts' < *Priteni*, and is closely related to the byform *Prydain* 'Britain'; compare also Greek Πρεττανοι *Prettanoi* 'the BRITONS' and the name BRITAIN itself. The group name is derived from Celtic *kʷritu-* 'form, artefact', OIr. *cruth*, W *pryd*; cf. also W *prydydd* 'master poet, i.e. fashioner of forms'. The position of PRYDAIN and *Prydyn* in Welsh is that of a relic, its old meaning as the name of a people surviving only in the unconquered outlands beyond the Roman walls. In contrast, Gaelic *Cruithin*, *Cruithni* refers to an incomplete adstratum in Ireland, applied only to tribes on the northern and eastern maritime fringes of Ulaid (as well as to the Picts of Britain). From a purely linguistic point of view, *Cruithin* could be either the cognate of Welsh *Prydyn* or a borrowing between the Celtic languages as late as, say, the taking over of Latin *planta* to give OIr. *cland* 'children, descendants', at which time foreign *p* was still regularly taken over as Gaelic *q*, whence Old Irish *c*. If the Gaelic plural *Cruithnigh* /k′r′iːn′ij/ had also been used to mean 'the Britons' (i.e. BRYTHONIC Celts living south of the Forth–Clyde isthmus), this could account for the *Creenies*, alternatively known as *Gossocks* (cf. Welsh *gwasog* 'servile person') in medieval Galloway; see Watson, *Celtic Place-Names of Scotland* 178. In the later 20th century, some Protestant writers in Northern Ireland, for example Ian Adamson, have revived the idea of a Cruithnean ethnic identity as an ancient and indigenous, but non-Gaelic, cultural group.

A crwth displayed on a Welsh dresser

FURTHER READING
BRITAIN; BRITONS; BRYTHONIC; ÉRIU; MAG ROTH; PICTISH KING-LIST; PICTS; PRYDAIN; TEAMHAIR; ULAID; Adamson, *Cruithin*; Byrne, *Irish Kings and High-Kings* 106–29; Hall, *Cruthin Controversy*; Jackson, *Scottish Historical Review* 33.14ff.; Watson, *Celtic Place-Names of Scotland* 178.

JTK

Crwth is a Welsh term for a plucked and, from about the 11th century, a bowed 3- to 6-string lyre. The rectangular-shaped body, including the neck, is carved from a single block of sycamore. The back and pine soundboard are flat. Set obliquely, the bridge has one foot on the soundboard while another extends through a sound-hole making contact with the back, thus acting as a soundpost. The tuning of three octave pairs

(g g' c" c' d' d")

recorded by Barrington (1770) corresponds with information gleaned from 16th-century poetry and treatises on *cerdd dant* (see WELSH POETRY; WELSH MUSIC). Two strings lie to the left of the flat fingerboard and can be bowed as drones or plucked by the thumb of the left hand since the instrument, held against the chest, is supported by a strap around the player's neck. A flat bridge means that all six strings can be played simultaneously.

That a forerunner of the *crwth* existed in the early CELTIC COUNTRIES is suggested by vocabulary. *Crot* translates Latin *cithara* (a lute-like instrument) in the 8th-century Old Irish Würzburg GLOSSES, and Venantius Fortunatus (*c.* AD 540–*c.* 600) mentions an instrument he calls a *chrotta Britanna*, as distinct from both the Roman lyre and barbarian harp. The late 12th-century Middle English borrowing *crouthe* marks the popularity of the *crwth* in England up to the mid-14th century. However, by the 15th century it had become confined to Wales (CYMRU) and the border, where it shared with the HARP recognition as one of the two instruments suitable to accompany the performance of CERDD DAFOD. Essentially a medieval instrument, the *crwth* could not easily adapt to the new fashionable dance music of the Elizabethan court which became increasingly popular among the Welsh gentry as their traditional patronage of *cerdd dafod* waned. Although still played by a lower class of musician, the *crwth* was gradually displaced by the Italian violin whose bright sound and wider range enabled it to play fast dance music with a choice of keys. By the 18th century the *crwth* was an object of antiquarian curiosity, and three instruments survive from this period. A recent revival of interest has led to the exploration of early performance practices.

FURTHER READING
CELTIC COUNTRIES; CERDD DAFOD; CYMRU; GLOSSES; HARP; WELSH MUSIC; WELSH POETRY; Barrington, *Archaeologia* 3.30–4; Jarman, *Llên Cymru* 6.154–75; Miles, 'Swyddogaeth a Chelfyddyd y Crythor'; Miles & Evans, *New Grove Dictionary of Music and Musicians* s.v. crwth; Vendryès, *Léxique étymologique d'irlandais ancien* s.v. crott.

Bethan Miles

Cú Chuimne

Cú Chuimne (†747) was an Irish scholar and poet, connected with Iona (EILEAN Ì). Reputedly a pupil of ADOMNÁN, Cú Chuimne is the author of a theologically astute Latin hymn of praise to the Blessed Virgin Mary, *Cantemus in omne die*. According to one manuscript, he was one of the two architects of the important Irish compendium of ecclesiastical legal tradition, COLLECTIO CANONUM HIBERNENSIS. In literary tradition, he led a dissolute life, before reforming and returning to scholarship. *Cú Chuimne* is an Old Irish name meaning 'hound of memory', probably referring to the calling of a scholar.

PRIMARY SOURCES
ED. & TRANS. Bernard & Atkinson, *Irish Liber Hymnorum* 1.33–4, 2.34–5; Clancy & Márkus, *Iona* 177–92.

FURTHER READING
ADOMNÁN; COLLECTIO CANONUM HIBERNENSIS; EILEAN Ì; IRISH; IRISH LITERATURE; O'Dwyer, *Mary*.

Thomas Owen Clancy

Cú Chulainn

Cú Chulainn, or Sétantae as he was called as a boy, is the principal warrior of the ULSTER CYCLE of early IRISH LITERATURE. Several of the stories in the Cycle are concerned with aspects of his extraordinary life and in this conform closely to the pattern known as the international heroic biography (Ó Cathasaigh, *Heroic Biography of Cormac mac Airt*). His birth is recounted in *Compert Con Culainn* (The conception of Cú Chulainn). While Dechtine, the sister (or daughter) of King CONCHOBAR mac Nesa of the ULAID is his mother, we learn that he had a divine father, LUG, and a terrestrial father, Sualtaim, and yet the Ulaid suspected that he had been conceived through a drunken incestuous encounter between Conchobar and his own sister. Ambiguity about the circumstances of his birth, inherent in this 'triple conception' marks him out as a person set apart from others.

In a section of TÁIN BÓ CUAILNGE ('The Cattle Raid of Cooley'), entitled *Macgnímrada Con Culainn* ('The Boyhood Deeds of Cú Chulainn'), his precocious exploits as a boy and the manner in which he gained his warrior name are recalled by some of the Ulster warriors. His encounter with Culann's monstrous hound may be taken to correspond to the hero's struggle with an OTHERWORLD monster in the international biographical pattern. His successful wooing of Emer daughter of Forgall Monach, followed by his training abroad in martial arts at the hands of the Amazonian Scáthach, is told in TOCHMARC EMIRE ('The Wooing of Emer'). This tale also contains *Verba Scáthaige* (The words of Scáthach), the prophetic poem uttered by his mentor, the instructress-in-arms Scáthach, which is also found independently and is considered to be one of the oldest compositions of the Cycle. Closely related to *Tochmarc Emire* is the short tale AIDED ÉNFIR AÍFE (The violent death of Aífe's one 'man' [i.e. son]), which tells how Cú Chulainn slew his only son in single combat. The combat of father and son, or of brother with brother, is a theme found in other traditions, most notably in the struggle between Sohrab and Rustem in the Persian *Shahnama*, or in that between Hadubrand and Hildebrand in the German *Hildebrandslied*. The theme occurs also in ARTHURIAN literature in the story of ARTHUR killing his son Amr which is alluded to in HISTORIA BRITTONUM and the MEDRAWD legend. It is uncertain whether the presence of this theme in the Irish saga is due to later borrowing from another tradition, or whether it reflects a shared inherited INDO-EUROPEAN motif.

Cú Chulainn's own death is related in BREISLECH MÓR MAIGE MUIRTHEIMNI (The great rout of Mag Muirtheimne). The earlier version of this tale is now fragmentary, and much of what survives is written in the somewhat obscure *rosc* style. Therefore, we are dependent on the later *Oidheadh Chon Culainn* (The violent death of Cú Chulainn) for a fuller account. This agrees with the earlier version in telling that Cú Chulainn was killed, not by the superior martial skill of his adversaries—the family of Calaitín—but by violating his *gessa* (taboos; see GEIS) and through magic. In some cases, violation of his taboos is unavoidable and death seems fated for him. On being mortally wounded by venomous spears, he ties himself upright to a pillar, and then slays an otter (*dobarchú* waterdog) which he sees drinking his blood. Just as his career as the warrior Cú Chulainn (the hound of Culann) had begun by killing Culann's hound, so also his final deed involves the killing of a canine creature.

While tales such as these deal with central aspects of the hero's life, there are many others in which Cú Chulainn also plays a leading rôle. He is the youthful warrior who stands alone against the might of the CONNACHT forces in *Táin Bó Cuailnge*, eventually winning the day for Ulster. He proves himself to be the bravest and most pre-eminent of the Ulster warriors in FLED BRICRENN, where he vanquishes his opponents CONALL CERNACH and Loegaire Buadach in a series of martial tests, culminating in a beheading contest arranged by the shadowy Munster hero, Cú Roí mac Dáiri. The latter succeeds in humiliating Cú Chulainn in combat as they both strive for the beautiful Bláthnat, as related in *Aided Chon Roí*. Cú Chulainn and Bláthnat, however, conspire to kill him later.

There are other tales in the Ulster Cycle in which Cú Chulainn's rôle is muted or in which he does not appear at all. In some cases this is due to chronology: the events related in the tale were conceived of as having taken place either before his birth or after his death, as, for instance, in *Compert Conchobuir* (The conception of Conchobar) or in *Aided Ailella ocus Conaill Cernaig* (The death of Ailill and of Conall Cernach). In these and other cases other Ulster heroes take centre stage. For example, Conall Cernach alone upholds the honour of the Ulstermen in SCÉLA MUCCE MEIC DÁ THÓ (Tidings of Mac Da Thó's pig).

Cú Chulainn's name, meaning 'hound of Culann', is transparently explained by the episode in the *Macgnímrada Con Culainn*. His boyhood name *Sétantae* may mean 'knower of the roads', but comparison has also been made with the ancient British tribal name *Setantii* in what is now Lancashire, north-west England, a derivation which would require a borrowing from BRITISH to GOIDELIC in the 2nd–6th centuries AD, that is, after

Goidelic had turned inherited Celtic *-nt-* > /*dd*/.

FURTHER READING
AIDED ÉNFIR AÍFE; ARTHUR; ARTHURIAN; BREISLECH MÓR MAIGE MUIRTHEIMNI; BRITISH; CONALL CERNACH; CONCHOBAR; CONNACHT; CÚ ROÍ; FLED BRICRENN; GEIS; GOIDELIC; HISTORIA BRITTONUM; INDO-EUROPEAN; IRISH LITERATURE; LUG; MEDRAWD; OTHERWORLD; SCÉLA MUCCE MEIC DÁ THÓ; TÁIN BÓ CUAILNGE; TOCHMARC EMIRE; ULAID; ULSTER CYCLE; Carney, *Proc. 6th International Congress of Celtic Studies* 113–30; Carney, *Studies in Irish Literature and History*; Mac Cana, *Celtic Mythology*; Mac Cana, *Learned Tales of Medieval Ireland*; Mallory, *Aspects of the Táin*; Mallory & Stockman, *Ulidia*; Ó Cathasaigh, *Heroic Biography of Cormac mac Airt*; Ó hUiginn, *Éigse* 32.77–87; Ó hUiginn, *Emania* 20.43–52; Ó hUiginn, *(Re)Oralisierung* 223–46; O'Keeffe, *Ériu* 1.123–7; Thurneysen, *Die irische Helden- und Königsage bis zum siebzehnten Jahrhunder*; Toner, *Ériu* 49.71–88.

Ruairí Ó hUiginn

Cú Roí mac Dáiri was a legendary Irish hero traditionally associated with Cathair Chon Roí (The fortress of Cú Roí), an inland promontory fort on the western edge of the Slieve Mish (Old Irish Slíab Mis) mountain range in Co. Kerry (Contae Chiarraí). He is usually depicted as a warrior king with magical abilities and frequently appears in the shape of an uncouth churl or ogre. Thus standing apart from other Irish heroes—who are more clearly idealized mortal warriors—Cú Roí has often been characterized by modern scholars as a 'demigod'.

Cú Roí plays a rôle in some of the oldest and best-known Irish heroic tales from the ULSTER CYCLE, among them MESCA ULAD ('The Intoxication of the Ulstermen'), TÁIN BÓ CUAILNGE ('The Cattle Raid of Cooley'), *Forfes Fer Fálchae* (The siege of the men of Fálchae), as well as the story of his tragic death, *Aided Chon Roí*. The latest of these describes how Cú Roí defeats and humiliates the greatest hero of the Ulster Cycle, CÚ CHULAINN, and is finally slain by the latter in a cowardly manner, through the involvement of a woman. The tale also provides the background to Cú Chulainn's own death, as described in BREISLECH MÓR MAIGE MUIRTHEIMNI (The great rout of Mag Muirthemne), since Cú Roí's son is the one who finally cuts off Cú Chulainn's head to avenge his father. *Aided Chon Roí* has been preserved in three medieval recensions, as an early modern Irish account in Seathrún CÉITINN's *Foras Feasa ar Éirinn*, and in various modern Irish versions from oral tradition, hence making its textual development especially interesting.

Cú Roí is an example of an Irish hero whose tradition spread beyond Ireland (ÉRIU). The episode in FLED BRICRENN ('Bricriu's Feast'), where Cú Roí features as an ogre challenging the Ulster heroes to a head-cutting contest in order to determine who is Ulster's greatest hero, served as a model for the similar episode in the Middle English Arthurian poetic narrative *Sir Gawain and the Green Knight* (see also HEAD CULT). The name of Gawain's supernatural opponent Sir Berkilak most probably derives from the Irish word *bachlach* 'churl', which is the word used to describe the guise assumed by Cú Roí in the beheading episode in *Fled Bricrenn*. The *Estoire*, an early version of the TRISTAN AND ISOLT tale, contains some parallels to *Aided Chon Roí*, and the important collection of early WELSH POETRY known as the Book of Taliesin (LLYFR TALIESIN) contains an eulogy for Cú Roí, *Marwnat Corroi m. Dayry* (The death-song of Cú Roí mac Dáiri), which is the only literary piece in early WELSH on an Irish subject. The fact that the same section of the Book of Taliesin also contains elegies for ALEXANDER THE GREAT and HERCULES in the traditional Welsh style shows that the Irish hero had likewise come to be viewed as a figure of some importance in international literature.

PRIMARY SOURCES
EDITION. Stokes, *Ériu* 2.1–14 (Eulogy of Cúrói).
ED. & TRANS. Best, *Ériu* 2.18–35; Henry, *ÉC* 31.79–94; Thurneysen, *ZCP* 9.189–234, 336.
TRANS. Tymoczko, *Two Death Tales from the Ulster Cycle*.

FURTHER READING
ALEXANDER THE GREAT; BREISLECH MÓR MAIGE MUIR-THEIMNI; CÉITINN; CÚ CHULAINN; ÉRIU; FLED BRICRENN; HEAD CULT; HERCULES; IRISH; LLYFR TALIESIN; MESCA ULAD; TÁIN BÓ CUAILNGE; TRISTAN AND ISOLT; ULSTER CYCLE; WELSH; WELSH POETRY; Baudiš, *Ériu* 7.200–9; Hellmuth, *Akten des Zweiten Deutschen Keltologen-Symposiums, Buchreihe der Zeitschrift für celtische Philologie* 17.65–76; Hellmuth, *Emania* 17.5–11; Hellmuth, *Fled Bricrenn* 56–69; Jacobs, *Fled Bricrenn* 40–55; Thurneysen, *Die irische Helden- und Königsage bis zum siebzehnten Jahrhundert*.

PSH

Cuilén Ring mac Illuilb was king of the SCOTS (*rí Alban*) 966–71. His Scandinavian epithet *Ring* ('ring', Old Norse *hringr*) reflects the Norse influence on the Scottish court in the 10th century. His father's name

Illulb was also of Scandinavian origin, corresponding to Old Norse *Indulf*. Cuilén seized power from DUB son of Mael Coluim, whom he killed in 966. Cuilén seems to have been denied the throne of YSTRAD CLUD (Strathclyde), although this compact kingdom had formed part of his father's territories. Cuilén died and his forces routed while fighting against Rhydderch (Radharc) son of Domnall of Strathclyde in 971.

FURTHER READING
ALBA; DUB; SCOTS; YSTRAD CLUD; Alan O. Anderson, *Early Sources of Scottish History AD 500 to 1286* 475–7; Smyth, *Warlords and Holy Men* 223–4.

PEB

Cúirt (court, pl. *cúirteanna*) was a formal meeting of amateur poets in Ireland in the 18th century. As the bardic schools collapsed in the 17th century for want of patrons and students (see BARDIC ORDER), *cúirteanna* replaced them as centres of poetic learning.

The *cúirteanna* were mostly confined to Munster (MUMU), with some similar gatherings in Ulster (counties Armagh/ARD MHACHA and Louth, see ULAID).

The Blarney *cúirt* (near Cork city/CORCAIGH) was founded soon after the death of this school's last BARD, Tadhg Ó Duinnín, by Diarmaid Mac Sheáin Bhuidhe Mac Cárrthaigh (c. 1632–1705).

Other well-known *cúirteanna* were those of Carrignavar, Co. Cork (Seán na Ráithíneach Ó Murchadha being chief), Sliabh Luachra near Killarney (Eoghan Ruadh Ó Súilleabháin), Rathluirc, Co. Cork (Seán Clárach Mac Domhnaill), Co. Louth (Pádraig Mac Giolla Fhiondain), Nobber, Co. Meath (Art Mac Cobhthaigh) and Sliabh gCua, Co. Waterford (Donncha Rua Mac Conmara).

Cynically modelled after the hated English court system, these courts appointed sheriffs (*sirriamaí*, sg. *sirriam*) and high sheriffs (*ard-shirriamaí*) who issued mock 'warrants' (*barántais*) as their bardic predecessors issued *gairmeanna scoile* (calls to school) to demand the presence of court members.

Cúirteanna might often involve mock or real contentions between the poets, as when Diarmaid Mac Cárrthaigh famously laments his dead mare in *An Fhalartha Ghorm* (The grey ambler), only to have other poets of the Blarney *cúirt* respond to the lament with jesting verse of their own.

While *cúirteanna* dealt mostly with minor matters, the poems record minor and major events of the period. The Gaelic insurrection of Scotland (ALBA) in 1745 is the subject of *Rosc Catha na Mumhan* (War song of Munster) by the Youghal poet Piaras Mac Gearailt (1702–95) and Aindrias Mac Craith (?1708–95) was exiled from Croom after angering the local priest in *Slán le Cromadh* (Farewell to Croom). A favourite *cúirt* poem-style was the AISLING—a dream allegory imagining ÉIRE as an abused woman praying for her liberation.

Without time for formal bardic schooling, the poets resorted to simpler poetic forms, and it is particularly out of *cúirteanna* that the AMHRÁN was popularized.

With the IRISH language in decline and literate speakers becoming ever scarcer, the *cúirteanna* had fallen into desuetude by the end of the 18th century.

PRIMARY SOURCES
De Brún, *Éigse* 21.66–71 ('Barántas' on mBliain 1714); Ó Cuív, *Éigse* 11.216–18 (Rialacha do Chúirt Éigse i gContae an Chláir); Ó Donnchadha, *Ámhráin Dhiarmada Mac Seáin Bhuidhe Mac Cárrthaigh*; Ó Donnchadha, *Seán na Ráithíneach*; Ó Foghludha, *Ámhráin Phiarais Mhic Gearailt*; Ó Foghludha, *Éigse na Máighe*; Ó Foghludha, *Seán Clárach 1691–1754*; Ó Muirgheasa, *Amhráin Airt Mhic Chubhthaigh agus Amhráin Eile*.
ED. & TRANS. Ó Floinn, *Maigue Poets / Filí na Máighe*.

FURTHER READING
AISLING; ALBA; AMHRÁN; ARD MHACHA; BARD; BARDIC ORDER; CORCAIGH; ÉIRE; IRISH; IRISH LITERATURE; MUMU; ULAID; Breatnach, *Studia Hibernica* 1.128–50; Corkery, *Hidden Ireland*.

Brian Ó Broin

Culbwch ac Olwen (Culhwch and Olwen) is the earliest extant ARTHURIAN tale in any language and the most linguistically and stylistically archaic sizeable specimen of Welsh prose. Closely parallel copies of the text survive in the two most famous manuscript collections of Middle Welsh prose tales, namely the White Book of Rhydderch (LLYFR GWYN RHYDDERCH) and the Red Book of Hergest (LLYFR COCH HERGEST). Standard editions (Welsh and English versions) by Rachel BROMWICH, D. Simon Evans, and Idris Foster did not appear until late in the 20th century, thereby greatly improving access relatively recently. At 1246 printed lines in these editions, the story is long. It is also complex. There is a frame tale—the wooing of Olwen, daughter of the giant Ysbaddaden, by Culhwch. Although it motivates the rest of the action and provides opportunities for a lyrical description of Olwen's beauty (lines 487–98) and grotesque humour with her father, this story is not central to the Welsh tradition, and its *dramatis personae* are chiefly known through this text. This part of the plot resembles a *tochmarc* or 'wooing' of the Irish sagas (cf., Edel, *Helden auf Freiersfüssen*) and has been analysed as a version of the tale 'Six Go Through the World' within the taxonomy of the international folktale (Jackson, *International Popular Tale and Early Welsh Tradition*).

Juxtaposed with the isolated story of Ysbaddaden's daughter is the great central hero of BRYTHONIC tradition ARTHUR, already *penn teyrneð yr ynys honn* 'chief of the chieftains of this island' (lines 142–3). These two strands come together early in the action when the magnificently attired, but unrecognized, Culhwch arrives at his first cousin Arthur's thronging court to ask his assistance in seeking Olwen. The anonymous storyteller/author takes full advantage of this situation, having Culhwch claim his boon in the name of a vast list of the heroes and ladies of Arthur's court, in which various traditional catalogues are interwoven with imaginative, and often humorous, inventions. There is a similar inventive pastiche, as the grotesque giant is later found and confronted and reels off a catalogue of difficult tasks (*anoetheu*, sing. ANOETH) which his prospective son-in-law must fulfil. These lead to a series of adventures—which overlap only partially with the list Ysbaddaden demanded—each of which could effectively stand on its own as an independent Arthurian tale. The longest of these is the hunt of the demon boar, TWRCH TRWYTH, and his piglets for the razor, scissors, and mirror needed to cut the giant's hair. Twrch Trwyth comes from Ireland (ÉRIU), swims across the Irish Sea, and is chased by Arthur and his men across a detailed terrain of south Wales (CYMRU), giving rise to several traditional place-names, before crossing the Severn estuary into Cernyw (KERNOW/Cornwall), Arthur's home country, for a climactic but inconclusive showdown with Arthur at the head of the mustered hosts of Dyfnaint (Devon) and Cernyw.

The tale's exuberant and eclectic character, its great lists of characters and tasks, the numerous naming tales and summarized traditional narratives brought in as asides render it a treasure trove of early Welsh tradition;

it is thus of comparable value to the TRIADS (Bromwich, TYP; see Edel, BBCS 30.253–67).

As discussed in the article on ARTHURIAN SITES, *Culhwch* shows some close points of comparison with HISTORIA BRITTONUM's topographical *mirabilia*, which include a reference to Arthur's hunt of the boar Troit in connection with the wondrous landmark named Carn Cabal, a name which, on the face of it, means 'horse's hoof', but is explained as 'the cairn named for Arthur's dog, Cafall'. Clearly, the Twrch Trwyth episode already existed in the 9th century, generating place-name lore, or perhaps affecting extant place-name lore, probably as an oral tale, but there is no hint that it had yet come together with the tale of the Giant's Daughter.

As a repository of early tradition, *Culhwch* has held great appeal for philological fossil hunters; in this vein, Jackson interpreted the giant's epithet *Penkawr* 'chief of giants' as containing a rare and archaic inflected genitive plural < Celtic **kawarom*, suggesting that the puzzling formula *teir Ynys Prydein* 'the three islands of BRITAIN' means Britain's southern two thirds, Britain beyond the Forth, and Ireland, and identified the place-name *Messur Pritguenn* 'measure of (Arthur's ship) Prydwen' in the Book of LLANDAF with the *Messur y Peir* 'measure of the cauldron' which occurs in a naming tale in *Culhwch* (*Ysgrifau Beirniadol* 12.12–23). An underlying theme in *Culhwch* of pigs as totem and nemesis has been explored by Hamp (ZCP 41.257–8) and Ford (*Celtic Language, Celtic Culture* 292–304). Koch has discussed the comparative Celtic affinities of the oath (*tyghaf tyghet* 'I swear a destiny', line 50) with which Culhwch's stepmother dooms him to the perilous quest for Olwen (ÉC 29.249–61).

Although *Culhwch* is freighted with tradition, Brynley F. Roberts, in a series of articles, has argued for the well-crafted literary qualities of the tale, seeing it as the work of a literate author as opposed to an oral story-teller, though one 'close to traditional modes of narration' (*Arthur of the Welsh* 77–80; *Craft of Fiction* 215–16).

Bromwich and Evans suggest that the extant version of *Culhwch* was most probably redacted in the last decades of the 11th century to *c.* 1100 (*Culhwch and Olwen* lxxxi–lxxxii). A similar date has been proposed by Roberts (*Arthur of the Welsh* 73; although he previously suggested *c.* 1050 in *Craft of Fiction* 214). But, according to Bromwich and Evans, the catalogues probably continued to take on new items between the period of composition and that of the extant 14th-century manuscripts (*Culhwch and Olwen* lxxii). Sims-Williams points to a close parallel with a datable text in the similar rôles of BEDWYR and CAI as Arthur's chief companions in *Culhwch*, the poem PA GUR YV Y PORTHAUR, and the Latin *Vita Cadoci* of Lifris of Llancarfan of *c.* 1100 (*Arthur of the Welsh* 39; see also CADOC). One way or another, a major qualitative gap in language as well as literary style between *Culhwch* and the Four Branches of the MABINOGI should be accounted for; for example, a word meaning 'said' *amkawð* occurs in *Culhwch* and virtually nowhere else. Studies by Arwyn Watkins, D. Simon Evans (*Ysgrifau Beirniadol* 13.101–13), and Mac Cana (*Ériu* 90–120; SC 14/15.174–87; *Studies in Brythonic Word Order* 45–80.), and the linguistic section of *Culhwch and Olwen* (xv–xxv) show ways in which the language of *Culhwch* agrees with Old Welsh usage, suggesting that the redaction belongs to the Late Old Welsh period, contrasting with the language of the Four Branches, which is so essential to Celtic scholars' description of the Middle Welsh linguistic stage as to be its definition.

PRIMARY SOURCES
EDITIONS. BROMWICH & Evans, *Culhwch ac Olwen*; Bromwich & Evans, *Culhwch and Olwen*.
TRANS. *Culhwch ac Olwen* is included in the following collections: Ford, *Mabinogi and Other Medieval Welsh Tales*; Gantz, *Mabinogion*; Gwyn Jones & Thomas Jones, *Mabinogion*.

FURTHER READING
ANOETH; ARTHUR; ARTHURIAN; ARTHURIAN SITES; BEDWYR; BRITAIN; BRYTHONIC; CADOC; CAI; CYMRU; ÉRIU; HISTORIA BRITTONUM; KERNOW; LLANDAF; LLYFR COCH HERGEST; LLYFR GWYN RHYDDERCH; MABINOGI; PA GUR YV Y PORTHAUR; TRIADS; TWRCH TRWYTH; WELSH; WELSH PROSE LITERATURE; Bromwich, TYP; Bromwich et al., *Arthur of the Welsh*; Edel, BBCS 30.253–67; Edel, *Helden auf Freiersfüssen*; D. Simon Evans, *Ysgrifau Beirniadol* 13.101–13; Ford, *Celtic Language, Celtic Culture* 292–304; Hamp, ZCP 41.257–8; Henry, SC 3.30–8; Jackson, *International Popular Tale and Early Welsh Tradition*; Jackson, *Ysgrifau Beirniadol* 12.12–23; Thomas Jones, *Nottingham Mediaeval Studies* 8.3–21; Koch, ÉC 29.249–61; Loomis, *Arthurian Literature in the Middle Ages*; Mac Cana, *Ériu*, 24.90–120; Mac Cana, *Mabinogi*; Mac Cana, SC 14/15.174–87; Mac Cana, *Studies in Brythonic Word Order* 45–80; Radner, CMCS 16.41–59; Brynley F. Roberts, *Arthur of the Welsh* 73–95; Brynley F. Roberts, *Craft of Fiction* 211–30; Brynley F. Roberts, *Guide to Welsh Literature* 1.203–43; Brynley F. Roberts, *Oral Tradition* 3.1/2.61–87; Sims-Williams, BBCS 29.600–20; Sims-Williams, *Sages, Saints and Storytellers* 412–26; Watkins, BBCS 34.51–60; Watkins, *Celtic Language, Celtic Culture* 247–252; Watkins, *Constituent Order in the Positive Declarative Sentence in the Medieval Welsh Tale 'Kulhwch ac Olwen'*; Watkins, SC 12/13.367–395; Watkins & Mac Cana, BBCS 18.1–25.

JTK

Culloden, battle of

The campaign of 1745–6, which ended in the battle of Culloden, was the final attempt of the last descendant of the Scottish Stuart dynasty, Charles Edward Stuart—'Bonnie Prince Charlie', 'The Young Chevalier' or 'The Young Pretender'—to regain the throne of Scotland (ALBA) and England. It followed in the wake of several earlier JACOBITE REBELLIONS, which had failed.

In 1744 it was decided that James Stuart's son, Prince Charles Edward Stuart, should use the Austrian wars of succession to make a bid for the throne of England and Scotland on behalf of his father. The assistance of a French force of 12,000 men had been promised, but the French fleet which had set out in support of Charles was scattered, with no replacement forthcoming. Prince Charles Edward Stuart decided to go it alone, landing on the west coast of Scotland with a handful of men and a shipful of weapons in July 1745.

A month later, over 1000 men had joined him, and at Glenfinnan on 19 August 1745 Charles proclaimed his father King James III of England and James VIII of Scotland. His army swiftly proceeded to the LOWLANDS, entering Edinburgh (DÙN ÈIDEANN) on 15 September 1745, cheered on by the crowds that lined the streets. Following an initial victory over government forces at Prestonpans (near Edinburgh) on 21 September 1745, he proceeded through England, badly overestimating the support he was likely to receive from Welsh and English Jacobites and from France. Although Charles and his army of about 5000 men went as far as Derby, he refrained from entering London, following the advice of Lord George Murray that a 30,000-strong government force would prove too powerful. His troops retreated to Scotland, winning the battle of Falkirk (between Glasgow and Stirling) on 17 January 1746, but moving on back into the HIGHLANDS. The greatly reduced force of 'Bonnie Prince Charlie' was finally vanquished by a 9000-strong government army at Culloden Moor (Scottish Gaelic Cùil Lodair) near Inverness on 16 April 1746. Prince Charles himself only escaped with the help of Lady Flora MacDonald of Uist (dressed as her maidservant Betty Burke) and other supporters.

If BANNOCKBURN was the highpoint of the Scottish fight for independence, Culloden for many represents the darkest hour of the Scottish nation. The ensuing brutal oppression of the Highland people and their culture, the execution of many Jacobite leaders, the imprisonment or deportation of thousands of their followers and, last but not least, 'Bonnie Prince Charlie' himself, became the stuff of national myth. The defeat of 1746 sounded the death-knell for the CLAN-system and the traditional way of living in the Highlands, marking a major milestone in the decline of the SCOTTISH GAELIC language, and setting back dreams of Scottish independence for centuries (see NATIONALISM; SCOTTISH PARLIAMENT).

FURTHER READING
ALBA; BANNOCKBURN; CLAN; DÙN ÈIDEANN; HIGHLANDS; JACOBITE POETRY; JACOBITE REBELLIONS; LOWLANDS; NATIONALISM; SCOTTISH GAELIC; SCOTTISH PARLIAMENT; Black, *Culloden and the '45*; Harrington, *Culloden, 1746*; Prebble, *Culloden*; Preston, *Road to Culloden Moor*; Sked, *Culloden*; Young & Adair, *Hastings to Culloden*.

MBL

Cumann Buan-Choimeádta na Gaeilge (The Society for the Preservation of the Irish Language, SPIL) was established in Dublin (BAILE ÁTHA CLIATH) in 1876. The founder members included An tAthair Eoin Ó Nualláin, Professor Brian Ó Luanaigh, P. W. Joyce, and Dáithí Ó Coimín. The aims of the society were to encourage those who could still speak the language to do so, to ensure that the language would be taught in schools in the IRISH-speaking areas (see EDUCATION), to provide books which would assist in the learning of the language, and to encourage the production of a Modern IRISH LITERATURE, 'original or translated'. It was also hoped that the Society might produce a journal, partly in Irish, to help it pursue its aims. In 1878 SPIL succeeded in having Irish recognized by the Commission of National Education as a subject for which result fees would be paid, as was already the case with Greek, Latin, and French. Another important achievement of the Society was the publication of inexpensive editions of Irish books. Between 1877 and 1879 SPIL produced a three-part language primer, based on the Irish lessons which Fr. Uileog de Búrc had published in *The Nation*; these booklets were followed by school editions of TÓRUIGHEACHT DHIARMADA AGUS GHRÁINNE ('The Pursuit of Diarmaid and Gráinne'), *Oidhe Chloinne Lir*

('The Violent Death of the Children of Lir'), *Oidhe Chloinne Tuireann* ('The Violent Death of the Children of Tuireann'), and *Oidhe Chloinne Uisnigh* ('The Violent Death of the Children of Uisneach').

Internal differences in the Society led to a split in 1879 and the dissenting members formed the Gaelic Union. In 1881 the new organization, in which Ó Coimín had a prominent rôle, decided to establish a journal, and in November 1882 the first issue of *Irisleabhar na Gaedhilge / The Gaelic Journal* appeared. This bilingual journal, which was taken over by CONRADH NA GAEILGE (The Gaelic League) in 1894, lasted until 1909. Its editors included Ó Coimín, Seán Pléimeann, Eoghan Ó Gramhnaigh, Eoin MacNEILL, Seosamh Laoide, and Tadhg Ó DONNCHADHA ('Torna'). Although the preservation of the language, rather than its restoration, was the aim of those who founded *The Gaelic Journal*, it has been claimed that the revival and reclamation of the Irish language owes much to the paper which, thanks to its enlightened editors, helped prepare the ground for the cultivation of modern Irish as a literary medium.

FURTHER READING
BAILE ÁTHA CLIATH; CONRADH NA GAEILGE; EDUCATION; IRISH; IRISH LITERATURE; LANGUAGE (REVIVAL); MACNEILL; Ó DONNCHADHA; TÓRUIGHEACHT DHIARMADA AGUS GHRÁINNE; Hyde, *Mise agus an Connradh go dtí 1905*; Ní Chiaragáin, *Index do Irisleabhar na Gaedhilge 1882–1909*; Ní Mhuiríosa, *Réamhchonraitheoirí*; Nic Pháidín, *Fáinne an Lae agus an Athbheochan 1898–1900*; Ó Conaire, *Comhar 39.4.10–15, Comhar 39.5.21–3*; Ó Conaire, *Studia Hibernica 29.117–56*; Ó Droighneáin, *Taighde i gcombair Stair Litridheachta na Nua-Ghaedhilge ó 1882 anuas*; Ó hAilín, *View of the Irish Language 91–100*; Ó Murchú, *Cumann Buan-Choimeádta na Gaeilge*; Power, *Studies 38.413–18*; Ryan, *Sword of Light*.

Pádraigín Riggs

Cumann na Scríbheann nGaedhilge (The Irish Texts Society)

Cumann na Scríbheann nGaedhilge (The Irish Texts Society) was founded in 1898 in London—which is still its main base—as an offshoot of the Irish Literary Society. Among the aims of the latter society, which had been founded in 1892, was 'the study of the IRISH language', and this was carried over into the objects of its daughter society, together with the publication and translation of texts in the Irish language. Douglas Hyde (Dubhghlas DE HÍDE) was the first president of the Society, a position which he held until his death in 1949. The first chairman of the Council was Frederick York Powell, and the first secretaries were Norma Borthwick and the Irish scholar, Eleanor Hull (1860–1935). Almost immediately, the Society took steps to provide a 'handy Irish dictionary', a task urged upon it by the Irish clergyman and language supporter, Eugene O'Growney (Ó Gramhnaigh; 1863–99). The result was the publication, in 1904, of *Foclóir Gaedhilge agus Béarla / An Irish–English Dictionary* by Fr. P. S. Dinneen (UA DUINNÍN; 1860–1934). This was superseded in 1927 by a greatly enlarged edition, still the most popular reference work of its kind (see DICTIONARIES AND GRAMMARS). Dinneen paid tribute to the Society as 'a distinctive university, unchartered and unendowed', in which he himself was the holder of a 'Chair'. In addition to the dictionary, Dinneen edited four of the Society's main series of volumes between 1900 and 1914, including three volumes of *Foras Feasa ar Éirinn*, Geoffrey Keating's History of Ireland (see CÉITINN). The achievements of this series, now at volume 55, have been described as unparalleled. It includes standard, multiple-volume editions of *Duanaire Finn* ('Lays of Fionn'), mainly by Gerard MURPHY, the poems of Dáibhí Ó BRUADAIR by J. C. McErlean, the poems of Tadhg Dall Ó hUIGINN by Eleanor Knott, and the *Leabhar Gabhála* (LEBAR GABÁLA ÉRENN, 'The Book of Invasions') by R. A. S. Macalister. These volumes, all still in print, were seen through the press by successive secretaries of the Society, notably Maurice O'Connell and, the unrelated, Noel O'Connell. The Society also publishes a subsidiary series, now at volume 13, which features new introductions to editions in the main series and proceedings of annual seminars on the same subject. The Society has also begun to publish a new *Historical Dictionary of Gaelic Placenames / Foclóir Stairiúil Áitainmneacha na Gaeilge* for the *Locus* Project, which is based in University College Cork (CORCAIGH).

PRIMARY SOURCES
Cork, University College, Boole Library, Archives of the Irish Texts Society.

FURTHER READING
CÉITINN; CORCAIGH; DE H-ÍDE; DICTIONARIES AND GRAMMARS; IRISH; IRISH LITERATURE; LEBAR GABÁLA ÉRENN; MURPHY; Ó BRUADAIR; Ó H-UIGINN; UA DUINNÍN; Ó Riain et al., *Historical Dictionary of Gaelic Placenames / Foclóir Stairiúil Áitainmneacha na Gaeilge*; Ó Riain, *Irish Texts Society*.
CONTACT DETAILS. The Irish Texts Society, c/o The Royal Bank of Scotland plc, Drummonds Branch, 49 Charing Cross, Admiralty Arch, London SW1A 2DX.

Pádraig Ó Riain

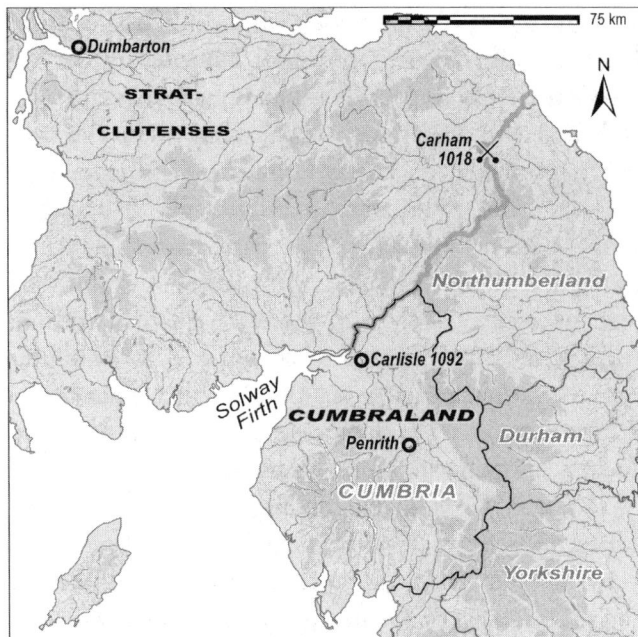

Cumbria: post-1974 county boundary in black, modern English–Scottish border in grey

Cumbria is today the name of the northernmost county on the west coast of England, bordering Scotland (ALBA). The modern county contains the historic pre-1974 counties of Cumberland, Westmorland, the north-westernmost part of Lancashire, and smaller parts of the old North Riding of Yorkshire. The corresponding English name is first attested in the Anglo-Saxon Chronicle as *Cumbraland* (945) and *Cumerland* (1000), that is, 'land of the *Cymry*, i.e. BRITONS'. The first element is a BRYTHONIC loanword, etymologically identical to CYMRU, the WELSH word for Wales. As the name indicates, this area was one of the last strongholds of Brythonic speech in Britain outside Cornwall (KERNOW) and Wales. This language was closely related to Early Welsh, and is usually called CUMBRIC by scholars; this term is also widely applied to Brythonic place-names and other linguistic evidence from northern England and southern Scotland generally, not just from Cumbria.

The kingdom of RHEGED—famed in early WELSH POETRY (see CYNFEIRDD; HEN OGLEDD; URIEN)—included part, or perhaps all, of present-day Cumbria, but its boundaries are highly uncertain. This kingdom came under Northumbrian domination in the 7th century, possibly during the reign of the expansionist ECGFRITH (670–85). Northumbrian English rule continued on both sides of the Solway Firth through the 8th century. There is no evidence that the Brythonic kingdom centred on Dumbarton extended as far south as the modern county of Cumbria before 900.

In sources of the 10th and 11th centuries Latin *Cumbria* is used, possibly interchangeably with *(Strat-) Clutenses* 'Strathclyde' (see YSTRAD CLUD), to signify a kingdom comprising the interior of what is now south-western Scotland and roughly the northern half of modern Cumbria as far as Penrith. It is not clear whether these references invariably meant one kingdom or sometimes one of two; if the first, the power of Strathclyde had probably pushed south.

We have little evidence to demonstrate how Brythonic Cumbria and its dynasty were at this period. JACKSON's theory that many of the Brythonic place-names of Cumbria belong to a secondary expansion or 're-conquest' of this time is possible, but uncertain (*Angles and Britons* 60–84). Only three rulers are specifically referred to as 'kings of the Cumbrians' in sources relating to the 10th century. Two of these have names that are probably Brythonic: an Owain, who reigned *c.* 915–*c.* 937, is mentioned by William of Malmesbury and Symeon of Durham; his son, DYFNWAL AB OWAIN (Dufnal, 'Donald'), died in Rome in 975 after leaving the throne. A king with the common Scottish name Mael Coluim, probably Dyfnwal's son, is mentioned by Florence of Worcester for 973. It is likely that the Cumbria ruled by these three included Strathclyde and parts of present-day English Cumbria.

Early in the next century we find Mael Coluim's brother with a Brythonic name—Owain the Bald (OWAIN AP DYFNWAL), mentioned by Symeon of Durham fighting on the side of MAEL COLUIM MAC CINAEDA of Scotland at the battle of Carham, south of the river Tweed in 1018. That this Owain is called King of Clutenses, rather than Cumbria, may be significant. He is the last known king of the dynasty of Strathclyde–Cumbria. Political control of the region in the 11th century was unsettled, with victories claimed for Scotland, England, and the earldom of Northumbria. In 1092 William II (Rufus) of England, William the Conqueror's son, took Carlisle, driving out its ruler Dolphin, son of an earl of Northumbria with the Brythonic name *Gospatric* 'servant of St

PATRICK' (see following article), and fixing the English–Scottish border at the Solway Firth, as today.

FURTHER READING
ALBA; BRITONS; BRYTHONIC; CUMBRIC; CYMRU; CYNFEIRDD; DYFNWAL AB OWAIN; ECGFRITH; HEN OGLEDD; JACKSON; KERNOW; MAEL COLUIM MAC CINAEDA; OWAIN AP DYFNWAL; PATRICK; RHEGED; URIEN; WELSH; WELSH POETRY; YSTRAD CLUD; Annable, *Later Prehistory of Northern England*; Jackson, *Angles and Britons* 60–84; Kirby, *Trans. Cumberland & Westmorland Antiquarian and Archaeological Society* 62.77–94; O'Sullivan, *Scandinavians in Cumbria* 17–35; Phythian-Adams, *Land of the Cumbrians*.

AM

Cumbric, as a linguistic term, refers to the BRYTHONIC spoken in the early Middle Ages in the area approximately between the line of the river Mersey and the Forth–Clyde isthmus. Evidence for Cumbric consists of the following: (i) proper names surviving through the medium of Welsh, English, Irish, or Latin texts; (ii) two legal terms in the 11th-century *Leges inter Brettos et Scotos* (Laws of the Britons and SCOTS)—*galnes, galnys* 'blood-fine' (Welsh *galanas*), *kelchyn* 'circuit' (Welsh *cylchyn*) (see Jackson, LHEB 9–10; Lapidge & Sharpe, *Bibliography of Celtic Latin Literature* 400–1200 item 1045); a third term, *mercheta* 'marriage fee', more probably derives from English or Norman French *marchet* 'market'; (iii) a few personal names in INSCRIPTIONS, but most of these are early and in ROMANO-BRITISH spelling; (iv) place-names borrowed into English; (v) probably the early Welsh poetry of the CYNFEIRDD set in north Britain.

In category (i) most of the names of north BRITONS, as found in pedigrees and annals, occur also in Wales (CYMRU): e.g. Old Welsh/Cumbric *Dumn(a)gual* (Mod. DYFNWAL), TEUDEBUR, *Elfin*, EUGEIN (Mod. *Owain*), CERETIC. However, there is a class of Brythonic male personal names that are rare in Wales, but common in north Britain; in these, *Gos*, var. *Cos* 'servant of' (Welsh *gwas*) is prefixed to the name of a saint: *Gos-patric, Gos-mungo, Gos-oswald*. That Celtic **wosto-* (Gallo-Roman *vassus*) became Cumbric *gos* is an interesting feature, but the variation of *gwa-* and *go-* is general throughout the Brythonic world—e.g. Welsh *golch* 'wash' = Breton *gwalc'h*—and does not have the character of a systematic sound law.

Category (v) above, the *Cynfeirdd* poetry, is the largest and potentially the most significant, but can only throw a slight and suggestive light on Cumbric. Although most modern scholars generally agree that some of this poetry was indeed composed in the HEN OGLEDD ('Old North') as opposed to in what is now Wales, and was perhaps even first transcribed in the north, how much of it has such a history and how faithful our copies are to northern originals are uncertain. If we had any Cumbric texts continuously transmitted in the north, these could then be a basis for finding orthographic, dialectal, and other Cumbric earmarks in Welsh manuscripts of *Cynfeirdd* poetry, but there are no such survivals, only Welsh copies. As it is, the most distinctive linguistic features of this corpus appear to be archaisms—throwbacks that were probably once found throughout the entire Brythonic world—rather than features of regional dialect. And we would expect regionalisms to be rare in formal court poetry anyway. Even so, possible Cumbric dialect features can occasionally be seen. For example, in the *Peis Dinogat* interpolation (LLYFR ANEIRIN 1101–17A), an informal song to a child which Gruffydd (*Celtic Language, Celtic Culture* 261–6) has shown to be set in the English Lake District in CUMBRIA, there are a number of singulative animal names in *penn* 'head': *penn ywrch* 'a roebuck', *penn gwythwch* 'a wild sow', *penn hyb* 'a stag', *penn grugyar* 'a grouse', *penn pysc* 'a fish'. Referring to a single animal in this way is otherwise found only in BRETON, and we have no evidence that the construction ever had any currency in the present-day Wales.

For the Brythonic place-names of southern Scotland (ALBA), see SCOTTISH PLACE-NAMES. Most place-names in northern England are of Norse or Old English origin. However, there is a scatter of Brythonic names throughout this extensive region, some of which clearly reflect a developed medieval language, much like Welsh, CORNISH, or Breton. For example, *Liscard* on the Wirral peninsula, recorded as *Lisenecark* in 1260, reflects Brythonic **Lis-an-Carrec* 'the court of the rock' (Welsh *llys y garreg*) with an example of the definite article in its original nasal form. The hill name *Penyghent* in west Yorkshire is attested as *Penegent* in 1307, reflecting **Penn-a-gënt* 'hill of the heathens' (Welsh *pen y gynt*), in which the definite article before a consonant is merely the obscure vowel, like Middle and Modern Welsh *y*.

In the northern half of the modern county of Cumbria (see map), the territory of the kingdom of

Cumbria in the 10th and 11th centuries, we find the densest distribution of Brythonic place-names in England outside Cornwall (KERNOW) and the Welsh border area, including the names of some of the most important places. For example, *Penrith*, the historic capital, means 'the main ford' (*Penred* in 1167, cf. Breton *Perret, Pen ret* in 871, and Welsh *Pen-rhyd*, formed from *pen* 'main, chief, head' + *rhyd* 'ford'), and *Carlisle* (Welsh *Caerliwelydd*) is derived from the British place-name *Luguvalion* (*Luguvallo* in the 3rd-century Antonine Itinerary). The river and lake name *Derwent* (near the setting of *Peis Dinogat*, see above) is based on the British **deru-* 'oak' (Welsh *derw*), and the mountain name *Blencogo* corresponds to Welsh *Blaen-cogau* 'foreland of cuckoos'.

Jackson proposed that Cumbric re-expanded into this area with the political control of Cumbria in the 10th century, following periods of Northumbrian and Norse dominance (*Angles and Britons* 60–84). Similarly, it is usually assumed that Cumbric speech survived more or less as long as, and wherever, rulers with Brythonic names ruled, for example, OWAIN AP DYFNWAL who ruled Strathclyde (YSTRAD CLUD) in the early 11th century. However, the usual pattern in the CELTIC COUNTRIES was for the older language to outlive the loss of sovereignty, sometimes by many centuries. Thus, Cumbric may have survived quite late in some areas, and a claim has been made that the 'shepherd's score', a special method of counting found in Cumbria and other parts of northern England, is a survival. In this system the numbers strongly parallel Welsh, for instance, *pimp* 'five', *dik* 'ten', *bumfit* 'fifteen', and Welsh *pump, deg, pymtheg*, although several words are clearly later rhyming creations: *yan* 'one', *tan* 'two', *tethera* 'three', *pethera* 'four', cf. Welsh *un, dau, tri, pedwar*. The system is not attested until the 18th century, and its ultimate origins may date to any time before that.

Although Cumbric is convenient shorthand for Brythonic evidence from northern England and southern Scotland and we have no acceptable replacement term, it would be misleading to think of it as a distinct language. Written Old WELSH, Old Breton, and Old Cornish of the 9th and 10th centuries are so similar as to be hard to distinguish from each other by linguistic criteria. If anything, Cumbric was even less different from Welsh than were the south-western dialects. Contemporary sources regard all four as the same language.

For BEDA there was one *lingua Brettonum* (*Historia Ecclesiastica* 1.1), and Latin texts from Wales and Brittany (BREIZH) use the term *Brit(t)annice* and *lingua Brit(t)annica* for the vernacular. The recent English term *Cumbric* is merely an Anglicization of the root and suffix which occur in the Welsh name for the Welsh language, i.e. *Cymraeg*, which, loaned into Old Irish as *Combrec*, was used in Irish GLOSSARIES for any Brythonic word. Furthermore, to say that the *Cynfeirdd* poetry was first composed in Cumbric and then 'translated' into Welsh is a not a good characterization of the transmission process as this is now understood. Thus, the main fact is the essential unity of Brythonic in the early Middle Ages, and Cumbric is more correctly a geographic rather than a linguistic term. The status of PICTISH as a language distinct from Brythonic remains unresolved, and will, of course, have a bearing on how we conceive of Cumbric and the Brythonic of north Britain.

FURTHER READING
ALBA; BEDA; BREIZH; BRETON; BRITONS; BRYTHONIC; CELTIC COUNTRIES; CERETIC; CORNISH; CUMBRIA; CYMRU; CYNFEIRDD; DYFNWAL; EUGEIN; GLOSSARIES; HEN OGLEDD; INSCRIPTIONS; KERNOW; LLYFR ANEIRIN; OWAIN AP DYFNWAL; PICTISH; ROMANO-BRITISH; SCOTS; SCOTTISH PLACE-NAMES; TEUDEBUR MAP BILI; WELSH; YSTRAD CLUD; Abalain, *Les noms de lieux bretons*; Annable, *Later Prehistory of Northern England*; Charles-Edwards, *Celtic World* 703–36; Gambles, *Lake District Place-Names*; Gruffydd, *Celtic Language, Celtic Culture* 261–6; Jackson, *Angles and Britons* 60–84; Jackson, LHEB; Lapidge & Sharpe, *Bibliography of Celtic Latin Literature* 400–1200; O'Sullivan, *Scandinavians in Cumbria* 17–35; Phythian-Adams, *Land of the Cumbrians*; Simpson & Roud, *Oxford Dictionary of English Folklore*.

JTK, AM

Cumméne Find (Cumméne the Fair, Cumméne mac Arnaine, Latin Cummeneus albus), seventh abbot of Iona (EILEAN Ì), was of COLUM CILLE's family and a nephew of Ségéne (5th abbot). He succeeded Abbot Suibne in 657, and died 24 February 669 (memorial in the *Martyrology of Tallaght*). The ANNALS record that he visited Iona's monastic *familia* in Ireland (ÉRIU) in 661, and he probably made a similar visitation to Iona's missions in England (see MONASTICISM). His abbacy saw a flowering of Iona's monastic culture: during his time we know that books were written there, its library was being built up and, probably, at this time the Book of DURROW, whose Eusebian Apparatus indicates great scholarship, was produced, if not there, then in a related monastery. But he also encountered some setbacks. In 664 the council called by King OSWYDD—who probably knew Cumméne—at Streanæshalch (Whitby) saw a break between Iona and churches which it had founded in England; and 664–8 was a period of devastating plague, although ADOMNÁN says that Iona itself escaped. It was Cumméne who received Bishop Colmán of LINDISFARNE back to Iona, en route to Inishboffin, after his argument for Iona's position was rejected at Streanæshalch.

Cumméne was the author of a *vita* of Colum Cille (probably entitled LIBER DE VIRTUTIBUS SANCTI COLUMBAE) and was therefore one of the first Irishmen, if not the first Irishman, to write HAGIOGRAPHY. Apart from one fragment (in a smaller script on page 108a of Schaffhausen, Gen. 1), this work is lost, but it underlies many chapters of Adomnán's *Vita Columbae*; from its reference to DOMNALL BRECC, king of the Irish in DÁL RIATA, it must have been written after 642. It is a definite possibility that Cumméne Find and the Cummian of *De Controversia Paschali* (written before 652) are identical—if so, Cumméne was in an Irish Columban monastery before becoming abbot. The reason given against the identification is that the author of the letter was so critical of Iona's Easter dating (see EASTER CONTROVERSY) that he could not have become abbot and let the practice continue; but it is equally possible that Cummian wrote so stridently to Ségéne of Iona (the letter indicates a close relationship) because of his concern about the practice of his own *familia*; and his duty to that *familia* could lead him to become its abbot, even knowing that in one aspect of their practice he had failed—as Adomnán later would fail—to convince his brethren.

PRIMARY SOURCES
ED. & TRANS. Alan O. Anderson & Marjorie O. Anderson, *Vita Columbae*.
TRANS. Sharpe, *Life of St Columba / Adomnán of Iona*.

FURTHER READING
ADOMNÁN; ANNALS; CHRISTIANITY; COLUM CILLE; DÁL RIATA; DOMNALL BRECC; DURROW; EASTER CONTROVERSY; EILEAN Ì; ÉRIU; HAGIOGRAPHY; LIBER DE VIRTUTIBUS SANCTI COLUMBAE; LINDISFARNE; MONASTERIES; MONASTICISM; OSWYDD; Herbert, *Iona, Kells, and Derry*; Walsh & Ó Cróinín, *Cummian's Letter*.

Thomas O'Loughlin

Cummíne Fota, St

Cummíne Fota, St (also Cummaine, Cuimine, Latin Cummenus or Cummianus Longus, 592–662) straddles the early Irish textual world as both an author and a fictionalized character. His reputation as a scholar (*sapiens*, ANNALS of Ulster 662) is fixed by his presumed authorship of the comprehensive penitential that goes under his name. Other Latin works have been attributed to him, with varying credibility: the hymn *Celebra Juda*, a commentary on Mark (see Bischoff, *Biblical Studies* 80–2), and the letter of *c.* 632 of 'Cummian' relating to the EASTER CONTROVERSY. There are some further indications of his involvement in native Irish law (Breatnach, *Peritia* 5.37). An elegy on the saint may be roughly contemporary with his death (Byrne, *Ériu* 31.111–22 but see Mac Eoin, *Ériu* 28.17–31). His associations are generally with west Munster (MUMU), and he is traditionally of the royal line of the Éoganachta Locha Léin (see ÉOGANACHT). His literary persona is quite the contrary: whilst displaying wisdom, sometimes unwittingly, he is depicted in various ways as a foolish saint, a fit companion for the holy fool COMGÁN MAC DÁ CHERDA. In some tales he is seen as a wandering, shiftless cleric, in others as a cruel and capricious confessor. The ultimate development of this quixotic persona is his transformation into the wise and witty swineherd Marbán, brother to king Guaire Aidne in the later medieval tale *Tromdámh Guaire* (Ó Coileáin, *Ériu* 28.54).

PRIMARY SOURCES
ED. & TRANS. Bernard & Atkinson, *Irish Liber Hymnorum* 1.16–21, 2.9–14 (*Celebra Iuda*); Bieler, *Irish Penitentials* 108–35 (Penitential of Cummean); Byrne, *Ériu* 31.111–22 (The lament for Cummíne Foto); Mac Eoin, *Béaloideas* 39–41.192–205 (The Life of Cuimine Fota); Mac Eoin, *Ériu* 28.17–31 (The lament for Cuimine Fota); Meyer, *Comrac Liadaine ocus Cuirithir / The Meeting of Liadáin and Cuirthir*; Migne, *Patrologia Latina* 87.589–644 (Commentary on Mark); O'Keeffe, *Ériu* 5.18–44 (Mac Dá Cherda and Cummaine Foda); Walsh & Ó Cróinín, *Cummian's Letter*.

FURTHER READING
ANNALS; COMGÁN MAC DÁ CHERDA; EASTER CONTROVERSY; ÉOGANACHT; IRISH; MUMU; Bischoff, *Biblical Studies* 73–160; Breatnach, *Peritia* 5.36–52; Clancy, 'Saint and Fool'; Clancy, *Ériu* 44.105–24; Clancy, *Satura* 20–47; Ó Coileáin, *Ériu* 25.88–125; Ó Coileáin, *Ériu* 28.32–70; Ó Cróinín, *Sages, Saints and Storytellers* 268–79.

Thomas Owen Clancy

Cunedda (Wledig) fab Edern/Cunedag

was, according to early Welsh sources, a chieftain from north BRITAIN who, in the 5th century, migrated to what is now Wales (CYMRU) and expelled the Irish who had settled in parts of GWYNEDD, DYFED, Cydweli, and Gŵyr (Gower). He figures also in this tradition as the father of seven sons who gave their names to territories in north and west Wales and as the progenitor of the first dynasty of Gwynedd, which continued in power until MERFYN Frych ap Gwriad (Old Welsh Mermin map Guriat) came to power in 825. HISTORIA BRITTONUM §14, as part of an account of the origins of the Gaels, relates:

The Maic Liethain (i.e. the Munster Uí Liatháin) were in possession of Dyfed and other regions, that is Gŵyr and Cydweli, until they were driven out by Cunedda and his sons from all the regions of Britain.

In *Historia Brittonum* §62, part of the 'Northern History', we are told:

MAELGWN (Mailcunus) the great king was reigning amongst the BRITONS, that is in the realm of Gwynedd, for his ancestor, i.e. Cunedda (archaic Old Welsh Cuneda), with his sons, whose number was eight, had come from the northern region, from the country called Manau Guotodin (see GODODDIN), 146 years before Maelgwn reigned, and they expelled the Irish from these regions with enormous slaughter, so that they never returned to inhabit them.

The Old Welsh GENEALOGIES in London, BL Harley MS 3859 supply the following information:

These are the names of the sons of Cunedda whose number was nine: Tybion (Old Welsh Tipi[p]iaun) the first born who died in the region that is called Manaw Gododdin and did not come with his father and his aforementioned brothers. Meirion (Meriaun) his brother divided the possessions with his brothers: ii. Osfael (Osmail), iii. Rhufon (Rumaun), iiii. Dunawd (Dunaut), v. Ceretic, vi. Abloyc, vii. Einion Yrth (Enniaun Girt), viii. Dogfael (Docmail), ix. Etern (Edern). These are their boundaries: from the river called the Dee (Dubr Duiu) to another called the Teifi (Tebi). And they held many regions on Britain's west coast.

The legend of lands founded by Cunedda and his sons

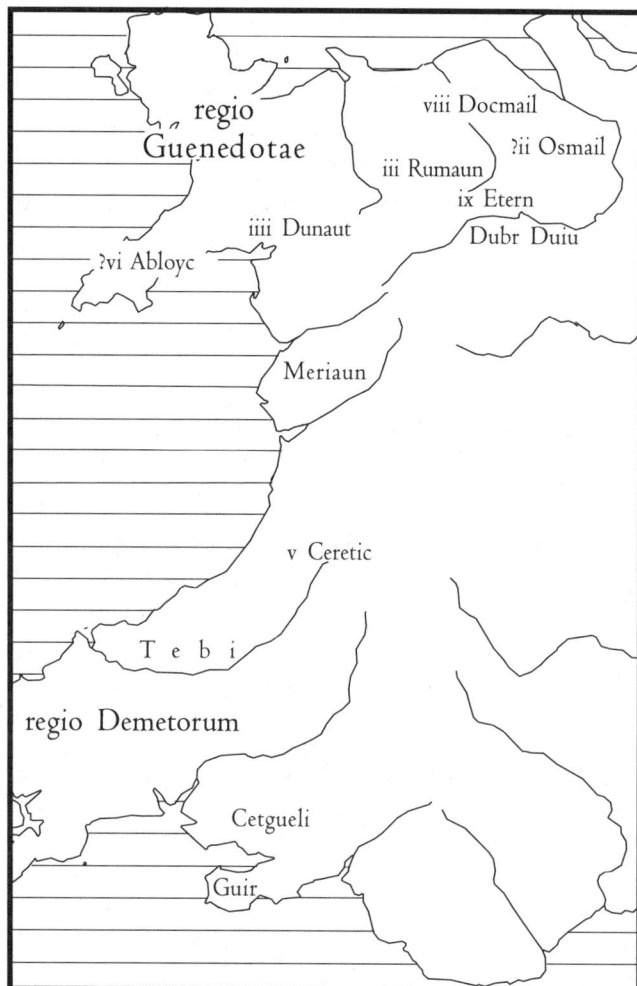

Some scholars (such as Nora K. Chadwick, *Celtic Britain* 66–8; Wendy Davies, *Wales in the Early Middle Ages* 89; Thomas, *Celtic Britain* 118) have preferred to view the story of Cunedda as essentially an origin legend rather than history. Conversely, Miller (BBCS 27.515–32) and Gruffydd (SC 24/25.1–14) have argued for a core of veracity in the story (cf. Alcock, *Economy, Society and Warfare* 92f.). The Irish settlements in late Roman to post-Roman Wales are essentially factual, as shown by OGAM inscriptions in Wales, place-name evidence (such as the derivation of the name of the Llŷn peninsula from Primitive Irish *Legenī, i.e. LAIGIN 'Leinstermen'), and doctrines of Irish dynastic orgins for Dyfed and BRYCHEINIOG. As to the district names, the pattern of derivation plainly shows names of territories deriving from those of men, four of whom bore Roman names in the manner characteristic of sub-Roman/Brythonic rulers of the 5th century: (1) *Meirion(n)ydd* 'land of Mariānus', (2) *Osfeiliawn* 'land of Osfael', (3) *Rhufoniawg* < *Rōmāniācon* 'estate of Rōmānus', (4) *Dunoding* 'progeny of Dōnātus', (5) CEREDIGION 'lands of CERETIC', (6) *Afloegiawn* 'lands of Afloeg' (a personal name possibly signifying an 'ex-layman' who retired to the church), (8) *Dogfeiling* 'progeny of Dogfael', (9) *Edeirniawn* 'lands of Aeternus'.

Taking the 146-year interval of *Historia Brittonum* §62 literally, this gives a date of AD 401 going back from Maelgwn's 547 obit in ANNALES CAMBRIAE, somewhat earlier if the beginning or middle of his reign was meant. However, counting generations in Gwynedd's genealogy, 146 years is rather long—though not impossible—between great-grandfather and great-grandson, therefore a heyday later in the 5th century is another possibility.

Another strand of evidence is the archaic Welsh elegy known as MARWNAD CUNEDDA (Death-song of Cunedda) in LLYFR TALIESIN. This poem is consistent with the Latin sources above in the hero's name (which repeatedly scans as early Brythonic *Cunedag*), his father's name, *Edern* < Latin *Aeternus*, and localization in 5th-century north Britain. However, the sons, the migration to Wales, and the war with the Irish do not figure at all in the elegy, raising the possibility that the foundation legend was possibly manufactured by Gwynedd propagandists, who wanted a famous northern ancestor, perhaps because CADWALLON was seeking to enforce claims on Northumbria in the period 632–5. However, it is also possible that the migration and Irish war did take place and the sons founded their kingdoms, but that these events were of insufficient interest and importance for the north British poet who produced *Marwnad Cunedda*.

To sum up, it seems likely that Cunedda was an early post-Roman north British leader and a focus of early literary activity. It is also likely that men with Latin and Brythonic names listed as his sons did found small kingdoms in north and west Wales in the early post-Roman period and that these displaced Irish lordships. An appropriate historical context for both circumstances can be seen as a struggle for control of the Irish Sea zone in the vacuum created by the withdrawal of Roman forces from SEGONTIUM and other bases in west Britain. Nonetheless, the poem *Marwnad Cunedda* leaves room to doubt whether Cunedda ever fought the Irish or migrated to Wales, in which case the sons need not be his real sons and the subsequent kings of Gwynedd, the Maelgyning (descendants of Maelgwn), may not, in fact, be descendants of Cunedda.

As a central figure within the scheme of Welsh royal pedigrees, Cunedda came to figure prominently also, by the 11th century and possibly earlier, in the genealogies of saints. In the TRIADS he is named as the founder of one of the three great kindreds of Welsh saints (Bromwich, TYP no. 81).

The name *Cunedag* is a Celtic compound. JACKSON argued that the preservation of the final lenited -*g* /γ/ implies that the spelling goes back to a written source of pre-*c.* 750 or probably earlier (*Celt and Saxon* 30); despite Dumville's counter-arguments (*Arthurian Literature* 6.18–19), Jackson was probably right. Several scholars have proposed that the first element is the rare Welsh poetic word *cun* 'lord', followed by an archaically retained composition vowel, thus going back to a BRITISH *Counodagos* (Jackson, *Celt and Saxon* 30), which would have to mean 'having good lords'. More probably, the first element, as in GILDAS's *Cuneglasus*, is the 6th- or 7th-century spelling of the extremely common name element Celtic *cuno-* 'dog' (Isaac, BBCS 38.100–1; Koch, *Gododdin of Aneirin* cxxi–cxxii). The name thus means 'having good hounds', 'hounds' being a common kenning for warriors. *Marwnad Cunedda* says of his war-band, 'his hounds (*cŵn*) will keep vigil at his frontier'; therefore, this is how the poet understood the name. We also seem to have the 9th-century Old Welsh spelling of the same name in the 'SUREXIT' MEMORANDUM as *Cinda*. The spelling *Cunedda*, though unhistorical, is by now well established.

The title *gwledig* 'sovereign' is commonly applied to Cunedda in the genealogies compiled in the Middle Welsh period, but it is not found in sources predating *c.* 1100. Thus, we may doubt that this was Cunedda's title and rank in the 5th century or that Gwynedd's first dynasty claimed it to be so.

PRIMARY SOURCES
MS. London, BL Harley 3859.
HISTORIA BRITTONUM §14, §62.

FURTHER READING
ANNALES CAMBRIAE; BRITAIN; BRITISH; BRITONS; BRYCHEINIOG; CADWALLON; CEREDIGION; CERETIC; CYMRU; DYFED; GENEALOGIES; GILDAS; GODODDIN; GWYNEDD; HEN OGLEDD; JACKSON; LAIGIN; LLYFR TALIESIN; MAELGWN; MARWNAD

CUNEDDA; MERFYN; OGAM; SEGONTIUM; 'SUREXIT' MEMO-
RANDUM; TRIADS; Alcock, *Economy, Society and Warfare among
the Britons and Saxons*; Bartrum, *Welsh Classical Dictionary* 151–
3; Bromwich, TYP; Nora K. Chadwick, *Celtic Britain*; Charles-
Edwards, *Celtic World* 703–36; Wendy Davies, *Wales in the Early
Middle Ages*; Dumville, *Arthurian Literature* 6.1–26; Gruffydd,
SC 24/25.1–14; Isaac, BBCS 38.100–1; Jackson, *Celt and Saxon*
20–62; Koch, *Gododdin of Aneirin*; Miller, BBCS 27.515–32;
Thomas, *Celtic Britain*.

JTK

Cunobelinos

Cunobelinos (r. *c.* AD 10–*c.* 42) was, according to
surviving evidence, the most powerful king in BRITAIN
to rule in the final century of independence between
CAESAR's expeditions of 55 and 54 BC and the invasion
of the Emperor Claudius in AD 43. His career may be
traced through both Roman notices and the sequence
of his massive and varied issues of COINAGE, minted
at both CAMULODŪNON and VERULAMION, as well as
the issues of other members of his own dynasty and
their rivals. On several of his coins Cunobelinos is
said to be the son of Tasciovanos (r. *c.* 15 BC–*c.* AD 10).
Some writers have lately written sceptically of this
statement, believing it to be a political claim to succession rather than a genealogical fact. However, in
the Old Welsh GENEALOGIES, he is *Cinbelin map Teuhant*,
and this must be taken as independent confirmation
since Tasciovanos is unknown apart from Iron Age coin
legends and Old Welsh *Teuhant* could only have developed from British *Tasciovanos* by continuous oral tradition; in other words, he could not have been taken into
Welsh tradition from some (now lost) Roman history.

The power of Cunobelinos sufficiently impressed
the Romans for Suetonius (*Caligula* §44) to refer to
him as *Britannorum rex* (king of the BRITONS). The
distribution of his coinage clearly implies a status as
the most powerful of the pre-Roman rulers, but Suetonius's assessment is too sweeping. The core area of
the coins are the tribal lands of the CATUVELLAUNI
and the TRINOVANTES north of the lower Thames. These
two old rivals had apparently merged as a single state.
From the beginning of his reign his coins appear heavily
south of the Thames in Kent, where issues of the
Atrebates had previously predominated. To the north,
his influence may be traced in a scatter of his coins in
the territory of the ICENI, but their own silver sequence
continued, including legends which are probably abbreviated names of their independent rulers (ANTED, AESU,
SAENU) as well as their tribal name, ECEN (Iceni). Further
to the margins, the coins of the Corieltauvi in the north
and the Durotriges and Dobunni in the west indicate
continued independence.

The end of Cunobelinos' reign heralded a period
of instability and increased Roman diplomatic and
military involvement. In AD 39/40 his son Adminios
(or Amminios) fell out with Cunobelinos and sought
refuge with the Emperor Gaius (Caligula), who made
preparations to invade Britain, but the troops assembled
at the Channel grew restive, which led to the famous
incident in which the erratic emperor ordered them to
collect sea shells. About this time, a chieftain called
Epaticcos son of Tasciovanos (thus apparently Cunobelinos's brother), minting coins derived from the issues
of Cunobelinos, appears around the Atrebatic centre
of CALLEVA, and in AD 42 Virica, king of the Atrebates,
fled to Rome, an incident which provided the
immediate opportunity for the Claudian invasion.
Cunobelinos was succeeded by two further sons,
Togodumnos and CARATĀCOS, who fought the Roman
invaders in the coming years, the latter being the longer
lived and more famous.

The name *Cunobelinos* is Celtic and means 'hound
of the god BELENOS'. It was a fairly popular name in
early Wales (CYMRU); the Old Welsh spellings *Conbelin*,
Cinbelin, and *Conuelin* occur. In the HISTORIA REGUM
BRITANNIAE of GEOFFREY OF MONMOUTH, Kim-
belinus son of Tenvantius (derived from Old Welsh
Cinbelin map Te(u)huant) figures accurately as one of
the last kings of Britain before the Claudian invasion.
In BRUT Y BRENHINEDD he is Kynuelyn uab Teneuan.
Geoffrey's Kimbelinus is the ultimate source of
Shakespeare's *Cymbeline*.

PRIMARY SOURCE
Suetonius, *Caligula*.

FURTHER READING
BELENOS; BRITAIN; BRITONS; BRUT Y BRENHINEDD; CAESAR;
CALLEVA; CAMULODŪNON; CARATĀCOS; CATUVELLAUNI; COIN-
AGE; CYMRU; GENEALOGIES; GEOFFREY OF MONMOUTH;
HISTORIA REGUM BRITANNIAE; ICENI; TRINOVANTES;
VERULAMION; Allen, *Britannia* 6.1–19; Bartrum, *Welsh Classi-
cal Dictionary* 154–5; Branigan, *Catuvellauni*; Cunliffe, *Iron Age
Communities in Britain*; Salway, *Oxford Illustrated History of Ro-
man Britain*; Van Arsdell, *Celtic Coinage of Britain*; Webster,
Rome Against Caratacus.

JTK

Cunomor/Conomor (*fl. c.* 550–*c.* 560) was a historical figure who ruled parts of Cornwall (KERNOW) and Brittany (BREIZH) at the period of the BRETON MIGRATIONS. His name is attested in early sources on both sides of the English Channel. It is derived from the BRITISH *Cunomāros 'having great hounds', *cunes 'hounds' being a common Celtic kenning for 'warriors' (cf. CUNEDDA).

Cunomor is mentioned in the contemporary *Historia Francorum* (History of the Franks; 4.4) by Gregory of Tours as Chonomor, where he is described as 'another count (*comes*) of that region', i.e. of Brittany. As Gregory explains, he hid the Breton chief Macliav from his enemies, concealing him in a tumulus with an air hole and saying that he was dead and buried under the mound. Macliav was the father of Waroch (*Historia Francorum* 5.19), the ruler also known as UUEROC, later Erec, the eponymous founder of the powerful Dark Age kingdom of Bro-Uueroc in south-east Brittany and, in later tradition, the enemy of Cunomor. Cunomor is mentioned in the 9th-century Breton Latin Life of St PAUL AURELIAN, written by Uurmonoc in 884. Uurmonoc describes a British king Marcus, also called Quonomorius. Cunomor is also mentioned in several other early saints' lives, including those of GILDAS and SAMSON.

In Cornwall, a stone from Castle Dore, near Fowey, bears what is probably a 6th-century inscription, reading:

[D]RVSTA
NVSHICIACIT
CVNO[M]ORIFILIVS,

'Here lies Drustan, Cunomorus' son'. If the reading *Drustanus* is correct and Uurmonoc's identification of Cunomor and Mark sound, the stone could be independent confirmation of historical figures known in the later Arthurian legend, Tristan (see TRISTAN AND ISOLT) and king Mark. *Cunomāros* gives the common early Welsh man's name Cynfawr, and the Welsh TRIADS contain a reference to a Kynvawr Catguduc; another genealogy refers to Gereint mab Erbin mab (*recte* grandson of) Kynvawr mab Tudwawl. (For the relationship between GERAINT and Erec/Gueroc, see TAIR RHAMANT; CHRÉTIEN DE TROYES.)

Over time in Brittany, the historical figure of Cunomor degenerated into the literary trope of a wicked king, cf. the rôle of King ARTHUR in the Life of Saint CADOC. Albert LE GRAND mentioned him in his 17th-century French-language *Vies des saints de la Bretagne armorique*, which had a strong influence on subsequent literary and oral tradition. In the Life of St Gildas, he describes Cunomor as '*Comte de Cornoüaille, un meschant et vicieux Seigneur, nommé Comorre*' (Count of KERNEV, a wicked and vicious lord, named Comorre). Comorre abducted and murdered Triphine, the daughter of Gueroc, the count of Vannes. Triphine was later brought back to life by Saint Gildas. Le Grand's story was adapted in the BRETON-language *Buez ar zent* (Lives of the saints). There, the story is told in the Life of Triphine and Comorre's son, Treveur (in the text, the names are spelled *Konomor, Trifina,* and *Tremeur*). Triphine was killed while she was pregnant, and Treveur was born after she was restored to life; Comorre was excommunicated and driven to the Menez Bre hills. In the 19th century Émile Souvestre collected a folk-tale in which Le Grand's story is mixed with elements of the Bluebeard tale (Aarne-Thompson type 312). In this version, the giant Comorre, king of Cornwall, has already slain four wives, fearing the outcome of a prophecy that he would be killed by his first-born son. While Comorre is away, Triphine discovers the tombs of the murdered women, and escapes with the help of the dead wives' four murder weapons. Comorre catches and beheads her, but Gildas brings her to life. Triphine gives birth to a son who is born able to speak. He asks for justice, whereupon Comorre's castle collapses upon him and kills him.

FURTHER READING
ARTHUR; BREIZH; BRETON; BRETON MIGRATIONS; BRITISH; CADOC; CHRÉTIEN DE TROYES; CUNEDDA; GERAINT; GILDAS; HAGIOGRAPHY; KERNEV; KERNOW; LE GRAND; PAUL AURELIAN; SAMSON; TAIR RHAMANT; TRIADS; TRISTAN AND ISOLT; UUEROC; Aarne & Thompson, *Types of the Folktale*; Bromwich, TYP; Dalton, *History of the Franks by Gregory of Tours*; Doble, *Saints of Cornwall 1*; Doble, *Lives of the Welsh Saints*; Le Grand, *Les vies des saints de la Bretagne armorique*; Marigo, *Buez ar zent*; Padel, *Arthur of the Welsh* 229–48; Radford, *Early Christian Inscriptions of Dumnonia*; Souvestre, *Le foyer breton 1*; Thomas, *And Shall These Mute Stones Speak?*
WEBSITE. www.ucl.ac.uk/archaeology/cisp/database (Celtic Inscribed Stones Project)

AM

Curetán/Curitan (**Boniface**) was the bishop of Rosemarkie (*Ros Maircnidh*), near Fortrose on the Black Isle in the Moray Firth, Ross-shire, *c.* 690–710.

He was one of the witnesses at the Synod of Birr (a monastic town in Co. Offaly, Ireland) in 697, which proclaimed the Old Irish *Lex Innocentium* (Law of the innocents) also known as CÁIN ADOMNÁIN ('Adomnán's Law'). This law held that women, children, and clerics should not participate in war as combatants or prisoners. Though Curetán's see was amongst the northern PICTS, his *Vita* (Life), in which he is called *Albanus Kiritinus Bonifacius*, says he was of Hebrew origin. According to his *Vita*, he was a contemporary of NECHTON SON OF DERELEI, king of the Picts (703–24), whom he is said to have baptized. An actual eastern connection for Curetán's cult might explain similarities in the iconography of the PICTISH Class II monuments at Nigg and Hilton of Cadboll (both near Rosemarkie) to that of Byzantine Christian art. Another possibility is that the tradition of Curetán's eastern background arose in the context of the EASTER CONTROVERSY, in which King Nechton had played an important part in bringing Pictland to Roman practice. The adherents of the Roman Easter attached special authority to the calendar doctrines of the Romans, Greeks, Egyptians, and Hebrews; a Dark Age Celtic churchman might thus be a 'Hebrew' by conviction. Curetán's name probably contains the Common Celtic diminutive suffix -*agnos*, Old Irish -*án*. The alternative *Boniface* is Latin.

St Boniface's day is the 16th of March, the date of the St Boniface Fair in Fortrose.

FURTHER READING
ADOMNÁN; CÁIN ADOMNÁIN; EASTER CONTROVERSY; NECHTON SON OF DERELEI; PICTISH; PICTS; Alan O. Anderson, *Early Sources of Scottish History AD 500 to 1286* 205, 211; Ní Dhonnchadha, *Peritia* 1.178–215; Skene, *Chronicles of the Picts* 1.277–8; Smyth, *Warlords and Holy Men* 127–8, 134; Watson, *History of the Celtic Place-Names of Scotland*.

PEB

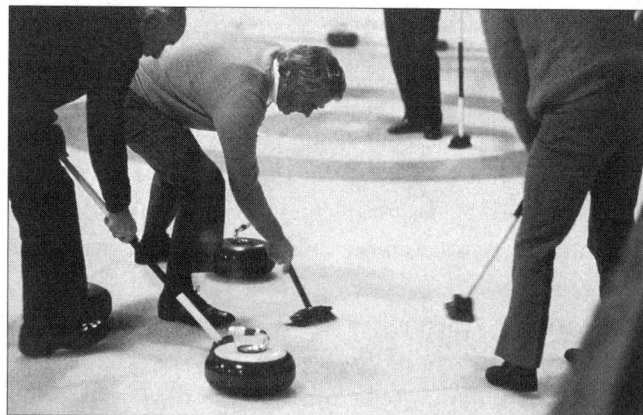

Curling players in Perth

stones over a sheet of ice towards a target or 'house', the object being to lay the stone as close to the centre as possible. With four players constituting a team, the stone is swept by two players directed by a 'skip', and the distinctive sound as it travels over the ice gives curling its nickname, 'the roaring game'. The Royal Caledonian Curling Club, founded as the 'Grand' Club in 1838, established itself as the ruling body, updating local rules and organizing national competitions. Outdoor curling, a feature of rural life in Scotland until the early 20th century, has been superseded by the modern indoor game on purpose-built rinks and is recognized as a major sport in many northern European countries and in North America.

FURTHER READING
ALBA; LOWLANDS; Kerr, *History of Curling*; Smith, *Curling*.

Jane George

Curling is a game played on ice and traditionally associated with Scotland (ALBA), but whose place and date of origin are uncertain. Visual evidence of games on ice appear in the 16th-century paintings of Pieter Breughel the Elder in Holland, and the terminology surrounding the game derives from the Continent. However, there can be no doubt that the game was nurtured, regulated and popularized in Lowland Scotland (see LOWLANDS) in the 19th century, and then exported to other countries. The game involves sliding

Cusantín mac Aeda (Constantine II), king of ALBA (900–43; †952), was the grandson of CINAED MAC AILPÍN. It is under Cusantín that the kingdom of the PICTS became the kingdom of Alba in contemporary annalistic records (see ANNALS). He inherited the beleaguered position of his predecessor and cousin DOMNALL MAC CUSANTÍN, during whose reign 'the Norse devastated Pictland'. In Cusantín's third year the Norse attacks began with raids on the royal city of Dunkeld (Dùn Chailleann) 'and all Alba', but in the following year he achieved a victory over them in

Strathearn. The year 906 saw the swearing of a compact, on the moot-hill at the royal monastery of Scone (Caiseal Creidhi), between Cusantín and his bishop, Cellach. The tone of this compact, as recorded in the CHRONICLE OF THE KINGS OF ALBA, is both self-consciously GAELIC, in keeping with the new Gaelic name of the Pictish kingdom, and redolent of the ideals of Christian kingship. In both the ritual and the renaming of the kingdom, scholars have begun to see in Cusantín 'the real father of the nation' (Woolf, *In Search of Scotland* 44). Cusantín has long been known to Anglo-Saxonists as the hoary-haired king of the SCOTS whose son died at the battle of Brunanburh in 937. This battle was a product of the king's multiple alliances, particularly with the king of York and Dublin/BAILE ÁTHA CLIATH, Ólafr Guthfrithsson (934–41). It brought him into conflict with the ascendant king in BRITAIN, ÆTHELSTAN of Wessex. Cusantín retired to the monastery of Cennrígmonaid (St Andrews) around 943, where he apparently became abbot of the Céili Dé community. A strange legend, however, has him coming out of retirement to lead a raid on the English instead of his successor, MAEL COLUIM MAC DOMNAILL. Both his long reign and aspects of his ecclesiastically-charged affairs speak of a lasting influence on the identity of the Gaelic kingdom of Alba.

FURTHER READING
ÆTHELSTAN; ALBA; ANNALS; BAILE ÁTHA CLIATH; BRITAIN; CHRONICLE OF THE KINGS OF ALBA; CINAED MAC AILPÍN; DOMNALL MAC CUSANTÍN; GAELIC; MAEL COLUIM MAC DOMNAILL; PICTS; SCOTS; Alan O. Anderson, *Early Sources of Scottish History AD 500–1286* 398–409, 425–51; Marjorie O. Anderson, *Kings and Kingship in Early Scotland* 251–2; Broun, *Spes Scotorum* 95–111; Hudson, *Kings of Celtic Scotland* 63–82; Hudson, *Scottish Historical Review* 77.129–61; Smyth, *Warlords and Holy Men* 197–210; Woolf, *In Search of Scotland* 42–5; Woolf, *Oxford Companion to Scottish History* 106.

Thomas Owen Clancy

Cusantín mac Cinaeda (Constantine I of Scotland), king of the PICTS (862–c. 876), was the son of CINAED MAC AILPÍN and the first of his generation to rule, succeeding his uncle, DOMNALL MAC AILPÍN. Cusantín's reign, like those of his contemporaries around Britain and Europe, saw a new vigour and purpose among Norse warlords, and east-central Scotland was battered several times during his

reign, with Ólafr and his army encamped in the heart of Pictland at one stage for three years. Cusantín seems to have slain Ólafr in 872 while the Norse king was collecting tribute from Pictland, no doubt continuing on from his sacking of Dumbarton Rock (Al Clut) and the subsequent ravaging of central Scotland. At this time Cusantín connived in the death of Arthgal map Dumnagual, king of the BRITONS OF YSTRAD CLUD, for reasons that we do not understand (Annals of Ulster 872). Attacks were renewed under Halfdan, and the battle of Dollar saw Cusantín defeated and the Norse once more occupying Pictland. There is some doubt about the date of Cusantín's death, whether it was 876 (Annals of Ulster 876) or 877 (see Duncan, *Kingship of the Scots 842–1292* 11); according to one kinglist, he died in Inverdovat, in Fife. His death appears to have unravelled the dynastic kingship for a time: his brother, Aed, was killed by allies after only a year, and Ciricius (Giric I), along with his foster-father EOCHAID SON OF RHUN, another grandson of Cinaed, seized the kingship for a decade, in a poorly understood interregnum. When contemporary ANNALS resume service for eastern Scotland upon the death in 900 of DOMNALL MAC CUSANTÍN, Cusantín's son, the kingdom he ruled was called ALBA (Annals of Ulster 900). With some justification, then, Cusantín and his brother Aed, although Gaels, may be seen as 'the last kings of the Picts' (Broun, *Oxford Companion to Scottish History* 106).

FURTHER READING
ALBA; ANNALS; BRITONS; CHRONICLE OF THE KINGS OF ALBA; CINAED MAC AILPÍN; DOMNALL MAC AILPÍN; DOMNALL MAC CUSANTÍN; EOCHAID SON OF RHUN; PICTS; YSTRAD CLUD; Alan O. Anderson, *Early Sources of Scottish History AD 500–1286* 1.296–312, 350–5; Marjorie O. Anderson, *Kings and Kingship in Early Scotland* 251–2; Broun, *Oxford Companion to Scottish History* 106; Broun, *Spes Scotorum* 95–111; Duncan, *Kingship of the Scots 842–1292* 11; Hudson, *Kings of Celtic Scotland* 49–54; Hudson, *Scottish Historical Review* 77.129–61; Mac Airt & Mac Niocaill, *Annals of Ulster (to A.D. 1131)* 866, 871, 872, 876; Miller, *Scottish Gaelic Studies* 19.241–5; Smyth, *Warlords and Holy Men* 197–210.

Thomas Owen Clancy

Cusantín mac Cuilén (Constantine III) was king of ALBA for a bare year and a half (995–7). Slain by his kinsmen and competitors, Cusantín was the last king of Alba from the dynastic segment descended from Aed mac Cinaeda mac Ailpín. His

death seems to have enabled a new family, the Clann Ruaidrí from whom Mac Bethad mac Findlaích was descended, to make claims to the kingship. His short reign helps to fix the date of a series of genealogies appended to Senchus Fer n-Alban as his genealogy, which takes his ancestry back to Cinaed mac Ailpín, and links this to the genealogies of the Cenél nGabráin (descendants of Aedán mac Gabráin). The decades of dynastic competition that preceded his reign may have given some urgency to the compilation of such genealogies.

FURTHER READING
Aedán mac Gabráin; Alba; Cinaed mac Ailpín; genealogies; Mac Bethad; Senchus Fer n-Alban; Alan O. Anderson, *Early Sources of Scottish History AD 500–1286* 517–18; Bannerman, *Studies in the History of Dalriada* 65–6; Hudson, *Kings of Celtic Scotland* 104–5; Woolf, *Scottish Historical Review* 79.145–64.

Thomas Owen Clancy

Custantin son of Uurguist (Cusantín mac Forgusa)

was king of the Picts *c.* 789–820. His reign has been championed in recent years as marking the zenith of Pictish power, a status partly owing to the recently discovered presence of his name (CUSTANTIN FILIUS FIRCUS) in an inscription on the magnificent and emblematic Dupplin cross (Forsyth, *From the Isles of the North* 237–44), from near the royal palace of Forteviot (Fothuir-tobaicht) in Strathearn. Until recently he was thought to have been of Gaelic descent, but this has been subject to reanalysis (Broun, *St Andrews Sarcophagus* 71–83). His family now emerges as a powerful and influential Pictish dynasty, perhaps related to kings earlier in the 8th century, whose lock on the kingship was only broken in the disastrous battle against the Norse in 839. Custantin's son, Domnall, would appear to have intruded into the kingship of Dál Riata for a time. It has also been argued (Clancy, *Scotland in Dark-Age Britain* 111–30) that Custantin was a patron of church reform. His connection with a Saint Constantine, found in contemporary Irish martyrologies, is uncertain (Dumville, *Scottish Gaelic Studies* 19.234–40), although one scribe plainly thought that it was the same person. His brother (Unuist), his son, and then his nephew succeeded him.

FURTHER READING
Constantine; Dál Riata; Gaelic; Picts; Unuist; Broun, *St*

Andrews Sarcophagus 71–83; Clancy, *Oxford Companion to Scottish History* 70; Clancy, *Scotland in Dark-Age Britain* 111–30; Dumville, *Scottish Gaelic Studies* 19.234–40; Forsyth, *From the Isles of the North* 237–44.

Thomas Owen Clancy

Cŵn Annwn

(the hounds of Annwn) is the Welsh name for the supernatural dogs documented in the folklore of all the Celtic countries. Spectral hounds fall into several categories: those identified primarily by sound are associated with the Wild Hunt, pursuing the souls of the dead across the sky. The sound of these hounds of hell has been identified with the call of the curlew or wild goose. Hearing or seeing them was an omen of ill luck or of death. The terrestrial hound was usually either a 'Barguest', a shape-changer that preferred a canine shape, or a 'black dog', usually pictured as a mastiff similar to a Newfoundland, but as large as a calf. The Scottish *cù sìth* (fairy hound) is dark green, the colour of the fairies, and the hounds of Arawn in Pwyll, if they are correctly identified as a type of 'black dog', were shining white with red ears, also otherworldly colours. The animals are sometimes headless or fire breathing. Although not exhaustively catalogued, they are associated with treasure in Ireland (Éire) and Brittany (Breizh), with standing stones in Wales (Cymru) and Cornwall (Kernow), and with other landmarks, such as the Moddey Dhoo (Black dog) of Peel Castle in Man (Ellan Vannin). They can function like the banshee (bean sí) in Cornish and Scottish tradition. They can also presage storms, as in Brittany, or mark the spot where a disaster occurred, as in Wheal Vor in Cornwall. Traditions vary as to whether black dogs are actively harmful, merely an omen of death, or benign. Other names for them are 'yell hounds' (Cornwall), *cŵn wybr* (sky hounds, Wales), *paotred* (boys or guys, Brittany). There is also a reference to *cŵn y nos* (dogs of the night) in the poetry of Dafydd ap Gwilym.

FURTHER READING
Annwn; Arawn; bean sí; Breizh; Celtic countries; Cymru; Dafydd ap Gwilym; Éire; Ellan Vannin; fairies; Kernow; Otherworld; Pwyll; Briggs, *British Folk-tales and Legends*; Briggs, *Dictionary of Fairies*; Brown, *Folklore* 69.175–92; Ford, *Mabinogi and Other Medieval Welsh Tales*; Palmer, *Folklore of (Old) Monmouthshire*; Palmer, *Folklore of Radnorshire*; Thompson, *Supernatural Highlands*.

AM

Cydymdeithas Amlyn ac Amig (The companionship of Amlyn and Amig) was a very popular tale throughout Europe in the Middle Ages. The Welsh version is contained in Oxford MS Jesus III (LLYFR COCH HERGEST 'The Red Book of Hergest'). There is also a copy of the 'Llyfr Coch' version in MS Llansteffan 148 or Shireburn D 3 in the hand of David Parry, *c.* 1697. The main theme of the story, which is common to all versions in various languages, is the remarkable friendship of two young men who are born on the same day and are so similar in appearance that it is difficult to distinguish one from the other. Their loyalty to each other forces them to make appalling choices, which cause them to deceive their feudal overlord, cheat in armed combat, kill a fellow courtier and commit the heinous crime of sacrificing two innocent children, so that one may be healed of his leprosy by being washed in their blood. In some versions of the tale they achieve martyrdom by fighting in a holy war.

The various texts of the Amlyn and Amig story are traditionally divided into two groups: the romantic and hagiographic, a distinction which is not entirely accurate, since there are Christian overtones in the so-called romance versions and residual pagan elements in the hagiographic. The oldest extant version is a Latin poem in hexameter verse composed *c.* 1090 by Radulphus Tortarius, a monk of Fleury, although the evidence of the opening lines suggests that the poet was versifying an international popular tale: *Historiam Gallus, breviter quam replico, novit, / Novit in extremo litore Saxo situs,* 'The Gaul knows the tale, which I am briefly telling, the Saxon in his remote shore knows it'. The immediate source of the hagiographic group is the 12th-century Latin prose tale *Vita Sanctorum Amici et Amelii carissimorum* (Kölbing, *Amis and Amiloun* xcvii–cx), but the more distant origins are rooted in folklore. Some of the hagiographic versions, including the Welsh, have an epilogue in which the two friends are killed in action, fighting on the side of Charlemagne against the king of Lombardy, who was in conflict with the Pope. They are buried in two separate churches in Mortara in northern Italy, but the following morning, the bodies are found lying side by side in the same tomb. It is thought that there was a tomb in the Church of St Albin in Mortara bearing the name *Aemelius*. This was then associated with the well-known tale of a man who was cured of his leprosy by being washed in the blood of his companion's children. The inscription *et Amicus*, 'and his friend', was added to the tomb, and Christianized elements were introduced into the original pagan tale, which was then used to entertain pilgrims and to advertise Mortara as a desirable stopping place on the way to Rome (Bédier, *Les légendes épiques* 181). The Welsh version is unique in using the order *Aemelius et Amicus (Amlyn ac Amic)*. The language and orthography suggest an early 14th-century date for the Welsh text; nevertheless, variations of style, syntax and orthography imply that the epilogue was composed by a different author from that of the main body of narrative. A Welsh analogue of the story is the 16th-century *Ystori Alexander a Lodwig* (Thomas Jones & Williams, SC 10/11.261–304). It also inspired Saunders Lewis to write his verse-play *Amlyn ac Amig* (1940), in which the premise that salvation may depend on committing a seemingly irrational and abhorrent act found a powerful expression.

PRIMARY SOURCES
MSS. Oxford, Jesus College III (LLYFR COCH HERGEST); Aberystwyth, NLW, Llansteffan 148 (Shireburn D 13).
ED. & TRANS. (into French) Gaidoz, RC 4.201–44.
EDITIONS. J. Gwenogvryn Evans, *Kymdeithas Amlyn ac Amic*; Jarman, *Chwedlau Cymraeg Canol* 136–41 (extract); Patricia Williams, *Kedymdeithyas Amlyn ac Amic*.

FURTHER READING
LEWIS; WELSH PROSE LITERATURE; Bédier, *Les légendes épiques*; Foster, *Amis and Amiloun*; Hemming, CMCS 32.57-94; Hofman, *Amis et Amiles und Jourdain de Blaivies*; Hume, *Journal of English and Germanic Philology* 69.89–107; Thomas Jones & Williams, SC 10/11.261–304; Kölbing, *Amis and Amiloun*; Kratins, PMLA 81.347–54; Leach, *Amis and Amiloun*; Poppe, BBCS 40.95–117; Patricia Williams, *Ysgrifau Beirniadol* 15.73–91.

Patricia Williams

Cyfarwydd is a Welsh term connected etymologically with 'knowledge', 'guidance', 'perception', as, for example, in Welsh *gwybod < gwydd-+bod* 'to know' and Old Irish *ro·fitir* 'knows', both from the PROTO-CELTIC root *wēd-/wid-* 'know, see' (cf. also DRUIDS; FEDELM). In the first attestation of the word in Old Welsh, its plural means specifically 'guides' with reference to traditional boundaries of a piece of land in a charter in the LICHFIELD GOSPELS: *imal-i tiduch cimarguithieit* 'as *cyfarwyddiaid* may lead you'. The *cyfarwydd* was therefore the 'guide', the 'well-informed person', the 'expert', and later the 'storyteller'. His relationship with the medieval poet is unclear. *Cyfarwyddyd*, meaning 'tale' or 'narrative', reflects the later semantic development of a noun which originally meant 'traditional lore' or 'traditional learning'. Two much-quoted sources suggest that poets would narrate *cyfarwyddyd* at court, and the term *cyfarwydd* (storyteller) may well be an occasional title that primarily denotes a function rather than a social or professional class. The storyteller is not listed among the 24 officers of the king's court in medieval Welsh LAW TEXTS, although the functions and status of the poet are described. Moreover, Welsh bardic TRIADS affirm a strong connection between poets and *cyfarwyddyd*, meaning traditional lore. We know little of the performance of the *cyfarwydd*—some sources suggest that he would narrate tales in the king's hall after a FEAST. His repertoire, together with the narrative techniques favoured by him, are reflected in the tales of the MABINOGI. According to GIRALDUS CAMBRENSIS in his DESCRIPTIO KAMBRIAE, one of the most famous storytellers of medieval Wales (CYMRU) was Bleddri.

FURTHER READING
CYMRU; DESCRIPTIO KAMBRIAE; DRUIDS; FEAST; FEDELM; GIRALDUS CAMBRENSIS; LAW TEXTS; LICHFIELD GOSPELS; MABINOGI; PROTO-CELTIC; TRIADS; Sioned Davies, *Crefft y Cyfarwydd*; Ford, SC 10/11.152–62; Mac Cana, *Learned Tales of Medieval Ireland*; Brynley F. Roberts, *Studies on Middle Welsh Literature*.

Sioned Davies

Cyfranc Lludd a Llefelys

Cyfranc Lludd a Llefelys (The adventure or encounter of Lludd and Llefelys) is a medieval Welsh prose tale (see WELSH PROSE LITERATURE) in which Lludd, king of BRITAIN, seeks the aid of his brother LLEFELYS, king of France, to rid his kingdom of three disastrous, supernatural 'oppressions' (Welsh *gormesoedd*; on the meaning of *gormes* and its etymology, see Sims-Williams, *History and Heroic Tale* 97–131). These *gormesoedd* are the race of CORANIAID, who can hear the slightest whisper and cannot, therefore, be overcome; a frightening cry every May Eve (*Calan Mai*; see CALENDAR), which makes all things and people barren; and the disappearance of prepared food and drink. Llefelys's cunning succeeds in overcoming all three. The cause of the cry is revealed as two DRAGONS fighting, and they are incarcerated in a stone chest (see DRAIG GOCH).

This episode, whether separately from the *Cyfranc* or not, is obviously related to the account in the 9th-century HISTORIA BRITTONUM §42 of the discovery of the beasts by GWRTHEYRN (Vortigern). The *Cyfranc* is an independent (incomplete) narrative in LLYFR GWYN RHYDDERCH ('The White Book of Rhydderch') and LLYFR COCH HERGEST ('The Red Book of Hergest'), but it first occurs as an insertion into a 13th-century Welsh translation of HISTORIA REGUM BRITANNIAE ('History of the Kings of Britain') of GEOFFREY OF MONMOUTH, where it is introduced as part of the stock in trade of the professional storyteller, the CYFARWYDD, and it is subsequently found in all later Welsh translations of the *Historia*. The context of the tale is the LEGENDARY HISTORY of Britain, and its origin is probably an account of successive mythological invaders, reflected in Triad 36 (see TRIADS; BROMWICH). It has also been interpreted as a triad of Dumézilian functions theorized as fundamental to inherited INDO-EUROPEAN social structure—the priestly or sovereignty function, physical force or the function of the warrior, fecundity and the food-producing function (on the mythological parallels, see further LLEFELYS; NŌDONS).

PRIMARY SOURCES
EDITIONS. Brynley F. Roberts, *Cyfranc Lludd a Llefelys*; Ifor Williams, *Cyfranc Ludd a Llevelys*.
TRANS. Ford, *Mabinogi*; Thomas Jones & Gwyn Jones, *Mabinogion*.

FURTHER READING
BRITAIN; BROMWICH; CALENDAR; CATH MAIGE TUIRED; CORANIAID; CYFARWYDD; DRAGONS; DRAIG GOCH; GEOFFREY OF MONMOUTH; GWRTHEYRN; HISTORIA BRITTONUM; HISTORIA REGUM BRITANNIAE; INDO-EUROPEAN; LEGENDARY HISTORY; LLEFELYS; LLYFR COCH HERGEST; LLYFR GWYN RHYDDERCH; NŌDONS; TRIADS; WELSH PROSE LITERATURE; Bromwich, TYP; Sims-Williams, *History and Heroic Tale* 97–131.

Brynley F. Roberts

Cymdeithas yr Iaith Gymraeg

Cymdeithas yr Iaith Gymraeg (The Welsh Language Society) was established as a direct action campaign group in 1962 with the objective of securing official status for WELSH on an equal footing with English in all spheres of public life in Wales (CYMRU). Its many achievements and the continuing influence of its policies in the wake of devolution (see CYNULLIAD CENEDLAETHOL CYMRU) make it one of the most successful language pressure groups in western Europe.

The Society was formed as a result of growing concerns about the spiralling decline of Welsh speakers since the Second World War and frustration with the apathy and inaction of the authorities to address the problem, as expressed in the celebrated radio lecture, TYNGED YR IAITH, by Saunders LEWIS. Disillusioned members of Plaid Cymru (The Party of Wales; see NATIONALISM) took up Lewis's challenge of organizing a campaign of civil disobedience on behalf of the language at the party's national conference in August 1962. Within months members of the new Society were deliberately breaking the law as a means of drawing attention to the inferior public status of Welsh.

The Society's principal method of campaigning was, and remains, non-violent direct action. The 1960s, an age of worldwide protest, provided abundant inspiration for civil disobedience in Wales. This direct action included protest marches, sit-ins, non-payment of various taxes and licences, and criminal damage. During the course of its campaign for bilingual road signs, hundreds of Society supporters set upon English-only signs, either painting them green or uprooting them completely. Supporters were prosecuted for various offences and many faced fines or imprisonment.

Despite the fact that the active membership base has been relatively limited (numbering no more than a few thousand even at its zenith in the 1970s), many of the Society's campaigns have attracted widespread popular support from disenchanted friends of the language, especially within the highly respected Welsh-speaking intelligentsia. It has received its most fervent support from students, with the result that the Society's membership has traditionally been young, well educated, and middle class. However, its choice of campaign methods and its irreverent disposition have not endeared the Society to all in Wales, with the result that official and public opinion towards the Society has frequently been unfavourable.

Policies quickly evolved from matters of language equality and increased public status for Welsh to encompass a wide range of issues, including EDUCATION, broadcasting, housing and planning policy, tourism, and economic development. The Society has developed an increasingly holistic approach to its interests, pursuing bold and radical policies to safeguard Welsh as a living community language. Despite unswerving opposition and disapproval from the establishment to its demands, many of the Society's policies have gradually been accepted as valuable contributions to the language debate. The Society has also been credited with wresting many concessions from successive governments of the United Kingdom in London, albeit grudgingly, including a plethora of official documents now available in Welsh; bilingual road signs; the Welsh-medium radio service (see MASS MEDIA) and the Welsh-medium television channel (see S4C); material status for Welsh in the land-use planning system; and two Welsh Language Acts (1967 and 1993) (see LANGUAGE [REVIVAL]).

PRIMARY SOURCE
LEWIS, TYNGED YR IAITH.

FURTHER READING
CYMRU; CYNULLIAD CENEDLAETHOL CYMRU; EDUCATION; LANGUAGE (REVIVAL); MASS MEDIA; NATIONALISM; S4C; WELSH; Cynog Davies, *Welsh Language Today* 266–86; Phillips, *Cof Cenedl* 13.165–95; Phillips, *Let's Do our Best for the Ancient Tongue* 463–90; Phillips, *Trwy Ddulliau Chwyldro*; Thomas, *Welsh Extremist*.

Dylan Phillips

Cymmrodorion, The Honourable Society of

Cymmrodorion, The Honourable Society of (lit. 'The society of the ancient or original inhabitants'; see below) was founded by Richard Morris (1703–79), who had settled in London (Welsh Llundain) as a jobbing clerk and accountant, aided by his home-keeping brothers, Lewis and William (see MORRISIAID MÔN). It was conceived as a patriotic and charitable association with the dedicated purpose of restoring the literary heritage of the nation. In the early years it took the form of a convivial club for gregarious exiles in the capital, with monthly meetings held in WELSH in a spirit of *undeb a brawdgarwch* (unity and fraternity). In what has been called the 'associational world' of early 18th-century London, the Society supplied the lack of any institution in or for Wales (CYMRU) that could salvage the cultural inheritance. Richard and William Morris were avid collectors of manuscripts, and their library of books was left to the Welsh School in London, where they remained until they were deposited in the British Museum in 1844.

In the second half of the 18th century the Cymmrodorion and the other London societies, the

Gwyneddigion (see EISTEDDFODAU'R GWYNEDD-IGION) and the Cymreigyddion, contributed substantially to the renaissance of Welsh learning and the Romantic revival. Membership of these societies was not mutually exclusive and many prominent literati, such as Owen Jones (Owain Myfyr, 1741–1814), co-editor of *The Myvyrian Archaiology of Wales*, and the polymath William Owen Pughe (1759–1835), belonged to more than one society. The more punctilious philologists and scholars of a later generation working in the same field came to regard the antiquarian theories and effusions of Pughe and Iolo Morganwg (Edward WILLIAMS) as charlatanry, but more recently historians have evaluated their contribution more generously. They are now seen as products of their age and circumstance who had a formative influence on the preservation and development of Welsh literary culture. The London Welsh societies were at first backward looking, although at the end of the century some of them tempered this conservatism with an active sympathy with the revolutionary movement in France. The Cymmrodorion were hostile to Methodism (see CHRISTIANITY), and therefore were not sympathetic to all developments in contemporary Wales, where the growth of Nonconformity led to a distancing from the influence of the degenerate life of the capital.

Richard Morris became president for life and ruled over the Society like a patriarch. He aimed to bridge social divisions in the cause of culture, so that the literati included the gentry of Wales and those professional men who had made distinguished careers in the capital. William Vaughan (1707–75) of Corsygedol, the first chief president (*penllywydd*), was succeeded by Sir Watkin Williams Wynn (1749–89), and then by the barrister Sir Watkin Lewes (1740–1821), Member of Parliament for the City of London and Lord Mayor in 1780. However, Morris's declared ambition to recruit 'all the aristocrats of Wales among us' was not completely fulfilled. His more scholarly brother Lewis proposed that the Society should found an academy, and his ambitious plans also included the establishment of a national library for Wales (see LLYFRGELL GENEDLAETHOL CYMRU). In its first phase (1751–87), the Society did not live up to this vision and it lapsed in 1785. Its collegiality had, however, anticipated the efforts at collaborative endeavour that were later to flourish within Wales.

A new chapter opened in the history of the London Welsh societies when the chapel took over from the tavern as the favoured place of meeting. The Welsh population of London was more representative of the homeland when the Cymmrodorion revived in 1820, largely at the initiative of *Yr Hen Bersoniaid Llengar* (The old literary clerics), as the sponsoring body of the eisteddfodau organized in Wales by the Cambrian Societies. The collaboration was soon undermined by disagreements over finance and different cultural values: the clerics distrusted the Anglicizing influence of the London Welshmen and their conception of the EISTEDD-FOD as an elaborate musical festival. The petition of the London Welshmen in 1829 against the proposal to discontinue the Courts of Great Sessions (a legal institution peculiar to Wales at the time) was organized by the Cymreigyddion. The petitioners did not succeed in dissuading Parliament from passing the act to abolish the courts in 1830, but the London Welsh societies helped to raise national consciousness about the identity of Wales as a distinct entity. Before being discontinued in 1843, the Cymmrodorion had an ambitious publishing programme and presented medals for poetry and prizes to pupils from Welsh grammar schools.

The Society was revived again in 1873 and has been in continuous existence ever since. Editions of historical texts and documents appeared as occasional publications in the Cymmrodorion Record Series from 1889, and the journal *Y Cymmrodor* was published regularly from 1877 to 1951. The *Bywgraffiadur* was published in 1953, followed by the English version, *The Dictionary of Welsh Biography down to 1940*, in 1959, under the joint editorship of Sir John Edward LLOYD and R. T. Jenkins, and *Atodiadau/Supplements* in Welsh and English have been printed subsequently. The *Transactions*, containing the texts of lectures delivered to the Society as well as commissioned and refereed articles, have appeared annually without interruption since 1893. The present Honorary Editor is Dr Peter R. Roberts.

In its modern phase the Society has continued to fulfil an enabling function in the promotion of Welsh causes in public affairs. Its initiatives in advancing educational reform led eventually to the founding of a university college for Wales at ABERYSTWYTH in 1872 and the passing of the Intermediate Education Act of 1889. In 1880 the National Eisteddfod Association was formed under its aegis (see EISTEDDFOD GENEDlaethol cymru). On the bicentenary of its foundation in 1951 it received a royal charter 'for the encouragement of Literature, Science and Art as connected with Wales'. The Society continues to act as a corporate sponsor of the arts, culture, and scholarship, and it has not outlived its usefulness in this rôle despite the growth of national institutions in Wales and a capital at Cardiff (Caerdydd). In 2001 it celebrated the 250th anniversary of its foundation in good health. By 1778 the membership totalled 228, with 136 'corresponding members' in Wales itself. For many years the members living in Wales have far outnumbered those resident in England, and yet the ambivalent reputation of élitism which the Cymmrodorion acquired in its early years as a body of the London Welsh has not been entirely lost to this day among some of their compatriots.

The word cymrodorion ('aborigines', singular cymrodor) is first attested in the 17th century. It is a compound of the word brodorion (singular brodor), which appears in the sense of 'natives' also for the first time in the modern period. Previously, brodorion had occurred in dialect as a plural of brawd 'brother'. In cymrodorion the compounding preposition cyf-, which usually means 'with', is felt as having the force of cyn- 'before, previous'. The double -mm- of Cymmrodorion was standard Welsh spelling before the 20th-century reforms (see further GPC, s.v. cymrodor).

FURTHER READING
Aberystwyth; Caerdydd; Christianity; Cymru; Eisteddfod; Eisteddfod Genedlaethol Cymru; Eisteddfodau'r Gwyneddigion; Lloyd; Llyfrgell Genedlaethol Cymru; Morrisiaid Môn; Welsh; Williams; Jenkins & Ramage, History of the Honourable Society of Cymmrodorion; Emrys Jones, Welsh in London; Lloyd & Jenkins, Dictionary of Welsh Biography Down to 1940.
CONTACT DETAILS. 30 Eastcastle Street, London W1N 7PD.

Peter R. Roberts

Cymru (Wales)

Cymru (Wales) is one of the six regions in which a Celtic language was spoken in modern times (see Ellan Vannin; Kernow) or is spoken to this day (see Alba; Breizh; Éire). Its eastern border with England roughly follows the 8th-century linear earthwork of Offa's Dyke (Clawdd Offa) from the mouth of the river Dee in the north to the Severn estuary in the south. To the north-west, west, and south the country is bounded by Liverpool Bay, the Irish Sea and the Bristol Channel. Its landmass covers 8015 square miles (20,758 km²). At the time of the latest census (2001) Wales counted 2,903,085 residents, represented in the British Parliament at Westminster by 40 Members of Parliament. The thirteen historic counties of Wales have twice been reorganized (in 1974 and 1996), and Wales is now subdivided into twelve counties and ten county boroughs, with its capital in Cardiff (Caerdydd). With the establishment of the National Assembly for Wales (Cynulliad Cenedlaethol Cymru) in 1999, Wales has gained a level of devolved political status within the United Kingdom (see nationalism; scottish parliament).

§1. WALES AND THE WELSH LANGUAGE

Due to its early incorporation into the English state and the resulting absence of national institutions, the native Celtic language assumed prime importance as the main national symbol in the 19th century. Welsh (Cymraeg) was spoken by 575,604 people (20.5% of the population) at the 2001 census, an increase of nearly 2% from the 508,098 speakers counted in 1991. Although this increase may partly be due to a rise in status, which made it desirable to claim knowledge of the language, it is still of huge symbolic importance since it represents the first increase in the total number of speakers for over a hundred years. The highest percentage of Welsh speakers within the population is found in the areas of the Welsh heartland (Y Fro Gymraeg) in the west and north of the country, but the highest numbers of speakers per square mile are found in the urban conurbations of south and north-east Wales. Unlike the other Celtic languages (with the exception, perhaps, of Breton), Welsh has succeeded in developing an urban base: it boasts a lively rock and pop scene and a film and television industry unmatched by most of the lesser-used languages of Europe (see welsh music; s4c; mass media). Its literary scene is vibrant (see welsh poetry; welsh prose literature). The main national festival, Eisteddfod Genedlaethol Cymru, held during the first week of August, attracts up to 200,000 people annually.

§2. EARLY HISTORY

Though there can be no absolute certainty about the distribution of languages in prehistoric times, it is

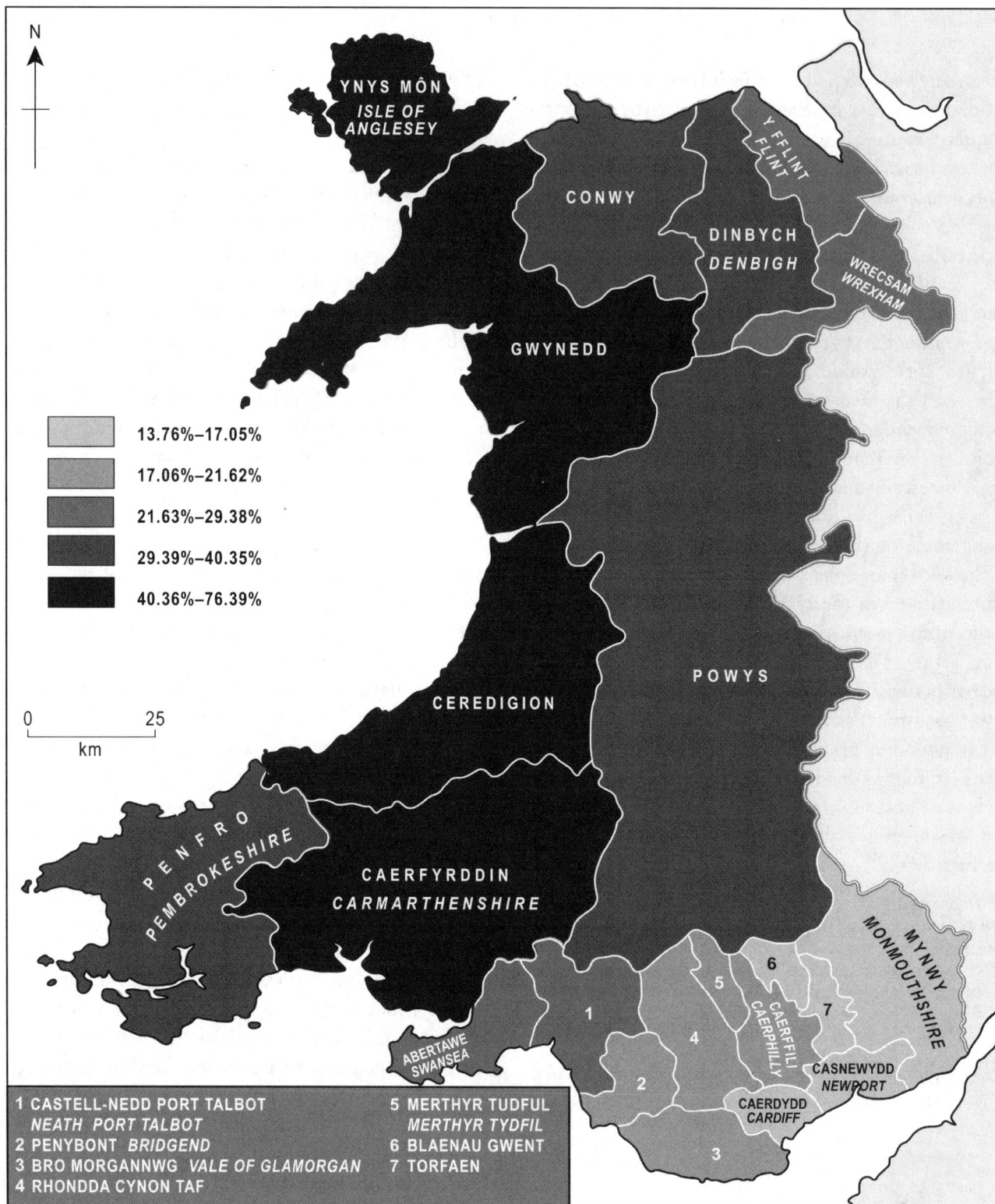

N

YNYS MÔN
ISLE OF ANGLESEY

CONWY

Y FFLINT
FLINT

DINBYCH
DENBIGH

WRECSAM
WREXHAM

GWYNEDD

13.76%–17.05%

17.06%–21.62%

21.63%–29.38%

29.39%–40.35%

40.36%–76.39%

POWYS

0   25
km

CEREDIGION

PENFRO
PEMBROKESHIRE

CAERFYRDDIN
CARMARTHENSHIRE

MYNWY
MONMOUTHSHIRE

6

5

CAERFFILI
CAERPHILLY

7

1

ABERTAWE
SWANSEA

4

CASNEWYDD
NEWPORT

2

CAERDYDD
CARDIFF

3

1 CASTELL-NEDD PORT TALBOT
  NEATH PORT TALBOT
2 PENYBONT *BRIDGEND*
3 BRO MORGANNWG *VALE OF GLAMORGAN*
4 RHONDDA CYNON TAF

5 MERTHYR TUDFUL
  MERTHYR TYDFIL
6 BLAENAU GWENT
7 TORFAEN

Contemporary Cymru/Wales: post-1996 counties and the Welsh language in the 2001 census. Percentages signify population over the age of 3 with one or more of the following skills: understanding spoken Welsh, speaking Welsh, reading Welsh, writing Welsh.

likely that Celtic-speaking groups were established in the area which was to become Wales as early as the Late Bronze Age (see LLYN FAWR). They entered history with the Roman conquest of parts of BRITAIN beginning in AD 43 and TACITUS's graphic description of the resistance which the Romans encountered. Within a a few years, the Romans were fighting in what is now Wales, facing the resistance spearheaded by CARATĀCOS (see also BOUDĪCA; CASSIVELLAUNOS; CUNOBELINOS; DRUIDS; MÔN). By the end of the 1st century, the tribes of Wales—the Deceangli, Demetae (see DYFED), Ordovices, and Silures—had been pacified, and Roman control was established within a quadrangle of major forts at Deva (see CAER) in the northeast, SEGONTIUM in the north-west, Moridūnum (see CAERFYRDDIN) in the south-west and Isca (CAERLLION) in the south-east. The period following the collapse of Roman power in Britain in AD 409/10 was marked by the rise of regional kingdoms (see ABERFFRAW; CERETIC; CUNEDDA; DEHEUBARTH; GWYNEDD; MATHRAFAL; POWYS) and the (re-)establishment of Christianity during the 'Age of Saints' in the 5th and 6th centuries (see HAGIOGRAPHY and saints' names). However, only a few rulers succeeded in uniting the country under a common overlord (cf. GRUFFUDD AP CYNAN; RHODRI MAWR), though there was a common legal and administrative system (see CANTREF; HYWEL DDA; LAW TEXTS). In the century following the Norman Conquest of England from 1066, Norman lordships penetrated most of south and west Wales; these areas and the parts of England nearest Wales became known as *Marcia Wallie* (the March of Wales). The last surviving Welsh kingdom, consisting of Gwynedd, Powys, and Deheubarth and recognized by Henry III in 1267, was bloodily subdued by Edward I in 1282, and LLYWELYN AP GRUFFUDD, the last 'Prince of Wales', was killed. Edward settled the question of Wales with the Statute of RHUDDLAN (1284) and an extensive programme of castle building. In 1301 he declared his first-born son, Edward II, Prince of Wales. Henceforth, the English king's first-born has assumed this title. A final nationwide rebellion against English rule (1400–15), mounted by OWAIN GLYNDŴR, proved unsuccessful. The ACTS OF UNION (1536–43) of Henry VIII made Wales an integral part of the emerging English central state, conferring upon Welshmen the same political rights as their English neighbours and evening out the

patchwork of native and Anglo-Norman administrative and legal practices that had arisen in post-conquest Wales. But Union was achieved with disregard of Welsh cultural identity, particularly in the linguistic sphere, declaring English the official language at a time when the BARDIC ORDER was in decline and the Welsh language in danger of disintegrating into a spectrum of dialects. It is thanks to the BIBLE translations that a new literary standard was created. From the mid-16th century, Welsh was the language of religion within the established Church and from the 17th century also the emerging Dissenting chapels (see CHRISTIANITY). Unlike Catholicism, they stressed the importance of individual study of the scripture, with the result that a much higher literacy rate existed within the population of Wales than was usual in late 18th-century Europe (see CIRCULATING SCHOOLS; HYMNS).

§3. INDUSTRIAL AND POST-INDUSTRIAL WALES
From *c.* 1770 onwards Wales experienced unparalleled demographic and industrial changes. Large numbers migrated from the rural areas into the coalfields of the south and north-east, taking their language and traditions with them to create vibrant urban, Welsh-speaking communities. A golden age of Welsh publishing ensued. However, from the 1880s, immigrants from England by far outnumbered those from Wales itself. Coupled with a hostile state EDUCATION system from 1870, the linguistic Anglicization of the industrial areas was speedy (see LANGUAGE [REVIVAL]). Welsh was increasingly seen as the language of rural life, confined to the western and northern areas and a marker of low social status. But the 19th century also saw the rise of NATIONALISM (see also CYMRU FYDD; ELLIS) and national institutions such as EISTEDDFOD GENEDLAETHOL CYMRU and GORSEDD BEIRDD YNYS PRYDAIN, as well as the emergence of political giants such as David LLOYD GEORGE. By the beginning of the 20th century a national library and museum had been founded (see AMGUEDDFEYDD; LLYFRGELL GENEDLAETHOL CYMRU). The south Wales valleys developed a strong tradition of political radicalism which still holds true.

Following the First World War, the Welsh economy all but collapsed with the decreasing demand for the coal and iron on whose export it had been so highly dependent. High unemployment well into the 1930s meant high rates of EMIGRATION, especially from the industrialized areas. Rural areas, though traditionally among the poorest in the United Kingdom, benefited from government subsidies. The Welsh economy only partly recovered after the Second World War, concentrating on low-skill high-technology jobs in the former coal and iron areas. The country still has a larger than average proportion of the population employed in agriculture, with sheep and cattle rearing dominant. Large stretches of mountain lands have been given over to timber production. Rural and coastal areas of Wales increasingly exploit their beauty and Celtic connections in order to promote tourism.

MBL

§4. THE NAME

Cymru 'Wales' is a modern respelling of *Cymry* 'Welsh people', plural of *Cymro* 'Welshman'. Middle Welsh *Kym(m)ry* had regularly meant both the people and the country. Etymologically, *Cymry* means people of the same *bro*, the latter signifying a compact home region; in BRETON, on much the same scale, *bro* means diocese. In an older Celtic sense, it is **kom- + mrugi-* 'persons within common borders'; cf. Old Irish *mruig* 'border'. The term *Cymry* first surfaces in MOLIANT CADWALLON, a poem set about 632/4 and addressed to the king of GWYNEDD. From this time onwards, the name *Cymry* gained ground at the expense of the term *Brython* 'BRITONS'. The corresponding language name *Cymraeg* is not attested as early as *Cymry*, but it does scan in early poetry in its trisyllabic Old Welsh form *Kymrä|ec* and is reflected in an Old IRISH loan-word *Combrēc*, found in the glossary of CORMAC UA CUILEANNÁIN and other early Irish glossaries. By the time the term *Cymry* had gained currency Anglo-Saxon rulers had already gained political control over most of the people and productive land of Britain. In the shift from the term *Brython* to *Cymry* it is not hard to see a new self-conscious minority status, a people made newly aware by changed reality that the limits of their ethnolinguistic group were no longer the seas encircling *Britannia* or *Ynys Prydein* 'Britain' (Charles-Edwards, *Celtic World* 703–36). That the cognate of *Cymry* has little or no currency in CORNISH and Breton strongly suggests that the term first arose after contact across the Severn Estuary had fallen off precipitously.

Wales. Old English *Wealas* 'Wales, the Welsh' has a general sense of 'foreigners', and was applied by Germanic peoples to ROMANO-CELTIC peoples of the former Roman Empire. Thus, German *Welsch* may signify French or Italian. The Germanic term seems to have been originally borrowed from the Celtic tribal name *Volcae*, a powerful group with branches in both southern GAUL and central Europe (where they would have had early contacts with Germanic groups). Celtic *Volcae* had meant 'beasts of prey, wolves' and probably also 'hawks', cf. Welsh *gwalch* (Jenkins, CMCS 19.55–67).

JTK

FURTHER READING
ABERFFRAW; ACTS OF UNION; ALBA; AMGUEDDFEYDD; BARDIC ORDER; BIBLE; BOUDĪCA; BREIZH; BRETON; BRITAIN; BRITONS; CAER; CAERDYDD; CAERFYRDDIN; CAERLLION; CANTREF; CARATĀCOS; CASSIVELLAUNOS; CERETIC; CHRISTIANITY; CIRCULATING SCHOOLS; CLAWDD OFFA; CORMAC UA CUILEANNÁIN; CORNISH; CUNEDDA; CUNOBELINOS; CYMRU FYDD; CYNULLIAD CENEDLAETHOL CYMRU; DEHEUBARTH; DRUIDS; DYFED; EDUCATION; ÉIRE; EISTEDDFOD GENEDLAETHOL CYMRU; ELLAN VANNIN; ELLIS; EMIGRATION; GAUL; GORSEDD BEIRDD YNYS PRYDAIN; GRUFFUDD AP CYNAN; GWYNEDD; HAGIOGRAPHY; HYMNS; HYWEL DDA; IRISH; KERNOW; LANGUAGE (REVIVAL); LAW TEXTS; LLOYD GEORGE; LLYFRGELL GENEDLAETHOL CYMRU; LLYN FAWR; LLYWELYN AP GRUFFUDD; MASS MEDIA; MATHRAFAL; MOLIANT CADWALLON; MÔN; NATIONALISM; ORDOVICES; OWAIN GLYNDŴR; POWYS; RHODRI MAWR; RHUDDLAN; ROMANO-CELTIC; S4C; SCOTTISH PARLIAMENT; SEGONTIUM; TACITUS; WELSH; WELSH MUSIC; WELSH POETRY; WELSH PROSE LITERATURE; Carter & Aitchison, *Geography of the Welsh Language*; Carter & Griffiths, *National Atlas of Wales*; Charles-Edwards, *Celtic World* 703–36; John Davies, *History of Wales*; R. R. Davies, *Age of Conquest 1063–1415*; D. Gareth Evans, *History of Wales 1815–1906*; Hume & Pryce, *Welsh and their Country*; Jenkins, CMCS 19.55–67; Jenkins, *Foundations of Modern Wales*; Jenkins, *Social History of the Welsh Language*; Beti Jones, *Etholiadau'r Ganrif / Welsh Elections 1885–1997*; Morgan, *Rebirth of a Nation*; Glanmor Williams, *Recovery, Reorientation and Reformation*; Gwyn A. Williams, *When Was Wales?*

Cymru Fydd was a patriotic movement, literally 'Wales will be' but known in English as Young Wales. It was formed in London (Welsh Llundain) in 1886, primarily by emigré Welshmen, on the model of Young Ireland, its programme appearing as 'a manifesto against old age'. It conceived its nationalist mission in terms of a native cultural and linguistic tradition, and consisted mainly of the Welsh intelligentsia. Its most prominent members included medieval historian John Edward LLOYD, Oxford don and littérateur Owen M. EDWARDS, journalist Thomas Edward ELLIS (who became Liberal Member of Parliament for his native

Merioneth in 1886), and barrister W. Llewelyn Williams. The latter asserted that the Cymru Fydd movement was concerned with 'true politics'.

The second branch of the society was formed, significantly, at Liverpool (Welsh Lerpwl), but the movement was notably slow to put down roots in Wales (CYMRU) itself; the branch established at Barry in 1891 was the first of its kind in south Wales. Thereafter, branches were set up in many parts of Wales, often closely linked with the traditional organization and personnel of the Liberal Party and the Nonconformist denominations (see CHRISTIANITY). The movement had published its own journal, *Cymru Fydd*, since January 1888, and won the backing of the Welsh popular press, particularly of the veteran Thomas Gee in *Y Faner* (The banner) and of the youthful David LLOYD GEORGE, elected Member of Parliament for the Caernarfon Boroughs in April 1890. Initially a cultural and educational movement, Cymru Fydd became, under the influence of T. E. Ellis and Lloyd George, a political campaign, with Ellis underlining 'the necessity of declaring for self-government'. Home rule thus became central to the Cymru Fydd programme, while Michael D. Jones and others even intended it to oust the Liberal Party and become an independent Welsh national party (see NATIONALISM).

The impact of the Cymru Fydd movement became apparent in the appointment of the Royal Commission on Land in Wales in 1892, the grant of a royal charter to a federal University of Wales in 1893, and the introduction of a succession of measures embodying the disestablishment of the Church in Wales (the denomination corresponding to the Church of England). But attempts to create a practical organization showed a distinct lack of direction. The efforts of its secretary, Beriah Gwynfe Evans, proved woefully inadequate. The movement was dealt a harsh blow in 1892 when T. E. Ellis accepted the position of junior whip in the parliament of Prime Minister Gladstone's fourth Westminster administration. From 1894 onwards it declined in the wake of Lloyd George's attempt to take over Cymru Fydd and fuse it with the Liberal Federations of North and South Wales. In August 1894 a meeting was convened at Llandrindod (Radnorshire / sir Faesyfed, now POWYS) to frame the constitution of a national Cymru Fydd league. William Jones, MP (Caernarfonshire / sir Gaernarfon), and John Herbert Lewis, MP (Flintshire/sir y Fflint), spearheaded the campaign at Westminster and throughout Wales, and a new nationalist journal—*Young Wales*—was launched in January 1895.

The agitation came to a head at the famous Newport (Casnewydd) meeting of January 1896, when a motion to unite the Liberal Federations of North and South Wales, proposed by the poet H. Elvet Lewis, was heavily defeated. At the root of the dissension was a glaring clash of interest between delegates representing the Anglicized southern ports of Cardiff (CAERDYDD), Newport, and Barry, and representatives of the remainder of Wales. In reality, many Liberals were indifferent to the national problems of Wales, with the possible exception of disestablishment of the Church.

Although Cymru Fydd branches survived in some towns and cities until the Second World War, after 1896 the ideal of Cymru Fydd was largely moribund—it became the victim of deep-rooted regional hostility and never succeeded in establishing a broad popular base. The skeleton of a Welsh National Federation survived the 1896 debâcle, but during the early and mid-20th century most Welsh politicians looked for success within the British political system. Welsh sectional, regional, linguistic, and class antagonisms lessened the appeal of a national political autonomy for Wales.

FURTHER READING
CAERDYDD; CHRISTIANITY; CYMRU; EDWARDS; ELLIS; LLOYD; LLOYD GEORGE; NATIONALISM; POWYS; George, *Cymru Fydd*; J. Graham Jones, NLWJ 29.435–53; Morgan, *Re-birth of a Nation*; Morgan, *Wales in British Politics*; Price, *Lloyd George*.
                                                    J. Graham Jones

Cynddelw Brydydd Mawr (*fl. c.* 1155–*c.* 1195)
is by far the most prolific of the Welsh court poets (GOGYNFEIRDD) whose work has survived: 3847 lines of his poetry have been preserved in 48 poems. He sang to the most important princes and noblemen of his age, most notably Madog ap Maredudd, prince of POWYS (†1160), OWAIN GWYNEDD (†1170), Owain Cyfeiliog (†1197), Lord RHYS AP GRUFFUDD of DEHEUBARTH (†1197) and, possibly, Llywelyn the Great (LLYWELYN AB IORWERTH, †1240).

Cynddelw was one of the most skilled and learned poets of this period. His poems contain a wealth of references to characters and incidents in Welsh history, mythology, the TRIADS, various story cycles such as the MABINOGI, and legends associated with ARTHUR and Merlin (MYRDDIN). Linguistically, he was extremely accomplished: he had a thorough command of the WELSH language and the intricacies of its sentence structure, and enjoyed playing with the meaning of words and their phonology. He also knew when to exercise restraint, and some of his most effective lines are very simple and direct, but often tinged with irony. After praising HYWEL AB OWAIN GWYNEDD for his prowess and cruelty on the battlefield, he states simply: *Calanmai celennig i frain* (On the calends of May, a gift for ravens). By referring to the enemy's corpses as a calends gift for the ravens, Cynddelw alludes to the patron's custom of bestowing gifts upon his poet on the calends of May.

His repertory was vast. As well as traditional eulogy and elegy to individuals sung on ENGLYN and AWDL metres, he praised retinues, sang two love poems, a long ode in praise of the monastery of MEIFOD and its patron saint, TYSILIO, two poems addressing the Godhead, a deathbed poem, appeasement poems, poems of thanks, personal *englynion* eulogizing the death of his son, Dygynnelw, an *englyn* to a monk from Strata Marcella (YSTRAD MARCHELL) who refused his request to be buried there, and also, possibly, an eulogy for his own cockerel.

His work is preserved in four medieval Welsh manuscripts: the Black Book of Carmarthen (LLYFR DU CAERFYRDDIN), the HENDREGADREDD MANUSCRIPT, NLW Peniarth 3 (see HENGWRT) and the Red Book of Hergest (LLYFR COCH HERGEST). Some poems have also been preserved in NLW 4973 in the 17th-century hand of Dr John Davies, Mallwyd; the medieval source for some of the poems in this early modern manuscript has been lost.

Little is known of Cynddelw's background. The epithet 'Prydydd Mawr' (great poet), which also occurs in the name of the 14th-century poet Trahaearn Brydydd Mawr, has generally been taken to refer to Cynddelw's poetic genius, but it could also refer to his physique. The 16th-century poet Wiliam Llŷn claimed that Cynddelw hailed from the commote (see CANTREF) of Mechain in Powys, and this would tie in with the fact that his earliest poems were addressed to Madog ap Maredudd of Powys and his family, and also with

the fact that he maintained his connection with Powys throughout his career. Unlike many of his contemporaries, it is probable that Cynddelw did not descend from a family of poets; his contemporary SEISYLL BRYFFWRCH reminds him of this in a poem which is preserved in the Hendregadredd Manuscript and which claims to be an *ymryson* (see YMRYSONAU) between the two for the *penceirddiaeth* (master-bardship; see BARDIC ORDER) of Madog ap Maredudd's court.

When Madog ap Maredudd died in 1160 it is presumed that Cynddelw became *pencerdd* (master-bard) of his chosen heir, Llywelyn, who was killed later in the same year. Powys was placed in a precarious situation, without a clear leader and with the *membra regis* vying against each other for supremacy, and it is possible that, during this unstable period, Cynddelw cast his lot with Owain Fychan, to whom he addressed a highly skilled ode echoing his elegy to Owain's father, Madog, in 1160. A short time later, however, it appears that he had moved north to GWYNEDD and associated himself with the powerful Owain Gwynedd, whose praises he sang until the death of his patron in 1170. In these poems, Cynddelw emphasizes Owain's superiority as ruler of his kingdom and as an effective battle leader. He was succeeded by his eldest son and heir, Hywel ab Owain Gwynedd, and it is assumed that Cynddelw became *pencerdd* to him upon his father's death. Cynddelw's longest poem—in which he refers to his patron as *brenin* and *rhi* (both words meaning 'king') and affirms his own exalted status as his poet—was addressed to Hywel. Later in 1170, however, Hywel was slain during a battle at Pentraeth, Anglesey (MÔN), by his half-brother, Dafydd, leaving Cynddelw bereft of his patron. Rather than remaining in Gwynedd and seeking the patronage of Dafydd and his brother Rhodri, he appears to have returned to Powys, where he composed an elegy upon the death of Iorwerth Goch, Madog ap Maredudd's half brother, in 1172. In 1179 Cynddelw sang a long and powerful elegy to Cadwallon ap Madog ab Idnerth of Maelienydd in southern Powys, the husband of Efa, daughter of Madog ap Maredudd. In 1187 Cynddelw mourned the killing of his former patron, Owain Fychan son of Madog ap Maredudd. During these years Cynddelw also praised Owain Cyfeiliog and his son, Gwenwynwyn. By the early 1190s, however, he was almost certainly in Deheubarth, singing the praises of Lord Rhys ap Gruffudd, but since no elegy by him has survived to either Lord Rhys or Owain Cyfeiliog, both of whom died in 1197, it is presumed that he predeceased them both.

PRIMARY SOURCES
MSS. Aberystwyth, NLW 4973, 6680 (HENDREGADREDD MANUSCRIPT), Peniarth 1 (LLYFR DU CAERFYRDDIN), Peniarth 3; Oxford, Jesus College 111 (LLYFR COCH HERGEST). EDITION. Nerys Ann Jones & Parry Owen, Gwaith Cynddelw Brydydd Mawr I & II.

FURTHER READING
ARTHUR; AWDL; BARDIC ORDER; CANTREF; DEHEUBARTH; ENGLYN; GOGYNFEIRDD; GWYNEDD; HENGWRT; HYWEL AB OWAIN GWYNEDD; LLYWELYN AB IORWERTH; MABINOGI; MEIFOD; MÔN; MYRDDIN; OWAIN GWYNEDD; POWYS; RHYS AP GRUFFUDD; SEISYLL BRYFFWRCH; TRIADS; TYSILIO; WELSH; YMRYSONAU; YSTRAD MARCHELL; Andrews, Llên Cymru 24.52–60; Charles-Edwards & Jones, Welsh King and his Court 191–221; Nerys Ann Jones, Ysgrifau Beirniadol 14.47–55; Nerys Ann Jones, Ysgrifau Beirniadol 20.90–107; Lloyd, BBCS 6.118–30; Lloyd, BBCS 7.16–23; Lloyd, ÉC 5.87–104; Lloyd, Llenor 11.172–87, 13.49–59; Parry Owen, Beirdd a Thywysogion 143–65; Parry Owen, Ysgrifau Beirniadol 14.56–86; Parry Owen, Ysgrifau Beirniadol 18.73–99; J. E. Caerwyn Williams, Court Poet in Medieval Wales esp. 140–64; J. E. Caerwyn Williams, Llên Cymru 11.3–94.

Ann Parry Owen

Cynddylan fab Cyndrwyn

(? †15 November 655) was a Welsh chieftain who is known to us primarily from two substantial pieces of early poetry: (1) MARWNAD CYNDDYLAN, a 71-line AWDL on his death addressed to an unnamed king of GWYNEDD at ABERFFRAW, whose attitude is that of a contemporary court poem and is widely accepted as authentic; (2) the 113 ENGLYNION of Canu Heledd (Poetry of HELEDD), whose attitude is also contemporary, but the dramatic persona is not that of a court poet, but rather Cynddylan's bereaved sister Heledd, wandering alone through the deserted ruins of the war-ravaged kingdom. This ENGLYN cycle is usually assigned to the 9th or 10th century.

Some details of the historical context can be gleaned from these poems. Both Marwnad Cynddylan and Canu Heledd refer to a place called Tren, probably the river Tern in central Shropshire (Welsh swydd Amwythig). A stray englyn from Canu Heledd states that Cynddylan was part of the coalition headed by PENDA at the battle of Cogwy or Maserfelth, where OSWALD of Northumbria was slain on 5 August 642 (BEDA, Historia Ecclesiastica 3.9). The site of this battle was most probably near Oswestry in Shropshire, where Oswald was killed

and crucified on 'Oswald's tree' (Welsh Croesoswallt). According to Marwnad Cynddylan, the hero answered the call to arms of mab Pyd, which refers to Panna son of Pyd, the latter being the Welsh name for Penda of Mercia, who is known to have had Welsh allies when he fought against the Northumbrians in the mid-7th century. Marwnad Cynddylan mentions a 'fight for the cattle (or the spoils) of Pennawg', which may refer to an attack known to have been made by Penda of Mercia and Welsh allies on the Northumbrian court at Bamburgh c. 650. The Marwnad describes a major, otherwise unknown, battle at Caerlwytgoed, the Roman fortified town of Lētocētum at Lichfield, Staffordshire. Canu Heledd describes desolation in several places for which probable locations can be found in Shropshire: including Pengwern (probably in Shrewsbury), Eglwysseu Bassa (Baschurch), Dinlleu Vreconn (the hill-fort of the Wrekin near Wroxeter), Romano-British Vriconium, and Ercal (High Ercall or Child's Ercall). There is some question as to whether these places represent a continuous recollection of the old pre-Anglo-Saxon landscape of what became western Mercia, or a later Brythonicizing of an already English countryside, in effect creative historical fiction. For example, Baschurch seems to be a purely English name and Eglwysseu Bassa a Welsh translation. Of course, it is possible that Cynddylan had ruled a linguistically mixed country in the 7th-century, including a community of Anglo-Saxon Christians.

Marwnad Cynddylan and Canu Heledd agree in portraying a military disaster in which Cynddylan fell, along with numerous noble kinsmen and comrades. The event itself is most plausibly identified with the battle of Winwæd, where Penda and all his many allies—called duces regii (royal generals) by Beda (Historia Ecclesiastica 3.27) and reges Brittonum (kings of the BRITONS) in HISTORIA BRITTONUM (§§64–5)—fell in battle against OSWYDD of Northumbria on 15 November 655. In the englynion, Cynddylan is once identified as ruler of POWYS. The royal lineage known as the Cyndrwynyn (progeny of Cynddylan's father, Cyndrwyn) do not seem to have survived into the 9th century, at which time Historia Brittonum (§§32–5) identified the kings of Powys as CADELLING, and ELISEG'S PILLAR traces the same group back to GWRTHEYRN. Marwnad Cynddylan mentions the Cadelling twice, viewing them with hostility, as if they were rivals.

FURTHER READING
ABERFFRAW; AWDL; BEDA; BRITONS; CADELLING; ELISEG'S
PILLAR; ENGLYN; ENGLYNION; GWRTHEYRN; GWYNEDD;
HELEDD; HISTORIA BRITTONUM; MARWNAD CYNDDYLAN;
OSWALD; OSWYDD; PENDA; POWYS; Bartrum, *Welsh Classical
Dictionary* 169–71; Wendy Davies, *Wales in the Early Middle Ages*;
Rowland, *Early Welsh Saga Poetry*; Stancliffe, *Oswald* 84–96;
Ifor Williams, *Canu Llywarch Hen*.

JTK

Cynfeirdd (sing. *cynfardd*) is a WELSH term usually translated as 'first poets' or 'early poets'. It is a modern coining and is first attested with *Y Kynveirdh Kymreig* (the Welsh *Cynfeirdd*) of the antiquarian Robert VAUGHAN of Hengwrt (1592?–1667) (see Morris-Jones, *Cymmrodor* 28.10; Jarman, *Cynfeirdd* 1). In current usage, *Cynfeirdd* can be used with both wider and narrower ranges of meaning. For example, the 9th-century Memorandum of the FIVE POETS is sometimes regarded as defining, as well as dating, the *Cynfeirdd* exactly—five named poets of the 6th century, of which only two, ANEIRIN and TALIESIN, have surviving works attributed to them. On the other hand, in attempting an overall scheme of the history of Welsh poetry, it is conventional to divide the Middle Ages into three sections: (1) *Cynfeirdd*; (2) GOGYNFEIRDD (rather early poets), broadly synonymous with the term *Beirdd y Tywysogion* (Poets of the Princes), from the later 11th century to sometime after the end of Welsh independence in 1282; (3) CYWYDDWYR, roughly synonymous with *Beirdd yr Uchelwyr* (Poets of the Nobility), from about 1300. Within such a scheme, a category of the 'later *Cynfeirdd*' emerges, including a diverse mass of anonymous material such as saga ENGLYNION, secular praise poetry, religious poetry, NATURE POETRY, PROPHECY—including ARMES PRYDEIN—and poems associated with MYRDDIN, and the so-called mythological poetry of LLYFR TALIESIN. For these works of the 'later *Cynfeirdd*', see these articles and WELSH POETRY [1].

Taken on its own, without context or qualification, *Cynfeirdd* poetry refers to a corpus of surviving early Welsh verse, showing degrees and varieties of linguistic archaism, mostly in the AWDL metre (long monorhyming stanzas), which take the attitude of contemporary court poetry celebrating (largely military) events of the mid-6th to mid-7th centuries. Though not so widely accepted, the list may also include one elegy, *Marwnad Cunedda*, to a 5th-century figure. This *Cynfeirdd* corpus may be itemized as follows, giving an indication of the era with which each poem's contents deal, and thus potentially when the poems might have been composed, if they had indeed been first created as occasional works contemporary to the events described. Each item is discussed at greater length in this Encyclopedia as noted.

1. MARWNAD CUNEDDA 'The elegy of CUNEDDA' [commemorating an occasion of AD 383×490]
2. The LLYFR ANEIRIN corpus, including:
    (i) The GODODDIN [Battle of CATRAETH, mid- to late 6th century]
    (ii) The *awdl* on the battle of Srath Carruin [December 642]
    (iii) 'Reciter's Prologue' [probably post-dating *obsesio Etin* 'the siege of DÙN EIDEANN/ Edinburgh' 638]
    (iv) The cradle song *Peis Dinogat* 'Dinogad's cloak'
3. TRAWSGANU CYNAN GARWYN [commemorating events of 575×610]
4. *Awdlau* addressed to URIEN Rheged [commemorating events of 570×595]
5. ENAID OWAIN AB URIEN 'The soul of Owain son of Urien' [commemorating events of 570×595]
6. *Awdlau* addressed to GWALLAWG fab Lleënnawg of ELFED [commemorating events of 570×610]
7. MOLIANT CADWALLON 'The praise of CADWALLON' [commemorating events of 630–4]
8. MARWNAD CYNDDYLAN 'The elegy of CYNDDYLAN' [commemorating events of 5 August 642– 15 November 655]

FURTHER READING
ANEIRIN; ARMES PRYDEIN; AWDL; CADWALLON; CATRAETH;
CUNEDDA; CYNDDYLAN; CYWYDDWYR; DÙN ÈIDEANN; ELFED;
ENAID OWAIN AB URIEN; ENGLYNION; FIVE POETS; GODODDIN;
GOGYNFEIRDD; GWALLAWG; LLYFR ANEIRIN; LLYFR TALIESIN;
MARWNAD CUNEDDA; MARWNAD CYNDDYLAN; MOLIANT
CADWALLON; MYRDDIN; NATURE POETRY; PROPHECY;
TALIESIN; TRAWSGANU KYNAN GARWYN; URIEN; VAUGHAN;
WELSH; WELSH POETRY [1]; Bromwich, BBCS 22.30–37;
Bromwich, *Beginnings of Welsh Poetry*; Bromwich & Jones,
Astudiaethau ar yr Hengerdd; Huws, *Llyfr Aneirin*; Jackson,
Gododdin; Jarman, *Aneirin*; Jarman, *Cynfeirdd*; Koch, *Gododdin of
Aneirin*; Koch, SC 20/21.43–66; Morris-Jones, *Cymmrodor* 28;
Brynley F. Roberts, *Early Welsh Poetry*; Ifor Williams, *Canu
Aneirin*; Ifor Williams, *Canu Taliesin*; Ifor Williams, *Poems of
Taliesin*.

JTK

Cynferching (Middle Welsh Kynuerchyn), 'the descendants of Cynfarch', refers to a post-Roman northern BRYTHONIC dynasty, known to both historical and legendary sources. Its most famous members were URIEN fab Cynfarch (Old Welsh Urbgen map Cinmarc) and Urien's son, Owain (see ENAID OWAIN AB URIEN). Both are prominent in the CYNFEIRDD poetry, saga ENGLYNION, and ARTHURIAN literature. Three other members of the family are mentioned in the 'Northern History' section of HISTORIA BRITTONUM: RHUN AB URIEN (Old Welsh Run), Rhun's son Royth, and Royth's daughter Rhieinfellt, wife of OSWYDD. The saga *englynion* mention Pasgen(t) son of Urien and Urien's sister, Efrddyl (also in TYP no. 70). Urien (Urbgen map Cinmarch) occurs in the Old Welsh GENEALOGIES in BL MS Harley 3859. The family is prominent in Middle Welsh genealogies, including figures unknown in the early poetry such as Urien's daughter, Morfudd, and another son, Cadell. In the Life of St CADOC, Henninni daughter of Cinmarch figures as the ancestress of Cadoc's mother, Guladus. Another son, Rhiwallawn, is known from the TRIADS (TYP no. 62). Since Cynfarch appears in the genealogies as a descendant of COEL HEN, the Cynferching figure as a subgroup of the larger north British lineage known as the Coeling (descendants of Coel Hen) in Welsh tradition. The Cynferching are first identified as a group distinct among the Coeling in a triad embedded in the Middle Welsh genealogical tract *Bonedd Gwŷr y Gogledd* (Descent of the men of the north). It is possible that they were only identified as a special subgroup as late as the 11th or 12th century because of the importance they had assumed in various branches of Welsh literature by that time. On the other hand, according to *Historia Brittonum*, Urien led a coalition to besiege the Angles on LINDISFARNE, which included three other chieftains, two of whom, GWALLAWG and Morgan (Old Welsh Morcant), were Coeling, but not Cynferching; Morgan then turned on Urien and assassinated him. Therefore, the group claiming descent from Coel had once formed a meaningful political block, which broke down in the later 6th century, after which emphasis on the later ancestor Cynfarch would have been more pertinent.

The name *Cynferching* is Celtic, reflecting a notional Old Celtic *Kunomarkigni* 'progeny of *Kuno-markos*', the latter name meaning 'warrior-stallion', literally 'hound-stallion'.

FURTHER READING
ARTHURIAN; BRYTHONIC; CADOC; COEL HEN; CYNFEIRDD; ENAID OWAIN AB URIEN; ENGLYNION; GENEALOGIES; GWALLAWG; HISTORIA BRITTONUM; LINDISFARNE; OSWYDD; RHUN AB URIEN; TRIADS; URIEN; Bartrum, EWGT; Bartrum, *Welsh Classical Dictionary* 174–5; Bromwich, TYP; Charles-Edwards, *Astudiaethau ar yr Hengerdd* 66–9; Miller, BBCS 26.255–80; Rowland, *Early Welsh Saga Poetry*.

JTK

cynghanedd

WELSH POETRY can be divided into two main categories, namely free metre poetry and strict metre, or *cynghanedd*, poetry. *Cynghanedd*, meaning harmony (from the roots *cyf-* 'with' + *can-* 'sing'), is a sophisticated form of alliteration, sometimes combined with internal rhyme. Welsh poetry and a rudimentary form of *cynghanedd* are as old as the language itself (see CYNFEIRDD; WELSH), and can be described as a language within a language.

The rules of *cynghanedd*, known as CERDD DAFOD (poetic art), were fully developed by the Middle Ages. *Cynghanedd* may well have had its roots in Celtic culture, since comparable patterns are found in the strict metres (*dán díreach*) of Irish (see IRISH LITERATURE) and SCOTTISH GAELIC POETRY, and, likewise, in Middle Breton (see BRETON LITERATURE) and Middle Cornish (see CORNISH LITERATURE). The characteristic structures shared by the traditional strict metres of the various Celtic poetic traditions can be understood as specific outgrowths of the cross-cultural fascination with euphony of rhyme and consonant harmony. The Welsh poetic tradition was, to a large extent, an oral tradition, and even today well-versed poets of the strict metre can immediately detect an error in a line of poetry.

One of the earliest of Welsh poets was the late 6th-century poet TALIESIN. In his book *Taliesin Poems*, Meirion Pennar quotes from one of Taliesin's battle poems: *Wedi boregad, briwgig* (in the early spelling of the manuscript *a gwedy boregat briwgic*), which he translates as 'after morning clash, they were tenderised meat'. Pennar draws attention to the alliterative effect of the corresponding consonants (d b r g / d b r g): 'You could hear the spurt of blood; the sheer violence of it all' (Pennar, *Taliesin Poems* 15).

The poetic art was taught to students (*ysbasiaid*) by experienced poets or scholars called *penceirddiaid* (see

BARDIC ORDER). So thorough was the study that years went by before a student was accepted as a master of the art. Today, *cerdd dafod* is introduced in schools as part of the Welsh literature curriculum, but is not taught as a special subject. Evening classes sponsored by Departments of Continuing Education in Welsh universities have been popular and successful, and many 20th-century *prifeirdd* (winners of the chair or crown at the National Eisteddfod of Wales, see EISTEDDFOD GENEDLAETHOL CYMRU) have attended such classes. Over the centuries, rural poets known as *beirdd gwlad* have mastered the art and transmitted it to younger poets.

During the 1970s, young poets such as Alan LLWYD and others brought a fresh impetus to the learning of *cynghanedd*, which led to the formation of a new society, Barddas (Poetic art), whose aims were to encourage a keen interest in this poetic form. The society established and publishes a bimonthly periodical, also called *Barddas*, which contains contemporary poetry and articles. The wide popularity of the radio programme *Talwrn y Beirdd* (Bardic contest), in which teams of poets compete against each other under the chairmanship of Gerallt Lloyd OWEN, also reflects the revival of interest in *cynghanedd*. Several textbooks on *cerdd dafod* have been published during recent years, but the standard reference work remains Sir John MORRIS-JONES's scholarly volume *Cerdd Dafod*, first published in 1925.

Any student of *cynghanedd* must first be acquainted with the normal accentuation of words. In most polysyllabic words in Welsh the accent or stress rests on the penultimate syllable (*goben*). Accented monosyllables are, of course, stressed on their final syllables. A 7-syllable line should have a natural break in the middle of the line, and all consonants before the penultimate accent in the first half of the line should correspond exactly to the consonants before the penultimate accent in the second half. The end of the first natural break is called *gorffwysfa* (rest), and the end of the second, which is the last word of the line, is the *prifodl* (main rhyme).

In writing a strict-metre poem there are scores of rules to be observed and numerous variations, but the three main types of *cynghanedd* are as follows.

§1. CYNGHANEDD GYTSAIN

In this form, the consonants correspond to each other in each half of the line, as described above. We may

take for example a line of *Cynghanedd Groes*, which is a subdivision of this class:

Gwaed y groes /a gwyd y graith (Ioan Madog)

The blood of the cross removes the scar.

Here the natural break in the line occurs after *groes* and the two main stresses fall on the accented one-syllable words, *groes* and *graith*. The consonants in each half correspond to one another, but those which come after the accented vowels of each half line (thus, *s* and *th* in this case) do not count.

A more sophisticated version of this type is known as *Cynghanedd Groes o Gyswllt*:

Y colyn cêl /yn y cwm

The hidden venom in the valley.

The natural break in this line is between *cêl* and *yn*, and the *c* and *l* in *cêl* have to be borrowed in order to complete the pattern (*c l n c*) in the second half of the line.

Another variation of this *Cynghanedd Gytsain* type is the *Cynghanedd Draws*, in which it may be necessary to ignore the middle order of consonants because of the natural break/pause in the line:

Myned /sydd raid /i minnau (Robert ap Gwilym Ddu)

I am compelled to depart.

The emphasis here is on *myned* and *minnau*, and the middle consonants (s dd r d) are ignored.

A further example based on this type is known as *Cynghanedd Draws Fantach*:

Bwlch ni ddangosai lle bu (T. Gwynn JONES)

No trace of where it was.

§2. CYNGHANEDD SAIN

This form consists of a combination of internal rhyme and alliteration. English-language poets who learned Welsh have made good use of this category, as we shall see below. Let us examine a line of this type:

Cleddau digon brau o bren (Lewys Glyn Cothi)

Flimsy wooden swords.

Note the internal rhyme in *cleddau* and *brau*, and also

the alliteration between *brau* and *bren*.

Another variation in this class is:

Trallodau, beiau bywyd (Edward Richard)

Trials and tribulations of life.

Since the accent is on the penultimate syllable, *beiau* and *bywyd* correspond correctly.

§3. CYNGHANEDD LUSG

This type of *cynghanedd* consists purely of internal rhyme and, although it is therefore the easiest of the *cynganeddion* to compose, it is very often the most pleasing to the ear:

Lle roedd sglein / ar bob ceiniog (Huw T. Edwards)

There was a gloss on every copper coin.

Note that the accented *ein* in the monosyllabic *sglein* rhymes with the accented penultimate syllable in *ceiniog*. The final unaccented syllable of a two-syllable word can also rhyme with the accented penultimate syllable, as in:

Pan feddwn dalent plentyn (Gerallt Lloyd Owen)

When I had a child's talent.

Many English-language poets have discovered and written lines in *cynghanedd* (see ANGLO-WELSH LITERA-TURE). It is evident from the following lines (both of which contain *Cynghanedd Sain*) that Dylan Thomas, although he never mastered the Welsh language, was aware of *cynghanedd*:

To the b*urn* and *turn* of *time*
When the morn*ing* was *walking* over the *war*.

Wilfred Owen, who had Welsh connections and spent his childhood holidays in Wales (CYMRU), also made use of *Cynghanedd Sain*:

The shad*ow* of the *morrow* weighed on *men*.

The first English-language poet to experiment with *cynghanedd* was William Barnes, who learned Welsh and also the rules of *cerdd dafod*. His well-known poem 'Linden Lea' contains a line of *Cynghanedd Groes*:

Do *lean down low* / in *Linden Lea*.

Coleridge also made good use of rhyme and allitera-tion in a manner reminiscent of Welsh *cynghanedd* in 'The Ancient Mariner':

The south wind blew,
the white foam flew
the furrow followed free,
we were the first ever to burst
into that silent sea.

Gerard Manley Hopkins was by far the most success-ful user of *cynghanedd* in English-language poetry. While at St Beuno College in St Asaph (Llanelwy) in north Wales, he learned Welsh and studied *cerdd dafod*. The following lines indicate how he introduced *cynghanedd* into his work:

I wake in the Midsummer not to call n*ight*, in the *white* and the *walk* of the morning . . . (*Cynghanedd Sain*).

And *fled* with a *fling* (*Cynghanedd Draws*) / of the *heart* to the *heart* of the *host* (*Cynghanedd Sain*).

Many English-language poets are indebted to Hopkins for introducing them to *cynghanedd*. Rayner Heppenstall, for example, has a fine example of *Cynghanedd Groes* in his poem 'Sebastian':

Peace to the hand, / pace to the heel.

Cynghanedd Lusg tends to evade English-language poets, probably because so many lines of English verse end with monosyllables and the unstressed final syllables of English polysyllables often have obscure vowels (unlike Welsh), and thus make unsatisfactory end rhymes. However, the following lines by John Tydu Jones are exceptions:

Home of the b*ard* and C*ardi*

and

Dew on the newb*orn* m*orning*.

FURTHER READING
ANGLO-WELSH LITERATURE; BARDIC ORDER; BRETON; BRETON LITERATURE; CERDD DAFOD; CORNISH LITERATURE; CYMRU; CYNFEIRDD; EISTEDDFOD GENEDLAETHOL CYMRU; IRISH LIT-ERATURE; JONES; LLWYD; MORRIS-JONES; OWEN; SCOTTISH GAELIC POETRY; TALIESIN; THOMAS; WELSH; WELSH POETRY; Donald Evans, *Poetry Wales* 14.1.86–94; Jon Meirion Jones, *Teulu'r Cilie*; Llwyd, *Poetry Wales* 14.1.23–58; Llwyd, *Trafod Cerdd Dafod y Dydd*; Morris-Jones, *Cerdd Dafod*; Parry, *History of Welsh Literature* 121–6; Pennar, *Taliesin Poems*; Rowlands, *Guide to Welsh Literature* 2.202–17; Stephens, NCLW.

Vernon Jones

Peter Hain (Labour), Richard Livsey (Liberal Democrats), Dafydd Wigley (Plaid Cymru), and Ron Davies (Labour) celebrating the victory for devolution in the Welsh referendum in 1997

Cynulliad Cenedlaethol Cymru (National Assembly for Wales) is the elected body which sits in Cardiff (CAERDYDD), the capital of Wales (CYMRU). On 1 July 1999, the Cynulliad took over the responsibilities of the Welsh Office for the regional government of Wales within the United Kingdom. In its function, it may be compared to the SCOTTISH PARLIAMENT, though its powers are more restricted.

Welsh nationalists from CYMRU FYDD to Plaid Cymru (see NATIONALISM) had campaigned for the devolution of government power to Wales since the end of the 19th century, but not until the latter decades of the 20th century did these initiatives bear fruit under Labour governments. Following a referendum in 1979, which failed to secure a majority in favour of devolution, and mounting pressure during the 1990s, a White Paper, *A Voice for Wales*, was published by the Labour government in July 1997. It proposed a second referendum, which was held on 18 September 1997, one week after the Scottish electorate had voted in favour of establishing a Scottish Parliament. In Wales 50.3% of the votes cast were in favour of an elected political body for the country, which was then set up by the

Government of Wales Act (1998). On 6 May 1999, the first elections for Cynulliad Cenedlaethol Cymru or the National Assembly for Wales were held, and the Cynulliad met for the first time on 12 May 1999. Unlike the Scottish Parliament, the Cynulliad is a fully bilingual body, where members are able to address the assembly in the WELSH language and in which minutes appear bilingually.

The brief of Cynulliad Cenedlaethol Cymru is to develop and implement policies which reflect the needs of the people of Wales and to allocate within Wales funds awarded by the Treasury of the UK government. To that extent, it is less powerful than the Scottish Parliament, which possesses tax-raising powers. Among the domains in which the Cynulliad exercises power are agriculture, economic development, EDUCATION and training, the environment, industry, local government, social security, and the Welsh language. So far, efforts have been made to develop educational and environmental policies distinctive to Wales, and to put some distance between Wales and Westminster. Nevertheless, the current popular perception is that devolved government has not yet won the hearts and minds of electors.

Cynulliad Cenedlaethol Cymru is composed of 60 members, of whom 40 represent constituencies and are elected directly. The remaining 20 members are elected in five larger electoral regions through the Additional Member System, which allocates four seats per region to the parties, depending on their share of the vote. The Cynulliad works through Subject Committees which reflect the balance of the political parties. In Regional Committees, members from each region assemble to lobby on behalf of their constituents. The rôle of the Committees is to advise the Cynulliad on the development and implementation of policies.

Elections are held every four years. At the election in 1999 the Labour Party won 28 seats, followed by Plaid Cymru with 18 seats, the Conservative Party with nine seats, and the Liberal Party with six seats. Since Labour failed to gain a majority, the Cynulliad became a genuine forum for all political parties in Wales. Following various reshuffles within the Labour Party, Rhodri Morgan became First Minister in 2000 and, under his leadership, in the elections of 2003 the Labour Party gained a slender overall majority, though the abysmally low turnout reflected the general indifference of the electorate to the outcome.

Although the first years of Cynulliad Cenedlaethol Cymru, the first Welsh parliament since that of OWAIN GLYNDŴR, have not been easy, it is clear that its existence has strengthened Welsh nationhood by providing a focus for its politics. A handsome new debating chamber is currently being built in Cardiff Bay, and this new building will further enhance the standing of the Assembly government within Europe. Working within the Cynulliad each party strives to develop a distinctive Welsh profile, and if the recommendations of the Richard Commission in 2004 are implemented the powers of the Cynulliad are likely to increase appreciably over the coming years.

PRIMARY SOURCES
HMSO, Voice for Wales; HMSO, Government for Wales Act (1998).

FURTHER READING
CAERDYDD; CYMRU; CYMRU FYDD; EDUCATION; NATIONALISM; OWAIN GLYNDŴR; SCOTTISH PARLIAMENT; WELSH; Andrews, Wales Says Yes; Richard Wyn Jones, Politics 19.37–46; Richard Wyn Jones & Trystan, Scotland and Wales 65–93; Richard Wyn Jones et al., Road to the National Assembly for Wales 159–74; Osmond, National Question Again; Taylor & Thomson, Scotland and Wales.
MBL

Cynwydion (Middle Welsh Kynnwydyon) is a name which occurs in Welsh GENEALOGIES for a north British dynasty of the post-Roman period. Its literal significance would be descendants of someone named Cynwyd (Old Welsh Cinuit), but it is possible that the ancestor figure was created to explain the group name, Celtic *Kunētiones; the singular Cunētio is attested as a ROMANO-BRITISH place-name.

The descent of this group, its membership, and historicity are murky and controversial owing to a discrepancy in the Welsh sources. In the Old Welsh genealogies in BL MS Harley 3859, there are three lineages descended from Cinuit map Ceretic Guletic, all through Cinuit's son Dumngual Hen (Dyfnwal the old): (1) the main royal line of Strathclyde (YSTRAD CLUD), (2) a collateral line of Strathclyde including the well-documented 6th-century king Riderch (RHYDDERCH HAEL), and (3) a line leading to Clitgno Eitin (Clydno of Edinburgh; MS [C]linog), the father of the most famous hero in the GODODDIN, Cynon fab Clydno. In the Middle Welsh Bonedd Gwŷr y Gogledd (Descent of the men of the north) several changes have occurred to harmonize the 12th-century state of traditions concerning the ancestry of Welsh kings, heroes, and saints. Thus, Cinuit map Ceretic and the main line of Strathclyde have vanished. The ancestor of Clydno Eidyn is now called Kynnwyd Kynnwydyon and has been made a descendant of the great northern patriarch COEL HEN, who was not Cinuit's ancestor in the Harleian genealogies. The fact that both Old Welsh Cinuit map Ceretic and Middle Welsh Kynnwyd Kynnwydyon occur a few generations back from Clydno Eidyn rules out the possibility of two 5th-century north British kings with the same name; rather, the genealogical doctrine had changed. Bonedd Gwŷr y Gogledd shows a weak historicity at several points; for example, AEDÁN MAC GABRÁIN of DÁL RIATA was garbled into 'Gauran mab Aedan' and given a bogus BRYTHONIC ancestry from Dyfnwal Hen. This may be mere ignorance or a desire to show that the current kings of Scotland were BRITONS. The expansion of pedigrees traced to Coel at this stage may likewise be a desire to simplify and systematize, but it should also be noted that the second dynasty of GWYNEDD claimed descent from Coel through the Llywarch Hen of the saga ENGLYNION and may have wished to be related to as many luminaries as possible. Furthermore, by the 10th and 11th centuries, a unified kingdom of Strathclyde/CUMBRIA —itself functioning increasingly as a subkingdom of ALBA (Scotland)—had expanded into old Coeling territory around Carlisle (Welsh Caerliwelydd), and the Welsh genealogists may thus have wished to make the descendants of Cynwyd a branch of the Coeling to legitimize this annexation.

FURTHER READING
AEDÁN MAC GABRÁIN; ALBA; BRITONS; BRYTHONIC; COEL HEN; CUMBRIA; DÁL RIATA; ENGLYNION; GENEALOGIES; GODODDIN; GWYNEDD; RHYDDERCH HAEL; ROMANO-BRITISH; WELSH; YSTRAD CLUD; Bartrum, EWGT; Bartrum, *Welsh Classical Dictionary* 185; Bromwich, TYP; Charles-Edwards, *Astudiaethau ar yr Hengerdd* 66–9; Miller, BBCS 26.255–80; Rowland, *Early Welsh Saga Poetry*.

JTK

Cywydd is a Welsh metrical form in use from the 14th century to the present day. The term is cognate with the Old Irish *cubaid* (whose meanings include 'a letter of the OGAM alphabet'), and originally meant 'harmony' or 'song'. Four types of *cywydd* are listed by EINION OFFEIRIAD in his account of the twenty-four metres (probably in the 1320s): *awdl-gywydd, cywydd deuair hirion, cywydd deuair fyrion,* and *cywydd llosgyrnog*.

The *awdl-gywydd* consists of units of two seven-syllable lines, the end of the first rhyming with the caesura of the second (*odl gyrch*), and the end of the second maintaining the main rhyme. Although little used by bardic poets it occurs in some free-metre verse of the early modern period, e.g.

O gwrthody, liw ewyn,
Gwas difelyn gudynnau,
Yn ddiwladaidd, da ei lên,
A'i awen yn ei lyfrau.
(Gruffydd & Ifans, *Gwaith Einion Offeiriad* 73)

The *cywydd llosgyrnog* is the most complex of the four, consisting of two, three or four eight-syllable lines with the *odl gyrch* followed by a seven-syllable line with the main rhyme (the *llosgwrn* 'tail'); it has been very little used. The following example is given in Einion Offeiriad's grammar:

Lliw eiry glennydd Mynydd Mynnau,
Lluoedd a'th fawl, gwawl gwawr Deau,
Llathrlun golau Oleuddydd;
Llifodd fy hoen o boen benyd,

Lluddiodd ym hun llun bun, lloer byd:
Lledfryd, nid bywyd, a'm bydd.
(Gruffydd & Ifans, *Gwaith Einion Offeiriad* 74)

The *cywydd deuair fyrion* consists of couplets of four-syllable lines and is also found in some early-modern free-metre poems, e.g.

Hardd-deg riain, hydwf, glwysgain,
Hoywliw gwenyg, buan debyg:
Hawdd dy garu, haul yn llathru.
(Gruffydd & Ifans, *Gwaith Einion Offeiriad* 72)

The only one of the four types commonly used by bardic poets was the *cywydd deuair hirion*, consisting of seven-syllable couplets with one line rhyming on a stressed syllable and the other on an unstressed one, and it is to this metre that the term *cywydd* normally refers. In fact, the example given in Einion Offeiriad's grammar does not feature the alternating stress pattern in the rhymes, and it has no CYNGHANEDD. This supports the theory that the *cywydd deuair hirion* derived from a simpler metre, known as the *traethodl*, which consisted of seven-syllable rhyming couplets and had no *cynghanedd*. (This metre was used by DAFYDD AP GWILYM, e.g. Parry, *Gwaith Dafydd ap Gwilym* 137). The rhyme-pattern may have been influenced by the final couplet of the ENGLYN *unodl union*.

The *cywydd* has no set length, and can range from as little as twelve lines to well over a hundred, but medieval *cywyddau* are usually around sixty lines. Dafydd ap Gwilym is the first poet known to have made extensive use of the *cywydd*, and it is likely that his love poems popularized the metre, e.g. *Cystudd y Bardd* ('The Poet's Affliction'):

Hoywdeg riain a'm hudai,
Hael Forfudd, merch fedydd Mai.
(Parry, *Gwaith Dafydd ap Gwilym* 276)

A sprightly, fair maid would entice me:
Bountiful Morfudd, god-daughter of May.
(Thomas, *Dafydd ap Gwilym: His Poems* 203)

Dafydd ap Gwilym may also have been responsible for introducing *cynghanedd* into the *cywydd*, although he quite often left the first line of the couplet without *cynghanedd*. He also used the *cywydd* for praise poetry of a very personal kind to Ifor Hael, but it seems to have been his younger contemporary IOLO GOCH who took the important step of composing traditional praise in the *cywydd* metre with full *cynghanedd*. The earliest datable *cywydd* of this sort is that to King Edward III *c*. 1350 (Johnston, *Gwaith Iolo Goch* 2–3). By the end of the 14th century the *cywydd* had become accepted as the standard metre for all kinds of bardic poetry, and it continued to be so until the demise of the bardic order in the 17th century. Revived by neo-classical poets in the 18th century, the *cywydd* tradition was maintained by the EISTEDDFOD, both as a discrete composition and as one of the AWDL metres, and it is used to good effect by present-day practitioners of the strict metres.

PRIMARY SOURCES
EDITIONS. Gruffydd & Ifans, *Gwaith Einion Offeiriad a Dafydd Ddu o Hiraddug*; Johnston, *Gwaith Iolo Goch*; Parry, *Gwaith Dafydd ap Gwilym*; Ifor Williams & Roberts, *Cywyddau Dafydd ap Gwilym a'i Gyfoeswyr*.
TRANS. Johnston, *Iolo Goch: Poems*; Thomas, *Dafydd ap Gwilym: His Poems*.

FURTHER READING
AWDL; CYNGHANEDD; CYWYDDWYR; DAFYDD AP GWILYM; EINION OFFEIRIAD; EISTEDDFOD; EISTEDDFOD GENED-LAETHOL CYMRU; ENGLYN; IOLO GOCH; OGAM; WELSH PO-ETRY; Morris-Jones, *Cerdd Dafod*; Parry, THSC 1939.209–31.

Dafydd Johnston

Cywyddwyr

§1. THE TERM
The WELSH plural noun *cywyddwyr* (sing. *cywyddwr*) refers to poets who composed *cywyddau*, i.e. poems in the CYWYDD metre, from the 14th to the 16th centuries. A compound of *cywydd* and *gwŷr* 'men' (sing. *gŵr* 'man'), the word means literally '*cywydd*-men' or 'composers of *cywyddau*'. The term *cywydd* properly refers to a group of metres, of which the *cywydd deuair hirion* was the one used by most of the *Cywyddwyr*.

When, in the latter half of the 18th century, the terms CYNFEIRDD, 'early poets', and GOGYNFEIRDD, 'rather early poets', began to be used by Lewis Morris (see MORRISIAID MÔN) and others to describe Welsh poets from the earliest times to the 14th century, the medieval term *Cywyddwyr* was added to indicate the third and last chronological stage of strict-metre poetry in Wales (CYMRU), beginning in about 1300 and declining shortly after the ACTS OF UNION of 1536 and 1543. However, this chronological division is somewhat misleading since not all 14th-century poets were *Cywyddwyr*; a few composed only in AWDL and ENGLYN metres, the traditional metres used by the

Cynfeirdd and *Gogynfeirdd*. The poets of the central and later medieval periods, comprising both *Cywyddwyr* and others, are sometimes described collectively as *Beirdd yr Uchelwyr*, or 'Poets of the Nobility'. Thus, the terms *Cywyddwyr* and *Beirdd yr Uchelwyr* overlap and are largely, but not precisely, synonymous.

Though the *cywydd* was revived by Edward WILLIAMS (Iolo Morganwg) at the end of the 18th century to form a key element in his vision of the modern EISTEDDFOD, and remains a central feature of *eisteddfod* competitions in Wales to this day, the term *Cywyddwyr* normally refers exclusively to poets of the central and late Middle Ages who composed in the *cywydd* metre.

§2. THE RISE OF THE CYWYDDWYR
The emergence of the *cywydd* metre as a prestige form of poetry, and hence the rise of the *Cywyddwyr* as poets who composed mainly or exclusively in this metre, occurred in the context of social and economic changes in Wales following the conquest of Gwynedd by Edward I in 1282–3. Before this date, court poetry (typically in the *awdl* and *englyn* metres) had been addressed to the ruling dynasties of Wales by the *Gogynfeirdd*, or *Beirdd y Tywysogion* 'Poets of the Princes', poets attached to the courts of the Welsh princes and lesser noblemen. Following Edward's suppression of the Welsh royal dynasties, the social and economic infrastructure of traditional court poetry largely disappeared. What arose in its place was a newly-empowered class of patrons, the *uchelwyr*, and a new prestige metre, the *cywydd*. The *Cywyddwyr* are therefore inseparable from the social group that supported them, the *uchelwyr*.

As the status of the *uchelwyr* improved from the late 13th century under English patronage, the leading fami-lies sought ways of establishing their class identity as the native élite in the post-1282 context. Offering sup-port to court poets, trained to sing the praises of the lord who supported them, was one of the means by which the *uchelwyr* asserted their place in the social hierarchy, while confirming their commitment to Welsh cultural practices. Until well into the 14th century, the *awdl* remained the dominant mode of praise poetry to patrons, and most of the *Cywyddwyr* composed in the *awdl* and *englyn* metres, as well as in the *cywydd* metre, in order to demonstrate their skills in all three of the major bardic metres.

The *cywydd*, among the simplest of the twenty-four

bardic metres and therefore apparently disdained by the *Gogynfeirdd*, was revived in the early 14th century as a useful medium for the new themes of love and nature influenced by English popular song. After the Black Death, which ravaged Wales in 1349 and accelerated the pace of change in the social order, the *cywydd*, polished by the addition of some of the ornamental features of the *awdl*, became fully established as the prestige form of *canu mawl*, or praise poetry. By the 15th century, the rapidly increasing pool of *uchelwyr* patrons, both secular and clerical, were receiving the praises of their poets in the form of *cywyddau*. The revival of the *cywydd* and its rôle in reinvigorating medieval Welsh court poetry is regarded by many modern critics as the major literary achievement of the medieval period in Wales.

It was not only the style of poetry which changed after 1282, but also the manner of its production and reception as well. Whereas the *Gogynfeirdd* were semi-permanent fixtures at the courts of the great princes of GWYNEDD, POWYS, and DEHEUBARTH, protected by the laws of the court (see LAW TEXTS), the *Cywyddwyr* tended to be more mobile and self-employed. Most of the major *Cywyddwyr* had multiple patrons, though these were often members of the same extended *uchelwyr* families. More significantly, the *Cywyddwyr* moved freely between the manor houses of their *uchelwyr* patrons and the growing towns of Wales, which provided new audiences among the burgesses and trade-enriched merchants, English as well as Welsh. Poems by DAFYDD AP GWILYM to Newborough and GUTO'R GLYN to Oswestry (Welsh Croesoswallt) are among the *cywyddau* which acknowledge the significance of urban life to the status and fortunes of the *Cywyddwyr* from the 14th century onwards. In many ways, as D. J. Bowen has claimed, the *cywydd* was a bourgeois form.

§3. SIGNIFICANT CYWYDDWYR

There are no surviving biographies of any of the *Cywyddwyr*, and information about their lives has to be inferred from references in the poetry and from what is known of their patrons. It seems fairly clear, however, that many of the *Cywyddwyr* belonged to the same socio-economic class as their patrons, being members of *uchelwyr* families who both supported and produced the professional poets of their age.

The earliest of the *Cywyddwyr* were composing at the same time as the last generation of *Gogynfeirdd* in the first half of the 14th century, and there is an obvious metrical and stylistic overlap between the older and newer forms of poetic composition. The first generation of *Cywyddwyr* included IOLO GOCH, Dafydd ap Gwilym, Llywelyn Goch ap Meurig Hen, Gruffudd Gryg, Madog Benfras, and Gruffudd ab Adda, some of the most innovative poets of the medieval period. This is the generation credited with turning the *cywydd* into a professional metre, suitable for court poetry, while continuing to compose in the *awdl* and *englyn* metres.

Of this early group, Dafydd ap Gwilym stands out as truly exceptional, not only for the number of poems attributed to him in manuscripts (currently stabilized at around 150 in the canon published by Thomas Parry in 1952) but also for the virtually unbroken manuscript record of his work after 1450 and for the many references to him as a revered poet by later generations of *Cywyddwyr*. Iolo Goch, whose more modest canon of 37 *cywyddau* has been edited by Dafydd Johnston, is another significant poet of the early period notable for his praise poems to leading Welsh figures of the day, including OWAIN GLYNDŴR.

Gruffudd Llwyd and his bardic apprentice, Rhys Goch Eryri, were both composing in the early years of the 15th century, each leaving a small surviving corpus of praise poems, love poems, and religious verse in both *cywydd* and *awdl* metres. But the dominant figure of the first half of the 15th century was SIÔN CENT, whose religious verse is deeply philosophical and didactic. His younger contemporary, on the other hand, Dafydd Llwyd of Mathafarn, whose work spans the middle and later decades of the century, developed the *cywydd* as a vehicle for reinterpreting the ancient Welsh art of PROPHECY, composing about 40 such *cywyddau brud* as well as some elegies and praise poems.

The second half of the 15th century produced some of the most prolific and accomplished praise-poets among the *Cywyddwyr*, including Guto'r Glyn, GUTUN OWAIN, DAFYDD NANMOR, LEWYS GLYN COTHI, Huw Cae Llwyd, Lewys Môn, and TUDUR ALED. Their patrons comprised the full range of the medieval Welsh gentry, both secular and religious, including the Fychan (Vaughan), Griffith, Pilston, and Tudor (TUDUR) families and senior members of the church. The tradition of love poetry established by the earlier generations was also strongly maintained by poets such as DAFYDD AB EDMWND, Bedo Brwynllys, and Bedo Aeddren. Dafydd ab Edmwnd was particularly known for his metrical innovations at the Carmarthen (CAERFYRDDIN) *eisteddfod* of *c.* 1451, insisting on strict CYNGHANEDD in the *cywydd* metres and increasing the complexity of many of the traditional twenty-four metres which formed the basis of the bardic system of training and grading. It was his pupil, Gutun Owain, a distinguished scholar and genealogist (see GENEALOGIES), who ensured that these changes were recorded in the 16th-century versions of the bardic grammar (see GRAMADEGAU'R PENCEIRDDIAID).

Dafydd ab Edmwnd was among the last of the great love-poets of the *Cywyddwyr*. Of the generation composing in the first half of the 16th century, Lewys Morgannwg (Llywelyn ap Rhisiart), a pupil of Tudur Aled, was one of the most prolific, with over a hundred of his *cywyddau* and *awdlau* surviving, mainly praise poetry and elegies. Gruffudd Hiraethog and his pupil, Wiliam Llŷn, also produced large numbers of *cywyddau* in praise of the Welsh gentry and were closely involved in discussions regarding regulations governing the BARDIC ORDER. By the end of the 16th century, the tradition of praise poetry was itself in decline, maintained only by a few pupils of Gruffudd Hiraethog, such as SIÔN TUDUR, who was both a poet and a member of the gentry and whose satires draw attention to the gradual decay of the bardic profession, and Simwnt Fychan, who is remembered not only for his poetry but for his re-working of the bardic regulations, *Pum Llyfr Cerddwriaeth*.

While poetry as a profession was dominated by males in medieval Wales, there are some surviving *cywyddau* and *englynion* attributed to a female poet, GWERFUL MECHAIN, who composed in the second half of the 15th century. As the daughter of Hywel Fychan of Powys, and therefore a member of a well-established family of *uchelwyr*, Gwerful belonged to the same social circle as many of the *Cywyddwyr* and their patrons, and was related by marriage to the poet Llywelyn ab y Moel. Among her surviving poems are a number of exchanges with Dafydd Llwyd of Mathafarn and Llywelyn ap Gutun, as well as the raunchy and humorous *cywyddau* for which she is particularly renowned.

§4. STYLE AND THEMES

The metre associated most closely with the *Cywyddwyr*, the *cywydd deuair hirion*, determined many of the stylistic possibilities of the poetry. Rhymed as a couplet (with rhyme between an accented and an unaccented final syllable), the metre lends itself to syntactic units of one couplet at a time, a style which became particularly refined in 15th-century praise poetry. Those poets of the 14th century, such as Dafydd ap Gwilym and Llywelyn Goch ap Meurig Hen, who continued to use the *awdl* metre for praise poetry alongside the *cywydd* metre, transferred modes of the *awdl* to the *cywydd*, including single-line sense units, alliteration at the beginning of a series of lines (*cymeriad*), and a series of repeated end-rhymes.

The 14th-century poets also tended to favour more complex syntactic units, often extending over several lines in counterpoint to the metrical logic of the couplet. Throughout the period of the *Cywyddwyr*, however, many poets used the couplet style to great effect, encapsulating neat and witty aphorisms within a single couplet or extending a dramatic comparison over a series of couplets. In general, the greater flexibility of the *cywydd* metre, compared to the *awdl*, encouraged a lighter and more humorous style of verse expressed through the innovative use of colloquial forms, compound words, and a highly figurative language of extended metaphor and imagery.

The *Cywyddwyr* practised a rhetorical and ornamental style that set their verse clearly apart from prose and from the simpler songs of minstrels and players. Apart from *cymeriad*, the most obvious adornment was *cynghanedd*, the system of consonantal repetition and internal rhyme applied to each line of verse in a number of variant patterns. For their rhetorical ornamentation, the *Cywyddwyr* drew on a common stock of European literary devices derived from Greek and Latin conventions, including metaphor, repetition, oxymoron, and paradox. Two devices particularly associated with the *Cywyddwyr* are *sangiad* and *dyfalu*. *Sangiad* corresponds to the Greek concept of 'parenthesis', and describes the insertion of additional phrases or asides, often in the form of a comment or value judgement, into a syntactic unit, a particularly helpful device in a strict syllabic metre governed by *cynghanedd*. The art of *dyfalu*, meaning 'to describe' or 'to deride', rests in the intricate development of a series of images and extended metaphors which either celebrate or castigate a person, animal or object. Dafydd ap Gwilym's poems to the wind (Parry,

Gwaith Dafydd ap Gwilym 117) and the mist (Parry, *Gwaith Dafydd ap Gwilym* 68) are frequently cited as classic examples of the technique of *dyfalu*.

The themes of the medieval *cywyddau* can be conveniently summarized as love, nature, religion, elegy, praise, and SATIRE, though most of the poems can be broadly categorized as either praise or satire. There are also a number of political poems, particularly the sub-genre known as the *cywyddau brud*, or prophetic poems (see PROPHECY). Many of the *Cywyddwyr* specialized in one type of poem rather than another, so that Dafydd ap Gwilym, Dafydd ab Edmwnd, and Bedo Brwynllys, for example, are famous for their love-poetry, while Iolo Goch, Tudur Aled, and Guto'r Glyn are particularly associated with praise poetry to patrons. The emergence of the *cywydd* metre is associated with lyric themes of love and nature, following trends from French and English verse, while the use of the *cywydd* for official praise poetry, taking over the function of the *awdl*, was commonplace by the 15th century. Prophetic poems, such as those by Dafydd Llwyd of Mathafarn, enjoyed a certain prominence during the 15th century in the context of the Wars of the Roses and the rise of the Tudor (Tudur) family.

Though satirical poems commonly appear in the form of *englynion*, especially in the 14th century, they were also composed as *cywyddau*. The *Cywyddwyr* directed their satire not only towards social groups regarded as inferior, such as itinerants, burgesses and English townspeople, but also towards each other. A number of *Cywyddwyr* exchanged colourful poems in the form of YMRYSONAU or 'contests' which included relentless satire and ridicule of the opponent, and may have formed part of the bardic competitions at which poets were graded. The *ymryson* between Dafydd ap Gwilym and Gruffudd Gryg in the 14th century, and one between Siôn Cent and Rhys Goch Eryri in the 15th century, both on the topic of what forms and subjects are proper to poetry, are among the best known. On the other hand, the *Cywyddwyr* also composed very moving elegies to each other, both before and after the actual death. Elegies to Dafydd ap Gwilym were composed by Iolo Goch, Madog Benfras, and his old opponent, Gruffudd Gryg, while Dafydd ap Gwilym composed elegies to Madog Benfras and Gruffudd Gryg, even though the latter was almost certainly alive at the time.

In both their language and themes, the *cywyddau* are

clearly marked as products of their cultural positioning, closely connected to both English and French literatures in the medieval period. The enormous increase of English loanwords into Welsh, compared to the earlier *Gogynfeirdd* period, indicates the expansion of English settlement after 1282 and the gradual emergence of English as a prestige language. Gruffudd Gryg is credited with the first borrowing of English 'hobby-horse' into Welsh (*hobi hors*) in his *ymryson* with Dafydd ap Gwilym, while Dafydd himself seems to have coined borrowings such as *acses* 'access', *butres* 'buttress' and *sercl* 'circle'. Many borrowings from English by the *Cywyddwyr* reflect their increasing contacts with towns, trade and urban culture in Wales, e.g. *cwrel* 'coral', *dwbled* 'doublet', *ffair* 'fair', *fflwring* 'florin', and *lifrai* 'livery'.

A number of *cywyddau* resemble French poetic genres, particularly the *débat* and *pastourelle*. There are many echoes of the *fabliau* style in some of the comic poems, and there is one example of an *aubade* or 'dawn song' in the Dafydd ap Gwilym corpus (Parry, *Gwaith Dafydd ap Gwilym* 129). The conventions of love, descriptions of a woman's beauty, and evocations of the natural world which characterize much of their work clearly show that these poets belonged to a contemporary tradition of courtly entertainment which owed much to European vernacular popular song, such as the Harley Lyrics in English and the work of the *trouvères* in northern France, as well as to the echoes of classical Latin rhetoric preserved in the medieval Latin verse of the *clerici vagantes*. In their development of sub-genres such as the *cywydd llatai*, however, where the poem describes a love-messenger, usually a bird or animal, sent to the poet's beloved, the *Cywyddwyr* showed that they were not merely imitators of a common style but could produce innovative interpretations of standard themes in the medium of their own native language and versification.

§5. PERFORMANCE

Medieval *cywyddau* were composed to be performed in public, and to be sung rather than recited. The evidence of the poems suggests that the *Cywyddwyr* normally performed their own work, accompanying themselves on a HARP or CRWTH, a stringed instrument, though the musical accompaniment may have been provided or amplified, at least on some occasions, by professional musicians. In his *cywydd* describing a song he composed for Dyddgu (Parry, *Gwaith Dafydd ap Gwilym* 142), Dafydd ap Gwilym claims to have written the music as well as the lyrics, while Iolo Goch, in his elegy for Dafydd, calls him *telyn llys a'i theulu* (harp of a court and its retinue; Johnston, *Iolo Goch: Poems* no. 21). A satire on the English burgesses of Flint (possibly by Tudur Penllyn) describes the poet singing an *awdl* at a wedding-feast in the town, while Dafydd ab Edmwnd's elegy for Siôn Eos, a harpist, alludes to the harpist playing both solo and as an accompanist to singers. These kinds of references to performance convey a general impresssion that the *Cywyddwyr*, as professional poets, formed a superior body among a variety of singers and musicians performing in the halls of the *uchelwyr*, to audiences of clerics, at celebratory gatherings such as fairs and wedding-feasts, and in public places in towns, such as taverns and market squares.

Not all *cywyddau*, however, were necessarily performed by the *Cywyddwyr* themselves, since there was a class of professional singers known as *datgeiniaid*, 'reciters'. These are mentioned in the earliest versions of the bardic grammar (see GRAMADEGAU'R PENCEIRDDIAID) as performers whose rôle is to enhance the songs they perform, and by the time the Statute of GRUFFUDD AP CYNAN was developed, in the 16th century, they are instructed to wait on the poets and to travel only in the company of a *pencerdd*, or master poet. Lewys Glyn Cothi describes sending a *datgeiniad* to sing to one of his patrons, Dafydd Llwyd ap Gruffudd, and Guto'r Glyn declares that Tomas ap Watcyn Fychan should have a hundred reciters to sing his praises. The *Cywyddwyr*, then, were often musicians and singers as well as poets, though they might be accompanied by professional musicians and singers, or even replaced by them.

§6. TRANSMISSION

The transmission of the poetry of the *Cywyddwyr* seems to have been almost entirely oral until the middle of the 15th century, when secular patrons began to commission manuscripts in significant numbers with the aim of recording what had become the mainstream tradition of bardic poetry. There are only two contemporary manuscript sources for any 14th-century *cywyddau*. The HENDREGADREDD MANUSCRIPT, dating from the early 14th century with additions up to the end of the century, is the earliest manuscript to contain some work of contemporary *Cywyddwyr*, Dafydd ap

Gwilym and Gruffudd Gryg, but it is their *awdlau* and *englynion* which are represented, including a series of *englynion* thought to be in Dafydd's own hand; there are only two fragments of anonymous *cywyddau*.

Another major repository of Welsh literature dating from the last quarter of the 14th century, the Red Book of Hergest (LLYFR COCH HERGEST), also contains examples of *awdlau* and *englynion* by poets who are better known as *Cywyddwyr*: IOLO GOCH, Gruffudd Gryg, and Llywelyn Goch. There is only one example of a *cywydd*, a love poem by Iolo Goch, which suggests that the manuscript's patron, Hopcyn ap Tomas, did not yet consider the *cywydd*, at least in the form of love poetry, to be a formal mode of verse. The third important manuscript collection of the late 14th century, the White Book of Rhydderch (LLYFR GWYN RHYDDERCH), which contains mostly prose works, includes a series of *englynion* by Dafydd ap Gwilym written on a blank page, but no evidence of the *cywydd*, despite its evident popularity as a cultural form.

The main period of manuscript transmission of the work of the *Cywyddwyr* came after 1450 and is notable for the number of versions written by the bards themselves. Important manuscripts from the second half of the 15th century include National Library of Wales (LLYFRGELL GENEDLAETHOL CYMRU) Peniarth MSS 48 and 57(i), the earliest manuscripts to contain *cywyddau* attributed to Dafydd ap Gwilym, and a number of autograph manuscripts of the work of Lewys Glyn Cothi, dating from the 1470s. Bards themselves often acted as scribes, writing down their own verse and that of their contemporaries. Gutun Owain (*fl.* 1450–98), a particularly prolific writer, recorded bardic grammars and chronicles as well as the poetry of his age. Other contemporary *Cywyddwyr* whose work survives in their own handwriting, mainly in NLW Peniarth MSS 54, 55 and 67, include Gwilym Tew, Hywel Dafi, Hywel Swrdwal, Huw Cae Llwyd, and Dafydd Epynt.

Sixteenth-century manuscripts containing *cywyddau* were mainly the work of Welsh humanist scholars such as Elis GRUFFYDD (*c.* 1490–*c.* 1558), Thomas Wiliems (†1622), Humphrey Davies (†1635), and Dr John Davies of Mallwyd (†1644). Anthologies from this period include NLW Llanstephan MS 6 (*c.* 1520) and British Library Additional MS 14997 (*c.* 1540). Many of them are laid out with titles, rubrics, and other indications that the contents were to be read as well as to be preserved for oral performance.

By the 17th century, the work of the *Cywyddwyr* was highly regarded among the native Welsh gentry as a mark of social status, and collections were made for the libraries of families such as the Wynns of Gwydir and the Vaughans of Corsygedol. Since PRINTING was still largely located in London and dominated by English-language publishing, Welsh texts continued to be hand-copied throughout the 18th century, generating a large corpus of manuscripts containing *cywyddau* which were copied and collected by scribes, clergy, and antiquarians. The Morris brothers of Anglesey (MORRISIAID MÔN), especially Lewis and William, were the most significant collectors and copyists of Welsh manuscripts in the 18th century, and made large collections of poems attributed to Dafydd ap Gwilym and other *Cywyddwyr*, forming the basis of the earliest printed editions in the latter part of the century.

§7. MAJOR CYWYDDWYR IN CHRONOLOGICAL ORDER

Dates indicate approximate lifespans and/or periods of activity as far as they can be documented.

DAFYDD AP GWILYM (*c.* 1315–*c.* 1350)
Madog Benfras (*c.* 1320–60)
Llywelyn Goch ap Meurig Hen (*c.* 1330–90)
Gruffudd ab Adda (*c.* 1340–80)
IOLO GOCH (*fl.* 1345–97)
Gruffudd Gryg (*fl.* 1357–70)
Rhys Goch Eryri (*c.* 1365–*c.* 1440)
Gruffudd Llwyd ap Dafydd ab Einion Llygliw (*c.* 1380–1410)
Dafydd Llwyd (of Mathafarn) (*c.* 1395–*c.* 1486)
SIÔN CENT (*fl. c.* 1400–30/45)
Llywelyn ab y Moel (*c.* 1400–40)
GUTO'R GLYN (*c.* 1418–*c.* 1493)
Ieuan ap Rhydderch (*c.* 1430–70)
Hywel Swrdwal (*c.* 1430–70)
Huw Cae Llwyd (*c.* 1430–1505)
Bedo Brwynllys (*c.* 1440–80)
Dafydd ap Maredudd ap Tudur (*c.* 1440–80)
Dafydd Epynt (*c.* 1440–80)
Gwilym ab Ieuan Hen (*c.* 1440–80)
Gwilym Tew (*c.* 1440–80)
Hywel Dafi (*c.* 1440–80)
DAFYDD NANMOR (*fl.* 1445–90)
LEWYS GLYN COTHI (*fl.* 1447–89)
Llawdden (*c.* 1450–80)

DAFYDD AB EDMWND (*fl.* 1450–97)
GUTUN OWAIN (*fl.* 1450–98)
Ieuan Brydydd Hir (*c.* 1450–1500)
Tudur Penllyn (*c.* 1460–85)
Ieuan Deulwyn (*c.* 1460–90)
Llywelyn ap Gutun (*c.* 1460–1500)
GWERFUL MECHAIN (*c.* 1460–*post* 1502)
Bedo Phylip Bach (*c.* 1460–1500)
TUDUR ALED (*c.* 1465–*c.* 1525)
Lewys Môn (*c.* 1465–1527)
Bedo Aeddren (*c.* 1480–1520)
Iorwerth Fynglwyd (*c.* 1480–1530)
Gruffudd ab Ieuan ap Llywelyn Fychan (*c.* 1485–1553)
Huw ap Dafydd (*c.* 1500–50)
Gruffudd Hiraethog (*c.* 1510–64)
Lewys Morgannwg (*c.* 1520–50)
SIÔN TUDUR (*c.* 1522–1602)
Simwnt Fychan (*c.* 1530–1606)
Wiliam Llŷn (*c.* 1535–80)
Edmwnd Prys (1543/4–1623)
Wiliam Cynwal (†1587/8)

PRIMARY SOURCES

MSS. Aberystwyth, NLW, Peniarth 48, 54, 55, 57(i), 67, Llanstephan 6 (*c.* 1520); London, BL Add. 14997 (*c.* 1540).
EDITIONS. Parry, *Gwaith Dafydd ap Gwilym*; G. J. Williams & Jones, *Gramadegau'r Penceirddiaid*.
NOTE: 'Cyfres Beirdd yr Uchelwyr', published by the University of Wales Centre for Advanced Welsh and Celtic Studies, is an ongoing project to edit the surviving works of the 'Poets of the Nobility'.
TRANS. Johnston, *Iolo Goch: Poems*.

FURTHER READING

ACTS OF UNION; AWDL; BARDIC ORDER; CAERFYRDDIN; CRWTH; CYMRU; CYNFEIRDD; CYNGHANEDD; CYWYDD; DAFYDD AB EDMWND; DAFYDD AP GWILYM; DAFYDD NANMOR; DEHEUBARTH; EISTEDDFOD; ENGLYN; GENEALOGIES; GOGYNFEIRDD; GRAMADEGAU'R PENCEIRDDIAID; GRUFFUDD AP CYNAN; GRUFFYDD; GUTO'R GLYN; GUTUN OWAIN; GWERFUL MECHAIN; GWYNEDD; HARP; HENDREGADREDD MANUSCRIPT; IOLO GOCH; LAW TEXTS; LEWYS GLYN COTHI; LLYFR COCH HERGEST; LLYFR GWYN RHYDDERCH; LLYFRGELL GENEDLAETHOL CYMRU; MORRISIAID MÔN; OWAIN GLYNDŴR; POWYS; PRINTING; PROPHECY; SATIRE; SIÔN CENT; SIÔN TUDUR; TUDUR; TUDUR ALED; WELSH; WELSH POETRY; WILLIAMS; YMRYSONAU; Bowen, BBCS 29.453–96; Bowen, *Beirdd yr Uchelwyr*; Bowen, *Llên Cymru* 9.46–73; Bowen, *Llên Cymru* 17.60–107; Bowen, *Ysgrifau Beirniadol* 11.63–108; Bromwich, *Aspects of the Poetry of Dafydd ap Gwilym*; Bleddyn Owen Huws, *Canu Gofyn a Diolch*; Daniel Huws, *Medieval Welsh Manuscripts*; Jarman & Hughes, *Guide to Welsh Literature 2*; J. Gwynfor Jones, *Concepts of Order and Gentility in Wales*; Matonis, BBCS 28.47–72; Parry, THSC 1936.143–60; Rowlands, *Poems of the Cywyddwyr*; J. E. Caerwyn Williams, *Court Poet in Medieval Wales*.

Helen Fulton

D

Dacians and Celts

Dacia was the ancient country north of the lower DANUBE, approximately coinciding with the territory of modern Romania. During the pre-Roman IRON AGE, its inhabitants were closely related to the Thracians, as can be seen from their linguistic and archaeological remains. Thrace (Thracia) was the ancient name of the country corresponding roughly to modern Bulgaria and European Turkey. The Thracian language was INDO-EUROPEAN, but distinct from Celtic; some scholars have seen a special connection between the extinct Thracian and the modern Indo-European language Albanian. The Dacians developed a distinctive civilization during the second Iron Age (from roughly 500 BC), which reached an advanced stage of development and a social structure capable of supporting a large centralized kingdom in the last two pre-Roman centuries (the 1st BC and the 1st AD). They founded an empire under the authority of king Burebista in the 1st century BC. This state was then conquered by the Roman emperor Trajan in AD 106.

During the second half of the 4th century BC, the cultural influence of the Celts appears in the archaeological records emanating from areas to the west (the middle Danube, ALPINE region, and north-west BALKANS), where Middle LA TÈNE material culture figured and where Celtic proper names were abundantly attested within the ancient period. This Celtic material appears in north-western and central Dacia and is reflected especially in burials (which have at the present time been more intensely researched and are consequently better known than the evidence from settlements).

Archaeological investigation, undertaken in the Celtic cemeteries of this period in western Dacia, has highlighted several Celtic warrior graves with military equipment (SWORDS, spears, battle knives). This material suggests the forceful penetration of a military élite within the region of Dacia, now known as Transylvania, bounded on the east by the formidable barrier of the Carpathian range. The relationship of these militaristic bearers of La Tène culture with the indigenous Dacians was not invariably hostile. A pattern of co-existence and fusion is seen in sites of the 3rd and 2nd centuries BC from Transylvania, revealing domestic dwellings where a mixture of Celtic and Dacian pottery was in use. Moreover, a number of graves of the Celtic type contain vessels of Dacian type. The presence of the Celts appears to have provided a catalysing factor for the intra-Carpathian Dacian civilization. In this period, these Dacians of Transylvania borrowed from the newcomers the potter's wheel, superior technology in metal work, and probably commenced the Dacian tradition of COINAGE. Certain types of Celtic jewellery—fibulae (brooches) and the distinctive Celtic neckrings known as TORCS—were also borrowed by the Dacians and adapted to local tastes.

The subsequent fate of the Celts in Transylvania remains uncertain. Evidence for definable La Tène groups peters out in the region in the 2nd century BC (most probably specifically after c. 150 BC). It is at about this time that Dacian culture underwent changes which led to its final mature phase, and the number of settlements attests to a growth in population and economic expansion. TROGUS POMPEIUS AND JUSTIN mention a rise in Dacian authority under the leadership of King Rubobostes, which possibly suggests the end of Celtic dominance in Transylvania, that is, that they were possibly thrust out of Dacia by the growing power of an indigenous dynasty. Alternatively, some scholars have proposed that the Transylvanian Celts remained, but merged into the local cultural context and thus ceased to be distinctive archaeologically. It is possible that both processes were partially responsible for the disappearance of La Tène material in Romania. The presence of the Celts in other parts of Dacia, further

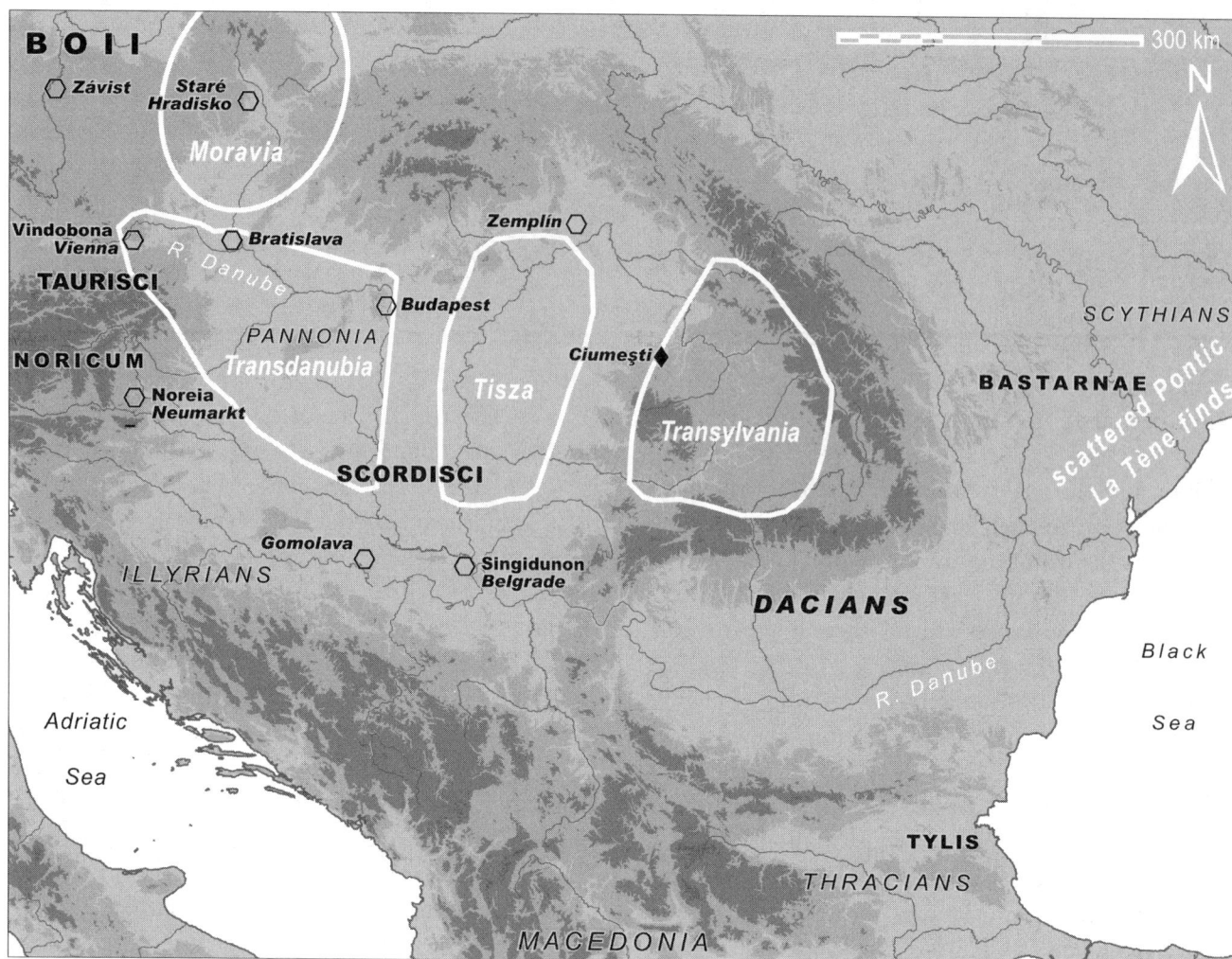

Celts and Dacians in eastern and central Europe: the areas outlined and labelled in white represent regional groups of eastern La Tène burials; hexagons represent oppida.

to the east (Moldova, Dobrogea) in areas associated with the group name Bastarnae, is controversial, but La Tène objects have been found there.

One pivotal historical episode was the defeat of several Celtic tribes by the Dacian king Burebista, probably around 60 BC, at which time his forces advanced to the middle Danube region. From this period, pottery of the Dacian type has been discovered in Celtic settlements in central Europe including Gomolava, Yugoslavia, and Budapest, Hungary. STRABO (*Geography* 7.3.11) tells the story of the destruction of the major central European Celtic tribes, the BOII led by Critasiros and the TAURISCI. Strabo also mentions the expeditions of Burebista against a group of Celts described as living among the Illyrians and the Thracians (probably the SCORDISCI). Archaeological discoveries in the settlements and the fortifications of the Dacians in the period of their kingdom (1st century

BC and 1st century AD) show that relations between the Dacians and the Celts from the regions north and west of Dacia continued. For example, in the Dacian sites from western and central Dacia, there are late La Tène-type painted ceramic imports, specifically vessels with coloured designs made by working graphite into the fabric, some imported, others made by Dacian potters imitating Celtic prototypes.

PRIMARY SOURCES
Izvoare privind istoria României 1; STRABO, *Geography* 7.3.11; Trogus Pompeius, *Philippic Histories* 24.4.5.

FURTHER READING
ALPINE; BALKANS; BOII; COINAGE; DANUBE; INDO-EUROPEAN; IRON AGE; LA TÈNE; SCORDISCI; SWORDS; TAURISCI; TORC; TROGUS POMPEIUS AND JUSTIN; Crişan, *Burebista and his Time* 16–23, 113–22; Rustoiu, *Les Celtes et les Thraco-Daces de l'est du bassin des Carpathes* 179–85; Sîrbu & Florea, *Les Géto-Daces* 189–91; Zirra, *Celts in Central Europe* 47–63; Zirra, *Dacia* new ser. 15.171–238.

Gelu Florea

Dafydd ab Edmwnd (*fl.* 1450–97) was a poet who hailed from Hanmer in Maelor Saesneg, northeast Wales (CYMRU). Like the Hanmer family itself, Dafydd was a descendant of Sir Thomas de Macclesfield, who settled in Wales following the conquests of Edward I. He was the owner of a mansion called Yr Owredd in Maelor Saesneg, though he seems to have spent much of his time at Pwllgwepra, Northop. His bardic teacher was probably Maredudd ap Rhys (*fl.* 1440–83). Dafydd, in turn, is credited with teaching both his relative TUDUR ALED and the poet-copyist GUTUN OWAIN.

As a comfortably placed *uchelwr* (nobleman), Dafydd was probably not financially dependent upon his craft, and this is possibly one reason why he has left relatively few elegies and eulogies. Among these, however, are some of the most memorable poems of his day. His CYWYDD advising Rhys Wyn ap Llywelyn from Botffordd in Anglesey (MÔN) not to marry an Englishwoman was seized upon by Saunders LEWIS as containing the most exciting political statement made by a Welsh poet during the period of the Wars of the Roses (*Meistri a'u Crefft* 128). Another key poem is his elegy to Siôn Eos, a harpist who killed a man in a brawl in Chirk (Y Waun). The poem is in part a complaint against English law, which saw Siôn hanged. The Welsh Law of HYWEL DDA, on the other hand, would have spared him.

Most of his poems, however, are love poems. In many ways they follow in the footsteps of DAFYDD AP GWILYM, though they tend to be more formal expositions of female beauty, and demonstrate Dafydd ab Edmwnd's mastery of the technical aspects of CERDD DAFOD. Indeed, his contribution to the rules of poetry was important (see BARDIC ORDER). In the EISTEDDFOD held at Carmarthen (CAERFYRDDIN) *c.* 1451, where he was awarded a silver chair, he was responsible for changes that resulted in the introduction of stricter metres and in stricter rules for CYNGHANEDD itself. Although these changes were criticized by later writers, they were probably designed to ensure that poetry remained a high-status craft whose requirements were demanding.

PRIMARY SOURCE
EDITION. Thomas Roberts, *Gwaith Dafydd ab Edmwnd*.

FURTHER READING
BARDIC ORDER; CAERFYRDDIN; CERDD DAFOD; CYMRU;
CYNGHANEDD; CYWYDD; CYWYDDWYR; DAFYDD AP GWILYM; EISTEDDFOD; GUTUN OWAIN; HYWEL DDA; LEWIS; MÔN; TUDUR ALED; WELSH POETRY; Lewis, *Meistri a'u Crefft* 124–31; Rowlands, BBCS 31.31–47; Rowlands, *Guide to Welsh Literature* 2.275–97.

Dylan Foster Evans

Dafydd ap Gwilym, regarded by his contemporaries as well as by modern critics as the foremost poet among medieval CYWYDDWYR, composed and performed poetry in the first half of the 14th century. There is little documentary evidence for his life, apart from the internal evidence of the poems. He was probably born *c.* 1315, in Brogynin, in the parish of LLANBADARN FAWR, near ABERYSTWYTH in CEREDIGION, and died *c.* 1350, possibly of the plague. Three of his contemporaries—Madog Benfras, Gruffudd Gryg, and IOLO GOCH—composed elegies on his death.

Born into a prominent family of *uchelwyr* (noblemen), Dafydd received his training in the art of CERDD DAFOD from his uncle, Llywelyn ap Gwilym, constable of Castellnewydd Emlyn in 1343, while enjoying a formal education at the Cistercian abbey of Strata Florida (YSTRAD-FFLUR) in Ceredigion (see CISTERCIAN ABBEYS IN WALES). References in the poems suggest that he travelled widely in Wales (CYMRU) during the 1330s and 1340s, performing his poetry for the *uchelwyr* and for clerical (and possibly monastic) audiences. Significant patrons include Ifor ap Llywelyn ('Ifor Hael') of Basaleg in MORGANNWG, and Ieuan Llwyd of Parcrhydderch in Ceredigion.

While upwards of 350 poems were attributed to Dafydd ap Gwilym by scribes of the 15th century and later, the canon of poems established by Thomas PARRY in *Gwaith Dafydd ap Gwilym* (Cardiff, 1952) numbers around 150. Most are in the CYWYDD metre, but the collection also includes poems addressed to patrons in the ENGLYN and AWDL metres. Dafydd is particularly renowned for his courtly love songs and nature poems, often with a deeply religious subtext, but his output also includes humorous narratives about failed love-trysts reminiscent of the *fabliau* genre. Examples of other French and English genres in his work, such as the *pastourelle*, the *aubade*, and the *serenade*, attest to his familiarity with European traditions of court poetry, while numerous folk-tale and popular allusions suggest the influence of sub-literary traditions associated with the *clêr*, the popular singers of medieval Wales.

Dafydd's contribution to the Welsh poetic tradition resides in his development of the *cywydd* metre as a stylish vehicle for court poetry; his assimilation of native Welsh traditions into the mainstream of European poetry; and the sheer range and quality of his verse, characterized by his versatile handling of CYNGHANEDD, the verbal wit of his puns and metaphors, and the seamless imagery of his poems of love and nature.

PRIMARY SOURCES
EDITIONS. Fulton, *Selections from the Dafydd ap Gwilym Apocrypha*; PARRY, *Gwaith Dafydd ap Gwilym*.
TRANS. Bromwich, *Dafydd ap Gwilym: A Selection of Poems*; Loomis, *Dafydd ap Gwilym: The Poems*; Thomas, *Dafydd ap Gwilym: His Poems*.

FURTHER READING
ABERYSTWYTH; AWDL; CERDD DAFOD; CEREDIGION; CISTERCIAN ABBEYS IN WALES; CYMRU; CYNGHANEDD; CYWYDD; CYWYDDWYR; ENGLYN; IOLO GOCH; LLANBADARN FAWR; MORGANNWG; WELSH POETRY; YSTRAD-FFLUR; Bromwich, *Guide to Welsh Literature* 2.95–125; Edwards, *Dafydd ap Gwilym: Influences and Analogues*; Fulton, *Dafydd ap Gwilym and the European Context*; Gruffydd, *Celtic Languages and Celtic Peoples* 425–42; Gruffydd, *Dafydd ap Gwilym*; Surridge, *Proc. First North American Congress of Celtic Studies* 531–43.

Helen Fulton

Dafydd Benfras

Dafydd Benfras (*fl.* 1220–58) was one of the medieval Welsh court poets known as the GOGYNFEIRDD, and is associated with the royal court of GWYNEDD in north Wales (CYMRU), where he sang to the major princes of the region between the second half of the reign of LLYWELYN AB IORWERTH and the early years of LLYWELYN AP GRUFFUDD. Although only 804 lines of his poetry have survived, he is regarded as one of the most accomplished poets of the period, his poems being well crafted and structured. He refers to himself as *pencerdd* (chief poet) and his poems exude the same self-confidence as seen (albeit to a greater extent) in the poetry of CYNDDELW Brydydd Mawr.

Apart from his association with Gwynedd, very little is known about Dafydd Benfras himself. (The epithet *penfras* literally means 'having a large head'.) BLEDDYN FARDD, Dafydd's contemporary and possible bardic pupil, wrote an elegy upon his death in which he refers to Dafydd as *un mab Llywarch* (the only son

of Llywarch), and it has been suggested that Dafydd Benfras might well have been the son of the poet LLYWARCH AP LLYWELYN, who was probably the chief poet of Llywelyn ab Iorwerth until *c.* 1220. However, this testimony contradicts that of a 16th-century genealogy in the hand of Gruffudd Hiraethog, which claims that Dafydd Benfras belonged to a family of poets from Anglesey (MÔN) and that he was the son of one Dafydd Gwys Sanffraid. Another genealogy from the same source claims that the important 14th-century Anglesey poet Gruffudd ap Maredudd was a direct descendant of Dafydd Benfras. An attempt has been made to reconcile these two conflicting accounts of Dafydd's lineage by suggesting that *mab Llywarch* could figuratively mean 'bardic pupil' or even 'foster son of Llywarch', but this is unlikely. One must, therefore, decide between the contemporary evidence of Bleddyn Fardd, and the later evidence of the genealogy of Gruffudd Hiraethog. The latter is supported by a strong association between Dafydd Benfras and Anglesey which is attested in the poems and in references to him by later poets. The most recent editor of the work of Dafydd Benfras tends towards this second view.

We learn from the elegy by Bleddyn Fardd that Dafydd Benfras died in south Wales and was buried in Llangadog, far from his homeland in Gwynedd:

> *Uthr gwynfan chwerw, herw hirwae:*
> *Eithr Gwynedd, ym medd, y mae.*

> Bitter [and] terrible lament, onslaught of long pain:
> He is in a grave outside Gwynedd.

No mention is made in the poem of Dafydd's poetic skills; rather he is praised for his valour on the battlefield and for his generosity as a patron.

Eleven of the twelve surviving poems of Dafydd Benfras are sung in one of the AWDL metres, the other being a series composed in the ENGLYN metre. Thematically they are sung in the TALIESIN tradition, expounding the traditional themes of valour on the battlefield and generosity in the court, and, as mentioned above, the princes of Gwynedd were his main patrons. No religious poems as such have survived, but his poems demonstrate that he was well versed in the traditions of the Bible and the Apocrypha, and in one poem he addresses both God and Llywelyn ab Iorwerth. One of his most notable poems is a series of *englynion* on the philosophical theme of the brevity of life, in which he reflects on the inevitability of the grave and the futility of all earthly wealth and ambition.

PRIMARY SOURCES
MSS. Aberystwyth, NLW 727, 4973, 6680 (HENDREGAD-REDD MANUSCRIPT), Peniarth 29 (Black Book of Chirk); Oxford, Jesus College III (LLYFR COCH HERGEST). EDITION. Costigan, *Gwaith Dafydd Benfras* 361–557. TRANS. Conran, *Welsh Verse* 160–1; Gwyn Williams, *Oxford Book of Welsh Verse in English* 30.

FURTHER READING
AWDL; BLEDDYN FARDD; CYMRU; CYNDDELW; ENGLYN; GOGYNFEIRDD; GWYNEDD; LLYWARCH AP LLYWELYN; LLYWELYN AB IORWERTH; LLYWELYN AP GRUFFUDD; MÔN; TALIESIN; Andrews et al., *Gwaith Bleddyn Fardd* 527–32; Bosco, *SC* 22/23.49–117; Bosco, *Ysgrifau Beirniadol* 13.70–92; Costigan et al., *Gwaith Dafydd Benfras* 361–557; Wiliam, *Trans. Anglesey Antiquarian Society and Field Club* 1980.33–5; Wiliam, *Trans. Anglesey Antiquarian Society and Field Club* 1985.109–11.

Ann Parry Owen

Dafydd Nanmor

was a Welsh poet (*fl.* 1445–90) from Nanmor near Beddgelert in Snowdonia (ERYRI), GWYNEDD. He was exiled from his native region about 1453 because of love poems which he addressed to a married woman known as Gwen o'r Ddôl. He seems to have spent the rest of his life in south-west Wales (CYMRU). His principal patrons were the Tywyn family near Cardigan (ABERTEIFI), and his praise poetry to them over three generations represents some of the clearest evidence of the values of *perchentyaeth* ('house-holdership'). The advice poem which he composed in his old age to the young Rhys ap Rhydderch celebrates the continuity of noble stock, drawing on imagery from the Chain of Being. Among his love poems two are outstanding: an elegy for an anonymous girl, and 'Gwallt Llio', a description of a girl's hair that uses the technique of *dyfalu* (meaning approximately 'poetic description', literally 'imagining, conjecture') to dazzling effect. His style is renowned for its epigrammatic clarity, and he was a virtuoso exponent of verse forms, including an *awdl enghreifftiol* using all twenty-four strict metres (see AWDL; CERDD DAFOD; CYWYDD; ENGLYN; EINION OFFEIRIAD). His work displays some Latin learning, and it is possible that the group of his poems in Peniarth MS 52 (see HENGWRT) is in his hand. He composed a number of

prophetic poems in support of the Lancastrian cause (see PROPHECY), and greeted the infant Henry Tudor (see TUDUR) as a future king soon after his birth in 1457. Some fifty of his poems survive, but the entire corpus has yet to be edited satisfactorily.

PRIMARY SOURCE
EDITION. Thomas Roberts & Williams, *Poetical Works of Dafydd Nanmor*.

FURTHER READING
ABERTEIFI; AWDL; CERDD DAFOD; CYMRU; CYWYDD; CYWYDDWYR; EINION OFFEIRIAD; ENGLYN; ERYRI; GWYNEDD; HENGWRT; PROPHECY; TUDUR; Lewis, *Meistri'r Canrifoedd* 80–92; Ruddock, *Dafydd Nanmor*.

Dafydd Johnston

Dagda

(Dagdae, Dagán) was one of the principal pre-Christian deities of Ireland (ÉRIU) commemorated in the MYTHOLOGICAL CYCLE of early IRISH LITERATURE, figuring in several texts as a leader or the king of the supernatural race, the TUATH DÉ, as in, for example, LEBAR GABÁLA ÉRENN ('The Book of Invasions') and the early tale DE GABÁIL IN T-SÍDA (Concerning the taking of the otherworld mound). The most extensive single surviving description of the Dagda is in CATH MAIGE TUIRED ('The [Second] Battle of Mag Tuired').

His name means 'good god' (< Celtic *Dago-dēwos), in the sense of technical competence and excellence of performance, and is often cited with the definite article, i.e. the Dagda. One of his alternative names, Eochaid Ollathair ('father of all' or 'great father'), invites parallels to the Norse god Òðin (also known as Alfǫðr, 'all-father'), who is similarly versatile. His rôle as a father-god can also be deduced from surviving descriptions of him, and he is the father of several important characters in the Mythological Cycle, most importantly OENGUS MAC IND ÓC, a god excelling in youth and beauty, and the goddess Bríg, also known as BRIGIT. The Dagda has been interpreted variously as a sky god, storm god, earth god, and the sun. He is shown in several tales to possess great sexual potency, mating with many different goddesses, including BÓAND (the mother of Oengus Mac ind Óc) and the MORRÍGAN in the *Metrical* DINDSHENCHAS. His children include Áed Menbhrec, Bodb Derg, Cermat, Mider, and Ainge. He is also described as a great warrior and skilful in magic. His characteristics suggest that the Dagda was a transfunctional deity associated with craft wisdom and bridging the distance between death and regeneration.

Even with all his powers, the Dagda is usually portrayed as gross and uncouth. Sent on behalf of the Túath Dé to the enemy camp in *Cath Maige Tuired*, he is mocked by the FOMOIRI, who force him to drink an enormous quantity of porridge that has been poured into a hole in the ground. His greed is such that he eats it all and scrapes the bottom of the hole with his finger to get the last of it. He travels on to the Sligo coast, his penis exposed and the great size of his belly impeding his progress. Despite his grossness, he manages to seduce the daughter of Indech, who afterwards agrees to perform spells against the Fomoiri, although the Dagda's earlier sexual encounter with the Mórrigan has effectively ensured victory for the Túath Dé.

The Dagda has two fabulous material attributes, a cauldron of plenty (see CAULDRONS), and a club that can kill the living and raise the dead. The latter has led to comparisons of the Dagda with Heracles and the Gaulish figure SUCELLUS. The club is so huge that it has to be dragged on wheels. Owing to these attributes, some early modern scholars tended to see in the Dagda a throwback to 'primitive' beliefs and virtues of the Stone Age. In the trifunctional school of interpretation of Indo-European myths based on the work of Dumézil, the Dagda has been seen as exemplifying the third social function of wealth and food production. His cauldron, together with his omniscience, suggests that the Dagda might also have been a Celtic god of the OTHERWORLD, and as such he has been identified with Donn and DīS PATER.

PRIMARY SOURCES
EDITION. Bergin, *Medieval Studies in Memory of Gertrude Schoepperle Loomis* 399–406 (How the Dagda got his Magic Staff).
ED. & TRANS. Gray, *Cath Muige Tuired*; Stokes, *Irische Texte* 3/2.354–7 (*Cóir Anmann*/Fitness of Names).

FURTHER READING
BÓAND; BRIGIT; CATH MAIGE TUIRED; CAULDRONS; DE GABÁIL IN T-SÍDA; DINDSHENCHAS; DĪS PATER; ÉRIU; FOMOIRI; IRISH LITERATURE; LEBAR GABÁLA ÉRENN; MORRÍGAN; MYTHOLOGICAL CYCLE; OENGUS MAC IND ÓC; OTHERWORLD; SUCELLUS; TUATH DÉ; Dumézil, *Jupiter, Mars, Quirinus*; O'Rahilly, *Early Irish History and Mythology* 318–20; Sjoestedt, *Gods and Heroes of the Celts* 38–44.

Victoria Simmons, Tom Sjöblom

Dál gCais (Middle Irish Dál Cais) is the name of an Irish kingdom and tribe of the early medieval period, centred on an area that is now eastern Co. Clare (Contae an Chláir). They first appear in the early 8th century as a branch of the population group known as Déisi Muman ('Déisi' or 'vassal tribes of Munster/MUMU'), settled on either side of the Shannon estuary. Those to the south and east of the river were known as the Déis Deiscirt and those to the north and west the Déis Tuaiscirt. By the beginning of the 9th century the lands of the Déis Deiscirt were overrun, probably by their neighbours to the west, the Uí Fidgenti, leaving the northern sub-kingdom standing alone.

The tribe is first referred to as the Dál gCais in 934, and the name can be seen as a by-product of innovative origin legend, which linked them with the previously dominant ÉOGANACHT federation. This legendary pedigree derived the Dál gCais kings from traditional heroes assigned to the prehistoric period and gave them claim to the kingship of CAISEL MUMAN: Dál gCais means 'people of Cas', named after Cormac Cas, son of Ailill Aulomm and brother of Éogan Már, legendary forefather and namesake of the Éoganacht tribes, who dominated Munster from the 6th to the 10th centuries. The creation of such a pedigree by the literary classes implies a political situation in which Dál gCais power had risen at the expense of the Éoganacht lineages. In the early 10th century other tribes of Clare, the Corca Mruad and Corca Baiscinn, came increasingly under the sway of the Dál gCais, who may also have extended their influence to the south of the Shannon estuary at this time. The 951 death notice of their king Cennétig mac Lorcáin in the ANNALS of Ulster calls him *rí Tuathmuman* ('king of Thomond, north Munster', approximately coextensive with the modern Co. Clare) and the Annals of Inisfallen, even more ambitiously, *rígdamna Cassil* 'royal heir of Caisel'.

It has been suggested that the rise of the Dál gCais at the expense of the Éoganacht was partly the result of machinations of the latter's traditional rivals, the Uí NÉILL kings of Tara (TEAMHAIR), whose natural self-interest was to keep the Munster leadership weak with competing claimants to the kingship of Caisel (Kelleher, *North Munster Studies* 230–41). However, as Ó Corráin points out (*Ireland before the Normans*), the impotence of the Éoganacht and the resulting political fragmentation of Munster can account for the success of Dál gCais without external factors. Arguing against an alliance with Tara at this period, Mael Sechnaill II of the southern Uí Néill invaded and laid waste Dál gCais territory in 950, when he also provocatively cut down the sacred tree (*bile*) at the royal inauguration site of Magh Adair.

The bitterness of the rivalry between the Dál gCais and the Éoganacht is reflected in the hostility in the hagiographic writings produced by the monks of their two main churches, at Killaloe (Cill Dalua) and Emly (Imleach) respectively. For instance, the Dál gCais saint Tairdelbach is described as smashing and burning the yew tree, the symbol of Emly and the Éoganacht (see Ó Corráin, *Ireland in Early Mediaeval Europe*).

The collapse of the Munster kingship in the mid-10th century was followed by a decade of sporadic warfare and constantly reconfiguring alliances, with the king of Dál gCais, Mathgamain mac Cennétig, and Mael Muad mac Brain of the Éoganacht Raithlinn the two main protagonists. By the end of this period Mathgamain, who had won the majority of direct encounters, appears to have been the *de facto* king of Munster. When Mathgamain was killed by Mael Muad following the treachery of his Uí Fidgenti allies, the kingship passed on to his brother, the renowned BRIAN BÓRUMA, who was to become the first convincing *Ard Rí na hÉireann* 'high-king of Ireland' from a dynasty other than the Uí Néill.

Following the death of Brian at the battle of Clontarf near Dublin (BAILE ÁTHA CLIATH) in 1014, the power of the Dál gCais—or Uí Briain 'O'Briens' as they were henceforth known—fell into eclipse for several decades, but revived under Tairdelbach Ua Briain who, under the patronage of the king of Leinster (LAIGIN), succeeded in wresting control of Munster from his uncle, Donnchad. Tairdelbach succeeded subsequently in bringing Meath (MIDE), Leinster, and Ulster (ULAID) under his lordship. This trend continued under his son Muirchertach, who further expanded this sphere of influence to include CONNACHT.

After the death of Muirchertach in 1118 the supremacy of the Uí Briain came to an end and their lordship shrank back to their hereditary lands in Thomond. Following the Anglo-Norman invasion (1169–), they defended their territory more effectively than most Gaelic lordships and were still a powerful

dynasty in the Tudor period (see TUDUR) when they became Earls of Thomond under the English policy of surrender and regrant.

A body of stories concerning the kings of the Dál gCais, the Dalcassian Cycle, is sometimes regarded as part of the KINGS' CYCLES (MacKillop, *Dictionary of Celtic Mythology* 113; Dillon, *Cycles of the Kings* 2). This material centres on the activities of Brian Bóruma and his son Murchad. Its prime source is the *Cogadh Gaedhel re Gallaibh* ('The War of the Gaedhil with the Gaill'), aiming to present the activities of Brian, especially at Clontarf, as patriotic and directed against the Norse rather than rival Irish warlords.

PRIMARY SOURCES
EDITION. Ó Donnchada, *An Leabhar Muimhneach*.
ED. & TRANS. Todd, *Cogadh Gaedhel re Gallaib*.

FURTHER READING
ANNALS; BAILE ÁTHA CLIATH; BRIAN BÓRUMA; CAISEL MUMAN; CONNACHT; ÉOGANACHT; ÉRIU; KINGS' CYCLES; LAIGIN; MIDE; MUMU; TEAMHAIR; TUDUR; UÍ NÉILL; ULAID; Byrne, *Irish Kings and High-Kings*; Dillon, *Cycles of the Kings*; Kelleher, *North Munster Studies* 230–41; MacKillop, *Dictionary of Celtic Mythology*; Ó Corráin, *Ireland before the Normans*; Ó Corráin, *Ireland in Early Mediaeval Europe*.

SÓF

Dál Riata (Dalriada, Early Old Irish Dál Réti) is the term universally used by modern scholars for the GAELIC-speaking kingdom which flourished in Argyll (Earra-Ghaidheal) between the 6th and 9th centuries AD. This name is, however, sparingly used in contemporary sources and its exact meaning and the chronology of its usage may be more complex than modern scholarship has allowed. Writing *c.* 730 the Northumbrian BEDA explained the presence of Gaelic speakers in Britain thus: 'These came from Ireland under their leader Reuda, and won lands among the Picts either by friendly treaty or by the sword. These they still possess. They are still called Dalreudini after this leader, *Dal* in their language signifying a part.' In Argyll, the 2nd-century *Geography* of PTOLEMY locates a tribe called 'Επιδιοι *Epidii*, a name probably related to the common Irish *Eochaid*. Middle Irish pedigrees of the kings of the SCOTS include an Eochaid Riada (known in some versions as Cairpre Rígfota) who, if we assign an average number of years to generations, would have ruled in the 2nd century

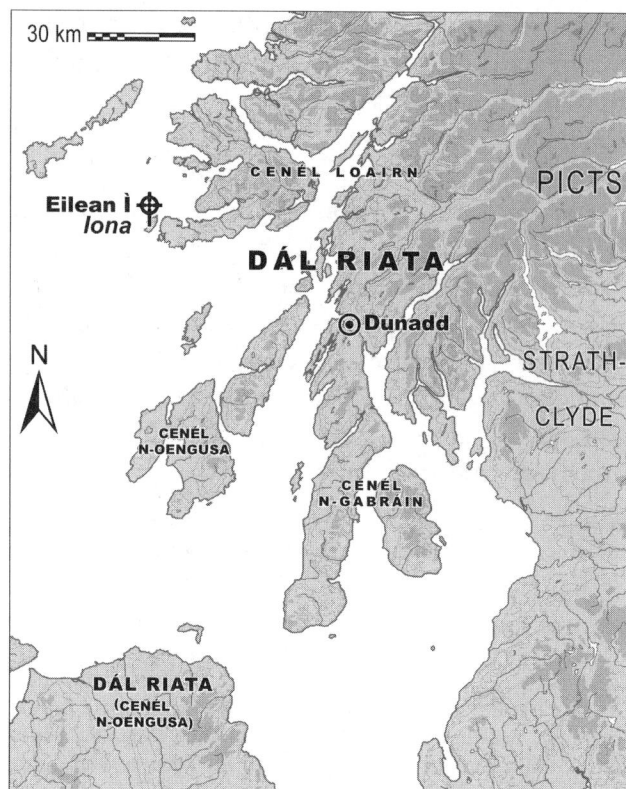

AD, but by the period of the texts (900–1200) the migration had been redated to the time of FERGUS MÓR MAC ERC whose obituary was noted in the ANNALS under the year 501. In its introductory passage the SENCHUS FER NALBAN claims that six of the thirteen sons of Erc settled in Scotland (ALBA), and this tale probably reflects the idea that there were six *cenéla* (kindreds) in Gaelic north Britain at the time this tract was originally compiled. The later portion of the tract, which deals with the military assessment of the 'three thirds of Dál Riata', names the three *cenéla* as Cenél nGabráin (based in Kintyre and Arran), Cenél Loairn (based in Mull and Lorne) and Cenél nOengusa. This last *cenél* was not descended from one of the six sons who were originally said to have settled in Scotland, but was principally located in Ireland (ÉRIU); however, a portion of them at the time of the text occupied at least part of Islay which, in the original scheme, had been assigned to the descendents of Fergus bec mac Erc. An additional unconnected tractate, *Cethri Prímchenéla Dáil Riata* (The four chief kindreds of Dál Riata), that appears to record information from *c.* 700, claims that the four 'chief kindreds' of Dál Riata were

the three named above plus Cenél Comgaill, a group whose territory had been assigned to Cenél nGabráin in the *Senchus*. What all this indicates is that the position of the constituent kindreds within Gaelic Argyll was fluid throughout the period and that the genealogical doctrines which explain these relationships were equally fluid. It is also clear that part of the kingdom of Dál Riata was in Ireland, but whether this was just the lands of Cenél nOengusa or whether all seven of the kindreds descended from the sons of Erc were regarded as having land in north-east Ireland is less clear. It may well be that the scheme presented in the early part of the *Senchus*—which related the descent not only of the thirteen sons of Erc but also of the eleven sons of his brother Olchú—had originally been designed to explain the relationship of a much larger group of peoples in the north of Ireland and their offshoot in Argyll, and that the idea of a sub-grouping, which became known as Dál Riata, was a later development.

Scholars are not in agreement as to the internal organization of Dál Riata. Some see it as a typical Irish overkingdom with each of the *cenéla* functioning as a TUATH in its own right with a local king and assembly, whilst others, influenced perhaps by the king-list prefixed to the later Scottish king-lists, believe it to have been a single kingdom ruled by a strong centralized monarchy. For most of the historical period, from the mid-6th century to the end of the kingdom in the 9th century, the kingship, or overkingship, was held by Cenél nGabráin, although in the decades around 700 Cenél Loairn was sometimes able to challenge this monopoly.

Dál Riata is most famous for playing host to St Columba (COLUM CILLE) and his foundation of Iona (EILEAN Ì). Because of this we are relatively well informed about the kingdom from the period of Columba's arrival (*c.* 563) through to the mid-8th century when a copy of the Chronicle kept at Iona was taken to Ireland, where it was eventually incorporated into the Irish World Chronicle, an important forerunner of surviving versions of the Annals. Columba's contemporary AEDÁN MAC GABRÁIN (r. 574–608) is the most famous of Dál Riatan kings, partly because he features significantly in the hagiographical record of the saint but also because he seems to have been the most successfully aggressive of the kings of Dál Riata, campaigning widely in northern Britain and establishing a regional hegemony in north-central Ireland. The large network of Irish cousins attributed to Dál Riata in the *Senchus* may reflect his ambitions in this area.

After the end of the extant Iona Chronicle coverage in the mid-8th century our understanding of the history of Dál Riata is reduced. In the 730s and 740s the Pictish king ONUIST son of Uurguist (Oengus son of Forgus) led a series of campaigns against the kingdom and some scholars see this as the effective end of its independent existence. By the middle of the 9th century a Cenél nGabráin dynast, CINAED MAC AILPÍN, made himself king of the PICTS and set the stage for the Gaelicization of all northern Britain. Precisely how this was achieved is far from clear. Equally the date of the disappearance of both Cenél nGabrain control over parts of Ireland and an independent kingdom in Argyll are unknown, but were presumably the results of the upheavals caused by the Vikings in the latter part of the 9th century.

FURTHER READING
AEDÁN MAC GABRÁIN; ALBA; ANNALS; BEDA; CINAED MAC AILPÍN; COLUM CILLE; EILEAN Ì; ÉRIU; FERGUS MÓR; GAELIC; ONUIST; PICTS; PTOLEMY; SCOTS; SENCHUS FER N-ALBAN; TUATH; Bannerman, *Studies in the History of Dalriada*; Dumville, *Rannsachadh na Gàidhlig 2000* 185–212; Dumville, *Scottish Gaelic Studies* 20.170–91; Sharpe, *Kings, Clerics and Chronicles in Scotland, 500–1297* 47–61.

Alex Woolf

in a rhetorical style absorbed from earlier praise poetry, peppered with learned Christian references and Latin words—some Gaelicized, and others kept in Latin form—and dense passages, often in grammatically dismembered form. Its justifiable fame rests not only on its somewhat rococo literary qualities, but also as the earliest testimony to the historical St Columba (see Herbert, *Iona, Kells, and Derry* 9–12; Charles-Edwards, *Early Christian Ireland* 285–90). It is also the first in a series of important praise poems to the saint emanating from the Columban *familia*. Dallán himself became a character in tales, some of them centred on the circumstances of the composition of the *Amrae* (Herbert, *Iona, Kells, and Derry* 'Preface'), held to be repayment for Columba's intervention to prevent a proposed banning of the overly powerful order of professional poets. In other tales he is identified with the chief poet Eochu Rígéces (King-poet), and in these his personality becomes that of a conservative guardian of a faded literary tradition and its élite.

PRIMARY SOURCES
ED. & TRANS. Clancy & Márkus, *Iona* 96–128; Stokes, RC 20.31–55, 132–83, 248–89, 400–37.

FURTHER READING
ADOMNÁN; COLUM CILLE; GAELIC; UÍ NÉILL; Charles-Edwards, *Early Christian Ireland*; Herbert, *Iona, Kells, and Derry*; Herbert, *Sages, Saints and Storytellers* 67–75; Ó hÓgáin, *Myth, Legend and Romance* 148–50.

Thomas Owen Clancy

Dallán Forgaill (the little blind one of the testimony) is the name given to a poet and character of early GAELIC literature. His real name may have been Eochu mac Colla, and he was perhaps from Co. Cavan (Contae an Chabháin), but there are conflicting traditions (see Clancy & Márkus, *Iona* 98). To him is attributed the Old Irish poem *Amrae Coluimb Chille*, an elegy on St Columba (COLUM CILLE), who died on 9 June AD 597. Details of the poem, such as a reference to its commission by 'Aed', probably the saint's cousin, King Aed mac Ainmirech (†598) of the Northern Uí Néill, and the absence of any trace of the legendary material found in St ADOMNÁN's *Vita Columbae* of *c.* 692, make it likely that *Amrae Coluimb Chille* is a genuine product of the immediate aftermath of the saint's death, though the poem awaits publication of a rigorous linguistic scrutiny. The poem is a tour de force, couched

Damona, a Gaulish goddess whose name may mean 'great/divine ox' (cf. Old Irish *dam* 'ox' and the goddess names EPONA, MATRONAE, NEMETONA, SIRONA) is attested independently and in dedications that link her with Apollo Borvon, Apollo Moritasgus, and Albius (Mars Albiorix?). A ritual precinct that encloses sacred springs and thermal baths at ALESIA preserved both a statuary head, thought to depict Damona wearing a crown wreathed with ears of grain, and fragments of a left hand holding a snake. Consistently associated with curative waters and probably honoured as a healer, Damona shares her attributes—the snake and grain—with Greek Hygeia and Demeter respectively.

INSCRIPTIONS (Partial listing)
DAMONAE AUG(USTAE), Bourbonne-les-Bains, France: CIL 13, no. 5921; *Revue Archéologique* new ser. 39 (1880) pl. 3 no. 8.

DEO APOLLINI MORITASG(US ET) DAMONAE, Alesia (Alise-Sainte-Reine), France: Le Gall, *Alésia* 150, 151.

DEO ALBIO ET DAMONAE, bronze vessel, Arnay-le-Duc/Chassenay, France: CIL 13, no. 2840.

DEO APOLLINI BORVONI ET DAMONAE, Bourbonne-les-Bains, France: CIL 13, no. 5911; Orelli et al., *Inscriptionvm Latinarvm* no. 5880 = *Revue Archéologique* new ser. 29 (1875) 69 = *Revue Archéologique* new ser. 39 (1880) 74 = *Mémoires de la Société des Antiquaires de France* 25 (1862) 71.

DEO BORVO(NI?) ET DAMONE, Bourbonne-les-Bains, France: CIL 13, no. 5920; *Revue Archéologique* new ser. 39 (1880) 22.

DEO BORVONI ET DAMON(AE), Bourbonne-les-Bains, France: CIL 13, no. 5918; *Revue Archéologique* new ser. 39 (1880) 26.

BORVONI ET DAMONAE, Bourbon-Lancy, France: CIL 13, no. 2806; *Mémoires de la Société des Antiquaires de France* 25.73 = *Revue Archéologique* new ser. 39 (1880) 77; Bourbonne-les-Bains, France: CIL 13, no. 5919; *Revue Archéologique* new ser. 39 (1880) 21.

BORMONI ET DAMONAE, Bourbon-Lancy, France: CIL 13, no. 2805; Orelli et al., *Inscriptionvm Latinarvm* no. 1974 = *Revue Archéologique* new ser. 39 (1880) 80–3.

BORVONI ET [DA]MONAE, Bourbonne-les-Bains, France: CIL 13, no. 5916; *Revue Archéologique* new ser. 39 (1880) 65 = *Mémoires de la Société des Antiquaires de France* 25 (1862) 70; *Revue Archéologique* new ser. 39 (1880) 84.

BORVONI ET DAMON(AE), Bourbonne-les-Bains, France: CIL 13, no. 5914; *Revue Archéologique* new ser. 39 (1880) 76; Bourbonne-les-Bains, France: CIL 13, no. 5917; *Bulletin de la Société des antiquaires de France* (1869) 124.

BORVONI IT DAMO(NAE), Bourbonne-les-Bains, France: CIL 13, no. 5915; *Revue Archéologique* new ser. 39 (1880) 23.

BO]RVONI ET [DAMONAE], Bourbon-Lancy, France: CIL 13, no. 2807; *Revue Archéologique* new ser. 39 (1880) 84.

IMAGES
Stone female head, retaining traces of polychrome, wearing a crown ornamented with ears of grain, left hand holding serpent, Musée Alesia, Alise-Sainte-Reine, France: Le Gall, *Alésia* 151; Thevenot, *Divinités et sanctuaries* 106.

FURTHER READING
ALESIA; EPONA; GAUL; MATRONAE; NEMETONA; SIRONA; Benoît, *Art et dieux de la Gaule* 73; DIL s.v. dam; D. Ellis Evans, *Gaulish Personal Names* s.v. Bor 154–6; Holder, *Altceltischer Sprachschatz* s.v. Borvo(n), Bormo, Damona; Le Gall, *Alésia* 148–53 et passim; Paulys *Real-encyclopädie* s.v. Albiorix, Bormanus, Bormo, Damona; Thévenot, *Divinités et sanctuaires de la Gaule* 104–7.

Paula Powers Coe

Dancing aboard the Bangor boat (1906)

The 'American Wake' from Riverdance

dances [1] Irish

Although dance and dancing must almost certainly have existed in early Ireland (ÉRIU), references to them are rare. Some dances came to Ireland with the Norman invasion in the 12th century and others were of earlier, presumably native, origin. Earlier use of words such as *cleasaíocht* (acrobatics) and *léimneach* (jumping; the cognate Middle Welsh *llamu* is also used for 'dancing'), indicate a form of dancing, but the modern Irish words for dance, *dámhsa* and *rince*, are loanwords, appearing in the 16th and 17th centuries respectively (cf. Welsh *dawnsio*).

The jig was well established in Ireland by the 18th century, towards the end of which the reel and hornpipe also became part of the dance and music repertoires in Ireland. These three are the most frequent dance rhythms of today, but slip jigs, double jigs, polkas, slides, and mazurkas are among the other popular dance steps current in Irish tradition.

Travelling dancing masters helped to increase the popularity of dancing, of particular dance forms and of various steps. These travelling dancing masters are well attested in many accounts and travelled from village to village, usually spending some weeks at each one. Normally, they stayed with a local family and, in return for bed and board, taught dancing free of charge to the members of the family.

Sets and half sets were the most popular dances throughout Ireland in the 19th and 20th centuries. Although they became less popular for many years, they regained their popularity in the 1980s and are now a vibrant part of traditional dance. They derive from the quadrille that was very popular in Paris during the time of Napoleon, and was brought to Ireland and England by the armies of the Duke of Wellington. The quadrille is based on a square dance of four couples and was developed to suit native Irish rhythms and music. The set dances contain several figures, and much of the nomenclature and movements recall their military origin. Many sets are associated with a particular region, e.g. 'The Mullagh Set' or 'The Conamara Set'.

Formerly, dances took place in peoples' homes, but by the middle of the 20th century the development of commercial dance halls and changes in lifestyle, travel, and communication saw the decline of the custom of the 'house dance'. The Irish word *céilí* means an informal social gathering in a neighbour's house, but since the beginning of the 20th century it has often come to be used to describe an organized dancing session. As part of a policy towards the re-establishment of the IRISH language and related culture, the Gaelic League (CONRADH NA GAEILGE) banned several dances because they were seen to represent foreign introductions, and was largely responsible for reviving older figure dances and creating newer dances for the *céilí*.

Solo or step dancing is found in all parts of Ireland (ÉIRE) and allows for a demonstration of the individual's creativity and artistry in footwork. Travelling dancing masters taught these dances from the early 18th century until well into the 20th century. During recent years, the older, freer forms of solo dance have been taught and displayed at summer schools and festivals, while at the same time modern displays such as 'Riverdance' have drawn on traditional step dance forms.

FURTHER READING
CONRADH NA GAEILGE; ÉIRE; ÉRIU; IRISH; IRISH MUSIC; Breathnach, *Folk Music and Dances of Ireland*; Brennan, *Story of Irish Dance*; Vallely, *Companion to Irish Traditional Music*.

Ríonach uí Ógáin

dances [2] Scottish

Indigenous Scottish dances include weapon dances, ritualistic dances, dramatic dances, social dances, and solo step dances.

Scottish weapon dances involved step dancing as part of mock battles with dirks or cudgels or dancing over dirks or crossed SWORDS, two swords for the Gille Calum solo sword dance (*Dannsa a' Chlaidhimh*) or four broadswords for the four-man Argyll broadswords. Ritualistic hilt-and-point sword dances performed in Perth (Peairt) in the 16th century and in Papa Stour in the Shetlands (Sealtainn) until the late 19th century symbolically slayed a hero as a sacrificial victim and then brought him back to life. These dances were related to the guisers' play (in which one character was wounded or slain, and then resurrected by a comic doctor), and morris dances.

The death-and-resurrection theme recurs in the widely known dramatic dance *Cailleach an Dùdain* ('The Old Woman of the Mill Dust'), performed to the tune of the same name played on pipes or fiddle or sung as *puirt-a-beul* ('mouth music'). The dancing and pantomime of a man and woman suggest simultaneously the manoeuvres of weapon play and the flirtations of a mating ritual. In one version, both are armed with sticks. In another, the man has a druidic or magic wand (*slachdan druidheachd* or *slachdan geasachad*). The man eventually kills the woman and then magically revives her limb by limb. The mill dust is the dark dust of a variety of oats that blackens the face when threshed, resembling the blackened or masked face of a morris dancer.

The manoeuvring for position recurs in dramatic dances that imitate the antics of cocks before mating or a cockfight and incorporate circling or swinging, e.g. in *Ruidhleadh nan Coileach Dubha* ('The Reel of the Black Cocks') and *Cath nan Coileach* ('Combat of the Cocks'), both from Barra (Barraidh).

Early social dances were communal ring dances, performed around a venerable object such as a sacred tree, a holy well, or a BELTAINE fire, and accompanied by communal dance-songs, called carols, or by BALLADS. A leader chanted a narrative line of a verse, and those in the ring responded in unison with the chorus as they danced around in a circle holding hands. The vocal solo and response form may derive from the communal work song. The SCOTTISH GAELIC-speaking areas also had ring dances of this type, e.g. *An Dannsa Mór* ('The Great Dance'), known on the Isles of Skye (An t-Eilean Sgitheanach) and Eigg (Eige).

The *Ruidhleadh Mór* ('The Big Reel') from Skye is similar to a ring dance in which the circling stops as the dancers drop hands and perform setting steps on the spot before continuing around in a circle. This type of dance may have been the progenitor of the uniquely Scottish social dance called the reel. The reel consists of a travelling figure alternating with setting steps danced on the spot and sometimes swinging. In the old west Highland circular reel for two couples, the travelling figure describes a circle. In the eastern HIGHLANDS and the LOWLANDS, the 'reel of three' used a weaving figure-8 pattern for a travelling figure and was replaced by a 'reel of four' with a figure 8 with an extra loop. Such reels also introduced the use of raised arms or arms akimbo during setting or swinging, snapping the fingers, and heuching (giving

'Gilli Challum' by Ronald Robert MacIan (1803–56)

a sudden yelp of glee). Dances were accompanied by BAGPIPE, FIDDLE, or, in the Highlands, *puirt-a-beul*.

The Scottish tunes and travelling steps used for reels were applied to the English country dances introduced into Scotland (ALBA) after 1700. The unique Scottish contribution to the figures of the country dances was the figure 'set to and turn corners and then reels of three with corners', which derived from the setting, swinging, and travelling patterns of the reel. The rhythmic pattern of the travelling step—step, close, step, hop—is the basis for any step or dance historically referred to as a *Schottische* (German for 'Scottish').

The devising and teaching of setting steps to dance in the reels led to the development of solo dances that emphasized the display of numerous steps choreographed to match a specific tune that gave the dance its name. The earliest of these dances still featured travelling steps in a circle interspersed with setting steps. Each turn of setting steps had a different variation at first and then ended with the same set of movements.

The earlier form of setting steps in the Highlands was low to the ground, shuffling and beating out the rhythm of the melody with the feet. The feet were parallel, the arms hung loosely at the side, and the subtle movements caused very little vertical movement. Later the shuffles and beats were extended into the kicks, rockings, sheddings, shakes, balances, and raised arm movements known in modern Highland dancing. The influence of dancing-masters trained in French ballet brought turnout, vertical lift, and balletic leg and arm movements into the step dances in Scotland.

The Highland emigrants (see EMIGRATION) to Cape Breton, Nova Scotia, Canada in the years 1784–1820 retained the older, close-to-the-floor tap-dance style. They took with them *Ruidhleadh Cheathrar* ('Foursome Reel'), also known as *Ruidhleadh Bheag* ('The Small Reel'), and the eight-handed reel, *Ruidhleadh Mór* ('The Big Reel'). The Foursome Reel is similar to the old west Highland circular reel described, the setting steps performed with the dancers in a straight line or in a square formation. In one form, the dancers swing each other instead of setting, and the travelling figure is performed by the diagonal pairs changing places. In the eight-handed reel, partners start facing each other in one large circle around the room. They set to and swing each other and, facing in the original direction, move on to the next person and do the same, and so on around the circle. Known as 'the wild eight', the dance was so boisterous in the mid-19th century that priests put a temporary ban on social dancing, and in some parish districts even went so far as to collect and destroy all the fiddles.

The older solo dances were forgotten in Cape Breton when reels gave way to French quadrilles, known as 'square sets', in 1890. In the revival of step dancing in solo dancing and within the square sets 60 years later, the steps consisted of very short sequences of movement assembled together extemporaneously rather than choreographed into longer segments with repetition to a specific tune.

Most of the competitive dances performed at HIGH-LAND GAMES are not traditional Highland dances, but were devised by Lowland dancing masters in the 1790s and the early 1800s. During the 1950s and 1960s Joan and Tom Flett collected social dances and solo step dances in Scotland that show the variety of dances and steps once extant before the introduction of modern dances after the First World War and the standardization of Highland dancing in 1955. Frank Rhodes, a colleague and co-writer with the Fletts, also collected dances in the Hebrides (Innse Gall) and in Cape Breton in the 1950s and 1960s and noted the similarities and differences between the two related traditions.

FURTHER READING
ALBA; BAGPIPE; BALLADS; BELTAINE; DRUIDS; EMIGRATION; FIDDLE; HIGHLAND GAMES; HIGHLANDS; LOWLANDS; SCOTTISH GAELIC; SWORDS; Bennett, *West Highland Free Press* 14/10/1994 (www.siliconglen.com /scotfaq/10_3.html); Cooke, *Fiddle Tradition of the Shetland Isles*; Donaldson, *Scottish Highland Games in America*; Emmerson, *Rantin' Pipe and Tremblin' String*; Emmerson, *Scotland Through Her Country Dances*; Emmerson, *Scottish Country Dance*; Emmerson, *Social History of Scottish Dance*; Joan F. Flett, *Social Dancing in England from the 17th Century*; Joan F. Flett & Thomas M. Flett, *Scottish Studies* 11.1–11, 125–47; Joan F. Flett & Thomas M. Flett, *Scottish Studies* 16.91–119, 17.91–107; Joan F. Flett & Thomas M. Flett, *Traditional Dancing in Scotland*; Joan F. Flett & Thomas M. Flett, *Traditional Step-Dancing in Lakeland*; Joan F. Flett & Thomas M. Flett, *Traditional Step-Dancing in Scotland*; Foss, *Notes on Evolution in Scottish Country Dancing*; Foss, *Roll Back the Carpet*; Fraser, *Airs and Melodies Peculiar to the Highlands of Scotland and the Isles*; Gibson, *Traditional Gaelic Bagpiping 1745–1945*; Hood, *Story of Scottish Country Dancing*; Lockhart, *Highland Balls and Village Halls*; MacDonald et al., *No Less, No More, Just Four on the Floor*; MacFadyen, *Album For Mrs Stewart*; MacFadyen & Adams, *Dance With Your Soul*; MacGillivray, *Cape Breton Ceilidh*; MacGillivray, *Cape Breton Fiddler*; MacInnes, *Companion Guide to Gaelic Scotland* s.v. 'dance in Gaelic society'; Milligan, *Won't You Join the Dance?*; Milligan & MacLennan, *Dances of Scotland*; Peel, *Dancing and Social Assemblies in York in the Eighteenth and Nineteenth Centuries*; Royal Scottish Country Dance Society, *Manual of Scottish Country Dancing*; Scottish Official Board of Highland Dancing, *Highland Dancing*; Seabright Productions, *Music in the Blood* (video); Sharp, *Country Dance Book*; Thurston, *Scotland's Dances*.
Susan Self

dances [3] Welsh

Like the traditional dances of most countries, those of Wales (CYMRU) have been handed down from generation to generation in specific localities or communities. Although many of the figures and steps used are common to traditional British dances, it is the recurrence of certain figures in the majority of Welsh dances that links them in what may be termed a Welsh tradition. Dances were, in the main, connected with the seasons or with annual festivities such as May Day (*Calan Mai*), MIDSUMMER'S DAY, harvest time, Hallowe'en (*nos Galan Gaeaf*), Christmas, and New Year (see further BELTAINE; CALENDAR; SAMAIN).

With the exception of the clog dancing tradition, which has survived unbroken, dancing all but disappeared in Wales during the religious revivals of the Nonconformist Protestant denominations in the 18th, 19th, and early 20th centuries (see CHRISTIANITY), but regained popularity later in the 20th century. The Welsh Folk Dance Society was formed in 1949, but there were some developments prior to this: 1918 saw the 'Llanofer reel', a dance devised at the country-house of Llanofer, Gwent, being recalled. A group of Llanofer children performing the reel were filmed by URDD GOBAITH CYMRU (The Welsh League of Youth) in 1933. Hugh Mellor collected a huge number of Welsh folk dances, and Gwennant Gillespie (née Davies), who joined the staff of Urdd Gobaith Cymru in 1943, played a major part, until her retirement 30 years later, in furthering folk dancing as an important part of the movement's activities. The driving force behind the folk dance revival in Wales, however, was Lois Blake, an Englishwoman who, in the 1930s,

Owen Huw Roberts dancing to the accompaniment of David Elio Roberts on the harp and Robert Ifor Roberts on the clarinet

moved from Liverpool (Welsh Lerpwl) to Llangwm, Denbighshire (sir Ddinbych). Having been a member of the English Folk Dance Society for some time, she was astonished to find that so few dances were being performed in Wales compared with other parts of Britain. She began teaching local children and adults to dance and carried out a vast amount of research into Welsh dances and dancing. At this time she met the well-known musician and publisher from Llangollen in north-east Wales, W. S. Gwynn Williams (1896–1978), who had himself undertaken a great deal of research into WELSH MUSIC and folk dancing, and together they published a series of dance manuals. Lois Blake and W. S. Gwynn Williams, along with Emrys Cleaver and Enid Daniels Jones, were the founder members of the Welsh Folk Dance Society and became, respectively, its first president, chairman, treasurer and secretary.

Lois Blake travelled widely, visiting libraries and museums within Wales and in other parts of Britain, and meeting people who were interested in Welsh folk dances and dancing. The 17th- and early 18th-century publications of John Playford (1623–86?) and John Walsh (†1736) included dances and music with definite Welsh associations and as a result they were regarded as part of the Welsh dance tradition. Details of the 'Llangadfan dances' were discovered in 1920 among the papers of Edward Jones (*c.* 1729–95). Lady Herbert Lewis provided information on the dance called 'Cadi

ha'. Lois Blake also met a remarkable lady by the name of Margretta Thomas, Nantgarw, south-east Glamorgan (MORGANNWG), who remembered the dances performed at fairs and festivals in that part of Wales. Her daughter, the dialectologist Dr Ceinwen H. Thomas, recorded the details and transferred them to Lois Blake, who arranged for the dances to be published. The work of discovering, interpreting and publishing dances continues to the present day, under the scrutiny of the editorial panel of the Welsh Folk Dance Society, and new dances, based on the Welsh dance traditions, are composed and published.

Over the years, mainly through the efforts of Urdd Gobaith Cymru and the Welsh Folk Dance Society, the number of dance parties across Wales has increased. Folk dancing has been recognized on a national level through the Urdd National Eisteddfod, the National Eisteddfod of Wales (EISTEDDFOD GENEDLAETHOL CYMRU), the *Cerdd Dant* Festival (*Gŵyl Gerdd Dant*), and the Llangollen International Musical Eisteddfod (EISTEDDFOD GERDDOROL RYNGWLADOL LLANGOLLEN), and increasing numbers of dance festivals, organized by the parties themselves, are held throughout Wales.

FURTHER READING
BELTAINE; CALENDAR; CHRISTIANITY; CYMRU; EISTEDDFOD GENEDLAETHOL CYMRU; EISTEDDFOD GERDDOROL RYNGWLADOL LLANGOLLEN; MIDSUMMER'S DAY; MORGANNWG; SAMAIN; URDD GOBAITH CYMRU; WELSH MUSIC; Blake, *Traditional Dance and Customs in Wales*; Blake, *Welsh Folk Dance*;

Blake, *Welsh Folk Dance and Costume*; Blake & Williams, *Llangadfan Dances*; Lile, *Troed yn ôl / Step in Time*; Mellor, *Welsh Folk Dances*; Alice E. Williams, *Welsh Folk Dancing Handbook*.

Glyn T. Jones

dances [4] Breton

In terms of its folk traditions, Brittany (BREIZH) is recognized as one of the more culturally conservative regions of France, though adherence to older forms of practice naturally varies in degree from area to area. In the Romance-speaking region of BREIZH-UHEL (Upper Brittany)—where the major towns were established—dances were borrowed from other cities very early and very thoroughly, thus contributing to the reinvigoration of the repertoire. Here, fragments taken from quadrilles or other figure dances mingled with older local traditions to create, by the early 19th century, a distinctive syncretized style. Dances such as *balanceuses*, *balancières*, *avant-deux* and *guedaines* have emerged as a result. Remnants of an earlier tradition have survived to this day in a vestigial *passe-pied*, and,

over towards the linguistic border, in several *branles*.

Traditional dance in the Breton-speaking region of BREIZH-IZEL (Lower Brittany) has retained far more of its original nature, though here too there is some element of change and renewal. The oldest types of dance known in Western European culture are round dances formed by a closed chain of an unlimited number of dancers, who circle with a single repeated step. These are still in use and are well represented in the countryside of the modern departments of Aodoù-an-Arvor (Côtes d'Armor), Penn-ar-Bed (Finistère) and Morbihan. The name usually given to these dances in Lower Brittany is of the type *-tro*, *an dro*, *dañs-tro*, based on the word *tro*, meaning 'turn'.

In general, the *dañs-tro* is followed immediately by another dance, the *bal* (Old French *baller* 'to dance'), which involves changing the arrangement of the dancers between a round and a procession, with additional separation into couples. In the suite which brings the two dances together, the large collective *dañs-tro* thus breaks up into a more personalized form of expression. The suite has two parts (*dañs tro*, *bal*) in most of

Traditional Breton dancing in Surzur (1939)

KERNEV and GWENED, but has three parts in Upper Kernev, which is traditionally more conservative than other regions. Its composition recalls the designation *trikory* (from *tri c'hoari* 'three games'), given at the turn of the 15th and 16th centuries to a dance-step from Lower Brittany.

This suite of dances fulfils two social functions at once, being both a pleasurable leisure exercise and a reinforcement of existing social networks. But it is also peculiarly flexible, adapting to the needs of the moment. With the exception that no one dances during Lent, the dance is not tied to the religious or secular calendar, nor even to a seasonal one. Instead, it is closely linked to marriage days and to certain kinds of rural labour. Ceremonial at moments during a wedding, it becomes practical when used to separate buckwheat, soften flax or tramp down the earthen floors of threshing-areas or new houses.

Far from being always the same, the composite dance-step of the *dañs-tro* differs from region to region. The musical beat may be 8-count or 4-count, less often 3- or 6-count, and the rhythm may change. The most westerly group covers all of Kernev, with significant extensions into LEON and Morbihan: the dance characteristic of this region is known by the French name *gavotte*. To the east, two other areas spread over the linguistic border. The first is restricted to Aodoù-an-Arvor, where the dance is called *dañs fañch* or *dañs plin* in the west, and *ronde* or *rond* in the east. The second is in the Morbihan, where the dance is known as *en dro* around Gwened and *tour*, *pilée* and *pilé-menu* further east.

Another type of dance, also very old, is performed in a northern zone stretching west to east, from Upper Leon, between the road from Landerne (Landerneau) to Montroulez (Morlaix) to the north of the Monts d'Arrée, and also at the western edge of TREGER which adjoins it. Here the main element of the ensemble is not the closed chain but the double front, one consisting of men, one of women, facing each other. Where the circular disposition of the *dañs tro* reveals its affiliation with round dances of the greater European tradition, the double front of the *dañs Leon* and the *dañs Treger* marks a radical distinction: it bears some resemblance to the 'longways for as many as will' of British tradition, which may have influenced it.

As practised by the last few generations of genuinely peasant communities, Breton dances could be accom-panied by instruments or voice, with some areas using both alternately: in some places, however, the arrival of instruments is relatively recent. In regions where musical instruments have been used for a long time the dances appear to have metamorphosed into new forms more readily. Thus in Lower Kernev and part of southern Gwened, the dances changed over time from a closed chain to an open chain, then to successively shorter chains ending up, in some cases, in couples.

Another form of renewal in the repertoire involves the recreation in a rural context of borrowed figures from urban dances. At least two of these new arrivals have become very widespread: the *jabadao* in the south, spreading in all directions from Quimper, and the *dérobée* in the north, spreading from Upper Brittany to Treger.

FURTHER READING
BREIZH; BREIZH-IZEL; BREIZH-UHEL; GWENED; KERNEV; LEON; TREGER; Kuter, *Breton Identity*.

Jean-Marie Guilcher

Danebury

The hill-fort of Danebury may be taken as representative of a series of successive stages in the social history of central southern BRITAIN in the pre-Roman Celtic IRON AGE. The site occupies a prominent position on the chalk downs of Hampshire, England. In its developed form, the main FORTIFICATION (the inner earthwork) enclosed an area of 5.3 ha (13 acres), which excavation showed to have been densely occupied. Outside the main defences, on the south-east side, the middle earthwork defined a corral attached to the fort. The whole complex lay within a much slighter ditched enclosure (the outer earthwork), which was probably of Late Bronze Age (*c.* 1200–*c.* 700 BC) date and represents the first stage in the definition of the hilltop.

Danebury has been the subject of a 20-year programme of excavations (1969–88), during which time 57% of the occupied interior (some 3 ha, 7 acres) has been totally excavated, resulting in a very large database—both structural and artefactual—reflecting on Iron Age society, economy and belief systems in southern Britain.

Occupation probably began in the late 6th or early 5th century BC with the construction of a palisaded enclosure occupying the hilltop, set within the Late

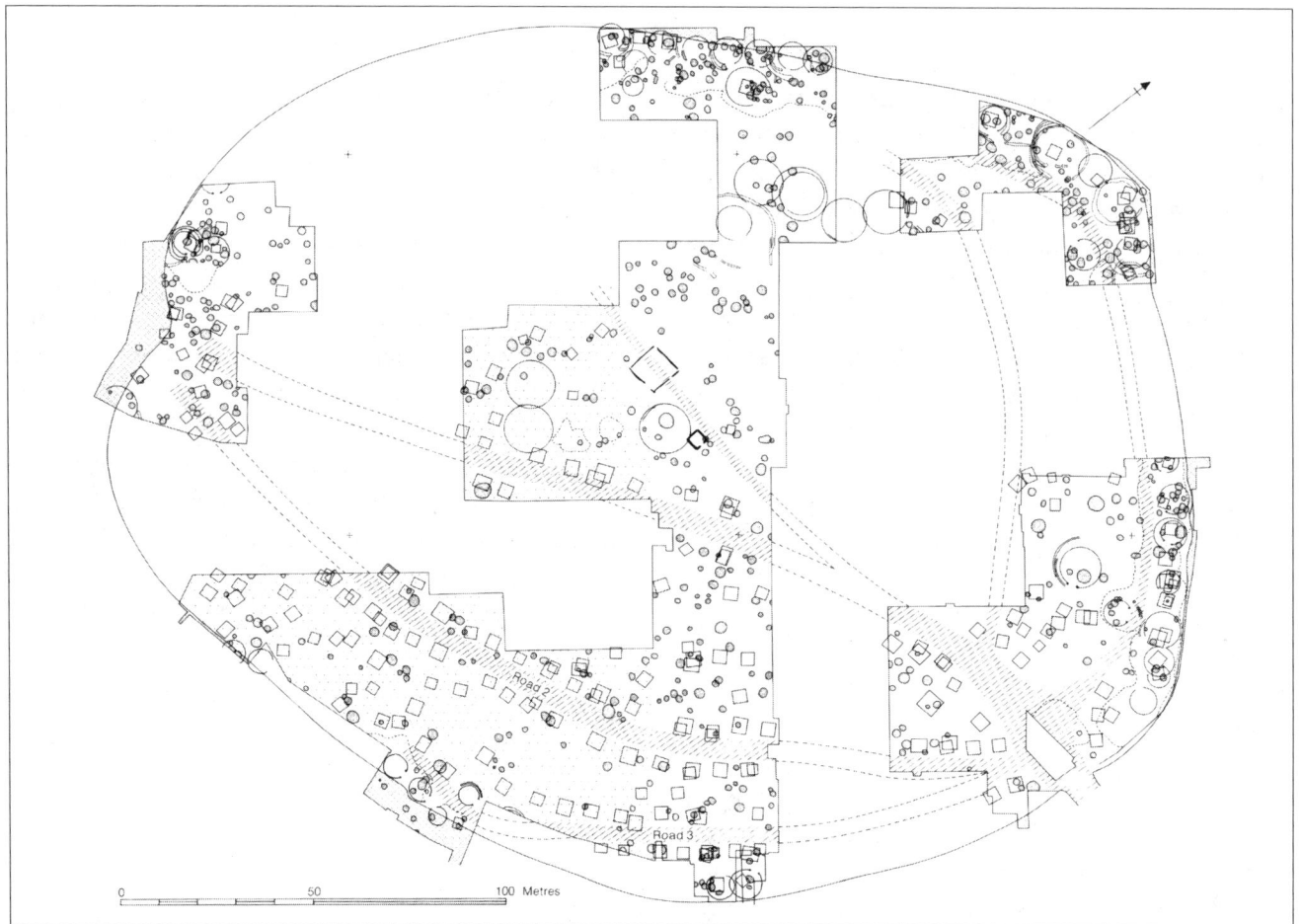

Danebury, late period, c. 350/300–c. 100 BC: excavated settlement area within the ramparts, showing roads, round houses, rectangular structures, and storage pits

Bronze Age ditched ENCLOSURE. Later in the 5th century the palisade was replaced with a rampart and ditch which had opposed entrances to the east and southwest. The rampart at this stage was faced with a vertical timber wall anchored back into the chalk-built rampart behind. In the middle of the 4th century BC there is some evidence of dislocation marked by a horizon of burning. This was followed by the refurbishing of the defences, now in glacis style (with a continuous steep slope from the crest of the rampart to the bottom of the ditch), and the blocking of the south-west entrance. The fort was intensively occupied in the 3rd and 2nd centuries BC, during which time its east entrance was strengthened on several occasions and provided with forward-projecting hornworks, creating a long corridor approach (and hence a defensive gauntlet for would-be attackers) to the gate itself which, in its later stages, was set within a gate tower. Occupation on a large scale came to an end in the early part of the first century

BC, at which time the gate was destroyed in an intense fire, quite possibly as the result of enemy raiding. Thereafter, the old enclosure continued to be used, though on a much reduced scale, into the early years of the first century AD.

The history of Danebury fairly reflects the history of central southern Britain in the Iron Age. In the 6th–5th centuries BC, hill-forts were appearing quite widely, and were often vertically walled and provided with opposed entrances. Many of these early hill-forts went out of use in the 4th century, while a much smaller number were strongly refortified with only one enhanced entrance. Forts of this kind, intensively occupied in the 3rd and 2nd centuries, are referred to as developed hill-forts. Extensive field surveys carried out in the vicinity of the developed hill-forts of Danebury and MAIDEN CASTLE suggest that for many kilometres around the landscape was devoid of rural settlement, the implication being that the population was now living within the forts.

Excavations inside Danebury showed that circular timber houses, streets, storage buildings and storage pits were already established in the 5th century, but the intensity of activity increased dramatically at the end of the 4th century, by which time a regular pattern of ROADS had developed and distinct zones of activity had been established. In the centre were buildings best interpreted as shrines, while houses occupied the peripheral space immediately behind the rampart. A main road ran across the centre of the site dividing an area dominated by storage pits from a zone of regularly arranged four- and six-post storage buildings.

Artefacts, animal bones and charred plant remains recovered from the excavations demonstrated the predominantly agricultural basis of the economy (see AGRICULTURE). Some items, such as salt, quern-stones, iron and bronze, were brought in from outside the region through exchange networks but, apart from iron-smithing and some bronze casting, there is little evidence of industrial activity within the settlement.

The belief systems of the community were amply demonstrated by the shrines in the centre of the fort and by special deposits (see HOARDS) placed in the grain storage pits when they had ceased to function as such. These special deposits, including animals, in whole or in part, grain, sets of tools, pots and human remains, were recovered from a high proportion of the pits and may well represent propitiatory offerings to the deities controlling the agro-pastoral cycle.

FURTHER READING
AGRICULTURE; BRITAIN; ENCLOSURE; FORTIFICATION; HOARDS; IRON AGE; MAIDEN CASTLE; ROADS; Cunliffe, *Danebury: Anatomy of an Iron Age Hillfort*; Cunliffe, *Danebury 1: Excavations 1969–1978, Site*; Cunliffe, *Danebury 2: Excavations 1969–1978, Finds*; Cunliffe & Poole, *Danebury 4: Excavations 1979–1988, Site*; Cunliffe & Poole, *Danebury 5: Excavations 1979–1988, Finds*; Cunliffe, *Danebury 6: Hillfort Community in Perspective*.

Barry Cunliffe

dánta grádha

The formal study of Irish courtly love poetry originates with the work of the Irish scholar T. F. O'Rahilly (Tomás Ó RATHILE). Between December 1915 and August 1916 he edited 37 poems in *New Ireland* under the general rubric 'Love Poems from Irish MSS'. These poems were published in book form in November 1916 as *Dánta Grádha: An Anthology of Irish Love Poetry*, with an introduction by another Irish scholar, Robin Flower (1881–1946). In 1925 O'Rahilly published *Laoithe Cumainn* (Love songs), a collection of 23 poems, including 15 from his previous work, but with no introductory essay. A year later, he published a second edition of *Dánta Grádha*, greatly expanded to 106 poems, 75 of which are anonymous. Of the 21 authors cited, some are little more than names to us. This volume also contained a substantial preface by the editor, and a complete recasting by Flower of his introductory essay.

Flower placed special emphasis on Gearóid Iarla (†1398), the first recorded poet of Norman descent to compose poetry in IRISH. Acquainted with both the French tradition of *amour courtois* and the Irish tradition of *bairdne* (bardic poetry), authors such as Gearóid Iarla were admirably placed for introducing COURTLY LOVE into Irish verse. Despite his emphasis on the French connection, Flower also underlined the close similarities between Irish courtly love poems and 16th-century English authors such as the Earl of Surrey and Thomas Wyatt the elder. In the later version of his essay, however, Flower gave much more prominence to the rôle of French literature, barely conceding the possibility of English influence. Normally a most perceptive critic, Flower was apparently caught up in the ideology of the emergent Irish Free State (see IRISH INDEPENDENCE MOVEMENT), finding it more acceptable to link the culture of Gaelic Ireland (ÉIRE) with Continental Europe than the recently departed enemy.

Flower's seminal essay dominated literary criticism of the *dánta grádha* until the final years of the 20th century. In recent years, a more nuanced approach has come to the fore, with Seán Ó TUAMA arguing for three periods of external influence on Irish courtly love poetry: (1) 1200–1400, French; (2) 1400–1550, French and English; (3) 1550 onwards, mainly English (*An Grá i bhFilíocht na n-Uaisle*). From this perspective, however, only Gearóid Iarla shows any possible trace of overt French influence. Given the late date of the bulk of these poems, it is more prudent to seek evidence for foreign influence in English, rather than French, sources, concentrating on poems in their totality rather than on mere thematic similarities. In fact, this approach has already yielded some very interesting results. Riocard do Burc's *Fir na Fódla ar ndul d'éag* (The men of Ireland after dying), for example, is a free adaptation of Ovid's *Non ego mendosos ausim defendere mores*, *Amores* 2.4. Instead of deriving directly from the Latin, however, Do Burc's version demonstrates familiarity with Sir John Harrington's translation, posthumously published in his *Epigrams* (1618), and subsequently reprinted in 1625 and 1633–4. The interest in Ovid is evidence of the RENAISSANCE interest in the classics, while the surname Do Búrc indicates a bilingual member of Old English stock (i.e. families in Ireland descended from the 12th-century Anglo-Norman invaders), ideally placed to mediate between the English and the Gaelic worlds. An amateur poet, Do Burc's foray into verse shows that the realm of love poetry offered the possibility of breaking down the barriers erected by the hereditary professional literary caste to protect their privileged status (see BARDIC ORDER).

Pádraigín Haicéad (1600–54) is another amateur poet of Old English stock whose love poems in stress metre to Máire Tóibín merit scrutiny. The fact that the lady is a historical figure leads us away from the medieval world into that of the Renaissance, with its emphasis on the dignity of the human person. One of his poems cleverly adapts Ovid's tale of the sun and the marigold to describe his relationship with Ms Tóibín, but it is Haicéad's failure to render the wordplay between *marigold* and *golden Marie* in Irish that ultimately reveals his source—a poem by one Charles Best, published in *A Poetical Rhapsody* (1602). Haicéad also composed moving and witty poems to his male friends very much in the style of Herrick and Carew. His contemporary Piaras Feiritéir (†1653), another poet of Old English stock, resembles even more closely the work of English cavalier poets in the poems of friendship he composed for both male and females.

Bilingual members of Old English stock were at a distinct advantage in enriching the Gaelic literary tradition with the current trends in contemporary English verse. Members of the Gaelic aristocracy in both Ireland and Scotland (ALBA) also turned their hands to amatory verse, in keeping with the prevailing fashion across western Europe. Understandably, the professional poets did not take kindly to outsiders invading their domain, and responded in kind. When they involved themselves in composing love poetry, however, they did so with a certain sense of irony and

wordplay, love for them being much more of a game rather than a matter of life and death. While Eochaidh Ó hEódhasa's *Ionmholta malairt bhisigh* (Change for the better should be praised) is usually interpreted as a light-hearted lament for the decline of classical syllabic poetry, it is equally possible to interpret Ó hEódhasa as claiming that amatory verse was both easier and more profitable than formal eulogy. The poem was composed around the time of the marriage of Rudhraighe Ó Domhnaill to Bridget Fitzgerald in 1603. Ó hEódhasa also composed a love poem to Bridget, pretending that it was written by his patron, Cúchonnacht Mag Uidhir. Bridget, in her turn, had a poem sent back to Ó hEódhasa, commissioning a professional poet or possibly composing it herself, in which she let Ó hEódhasa know in no uncertain terms that she had seen through his tricks. Ó hEódhasa replied in a final poem in which he plays both a male and a female rôle. This poem, a witty dialogue between two former lovers who have both betrayed each other, exhibits many of the characteristics of the answer-poem, a type of verse that came to the fore in the courts of James I and Charles I. The poetic interchange between Ó hEódhasa and Fitzgerald with the involvement of Ó Domhnaill and Mag Uidhir gives a very interesting insight into the recreational activities of the Gaelic aristocracy in the early 17th-century.

PRIMARY SOURCES
O'Rahilly, *Dánta Grádha*; O'Rahilly, *Laoithe Cumainn*.

FURTHER READING
ALBA; BARDIC ORDER; COURTLY LOVE; ÉIRE; GAELIC; IRISH; IRISH INDEPENDENCE MOVEMENT; IRISH LITERATURE; Ó RATHILE; Ó H-EÓDHASA; Ó TUAMA; RENAISSANCE; Mac Craith, *Lorg na hIasachta ar na Dánta Grá*; Ní Dhonnchadha, *Field Day Anthology of Irish Writing* 4.358–457; Ó Tuama, *An Grá i bhFilíocht na nUaisle*.

Mícheál Mac Craith

The **Danube** (**Dānuvius**) is the second longest river in Europe (2845 km from the confluence of the Brigach and the Breg; 2888 km from the source of the Breg). Its two headwaters, Brigach and Breg, have their origin in the Black Forest in south-west Germany, and join at Donaueschingen (Baden-Württemberg) to form the Danube. The river flows through south Germany, Austria, Slovakia, Hungary, Croatia, Serbia, Bulgaria, and Romania, before finally discharging into the Black Sea.

§1. DANUBIA IN THE IRON AGE AND ROMAN TIMES

The Greek historian HERODOTUS, wrote in the 5th century BC: '... the Ister [Danube], beginning in the land of the Celts (Κελτοί Keltoi) and the city of Pyrene, flows through the middle of Europe' (2.33). The location of Pyrene is unknown, but a confused reference to the Pyrenees has been suggested. In the IRON AGE (8th–1st century BC), the Upper Danube region was in the heartland of the HALLSTATT and LA TÈNE cultures, and many significant hill-forts and oppida (sing. OPPIDUM) have been found on the banks of the river, e.g. HEUNEBURG, MANCHING, KELHEIM. Place-name evidence in the Danube region points to an ancient Celtic-speaking population, with places such as Vienna (Vindobonā 'White or fair settlement'), Passau (ancient Boioduron 'Oppidum of the BOII, i.e. of the cattle lords)' and Lorch (Lauriācum 'Settlement of Laureus'), as well as SINGIDŪNON (modern Belgrade), bearing Celtic names. Most of the river-names in this region are also Celtic, e.g. the two headwaters Brigach and Breg (see BRIGANTES), the Inn, the Isar, and the Iller.

§2. THE NAME

In Roman records, Dānuvius at first referred only to the upper course of the river, with Ister as the name of the lower Danube. The latter is derived from Greek Ἴστερ, a name which was probably itself borrowed from the Thracian language. In modern European languages, the name is German Donau, Hungarian Duna, Serbo-Croatian and Slovak Dunav, and Romanian Dunărea. All of these forms (except Ister) imply an older *Dānouio-. The Welsh river-name Donwy reflects this same original form *Dānouio-, which is thus shown to have existed in PROTO-CELTIC. The English river-name Don is derived from a related Celtic *dānu-; the nearby town of Doncaster was ROMANO-BRITISH Dānum, Old Welsh Cair Daun. The name Danube has been connected with the Irish goddess Danu (see TUATH DÉ) and the Welsh mythological ancestress DÔN, but the three names are distinct: the Irish has a short a or short o, the Welsh a Celtic short o, and Danube < *Dānouio- a long ā.

Danube is probably derived from the INDO-EUROPEAN word *deh₂nu- 'river', from the root *deh₂- 'flow', cf. Vedic Sanskrit dānu- 'dripping fluid' (or 'gift'?), Ossetian don 'water, river'. It has been suggested that the name was an early loan into Celtic from its ancient neighbour to the east, the Iranian language of the Scythians of the eastern European and central Asiatic grasslands. (A kindred Iranian-speaking group, the Sarmatians, also penetrated ancient central Europe.) We have, for example, the Scythian tribal name Δαναοί Dana(v)i (reflecting Proto-Iranian *Dānav(y)a-). The Slavic river-names Don, Dniepr, and Dniestr are borrowings from Scythian *dānu, *dānu apara 'upper river', *dānu nazdya 'lower river'. Although these three river-names are loans from Scythian and the Danube also flows into the Black Sea, Welsh Donwy leaves no doubt that Celtic and Iranian had the same inherited river-name. Despite the views of earlier scholars such as Vasmer, who took Danube to be Iranian in origin, a Celtic source cannot be ruled out on linguistic grounds, and the name Dānuvius is first attested in the Celtic-speaking western region of the Danube basin. On the other hand, the lands north and west of the Black Sea are likely to have been home to early Indo-European-speaking groups in the 3rd millennium BC or even earlier, thus before the separation into the attested Indo-European branches or sub-families. Among place-names, river-names have a particularly high survival rate, for example, the many native American river-names in North America. Therefore, it is possible that Dānuvius is what is termed an 'Old European river-name' and predates the emergence of Celtic or Iranian as distinct dialects.

FURTHER READING
BOII; BRIGANTES; DACIANS; DÔN; HALLSTATT; HERODOTUS; HEUNEBURG; INDO-EUROPEAN; IRON AGE; KELHEIM; LA TÈNE; MANCHING; OPPIDUM; PROTO-CELTIC; ROMANO-BRITISH; SINGIDŪNON; TUATH DÉ; Ekwall, English River-Names 126–8; Förster, Zeitschrift für slavische Philologie 1.1–25; Holder, Alt-celtischer Sprachschatz; Mallory & Adams, Encyclopedia of Indo-European Culture 486–7; Pokorny, IEW 175; Rivet & Smith, Place-Names of Roman Britain 329; Schrijver, Studies in British Celtic Historical Phonology 294; Vasmer, Untersuchungen über die ältesten Wohnsitze der Slaven 60ff.

PEB, CW

Darogan yr Olew Bendigaid (The prophecy of the blessed oil), also known as Hystori yr Olew Bendigaid (The story of the blessed oil), is a prose political prophecy, probably of the first half of the 15th century. Peniarth 50 is the oldest surviving manuscript. It is possibly in the redactor's hand and written at Neath Abbey (Lloyd-Morgan, Archaeology and History of

Glastonbury Abbey 306–7; Lloyd-Morgan, THSC 1985.20). The redactor worked from an English Latin prophecy about Thomas Becket (archbishop of Canterbury, †1170). The blessed oil in question has been sent from heaven for anointing the rightful kings of England. In this Welsh adaptation, *England* is turned to *yr ynys honn* 'this island', the whole of BRITAIN, and established GLASTONBURY legends are used to put an ARTHURIAN frame around the story. Thus, the oil is brought to Britain by followers of Joseph of Arimathea, a principal figure in many versions of the GRAIL legend, and is later used by the semi-legendary 6th-century Archbishop Dubricius to consecrate ARTHUR. The oil, together with divine support, then enables Arthur to vanquish giants and to 'trample pagan Saxons underfoot' (Lloyd-Morgan, THSC 1985.16). The immediate political context for the text may reflect the fall and disappearance of the Welsh insurgent leader OWAIN GLYNDŴR (1408×1413), as suggested by Lloyd-Morgan (THSC 1985.20–2).

PRIMARY SOURCES
MSS. Aberystwyth, NLW, Peniarth 50.
EDITION. R. Wallis Evans, *Llên Cymru* 14.86–91.

FURTHER READING
ARTHUR; ARTHURIAN; BRITAIN; GLASTONBURY; GRAIL; OWAIN GLYNDŴR; Lloyd-Morgan, *Archaeology and History of Glastonbury Abbey* 301–15; Lloyd-Morgan, *Llên Cymru* 14.64–85; Lloyd-Morgan, THSC 1985.9–26.

JTK

Davies, James Kitchener (1902–52) was born
in Llwynpiod, Cardiganshire (now CEREDIGION), Wales (CYMRU), and educated in the same county at Tregaron and ABERYSTWYTH. He spent his working life as a secondary school teacher in the Rhondda, Glamorgan (MORGANNWG), where he was active in local politics as a nationalist (see NATIONALISM) and as a lay preacher and WELSH-language campaigner until his death from cancer.

All Kitchener's important work is associated either with the Rhondda or with the area around Tregaron: the controversial play, *Cwm Glo* (Coal valley, 1934–5), described conditions in the Rhondda coalfield in the 1920s; his verse play, *Meini Gwagedd* (Stones of vanity, 1944), presented the harsh reality of rural life he had known as a child; the dramatic monologue, *Sŵn y Gwynt*

sy'n Chwythu (The sound of the wind that blows, 1952), reflects on the spiritual meaning of the wind, which penetrates the thick hedges of his Cardiganshire childhood and sweeps across the industrial Rhondda, a community stripped of all protection (see also WELSH DRAMA; WELSH POETRY).

If the strongest early influence on Kitchener's thought was the socialist Robert Owen, the formative experience was being exiled to England at the age of seven after the death of his mother, reinforced when his father sold the family home and moved to south Wales. This was unquestionably the source of the self-alienation which underlay the critical, analytical spirit which characterized his work.

PRIMARY SOURCES
EDITION. Mair I. Davies, *Gwaith James Kitchener Davies*.
SELECTIONS. Rhys & Thomas, *James Kitchener Davies: Detholiad o'i Waith*.

FURTHER READING
ABERYSTWYTH; CEREDIGION; CYMRU; MORGANNWG; NATIONALISM; WELSH; WELSH DRAMA; WELSH POETRY; Clancy et al., *Poetry Wales* 17.3.9–64; Glyn Jones & Rowlands, *Profiles*; Thomas, *James Kitchener Davies*; Ioan Williams, *Kitchener Davies*; Ioan Williams, *Planet* 30, 1976, 44–50; Ioan Williams, *Poetry Wales* 16.4.104–11.

Ioan Williams

Davitt, Michael (1846–1906) was born in Straide,
Co. Mayo (Contae Mhaigh Eo), in the west of Ireland (ÉIRE), on 25 March 1846. This was in the middle of the potato FAMINE, which was particularly acute in Mayo. Davitt was reared in Haslingden, Lancashire, England, following his family's eviction from their smallholding in 1852. As a child labourer in a mill in England, he lost his right arm. Davitt joined the Irish Republican Brotherhood in 1865 and was imprisoned for treason felony in connection with arms smuggling between 1870 and 1877. Land reform was the great passion of Davitt's life. After a sojourn in America, he established the Irish National LAND LEAGUE on 21 October 1879 in order to promote the cause of the tenant farmers (see LAND AGITATION). In 1881 he was elected a Member of Parliament (UK) for Co. Meath (Contae na Mí) while in Portland Prison, but he was not allowed to take his seat. From mid-1882 he advocated land nationalization rather than peasant proprietorship.

Davitt was deeply committed to a non-sectarian and inclusive Irish NATIONALISM. He served as Home Rule Member of Parliament in Westminster, initially for North-east Cork (Corcaigh) and later for South Mayo, from 8 February 1893 to 25 October 1899, when he resigned in protest against the Boer War in South Africa. He was passionate about social justice and social reform, about the cause of the working man and of organized labour, and was an early supporter of the Labour Party in Britain. Davitt was international in his thinking and in his social radicalism. He travelled and lectured widely, including several visits to Russia in the period 1903–5, and was an influential journalist and writer. He died of blood poisoning in Dublin (BAILE ÁTHA CLIATH) on 30 May 1906 and was buried in his native Straide.

PRIMARY SOURCE
Davitt, *Fall of Feudalism in Ireland*.

FURTHER READING
BAILE ÁTHA CLIATH; EMIGRATION; ÉIRE; FAMINE; LAND AGITATION; LAND LEAGUE; NATIONALISM; Cashman, *Life of Michael Davitt*; King, *Michael Davitt*; Moody, *Davitt and Irish Revolution 1846–82*; Skeffington, *Michael Davitt*; Travers, *Famine, Land and Culture in Ireland 83–100*.

Laurence M. Geary

De Bhaldraithe, Tomás

De Bhaldraithe, Tomás (1916–96) was a pioneering expert in Modern IRISH dialects, a renowned lexicographer (see DICTIONARIES AND GRAMMARS), and an editor of numerous important Modern Irish texts. A native of Ballinacor, Co. Limerick (Contae Luimnigh), he was educated in Dublin (BAILE ÁTHA CLIATH) at Belvedere College, by the Jesuits, and at University College Dublin, where he graduated in French and Irish in 1937. During a scholarship year (1938–9) spent at the Sorbonne, De Bhaldraithe's interest in dialectology was developed under the influence of his professors, Joseph VENDRYÈS and Marie Sjoestedt Jonval (author of *Description d'un parler irlandais de Kerry* [1938]). Returning to Ireland (ÉIRE) at the outbreak of the Second World War, he spent two years (1939–41) carrying out field research as part of a detailed study of the Irish of Conamara (see GAELTACHT). The results of this work were published in a series of articles ('Cainteanna as Cois Fhairrge') in *Éigse* 3–5 (1942–7) and in two ground-breaking

monographs, *The Irish of Cois Fhairrge, Co. Galway: A Phonetic Study* (1945) and *Gaeilge Chois Fhairrge: An Deilbhíocht* [morphology] (1953). These works, as well as De Bhaldraithe's congenial association with his informants and their locale, did much to enhance the regard for 'Conamara Irish' among academics. After receiving his doctorate in 1942, De Bhaldraithe was a scholar at the Dublin Institute for Advanced Studies (INSTITIÚID ARD-LÉINN, 1942–3) and an assistant in the Department of Modern Irish in University College Dublin (1943–6). During this period, he was also a founding member of An Chomhchaidreamh, an organization of young, progressive language activists, and the vice-editor of their journal, COMHAR (1942–). De Bhaldraithe's abiding interest in Modern IRISH LITERATURE was manifest in several editions he produced over the years, most notably: *Nuascéalaíocht 1940–1950*, *Scothscéalta le Pádraic Ó Conaire* (1956), *Seacht mBua an Éirí Amach* [Pádraic Ó CONAIRE] (1967), and *Cín Lae Amhlaoibh* [Amhlaoibh Ó SÚILLEABHÁIN] (1970).

As a lecturer in University College Dublin from 1946 until 1960, De Bhaldraithe devoted himself to the compilation of his *English–Irish Dictionary* (1959). Despite its age, 'De Bhaldraithe's dictionary' remains an indispensable tool for users of the Irish language. In 1954 he established the university's dialect archive. De Bhaldraithe was Professor of Modern Irish at University College Dublin from 1960 to 1978, during which time he served as the advisory editor for the Irish–English Dictionary Project (resulting in the publication of Niall Ó Dónaill's *Foclóir Gaeilge–Béarla* in 1977) and completed his editions of *Cín Lae Amhlaoibh* (1970) and *Seanchas Thomáis Laighléis* (1977), 'GAELTACHT AUTOBIOGRAPHIES' of great linguistic, historic, and sociological interest. From 1978 until his retirement in 1986, De Bhaldraithe was Professor of Irish Dialectology at University College Dublin. During this period he directed several lexicographical projects and completed his own *Foirisiún Focal as Gaillimh* (1985), an invaluable lexicon for students of Co. Galway Irish and its literature.

With his sudden death at a public occasion on 24 April 1996, CELTIC STUDIES lost a great scholar whose work affirmed the relevance of the field to the life of the Irish nation. His greatest contribution was to make the fruits of linguistic and lexicographical research readily available to students of Irish language and literature, and to the Irish-speaking communuity at large. Tomás de Bhaldraithe served on the Board of Directors of the Dublin Institute for Advanced Studies from 1961 until 1996. He had also been a member of the Royal Irish Academy (ACADAMH RÍOGA NA HÉIREANN) since 1952, and served as the society's vice-president in the periods 1965–6 and 1981–3.

SELECTION OF MAIN WORKS
Irish of Cois Fhairrge, Co. Galway (1945); *Gaeilge Chois Fhairrge* (1953).
EDITIONS. *Nuascéalaíocht 1940–50* (1952); *Scothscéalta le Pádraic Ó Conaire* (1956); *English–Irish Dictionary* (1959); *Seacht mBua an Éirí Amach / Pádraic Ó Conaire* (1967); *Cín Lae Amhlaoibh / Amhlaoibh Ó Súilleabháin* (1970); *Seanchas Thomáis Laighléis* (1977); *Clocha ar a Charn / Pádraic Ó Conaire* (1982); *Foirisiún Focal as Gaillimh* (1985).
ED. & TRANS. *Diary of Humphrey O'Sullivan 1827–1835* (1979).
BIBLIOGRAPHY OF PUBLISHED WORKS. Gunn, *Féilscríbhinn Thomáis de Bhaldraithe* 153–63.

FURTHER READING
ACADAMH RÍOGA NA H-ÉIREANN; BAILE ÁTHA CLIATH; CELTIC STUDIES; COMHAR; DICTIONARIES AND GRAMMARS; ÉIRE; GAELTACHT; GAELTACHT AUTOBIOGRAPHIES; INSTITIÚID ARD-LÉINN; IRISH; IRISH LITERATURE; Ó CONAIRE; Ó SÚILLEABHÁIN; VENDRYÈS; Mac Aonghusa, *Tomás de Bhaldraithe*; Watson, *Féilscríbhinn Thomáis de Bhaldraithe*.

William J. Mahon

De Blácam, Aodh
(Hugh Blacam) was a 20th-century Irish journalist, critic, and fiction writer. He was born in London in 1890 and died in Dublin (BAILE ÁTHA CLIATH) in 1951. Having learned IRISH from the essayist Robert Lynd (1879–1949), De Blácam moved to Ireland (ÉIRE) to work as a journalist. He became an active member of Sinn Féin and began writing on nationalist issues (see NATIONALISM). In his work, which encompasses literary history, novels, short stories, and poetry, De Blácam draws on Irish myth and history, while strongly advocating the return of Gaeldom. Among his works is the heavily auto-biographical *Holy Romans* (1920), a novel about an Ulster Protestant brought up in London, who becomes a Roman Catholic and Irish nationalist. De Blácam's *Gaelic Literature Surveyed* (1929), which gives an account of the history of Irish-language literature and puts it in a framework of reference to important works in ANGLO-IRISH LITERATURE, is still considered an important critical evaluation of GAELIC literature.

SELECTION OF MAIN WORKS
COLLECTIONS OF SHORT STORIES. *The Ship that Sailed Too Soon* (1919); *Patsy Kehoe, Codologist* (1922).
LITERARY WRITINGS. *Gaelic Literature Surveyed* (1929); *Black North* (1938).
NOVELS &C. *Holy Romans* (1920); *Druid's Cave* (1921).
POETRY. *Dornán Dán* (1917); *Songs and Satires* (1920).

RELATED ARTICLES
ANGLO-IRISH LITERATURE; BAILE ÁTHA CLIATH; ÉIRE; GAELIC; IRISH; IRISH LITERATURE; NATIONALISM.

PSH

De Clare, Richard
(known as Strongbow, c. 1130–76) was a Norman nobleman from Wales (CYMRU). His father, Gilbert de Clare (also known as Strongbow), was earl of Pembroke (Penfro). Richard succeeded his father in 1148, but Henry II of England stripped De Clare of his title upon the king's accession in 1154. De Clare's involvement with the affairs of Ireland (ÉRIU) began when Diarmait Mac Murchada (Anglicized as Dermot MacMurrough), the exiled king of Leinster (LAIGIN), came to Britain with the permission of Henry II to seek military aid.

There are two near-contemporary sources: Gerald of Wales (GIRALDUS CAMBRENSIS) wrote a history called *Expugnatio Hibernica* ('The Conquest of Ireland'), composed in the 1180s, and there is an Old French (specifically, Hiberno-Norman) *chanson de geste* usually entitled 'The Song of Dermot and the Earl'. The *chanson de geste* is preserved in a single manuscript, written between 1226 and 1230. According to these sources, De Clare contracted with Mac Murchada to offer military assistance in return for the hand of Mac Murchada's daughter Aífe (modern Irish Aoife, sometimes Anglicized as Eve) and succession to the kingship of Leinster. De Clare and Mac Murchada landed at Wexford in 1170. They took the city, and managed to reconquer and hold Leinster. When Mac Murchada died the following year, Strongbow used both his marriage and his military might to establish himself king of Leinster. Henry II, displeased with the *de facto* independent Norman kingdom that resulted, came to Ireland himself. De Clare acknowledged Henry as his overlord, and after handing over Dublin (BAILE ÁTHA CLIATH), Wexford (LOCH GARMAN) and other coastal towns, was recognized as Lord of Leinster.

The family takes its name from their estates at Clare in Suffolk, England. The name is sometimes spelled De Claire, an incorrect etymology involving the French word *claire* 'clear, bright'. County Clare in Ireland is named after Thomas de Clare, a descendant of Richard's cousin Roger, earl of Hertford.

FURTHER READING
BAILE ÁTHA CLIATH; CYMRU; ÉRIU; GIRALDUS CAMBRENSIS; LAIGIN; LOCH GARMAN; Conlon, *Song of Dermot and Earl Richard Fitzgilbert*; Connolly, *Oxford Companion to Irish History*; Duffy, *Ireland in the Middle Ages*; Foster, *Oxford History of Ireland*; Mills, *Oxford Dictionary of English Place-Names*; Roche, *Norman Invasion of Ireland*.

AM

De Gabáil in t-Sída (Concerning the taking of the otherworld mound) is a brief text, linguistically of Old IRISH date, which occurs in the Book of Leinster (LEBOR LAIGNECH). It throws light on the early development of several doctrines that find fuller expression in the longer later texts of the MYTHO-LOGICAL CYCLE and Irish LEGENDARY HISTORY, including ideas about Ireland's supernatural race, the TUATH DÉ, the conquest of Ireland (ÉRIU) by the sons of MÍL ESPÁINE, and the nature and origin of the OTHERWORLD of the síd mounds.

At the opening of the narrative there is a convergence of the themes of the fertility of the land and the foundation of GAELIC Ireland. The underlying idea is that the first Irishmen skilfully manipulated social exchange with the gods so as to subordinate them and be entitled to ongoing sustenance in return:

There was a wondrous king over the Tuatha Dé in Ireland, Dagán by name [i.e. 'the DAGDA']. Great was his power, even over the sons of Míl after they had seized the land. For the Tuatha Dé blighted the grain and milk of the sons of Míl until they made a treaty [*cairdes*] with the Dagda. Thereafter they preserved their grain and their milk for them.

The permanence of the *cairdes*, and the formal division of Ireland into a mortal surface world and the world of the *síd* for the Tuath Dé is made explicit in a version of the same events related at the beginning of MESCA ULAD ('The Intoxication of the Ulstermen').

In *De Gabáil in t-Sída*, there follows a second episode, a flashback deep into the pre-mortal mythological age,

concerning the control of time by the inhabitants of the *síd* mounds:

Great too was his [i.e. the Dagda's] power when he was king in the beginning; and it was he who divided the *síde* among the Fir Dé ['men of the gods']: LUG son of Eithliu in Síd Rodrubán, Ogma in Síd Aircheltrai, the Dagda himself however had Síd Lethet Lachtmaige . . .

They say, however, that Síd in Broga [i.e. the megalithic tomb called Newgrange/BRUG NA BÓINNE] belonged to him at first. [OENGUS MAC IND ÓC] came to the Dagda seeking territory when he had made the division to everyone; he was a foster son of Midir of Brí Léith and of Nindid the prophet.

'I have nothing for you,' said the Dagda. 'I have finished the distribution.'

'Obtain for me then,' said the Mac Óc, 'just a day and a night in your own dwelling.' That was granted to him then.

'Now go to your house,' said the Dagda, 'for you have used up your time.'

'It is plain,' he said, 'that the whole world is day and night, and that is what was granted to me.'

Then Dagán departed from there, and the Mac Óc remained in his *síd*.

(Trans. Koch & Carey, *Celtic Heroic Age* 145)

This story is intriguing when we consider that many of these prehistoric burial monuments incorporate alignments with astronomical calendar events such as the solstices and equinoxes. The burial shaft at Newgrange, in particular, is illuminated only at daybreak on the shortest day of the year and a few days before and after it. Thus, the idea of tricky extension of a single day into eternity at this site had some four millennia of precedent behind it when our tale was written (see Carey, *Proc. Harvard Celtic Colloquium* 10.24–36).

Among the medieval Irish literati, *De Gabáil in t-Sída* was counted as one of the *remscéla* (fore-tales) of TÁIN BÓ CUAILNGE (Mac Cana, *Learned Tales of Medieval Ireland* 89), perhaps because a version of the same events is recounted in the ULSTER CYCLE saga, *Mesca Ulad*.

PRIMARY SOURCES
EDITION. Hull, ZCP 19.53–8.
TRANS. Koch & Carey, *Celtic Heroic Age* 145.

FURTHER READING
BRUG NA BÓINNE; DAGDA; ÉRIU; GAELIC; IRISH; LEBOR
LAIGNECH; LEGENDARY HISTORY; LUG; MESCA ULAD; MÍL
ESPÁINE; MYTHOLOGICAL CYCLE; OENGUS MAC IND ÓC;
OTHERWORLD; SÍD; TÁIN BÓ CUAILNGE; TUATH DÉ; ULSTER
CYCLE; Carey, *Proc. Harvard Celtic Colloquium* 10.24–36; Koch,
Emania 9.17–27; Mac Cana, *Learned Tales of Medieval Ireland*.

John Carey, JTK

De hÍde, Dubhghlas (Douglas Hyde)

(1860–1949) was a pioneering scholar of the Irish language, literature, and history, and first President of
Ireland (ÉIRE). Hyde was tutored at home in Frenchpark, Co. Roscommon (Contae Ros Comáin), by his
father, an Anglican clergyman, and became expert in
Hebrew, Greek, and Latin. He learned IRISH from the
farmers in their district. With a view to the Anglican
priesthood, Hyde entered Trinity College Dublin
(BAILE ÁTHA CLIATH), adding German and French to
his languages. He won the university's gold medal for
modern literature in 1884, gaining a BA in that subject.
In 1886 he was awarded an LLD from Trinity College,
also winning a prize in theology. Having already published extensively, including two sets of GAELIC stories
collected from elderly Irish speakers, mostly of the
Roscommon area, Hyde was Professor of Modern
Languages at the University of New Brunswick in
Canada from 1891 to 1892. On returning to Ireland he
was appointed president of the National Literary
Society, and his inaugural speech, 'The Necessity of
De-Anglicising Ireland', which was published as a
pamphlet, greatly influenced the burgeoning Gaelic
movement. The following year (1893), he published the
well-received *Abhráin Grádh Chúige Connacht / The Love
Songs of Connacht*, and was subsequently appointed
president of CONRADH NA GAEILGE (The Gaelic
League) at its founding. Under Hyde's leadership, the
League virtually steered Gaelic culture in Ireland for
more than two decades. It was principally through his
unusual Hiberno-English translations of Irish songs
that he became known to W. B. YEATS, Lady GREGORY,
J. M. Synge and others of the Irish literary revival, who
were actively seeking a uniquely Irish idiom for their texts
(see LANGUAGE [REVIVAL]; IRISH LITERATURE).

The songs and stories of CONNACHT were to remain
a subject close to Hyde's heart, and he published widely
on this subject, developing a particular interest in
religious and love poetry. His 1906 volume—*Abhráin
Diadha Chúige Connacht / The Religious Songs of
Connacht*—remains highly respected.

In 1899 Hyde's very influential *Literary History of
Ireland* was published, detailing Gaelic literature from
the earliest times to the 18th century. Also in this year,
as president of the Irish Texts Society (CUMANN NA
SCRÍBHEANN NGAEDHILGE), he edited and translated
*Eachtra Cloinne Rígh na hIoruaidhe / The Adventures of the
Children of the King of Norway*. In 1917 he edited and
translated *Gabháltais Shearluuis Móir / The Conquests of
Charlemagne* for the same society.

Hyde's play *Casadh an tSúgáin* (translated into English
as *The Twisting of the Rope* by Lady Gregory) was performed by the Gaelic League's amateur dramatic society at the Gaiety Theatre, Dublin, in 1901. It was the
first dramatic work to be produced in Modern Irish
(see IRISH DRAMA). With the assistance of W. B. Yeats
and Lady Gregory, Hyde wrote a number of Irish plays
over the next decade, tailoring them for production by
activists.

Hyde toured America in 1905 on an enormously
successful fundraising tour for the Gaelic League. He
published an account of the journey in 1937.

In 1908 Hyde was appointed Professor of Modern
Irish at University College Dublin, and remained in
the post until his retirement in 1932.

Hyde resigned from Conradh na Gaeilge in 1915 after
an acrimonious Ard-Fheis (AGM) in which Patrick
Pearse (Pádraig MAC PIARAIS) spearheaded a move to
alter the organization's constitutional goal to 'an
Ireland, free and Gaelic'. He devoted himself for some
years thereafter to the Celtic Congress, an organization
whose goal was to unite the Celtic nations of north-
western Europe (see PAN-CELTICISM).

Hyde served as a senator in Seanad Éireann (the Irish
senate) from 1925 until 1938. When the redrafted Irish
constitution of 1937 created the office of President,
Hyde's nomination for the office was unanimously
supported. Despite a stroke in 1940 he remained
President until 1945, living afterwards in a state-
provided house in the Phoenix Park, Dublin, called
Ratra after his beloved home in Frenchpark, Co.
Roscommon, which the Gaelic League had bought for
him after his American tour.

SELECTION OF MAIN WORKS
Literary History of Ireland (1899).

SELECTION OF PLAYS. Gareth W. Dunleavy & Janet E. Dunleavy, *Selected Plays of Douglas Hyde*.
ED. & TRANS. *Abhráin Grádh Chúige Connacht/Love Songs of Connacht* (1893); *Giolla an Fhiugha, Eachtra Cloinne Rígh na hIoruaidhe/Lad of the Ferule, Adventures of the Children of the King of Norway* (1899); *Abhráin Diadha Chúige Connacht/ Religious Songs of Connacht* (1906); *Gabháltais Shearluuis Móir/ Conquests of Charlemagne* (1917).

FURTHER READING
BAILE ÁTHA CLIATH; CONNACHT; CONRADH NA GAEILGE; CUMANN NA SCRÍBHEANN N-GAEDHILGE; ÉIRE; GAELIC; GREGORY; IRISH; IRISH DRAMA; IRISH LITERATURE; LANGUAGE (REVIVAL); MAC PIARAIS; PAN-CELTICISM; YEATS; Coffey, *Douglas Hyde*; Daly, *Young Douglas Hyde*; Janet E. Dunleavy & Gareth W. Dunleavy, *Douglas Hyde*; Ó Glaisne, *Dúbhglas de h-Íde 1860–1949*.
BIBLIOGRAPHY OF PUBLISHED WORKS. O'Hegarty, *Bibliography of Dr. Douglas Hyde*.

Brian Ó Broin

De Paor, Liam

(1926–98) was an Irish archaeologist and historian. Born in Dublin (BAILE ÁTHA CLIATH), he was educated at University College Dublin, where he later became lecturer. He collaborated with his wife, Máire (1925–94), on the volume *Early Christian Ireland* (1958), and in 1964 spent a year in Nepal as UNESCO adviser on historic monuments.

He wrote a regular column entitled 'Roots' for the *Irish Times*, and a collection of some of his most important essays on political and national issues was published as *Landscape with Figures: People, Culture and Art in Ireland and the Modern World* (1998).

SELECTION OF MAIN WORKS
(with Máire De Paor) *Early Christian Ireland* (1958). *Divided Ulster* (1970); *Portrait of Ireland* (1985); *Peoples of Ireland* (1986); *Tom Moore and Contemporary Ireland* (1989); *Unfinished Business* (1990); *Saint Patrick's World* (1993); *Ireland and Early Europe* (1997); *Landscape with Figures* (1998).

RELATED ARTICLES
BAILE ÁTHA CLIATH; NATIONALISM.

PEB

De Paor, Louis

(1961–), Irish-language poet, author, and editor, was born in Cork city (CORCAIGH) and graduated from University College Cork in 1981. His Ph.D. on the short stories of Máirtín Ó CADHAIN was published as *Faoin mBlaoisc Bheag Sin* (Inside that little skull; 1991). He jointly edited *Coiscéim na hAoise Seo* (A step forward in our time; 1991) with Seán Ó TUAMA and also edited two issues of INNTI (12

and 13). He lived in Australia from 1987 to 1996, where two bilingual collections of his poetry were published: *Aimsir Bhreicneach / Freckled Weather* (1993) and *Gobán Cré is Cloch / Sentences of Earth and Shore* (1996). De Paor belongs to the Cork *Innti* school of poetry—his style and language clearly influenced by Seán Ó RÍORDÁIN, Seán Ó Tuama, Michael DAVITT, and Liam Ó MUIRTHILE. In 2000, he received the Lawrence O'Shaughnessy poetry award.

SELECTION OF MAIN WORKS
Próca Solais is Luatha (1988); *Faoin mBlaiosc Bheag Sin* (1991); *Tríocha Dán* (1992); *Aimsir Bhreicneach / Freckled Weather* (1993); *Gobán Cré is Cloch / Sentences of Earth and Shore* (1996); *Seo, Siúd agus Uile* (1996); *Corcach agus Dánta Eile* (1999); *Agus Rud Eile* (2002).
ED. (with Ó Tuama). *Coiscéim na hAoise Seo* (1991).

RELATED ARTICLES
CORCAIGH; DAVITT; INNTI; IRISH; IRISH LITERATURE; Ó CADHAIN; Ó MUIRTHILE; Ó RÍORDÁIN; Ó TUAMA.

Pádraigín Riggs

De raris fabulis

§1. INTRODUCTION

Oxford, Bodleian Library MS 572, also known as *Codex Oxoniensis Posterior*, is dated on palaeographical grounds to the second quarter of the 10th century (Madan & Craster, *Summary Catalogue of Western Manuscripts in the Bodleian Library at Oxford* 2.170–4). The manuscript contains a scholastic colloquy, *De raris fabulis* (Concerning uncommon stories), which possibly originated as a 9th-century text (Dumville, *Anglo-Saxon Glossography* 66). Since it has been claimed that the colloquy contains GLOSSES in two early Neo-BRYTHONIC languages (WELSH and CORNISH)—and there has been a fair amount of attendant controversy on the subject over the years—the text is significant for CELTIC STUDIES. It is a key-case study in the problem of distinguishing the Welsh, Cornish, and BRETON languages of the early Middle Ages.

The colloquy has been edited several times and has drawn the attention of students of various disciplines. The text is also of great importance for the analysis of contemporary Latin learning in Britain, since the scholastic colloquy was a form frequently used in the Middle Ages, both for elementary instruction and as a means of acquiring a learned vocabulary. It has been argued that the origin of this genre can be found in the bilingual phrasebooks of late antiquity, and several Latin colloquies are attested in the manuscripts of pre-Norman Britain. The colloquy is written in the form of a dialogue, which could also allow word substitutions within one syntactic pattern, e.g. 'Good morning, students, go to the river / to the spring / to the well'. Brythonic glosses (in ink), alongside the numerous Latin glosses, are found both incorporated into the main text and between the lines.

§2. OLD WELSH OR OLD CORNISH

The Celtic glosses were at one time considered to be Cornish—basically due to peculiarities of orthography—after H. Bradshaw's *Collected Papers*, and the Brythonic words were treated in various dictionaries as Old Cornish (e.g. Loth, *Les mots latins dans les langues brittoniques*, which is still usable). However, in 1893 J. LOTH published a small note in which he reconsidered the linguistic aspect of the problem (RC 14.70), and now most of the Brythonic words are considered to be Old Welsh. The greatest number of examples could be as easily Old Welsh as Old Cornish, since the two languages remained very similar at this period—for example, *selsic* 'sausage', *tarater* 'awl', *ord* 'sledge hammer', *creman* 'sickle', *arater* 'plough', *iou* 'yoke', *notuid* 'needle', *bendat* 'grandfather', *henmam* 'grandmother', *modreped* 'aunts', *guin* 'WINE', *med* 'mead', *fruidlonaid* 'fertility'. However, a few words must be Welsh and cannot be Cornish, since they show an older Neo-Brythonic stressed long ō becoming a Welsh diphthong *au* (later Welsh *aw*); this never happened in Cornish. Thus, for example, *guerclaud* 'enclosed field', *brachaut* 'a type of alcoholic drink', *plumauc* 'a type of furniture stuffed with feathers'. On the other hand, the list of the entries which had been believed to show Cornish characteristics is not extensive and open to question. According to Jackson (LHEB 55), this Cornish group includes: *iot* glossed *pultum* 'porridge' (Modern Welsh *uwd*—we might expect Old Welsh **iut*—Latin *pulsus*), *iotum* glossed *ius* 'juice', *tarater* glossed *scapa uel rostrum* (*i.foratorium*) (all on fo. 42a), and *torcigel* glossed *uentris lora* (fo. 43a). Jackson also notes that the letter '*e* is used for [ə], *b d g* for lenited *p t c*, and *d* for *th*, more often than is normal in OW'; in fact, this is a groundless argument—all these features are very common in Old Welsh. J. Loth's conclusion was that: '*Ces gloses ne proviennent probablement pas du pays de Galles actuel, mais*

d'un territoire limitrophe, rattaché linguistiquement à la principauté, comme le territoire du Gloucestershire ou du Somersetshire' (These glosses probably do not originate from Wales itself, but from some bordering region, linked linguistically to Wales, such as the region of Gloucestershire or Somerset). This theory was rejected by Jackson (LHEB 56) on historical grounds; by this date, Gloucestershire and Somerset were—Jackson believed—English speaking. Jackson proposed that it was 'most probable that the text and glosses were written by a Cornishman in Wales or a Welshman in Cornwall'. He concluded: 'Since the script is Continental it is more likely to have been written in Cornwall, where the Continental hand was already in use in the early tenth century'. Since the text is apparently a copy from an earlier exemplar (on the layers see Lapidge, *Proc. 7th International Congress of Celtic Studies* 94–5; Porter, *Anglo-Saxon Conversations* 21–2), it could also be the case that the original was written at a Welsh scriptorium, and then changed in the style of the script and perhaps also minimally in the features of its Brythonic dialect when later copied outside Wales.

§3. OLD ENGLISH GLOSSES

The presence of several Old English glosses on fo. 42a–b, some of which were considered by H. H. E. Craster (RC 40.135–6) and edited by H. D. Meritt (*Old English Glosses* 57), makes this text of interest to Anglo-Saxon studies. The hand which was responsible for these dry-stylus glosses (scratched into the parchment without ink), and which is different from the main hand of the manuscript—but almost contemporary with it—is also accountable for the two glosses which were formerly considered Brythonic, but which are, in fact, Latin and (very probably) Anglo-Saxon, respectively. The use of more than one vernacular language for glossing this text suggests that this colloquy came from an area or monastery where both Brythonic and Old English were in use. The pro-Brythonic orientation of the text can be deduced from the fragment which occurs on fos. 45b–46a and which relates the British victory over the English.

§4. INCONCLUSIVE CASE FOR IRISH INFLUENCE

The text abounds in the so-called 'Irish symptoms' and Hiberno-Latin spelling features, such as *ti* for *si* (*ecletia*), interchange of *i/e*, *u/o*, *b/p* (as in *peregrinus*, *insola, cubis*, see Lapidge, *Proc. 7th International Congress of Celtic Studies*, 95); however, all these features are also found in Latin manuscripts from Wales (Lindsay, *Early Welsh Script*; Charles-Edwards, *Studia Hibernica* 20.151). In the introduction to W. H. Stevenson's edition (*Early Scholastic Colloquies* ix), Lindsay drew attention to the phrase *non difficile*, which occurs several times in the text and which he considered 'a Latin version of the normal Old Irish preface to the answer of a question', i.e. Old Irish *ní annsae* 'not difficult'. If so, this detail might point to an Irish connection. However, as Jackson showed (LHEB 55), a similar phrase with the same rhetorical function occurs in the Old Welsh COMPUTUS FRAGMENT, namely *nit abruid* 'not difficult'; cf. Charles-Edwards, *Studia Hibernica* 20.151.

PRIMARY SOURCES

MS. Oxford, Bodleian Library 572 (*Codex Oxoniensis Posterior*). EDITIONS. Stevenson, *Early Scholastic Colloquies* 1–11; Stokes, *Trans. Philological Society* 1860/1.238–44, 293; Zeuss, *Grammatica Celtica* 1091–6.
See also La Villemarqué, *Archives des Missions scientifiques et littéraires* 5.272, plate 3, for a facsimile edition of part of the folio.

FURTHER READING

BRETON; BRYTHONIC; CELTIC STUDIES; COMPUTUS FRAGMENT; CORNISH; GLOSSES; IRISH; LOTH; WELSH; WINE; Bradshaw, *Collected Papers*; Charles-Edwards, *Studia Hibernica* 20.151; Craster, RC 40.135–6; Dumville, *Anglo-Saxon Glossography* 59–76; Falileyev, *Ireland and Europe in the Early Middle Ages* 6–13; Falileyev & Russell, *Yr Hen Iaith* 95–101; Gwara, *Latin Colloquies from Pre-Conquest Britain* 1–26; Gwara & Porter, *Anglo-Saxon Conversations* 1–76; Jackson, LHEB 54–6; Lapidge, *Insular Latin Studies* 45–82; Lapidge, *Proc. 7th International Congress of Celtic Studies*, 91–107; Lindsay, *Early Welsh Script* 26; Loth, *Les mots latins dans les langues brittoniques*; Loth, RC 14.70; Madan & Craster, *Summary Catalogue of Western Manuscripts in the Bodleian Library at Oxford* 2; Meritt, *Old English Glosses*; Porter, *Neophilologus* 81.467–80.

Alexander Falileyev

De Valera, Eamon (Irish Éamonn; 1882–1975)

was, arguably, the most influential politician in 20th-century Ireland. One of the leaders of the Easter Rising and the Irish War of Independence (see IRISH INDEPENDENCE MOVEMENT), he became the longest-serving Taoiseach (Prime Minister) of Dáil Éireann, the parliament of Saorstát na hÉireann (Irish Free State), holding office from 1932 until 1948, and returning from 1951 to 1954. From 1959 until 1973 he served as Uachtarán na hÉireann, President of the Republic of Ireland. De Valera led Ireland on the road to independence and successfully negotiated its difficult early relationship with the United Kingdom. He established his country's independence by preserving its neutrality during the Second World War, and concentrating afterwards on gaining international recognition for ÉIRE.

Born Edward de Valera in New York on 14 October 1882, he came to Co. Limerick (Contae Luimnigh) in 1885 to be brought up by his grandmother. In 1898 he won a scholarship to Blackrock College, Dublin (BAILE ÁTHA CLIATH), and in 1901 he accepted a post as mathematics teacher at Rockwell College, Co. Tipperary (Contae Thiobraid Árainn). He changed his name to Éamonn when he joined CONRADH NA GAEILGE in 1908, marrying one of his Irish teachers, Sinéad Flanagan, in 1910. Enrolment in the language organization, as for Michael COLLINS and Patrick Pearse (Pádraig MAC PIARAIS), was his first step on the path to Irish national politics. In 1913 he attended the foundation meeting of the Irish Volunteer Force (see IRISH REPUBLICAN ARMY), set up in response to the unionist Ulster Volunteer Force formed earlier that year. During the Easter Rising he was in charge of the third battalion of the Irish Volunteers, the last to surrender to British troops on 30 April 1916. Although sentenced to death, along with the other leaders of the Rising, he was spared, probably because he had been born in the USA. As the only survivor, he quickly gained a prominent place in politics when released from prison in June 1917: he won the East Clare by-election, and was elected President of Sinn Féin and the Irish Volunteers. Re-arrested for his alleged part in the 'German plot' in May 1918, he escaped from Lincoln prison in England, with the help of Michael Collins, to become Príomh Aire (President) of the first Dáil Éireann in April 1919. He spent most of the War of Independence in the USA raising support for the Dáil, but negotiated the truce that ended it on 11 July 1921. His subsequent negotiations for independence, however, failed and he decided not to join the second delegation, headed by Arthur Griffith (see Ó GRÍOFA), which eventually signed the first Anglo–Irish Treaty on 6 December 1921. When the treaty was accepted by the Dáil, de Valera resigned as President and supported the anti-treaty forces in the ensuing civil war, although he later tried to end the military conflict.

De Valera's rise to political power in the Free State began with his resignation in 1926 from Sinn Féin and the foundation of his own party, Fianna Fáil. It won the general election of 1932, ushering in his long term as Taoiseach. He set about realizing his vision of a truly free Ireland, removing the oath of allegiance (to the English Crown) and the office of (the British) Governor General. In 1937, he introduced a new constitution, Bunreacht na hÉireann, which, among other things, changed the name of the country to Éire, gave both IRISH and English official status, claimed jurisdiction over the whole island, and laid the foundations for the Irish Republic which was declared in 1949. With the 1938 Anglo–Irish agreement, which followed the 'economic war' between Britain and the Free State, he wrung important economic concessions from Britain. During the Second World War, he persevered with the difficult task of preserving neutrality. The period after the war saw him hard at work raising Éire's international profile and preparing the ground for the country's entry to the European Economic Council (now the European Union) in 1972. Retiring from his office as President in 1973, he died in 1975.

Tragically, de Valera failed in the two tasks closest to his heart. Despite providing considerable public support for Irish-medium EDUCATION, as well as his enthusiastic personal support for the Irish language, his policies did not reverse its decline (see LANGUAGE [REVIVAL]); nor did he succeed in ending the partition of Ireland, though the enduring idea of Ireland as a single cultural and historical entity owes much to de Valera's efforts.

Eamon de Valera's wife, Sinéad (1879–1975), is best known as an author and translator of folk and fairy tales in both English and Irish, primarily aimed at children. Her most popular works include Coinneal na Nodlag agus Sgéalta Eile (The Christmas candle and other stories; 1944) and Áilleacht agus an Beithidheach (Beauty and the beast; 1946).

Their son, Rúaidhrí or Ruary de Valera (1916–78), succeeded Seán Ó Ríordáin as Chair of Celtic Archaeology at University College Dublin in 1957. He was appointed Place-names Officer with Suirbhéireacht Ordanáis Éireann (Ordnance Survey Ireland) in 1946, and Archaeology Officer in 1947, posts which he held until 1957. Together with Seán Ó Nualláin, he wrote the Survey of the Megalithic Tombs of Ireland vols. 1–4 (1961–83).

SELECTION OF MAIN WORKS
EAMON DE VALERA. Recent Speeches and Broadcasts (1933); Unity of Ireland (1939); Peace and War (1944).
SINÉAD DE VALERA. Buaidhirt agus Bród (1935); Lá Bealtaine (1936); Teach i n-Áirde (1936); Coinneal na Nodlag agus Sgealta Eile (1944); Áilleact agus an Beithidheacht (1946); Oilibhéar Beannaithe Plongcéad (1948); Irish Fairy Tales (1973); More Irish Fairy Tales (1979).
RUAIDHRÍ DE VALERA (with Ó Nualláin), Survey of the Megalithic Tombs of Ireland.

FURTHER READING
BAILE ÁTHA CLIATH; COLLINS; CONRADH NA GAEILGE; EDUCATION; ÉIRE; IRISH; IRISH INDEPENDENCE MOVEMENT; IRISH REPUBLICAN ARMY; LANGUAGE (REVIVAL); MAC PIARAIS; Ó GRÍOFA; Ó RÍORDÁIN; Bowman, De Valera and the Ulster Question; Boyce, Ireland 1828–1923; Brown, Ireland; Coogan, De Valera; Douglas, President de Valera and the Senate; Dwyer, Eamon de Valera; Dwyer, Michael Collins and the Treaty; Edwards, Éamon de Valera; Fitzgibbon, Life and Times of Eamon de Valera; Kehoe, History Makers of 20th Century Ireland; Longford & O'Neill, Eamon de Valera; Lyons, Ireland Since the Famine; MacManus, Eamon de Valera; Severn, Irish Statesman and Rebel; Travers, Eamon de Valera; Younger, State of Disunion.

MBL

Dean of Lismore, Book of the, is the most important manuscript of late medieval GAELIC poetry in Scotland (ALBA). Compiled between the years 1512 and 1526, primarily by the brothers Seamus MacGriogair (James MacGregor, the eponymous Dean) and Donnchadh MacGriogair, the work represents an effort of collection begun the generation before by Fionnlagh Mac an Aba, whose exhortatory poem to the brothers' father, Dubhghall MacGriogair of Fortingall, is included in the collection (Watson, Scottish Verse from the Book of the Dean of Lismore 2–5). Seamus MacGriogair was a notary public at a time when Scots law was dominated by the Lowland SCOTS language, and it is this cultural intersection which has given the manuscript its current rather intractable form. The Gaelic poems included in it are transliterated into an orthography based essentially on that of Lowland Scots. This orthography has proved to be the greatest single obstacle to editing the poetry, especially since most of it is uniquely preserved here. On the other hand, the orthography provides copious evidence for Gaelic dialects and historical morphology. Moreover, the manuscript contains not only Gaelic poetry but also poetry and prose in Scots, and some material in Latin.

The collection is testimony to two main strands of

tradition. The most important for SCOTTISH GAELIC is the light it sheds on the vibrant and often unorthodox poetic scene in Perthshire and Argyll during the late 15th and early 16th centuries, particularly evidenced by the work of Donnchadh CAIMBEUL of Glenorchy and others belonging to the circle of the Campbells and the MacGregors (see MACGREGOR POETRY). Despite these links, it also contains poetry connected with the Clann Domhnaill (Clan Donald) LORDSHIP OF THE ISLES, including significant items related to its declining years in the 1490s. The other strand includes a large number of classical Irish poems (see IRISH LITERATURE [3]), some found uniquely here, including many by the Ó DÁLAIGH FAMILY, and this suggests that material from one or more earlier manuscripts is incorporated in the Dean's Book.

The Book is also omnivorous in its approach to verse. Alongside classical Irish poetry of the highest order, both from Scotland and Ireland (ÉIRE), we have grimly scatological material, effecting love poetry in the courtly mode, heroic BALLADS, philosophical pieces and allegories. From the Dean's Book we also have poetry by at least four women, which must be balanced by the dedicated misogyny of other items.

A full edition of the contents is still awaited, though much has appeared in the form of either transcriptions (Quiggin, *Poems from the Book of the Dean of Lismore*), or full editions into conventional Gaelic orthography (Bergin, Gillies, Meek, Ross, Watson).

PRIMARY SOURCES
ED. & TRANS. Bergin, *Irish Bardic Poetry*; Gillies, *Scottish Gaelic Studies* 13.18–45, 263–88, 14.59–82; Meek, *CMCS* 34.1–50; Meek, 'Corpus of Heroic Verse in the Book of the Dean of Lismore'; M'Lauchlan, *Dean of Lismore's Book*; Quiggin, *Poems from the Book of the Dean of Lismore*; Ross, *Heroic Poetry from the Book of the Dean of Lismore*; Watson, *Scottish Verse from the Book of the Dean of Lismore*.

FURTHER READING
ALBA; BALLADS; CAIMBEUL; ÉIRE; GAELIC; IRISH LITERATURE [3]; LORDSHIP OF THE ISLES; MACGREGOR POETRY; Ó DÁLAIGH FAMILY; SCOTS; SCOTTISH GAELIC; SCOTTISH GAELIC POETRY; Gillies, *Companion to Gaelic Scotland* 293–4; Gillies, *History of Scottish Literature* 1.245–61; Gillies, *Scottish Studies* 21.35–53; Meek, *Bryght Lanternis* 387–404; Meek, *Companion to Gaelic Scotland* 294–5; O'Rahilly, *Scottish Gaelic Studies* 4.31–56; Thomson, *Companion to Gaelic Scotland* 59–60, 292–3; Thomson, *Introduction to Gaelic Poetry*; Thomson, *Scottish Studies* 12.57–78.

Thomas Owen Clancy

Deane, Seamus (1940–) is an (English-language) Irish poet, novelist and scholar. He was born in Derry/Londonderry (DOIRE) and educated in Belfast (Béal Feirste) and Cambridge. He taught Modern English and American literature at the National University of Ireland, Dublin (BAILE ÁTHA CLIATH) and is now the Keogh Professor of Irish Studies at the University of Notre Dame, Indiana, USA. His poetry reflects his experiences in the divided society of Northern Ireland, and combines an emotional involvement with intellectual argument and historical and cultural awareness. His scholarly interests concern Irish cultural identity and its resonance in the literature.

SELECTION OF MAIN WORKS
While Jewels Rot (1967); *Gradual Wars* (1972); *Rumours* (1977); *Civilians and Barbarians* (1983); *History Lessons* (1983); *Heroic Styles* (1984); *Celtic Revivals* (1985); *Short History of Irish Literature* (1986); *Irish Writers 1886–1986* (1986); *Selected Poems* (1988); *French Revolution and Enlightenment in England* (1988); *Reading in the Dark* (1996); *Strange Country* (1997).

RELATED ARTICLES
BAILE ÁTHA CLIATH; DOIRE; IRISH LITERATURE [7].

PSH, PEB

Déchelette, Joseph (1862–1914) was a pioneering French archaeologist, whose *Manuel d'archéologie préhistorique celtique et gallo-romaine* provided an original synthetic overview of the great discoveries made during his lifetime in the study of the IRON AGE in GAUL and central Europe. He elucidated the chronological sequence of cultures that culminated in the civilization of the vast late LA TÈNE *oppida* of the century before CAESAR's conquest (see OPPIDUM). He was the founder of the Musée Joseph Déchelette in Roanne (Loire), France, which holds an important collection of Gaulish, Gallo-Roman, and Roman artefacts. He was killed in the First World War at the height of his career.

SELECTION OF MAIN WORKS
Les vases céramiques ornés de la Gaule romaine (1904); *Manuel d'archéologie préhistorique celtique et gallo-romaine* (1908–14).

RELATED ARTICLES
CAESAR; GAUL; HALLSTATT; IRON AGE; LA TÈNE; OPPIDUM.

PEB

Book of Deer: seated figure with sword, Cambridge University Library MS Ii.6.32 fo. 4v.

Deer, Book of, is an insular gospel book, which was probably originally copied and illustrated in the 9th or 10th century, and was in the possession of the religious community of Deer, in Buchan, north-east Scotland (ALBA), by the 11th century. It cannot be certain that the gospel book itself is a product of a Scottish scriptorium, though some have thought it likely (Geddes, *Proc. Society of Antiquaries of Scotland* 128.537–49; Marner, *Medieval Archaeology* 46.1–28). The illustrations are in a calligraphic, cartoon-like style, which has won few admirers from insular art historians used to the major gospel books, but deserves assessment in its own right. Other contents, additional to the fragmentary synoptic gospels and complete copy of John, are of signal importance. One is a liturgy for the anointing of the sick and dying, of a sort found in Ireland (ÉRIU) in the company of gospel books, which has suggested a relationship between these books and aspects of pastoral care. The most discussed aspect of the Book of Deer, however, is its collection of property records, dating from the early 12th century, the latest from *c.* 1150, the earliest set being retrospective, and recording grants dating back to the 10th century. With one exception, these records are in the vernacular, and reveal some emergent signs of a local Scottish dialect of GAELIC; indeed, they are our earliest witness to it. There are also important and unique references to social institutions, such as the high grades of leadership *mormaer* (a term of PICTISH or BRYTHONIC origin) and GOIDELIC *toísech*, the land unit called the *dabach*, and other items, which have allowed historians to investigate something of the Gaelic world of 10th–12th century eastern Scotland. It is also a window, albeit a narrow one, on ecclesiastical houses and their patronage during this latter part of the early Middle Ages, prior to the major monastic transformation which would see Deer itself turned into a parish church, and later a colony of Cistercians develop a new community under the old name.

PRIMARY SOURCES
MS. Cambridge, University Library Ii.6.32.
EDITION. Stuart, *Book of Deer*.
ED. & TRANS. Jackson, *Gaelic Notes in the 'Book of Deer'*.

FURTHER READING
ALBA; BRYTHONIC; ÉRIU; GAELIC; GOIDELIC; PICTISH; Forsyth, *Studies in the Book of Deer*; Geddes, *Proc. Society of Antiquaries of Scotland* 128.537–49; Marner, *Medieval Archaeology* 46.1–28.

Thomas Owen Clancy

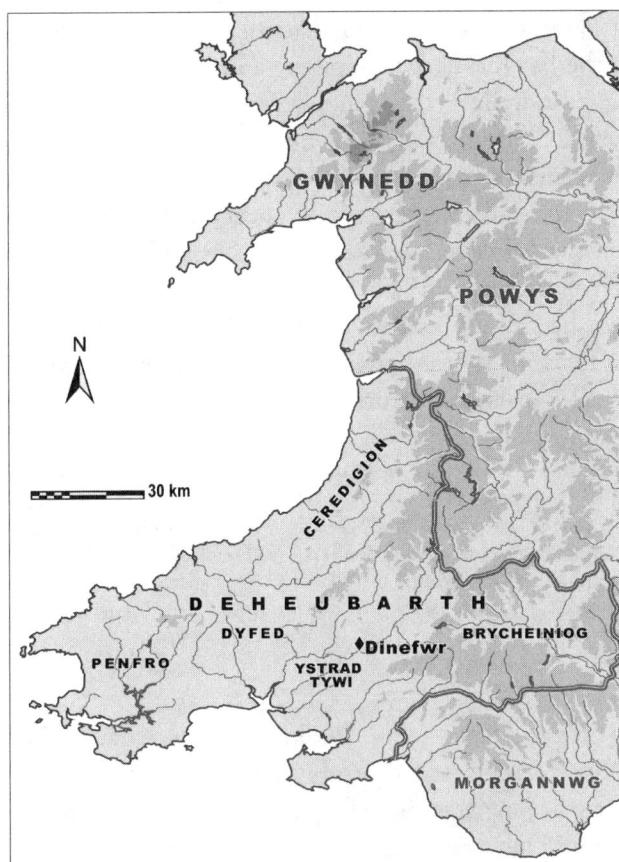

Deheubarth, its constituent regions, neighbouring kingdoms, and approximate mid 11th-century boundaries

Deheubarth, meaning 'southern (*deheu*) part (*parth*)', was one of the traditional Welsh kingdoms of the early Middle Ages. Established in the 10th century by HYWEL DDA, it consisted mainly of the territories of the earlier territorial entities of DYFED, Ystrad Tywi, Penfro, CEREDIGION, and BRYCHEINIOG. Its main court was at Dinefwr. From the central Middle Ages until the Anglo-Norman encroachments of the 12th and 13th centuries, Deheubarth was one of the main political units of Wales (CYMRU) (besides GWYNEDD, POWYS, and MORGANNWG) and the rulers of Deheubarth were often in a position to compete with those of Gwynedd for hegemony in Wales. From the late 11th century, Deheubarth came increasingly under the pressure of Norman power based in England and was repeatedly subjected to raids and Norman overlordship. Deheubarth experienced a renaissance under

Lord RHYS AP GRUFFUDD (r. 1155–97). It was partly conquered by LLYWELYN AP GRUFFUDD in 1263 before it became part of the Principality of Wales (*Pura Wallia*) in 1282 after the conquest and death of the last independent Welsh prince, Llywelyn ap Gruffudd of Gwynedd.

FURTHER READING
BRYCHEINIOG; CEREDIGION; CYMRU; DYFED; GWYNEDD; HYWEL DDA; LLYWELYN AP GRUFFUDD; MORGANNWG; POWYS; RHYS AP GRUFFUDD; John Davies, *History of Wales*; John Davies, *Making of Wales*; R. R. Davies, *Age of Conquest*; Pryce, WHR 13.265–81; Rees, *Guide to Ancient and Historic Wales: Dyfed*.

PEB

Deiniol, St, was bishop of BANGOR (GWYNEDD) and patron of its cathedral where pilgrims visited his miraculous image. ANNALES CAMBRIAE records the death of Deiniol ('Daniel', feast-day 11 September) in the year 584, calling him *Daniel Bancorum* ('Deiniol of the Bangors'), thus implying a link to BANGOR IS-COED as well. A 12th-century text locates him at the Synod of Brefi (545) with David (DEWI SANT) and Dubricius, and among witnesses to a supposed grant to KENTIGERN by MAELGWN Gwynedd (†*c*. 547). The fact that three of the twelve churches under Deiniol's patronage are located in Flintshire supports traditions that he trained at Bangor Is-coed on the river Dee under his north British father, Abbot Dunawd, brother-in-law of Brochfael, king of POWYS.

FURTHER READING
ANNALES CAMBRIAE; BANGOR (GWYNEDD); BANGOR IS-COED; DEWI SANT; HAGIOGRAPHY IN THE CELTIC COUNTRIES [3]; KENTIGERN; MAELGWN; POWYS; Baring-Gould & Fisher, *Lives of the British Saints*; Henken, *Traditions of the Welsh Saints*; HENKEN, *Welsh Saints*.

Graham Jones

Denez, Per (1921–) is known primarily for his contributions to the study and promotion of the BRETON language, especially the dialect of the region around Douarnenez in KERNEV. Born Pierre Denis in Rennes (ROAZHON), he began to study Breton by correspondence when he was a teenager. After suffering from tuberculosis as a young man, he became an academic, first in the department of English and then the department of Breton at the University of Rennes II. Per Denez founded a number of journals (*Ar Vro* 'The country', HOR YEZH 'Our language') and a press (Mouladurioù Hor Yezh 'Our language publishers'), and has published dictionaries and several other reference works, as well as poetry and prose fiction such as *Diougan Gwenc'hlan* (The prophecy of Gwenc'hlan). His bilingual Breton textbook, *Brezhoneg . . . Buan hag Aes: le breton vite et facilement* (Breton . . . quickly and easily) has been translated into several languages, including English, German, and WELSH.

SELECTION OF MAIN WORKS
Brezhoneg . . . Buan hag Aes: le breton vite et facilement (1972); *Geriadur brezhoneg Douarnenez* (1981); *Brittany* (1998).
TRANS. *Beginner's Course in Breton*; *Bretonisch schnell und mühelos*; *Cyflwyno'r Llydaweg*.
NOVEL. *Diougan Gwenc'hlan* (1979).

FURTHER READING
BRETON; DICTIONARIES AND GRAMMARS [5]; HOR YEZH; KERNEV; ROAZHON; WELSH; Gohier & Huon, *Dictionnaire des écrivains d'aujourd'hui en Bretagne*; Hervé, *Breizh ha poblou Europa* 13–16.

AM

Derdriu/Deirdre, the beautiful daughter of the storyteller Feidlimid mac Daill, was the focus of the tragic love triangle involving the young hero Noísiu mac Uislenn and CONCHOBAR, king of ULAID. In this basic narrative structure, the story is closely comparable to several unhappy love stories from the Celtic world, such as the early Modern Irish TÓRUIGHEACHT DHIARMADA AGUS GHRÁINNE ('The Pursuit of Diarmaid and Gráinne'), TRISTAN AND ISOLT in ARTHURIAN literature, and PLUTARCH's accounts of the much admired Galatian high priestess CAMMA. The earliest of the surviving versions of Derdriu's story, and, artistically, one of the finest and most enduring, is the saga in Old Irish, LONGAS MAC NUISLENN ('The Exile of the Sons of Uisliu'), the subject of its own Encyclopedia entry. *Longas Mac nUislenn* provides pivotal background to the central saga TÁIN BÓ CUAILNGE, and explains why the Ulster heroes were divided in their time of urgency; Derdriu is discussed in this context in ULSTER CYCLE §3. While the popularity of the Ulster Cycle tended in general to be eclipsed by FIANNAÍOCHT in the early modern Gaelic world, the tale of Derdriu remained popular, and this accounts for the international popularity of the name Deirdre today. On the 18th-century Irish *Imeacht Dheirdre le Naoise* (The elopement of Deirdre with Noísiu), see IRISH LITERATURE [4] §3. An oral Scottish Gaelic version was collected, translated, and published by Alexander Carmichael. The demythologized *Deirdre of the Sorrows* by the Anglo-Irish playwright J. M. Synge (1871–1909) was first performed in 1910. On the drawing *Deirdre of the Sorrows* by the Scottish artist John Duncan, see ART, CELTIC-INFLUENCED [2] §2. The name *Derdriu* is given and explained in *Longas Mac nUislenn* by the druid CATHBAD, as the unborn girl is heard crying out forebodingly in her mother's womb, 'It is well that the child may cry (*ro-derdrestar*)'. This verb is otherwise unattested, but the meaning is clear in context; it is probably related to Old Irish *dord* 'a noise, murmuring', *dordaid* 'to make a noise', and perhaps also *derdan* 'storm'.

PRIMARY SOURCES
LONGAS MAC N-UISLENN.
TRANS. Carmichael, *Deirdire, and The Lay of the Children of Uisne*.
PLAY. Synge, *Deirdre of the Sorrows*.

FURTHER READING
ART, CELTIC-INFLUENCED [2]; ARTHURIAN; CAMMA; CATHBAD; CONCHOBAR; FIANNAÍOCHT; IRISH LITERATURE [4]; PLUTARCH; TÁIN BÓ CUAILNGE; TÓRUIGHEACHT DHIARMADA

AGUS GHRÁINNE; TRISTAN AND ISOLT; ULAID; ULSTER CYCLE; Herbert, *Proc. 2nd North American Congress of Celtic Studies* 53–64; Vendryès, *Lexique étymologique d'irlandais ancien s.v. derdrethar.*

JTK

Descriptio Kambriae ('The Description of Wales') is a portrayal of contemporary Welsh social life and mores by Gerald of Wales (GIRALDUS CAMBRENSIS), written in Latin. In this, one of his earliest works (1194), Gerald reveals his deep knowledge of the historical and regional geography of Wales (CYMRU). His analysis of features of the Welsh character is descriptive and shrewd, critical and complimentary. Always conscious of his descent from Norman Marcher lords and Welsh princes, Gerald attempts to be unbiased and dispassionate. The first book of the *Descriptio* gives a résumé of Welsh history and then portrays the admirable qualities of the Welsh. Simple folk following a rural life, they are of noble descent, courageous, hospitable, witty, and they delight in rhetorical skills. His scholastic training leads him to present the antithesis; the Welsh are fickle, inconstant, easily discouraged, prone to plunder, perjury, and to sexual sins, and they foolishly follow a system of inheritance that leads to fratricide and feuding. Gerald ends by giving advice to the English on how they should overcome and rule the Welsh. In the first edition this entailed devastating and recolonizing the whole country or making it an unpopulated forest and game preserve, but this cynical, jaundiced section was removed in a later edition, *c.* 1215. However, Gerald also advised the Welsh how they could withstand English invasion. The work has a symmetrical, antithetical structure, but although Gerald strives to be objective, his Welsh sympathies are unmistakable.

Since Gerald set considerable store by the value of political PROPHECY it is significant that the work ends with the prophecy of 'the old man of Pencader' to Henry II, that the Welsh, and none other, will be answerable for this piece of land on Judgement Day. The *Descriptio* is unique as a consciously written description of contemporary Welsh custom, manners, and society. It reveals Gerald at his disciplined best as a writer, but although he wrote as an experienced observer of Welsh life, he sometimes misinterprets what he sees and the formal, rhetorical pattern that he chose

for his book occasionally leads him to overemphasize some features. As a result, his description must be used with care.

PRIMARY SOURCES
EDITION. Brewer et al., *Giraldi Cambrensis Opera.*
TRANS. Hoare, *Itinerary of Archbishop Baldwin through Wales/Giraldus Cambrensis*; Thomas Jones, *Gerallt Gymro*; Thorpe, *Journey through Wales/Gerald of Wales.*

FURTHER READING
CYMRU; GIRALDUS CAMBRENSIS; PROPHECY; Bartlett, *Gerald of Wales, 1146–1223*; J. Conway Davies, *Journal of the Historical Society of the Church in Wales* 2.46–60; R. R. Davies, WHR 12.155–79; Holmes, *Medievalia et Humanistica* 1.217–31; Thomas Jones, NLWJ 6.117–48, 197–222; Pryce, WHR 13.265–81; Brynley F. Roberts, *Gerald of Wales.*

Brynley F. Roberts

Dewi Sant (**St David**) is remembered as a founder and a practitioner of ascetic monasticism. He is both patron saint of Wales (CYMRU) and symbol of the Welsh nation. The link between the two lies in the successful development of his cult.

An important expression of the cult of Dewi was a Life, composed in Latin by RHYGYFARCH, son of Sulien, in the late 11th century. It has been seen as an apologia for the antiquity, orthodoxy, and independence of the church and cult of Dewi in the face of the advancing Normans. There are various recensions and versions of the Life, including one by GIRALDUS CAMBRENSIS, and there is also a Welsh-language version composed in the 14th century. Together, they tell of the conflict and miracle surrounding the birth, youth, and ministry of Dewi. He was the result of a rape committed by Sant, a prince of CEREDIGION, on a nun called Nonnita (Welsh Non). His future significance had been communicated thirty years before by angels, both to Sant and to PATRICK, who was warned to move to Ireland (ÉRIU) and leave Vallis Rosina (Welsh Glyn Rhosyn) to Dewi. His birth, supposedly on the site of the ruined St Non's chapel, was marked by a violent thunderstorm. A stream of clear water burst forth for his baptism at Porth Clais which gave his sight back to a blind man. Dewi's education took him to Henfynyw (near Aberaeron in Ceredigion), and then to the unknown Winctilantquendi under Paulinus (probably not the apostle of Northumbria of that name). He is said to have founded twelve monasteries in various parts of Wales and what was to become

England, many of which patently had no connection with him, e.g. Repton and BATH. He founded his own monastery at Vallis Rosina, thought to be the Alun valley in which lies the present cathedral associated with Dewi. Here, he and his companions, having survived conflict with Boia, the local chieftain, and his wife, who were opposed to the settlement of Dewi and his community in the valley, followed a life of extreme austerity, dividing their time between worship, study and toil, eschewing the use of draught animals to till the fields, and living on a meat-free diet of bread, herbs, and water. Dewi's sobriquet of *Aquaticus* (Welsh *Dyfrwr*) is probably due not only to his diet but also to his daily habit of standing up to his neck in cold water to subdue the flesh. In company with two companions, TEILO and Padarn, he was urged in a vision to go to Jerusalem where the Patriarch made him archbishop and bestowed gifts on the three; Dewi's gifts included a tunic, a bell and a portable altar. After his return he was summoned to (Llanddewi) Brefi to address a synod of bishops called to defend the church against the Pelagian heresy (see PELAGIUS). Here, the ground is said to have risen under his feet in order that he could be heard, and a dove, the symbol of the Holy Spirit, rested on his shoulder.

The time of his death was made known to him in an angelic vision. The tradition has been handed down that he died on Tuesday, 1 March, either 588 or 602 AD. In the ANNALES CAMBRIAE the year of his death notice corresponds to 601 or (by another reckoning) 603. In the Irish ANNALS of Inisfallen his death is put at 589, but neither source would be precisely accurate to the year for this period; the modern 'anno domini' dating is a secondary imposition onto older chronological reckonings. The 1 March date for Dewi's death is found already in our oldest source on the subject, the early 9th-century Irish Martyrology of OENGUS CÉILE DÉ.

The name *Dewi* reflects an early borrowing into Brythonic of the biblical name *David*. The names of Old Testament kings had become popular in Wales in the 6th century; Welsh kings named *Selyf* 'Solomon' and *Sawel* 'Samuel' were contemporaries of Dewi.

In early sources, the church of St David's, Pembrokeshire (Tyddewi, sir Benfro) is called Old Welsh *Miniu* (*Mynyw* in Modern Welsh spelling) and Old Irish *Cell Muini*. In the *Annales Cambriae*, Mynyw is regarded as the seat of a bishop in notices from the 9th century. These are almost certainly contemporary records. The scarcity of earlier notices is not an argument against the earlier episcopal status of St David's, since the interest of *Annales Cambriae* in the 7th and 8th century are mostly in north Britain, rather than Wales.

PRIMARY SOURCES
MS. London, BL, Cotton Vespasian A.xiv.
EDITIONS. D. Simon Evans, *Buched Dewi*; James, *Rhigyfarch's Life of St David*; Wade-Evans, *Vitae Sanctorum Britanniae et Genealogiae* 150–70.

FURTHER READING
ANNALES CAMBRIAE; ANNALS; BATH; CEREDIGION; CYMRU; ÉRIU; GIRALDUS CAMBRENSIS; OENGUS CÉILE DÉ; PATRICK; PELAGIUS; RHYGYFARCH; TEILO; Baring-Gould & Fisher, *Lives of the British Saints*; Bowen, *St David of History*; Dumville, *Saint David of Wales*; D. Simon Evans, *Welsh Life of St David*; Henken, *Traditions of the Welsh Saints*; Wade-Evans, *Life of St David*.

J. Wyn Evans

Dewr, Deifr

Dewr, Deifr (Old Welsh Deur, Old English Dere, Latin and Modern English Deira) is the name of a kingdom of the post-Roman period in what is now east and north-east Yorkshire, between the Humber estuary and the river Tees. Historically, Deira is known to us only as an Anglo-Saxon kingdom, and, from the time of ÆTHELFRITH (r. 592–617), it functioned mainly as a subkingdom within the dominant northern English overkingdom of Northumbria. The name is probably of BRYTHONIC origin and therefore it is likely that an undocumented Celtic polity in the area had been Anglicized through settlement and/or conquest (see ANGLO-SAXON 'CONQUEST'). However, the boundaries of early medieval Deira do not correspond closely to those of known Romano-British divisions, such as the CIVITAS of the Parisi or that of the BRIGANTES, nor to the *territorium* of the town and legionary fortress of York, which served in the late Roman period as the headquarters of the important command of the *Dux Britanniarum*. A 5th- to 7th-century pagan Germanic cemetery, containing thousands of burials and covering over 30 acres (12 ha), was situated at Sancton, a short distance east of the Roman road running north from the fortified town at Brough-on-Humber/Petuaria Parisiorum. There is evidence of pagan Anglo-Saxon settlement elsewhere along the line of this road and near York itself with some material as far to the north-west as Catterick (CATRAETH).

The first well-documented Deiran king is EADWINE son of Ælle (r. 617–33), who ruled the whole of Northumbria, annexed the Brythonic kingdom of ELFED west of Deira, accepted Christianity from Paulinus in 627, and was overthrown and killed by CADWALLON. According to HISTORIA BRITTONUM, the north Briton RHUN AB URIEN (Old Welsh Run map Urbgen) had been instrumental in the conversion of Northumbria. A genealogy of Eadwine which goes back to the Germanic god Woden occurs in both *Historia Brittonum* (§61) and in English sources. Six generations before Eadwine in the *Historia Brittonum* list there is a reference to Soemil with the note that he first separated Deur from Bernech (Mod. BRYNAICH). It is not certain what the note means. Soemil would have lived in the 5th century, long before the English kept records. By the time the genealogy was compiled, the Bernician dynasty ruled Deira within a united Northumbria; perhaps the note is a claim that this was the original situation and that Deira had only temporarily broken away. In any event, there is no certainty regarding when Eadwine's ancestors—or any other Anglo-Saxons—first established themselves as kings of Deira. Some Romano-British survival and fusion with the Angles seems likely, at Catterick and York for example. In the more archaic B texts of the GODODDIN, the Deirans are the main enemies of the northern attackers on Catraeth and the Bernicians are not mentioned. In Welsh heroic poetry, references to Deira are sometimes ambiguous, as the name *Dewr* is homophonous with *dewr* 'bold'. The etymology of *Dewr* is not certain, but the byform *Deifr* makes good sense as the reflex of British **Dubria* 'land of waters'.

FURTHER READING
ÆTHELFRITH; ANGLO-SAXON 'CONQUEST'; BRIGANTES; BRYNAICH; BRYTHONIC; CADWALLON; CATRAETH; CIVITAS; EADWINE; ELFED; GODODDIN; HISTORIA BRITTONUM; RHUN AB URIEN; Blair, *Anglo-Saxon Northumbria*; Dark, *Civitas to Kingdom*; Dumville, *Early Welsh Poetry* 1–16; Dumville, *Origins of Anglo-Saxon Kingdoms* 213–22; Higham, *Kingdom of Northumbria*; Jackson, *Gododdin*; Koch, *Gododdin of Aneirin*; Miller, *Anglo-Saxon England* 8.35–61; Myres, *English Settlements*.

JTK

Dialog etre Arzur Roue d'an Bretounet ha Guynglaff (The dialogue between Arthur, king of the Bretons, and Guynglaff) is a poetic prophecy in Middle Breton and perhaps the most important piece of popular verse to survive in the BRETON language from this period. It survives only in poor 18th-century copies at multiple removes from the original (Piriou, *Actes du 14e Congrès* 2.474–5), which, according to Piette and Fleuriot, was composed *c.* 1450 (*Llên Cymru* 8.190; *Histoire littéraire* 1.157–8). One copy of 1710 has survived from a manuscript dated 1619. The *Dialog* contains 247 verse lines, but the form is so corrupt that it is certain that it is not the original composition. It tells how ARTHUR once caught the prophet Guynglaff (var. *Guiclan*, Modern *Gwenc'hlañ*) and forcefully pleaded with him. Guynglaff yielded and told Arthur what would happen before the world came to an end. There follow prophecies for the years 1470 to 1476 and 1486 to 1488, and generalities about the wars with the English and destructions committed by them. The fact that most of what was predicted never happened implies that the prophecies were composed before 1470 and that they embody wishful thinking about the future. There clearly have been later modifications; e.g., some of the prophecies can be related to events in the later 16th century (Piriou, *Actes du 14e Congrès* 2.478–80). Fleuriot proposed that the prophetic wildman of the woods, Guynglaff, is an avatar of the Brittonic MYRDDIN figure (*Histoire littéraire* 157–8; Piriou, *Actes du 14e Congrès* 2.477). Guynglaff can thus be viewed as the literary 'missing link' between the medieval ARTHURIAN prophet Merlin (Myrddin) and the prophet *Roue Stefan* (King Stephen) of Modern Breton folklore. Piriou interprets the name *Guynglaff* as meaning 'blessed sick man' and presents some indirect evidence for the idea of epilepsy as a disease accompanied by supernatural powers (Piriou, *Actes du 14e Congrès* 2.492–3).

This is the oldest surviving Arthurian text written in Breton, and it is disappointing that it reveals little of the substance of the Breton Arthurian tradition. However, the consistent pattern in which Arthur is closely linked with a poet and visionary such as Merlin is noteworthy.

FURTHER READING
ARTHUR; ARTHURIAN; BRETON; BRETON LITERATURE [1]; ERNAULT; MYRDDIN; Ernault, *Annales de Bretagne* 39.18–30; Fleuriot, *Histoire littéraire et culturelle de la Bretagne* 1.153–72; Largillière, *Annales de Bretagne* 38.627–74; Le Goaziou, *La longue vie de deux 'colloques françois et breton'*; Piette, *Llên Cymru* 8.183–90; Piriou, *Actes du 14e Congrès International Arthurien* 2.473–99.

Gwenaël Le Duc, JTK

Dian Cécht is an Irish supernatural being or deity, the physician of the Tuath Dé. His name is subject to a variety of interpretations, but may be a combination of the Old Irish common words *dían* 'swift' and *cécht*, glossed as 'power'. He appears in the Mythological Cycle of medieval Irish tales.

In Cath Maige Tuired ('The [Second] Battle of Mag Tuired'), Dian Cécht is given as Lug's paternal grandfather, and he is called the son of the Dagda in the prose Dindshenchas. Dian Cécht's children are also associated with medicine, especially his daughter Airmed and his son Miach. Both names are Old Irish common nouns, the names of dry measures (but note the similarity of Miach's name with the Middle Irish word *midach* 'doctor', an early borrowing from the Latin *medicus*).

In a battle against the demonic invaders, the Fomoiri, in *Cath Maige Tuired*, the three physicians and another of Dian Cécht's children, Ochtríuil, cast the mortally wounded warriors into a well called *Sláine* 'health', and they emerge alive and healthy. This may be a metaphor, as the healing is explicitly attributed to the doctors' incantations, but given the mythological context it is more likely to be a reference to the cauldron of regeneration of Celtic mythology (see CAULDRONS).

Dian Cécht forges an artificial fully functioning silver hand for Nuadu (see NŌDONS), who had lost his original hand in battle. Miach healed Nuadu completely, and Dian Cécht then killed Miach in a series of ever more severe wounds. Miach healed the first three, but could not heal the removal of his brain. After his death, 365 healing herbs grew out of his body. They were gathered and sorted by Airmed according to what they healed, but Dian Cécht mixed them up.

Dian Cécht is also invoked in a medico-legal text, *Bretha Déin Chécht*, which begins *Bretha dein checht o legib* 'The judgements of Dian Cécht concerning doctors'. The medical lore contained therein is all of eastern origin, mostly Arabic and Greek.

PRIMARY SOURCES
EDITION. Binchy, 'Bretha Déin Chécht', *Ériu* 20.1–65.
ED. & TRANS. Gray, *Cath Maige Tuired*.

RELATED ARTICLES
CATH MAIGE TUIRED; CAULDRONS; DAGDA; DINDSHENCHAS; FOMOIRI; IRISH; LUG; MYTHOLOGICAL CYCLE; NŌDONS; TUATH DÉ.

AM

Diarmaid ua Duibhne is an Irish legendary figure best known through stories of his elopement with Gráinne, the betrothed of Finn mac Cumaill (see FIANNAÍOCHT; TÓRUIGHEACHT DHIARMADA AGUS GHRÁINNE). Fostered by the love-god Aonghus Óg (Early Irish Oengus Mac ind Óc) of the Tuath Dé, Diarmaid was half-brother to a boy who was transformed into a boar fated to kill him. Diarmaid had a *ball seirce* (love spot) which made him irresistible to women. Gráinne, daughter of Cormac mac Airt, the legendary king of Tara (Teamhair), drugged the celebrants at her wedding to Fionn and put Diarmaid under a GEIS (sworn promise) to elope with her. The enraged Fionn and the Fianna (war-band) pursued the pair for 16 years before making peace. Years later, while hunting with the Fianna, Diarmaid was gored by the boar and left to die by Fionn.

FURTHER READING
CORMAC MAC AIRT; FIANNAÍOCHT; FINN MAC CUMAILL; GEIS; OENGUS MAC IND ÓC; TEAMHAIR; TÓRUIGHEACHT DHIARMADA AGUS GHRÁINNE; TUATH DÉ; Breatnach, *Studies* 47.90–7; Cormier, *Speculum* 51.589–601; Krappe, *Folklore* 47.347–61; Meek, *Celtica* 21.335–61; Ní Shéaghdha, *Tóruigheacht Dhiarmada agus Ghráinne*.

Brian Ó Broin

Diarmait mac Cerbaill was, according to the Irish ANNALS, king of Tara (Teamhair) between 544 and 565 and, according to the GENEALOGIES, great-great-grandson of Niall Noígiallach (Niall of the nine hostages), namesake and traditional founder of the dominant dynastic federation of early medieval Ireland (Ériu), the Uí Néill. The southern subgroups of the Uí Néill claimed descent from Diarmait: Síl nAedo Sláine (descendants, lit. seed, of Aed Sláine), centred in Brega in east-central Ireland, and traced their ancestry to Diarmait's son Aed Sláine (†604), whereas Cland Cholmáin (the children of Colmán), further west in Mide around Uisnech, descended from a second son, Colmán Már (†555/8).

The historicity of Diarmait is assured; Smyth has argued that the annals naming him are among the first contemporary entries (PRIA C 72.1–48). Writing in the 690s, Adomnán regards Diarmait's progeny as having been granted by God the prerogative of the kingship of all Ireland (*totius Euerniae*; *Vita Columbae* 1.14). This is a significant admission since Colum

CILLE and Adomnán himself belonged to the northern Uí Néill lineage of Cenél Conaill, and he does not speak in such terms of his own closer relations, DOMNALL MAC AEDO and his grandson, Loingsech mac Oengusso (†704), though both were *rex Hibernie* (king of Ireland) according to the annals. Evidently, Diarmait's pre-eminence was recognized in both the north and the south, though interestingly the annals record only defeats on the battlefield for him. BINCHY attached special significance, as a milestone in the passing of pagan institutions, to the fact that Diarmait is explicitly named in the Annals of Tigernach as the last king to celebrate the *Feis Temro* (Feast of Tara), understood as both a fertility ritual and an inauguration of kingship, in 558 or 560 (*Studia Hibernica* 8.49–59). Diarmait developed as a central figure in the Middle Irish KINGS' CYCLES (§3). In HAGIOGRAPHY, a number of stories show Ruadán and other saints in hostile opposition to Diarmait, which, taken together with Adomnán's claim and the record of the *Feis Temro*, presents a mixed tradition for the king's Christianity. Diarmait was killed by Aed Dub mac Suibni, king of the CRUITHIN and overking of ULAID. There are several versions of his death-tale; these include the theme of a prophesied, difficult-to-achieve death, in this case involving a shirt made of linen from a single flax seed. In the version in British Library MS Egerton 1782, the theme of a multiple death is developed: Diarmait is pierced by Aed's spear, then the house is burnt around him, he drowns in an ale vat (cf. WATERY DEPOSITIONS §3), and the roof falls on his head.

PRIMARY SOURCE
Koch & Carey, *Celtic Heroic Age* 212–16 ('Death of Diarmait', two versions).

FURTHER READING
ADOMNÁN; AED SLÁINE; ANNALS; BINCHY; COLUM CILLE; CRUITHIN; DOMNALL MAC AEDO; ÉRIU; GENEALOGIES; HAGIOGRAPHY; KINGS' CYCLES; LEGENDARY HISTORY §3; MIDE; NIALL NOÍGIALLACH; TEAMHAIR; UÍ NÉILL; UISNECH; ULAID; WATERY DEPOSITIONS §3; Binchy, *Ériu* 18.113–38; Binchy, *Ireland in Early Mediaeval Europe* 165–78; Binchy, *Studia Hibernica* 8.49–59; Byrne, *Historical Studies* 5.37–58; Byrne, *Irish Kings and High-Kings*; Smyth, PRIA C 72.1–48.

JTK

dictionaries and grammars [1] Irish

§1. DICTIONARIES

For approximately a thousand years IRISH lexicographers concerned themselves with the words of their own language, which they explained in monolingual GLOSSARIES, often with supposed etymologies or providing native or foreign etymologies for more common words. The earliest of these is O'Mulconry's Glossary (*Descriptio de Origine Scoticae Linguae*), written between AD 650 and 750. Other early medieval Irish glossaries include the famous SANAS CHORMAIC of *c.* 900.

In the 17th century Irish scholars determined that their country should have dictionaries and grammars. The Irish Franciscans in Louvain published firstly Micheál Ó CLÉIRIGH's *Foclóir nō Sanasán Nua* (1643), a traditional glossary. However, their efforts to publish a large Latin–Irish dictionary came to nothing, although we have notice of a substantial work begun by Baothghalach Mhac Aodhagáin, who died in 1654, and supplemented by a Fr. Ó Cuirnín. In 1671 this dictionary was felt to be incomplete, and was never published. It is now lost.

In 1662, another Franciscan, Risdeard Pluincéad, completed a large manuscript Latin–Irish dictionary in the friary of Trim (Baile Átha Troim). It was borrowed by the Welsh linguist and scholar Edward LHUYD for use in the first Irish–English dictionary, included in Lhuyd's *Archaeologia Britannica* (1707), and in the 'Comparative Vocabulary' section of the same.

A manuscript trilingual dictionary by Froinsias Bhailis (Francis Walsh), *Dictionarium Latino–Anglo–Hibernicum*, was completed by Tadhg Ó Neachtain in 1729. The next published Irish dictionary was *The English Irish Dictionary / An Foclóir Béarla Gaoidheilge* (Paris, 1732) by Conchobhar Ó Beaglaoich, assisted by Aodh Buidhe Mac Cruitín. Tadhg Ó Neachtain's large manuscript *Foclóir Gaeilbhéarlach* was completed in 1739. *Mémoires sur la langue celtique* by M. Bullet in 1753 contained an Irish–French dictionary. A large and neglected English–Irish manuscript dictionary was completed in 1760 by a Mr Crab, a schoolmaster from Ringsend in Dublin (BAILE ÁTHA CLIATH). In 1768 Bishop John O'Brien published his *Foclóir Gaoidhilge–Sax-Bhéarla*, again in Paris, which included readings and misreadings from the LEABHAR BREAC, some entries on place-names and many plant names.

The most notable dictionary of the 19th century was by Edward O'Reilly, first published in 1817 with subsequent editions, including one with a supplement of archaic manuscript words brought out by John O'Donovan in 1877. Thomas de Vere Coneys's dictionary of 1849 is based mainly on the 19th-century editions of Bedell's Irish BIBLE.

The first published dictionary to do justice to the spoken language was that of Fr. Patrick S. Dinneen (UA DUINNÍN) in 1904; a much-extended version appeared in 1927, published by the Irish Texts Society (see CUMANN NA SCRÍBHEANN N-GAEDHILGE). This remains the most useful dictionary to scholars and readers of 18th- and 19th-century literature. Tadhg O'Neill-Lane produced a small English–Irish dictionary in 1904 and a large one in 1916. Lambert McKenna (MAC CIONNAITH) compiled a useful English–Irish dictionary in 1935, indicating sources. In 1957 An Gúm (the Department of Education) produced an English–Irish dictionary which provided much-required technical vocabulary, but it ignored the existence of dialect and register. This has since been supplemented by several technical dictionaries, and work on its replacement has been begun by FORAS NA GAEILGE.

In 1977 An Gúm produced a well-laid-out Irish–English dictionary. Words and meanings which do not occur in spoken Irish are marked 'Lit.', the only concession to regional or temporal variation.

In 1975 the Royal Irish Academy (ACADAMH RÍOGA NA HÉIREANN) concluded its (Contributions to a) Dictionary of the Irish Language (DIL), the first volume of which was edited in 1913 by Karl Marstrander. This is a large historical citation dictionary, based mainly on Old and Middle Irish materials, and was a momentous advance in Irish lexicography.

In 1978 work began on a similar project for Modern Irish—An Foclóir Nua-Ghaeilge—with Tomás DE BHALDRAITHE as general editor. The project has been badly under-resourced, and is currently confined to compiling a machine-readable corpus of Modern Irish to be published on CD-ROM.

LATE MANUSCRIPT IRISH DICTIONARIES
Bhailis, Froinsias & Tadhg Ó Neachtain, Dictionarium Latino-Anglo-Hibernicum (Dublin, Marsh's Library, Z3.1.13), 649 fos., 1712; Crab, [Irish–English] (Dublin, Royal Irish Academy 1155–57 [24 Q 19–21]), 900 fos., c. 1760; Mac Ádhaimh, Roibeard, [English–Irish] (Belfast, Queen's University Library), 1,388 pp., c. 1850; Ó Neachtain, Tadhg, Foclóir Gaeilbhéarlach (Dublin, Trinity College 1290 [H.I.16]), 1739; O'Connell, Peter, 'An Irish-English Dictionary' (London, BL, Egerton 83), 330 fos. in rough draft autograph, 631 in neat copy by J. O'Donovan, 1826; Pluincéad, Risdeard, Vocabularium Latinum-Hibernum/Foclóir Laidne agus Gaoidheilge (Dublin, Marsh's Library, Z4.2.5), 832 pp., 1662.

HISTORIC DICTIONARIES
Bullet, Mémoires sur la langue celtique; Coneys, Foclóir Gaoidhilge–Sacs-béarla; Connellan, English–Irish Dictionary; Foley, English–Irish Dictionary; Fournier d'Albe, English–Irish Dictionary and Phrase Book; Lhuyd, Archaeologia Britannica 1 (includes Foclóir Gaoidhbilge-Shagsonach and 'A Comparative Vocabulary'); Ó Beaglaoich & Mac Cuirtín, English Irish Dictionary / An Foclóir Béarla Gaoidheilge; Ó Cléirigh, Foclóir nó Sanasán Nua; O'Brien, Foclóir Gaoidhilge–Sax-Bhéarla; O'Reilly, Irish–English Dictionary.

MODERN DICTIONARIES
De Bhaldraithe, English–Irish Dictionary; Dinneen, Foclóir Gaedhilge agus Béarla / Irish–English Dictionary; Mac Cionnaith, Foclóir Béarla agus Gaedhilge / English–Irish Dictionary; McKenna, English–Irish Phrase Dictionary; Ó Dónaill, Foclóir Gaeilge Béarla; O'Neill-Lane, Lane's English–Irish Dictionary/Foclóir Béarla–Gaedhilge; O'Neill-Lane, Larger English–Irish Dictionary/Foclóir Béarla–Gaedhilge; Royal Irish Academy, Dictionary of the Irish Language (DIL).

DIALECT DICTIONARIES
See lists at:
www.ria.ie/projects/fng/index.html
www.celt.dias.ie/publications/cat/cat_e.html#E.4

WEBSITES
www.focloir.ie
www.ria.ie/projects/fng/index.html
www.celt.dias.ie/publications/cat/cat_e.html#E.4

FURTHER READING
ACADAMH RÍOGA NA H-ÉIREANN; BAILE ÁTHA CLIATH; BIBLE; CUMANN NA SCRÍBHEANN N-GAEDHILGE; DE BHALDRAITHE; FORAS NA GAEILGE; GLOSSARIES; IRISH; LEABHAR BREAC; LHUYD; MAC CIONNAITH; Ó CLÉIRIGH; O'DONOVAN; SANAS CHORMAIC; UA DUINNÍN; Abbott, Hermathena 13.15–25, 332–53; Coombes, Bishop of Penal Times; De Bhaldraithe, Dán do Oide 21–37; De Bhaldraithe, Maynooth Review 6.1.3–15; De Bhaldraithe, Teangeolas, Earrach 1987.19–25; Harrison, Féilscríbhinn Thomáis de Bhaldraithe 48–69; Morley, An Crann os Coill 104–10; Ó Cearbhaill, Glór na Féile, Iris na Féile 1979.65–9; Ó Murchú, Cás na Gaeilge 1952–2002.

§2. GRAMMARS

AURAICEPT NA NÉCES ('The Scholars' Primer'), the earliest IRISH grammar, belongs to the Old Irish period, possibly as early as the 7th century. It was later augmented by commentary.

Irish bardic poets must have met prior to AD 1200 and agreed the rules of standard language to be used while composing poetry in the strict syllabic metres (see BARDIC ORDER). These observations have been preserved in later manuscripts known as the Irish Grammatical Tracts, and Bardic Syntactial Tracts. Three parts of speech were recognized: *focal* a concrete noun; *pearsa* an abstract noun (*pearsa lóir*), verbal noun or verb; and *iairmbéarla* a particle or unstressed word.

The German planter Sir Mathew de Renzy attempted to publish as his own an Irish grammar and prosody, now known as *Graiméar Uí Mhaolchonaire* from the author of the best surviving copy, which had been composed by Tadhg Óg, son of Tadhg Dall Ó hUiginn, until challenged by its true author. *Rudimenta Grammaticae Hibernicae* is a grammar and prosody written by Bonabhentúra Ó hEódhasa, OFM (†1614), for the use of his fellow Franciscans in Louvain, to whom he was teaching Irish. The grammar is in Latin, the prosody in Irish. The 17th-century grammars divide nouns into a five-declension system based on Latin.

In 1677 Fr. Francis O Molloy, OFM, published *Grammatica Latino–Hibernica* in Rome; it is defective in paradigms verbal and nominal. H. Mac Curtin (Aodh Buidhe Mac Cruitín) published in Lovain in 1728 an Irish grammar in English, the first really useful grammar for a learner of Irish, which he had plagiarized from the aforementioned Fr. Froinsias Bhailis, OFM, lexicographer, who had completed it in 1713. This was republished in 1732, along with the dictionary of Ó Beaglaoich and Mac Cruitín.

In 1808 William Neilson published his *Introduction to the Irish Language*, which dealt with Ulster Irish, and William Halliday his *Uraicecht na Gaedhilge: a Grammar of the Gaelic Language*. These were followed in 1809 by the Revd Paul O'Brien's *A Practical Grammar of the Irish Language*. In 1845 John O'DONOVAN published *A Grammar of the Irish Language*, which attempts to deal with all periods from Middle Irish to modern dialects.

The 20th century saw grammars intended for schools, notably by the Christian Brothers, who first published *Graiméar na Gaedhilge* in 1901. Also of note are the work of Fr. Gerald O'Nolan and the syntactical studies of Cormac Ó Cadhlaigh. In 1945 the spelling of Irish was reformed and the principles published in *Litriú na Gaeilge* by Rannóg an Aistriúcháin. In 1958 a standard grammar followed, *Gramadach na Gaeilge agus Litriú na Gaeilge: an Caighdeán Oifigiúil*, to be taught in schools and used in Government publications.

Stair na Gaeilge, edited by K. McCone and others, contains most useful grammars of Middle, Classical, Post-classical Irish and modern dialects.

In Early Irish, Johann Kaspar ZEUSS extracted from the study of Old Irish and other Celtic GLOSSES his *Grammatica Celtica* (1853). In 1908 J. VENDRYÈS produced *Grammaire du vieil-irlandais* and in 1909 Rudolf THURNEYSEN his *Handbuch des Alt-Irischen*. A revised edition of this appeared in English in 1944 as *A Grammar of Old Irish*, and remains the indispensable Old Irish grammar.

GRAMMARS
Ahlqvist, *Early Irish Linguist*; Bergin, *Irish Grammatical Tracts 1–5*; Bráithre Críostamhla, *Graiméar na Gaedhilge*; *Gramadach na Gaeilge agus litriú na Gaeilge*; Halliday, *Uraicecht na Gaedhilge*; Mac Aogáin, *Graiméir na mBráthar Mionúr*; Mac Curtin, *Elements of the Irish Language Grammatically Explained in English*; McKenna, *Bardic Syntactical Tracts*; Neilson, *Introduction to the Irish Language*; O'Brien, *Practical Grammar of the Irish Language*; Ó Cadhlaigh, *Ceart na Gaedhilge*; Ó Cadhlaigh, *Gnás na Gaedhilge*; O Molloy, *Grammatica Latino–Hibernica*; O'Nolan, *New Era Grammar of Modern Irish*; O'Nolan, *Studies in Modern Irish 1–4*; Rannóg an Aistriúcháin, *Litriú na Gaeilge*; Thurneysen, *Grammar of Old Irish*; Thurneysen, *Handbuch des Alt-Irischen*; Vallancy, *Grammar of the Iberno-Celtic, or Irish Language*; Vendryès, *Grammaire du vieil-irlandais*; Zeuss, *Grammatica Celtica*.

DIALECT GRAMMARS
www.celt.dias.ie/publications/cat/cat_e.html#E.2

FURTHER READING
AURAICEPT NA N-ÉCES; BARDIC ORDER; GLOSSES; IRISH; O'DONOVAN; Ó H-UIGINN; THURNEYSEN; VENDRYÈS; ZEUSS; Bergin, *Native Irish Grammarian*; Harrison, *Féilscríbhinn Thomáis de Bhaldraithe 48–69*; McCone et al., *Stair na Gaeilge*; Morley, *An Crann os Coill 95–100*; Ó Cuív, *Celtica 10.114–40*.

Seán Ua Súilleabháin

dictionaries and grammars [2] Scottish Gaelic

The first major dictionary to mention the language is that of Edward LHUYD, the well-known Celtic polymath, when he published *Archaeologia Britannica* in 1707 with its inclusion of an IRISH–English dictionary and, as an Appendix to this, added a number of words from SCOTTISH GAELIC. The work included a 'brief introduction' to the 'Irish or Ancient Scottish language', in which the language is that of the late Classical period in Irish, with a spelling and letter shapes deriving from this. Robert Kirk published several word lists in 1702, and by so doing provided subsequent dictionary makers with some source materials and effectively founded the history of GAELIC dictionary making, although his 'vocabulary and orthography were judged to be over-influenced by literary Irish' (Sanderson, *Secret Commonwealth by Robert Kirk* 8). The total number of words in one list was 430, and it was based on an earlier multilingual school dictionary, the *Dictionariolum Trilingue* of John Ray, where Kirk substituted words of Perthshire dialect for Latin words in that listing.

The first dictionary was published in Edinburgh (DÙN ÈIDEANN) by Alexander McDonald (Alistair MacDomhnuill) as a 'Gaelic and English Vocabulary'. This appeared in 1741 and was taken from a school dictionary intended to provide instruction in English and Latin. McDonald retained the English and substituted Gaelic for the Latin. The work is organized into sections on general semantic categories, in parallel columns and with no alphabetization of either column, in a total of 161 pages. It contains an Appendix of 30 pages where McDonald adds new 'words and terms that most frequently occur in Divinity', collected 'from the Irish Confession of Faith . . . Book of Common Prayer in Irish' (A. MacDonald, *Galick and English Dictionary* 162), and this Gaelic–English dictionary section is organized alphabetically by the Gaelic headword. He had worked on behalf of the Society for Propagating Christian Knowledge as a schoolmaster in Argyllshire, and his Appendix supplied Gaelic explanations for a number of words, for example, 'probationer' defined as 'someone who can prove himself in his learning'.

A total of nine Gaelic–English dictionaries appeared over the late 18th and 19th centuries, and the culmination of this lexicographical activity was the Gaelic–English dictionary of Edward Dwelly which appeared in 1909, and which has served as the reference point for all subsequent smaller dictionaries, since he included materials from most preceding works. It also includes a 'summary of a concise Gaelic grammar', and there have been few published separate grammars until very recently with *Gràmar na Gàidhlig*.

The paucity of new terminology has long been a bane of Gaelic, and several attempts have been made to counter this, the most recent being *Faclair na Pàrlamaid/ Dictionary of Terms* (See www.scotland.gov.uk/ dictionary/_bin/).

Two threads wrap through the history of these dictionaries and grammars: the presence of Gaelic in a multilingual society in Scotland (ALBA), and the effects of the Reformation on this society (see CHRISTIANITY).

The results have meant that by the post-1600 period we find an increasing appearance of English borrowings, and an ever-present desire to avoid, as far as possible, connections with Irish, which is taken as a Roman Catholic—and hence foreign—influence.

DICTIONARIES AND GRAMMARS
Armstrong, *Gaelic Dictionary in Two Parts*; Byrne, *Gràmar na Gàidhlig*; Calder, *Gaelic Grammar*; Clyne, *Appendix to Dwelly's Gaelic–English Dictionary*; Dwelly, *Illustrated Gaelic–English Dictionary*; Highland Society, *Dictionarium Scoto–Celticum*; Lhuyd, *Archaeologia Britannica*; MacAlpine, *Pronouncing Gaelic–English Dictionary*; MacAlpine, *Pronouncing Gaelic–English Dictionary, with Grammar*; Macbain, *Etymological Dictionary of the Gaelic Language*; A. MacDonald, *Galick and English Dictionary*; MacEachen, *Faclair Gaidhlig is Beurla*; MacFarlan, *New Alphabetic Vocabulary Gailic and English*; MacFarlane, *New and Copious English and Gaelic Vocabulary*; MacLeod & Dewar, *Dictionary of the Gaelic Language*; McNeir, *Faclair na Pàrlamaid*; Nicolson, *Scottish Historical Library*; Shaw, *Galic and English Dictionary*.

WEBSITE
www.scotland.gov.uk/dictionary/_bin/

FURTHER READING
ALBA; CHRISTIANITY; DÙN ÈIDEANN; GAELIC; IRISH; LHUYD; SCOTTISH GAELIC; Black, *Scottish Gaelic Studies* 14.2.1–39; Campbell, *Scottish Gaelic Studies* 6.27–42; Campbell, *Scottish Gaelic Studies* 9.89–90; Campbell, *Gaelic Words and Expressions from South Uist and Eriskay*; Campbell & Thomson, *Edward Lhuyd in the Scottish Highlands*; Durkacz, *Decline of the Celtic Languages*; Kirk, *Secret Commonwealth*; K. MacDonald, *Trans. Gaelic Society of Inverness* 50.1–19; McLeod, *Faclair na Pàrlamaid*; Thompson, *Trans. of the Gaelic Society of Inverness* 53.51–69.

Cathair Ó Dochartaigh

dictionaries and grammars [3] Manx

Although the MANX Gaelic corpus includes texts dating to the 17th century, the first printed work did not appear until 1707. It is therefore not surprising that the earliest dictionaries and grammars were not published until the beginning of the 19th century. One of the earliest grammars was produced by John Kelly, whose *A Practical Grammar of the Antient Gael[i]c; or Language of the Isle of Mann, Usually Called Manks* was published in 1804. Kelly also planned an ambitious trilingual dictionary around 1805, but failed to publish after a fire at the printing office destroyed sections of it. Copy proofs for one section at least survive in the archives of the Manx Museum. Robert Thomson notes that there is some correspondence with Shaw's Gaelic dictionary (1780) (see DICTIONARIES AND GRAMMARS

[2] SCOTTISH GAELIC), which Kelly is known to have owned. Kelly's Manx–English dictionary was not published until 1866 in the Manx Society's series of publications, edited by the Revds Gill and Clarke.

The first half of the 19th century also saw the production of what has become the seminal Manx–English dictionary. Compiled by Archibald Cregeen and published on the Isle of Man (ELLAN VANNIN) in 1835, it was regularly reprinted throughout the 20th century. The main criticism remains Cregeen's predilection for classing nouns as feminine, a tendency which has been corrected by later dictionaries.

With the founding of Yn CHESHAGHT GHAILCK-AGH, the Manx Language Society, in 1899, antiquarian activity focused once more on Manx Gaelic. Edmund Goodwin's *Lessoonyn ayns Chengey ny Mayrey Ellan Vannin* (1901) was reprinted as *First Lessons in Manx* (1947) and later revised by Thomson. It continues to be regarded as one of the most important primers for the language. Until John Joseph (J. J.) Kneen's *A Grammar of the Manx Language* (1931), written in 1909–10 with the assistance of Professors E. C. Quiggin and Carl Marstrander, Goodwin's slim volume remained the first point of grammatical reference. Kneen's work on the language continued, producing a further volume on Manx Gaelic usage, *Manx Idioms and Phrases* (1938), and, in conjunction with the *Mona's Herald* newspaper, an *English–Manx Pronouncing Dictionary* (1938).

The latter half of the 20th century saw significant developments in the publication of reference books for Manx Gaelic. Originally intended in the 1950s as a Manx–English Dictionary combining the work of Kelly and Cregeen with a reverse of Kneen's dictionary, *Fargher's English–Manx Dictionary* (1979) was an attempt to 'provide some sort of basic standard upon which to build the modern Manx language of today and tomorrow' (vi). It followed patterns established in DE BHALDRAITHE's *English–Irish Dictionary* (1959).

George Broderick's study of the spoken language of the last native speakers resulted in a three-volume work published by Niemeyer (1984–6), *A Handbook of Late Spoken Manx*, comprising a grammar, a dictionary, and phonology.

In 1986, Manx Gaelic was added to the popular Usborne *First Thousand Words in . . .* series, adapted by Robert Thomson, Pat Burgess, Adrian Pilgrim and Audrey Ainsworth.

Phil Kelly, Manx Language Officer for the Department of Education, together with Mike Boulton and F. Craine, produced a reverse of Fargher's Dictionary (1991), which was revised and reprinted by Kelly in 1993. It was accompanied by a two-volume *Manx Usage* in 1993. Crucially for the internet age, Kelly's and other dictionaries have been made available online in searchable form.

An entry on dictionaries and grammars would not be complete without recognition of the work of teachers at a grass-roots level from the late 19th century to the present. There has been a succession of published and privately published lessons and exercises in Manx Gaelic which have inspired many learners of the language (see EDUCATION; LANGUAGE [REVIVAL]).

DICTIONARIES
Amery, *First Thousand Words in Manx*; Cregeen, *Dictionary of the Manks Language*; Fargher, *Fargher's English–Manx Dictionary*; John Kelly, *Fockleyr Manninagh as Baarlagh*; Phil Kelly, *Fockleyr Gaelg–Baarle*; Kneen, *English–Manx Pronouncing Dictionary*; Kneen, *Manx Idioms and Phrases*; Wood, *Focklioar Giare, Gaelg-Baarle*.
WEBSITES. www.embedded-systems.ltd.uk/ManxStart.html; www.gaelg.iofm.net/DICTIONARY/dict/index.html; www.gaelg.iofm.net/DICTIONARY/dict2/index.html.

GRAMMARS
Broderick, *Handbook of Late Spoken Manx*; John Kelly, *Practical Grammar of the Antient Gael[i]c*; Phil Kelly, *C'red*; Phil Kelly, *Manx Usage*; Kneen, *Grammar of the Manx Language*; Thomson & Pilgrim, *Outline of Manx Language and Literature*.
WEBSITE.
www.gaelg.iofm.net/GRAMMAR/GRAMMAR.html.

PRIMERS &C
Douglas, *Beginning Manx Gaelic*; Goodwin, *Lessoonyn ayns Chengey ny Mayrey Ellan Vannin*; Stowell, *Yn Chied Lioar Gailckagh*; Thomson, *Lessoonyn Sodjey 'sy Ghailck Vanninagh*.

RELATED ARTICLES
CHESHAGHT GHAILCKAGH; DE BHALDRAITHE; DICTIONARIES AND GRAMMARS [2]; EDUCATION; ELLAN VANNIN; MANX; LANGUAGE (REVIVAL).

Breesha Maddrell

dictionaries and grammars [4] Welsh

The first printed Welsh dictionary was a Welsh–English dictionary, misleadingly titled *A Dictionary in Englyshe and Welshe* (1547), by William SALESBURY, translator of the Book of Common Prayer and the New Testament. He also produced an introduction to Welsh pronunciation (1550, 1567).

Three grammars were published during the 16th century. The first (1567–*post* 1584), by Gruffydd Robert (*fl.* 1558–98), is a classic of Welsh prose, which contains among other things a discussion of the Latin element in Welsh. The second (1592), in Latin, by Siôn Dafydd Rhys (John Davies of Brecon, 1534–*c.* 1619) draws on GRAMADEGAU'R PENCEIRDDIAID and, like them, is heavily influenced by Latin grammar. The third (1593), also in Latin, was by Henry Salesbury (1561–?1637), who also compiled an unpublished Welsh–Latin dictionary.

The greatest Welsh scholar until modern days was John Davies (*c.* 1567–1644) of Mallwyd, editor of the 1620 BIBLE, whose grammar (in Latin) (1621) and Welsh–Latin Latin–Welsh dictionary (1632) are among the most influential works of Welsh scholarship. The Latin–Welsh section is based upon an unpublished translation by Thomas Wiliems (1545/6–1622) of Thomas Thomas's standard Latin–English dictionary. The Welsh–Latin section formed the basis of the small Welsh–English dictionary with Welsh synonyms by Thomas Jones (1648–1713) the almanac-maker, published in 1688, and the Welsh–English dictionary (1753) of Thomas Richards (1709/10–90), which also contained a grammar based on that of Davies.

John Roderick (Siôn Rhydderch, 1673–1735), the almanac-maker, published the first English–Welsh dictionary (1725), and a grammar written in Welsh (1728) based upon *Gramadegau'r Penceirddiaid* and Siôn Dafydd Rhys's grammar. William Gambold (1672–1728) published the first Welsh grammar written in English in 1727, but failed to publish his Welsh–English English–Welsh dictionary, the latter part of which was used by John Walters (1721–97) in the compilation of his comprehensive English–Welsh dictionary (1770–94), directly or indirectly a major influence on all subsequent English–Welsh dictionaries.

The greatest influence on 19th-century Welsh was William Owen Pughe (1759–1835), the knowledgeable but incredibly idiosyncratic editor of a Welsh–English dictionary (1793–1803) and grammar (1803). Many dictionaries and grammars were published during the century, most of them extremely derivative. The standard grammar was that of Thomas Rowland (1824–84), published in 1853, which was valuable but remained heavily influenced by Pughe. D. Silvan Evans (1818–1903) edited a large two-volume English–Welsh dic-

tionary (1847–58), and a historical Welsh–English dictionary (1887–1906), which, however, only reached the word *ennyd*. The fate of the comprehensive work by John Lloyd-Jones (1885–1956) on the vocabulary of early WELSH POETRY (1931–63) was somewhat better: it was published as far as the word *heilic*.

Edward Anwyl (1866–1914) published *A Welsh Grammar for Schools Based on the Principles and Requirements of the Grammatical Society* (1898–9), and later aided his brother, J. Bodvan Anwyl (1875–1949), with the initial revision of William Spurrell's Welsh–English (1848) and English–Welsh dictionaries (1850). These and later revisions were the standard dictionaries of the first half of the 20th century and remain valuable to this day. The work of O. H. Fynes-Clinton (1869–1941) on *The Welsh Vocabulary of the Bangor District* (1913) was a milestone in the study of Welsh phonetics and lexis.

Grammatical activity flourished during the 20th century. The most important grammar was undoubtedly John MORRIS-JONES's historical and comparative grammar of 1913, which however dealt only with phonology and 'accidence' (morphology). An unfinished draft of the section on syntax was published posthumously (1931). Morris-Jones's work exerted a powerful influence on subsequent grammars, the most important of which were those of Stephen J. Williams (1896–1992) on standard Modern Welsh and D. Simon Evans (1921–98) on Middle Welsh. Morris-Jones's work was complemented by the monographs of Melville Richards (1910–73) on the syntax of the sentence and T. J. Morgan (1907–86) on the mutations.

The second half of the century saw the publication of work on previously unstudied topics, covering a broader range of varieties and registers of Welsh, and the use of new methods and models of linguistics. Especially noteworthy among these are *Ieithyddiaeth* (Linguistics, 1961) by T. Arwyn Watkins, and Ceinwen H. Thomas's phonology, grammar, and glossary of her native dialect of Nantgarw in south-east Glamorgan (MORGANNWG, 1993), the glossary bearing comparison with that of Fynes-Clinton. The greater emphasis on the teaching of Welsh also led to the production of a large number of popular didactic works and of dictionaries. In the latter field H. Meurig Evans has been particularly active.

Twentieth-century lexicography also encompassed work in the field of terminology, and bilingual dictionaries. The last decade has seen the production of electronic dictionaries and spelling-checkers and the completion of two of the most important and influential projects in the history of the Welsh language: *The Welsh Academy English–Welsh Dictionary* (1995) and *Geiriadur Prifysgol Cymru / A Dictionary of the Welsh Language* ([GPC] 1950–2002), the standard historical Welsh dictionary, as well as the publication of a third standard work, Peter Wynn Thomas's Welsh grammar (1996).

MANUSCRIPT DICTIONARIES
Aberystwyth, NLW 13215, pp. 315–400 (*Geiria Tavod Comroig Hoc est Vocabvlarivm Lingvae Gomeritanae . . .* per Henricum Salesbury), Llanstephan 189 (*Lexicon Cambro-Britannicum*), Llanstephan 190 (The Welsh–English Dictionary), Peniarth 228 (*Dictionarium Latino-Cambricum* by Sir Thomas Wiliems); Oxford, Jesus College 16 (Welsh–English–Latin Dictionary).

HISTORIC DICTIONARIES
Anwyl, *Geiriadur Cymraeg a Saesneg / Spurrell's Welsh–English Dictionary*; Anwyl, *Geiriadur Saesneg a Chymraeg / Spurrell's English–Welsh Dictionary*; John Davies, *Antiquae Linguae Britannicae . . . Dictionarium Duplex*; D. Silvan Evans, *Dictionary of the Welsh Language / Geiriadur Cymraeg*, Parts 1–5, A–Ennyd; D. Silvan Evans, *English and Welsh Dictionary*; Thomas Jones, *Y Gymraeg yn ei Disgleirdeb, neu Helaeth Eir-lyfr Cymraeg a Saesneg*; Pughe, *Geiriadur Cynmraeg a Saesoneg / Welsh and English Dictionary*; Rhydderch, *English and Welch Dictionary / Y Geirlyfr Saesneg a Chymraeg*; Richards, *Antiquae Linguae Britannicae Thesaurus: being a British, or Welsh–English Dictionary*; Salesbury, *Dictionary in Englyshe and Welshe*; Spurrell, *English–Welsh Pronouncing Dictionary / Geiriadur Cynaniaethol Saesonaeg a Chymraeg*; Spurrell, *Geiriadur Cymraeg a Saesonaeg, ynghyd â grammadeg o iaith y Cymry / Dictionary of the Welsh Language . . . to which is Prefixed a Grammar of the Welsh Language*; Walters, *English-Welsh Dictionary*.

DIALECT DICTIONARY
Fynes-Clinton, *Welsh Vocabulary of the Bangor District*.

MODERN DICTIONARIES
CysGair: Y Geiriadur Saesneg a Chymraeg ar gyfer Windows / English and Welsh Dictionary for Windows; *CySill: Welsh Spelling and Grammar Checker*; Meirion Davies et al., *Geiriadur Ffrangeg–Cymraeg, Cymraeg–Ffrangeg / Dictionnaire français–gallois, gallois–français*; H. Meurig Evans & Thomas, *Y Geiriadur Mawr / Complete Welsh–English, English–Welsh Dictionary*; Greller et al., *Geiriadur Almaeneg–Cymraeg, Cymraeg–Almaeneg / Wörterbuch Deutsch–Walisisch, Walisisch–Deutsch*; Griffiths & Jones, *Geiriadur yr Academi / Welsh Academy English–Welsh Dictionary*; Lloyd-Jones, *Geirfa Barddoniaeth Gynnar Gymraeg, Rhannau 1–8, A–Heilic*; Prifysgol Cymru, Bwrdd Gwybodau Celtaidd, *Geiriadur Prifysgol Cymru / Dictionary of the Welsh Language* [GPC]; Prys & Jones, *Y Termiadur Ysgol: Standardized Welsh Terminology for the Schools of Wales*; Thomas, *Geiriadur Lladin–Cymraeg*; Jac L. Williams, *Geiriadur Termau / Dictionary of Terms*.

HISTORIC GRAMMARS
Anwyl, *Welsh Grammar for Schools Based on the Principles and Requirements of the Grammatical Society*; John Davies, *Antiquae*

Linguae Britannicae . . . Rudimenta; Gambold, *Welsh Grammar*; Pughe, *Grammar of the Welsh Language*; Rhydderch, *Grammadeg Cymraeg*; Rhys, *Cambrobrytannicae Cymraecaeve Linguae Institutiones et Rudimenta*; Robert, *Dosparth Byrr ar y Rhann Gyntaf i Ramadeg Cymraeg*, repr. G. J. Williams (ed.), *Gramadeg Cymraeg gan Gruffydd Robert*; Rowland, *Grammar of the Welsh Language*; Henry Salesbury, *Grammatica Britannica*; William Salesbury, *Briefe and a Playne Introduction, Teachyng How To Pronounce the Letters in the British Tong*; William Salesbury, *Playne and a Familiar Introductiō, Teaching How To Pronounce the Letters in the Brytishe Tongue*.

MODERN GRAMMARS AND STUDIES
Awbery, *Syntax of Welsh*; D. Simon Evans, *Gramadeg Cymraeg Canol*; D. Simon Evans, *Grammar of Middle Welsh*; Fife, *Semantics of the Welsh Verb*; Morris Jones & Thomas, *Welsh Language*; Morgan, *Y Treigladau a'u Cystrawen*; Morris-Jones, *Welsh Grammar, Historical and Comparative: Phonology and Accidence*; Morris-Jones, *Welsh Syntax—An Unfinished Draft*; Richards, *Cystrawen y Frawddeg Gymraeg*; Thomas, *Tafodiaith Nantgarw*; Thomas, *Gramadeg y Gymraeg*; Watkins, *Ieithyddiaeth*; Stephen J. Williams, *Elfennau Gramadeg Cymraeg*; Stephen J. Williams, *Welsh Grammar*; Willis, *Syntactic Change in Welsh*.

FURTHER READING
BANGOR; BIBLE; EDUCATION; GRAMADEGAU'R PENCEIRDDIAID; MORGANNWG; MORRIS-JONES; SALESBURY; WELSH; WELSH POETRY; WELSH PROSE LITERATURE; Bevan, THSC 1994.27–39; Burdett-Jones, *Nation and its Books* 75–81; Caryl Davies, *Adfeilion* 153–69; Emanuel, SC 7.141–54; Heinz, *Welsh Dictionaries in the Twentieth Century*; Huws, *Y Casglwr* 42.20; Menna Elisabeth Morgan, 'Agweddau ar Hanes Geiriaduraeth Gymraeg'; T. J. Morgan, *Llên Cymru* 9.3–18; Parry, BBCS 6.55–62, 225–31; Watkins, *Celtic Studies in Wales* 143–82; J. E. Caerwyn Williams, *Geiriadurwyr y Gymraeg yng Nghyfnod y Dadeni*; J. E. Caerwyn Williams, SC 16/17.280–316.

Gareth A. Bevan

dictionaries and grammars [5] Breton

The earliest BRETON lexicography, as in the other CELTIC LANGUAGES, is in the form of occasional Old Breton glosses of Latin words found from the 9th century onwards (see BRETON LITERATURE). The function of these glosses, however, was utilitarian rather than systematic, and the first serious attempt to record the Breton language in a form useful for non-Breton speakers was the late medieval CATHOLICON, a trilingual Breton–French–Latin dictionary. This work, first printed at the end of the 15th century, was not superseded until the work of Julian MAUNOIR (1606–83) in the 17th century. In 1659 he published *Le sacré collège de Jésus* (The sacred school of Jesus), a catechism in Breton which included a Breton dictionary and grammar. Most of the works on the Breton language at this stage were produced by the clergy, many of whom needed to learn Breton in order to be able to communicate with their parishioners. *Brezhoneg beleg* 'priest-Breton' is the name given to this clerical stage of Breton codification and production. Louis Le Pelletier (1663–1733) and Jean-François Le Gonidec (1775–1838) were important lexicographers of the period; both produced grammars, along with their dictionaries, and Le Gonidec also published Breton manuscripts.

The codification of Breton has been beset from the beginning by difficulties of orthography, both in representing the sounds of the language where divergent from Latin and French, and in representing the BRETON DIALECTS where divergent from each other. Both Le Pelletier and Le Gonidec used a Breton alphabetical order where the sounds of the letters determined their placement, following the traditional Latin order. As set out in *Yezhadur bras ar brezhoneg* (The big grammar of Breton), it is A B K D E F G H CH C'H I Y J L M N O P R S T U V W Z. This has largely been superseded by one which conforms more closely to the conventional order of the letters, regardless of sound: A B CH C'H D E F G H I J K L M N O P R S T U V W Y Z. (While EU, GN, NG, LH, and OU, and sometimes GW and ZH, are considered to be single letters in Breton, they are not treated that way for alphabetization purposes.) In 1744 Abbé Armeyrie published a Breton dictionary based on the dialect of Vannes (see GWENED). The controversy over which dialect(s) to represent, and which spelling system with which to represent it/them, has not been solved. The best guide to the diversity of Breton is Francis Favereau's 1997 dictionary and grammar, which uses the international phonetic alphabet to indicate the pronunciation in various dialects.

Most Breton dictionaries and grammars have been aimed at a French-speaking audience, but as early as 1903 J. Percy Treasure published an English-language grammar of Breton in Wales (CYMRU), and many of the publications dealing with Old and Middle Breton have been in English. The most important introduction to Middle Breton, Henry LEWIS and J. R. F. Piette's *Llawlyfr Llydaweg Canol* (Handbook of Middle Breton), first published in 1922, has been reprinted in Welsh and translated into German with additions and corrections, but has never been published in English or French. The late 1980s and 1990s saw the beginning of

a wider interest in the Breton language, with dictionaries in German, Irish, Spanish, Welsh, and a number in English becoming available, as well as translations of Breton-language textbooks (see Per DENEZ). Also in this period, Yann Lagadeg and Martial Ménard published the first monolingual dictionary of modern Breton, *Geriadur brezhoneg gant skoueriou*. This period, too, has witnessed an increase in the user-friendliness of the dictionaries. Keys to pronunciation, usage, and grammar, absent or sparse in the early dictionaries designed for people living in Breton-speaking areas, are becoming standard.

HISTORIC DICTIONARIES

Armeyrie, *Dictionnaire françois–breton ou françois–celtique du dialecte de Vannes*; De Rostrenen, *Dictionnaire françois–celtique ou françois–breton*; Le Gonidec, *Dictionnaire breton-français*; Le Gonidec, *Dictionnaire celto–breton ou breton–français*; Le Gonidec, *Léorik a zo enn-han ann darnvuia euz ar geriou brezonnek ha gallek*; Le Gonidec, *Vocabulaire français–breton*; Le Pelletier, *Dictionnaire de la langue bretonne*; Maunoir, *Les dictionnaires français–breton et breton–français*; Maunoir, *Le sacré collège de Jésus*.

MODERN DICTIONARIES

Andouard, *Geriadur iwerzhoneg–brezhoneg gant lavarennou*; Ar Porzh, *Geriadur brezhoneg–saozneg gant skoueriou/Breton–English Dictionary with Examples, A–G*; Conroy, *Breton–English/English–Breton: dictionary and phrasebook*; Cornillet, *Geriadur brezhoneg-alamaneg/Bretonisch–Deutsches Wörterbuch*; Delaporte, *Elementary Breton–English English–Breton Dictionary/Geriadurig brezhoneg–saozneg saozneg–brezhoneg*; Denez, *Geriadur brezhoneg Douarnenez/Dictionnaire du breton parlé a Douarnenez*; Ernault, *Gériadurig brezhoneg–galleg/Vocabulaire breton–français*; Ernault & Le Goff, *Dictionnaire breton–français du dialecte de Vannes*; Fleuriot, *Dictionary of Old Breton/Dictionnaire du vieux breton*; Favereau, *Dictionnaire du breton contemporain/Geriadur ar brezhoneg a-vremañ*; Fulub, *Diccionario básico español–bretón/Geriadur diazez brezhoneg–spagnoleg*; Hemon, *Dictionnaire breton–français*; Hemon, *Dictionnaire français–breton*; Hemon, *Geriadur istorel ar brezhoneg* [Middle Breton]; Kadored et al., *Geriadur bihan brezhoneg–galleg, galleg–brezhoneg*; Lagadeg & Ménard, *Geriadur brezhoneg gant skoueriou ha troiennou*; Le Gléau, *Dictionnaire classique français–breton*; Vallée, *Grand dictionnaire français–breton*; Rita Williams, *Geriadur brezhonek–kembraek*; Rita Williams, *Geiriadur Bach Llydaweg–Cymraeg*.

HISTORIC GRAMMARS

Hingant, *Élements de la grammaire bretonne*; Le Clerc, *Grammaire bretonne du dialecte de Tréguier*; Le Gonidec, *Grammaire celto-bretonne*; Treasure, *Introduction to Breton Grammar*.

MODERN GRAMMARS

Desbordes, *Petite grammaire du breton moderne*; Favereau, *Grammaire du breton contemporain*; Fleuriot, *Le vieux breton*; Guillevic & Le Goff, *Grammaire bretonne du dialecte de Vannes*; Hemon, *Breton Grammar*; Hemon, *Historical Morphology and Syntax of Breton*; Hemon, *Yezhadur istorel ar brezhoneg*; Kervella, *Yezhadur bras ar brezhoneg*; Lewis & Piette, *Llawlyfr Llydaweg Canol*; Lewis & Piette, *Handbuch des Mittelbretonischen*; Press, *Grammar of Modern Breton*; Trépos, *Grammaire bretonne*; Vallée, *Grammaire française et grammaire bretonne*.

FURTHER READING
BRETON; BRETON DIALECTS; BRETON LITERATURE; CATHOLI-
CON; CELTIC LANGUAGES; CYMRU; DENEZ; GWENED; LEWIS;
MAUNOIR.

                                                      AM

dictionaries and grammars [6] Cornish

Cornish studies have benefited from a long history
of collecting and publishing vocabularies, with much
work being done by those who wish to revive the
language; however, there remains a need for a scholarly
historical dictionary, and even for a dependable dictionary of any kind without any reconstructed or conjectured forms.

§1. MANUSCRIPT GLOSSARIES

The earliest CORNISH dictionary could be said to be
the Old Cornish VOCABULARIUM CORNICUM, a
Cornish adaptation of Ælfric's Old English–Latin
thematic glossary, preserved in the early 12th-century
British Library MS Cotton Vespasian A.xiv, fos. 7a–
10a. This was followed, half a millennium later, by
several antiquarian GLOSSARIES such as those in BL
Add. 28554 (the Gwavas Manuscript), National Library
of Wales MS, Bodewryd 5 (Hawke, Cornish Studies, 2nd
ser. 9.83–104), Thomas Tonkin's manuscript vocabulary in the so-called 'Bilbao Manuscript' (later
published by William Pryce in 1790), the huge, yet
extraordinarily misinformed, An Lhadymer ay Kernou by
William Hals (BL Add. 71157), William Borlase's
vocabulary (published in 1754 and 1769), Edward
LHUYD's MS notebook, which accompanied him on
his travels to Cornwall (NLW, Llanstephan 84) and
which later supplied some of the material for the
published vocabulary (1707), and, following in the same
tradition, the extensive manuscript vocabularies prepared (but never published) by Charles Rogers, a
Plymouth chemist (Rogers MS, 1861) and the Revd John
Bannister (preserved in the Egerton MSS).

§2. PRINTED DICTIONARIES

The earliest printed dictionary of Cornish, compiled
by Lhuyd and his team from evidence gathered from
his field-trip to Cornwall (KERNOW) in 1700 and from
copies he had made of several of the Middle Cornish
texts, was published in his Archæologia Britannica in 1707,
as 'A Comparative Vocabulary of the Original Languages of Britain and Ireland'. Much other Cornish
vocabulary is to be found in several other sections.
Despite being resident in west Cornwall, William
Borlase's Cornish–English vocabulary of 1754 (pp. 376–
413) is largely a derivative work with much input from
Lhuyd's work. A revised second edition was published
in 1769 (pp. 415–64). William Pryce's Archaeologia
Cornu–Britannica of 1790, which contains an extensive
'Cornish–English Vocabulary', draws on both Lhuyd
and Borlase, but is derived chiefly from the unpublished
work of Thomas Tonkin and William Gwavas.

The first attempt at a historical dictionary of Cornish was the Lexicon Cornu-Britannicum of Canon Robert
Williams, published in parts between 1861 and 1865.
This work cites examples from the Cornish plays, with
references and cognates from the other Celtic languages.
It suffers somewhat from the author's mistaken attempt
to align the orthography of Cornish with that of
WELSH, but nevertheless remains a useful reference
today. Unfortunately, it just predated the (re)discovery
of BEUNANS MERIASEK (ed. Stokes), rendering it
incomplete almost as soon as it was published, and
necessitating Stokes's glossary to the play (Archiv für
celtische Lexikographie 1.101–42) following his supplement
to the Lexicon (Stokes, Cornish Glossary) and Joseph
LOTH's extensive 'Remarques et corrections au Lexicon
Cornu–Britannicum de Williams' (RC 23.237–302). Joseph
Cuillandre, having collected extensive materials for
an historical dictionary of Cornish and having
published just a few lexical notes in the Revue Celtique,
died before the work could be completed. Frederick
Jago, having already published The Ancient Language, and
the Dialect of Cornwall: with an Enlarged Glossary of
Cornish Provincial Words in 1882, proceeded to 'reverse'
the Lexicon, resulting in his English–Cornish Dictionary
of 1887, which, whilst a less scholarly work than that
of Williams, does include some independent matter,
mostly collected from Penwith fishermen who still
had some knowledge of the language.

Robert Morton NANCE, who inherited Henry
Jenner's rôle as the leader of the Cornish language
revival (see LANGUAGE [REVIVAL]), devoted years of
study to the entire known corpus of CORNISH
LITERATURE, culminating in his much condensed Gerlyver
Noweth Kernewek ha Sawsnek: A New Cornish–English
Dictionary of 1938, being a much more comprehensive

counterpart to his slightly earlier *English–Cornish Dictionary* (Nance & Smith, 1934). Although much smaller than Williams's *Lexicon*, the 1938 dictionary remains an indispensable work, marred (from the scholar's standpoint) only by the inclusion of many unmarked conjectural forms based on Welsh or BRETON. The fact that they were unmarked seems to have been an oversight on Nance's part, as his draft revision in the (uncatalogued) papers of the Nance Bequest at the Courtney Library of the Royal Institution of Cornwall adds asterisks to most, if not all, of these conjectural forms, as well as a mass of further material from the 'TREGEAR HOMILIES' and other sources. Lack of funds ensured that all further editions (English–Cornish, 1952; Cornish–English, 1955, 1967, 1976; combined English–Cornish and Cornish–English, 1978) of both dictionaries omitted much of the material which would have been the most valuable for scholarly purposes. The 1938 dictionary has been reprinted (together with the English–Cornish edition of 1952) several times, as *Gerlyver Noweth Kernewek–Sawsnek ha Sawsnek–Kernewek* (1990, 1999). Nance also published several glossaries, including 'A Glossary of Celtic Words in Cornish Dialect' (1923) and, posthumously, *A Glossary of Cornish Sea-words* (1963), which is of particular importance to lexical studies. Martyn Wakelin studied the Cornish element in the English dialect of Cornwall in a useful volume published in 1975, but omitted the majority of the evidence by concentrating on the very narrow brief of the Leeds Survey of English dialects. Much useful lexical information is contained in Oliver Padel's important *Cornish Place-Name Elements* (1985).

§3. RECENT DICTIONARIES

There has been something of a spate of Cornish dictionaries recently, partly encouraged by the internal divisions within the revival movement which have spawned several orthographical systems, necessitating their respective dictionaries. The proponents of Kernewek Kemmyn (Common Cornish) have produced two new dictionaries based on a reappraisal of the existing texts, but retaining most of the semantic information from Nance's dictionaries. George's 'Gerlyver Meur' Cornish–English version (1993) is the most useful for scholarly purposes since it gives an indication of attestation and occurrence (see N. J. A.

Williams, *Cornish Studies*, 2nd ser. 9.247–311), and his 'Gerlyver Kres' is a condensed two-way version (1998). Richard Gendall has produced a series of dictionaries based exclusively on his extensive study of the evidence of the Modern period of the language and the Cornish survivals in the English dialect of Cornwall, with brief details of attestation. Nicholas Williams (2000) has produced the most comprehensive English–Cornish dictionary published to date (with online addenda, including the new evidence from BEUNANS KE), based on his own 'Unified Cornish Revised' version of the language, but with no details of attestation or authenticity, making it the least useful of the recent works from a scholarly point of view.

§4. GRAMMARS

Lhuyd was the first to systematically describe the grammar of Cornish in his *Archaeologia Britannica* (pp. 222–53), forming the basis for a number of subsequent works such as William Pryce's *Archaeologia Cornu–Britannica* of 1790. Edwin Norris reappraised the grammar in his *Sketch of Cornish Grammar*, which is more commonly found as part of *The Ancient Cornish Drama*, his edition of the ORDINALIA and VOCABULARIUM CORNICUM. Henry Jenner attempted to simplify the grammar of (predominately) Modern Cornish in his *A Handbook of the Cornish Language* for those interested in learning the language in the early days of the revival movement, beginning a long tradition of revivalist grammatical works, which generally tend to simplify and generalize, although they can be useful from a scholarly viewpoint. Henry LEWIS published the standard grammar of Middle Cornish in 1923, with a substantially revised edition appearing in 1946. Unfortunately, Lewis chose to ignore most of the valuable corrections and criticism communicated to him by the revivalists A. S. D. Smith and R. Morton Nance (posthumously published in 1968). The 1946 edition has been translated into German by Stefan Zimmer and into Dutch by Lauran Toorians, and an English translation by Glanville Price is in preparation. Smith's *Cornish Simplified* contains much useful information, although primarily intended for learners of Revived Cornish. Four valuable cyclostyled supplements to it, which were originally compiled by Smith in 1954–63, were published by E. G. R. Hooper in emended form as a single volume in 1984. Iwan

Wmffre's *Late Cornish* (1998) treats the grammar of Modern Cornish. Wella Brown's *A Grammar of Modern Cornish* is the most comprehensive grammar of the revived language, but Lewis's *Llawlyfr* remains the standard scholarly work.

MANUSCRIPT GLOSSARIES
Aberystwyth, NLW, Bodewryd 5 (ed. Hawke, *Cornish Studies*, 2nd ser., 9.83–104), Llanstephan 84; Bilbao, Biblioteca de la Disputación Foral de Bizkaia, Bnv-69, (The Bilbao MS); London, BL, Add. 28554, fos. 119v–125r, Add 71157, Cotton Vespasian A.xiv, fos. 7a–10a, Egerton 2328, 2329 (Bannister); Oxford, Bodleian Library, Corn. d. 1 (The Rogers MS).

HISTORIC DICTIONARIES &C.
Borlase, *Observations on the Antiquities, Historical and Monumental, of the County of Cornwall*; Cuillandre, RC 48.1–41, 49.109–31; Jago, *Ancient Language and the Dialect of Cornwall*; Jago, *English–Cornish Dictionary*; Lhuyd, *Archaeologia Britannica* 1; Loth, RC 23.237–302; Nance, *Cornish–English Dictionary*; Nance, *English–Cornish and Cornish–English Dictionary*; Nance, *Gerlyver Noweth Kernewek ha Sawsnek / New Cornish–English Dictionary*; Nance, *Gerlyver Noweth Kernewek–Sawsnek ha Sawsnek–Kernewek*; Nance, *Glossary of Celtic Words in Cornish Dialect*; Nance, *Glossary of Cornish Sea-words*; Nance & Smith, *English–Cornish Dictionary*; Pryce, *Archaeologia Cornu-Britannica*; Stokes, *Archiv für celtische Lexikographie* 1.101–42; Stokes, *Cornish Glossary*; Robert Williams, *Lexicon Cornu–Britannicum*.

MODERN DICTIONARIES
Gendall, *New Practical Dictionary of Modern Cornish*; Gendall, *Students' Dictionary of Modern Cornish*; George, *Gerlyver Kernewek Kemmyn: An Gerlyver Kres, Kernewek–Sowsnek, Sowsnek–Kernewek*; George, *Gerlyver Kernewek Kemmyn: An Gerlyver Meur, Kernewek–Sowsnek*; N. J. A. Williams, *English–Cornish Dictionary / Gerlyver Sawsnek–Kernowek*.

GRAMMARS &C.
Brown, *Grammar of Modern Cornish*; Jenner, *Handbook of the Cornish Language*; Lewis, *Handbuch des Mittelkornischen*; Lewis, *Handboek voor het Middelcornisch*; Lewis, *Llawlyfr Cernyweg Canol*; Lhuyd, *Archaeologia Britannica* 1; Norris, *Ancient Cornish Drama* [includes Sketch of Cornish Grammar]; Norris, *Sketch of Cornish Grammar*; Pryce, *Archaeologia Cornu-Britannica*; Smith, *Cornish Simplified*; Smith & Nance, *Comments on 'Llawlyfr Cernyweg Canol' Henry Lewis*; Wmffre, *Late Cornish*.

FURTHER READING
BEUNANS KE; BEUNANS MERIASEK; BRETON; CORNISH; CORNISH LITERATURE; GLOSSARIES; KERNOW; LANGUAGE (REVIVAL); LEWIS; LHUYD; LOTH; NANCE; ORDINALIA; TREGEAR HOMILIES; VOCABULARIUM CORNICUM; WELSH; Jenner, *Journal of the Royal Institution of Cornwall* 21.421–37; Mills, 'Computer Assisted Lemmatisation of a Cornish Text Corpus for Lexicographical Purposes'; Padel, *Cornish Place-Name Elements*; Wakelin, *Language and History in Cornwall*; N. J. A. Williams, *Cornish Studies*, 2nd ser. 9.247–311.

Andrew Hawke

Dillon, Myles (1900–72) was a prolific Irish scholar who is probably best known for his work on the prose literature of early Ireland (ÉRIU). His publications demonstrate the breadth of his interests and expertise, and include several highly original comparative studies of Celtic and INDO-EUROPEAN languages and traditions. Dillon was born in Dublin (BAILE ÁTHA CLIATH) and died there, but he also spent significant periods abroad. He studied under Douglas Hyde (DE HÍDE) and Osborn Bergin (Ó HAIMHIRGÍN) at University College Dublin, and went on to teach in Ireland (ÉIRE), America, and Scotland (ALBA). As the Director of the Dublin Institute for Advanced Studies (INSTITIÚID ARD-LÉINN), Dillon was prominent in promoting the Institute's function as an academic publishing house. He was also assistant editor of the early Irish dictionary (see DICTIONARIES AND GRAMMARS) published by the Royal Irish Academy (ACADAMH RÍOGA NA HÉIREANN), and contributed to the *Catalogue of Irish Manuscripts* in the British Museum.

SELECTION OF MAIN WORKS
Cycles of the Kings (1946); *Early Irish Literature* (1948); *Celt and Hindu* (1973); *Celts and Aryans* (1975).
(with Nora K. Chadwick) *Celtic Realms* (1967).
(with Ó Cróinín) *Teach Yourself Irish* (1961).
ED. *Serglige Con Culainn* (1953); *Early Irish Society* (1954); *Irish Sagas* (1959); *Lebor na Cert / Book of Rights* (1962); *Stories from the Acallam* (1970); *There was a King in Ireland* (1971).

BIBLIOGRAPHY OF PUBLISHED WORKS
Baumgarten, *Celtica* 11.1–14.

FURTHER READING
ACADAMH RÍOGA NA H-ÉIREANN; ALBA; BAILE ÁTHA CLIATH; DE H-ÍDE; DICTIONARIES AND GRAMMARS; ÉIRE; ÉRIU; INDO-EUROPEAN; INSTITIÚID ARD-LÉINN; IRISH; IRISH LITERATURE; Ó H-AIMHIRGÍN; Fischer & J. Dillon, *Correspondence of Myles Dillon 1922–1925*.

PSH

Dinas Basing, Abaty (Basingwerk Abbey), Flintshire (sir y Fflint), north-east Wales (CYMRU), was an abbey of the Savignac order founded in 1131, probably by Ranulf II, earl of Chester (CAER). Building began on the present site c. 1157, and the surviving buildings date from the 13th century. The Book of Aneirin (LLYFR ANEIRIN), transcribed in the later 13th century, and the Welsh text of the Black Book of Basing have been associated with the abbey's scriptorium. Basingwerk was for a time the home of the Welsh poet GUTUN OWAIN (*fl.* 1450–98), and part of the Black Book is in his hand. The abbey possessed the manor of Holywell (Treffynnon), and the shrine of St Winifred, with its well-chapel, was under its control.

FURTHER READING
CAER; CYMRU; GUTUN OWAIN; LLYFR ANEIRIN; Cowley, *Monastic Order in South Wales 1066–1349*; Hubbard, *Clwyd*; Owen, *Journal of the Flintshire Historical Society* 7.47–89; Taylor, *Basingwerk Abbey, Flintshire*; D. H. Williams, *Welsh Cistercians: Aspects of their Economic History*; D. H. Williams, *Welsh Cistercians*.

John Morgan-Guy

Dinas Emrys is a craggy hilltop with ruined FORTIFICATIONS which rises about 70 m above the Glaslyn valley in north Wales (CYMRU), and is thus in a good position to overlook and control one of the main routes into Snowdonia (ERYRI) from the south. Steep natural defences on the north and west, augmented by encompassing stone ramparts that stand about 3 m high where intact, enclose an area of roughly 1.2 ha (3 acres). The occupation debris is of mixed date, including late Roman and early post-Roman material. For example, an amphora (large ceramic WINE vessel, type Biv) from the eastern Mediterranean of the 5th or 6th century AD reveals that the site was a post-Roman aristocratic residence as well as a military strongpoint.

GIRALDUS CAMBRENSIS refers to *Dynas Emereis* (Citadel of Ambrosius) in north Wales in his *Itinerarium Kambriae* (1191). In the Middle Welsh mythological tale CYFRANC LLUDD A LLEFELYS, *Dinas Emreis*, previously known as *Dinas Ffaraon Danðe* (Citadel of fiery Pharaoh), figures as the place where the slumbering dragons were entombed in BRITAIN's remote pre-Roman past (see also DRAIG GOCH). The story thus ties in with that of the release of the DRAGONS in the presence of GWRTHEYRN and the wonder child AMBROSIUS during the building of a stronghold on a summit; the earliest surviving version is in the 9th-century Welsh Latin HISTORIA BRITTONUM. In this source, the place is said to be in Snowdonia (Old Welsh Heriri). It is thus likely, but not certain, that the tale's localization at Dinas Emrys had already taken place.

In the enclosed area on the hilltop there is a man-made pool or cistern, somewhat under 10 metres square. It has been suggested that this feature inspired the pool surrounding the sleeping dragons in *Historia Brittonum*. Although this is possible, evidence for this feature suggests a date in the central Middle Ages. Nonetheless, the medieval redigging of the Dark Age fort's cistern cannot be ruled out.

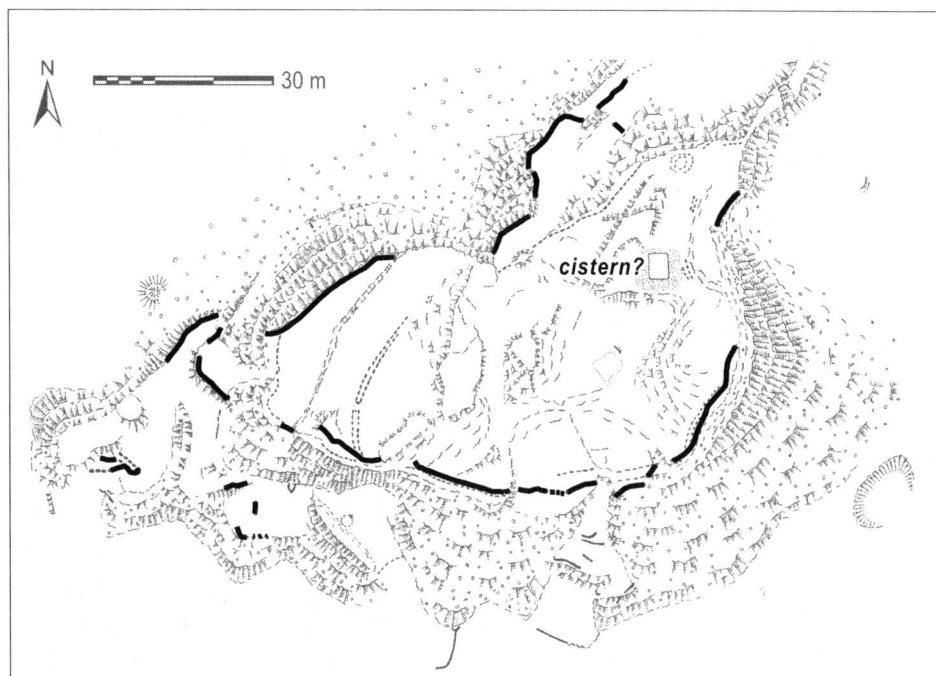

Plan of the fortified hilltop of Dinas Emrys

FURTHER READING
AMBROSIUS; BRITAIN; CYFRANC LLUDD A LLEFELYS; CYMRU;
DRAGONS; DRAIG GOCH; ERYRI; FORTIFICATION; GIRALDUS
CAMBRENSIS; GWRTHEYRN; HISTORIA BRITTONUM; WINE;
Alcock, *Arthur's Britain*; Alcock, *Economy, Society and Warfare
among the Britons and Saxons*; Edwards & Lane, *Early Medieval
Settlements in Wales* 54–7; Savory, *Archaeologia Cambrensis* 109.13–
77.
                                                                                    JTK

dindshenchas

The Irish term *dindshenchas*, later *dinnsheanchas*, means 'lore of high places'. Some of the lore clearly began as mythology, for example, the list of landscape features at the end of TÁIN BÓ CUAILNGE ('The Cattle Raid of Cooley'), caused by the fight to the death of two supernatural bulls (Patricia Kelly, *Aspects of the Táin* 76). However, the names and features mentioned differ between the two main versions, probably reflecting the storyteller's desire to make his tale relevant to his hearers (Ó hUiginn, *Aspects of the Táin* 44–9). In an earlier scene (O'Rahilly, *Táin Bó Cúailnge* I l. 699), the hero CÚ CHULAINN stands on a hill and gets his charioteer to identify to him each *prímdún* (chief fort) they can see between Tara (TEAMHAIR) and KELLS (Ceanannas).

Such a triangulation of Ireland (ÉRIU) was important for a society which needed to know where the boundaries of each local kingdom or TUATH ran, since ordinary people (unlike poets, lawyers, and clerics) lost status, and thus legal protection, in another's territory. Hills often marked the boundaries between territories, and because of the view this gave them were favoured as sites for ritual (e.g. *glám dícenn* 'endless revilement', supposedly fatal to the victim; Thurneysen, *Irische Texte* 3.1.96–7, trans. Stokes, RC 12.119–20; see also SATIRE) or for assembly (*Ualand*; Dillon, *Ériu* 11.50, trans. 61–2). An official in the church of Armagh (ARD MHACHA) in the 12th century was called *príomhchríochaire* (chief boundary keeper) (O'Donovan, *Annála Ríoghachta Éireann/Annals of the Kingdom of Ireland by the Four Masters* AD 1136; Pettiau, *Armagh* 127).

After their 8th year of study Irish poets were expected to be able to narrate all the traditional stories and explain the origin of place-names (*Dá ernail déc na filidheachta*; Thurneysen, *Irische Texte* 3.1 §2). An early story tells how MONGÁN mac Fiachna embarrassed his father's poet, Eochu Rígéigeas, for exclaiming: '*Sochaide lasa ndéntar rátha … co nach talla for menmain*', 'So many build castles … that they do not all find room in the memory' (Knott, *Ériu* 8.157, 159).

Another revealing story concerning poets, place-names, and heights is to be found in Edward Gwynn's edition of the *Metrical Dindshenchas* (3.532–3, introductory tale to p. 304, the poem on Echtge). Following the death of Flann mac Lonáin (?–896), his harper Ilbrechtach served another CONNACHT poet Mac Liac. He liked to go visiting south across Slieve Aughty to Limerick (Luimneach),

carrying with him 12 bottles (*putraic*) and suitable victuals thereto. For there are 12 points of view in Slieve Aughty and he used to drink a bottle at each of them.

As they rested at one viewpoint, Mac Liac commented how good it would be to know the stories of every place they could see. Ilbrechtach unwisely replied that his late master knew them all. He was made to fast until the soul of Mac Lonáin appeared and gave Mac Liac the knowledge to compose the poem on Echtge.

A Mac Liacc (†AD 1016) is one of the named authors of *dindshenchas* poems, along with Cinaed ua hArtacáin (†974) and Cúán ua Lothcháin (†1024). A collection made in the 11th century appears in many important Irish manuscripts, and has been edited in 5 volumes by Edward Gwynn. There are also anonymous prose pieces on many of the names, edited from collections in different manuscripts by Whitley STOKES (*Folklore* 3.467–516; *Folklore* 4.471–97; RC 15/16). It is evident that later recensions were intended to include both verse and prose (Gwynn, *Metrical Dindsenchas* 4.92; Bowen, SC 10/11.113). Bowen lists articles on 218 different names, some of which are paralleled in surviving tales. The explanations are sometimes stories, sometimes etymological.

Many of the stories deal with mythological traditions and the people of the SÍD (a fairy rath or fort). As Máirín O Daly points out, there are far more allusions to the ULSTER CYCLE and the FINN MAC CUMAILL Cycle (FIANNAÍOCHT) than to the KINGS' CYCLE (O Daly, *Early Irish Poetry* 59–60). However, some saints appear—COLUM CILLE in the stories of *Coire Breccáin* and *Ailech*, and PATRICK in those of *Sliab Fuait*, *Brí Graige*, *Findloch Cera*, and *Tailtiu*. Many of the *dindshenchas* poems also end with religious quatrains praising the coming of CHRISTIANITY, prompting Tomás Ó Concheanainn (*Ériu* 33.98) to attribute the latest recension to the poet Cuan Ó Lochán. Many of these final verses provide an additional *dúnadh* (closing echoing the first line) to a poem that already has one (Gwynn, *Metrical Dindshenchas* 4.16, 18, 76, 88, 90, 130), clear evidence for recomposition by a second poet.

Baumgarten has written about the place-name lore pervasive in secular literature as part of narrative style. The place-name *Adarca Iuchna* (the horns of Iuchna) plays a pivotal rôle in the story of Finn mac Cumaill's death. Finn drank from a well here, inadvertently breaking a taboo (GEIS) never to drink from a horn. Baumgarten also gives from ACALLAM NA SENÓRACH (Dialogue of [or with] the old men) two versions of an itinerary, which provides information and stylistic enrichment by its references to place-names, their alternatives, and their stories.

Stories based on place-names continued in Irish oral tradition in modern times. An example from Donegal (Tír Chonaill) explains *Loch Finne*, *Mín-an-áil*, and *Loch Muc* from the hunt for a monster sow (Joyce, *Origin and History of Irish Names of Places* 174–5) and a story from Co. Down (Contae an Dúin) includes the English house-name Mount Panther among place-names commemorating the chase of a magic cat (Fr [J.] O'Laverty, quoted by Hyde, *Ulster Journal of Archaeology* 2nd ser. 3.264 n.1).

Place-name lore analogous to Irish *dindshenchas* is also a feature of early Welsh literature. Many names are given explanatory stories or etymologies in, for example, the 9th-century Welsh Latin HISTORIA BRITTONUM and the Middle Welsh tales of the MABINOGI.

PRIMARY SOURCES
O'Donovan, *Annála Ríoghachta Éireann*; Gwynn, *Metrical Dindshenchas*.

FURTHER READING
ACALLAM NA SENÓRACH; ARD MHACHA; CHRISTIANITY; COLUM CILLE; CONNACHT; CÚ CHULAINN; ÉRIU; FIANNAÍOCHT; GEIS; HISTORIA BRITTONUM; KELLS; KINGS' CYCLE; MABINOGI; MONGÁN; PATRICK; SATIRE; SÍD; STOKES; TÁIN BÓ CUAILNGE; TEAMHAIR; TUATH; ULSTER CYCLE; Arbuthnot, *Ériu* 50.79–86; Baumgarten, *Heroic Process* 1–24; Baumgarten, *Ériu* 41.115–22; Bowen, SC 10/11.113–37; Dillon, *Ériu* 11.42–65; Hyde, *Ulster Journal of Archaeology* 2nd ser. 3.258–71; Joyce, *Origin and History of Irish Names of Places*; Kelly, *Aspects of the Táin* 69–102; Knott, *Ériu* 8.155–60; Ó Concheanainn, *Ériu* 33.85–98; Ó Daly, *Early Irish Poetry* 59–72; Ó hUiginn, *Aspects of the Táin* 29–67; O'Rahilly, *Táin Bó Cúailnge, Recension 1*; Pettiau, *Armagh* 121–86;

Stokes, RC 12.52–130, 306–8; Stokes, *Folklore* 3.467–516; Stokes, *Folklore* 4.471–97; Stokes, RC 15.272–336, 418–84, 16.31–83, 135–67, 269–312; Thurneysen, *Irische Texte* 3.1.96–7.

Kay Muhr

Diodorus Siculus (the Sicilian Διόδορος) was a Greek author from Agyrion in Sicily who wrote a world history, known as *The Historical Library* (Βιβλιοθήκη), between *c.* 60 and *c.* 30 BC. It survives in sizeable fragments. This work is important to CELTIC STUDIES because it preserves material attributed to the lost Celtic ethnography of POSIDONIUS, based on first-hand experience in GAUL in the earlier 1st century BC. Diodorus' fidelity to his source can be judged from his handling of his other sources and also from Posidonian passages paralleled by STRABO. Diodorus is thus one of the more important of the extant GREEK AND ROMAN ACCOUNTS of Celtic life in pre-Roman Gaul, and includes the following points (which are discussed more fully elsewhere in this Encyclopedia): an often-cited formulation on the learned classes, the BARDS and DRUIDS (31); a passage suggesting that the Gauls believed in REINCARNATION; a reference to the use of the CHARIOT in warfare by the Gauls (29.1); an origin legend of the Gauls claiming descent from HERCULES (5.24); an explanation of the mixed origins of the inhabitants of CELTIBERIA (5.33); an account of the Gauls' invasion of ROME under BRENNOS OF THE SENONES and the origins of the Celts in ITALY (14); and an account of the Gauls' invasion of Greece under BRENNOS OF THE PRAUSI, showing a parallel with the Welsh legendary hero BRÂN FAB LLŶR (22.9).

PRIMARY SOURCES
ED. & TRANS. Oldfather et al., *Diodorus Siculus*; Tierney, PRIA 60 C.5. 189–275 (excerpts).
TRANS. Koch & Carey, *Celtic Heroic Age* 12–15 (excerpts).

RELATED ARTICLES
BARD; BRÂN; BRENNOS OF THE PRAUSI; BRENNOS OF THE SENONES; CELTIBERIA; CELTIC STUDIES; CHARIOT; DRUIDS; GAUL; GREEK AND ROMAN ACCOUNTS; HERCULES; ITALY; POSIDONIUS; REINCARNATION; ROME; STRABO.

JTK

Dīs Pater was the Roman god of wealth and the underworld, the realm of the dead, and was identified with the Greek Hades, also called Pluto (Πλούτων).

In *De Bello Gallico* (6.18) CAESAR stated that all the Gauls believed that they were descended from Dīs Pater, as was taught to them by the DRUIDS. The Latin word *dis* has two meanings: 'the rich one' or 'deity'. In the latter, generic sense, *diespiter* was often used for Jupiter, although Caesar refers to the two separately. It is unclear which of the Gaulish gods Caesar meant here. Mythological figures attested in inscriptions who *might* match the identification are SUCELLUS and Smertrius. In Irish tradition, the supernatural Donn mac Míled, who figures in LEGENDARY HISTORY as the first of the ancestral Gaels to die in Ireland and as the keeper of the house of the dead *Tech Duinn* (Donn's house), is a comparable figure (see also LEBAR GABÁLA; MÍL ESPÁINE).

RELATED ARTICLES
CAESAR; DRUIDS; GAUL; LEBAR GABÁLA; LEGENDARY HISTORY; MÍL ESPÁINE; SUCELLUS.

PEB

of Ariovistus, who was by then threatening the whole of Gaul. Moved by this speech, Caesar later fought and crushed the Germani in Gaul, though Ariovistus himself escaped across the Rhine. Dīviciācos was then restored to power.

Cicero (106–43 BC) states that he had met 'Diviciacus Aeduus', and describes him as a druid who claimed special knowledge of the natural world, including skills of PROPHECY (*De Divinatione* 1.41.90). We may conclude that the *vergobreti* and DRUIDS of Gaul had overlapping educational qualifications, or at least were not rigidly separate classes.

On the name *Dīviciācos*, see the following article.

PRIMARY SOURCES
CAESAR, *De Bello Gallico*; Cicero, *De Divinatione*.

FURTHER READING
AEDUI; ARVERNI; DĪVICIĀCOS OF THE SUESSIONES; DRUIDS; GAUL; HELVETII; PROPHECY; RHINE; D. Ellis Evans, *Gaulish Personal Names* 81–3.

JTK

Dīviciācos of the Aedui

Dīviciācos of the Aedui (*fl.* 58 BC) was a key figure in the events of the Roman conquest of GAUL and is mentioned many times in CAESAR's *De Bello Gallico*. He was Caesar's trusted friend, a pro-Roman tribal leader, holding the title *vergobretos* (translated by Caesar *magistratus*), elder brother and rival of the zealously anti-Roman Dumnorīx, ally of the HELVETII. In 61 BC he unsuccessfully asked the Roman Senate for aid against Ariovistus of the Germani. 'Diviciacus' gave the history of his desperate situation in a speech delivered in 58 BC to an assembly of Gaulish tribal leaders and Romans, as quoted by Caesar, who was present (*De Bello Gallico* 1.3.31). There had been two major tribal coalitions in Gaul: one led by the powerful AEDUI with numerous allied tribes and a second led by the ARVERNI. The balance shifted when the Arverni and the Sequani invited the Germani from east of the RHINE as paid allies. The Aedui were heavily defeated, forced to swear an oath declaring perpetual submission to the Sequani by giving them hostages and receiving none in return, and compelled not to seek assistance from their Roman allies. However, Dīviciācos himself was free to speak since he had neither taken the oath nor given hostages. Within a short period of time the Sequani had lost a third of their territory to the Germani from across the Rhine under the leadership

Dīviciācos of the Suessiones

Dīviciācos of the Suessiones ruled this tribal group of the BELGAE in north-east GAUL *c.* 100 BC. According to CAESAR (*De Bello Gallico* 2.4), there was still living memory of Diviciacus in the 50s BC to the effect that he had been the most powerful chief in Gaul and had also ruled in BRITAIN. While Caesar probably selected these details to provide a precedent for his own intended extension of the Roman conquest of Gaul into Britain, north-east Gaul and south-east Britain do resemble a single cultural province at the relevant period with regard to COINAGE and other features of high-status material culture of the ruling élite. We also have examples from a slightly later period of kings, tribes, and kingdoms astride the Channel, for example, Caesar's contemporary and inconstant ally, Commios of the Gaulish and British Atrebates.

South Belgic coinage inscribed DEIVICIAC is probably that of a later king of the same name. As well as DĪVICIĀCOS OF THE AEDUI, the name is also attested in INSCRIPTIONS from Lyon (LUGUDŪNON) as DIVICIAC[VS] (CIL 13, no. 2081) and Mainz (Moguntiācon) as genitive DIVICIACI. *Dīviciācos* is a Celtic masculine adjective used as a noun, probably based on the PROTO-CELTIC compound verb **di-wik-* reflected in Old Irish *di-fich-* 'fight back, avenge', Early Welsh *diwg*, thus meaning 'he who fights back, avenges'. Derivation from Celtic *dēvo-*, Gaulish *dīvo-* 'god' is less likely.

PRIMARY SOURCES
CAESAR, *De Bello Gallico* 2.4; CIL 13, no. 2081.

FURTHER READING
BELGAE; BRITAIN; COINAGE; DĪVICIĀCOS OF THE AEDUI; GAUL; INSCRIPTIONS; LUGUDŪNON; PROTO-CELTIC; Cunliffe, *Iron Age Communities in Britain*; D. Ellis Evans, *Gaulish Personal Names* 82–3.

JTK

Divination, the foretelling of the future, can be done by reading the signs of the unmanipulated environment, or by performing an action and interpreting the results. The DRUIDS were said to practise a variety of divination rituals, including a method that involved observing the death throes of a human SACRIFICE (DIODORUS SICULUS 5.31). Medieval Celtic narrative includes many descriptions of divinatory behaviour. The best known is the *tarbfeis* (see FEIS), found in SERGLIGE CON CULAINN ('The Wasting Sickness of Cú Chulainn') and TOGAIL BRUIDNE DA DERGA ('The Destruction of Da Derga's Hostel'), in which a dream of the future king follows eating the flesh of a white bull. The same tradition may be reflected in the Welsh Dream of Rhonabwy (BREUDDWYD RHONABWY), in which the protagonist falls asleep on an ox-hide and dreams of the glorious ARTHURIAN past.

Divination, often performed playfully, continues to the present day. Hallowe'en, weddings, and funerals are held to be especially propitious for foretelling future marriages or deaths, but most saints' days have been associated with weather omens, and every major festival includes divination traditions (see CALENDAR). In Wales (CYMRU), a man could identify a future sweetheart on St John's Eve by walking around a church, plunging a knife into the keyhole of the door and saying, 'Here is the knife, where is the sheath?' (Owen, *Welsh Folk Customs* 111). An Irish Candlemas custom was to light a candle for each member of the family, who would die in the order in which the candles burned out (Wilde, *Ancient Cures, Charms, and Usages of Ireland* 63).

For Celtic literary genres foretelling future events, particularly in the realms of politics and warfare, see PROPHECY.

FURTHER READING
ARTHURIAN; BREUDDWYD RHONABWY; CALENDAR; CYMRU; DIODORUS SICULUS; DRUIDS; FEIS; PROPHECY; SACRIFICE; SERGLIGE CON CULAINN; TOGAIL BRUIDNE DA DERGA; Griffith, *Early Vaticination in Welsh*; Owen, *Welsh Folk Customs*; Jane Francesca Wilde, *Ancient Cures, Charms, and Usages of Ireland*.

Victoria Simmons

Doire (**Derry/Londonderry**) is a district, county, and city on the river Foyle, about 6.5 km (4 miles) from Lough Foyle in Northern Ireland. Contemporary Irish annal notices concerning Derry begin in the 8th century, but the 7th-century *Vita Columbae* of ADOMNÁN indicates that Daire Calgaig was a significant landfall for travellers to and from Iona (EILEAN Ì); that place-name means 'the oak-wood of Calgach', and contains a personal name meaning 'swordsman' (cf. the Calgācus, who led the CALIDONES against AGRICOLA). This was the place later known as Daire Coluim Cille, i.e. modern Derry. It is thus possible that Daire Calgaig had been the site of a foundation by COLUM CILLE (St Columba) before his departure from Ireland (ÉRIU) to Iona in 563. While the ANNALS record a regular succession of monastic officials throughout the centuries, the main period of Derry's prominence was in the 12th century. Assisted by the political success of its royal patrons, the Mac Lochlainn dynasty, and by alliance with Irish church leadership in Armagh (ARD MHACHA), Derry supplanted KELLS (Ceanannas) as head of the Columban monastic *familia* c. 1150. These events are reflected in the composition of a new Irish-language version of the Life of the founder, which combined traditions from *Vita Columbae* with the assertion of Derry's preeminence among Colum Cille's churches. In 1613 a charter of James I granted rights to Derry to a number of London mercantile companies, resulting in the well-known name Londonderry, still favoured among Northern Ireland's Protestant community. The architecturally significant remains of the Renaissance walled town, with still impressive city fortifications, also date from this period. The partition of Ireland in 1920 placed the border between the city and part of its economic region, including Irish-speaking north Donegal (Tír Chonaill). Derry has figured importantly in the sectarian 'troubles' of 1968–94 and was the scene of such historical milestones as the Catholic civil rights march of 5 October 1968 and the 'Bloody Sunday' shootings of 30 January 1972, in which 13 unarmed demonstrators were killed by the British Parachute Regiment (another subsequently died) and twelve were wounded. In the 2001 census the city's population was approximately 84,000 and that of the traditional county (Contae Dhoire) around 233,500.

FURTHER READING
ADOMNÁN; AGRICOLA; ANNALS; ARD MHACHA; CALIDONES; COLUM CILLE; EILEAN Ì; ÉIRE; ÉRIU; KELLS; Herbert, *Iona, Kells, and Derry*; O'Brien, *Derry and Londonderry*; Lacey, *Colum Cille and the Columban Tradition* 81–91.

Máire Herbert

Domhnall Ó Duibhdábhoireann, Book of

(London, British Library, Egerton 88), is one of the most important medieval Irish legal manuscripts. It was written between 1564 and 1570 for the lawyer Domhnall mac Aodha Uí Dhuibhdábhoireann (O'Davoren), a member of the legal family of Cahermacnaghten, Co. Clare (Contae an Chláir). The manuscript was for the most part compiled at Park, at the Mac Aedhagáin legal school, in north-east Co. Galway (Contae na Gaillimhe). Typically for a law-book, the manuscript contains little ornamentation. The scribes of the manuscript frequently took turns at writing; since this work stretched over a length of time, significant changes in the penmanship of the individual scribes also occur. An authoritative analysis of the distribution of hands was recently published by W. O'Sullivan (*Celtica* 23.276–99). He demonstrated that, apart from the lawyer himself, a further 21 scribes were involved, several of whom were Domhnall's kinsmen. Identification of the names of most of these scribes was made possible by the numerous marginal notes in the manuscript, which also mention the time of their writing and include personal comments.

Several folios of the manuscript became detached during the 18th century, and they now comprise Copenhagen, Royal Library, Ny kgl. Saml. MS 261b, fos. 1–6 and Dublin, Royal Irish Academy MS 1243 (23 Q 6), fos. 33–52. The resulting diminished codex was one of the 191 manuscripts collected by the Irish scholar James Hardiman (*c.* 1790–1855) in the first quarter of the 19th century and purchased by the British Museum in 1832 from the bequest of Francis Henry Egerton, eighth earl of Bridgewater (1756–

Derry/Londonderry, Iona, Kells, and Armagh: modern county outlined in black, Northern Ireland border grey on white

1829). It reached its present location in such disarray that the Irish historian Eugene O'CURRY (1796–1862) was employed in 1849 to place the folios into the order in which they are presently bound.

The majority of texts in the manuscript are LAW TEXTS, for example, SENCHAS MÁR (The great tradition); these texts often consist of short extracted passages on a number of themes, complemented by a comprehensive commentary, rather than full editions. This suggests that Ó Duibhdábhoireann intended his book for practical use in his legal practice. Some literary texts were also included, including a dossier on the legendary Irish hero Cú Roí mac Dáiri, which indicates that Ó Duibhdábhoireann also had literary interests.

PRIMARY SOURCE

MS. London, BL, Egerton 88; Copenhagen, Royal Library, Ny kgl. Saml. 261b, fos. 1–6; Dublin, Royal Irish Academy 1243 (23 Q 6), fos. 33–52.
DESCRIPTION. British Museum, *Catalogue of Irish Manuscripts* 1.84–141.

FURTHER READING

CÚ ROÍ; IRISH; LAW TEXTS; O'CURRY; SENCHAS MÁR; Kelly, *Guide to Early Irish Law*; Ó Concheanainn, CMCS 16.1–40; O'Sullivan, *Celtica* 23.276–99; Smith, ZCP 19.111–16; Stern, ZCP 2.323–72; Stokes, ZCP 4.221–33.

PSH

Dòmhnall Ruadh Chorùna

(Donald MacDonald, 1887–1967), Gaeldom's foremost First World War poet, spent most of his life in his native North Uist (Uibhist mu Thuath). He composed over 60 songs, all to traditional airs and metres, the earliest and most famous of which date from his time in the trenches of France or the immediate post-war years. It is their complex, honest mix of emotions and their journalistic eye for detail which give these songs their power: veering from bravado to pathos, from humanity to savagery within the same piece, accepting the need for killing but bearing witness to the terrible waste, loyal to the regimental *esprit-de-corps*, but undeluded about the British ruling classes. *Òran Arras* (Song of Arras) is astonishing in its artistry, its English coda 'march at ease' reverberating from verse to verse with unresolved degrees of pathos and irony. Technically much more intricate, *Nam Bithinn Mar Eun* (If I were a bird) also shows originality when it interrupts its lyricism halfway with 'the stench of death' and ends on the chilling image of the gas mask. MacDonald's most popular song is his only romantic work, *An Eala Bhàn* (The white swan). Many of the post-war songs are on local themes of praise, social change or morality. Although there are notable flashes of humour, a strong philosophical note sounds throughout his work.

PRIMARY SOURCE

ED. & TRANS. Dòmhnallach, *Dòmhnall Ruadh Chorùna*.

FURTHER READING

SCOTTISH GAELIC POETRY; Black, *An Tuil* 739–41.

Michel Byrne

Domnall Brecc,

Welsh *Dyfnwal Frych*, was king of the Scottish DÁL RIATA (r. 629–† December 642) and grandson of AEDÁN MAC GABRÁIN. He was a major, though largely unsuccessful, military leader in both north BRITAIN and Ireland (ÉRIU) and came to figure importantly in early Irish, Hiberno-Latin, and Welsh literature. The defeat of Domnall Brecc in alliance with Congal Caech of ULAID by DOMNALL MAC AEDO in 637 was viewed in the LIBER DE VIRTUTIBUS SANCTI COLUMBAE (The book of miracles of St Colum Cille) of CUMMÉNE FIND as a decisive negative turning point for Dál Riata, after which it was dominated by 'foreigners', probably meaning the sons of ÆTHELFRITH, kings Oswald (†642) and OSWYDD (†670) of Northumbria. Domnall Brecc was killed at the battle of Srath Caruin (Strathcarron) in central Scotland (ALBA) by the Brythonic king, EUGEIN map Beli (grandson of Neithon). The event is described in a Welsh AWDL, versions of which occur in the hands of both scribes A and B of LLYFR ANEIRIN (B1.1 = A.78, translated below). Domnall Brecc's death, which is noted to the month in the ANNALS of Ulster, is the only closely datable event mentioned in the GODODDIN corpus.

> I saw an array that came from Kintyre,
> who brought themselves as a sacrifice to a
>   holocaust.
> I saw a second [array] who had come down
>   from their settlement,
> who had been roused by the grandson of
>   Neithon.
> I saw mighty men who came with dawn.
> And it was Dyfnwal Frych's head that
>   the crows gnawed.

Old Irish *Domnall*, Welsh *Dyfnwal*, is a Common Celtic compound name < **Dumno-ualos* 'world-wielder'. The epithet *Brecc/Brych* means 'freckled' or 'pock-marked'.

FURTHER READING

AEDÁN MAC GABRÁIN; ÆTHELFRITH; ALBA; ANNALS; AWDL; BRITAIN; COLUM CILLE; CUMMÉNE FIND; DÁL RIATA; DOMNALL MAC AEDO; ÉRIU; EUGEIN; GODODDIN; LIBER DE VIRTUTIBUS SANCTI COLUMBAE; LLYFR ANEIRIN; MAG ROTH; OSWALD; OSWYDD; ULAID; Marjorie O. Anderson, *Kings and Kingship in Early Scotland*; Bannerman, *Studies in the History of Dalriada*; Koch, *Gododdin of Aneirin*; Smyth, *Warlords and Holy Men*; Ann Williams et al., *Biographical Dictionary of Dark Age Britain* 102.

JTK

Domnall mac Aedo maic Ainmirech
(†642) was king of Tara (TEAMHAIR) and the first
ruler to be called *rex Hibernie* (king of Ireland) in
contemporary Irish ANNALS. He was a member of
the Northern Uí NÉILL dynasty, specifically its Cenél
Conaill branch. Thus, his hereditary lands were
situated in the northern province of Ulster, present-
day Co. Donegal in particular, and he was a close
relative of St COLUM CILLE and many of the other
early abbots of Iona (EILEAN Ì). In 637 Domnall
defeated the coalition of Congal Caech ('Congal the
One-eyed'), Cruithnean king of ULAID, and
DOMNALL BRECC of the Scottish DÁL RIATA at the
battle of MAG ROTH (Moira, Co. Down) (ADOMNÁN,
Vita Columbae 3.5; Byrne, *Irish Kings and High-Kings* 112–
13; Charles-Edwards & Kelly, *Bechbretha* 126–31; Sharpe,
Life of St Columba 359–60). Congal was killed at Mag
Roth. In this clash, the church of Iona sided with
their Gaelic kin (i.e. Domnall mac Aedo's party) over
their Gaelic neighbours and traditional patrons in Dál
Riata; we can infer this from the surviving fragment
of the LIBER DE VIRTUTIBUS SANCTI COLUMBAE of
Cumméne, seventh abbot of Iona (657–69), a Cenél
Conaill man himself. Congal Caech figures in the
Irish king-lists as *Rí Temro* (king of Tara) preceding
Domnall mac Aedo. Domnall's ascent thus represents
a decisive turning point, as a major loss of political
power for the CRUITHIN and Ulaid on the one hand,
and a major step towards the permanent consolidation
of the kingship of Tara by the Uí Néill on the other
as an incipient high-kingship of Ireland.

The next king to be given the title *rex Hibernie* in the
annals is Domnall mac Aedo's grandson, Loingsech mac
Oengusso, who died in 704. The latter was a witness to
CÁIN ADOMNÁIN ('Adomnán's Law') in 697, in which
his title is given in its Irish form (*Rí Érenn*). Domnall is
also styled *rex Scottorum* (king of the Scots, i.e. 'the Irish')
in a synchronistic poem that Ó Cróinín has argued to
be contemporary with Domnall's life (*Peritia* 2.79–80).
A 'Domnall' also occurs in the correct position in the
probably 7th-century list of kings of Tara in *Baile Chuind*
'CONN CÉTCHATHACH's Ecstasy' (ed. Murphy, *Ériu*
16.149). Yet, remarkably, neither of these Northern
Uí Néill overkings is described by their kinsman
Adomnán as high-kings, a status he reserves for
DIARMAIT MAC CERBAILL, AED SLÁINE, and
OSWALD. Instead, Domnall mac Aedo is called

merely *rex valde famosus* 'a very famous king' (*Vita
Columbae* 1.10; cf. Charles-Edwards & Kelly, *Bechbretha*
127f). One possible conclusion is that Adomnán
anticipated that some of his intended audience would
have rejected Iona's claims that Domnall and
Loingsech were national high-kings. On the name, see
DOMNALL BRECC; DOMNALL MAC AILPÍN.

FURTHER READING
ADOMNÁN; AED SLÁINE; ANNALS; CÁIN ADOMNÁIN; COLUM
CILLE; CONN CÉTCHATHACH; CRUITHIN; DÁL RIATA;
DIARMAIT MAC CERBAILL; DOMNALL BRECC; DOMNALL MAC
AILPÍN; EILEAN Ì; LIBER DE VIRTUTIBUS SANCTI COLUMBAE;
MAG ROTH; OSWALD; TEAMHAIR; UÍ NÉILL; ULAID; Alan O.
Anderson & Marjorie O. Anderson, *Adomnán's Life of Columba*;
Byrne, *Irish Kings and High-Kings*; Charles-Edwards & Kelly,
Bechbretha; Herbert, *Iona, Kells, and Derry*; Murphy, *Ériu* 16.145–
51; Ní Dhonnchadha, *Peritia* 1.178–215; Ó Cróinín, *Peritia* 2.74–
86; Sharpe, *Life of St Columba*.

JTK

Domnall mac Ailpín, known as Donald I King
of the SCOTS (r. 858–62), was the son of AILPÍN MAC
ECHACH and brother of CINAED MAC AILPÍN whom
he succeeded as king of the PICTS and Scots. It is often
assumed that he was the son of a Norse woman because
his dynasty came to power through the assistance of
Norsemen. He imposed the laws of DÁL RIATA on
the Picts as well as the Scots and is called king of the
Picts in the ANNALS of Ulster, thus reflecting the recent
domination of Pictland by his brother Cinaed.
Domnall mac Ailpín was probably assassinated in 862.
He is buried on Iona (EILEAN Ì). His name, the source
of the English name *Donald*, is Celtic and cognate with
Old Welsh and CUMBRIC *Dumngual*, all of which derive
from Celtic **Dumno-ualos*. *Domhnall* has been a common
man's name in Ireland (ÉIRE) and Scotland (ALBA) at
all historically documented periods.

FURTHER READING
AILPÍN MAC ECHACH; ALBA; ANNALS; CINAED MAC AILPÍN;
CUMBRIC; DÁL RIATA; EILEAN Ì; ÉIRE; PICTS; SCOTS; Alan O.
Anderson, *Early Sources of Scottish History AD 500 to 1286* 1.290–
2; Marjorie O. Anderson, *Kings and Kingship in Early Scotland*;
Smyth, *Warlords and Holy Men* 190–1.

PEB

Domnall mac Cusantín, known as Donald II
of Scotland (ALBA), ruled from 889 to 899. He was

the son of CUSANTÍN MAC CINAEDA (Constantine I of Scotland) and the grandson of CINAED MAC AILPÍN, the famous first Gaelic king of the PICTS and SCOTS. Domnall is the first historical ruler to be described as *Rí Alban* (king of Scotland) in the ANNALS of Ulster (in his death notice). His predecessors were referred to as 'kings of the Picts'. His reign is in this way a significant milestone in the emergence of the Scottish identity of north Britain. He has also been seen as a key figure in the incorporation of the old Brythonic kingdom of Strathclyde (YSTRAD CLUD)/CUMBRIA into Scotland. Domnall restored the rule of Cinaed mac Ailpín's dynasty over Alba. His possible rôle in banishing the native aristocracy from Strathclyde is suggested by records which show that some of them appear in GWYNEDD, north Wales (CYMRU), *c.* 890 and the native dynasty peters out at about that time. Domnall was also the ancestor of a new dynasty who came to power over Strathclyde/Cumbria and ruled there until the 11th century as sub-kings under the kings of Alba. During his reign, Alba lost the archipelago of Orkney (Arcaibh) to the Vikings under King Harold Fairhair of Norway, who also gained ground on the facing mainland in Caithness (Gallaibh) and attacked Dunottar Castle near Stonehaven (Caladh nan Clach /Sròn na h-Aibhne). Domnall died in 899 and was buried on Iona (EILEAN Ì). On the name, see DOMNALL BRECC; DOMNALL MAC AILPÍN.

FURTHER READING
ALBA; ANNALS; CINAED MAC AILPÍN; CUMBRIA; CUSANTÍN MAC CINAEDA; CYMRU; DOMNALL BRECC; DOMNALL MAC AILPÍN; EILEAN Ì; GWYNEDD; PICTS; SCOTS; YSTRAD CLUD; Alan O. Anderson, *Early Sources of Scottish History AD 500 to 1286* 1.395–6; Smyth, *Warlords and Holy Men* 216–17; Ann Williams et al., *Biographical Dictionary of Dark Age Britain* 103.

PEB

Domnonia (French *Domnonée*) is the name of an early Breton principality, whose rulers were viewed as kings (*reges*) by some Breton sources, but as counts (*comites*) by the Merovingian Franks. One of its best documented rulers and monastic founders is IUDIC-HAEL, who flourished in the first half of the 7th century. Although the exact extent of Domnonia is uncertain and probably varied over time, it comprised roughly the northern half of Brittany (BREIZH), i.e.

the regions which are now the Côtes-d'Armor (Aodoù-an-Arvor) and the northern parts of Finistère (Penn-ar-Bed). The name continues the tribal name *Dumnonii* (< Celtic *dubno-*/*dumno-* 'deep, the world'), who also gave their name to Devon (Welsh *Dyfnaint*) in England. Domnonia was probably settled, at least in part, from insular Dumnonia (see BRETON MIGRATIONS). It is likely that British and Armorican DUMNONIA functioned at times as a single sea-divided sub-Roman CIVITAS and then as an early medieval kingdom. Another British tribe and Romano-British *civitas*, the *Cornovii*, gave its name to south-west Brittany (Cornouaille /KERNEV), as well as to the territory west of Devon in England (Cornwall/KERNOW). Domnonia is mentioned in the Life of St UUINUUALOE 1.1 as 'a country notorious for its sacrileges, unlawful feastings and adulteries'. Unlike the long-lived Kernev, Domnonia was not significant in the political or diocesan divisions of Brittany after the early Middle Ages and thus parallels the early submergence of insular Dumnonia east of the river Tamar within Anglo-Saxon Wessex.

FURTHER READING
BREIZH; BRETON MIGRATIONS; CIVITAS; DUMNONIA; IUDIC-HAEL; KERNEV; KERNOW; UUINUUALOE; Balcou & Le Gallo, *Histoire littéraire et culturelle de la Bretagne* 1; Baring-Gould, *Book of Brittany*; Chédeville & Guillotel, *La Bretagne des saints et des rois, Ve–Xe siècle*; Giot et al., *British Settlement of Brittany*.

AM

Dôn figures as the ancestress of three central characters in the Middle Welsh tale known as MATH FAB MATHONWY or, alternatively, as the Fourth Branch of the MABINOGI—ARIANRHOD, Gilfaethwy, and GWYDION. In the early Welsh ARTHURIAN prose tale CULHWCH AC OLWEN, Dôn is named as the mother of the supernatural ploughman Amaethon mab Don (< *Ambaχtonos* 'ploughman-god') and the supernatural smith Gouannon mab Don (< *Gobannonos* 'smith-god'; see GOFANNON FAB DÔN). In the early 11th-century Breton Latin Life of St IUDIC-HAEL, the legendary poet TALIESIN also figures as the son of Dôn, *Taliosinus bardus filius Donis*; Taliesin is likewise connected with Dôn and other figures of the Fourth Branch in the mythological poem *Kadeir Kerrituen* (The chair of Ceridwen) in LLYFR TALIESIN. In the TRIADS (TYP no. 35), Arianrhod is once called the daughter of Beli;

therefore BELI MAWR had perhaps figured as Dôn's consort. The GENEALOGIES of the 'Hanesyn Hen' Tract contain a list of *Plant Don o Arvon*, which indicates that her progeny had come to be localized in north Wales (CYMRU) as in the Fourth Branch.

In many modern discussions of Celtic mythology, Dôn is linked with the eponym of the mythological race of early IRISH LITERATURE, Tuatha Dé Danann (see TUATH DÉ) and the goddess of the river DANUBE (see Gruffydd, BBCS 7.1–4). However, these equations are phonetically unworkable: a cognate of Middle Irish *Danu*, BRITISH **Donū* or **Danū* would necessarily give Welsh ***Dyn* or ***Dein*. The authenticity and antiquity of Middle Irish *Danu* itself has been questioned by Carey (*Éigse* 18.291–4). Carey has elsewhere offered an interpretation of *Math* as a pre-Christian creation myth (*Journal of the History of Religions* 31.24–37), which suggests another possible etymology for the name Dôn, i.e. that it is the cognate of Old Irish genitive, dative, and accusative singular *don* 'place, ground, earth', the cognate of Greek nominative *khthōn* χθών, genitive *khthonós* χθονός 'the earth'. (There is no surviving attestation of the expected Old Irish nominative **dú*.) Welsh *Dôn* occurs only as semantic genitive, mostly preceded immediately by *merch* 'daughter', *mab* 'son', or *plant* 'children'. Thus, *Plant Dôn* as 'Children of the Earth' would be parallel to a second great mythological family in the Mabinogi, namely the children of LLŶR; cf. Old Irish *ler*, genitive *lir* 'sea'. They would also be comparable to the Titans of Hesiod who were likewise 'children of the earth' and primeval beings of the mythical age. Such a name would originally have resonated meaningfully with the COMMON CELTIC word for 'human being', namely **(g)donios* (lit. 'earthling'), whence Irish *duine*, Welsh *dyn*, Breton *den*.

FURTHER READING
ARIANRHOD; ARTHURIAN; BELI MAWR; BRITISH; COMMON CELTIC; CULHWCH AC OLWEN; CYMRU; DANUBE; GENEALOGIES; GOFANNON FAB DÔN; GWYDION; IRISH; IRISH LITERATURE; IUDIC-HAEL; LLYFR TALIESIN; LLŶR; MABINOGI; MATH FAB MATHONWY; TALIESIN; TRIADS; TUATH DÉ; Bartrum, *Welsh Classical Dictionary* 204; Bromwich & Evans, *Culhwch and Olwen* 121–2; Carey, *Éigse* 18.291–4; Carey, *Journal of the History of Religions* 31.24–37; Gruffydd, BBCS 7.1–4; Gruffydd, *Math vab Mathonwy*; Hughes, *Math uab Mathonwy*; Koch, *Proc. Harvard Celtic Colloquium* 9.2–11.

JTK

Donnán, St (†617) is associated with the island of Eigg in the Small Isles off the western coast of Scotland (ALBA). Our historical knowledge of this saint is limited to the brief mention in the main hand of the ANNALS of Ulster (617.1), *combustio martirum Ega* 'the burning of the martyrs of Eigg', augmented by the later hand which adds 'the burning of Donnán of Eigg on the 17 April, with one hundred and fifty martyrs'. Various modern attempts to make this the early work of Vikings are highly fabulous: the culprits are more likely to have been local, perhaps unchristianized, secular powers. The ethnicity of Eigg (Pictish or Gaelic) prior to its monastic colonization is uncertain. The early 9th-century Martyrology of Tallaght preserves the names of 52 martyrs, including Donnán, which seems a more credible figure (Best & Lawlor, *Martyrology of Tallaght* 33). Two legends are preserved in the later notes to the Martyrology of OENGUS CÉILE DÉ. One explains that a rich woman, jealous of the land of Donnán and his monks, had brigands come and slaughter them; the other tells how COLUM CILLE refused to be Donnán's soul-friend because he would not be patron to people on their way to 'red martyrdom' (Stokes, *Félire Óengusso Céli Dé* 114–17). Another note, appended to both martyrologies, says that 'Stephen and Laurence and George . . . and all the martyrs of the world' were celebrated on Donnán's feast-day (Best & Lawlor 106–7; Stokes 114–15), and it may be that Donnán, as an actual Gaelic martyr, acquired a special interest. His kneecap is found in a strange relic-listing poem of, perhaps, the 8th century (Carney, *Celtica* 15.25–41).

Donnán's monastery was probably at the site of Kildonan on Eigg, from where there is an impressive collection of early medieval sculpture (Fisher, *Early Medieval Sculpture* 92–4). Eigg certainly continued as an active monastery into the 8th century, as shown by the obituaries of two ecclesiastical figures in the Annals of Ulster (725.7; 752.2). The cult of Donnán is fairly widely distributed throughout the Hebrides and down the west coast of Scotland as far as Wigtownshire (Watson, *History of the Celtic Place-Names of Scotland* 283, 165), and it may owe its popularity to the Scandinavian settlers of this region, later converted to Christianity and GAELIC speech, for whom the legend of a saint burned with his followers in a church may have stirred recollections of the life from which they had turned.

PRIMARY SOURCES
ED. & TRANS. Best & Lawlor, *Martyrology of Tallaght* 33, 106–7; Carney, *Celtica* 15.25–41 (*A maccucán, sruith in tíag*); Mac Airt & Mac Niocaill, *Annals of Ulster (to A.D. 1131)* 617.1, 725.7, 752.2; Stokes, *Félire Óengusso Céli Dé* 107, 114–17.

FURTHER READING
ALBA; ANNALS, COLUM CILLE; GAELIC; OENGUS CÉILE DÉ; Fisher, *Early Medieval Sculpture in the West Highlands and Islands* 92–4; A. D. S. Macdonald, *Scottish Archaeological Forum* 5.57–64; Sharpe, *Life of St Columba* 369–70; Smyth, *Warlords and Holy Men* 107–12; Watson, *History of the Celtic Place-Names of Scotland*.

Thomas Owen Clancy

Dorbbéne (†713) was an abbot of Iona (EILEAN Ì) and a scribe. The earliest manuscript of ADOMNÁN's *Vita Columbae* (Life of COLUM CILLE) contains a colophon noting that the scribe was one Dorbbéne. This is almost certainly the man who, according to the ANNALS of Ulster (713.5), became head of the monastery of Iona in June AD 713, and died five months later on Saturday, 28 October AD 713. His genealogy indicates that he was a descendant of the Cenél Conaill branch of the Northern UÍ NÉILL dynasty, and hence a distant cousin of Adomnán and Colum Cille. The peculiar wording of his obituary, with its description of his holding the *kathedra Iae* and its *primatus*, have led to some discussion about the meaning of these terms, and whether Dorbbéne was not also a bishop. This now seems less radical a suggestion than it would once have been, as episcopal holders of the Iona abbacy are gradually uncovered (Bourke, *Innes Review* 49.77–80; Bourke, *Innes Review* 51.68–71; Márkus, *Spes Scotorum* 115–38). Dorbbéne's succession interrupts the abbacy of DÚNCHAD, and it may be that it was in some way caught up with internal Iona politics concerning the dating of Easter (see EASTER CONTROVERSY), which remained unresolved until AD 716.

PRIMARY SOURCES
MS. Schaffhausen, Stadtbibliothek Generalia I.
ED. & TRANS. Alan O. Anderson & Marjorie O. Anderson, *Adomnán's Life of Columba*; Best & Lawlor, *Martyrology of Tallaght* 85; Mac Airt & Mac Niocaill, *Annals of Ulster (to A.D. 1131)* 713.5.

FURTHER READING
ADOMNÁN; ANNALS; COLUM CILLE; DÚNCHAD MAC CINN-FHAELAD; EASTER CONTROVERSY; EILEAN Ì; UÍ NÉILL; Bourke, *Innes Review* 49.77–80; Bourke, *Innes Review* 51.68–71; Harvey, *Celtica* 21.178–90, 22.48–63; Herbert, *Iona, Kells, and Derry* 58–9; Márkus, *Spes Scotorum* 115–38; Sharpe, *Life of St Columba* 75–6, 235–6, 378.

Thomas Owen Clancy

Douglas, Mona (1898–1987) was an influential cultural revivalist and a prolific collector of MANX MUSIC and dances, songs in the MANX language, and other Manx folk traditions (see FOLK-TALES). Childhood illnesses led to an unconventional upbringing which gave Mona Douglas a voracious appetite for poetry and literature. She began collecting folklore and music while still in her teens, and published her first collection of poetry in 1915. Her lifelong association with Celtic organizations began in 1917 when she was appointed Honorary Secretary of the Manx Society (Yn CHESHAGHT GHAILCKAGH) and admitted to GORSEDD BEIRDD YNYS PRYDAIN at the National Eisteddfod of Wales (EISTEDDFOD GENEDLAETHOL CYMRU). She worked in Wales (CYMRU) and in London during the 1920s, but returned to the Isle of Man (ELLAN VANNIN) in 1933. She combined farming with her post as a rural librarian, somehow finding time to write and publish poetry and articles on Manx traditional culture, and to collect and teach Manx music and dance. After her retirement she became a full-time journalist. She was the driving force in organizations such as Aeglagh Vannin (Manx youth), Ellynyn ny Gael (Manx arts) and in 1977 she revived the Manx traditional festival, Yn CHRUINNAGHT. In recognition of her work she received several honours and awards, including the Manannan Trophy (1972), presidencies of the Celtic Congress (see PAN-CELTICISM) and the Pan-Celtic Festival in Killarney (1980), first Manx delegate to the Welsh National Eisteddfod (1981), Member of the British Empire (1982), patron of the Manx Heritage Foundation (1986), and, posthumously, the Reih Bleiney Vanannan.

PRIMARY SOURCES
SELECTION OF MAIN WRITINGS
Manx Song and Maiden Song (1915); 'Folk-lore Notes, Lezayre', *Mannin* 7.416–18 (1916); *Twelve Manx Folk Songs* (1928–57); (with A. Foster) *Five Manx Folk Dances* (1936); 'Manx Folk Dances: their Notation and Revival', *Journal of the English Folk Dance and Song Society* 3.110–16 (1937); 'The Manx Dirk Dance as Ritual', *Journal of the International Folk Music Council* 9.31–3 (1957); '"A Chiel' Amang 'Em": Memories of a Collector on the Isle of Man', *Journal of the English Folk Dance and Song Society* 8.156–9 (1958); *Christian Tradition in Mannin* (1965);

This is Ellan Vannin (1965); *This is Ellan Vannin Again* (1966); *They Lived in Ellan Vannin* (1968); 'The Wise Woman', *Manninagh* 1 (1972); 'Hunting the Dance in Mann', *Manninagh* 3.38–41 (1973); *Folksongs of Britain and Ireland* 179–202 (1975); *Manx Folk-song, Folk Dance, Folklore* (1994).

FURTHER READING
CHESHAGHT GHAILCKAGH; CHRUINNAGHT; CYMRU; EISTEDDFOD GENEDLAETHOL CYMRU; ELLAN VANNIN; FOLK-TALES; GORSEDD BEIRDD YNYS PRYDAIN; MANX; MANX MUSIC; PAN-CELTICISM; Bazin, *Mona Douglas*; Giovannelli, *Exile on an Island*.

Fenella Bazin

Dragons are fictitious monsters, typically lizard-like or serpentine in appearance. Originating in mythic symbolism and narrative, they are also popular adversaries in legend and FOLK-TALES. Dragon beliefs are found across Eurasian cultures, including biblical tradition. Although most of the dragon words in the CELTIC LANGUAGES are borrowed (e.g. Old Irish *drauc* and Welsh *draig* from Latin *dracō*, itself borrowed from Greek δράκων *drákōn*), this does not necessarily mean that dragon lore was not long-established among the Celts, since these imports may have replaced tabooed native words. The ram-horned serpent on the Iron Age GUNDESTRUP CAULDRON is one of a number of fantastic images on ritual objects and other ornamented works that may be meant to be a dragon (see further ART, CELTIC-INFLUENCED [1]). Dragons have been interpreted as representing both elemental forces and the blockage of creative influences (hence the dragon who guards a treasure). In folk-tale and legend they may also function quite simply as a needed ordeal for the hero, and they have often become focuses of affection and local identity. Geographical features, such as Cnoc-na-Cnoimh (Hill of the worm) in Sutherland, might be explained as being the result of the dragon's activities or death struggles. Ritually quarrelling dragons are found in the traditions of both Wales (CYMRU)—in HISTORIA BRITTONUM and CYFRANC LLUDD A LLEFELYS—and early Ireland (ÉRIU), e.g. the swineherds of TÁIN BÓ CUAILNGE's *De Chophur in Dá Mucado* (Of the *cophur* of the two swineherds). More conventionally, a hero fought a dragon—folk-motif B11.11. The hero PEREDUR of ARTHURIAN romance encountered two treasure-guarding dragons, and the hero of the *Táin Bó Fraích* ('The Cattle Raid

of Froech') killed a water-dragon (*béist*, *míl*) in order to obtain some magic berries. Less successful was FINN MAC CUMAILL's son Dáire, who was swallowed by a dragon, but managed to cut himself (and the dragon's other victims) free. While several saints, including Armel, Beircheart, Carantoc, COLUM CILLE, Ciaran, PETROC, and SAMSON defeated dragon-like monsters, many dragon-slayers of local tradition—such as the lazy braggart Assipattle, who slew the Stoor Worm (Marwick, *Folkore of Orkney and Shetland* 139–44)—were farmers and labourers. Not all dragon imagery invoked evil. Dragon insignia were used in battle by the Celts of late antiquity and associated with qualities of leadership. The best-known legendary example is ARTHUR, who was provided by GEOFFREY OF MONMOUTH with dragon devices for his battle gear and a father named UTHR BENDRAGON. The DRAIG GOCH, a beloved national symbol of the Welsh, is quite different from the *gwiber* (from Latin *vipera* 'viper'), a snake that was transformed into a troublesome winged serpent after drinking the milk of a woman and eating consecrated bread (Owen, *Welsh Folk-lore* 349). But there were also Welsh serpents which attached themselves to families and brought good luck and wealth (Simpson, *British Dragons* 36). The teasing snapdragons used in local pageants were an English phenomenon, but Simpson detects a dragon-like nature to the famous hobby-horses of Minehead (Somerset) and Padstow (Cornwall) (*British Dragons* 114); the latter town was named after St Petroc. Dragons could also be employed as nursery bogeys to frighten children away from the dangerous pits and ponds where they were said to dwell.

FURTHER READING
ART, CELTIC-INFLUENCED [1]; ARTHUR; ARTHURIAN; CELTIC LANGUAGES; COLUM CILLE; CYFRANC LLUDD A LLEFELYS; CYMRU; DRAIG GOCH; ÉRIU; FINN MAC CUMAILL; FOLK-TALES; GEOFFREY OF MONMOUTH; GUNDESTRUP CAULDRON; HISTORIA BRITTONUM; PEREDUR; PETROC; SAMSON; TÁIN BÓ CUAILNGE; UTHR BENDRAGON; Campbell, *Celtic Dragon Myth*; Marwick, *Folklore of Orkney and Shetland*; Owen, *Welsh Folklore*; Simpson, *British Dragons*; Watkins, *How to Kill a Dragon*.

Victoria Simmons

The **Draig Goch** (Red Dragon) is the national symbol of Wales (CYMRU). Its four-legged, barb-tailed, winged image is found on the Welsh flag, as well as on

Welsh singer Shirley Bassey performing in a dress incorporating the Welsh flag

product labels, advertising, and tourist memorabilia. Dragons were already popular Roman and Germanic military emblems in late antiquity. The Welsh word *draig* (Middle Welsh *dreic*) is an early loanword (see DRAGONS), and GILDAS refers to MAELGWN as *insularis draco* (dragon of the isle), which might have been one of the king's honorific titles or a term of abuse from his critic. Early WELSH POETRY identifies dragons with the virtues of warriors and leaders. The red dragon appears as a symbol of Brythonic identity (in opposition to the Anglo-Saxon invaders) in the story of GWRTHEYRN's castle in the early 9th-century HISTORIA BRITTONUM, in which a red dragon defeats a white one, a motif repeated in the Middle Welsh prose tale CYFRANC LLUDD A LLEFELYS. GEOFFREY OF MONMOUTH closely associated ARTHUR with dragons, and by the mid-13th century the Norman kings were co-opting both traditions as emblems of their own Britishness. Lofmark suggests that it is only the rise of the cult of St George which kept the red dragon from becoming a national emblem of England. By the mid-15th century the sons of Owain Tudor were employing the red dragon as heraldic devices, and Henry Tudor used a red dragon on a green and white field as one of his battle standards at the Battle of Bosworth in 1485 (see TUDUR). After the Stuart unicorn supplanted the Tudor dragon, the latter became increasingly rare as a royal or national symbol of England or Great Britain. Neither was it used as an emblem by important Welsh families (Lofmark, *History of the Red Dragon* 72), but it remained important enough as a symbol of Wales to be chosen for the royal badge for Wales in 1807. It continued to represent the Welsh on various royal insignia and flags until 1959, when the present red dragon on a green and white field was established as the national flag of Wales. The Red Dragon remains a symbol for both militant Welshness and for the Wales of the tourist.

FURTHER READING
ARTHUR; CYFRANC LLUDD A LLEFELYS; CYMRU; DRAGONS; GEOFFREY OF MONMOUTH; GILDAS; GWRTHEYRN; HISTORIA BRITTONUM; MAELGWN; TUDUR; WELSH POETRY; Lofmark, *History of the Red Dragon*; Stephens, NCLW 620.

Victoria Simmons

Drest/Drust was the name of a king of the PICTS *c.* 724–9. The extant notices reflect a turbulent career, preoccupied with factional rivalry. According to the PICTISH KING-LIST, he ruled for five years, intermittently or jointly with his predecessor, NECHTON SON OF DERELEI. He probably compelled Nechton to retire to a monastery in 724, but was replaced by him again in 726 and, then, having overthrown Nechton for a second time, took him captive. Drest was driven out of Pictland by another rival, ELPIN, also in 726. He returned in 727, but was defeated by a fourth claimant, ONUIST son of Uurguist, who finally slew Drest in the battle of Druim

Derg Blathuug (the red ridge of 'Blathuug', site unknown) on 12 August 729, according to the ANNALS of Clonmacnoise.

Though Drest was a common Pictish name, it is this particular ruler who is sometimes identified as the historical basis of the Welsh legendary figure Drystan ap Tallwch, the figure on which the famous international legend of TRISTAN AND ISOLT (see also DRYSTAN AC ESYLLT) has been modelled. *Drust* is the form of the name found in texts which use Gaelic or Gaelicized spellings. *Drest* presumably reflects a native PICTISH or north BRYTHONIC pronunciation.

FURTHER READING
ANNALS; BRYTHONIC; DRYSTAN AC ESYLLT; ELPIN; NECHTON SON OF DERELEI; ONUIST; PICTISH; PICTISH KING-LIST; PICTS; TRISTAN AND ISOLT; Marjorie O. Anderson, *Kings and Kingship in Early Scotland* 173; Smyth, *Warlords and Holy Men* 73–4.

PEB

Drest/Drust son of Donuel, king of the PICTS c. 663–72, succeeded his brother Gartnait in 663. It is unclear whether their father, given as *Donuel* in the PICTISH KING-LIST and as *Domnall* in contemp-orary Irish ANNALS, was DOMNALL BRECC of DÁL RIATA. The two brothers paid tribute to OSWYDD of Northumbria, and rebelled against the Northumbrians after Oswydd's death in 670. According to the Annals of Tigernach, Oswydd's son ECGFRITH subdued the Picts and expelled Drest in 672. There is a slight discrepancy concerning the length of Drest's reign: the Pictish king-list records a six- or seven-year reign, whereas the contemporary annals give eight to nine years. The name *Drest*, also spelled *Drust, Drost*, was common among the Pictish rulers, as was its diminutive *Drustan* or *Drosten*. Forms of the latter were widespread in the Celtic countries during the early Middle Ages (see further DRYSTAN AC ESYLLT). His father's name *Donuel* is Celtic and possibly specifically the PICTISH form cognate with Old Irish *Domnall*, Old Welsh and Cumbric *Dumngual*, all from Celtic **Dumno-ualos*. *Donuel* might be an inflected genitive form of the Pictish nominative **Donual*, thus corresponding exactly to Old Irish *Domnaill*. On the common Gaelic name *Domhnall*, see further DOMNALL BRECC; DOMNALL MAC AILPÍN.

FURTHER READING
ALBA; ANNALS; CUMBRIC; DÁL RIATA; DOMNALL BRECC; DOMNALL MAC AILPÍN; DRYSTAN AC ESYLLT; ECGFRITH; ÉRIU; OSWYDD; PICTISH; PICTISH KING-LIST; PICTS; Marjorie O. Anderson, *Kings and Kingship in Early Scotland* 172; Smyth, *Warlords and Holy Men* 62, 70.

PEB

druids [1] accounts from the classical authors

§1. INTRODUCTION

We have no written accounts by the pre-Christian druids describing their own beliefs or system of learning. It is highly unlikely that any such texts ever existed in GAUL and improbable likewise for the rest of the pre-Christian Celtic world, in the light of what CAESAR said (*De Bello Gallico* 6.14; see also LITERACY §2):

> [The druids] are said to commit to memory a great number of verses. And they remain some 20 years in training. Nor do they judge it to be allowed to entrust these things to writing, although in nearly the rest of their affairs, and public and private transactions, Greek letters are used. It seems to me there are two reasons this has been established: neither do they wish the common people to pride themselves in the training nor those who learn to rely less on memory, since it happens to a large extent that individuals give up diligence in memory and thorough learning through the help of writing.

Thus, the classical sources have special value as the only literary evidence for the druidical order and its beliefs from a period when pagan Celtic religion was alive. For an overview of this material, see GREEK AND ROMAN ACCOUNTS (§10). By contrast, the druids of early Irish and Welsh literature are a marginal and largely fictional presence.

§2. DRUIDS AS PHILOSOPHERS

What is perhaps the oldest instance of this idea was ascribed to ARISTOTLE (see entry) by Diogenes Laertius, included in a list of classes of learned sages among other barbarian (i.e. non-Graeco-Roman) peoples. A similar list is given by Dion Chrysostom (*Orations* 49), who goes on to maintain that druids wielded great power over Celtic kings.

The druids figure as one within a three-fold distinction of Celtic men of learning in DIODORUS

SICULUS (5.31), probably deriving from POSIDONIUS:

> They have lyric poets called bards, who, accom-panied by instruments resembling lyres, sing both praise and satire. They have highly honoured philosophers and theologians [those who speak about the gods] called druids. They also make use of seers, who are greatly respected.

Also drawing on Posidonius, STRABO (4.4.4) gives a version of the same formulation:

> As a rule, among all the Gallic peoples three sets of men are honoured above all others: the bards, the *vātes*, and the druids. The bards are singers and poets, the *vātes* overseers of sacred rites and philosophers of nature, and the druids, besides being natural philosophers, practice moral philosophy as well.

The 4th-century Roman historian Ammianus Marcellinus (15.9.8) repeats this threefold division.

That the philosophy of the druids was specifically akin to that of Greek Pythagoras (recognized for an emphasis on mathematical patterns and a belief in RE-INCARNATION) is stated by Hippolytus (*Philosophumena* 1.25), Clement of Alexandria (*Stromata* 1.15.70.), and Valerius Maximus (2.6.10).

§3. DRUIDIC AFTERLIFE BELIEFS

See REINCARNATION; GREEK AND ROMAN ACCOUNTS §§10, 12. LUCAN (*Pharsalia* 1.450–58) tells specifically of a druidic doctrine of an afterlife in an OTHERWORLD.

§4. DRUIDIC SCIENCE AND NATURAL MAGIC

The idea that the druids maintained the Celtic CALENDAR and understood the workings of the cosmos is widespread amongst the classical writers, thus Pomponius Mela (*De Situ Orbis* 3.2.18–19):

> [The druids] claim to know the size of the earth and cosmos, the movements of the heavens and stars, and the will of the gods. They teach, in caves or hidden groves, many things to the nobles in a course of instruction lasting up to twenty years.

A number of details occur uniquely in the *Natural History* of PLINY—druidical beliefs regarding medicinal plants, their uses, and various harvesting rituals, including the great reverence for mistletoe and the oak trees on which it grew and the elaborate rite in gathering it:

> . . . they lead forward two white bulls with horns bound for the first time. A priest in white clothing climbs the tree and cuts the mistletoe with a golden sickle, and it is caught in a white cloak. They then sacrifice the bulls while praying that the god will grant the gift of prosperity to those to whom he has given it. They believe that mistletoe, when taken in a drink, will restore fertility to barren animals, and is a remedy for all poisons. (*Natural History* 16.24)

There is also the curious description of an egg-like object, called an *anguinum*, made from the venom of snakes, reminiscent of the *mân macal* or *glain y neidr* (jewel of the snake) of Welsh folk tradition: 'The Druids value it highly: it is praised as insuring success in litigation and in going to audiences with kings' (*Natural History* 29.52).

§5. DRUIDS AS JUDGES

Caesar (*De Bello Gallico* 6.16) emphasizes the judicial function of the druids and interestingly states that execution of criminals and sacrifice of captives were functionally interchangeable in that both were believed to please the gods. DĪVICIĀCOS OF THE AEDUI was both a *vergobretos* or supreme tribal magistrate and a druid.

§6. DRUIDS AS PROPHETS

This is a recurrent theme, and there are specific anec-dotes recorded by Lampridius (*Alexander Severus* 59.5) and Vopiscus (*Numerianus* 14; *Aurelianus* 63.4.5), which seemingly confirm druidical foresight with the sub-sequent history of the Roman Empire; see PROPHECY, cf. DĪVICIĀCOS OF THE AEDUI.

§7. DRUIDS AS HISTORIANS

On the druidic doctrine of the origins of the peoples of Gaul preserved by Ammianus Marcellinus (15.9), see LEGENDARY HISTORY §2 (cf. BELGAE; FLOOD LEGENDS). Another origin legend ascribed to the druids is that the Gauls were all descended from the god corresponding to the Roman DĪS PATER, god of death and the underworld, according to Caesar (*De Bello Gallico* 6.18).

§8. THE STATUS OF THE DRUIDS

According to Caesar, the status of the druids was

comparable to that of the *equites* of Gaul. We may take the latter to mean approximately 'warrior aristocracy':

> The Druids retire from war nor are they accustomed to any taxes. They have immunity from military service and are exempt from all lawsuits. (*De Bello Gallico* 6.14)

The picture of an élite status, free from the usual obligations and limitations of a Gaulish tribesman, is further enhanced by Caesar's description of their annual assembly, implying a nascent national learned and judicial class which transcended tribal divisions:

> At a certain time of the year they sit down in a con-secrated place in the territory of the Carnutes [around modern Chartres, France], which region is believed to be the centre of all Gaul. To this place all come from everywhere who have disputes and the Druids bring forth their resolutions and decisions. (*De Bello Gallico* 6.13)

Both the high honour and extra-tribal status of the druids is illustrated by the following account recorded by Diodorus (5.31):

> Often when two armies have come together with swords drawn these men [the druids and bards] have stepped between the battle-lines and stopped the conflict, as if they held wild animals spellbound. Thus, even among the most brutal barbarians, angry passion yields to wisdom and Ares stands in awe of the Muses.

Explaining that the druids were considered the best of men, Strabo (4.4.4) gives much the same account; the common source is probably Posidonius.

§9. ROMAN REPRESSION OF DRUIDISM

According to Strabo (4.4.5), the Romans put an end to human SACRIFICE by the druids of Gaul. The sources are consistent in portraying the druids as taking part in sacrifice of all sorts (e.g. Diodorus Siculus 5.31), much of it described as inhumane in terms meant to shock readers and thus justify repression. Unspecified general repression of druidism occurred in Gaul under the emperors Augustus (r. 30 BC–AD 14) and Claudius (r. AD 41–54), according to Suetonius (AD 69–c. 140; *Claudius* 25).

§10. DRUIDS IN BRITAIN

According to Caesar (*De Bello Gallico* 6.13):

> It is believed the training for druids was discovered in Britain and from there it was transferred into Gaul. And now those who wish to learn the matter carefully depart for Britain for the sake of learning.

This passage has given some writers reason to believe that druidism might have been a pre-Celtic religion which later spread from the Atlantic periphery to the Continental heartland of the ancient Celtic world, but this statement was probably at least partly motivated by Caesar's wish to justify an extension of the Roman invasion of Gaul into Britain. In the next century the British druids of Anglesey (MÔN) were perceived by the Romans as an anti-Roman unifying force and were accordingly targeted; cf. also BOUDĪCA; CARATĀCOS. The storming of Anglesey in AD 60 is vividly described by TACITUS (*Annals* 14.30):

> Women in black clothing like that of the Furies ran between the ranks. Wild-haired, they brandished torches. Around them, the druids, lifting their hands upwards towards the sky to make frightening curses, frightened [the Roman] soldiers with this extraordinary sight. And so [the Romans] stood motionless . . . Then their commander exhorted them and they urged one another not to quake before an army of women and fanatics. They carried the ensigns forward, struck down all resistance . . . After that, a garrison was imposed on the vanquished and destroyed their groves, places of savage superstition. For they considered it their duty to spread their altars with the gore of captives and to communicate with their deities through human entrails.

§11. DRUIDS IN GALATIA

Although there is no direct documentary evidence, the related etymologies of the name of the Galatian tribal meeting-place *Drunemeton* [see NEMETON] and *druid* (see DRUIDS [2]), as well as the similarity of the Dru-nemeton and Carnutian assemblies and the judicial function of the Galatian tetrarchs, has led some modern writers to infer the presence of the order there; see GALATIA.

PRIMARY SOURCES
CAESAR, *De Bello Gallico*; DIODORUS SICULUS, *Historical Library*; PLINY, *Natural History*; Pomponius Mela, *De Situ Orbis*;

STRABO; TACITUS, *Annals*.

TRANS. Koch & Carey, *Celtic Heroic Age* 5–50.

FURTHER READING

ARISTOTLE; BELGAE; BOUDĪCA; CALENDAR; CARATĀCOS; DĪS PATER; DIVICIĀCOS OF THE AEDUI; DRUIDS [2]; FLOOD LEGENDS; GALATIA; GAUL; GREEK AND ROMAN ACCOUNTS; LEGENDARY HISTORY; LITERACY; LUCAN; MÔN; NEMETON; OTHERWORLD; POSIDONIUS; PROPHECY; REINCARNATION; SACRIFICE; Nora K. Chadwick, *Druids*; De Vries, *La religion des Celtes*; Kendrick, *Druids*; Mac Cana, *Celtic Mythology*; Piggott, *Druids*; Rankin, *Celts and the Classical World*; Rankin, *Celtic World* 21–33; Ross, *Celtic World* 423–44; Tierney, PRIA C 60.189–275; Zwicker, *Fontes Historiae Religionis Celticae*.

JTK

druids [2] romantic images of

The largest body of images of druids has come from Britain, and seminal to it was the engraving published in Aylett Sammes's *Britannia Antiqua Illustrata, or, The Antiquities of Ancient Britain* (1676). The picture was formed by a process of conflating classical descriptions and archaeological finds with extant iconographies of appropriate other types (such as wild men and holy men), who lent themselves to be reinterpreted as druids. Thus, Conrad Celtes's description of carvings found at the Fichtelberg in Saxony, Germany, recycled by John Selden in *Jani Anglorum Facies Altera* (1610), were grafted onto depictions of wild men, green men, and Christian hermits. Descriptions of pageants and theatricals in England make it clear that the visual representation of the WILD MAN or Ancient Briton was well established in the 16th century, and one of the earliest surviving images specifically identified as a druid, a design by Inigo Jones for Lodowick Carlell's *The Passionate Lovers* (1638), emanates from this performance tradition. Visualizations of Christian hermits, such as that engraved after Marten de Vos for *Solitudo, sive vitae Patrum Eremicolarum* (Solitude, or lives of the hermit fathers; 1594) seem to have been particularly influential, but Continental imaging of the druid himself was generally savage, as in the title-page of Schedius's *De Dis Germanis* (On the German gods; 1648). However, for English speakers, the location of the archetypical druid in Anglesey (MÔN), Wales, by Henry Rowlands in *Mona Antiqua Restaurata* (Ancient Mona restored; 723) had the most important consequences. Rowlands' image, though dependent on that published by Sammes, removed the druid's book with its Christian resonance and replaced it with an oak branch as a symbol of ancient and internalized wisdom—a shift of meaning to which Rowlands was presumably sensitized by his familiarity with the oral tradition of WELSH POETRY.

Subsequent imaging of druids, especially in the hands of Romantics, centred on concepts of ancient BRITAIN, and in particular of Wales (CYMRU), whose poetic and musical tradition came to be regarded as a living archaeology of the more benign aspects of druidical behaviour. Thomas Gray's poem 'The Last Bard' (1757) was based on mythical events in the 13th century, but in the flood of visual images that it released the bard was distinguished from the druid only by the addition of a HARP. Images of druid-bards continued from Thomas Jones's version of 1774 to that of John Martin in 1817.

William Blake's idiosyncratic visualizations of druidism emanated from a complex and highly personal theology. On the other hand, more widely distributed printed images—notably De Loutherbourg's *The Last Bard* (1784), and the sartorial splendour of Meyrick and Smith's return to the 'scientific' study of the subject, *The Costume of the Original Inhabitants of the Islands of Britain* (1815)—stimulated the production of a plethora of kitsch objects. The escape of the druid from intellectual to popular culture was most publicly manifested in 'Druid Inn' pub signs, the most notable of which is at Pontypridd in south Wales—the successor to the local hostelry of Dr William Price (1800–93), the celebrity of whose druidical costume had an appropriate outcome in his influence on the promotion of cremation as a self-conscious break with Christian funerary customs.

The more anti-social aspects of druidical behaviour presented a difficulty for 19th-century English society with its self-image of the world's exemplar of Christian virtues. The continued fascination with the subject was therefore focused on imaging the first contacts between Christian missionaries and disgruntled pagans. The most celebrated of this pious genre was Holman Hunt's *A Converted British Family Sheltering a Christian Priest from the Persecution of the Druids* (1850), but the moral and political potential of the subject had been realized earlier in the commission to Vincent Waldré to paint *St Patrick Lighting the Paschal Fire on the Hill of Slane* for Dublin Castle (see BAILE ÁTHA CLIATH), the home of the Anglicized

ASCENDANCY. The picture was appropriately completed at about the time of the ACT OF UNION of 1800. Exploiting political potential in the opposite direction, Bellini's opera *Norma* (1831), set in GAUL, seemed to encourage ideas of national resurgency and provided splendid opportunities for druidical design in productions all over Europe and the United States.

The theatricality of the druid has provided a recurrent context for his imaging. The work of Iolo Morganwg (Edward WILLIAMS), familiar to William Blake, provided the source for the on-going *gorseddic* pageants of the Celtic nations. Though a forced marriage, the union of Iolo's GORSEDD BEIRDD YNYS PRYDAIN with the EISTEDDFOD movement in Wales in 1819 was a success. In the regalia and robes designed by the Bavarian-born Hubert von Herkomer and the Welsh sculptor William Goscombe John (1860–1952), the archdruid Hwfa Môn (Rowland Williams, 1823–1905) became a living art object and icon.

FURTHER READING
ACT OF UNION; ASCENDANCY; BAILE ÁTHA CLIATH; BRITAIN; CHRISTIANITY; CYMRU; EISTEDDFOD; EISTEDDFOD GENEDLAETHOL CYMRU; GAUL; GORSEDD BEIRDD YNYS PRYDAIN; HARP; MÔN; WELSH POETRY; WILD MAN; WILLIAMS; Lord, *Imaging the Nation*; Piggott, *Druids*; Smiles, *Image of Antiquity* 75–111.

Peter Lord

Welsh Archdruid Hwfa Môn in the habit designed by Sir Hubert von Herkomer (c. 1895)

druids [3] the word

The oldest attestation of the word can be found in Latin *druides* (pl.), which is probably a loan from GAULISH. It is also found in Old Irish *druí* and early Welsh *dryw* (LLYFR TALIESIN, in a copy of the Middle WELSH period of a poem of Old Welsh date). All these forms are derived from PROTO-CELTIC **dru-wid-s*, pl. **druwides* 'oak-knower', as PLINY the Elder had already noted. The Old English word *drȳ* for a magician or wizard is a borrowing from Celtic (it is uncertain whether it was borrowed from IRISH or BRYTHONIC).

§1. DRUID = WREN

Both Irish *druí* and Welsh *dryw* could also be used to signify the wren. Besides these, we find BRETON *drew* 'merry, cheerful' (derived from 'wren') and Middle Irish *dreän* 'wren'. At first sight, it would seem strange that the word for wren could be the same etymologically as the word for druid, but, in fact, the wren was one of the prophetic birds, along with the raven, according to both Irish and Welsh tradition.

§2. FURTHER BRYTHONIC FORMS

Middle and Modern Welsh *derwydd* (also attested in texts of Old Welsh date such as ARMES PRYDEIN) and Old Breton *dorguid* (or *darguid*) seem to reflect an analogical reformation of inherited Proto-Celtic **dru-wid-* to **daru-wid-*, so that the form now contains a form of the word for 'oak' more recognizable in BRITISH, as in Welsh *dâr* 'oak tree' < **daru-*. Alternatively, the reformation could have been based on the stem form **deru-* that is found in Old Welsh *deruen(n)*, Modern *derwen* 'oak tree', also in the ROMANO-BRITISH place-name *Deruentio* and Old Irish *derucc* 'acorn' (< Proto-Celtic **deru-knut-* 'oak-nut'), or with the **doru-* that is very well attested outside Celtic (e.g. Greek δόρυ *dóry* 'tree trunk, wood' and Vedic Sanskrit *dắru-*). In other words, the reformation was based on a popular understanding of the correct etymology.

RELATED ARTICLES
ARMES PRYDEIN; BRETON; BRITISH; BRYTHONIC; GAULISH; IRISH; LLYFR TALIESIN; PLINY; PROTO-CELTIC; ROMANO-BRITISH; WELSH.

CW

Drunkenness

Drunkenness as the result of consumption of alcohol is a common phenomenon the world over, but the Celts have been stereotyped as excessively prone to drunkenness from classical to modern times. The Celtic stereotype in GREEK AND ROMAN ACCOUNTS was founded on ancient perceptions of the Barbarian 'other' (that is, 'people unlike ourselves' from the writers' point of view), and accounts of drunkenness are not necessarily based on authentic observations of Celtic behaviour, although alcohol was certainly consumed in quantity on festive occasions (see FOODWAYS; WINE).

Alcohol was a standard feature of a FEAST, and many literary narratives were propelled by the excessive consumption of alcohol. The ULSTER CYCLE tale MESCA ULAD ('The Intoxication of the Ulstermen') recounts CÚ CHULAINN's journey with his companions across the breadth of Ireland (ÉRIU) on account of his drunkenness. Although this tale is comic, the magnitude of the journey and the changes wrought on Ireland's topography can also be read as mythic. The figure of MEDB may be another aspect of the cosmic importance of drunkenness; her name (Celtic *medwā 'intoxicating' f.) is cognate with Welsh meddw and Breton mezv, both of which mean 'drunk, intoxicated' and are also cognate with English mead. Her name may reflect a rôle derived from the SOVEREIGNTY MYTH—a goddess whose prerogatives included the distribution of alcohol. In a Christian context, this can be seen reflected in the figure of Saint BRIGIT, whose miracles involve the production of ale.

The capacity and opportunity to drink large quantities of alcohol are seen as heroic. For example, much of the GODODDIN, an early Welsh poem, is devoted to the glories of the mead-feasts for the year prior to the battle. The chieftain's hospitality and ability to provide his warriors with enough alcohol to keep them pleasantly drunk for a year was seen as a testament to his worthiness as a leader.

The tradition also contains humorous and negative references to drinking. In the Welsh dialogue *Selyf a Marcholffus*, Marcholffus describes his wife's pedigree, including:

Tromddiod oedd vam Medd-dod,
Medd-dod oedd vam Meddw,
Meddw oedd vam Meddwen,
Meddwen oedd vam Meddwach,
Meddwach oedd vam Meddwaf oll.

Heavy drinking was Drunkenness's mother,
Drunkenness was Drunk's mother,
Drunk was Drunken Maiden's mother,
Drunken Maiden was the mother of Drunker,
Drunker was the mother of Drunkest of all).

FURTHER READING
BRIGIT; CÚ CHULAINN; ÉRIU; FEAST; FOODWAYS; GODODDIN; GREEK AND ROMAN ACCOUNTS; MEDB; MESCA ULAD; SOVEREIGNTY MYTH; ULSTER CYCLE; WINE; Gantz, *Early Irish Myths and Sagas*; Jarman, *Aneirin*; Lewis, BBCS 6.314–23; Mac Cana, *Celtic Mythology*.

AM

Drystan ac Esyllt

The famous international tragic medieval love story of TRISTAN AND ISOLT is covered in a separate article. This entry treats Welsh versions of the tale, its Celtic origins and affinities.

§1. WELSH VERSIONS

There is no complete and coherent medieval Celtic version of the Tristan story. The Welsh Tristan fragments comprise: (1) a poem or fragments of two poems in LLYFR DU CAERFYRDDIN (Jarman, 74); (2) allusions in the Welsh triads to the three characters of the triangle—Drystan (Bromwich, TYP nos. 19, 21, 26, 41, 71, 72, 73, 80), Esyllt (nos. 26, 71, 80), and March (nos. 14, 26, 71, 73); (3) allusions by poets to Drystan and Esyllt, beginning with the GOGYNFEIRDD of the 13th century and more commonly by the CYWYDDWYR of the 14th to the 16th century; (4) *Ystorya Trystan* (The tale of Tristan), a mixed prose-verse text which occurs only in 16th- to 18th-century manuscripts (Bromwich, *Arthur of the Welsh* 209). In her edition of these poem(s), BROMWICH's discussion underscores the uncertainty of the relationship of the text to the Tristan story, despite containing the names *D(i)ristan* and *March*. As to the date of the original, she draws attention to the retention of the verbal noun ending *-if* (proved by internal rhyme). This form was already shortened to *-i* in the Old Welsh COMPUTUS Fragment of the late 9th to the mid-10th century, and therefore this poem is likely to be of Old WELSH date.

Newly discovered texts of *Ystorya Trystan* have been edited by Rowland and Thomas (NLWJ MS 22.241–53). A separate history and authorship for the prose and verse portions are likely, and sharp differences distinguish these Welsh versions from the Continental Tristan romances (Rowland, *Early Welsh Saga Poetry* 252–4).

§2. CELTIC ORIGINS AND AFFINITIES

Celtic origin of the Tristan story is not in doubt, as confirmed by the fact that the principal characters of the love triangle (Drystan, Esyllt, and March, in their Welsh forms) bear names of Celtic, specifically BRYTHONIC, origin (Bromwich, *Arthur of the Welsh* 209). However, a different sort of Celtic origin—Pictish-plus-Old Irish—is also widely accepted (Bromwich, THSC 1953.32–60; Newstead, *Arthurian Literature in the Middle Ages* 122–33; Pearce, *Folklore* 85.145–63). It is possible that the story circulated in the Celtic world and accumulated local elements, in Pictland and Cornwall, for example, perhaps assimilating characters to local heroes with similar names. The Pictish/Irish-origin theory rests mainly on the recurrence of the names *Drust(an)* and *Talorg(en)* in the PICTISH KING-LIST (see also DREST; Marjorie O. Anderson, *Kings and Kingship in Early Scotland*) and the similarity between this love triangle and certain Irish tales, chiefly TÓRUIGHEACHT DHIARMADA AGUS GHRÁINNE ('The Pursuit of Diarmaid and Gráinne'). The PICTISH name *Drust(~)* is the cognate of Welsh *Drystan* (later *Tristan* in the romances). Pictish *Talorg(~)*, *Talorc-* has been taken as similar to *Tallwch*, Drystan's father's name in the Welsh sources. The difficulties with taking these names to be a decisive parallel are that nothing similar to *Talorc/Tallwch* occurs in the Continental or English versions of the story and that Pictish *Talorc* and Welsh *Tallwch*, though similar, are not exact cognates. *Talorc* would probably have been understood as a compound meaning 'Pig-brow', although the actual etymology is unclear, and *Tallwch* as Welsh *tâl* 'brow' + *hwch* 'swine, sow'. As Drystan son of Tallwch appears in the Welsh TRIADS as one of

the 'Three Powerful Swineherds', where he is connected with ARTHUR (Bromwich, TYP 44–8), an underlying Pictish dynastic tale is not necessary to explain the unique name *Tal-hwch*. The comparable Irish love story of Diarmaid and Gráinne does not appear as a written text until the Early Modern IRISH period and therefore would be too late to be the source of the Tristan tales. The reverse relationship is possible, i.e. deriving *Tóruigheacht Dhiarmada agus Ghráinne* from the Brythonic tale, at least partly (Bromwich, *Arthur of the Welsh* 222–3). A second Irish parallel involves a monster-slaying episode in TOCHMARC EMIRE ('The Wooing of Emer') in the ULSTER CYCLE. Although *Tochmarc Emire* is early enough, the episode has no echoes in the Welsh Tristan material.

The Cornish connections of the Tristan story seem to have more in their favour than the Pictish theory (Padel, CMCS 1.53–82). Key points in the case for a Cornish Tristan include the 5th- to 7th-century inscribed memorial to DRVSTA(N)VS CVNOMORI FILIVS 'Drystan son of CUNOMOR' (Fleuriot, *Histoire littéraire et culturelle de la Bretagne* 1.127–9), near the locale of the tale in Béroul's 12th-century French version of the romance at Castle Dore (cf. ARTHURIAN SITES), and the Old CORNISH place-name *Hryt Eselt* (Isold's ford) in a 10th- or 11th-century Anglo-Saxon charter, probably reflecting an older form of one of the two episodes set at fords in Béroul's version. Béroul's Tristan geography, Lantien (now Castle Dore), was a pre-Roman IRON AGE site and therefore could not possibly have been the actual stronghold of a historical Dark Age Marc Cunomor (Padel, *Arthur of the Welsh* 240–3).

PRIMARY SOURCES

EDITIONS. Cross, *Studies in Philology* 17.98–110; Jarman, *Llyfr Du Caerfyrddin* 74; E. D. Jones, BBCS 13.25–7; Rowland & Thomas, NLWJ 22.241–53; Ifor Williams, BBCS 5.115–29. ED. & TRANS. Bromwich, SC 14/15.54–69. TRANS. Thomson, *Tristan Legend* 1–5.

FURTHER READING

ARTHUR; ARTHURIAN; ARTHURIAN SITES; BROMWICH; BRYTHONIC; COMPUTUS; CORNISH; CUNOMOR; CYWYDDWYR; DREST; GOGYNFEIRDD; IRISH; IRON AGE; KERNOW; LLYFR DU CAERFYRDDIN; PICTISH; PICTISH KING-LIST; TOCHMARC EMIRE; TÓRUIGHEACHT DHIARMADA AGUS GHRÁINNE; TRIADS; TRISTAN AND ISOLT; ULSTER CYCLE; WELSH; Marjorie O. Anderson, *Kings and Kingship in Early Scotland*; Bromwich, *Arthur of the Welsh* 209–28; Bromwich, THSC 1953.32–60; Fleuriot, *Histoire littéraire et culturelle de la Bretagne* 1.127–9; Newstead, *Arthurian Literature in the Middle Ages* 122–33; Padel, *Arthur of the Welsh* 229–48; Padel, CMCS 1.53–82; Pearce, *Folklore* 85.145–63; Rowland,

Early Welsh Saga Poetry 252–4; Sterckx, *Bretagne et pays celtiques* 403–13.

         JTK

Marjorie O. Anderson, *Kings and Kinship in Early Scotland*; Smyth, *Warlords and Holy Men* 223–5; Ann Williams et al., *Biographical Dictionary of Dark Age Britain* 105.

         JTK

Dub mac Mael Choluim was the great-great-grandson of CINAED MAC AILPÍN (regarded as the founder of the kingdom of ALBA) and was himself king of Scotland (*rí Alban*) from 962 to 966. He had previously been king of Strathclyde (YSTRAD CLUD; see also CUMBRIA), where he was succeeded by DYFNWAL AB OWAIN. What is known of Dub's career illustrates how the old Brythonic polity of Strathclyde functioned at this period as a sub-kingdom of Gaelic-dominated Alba. It also shows the instability of succession within the tandem dynasties: Dub was driven from the throne by CUILÉN RING, a member of a rival branch of Cinaed's descendants. Soon after, he was killed by another rival party in Moray (Moireibh) and buried on Iona (EILEAN Ì).

    The name *Dub* is GAELIC (Modern *Dubh*), from a Celtic root meaning simply 'black' or 'black-, dark-haired', Welsh, Cornish, and Breton *du*.

FURTHER READING
ALBA; CINAED MAC AILPÍN; CUILÉN RING; CUMBRIA; DYFNWAL AB OWAIN; EILEAN Ì; GAELIC; YSTRAD CLUD;

Dubhadh (Early Irish Dubad, also Síd mBresail, English Dowth) is an ancient circular mound roughly 85 m (280 feet) in diameter and originally about 16 m (50 feet) high. It lies somewhat over 2 km east northeast of a similar structure at Newgrange (Early Irish BRUG NA BÓINNE, also Síd in Broga). Dowth is situated in the valley of the Boyne (Old Irish BÓAND) in Ireland's east midlands. The mound of Dowth, like Newgrange and a third similar tomb nearby at Knowth, is on a hilltop and is thus visible on the horizon at a distance. Two megalithic passage graves have been located in the south-western sector of the mound. Like its sister tumuli, Dowth is probably a structure of the Neolithic period, dating to *c.* 3000 BC or a few centuries before.

    Dowth, like Newgrange, is prominent in early IRISH LITERATURE. The two sites are named together in the ULSTER CYCLE tale TOCHMARC EMIRE ('The Wooing of Emer'; §§17, 40), where CÚ CHULAINN's figurative description of a journey 'between the god and his

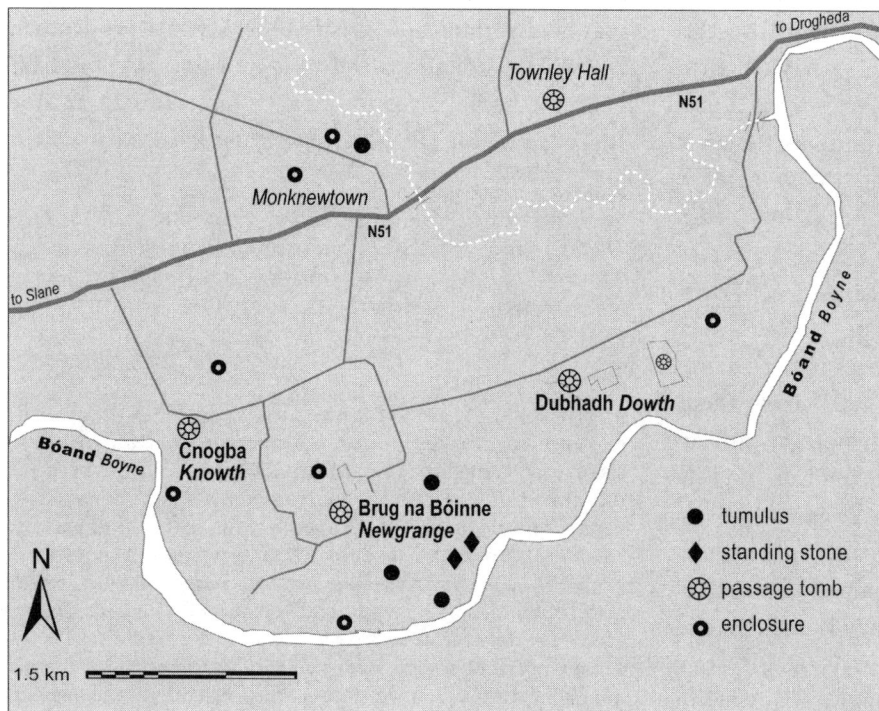

Map showing the relationship of the main monuments in the Boyne Valley, Co. Meath

prophet' (*etir in dia 7 a fáith*) is later explained as between 'Newgrange and Dowth' (*etir cnoc Síde in Broga . . . 7 Síth mBresail*), i.e. the residences of the mythological figures OENGUS MAC IND ÓC and Bresal Bófháith. In a collection of DINDSHENCHAS in a verse attributed to a poet named Flann (probably FLANN MAINISTREACH), the mound of Dubad and its name are explained as the work ordered by a king from Ireland's remote mythological past, here called Bresal Bódíbad. Bresal sought to build a tower to reach heaven, like the Tower of Babel, as Flann notes. He compels the men of Ireland to work raising the tower for a single day, and Bresal's sorceress sister casts a spell to fix the sun in the sky so that this one day lasts indefinitely. But Bresal is overcome with sinful lust and has sex with his sister, thus ruining the spell. The sun goes down, and the workers go home. Hence the name Dubad, meaning 'blackening' or 'darkening'. As with the early legends connecting Newgrange with Oengus Óc and the DAGDA, the *Dinshenchas* of Dowth combines the themes of the magical manipulation of time that make one day eternity and sexual transgression. O'Kelly (*Newgrange*) and Carey have suggested that these tales reflect the beliefs of the megalith builders of prehistoric Ireland (ÉRIU).

PRIMARY SOURCES
(Dindshenchas of Dowth)
ED. & TRANS. Gwynn, *Metrical Dindsenchas* 4.270–2.
TRANS. Koch & Carey, *Celtic Heroic Age* 144–5.

FURTHER READING
BÓAND; BRUG NA BÓINNE; CÚ CHULAINN; DAGDA; DINDSHENCHAS; ÉRIU; FLANN MAINISTREACH; IRISH LITERATURE; OENGUS MAC IND ÓC; TOCHMARC EMIRE; ULSTER CYCLE; Carey, *Proc. Harvard Celtic Colloquium* 10/11.24–36; Eogan, *Knowth*; Harbison, *Pre-Christian Ireland*; O'Kelly, *Newgrange*.

                                                              JTK

Duchcov, in the Czech Republic, is the site of one of numerous examples of WATERY DEPOSITIONS known from the Celtic world. In a hot spring, the *Riesenquelle* (giant spring), in the township of Lahošt, north of Duchcov (then still known by its German name Dux), a bronze cauldron containing hundreds of fibulae and numerous other metal items was discovered. Most of these finds date to the late 4th and 3rd centuries BC, the LA TÈNE B period (Kruta, *Celts* 295; see also CAULDRONS).

The numerous characteristic fibulae with knob-decorated back-bent foot were recognized early as a diagnostic find of the La Tène B period, which led R. Beltz (*Latènefibeln* 676) to name fibulae of this style as Type Dux (now more commonly referred to as Duchcov). They represent a development from the wire fibulae of the La Tène A period, and lead on to the typical middle La Tène fibulae with a back-bent foot attached to the bow which were characteristic of the La Tène C period. Together with fibulae of the MÜNSINGEN type, they are the main type of fibula used in the La Tène B period (*c.* 350–*c.* 250 BC).

Since little else, other than that they were found in this hot spring, is known of the circumstances of the find, not much can be said about the purpose of their deposition, except that it fits well into the pattern of other La Tène period watery depositions. A votive offering for a god or goddess associated with the spring—given that it was a hot spring, probably one that was ascribed the power of healing, like similar finds at the hot springs in Aquae Sulis (BATH)—is a distinct possibility, but, due to the lack of written evidence, cannot be proved conclusively.

FURTHER READING
BATH; CAULDRONS; LA TÈNE; MÜNSINGEN; WATERY DEPOSITIONS; Beltz, *Zeitschrift für Ethnologie* 43.663–943; Kruta, *Celts* 295; Kruta, *Le trésor de Duchcov dans les collections tchécoslovaques*.

                                                              RK

Dumnonia is the Latinized name for a British kingdom which was located in the present English counties of Cornwall (KERNOW), Devon and part of Somerset. It is named after the P-CELTIC tribe, the Dumnonii or Damnonii (Δουμνονιοι in PTOLEMY), which resided in this area from before the time of the Roman conquest. The eastern borders of the kingdom were probably delimited by the river Parret in the north. In the early medieval period, under constant pressure from the English kingdom of Wessex, this eastern border receded westwards until the whole of Somerset and Devon was eventually lost by the 9th century (cf. ANGLO-SAXON 'CONQUEST').

The difficulty in identifying a capital for post-Roman Dumnonia may therefore result from the fact that there was no one capital for any sustained period of time, the centre of power moving due to territorial contraction. A number of sites, including TINTAGEL

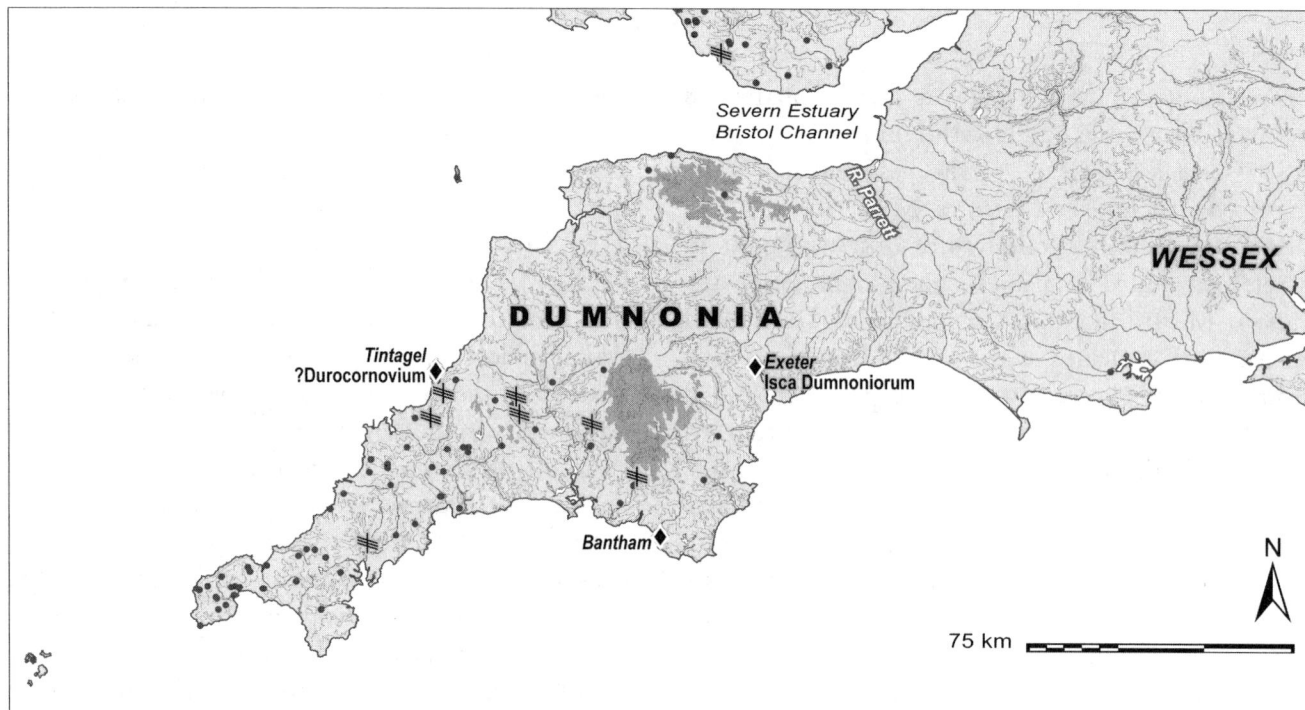

Post-Roman Dumnonia: the location of Early Christian inscribed stones are shown with black dots; the ogam symbol identifies sites of inscriptions in the Irish ogam script

(possibly the ROMANO-BRITISH Durocornovium) and Exeter (Isca Dumnoniorum) may all have been power centres of the kingdom at one time or other.

A post-Roman return by the Dumnonii to a self-governing British kingdom may have been more swiftly and more naturally achieved than elsewhere because, like most of Wales (CYMRU), the civil power of Rome had failed to impose itself strongly on the region following military conquest. In both areas, this fact may be related to the prevalence of a system of smaller dispersed settlements which, unlike the more central-ized south-eastern British tribal kingdoms, did not lend itself to Roman administration, modelled as it was on the Mediterranean city state.

Archaeological research gives the surprising indica-tion that Dumnonia became more Romanized in the post-Roman period than it had been during the *Pax Romana*. Close trading links with GAUL and the Mediterranean, the use of Latin in INSCRIPTIONS, and the adoption of Christian burial practice are among cited indications of this (Dark, *Britain and the End of the Roman Empire* 155–8). The aforementioned trading links are most notably proved by the sites of Tintagel and Bantham, where large quantities of Mediterranean amphorae have been recovered. As in prehistory and the

Roman period, it is likely that Cornish tin played an important part in this trade. Several OGAM stones in the western part of the kingdom are also indicative of a strong cultural contact with Ireland (ÉRIU).

As is the case with many of the post-Roman British kingdoms, very little is known about the history of Dumnonia. GILDAS (*De Excidio Britanniae* §28), writing *c*. AD 550, mentions one Constantine of 'Damnonia' among five British kings of this time, and king-lists for the kingdom which cover the period from the late 5th to about the 9th century survive in some medieval Welsh sources. There is also an indication from such sources that a considerable body of Dumnonian legend/pseudo-history existed, much of which has since been lost, but some of which (such as the legend of TRISTAN AND ISOLT; see also DRYSTAN AC ESYLLT) was incorporated into Welsh tradition.

Precisely how closely this territory was linked with its namesake in Brittany, DOMNONIA, is not certain. Linguistic evidence suggests that many or most of the British immigrants of the post-Roman period who crossed south over the Channel were from Dumnonia (see Jackson, LHEB 3–30). The king-lists for the two areas share several names, for example, CUNOMOR, but it is difficult to assess whether any king held power concurrently in both regions, and Thomas thinks this is unlikely (*Celtic Britain* 66; see also BRETON MIGRATIONS). The language of Dark Age Dumnonia can be called 'Primitive CORNISH', following the terminology established by JACKSON in *Language and History in Early Britain* (LHEB), though it needs to be borne in mind that at this period there was minimal linguistic difference between Cornish and WELSH, and still less between Cornish and BRETON.

The name, whence Welsh *Dyfnaint* 'Devon', is Celtic, based on the well-attested PROTO-CELTIC root *dumno~*, reflected in Old Irish *domon* and Welsh *dwfn*, meaning both 'deep' and 'world'. The name may have had significance in the ideological claims of the ancient tribe, but it may also have arisen because their territory was the first mainland to be reached from the Continent by the western sea route. There was an ancient tribe with the same name in present-day west-central Scotland (ALBA), around the Clyde estuary (see YSTRAD CLUD). The FIR DOMNANN which were prominent in Irish LEGENDARY HISTORY share the same name and may reflect an old branch of the same tribal group. The by-form *Damnonii* is old and may, if not purely scribal, indicate that the vowel of the first

syllable was unaccented and could already be pronounced with an 'obscure' sound as in the Welsh. Gildas probably selected the by-form *Damnonia* as a pun on 'damnation' to castigate the tyrant Constantine.

FURTHER READING
ALBA; ANGLO-SAXON 'CONQUEST'; BRETON; BRETON MIGRATIONS; CORNISH; CUNOMOR; CYMRU; DOMNONIA; DRYSTAN AC ESYLLT; ÉRIU; FIR DOMNANN; GAUL; GILDAS; INSCRIPTIONS; JACKSON; KERNOW; LEGENDARY HISTORY; OGAM; P-CELTIC; PROTO-CELTIC; PTOLEMY; ROMANO-BRITISH; TINTAGEL; TRISTAN AND ISOLT; WELSH; YSTRAD CLUD; Dark, *Britain and the End of the Roman Empire*; Pearce, *Kingdom of Dumnonia*; Jackson, LHEB; May & Weddell, *Current Archaeology* 178.420–2; Rivet & Smith, *Place-Names of Roman Britain* 342-4; Thomas, *Celtic Britain*.

SÓF

Dún Ailinne was the legendary seat of the kings of Leinster (LAIGIN). It is mentioned as the site of a battle for the Leinster kingship in 728 and again *c.* 800. *Félire Oengusso* (see OENGUS CÉILE DÉ) contrasts the ancient and deserted pagan capital of the Leinstermen with the thriving Christian monastery of Kildare (Cill Dara). The site was first identified with the modern Knockaulin, Co. Kildare (Cnoc Ailinne, Contae Chill

Sketch plans of the final two stages ('Rose' on the left and 'Mauve') of the circular Iron Age ceremonial structures (henges) atop Dún Ailinne; the small circular structure at the centre of the Mauve plan has been interpreted as the base of a tower

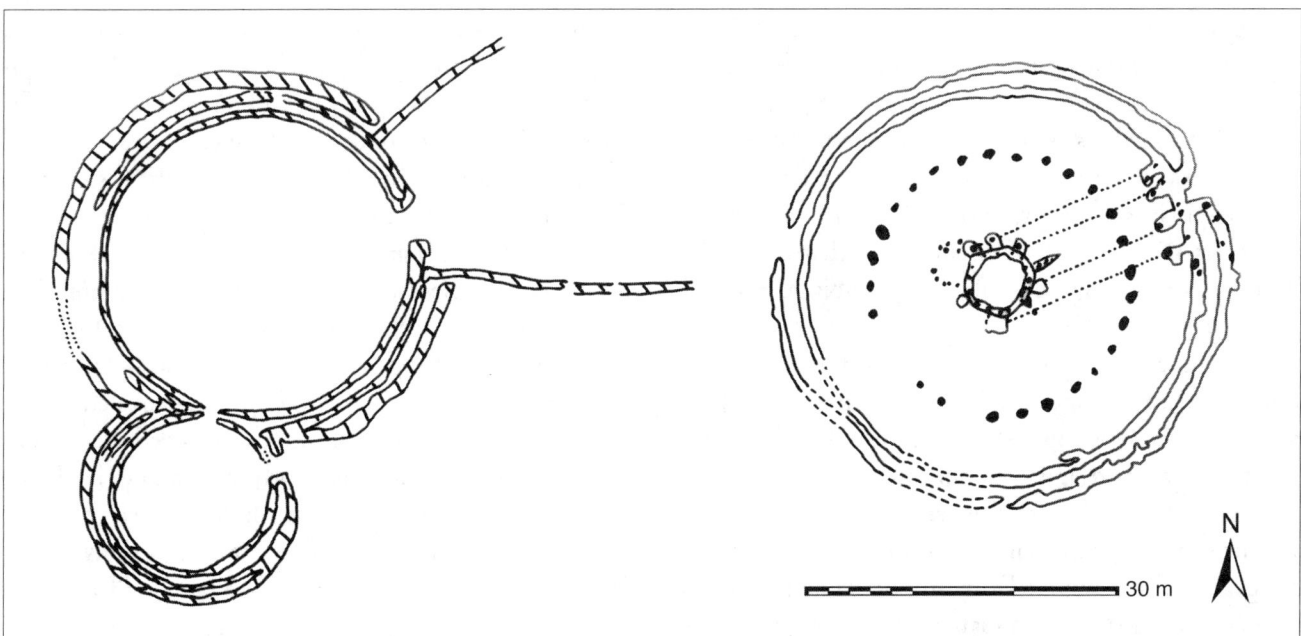

Dara), by John O'Donovan, and this identification has not been challenged. The site was excavated during the period 1968–75.

Dún Ailinne occupies a hilltop and shows traces of occupation during the Neolithic (a circular ditched enclosure, Neolithic pottery, flint artefacts) and the Early Bronze Age (a food vessel). The main period of occupation is associated with the later Iron Age occupation, where it is stratified into three main phases, labelled by modern archaeologists as White, Rose, and Mauve. The White phase is marked by a circular slot about 22 m across which held timber uprights. This was immediately followed by the Rose phase, which saw the erection of two adjoining triple-slotted enclosures. The smaller of these enclosures was approached by a door to its north-east, while the much larger northern enclosure was fronted by palisades which formed a long funnel-shaped entrance. These structures were subsequently dismantled to make way for the Mauve phase structure: a large (42 m diameter) double-slot outer enclosure which surrounded a middle ring (25 m diameter) of timber uprights and then a central structure that has been interpreted as a tower that may have stood 9 m high. The site is enclosed by an external bank and an internal ditch, the type of hengiform arrangement encountered on other 'royal' sites of the period, e.g. Tara (Teamhair), Navan (Emain Machae). Radiocarbon dates suggest that the main period of the site spanned from the 5th century BC to the 3rd century AD, but that the three main Iron Age phases, which saw the deliberate dismantling of prior structures, may have lasted only decades rather than centuries.

Finds from the site include an iron sword and an iron spearhead, bronze fibulae and glass beads. The faunal remains were primarily of cattle and swine, and their slaughter patterns suggested that they were killed in the spring and autumn, possibly as part of seasonal feasts.

There are several striking architectural similarities between Dún Ailinne and Emain Machae. Both sites see a phase where triple-slotted figure-of-eight structures were erected and then followed by the building of a circular timber enclosure about 40–42 m in diameter with a main central feature (a post at Emain Machae and a 'tower' at Dún Ailinne). The interpretation of these features is a matter of some dispute since

the Dún Ailinne timber structures have been generally reconstructed as open-air (unroofed) timber-built 'arenas' for ceremonial activity, while those at Emain Machae have been seen as roofed buildings. Nevertheless, the broadly similar sequence of comparable structures does suggest the widespread adoption of related ritual architecture, and perhaps beliefs, during the first centuries BC.

FURTHER READING
EMAIN MACHAE; ENCLOSURES; FEAST; IRON AGE; LAIGIN; O'DONOVAN; OENGUS CÉILE DÉ; SWORD; TEAMHAIR; Lynn, *Emania* 8.51–6; Wailes, *Emania* 7.10–21.

J. P. Mallory

Dún Aonghasa

The great stone enclosure of Dún Aonghasa is located on a cliff 87 m (about 270 feet) above the sea on Inis Mór, the largest of the Aran Islands (Oileáin Árann) situated in Galway Bay, off the west coast of Ireland (Éire). The site comprises an inner stone fort with two outer walls, fragments of a third, and a *chevaux-de-frise* (a broad band of relatively jagged upright stones placed to hinder access to the inner enclosure). The outermost defences enclose 5.7 ha (about 13 acres). The innermost enclosure is now open to the Atlantic along its southern side, and was probably originally protected by, at least, a low stone wall. All the ramparts are of dry-stone construction (that is, without mortar), the innermost surviving to 4.9 m in height, over 5 m thick, and with a slight external batter (that is, a broadening of the base for increased stability). Access to the interior was provided by a low, narrow, lintelled entrance (that is, with a horizontal stone beam) to the north-east.

The site was partially excavated by the Western Stone Fort project of the Discovery Programme (An Clár Fionnachtana) between 1992 and 1995. Occupation evidence dating from the Irish Middle and Late Bronze Age (c. 1400–c. 600 BC) was uncovered in the inner and middle enclosures, and included the remains of circular hut foundations, work areas, and walls. These dates came as something of a surprise, since previous thinking had tended to assign the site entirely to the Irish Iron Age (c. 600 BC–c. AD 400). Hut 1, for example, measured 4.8 m in diameter, and survived as

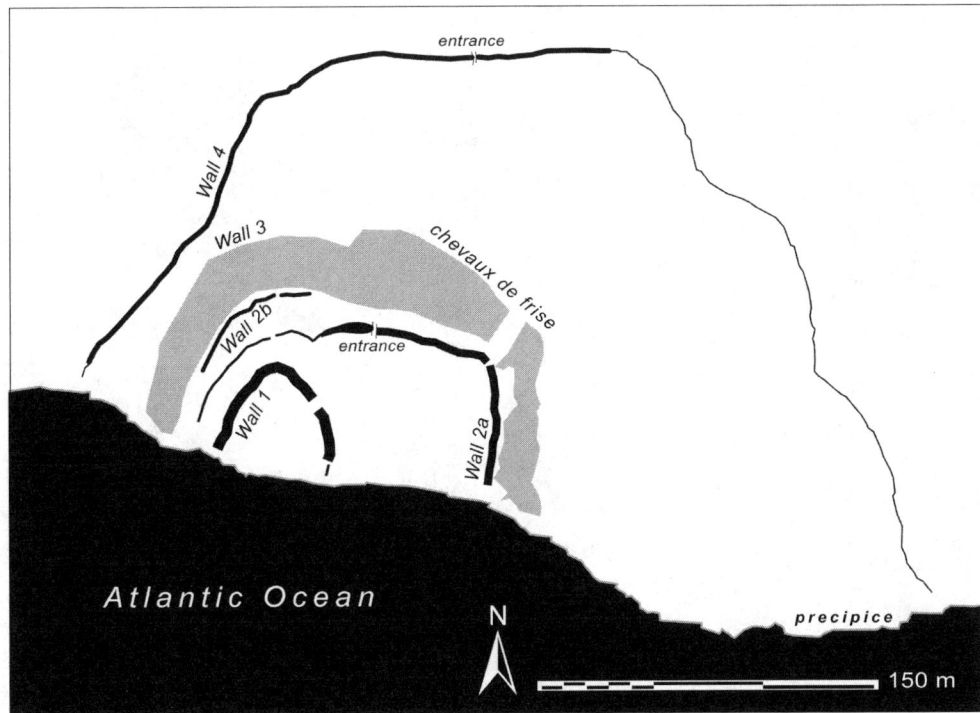

Plan of the fortifications at Dún Aonghasa, Inis Mór

low lines of foundation edging stones, part of a paved floor, and a stone-lined hearth. Evidence of habitation included limpet shells, animal bones, sherds of coarse pottery, clay mould fragments, and two clay crucibles for smelting bronze. This material was radiocarbon dated to 1063–924 BC (as recalibrated with reference to tree-ring dating), while earlier occupation material beneath the floor and running beyond the walls was dated *c.* 1300–*c.* 1000 BC. Not all of the structures identified were in use at the same time, though they do date to the general period of *c.* 1000–*c.* 800 BC.

When the innermost rampart was investigated, it was discovered that it consisted of a series of vertical stone walls. The first wall was double-faced with a rubble core, with additional 'skins' or faces added at later stages, gradually increasing the width. The core wall enclosed the original Bronze Age settlement. The additions to the original wall and the construction of the outer defences and ramparts remain undated.

The excavations also revealed that the economy of the site was based on sheep rearing, with the sheep primarily exploited for their meat rather than their wool. Cattle were the second most important domestic species, and pig bones were also recovered. Crucibles and moulds reflected the production of bronze SWORDS, spearheads, rings/ bracelets and pins which, in conjunction with the impressive setting and imposing defences, reflect the status and importance of the site

and its inhabitants.

Today, Dún Aonghasa is a major tourist attraction in an IRISH-speaking (GAELTACHT) area. The site, however, does not figure in the folklore of the island. It is thus not clear whether the place-name, meaning 'the fort of Aonghus', refers to the early supernatural hero OENGUS MAC IND ÓC of the TUATH DÉ, who is also associated with the great prehistoric monument BRUG NA BÓINNE (Newgrange), a more obscure Oengus of the FIR BOLG of LEGENDARY HISTORY, or some other figure with the same common Irish man's name.

FURTHER READING
BRUG NA BÓINNE; ÉIRE; ENCLOSURES; FIR BOLG; FORTIFICATIONS; GAELTACHT; IRISH; IRON AGE; LEGENDARY HISTORY; OENGUS MAC IND ÓC; OILEÁIN ÁRANN; TUATH DÉ; Cotter, *Discovery Programme Reports* 1.1–19; 2.1–11; 4.1–14; Cotter, *Excavations 1995* 36–7; Waddell, *Prehistoric Archaeology of Ireland* 218–21.

Michelle Comber

Dùn Èideann (Edinburgh)

Although it has an ancient pedigree, Edinburgh did not become Scotland's leading burgh until the 12th century, when the combination of a major royal castle, the wealthy Holyrood Abbey, and a vibrant market created the economic and political conditions for

Aerial view of Edinburgh Castle and the central city

success. At the heart of Edinburgh is the castle, perched upon an extinct volcano and towering over the surrounding settlement. Archaeological excavations have recovered occupation debris dating back to *c.* 800 BC (Driscoll & Yeoman, *Excavations within Edinburgh Castle 1988–91*). It is presumed that a hill-fort preceded the castle defences, though no prehistoric ramparts are visible today. A range of imported Roman goods dating to the 2nd and 3rd centuries AD are interpreted as an indication that the settlement was economically and politically important, perhaps serving as the regional centre for LOTHIAN.

In the early medieval poetic tradition preserved in the GODODDIN elegies Din Eidyn is identified as the seat of a great 6th-century king of the north BRITONS, but there are major problems with reading this poetry as straight political history. The first secure historical event is a siege of 'Etin' noted in an annal under AD 638, probably derived from a contemporary record made at Iona (EILEAN Ì; see also ANNALS). This

notice has usually been seen in the context of the conquest of the Lothians by the Angles of North-umbria. In 934 Edinburgh is mentioned in relation to ÆTHEL-STAN's northern raid, and later the fortress of Eden was abandoned to the SCOTS (between 954 and 962). From this point onwards, the castle served as a major Scottish royal centre, increasing in importance during the 11th and 12th centuries. The earliest surviving building in the castle is a chapel dedicated to St Margaret, which has been identified as part of a tower built by David I (1124–53).

During the Wars of Independence the castle was held by the English for 17 years until it was captured and slighted by Robert de BRUCE in 1314. The restoration of the castle as a royal palace was undertaken by David II in 1356, and the castle remained a major royal residence until the early 16th century. Although the royal residence was then superseded by Holyrood Palace, the castle remained an important military stronghold until the 18th century, as can be seen from the impressive artillery defences. Today, there is still a token military presence in the castle.

Edinburgh developed into the most prosperous burgh in Scotland (ALBA). The castle stood at one end of the long High Street, the Royal Mile, which terminated at Holyrood Abbey. The core of medieval Edinburgh survives intact, thanks to the 18th-century creation of the Georgian new town to the north of the High Street. Midway along the High Street, in the heart of the medieval market, is Parliament Square, where legal buildings surround St Giles, the greatest parish church to be built in medieval Scotland. Throughout the medieval and post-medieval periods Edinburgh was the acknowledged administrative centre of Scotland, even if by the 16th century the royal presence was less regular. This is a position it retained even prior to the reinstatement of the SCOTTISH PARLIAMENT in 1998.

FURTHER READING
ÆTHELSTAN; ALBA; ANNALS; BRITONS; BRUCE; EILEAN Ì; GODODDIN; LOTHIAN; SCOTS; SCOTTISH PARLIAMENT; Driscoll and Yeoman, *Excavations within Edinburgh Castle 1988–91*; MacIvor, *Edinburgh Castle*; Royal Commission on the Ancient and Historical Monuments of Scotland, *Inventory on the Ancient and Historical Monuments of the City of Edinburgh*.

Stephen Driscoll

Dúnchad mac Cinnfhaelad (710–17) succeeded Conamail as eleventh abbot of Iona (EILEAN Ì), after the founder COLUM CILLE (†597). Like the founder himself, Dúnchad was of royal Irish descent and belonged to the Cenél Conaill sub-branch of the powerful northern UÍ NÉILL dynasty. He was a key figure in the history of Iona, since the monastery had been the chief intellectual centre which promoted the insular position in the EASTER CONTROVERSY, and influenced adherents in Ireland (ÉRIU), DÁL RIATA, the kingdom of the PICTS, and Anglo-Saxon Northumbria. The Irish ANNALS record that in 716—during Dúnchad's abbacy and presumably as a result of his decision—Iona changed its reckoning of Easter, thus conforming with Rome and Canterbury. The fact that Dúnchad was a close relative of the founder and of the principal secular patrons of the monastery was probably a key factor in giving him the power to take this precipitous and long-delayed step. In September 716

a co-abbot named Faelchú was installed alongside Dúnchad, a fact which could be taken to mean either that his authority had been weakened by his controversial stand or that his health was already failing, since he died the following spring. Later in 717 NECHTON SON OF DERELEI, king of the Picts, expelled the Columban clergy from Pictland to Iona. Whatever the exact impetus for this momentous event, it appears that the death of Dúnchad had left Iona in a weakened position *vis-à-vis* its daughter houses and at least some of its traditional royal patrons in north BRITAIN. On the name *Dúnchad*, see DÚNCHAD MAC CRINÁIN. *Cenn Faelad* (genitive *Cinn Fhaelad*) is a common Old Irish man's name, meaning lit. 'head of wolves', probably figuratively 'leader of warriors'.

FURTHER READING
ANNALS; BRITAIN; COLUM CILLE; DÁL RIATA; DÚNCHAD MAC CRINÁIN; EASTER CONTROVERSY; EILEAN Ì; ÉRIU; NECHTON SON OF DERELEI; PICTS; UÍ NÉILL; Alan O. Anderson & Marjorie O. Anderson, *Adomnán's Life of Columba* 98–9; Reeves, *Life of St Columba* 379–81; Sharpe, *Life of St Columba / Adomnán of Iona* 75–6.

PEB, JTK

Dúnchad mac Crináin, known as Duncan I, king of Scotland (ALBA) 1034–40, was a pivotal figure during a turbulent and formative period of Scottish history. He was the last recorded king of the BRITONS of Strathclyde (YSTRAD CLUD) and the last king of Strathclyde-Cumbria, which apparently ceased to be a distinct political entity and merged with Alba in 1034. It is noteworthy that there is in fact a cognate Welsh name, which was in use among the northern Britons, namely the Old Welsh masculine name *Dinacat*, later *Dingad* (*Dinogat* occurs in LLYFR ANEIRIN) from a Common Celtic compound *$Dūno\text{-}catus$* 'having a fort in battle'. Therefore, *Dúnchad* is not certainly a Gaelic, as opposed to a Gaelicized BRYTHONIC, name. Dúnchad succeeded his grandfather MAEL COLUIM MAC CINAEDA (Malcolm II) in 1034 as king of Alba. In order to pave the way for his grandson, Mael Coluim had tried to eliminate all opposition by killing the possible rival candidates for the throne. Dúnchad's succession was challenged by MAC BETHAD son of Findlaech (Macbeth), whose claim to the kingship of Alba may have relied on, or been strengthened through, his wife Gruoch, the grand-daughter of CINAED MAC DUIB (Kenneth III). Mac Bethad's own hereditary office was as *mormaer* ('earl') of Moray (Moireibh), a house that had also a claim to the throne of Alba. Dúnchad was defeated and slain in combat with Mac Bethad's army in 1040. He was the father of MAEL COLUIM MAC DONNCHADA (Malcolm III 'Canmore'), who defeated and killed Mac Bethad in 1057 and became unrivalled king of Alba in 1058, after defeating and killing the challenger, Mac Bethad's stepson LULACH.

FURTHER READING
ALBA; BRITONS; BRYTHONIC; CINAED MAC DUIB; LLYFR ANEIRIN; LULACH; MAC BETHAD; MAEL COLUIM MAC CINAEDA; MAEL COLUIM MAC DONNCHADA; SCOTS; YSTRAD CLUD; Alan O. Anderson, *Early Sources of Scottish History AD 500 to 1286* 571–82; Barrow, *Scottish Genealogist* 25.98; Duncan, *Scotland* 99–100; Skene, *Celtic Scotland* 399–405; Ann Williams et al., *Biographical Dictionary of Dark Age Britain* 106–7.

PEB

Dúnchath mac Conaing was the ruler of the Scottish kingdom DÁL RIATA *c.* 650–4. According to SENCHUS FER N-ALBAN (Tradition of the men of Scotland), the ANNALS of Ulster and the Annals of Tigernach, he was the grandson of the powerful and aggressive king AEDÁN MAC GABRÁIN. Dúnchath was killed in 654 at the battle of Ráith Ethairt (alternatively Srath Ethairt, site unknown), fighting against TALORCEN SON OF EANFRITH, a Pictish king and a member of the Anglo-Saxon royal house of Bernicia (BRYNAICH). Dúnchath's name (var. *Dúnchad*) is of Celtic origin (see DÚNCHAD MAC CRINÁIN). His father's name *Conaing* is a borrowing from Old English *cyning* 'king' and reflects the international political aspirations of the Cenél nGabráin dynasty of Dál Riata (i.e. Aedán mac Gabráin's progeny).

FURTHER READING
AEDÁN MAC GABRÁIN; ANNALS; BRYNAICH; DÁL RIATA; DÚNCHAD MAC CRINÁIN; SENCHUS FER N-ALBAN; TALORCEN SON OF EANFRITH; Bannerman, *Studies in the History of Dalriada* 103; Ann Williams et al., *Biographical Dictionary of Dark Age Britain* 107.

JTK, PEB

Duns are a type of Scottish Late IRON AGE defended settlement which appear to have been constructed from the final centuries BC onwards. Excavations at Balloch

Hill Dun, Argyll (Earra-Ghaidheal), moved the chronology of duns back several centuries, i.e. to the period from the 6th to the 1st century BC. These monuments were used, and in some cases reused, until the beginning of the medieval period; e.g. the dun at Ardifuir, Argyll, was reoccupied by metalworkers in the 5th or 6th century AD. Duns consist basically of small dry-stone built ENCLOSURES, usually with a fairly small internal area (less than 0.3 ha or one acre), but occasionally bordering on the size of small hill-forts. They are often sub-circular or oval in plan, but vary widely in their range of shapes and situations. They are sometimes seated upon coastal promontories (e.g. Dun Grugaig, Skye [An t-Eilean Sgitheanach]; Ness of Burgi, Shetland [Sealtainn]), thus forming what is known elsewhere on the Atlantic fringe as a cliff castle or promontory fort. Duns are also sometimes situated on the summit of hills (e.g. Dun Gerashader, Skye), but they are just as often to be found in places which are not notable for their defensive qualities. It has been noted that duns can be further divided into two types, i.e. enclosures and houses, the latter being roofed over. The walls tend to be high (up to *c.* 3 m) and quite thick. Duns are most plentifully distributed along the western seaboard from Skye and North and South Uist (Uibhist) in the north to Kintyre (Ceann Tíre) and Arran (Arainn) in the south. Like the BROCHS, with which they partially overlap in both distribution and construction, they are considered to be the defended homesteads of small farming groups, equivalent to the rounds and raths found in the more southerly parts of the Atlantic zone during this period. Indeed, their appearance and interpretation is very similar to that of the *caiseal* (stone-built ring-fort, see CASHEL) of the western coast of Ireland (ÉRIU) in particular. As is the case with brochs, duns are now viewed more in terms of the common features, purpose and origins they share with other defended settlements of the Atlantic zone during this period, rather than their singularity.

The term *dun* is a borrowing from Scottish Gaelic *dùn* 'hillock, fort, castle, &c.', which is Common Celtic; cf. Irish *dún*, and the now obsolete Welsh and Breton *din*, common in place-names. Forts and fortified towns with names in Celtic *-dūnon* (Latinized *-dūnum*) were common throughout the ancient Celtic world: e.g. CAMULODŪNON, LUGUDŪNON, SINGIDŪNON. The

Ness of Burgi fort, mainland Shetland, looking south over rock chasm to outer defences with blockhouse to rear. The outer wall shows in section above the chasm.

noun is probably related to the Gaelic verb *dùnadh* 'act of shutting, closing'.

FURTHER READING
ALBA; BROCHS; CAMULODŪNON; CASHEL; ENCLOSURES; ÉRIU; IRON AGE; LUGUDŪNON; SINGIDŪNON; Cunliffe, *Facing the Ocean*; Darvill, *Prehistoric Britain*; Lloyd Laing & Jennifer Laing, *Picts and the Scots*; MacSween & Sharp, *Prehistoric Scotland*.

SÓF

Dürrnberg bei Hallein is an important early centre of SALT mining in central Europe which was in use during the pre-Roman IRON AGE. The Dürrnberg complex has been the source of numerous and rich finds from graves and settlements dating from the HALLSTATT and earlier LA TÈNE periods. In the development of modern archaeology, materials from the site have been important in defining the characteristic material culture for a key period in a core area of Celtic-speaking west-central Europe.

§1. TOPOGRAPHY AND RESEARCH HISTORY
The Dürrnberg is situated south-west of Salzburg on the border between Germany and Austria. From the end of the 12th century AD until the cessation of commercial salt mining in 1989, the salt of the Dürrnberg mines was the most important economic factor in the Salzburg region. The site extended over an area of 2 km², mostly on what is now Austrian territory, but extending into Bavaria. The landscape is characterized by a series of small valleys and hilltops, mainly centred around the 802 m high Moserstein

Fig. 1: Overall view of Dürrnberg with the modern village and church on Lettenbichl and Moserstein; the Steigerhaushügel and the Ramsautal are in the foreground

Fig. 2: Beaked flagon of grave 112, excavated in 1932 by O. Klose

(Fig. 1). In prehistoric times the Raingraben valley provided the chief access to the Dürrnberg, protected by a hill-fort on the Ramsaukopf, which encloses the area on the eastern side.

The archaeological material from the Dürrnberg is extremely rich and originated from an outstanding range of different sources: graves, settlements, and the salt mines themselves. Each of these has produced a different selection of the material culture itself, in varying degrees of preservation, with the best preservation of organic materials due to salt in the mines and in waterlogged terrain in the settlements, mining entrances, and sometimes in wooden chambers.

During what may be regarded as the beginning of the modern discovery of the ancient salt mines of Dürrnberg, we have records that two miners' bodies were discovered in the mines in AD 1577 and 1616. These finds—popularly known as the 'men in the salt'—were made in the so-called *Heidengebirge* (pagan rock). From this time onwards, the miners began to be aware that the remains from the site belonged to an earlier epoch, referred to in popular tradition as a time 'some hundred years ago among the pagans'.

In 1831/3 Andreas Seethaler, a high-ranking official in the salt mines, described in his *Die allersten Celtischen und Römischen Alterthümer am Dürrnberg und zu Hallein an der Salza in Verbindung mit ihren Salinen* (The first Celtic and Roman antiquities on Dürrnberg and in Hallein at the Salzach in connection with the salt mines) a grave found on the Hallersbichl and gave a first overview of prehistoric sites (Penninger, *Die Kelten in Mitteleuropa* 150–8). Later in the 19th century, despite a couple of attempts to establish regular archaeological excavations on Dürrnberg, there were no successes comparable to those of the better-known Hallstatt, some 50 km to the east. This work had to wait until the first half of the 20th century when Martin Hell, Olivier Klose and, after the Second World War, Ernst Penninger worked on the site. Archaeological research increased during this period, and was especially stimulated by important finds such as the well-known bronze beaked flagon found by Klose in a CHARIOT burial in 1932 (Fig. 2). The second chariot grave 44/2 was discovered in 1954 by Penninger at the plateau of the Moserstein.

Two events accelerated and supported these efforts. First, a new all-weather road was built from Hallein to Dürrnberg between 1978 and 1982, which necessitated a large-scale rescue excavation, and doubled previous archaeological discoveries in a very short time. Secondly, a major international exhibition was held in 1980 in the local Keltenmuseum, entitled 'The Celts in Central Europe' (*Die Kelten in Mitteleuropa*). This superseded the first publications dealing with finds made prior to 1974. The need for a permanent archaeological research facility was then recognized, and a local research centre, the Österreichisches Forschungszentrum Dürrnberg (Austrian Dürrnberg Research Centre) was established in 1984 in the Keltenmuseum. Since that time, research projects and year-round archaeological work has led to large-scale excavations, especially in the various small-scale cemeteries. At the same time, work was also carried out on the settlement areas. Recently, in co-operation with several other institutions, the ancient salt mines themselves have been the subject of intensive investigation.

FURTHER READING

CHARIOT; HALLSTATT; IRON AGE; LA TÈNE; SALT; Barth, *Mitteilungen der Gesellschaft für Salzburger Landeskunde* 115.313–20; Dobiat & Stöllner, *Archäologisches Korrespondenzblatt* 30.65–84; Dobiat et al., *Archäologisches Korrespondenzblatt* 27.93–102, 28.555–74; Klose, *Mitteilungen der Anthropologischen Gesellschaft Wien* 56.346–50; Klose, *Wiener Prähistorische Zeitschrift* 19.39–81; Klose, *Wiener Prähistorische Zeitschrift* 21.83–107; Moosleitner et al., *Der Dürrnberg bei Hallein 2*; Pauli, *Der Dürrnberg bei Hallein 3*; Penninger, *Der Dürrnberg bei Hallein 1*; Penninger, *Die Kelten in Mitteleuropa* 150–8; Penninger, *Mitteilungen der Gesellschaft für Salzburger Landeskunde* 101.167–71; Penninger, *Mitteilungen der Gesellschaft für Salzburger Landeskunde* 106.17–20; Stöllner, *Archäologisches Korrespondenzblatt* 21.255–69; Stöllner, *Der Anschnitt* 47:4/5.126–34; Stöllner, *Der prähistorische Salzbergbau am Dürrnberg bei Hallein 1*; Stöllner, *Die Kelten in den Alpen und an der Donau* 225–43; Stöllner, *Salzburg Archiv* 12.17–40; Zeller, *Archäologische Berichte aus Sachsen-Anhalt* 1.293–357; Zeller, *Die Räter* 287–92; Zeller, *Salz* 104–26; Zeller, *Salzburg Archiv* 10.5–16; Zeller, *Salzburg Archiv* 10.17–24; Zeller, *Salzburg Archiv* 12.1–16; Zeller, *Salzburg Archiv* 14.esp. 44 ff.; Zeller, *Salzburg Archiv* 20.19–30; Zeller, *Salzburg Archiv* 23.5–26; Zeller, *Studien zu Siedlungsfragen der Latènezeit* 199–204.

§2. SALT MINING

The SALT deposits of the Dürrnberg consist of the so-called *haselgebirge* (hazel mountains), a mixture of 40% to 95% pure salt (sodium chloride) together with clay and anhydrite or gypsum. The deposit was pushed upwards by tectonic movements during the formation of the northern calcareous Alps; these mainly overlay underground salt deposits. The whole deposit is covered by a layer of clay with a thickness of around 20–40 m, which protects the salt deposit against further leaching by fresh water. On top of the malleable and movable salt deposits, and causing even tectonic pressure on the salt, there are a number of calcareous outcrops. In central position is the Hahnrainkopf (1026 m). At the foot of the Hahnrainkopf are a couple of brine springs, which were presumably responsible for the discovery of the underground salt deposits by HALLSTATT-period Celtic miners in the 6th century BC. The prehistoric mining areas were mainly distributed around this hilltop because easy access to the salt was possible by shafts cut down diagonally from the slopes of the Hahnrainkopf. Until it was possible to carry out commercial mining in larger galleries, the prehistoric miners continuously had to extend the shafts in order to access new deposits. Our knowledge about the ancient working areas is in fact mainly based on mining in the historic period; mining exploited the salt deposits from the 13th century until 1989 (Stöllner, *Der prähistorische Salzbergbau am Dürrnberg bei Hallein 1*).

On the basis of the reports of miners in the historic period as well as of modern underground research, it is possible to reconstruct a rough overview of the prehistoric mines and to distinguish no fewer than twelve different mines, two of which had been worked simultaneously, especially in the Early LA TÈNE period. Research in the 1990s has modified the older views of Schauberger. The current archaeological record allows the reconstruction of large working galleries, in some cases more than 30 m wide, 4–10 m high and up to 200 m long. These galleries follow the salt by the

Fig. 3: Implements including beechwood handles, a whetstone, and an iron pick from the Iron Age salt-mines

construction of roughly diagonal chambers in which the IRON AGE miners retrieved salt by hacking out large lumps. Organic material is preserved in remarkable condition through the saline environment, resulting in a mass of information concerning the tools (Fig. 3), the distribution of labour, and the clothes of the miners. Knowledge of their health and diet is based on the analysis of coprolites or paleofaeces, i.e. petrified excrement. On the basis of these data, one may suppose that the mining community consisted of a poorer and socially less favoured stratum of the contemporary Iron Age community. In addition, the small size of some shoes found in the shafts offers evidence for the employment of children in the mines. Contrary to the views of Schauberger and Pauli (cited below), the working groups in the mines must have been of considerable size, especially when taking into consideration the short period of time during which the chambers were worked. This can be calculated on the basis of some new dendrochronological dates (i.e. dates based on counting tree rings) from three such mining chambers which have been examined thoroughly. The working processes and the implements used provide evidence of distinctive and specialized professions: hewers, hauliers, carpenters, and the like. Besides natural ventilation, there is evidence of artificial thermal ventilation by heating the air through fire and the hundreds of wooden tapers which provided the main source of illumination below ground.

Further salt processing was presumably done on the dumped waste material in front of the mine entrances, either to purify and process rock salt as a trade product or to use it for leatherwork and curing meat. None of the ancient mining entrances identified so far have been sufficiently explored. Radiocarbon and dendrochronological (tree-ring) dates support the view that the mines were in use during the whole Celtic settlement period on the Dürrnberg, between the 6th and 1st centuries BC. Some of the richer parts of the salt deposits seem to have been exploited at more than one period. There could well be evidence for further small-scale activities during the Roman period.

FURTHER READING
HALLSTATT; IRON AGE; LA TÈNE; SALT; Aspöck et al., *Mitteilungen der Anthropologischen Gesellschaft Wien* 103.41–7; Barth, *Festschrift zum 50jährigen Bestehen des Instituts für Ur- und Frühgeschichte der Leopold-Franzens-Universität Innsbruck* 25–36; Barth, *Mitteilungen der Gesellschaft für Salzburger Landeskunde* 115.313–20, fig. 3; Barth et al., *Mitteilungen der Anthropologischen Gesellschaft Wien* 105.45–52; Brand, *Zur eisenzeitlichen Besiedlung des Dürrnberges bei Hallein*; Hundt, *Jahrbuch des Römisch-Germanischen Zentralmuseums, Mainz* 8.7–25; Klose, *Mitteilungen der Anthropologischen Gesellschaft Wien* 56.346–50; Pauli, *Der Dürrnberg bei Hallein* 3; Schatteiner, *Salz macht Geschichte* 125–33; Schauberger, *Die vorgeschichtlichen Grubenbaue im Salzberg Dürrnberg/Hallein*; Stöllner, *Der prähistorische Salzbergbau am Dürrnberg bei Hallein* 1.

§3. SETTLEMENTS

Stray finds offer evidence of exploitation of the natural brine springs since the Middle Neolithic (roughly 4th millennium BC) and may suggest the presence of sporadic settlements. A permanent settlement had been established, based on the mining of underground salt, though not earlier than the late HALLSTATT period (Ha D1, earlier 6th century BC). There were close relations with the nearby hill-fort on the Hellbrunnerberg, a rich and therefore presumably chieftainly centre just south of the site of the modern city of Salzburg, especially in the early period. There exists only a slight scattering of Hallstatt finds combined with a RITUAL place for burnt-offerings (German *Brandopferplatz*) on the nearby Hallersbichl as well as some tomb-groups surrounding this early settlement. In the latest phase of the Hallstatt Iron Age (D3, *c.* 500 BC) and at the beginning of LA TÈNE A (first half of the 5th century BC) several important changes may have led to a regional concentration of the settlement activities on the Dürrnberg. A large trade and crafts settlement was established around the Ramsautal, the hill-fort on the Ramsaukopf and on the Moserstein. At the same time, the rich settlement on the Hellbrunnerberg was abandoned. Subsequently, settlement was concentrated on the Dürrnberg itself. From this time onwards, the complex craft and trade centre on the Dürrnberg existed, linked with the Salzach valley by a settlement which has been located below the modern town of Hallein. Even in this period, between the 5th and the 3rd centuries BC, the settlement area extended as far as the German side of the present international border. In the second part of the 4th and the beginning of the 3rd centuries BC, the settlement suffered a decline. Mud avalanches in the mine and regular flooding in the Ramsautal may indicate land exhaustion caused by intensive mining and other human activities on the Dürrnberg. In later centuries and into Roman times we see again a restricted core settlement on the Moserstein which reveals by then the decreased importance of the Dürrnberg.

Despite early investigations by Martin Hell and an excavation on the Hinterramsau, until the late 1970s there had been only restricted knowledge about settlement structure and construction techniques. In advance of the construction of the Dürrnbergstrasse, large cemeteries and even a couple of houses—well-preserved in some parts—and settlement quarters were discovered and excavated in and around the Ramsautal. This allowed a new insight into the nature of IRON

AGE habitations on the Dürrnberg. The waterlogged conditions of the Ramsautal valley offered optimal conditions for recovering an extended settlement which exhibited a range of craft activities and which existed between the 5th and the 3rd centuries BC. Small-scale excavations have also brought to light a couple of well-preserved large houses up to 15 m in length. These houses were constructed on raised areas of dry land and were settled and rebuilt over generations. These more or less dry dwelling areas were secured by drains and wickerwork fences against the permanent moisture of the swampy area. The house constructions and their stratigraphy (i.e. their sequenced layers corresponding to successive time periods) show that living and craft activities were carried out in the same house-units, presumably over several generations, by the same families, or at least by related social groups. Besides bronze casting and iron working, there is evidence for meat processing and tanning, glass production, woodworking carpentry, tool making, lathes, pottery, and others. We must presume that these specialists worked not only for the community on the Dürrnberg, but also for the immediate hinterland where similar finished products have been found. The results of the excavations at the Ramsautal have also provided insights into the complex economic relations between the salt-mining centre of the Dürrnberg and its supporting region. This was situated in the Salzach valley and basin and in the Inn-Salzach area of the Bavarian and Salzburg Alpine promontory, which had the closest cultural links with Dürrnberg. There is also evidence of economic contacts with the ALPINE hinterland, especially with the Fritzens-Sanzeno culture, where pottery and brooches point to a fluctuating exchange of people such as seasonal workers and of trade goods, e.g. sheep, between those regions.

In addition, there are many examples of long-distance trade in rare raw materials such as amber, silk, and coral, as well as luxury goods found in the rich Dürrnberg graves—Etruscan and Greek vessels of pottery and bronze and even WINE from south of the Alps. Some graves can be interpreted as being those of traders, one of them presumably having come from the area of the Veneti and the head of the ADRIATIC.

FURTHER READING
ADRIATIC; ALPINE; HALLSTATT; IRON AGE; LA TÈNE; RITUAL; WINE; Brand, *Zur eisenzeitlichen Besiedlung des Dürrnberges bei*

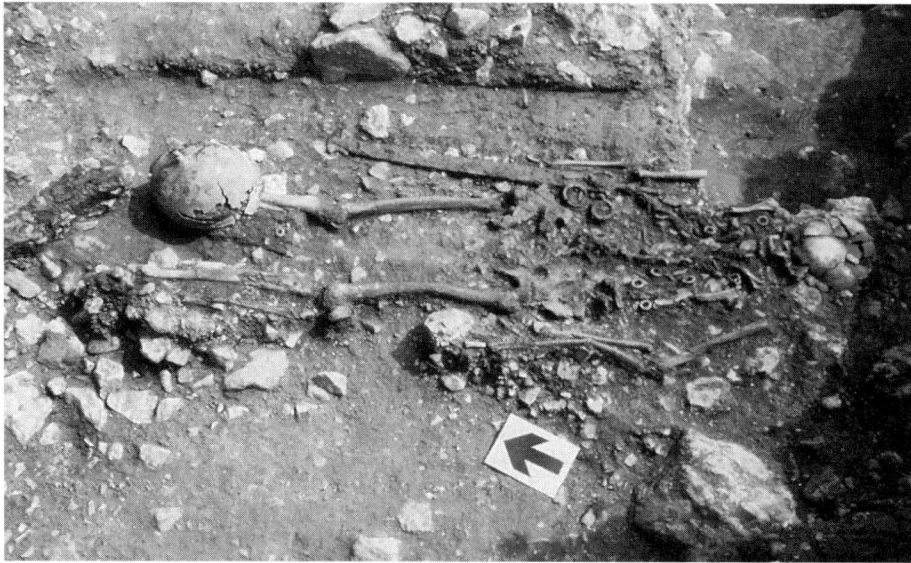

Fig. 4: Early La Tène warrior-grave 145 with a sword on the right side and helmet at the feet

Hallein; Groenman-van Waateringe & Stöllner, *Patina* 291–304; Hell, *Mitteilungen der Anthropologischen Gesellschaft Wien* 56.320–45; Hell, *Wiener Prähistorische Zeitschrift* 3.57–70; Hell, *Wiener Prähistorische Zeitschrift* 20.112–47; Hell, *Wiener Prähistorische Zeitschrift* 23.42–72; Irlinger, *Der Dürrnberg bei Hallein* 4; Maier, *Germania* 52.326–47; Megaw et al., *Germania* 68.509–49; Moosleitner, *Archaeologia Austriaca* 56.13–20; Moosleitner, *Germania* 57.53–79; Moosleitner, *Jahresschrift des Salzburger Museums C.A.* 1969.103–9; Moosleitner et al., *Der Dürrnberg bei Hallein* 2; Pauli, *Der Dürrnberg bei Hallein* 3; Penninger, *Germania* 38.353–63; Penninger, *Mitteilungen der Gesellschaft für Salzburger Landeskunde* 106.17–20; Pucher, *Archäozoologische Untersuchungen am Tierknochenmaterial der keltischen Gewerbesiedlung im Ramsautal auf dem Dürrnberg*; Stöllner, *Archäologie in Salzburg* 3/1–2; Stöllner, *Archäologisches Korrespondenzblatt* 21.255–69; Stöllner, *Der prähistorische Salzbergbau am Dürrnberg bei Hallein* 1; Stöllner, *Die Kelten in den Alpen und an der Donau* 225–43; Zeller, *Archäologische Berichte aus Sachsen-Anhalt* 1.293–357; Zeller, *Die Räter* 287–92; Zeller, *Studien zu Siedlungsfragen der Latènezeit* 199–204.

§4. LATE HALLSTATT AND LA TÈNE GRAVES

The cemeteries spread over the whole area of the Dürrnberg in the early settlement phases were concentrated especially in three areas: the graves of the Eislfeld (around 80–100 graves); the graves of the Simonbauernfeld (a smaller grave group); and a larger group on the Hexenwandfeld. At the beginning of the IRON AGE occupation one can detect groups of 'founders' graves'. With the changes at the beginning of the 5th century BC new cemeteries were established, some devoted to warriors or other richer graves (Gratzenfeld-Putzenfeld, Kammelhöhe/Sonneben, Moserstein-Plateau Kurgarten, Osthang-Moserstein, Römersteig, Steigerhaushügel). Secondary burials of the Early LA TÈNE period can be observed in older burial mounds first built in the 6th century, especially on the Eislfeld.

Graves of La Tène Bii (*c.* 350–*c.* 150 BC) and La Tène C (*c.* 250–*c.* 150 BC) are normally rare, especially in the older HALLSTATT burial-mounds, but are more common in the north-eastern zone of Dürrnberg, where new cemeteries have been found. In some cases we have new grave-groups and single graves from the 3rd and 2nd centuries, and sometimes very rich SWORD graves with wagon-fittings or rich women's graves which reveal that some kind of local upper class still existed at that time. The burial rate seems to have been continuously reduced from the 4th century, contrary to what can be deduced from the settlement evidence—the latter shows continual prosperity in the later phases of the Early and especially in the Middle La Tène periods (*c.* 350–*c.* 150 BC). Finally, evidence for graves of the latest settlement phases is still lacking, which is not surprising when set against the background of Late La Tène civilization in southern Germany.

Normally, the cemeteries or clusters of graves were situated on steep slopes or on obviously selected and clearly visible sites close to the settlements, especially around the major areas of population such as Moserstein or Ramsautal. It must be doubted whether the graves always were covered with mounds, especially in the case of the more recent graves constructed in calcareous gullies (German *Karrenrinnen*). Some graves seem to have been constructed with an eye to being accessible for later RITUAL practices—perhaps this was also a reason for locating them close to settlements and working areas.

The normal practice for the construction of graves was to build rectangular wooden chambers covered by stones, inside which one or more persons were buried, cremated, or inhumed in an extended position. In some burials the chambers were used for two individuals, presumably indicating some sort of relationship, such as kinship. These multiple graves, together with gifts of amulets and brooches with elaborate decoration, exhibit a range of fanciful forms of clear symbolic importance and are a prominent feature of the Dürrnberg burials. Recent research has provided detailed information about burial customs and has produced further evidence of the building of new chambers over old ones. Up to four distinct layers are known. Secondary burial activities—the construction of a new chamber or a succeeding funeral—did not always leave the prior burial undisturbed. Some burial goods were removed and the earlier skeletons disarticulated. Later disturbance of earlier burial is frequently observed and may have had its origin in robbery or—more likely—in some kind of ritual practice involving two-stage burial.

The dead were normally equipped with drinking vessels and other dishes as well as the remains of joints of meat (pig, cattle, and sheep or goat; the latter two animals are not easy to distinguish archaeologically). This indicates a funerary FEAST as part of the rite of passage into the OTHERWORLD. In addition, there are single-edged knives (German *Hiebmesser*), shears, and status symbols such as wagons, weapons, complex belts, and special luxury items in richer and socially higher ranked graves.

From Hallstatt D (roughly 6th century BC) on, spears and axes appear in the personal equipment of men's graves, sometimes combined with some sort of status weapons like daggers, helmets, and swords with richly decorated scabbards. Rich costume articles, e.g. bracelets, anklets, beads, amulets, belts, and a substantial number of brooches are noticeable for women and also in the richer children's graves, even those of the very young. These are known in considerable numbers and with a wide range of grave goods, indicating some sort of local aristocracy. These rich graves of minors are in contrast to the unaccompanied infants' and neonatal burials close to and even in the floors of houses found in the Ramsautal and other settlement areas (Fig. 4).

Other, more outstanding, status symbols are known from rich male or female graves situated in special areas in the cemeteries, such as parts of wagons (graves 44/2, 112), a large bronze situla ('wine' bucket) of local manufacture and a bronze 'pilgrim flask' copying southern forms (44/2), the famous bronze Celtic beaked flagon (grave 112, see Fig. 2 above), a miniature golden boat (grave 44/1, Fig. 5), splendid axes (graves 46/2, 88), and imports from the Mediterranean world (graves 59, 44/2, Fig. 6;). Rings of gold may have been special gifts, and likewise large dress pins with double spiral heads. Even more exotic are ritual wands or sceptres and even a cowrie shell (grave 44/2). The social system of the Dürrnberg seems to have been more differentiated than was previously thought. Between the working population in the mines on the one hand and what is represented in the graves on the other, it is very unlikely that the whole population is represented in the latter. The cemeteries represent a cross-section of the higher class and more wealthy sections of a settled population. So far we cannot identify miners, seasonal workers, and craftspeople from

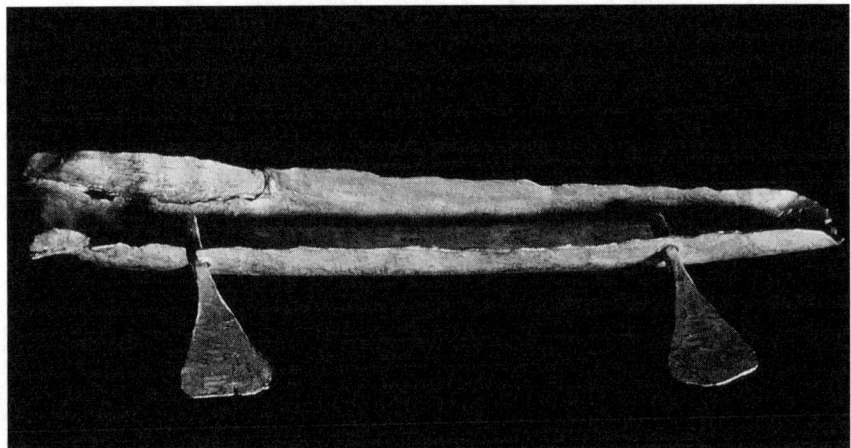

Fig. 5: Small golden votive boat from grave 44/1 as a sign of the salt trade on the river Salzach

grave-goods or on the basis of pathological evidence.

FURTHER READING
CHARIOT; FEAST; HALLSTATT; IRON AGE; LA TÈNE;
OTHERWORLD; RITUAL; SALT; SWORDS; Bergonzi, *Popoli e facies
culturali celtiche a nord e a sud delle Alpi dal V al I secolo a. C.* 49–
58; Brand, *Zur eisenzeitlichen Besiedlung des Dürrnberges bei Hallein*;
Moosleitner, *Arte protoceltica a Salisburgo*; Moosleitner et al.,
Der Dürrnberg bei Hallein 2; Pauli, *Der Dürrnberg bei Hallein 3*;
Pauli, *Keltski voz* 89–97; Stöllner, *Germania* 76.59–168; Zeller,
Archäologische Berichte aus Sachsen-Anhalt 1.293–357; Zeller, *Die
Kelten in Mitteleuropa* 159–81; Zeller, *Salzburg Archiv* 23.5–26;
Zeller, *Studien zu Siedlungsfragen der Latènezeit* 199–204.

§5. CULTURAL LINKS

Dürrnberg and its northern ALPINE extension, the
Inn-Salzach-region, are closely linked by culture. The
connections are manifested in burial customs such as
specific grave-goods in women's burials and in a widely
comparable material culture. This may be due to the
dependence of the mining society on an external supply
of food and raw materials. The interaction between
the Hellbrunnerberg and Dürrnberg is clearly demon-
strable. We may postulate an important settlement in
the Salzach valley which served as trading post, market,
and administrative centre. At the beginning of the 5th
century BC the Hellbrunnerberg settlement vanished

just at a time when the settlement of the Dürrnberg
was flourishing. Regional resettlement seems most
likely, supported by connections in the settlement
dynamics of the Salzburg basin and beyond. From
the beginning of the 6th century BC the area was
culturally linked with other Eastern Alpine regions
within the East Hallstatt province. From the middle
of the 6th century BC, however, connections with the
West Hallstatt province began to increase, and were
marked by changes in dress ornaments, burial rites,
and pottery forms. It seems to be a coincidence rather
than the result of any direct cultural influence that
these changes are contemporary with the establishment of the IRON AGE complex on the Dürrnberg
and its flourishing development in the second half
of the 6th century BC. From then onwards, the area
was a closely connected subzone of the West Hallstatt
province. There are many reasons for believing that
this situation was responsible for the important rôle
which Dürrnberg played in the development of LA
TÈNE culture at the beginning of the 5th century—a
time when Dürrnberg reached its climax. The Celtic
migrations in the 4th and 3rd centuries BC also changed
the cultural and the basic economic relations of
Dürrnberg. Connections with the Carpathian basin and
the Alpine hinterland were apparently stronger in the
4th and the 3rd centuries. Late La Tène culture (*c.* 150–*c.*
15 BC) was more influenced by the culture of the late
Celtic *oppida* in southern Germany than by NORICUM
in the emerging Roman Empire (see OPPIDUM).

*Fig. 6: Mediterranean Imports from the Dürrnberg: Etruscan
Stamnos from grave 63; Attic cup from grave 44/2*

FURTHER READING
ADRIATIC; ALPINE; DACIANS; IRON AGE; LA TÈNE; NORICUM;
OPPIDUM; WINE; Brand, *Zur eisenzeitlichen Besiedlung des
Dürrnberges bei Hallein*; Groenman-van Waateringe & Stöllner,
Patina 291–304; Irlinger, *Der Dürrnberg bei Hallein 4*; Moosleitner,
Germania 57.53–79; Pauli, *Der Dürrnberg bei Hallein 3*; Pauli,
Hamburger Beiträge zur Archäologie 2.2.273–89; Stöllner,
Archäologie in Salzburg 3/1–2; Stöllner, *Der prähistorische
Salzbergbau am Dürrnberg bei Hallein 1*; Zeller, *Archäologische
Berichte aus Sachsen-Anhalt* 1.293–357; Zeller, *Salz* 104–26.

Thomas Stöllner (and thanks to Kurt Zeller)

Durrow, Book of (Dublin, Trinity College MS
57 [A. 4. 5]), is most likely the earliest extant essentially
complete illuminated insular gospel book. Besides its
text of St JEROME's Latin version of the Gospels and
various preliminaries (including framed canon tables,

fos. 8–10) written in a fine Irish majuscule script, the manuscript contains six carpet pages (pages covered with ornament but without text) and five pages displaying symbols of the evangelists. Elaborately decorated initials open each of the four Gospels and an important text in Matthew, and smaller decorated initials are used for the preface and the list of chapters. For several reasons, including ill treatment over the centuries, the codex is mainly a collection of single leaves, and when it was rebound in 1954 an attempt was made to adjust the order of several of the carpet pages and one of the evangelist symbol pages that were clearly out of place. This rearrangement left St Matthew's Gospel without a carpet page and although suggestions have been made that one or another of the surviving carpet pages once prefaced Matthew, it is more likely that its carpet page is simply lost. If so, allowing for pagination change after fo. 21v, the original arrangement of the major decorated pages was as follows: fo. 1v, a carpet page with a large double-barred cross; fo. 2r, a page presenting the four evangelist symbols around an interlaced cross; fo. 3v, a carpet page with trumpet spirals before the prefaces; fo. 21v, the Man, symbol of Matthew; the lost carpet page (that would have been fo. 22r); fo. 22r, the Matthew incipit; fo. 84v, the Eagle, symbol of Mark; fo. 85v, a carpet page with interlace roundels and a small central cross; fo. 86v, the Mark incipit; fo. 124v, the Calf, symbol of Luke; fo. 125v, a carpet page with interlace and geometric patterns; fo. 126v, the Luke incipit; fo. 191v, the Lion, symbol of St John; fo. 192v, a carpet page with panels depicting biting animals framing a small circled central cross; fo. 193v, the John incipit; and fo. 248r, a carpet page with a lattice-like design.

The order of equivalence followed by the individually pictured evangelist symbols is not the canonical Latin order established by St Jerome but most likely depends on that which was set out in the 2nd century by St Irenaeus. The symbol type of the four symbols page (fo. 2r) and those separately depicted are also quite unusual, the first possibly partially inspired by Coptic example, and the second—lacking the usual wings, halos and attributes—related to a type known as 'terrestial' found in the mid-6th century at San Vitale, Ravenna.

There are two inscriptions by the scribe of the Book of Durrow on fo. 247v, the second of which refers to the writer as St Columba (COLUM CILLE). On fo. 248v there is an 11th- or 12th-century addition recording a legal transaction concerning the monastery of Durrow, Co. Offaly (Darmhaigh, Contae Uíbh Fhailí), and on fo. IIv there is an inscription, added in the 17th century by the antiquarian Roderick O'Flarety, taken from the *cumdach* (book shrine), now lost, in which the manuscript had been placed at Durrow by Flann mac Mael Sechnaill, king of Ireland (ÉRIU), during the late 9th or early 10th century. Further evidence suggests that the book was at Durrow in the early 17th century, and was still revered as the Book of Colum Cille. Nevertheless, by the 1930s scholars began to question its attribution to the hand of Columba and its Durrow provenance. Indeed, the character of its script and its repertoire of Celtic, Anglo-Saxon, and Mediterranean ornamental patterns and iconographic formulations led a number of scholars to place its creation in Northumbria some time during the 7th century. Its date and place of manufacture remain difficult to establish and the manuscript remains the centre of an ongoing controversy regarding the relative importance of North-umbria and Ireland in the development of 7th- and 8th-century insular script and manuscript decoration.

In recent years, scholarly opinion has shifted from the Northumbrian thesis to the view that the Book of Durrow was created by Irish monks in a Columban scriptorium (manuscript-production centre), with two proposals emerging as most developed and credible. The first hypothesis rests mainly on palaeographic evidence which connects the book with the monastery of Rath Melsigi in Co. Carlow (Contae Cheatharlaigh), where the Anglo-Saxon missionary Willibrord spent several years before travelling to the Continent in 690. Manuscripts from Echternach associated with Willibrord have scribal similarities with the Book of Durrow, and this and other palaeographic evidence has led to the conclusion that the script developed at Rath Melsigi was employed in the creation of our manuscript at Durrow, probably early in the 8th century. The second theory depends upon recognition of an iconographic contiguity between the facing miniatures opening the codex—the cross-carpet page (fo. 1v), and the four evangelist symbols page (fo. 2r)—leading to the conclusion that these pages were intended to call to mind images of adjacent *loca sancta* (holy places) of the Holy Sepulchre in Jerusalem and the Easter rites they helped to inspire. The John carpet page (fo. 192v),

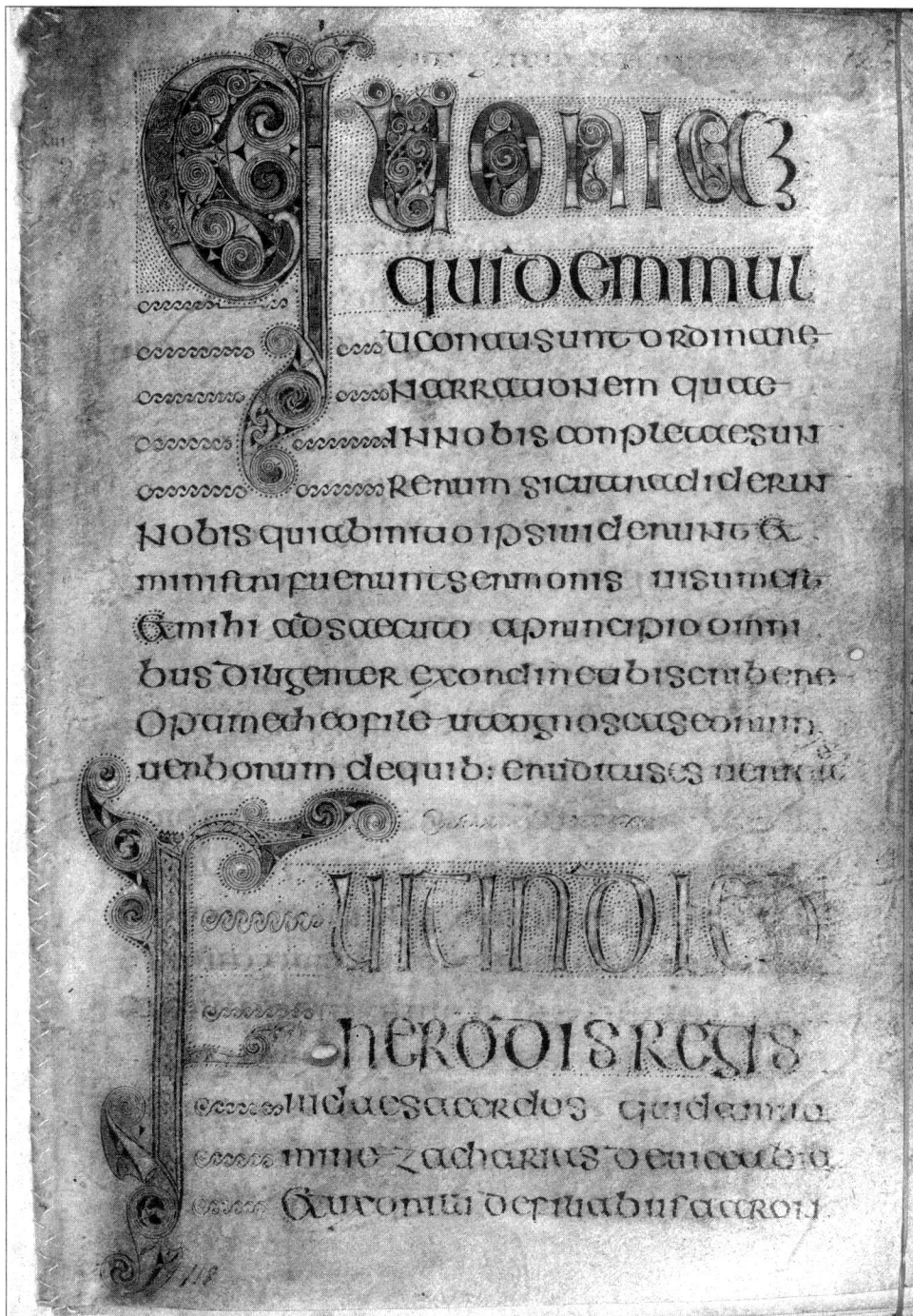

Book of Durrow, opening of the Gospel of St Luke, fo. 126r, showing decorated oversize initials

is seen as making similar reference to the Holy Sepulchre, and supports the thesis of a dominant Easter programme developed for the codex by ADOMNÁN, ninth abbot of the Columban monastery of Iona (EILEAN Ì), and a date for its creation on Iona of *c.* 685. Since it has also been postulated that the Book of KELLS employs a more subtle and elaborate version of Durrow's Easter programme, this iconographic relationship associates the two manuscripts even more intimately than previously documented textual links and strengthens the possibility that they were both a product of the Iona scriptorium.

PRIMARY SOURCE
FACSIMILE. Luce et al., *Evangeliorum Quattuor Codex Durmachensis.*

FURTHER READING
ADOMNÁN; COLUM CILLE; EILEAN Ì; ÉRIU; JEROME; KELLS; Meehan, *Book of Durrow*; O Cróinin, *Peritia* 3.17–49; Stevick, *Earliest Irish and English Bookarts*; Werner, *Anglo-Saxon England* 26.23–39; Werner, *Art Bulletin* 72.174–223.

Martin Werner

Duval, Añjela (1905–81) spent her life on the smallholding where she was born in Traoñ an Dour, Ar C'houerc'had (Le Vieux Marché), in northern Brittany (BREIZH):

Me zo ganet en un ti plouz
'Kreiz ar maezioù glas ha didrouz
E koantañ traonienn zo 'n Treger
Ma red enni sioul al Leger.
Ar barzh paour, 1964 (The poor poet; *Añjela Duval* 224)

I was born in a thatched house
Deep in the green and noiseless countryside
In the prettiest valley in Treger
Where the Leger silently flows.

Becoming an only child after the early death of two elder siblings, Charlez and Maïa (*Stourm a ran* 77; *Kan an Douar* 30–3), she soon established an intimate relationship with nature: 'Trees of my childhood years, tell me now, where does my deep love of you come from?' (*Traoñ an Dour* 68). Communion with the earth permeates her work: 'While your eyes can see nature's thousand wonders, while the tang of earth freshly ploughed and the delicate fragrance of the willow quickens your senses, do not say that age is a heavy burden' (*Stourm a ran* 116).

Añjela Duval turned to poetry at the age of 56: 'My beloved parents died in turn of old age, and one day I found myself alone in my home. And alone in winter by the fire after supper, instead of singing I just pined, my heart full of grief. For years I fought with sickness and despair' (*Kan an Douar* 64).

Then, in 1961, she received a valuable gift of books and journals containing most Breton writing since the 1920s. The corpus included creative works, dictionaries and grammars, largely products of the Gwalarn school whose founder Roparz HEMON was exiled in Ireland: 'But one day (such a wonder!), flown from Ireland, echoes of your monumental songs come to stir my heart' (*Kan an Douar* 65). The marriage of popular idiom to the substance of the written word, fuelled by an immense need for personal expression, then resulted in a unique body of work which continues to inspire the Breton language movement.

Twin themes in Duval's poetry are the demise of Breton civilization and the rise of French hegemony. Treatment of the first transports us into a world which has vanished, and the many glimpses afforded of this world ensure the endurance of the work as a social document. In 'Va c'hêriadenn' (My village) she says: 'The village has fallen silent, its face is the colour of death, its heart has ceased to beat. The cockerel is silent at daybreak, silent the clatter of wheels along the lane, the cart-driver's whip is silent (and his swearing!). Silent the neighing mare as she returns to her foal, the bull's droning bellow is silent, no cow lowing with heavy udder, the fields are fallow!' (*Kan an Douar* 114).

Añjela Duval greets the rise of French hegemony with dismay, indignation, outrage and desperation. The opening poem of *Kan an Douar*, 'Ne gavan ket plijus' (I don't like), makes the point: 'I loathe the sight of my country's old people pining in homes for the toil they once knew, and the young mothers of my country speaking the language of the oppressor to their babies' (*Kan an Douar* 17). By 1981 these and similar sentiments have been distilled: 'I will have seen . . . the stone houses ruined . . . the hedgerows levelled along with their chestnut, beech and oak . . . the pathways choked with briars . . . the Breton names of the fields erased from the signposts, Breton children become French, deaf and mute among the old people, and strangers in their own country' (*Stourm a ran* 136).

The imminent collapse of the BRETON language casts a long shadow in Añjela Duval's work. She writes in strident tones on the subject. It is 'a crime to break the golden chain' of the language (*Stourm a ran* 127). French is '. . . no more than a corrupt Latin spoken by the soldiers and servants of Caesar' (*Stourm a ran* 61). 'The Celts have become Romans thanks to the cursed French' she writes (*Stourm a ran* 112).

The words *gouenn* 'race' and *gwad glan* 'pure blood' occur frequently. She also says: 'Ancestors of my forefathers from the Celtic Eden, see my tears spill on your ruined edifices' (*Traoñ an Dour* 109). And: 'In the eyes of God, in the eyes of the world, we are Bretons, we are Celts!' (*Traoñ an Dour* 99).

Añjela Duval never married. The fact that she was childless created a vacuum in her personal life: 'Who will carry on my anthem when I am gone?' she asks. 'Who will take up my arms as I have borne no son?' (*Stourm a ran* 93). Young Breton activists became her adopted sons. One she calls 'Yann-Kael [Kernalegen], child of my heart' (*Stourm a ran* 107). 'Our martyrs Yann-Vari and Yann-Kael' (*Stourm a ran* 110), she wrote, after he and another were killed in 1976 during a bomb attack they were carrying out.

'The Faith. The Country. The Country's Land. All three are endangered', writes Añjela Duval (*Stourm a ran* 133). This trinity is at the heart of her verse: 'My song is a song of pity for the small farmers of my country. I proclaim my contempt for those who betray my land . . . the sacred Land of our Fathers' (*Traoñ an Dour* 108). The industrialization of farming angers her: 'So as to increase the work done by machine, the dumb beast must be contaminated' (*Stourm a ran* 117).

Ironically, Añjela Duval wrote in an idiom obscure to Breton speakers. Her language incorporated neologisms and archaisms which put her work beyond her fellows and neighbours. It has thus remained inaccessible to 'My brothers in toil: the small farmers' (*Stourm a ran* 59).

Her legacy is the culmination of great endeavour and it represents a considerable human achievement. Añjela Duval is of unrivalled stature in Breton-language literature in the latter part of the 20th century.

SELECTION OF MAIN WORKS
Kan an Douar (1973); *Traoñ an Dour* (1982); *Me, Añjela* (1986); *Stourm a ran war bep tachenn* (1998); *Añjela Duval* (2000).

FURTHER READING
BREIZH; BRETON; BRETON LITERATURE; HEMON; Timm, *Modern Breton Political Poet, Añjela Duval*.

Diarmuid Johnson

Early medieval Dyfed, Ystrad Tywi, and Ceredigion, cantrefi, and political centres

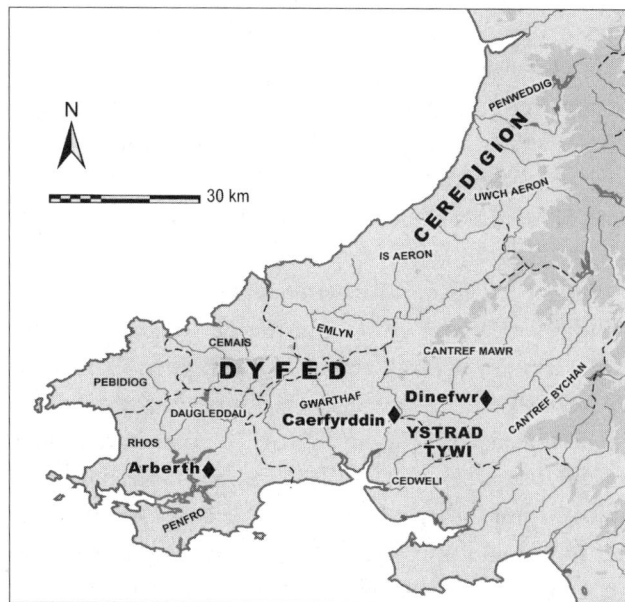

Dyfed is unique among the regions and medieval kingdoms of what is now Wales (CYMRU) in continuing, in name and approximate geographic limits, what was a CIVITAS of Roman Britain and a Celtic tribe of the pre-Roman IRON AGE. In this respect, Dyfed is comparable to the post-Roman kingdoms of DUMNONIA in south-west BRITAIN and GODODDIN in the northeast. The tribal name *Demetae*, from which the Welsh *Dyfed* derives, is recorded in the *Geography* of PTOLEMY as Δημηται *Dēmētae*, though the two long vowels for short seem to be an error based on copying from source in Roman script (in which long and short *e* are not distinguished). Although the etymology is uncertain (Rivet & Smith, *Place-Names of Roman Britain* 333), a connection with Welsh *dafad* 'sheep', in the sense of 'tame, domestic', is possible.

In Roman times the tribal *caput* was the town of Moridūnon (Sea-fort), now Carmarthen (CAERFYRDDIN), preserving the old name with *caer* 'fortified town' prefixed. Somewhat paradoxically, the post-Roman dynasty of Dyfed did not arise from the old ROMANO-BRITISH aristocracy, but rather from an intrusive Irish group known as the Déisi (who probably arrived in the 5th century), whose collaterals in Ireland were based in the counties of Waterford (Port Láirge) and Meath (Old Irish MIDE). Tracing them in early Ireland (ÉRIU) is further complicated by the common noun *déisi* 'vassals'. The evidence for this migration is an Old Irish text, probably dating from the 8th century, usually called the 'Expulsion of the Déisi', which refers to their destination as *crich Demeth* 'the region of Dyfed' (see Dillon, *Celtica* 12.1–11; Ó Cathasaigh, *Éigse* 20.1–30; Coplestone-Crowe, SC 16/17.1–24). The tale includes a pedigree of the kings of Dyfed which corresponds closely with that found in the Old Welsh GENEALOGIES found in British Library MS Harley 3859. In fact, the name forms in the Irish list, e.g. *Goirtibe[r]* = Old Welsh *Guortepir*, show clear signs of being derived from Welsh rather than having developed continuously in an independent Irish tradition. The foundation legend is broadly confirmed by the concentration of Primitive Irish OGAM inscriptions and place-name elements of Irish origin (e.g. *meidir* 'road' < Ir. *bóthar*, *cnwc* 'hillock' < *cnoc*) in south-west Wales (see Richards, *Journal of the Royal Society of Antiquaries of Ireland* 90.133–62).

In the 6th century GILDAS denounced Dyfed's

reigning ruler Vorteporius as *tyrannus Demetarum* 'tyrant of the Demetae' (*De Excidio Britanniae* §31). This is the same man as the Guortepir of the genealogy and probably the same as the (Latin genitive) VOTEPORIGIS PROTICTORIS, ogam genitive VOTECORIGAS, named on a famous inscription from near Carmarthen. The Romanization of Dyfed's dynasty is reflected in the Old Welsh genealogy, where descent is claimed from *Maxim guletic* (MACSEN WLEDIG), and we find among the early names Roman titles such as *Triphun* < *tribunus*, as well as *Protector*, as on the Voteporix stone.

Another interesting detail is that the tribal name itself occurs as the ancestral name *Dimet* along with the rhyming doublet *Nimet* 'Man of privileged rank' (see NEMETON). The 7th- or 8th-century Life of St SAMSON uses the place-name *Demetia*. ANNALES CAMBRIAE refers to *Demetica regio* in an entry of 645, and this is also the Latinized form in ASSER's Life of ALFRED THE GREAT.

Dyfed figures as the chief setting of the first and third Branches of the MABINOGI, PWYLL and MANAWYDAN. The kingdom is said to have had a main court at ARBERTH (now Narberth, Pembrokeshire) and comprised seven hundreds (see CANTREF): Cemais, Pebidiog, Rhos, Daugleddau, Penfro, Cantref Gwarthaf, and Emlyn. Pwyll's son and successor PRYDERI is said to have added to his legacy the three *cantrefi* of Ystrad Tywi and the four of CEREDIGION. This legendary expansion probably reflects a historical development seen in 11th-century sources whereby a larger political entity comes to be called DEHEUBARTH 'southern region' or *dextralis pars Britanniae*, with its royal centre at Dinefwr.

Dyfed re-emerged with the consolidation of Cardiganshire, Carmarthenshire, and Pembrokeshire (sir ABERTEIFI, sir Gaerfyrddin, sir Benfro) in the local government reorganization of 1974. These three pre-1974 counties came back into being in 1993, but the official name of the old Cardiganshire is now Ceredigion.

PRIMARY SOURCES
EDITION. Bartrum, EWGT.
ED. & TRANS. (Expulsion of the Déisi) Hull, ZCP 24,266–71; Hull, ZCP 27.14–63; Meyer, *Ériu* 3.135–42; Pender, *Féilscríbhinn Torna* 209–17.

FURTHER READING
ABERTEIFI; ALFRED THE GREAT; ANNALES CAMBRIAE; ARBERTH; ASSER; BRITAIN; CAERFYRDDIN; CANTREF; CEREDIGION; CIVITAS; CYMRU; DEHEUBARTH; DUMNONIA;

ÉRIU; GENEALOGIES; GILDAS; GODODDIN; IRON AGE; MABINOGI; MACSEN WLEDIG; MANAWYDAN; MIDE; NEMETON; OGAM; PRYDERI; PTOLEMY; PWYLL; ROMANO-BRITISH; SAMSON; Coplestone-Crowe, SC 16/17.1–24; Dillon, *Celtica* 12.1–11; Mac Cana, *Y Gwareiddiad Celtaidd* 153–89; Miller, SC 12/13.33–61; Ó Cathasaigh, *Éigse* 20.1–30; Richards, *Journal of the Royal Society of Antiquaries of Ireland* 90.133–62; Rivet & Smith, *Place-Names of Roman Britain*.

JTK

Dyfnwal ab Owain/Domnall mac Eogain

was king of Strathclyde (YSTRAD CLUD) *c.* 962–75. In Irish sources his title is given as *Rí Bretan* 'King of the Britons'. He became king when DUB mac Mael Choluim left the throne of Ystrad Clud to become king of the Scots in 962. He prevented CUILÉN RING mac Illuilb from taking the kingship of Ystrad Clud, and his son Rhydderch slew Cuilén in 971. He was one of the eight northern rulers who took part in the act of submission to Edgar, king of the English, at Chester (CAER) in 973. He then seems to have abdicated in favour of his son Mael Coluim, whose reign was brief and unremarkable. Dyfnwal died after entering a monastery on a pilgrimage in 975. On Old Welsh and Cumbric *Dumngual* and the Gaelic cognate *Domhnall*, see DOMNALL BRECC; DOMNALL MAC AILPÍN. For his father's name, see ENAID OWAIN AB URIEN. Since both his name and patronym exist in BRYTHONIC and GAELIC forms, they are ambiguous in determining his cultural origin.

FURTHER READING
ALBA; BRYTHONIC; CAER; CUILÉN RING; CUMBRIC; DOMNALL BRECC; DOMNALL MAC AILPÍN; DUB; ÉIRE; ENAID OWAIN AB URIEN; GAELIC; YSTRAD CLUD; Alan O. Anderson, *Early Sources of Scottish History AD 500 to 1286* 1.478, 480; Smyth, *Warlords and Holy Men* 224, 226–7.

PEB

Dyfnwal ap Tewdor

(†760) was a king of Dumbarton (see YSTRAD CLUD) documented in early Welsh sources. 'Dumnagual map Teudebur' is listed as a ninth-generation descendant of Cinuit map Ceretic Guletic, probably the eponym of the CYNWYDION dynasty, in the Old Welsh GENEALOGIES in British Library MS Harley 3859, and the death of 'Dunnagual filius Teudubr' is noted in ANNALES CAMBRIAE. These records imply significant channels for written records from north Britain to Wales (CYMRU) during the 8th and 9th centuries. Dumbarton (Dùn Breatann) was under heavy military pressure during Dyfnwal's reign. Kyle (Cuil) in present-day Ayrshire fell to Eadberht (†768) of Northumbria and, according to the *Historia Regum* attributed to Symeon of Durham, Eadberht in alliance with ONUIST son of Uurguist of the PICTS captured Dumbarton itself on 1 August 756. Since *Annales Cambriae* 760 coincidentally notes a *Gueith Hirford* (battle of Hereford) between the BRITONS and the Saxons, some later historians have taken this and the death notice as one entry, i.e. that Dyfnwal fell at Hereford.

On the Celtic origins of the name *Dyfnwal*, cf. DOMNALL BRECC; DOMNALL MAC AILPÍN. The spelling *Dumnagual*, which preserves the vowel quality of the first syllable of COMMON CELTIC **Dumno-ualos* and the unaccented vowel between the elements, is conservative and probably the 8th-century spelling. *Teudubr* appears, rather oddly, to be a compound of *tew* 'stout, fat' and *dŵr* 'water', both native Celtic words, but a Brythonic adaptation of Latin *Theodorus*, Greek Θεόδωρος, is possible; cf. Welsh *Tewdws* ~ Latin *Theodosius*.

FURTHER READING
ANNALES CAMBRIAE; BRITONS; BRYTHONIC; COMMON CELTIC; CYMRU; CYNWYDION; DOMNALL BRECC; DOMNALL MAC AILPÍN; GENEALOGIES; ONUIST; PICTS; YSTRAD CLUD; Bartrum, *Welsh Classical Dictionary* 213; Kirby, *Trans. Cumberland and Westmorland Antiquarian and Archaeological Society* 62.77–94; Ann Williams et al., *Biographical Dictionary of Dark Age Britain* 106.

JTK

E

Eadwine/Edwin, revered as a saint, was the Anglo-Saxon king of Northumbria (northern England) during the years 617–33. His hereditary base was the kingdom of DEWR (English and Latin Deira) in southern Northumbria, but he came to power by defeating and killing ÆTHELFRITH, the pagan king of BRYNAICH (Bernicia, northern Northumbria) at the battle of the river Idle. He then ruled lands on both sides of HADRIAN'S WALL as a single kingdom. Born a pagan himself, Eadwine, along with many of his Anglo-Saxon subjects, accepted CHRISTIANITY from the Roman missionary Paulinus in 627 or 628, becoming Northumbria's first Christian ruler.

From the standpoint of CELTIC STUDIES, Eadwine's reign is noteworthy for numerous and high-level relations with Wales (CYMRU) and the BRITONS of the North (see HEN OGLEDD), both friendly and hostile, as well as several mentions in early Welsh literature. One of his important palaces was a royal centre of pre-English origin at Yeavering in the Upper Tweed valley.

§1. EADWINE AND ELFED

Before Eadwine came to power he lived as an exile, pursued by his ruthless and powerful rival Æthelfrith. In this same period, Eadwine's nephew Hereric was living under the protection of the Brythonic king Cerdig (CERTIC), probably the ruler of this name known to have been in power in ELFED (Elmet, in what is now West Yorkshire, England) at that time. At Cerdig's court, Hereric was assassinated by poison (BEDA, *Historia Ecclesiastica* 4.23), most probably at the instigation of Æthelfrith. Early in his reign, Eadwine occupied Elfed and expelled its hereditary king Cerdig *c.* 617. This may be the same 'Ceretic' as the one whose death is recorded at a year corresponding to AD 616 or 618 in ANNALES CAMBRIAE.

§2. EADWINE AND THE CYNFERCHING DYNASTY OF RHEGED

Although Beda credits the act to Paulinus, HISTORIA BRITTONUM (§63) describes Eadwine's baptism as follows:

> Eadguin himself was baptised the following Easter, and 12,000 people were baptised with him. If anyone wishes to know who baptised them, Run son of Urbgen [RHUN AB URIEN] baptised them, and for forty days he did not cease in baptising the whole rapacious race and through his teaching many believed in Christ. (Koch & Carey, *Celtic Heroic Age* 302)

Whether this account is true or not, it makes the claim that the native Brythonic Christian rulers of what was to become Anglo-Saxon Northumbria were responsible for the king and his people becoming Christians.

Evidence from the English side that Eadwine enjoyed harmonious relations with at least some of his north British Welsh subjects is implied by two details recounted by Beda. First, Eadwine's subjects (even a woman with a newborn child) could travel from sea to sea within his vast kingdom in safety. Second, the king had placed stands with bronze hanging bowls at springs found at roadsides so that travellers might refresh themselves (Beda, *Historia Ecclesiastica* 2.16). These bowls have been taken as referring to objects of a Celtic type, of which several 6th- and 7th-century examples have been found at Anglo-Saxon sites. Although Beda must be understood as taking pains to portray Eadwine as an ideal Christian ruler, these stories are consistent with the testimony of *Historia Brittonum* that RHEGED's royal family and church enjoyed excellent relations with this English king.

§3. EADWINE AND GWYNEDD

According to Welsh tradition, in his youth Eadwine had been in FOSTERAGE at the court of GWYNEDD. While this is not impossible, given his years of exile, driven out of Northumbria by Æthelfrith, the story cannot be confirmed in an early and credible source. According to Beda (*Historia Ecclesiastica* 2.9), Eadwine exacted tribute from Anglesey (MÔN) and the Isle of Man (ELLAN VANNIN) at the height of his power, which would imply that he had imposed himself as military overlord over the kings of Gwynedd—CADFAN and his son CADWALLON.

Moliant Cadwallon ('In Praise of Cadwallon') refers to Eadwine as ruling over Brynaich as *Tad rwy tuylluras* 'a father of excessively great deception'. As shown by the poem's editor, R. Geraint Gruffydd, the poet's attitude reflects the situation of 633, immediately preceding the campaign season in which Cadwallon overthrew Eadwine. The meaning of the line may be that, as a Deiran, Eadwine lacked a legitimate hereditary claim to Brynaich, as far as the court of Gwynedd was concerned. Gwynedd's first dynasty itself claimed a northern descent from CUNEDDA, and therefore put forward its own claim to Brynaich as a sounder one. It was not an idle boast. Cadwallon conquered and ruled Northumbria for a period of a year, as recounted by *Historia Brittonum* (§61):

> Osfird and Eadfird were two sons of Edgu[*in*] [Eadwine], and with him they fell in the battle of Meicen [Old English Haethfelth, 12 October 633], and the kingship was never revived from their lineage, for none from their line escaped from that battle, but rather they all were killed with him by the army of Catguollaun [Cadwallon], the king of the realm of Guenedota [Gwynedd]. (Koch & Carey, *Celtic Heroic Age* 302)

Moliant Cadwallon also pointedly mentions GWALLAWG (of Elfed) as the hero or instigator of the battle of CATRAETH, a site which significantly also figured as one of Eadwine's royal residences. The poem also anticipates *o Gymru dygynneu tân yn tir Elued* 'kindling fire in Elfed's land by the Welsh', suggesting that Eadwine's annexation of Elfed and expulsion of Cerdig (who was probably Gwallawg's son) were issues used to justify Cadwallon's successful campaign in Northumbria. The poem also mentions [*c*]*yfŵyre gynne Efrawc* 'the mustering for the burning of York'. Interestingly, the poem urges destruction in southern Northumbria, in and around Eadwine's hereditary lands, but speaks of his illegitimacy in the north, in Brynaich. Apparently, a

political distinction is being made in the motives for Gwynedd's invasion of Eadwine's united Northumbria. The archaeologically revealed destruction of Eadwine's court at Yeavering probably occurred in 633/4 as part of Cadwallon's invasion. A fragment of another Welsh poem about Cadwallon, *Gofara Braint* (The river Braint floods), claims that Eadwine's head was brought to Gwynedd's court at ABERFFRAW.

If the story (§2 above) of Rhun son of Urien baptizing Eadwine in 628 is factual, it seems unlikely that URIEN's dynasty, the CYNFERCHING, had joined with Cadwallon in Eadwine's destruction in 633–34; more probably what remained of Rheged supported Northumbria or remained neutral.

PRIMARY SOURCES
BEDA, *Historia Ecclesiastica* §§57–65.
EDITION. Gruffydd, *Astudiaethau ar yr Hengerdd* 25–43 (*Moliant Cadwallon*; *Gofara Braint*).

FURTHER READING
ABERFFRAW; ÆTHELFRITH; ANNALES CAMBRIAE; BRITONS; BRYNAICH; CADFAN; CADWALLON; CATRAETH; CELTIC STUDIES; CERTIC; CHRISTIANITY; CUNEDDA; CYMRU; CYNFERCHING; DEWR; ELFED; ELLAN VANNIN; FOSTERAGE; GWALLAWG; GWYNEDD; HADRIAN'S WALL; HEN OGLEDD; HISTORIA BRITTONUM; MÔN; RHEGED; RHUN AB URIEN; URIEN; Charles-Edwards, *Celtica* 15.42–52; Higham, *Kingdom of Northumbria*; Higham, *English Empire*; Wallace-Hadrill, *Bede's Ecclesiastical History of the English People*.

JTK

Easter controversy

§1. INTRODUCTION

One might expect that the conversion of the pagan Anglo-Saxons, which began in 597, could have led to a cultural *rapprochement* with the BRITONS, who had possessed Christian institutions for centuries, since the later ROMANO-BRITISH period, as well as with the Irish and the PICTS, who had also become Christians before the English. For a variety of reasons, discussed in the entries on AUGUSTINE, BEDA, CAER, CHRISTIANITY, this unified insular church never came about. Perhaps the single most important schismatic issue was the reckoning of Easter, which raged from the late 6th century to the late 8th century. It would be an oversimplification to identify one Easter computus as Celtic and the opposing system as Roman/Anglo-Saxon. At various times and places, we find particular groups of English, Britons, Gaels, and Picts using the insular reckoning—an 84-year cycle attributed to the 3rd-century Syrian bishop, Anatolius of Laodicaea, in which Easter could not occur before 25 March, reckoned as the spring equinox. At other times, or in other places at the same time, the same groups followed Roman practice—a 19-year cycle attributed to Victorius in which Easter could occur as early as the more astronomically accurate equinox of 21 March. For over a century, this became the prime issue separating the English from the Brythonic church. To modern readers, the date of a movable holiday—which often coincided in both systems, anyway—may seem a trivial matter, but, for medieval cosmology, Easter—the resurrection of Christ—was the annual triumph of light over darkness and life over death. To calculate it incorrectly was to misunderstand fundamentally God's creation. Furthermore, the Easter computus was the centrepiece of early medieval astronomy, earth science, and timekeeping. It is thus no coincidence that Beda was simultaneously the leading proponent of the Roman computus (which eventually prevailed) and the greatest historian and scientist of the early Middle Ages, who unreservedly hated the Britons as heretics, and wrote his *Historia Ecclesiastica* with this bias.

§2. ST PATRICK'S COMPUTUS

During the 6th and earlier centuries, there had been competing systems, without any one of them achieving universality. Cummian (cf. CUMMÉNE FIND), in his letter arguing for the Roman Easter to Abbot Ségéne of Iona (EILEAN Ì), surveyed several Easter cycles. The first is attributed to *sanctus Patricius papa noster* (St Patrick our senior bishop). Another 7th-century Irish text contains the prologue of a computus ascribed to a Patricius. It was a 19-year cycle of the Alexandrian type sanctioned by the Nicene Council of 325 (Walsh & Ó Cróinín, *Cummian's Letter* 190). This cycle was observed by some Western churches in 384 and 387 (Ó Cróinín, *Peritia* 5.279–80; cf. Charles W. Jones, *Bedae Opera de Temporibus* 35–6). It was explained and defended at length by St Ambrose of Milan in a letter of 386 (McLynn, *Ambrose of Milan* 280–1; cf. Jones, *Bedae Opera de Temporibus* 35–7). At the time, the 'Romano-Briton' Magnus Maximus (MACSEN WLEDIG) ruled BRITAIN, GAUL, and Spain. A fanatical orthodox Christian, Maximus was eager to accede to Ambrose, who came to him as emissary of the rival emperor Valentinian II in

384×386 (Stancliffe, *St. Martin and his Hagiographer* 283); Maximus and his British following would no doubt have heeded Ambrose's letter of 386. Thus, it is not surprising that PATRICK—a son of the Romano-British élite and a third-generation Christian—used this Alexandrian computus.

§3. COLUMBANUS

By the beginning of the 7th century, Continental Roman Christians were agreed on the method of Victorius, while the Britons and Irish used a different, older 84-year cycle. COLUMBANUS, an Irish monastic leader who was working on the Continent, wrote to Pope Gregory the Great on the Easter question in 600:

> Why then, with all your learning . . . do you favour a dark Easter? I am surprised, I must confess, that this error of Gaul has not long since been scraped away by you, as if it were a warty growth; unless perhaps I am to think, what I can scarce believe, that while it is patent that this has not been righted by you, it has met with approval in your eyes . . . For you must know that Victorius has not been accepted by our teachers, by the former scholars of Ireland, by the mathematicians most skilled in reckoning chronology, but has earned ridicule or indulgence rather than authority. (Letter i, Walker, *Sancti Columbani Opera* 4–7)

In 603 Columbanus wrote to a hostile synod in Gaul in defence of the insular Easter, pleading 'we are all joint members of one body, whether *Galli*, *Britanni*, or *Iberi* [Irish]' (Letter ii, Walker, *Sancti Columbani Opera* 22–3).

§4. CUMMIAN'S LETTER

According to BEDA (*Historiae Ecclesiastica* 2.19), Pope Honorius I (625–38) wrote to the Irish (*Scotti*) exhorting them not to believe that their own small number at the extreme ends of the earth was wiser than the rest of the churches of the world in the matter of reckoning Easter.

Some southern Irish churches had adopted the Roman Easter by 632/3. Following a synod held by this group at Mag Léne, Cummian, one of their leaders, as noted above, wrote a letter to the abbot of Iona, the intellectual stronghold of the insular Easter. The letter argued for the Roman Easter on the basis of the superior authority of the *tres linguae sacrae*, the three sacred languages—Hebrew, Greek, and Latin—and the intellectual insignificance and geographic marginality of the Irish and Britons (Walsh & Ó Cróinín, *Cummian's Letter*). In the 7th-century computus which Ó Cróinín has attributed to 'the circle of Cummianus', a similar theme of authoritative *principales linguae* (excluding BRYTHONIC and IRISH) is cited to justify the Roman Easter (PRIA C 82.405–30). Thus, the Easter issue had implicitly spawned an attack on learning in Irish or WELSH. 'Beccanus solitarius', who (along with Ségéne) was one of the addressees of Cummian's letter, was probably Beccán mac Luigdech who composed two 7th-century poems in Irish —*Fo réir Choluimb* (Bound to Colum) and *Tiugraind Beccáin* (The last verses of Beccán)—praising Iona's founder, COLUM CILLE (Walsh & Ó Cróinín, *Cummian's Letter* 7–15; Clancy & Márkus, *Iona* 129–34).

In 640 Pope elect John IV wrote to Ségéne and other Irish church leaders pressing the same point (letter preserved by Beda, *Historiae Ecclesiastica* 2.19).

§5. STREANÆSHALCH AND ITS AFTERMATH

In 664, at a council held at Streanæshalch (often called the 'Synod of Whitby'), Northumbria's church—which owed its foundation to Iona—accepted the Roman Easter. Colmán, the Irish abbot of LINDISFARNE, withdrew to Ireland (ÉRIU), by way of Iona (see CUMMÉNE FIND). Also present were the noble Anglo-Saxon Bishop Wilfrid, a strong adherent of the Roman side, and his patron, Prince ALCHFRITH. Presiding was Alchfrith's father, King OSWYDD, who, Beda tells us, supported the Insular Easter because he had been educated by the Irish and spoke their language perfectly. Beda writes that some churches of the Britons adopted the Roman Easter after the battle of NECHTANESMERE in 685, but does not say which ones. Before Iona came into conformity in 716, most non-Columban Irish foundations, including Armagh (ARD MHACHA), had followed the Roman Easter for some decades. ADOMNÁN, the abbot of Iona, accepted the Roman Easter before his death (†704). St ELFODDW was responsible for finally changing the reckoning in Wales (CYMRU) in 768, according to ANNALES CAMBRIAE. The Old Welsh COMPUTUS Fragment is a commentary on Beda's Victorian computus.

§6. TALIESIN, URIEN, CATRAETH, AND EASTER

In *Yspeil Taliessin, Kanu Vryen* (Spoils of Taliesin, poetry of URIEN), an early Welsh poem in LLYFR TALIESIN,

there is a description of the poet and his patron at Easter:

> On Easter, I saw the great light and the abundant fruits.
> I saw the leaves that shone brightly, sprouting forth.
> I saw the branches, all together in flower.
> And I have seen the ruler whose decrees are most generous:
> I saw Catraeth's leader over the plains.
> (Koch & Carey, *Celtic Heroic Age* 364)

This description is unique in the CYNFEIRDD poetry. Points are being made, surely intentionally: Urien and his bard are overtly Christians; they observe the true Easter in which light has triumphed over darkness and all the plants are in flower—thus life has triumphed over death. Furthermore, the place was one of great Christian sanctity and priority in Northumbria—at CATRAETH (Catterick) thousands were baptized in 627, and when most of the kingdom relapsed into paganism during CADWALLON's invasion (633–5) the Roman mission continued under *Iacobus diaconus* ('James the Deacon') in the neighbourhood of Catterick. Thus, the poet has placed Urien and his own persona on the right side of two major crises in Northumbria's 7th-century church.

PRIMARY SOURCES
EDITION. Charles W. Jones, *Bedae Opera de Temporibus*.
ED. & TRANS. Clancy & Márkus, *Iona* (*Fo réir Choluimb; Tiugraind Beccáin*); Walker, *Sancti Columbani Opera*; Walsh & Ó Cróinín, *Cummian's Letter*.
TRANS. Koch & Carey, *Celtic Heroic Age* 364.

FURTHER READING
ADOMNÁN; ALCHFRITH; ANNALES CAMBRIAE; ARD MHACHA; AUGUSTINE; BEDA; BRITAIN; BRITONS; BRYTHONIC; CADWALLON; CAER; CATRAETH; CHRISTIANITY; COLUM CILLE; COLUMBANUS; COMPUTUS; CUMMÉNE FIND; CYMRU; CYNFEIRDD; EILEAN Ì; ELFODDW; ÉRIU; GAUL; IRISH; LINDISFARNE; LLYFR TALIESIN; MACSEN WLEDIG; NECHTANESMERE; OSWYDD; PATRICK; PICTS; ROMANO-BRITISH; URIEN; WELSH; WELSH POETRY; McLynn, *Ambrose of Milan*; Ó Cróinín, PRIA C 82.405–30; Ó Cróinín, *Peritia* 5.276–83; Stancliffe, *St. Martin and his Hagiographer*.

JTK

Ecgfrith (r. 670–†20 May 685), son of OSWYDD, nephew of OSWALD, younger half-brother of ALCHFRITH and FLANN FÍNA, was king of Northumbria. His relations with his neighbours—BRITONS, Irish, and

PICTS—were characterized by aggression and oppression, and ultimately led to disaster and a long-term lessening of Anglo-Saxon influence in the CELTIC COUNTRIES, in the context of a general weakening of Northumbrian power. The near-contemporary Life of Wilfrid by Eddius Stephanus shows that Ecgfrith violently expropriated the church lands of the Britons in the Pennines in the period 671×678:

Then St Wilfrid the Bishop stood in front of the altar, and, turning to the people, in the presence of the kings [Ecgfrith and Ælfwini], read out clearly a list of the lands which the kings, for the good of their souls, had previously, and on that very day as well, presented to him . . . and also a list of the consecrated places in various parts which the British clergy had deserted when fleeing from the hostile sword wielded by the warriors of our own nation . . . these are the names of the regions: round [?]Ribble and Yeadon and the region of Dent and Catlow [*iuxta Rippel et Ingaedyne et in regione Dunutinga et Incaetlaevum*] and other places. (Colgrave, *Life of Bishop Wilfrid/Eddius Stephanus* 36–7; regarding possible uncertainties on some of the place-names, see Sims-Williams, *Journal of Ecclesiastical Studies* 39.2.180–3)

As Smyth argues (*Warlords and Holy Men* 24–5; cf. Koch, *Gododdin of Aneirin* cxvi–cxvii), these confiscated lands probably belonged to the Christian BRYTHONIC kingdoms of ELFED and RHEGED. A comparable and broadly contemporary confiscation of Rheged church lands was Ecgfrith's grant of Cartmel (now south-west CUMBRIA) to St Cuthbert, giving him *omnes Britannos cum eo*, which is described in *Historia de sancto Cuthberto* (Jackson, LHEB 217, 241; Thacker, *St Cuthbert* 116). In 678 Ecgfrith imposed a puppet king and an English bishop, Trumwine, on the Picts (BEDA, *Historia Ecclesiastica* 6.12). In a passage concerning events of 679, we see that Wilfrid and his patron, Ecgfrith, had expanded their claim:

Wilfrid, Bishop of York, beloved of God, appealing to the Apostolic See . . . has confessed the true and catholic faith for all the northern part of Britain and Ireland, and for the islands which were settled by the peoples of the English and the Britons and also of the Irish and of the Picts and confirmed it

with his signature. (Colgrave, *Life of Bishop Wilfrid / Eddius Stephanus* 114)

The rationale behind these claims must be that Northumbria did not regard itself to be divorced from the churches founded by COLUM CILLE, but rather that York was now empowered by default to lead the Columban federation, since Northumbria was orthodox but the mother church remained schismatic in the EASTER CONTROVERSY. This papally endorsed claim served as the charter for Ecgfrith's unprecedented and horrific attack on Brega in the Irish midlands in June 684. Beda and the Irish ANNALS concur that many churches were destroyed at that time (*Historia Ecclesiastica* 6.26; Annals of Ulster 684: *Saxones Campum Bregh uastant 7 aeclesias plurimas in mense Iuni*). Beda attributes Ecgfrith's downfall not to the Picts who actually killed him, but to the prayers of the Irish for vengeance (*Historia Ecclesiastica* 6.26). In 686 ADOMNÁN negotiated with Ecgfrith's successor, Flann Fína mac Ossu/Aldfrith, for the return of sixty captives taken during the incursion. It is likely that Ecgfrith's ravaging of Brega served as some sort of impetus for the humanitarian concerns of CÁIN ADOMNÁIN ('Adomnán's Law') of 697. On 20 May 685, at NECHTANESMERE (possibly modern Dunnichen) in Pictland, the Northumbrian king and most of his army were wiped out by the Pictish BRUIDE MAC BILI, king of Fortrinn (*Historia Ecclesiastica* 6.26; Annals of Ulster 686 [=685]; HISTORIA BRITTONUM §57). Bishop Trumwine fled to Whitby as the hostile forces advanced (*Historia Ecclesiastica* 6.26). Beda describes the long-term political consequences of the battle:

From that time the hope and strength of the dominion of the English began to ebb and flow away. For the Picts took possession of their country which the English had held; and the Gaels who were in Britain; and some part of Britons recovered their freedom, which they have now enjoyed for approximately forty-six years. [Beda was writing in 731.] Many of the English folk were either slain by the sword, or taken into slavery, or took flight from the land of the Picts.

PRIMARY SOURCES
Colgrave, *Life of Bishop Wilfrid / Eddius Stephanus*; Wallace-Hadrill, *Bede's Ecclesiastical History of the English People*.

FURTHER READING
ADOMNÁN; ALCHFRITH; ANNALS; BEDA; BRITONS; BRUIDE
MAC BILI; BRYTHONIC; CÁIN ADOMNÁIN; CELTIC COUNTRIES;
COLUM CILLE; CUMBRIA; EASTER CONTROVERSY; ELFED;
FLANN FÍNA; HISTORIA BRITTONUM; NECHTANESMERE;
OSWALD; OSWYDD; PICTS; RHEGED; Blair, *World of Bede*;
Higham, *Kingdom of Northumbria*; Jackson, *Celt and Saxon* 20–
62; Jackson, *LHEB*; Kirby, *Trans. Cumberland and Westmorland
Antiquarian and Archaeological Society* new ser. 62.77–94; Koch,
Gododdin of Aneirin; Mac Lean, *Ruthwell Cross* 49–70; Moisl,
Peritia 2.103–26; Sims-Williams, *Journal of Ecclesiastical History*
39.163–83; Smyth, *Warlords and Holy Men*; Stancliffe &
Cambridge, *Oswald*; Thacker, *St Cuthbert*; Wormald, *Anglo-
Saxons* 70–100.

                                                    JTK

Echtrai (sing. *echtrae*, Modern Irish *eachtraí, eachtra*),
usually translated as 'adventures', constitute one of the
traditional Irish tale types. One should include in the
definition that the *echtrai* usually involve a lone hero
encountering supernatural or otherworldly challenges
(see IRISH LITERATURE [1] §§3–4). The term's etymological sense of 'going outside' or 'outing' (< Celtic
*$eχst(e)rio$-) is also meaningful. For example, in *Echtrae
Nerai* ('The Adventure of Nera'), which is part of the
ULSTER CYCLE (§4) and a *rem-scél* or 'fore-tale' of TÁIN
BÓ CUAILNGE, the action begins on a SAMAIN night at
the court of MEDB and Ailill at CRÚACHU, when Nera
is challenged to go out to put a withe around a hanged
captive outside. The presumably dead captive then
speaks, sending Nera on a series of strange and horrific
adventures into the OTHERWORLD (§3) and complete
disjunction from earthly time (Carey, *Ériu* 39.67–74).
Within the medieval Irish TALE LISTS, there are 14 *echtrai*
in the A list and ten in B, but they have only three in
common (Mac Cana, *Learned Tales of Medieval Ireland*):
Echtrae Nerai, Echtra Crimthainn Nia Náir (The adventure
of Crimthann Nia Náir), and *Echtra Con Culainn* (The
adventure of CÚ CHULAINN); the last does not survive,
at least under this name. Early Irish writers did not
apply the term with precision. As discussed by
Dumville (*Ériu* 27.73–94), there is an overlap
especially between *echtrai* and IMMRAMA (voyage tales;
see also VOYAGE LITERATURE). As well as the maritime element, the *immrama* also more usually include
overt Christian themes than do *echtrai*. However, the
oldest extant *eachtrae, Echtrae Chonlai* (The adventure
of Conlae, discussed in VOYAGE LITERATURE §2),
which is one of the early texts derived from CÍN

DROMMA SNECHTAI, is in fact a voyage tale with
Christian themes. On the relationship of *Echtrae Brain*
(Adventure of Bran) and the extant voyage tale
IMMRAM BRAIN, see BRAN MAC FEBAIL. *Echtra Mac
nEchach Muig-medóin* ('The Adventure of the Sons of
Eochaid Muigmedón'), an 11th-century foundation
legend of the great UÍ NÉILL dynasty, is one of the
most famous surviving examples of the Celtic
SOVEREIGNTY MYTH (see also LEGENDARY HISTORY
§2; cf. ARTHURIAN LITERATURE [6] §4). In it, Níall
and his brothers are lost and weary after hunting (a
common plot device); one brother after another goes
out seeking water and confronts a hideous hag at the
well who asks each of them for a kiss; Níall at last
kisses and lies with her, at which point she is transformed into the beautiful personification of the
sovereignty of Ireland (ÉRIU), conferring the right
to rule on Níall and his progeny forever. On *Echtra
Fergusa maic Léiti* (The adventure of Fergus son of
Léite), see LUCHORPÁN. The *echtrae* genre continued
into the later Middle Ages and modern times,
becoming influenced by the international chivalric
romance (see IRISH LITERATURE [4] §3).

PRIMARY SOURCES
TRANS. Koch & Carey, *Celtic Heroic Age* 127–32 (*Echtrae Nera*),
184–7 (*Echtra Chorbmaic Uí Chuinn* 'The adventure of Cormac
grandson of Conn'), 203–8 (*Echtra Mac nEchach*).

FURTHER READING
ARTHURIAN LITERATURE [6]; BRAN MAC FEBAIL; CÍN
DROMMA SNECHTAI; CRÚACHU; CÚ CHULAINN; ÉRIU;
IMMRAM BRAIN; IMMRAMA; IRISH LITERATURE; LEGENDARY
HISTORY; LUCHORPÁN; MEDB; OTHERWORLD; SAMAIN;
SOVEREIGNTY MYTH; TÁIN BÓ CUAILNGE; TALE LISTS; UÍ
NÉILL; ULSTER CYCLE; VOYAGE LITERATURE; Carey, *CMCS*
30.41–65; Carey, *Ériu* 39.67–74, 40.194; Dumville, *Ériu* 27.73–
94; Mac Cana, *Learned Tales of Medieval Ireland*.

                                                    JTK

Edgeworth, Maria (1768–1849) was a product
of the Anglo-Irish ASCENDANCY and an important
novelist who wrote on Irish themes. Her work is of
interest to CELTIC STUDIES for several reasons. It
reflects, in conscious and systematic detail, the spoken
English of pre-FAMINE rural Ireland (ÉIRE), inci-
dentally revealing much influence from spoken IRISH
(see Flynn, *Proc. Harvard Celtic Colloquium* 2.115–86). It
also reflects an important early stage in the formation
of an Irish national consciousness and national litera-

ture in English (see NATIONALISM). She also contributed negatively to the formation of a stereotype of the native Irish population in English literature.

Edgeworth was born in England and moved to Ireland in 1782 to live with her father in Edgeworthstown. Apart from occasional travels in Britain and continental Europe, she lived in Ireland until her death in 1849. Biographers frequently remark on the impact of the 1798 Irish uprising on Edgeworth (see TONE; ACT OF UNION), particularly her exposure to the casualties of the uprising, and, later, her family's attempts to alleviate the suffering caused by the Famine of 1845. A writer almost as prolific as Lady Morgan (Sydney OWENSON), to whom she was (and is) often compared, Edgeworth published over two dozen volumes between 1795 and 1848, many of which went through multiple editions.

Education is a recurring concern in Edgeworth's work. Her father, Richard Lovell Edgeworth, was an education theorist and inventor. Until his death in 1817, Edgeworth collaborated with her father on several educational tracts, and also applied their principles in her fiction. Most of the fictional volumes are for children, making Edgeworth a key voice in the early history of children's literature, as well as a popular children's writer in her time. But she also wrote educational fiction for other groups, including the newly literate lower classes, in volumes such as *Popular Tales*. Her novels also frequently draw on didactic themes; *Ennui*, for instance, a novel in the first series of *Tales of Fashionable Life*, focuses on the re-education of the protagonist. Typically in such tales, benevolent elders reward dutiful subordinates, fostering behaviour which is shaped by a strong work ethic and a high regard for authority.

While many of her works for adults fall into the category of the novel of manners, and therefore bear comparison with Jane Austen's novels, Edgeworth was also a significant voice on the representation of Ireland. Her first and most-discussed novel, *Castle Rackrent* (1800), is notable for its representation of Hiberno-English dialect in both the text and an appended 'Glossary'. As Marilyn Butler notes, however, 'Irish traditions meant to the Edgeworths the survival of irrational and inefficient habits: they thought that extensive education among all classes was the best remedy for tradition' (*Maria Edgeworth* 364). Works such as

The Essay on Irish Bulls (1802), *Castle Rackrent*, and *Ennui* (1809) suggest that some of the effects of such traditions are attractive-imaginative phraseology, a commitment to the local authority, but these are largely infantilized attributes and participate in the emerging stereotype of the Irish as lively in unproductive ways and with the ever-present risk that this liveliness would become unruliness.

Because of the ethnographic dimension of her Irish work and an attendant concern with the ways in which a culture enters modernity, Edgeworth is also frequently grouped with authors of the national tale, especially Lady Morgan and Sir Walter SCOTT. Scott was a friend and long-time correspondent, and several critics have traced a mutual influence, but Edgeworth found 'comparisons' of her work to that of her fellow Irish novelist Morgan 'odious', and echoes the conservative reviews in her description of Morgan's work: 'a shameful mixture . . . of the highest talent and lowest malevolence'; 'impropriety—& disregard of the consequences of what she writes' (*Maria Edgeworth* 448). The national tales which these writers produced are quite different, employing different notions of modernity as well as widely separated political perspectives. But they collectively register an early 19th-century concern with bridging the gap between the English metropole and the so-called 'Celtic periphery' in the wake of the 1800 Act of Union.

PRIMARY SOURCES
Castle Rackrent (1800); *Essay on Irish Bulls* (1802); *Popular Tales* (1804); *Tales of Fashionable Life* (1809–12).

FURTHER READING
ACT OF UNION; ANGLO-IRISH LITERATURE; ASCENDANCY; CELTIC STUDIES; ÉIRE; FAMINE; IRISH; NATIONALISM; OWENSON; SCOTT; TONE; Butler, *Maria Edgeworth*; Deane, *Strange Country*; Dunne, *Maria Edgeworth and the Colonial Mind*; Flynn, *Proc. Harvard Celtic Colloquium* 2.115–86; Hollingworth, *Maria Edgeworth's Irish Writing*; Kowaleski-Wallace, *Their Father's Daughters*; Myers, *Nineteenth-Century Contexts* 19.373–412; Tracy, *Nineteenth-Century Fiction* 40.1–22.

Julia M. Wright

education in the Celtic languages [1] Irish medium

§1. INTRODUCTION

IRISH-medium education is provided in two jurisdictions: the Republic of Ireland (ÉIRE) and Northern Ireland. In the Republic of Ireland, Irish-medium education takes two forms—in the remaining GAELTACHT (Irish-speaking) regions, Irish-medium education is intended to be L1 (first-language) medium instruction, whereas the Gaelscoil (Irish-medium schooling) movement in non-Gaeltacht areas of the Republic of Ireland and in Northern Ireland is following a total immersion model with the vast majority of students having English as a home language.

§2. PRESCHOOL EDUCATION

Irish-medium preschools (naíonraí, sing. naíonra) are part of a national, primarily community and voluntary based, movement. Most naíonra leaders (stiúrthóirí, sing. stiúrthóir) work on a part-time basis and are dependent mainly on contributions (fees) from parents for their income (Hickey, An Luath-Thumadh in Éirinn / Early Immersion Education in Ireland). The first naíonra opened in 1968, and in 1974 a representative organization for naíonra stiúrthóirí was established. In 1978 the name of this organization was changed to Na Naíonraí Gaelacha (the Gaelic preschools), to highlight the pedagogical approach advocated—a combination of the positive aspects of both the preschool and playgroup models (Hickey, An Luath-Thumadh in Éirinn / Early Immersion Education in Ireland). In the same year, a national organization for the promotion of preschooling through the medium of Irish, An Comhchoiste Réamh-scolaíochta, was established as a joint venture between Na Naíonraí Gaelacha and Bord na Gaeilge, the state board with responsibility for the Irish language.

An Comhchoiste Réamhscolaíochta employs a total of 15 advisors on a full- and part-time basis, who provide advice and support for naíonra stiúrthóirí. They run a short foundation-level course for stiúrthóirí on an annual basis and since 2000 have been running a part-time FETAC (Further Education and Training Awards Council) validated certificate course in childcare through the medium of Irish. An Comhchoiste also provides financial support to naíonraí in the form of grant-aid ranging from €1,810 to €10,800 per annum, depending on the number of children attending the naíonra. Naíonraí in Gaeltacht areas receive similar levels of support from Údarás na Gaeltachta (the Gaeltacht development authority). They also receive administrative support in relation to taxation and the handling of employment and personnel matters from Seirbhísí Naíonraí Gaeltachta Teo. (Gaeltacht

	Naíonra Centres	Stiúrthóirí (Naíonra Leaders)	Stiúrthóirí Cúnta (Assistants)	Children
Gaeltachtaí (Irish-speaking regions)	69	70	78	1,152
English-speaking regions	141	156	28	2,348
Republic of Ireland (Total)	210	226	106	3,500
Northern Ireland	37	37	76	848
Total	247	263	182	4,348

Table 1: Statistics relating to Naíonra in 2002–03 (source: An Comhchoiste Réamhscolaíochta, Seirbhísí Naíonraí Gaeltachta Teo. & Comhairle na Gaelscolaíochta)

Naíonra Services Ltd.), a subsidiary company of Údarás na Gaeltachta. In Northern Ireland, sources of funding for naíonraí include the Education and Library Boards and the Department of Education, and Altram acts as a representative and support body for the naíonraí. In recent years, some naíonraí in the Republic of Ireland have received capital and staffing funding under the Department of Justice, Equality and Law Reform's Equal Opportunities Childcare Programme for 2000–2006, which aims to increase the provision of preschool childcare services generally. However, lack of funding is still the major challenge facing the sector, with its consequent effects on the provision of suitable facilities and on the recruitment and professional development of staff.

§3. PRIMARY LEVEL EDUCATION
(AGES 4–12 YEARS)

Schools in Gaeltacht regions generally teach through the medium of Irish at both primary and second level. The number of primary level Gaeltacht schools is 108, with a total number of 7507 pupils (Department of Education and Science, 1999/2000). Because of the rural nature of the Gaeltacht, the majority of these schools are small, with more than 50% of them having only three teachers or less.

Outside the Gaeltacht regions, the 1950s and 1960s saw a drastic reduction in the number of Irish-medium

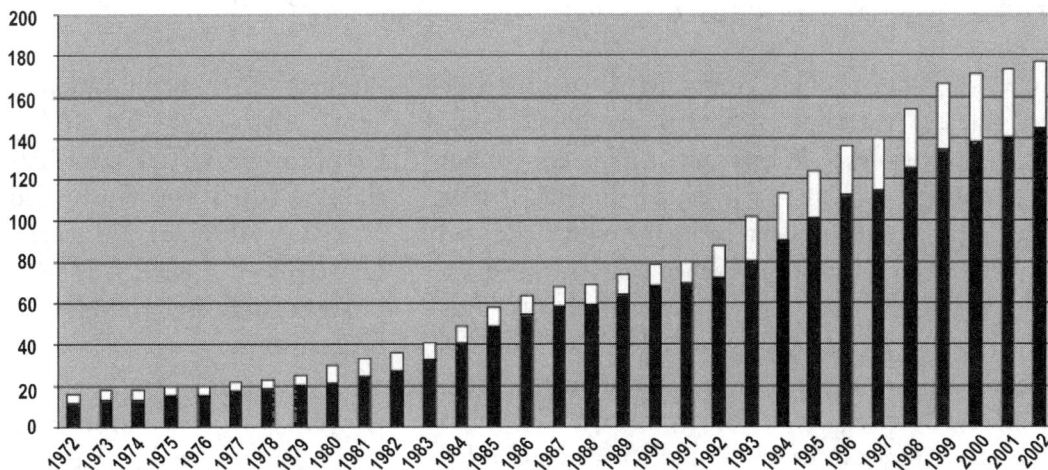

Table 2: Growth of the number of Irish-medium schools (vertical axis) outside the Gaeltacht regions, 1972–2002, primary schools in black, secondary in white (source: Gaelsoileanna)

schools. From 1972 onwards, however, a parent-based movement led to renewed interest and growth in Irish-medium schooling (see Table 2). Gaelscoileanna (Gael-schools) in the Republic of Ireland, and Gaeloiliúint (Gaelinstruction) in Northern Ireland act as representative and promotional bodies for Irish-medium schools in each jurisdiction respectively.

Current demographic trends suggest that the number of pupils receiving Irish-medium schooling in Gaeltacht areas will decrease, or at best, remain static in the future. The potential for growth in the Irish-medium school sector in non-Gaeltacht areas is still great, however, given that only 6% of primary level students are currently attending Irish-medium schools despite the fact that the potential demand at primary level is in the region of 30% (Ó Riagáin & Ó Gliasáin, *National Survey on Languages*).

Current challenges facing the sector include the supply of teachers qualified to teach through the medium of Irish, the provision of Irish-medium textbooks and other teaching resources, and planning issues relating to the establishment of new schools. Gaeltacht schools face additional challenges. With the continued shift of language patterns in Gaeltacht areas from Irish to English, Gaeltacht schools have to deal with a mixed intake of pupils, some who are native speakers of Irish and others who are not. A lack of forward language planning has left such schools struggling to deal with a complex linguistic situation without the resources, in terms of personnel and training, to do so.

§4. SECOND-LEVEL EDUCATION
(AGES 12–18 YEARS)

In Gaeltacht areas, 20 second-level schools currently teach through the medium of Irish, with a total of 3340 pupils attending them (Department of Education and Science, 1999/2000). In non-Gaeltacht areas, the number of students receiving Irish-medium schooling has shown a steady increase in the period from 1972 to

	Schools	Pupils	Teachers	Families
Republic of Ireland	119	21,894	1,065	14,920
Northern Ireland	25	1,996	120	1,462
Total	144	23,890	1,185	16,382

Table 3: Statistics for Irish-medium primary schools outside the Gaeltacht regions in 2002–03 (source: Gaelsoileanna)

	Schools	Pupils	Teachers	Families
Republic of Ireland	30	5,213	486 (+45 part-time)	3,796
Northern Ireland	3	427	47	300
Total	33	5,640	533 (+45 part-time)	4,096

Table 4: Statistics for Irish-medium second-level schools outside the Gaeltacht regions in 2002–03 (source: Gaelsoileanna)

2002 (see Table 2). This growth has been driven by the increased participation in Irish-medium schooling at primary level. Where initial numbers are not large enough to justify the establishment of new schools on an independent basis, the model adopted has been to establish semi-independent Irish-medium units within existing English-medium schools. This model has, so far, not proved completely satisfactory. While the percentage of students continuing in Irish-medium schooling from primary to second level is high in some cases, the overall percentage is regarded as disappointing. Research is currently underway into the reasons for this.

§5. THIRD LEVEL SECTOR

The National University of Ireland, Galway (Ollscoil na hÉireann, GAILLIMH) has a legislative responsibility in relation to university education through the medium of Irish, and currently offers a range of courses and modules through the medium of Irish at diploma, degree and postgraduate level. These include an MA in Translation Studies and Higher Diplomas in Education, Applied Communications and in Information Technology. A limited range of options is available through Irish for students at undergraduate level in several disciplines. Figures for the 2001–2 academic year show that a total of 218 students were following all or some of their studies through the medium of Irish. In its recently published strategic plan for the period 2003–8, the University has announced its intention of establishing an Irish-medium academy, Acadamh na hOllscolaíochta Gaeilge, which will have as its remit the development of Irish-medium teaching and research activities both on campus and in its three Gaeltacht centres. The focus of the new academy will be to provide for the specific needs of Irish speakers and Gaeltacht communities through the development of teaching and research activities in subject areas that are seen as being of strategic importance to their future development.

Fiontar (enterprise), the Irish-medium unit in Dublin City University offers two undergraduate programmes: a BSc in Finance, Computing and Enterprise and a BSc in Entrepreneurship with Computing/Applied Irish, and an MSc/Graduate Diploma in Business and Information Technology. Galway–Mayo Institute of Technology offers an Irish-medium BA in Business and Communication Studies, and the Letterkenny Institute of Technology offers a National Certificate in Office Information Systems. Teacher-training education is provided through Irish in St Mary's College of Education, Marino, and the University of Limerick is proposing to offer a new postgraduate programme in sociolinguistics in September 2003.

§6. LEGISLATIVE AND LEGAL DEVELOPMENTS

The legal and legislative provision for Irish-medium education has improved considerably in recent years. In the Republic of Ireland, the Education Act of 1998 contains several provisions relating to Gaeltacht and Irish-medium schools, including provision for the establishment of a state-sponsored support body for Irish-medium schools—An Chomhairle um Oideachas Gaeltachta agus Gaelscolaíochta (The Council for Gaeltacht and Gaelscoil Education). In Northern Ireland, provisions supportive of Irish-medium education in the Good Friday Agreement have led to the Education (Northern Ireland) Order 1998, which places a statutory duty on the Department of Education to encourage and facilitate Irish-medium education. In response to this, following consultation with interested parties, the Department established the promotional body Comhairle na Gaelscolaíochta (The Gaelschooling Council) in August 2000. with the remit of promoting and supporting the strategic development of Irish-medium education in Northern Ireland.

PRIMARY SOURCES
Hickey, *An Luath-Thumadh in Éirinn*; Ollscoil na hÉireann, Gaillimh (National University of Ireland, Galway), *Plean Straitéiseach do OÉ, Gaillimh 2003–2008*; Ó Riagáin & Ó Gliasáin, *National Survey on Languages 1993*; Roinn Oideachais agus Eolaíochta (Department of Education and Science), *Tuarascáil Staitisticiúil 1999/2000*.

LEGISLATIVE PROVISIONS
Education Act, 1998; *Statutory Instrument 1998 No. 1759 (N.I. 13), Education (Northern Ireland) Order 1998*.

FURTHER READING
ÉIRE; GAELTACHT; GAILLIMH; IRISH; Hickey et al., *Luathoideachas trí Ghaeilge sa Ghaeltacht*; Kirk & Ó Baoill, *Language Planning and Education: Linguistic Issues in Northern Ireland, the Republic of Ireland and Scotland*; Mercator-Education, *Irish Language in Education in Northern Ireland*; Mercator-Education, *Irish Language in Education in the Republic of Ireland*; Muintearas, *Gnéithe den Oideachas sa Ghaeltacht: Impleachtaí Polasaí*.

BIBLIOGRAPHY. O'Connor, *Innéacs Taighe*.

WEBSITES
www.gov.ie/oireachtas/frame.htm
www.legislation.hmso.gov.uk/si/si1998/19981759.htm
www1.fa.knaw.nl/mercator/regionale_dossiers/regional_
dossier_irish_in_ireland.htm)
www1.fa.knaw.nl/mercator/regionale_dossiers/regional_
dossier_irish_in_northernireland.htm

MAIN CONTACT ORGANIZATIONS

REPUBLIC OF IRELAND
An Chomhairle um Oideachas Gaeltachta agus Gael-
scolaíochta, 22 Plás Mhic Liam, Baile Átha Cliath 2.
An Comhchoiste Réamhscolaíochta, 7 Cearnóg Mhuirfean,
Baile Átha Cliath 2.
GAELSCOILEANNA, 7 Cearnóg Mhuirfean, Baile Átha
Cliath 2.
www.iol.ie/gaelscoileanna

NORTHERN IRELAND
Comhairle na Gaelscolaíochta, Teach an Gheata Thiar, 4 Sráid
na Banríona, Béal Feirste BT1 6ED.
www.comhairle.org
ALTRAM, 34a Corrán Uíbh Eachach, Béal Feirste BT12 6AW.
Gaeloiliúint, 216, Bóthar na bhFál, Béal Feirste BT12 6AT.

Seosamh Mac Donnacha

education in the Celtic languages [2] Scottish Gaelic medium

Education through the medium of SCOTTISH GAELIC was formally introduced into state education in Scotland (ALBA) in 1975. The previous year had seen a major reorganization of local government and the creation of a single local authority for the Outer Hebrides (Innse Gall). The new council, Comhairle nan Eilean, adopted a bilingual policy and initiated a bilingual education project which was partly funded by central government.

§1. HISTORY OF PROVISION
Prior to the introduction of the project, the use of Gaelic as a medium of instruction had been informal, unofficial and sporadic, and had been tolerated rather than encouraged. No provision was made for Gaelic in the 1872 Education Act which established state education in Scotland. This was despite the fact that around 250,000 of the population could speak Gaelic and that the language had been used as a medium of instruction in many of the previously independent schools run by churches and various societies. Official disdain for the language was reflected in the appoint-

ment of monoglot English-speaking teachers in Gaelic-speaking areas and the not infrequent practice of administering corporal punishment to children for speaking Gaelic in school.

§2. THE BILINGUAL EDUCATION PROJECT
The Bilingual Education Project began as a pilot, but was extended in phases to all schools in the Outer Hebrides. The project was not only pioneering in linguistic terms, but also adopted an innovative approach in curricular areas such as environmental studies. By the early 1980s, however, parents and language activists were voicing concern about the ability of this particular model of bilingual teaching to deliver linguistic competence in Gaelic comparable to that in English. Similar concerns were being expressed about a second bilingual scheme being trialled in primary schools in the Isle of Skye (Sgiathanach) by the Highland Regional Council. There was mounting concern about the rapid erosion of the language among young people, and a growing conviction that greater use of Gaelic as a teaching medium was required to stem this decline. Gaelic-medium playgroups were set up in various parts of the country and they laid the foundation for the development of Gaelic-medium education in primary schools.

§3. PRIMARY EDUCATION
Provision in the primary sector was instituted in 1985 with the opening of Gaelic-medium units in schools in Glasgow (GLASCHU) and Inverness (Inbhir Nis). The success of these units and the spread of Gaelic-medium playgroups fuelled demand for provision in other areas, and by 2003–4 there were 1972 pupils engaged in Gaelic-medium education in 60 schools. Of these, 49 are located in the HIGHLANDS and Islands, and almost all of the schools have parallel Gaelic-medium and English-medium streams. The first all-Gaelic school in Scotland opened in Glasgow in 1999 and 5 primary schools in the Hebrides, in which the Gaelic-medium stream predominates, have been designated Gaelic schools by the local authority.

Most pupils in Gaelic-medium education in urban areas come from non-Gaelic-speaking homes, although many have a Gaelic or Highland family background. A two-year immersion programme in the language is a feature of the curriculum in all Gaelic-medium schools, and Gaelic is the main language of instruction in primaries at ages 3–7, although the balance of language use varies across education authorities and across the stages of the primary curriculum. All schools are bound by the National Curriculum Guidelines for ages 5–14, which specify that Gaelic-medium education should aim 'to bring pupils to the stage of broadly equal competence in Gaelic and English, in all skills, by the end of Primary 7'.

§4. SECONDARY EDUCATION

Gaelic first became an officially recognized medium of instruction in secondary schools in 1983, when the Bilingual Project in the Western Isles was extended to two secondary schools in Lewis (Leòdhas). The initial pilot project concentrated on the teaching of social subjects through the medium of Gaelic, and this focus was maintained beyond the project stage.

The first provision for pupils transferring from Gaelic-medium classes in primary schools was made in 1988 at Hillpark Secondary in Glasgow. By 2003–4, there were 15 schools providing some form of Gaelic-medium education to just over 300 pupils in various parts of Scotland. Gaelic-medium education in most secondary schools is limited to two or three school subjects, of which History is the most widely available. The subjects on offer vary from school to school, according to the availability of Gaelic-speaking subject teachers. The Scottish Qualifications Authority (SQA) offers Gaelic versions of the national Standard Grade examinations in history, geography, and mathematics in the Fourth Year, and it is anticipated that other subjects will, in the near future, be added to those currently available. Gaelic-medium pupils also study the language as a subject, and take the certificate Gàidhlig course designed for fluent speakers.

§5. TERTIARY AND HIGHER EDUCATION

Gaelic-medium education is not confined to the school sector. In the tertiary and higher sectors, some of the colleges of the University of the Highlands and Islands make provision for the language as a medium of instruction. The Gaelic College—SABHAL MÒR OSTAIG—on Skye offers a range of certificate, diploma, degree and postgraduate courses taught through the medium of Gaelic. Lews Castle College also provides some courses in Gaelic at campuses in Stornoway (Steòrnabhaigh) and Benbecula (Beinn nam Faodhla).

§6. FUTURE PROSPECTS

Gaelic education has recently been made a national priority by the Scottish Executive (see SCOTTISH PARLIAMENT), and the requirement this places on local authorities to produce development plans and progress reports may help overcome two of the major difficulties experienced in Gaelic-medium education at present—a lack of overall planning and a shortage of teachers. Despite these shortcomings, Gaelic-medium education has been described, with some justification, as 'one of the success stories of recent Scottish education' by the General Teaching Council of Scotland.

PRIMARY SOURCES
Scottish Office Education Department, *Curriculum and Assessment in Scotland: National Guidelines*; General Teaching Council for Scotland, *Teaching in Gaelic Medium Education*; HM Inspectors of Schools, *Provision for Gaelic Education in Scotland*.

FURTHER READING
ALBA; GLASCHU; HIGHLANDS; SABHAL MÒR OSTAIG; SCOTTISH GAELIC; SCOTTISH PARLIAMENT; Dunn & Robertson, *Gaelic and Scotland* 44–55; Johnstone, *Impact of Current Developments to Support the Gaelic Language*; Johnstone et al., *Attainments of Pupils Receiving Gaelic Medium Primary Education in Scotland*; MacIver, *Language Planning and Education* 56–60; MacKinnon, *Gaelic*; M. MacLeod, *Trans. Gaelic Society of Inverness* 43.305–34; W. McLeod, *Gaelic-medium Education Provision* 118–32; Murray & Morrison, *Bilingual Primary Education in the Western Isles, Scotland*; Robertson, *Gaelic*; Robertson, *Home Language and School in a European Perspective* 67–82; Robertson, *Language Planning and Education* 76–81; Robertson, *Other Languages of Europe* 83–101; Robertson, *Scottish Education* 250–61; Smith, *Trans. Gaelic Society of Inverness* 51.1–67.

Boyd Robertson

education in the Celtic languages [3] Manx medium

In 1996 the first regular Manx preschool group was established in Braddan by Mooinjer Veggey (the little people), with six children learning MANX through play, songs, stories, and activities. Mooinjer Veggey expanded rapidly and by April 2002 it had four groups with over 80 children registered. Also in 1996, following pressure from parents of bilingual (Manx/English) children, the Department of Education agreed on a trial basis to provide a half-day a week language session taught primarily through Manx. This has been well supported, with around 20 children attending regularly.

In November 1999 parents of children at Mooinjer Veggey and the half-day class formed Sheshaght ny

Paarantyn (SnyP, Parents for Manx-medium Education) with the specific aim of lobbying the Manx Government for the establishment of full-time Manx-medium primary education. SnyP worked tirelessly over the next 18 months, meeting various politicians and government officials and building support until, in April 2001, the Isle of Man Department of Education agreed that full-time Manx-medium education would be offered.

In September 2001 a Manx-medium class opened in Ballacottier Primary School, Douglas (Doolish), with nine pupils between 4 and 5 years old. The class proved to be extremely successful and it is envisaged that it will develop into a dedicated Manx-medium school. Support for the class from parents remains strong, but finding sufficient resources and teachers may prove difficult in the future.

RELATED ARTICLES
ELLAN VANNIN; MANX.

Phil Gawne

education in the Celtic languages [4] Welsh medium

The growth of WELSH-medium education—instigated by inspirational pioneers, and secured by dedicated teachers and committed parents—is one of the minor miracles of modern Europe. Education is the chief focus of the language struggle. It remains the central pillar of contemporary language transmission and offers a model that has been emulated in bilingual contexts worldwide.

The Butler Education Act of 1944 permitted Local Education Authorities to establish designated Welsh-medium schools, the first of which opened in Llanelli in 1947. By the early 1950s there were 15 designated schools, underpinned by a network of voluntary Ysgolion Meithrin (nursery schools), mainly in Anglicized areas. Parental pressure led to the establishment of Welsh-medium secondary schools in Rhyl (Ysgol Glan Clwyd, 1956), in Mold/Yr Wyddgrug (Ysgol Maes Garmon, 1962) and in Pontypridd (Ysgol Rhydfelen, 1962), and Ysgol Ystalyfera in the upper Swansea valley in 1967. Subsequently, a wide variation in the national pattern of bilingual teaching emerged, ranging from complete Welsh-medium to differing proportions of Welsh and English within the curriculum and subjects, dependent on both the sociolinguistic context of the catchment area and the Local Education Authority's language policy.

For 20 years, the acclaimed educational and sociocultural achievements of such schools led to a steady growth in bilingual provision characterized by an increasing number of children from non-Welsh-speaking homes. The Conservative Government's creation of a National Curriculum for Wales via the 1988 Education Act resulted in Welsh becoming a core subject, together with English, mathematics, and science, in all schools. The 1988 Act had far-reaching consequences. Welsh-medium education benefited from the additional resources expended on teacher training and the development of teaching materials in the 445 designated Welsh-medium schools (25.9% of the 1718 schools in 1990). English-medium schools also saw a significant growth in the teaching of Welsh. In 1990 barely half (50.7%, 870) the schools had classes where Welsh was taught as a second language. By 1997 this proportion had risen to 67.6% (1136). The Welsh Language Act of December 1993 further strengthened such trends by charging the statutory Welsh Language Board (BWRDD YR IAITH GYMRAEG) with a strategic responsibility for Welsh and ensuring that Local Education Authorities implement their agreed Welsh Language Education Schemes.

Consequent to these legislative reforms, the percentage of primary schoolchildren speaking Welsh fluently increased from 13.1% in 1986/7 to 16.0% in 1998/9. However, the percentage of primary schoolchildren speaking Welsh at home fell over the same period from 7.3% to 6.3%. In January 1999, 13.3% of secondary school pupils in Years 7 to 11 (the compulsory school age) were taught Welsh as a first language; the percentage has increased virtually every year since 1977/8, when the comparable figure was 9.3%. By 1999, 14.6% of pupils in Year 7 were being taught Welsh as a first language.

In 2001–2 there were 445 Welsh-medium primary schools, constituting 27% of the 1631 primary schools. A further 82 schools, 5% of the total, used Welsh as a teaching medium to some extent. In the remaining 1133 schools, 68% of all primary schools, Welsh was taught as a second language to 223,786 pupils. The number of full- and part-time primary teachers teaching through the medium of Welsh was 2812, while 8277 teachers taught it as a second language.

Also in 2001–2, there were 52 Welsh-medium secondary schools—22% of the total number of 229 secondary schools—who taught 37,389 pupils, 20% of the 186,081 secondary pupils. The number of secondary pupils taught Welsh as a first language was 26,135, and those taught Welsh as a second language numbered 157,300. The number of secondary teachers teaching through the medium of Welsh was 1802, while 772 teachers taught Welsh as a second language. The range and quality of bilingual material to sustain the teaching of specialist topics has grown tremendously, thanks largely to the commissioning policy of ACCAC (Qualifications, Curriculum and Assessment Authority for Wales), the publishing programmes of the Welsh Joint Education Committee and the innovative resources provided by Acen (established in 1989 as a project within S4C, the Welsh television channel, to teach Welsh to adults) and a plethora of small, independent media and publishing companies.

Yet, despite such incremental growth, the lack of continuity of provision at each successive level in the educational system has diminished the effectiveness of national bilingual strategies. At the base of the pyramid in 2002, 13,349 children attended Mudiad Ysgolion Meithrin Welsh-medium playgroups, taught by 1,028 playgroup leaders and supported by a national network of Cylchoedd Ti a Fi (parent and toddler groups). At primary-school level, the percentage which can speak Welsh fluently continues to rise, but, when they transfer to high school, Baker and M. P. Jones (*Language Revitalization* 131) argue that around 40% of such secondary school pupils move from a first-language to a second-language category.

In addition, the lack of adequate investment in bilingual teacher training and the patchy recruitment of *athrawon bro* (peripatetic Welsh teachers) have weakened the firm bilingual foundations laid in the earlier years, as has the need to widen access to Centres for Latecomers, to avoid duplication in the provision of teaching resources, to strengthen Welsh for Adults provision, and to develop bilingual software and resources for IT and Special Educational Needs. Vacillation over the post-16 bilingual policies pursued by ELWa (Education and Learning Wales) and the absence of an effective national strategy, together with a lack of adequate funding and training in Welsh-medium higher education provision, have also impeded the effectiveness of Welsh-medium education.

By 2003, the educational policy reforms announced by the National Assembly for Wales (Cynulliad Cenedlaethol Cymru), together with its adoption of holistic programmes to realize its declared ambition of creating a bilingual Wales (Cymru), had not yet assuaged the fears of critics who argued that Welsh-medium education was in crisis, especially in the post-16 sector. Because the bilingual infrastructure was so underdeveloped and the vocational element almost non-existent, many opportunities were being lost for the effective training of a bilingual workforce. In order to sustain the momentum generated so assiduously by countless thousands of committed individuals, the Government of Wales is being urged to engage in a historically unprecedented and sustained level of investment in Welsh-medium education at all levels. Anything less would render the aim of creating a bilingual Wales within the medium term an unsustainable programme, open to charges of political self-deception.

FURTHER READING
BWRDD YR IAITH GYMRAEG; CYMRU; CYNULLIAD CENEDLAETHOL CYMRU; LANGUAGE REVIVAL; S4C; WELSH; Baker & Jones, *Encyclopedia of Bilingualism and Bilingual Education*; Baker & Jones, *Language Revitalization* 116–37; Bwrdd yr Iaith Gymraeg / Welsh Language Board, *Addysg Gymraeg a Dwyieithog yng Nghymru / Welsh Medium and Bilingual Education in Wales*; Stevens, *Meithrin*; Iolo Wyn Williams, *Addysg Gymraeg Ddoe a Heddiw*.

Colin H. Williams

education in the Celtic languages [5] Breton medium

Despite official French attitudes towards its regional languages in the 19th century, there is evidence, as bilingual textbooks testify, that the BRETON language was used as the teaching medium in some small private schools during this period. In addition to this, religious instruction, mainly in the form of catechism, was taught through the medium of Breton in many areas of Lower Brittany (BREIZH-IZEL) well into the 20th century. With the passing of the Jules Ferry Laws in 1881–9, however, the French government's policy regarding the medium of instruction was hardened to such an extent that the Breton language was persecuted in schools.

The 20th century witnessed active campaigning by various associations for Breton to be taught in schools. One of these, ABES (Ar Brezoneg er Skol 'Breton in Schools', founded in 1934), collected votes from more than 200 *communes* in 1936 in support of a motion calling for Breton in schools. Another movement was Ar Falz (The sickle), an association of lay teachers led by Yann Sohier (1901–35) who founded the monthly bulletin of the same name in 1933.

It was during the Vichy regime, in 1941, that the then Minister for Education, Jerôme Carcopino, passed a declaration lifting the ban on Breton in schools. Thus, this turbulent time saw the first true attempt at Breton-medium education, made by Sohier's successor, Yann Kerlann (Jean Delalande 1910–69), when he founded a residential school with nine pupils at Plestin-les-Grèves in 1942. This independent venture, funded entirely by voluntary contributions, taught all subjects through the medium of Breton until its closure in June 1944. Despite the subsequent illegality of Vichy declarations, the status of Breton in education was reaffirmed by the Deixonne Law of 1950–1, which authorized the teaching of regional languages in secondary schools.

Armañs ar C'halvez (Armand Le Calvez 1921–72) also founded a short-lived private school, Skol Sant-Erwan, in Plouézec in 1957, but it was not until 1977 that Breton-medium education truly gained momentum when, through the co-ordinated efforts of parents and teachers, the first Diwan (Germination) school was opened. The number of pupils attending these Breton-medium schools steadily increased each year, so that by the academic year 2000–1 there were 2414 pupils attending 30 nursery schools, 28 primary schools, 4 *collèges*, and 1 *lycée*. In 1997 the first batch of pupils sat their *baccalauréat* examination, having received all their schooling in Breton. Diwan schools are presently on the verge of being integrated into the French state system.

Children other than Diwan pupils can also receive their education through the medium of Breton, since there are bilingual schools and bilingual streams within both the public and Catholic (private) education systems. State bilingual schools and streams are supported by the parents' movement Div Yezh (Two languages), while Dihun (Awake!) represents the parents that are involved in Catholic Breton-medium education. The publication of textbooks and audio-visual materials for use in Breton-medium education is the responsibility of TES (Ti-embann ar Skoliou Brezhonek 'The Breton schools publishing house') based in Saint-Brieuc (Sant-Brieg).

FURTHER READING
BREIZH; BREIZH-IZEL; BRETON; LANGUAGE (REVIVAL); Faverau, *Bretagne contemporaine*; Mercator-Education, *Breton*; Skol Vreizh, *Histoire de la Bretagne et des Pays Celtiques 5*.

Gwenno Sven-Myer

education in the Celtic languages [6] Cornish medium

There is no Cornish Language Act, nor do CORNISH language, CORNISH LITERATURE or history feature in the National Curriculum of the United Kingdom. Education in Cornish has therefore, since the revival of the mid-19th century onward, been suppressed and underfunded. Provision is piecemeal at best, and non-existent at worst. Most people learn Cornish as adults at evening classes or studying independently on their own. There are a growing number of families who speak Cornish exclusively at home, but there are no facilities and few resources at present for such children to be educated in that medium.

Instruction in Cornish has therefore been dependent upon interested individuals working with the education system, most notably E. G. R. Hooper. Robert Morton NANCE's *Cornish for All* (1929) and A. S. D. Smith's *Cornish Simplified* (1939) were the standard textbooks for many years, followed by Richard Gendall's *Kernewek Bew* (Living Cornish, 1972). Other influential educators were Crystan Fudge, Graham Sandercock, Wella Brown, and Neil Kennedy. Subscribed magazines form a staple educative device within the learning community.

At the beginning of the 21st century, most primary schools in Cornwall (KERNOW) undertake some commitment to teaching core words and phrases in the Cornish language, but since the early 1990s there no longer exists a General Certificate of Secondary Education (GCSE) in the Cornish language. Secondary provision is extremely poor, though some schools do provide limited Cornish studies. Examinations in the

Cornish language are held by the Cornish Language Board, though these are almost exclusively in *Kemmyn* (one of the competing standard forms of revived Cornish). Grade Four guarantees bardic acceptance into the Cornish GORSETH. By means of annual competitions, the Gorseth supports language development, but, for the most part, these are outmoded and ineffective. The best practice is seen in work on 'non-standard' speech in schools, on the Internet, and in television programmes such as *Kernopalooza!* (1998; see MASS MEDIA).

PRIMARY SOURCES
Gendall, *Kernewek Bew*; Nance, *Cornish for All*; Smith, *Cornish Simplified*.

FURTHER READING
CORNISH; CORNISH LITERATURE; GORSETH; KERNOW; LANGUAGE (REVIVAL); MASS MEDIA; NANCE; Brown, *Skeul an Yeth: A Complete Course in the Cornish Language*; Fudge & Sandercock, *Kernewek Mar Plek!* Gendall, *Cornish Language Around Us*; Kennedy, *Deskans Noze: A Cornish Course for Beginners*.

Alan M. Kent

Edwards, Sir Owen M.

Edwards, Sir Owen M. (1858–1920) was arguably the most important cultural figure in Wales (CYMRU) on the eve of the 20th century. A native of Llanuwchllyn, Merioneth (Meirionnydd), he was educated at the local church school, and at Ysgol Tŷ-tandomen and the Theological College, Bala. He studied at the University College of Wales, ABERYSTWYTH, the University of Glasgow (GLASCHU), and Balliol College, Oxford (Welsh Rhydychen). After graduating in 1887 he travelled on the Continent, and in 1889 he was appointed Fellow and Tutor in History at Lincoln College, Oxford. Following the death of Thomas Edward ELLIS, he was elected Member of Parliament for Merioneth (1899–1900). He returned to Llanuwchllyn in 1907 on his appointment as Chief Inspector of Schools of the Welsh Board of Education.

Edwards was the catalyst who opened up a new period in the history of Welsh creative writing by liberating Welsh prose from the artificiality imposed upon it by the lexicographer William Owen Pughe (1759–1835) and his followers. He was an indefatigable publisher, writer, and editor. He provided his fellow-countrymen with attractive, affordable reading material, and acquainted them with the history and traditions of Wales. He was also a pioneer in the field of children's literature, and through his books and the influential periodical *Cymru'r Plant* (1892–1920) he changed the content and style of the genre for young Welsh readers. He also had a lasting influence on EDUCATION in Wales. He campaigned successfully for Welsh-medium teaching and for a syllabus that reflected Wales's rich heritage. His motto was '*codi'r hen wlad yn ei hôl*' (to raise the old country to its former glory). This he did by stimulating a far-reaching cultural and national renaissance in the Wales of his period.

SELECTION OF MAIN WORKS
TRAVEL, ESSAYS AND HISTORY. *Tro yn yr Eidal* (1888); *O'r Bala i Geneva* (1889); *Tro yn Llydaw* (1890); *Ystraeon o Hanes Cymru* (1894–5); *Hanes Cymru* (1895, 1899); *Cartrefi Cymru* (1896); *Er Mwyn Iesu* (1898); *Wales* (1901); *Clych Atgof* (1906); *Short History of Wales* (1906).
BOOKS FOR CHILDREN. *Llyfr Del* (1906); *Yr Hwiangerddi* (1911); *Llyfr Nest* (1913).
SERIES. *Cyfres y Werin* (1888); *Llyfrau'r Bala* (1889); *Cyfres y Llyfrau Bach* (1892–5); *Cyfres Urdd y Delyn* (1897); *Cyfres Clasuron Cymru* (1898–1901); *Cyfres y Fil* (1901–16); *Llyfrau Ab Owen* (1905–14).
ED. *Gwaith Barddonol Islwyn* (1897).
PERIODICALS. *Cymru Fydd* (1889–91); *Cymru* (1891–1920); *Cymru'r Plant* (1895–8); *Y Llenor* (1895–8); *Heddyw* (1897–8).

FURTHER READING
ABERYSTWYTH; CYMRU; EDUCATION; ELLIS; GLASCHU; WELSH PROSE LITERATURE; Hazel Walford Davies, *Llythyrau Syr O. M. Edwards ac Elin Edwards 1887–1920*; Hazel Walford Davies, *O. M. Edwards*; Hazel Walford Davies, *Syr O. M. Edwards*; Gruffydd, *Owen Morgan Edwards*; G. A. Jones, *Bywyd a Gwaith Owen Morgan Edwards 1858–1920*.

Hazel Walford Davies

Efengyl Nicodemus

Efengyl Nicodemus (The gospel of Nicodemus) is a Middle Welsh translation of the Christian Latin apocryphal text *Evangelium Nicodemi*. It elaborates on the biblical account of the Crucifixion and Christ's descent into hell. The earliest Welsh translation can be found in the White Book of Rhydderch (LLYFR GWYN RHYDDERCH, NLW Peniarth 5).

PRIMARY SOURCES
MSS. Aberystwyth, NLW, Peniarth 5 (LLYFR GWYN RHYDDERCH, *c.* 1350), Llanstephan 27 (*c.* 1400), Llanstephan 2 (*c.* 1450–1500).
EDITION. J. E. Caerwyn Williams, BBCS 14.257–73.

FURTHER READING
D. Simon Evans, *Medieval Religious Literature*; Mittendorf, *Übersetzung, Adaptation und Akkulturation im insularen Mittelalter*

259–88; Owen, *Guide to Welsh Literature* 1.248–76 [esp. 250–9]; J. E. Caerwyn Williams, *Proc. 2nd International Congress of Celtic Studies* 65–97; J. E. Caerwyn Williams, *Y Traddodiad Rhyddiaith yn yr Oesau Canol* 312–59, 360–408.

Ingo Mittendorf

Efnisien (Middle Welsh Efnyssyen) figures in the wonder-tale *Branwen* in the MABINOGI as the son of Euroswydd by Penarddun, daughter of BELI MAWR son of Mynogan; thus, Efnisien was the maternal half-brother of the protagonists Branwen and her brother Bendigeidfran. For a summary of the story and Efnisien's pivotal destructive part in it, see BRANWEN ferch LŶR; cf. BRÂN fab LLŶR. Efnisien dies in the final climactic and mutually destructive battle between the Irish and the BRITONS. Regretting the carnage he has caused and his inability to help his own people, he has himself thrown into the *pair dadeni* (cauldron of rebirth; see CAULDRONS), with which the Irish warriors are revivifying their comrades, stretches out to rend the cauldron, and dies, breaking his heart in the feat. Mac Cana saw in Efnisien's rôle as troublemaker an explicit functional analogue with that of BRICRIU in the early Irish tale FLED BRICRENN ('Bricriu's Feast') in the ULSTER CYCLE, and thus possibly an example of direct borrowing from Irish narrative tradition into the Welsh. However, there is a major difference in that Efnisien's outrageous provocations are consistently motivated by his problematical sense of his own honour owing to his maternal link to the royal lineage within a patriarchal society (cf. Ó Cathasaigh). Bricriu, on the other hand, lacks Efnisien's dynastic motivation and appears to be a troublemaker by nature. Consequently, Efnisien's spectacular mutilations and murders have an air of tragic inevitability, which contrasts with the burlesque quality of the strife incited by Bricriu.

The name *Efnisien* is Celtic and is a negated form of that of his good brother, NISIEN.

FURTHER READING
BELI MAWR; BRÂN; BRANWEN; BRICRIU; BRITONS; CAULDRONS; FLED BRICRENN; MABINOGI; NISIEN; ULSTER CYCLE; Bartrum, *Welsh Classical Dictionary* 507; Mac Cana, *Branwen*; Ó Cathasaigh, *Peritia* 5.128–60.

JTK

Éigse (Learning/Poetry), subtitled 'A Journal of Irish Studies', is one of the main specialist Irish journals dealing with CELTIC STUDIES. It is dedicated to all aspects and periods of IRISH and its literature. Numerous and extensive reviews of books (*Léirhmheas*) in its field are a regular feature. It was established in 1939 and is published for the National University of Ireland in Dublin (BAILE ÁTHA CLIATH). *Éigse* has been edited by the prominent Irish scholars, Gerard MURPHY, Brian Ó Cuív, Tomás Ó Concheanainn, and Pádraig Breatnach. The journal has been published in single annual volume format (no sub-parts) since the mid-1980s. Contributions are written in English or Irish.

RELATED ARTICLES
BAILE ÁTHA CLIATH; CELTIC STUDIES; ÉIRE; IRISH; IRISH LITERATURE; MURPHY.
CONTACT DETAILS. *Éigse*, The National University of Ireland, 49 Merrion Square, Dublin 2, Éire.

PSH

Eilean Ì (Iona, also called simply Ì in Gaelic) is an island of the Inner Hebrides (Innse Gall) in Scotland, separated from the Island of Mull by the Sound of Iona. The island is only about 12 km² (4.5 m²), but was an important religious and cultural focal point during the Middle Ages, taking advantage of its geographically central position between Ireland (ÉRIU) and Gaelic Scotland. Iona was instrumental, likewise, in the Christianization of the PICTS in the later 6th century and the second conversion of Anglo-Saxon Northumbria in 635. According to the ANNALS, it was in 563 that COLUM CILLE (Columba; †597), the famous Irish saint of Northern UÍ NÉILL royal lineage, founded a monastery on the island, which was to become pivotal in the establishment and the spread of the Celtic church (see CHRISTIANITY [2]). The island is also said to have been the location of the martyrdom of Blathmac, the monk who refused to reveal the location of Colum Cille's shrine.

As an unrivalled centre of learning in the early Middle Ages, the monastic scriptorium (manuscipt-production centre) on Iona produced several important documents, among them some of the earliest keeping of regular contemporary records in Britain, probably from the 6th century, leading to the compilation of the Iona Chronicle (*c.* 686–*c.* 740), now recognized as the basis for the early Irish annals. The intellectual self-confidence of the scholars of 7th-century Iona, especially in matters of the calendar and record keeping, was an important factor in fuelling the EASTER CONTROVERSY, a controversy that Iona ultimately lost. This led to a sharp decline in its influence in Northumbria (after the council of Whitby in 664) and, in the early 8th century, in Pictland, as well as setbacks in the careers of ADOMNÁN and other leaders of the community. Although the case for the place of origin of the most famous illuminated gospel book, the Book of KELLS, remains controversial, evidence favours its being begun at Iona towards the end of the 8th or the opening years of the 9th century.

Iona was an important centre of medieval sculpture, and the island boasts the highest concentration of carved stone monuments anywhere in the Celtic world. Among them are the large, free-standing HIGH CROSSES, which begin to appear from around AD 800. It is likely that the Iona School is to be credited with having first placed a stone circle around the top part of a stone cross, the design feature now generally regarded as defining the 'Celtic cross'.

Unfortunately, Iona's central (and exposed) maritime position made the island an easy target for numerous attacks by Vikings and Irish kings between the late 8th and 10th centuries. A third and particularly devastating Viking raid occurred in 807. At the beginning of the 9th century a new Columban monastery was founded at Kells, Co. Meath (Cenannas, Contae na Mí), Ireland, and Iona was gradually losing its position as the main focus of the 'familia' of foundations of Colum Cille and his successors in favour of this new foundation. This shift is illustrated by the moving of the saint's relics to Kells in 877, which may also have been the time when the Book of Kells arrived on the site from which it is named, although the manuscript had possibly already left Iona in the wake of the raid of 807.

Although the importance of Iona waned in Ireland after the series of Viking raids in the early 9th century, its prestige rose in north Britain with the formation of the Gaelic kingdom of ALBA in the mid- and later 9th century. Since Iona was physically situated alongside or even within the territory of the old kingdom of Scottish DÁL RIATA and their early kings, such as AEDÁN MAC GABRÁIN, were closely associated

with Colum Cille and his successors, the kings of Scotland, many of whom were buried at Iona, especially revered the holy site as connected with the origins of their dynasty.

During the mid-20th century, a Christian group, the Iona Community, rebuilt the ancient buildings on the island so that they could once again be used for worship. Although the abbey on Iona was consecrated in 1959 by the Church of Scotland, the project is ecumenical and attracts visitors from all Christian backgrounds.

FURTHER READING
ADOMNÁN; AEDÁN MAC GABRÁIN; ALBA; ANNALS; CHRISTIANITY; COLUM CILLE; DÁL RIATA; EASTER CONTROVERSY; ÉRIU; HIGH CROSSES; KELLS; MONASTERIES; MONASTICISM; PICTS; UÍ NÉILL; Bannermann, *Studies in the History of Dalriada*; Clancy & Márkus, *Iona*; Ferguson, *Chasing the Wild Goose*; Herbert, *Iona, Kells, and Derry*; McNeill, *Iona*.

PSH

Einion Offeiriad (Einion the Priest, *fl. c.* 1320– *c.* 1349) was a beneficed clergyman who was also the author of the first recension of the Welsh 'bardic grammar' (see GRAMADEGAU'R PENCEIRDDIAID). Nothing is known of his parentage and education, but he may have been preferred early by the powerful magnate Sir Gruffudd Llwyd to the rectory of Llanrug near Caernarfon, north Wales (CYMRU). Soon, however, he transferred his allegiance to an even more powerful magnate, Sir RHYS AP GRUFFUDD, and it was stated by the antiquary Robert VAUGHAN of HENGWRT in the early 17th century that Einion's grammar was composed 'in honour and for the praise of Rhys ap Gruffudd'; indeed, Einion's only surviving poem is a well-crafted AWDL in praise of Rhys. Rhys's power base lay chiefly in south-west Wales, and Einion was seemingly given land by him in both CEREDIGION and Carmarthenshire (sir Gaerfyrddin); he may have held church livings there as well. He died *c.* 1349, perhaps as a result of the first epidemic of the Black Death.

His grammar, written in WELSH, probably *c.* 1320, draws heavily on both elementary Latin learning (as represented by the Late Roman grammars of Donatus and Priscianus) and the oral instruction imparted by the Welsh master-poets to their apprentices (see BARDIC

ORDER). However, Einion himself probably composed the sections on the twenty-four metres (including three devised by him) and on the duties of the professional poets.

PRIMARY SOURCES
MS. Oxford, Balliol College 353, fos. 108r–123v.
EDITIONS. Gruffydd & Ifans, *Gwaith Einion Offeiriad a Dafydd Ddu o Hiraddug*; G. J. Williams & Jones, *Gramadegau'r Penceirddiaid*.

FURTHER READING
AWDL; BARDIC ORDER; CEREDIGION; CYMRU; CYNGHANEDD; CYWYDDWYR; ENGLYN; GRAMADEGAU'R PENCEIRDDIAID; HENGWRT; RHYS AP GRUFFUDD; VAUGHAN; WELSH; Bromwich, *Ysgrifau Beirniadol* 10.157–80; Daniel, *Ysgrifau Beirniadol* 13.178–209; Gruffydd, PBA 90.1–28; Ceri W. Lewis, *Guide to Welsh Literature* 2.44–94; Saunders Lewis, *Gramadegau'r Penceirddiaid*; Lynch, *Dwned* 4.59–74; Matonis, BBCS 36.1–12; Matonis, *Celtic Language, Celtic Culture* 273–9; Matonis, *Modern Philology* 79.121–45; Matonis, ZCP 47.211–14; Parry, PBA 47.177–95; Poppe, BBCS 38.102–4; Poppe, *Historiographia linguistica* 18.269–80; Poppe, NLWJ 29.17–38; Smith, BBCS 20.339–47.

R. Geraint Gruffydd

Éire (Ireland) lies west of Scotland (ALBA), the Isle of Man (ELLAN VANNIN), Wales (CYMRU) and England, separated from them by the North Channel, the Irish Sea and St George's Channel. It is home to the IRISH language and measures 84,429 km² (32,598 square miles).

§1. POLITICAL DIVISION

Over 80% of Ireland's land mass is taken up by the Republic of Ireland, Poblacht na hÉireann (also Éire for short, which can also mean the whole island), which covers 70,285 km² (27,137 square miles) and is subdivided into four traditional provinces and 26 counties. Its capital is Dublin (BAILE ÁTHA CLIATH), on the east coast. In 2002 there were 3,917,336 inhabitants (Central Statistics Office Ireland, www.cso.ie) in the Irish Republic, of whom over 93% were Roman Catholics. The six counties in the north-east of the traditional nine-county province of Ulster (Ulaidh, earlier ULAID), i.e. the remaining 20% of Ireland (14,147 km², 5462 square miles), were partitioned off through the British Government of Ireland Act in 1920. Known as Northern Ireland, with the capital in Belfast (Béal Feirste), they remain part of the United Kingdom. At the last British census taken in 2001,

Northern Ireland had 1,685,267 inhabitants, of whom 40% were Roman Catholics and 60% belonged to various Protestant denominations (Northern Ireland Statistics & Research Agency, *Census 2001 Output* www.nisra.gov.uk/Census). It would be misleading to take these figures as indicating that 100% of Northern Ireland's population in 2001 professed and practised a religion and willingly identified with one of the sectarian communities; respondents to census questionnaires were not permitted to opt out of religious affiliation, and those who left this section of the form blank were controversially assigned to the figures of the Catholic or Protestant community on the basis of such factors as surname and address. Both the current predominance of Protestantism in the north-east of the island, which ultimately led to partition, and the decline of the Irish language are deeply rooted in the history of Éire and its cultural and political contacts with its English neighbour (see below).

§2. THE IRISH LANGUAGE

Ireland's Celtic language, Irish, closely akin to SCOTTISH GAELIC and MANX, is spoken as a native language in western parts of the island known as the GAELTACHT areas. In 1996, 1,430,205 people (about 30% of the population) in the Irish Republic—where it is the official language—claimed to be Irish speakers (Central Statistics Office Ireland, www.cso.ie). In Northern Ireland, 167,490 people, i.e. 10.35% of the population, claimed some knowledge of the Irish language in 2001 (Northern Ireland Statistics & Research Agency, *Census 2001 Output* www.nisra.gov.uk/Census). Following the FAMINE, numbers of Irish speakers fell rapidly—from 1,077,087 in 1861 (the first census to include the language) to 540,802 in 1926, but organizations such as CONRADH NA GAEILGE contributed to its revival (see LANGUAGE [REVIVAL]). It now has its own MASS MEDIA, and FORAS NA GAEILGE, a central language board, furthers its use, but its continued survival as a mother tongue cannot be taken for granted. Ireland and the Irish are secure in their national identity, which is expressed through the existence of Poblacht na hÉireann and through a host of national customs and traditions (see BAGPIPE; BODHRÁN; GAMES; HURLING; IRISH MUSIC) and a lively ANGLO-IRISH LITERATURE. Anglo-Irish authors such as James JOYCE and William Butler YEATS are as prominent in

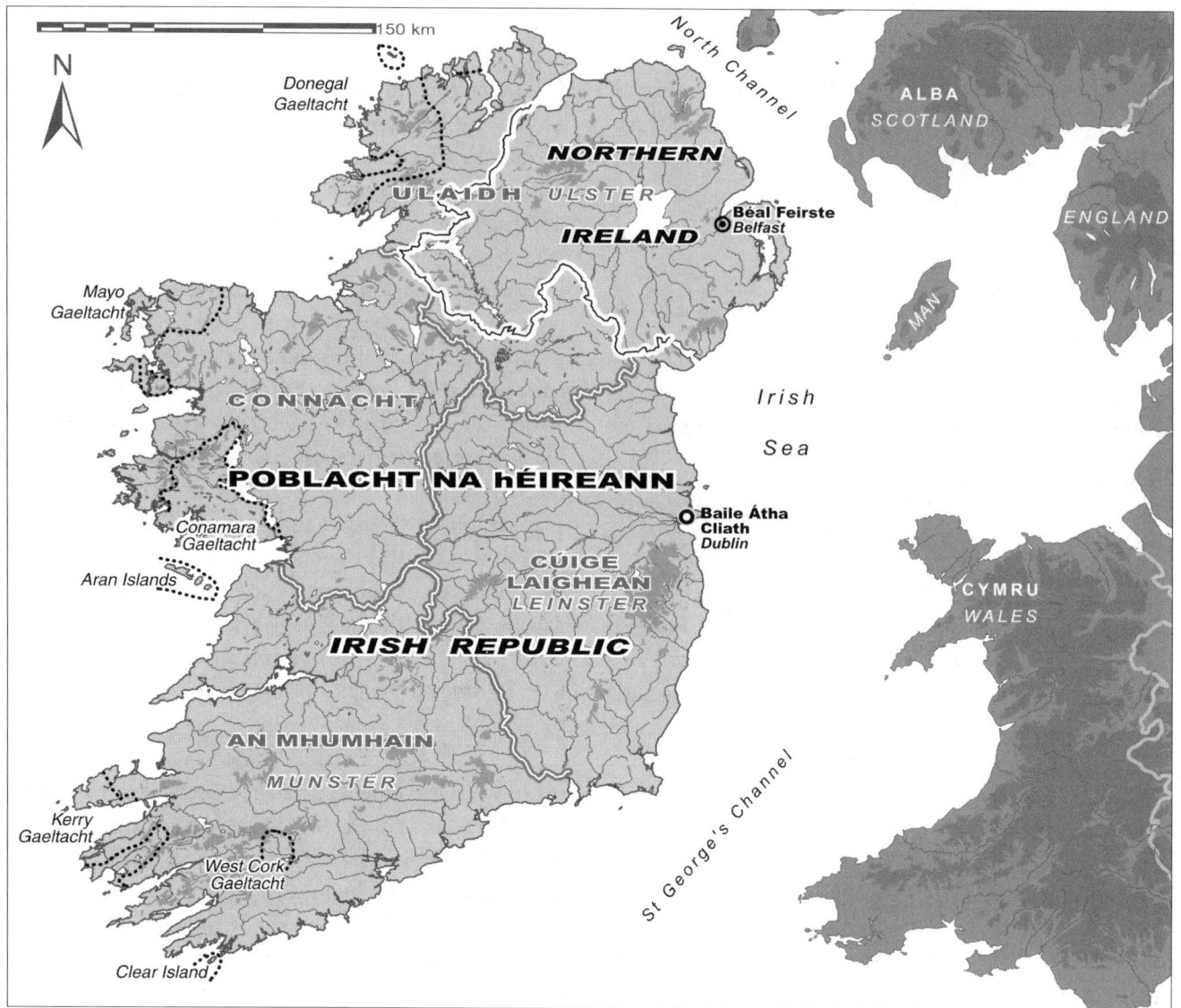

Contemporary Ireland (Éire) and western Britain, showing the traditional provinces, the border between the Republic and Northern Ireland (black on white), and Gaeltacht (Irish-speaking) areas

the formation of Irish national identity and culture as are Irish Gaelic writers and poets such as Peig SAYERS and Máire MHAC AN TSAOI. The breadth of available national symbols and the distinctiveness and worldwide recognition of Anglo-Irish literature may explain why the Irish language and Irish literature are not as important to the Irish as, for instance, WELSH and its literature are for Welsh identity.

§3. THE CENTRAL AND LATER MIDDLE AGES
An outline of Ireland's past down to the Anglo-Norman incursions is given in the article on ÉRIU. It was over a hundred years before the Norman Conquest of England spilled over into Ireland. With mixed

Norman, English, and Welsh forces, Richard DE CLARE, 'Strongbow', intervened on the side of the deposed king of Leinster (Laighin < LAIGIN), Diarmait Mac Murchada, in 1169. The English King Henry II landed in October 1171 to reconfirm conquest and nominally to oversee ecclesiastical reforms as authorized in the papal bull *Laudabiliter* (1155). Over the next hundred years, Anglo-Norman families such as the earls of Kildare, of Desmond and of Ormond (representing the Leinster Fitzgeralds, the Munster Fitzgeralds and the Butlers) built up huge estates. Often assimilated to Gaelic cultural norms through intermarriage and other contacts, from time to time anti-Irish legislation, such as the Statutes of KILKENNY, was passed in order to reconfirm the Anglo-Norman aristocracy's originally distinct status. There is little evidence, however, that such legislation enjoyed much success outside an area around Dublin known as the Pale. In time, those families became known as the 'Old English', but some of them came to identify with the native Irish. The 14th century also saw a reassertion of Gaelic power over parts of Ulster, Connacht and Leinster, which went hand in hand with a flowering in IRISH LITERATURE and law in the 'Classical Modern Irish' period (*c.* 1200–*c.* 1600).

§4. PLANTATION AND OPPRESSION OF THE CATHOLIC POPULATION

In the 15th century, the English Crown introduced a policy of 'Surrender and Regrant' of lands by the king.

Many Gaelic lords submitted, hoping to receive a modicum of protection, hardly realizing that they would then hold their lands courtesy of the English Crown. Henry VII's 'Poyning's Law' (1495) provided that future Irish parliaments and legislation had to receive prior approval from the English Privy Council. Having abolished the MONASTERIES and established a Protestant 'Church of Ireland' in 1537, Henry VIII proclaimed himself king of Ireland in 1541 and formally annexed the country to England. However, whereas England was becoming a Protestant nation, the majority of the Irish remained Catholic and refused the imposition of Protestantism, often seeking a last resort in rebellion (see BIBLE; CHRISTIANITY; RENAISSANCE).

The Elizabethan plantation of parts of Ireland laid the foundations for the Protestant ASCENDANCY of

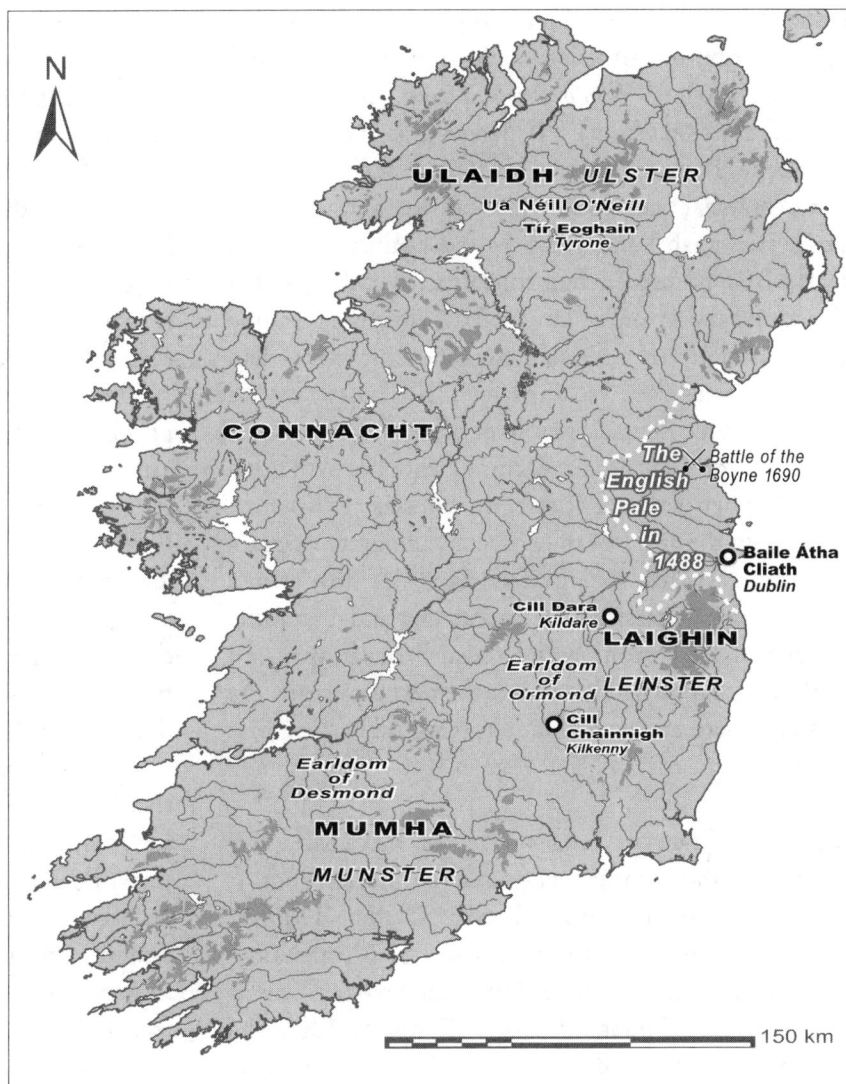

Late medieval and early modern Ireland —places mentioned in the text

the Anglo-Irish landlord class which was to dominate life in Ireland down to the 20th century. English settlers were rewarded with Irish land for loyalty to the Crown in the Desmond Rebellions (1569–73, 1579–83) and Nine Years War (1594–1603), which occurred during the reign of Elizabeth I. Irish land was advertised in gentry circles, and taken up by the younger sons who would otherwise have gone empty-handed. Following the Flight of the Earls (1607), when the last truly great Gaelic lord, Hugh O'Neill (Aodh Ruadh), earl of Tyrone in Ulster, left Ireland for Spain with a small party of followers, it was clear that the dominant force in future Ireland would be English and Protestant. Under King James I, large parts of Ulster were settled by Scottish and English Protestants. When Oliver Cromwell crushed the 1649–50 rebellion during the English Civil Wars, with the loss of hundreds of thousands of lives, the subsequent distribution of lands among his soldiers and officers rounded off the process of redistribution of Irish lands among English and Scottish settlers. When the deposed James II (see JACOBITE REBELLIONS) was defeated at the battle of the Boyne (Bóinn; cf. BÓAND) in 1690, it only confirmed a process that had been underway for a century. By 1704, the harsh Penal Laws passed against Catholics by the Irish parliament had consolidated and expanded Protestant ownership of land and deprived the Catholic population of any political power they might have had left. Catholics were excluded from parliament by the introduction of unacceptable oaths and declarations; they were forbidden to own arms or a horse worth more than £5; they were not allowed to run schools, to vote, to serve in the army, or to engage in commerce or practise law. Less than 10% of Irish land was now owned by Catholics. Classical Gaelic learning and literature, robbed of its patronage and social base, disappeared with the Irish-owned lands. For the next 200 years, the Irish language and an oral literature would be kept alive by the lower orders in the western half of the island.

§5. UNION, FAMINE, AND NATIONAL REAWAKENING
Thus, the 18th century witnessed the Ascendancy at the height of its power. Trinity College Dublin, founded in 1593 for the education of Protestants, produced such figures as Jonathan Swift, Thomas MOORE, and Theobald Wolfe TONE. Dublin, the capital, was expanded to a grand plan, and the many

Georgian mansions which are the pride of the Irish tourist industry were built. The Catholic population and members of radical Protestant denominations who were similarly oppressed formed secret societies such as the United Irishmen. Although the great 1798 rebellion led by Wolfe Tone was crushed, it resulted in the abolition of the Irish parliament and the full incorporation of Ireland into the English state by the ACT OF UNION passed in 1800. The new political unit was named the United Kingdom of Great Britain and Ireland, a term which survives in the current name of the United Kingdom of Great Britain and Northern Ireland. Members of Parliament now went to take their seats in London, which deprived the country of a permanent Protestant leadership for half of the year. Based in London, the upper classes began to feel more British than Irish; they became absentee landlords, and Protestantism became almost identical with Unionism. On the other hand, following the election of the Catholic Daniel O'Connell to a parliamentary seat and the emancipation of the Catholic population in 1829, an era began which would end with independence for most of the island. The Young Ireland movement of the 1840s, led by Thomas Davis through the pages of his paper, *The Nation*, and its unsuccessful rising of 1848, was a first expression of the movement for the repeal of the Union with Britain, which would grow into the independence movement.

Unification with Britain also brought new economic problems, as the value of agricultural produce and real estate plummeted. Too many people relied solely on the potato as their staple crop and diet, with the result that the onset of potato blight led to famine and EMIGRATION on an unprecedented scale. Between 1846 and 1851 almost half the population either starved to death or emigrated—a catastrophe which left the country paralysed for 20 years afterwards and which, to this day, has left deep scars in the Irish national psyche.

The 1860s saw a revival of national aspirations with the rise of Fenianism both in Ireland itself and among the Irish diaspora in Britain and the New World. The secret Fenian organization, the Fianna, aimed to secure political independence by injuring English interests, and staged another unsuccessful uprising in 1867. However, with the disestablishment of the Church in Ireland in 1869 and the 1870 Irish Land Act, the first concessions were made to Irish interests (see DAVITT;

LAND AGITATION; LAND LEAGUE). The national movement acquired a more constitutional character, with Charles Stewart PARNELL achieving substantial power through the Irish parliamentary party at Westminster, forcing the introduction of Home Rule bills and the passing of further Land Acts in the British parliament between 1880 and 1893. With Parnell's death, cultural nationalism developed alongside enthusiasm for preserving and reviving the Irish language, finding expression in the foundation of Conradh na Gaeilge and other organizations. These developments vastly increased support for the IRISH INDEPENDENCE MOVEMENT, led by men such as Michael COLLINS, Èamonn DE VALERA, and Art Ó GRÍOFA, with independence finally achieved in 1921.

§6. THE 20TH CENTURY: POBLACHT NA H-ÉIREANN
During the Irish War of Independence (1919–21) British forces were fought to a standstill by the guerrilla troops of the IRISH REPUBLICAN ARMY (IRA). The aftermath of this was the partitioning of Northern Ireland and the establishment elsewhere on the island of an independent state. The first name of the Irish state, adopted in 1922 after negotiations with the British Government granted independence to Ireland, was Saorstát na hÉireann or the Irish Free State. However, members of the government still had to swear an oath of allegiance to the British Crown, and the new state, as a dominion, remained part of the British Empire. These were two of the factors which contributed to a split in the IRA, and the subsequent short, but bloody, Civil War (1922–3) between the two factions. An uneasy peace was achieved in the fledgling state following the victory of those who supported the Anglo-Irish Treaty. A new constitution adopted in 1937 changed the name of the country to Éire (the ancient Celtic name of the island; see ÉRIU) and asserted its autonomy from the United Kingdom. On 18 April 1949, the country officially became a republic, changing its official name to Poblacht na hÉireann, Republic of Ireland, keeping Éire for short reference.

Poblacht na hÉireann is a parliamentary republic governed by the Oireachtas, a parliament consisting of the directly elected Dáil Éireann (166 members) and the Seanad (60 members), which is nominated by grand electors. The head of government is the Taoiseach or Prime Minister, and the head of state is the President (Uachtarán), elected directly every 7 years. Poblacht na hÉireann is a member of the United Nations and the European Union. The first official language of the Republic is Irish (Gaeilge), with English named as a second official language.

Following the Second World War, with emigration again rising, the protectionist high tariff policy pursued by Éire was abandoned and successive programmes of economic expansion put into place. The result has been a mixed-market economy—largely based on AGRICULTURE, chemical industries, high technology and services—which boomed since the 1990s. In particular, the development of the high technology sector, with Éire currently one of the world's leading exporters of computer software, has led to it being labelled the 'Celtic Tiger'. Like most other members of the European Union, the country introduced the Euro as its currency in 1999, replacing the punt (Irish pound).

§7. THE 20TH CENTURY: NORTHERN IRELAND
The forced plantations of English and Scottish Protestant settlers laid the foundation for the division of Ireland in the early 20th century and the current distribution of the religious denominations in Northern Ireland. The political loyalties within Northern Ireland have historically followed religious lines. The mostly Protestant 'Unionists' campaign for maintaining the union with the United Kingdom and, comprising about 60% of the population, are still in the majority. The 'nationalists' are mostly Catholics, with the political label signifying a preference for the six counties of Northern Ireland to be reunited with the rest of Ireland (see NATIONALISM). The terms 'loyalist' and 'republican', in a Northern Irish context, designate political and paramilitary groups which can be broadly viewed as more extreme unionists and more extreme nationalists, respectively, again tending to follow the Protestant–Catholic divide.

Following the Act of Union, Protestants came to feel more and more part of the United Kingdom, which led to attempts to block home rule legislation from the 1870s onwards. An organization in defence of the Protestant Ascendancy, the Orange Order, founded in 1795, was already in existence. It survives in Northern Ireland to this day, and its annual processions are often the starting point for sectarian violence. When Home Rule for the whole of Ireland was mooted in 1912,

Protestant Unionists led by Sir Edward Carson reacted by forming the 'Solemn League and Covenant to resist Home Rule' and establishing the Ulster Volunteer Force (UVF), an armed secret organization whose descendants still exist. Aware of the support Home Rule enjoyed in most of the island following the abortive Easter Rising (1916), Unionists began to restrict their demands to keeping Ulster within the United Kingdom, thus precipitating the partition of the island. In 1920 the Northern Irish political unit within the UK was created, which, especially under its first Prime Minister, Sir James Craig (1921–40), pursued a policy of strict Protestant leanings. It discriminated against the Catholic minority who lived within its borders and failed to restrain violence against them. In the 1960s a Catholic civil rights movement—emulating the African-American Civil Rights movement—arose, and sectarian violence began to increase. Violence against Catholics by the revived Ulster Defence Association (UDA) and the UVF led to a vast influx of recruits to the IRA, which had been in decline for some decades. British troops began to occupy the region in early 1969, ostensibly to 'keep the peace', but their very presence played a central rôle in fanning the violence between Protestants and Catholics which developed in the following decades. In March 1972, the Northern Irish parliament was suspended, following the escalation of communal violence between Catholics and Protestants, and direct British rule introduced. Following several failed initiatives in the 1970s and 1980s, a ceasefire was agreed between the IRA and the Unionist paramilitary groups in 1994, and discussions involving the Irish Republic were resumed in 1996. On 10 April 1998, the Belfast Agreement, or Good Friday Agreement, established a new 108-member Northern Ireland Assembly in Belfast, which was obliged to include both Protestants and Catholics in its executive and pass legislation only if factions of both agreed. Since the Good Friday Agreement, troops have been withdrawn and a new police force—Police Service of Northern Ireland—has been created. Between 1972 and 2000, over 3600 people were killed by sectarian violence and/or British troops in Northern Ireland.

The rapid industrialization of the region around Belfast in the 19th century, with textile industries, heavy engineering and shipping dominant, attracted a population that could not be sustained when those industries began to decline in the 20th century. Foreign companies have been slow to invest because of the political violence. Hence, the region is economically unstable, with the service sector its most important employer.

FURTHER READING
ACT OF UNION; AGRICULTURE; ALBA; ANGLO-IRISH LITERATURE; ASCENDANCY; BAGPIPE; BAILE ÁTHA CLIATH; BIBLE; BÓAND; BODHRÁN; CHRISTIANITY; COLLINS; CONRADH NA GAEILGE; CYMRU; DAVITT; DE CLARE; DE VALERA; ELLAN VANNIN; EMIGRATION; ÉRIU; FAMINE; FORAS NA GAEILGE; GAELTACHT; GAMES; HURLING; IRISH; IRISH INDEPENDENCE MOVEMENT; IRISH LITERATURE; IRISH MUSIC; IRISH REPUBLICAN ARMY; JACOBITE REBELLIONS; JOYCE; KILKENNY; LAIGIN; LAND AGITATION; LAND LEAGUE; LANGUAGE (REVIVAL); MANX; MASS MEDIA; MHAC AN TSAOI; MONASTERIES; MOORE; NATIONALISM; Ó GRÍOFA; PARNELL; RENAISSANCE; SAYERS; SCOTTISH GAELIC; TONE; ULAID; WELSH; YEATS; Bardon, *History of Ulster*; Bew et al., *Northern Ireland 1921–1994*; Boyce, *Nineteenth-century Ireland*; Brown, *Ireland*; De Breffny, *Ireland*; Dillon, *Early Irish Society*; Edwards, *Atlas of Irish History*; Edwards, *New History of Ireland*; Foster, *Modern Ireland 1600–1972*; Freeman, *Ireland*; Keogh, *Twentieth-century Ireland*; Lalor, *Encyclopaedia of Ireland*; Lyons, *Ireland since the Famine*; McMahon, *Short History of Ireland*; Mansergh, *Irish Question 1840–1921*; Moody et al., *New History of Ireland*; Ó Gráda, *Ireland*; O'Leary & McGarry, *Politics of Antagonism*; Ó Murchú, *Irish Language*; Otway-Ruthven, *History of Medieval Ireland*; Ranelagh, *Short History of Ireland*; Richter, *Medieval Ireland*; Robinson, *Plantation of Ulster*; Walker, *Parliamentary Election Results in Ireland 1801–1922*.
WEBSITES. www.cso.ie; www.nisra.gov.uk/Census
MBL

An **eisteddfod**, derived from the Welsh verb *eistedd* 'to sit', was from the beginning literally a 'sitting together', a session (probably competitive from its inception) of bards and minstrels intent on demonstrating their artistic skills in the presence of a noble patron.

The first recorded eisteddfod as recounted in Brut y Tywysogyon took place in the castle in Cardigan (Aberteifi) at Christmastide 1176, when Lord Rhys ap Gruffudd of Deheubarth presided as bards and minstrels competed for the two prime Chair awards. This eisteddfod, it is said, was proclaimed a year in advance 'throughout Wales (Cymru), England, Scotland (Alba), Ireland (Ériu) and the other islands', giving reason to believe that it was on a scale hitherto unknown. Seen in the light of J. E. Caerwyn Williams's argument that Lord Rhys could have been impressed by the competitive 'puys' in France, the 1176 eisteddfod assumes even greater significance as a cultural institution compounded of traditional practice and foreign influence.

Between 1176 and the middle of the 16th century huge and inexplicable gaps in the eisteddfod timeline leave us with no more than three eisteddfodau of whose authenticity we can be sure. Gruffudd ap Nicolas (*fl.* 1425–56), a worthy successor to Lord Rhys, presided over an eisteddfod held in Carmarthen (CAERFYRDDIN) *c.* 1451, and the Mostyn family in Flintshire (sir y Fflint) acted as patrons for two eisteddfodau held in Caerwys in 1523 and 1567, both of which received royal assent. All three would come to be seen by future embattled *eisteddfodwyr* as representing a golden age, but in fact they marked the inevitable demise of an age-old BARDIC ORDER. Their main purpose was to secure the status of the professional bards and minstrels who had been tutored and licensed to practise their art against the trespass of 'rogues and vagabonds', but the forces of social change were to prove irresistible. The bardic tradition petered out in the late 17th century.

In the 18th century a fistful of devotees kept alive, mainly in north Wales, a wan, tavern-housed eisteddfod culture. But 1789 would change everything. Prompted by Thomas Jones, a Corwen-born exciseman, the London-based Gwyneddigion Society responded to a call for a renewed patronage and in September of that year a Gwyneddigion-directed eisteddfod at Bala (see EISTEDDFODAU'R GWYNEDDIGION) provided a blueprint for the modern institution which, facilitated by the coming of the railways, would thereafter be at the heart of Welsh culture at local and national level.

With the end of the Napoleonic wars the eisteddfod movement made rapid progress. A band of patriotic clerics succeeded in establishing provincial societies, which between 1819 and 1834 held ten ambitious 'eisteddfodau' that attracted the support of 'the best people'. They were followed by ten spectacular eisteddfodau promoted by the Abergavenny (Y Fenni) Cymreigyddion Society between 1835 and 1853 (see EISTEDDFODAU'R FENNI), which attracted the interest of Continental Celtic scholars and by 1858, when the Revd John Williams (Ab Ithel, 1811–62) organized what was to be a fractious but epochal eisteddfod at Llangollen, the country was ripe for a properly constituted National Eisteddfod (see EISTEDDFOD GENEDLAETHOL CYMRU).

FURTHER READING
ABERTEIFI; ALBA; BARD; BARDIC ORDER; BRUT Y TYWYSOGYON; CAERFYRDDIN; CYMRU; DEHEUBARTH; EISTEDDFOD GENEDLAETHOL CYMRU; EISTEDDFODAU'R FENNI; EISTEDDFODAU'R GWYNEDDIGION; ÉRIU; RHYS AP GRUFFUDD; WILLIAMS; Bowen, *Barn* 142.441–8; Edwards, *Eisteddfod*; Edwards, *Yr Eisteddfod: Cyfrol Ddathlu Wythganmlwyddiant yr Eisteddfod 1176–1976*; Foster, *Twf yr Eisteddfod*; Morgan, *Iolo Morganwg*; Ramage, *Gwŷr Llên y Ddeunawfed Ganrif* 198–206; Ramage, *Gwŷr Llên y Bedwaredd Ganrif ar Bymtheg* 151–63; Gwyn Thomas, *Eisteddfodau Caerwys*; Mair Elvet Thomas, *Afiaith yng Ngwent*; G. J. Williams, *Agweddau ar Hanes Dysg Gymraeg*; J. E. Caerwyn Williams, *Yr Arglwydd Rhys* 94–128.

Hywel Teifi Edwards

Eisteddfod Genedlaethol Cymru (National Eisteddfod of Wales) made its first appearance in 1861 in Aberdare (Aberdâr). A general meeting of *eisteddfodwyr* at the stormy Llangollen EISTEDDFOD of 1858 decided that the time was ripe for a fully-fledged annual national festival. In 1860, at the Denbigh/Dinbych eisteddfod, an association known as 'Yr Eisteddfod' was formed and an executive council was subsequently elected to promote a series of 'Nationals' at Aberdare (1861), Caernarfon (1862), Swansea/ ABERTAWE (1863), Llandudno (1864), ABERYSTWYTH (1865), Chester (1866), Carmarthen/ CAERFYRDDIN (1867) and Rhuthun (1868). Overcome with debts, 'Yr Eisteddfod' folded in 1868, but in 1880 Sir Hugh Owen inspired the creation of the National Eisteddfod Association, and the current ongoing series of 'Nationals' got underway at Merthyr Tudful in 1881. With the exception of 1914, for obvious reasons, it proved to be an unbroken series, a 'Radio eisteddfod' triumphing over hostilities in 1940.

In 1937 a more amicable relationship between the Eisteddfod Association and the GORSEDD BEIRDD YNYS PRYDAIN (Gorsedd of Bards) resulted in a new constitution and the creation of the National Eisteddfod Council, which, in turn, gave way in 1952 to the Court of the National Eisteddfod as the ultimate authority over eisteddfod proceedings. The Council functions as its executive and, through its sub-committees, secures a sound working relationship with representatives of the locality hosting the 'National'. The appointment of two full-time organizers in 1959 to serve north and south Wales, followed in 1978 by a full-time director based in Cardiff (CAERDYDD), revo-

Eisteddfod Genedlaethol Cymru (National Eisteddfod of Wales) 1913

lutionized eisteddfod administration and facilitated the organizing of a festival which currently attracts around 150,000 people at a cost of some two million pounds, defrayed, in the main, by central and local government grants, public subscription and local fundraising.

A peripatetic institution since its inception, now alternating only between north and south Wales, the location of the 'National' has long been a place of pilgrimage for Welsh people addicted to its mix of culture and *hwyl* (fun). Arguments in the wake of many a sodden festival for mooring it permanently to a professionally prepared site have not prevailed against the many who are convinced that, deprived of the attractions of differing geographical and cultural contexts, the 'National' would be much impoverished. Added to which is the obvious fact that its missionary rôle as a prime exhibitor of Welsh culture would be seriously curtailed. Notwithstanding the excellent television and radio coverage of its proceedings (see MASS MEDIA; S4C), nothing can compare with the actual presence of the 'National' in one's neighbourhood.

Today, it is generally accepted that the National

Eisteddfod, held regularly during the first full week in August since 1918, exists to celebrate and foster WELSH-language culture. It was not always so. Rapidly Anglicized in the 1860s by would-be progressives who could see no utilitarian value in the mother tongue, the 'National' marginalized the Welsh language for the better part of a century. It took the revised constitution of 1937 to turn the tide by making Welsh the official language of its proceedings, and since 1950 when the 'All-Welsh rule', or the 'Welsh principle' as Cynan (Albert Evans-Jones, 1895–1970) described it, came into force, the 'National' has been true to its commission. It exists to convince a people, too many of whom are still bedevilled by a sense of cultural inferiority, that their language is indeed rich enough to meet the demands of modern life, and to provide a many-faceted opportunity for its enjoyment. And it challenges people to put to work throughout Wales (CYMRU) the creative vigour inherent in the Welsh language.

The National Eisteddfod has proved to be a launching pad for many successful careers. Its coming in 1861 coincided with the flowering of 'The Land of

Song', and singers of international repute, from Edith Wynne in the Victorian heyday to Bryn Terfel in our times, have been indebted to it. Chaired and crowned poets over the years have left their mark on Welsh literature (see WELSH POETRY), and winners of the Prose Medal and the Daniel OWEN Memorial Prize for novelists are likewise influential (see WELSH PROSE LITERATURE). By now, major awards are given for excellence in all the arts, there has been a concerted effort to encourage a greater interest in the sciences, scholarships are awarded to successful young contestants who wish to pursue careers in music and drama, and much more besides (see WELSH MUSIC; WELSH DRAMA). Down to the 1950s a 'National Winner' was a figure to be reckoned with in Wales. By today, he or she may not trail such a visible cloud of glory, but it still pays to win at the 'National'. It still matters to many people.

Critics of a stern countenance have frequently railed against the shortcomings of eisteddfod culture. Competition is said to be inimical to art; the vagaries of adjudication make a mockery of standards; tribal triumphs feed mere self-satisfaction. There have even been calls to translate the 'National' into an academy

Welsh-language poet and rock musician Twm Morys winning the Chair at the 2003 National Eisteddfod in Meifod, Powys

for the few who take their culture seriously. Nevertheless, it has kept to its brief as a popular festival whose competitions over the years have stimulated many fine performers and memorable performances in a context that encourages displays of egalitarian enthusiasm. It excites debate about literature, music, drama, and art; it allows the young, particularly since the coming of 'Maes B' (The B field), to revel in their pop culture and ward off eisteddfod sclerosis with a regular fix of irreverence. Its history is an unfailing source of legendry and exploits that grow ever more fabulous in recollection. Deprived of the 'National', Welsh culture would lose the major traditional signifier of its distinctiveness. It is irreplaceable.

In the past it has also served Wales well as a forum for debating national concerns, as an arena for protest and dissent, and as a platform for demonstrating a will to prosper. Supported as it now is by the National Assembly (see CYNULLIAD CENEDLAETHOL CYMRU), its continued success will still depend to a great extent on its readiness to agitate for the enlargement of a Welsh-speaking Wales. For far too long after 1861 it betrayed its purpose in pursuit of the patronizing commendation of 'onlooking nationalities', but it survived its self-betrayal to help reinvigorate the language which has been the tap-root of the Welsh experience for most of two millennia. As long as it continues to do so spiritedly it will not lack support.

FURTHER READING
ABERTAWE; ABERYSTWYTH; CAERDYDD; CAERFYRDDIN; CYMRU; CYNULLIAD CENEDLAETHOL CYMRU; EISTEDDFOD; GORSEDD BEIRDD YNYS PRYDAIN; MASS MEDIA; OWEN; S4C; WELSH; WELSH DRAMA; WELSH MUSIC; WELSH POETRY; WELSH PROSE LITERATURE; Gwynn ap Gwilym, *Eisteddfota 2*; Ifor ap Gwilym, *Eisteddfota 3*; Edwards, *Gŵyl Gwalia*; Gruffydd, *Nodiadau'r Golygydd 27–69*; Jenkins, THSC 1933/5.139–55; Jenkins & Ramage, *History of the Honourable Society of Cymmrodorion*; Llwyd, *Eisteddfota*; Miles, *Royal National Eisteddfod of Wales*; Parry, *Eisteddfod y Cymry*.

Hywel Teifi Edwards

88) and W. S. Gwynn Williams (1896–1978) who, with a dedicated team of volunteers, arranged the first festival in 1947.

A celebration of international song and dance, the festival was seen as a modest means of bringing back together international communities torn apart by six years of war. The whole ethos is based on friendly competition between folk-dance and choral groups, both youth and adult. Only very minimal token prize money is offered, for the winning of an EISTEDDFOD trophy is reckoned to represent the true value of success.

The festival is organized by a large team of volunteers, apart from five full or part-time staff, and is now traditionally held during early July. Competitors are traditionally housed with local residents for the whole week, with many giving special performances for the residents of the neighbouring communities in which they stay. Nowhere else in the world can be found such a divergence of global cultures as in Llangollen during the eisteddfod.

The dedication of these competitors is also worthy of mention, with groups travelling for many days by coach in order to compete in one of the competitions. The popularity of the festival remains undiminished after over half a century, with an astounding 114 different countries being represented since 1966.

An impressive number of international celebrities have also performed at the Llangollen International Musical Eisteddfod. Some, such as Pavarotti, competed at the festival with their hometown groups, many years before giving a solo concert, while other soloists include Placido Domingo, Bryn Terfel, Yehudi Menuhin and Julian Lloyd Webber.

FURTHER READING
CYMRU; EISTEDDFOD; Attenburrow, *Fifty Glorious Weeks*.

Nigel Davies

Eisteddfod Gerddorol Ryngwladol Llangollen (International Musical Eisteddfod)

Born out of the devastating years of the Second World War, the Llangollen International Musical Eisteddfod was the inspiration of Harold Tudur (1908–

Eisteddfodau'r Fenni (Abergavenny eisteddfodau)

were a series of eisteddfodau organized between 1834 and 1854 by Cymdeithas Cymreigyddion y Fenni (the Abergavenny Cymreigyddion Society) under the patronage and leadership of Lady Augusta HALL and Thomas PRICE.

Through their essay competitions, Eisteddfodau'r

Fenni fostered the study of the WELSH language, literature, and customs. They inspired the young Augusta Hall, for instance, to compose her famous essay on 'The Advantages Resulting from the Preservation of the Welsh Language and National Costumes of Wales' (see MATERIAL CULTURE) and also Thomas Stephens to produce important volumes such as *The Literature of the Kymry* (1849). As Thorne has shown (NLWJ 27.97–107), these eisteddfodau also assisted in the development of comparative linguistics in Wales (CYMRU). They are also relevant to PAN-CELTICISM, since it was at Abergavenny that representatives of two CELTIC COUNTRIES first assembled to celebrate their common ancestry and to make it a base for cooperation (see also LA VILLEMARQUÉ). Most importantly, Eisteddfodau'r Fenni developed the foundations on which EISTEDDFOD GENEDLAETHOL CYMRU would be created from the 1850s onwards.

FURTHER READING
CELTIC COUNTRIES; CYMRU; EISTEDDFOD; EISTEDDFOD GENEDLAETHOL CYMRU; HALL; LA VILLEMARQUÉ; MATERIAL CULTURE; PAN-CELTICISM; PRICE; WELSH; WELSH LITERATURE; Jenkins & Ramage, *History of the Honourable Society of Cymmrodorion*; Ley, *Arglwyddes Llanofer*; Thomas, *Afiaith yng Ngwent*; Thorne, NLWJ 27.97–107.

MBL

Eisteddfodau'r Gwyneddigion

The Gwyneddigion was a literary society, with some philanthropic functions, which was founded in 1770 by a group of London Welshmen—Owen Jones (Owain Myfyr), Robert Jones (Robin Ddu yr Ail o Fôn), and John Edwards (Siôn Ceiriog). The name refers to the north Walian region and medieval principality of GWYNEDD. The society became the focus of the cultural life of the Welsh literati in London (Welsh Llundain), especially during the closing years of the 19th century. They appealed to a more plebeian audience than the rather more rarefied Honourable Society of CYMMRODORION. The most prominent members, including Owen Jones (1741–1814) and William Owen Pughe (1759–1835), did much to preserve and publish early Welsh texts in works such as *Barddoniaeth Dafydd ab Gwilym* (The poetry of DAFYDD AP GWILYM, 1789) and *The Myvyrian Archaiology of Wales* (1801–7). The Gwyneddigion came to be regarded as arbiters in matters of Welsh literature and learning, not only in London, but also in Wales (CYMRU) itself.

The institution of the EISTEDDFOD (bardic competition) had declined since the days of the professional bardic system of the Middle Ages (see BARDIC ORDER), but minor eisteddfodau were still being held in the 18th century. In 1789 Thomas Jones, an exciseman from Corwen, Merioneth (sir Feirionnydd), contacted the Gwyneddigion to seek their patronage for a local eisteddfod to be held at Corwen in May 1789. The society was supportive, but laid down stringent conditions in an attempt to regularize the amateur and rather chaotic local eisteddfodau and give them greater dignity and order. The Gwyneddigion decided to play no active rôle in the Corwen eisteddfod, but agreed to support an eisteddfod to be held in Bala (Meirionnydd, now Gwynedd) in September 1789. Thomas Jones, however, deliberately exaggerated the society's intentions, in an attempt to give the Corwen eisteddfod enhanced status, publicizing it as being under the aegis of the Gwyneddigion. The chair (as a token of the best poetry in the strict metres) was awarded at Corwen to Walter Davies (Gwallter Mechain, 1761–1849), with the Gwyneddigion as adjudicators (judges).

Rumours soon circulated that there had been some rather suspicious dealings in the chair competition and that, although the poems were supposed to have been composed *ex tempore*, Gwallter Mechain had been given the subjects beforehand. Letters preserved in the National Library of Wales (LLYFRGELL GENEDLAETHOL CYMRU) prove that there was indeed collusion between the adjudicators and Gwallter Mechain.

The Gwyneddigion openly patronized the Bala eisteddfod. Gwallter Mechain once more succeeded in currying favour with the society and won the main prize. The Bala eisteddfod did have one important development in that it produced what was probably the first official published adjudication. A judgement with explanatory literary criticism is now an essential feature of the National Eisteddfod of Wales (EISTEDDFOD GENEDLAETHOL CYMRU). The Gwyneddigion also urged the poets to break away from the confines of the more restrictive strict metres in order to promote the concept of a classical Christian epic poem as advocated by Goronwy Owen (see WELSH POETRY).

Eisteddfodau'r Gwyneddigion had a relatively short life, and they lost their impetus when Thomas Jones left Wales in 1795. The eisteddfod increasingly became a source of entertainment rather than the sober breeding ground for poets which the Gwyneddigion had envisaged.

FURTHER READING
BARDIC ORDER; CYMMRODORION; CYMRU; DAFYDD AP GWILYM; EISTEDDFOD; EISTEDDFOD GENEDLAETHOL CYMRU; GWYNEDD; LLYFRGELL GENEDLAETHOL CYMRU; WELSH; WELSH POETRY; Carr, *William Owen Pughe*; Edwards, *Yr Eisteddfod*; Leathart, *Origin and Progress of the Gwyneddigion Society of London*; Ramage, *Twf yr Eisteddfod* 9–28; G. J. Williams, *Llên Cymru* 1.29–47, 113–25; G. J. Williams, *Llenor* 14.11–22, 15.88–96.

Glenda Carr

Elfed/Elmet is the name of an early medieval BRYTHONIC kingdom in what is now south-west Yorkshire, north-central England. It is particularly noteworthy as a Celtic kingdom situated well to the east of the latter-day frontiers of Wales (CYMRU) and Cornwall (KERNOW) and south of that of Scotland (ALBA), and yet it survived late enough to be well documented in the period when its Anglo-Saxon neighbours were becoming literate Christians. That Elfed is known only through the fortuitous survival of disparate bits of evidence alerts us to the likelihood that other Brythonic kingdoms, for which we have no extant historical records, survived into the 7th century in what are now core areas of England. We have three primary sources of evidence for Elfed: (1) place-names, (2) references in early WELSH POETRY, and (3) historical notices relevant to the kingdom's annexation by Northumbria, which are discussed in this Encyclopedia's entries on Elfed's last ruler CERTIC and the expansionist EADWINE of Northumbria (†633).

§1. PLACE-NAME EVIDENCE
Elfed is the modern Welsh form; the older form *Elmet* is preserved in several English place-names between the rivers Wharfe and Don in south Yorkshire, including

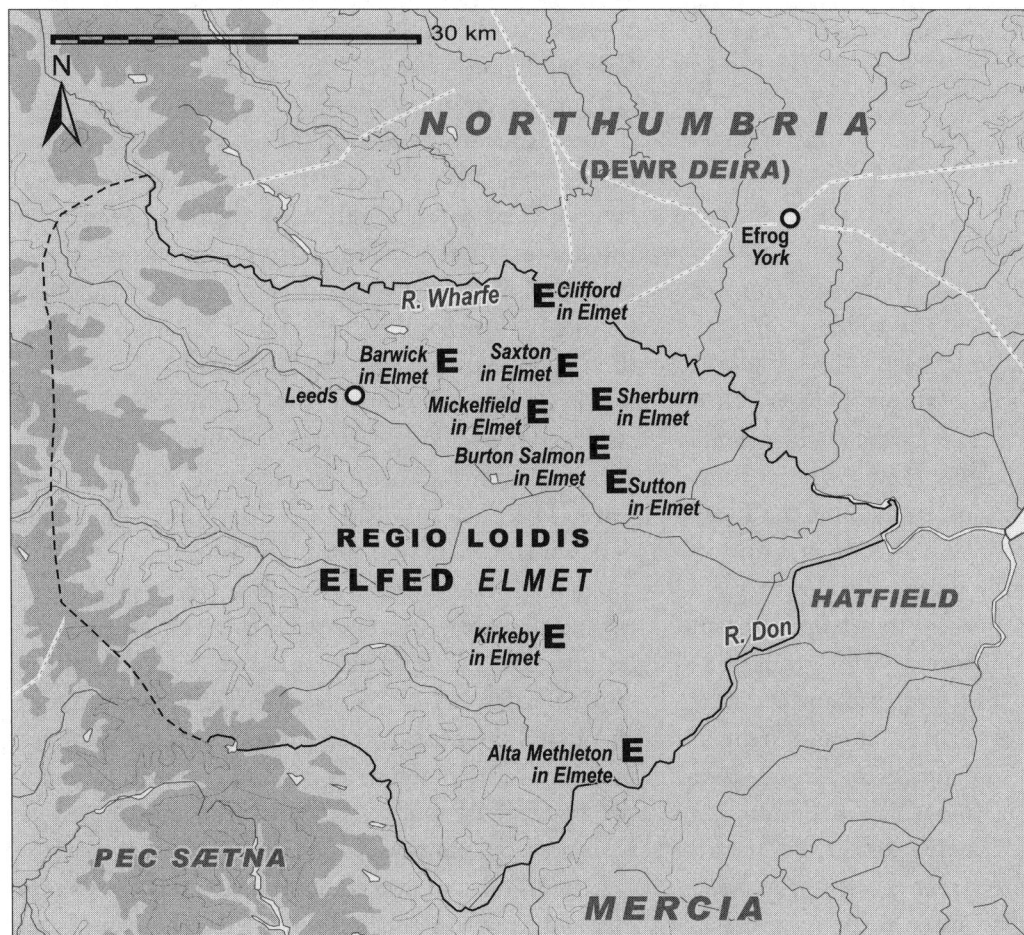

Elfed (Elmet) and neighbouring regions: 'in Elmet' place-names marked with bold E, approximate limits of the kingdom before 7th-century annexation by Northumbria in black (less certain western boundary dashed), Roman roads white with thin dashed line

Barwick in Elmet, Burton Salmon in Elmet, Clifford in Elmet, Mickelfield in Elmet, Sherburn in Elmet, and Sutton in Elmet. A grant of 1361 speaks of 'Kirkeby in Elmet', referring to present-day South Kirkby, south of Leeds, and a record of 1281 mentions an *Alta Methleton in Elmete*, probably modern High Melton, west of Doncaster. The Anglo-Saxon tribute list known as the Tribal Hidage places the *Elmed sætna* (Elmet dwellers) between the *Pec sætna* (dwellers in the Peak [District]) and the inhabitants of Lindsey and Hatfield, thus indicating an extensive landlocked territory astride the strategic frontier of the great kingdoms of Mercia and Northumbria. According to BEDA, a district called *regio Loidis* (which gives its name to modern Leeds) included *silva Elmete* (the wood of Elmet; *Historia Ecclesiastica* 2.14), and many scholars have concluded that Loidis and Elmet were two names for more or less the same place. Both names are probably Celtic. There is also an Elfed in south Wales. More probably referring to the Pennine kingdom is a 5th- or 6th-century inscribed stone from the church of Llanaelhaearn in GWYNEDD: ALIORTVS ELMETIACO HIC IACET 'here lies Aliortus of Elfed'.

§2. ALLUSIONS TO ELFED IN POETRY

Of the praise poems in the AWDL metre in the Book of Taliesin (LLYFR TALIESIN), two are addressed to a Dark Age north British ruler named GWALLAWG. He is described in one as *a·eninat yn ygnat ac Eluet*, probably to be translated 'who has been anointed magistrate of Elfed', suggesting the legitimacy of a church ceremony. A Madawg Elfed occurs among the heroes of the GODODDIN. The epithet could simply mean 'Madawg from Elfed' but, as with the style of OWAIN GWYNEDD or URIEN RHEGED, it could naturally be understood as 'Madawg, ruler of Elfed'. Given the proximity of the Gododdin's enemies in Deira (DEWR) and the battle site of CATRAETH to Elfed, it would hardly be surprising had the leadership of the kingdom been involved, or even at stake, in that conflict. In MOLIANT CADWALLON, 'the land of Elfed' is again mentioned, this time as a place of imminent conflagration, along with recollections of Gwallawg and 'the great mortality of Catraeth'. This poet saw connections between 6th-century events in the Pennines and CADWALLON of Gwynedd's invasion of Northumbria in 633–5. Presumably, he wanted his

audience to remember that the BRITONS had great champions and legitimate rulers in the region not long before. The claim was not soon forgotten by Welsh poets: also in *Llyfr Taliesin* is a 10th-century PROPHECY concerned with the messianic return of CADWALADR, Cadwallon's son, whose anticipated deeds include operations beyond the Solway Firth (Merin Rheged) and ruling Elfed (proved by rhyme).

FURTHER READING
ALBA; AWDL; BEDA; BRITONS; BRYTHONIC; CADWALADR; CADWALLON; CATRAETH; CERTIC; CYMRU; DEWR; EADWINE; GODODDIN; GWALLAWG; GWYNEDD; KERNOW; LLYFR TALIESIN; MOLIANT CADWALLON; OWAIN GWYNEDD; PROPHECY; RHEGED; URIEN; WELSH POETRY; Bartrum, *Welsh Classical Dictionary* 237; Bromwich, *Beginnings of Welsh Poetry*; Bromwich, TYP 308; Gruffydd, SC 28.63–79; Hind, BBCS 28.541–52; G. R. J. Jones, *Northern History* 10.3–27; Rowland, *Early Welsh Saga Poetry*; Taylor, *Medieval History* 2/1.111–29.

JTK

Elfoddw, St (Old Welsh Elbodug; †809) is called *archiepiscopus Guenedotae* (archbishop of GWYNEDD) in his death notice in ANNALES CAMBRIAE. At 768 in *Annales Cambriae*, it is stated that he changed the BRITONS' reckoning of Easter, and this is usually taken as signifying the last insular churches coming into conformity with Roman practice at that time (see EASTER CONTROVERSY; CHRISTIANITY). Those texts of HISTORIA BRITTONUM which are attributed to Nennius call him *sancti Elbodugi discipulus* (disciple of St Elfoddw). Taken together, this evidence suggests that, because Elfoddw was responsible for a major reform of the calendar in the Welsh church, he was also a key figure for the keeping of historical records in Wales (CYMRU) in the early Middle Ages. It is possible that the 8th-century bishops Elvogus of LLANDAF and Eluoed of St David's (Tyddewi) are the same person.

Old Welsh *Elbodug* is a Celtic compound name deriving from PROTO-CELTIC *elu-* 'many' and *bodwo-* 'crow', which was also a divine name; cf. Old Irish BODB.

FURTHER READING
ANNALES CAMBRIAE; BODB; BRITONS; CHRISTIANITY; CYMRU; EASTER CONTROVERSY; GWYNEDD; HISTORIA BRITTONUM; LLANDAF; PROTO-CELTIC; Bartrum, *Welsh Classical Dictionary* 239; Nora K. Chadwick et al., *Studies in the Early British Church* 29–120; Miller, *Saints of Gwynedd*; Ann Williams et al., *Biographical Dictionary of Dark Age Britain* 132–3.

JTK

Elidir Sais was one of the Poets of the Princes (Welsh *Beirdd y Tywysogion*; see GOGYNFEIRDD). He was active by 1195 and was still alive *c.* 1246. He was a native of Anglesey (MÔN), and it is possible that his father was the court poet GWALCHMAI AP MEILYR, since Gwalchmai had a son named Elidir. The reason for the epithet *Sais* 'Englishman' is not known, but speculation has focused around either exile in England or ability in English, and possibly both. Most of Elidir's extant poems are religious in theme. Two are short prayers for salvation; another contrasts God's bounty with human sinfulness, asserts the value of composing poetry to God, and concludes with another plea for heaven. In a predominantly homiletic poem, confession is mixed with warnings of Judgement and the need to be reconciled with God before death, for every sin will be measured. Another poem urges penance, recounts the events of Holy Week, and ends with a prayer. Yet another describes the fall of Jerusalem to Saladin in 1187 as an 'oppression' caused by God, and associates it with the exile of Dafydd ab Owain, once ruler of GWYNEDD, from Wales (CYMRU). Faith in God is reasserted at the end, implying that both wrongs will be amended. Elidir's elegy for Dafydd's brother Rhodri is also strongly religious in content, and there are two other elegies to prominent Gwynedd noblemen, and a *dadolwch*, or poem pleading for reconciliation, to LLYWELYN AB IORWERTH. Here, Elidir contrasts his unnatural separation from favour with gnomic references to the undisturbed rhythms of nature and society, and Llywelyn is warned to do his duty by fighting the English rather than invading neighbouring territories. A series of laudatory *englynion* (see ENGLYN) is attached to the end of the poem.

PRIMARY SOURCES
EDITION. J. E. Caerwyn Williams et al., *Gwaith Meilyr Brydydd* 315–423.
TRANS. Costigan, *Defining the Divinity.*

FURTHER READING
CYMRU; ENGLYN; GOGYNFEIRDD; GWALCHMAI AP MEILYR; GWYNEDD; LLYWELYN AB IORWERTH; MÔN; McKenna, *Medieval Welsh Religious Lyric.*

Barry J. Lewis

Elis, Islwyn Ffowc (1924–2004) was a major 20th-century writer of prose fiction in the WELSH language. He was born at Wrecsam, Denbighshire (sir Ddinbych) and raised in the vale of Ceiriog in northeast Wales (CYMRU). He first came to prominence as the winner of the Prose Medal at the 1951 National Eisteddfod at Llanrwst (see EISTEDDFOD GENEDLAETHOL CYMRU) with *Cyn Oeri'r Gwaed* (Before the blood cools), a volume of romantic and lively essays, but he is best known as a pioneering Welsh novelist.

When *Cysgod y Cryman* (Shadow of the sickle) was published in 1953, the public were enchanted by the professionalism and novelty of a young author who, for the first time in Welsh, dealt with the social issues of the day. He depicted the inevitable conflict between old and new in the aftermath of the Second World War, thrilling many generations with his narrative skills and panoramic canvas.

In 1955 he ventured to experiment further with the publication of *Ffenestri tua'r Gwyll* (Windows towards the dusk), a dark, modern psychological novel which disturbed rather than entertained its readers; it was a novel before its time, and was not fully appreciated by the reading public. This seems to have prompted the author to return to Lleifior, the flourishing farm of his first novel, and *Yn ôl i Leifior* (Return to Lleifior) was published the following year, satisfying the general public's need for an emotional family tale in a real society. From then on, Elis dedicated himself to producing a more accessible literature, at times experimental in form, missionary and politically challenging, but rather more reluctant to plunge to the psychological depths of his characters.

The main aim of his prophetic novel, *Wythnos yng Nghymru Fydd* (A week in the new Wales, 1957), which urged his readers to campaign for a successful Wales in which the Welsh language will flourish, is to convey a political message. This volume was also an important milestone in the development of political and prophetic prose in Welsh (see PROPHECY). The following year saw the publication of *Blas y Cynfyd* (A taste of prehistory), a light novel in which family and nationalist elements were interwoven. Once again, the message was simple but the plot complicated, reflecting the careful plotting of the serial radio drama on which it was based (see MASS MEDIA).

Islwyn Ffowc Elis broke new ground once again in *Tabyrddau'r Babongo* (The drums of the Babongo, 1961), a farcical satire based in Africa. The ingenuity, humour and novelty of this thought-provoking novel won him an Arts Council of Wales award in 1962. It was he who also wrote the first Welsh science-fiction thriller, *Y Blaned Dirion* (The gentle planet, 1968). In 1970 and 1971 he published two short novels, *Y Gromlech yn yr Haidd* (Stones in the barley) and *Eira Mawr* (White-out), in a further attempt to reach a wider audience. Over the years he also published numerous essays and discerning articles of literary criticism.

Islwyn Ffowc Elis was acknowledged as a versatile author who took the Welsh novel to new and exciting directions. It is sometimes claimed that some tensions existed between the serious writer in him on the one hand and the entertainer and missionary on the other, and that his desire to widen the circle of readers in Welsh suppressed his literary skills at times. However, his varied collection of short stories, *Marwydos* (Embers, 1974), is a psychologically complex, discerning composition, which shows that he had the ability to combine all these elements in an ingenious way.

PRIMARY SOURCES
NOVELS. *Cysgod y Cryman* (1953); *Ffenestri tua'r Gwyll* (1955); *Yn ôl i Leifior* (1956); *Wythnos yng Nghymru Fydd* (1957); *Blas y Cynfyd* (1958); *Tabyrddau'r Babongo* (1961); *Y Blaned Dirion* (1968); *Y Gromlech yn yr Haidd* (1970); *Eira Mawr* (1971). SHORT STORIES. *Marwydos* (1974). ESSAYS. *Cyn Oeri'r Gwaed* (1952); 'The Modern Novel in Welsh', *Anglo-Welsh Review* 15/36.20–6 (1958); [Biographical Essay], *Artists in Wales* 143–58 (1971;); 'Creu Ysgrif', *Ysgrifennu Creadigol* 75–84 (1972); *Naddion* (1998).

FURTHER READING
CYMRU; EISTEDDFOD GENEDLAETHOL CYMRU; MASS MEDIA; PROPHECY; WELSH; WELSH PROSE LITERATURE; Brown, *Anglo-Welsh Review* 9/24.30–8; Chapman, *Islwyn Ffowc Elis*; Chapman, *Rhywfaint o Anfarwoldeb*; George, *Barn* 312.13–16, 22; George, *Islwyn Ffowc Elis*; Glyn Jones & Rowlands, *Profiles* 136–43; John Maxwell Jones, *Islwyn Ffowc Elis*; R. M. Jones, *Llenyddiaeth Gymraeg 1936–1972* 256–62; Ioan Williams, *Y Nofel* 34–9.

Delyth George

Eliseg's Pillar is a broken stone pillar, originally about 3.6 m (12 ft) high, located in Llandysilio-yn-Iâl near Llangollen, Denbighshire (sir Ddinbych). It has a lengthy Latin inscription, with Old WELSH names, dating to the earlier 9th century, which gives the genealogy of the kings of Powys (Old Welsh POUOIS) and a unique version of their origin legend. The inscription was commissioned by king Cyngen (Old

Welsh CONCENN) and commemorates his great-grand-father Elise (ELISEG), who is said to have taken the land from the English (ANGLI) by the sword. The genealogical sequence CONCENN FILIUS CATTELL . . . FILIUS BROHCMAIL . . . FILIUS ELISEG . . . FILIUS GUOILLAUC at the top of the inscription parallels exactly *Cincen map Catel map Brocmayl map Elitet map Guilauc* in the Old Welsh Powys GENEALOGIES in BL MS Harley 3859. Further down in the inscription, passers-by are invited to pray for Eliseg's soul, not an uncommon device in an early medieval commemorative inscription. It goes on to state that St Germanus blessed BRITU the son of GUARTHI[GIRN] (i.e. Vortigern/GWRTHEYRN) and SE[V]IRA the daughter of MAXIMUS (i.e. MACSEN WLEDIG); this seems to be the account of the founda-tion of the line. We have a similar, but different, story of Germanus, Guorthigirn, and his son in HISTORIA BRITTONUM, as well as an account of the descent of the kings of Powys from a virtuous commoner named Cadell (see CADELLING). Evidently, more than one doc-trine was current in the 9th century. The pillar's origin legend is particularly ambitious in claiming descent from two rulers regarded as having held authority over the whole of BRITAIN before the *adventus Saxonum* (arrival of the Anglo-Saxons), and was evidently intended to justify the legitimacy of Eliseg's taking the area by force from the English. The stonecutter identifies himself as CONMARCH, thus bearing the same name as the eponym of the CYNFERCHING. The pillar is now in many parts illegible; readings rely on a transcription made by Edward LHUYD in 1696.

FURTHER READING
BRITAIN; CADELLING; CYNFERCHING; GENEALOGIES; GWRTHEYRN; HISTORIA BRITTONUM; LHUYD; MACSEN WLEDIG; POWYS; WELSH; Bartrum, EWGT 1–3; Wendy Davies, *Wales in the Early Middle Ages*; Dumville, *Early Welsh Poetry* 1–16; Macalister, *Corpus Inscriptionum Insularum Celticarum* 2.145–9; Nash-Williams, *Early Christian Monuments of Wales* 123–5.

JTK

Ellan Vannin (Isle of Man)

§1. GENERAL BACKGROUND

The Isle of Man is not part of the modern political state of the United Kingdom, nor of Great Britain—either in the sense of being part of the island of

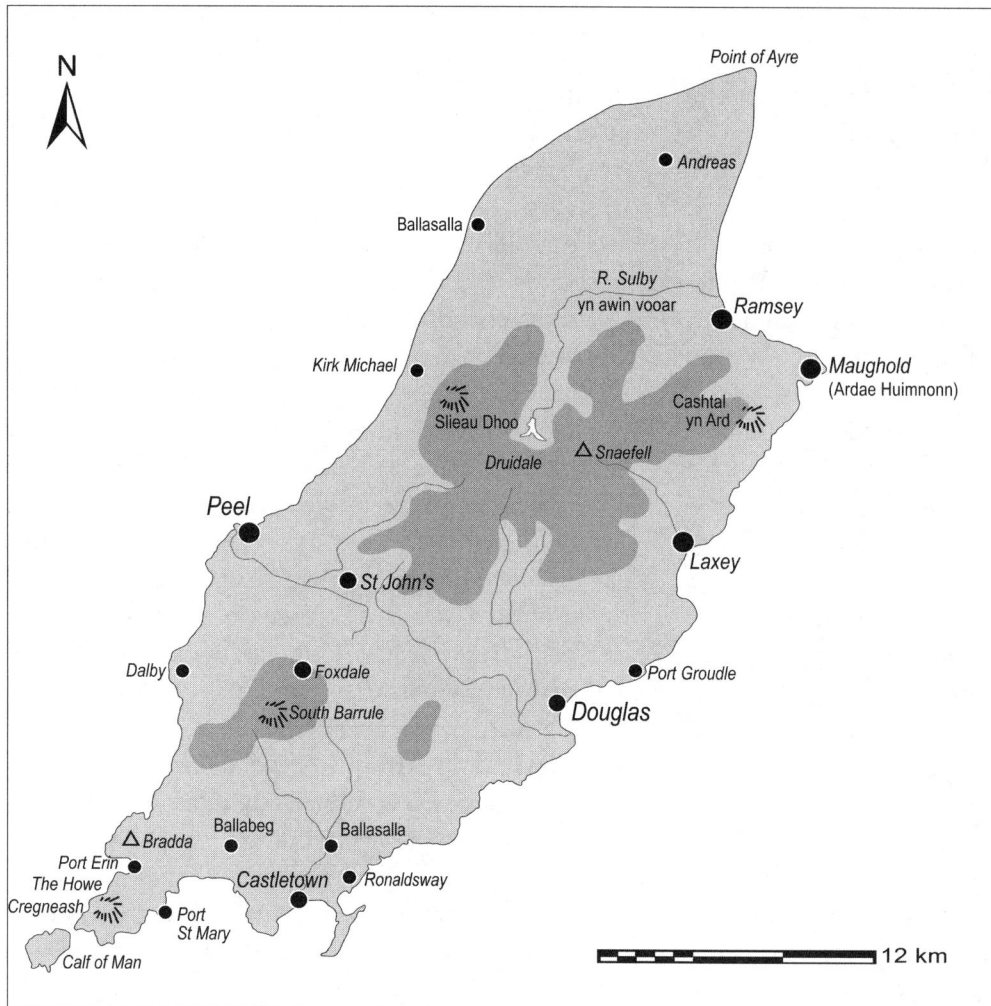

N

Point of Ayre

Andreas

Ballasalla

R. Sulby
yn awin vooar

Ramsey

Kirk Michael

Maughold
(Ardae Huimnonn)

Slieau Dhoo

Cashtal
yn Ard

Druidale

△ Snaefell

Peel

St John's

Laxey

Dalby

Foxdale

Port Groudle

South Barrule

Douglas

△ Bradda

Ballabeg

Ballasalla

Port Erin
The Howe
Cregneash

Castletown

Ronaldsway

Port
St Mary

Calf of Man

12 km

BRITAIN or as the term is sometimes used synonymously for the UK. Man is a self-governing British Crown dependency and a member of the British Commonwealth. It recognizes the Queen or King of England, who, as sovereign, retains the title Lord of Man. The constitutional status and history of Man is discussed in detail in §8 below. Castletown was the ancient capital, but in the 1870s the Administration moved to Douglas, which then became the modern capital.

The Isle of Man is geographically part of the British Isles (the archipelago of Britain, Ireland/ ÉIRE, and smaller islands off Europe's Atlantic north-west). It is situated in the centre of the Irish Sea, approximately 26 km south of Burrow Head (Scotland/ALBA), 43 km south-west of St Bees Head (Cumbria, England), and 43 km east of Strangford Lough (Ireland). It is approximately 53 km long and 19 km wide, and its area is 365 km². At the south-western extremity is an islet called the Calf of Man, containing about 324 ha (about 700 acres) which is now a bird sanctuary.

A chain of mountains extends from north-east to south-west, the highest of which is Snaefell (620 m). These mountains are broken by a central valley which runs between Douglas and Peel. This was of great importance in the past, for it divided the island into two distinct portions, the 'north-side' and the 'south-side'. The northern plain, which extends from Ramsey to the Point of Ayre, is sandy in character and is relieved only by a low range of hills, the highest of which is only 82 m. Streams radiate from Snaefell, winding their way to the sea from all sides, forming narrow winding glens, which are studded with mainly fir, sycamore and mountain ash, interspersed with patches of gorse, heather and fern, which provide a striking and beautiful contrast to the bare mountain tops, although much planting of coniferous trees has taken place on the slopes during the 20th century.

The geology of the Isle of Man contains old stratified rocks traversed by numerous metalliferous lodes, some of them proving to be extremely productive, the most important being the silver-lead and zinc lodes in the Laxey and Foxdale areas. Copper and iron ore were also found at Bradda and Maughold and elsewhere, but they were of comparatively small quantities. The Laxey Wheel, the largest working water-wheel in the world, was built in 1854 to pump water from the Laxey mines. Since the closure of the mines in 1929 it has not been required for this purpose. In 1965 it was bought by the Manx government and is now maintained as a working tourist attraction.

Much of the coastline of the Isle of Man is very rugged and steep, especially between Peel and the south, and between Ramsey and Castletown on the east coast. The main bays are on this coast—Ramsey, Laxey, Douglas, Castletown, and Port St Mary—the only two on the west coast being Port Erin and Peel. In the south of the island between Scarlett and Port St Mary the rock formations provide evidence that volcanic action has taken place.

As to its climate, the island is affected by its situation, being exposed on the south-west to the full force of heavy Atlantic gales, but it is also influenced by the warm Gulf Stream, and as a result the winters are relatively mild.

The earliest known inhabitants of the Isle of Man have been identified as Middle Stone Age hunter-gatherers from *c.* 7000 BC. Dating from the Copper and earlier Bronze Ages, *c.* 2500–*c.* 1500 BC, are the great stone circles, which usually contain within their precincts rough cists (stone-lined single graves of small dimensions). The Meayl Circle at Cregneash and Cashtal yn Ard at Maughold are good examples of these megaliths (large-stone monuments). See further §3 Prehistory, below.

There are numerous early medieval monuments on the Isle of Man, including early Celtic keeills (small chapels) and sculptured crosses (see HIGH CROSSES). About a quarter of these crosses have inscriptions in early GOIDELIC, written in the OGAM script. In general, the stone crosses were rectangular in shape, some with rounded upper corners, and some, called wheel crosses, with the whole head rounded.

The arrival of the Vikings towards the end of the 8th century had an immense effect on the history and culture of the Isle of Man. Coming from Norway, the links between the two countries have survived up to the present time in the form of the Isle of Man's

parliamentary system which has existed for well over a thousand years, being the oldest continuous parliament in the world. An annual open-air assembly of all the freemen at some central place where new laws were announced and disputes settled was an essential feature of the Norse system, and such an assembly was called the 'thing'—the Manx Parliament is called TYNWALD, the first part based on this word and the second on the Norse word *vollr* meaning field or meeting-place. This open-air meeting is still held annually on 5 July (old MIDSUMMER'S DAY) on Tynwald Hill at St John's, which is situated near the centre of the island.

For administrative and political purposes, the Isle of Man is divided into six ancient sheadings (Manx *seden* i.e. six). There are 17 ecclesiastical parishes within these sheadings and, with the exception of Marown, all of these touch the sea.

During the 19th century the main industries were farming, fishing (§10 below), and mining (§11 below), the majority of the land being cultivated, and at one

View of the five burial chambers of Cashtal yn Ard, Maughold

time there were over 700 boats in the Manx fishing fleet. During the 20th century, although farming and fishing were still important, the tourist industry flourished despite the interruptions caused by two world wars but, with the introduction of wider air travel since the Second World War, more and more people seek the sun outside the British Isles, thus causing a significant decline in the tourist trade. To counter the effects on the Manx economy, the government encouraged development in the manufacturing industries and the finance sector, and this sector is the major factor in the tremendous economic growth which has taken place in the latter part of the 20th century. As a result, there are better opportunities for employment, and many people have had to be recruited from outside the island, creating a large increase in the population, which, at the 2001 census, had risen to 76,535. Manx-born residents are now in the minority.

In Viking times, the coat of arms of the Isle of Man was a ship with sails furled, but after the Viking era ended this was changed to the three legs emblem, the earliest known examples being on the Manx Sword of State (*c.* AD 1230) and the 14th-century Maughold Cross. Since 1996, a peregrine falcon and a raven have been added as supports on either side of the shield, alluding to the custom of giving two falcons to each English monarch on coronation day. The motto that forms part of the coat of arms is *Quocunque jeceris stabit* (it will stand wherever you throw it).

Victor Kneale

§2. THE CELTICITY OF THE ISLE OF MAN
The date of the arrival of Celtic speech in Man is uncertain. Man was never incorporated into the Roman Empire, but the island was noted in GREEK AND ROMAN ACCOUNTS, where it was called variously *Monapia*, Μοναοιδα *Monaoida*, Μοναρινα *Monarina*, *Manavi, Mevania* (Rivet & Smith, *Place-Names of Roman Britain* 410–11). The Old Irish and Old Welsh names for the Isle of Man—*Mano* and *Manau*—also occur for an ancient district in north Britain along the lower river Forth (Foirthe; see GODODDIN). The name is probably connected with that of the island of MÔN (Anglesey), and possibly with the Celtic root reflected in Welsh *mynydd*, Breton *menez*, Scottish Gaelic *monadh* 'mountain' (on the INDO-EUROPEAN, see §5 below). Both *Manann* and *Manau* are associated with an early

mythological figure connected with seafaring, Irish MANANNÁN and Welsh MANAWYDAN. From the early post-Roman centuries there is inscriptional evidence for Celtic of both the Goidelic and BRYTHONIC type on the island. The second dynasty of GWYNEDD in Wales (CYMRU) was founded by MERFYN Frych in 825; his father Gwriad is probably commemorated as Old Welsh GURIAT on an inscribed cross on Man, and the dynasty probably came from Man. The MANX language is a Celtic language of the Goidelic type, i.e. GAELIC. Although the Viking era had a great impact on the Isle of Man and there are several place-names of Norse origin such as *Snaefell* (snow mountain) on Man, Norse speech failed to survive on the island. The majority of place-names (see §5 below) and family names of Manx-born families are of Celtic origin. Manx was widely spoken on the island until the later 19th century, but since then it has rapidly declined, although in recent years efforts have been made to encourage its use, and it is now an optional subject in the schools (see EDUCATION). In Manx, an affectionate pet name *Ellan Vannin Veg Veen* (the dear little Isle of Man) is current for the island. According to traditional accounts, CHRISTIANITY was brought to the Isle of Man by the disciples of St PATRICK, and there are a number of place-names associated with him, for example, St Patrick's Isle, St Patrick's Well, St Patrick's Chair, St Patrick's Footsteps. Since 1977, Yn CHRUINNAGHT (The gathering) has been held annually as a self-consciously Celtic Manx national festival.

FURTHER READING
ALBA; BRITAIN; BRYTHONIC; CHRISTIANITY; CHRUINNAGHT; CYMRU; EDUCATION; ÉIRE; GAELIC; GODODDIN; GOIDELIC; GREEK AND ROMAN ACCOUNTS; GWYNEDD; HIGH CROSSES; MANANNÁN; MANAWYDAN; MANX; MANX SURNAMES; MERFYN; MIDSUMMER'S DAY; MÔN; OGAM; PATRICK; TYNWALD; Rivet & Smith, *Place-Names of Roman Britain* 410–11.

Victor Kneale, JTK

§3. PREHISTORY
Evidence from over 40 sites for the first Mesolithic (Middle Stone Age) hunter-gatherers who had arrived by around 7000 BC consists almost entirely of microlithic flint tools, similar to implements recovered from much of north-west Atlantic Europe (McCartan, *Recent Archaeological Research on the Isle of Man* 5–11). Between 5000 and 4000 BC these earliest inhabitants were apparently replaced by groups using much heavier tools

and weapons, which represent local developments in Man and Ulster (Ulaidh; earlier ULAID). They were also essentially hunter-gatherers, but pollen evidence shows that they had a greater impact on the landscape. They burned woodland clearings to encourage game, and eventually adopted cereal cultivation—a Manx site, at Ballachrink, Andreas, has the earliest pollen evidence (5,925±60 BP) for the use of cereals in the British Isles.

By around 3000 BC knowledge of AGRICULTURE, pottery, and polished stone tools—the Neolithic (New Stone Age)—had arrived (Burrow, *Recent Archaeological Research on the Isle of Man* 27–38). Manx inhabitants began to construct large megalithic tombs in which to bury their dead (Henshall, *Man and Environment in the Isle of Man* 1.171–6). The form and ritual associated with these monuments is so close to that visible on tombs in Ulster and south-west Scotland as to suggest that the island was part of a coherent local socio-economic system.

The Late Neolithic (or 'Ronaldsway neolithic') on Man saw a remarkable set of insular developments, unparalleled elsewhere (Burrow, *Proc. Prehistoric Society* 65.125–43). Between around 2800 and 2200 BC distinctive pottery (the Ronaldsway urns), flintwork (the hump-backed scraper and lozenge-shaped arrowhead), incised slate plaques, and the local exploitation of a local rock source for the production of the unique 'roughened-butt' axes were all characteristic.

If Ronaldsway provided evidence for a period of isolation and indigenous development, during the earlier Bronze Age (*c.* 2200–1500 BC) the island returned to the main stream (Woodcock, *In Search of a Cultural Identity*). Most of the types of ritual site, burials, pottery and flint artefacts present around the rest of the Irish Sea occur, often in quantity. The specific links are with Ireland (ÉRIU), especially the north-east. By this period a majority of the Manx lowlands had been cleared for the plough and significant inroads were being made into the uplands (Chiverrell et al., *Geomorphology* 40.219–36).

At some time during the Later Bronze Age (*c.* 1500–750 BC) a massive dominant hill-fort was constructed on South Barrule, the highest land in the south of the island. Flat cemeteries with cordoned urns became the norm. Bronze tools and implements were used in greater numbers and appear to show closer relationships with Britain.

The IRON AGE on Man runs from after 750 BC up to the arrival of CHRISTIANITY by around AD 500 (Gelling, *Man and Environment in the Isle of Man* 1.233–43). Until the 1st century of our era, sites, monuments and artefacts are rare. There is no pottery or metalwork. Settlement sites have been located on marginal land on the flanks of Slieau Dhoo in Kirk Michael and beneath the medieval walls of Peel Castle. Some of the 20 or so promontory forts date from this period (see FORTIFICATION).

During the 1st century, almost certainly due to the proximity of the Roman military, there seems to have been a period of prosperity. A number of very large circular timber houses were built, especially in the south of the island, that show direct contacts with the Empire, with metal and glass artefacts from far afield (Bersu, *Three Iron Age Round Houses in the Isle of Man*).

FURTHER READING
AGRICULTURE; CHRISTIANITY; ÉRIU; FORTIFICATION; INDO-EUROPEAN; IRON AGE; ULAID; Bersu, *Three Iron Age Round Houses in the Isle of Man*; Burrow, *Recent Archaeological Research on the Isle of Man* 27–38; Burrow, *Neolithic Culture of the Isle of Man*; Burrow, *Proceedings of the Prehistoric Society* 65.125–43; Burrow & Darvill, *Antiquity* 71.412–19; Chiverrell et al., *Geomorphology* 40.219–36; Chiverrell et al., *Recent Archaeological Research on the Isle of Man* 321–36; Clark, *Proc. Prehistoric Society* 1.70–92; Darvill, *Recent Archaeological Research on the Isle of Man* 13–26; Davey et al., *Recent Archaeological Research on the Isle of Man* 39–62; Freke, *Proc. Isle of Man Natural History and Antiquarian Society* 9.491–500; Garrad, *Recent Archaeological Research on the Isle of Man* 75–80; Gelling, *Man and Environment in the Isle of Man* 1.233–43; Gelling, *Prehistoric Man in Wales and the West* 285–92; Gelling, *Proc. Prehistoric Society* 24.85–100; Henshall, *Man and Environment in the Isle of Man* 1.171–6; Innes et al., *Journal of Quaternary Science* 18.603–13; McCartan, *Proc. Isle of Man Natural History and Antiquarian Society* 10.2.87–117; McCartan, *Recent Archaeological Research on the Isle of Man* 5–11; Woodcock, *Recent Archaeological Research on the Isle of Man* 121–37; Woodcock, 'In Search of a Cultural Identity'; Woodman, *Man and Environment in the Isle of Man* 1.119–39.

P. J. Davey

§4. THE ISLE OF MAN IN EARLY IRISH LITERATURE
Although Man did not produce any literary texts during the early Middle Ages which have survived, the island belonged to a literate early Christian Gaelic world and is often mentioned in early Irish texts. As well as its usual Old Irish name (*Mano*, genitive *Manann*), it also had literary place-names such as *Inis Falga* and *Emain Ablach* (Emain of the apples, cf. Welsh *Ynys Afallach* AVALON). Despite the Isle of Man's close geographical proximity to the east coast of Ireland and the south-west of Scotland—lying within sight of both, it usually

appears as a markedly exotic location in medieval Gaelic literature. Although it is mentioned in the ANNALS as an important prize in the territorial ambitions of various Irish and Scottish dynasties from the 6th century and its naturally strategic location for control of the facing coasts, in most of the tales it is a place associated with magic and isolation rather than with conquest and secular power politics. In other tales, which probably extrapolate the LORDSHIP OF THE ISLES back into the mythic past of the region, Man is a centre of power from which a high-king comes to make a circuit and to arrange the affairs and households of a disorderly Ireland. Another notable feature of its appearance in most of the tales is a lack of detail in the descriptions of the island. While medieval Gaelic literature is rich in onomastics, there is seldom a mention of particular locations on the Isle of Man, and our impressions of the island, based on the tales, are of a dark and misty place, beetling with tall craggy cliffs, and populated by very few and rather strange creatures. In this respect, the Man of the Irish sagas is similar, in its marked resemblance to the OTHERWORLD, to ALBA (Britain or north Britain) as it figures in the same corpus, even though Alba was from c. AD 845 the united kingdom of PICTS and SCOTS and a constant political reality in the Gaelic world. LOCHLANN is also comparable in seeming at times to be an Otherworld, but at other times a real Scandinavia.

There are consistencies then, as well as contradictions, in the portrayal of the Isle of Man in medieval Gaelic literature. It is sometimes presented as marginal and sometimes as central to the mythical geography of the culture. One of its most important and consistent associations in the tales is with the character MANANNÁN mac Lir, the sometime god of the Irish Sea. The Isle of Man, according to the authority of texts such as SANAS CHORMAIC ('Cormac's Glossary') and *Tochmarc Luaine* (The wooing of Luan), and to the meaning of his very name 'the little one of Man', is the home of Manannán. But the relationship between the character and the island is more complex than that between a man and his homeland. In some cases, Manannán even seems to be a personification of the island, and the association with Manannán is central to Man's place in medieval Gaelic literature.

Nevertheless, Man is not Manannán's only home, and Manannán is not the only important character to be associated with the Isle of Man. There are also connections between the magically powerful Midir, Cú Roí mac Dáiri, the smith Culann (CÚ CHULAINN's namesake) and the Isle of Man. Culann is located on the Isle of Man in versions of the boyhood deeds of Cú Chulainn, and it is to Man that CONCHOBAR goes in order to have Culann forge his battle armour. When, with the help of the magically powerful armour, Conchobar takes the kingship of Ulster (ULAID), he brings Culann from Man to live in honour in Ireland. Another reference to the Isle of Man occurs in *Aided Chon Roí* (The death of Cú Roí). In this story Midir is the king of the Isle and Cú Roí is the king's enemy who conspires, along with the Ulstermen, to raid the king's palace and steal his jewels. The Isle of Man in both these tales is associated with supernatural power, which is imported into Ireland, but it is only briefly mentioned, and its association with Cú Roí and Culann is exceptional. The supernatural power that flows from the island, however, is characteristic of its presentation in other tales as well. The Isle of Man appears to be far enough away from Ireland to be exotic and magical, but, at the same time, close enough to be a repository of Gaelic culture—the rich and strange people and things which are located there are clearly Gaels rather than foreigners.

This combination of exotic and mysterious marginality and cultural centrality is also characteristic of the Isle of Man in the story of the journey of SENCHÁN TORPÉIST, the legendary poet and tradition bearer. There are a number of versions of an episode in which Senchán travels to the Isle of Man in search of a poetess who had gone on a circuit of Ireland, Scotland, and Man. Kuno MEYER included three versions of this story in his edition of *Sanas Chormaic*, and Senchán and his troops find her on the Isle of Man later on in all three versions of the episode.

In contrast to the brevity of the above references, one of the most extensive poetic uses of the Isle of Man in all medieval Gaelic literature occurs in a poem in praise of Raghnall, king of Man and the Isles (1187–1229). Raghnall was the great-grandson of Gofraidh Crobh-bhán, or Gofraidh Mérach as he is named in this poem. In 1187 Raghnall took over a kingdom which had been founded by his grandfather on the Isle of Man, but which also, at times, incorporated Dublin (BAILE ÁTHA CLIATH) and some of the Hebrides.

Raghnall had strong Norse connections and is noted for his military prowess in *Orkneyinga Saga*.

Other Gaelic poems, including some written in praise of Feargal O'Reilly (†1291) found in the Book of the DEAN OF LISMORE, contain references to Manannán, and by implication to the Isle of Man. Most of these poems read as long excuses for the poet to show off his knowledge of tradition.

PRIMARY SOURCES
EDITIONS. Best, *Ériu* 2.20–31 (*Aided Chon Roi*); Best, *Ériu* 3.149–73 (Adventures of Art Son of Conn, and the Courtship of Delbchaem); Breatnach, *Celtica* 13.1–31 (*Tochmarc Luaine ocus Aided Athairne*); Carney, *Poems on the O'Reillys* 106; Clancy et al., *Triumph Tree*; Keating, *Foras Feasa ar Éirinn*, vol. 2, chap. 36; Dobbs, ZCP 18.189–230 (*Altrom Tige Dá Medar*); Duncan, *Ériu* 11.184–225 (*Altrom Tige Dá Medar*); Gantz, *Early Irish Myths and Sagas* 256; Gwynn, *Poems from the Dindshenchas* 274; Joynt, *Tromdámh Guaire*; Macalister, *Lebor Gabála Érenn*, pts. 1–4; Mac Giolla Léith, *Oidheadh Chloinne hUisneach*; M'lauchlan, *Dean of Lismore's Book* 102; Mac Mathúna, *Immram Brain*; Mac Neill & Murphy, *Duanaire Finn* 1.19 & 116; Meyer, *Sanas Cormaic*; Meyer & Nutt, *Voyage of Bran*; Ó Cuív, *Éigse* 8.283–301 (Poem in praise of Raghnall); O'Curry, *Atlantis* 4.113–240 (*Tri Thruaighé na Scéalaigheachta*); O'Grady, *Silva Gadelica* 277, 482ff. (Kern in the Narrow Stripes); Stokes, *Annals of Tigernach*; Stokes, *Irische Texte* 3/1.193–9 (*Cuach Cormaic*); Stokes, RC 15.448–50 (Findglais, The Rennes Dindshenchas); Stokes, *Three Irish Glossaries* 418; Stokes, RC 24.270–87 (*Tochmarc Luaine ocus Aided Athairne*).

FURTHER READING
ALBA; ANNALS; AVALON; BAILE ÁTHA CLIATH; CONCHOBAR; CÚ CHULAINN; CÚ ROÍ; DEAN OF LISMORE; ÉRIU; LOCHLANN; LORDSHIP OF THE ISLES; MANANNÁN; MEYER; OTHERWORLD; PICTS; SANAS CHORMAIC; SCOTS; SENCHÁN TORPÉIST; ULAID; Duffy, *Ireland in the Middle Ages* 42; Fell et al., *Viking Age in the Isle of Man*; MacCana, *Learned Tales of Medieval Ireland*; McCone, *Pagan Past and Christian Present in Early Irish Literature* 152–3; Megaw, *Early Cultures of North-West Europe* 143–71; Mercier, *Irish Comic Tradition* 23; Moore, *Folklore of the Isle of Man* 8; Ó Corráin, *Ireland before the Normans* 62–3; Ó hÓgain, *Myth, Legend & Romance* 357; Spaan, *Folklore* 76.177; Wagner, ZCP 38.1–28; Wait, *Ritual and Religion in Iron Age Britain* 217–20; Wooding, *Otherworld Voyage in Early Irish Literature*.

Charles W. MacQuarrie

§5. PLACE-NAMES OF THE ISLE OF MAN

Early names, general. Only a few names are found in Man which definitely predate the arrival of Scandinavian (from the 9th century onwards). They include the name of the island itself: Man, probably from the INDO-EUROPEAN root **men-* 'rise', for example, a hill or mountain rising out of the water on the horizon; so is Man seen from the surrounding areas (cf. §2 above). *Douglas*, Irish *Dubhghlais*, PROTO-CELTIC

*duboglassio 'dark water', Welsh *du*, Irish *dubh* 'black, dark', with Welsh *glais*, Irish *glas*, *glais(e)* 'water, stream', is a name frequently found in the western areas of the British Isles, particularly in Ireland, Scotland, and western England. In Wales it appears as *Dulas*, and in south-west England as *Dawlish*, *Dowles*, *Dowlish*, *Develish*, &c. The name *Rushen*, Irish *roisean*, is a diminutive form of *ros* 'moor, heath, hill, headland, swamp, wood, &c.', and is an element also commonly found in the British Isles. The element *ard* normally means 'height', but in the parish of Maughold in the north-east of Man it may have the meaning 'headland', cf. Irish *aird*, originally referring to Maughold Head but later to the adjacent rounded hill of 'the Ards'. The name of Maughold Head appears in the Book of ARMAGH as *Ardae Huimnonn* (correctly *ardaí ?Manann*) 'the heights of Man' and could very well be considered as pre-Scandinavian. Other contenders would include *Appyn*, Scottish Gaelic *apuinn* 'abbeyland' (of which there are a few examples), and may refer to the early Christian period of Manx history (6th–7th centuries). The element is also common in Scotland. Finally, there are one or two names in *be-*, *bi-*, *ba-*, e.g. Bemahague, Billown, Balthane, probably representing names in Irish *both* 'hut, hermitage' plus a personal name—*both mo Thaidhg* 'my Tadg's hut', *both ghille Eòghainn* 'hut of the tonsured servant of John', *both Ultáin* 'Ultan's hut', i.e. names from the early Christian period.

River names. It is noteworthy that there are no old river names attested in Man of the type found in Britain or Ireland, e.g. *Dee* < f. of Celtic **dēwos* 'god', *Boyne* < *Buvinda* 'having white cows' or 'as white as a cow' (see BÓAND). The longest river in Man, the Sulby river, is some 22 km long and is known in MANX as *yn awin vooar* (Irish *an abhainn mhór*) 'the big river', and as such in English among the Manx people themselves. There is also the *awin ruy* (Irish *abhainn* + *ruaidh*) 'red river'. However, apart from Douglas, there is no trace in Man of the pre-Germanic British or Old European river names commonly found in Britain and Ireland.

Names of ancient monuments. Another category conspicuous by its absence—completely in this case—is meaningful sets of names for prehistoric monuments, e.g. graves, fortifications, &c. In Ireland and Scotland, such artefacts—fortifications in particular—bear names which make clear that the local population fully understood their function, e.g. *dún, ráth, lios, caiseal, cathair*. In Man, such monuments, as well as large rocks, would all be termed *cashtal* (Irish *caiseal*) 'fortification'. The other elements are lost to Manx nomenclature.

Goidelic names. As with GOIDELIC names in Galloway (Gall Ghàidhil) in south-west Scotland which contain the place-name elements *sliabh* 'mountain, moor-hill' and *carraig* 'rock', names of this type in Man seem to date from the earliest Goidelic settlements on the island *c.* AD 500 and thereafter, e.g. *Slieau Dhoo* 'black mountain' (Irish *sliabh dubh*), *Carrick* '(the) rock' (Irish *carraig*). Names consisting solely of a noun (without the definite article), for example, *Rushen, Ard, Carrick*, would comprise the oldest names in Man. Names comprising a noun with the definite article, e.g. *Niarbyl*, from *yn arbyl* (Irish **an earball*) 'the tail' (rock formation—unless this is a prepositional form, *in earball* 'at the tail'), would be the next oldest, but are also seldom attested. Nevertheless, they are pre-Scandinavian. Names such as *Purt ny Hinshey, Cashtal yn Ard, Cronk y Voddy*, &c., have the form definite noun plus dependent definite noun in the genitive, and are in reality phrasal names. Names of this type, which are also to be seen in Ireland and Scotland, are relatively recent creations (12th/13th century), though they are occasionally attested in the 9th century outside Man. They form the overwhelming majority of Gaelic names in Man and in their present form are unlikely to be pre-Scandinavian, but may be reformations of earlier names.

Names in *balla* (Irish *baile*) 'settlement, farm, village, town' are the most common name type in Man. Except possibly for one or two examples, the general distribution of names in *balla*- seems to be post-Scandinavian. In Ireland, it can be shown that such names became much more common after *c.* 1150, possibly as result of Anglo-Norman influence where *baile* may be a translation of Latin *villa*. In Man, the first attestation of *balla*- is to be found *c.* 1280 in the Limites or Abbeyland Bounds attached to the Chronicles of Man, e.g. *Balesalach* (*Ballasalla*). However, most of the *balla*-names seem to be quite late. The earliest would be descriptive—*balla* plus adjective, e.g. *Ballabeg* 'little farm, &c.' (Irish *baile beag*), then geographically descriptive, with an attached noun in the genitive, e.g. *Ballacurree* (nominative *Curragh*) 'marsh farm' (Irish *baile curraigh*

[*currach*]), and later with a personal name or surname as the specific, e.g. *Ballakelly* 'Kelly's farm' (Irish *baile (mh)ic Ceallaigh*), *Ballacorlett* 'Corlett's farm', a Manx surname containing Irish *mac* (*mhic*) plus the Scandinavian personal name *Thorljótr* (see MANX SURNAMES).

Scandinavian names. Many of the prominent natural features in Man, for example, valleys, mountains, coastal rocks, &c., bear Scandinavian names, e.g. valleys: *Cardle* < *kvernárdalr* 'mill river dale', *Eskdale* < *eskedalr* 'ashdale' (the older name for Dhoon Glen), *Groudle* < *grafdalr* 'narrow dale'; mountains: *Snaefell* 'snow mountain' (though this may be a translation of Irish *sliabh sneachta*, found also in Donegal), *Greeba* < *gnípa* 'summit', *Barrule* < *vörðufjall* 'cairn mountain'. Ramsey < *hrams-á* 'wild garlic river' and *Laxey* < *laxá* 'salmon river' are originally river names transferred to settlements. Many headlands and peninsulas bear Scandinavian names: *The Howe* (< *höfuð* 'hill, headland' or *haugr* 'hill, mound'), *Cregneash* < *krók-nes* 'crooked (indented coastline) promontory'. There are some 28 *vík*-names, e.g. *Fleshwick* < *flesja(r)-vík* 'green (grassy) spot creek', and 26 *by*-names (probably bestowed by immigrants originally from the Danelaw in England), e.g. *Dalby* < *dalr-by*) 'dale farm', *Sulby* < *súla-by* 'farm by the cleft fork (in a river)'. The element *staðir* 'farm' also occasionally appears, e.g. *Leodest* < *Ljótólfsstaðir* 'Ljótólf's farm', *Aust* < *Auðolfsstaðir* 'Auðolf's (Adolf's) farm'.

'*Inversion compounds*' are formed from two elements from one language, but set together according to the syntax of another language, and as such are a result of language contact, e.g. *Dreemlang* 'long ridge', i.e. Manx *dreeym* (Irish *driom*), with English dialect *lang* 'long', but in Gaelic word-order, viz. 'ridge long'. Scandinavian names of this type are scarce, but one or two examples are attested, e.g. *Toftar Asmund* (*c.* 1280) 'Asmund's hillocks' < Old Norse *toftir* 'hillocks' with the Scandinavian personal name *Ásmundr*, but *Ásmundar-toftir* in normal Scandinavian word-order, and *Crosyvor* 'Ivar's cross' (*c.* 1280) (with Scandinavian *kross* as a borrowing from Irish *cros*, itself a borrowing from Latin *crux*), Irish *cros-Íomhair*, Scandinavian *Ivars-kross*. The evidence for inversion compounds is scant, and as a result little can be said about them, other than that they appear to be a development of the later Scandinavian period in Man (*c.* 13th century and possibly later).

English names. Castletown and Peel are English. The name Castletown itself is first attested as *casteltown* in 1511. In the Abbeyland Bounds of *c.* 1280 Castletown appears as *uillam* (accusative case) *castelli*, which in all probability is a translation of Irish *baile a' chaistil* (*caisteal*), Manx *balley y chashtal*, although it is not known what the local people in fact called this town. Peel is first evidenced in 1595. Prior to that it was known as *Holmtown* (1417) 'island town' (< Old Norse *holmr* 'island' with Middle English *toun*, referring to the small island of St Patrick's Isle at the mouth of Peel harbour). Peel is Middle English *pele* (< Medieval Latin *pela, palus*) 'palisade, fortification' (referring to the same on St Patrick's Isle) and, like *Holmtown*, is probably an independent name bestowed upon the town by the English (garrison) inhabitants, and not a translation from the Manx, i.e. *Purt ny Hinshey* 'harbour of the island (St Patrick's Isle)', Irish *port na h-inse*. The use of the French definite article *le(s)*, as in *Le Calf* (1511) 'the Calf of Man (island)', *Lezayre* 'the Ayre' would date back to early English influence of the 14th century, cf. *Newton-le-Willows*, in Cheshire, &c.

Kirk-names. The parish names in Man comprise the element *kirk* plus the name of the saint to whom the parish church is dedicated, in Gaelic word-order—Kirk Maughold, Kirk Lonan, Kirk Braddan, &c. (although Kirk falls away in everyday speech). Originally, the element is Old Norse *kirkja* 'church', and the parish formation in Man seems to be part of a general development which was taking place in adjacent territories, e.g. northern England and south-western Scotland, where (in Galloway at any rate) Old Norse *kirk* has replaced earlier Irish *cill* (see also below) but retained the Gaelic word order. The development in Man seems to be similar and to have taken place around the same time (13th century).

In Manx, the generic for church is *keeill* (Irish *cill*) and this is the normal word for a ruined church or cell of the early Christian period. Many of these *keeills*, however, are of a later date, probably of the late Scandinavian period (13th century). In place-names, the element is used to denote small churches or chapels, e.g. *Keeill Woirrey* 'St. Mary's Church' (Irish *cill Mhoire*). In the genitive, it is found in such names as *Ballakilley* 'church farm' (Irish *baile cille*), *Lag ny Killey* 'the church hollow' (Irish *lag na cille*). Although CHRISTIANITY

established itself in Man in the 6th/7th centuries and the building of cells or churches was set in motion to serve the new cult, it is not very probable that the present-day ruined *keeills* and the names attached to them survived in the memory of the Manx people from the beginning, right through the Scandinavian period to the present day, when older pre-Scandinavian settlement names have not survived.

FURTHER READING
ARMAGH; BÓAND; CHRISTIANITY; GOIDELIC; INDO-EUROPEAN; IRISH; MANX; MANX SURNAMES; PROTO-CELTIC; Andersen, *Viking Age in the Isle of Man* 147–68; Broderick, *Akten des Ersten Symposiums Deutschsprachiger Keltologen* 57–65; Broderick, *Bulletin of the Ulster Place-Name Society* 2nd ser. 2.20–3; Broderick, *Bulletin of the Ulster Place-Name Society* 2nd ser. 3.13–15; Broderick, *Bulletin of the Ulster Place-Name Society* 2nd ser. 3.40–1; Broderick, *Cronica Regum Mannie et Insularum*; Broderick, *Place-Names of the Isle of Man*; Brooke, *Trans. Dumfriesshire and Galloway Natural History and Antiquarian Society* 58.56–71; Davey, *Man and Environment in the Isle of Man*; Fell et al., *Viking Age in the Isle of Man*; Fellows-Jensen, *Man and Environment in the Isle of Man* 1.315–18; Fellows-Jensen, *Viking Age in the Isle of Man* 37–52; Fellows-Jensen, *Nomina* 24.33–46; Flanagan, *Bulletin of the Ulster Place-Name Society* 2nd ser. 1.8–13; Flanagan, *Bulletin of the Ulster Place-Name Society* 2nd ser. 3.16–29; Flanagan, *Nomina* 4.41–5; Gelling, *Journal of the Manx Museum* 7/86.130–9, 7/87.168–175; Gelling, *Language Contact in the British Isles* 140–55; Gelling, *Man and Environment in the Isle of Man* 1.251–64; Kneen, *Place-Names of the Isle of Man*; Marstrander, *Norsk Tidsskrift for Sprogvidenskap* 6.40–386; Marstrander, *Norsk Tidsskrift for Sprogvidenskap* 7.287–334; Megaw, *Scottish Studies* 20.1–44; Rockel & Zimmer, *Akten des Ersten Symposiums Deutschsprachiger Keltologen*; Thomson, *Man and Environment in the Isle of Man* 1.319–21; Ureland & Broderick, *Language Contact in the British Isles*.

George Broderick

§6. MATERIAL CULTURE IN THE HIGH MIDDLE AGES (11TH TO MID-16TH CENTURY)

Introduction. The late 11th-century Norse Kingdom of the Isles created a distinctive Norwegian/Celtic cultural entity in the northern Irish Sea. A complex of settlement patterns, tenurial systems and agricultural practices, some Scandinavian, some IRON AGE in origin, created a Manx material culture appropriate to a maritime capital. The evidence comes from rare documentary sources, architecture, and archaeology.

Settlement and tenure. Medieval settlement was disbursed; there were no villages or urban centres. Land division was based upon a primary unit known as the treen, which was subdivided into quarterlands and progressively grouped upwards into parishes and sheadings (E. Davies, *Trans. Institute of British Geographers* 22.97–116).

In 1500 around 53,000 acres were enclosed (cf. Talbot, *Manorial Roll of the Isle of Man 1511–1515*). Lowland wetlands provided fuel, fish, and wildfowl, and the uplands grazing, fuel, and other raw materials.

Archaeological evidence. Three high-status sites dominate—Peel Castle (Freke, *Excavations on St Patrick's Isle, Isle of Man*), Castle Rushen (Davey et al., *Excavations in Castletown, Isle of Man, 1989–92*) and Rushen Abbey (Butler, *Journal of the British Archaeological Association* 141.60–104; Davey, *Rushen Abbey*). There is no evidence for the nature of settlement or the quality of life beyond these centres of power. None of the 700 or so quarterland farms—the backbone of Manx social and economic life—has been excavated.

The copper alloy finds consist for the most part of wire pins and needles, lace chapes, and dress accessories such as strap ends and belt fittings, with some evidence for the local repair of bronze vessels. Iron artefacts occur even less frequently. Even at Peel, only seven items were recovered—a very small proportion of the iron objects actually in use at any time in the medieval period. These vestigial assemblages establish that, at the main sites, metal was in widespread use for a range of purposes. They exhibit no particularly insular features and lie within the mainstream of the available technologies within the British Isles. The presence of a smelt for lead and possibly silver, owned by Furness Abbey, together with a number of iron working sites, show that the mineral resources of the island were being widely exploited.

Medieval glass is even more rare. Four sherds from a crumbling potash glass vessel were found at Peel, together with some 220 sherds of extremely weathered window glass, including ten with traces of grisaille decoration. Many fragments of window glass, fragments of a urinal and a lamp were recovered from Rushen Abbey, the latter within a burial.

Peel Castle has provided a wide range of information about the exploitation of natural resources, especially animals, birds, and fish. Cattle form by far the largest group of animal bones, followed by sheep and pigs with a few horse, deer and dog bones. In contrast, of the 45 species of birds, only five were domesticated, yet at least 38 of them, mostly seabirds, formed part of the human diet. Fish were also important in the Manx economy, as is clear from the complex system of herring tithes. The 28 species identified at Peel imply both deep-sea and inshore fishing. Shellfish were also consumed in quantity. Manx medieval society not only relied on domesticated animals and birds, but exploited local populations of wild birds, fish, and shellfish to a high degree.

No medieval plant remains were recovered from either Peel or Castletown. At Rushen Abbey, trial trenches produced charred grains of wheat, barley, and oats. Documentary sources suggest that cereal production, especially of wheat, was an important element in Manx medieval AGRICULTURE. The limited surviving contemporary pollen evidence paints the same picture (Innes, *Dhoo Valley, Isle of Man* 11–13).

Locally handmade cooking wares continued in production until late in the 16th century (Davey, *Proc. Isle of Man Natural History and Antiquarian Society* 11/1.91–114). The island also received considerable quantities of imports from Britain and the Continent. The very limited evidence from other lower status sites suggests that, although imports were in general circulation, they were present in very small numbers outside the major centres.

Money. Although the five medieval coin hoards and rare single finds might imply a restricted use of currency, a number of factors suggest that money was in general use. The synodal statutes from the 13th and 14th centuries show that tithes, payable by the majority of the farms, were valued in monetary terms. Although payments in kind were also acceptable, it is clear from the records of episcopal payments of papal taxation that commodities such as sheep, honey or grain must have been cash convertible, as the diocesan valuation, at 660 florins for an incoming bishop, was a significant one

Peel Castle, Isle of Man

in regional terms (Storm, *Exactions from the Norwegian Church Province*). The money was generally paid late, and in instalments, but it was paid.

Architecture. The few surviving medieval buildings give some indication of economic activity. The 13th-century cathedral of St Germans at Peel is the pre-eminent ecclesiastical structure. Similar, good quality workmanship is in evidence at several chapels and parish churches. At Rushen Abbey most of the architectural fragments recovered from the excavations appear to be using imported sandstones, while the principal walls used finely dressed local limestone. Although the masons may have been brought in specially, the number of phases of workmanship in these structures implies resident skills in the Manx population. The buildings display competent lead working, slating, carpentry and glazing of a quality equivalent to their architecture and status. The bishop's tower-house at Bishopscourt is the only domestic building to survive.

Manx medieval landscape and society in an Irish Sea context. The Isle of Man had neither the open-field systems of north-west England (Youd, *Trans. Historical Society of Lancashire and Cheshire* 113.1–41) and lowland north Wales (Glanville R. J. Jones, *Archaeology of Clwyd* 186–202) nor the planned landscapes of Anglo-Norman Ireland (Mitchell & Ryan, *Reading the Irish Landscape*). There were no towns or villages. The beginnings of nucleation around the two medieval castles and at Ballasalla seem to date from the 15th century at the earliest. The parish churches are diminutive affairs—simple, single-celled extensions of pre-existing keeills. Only the cathedral of St Germans at Peel Castle is aisled. Two possible mottes and baileys are the only examples of a type of structure common in adjacent areas. There are neither moated sites—a major feature in south-east Ireland (Mitchell & Ryan, *Reading the Irish Landscape*), north-west England (Newman, *Archaeology of Lancashire*), and north Wales (Spurgeon, *Archaeology of Clwyd* 157–72)—nor manor houses. Instead, the island was owned and administered as a single entity by its kings and lords. The lack of moated sites and manors is a clear indication that society was much less vertically structured than, for example, in neighbouring areas of England—a feature of Manx social life that persists today.

PRIMARY SOURCE
Talbot, *Manorial Roll of the Isle of Man 1511–1515*.

FURTHER READING
AGRICULTURE; IRON AGE; Butler, *Journal of the British Archaeological Association* 141.60–104; Cheney, CMCS 7.63; Davey, *Rushen Abbey*; Davey et al., *Excavations in Castletown, Isle of Man, 1989–92*; Davey, *Proc. Isle of Man Natural History and Antiquarian Society* 11.1.91–114; E. Davies, *Trans. Institute of British Geographers* 22.97–116; Freke, *Excavations on St Patrick's Isle, Isle of Man 1982–88*; Innes, *Dhoo Valley, Isle of Man*; Glanville R. J. Jones, *Archaeology of Clwyd* 186–202; Mitchell & Ryan, *Reading the Irish Landscape*; Newman, *Archaeology of Lancashire*; Spurgeon, *Archaeology of Clwyd* 157–72; Storm, *Exactions from the Norwegian Church Province*; Youd, *Trans. Historical Society of Lancashire and Cheshire* 113.1–41.

P. J. Davey

§7. TRADITIONAL MAN-MADE LANDSCAPE DIVISIONS

The primary divisions of farmland were the 'treens', which are commonly believed to have been later subdivided into 'quarterlands'. The uplands, together with inaccessible river gullies and marsh, were set aside as unenclosed 'commons', although all were susceptible to improvement and absorption into farmland as 'intack', having been 'taken in' from the unenclosed lands. These terms are a mixture of MANX and English, and first come into the written record in the early manorial rolls of *c.* 1540. The treens have several times been associated by scholars with the distribution of early medieval chapels (Manx KEEILLS), although this has been shown to be sufficiently inconsistent to call such a link into question. No chronology yet exists to demonstrate whether all *keeills* are of a similar date.

More effective is to contemplate the landscape as having been divided, largely equitably, on the basis of its topography. This is particularly clear where the land rises gradually from seashore to upland, as here the treens, and the quarterlands within them, stretched from the coast to the edge of the commons, from which they were separated by a mountain hedge. The treens were frequently divided from each other by watercourses, and reliance was clearly placed upon natural barriers providing the limits of a holding. These traditional landholdings thus had access to the shore for fishing, seaweed, and flotsam; to wells and watercourses for water-supply; and to the upland commons for seasonal grazing, turf (peat) and stone, while at the same time sharing the most, and least, fertile soils.

The system shows signs of most adaptation in those areas where considerable land improvement has had to be made, and also where coastal erosion has either removed or added land. Such physical and adminis-

Druidale keeill, Michael, following excavation

trative changes hint at the considerable antiquity of the system as originally conceived. Demand for land resulted in the absorption of common land up-slope of original holdings. Here, the mountain hedge formerly defining the top of a holding became a subsidiary boundary, and a new mountain hedge had to be constructed.

The earliest extant Manx statutes from the 15th century allowed the creation of boundaries surrounding landholdings and from late in the next century included regulations—heights and materials—for their construction. These laws demonstrate a preoccupation with controlling the movements of livestock and of preserving crops from animal damage. It is considered probable, however, that enclosure did not become the norm until the 17th century. The characteristic Manx field boundary—a 'sod hedge'—is made from a combination of stone and earth, and could be quite large, but it is noticeable that later boundaries relating to the expansion of landholdings were often insubstantial and more heavily reliant on a vegetative topping

of gorse to render them stock-proof (European gorse, *Ulex europaeus*, may have been introduced specifically for this purpose). A correlation between hedge age and the number per unit length of hedgeline of bramble sub-species has been cited as a possible dating medium, though this has not been tested extensively. Considerable areas of the traditional field pattern survive, although some farms were improved during the 1840s, and modern agricultural efficiency saw the removal of more boundaries, particularly in the 1980s. Stone walls were built to enclose new intack during the 19th century, as well as to divide the commons following disafforestation in the 1860s. This type of boundary, often built by imported labour (for instance from modern CUMBRIA), marks a complete change from the customary indigenous boundary construction, and is highly diagnostic.

Sources of water are traditionally closely associated with pagan Celtic religion and subsequently with the early Christian church (see CHRISTIANITY). Holy wells—their water believed to be good for eye, digestive and skin complaints—were remembered, and continued to be used into the 20th century, and some are quite close to the early medieval chapels, perhaps hinting at possible association.

But closely associated with water sources are the traditional habitation sites. Fewer and fewer farmsteads survive unaltered by modern agriculture and conversion. Among those that do, there are few of the single-storey, two-roomed cottages with a hearth in each gable, except at the village folk museum of Cregneash, and virtually none of the earlier, single-roomed, central hearth cottages which would have been more closely comparable with Scottish blackhouses.

RELATED ARTICLES
AGRICULTURE; CHRISTIANITY; CUMBRIA; KEEILL; MANX.

Andrew Johnson

§8. THE MANX CONSTITUTION

The Isle of Man is a dependent territory of the United Kingdom, having full internal self-government. Its constitutional history is unique. Its legislature and customary law can be traced back to the kingdom of Man and the Isles, established by the Norsemen in the 10th century. In consequence, the Isle of Man justifiably claims to have the world's oldest parliament.

The Norse kingdom. The origins of the Norse KINGDOM OF MAN and the Isles are obscure, but it was well established by the 11th century. It was not a wholly independent kingdom, since the kings of Man owed allegiance to the kings of Norway, who regarded Man as one of their territories. The kingdom included all the Hebrides of present-day Scotland until 1156, and thereafter only the Western Isles. An important feature of the Norse kingdom was the annual open-air assembly known as TYNWALD, presided over by the king and attended by his officers, including the two deemsters who were the guardians of the customary law, and representatives of the people. Tynwald was primarily a judicial body, at which the customary law was also proclaimed. The customary law, about which little is known, was probably introduced by the Norse settlers. Elements of Norse udal tenure survived in Manx customary law to the 20th century.

Scottish rule. In 1266, by the Treaty of Perth, Magnus, king of Norway, sold Man and the Western Isles to Alexander, king of the SCOTS, for 4,000 marks and an annual payment of 100 marks. The Treaty provided that the people of Man should be subject 'to the laws and customs' of Scotland. Had the Treaty been fully implemented, Man would have been absorbed into the kingdom of Scotland. However, Scottish rule was short-lived.

Rule of the Montacutes. Between 1290 and 1333 control of Man passed to and fro between the Scots and the English during the Anglo-Scottish wars. However, following the battle of Halidon Hill in 1333, English control of Man was finally established, and Edward III then granted to Sir William de Montacute, who claimed Man by right of descent from the Norse kings, 'all the rights and claims which we have, have had, or in any way could have, in the Isle of Man . . . so that neither we, nor our heirs, nor any other in our name, shall be able to exact or dispose of any right or claim in the aforesaid Island.' The grant by Edward III effectively restored the Norse kingdom, but without the Western Isles. Sir William de Montacute, who had been created Earl of Salisbury in 1337, died in 1344 and was succeeded by his son who, in 1392, sold Man to Sir William Le Scroop. In 1399 Le Scroop was beheaded by Henry IV and Man then came into the absolute possession of the English Crown. It has remained a possession of the Crown ever since.

Rule of the Stanleys. In 1406 Man was granted by Henry IV to Sir John Stanley, his heirs and assigns, on the service of rendering two falcons on paying homage, and two falcons to all future kings of England on the day of their coronation. Thereafter, for over 350 years, the descendants of Sir John Stanley were the hereditary kings of Man, or 'Lords' as they were styled after 1504, until, in 1765, the second Duke of Atholl sold Man to the English Crown for £70,000. The REVESTMENT Act 1765 (of Parliament) provided that the Isle of Man should be 'unalienably vested' in His Majesty, his heirs, and assigns.

Throughout the period from 1406 to 1765 the kings or lords of Man rarely visited the island. They ruled through the captains or governors whom they appointed. Although the customary laws were respected and Tynwald continued to meet, English influence was pervasive. English was the language of government, although MANX Gaelic remained the language of the people until the beginning of the 19th century. The

Stanleys established courts on the English model, alongside the deemsters' courts in which the customary law was administered. The two systems gradually converged, but were not brought together until 1883.

During the 17th century Tynwald began to enact legislation in a recognizably modern form. Tynwald comprised the Governor and the principal officers, including the deemsters and the bishop, who formed the Lord's Council, later to become the Legislative Council, together with the twenty four 'Keys', originally a kind of jury, but later to be regarded as the representatives of the people, although generally appointed by the Lord. In the 18th century the Keys became the 'House of Keys' and elected a Speaker, emulating the House of Commons. Bills passed by Tynwald did not become law until approved by the Lord.

The Revestment and direct rule. The Revestment in 1765 did not affect the constitutional status of Man, except that the Governor and other principal officers were now appointed by the Crown, rather than the Lord, and the assent of the Crown rather than the Lord was required before a Bill passed by Tynwald became law. Tynwald continued to meet and enact laws. The courts continued to administer the customary law, although increasingly English legal precedents were relied on by the Manx courts, with the result that during the 19th century Manx law was to a great extent assimilated to English law.

However, after 1765 the British Government assumed complete control of the island's finances. The island's revenue, mainly customs duties, was remitted to London and, although it had been intended to manage the Manx revenue as a separate fund, in time it was treated as part of the revenue of the United Kingdom. Public expenditure had to be approved by the Treasury in London. In addition, the Governor was answerable to the Home Secretary, and the Home Office in London thus exerted effective control over the island's affairs. In form and in fact the Governor, or Lieutenant Governor as he was now styled, was the government. He presided over the Legislative Council and Tynwald, and was also the senior judge of the island's courts. For most of the 19th century, the island was largely governed by a form of direct rule from London, and was, for many purposes, treated as though it were part of the United Kingdom. Although Tynwald continued

to enact legislation, increasingly Acts of the Westminster Parliament, which had had the power to legislate for the Isle of Man since the 14th century, were applied to the island.

Reforms of 1866. In 1866 the British Government agreed to allow Tynwald some control over public expenditure, and at the same time the House of Keys became an elected body and ceased to have judicial functions. In addition, Tynwald began to perform an administrative rôle by creating statutory committees to undertake specific functions. A Committee of Highways had been established in 1776 by Act of Tynwald, but by the end of the 19th century there were eleven such bodies, which became known as Boards of Tynwald. Subsequently, many other boards were formed as government assumed responsibility for new matters. The significance of these boards was that they were a form of local government, largely independent of the Governor. Local authorities were also created for the towns, villages, and parishes in the latter part of the 19th century.

20th century. In the 20th century the Manx constitution developed and changed in many ways, of which the following were the most significant:

(1) The House of Keys became the dominant element in Tynwald. Starting in 1919, the official members of the Legislative Council were progressively replaced by members elected by the House of Keys, which was itself given power, by Act of Tynwald, to override the Legislative Council.

(2) The British Government relinquished all control over the island's finances in 1958, leaving Tynwald in control of both taxation and expenditure.

(3) Between 1961 and 1992 almost all the executive functions of the Governor were transferred to other bodies answerable to Tynwald. The Governor retains certain constitutional functions and appoints, or advises on the appointment of, the judiciary, and is the representative of the Crown on the island.

(4) In 1986–7 the Boards of Tynwald were replaced by nine Government Departments, each headed by a Minister nominated by the Chief Minister, who is himself appointed by the Governor on the nomination of Tynwald. The Chief Minister and the Ministers, who must all be members of Tynwald, constitute the Council of Ministers, in effect the Cabinet of the

Manx Government.

(5) Since 1945 nearly all the functions that had been exercised by the British Government in the Isle of Man at one time or another, including those relating to the post office, customs and excise, telecommunications, merchant shipping, minerals, and the territorial sea, have been transferred to the Manx Government. The British Government is now only responsible for defence and foreign affairs and for the ultimate good government of the island.

(6) Parliament now enacts laws for the Isle of Man only in very limited circumstances. Tynwald has assumed responsibility for legislating on nearly all matters. Moreover, Tynwald is now recognized as having co-ordinate legislative powers with Parliament, so that Acts of Tynwald, which have received the Royal Assent, may repeal or amend Acts of Parliament extending to the Isle of Man.

(7) In 1972, when the United Kingdom joined the European Economic Community (EEC), the Isle of Man was excluded from the Treaty of Accession, except for free trade in goods and for certain other limited purposes.

(8) While the British Government retains responsibility for the island's international affairs, the Manx Government is now permitted to take part in international negotiations in regard to matters which directly affect the island.

Summary. The fundamental status of the Isle of Man as a separate legal jurisdiction, with its own government, legislature, courts and law, has not changed since the Norse kingdom came to an end in 1266. Man has never been part of England or of the United Kingdom, but it has never been an independent state in its own right. Since 1399 Man has been a possession of the English Crown. In the 20th century direct rule from London, which was imposed in 1765, was replaced by full internal self-government. However, the relationship of Man to the United Kingdom is still susceptible to change and will no doubt continue to change in the light of new circumstances as they arise.

FURTHER READING
ALBA; KINGDOM OF MAN; MANX; REVESTMENT; SCOTS; TYNWALD; Dickinson, *Lordship of Man under the Stanleys*; Kinvig, *Isle of Man*.

T. W. Cain

§9. WOMEN'S VOTE (1881)

In the early months of 1881 TYNWALD (see previous section) amended the law as to the election of Members of the House of Keys, and delivered the first instalment of women's suffrage to vote in parliamentary elections within the British Isles.

The Election Bill was introduced into the House of Keys only 13 years after the historic passing of the House of Keys Election Act of 1866, which ended the ancient system of a non-elected, self-selecting oligarchy by enfranchising male ratepayers who held property valued at £8, around 8% of the island's 53,000 population.

The second Bill, introduced into the Keys on 5 November 1880, proposed to give the vote to every male person of full age who was not subject to any legal incapacity. However, the Manchester National Society for Women's Suffrage reasoned that by deleting the word 'male', women would receive the vote also. The Society organized public meetings on the Isle of Man to promote the issue, and public and press support grew to the extent that at the last such meeting a resolution proposing the extension of the vote to women was approved unopposed.

Public support proved crucial in persuading the Keys in favour of the Isle of Man becoming the first country in the world to legislate to give *all* women the vote in national elections. The House carried the motion, 16 to 3. The action of the Keys was widely applauded. Citing the example, campaigners in the UK voiced the hope that 'the House of Commons will not be less just in dealing with the claims of women ratepayers . . . than its sister assembly, the House of Keys'.

However, when the Bill was sent to the island's second chamber—the Council, the Lieutenant Governor, on the instruction of the British Government, advised that they could not endorse the Keys' decision because it would never receive Royal assent. Following political posturing, the Keys submitted to the Council, but took the unprecedented step of unanimously approving the following resolution:

Resolved; that whilst accepting the proposition of the Council to confer the electoral franchise on female owners of real estate, and to exclude female occupiers, this House considers it right to record that their agreement to this proposal is solely with the object of securing the partial concession made by the Council towards female suffrage, instead of being compelled to lose the benefit of the proposed new Election Bill altogether; and that the opinion already expressed by the House, that male and female occupiers are equally entitled to vote, remains unaltered.

Thus the right to vote was extended to unmarried women and widows who owned property, comprising around 11% of the electorate. In the UK women had to wait until 1918 for the same right.

PRIMARY SOURCES
MSS. Douglas, Manx National Heritage Library 9191 (Journals of the House of Keys), 9845 (Government Office Papers). EDITION. Gill, *Statutes of the Isle of Man 3–5*.

Roger Sims

§10. FISHING

The traditional Manx fishery was based on the exploitation of herring and cod spawning and nursery areas of the north Irish Sea on either side of the island. Along with AGRICULTURE, fishing was of prime importance in the economy, with the two being closely linked. Seventeenth-century fishing regulations indicate the long-established responsibility of quarterland or more substantial farmers to have their boats with stipulated amounts of net in readiness for the annual mustering of the herring fleet (Gill, *Statutes of the Isle of Man, s.a.* 1610, 1613). Smaller farmers and crofters relied on the 'harvest of the sea' and were an important element in fishing crews until the later 19th century. The herring catch was of supreme importance and drift-net fishing continued to be used until the 1930s. Herring fishing played an important rôle in the island's commercial life, e.g. in the period *c.* 1770–*c.* 1840 when trade in red herrings to the Mediterranean and Caribbean replaced the now suppressed SMUGGLING.

Until the later 18th century open boats of 5–7 tons with four sweeps and a square sail, known as 'herring scoutes', were the standard vessels (Megaw, *Journal of the Manx Museum* 5/64.15–16). The improved 19th-century boats owed much to Cornish designs. Two-masted dandy smacks or buggers were widely adopted from *c.* 1830. In the 1870s the finest Manx sail fishing boats, known as 'nickeys', again derived from Cornwall (KERNOW), though local shipbuilders made modifications. These vessels were 13.5–16.5 m long with a beam of 4.5 m and suitable for the more exposed conditions of the Kinsale fishing. The last of the sail fishing boats were the 'nobbies'. Light rigged and smaller than the 'nickeys', they were typical of the declining Manx herring fishing after 1900.

The zenith of Manx fishing was attained in the 1880s. At that time, it was estimated that 13,000 out of a population of 53,000 were either directly or indirectly dependent on fishing (*Official Catalogue of the Great International Fisheries Exhibition*). Many fishermen of this era had an almost year-long commitment to their calling, although this made them more vulnerable than the crofter-fishermen when the shoals were absent, as during much of the 1890s. From the early 1860s many Manx boats joined in the spring mackerel fishing off southern Ireland (ÉIRE), particularly out of Kinsale. At the end of June they would return to fish for herring in home waters, or further afield out of Lerwick in the Shetlands. The autumn fishing off the east coast of Ireland often followed. Deep-sea long-line cod fishing was a late winter activity.

The present status of Manx fishing reflects profound changes following an early 20th-century decline in the herring fishery. Steam drifters from outside the island dominated the market and supplied the curers and kipperers who had from the 1890s become the main fish processors. From the 1930s traditional drift-net fishing was replaced first by ring-netting and later by trawling. Drastic depletion of fish stocks followed the exploitation of the spawning grounds to the east of the island by pickle curers and Klondykers in the 1970s. Ensuing fishing quotas have severely curtailed herring fishing to the extent that the formerly popular undyed Manx kipper is now difficult to obtain. By the 1990s fishing and farming together produced a mere 2% of Manx national income. A new fishing resource discovered close to Port Erin in 1937 in the form of scallops is the target catch of what remains of the Manx fishery. 90% of all fish landed is now scallops and queen scallops which occur over much of the north Irish Sea. The University of Liverpool's Marine Laboratory at Port Erin carries out biological sampling and other research relevant to the conservation of both herring and scallop stocks.

PRIMARY SOURCES
Gill, *Statutes of the Isle of Man 1*; *I.O.M Government Annual Reports on the Fisheries*; *Official Catalogue of the Great International*

Fisheries Exhibition; Statistical Abstract of the Isle of Man.

FURTHER READING
AGRICULTURE; ÉIRE; KERNOW; SMUGGLING; Killip, *Journal of the Manx Museum* 6/75.35–7; Megaw, *Journal of the Manx Museum* 5/64.15–16; Smith, *Short History of the Irish Sea Herring Fishery.*

F. J. Radcliffe

§11. MINING

Significant lead-zinc-copper vein deposits have been mined within a strike-parallel zone along the NE–SW axis of the Ordovician rocks of the Manx Group. The veins are typically associated with steeply inclined faults in these rocks, although veins in the Foxdale area pass into a granite host at depth. Ferrous metal in the form of hematite was also mined in the Maughold area.

Copper and iron staining on coastal rocks would have encouraged prehistoric mining. The first documented reference is a charter of 1246 authorizing the Cistercian monks of Furness to mine, transport, and sell minerals from the island. The Derby and Atholl Lords of Man entered into a succession of business partnerships with entrepreneurs from outside the island. The Crown purchase of the remaining feudal rights of the last Lord in 1829 stimulated a new interest in mining (Belchem, *New History of the Isle of Man* 214). Cornish expertise and labour played important rôles in Manx mining. The Manx mines, which truly came to fruition in the period *c.* 1830–90, were outstanding for a time among British sources of lead and zinc. Manx zinc output was probably equal to a fifth of all the zinc produced in the British Isles and in the region of 5% of all lead. In the period 1870–90 the two main centres, Foxdale and Laxey, were together employing up to a thousand men and boys. Significant amounts of silver also came from these centres. Laxey Mine achieved maximum zinc production in 1875 and a lead maximum in 1876. Foxdale achieved lead maxima in 1885 and 1891 (Lamplugh, *Geology of the Isle of Man*).

Overseas competition and exhaustion of the veins led to rapid decline with little significant production after 1920. The veins were steep and faulting was widespread. In the later stages, depths in excess of 650 m were reached and operations became very expensive. Since the island has no coal mines, much ingenuity was applied to the collection of water and the creation of hydraulic appliances. Local smelting had been characteristic of the 18th century, but all ores were exported for this process during the main period of mining.

The Great Laxey Wheel (or Lady Isabella), erected in 1854 to drain the Laxey mine, epitomized the optimism of the period when the speculative banker G. W. Noble was chairman of the mine and the Cornishman R. Rowe the mine's captain. This remarkable pitch back-shot wheel with a diameter of 22.1 m was the largest to be constructed at that time. Its designer was a local man, Robert Casement. Water from a wide catchment area, collected in a hillside cistern, ascended a stone-built tower to turn the wheel. Power from the wheel was transferred via the crank along the top of a *c.* 410 m stone viaduct by means of a sectional timber beam running on bogies. An inverted T-shaped rocker changed the horizontal movement of the viaduct rod to the vertical movement of the pump rods. The wheel is the island's most famous example of industrial archaeology.

PRIMARY SOURCES
Annual Reports of Inspectors of Mines from 1850, POWE 7, Public Record Office, Kew.

FURTHER READING
Belchem, *New History of the Isle of Man* 5; Chadwick et al., *Geology of the Isle of Man and its Offshore Area*; Cumming, *Isle of Man* 308–10; Dickinson, *Lordship of Man under the Stanleys*; Garrad et al., *Industrial Archaeology of the Isle of Man*; Hollis, *British Mining* 34.49–54; Jespersen, *Lady Isabella Waterwheel of the Great Laxey Mining Company*; Lamplugh, *Geology of the Isle of Man*; Mathieson, *Proc. Isle of Man Natural History and Antiquarian Society* 5.555–70; Megaw, *Journal of the Manx Museum* 7/77.105–7.

F. J. Radcliffe

Ellis, Thomas Edward (1859–99) was an

important Liberal politician and British parliamentarian who was influential in effecting numerous reforms beneficial to his native Wales (CYMRU). Ellis was born at Cynlas, Cefnddwysarn, near Bala in Merioneth (sir Feirionnydd), north Wales, and was educated locally at Bala grammar school, the fledgling University College of Wales, ABERYSTWYTH, and New College, Oxford. During his Oxford days he became an active member of the Essay Society, participated fully in social and political activities, and served on the Standing Committee of the Oxford Union Society. After graduating in Modern History in 1884 he worked briefly as a tutor to the Cory family of St Mellons, and in 1885 accepted a position as private secretary to the industrialist Sir John Brunner, the Liberal Member of Parliament for Norwich, whom he assisted in his political activities. At the same time Ellis engaged in regular journalism, contributing pungent columns to the *South Wales Daily News* and other newspapers. In 1886 he was elected the Liberal Member of Parliament for his native Merioneth, immediately earning a reputation at Westminster as a champion of the national rights of Wales, and helping to press for the passage of the Welsh Intermediate Education Act of 1889. He was also one of the most prominent members of the CYMRU FYDD movement, founded in 1886.

His health had already begun to fail when he was taken ill with typhoid fever while on a visit to Egypt in 1889–90, following which he was presented with an impressive national testimonial. When W. E. Gladstone returned to power in 1892 he offered T. E. Ellis the position of Liberal junior whip. After prolonged heart-searching, he accepted, a move which caused much bad feeling in Liberal Wales. Although now hamstrung by the constraints of office, he helped to press for the appointment of the Royal Commission on Land in Wales in 1892 and for the introduction of measures for the disestablishment of the Church in Wales, since most of the population in Wales belonged to Nonconformist denominations (see CHRISTIANITY). In 1894 the Prime Minister, the Earl of Rosebery, promoted him to be his party's chief whip, a position he held until 1896. Ellis was prominent in the educational administration of Wales, and was a notably cultured, well-read, erudite individual. He married Annie J. Davies of Cwrt-mawr, Llangeitho, Cardiganshire (now CEREDIGION), in 1898, and died at the age of 40 at Cannes in France.

FURTHER READING
ABERYSTWYTH; CEREDIGION; CHRISTIANITY; CYMRU; CYMRU FYDD; NATIONALISM; Mari Ellis, *Y Golau Gwan*; T. I. Ellis, *Thomas Edward Ellis*; J. Graham Jones, *Journal of the Merioneth Historical and Record Society* 12.366–83; J. Graham Jones, *Journal of the Merioneth Historical and Record Society* 13.53–72; Wyn Jones, *Thomas Edward Ellis 1859–1899*; Masterman, *Forerunner*.

J. Graham Jones

Elpin/Ailpín was the name of a king who ruled over the PICTS in the period 726–8. In the SCOTTISH KING-LISTS a ruler of DÁL RIATA with this name occurs for about the same period. The name itself is of

interest for two reasons. First, since it contains a *p*, it is clearly not GOIDELIC in origin, but rather PICTISH or BRYTHONIC (see also Q-CELTIC; P-CELTIC). The corresponding Brythonic name *Elffin* is recorded in the early medieval kingdoms of GWYNEDD in Wales (CYMRU), and YSTRAD CLUD and RHEGED in north BRITAIN. Secondly, CINAED MAC AILPÍN was the famous first Scottish king of the united kingdom of Picts and SCOTS from about 843. Therefore, this patronym and its earlier currency among the kings of the Picts—one of whom also became king of the Scots—suggests some sort of Pictish (or Brythonic) background or acculturation for the founders of the united kingdom of ALBA. According to the PICTISH KING-LIST, Elpin ruled together with DREST for five years. In the ANNALS of Ulster it is noted that Elpin was defeated, with heavy losses, by 'Oenghus' (probably ONUIST son of Uurguist) in a Pictish internecine battle at Monid Croib (probably Moncrieffe Hill, Perthshire) in 727 (= 728) and again in the same year at a 'Castellum Credi', where he was put to flight.

FURTHER READING
ALBA; ANNALS; BRITAIN; BRYTHONIC; CINAED MAC AILPÍN; CYMRU; DÁL RIATA; DREST; GOIDELIC; GWYNEDD; ONUIST; P-CELTIC; PICTISH; PICTISH KING-LIST; PICTS; Q-CELTIC; RHEGED; SCOTTISH KING-LISTS; SCOTS; YSTRAD CLUD; Marjorie O. Anderson, *Kings and Kingship in Early Scotland* 112, 177–9, 182–4; Smyth, *Warlords and Holy Men* 72–5; Ann Williams et al., *Biographical Dictionary of Dark Age Britain* 45.

PEB

Emain Machae, the legendary capital of ULAID and the court of King CONCHOBAR and the ULSTER CYCLE heroes in early Irish tradition, is identified with Navan Fort, which is situated 2.6 km west of Armagh (ARD MHACHA). Navan Fort is the most prominent monument in an archaeological complex of sites dating from the Neolithic to the early medieval period. Other major monuments include Haughey's Fort, Loch na Séad (Loughnashade) and the King's Stables. The site has been variously identified with either the Ισαμνιον *Isamnion* or northern Ρεγια *Regia* of PTOLEMY's 2nd-century map of Ireland (ÉRIU).

The earliest evidence for settlement within the complex is to be found on the drumlin (glacial oval hill) on which Navan Fort was later constructed. It consisted

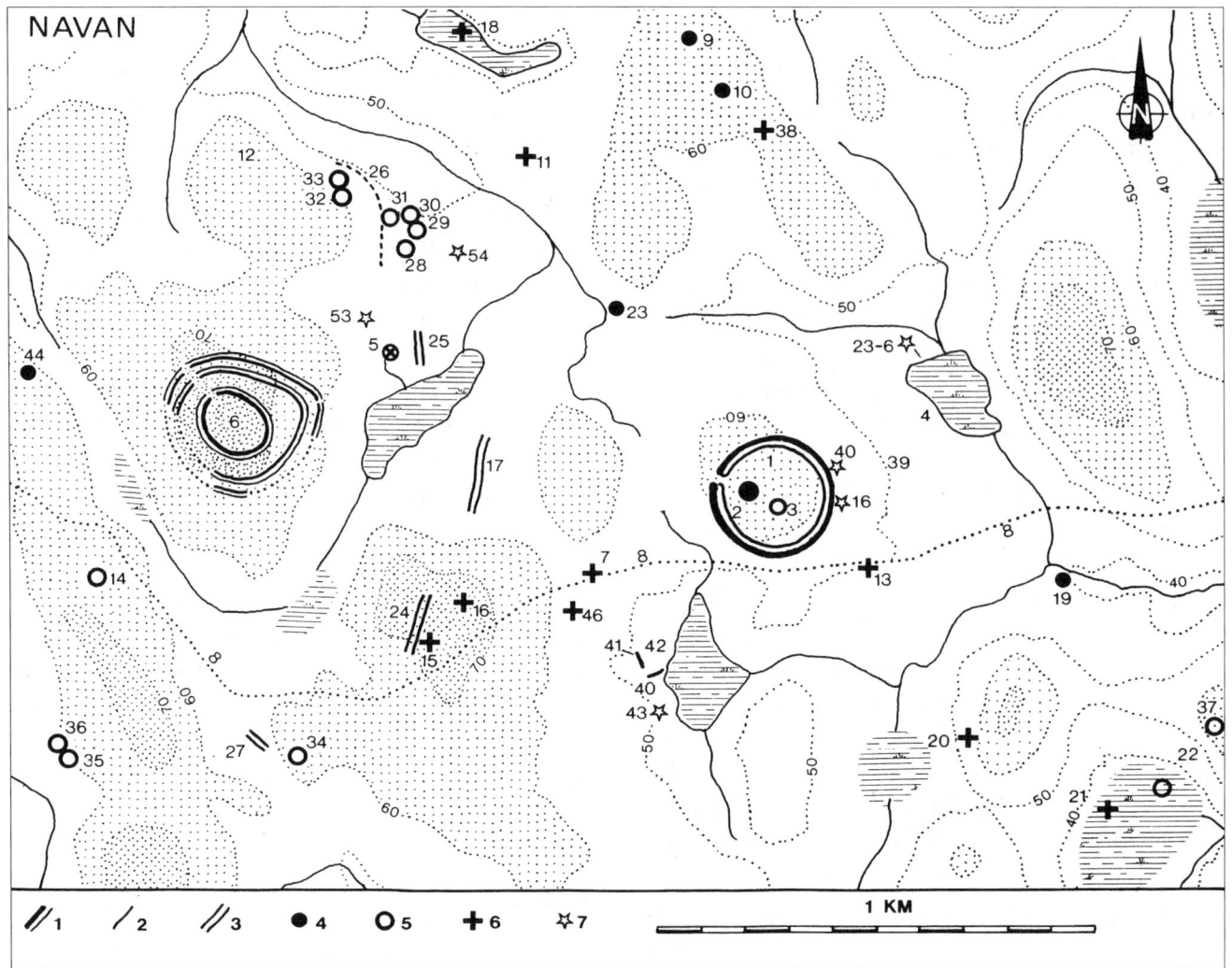

NAVAN

Key symbols: //1 /2 //3 ●4 ○5 +6 ☆7

1 KM

The Navan Complex near Armagh, Northern Ireland: antiquities in the landscape and ancient extent of bogs and lakes. Key: 1=bank-and-ditch; 2=linear-ditch; 3=double linear-ditch; 4=mound; 5=ring-ditch; 6=other type of site; 7=find spot. The large circular monument near the centre of the map is Navan Fort (Emain Machae). Loch na Séad is the lake to its north-east. The roughly circular trivallate hill-fort a kilometre to the west is the Late Bronze Age Haughey's Fort. The artificial ritual pool known as the King's Stables is on its north-east (site 5). Armagh is a short distance beyond the map's eastern edge.

of a series of pits containing Neolithic pottery and flint tools. Soil accumulated over this layer, and it was ploughed during the Bronze Age. Then, at approximately 1000 BC, there is abundant evidence for Later Bronze Age activity within the complex. At Navan a circular enclosure, some 46 m across, was made which consisted of a ring ditch (*c.* 5 m across and 1 m deep) and a series of internally erected timber posts. This structure is believed to have been used for a RITUAL function, in the absence of a more plausible explanation. For this period, far greater activity was found at Haughey's Fort, west of Navan Fort. This is a Late Bronze Age hill-fort, surrounded by three ditches, and enclosing a maximum area of *c.* 340 m by 310 m. The interior of the site has revealed the presence of two large circular timber structures and a series of pits and stakeholes. The pits have yielded small fragments of gold, bronze, glass beads, coarse pottery, animal bones, and charred barley seeds. The waterlogged ditches preserved the remains of bones, wood—both artefacts and the natural remains of trees and bushes from the vicinity of the ditches, seeds, pottery, and about 80 species of beetles. The economy of Haughey's Fort was based primarily on barley cultivation and the raising of cattle and swine; other domestic livestock was minimally present. Several dog skulls were recovered, and these are the largest known from prehistoric Ireland.

At the foot of the hill on which Haughey's Fort is situated lies the site known as the King's Stables. This is a circular embanked enclosure whose bottom had been hollowed out in the Late Bronze Age to form an artificial pool. Within it were found animal remains, some articulated as if either the entire animal or large portions of it had been deposited. Also recovered was the front portion of the skull of a young human male (see SACRIFICE; WATERY DEPOSITIONS).

Both Haughey's Fort and the King's Stables date to c. 1000 BC, and they appear to form an associated complex of sites which included elements of occupation (Haughey's Fort) and ritual (both Haughey's Fort and the King's Stables). Given the later developments at nearby Navan Fort, it has been suggested that Haughey's Fort served as a major tribal centre in Late Bronze Age Ireland, but it was probably abandoned by c. 900 BC as the centre shifted to Navan.

By c. 400 BC Navan Fort began to see a sequence of major architectural changes. Within the area of the earlier ditched enclosure was erected a series of figure-of-eight structures which consisted of a smaller round house, about 10–12 m in diameter, attached to a larger enclosure, some 20–25 m across and entered by way of a fenced walkway. Finds associated with these structures, which were regularly renewed, include coarse ceramics, a few bronze objects and the skull of a barbary ape—the latter seen as evidence for a distant gift exchange from North Africa along ocean trade routes across Europe's Atlantic Zone (remains of another ape have been recovered from a LA TÈNE site in Luxembourg).

At approximately 100 BC Navan underwent two major architectural changes. The occupants of the site surrounded the top of the hill with a hengiform enclosure, i.e. they encircled the hill with a large outer bank and an inner ditch. The earlier figure-of-eight structures were cleared away and replaced by a single circular building, constructed of c. 269 upright oak posts, which measured 40 m in diameter, hence the 'Forty Metre Structure'. The massive central post has been dated by tree rings to 95 BC. There is debate as to whether or how this structure may have been roofed, but it is presumed to be some form of large ritual building. No finds were associated with its floor. While the posts were still standing, possibly soon after they had been erected, the structure was transformed in three

acts. The first involved filling the entire 'Forty-Metre Structure' with limestone boulders up to almost 3 m in height. Then the timber along the outer edge of the structure was burnt (several large charred oak beams were recovered from the bottom of the outer ditch) and, finally, sods were imported to cap the cairn and form an earthen mound some 5 m high.

Also within the main enclosure, excavations revealed the remains of three more circular wall-slots and a larger triple-ringed timber enclosure. These were cut through by a ditch whose later fill revealed an early medieval brooch.

At the foot of Navan Fort lies Loughnashade (Loch na Séad), a small lake that now occupies only one acre (0.4 ha), but probably spread over five acres (2 ha) during the heyday of Navan. In the late 18th century its boggy shoreline yielded four large bronze horns (see CARNYX), decorated in the La Tène style and probably contemporary with the 'Forty Metre Structure' and the outer bank and ditch. The practice of depositing musical instruments in bodies of water is well represented across north-west Europe during the Later Bronze Age and the IRON AGE.

The Navan complex provides numerous major issues of interpretation. The monumentality of the site suggests its ritual, if not political, importance in Iron Age Ireland. There are problems with reconciling this with its rôle as a later historical royal site, or rather a pseudo-historical royal site, since the earliest historical references to it as a capital of the Ulstermen appear long after its archaeological heyday. The proximity of Armagh, the traditional primatial see of St PATRICK, and the preservation of the name of the territorial goddess MACHA in the two place-names has inspired much speculation concerning a possible key rôle for greater Navan in the transition from pagan to Christian Ireland. The creation and encasement of the 'Forty Metre Structure' has invited much speculation: a timber temple, an OTHERWORLD structure (see also SÍD) intended to be set encased in stone, an attempt to replicate a megalithic monument (a passage tomb is known from the main Iron Age enclosure at Tara [TEAMHAIR]), or an attempt to symbolize within a single monument the three Celtic (and Indo-European) social strata of the Dumézilian theory. In terms of formal architecture, the 'figure-of-eight' houses and ENCLOSURES are best paralleled at other

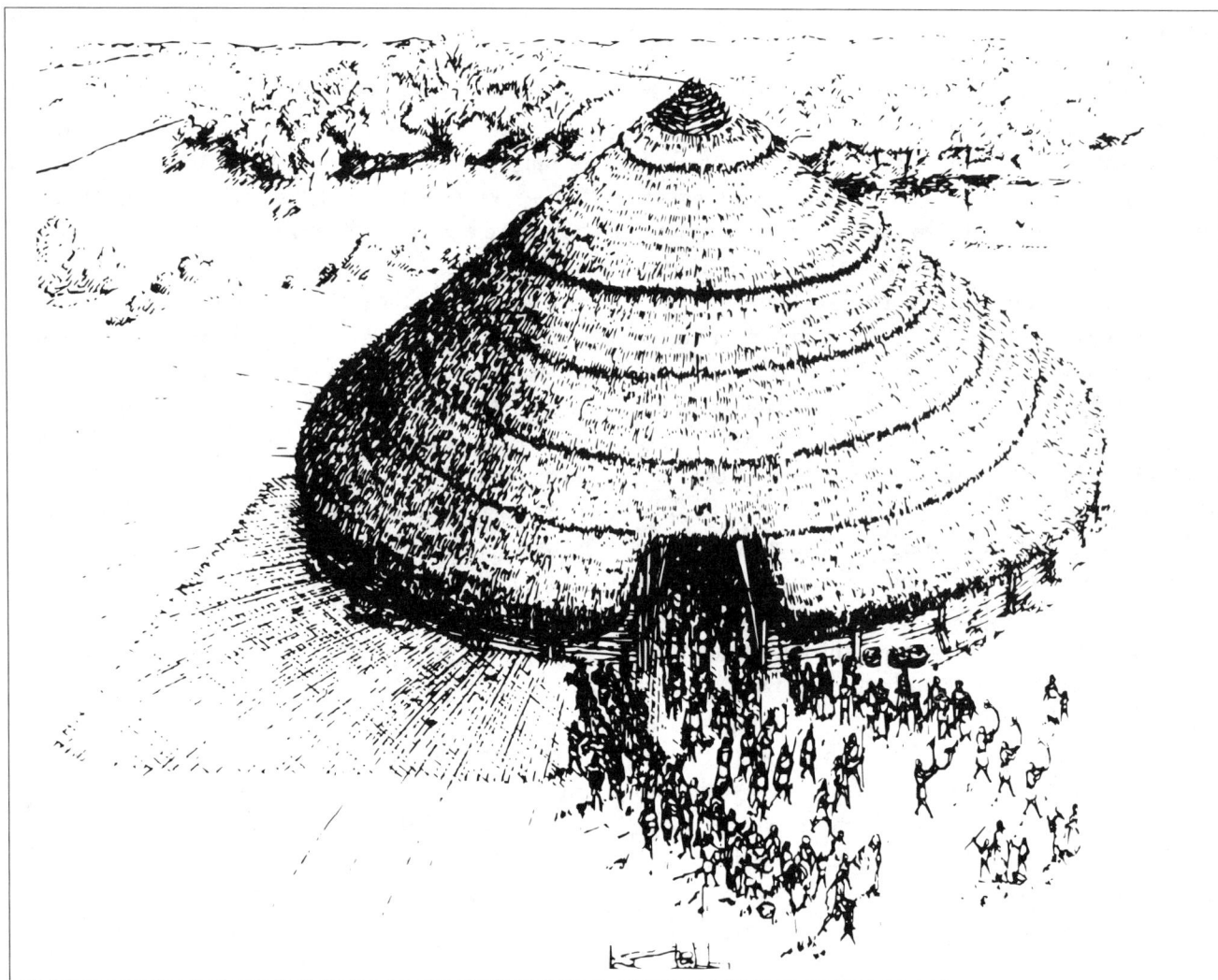

Reconstruction of the 'Forty-Metre Structure' at Navan (Emain Machae), as it would have appeared c. 95 BC, with conjectural roof, before it was intentionally destroyed and capped with a cairn

so-called royal sites, such as DÚN AILINNE and Tara; a large circular post-built structure of Iron Age date is also known from Dún Ailinne.

FURTHER READING
AGRICULTURE; ARD MHACHA; CARNYX; CONCHOBAR; DÚN AILINNE; ENCLOSURES; ÉRIU; IRON AGE; LA TÈNE; MACHA; OTHERWORLD; PATRICK; PTOLEMY; RITUAL; SACRIFICE; SÍD; TEAMHAIR; ULAID; ULSTER CYCLE; WATERY DEPOSITIONS; Waterman & Lynn, *Excavations at Navan Fort 1961–71*.

J. P. Mallory

Emania is an Irish journal established by J. P. Mallory in 1986 as the Bulletin of the Navan Research Group at Queen's University, Belfast (see EMAIN MACHAE). The articles, all of which are written in English, deal mainly with archaeology of the Irish Late Bronze Age, IRON AGE, and early Middle Ages, as well as IRISH and INDO-EUROPEAN historical linguistics, and the study of early IRISH LITERATURE, especially the ULSTER CYCLE, including some edited texts and translations of primary Old and Middle Irish sources. *Emania* is usually published annually and each issue has a particular thematic 'focus'. It publishes new work rapidly and is aimed at a mixed readership of professionals and interested non-specialists.

RELATED ARTICLES
EMAIN MACHAE; INDO-EUROPEAN; IRISH; IRISH LITERATURE; IRON AGE; ULSTER CYCLE.
CONTACT DETAILS. *Emania*, Department of Archaeology, The School of Geosciences, Queen's University, Belfast BT7 1NN, Northern Ireland.

PSH

emigration and the Celtic countries

§1. IRELAND

See CELTIC LANGUAGES IN AUSTRALIA; CELTIC LANGUAGES IN NORTH AMERICA §1.

§2. SCOTLAND

See CELTIC LANGUAGES IN AUSTRALIA; CELTIC LANGUAGES IN NORTH AMERICA §2–3.

§3. MAN

The 18th century saw the widespread emigration of young adults from the Isle of Man (ELLAN VANNIN), in spite of legislation in 1655 requiring the Governor's permission to do so. From the 1820s favourable reports from pioneering emigrants to Cleveland, Ohio, resulted in group migration, effectively establishing MANX-Gaelic-speaking communities in the area (cf. CELTIC LANGUAGES IN NORTH AMERICA).

In 1845 potato blight affected Manx farming communities, and the total loss of the crop in the following year, coupled with news of gold finds in America and Australia, resulted in a further burst of emigration between 1847 and 1851. Alongside the 19th century's general movement from rural to urban areas, improvements to transport links with the large north of England labour market served to attract Manx emigrants. The late 19th century encouraged emigration from the declining Manx mining industry to South Africa, Australia, the USA, and Canada.

The 20th century witnessed successive bursts of emigration due to economic pressures—most notably during the 1950s and 1970s. The latter period proved particularly problematic for the Manx Government, who introduced measures to attract new residents, resulting in a nationalist backlash (see NATIONALISM). The almost full labour market provided by the success of the finance sector reduced the need for the young working population to emigrate en masse.

The existence of Manx societies in Cleveland, Queensland, New Zealand, Dubai, and London, for example, shows the continued desire of the Manx diaspora to identify with the Isle of Man.

FURTHER READING
AGRICULTURE; CELTIC LANGUAGES IN NORTH AMERICA; ELLAN VANNIN; MANX; NATIONALISM; Belchem, *New History of the Isle of Man 5*; Coakley, www.isle-of-man.com/manxnotebook/famhist/genealgy/bsps1.htm.

Breesha Maddrell

§4 .WALES

The movement of Welsh people to settle overseas has been smaller in scale than that from Ireland (ÉIRE) and Scotland (ALBA). Nor has it been as prominent a feature of the history of Wales (CYMRU) as internal migration to England. Nevertheless, people have emigrated from Wales since at least the 17th century. (An even earlier migration was claimed in the legend that Prince MADOG AB OWAIN GWYNEDD, and his followers settled in America in the late 12th century.) A period of significant migration during the late 17th and early 18th century was followed by a longer, more voluminous, and almost continuous phase between the 1790s and the early 1930s. The outward movement has continued since 1945, though on a smaller scale compared to the late 19th-/early 20th-century peak. Welsh emigrants have been notably diverse in terms of their geographical, social and occupational origins, their motives in emigrating and the destinations they have chosen. Wherever they have settled in significant numbers, they have rarely encountered hostility, and they have usually earned recognition as a small, but distinctive and locally influential group.

The absence or unreliability of statistical records make it difficult to make an accurate assessment of the actual number of emigrants, but it is certain this was higher than the recorded figures suggest. In the 19th century, when systematic records of emigration began to be kept by many countries, the British government did not differentiate between emigrants from England and Wales, whilst in the receiving countries many Welsh were classed as English. Extant official records state that at the end of the 19th century about 100,000 people who had been born in Wales were living in the USA, 13,500 in Canada, and 13,000 in Australia. The majority of Welsh emigrants have settled in what became the USA, but in the early 20th century greater numbers of Welsh people were moving within the British Empire, especially to Canada. During the last half-century, Canada and Australia have been the main destinations.

Like all emigrants, those from Wales have been stimulated to move by a combination of factors, among them personal considerations peculiar to each individual emigrant. To some, emigration has been a means of escaping severe economic distress and perceived or real cultural, religious, and political oppression within Wales. To others, perhaps the majority, the search for a new life overseas has been a calculated quest for greater opportunities, a better life and even for adventure. It is likely that 19th-century Welsh emigrants were strongly influenced by economic considerations, often a combination of difficult conditions at home and the attractions of land or the higher wages overseas that skilled Welsh industrial workers could command. Other reasons have also been significant at various times. Many of the Baptists, Quakers, and Anglicans from mid and west Wales who settled in the Philadelphia area in the late 17th century were at the same time fleeing from religious persecution and attracted by the Pennsylvania colony's principles of religious freedom and toleration. Welsh people have also emigrated for political, cultural, and what might be termed nationalistic reasons (see NATIONALISM). Notable examples here are the various attempts to set up a new Wales in the American Colonies, prior to the American War of Independence, as well as the permanent *Gwladfa* in PATAGONIA, Argentina. The latter, established in 1865 in the Chubut valley, was founded in order to establish a proto-Welsh-language State free from English incursion. During its years of expansion between 1865 and 1914 the colony attracted between 3,000–4,000 Welsh people.

Nonconformist religion, *eisteddfodau* (sing. EISTEDDFOD) and choral societies have played a formative rôle in most Welsh immigrant communities, whilst in the USA and Patagonia Welsh newspapers were, and remain, important vehicles for maintaining Welsh ethnic networks and promoting activities. The flowering of Welsh-language culture overseas was largely, though by no means exclusively, due to the efforts of first generation settlers (see CELTIC LANGUAGES IN NORTH AMERICA §4). Attitudes towards the desirability of becoming fully absorbed into the host societies varied greatly, whilst the processes of adaptation and adjustment were complex and differed in pace and scale depending on local conditions. In time, usage of Welsh declined, churches closed and *eisteddfodau* became rarities. But since the 1970s, there has been an unmistakable expansion of Welsh ethnic awareness overseas and greater interest in Wales and a Welsh heritage, especially among the younger generation. This revival has manifested itself in the growing popularity of events such as the annual Welsh hymn-singing gathering, the North American Cymanfa Ganu and the closer ties between Wales and the Welsh in Patagonia.

FURTHER READING
ALBA; CELTIC LANGUAGES IN NORTH AMERICA; CYMRU; ÉIRE; EISTEDDFOD; MADOG AB OWAIN GWYNEDD; NATIONALISM; PATAGONIA; Berthoff, *British Immigrants in Industrial America*; Chamberlain, *Welsh in Canada*; Conway, *Perspectives in American History* 7.177–271; Hywel M. Davies, *Transatlantic Brethren*; Dodd, *Character of Early Welsh Emigration to the United States*; Edwards, *Eisteddfod Ffair y Byd, Chicago 1893*; H. Hughes, THSC new ser. 7.112–27; Aled Jones & Bill Jones, *Welsh Reflections*; Bill Jones, *Llafur* 8.2.41–62; Bill Jones, WHR 20.2.283–307; Robert Owen Jones, *Iaith Carreg fy Aelwyd* 281–305; Robert Owen Jones, *Language and Community in the Nineteenth Century* 287–316; William D. Jones, *Wales in America*; Knowles, *Calvinists Incorporated*; Knowles, *Nested Identities* 282–99; Lloyd, *Australians from Wales*; Thomas, *Hanes Cymry America*; David Williams, BBCS 7.396–415, 8.160; Glyn Williams, *Desert and the Dream*; Glyn Williams, *Welsh in Patagonia*; Gwyn A. Williams, *Madoc*; Gwyn A. Williams, *Search for Beulah Land*.

Bill Jones

§5. BRITTANY
See CELTIC LANGUAGES IN NORTH AMERICA §5.

§6. CORNWALL
Emigration may be seen as part of the ongoing experience of the Cornish people from the earliest times to the present, broadly related to 'push' factors in Cornwall (KERNOW), such as famine and economic decline, and 'pull' factors in other territories, such as mineral rewards. The earliest historically documented emigration experience for the Cornish was the number of south-western BRYTHONIC-speaking peoples who emigrated to Brittany (BREIZH), generally explained (dating from the 6th-century account of GILDAS) as motivated primarily by the pressure from Saxon invaders from the east (see BRETON MIGRATIONS). This age-old movement of peoples between Cornwall and Brittany continued until the Reformation. Over time, emigration out of Cornwall into the rest of the islands of BRITAIN and Ireland (ÉIRE) also occurred, most often where technical prowess in hard-rock mining was required, as in parts of Ireland, and the coal-mining regions of Wales (CYMRU) and England.

On the American continent, the Cornish—some of whom were possibly CORNISH speakers—were among the first waves of 16th-century settlers who travelled across the Atlantic, helping to found the famous Roanoke colony of 1585–6. More of a presence was made, however, in the 18th and 19th centuries in the opening up of the mining frontier as it moved westwards. Initially, the Cornish settled much of the midwest, mining first copper in the Upper Peninsula of Michigan and lead in Wisconsin and Illinois, but then moved westwards, into territories such as Montana, Arizona, and New Mexico, eventually making for the 1849 gold-rush in California.

Twenty-four years before the California gold-rush, Cornish miners went to Mexico to open the silver mines of Pachuca and Real del Monte. So-called 'Cousin Jacks and Jennies' also travelled to South Africa to mine copper, diamonds, and gold, playing an active part in the Zulu and Boer wars before the Union of South Africa was formed. Chile, Peru, New Zealand, and Canada were other favourites of the Cornish, who often travelled for farming opportunities as well.

Territories such as South Australia, founded in 1836, became important destinations for the Cornish, since, alongside copper mining, they offered religious freedom. The potato blight of 1845–6, though well documented in Ireland and Scotland (ALBA), had an impact in Cornwall too, causing massive emigration in the 1840s (see FAMINE). Around a third of the entire population of Cornwall had gone overseas by the end of the 19th century, and by this time the maxim that 'wherever in the world was a hole in the ground one was likely to find a Cornishman' seemed entirely true. This had a massive social effect on Cornwall; many Anglo-Cornish writers, such as Robert Stephen Hawker (1803–75) and the Hocking siblings, documented the process. A. L. Rowse (1903–97) was to comment: 'Not one is left in this country: all of them gone abroad, not to return, the home broken up' (Rowse, *Cornish Childhood* 23).

In the face of globalization in the 20th century there has been much rediscovery and reassertion of Cornishness in the territories of the Cornish diaspora, with a growing number of societies and gatherings in key locations of past and present Cornish activity, such as Mineral Point (where Cornish miners' cottages are preserved), Grass Valley (where male-voice choirs persist), Pen Argyl and Butte in the United States, and Burra and Moonta in South Australia. In such places, Cornish culture proliferates and festivals like the Australian Kernewek Lowender (Cornish enjoyment) unite aspects of pre-industrial, industrial, and post-industrial Cornish cultural identity, including an appreciation of a Celticity which links these traditions to those of the other CELTIC COUNTRIES.

FURTHER READING
ALBA; BREIZH; BRETON MIGRATIONS; BRITAIN; BRYTHONIC; CELTIC COUNTRIES; CORNISH; CYMRU; ÉIRE; FAMINE; GILDAS; KERNOW; Dawe, *Cornish Pioneers in South Africa*; Fiedler, *Mineral Point*; Kent, *Pulp Methodism*; McKinney, *When Miners Sang*; Payton, *Cornish Miner in Australia*; Payton, *Cornish Overseas*; Rowe, *Hard-Rock Men*; Rowse, *Cornish Childhood*; Rowse, *Cornish in America*; Todd, *Search for Silver*.

Alan M. Kent

Emvod Etrekeltiek an Oriant (Festival Interceltique de Lorient)

For over thirty years, each August the Interceltic Festival in Lorient (An Oriant), Morbihan, Brittany (BREIZH), has attracted a worldwide audience of all ages to enjoy the diverse music of the Celtic lands on the European Atlantic periphery. The festival in Lorient evolved from the earlier Festival des Cornemuses, a Breton piping and pipe-band championship, first held in Brest in 1953, which was moved to Lorient in 1971 in an attempt to reinvigorate the championships and encourage international participation (see BAGPIPE; BINIOU).

The Scottish Highland bagpipe (BINIOU *braz*) began to be used by Breton musicians at the end of the 19th century. Breton cultural activist Polig Montjarret founded pipe bands (*bagadoù*) during and after the German occupation of the Second World War in order to increase the number of traditional music players. Earlier, pairs of musicians had used the medieval Breton *bombard* along with the high-pitched *biniou kozh* (small pipes, lit. 'old bagpipe') to accompany dance music. However *bombard*, *biniou braz*, and drums produced a better balance in a larger band. The adoption of Scots and Irish pipe tunes aided the Breton musical revival, and led directly to the development of an inter-cultural 'Celtic music'.

The Festival des Cornemuses in Lorient invited musicians from the six CELTIC COUNTRIES and from the Celtic diaspora in the New World, as well as the Spanish regions of GALICIA and Asturias, which sometimes claim Celtic cultural heritage and have lively contemporary piping traditions. This helped to promote Brittany's distinctive Celtic identity which had survived hostility from the centralized French State and media.

As an inclusive, attractive spectacle, Emvod Etrekeltiek an Oriant augments traditional music with jazz, rock, and classical forms in its open-air and indoor concerts, parades, lectures, informal sessions, and communal dance. Major new works have been commissioned—a good example of which is the 1983 Lorient Festival Suite, which Shaun Davey composed for solo traditional players, singers and orchestra. It became *The Pilgrim*, and has been played in several countries with a reprise at Lorient in August 2001.

The port of Lorient was extensively rebuilt following the Second World War, and provides ideal open-air spaces, excellent access and accommodation. From the first Friday to the second Sunday in August, Lorient has attracted upwards of 500,000 spectators in recent years. To reach such levels of popularity is as much a tribute to its organization as to its concept. From the start, a small core of professional organizers called on a loyal cohort of voluntary helpers numbering several hundreds. They come from the participating Celtic lands, and organize the transportation, feeding, accommodation and, above all, performances by musicians, lecturers, exhibitors, and film makers, now numbering 4500 each year.

While younger events such as Celtic Connections in Glasgow (GLASCHU) and Celtic Colours in Cape Breton, Nova Scotia, Canada, feed from it, Emvod Etrekeltiek an Oriant is the prime showcase for listening to the songs which perpetuate the 'pure' traditions of the individual Celtic countries and the instrumental music which, through cross-fertilization, created the new self-aware phenomenon of 'Celtic music'. The piping competitions are as keenly contested today as formerly, and the festival has played a key rôle in defining, disseminating, and enhancing the prestige of a distinctive and eclectic modern Celtic culture.

FURTHER READING & SOUND RECORDINGS
BAGPIPE; BINIOU; BREIZH; BRETON MUSIC; CELTIC COUNTRIES; GALICIA; GLASCHU; Becker & Le Gurun, *La Musique Bretonne*; Davey, *Pilgrim* (CD); Hirio, *Festival Interceltique de Lorient – 25 ans* (CD); *How to Be Celtic*; Morvan et al., *Bretagne*; Pichard & Plisson, *Musique des mondes celtiques*.

Rob Gibson

Enaid Owain ab Urien (The soul of Owain son of URIEN; MS *Eneit Owein ap Vryen*; also known as

Marwnad Owain) is an early Welsh poem attributed by many modern scholars to the historical 6th-century poet TALIESIN, partly on the basis of the subject matter—the poem commemorates a 6th-century northern BRYTHONIC hero—and partly on its inclusion in the LLYFR TALIESIN manuscript. Consistent with details found in other poems in this manuscript, as well as in the saga ENGLYNION on Urien and his sons, Owain is identified as lord of RHEGED and probably also the northern country of Llwyfenydd (MS *vб lleweny6*). His enemies are the men of England (Lloegr), and he is said to have slain Fflamddwyn (Flamebearer), a nickname that appears elsewhere in *Llyfr Taliesin*, apparently referring to an Anglo-Saxon leader of BRYNAICH. Vivid imagery includes a description of 'England's broad host asleep with light in their eyes'.

Several details suggest that *Enaid Owain* is late in the CYNFEIRDD corpus. First, the word *eneit*, the poem's keynote, means 'soul' in a thoroughly Christianized sense, not the older meaning 'life force' attested elsewhere. Metrically, it is a near flawless example of the *awdl-gywydd* metre of the canonical twenty-four metres of the later medieval period: fourteen-syllable lines with a break regularly falling at the word-final seventh syllable and marked by internal rhyme. The third line (of a total of eleven) is the only exception: both feet are six syllables. In line 6, the internal rhyme is *Fflamddwyn* : *fwy n/oc* 'more than', which would not have been possible in the 6th century, though viable by the 8th.

The poem's content is essentially a prayer for the hero's soul. The poet does not adopt the explicit attitude of singing on the occasion of Owain's death. Since Owain is otherwise famous in early WELSH POETRY, and eventually became one of the great heroes of international ARTHURIAN literature (cf. TAIR RHAMANT), concern for his soul among Christian men of letters might have inspired this polished poem a century or more after his death. Compare, for example, the 9th-century ELISEG'S PILLAR, where Cyngen of POWYS invites passers-by to pray for the soul of his great-grandfather, the warrior-king Elise.

PRIMARY SOURCES
EDITIONS. Ifor Williams, *Canu Taliesin*; Ifor Williams, *Poems of Taliesin*.
ED. & TRANS. Pennar, *Taliesin Poems* 101–6.
TRANS. Clancy, *Earliest Welsh Poetry* 31–2; Conran, *Welsh Verse* 112; Gwyn Jones, *Oxford Book of Welsh Verse in English* 2; Koch & Carey, *Celtic Heroic Age* 368.

MODERN WELSH VERSION. Thomas, *Yr Aelwyd Hon* 37.

FURTHER READING
ARTHURIAN; BRYNAICH; BRYTHONIC; CYNFEIRDD; ELISEG'S
PILLAR; ENGLYNION; LLYFR TALIESIN; OWAIN AB URIEN;
POWYS; RHEGED; TAIR RHAMANT; TALIESIN; URIEN; WELSH
POETRY; Bromwich, *Beginnings of Welsh Poetry*; Rowland, *Early
Welsh Saga Poetry*.

JTK

Enclosures are an archaeological feature of IRON AGE settlements, highly characteristic of, but hardly limited to, ancient Celtic-speaking areas. This general term functions as an umbrella to cover several sub-categories—VIERECKSCHANZEN (rectangular enclosures), hill-forts, cattle stockades, and other areas of land delimited by earthworks, most commonly a bank and a ditch. The bank was often topped by a wooden palisade, and sometimes the outer face was retained and made sharply vertical with dry-stone masonry (i.e. without any mortar or cement; see FORTIFICATION).

In the eastern LA TÈNE area (present-day south Germany, Austria and the Czech Republic), most enclosures were *Viereckschanzen*, whose functions are still unclear. Further west, in GAUL, alongside other types of enclosures, there are also examples of *Viereckschanzen*, which seem to have counterparts in the south of England. In southern England and the western La Tène zone of the Continent, hill-forts and oppida (sing. OPPIDUM), also occur, with some large oppida also in central Europe (e.g. STARÉ HRADISKO); these are essentially fortified towns. Some *Viereckschanzen* seem to have had a ritual function (see FANUM). However, recent research and analysis suggest that most of them were fortified farmsteads rather than sanctuaries.

FURTHER READING
BOPFINGEN; FANUM; FORTIFICATION; GAUL; HOCHDORF; IPF;
IRON AGE; LA TÈNE; MANCHING; OPPIDUM; RIBEMONT-SUR-
ANCRE; ROQUEPERTUSE; STARÉ HRADISKO; VIERECK-
SCHANZEN; Cunliffe et al., *Archaeology*; Hayes, *Archaeology of
the British Isles*; Piggott, *Ancient Europe from the Beginnings of
Agriculture to Classical Antiquity*.

PEB

Englyn is a type of Welsh metre. Eight different kinds of *englynion* are listed among the traditional twenty-four strict metres, all with obligatory CYNGHANEDD (systematic line-internal sound correspondences) from the 14th century onwards (see AWDL; CERDD DAFOD; CYWYDD; EINION OFFEIRIAD). Two of these metres have only three lines—the *englyn milwr* (lit. 'soldier *englyn*') and the *englyn penfyr* (lit. 'short-end *englyn*') which are characteristic of the saga, gnomic, and NATURE POETRY of the 9th and 10th centuries (see ENGLYNION). It is not impossible that some examples, such as the *englynion* in the GODODDIN, might be older than this. The following famous example of the *englyn penfyr* (in which medieval spelling is retained) is from the HELEDD cycle:

Stauell Gyndylan ys tywyll heno,
Heb dan, heb gannwyll.
Namyn Duw, pwy a'm dyry pwyll?

Cynddylan's hall is dark tonight,
Without fire, without candle.
But for God, who will give me sense?

Of the four-line *englynion*, by far the most common from the 12th century onwards is the *englyn unodl union*. This famous example by TUDUR ALED (*c.* 1500) illustrates the syllabic structure—10, 6, 7, 7—and the *gair cyrch* which follows the main rhyme of the first line (like the *englyn penfyr*):

Mae'n wir y gwelir argoelyn—difai
  Wrth dyfiad y brigyn
    A hysbys y dengys dyn
    O ba radd y bo'i wreiddyn.

It is true that one sees a faultless sign
In the growth of the shoot;
And man manifestly shows
From what grade his root is.

The first two lines are known as the *paladr* (lit. 'spearshaft' or 'ray'), and the last two as the *esgyll* (lit. 'wings'). The *esgyll* is equivalent to the *cywydd* couplet, and has the same rhyming pattern—one stressed syllable and the other unstressed, thus often involving vowels of different phonetic length. Reversing the order of *paladr* and *esgyll* gives the much less common *englyn unodl crwca*.

The *englyn cyrch* is characterized by the *odl gyrch* which rhymes the end of the third line with the caesura of the fourth, and corresponds to the *triban* ('three prominences') in the free metres. Three other kinds of *englyn* use *proest* or assonantal rhyme (like consonants, but not identical vowels), and are distinguished by the types of vowels used, *proest dalgron* for simple vowels, *lleddfbroest* for diphthongs, and *proest gadwynog* ('chained *proest*') where alternate lines have full rhymes. *Englynion proest* are very common in the *awdlau* of the Poets of the Nobility (see CYWYDDWYR; WELSH POETRY).

From the earliest period *englynion* were normally used in extended series known as *cyngogion*, and later as a *cadwyn* or chain, linked by *cyrch-gymeriad* repeating a word or sound from the end of one line to the beginning of the next. In the work of the Poets of the Princes of the 12th and 13th centuries (see GOGYN-FEIRDD) the *englynion* series seems to have been an alternative form to the *awdl*, and although it has been argued that the *englyn* was of a lower status and was used originally by the *bardd teulu* ('household bard'; see BARDIC ORDER), there is no firm evidence to support such a view. There are isolated instances of the use of *englynion* within *awdlau* by the Poets of the Princes, and this practice spread rapidly in the 14th century to become standard practice in the *awdlau* of the Poets of the Nobility. In the same period the single *englyn unodl union* came to be used as a form of epigrammatic expression, as seen in the example quoted above, and it was also used to good effect in bardic debates (YMRYSONAU) and flytings. The *englyn* has remained popular with folk poets from the 18th century until the present day, as many commemorative verses on gravestones throughout Wales (CYMRU) attest, and it is the mainstay of the contemporary flourishing of strict-metre poetry.

FURTHER READING
AWDL; BARDIC ORDER; CERDD DAFOD; CYMRU; CYNGHANEDD; CYWYDD; CYWYDDWYR; EINION OFFEIRIAD; ENGLYNION; GODODDIN; GOGYNFEIRDD; HELEDD; NATURE POETRY; TUDUR ALED; WELSH POETRY; YMRYSONAU; Nerys Ann Jones, *Beirdd a Thywysogion* 288–301; R. M. Jones, *Ysgrifau Beirniadol* 12.250–93; Llwyd, *Ynglŷn â Chrefft Englyna* 15–53; Morris-Jones, *Cerdd Dafod*.

Dafydd Johnston

***Englynion*, saga,** is a term which describes a sizable body of early WELSH POETRY composed in the three-line metre known as the earlier type of ENGLYN; their metrical form is described in that article.

§1. THEMATIC CONTENT AND LITERARY FUNCTION
Although the early *englynion* are used for a wide range of subject matter (see below), themes of martial heroism viewed with the attitude of the grief and nostalgia of bereaved survivors have particular prominence in this material. In their concern with the values and HEROIC ETHOS of the war-band and looking to a heroic age set in 6th- and 7th-century BRITAIN, the saga *englynion* offer many points of commonality with the poetry in the AWDL metres attributed to the CYNFEIRDD. However, readers will perceive obvious differences. Whereas the attitude of the *awdlau* of ANEIRIN and the other *Cynfeirdd*, like those of the GOGYNFEIRDD of the 12th and 13th centuries, are intelligible as the sentiments of court poets, composed and performed for specific noble patrons for specific public occasions, the personas of the poets of saga *englynion* are felt more as characters in stories, as opposed to functionaries upholding a real social order at a particular point in history. These poetic personas, such as Llywarch Hen or HELEDD, are highly developed, emotionally and psychologically. And they are often in isolation, not declaiming their verses before the throng in the court, but in rude circumstances, in hardship, often out of doors, looking back, literally or in the imagination, over their former aristocratic way of life and residence, now ruined and desolate. Owing to these factors and also to the fact that dramatic *englynion* are sometimes spoken by leading characters in the prose tales—such as ARTHUR in CULHWCH AC OLWEN or GWYDION in MATH FAB MATHONWY, Ifor WILLIAMS influentially argued that these *englynion* represented a residue of dramatic verse dialogue in works that had been originally performed as lengthy narrative sagas of mixed prose and poetry. This theory finds a measure of support in the analogy of the early Irish ULSTER CYCLE, tales that are mostly prose, but include dramatic speeches by the leading characters in the metrical *rosc* style. Although Ford rejected this 'lost prose matrix' theory, we have to assume that a traditional narrative background was understood by the audience in order to appreciate the tragic destinies of the characters speaking the verses.

§2. AUTHORSHIP AND DATING
Since Llywarch Hen and Heledd appear to us to be more literary creations than real poets and neither is

named in the Memorandum of the FIVE POETS, the saga *englynion* are generally regarded as anonymous compositions, and may, in part, be growths of cumulative tradition. The fictionalization of the settings means that attempting to date these cycles according to the events and persons described is at best complicated and probably inappropriate. Although the main manuscripts for the corpus (LLYFR COCH HERGEST, LLYFR DU CAERFYRDDIN, NLW Peniarth 111, NLW 4973a and 4973b, BL Additional MS 31055(T)) are mostly of the central or later Middle Ages, it is generally accepted that texts were composed during the Old Welsh period (AD *c.* 800–1100), a conclusion supported by fairly numerous throwbacks in the text and the language of the extant copies, as well as the fact that a newer form of the *englyn* (with four lines) became popular in the 12th century. One precious survival proves that *englynion* of this general type were being composed and committed to writing in Old Welsh, namely the three *englynion* in the Cambridge JUVENCUS manuscript of *c.* AD 900, in which a chieftain glumly broods over his drink, his retinue reduced to a single Frank, presumably an ignoble foreign mercenary.

Ni·canam, ni·guardam, ni·cuasam henoid,
cet iben med nouel,
mi a–m·Franc d'am an patel.

I do not sing, I do not laugh, I do not . . . tonight, though we drank fresh mead, my Frank and I, around our bowl.

§3. THE LLYWARCH HEN CYCLE

Consisting of 303 lines in Rowland's edition, the central figure and main speaker is Llywarch the Old (or the Ancestor). He presents himself as an aged noble warrior, whose twenty-four sons have all been killed in battle, for which he now feels guilt. On the basis of internal evidence we can see that at least one reason for his responsibility is that he inculcated the heroic ideal in them and urged them to fight for honour and to protect the homeland. The sons whose heroism and doom receive the most attention are Gwên, Pyll, and Maen. The recurrent sense of personal doom is epitomized in the *englyn*:

Truan a dynghet a dynget y Lywarch,
yr y nos y ganet,
hir gnif heb escor lludet.

It was a doomed man's destiny that was destined to Llywarch, since the night he was born, long labour, without deliverance from exhaustion.

The theme of 'dooming a destiny' also occurs in *Culhwch* and *Math*, and has resonances elsewhere in Celtic tradition. The Llywarch *englynion* repeatedly allude to URIEN of RHEGED and his family (his sons and his sister Efrddyl), and the descent of both Llywarch and Urien from the common ancestor COEL HEN is found in the Middle Welsh GENEALOGIES known as *Bonedd Gwŷr y Gogledd* (Descent of the men of the north). However, most of the geographical associations belong, not to north Britain, but to eastern Wales (CYMRU) and the border area, and on this basis Sims-Williams proposes that the cycle took shape at the Viking-age royal crannog (artificial island) at Llangors in BRYCHEINIOG (CMCS 26.27–63).

The name *Llywarch* is Celtic; for the etymology, see LLYWARCH AP LLYWELYN.

§4. THE HELEDD CYCLE

The main discussions are in the articles CYNDDYLAN and HELEDD. In 339 surviving lines, the poetic persona is interestingly female—Heledd, the sister of the fallen hero Cynddylan, who laments her brother and his ruined kingdom, mostly in present-day Shropshire (swydd Amwythig) in England. *Canu Heledd* includes the hauntingly memorable and often quoted imagery, including *Stauell Gynddylan ys tywyll heno* (Cynddylan's hall is dark tonight) and descriptions of screaming bloody eagles devouring Cynddylan's corpse.

§5. THE URIEN ENGLYNION

Comprising 177 lines, these verses are also discussed in the article on URIEN. Although King Urien and his family are the subject, he is not the poetic persona, and it is not clear who is speaking. Thirty-six lines describe the ruined and overgrown hearth of what had been the court of Rheged. Forty-two lines are delivered by a poet in the macabre situation of carrying Urien's severed head; another 30 lines describe Urien's decapitated corpse. In the former, there is much penetrating wordplay on the multiple senses of *pen* (head, chief, leader) and *porthi* (carry, support [e.g. of a poet by his patron]). The situation is reminiscent of that in BRANWEN, in which seven survivors, including the poet

TALIESIN, return from Ireland with the severed head of their king, BRÂN, and the *englynion* may intentionally echo this story:

> Penn a borthaf ar vyn tu,
> penn Uryen llary—llywei llu—
> ac ar y vronn wenn vran ôu.

The head I carry at my side, head of generous Urien—he used to lead a host, and on his white breast (*bron wen*) a black crow (*brân*).

The poet is convulsed by guilt, but is not necessarily the killer. It is likely that the Urien *englynion* reflect the same story as that which occurs in HISTORIA BRITTONUM (§63), where Urien is said to have been assassinated by his own ally and kinsman Morgan (Old Welsh Morcant) while besieging the Anglo-Saxons on LINDISFARNE. The *englynion* do agree with this account in as much as the event is said to have taken place in BRYNAICH and specifically at Aber Lleu, which could mean the mouth of the river Low, very close to Lindisfarne (Sims-Williams, CMCS 32.25–56). Since their setting and personnel are entirely northern, the Urien *englynion*, unlike the Llywarch Hen and Heledd cycles, raise the question whether the genre of the sagas originally developed in what is now Wales or in Dark Age north Britain. The fact that the GODODDIN includes two *englynion*, one seeming to be a stray from the Llywarch Hen cycle, is certainly relevant to the issue, but is not immediately decisive one way or the other.

§6. SOME OTHER TYPES OF EARLY ENGLYNION

The three-line *englyn* was used for religious poetry as early as the group of nine found in the JUVENCUS manuscript. This is a copy of *c.* 900, and scribal errors indicate that there was an even earlier written original, though not necessarily much earlier. The verses on the death of GERAINT at the battle of Llongborth differ from the foregoing cycles in that the poetic persona is not more developed or psychologized than that of, say, ANEIRIN in the *Gododdin*. A catalogue poem listing the battles of CADWALLON is of uncertain historical value. The *englyn* is the usual vehicle for the large body of early Welsh NATURE POETRY, and the fact that the Llywarch and Heledd cycles often express the churning thoughts and observations of their personas while in isolation out of doors suggests how the saga and

nature-poetry genres came to overlap. A similar affinity helps to explain why the *englyn* is often the vehicle for gnomes or expressions of eternal truths (thus comparable to Irish WISDOM LITERATURE), occurring sometimes within the saga material, as statements of resigned destiny, but also in the nature poetry and other contexts. *Englynion y Beddau* ('Stanzas of the Graves', ed. Thomas Jones) occur as 228 lines in *Llyfr Du Caerfyrddin*. Listing the graves of heroes, it is a catalogue of heroic tradition and place-name lore. As such, these verses are a valuable source for early Welsh tradition, including allusions to many stories otherwise lost, in this respect similar to the TRIADS and the catalogues in CULHWCH AC OLWEN. As in the Geraint *englynion*, the *Beddau* stanzas contain an early allusion to ARTHUR (see also ANOETH). BEDWYR is also named, and there is an allusion to the battle of CAMLAN.

For a variety of purposes, many of the major poets of Wales in the central and later Middle Ages continued to use the *englyn* (usually the four-line form), including several whose *englynion* are mentioned in other articles in the Encyclopedia: CYNDDELW (see also BARDIC ORDER [2] §7); DAFYDD AP GWILYM; BLEDDYN FARDD; CASNODYN; DAFYDD BENFRAS; ELIDIR SAIS; GWERFUL MECHAIN; LLYWARCH AP LLYWELYN; SEISYLL BRYFFWRCH. *Englynion* were commonly mixed with *awdlau* within a single poem in the works of the GOGYNFEIRDD.

PRIMARY SOURCES
MSS. Aberystwyth, NLW 4973a and 4973b, Peniarth III; London, BL Add. 31055 (T).
EDITIONS. Rolant, *Llywarch Hen a'i Feibion*; Ifor Williams, *Canu Llywarch Hen*.
ED. & TRANS. Ford, *Poetry of Llywarch Hen*; Thomas Jones, PBA 53.97–137 (*Englynion y Beddau*); Rowland, *Early Welsh Saga Poetry*.

FURTHER READING
ANEIRIN; ANOETH; ARTHUR; AWDL; BARDIC ORDER; BEDWYR; BLEDDYN FARDD; BRÂN; BRANWEN; BRITAIN; BRYCHEINIOG; BRYNAICH; CADWALLON; CAMLAN; CASNODYN; COEL HEN; CULHWCH AC OLWEN; CYMRU; CYNDDELW; CYNDDYLAN; CYNFEIRDD; DAFYDD AP GWILYM; DAFYDD BENFRAS; ELIDIR SAIS; ENGLYN; ÉRIU; FIVE POETS; GENEALOGIES; GERAINT; GODODDIN; GOGYNFEIRDD; GWERFUL MECHAIN; GWYDION; HELEDD; HEROIC ETHOS; HISTORIA BRITTONUM; JUVENCUS; LINDISFARNE; LLYFR COCH HERGEST; LLYFR DU CAERFYRDDIN; LLYWARCH AP LLYWELYN; MATH FAB MATHONWY; NATURE POETRY; RHEGED; SEISYLL BRYFFWRCH; TALIESIN; TRIADS; ULSTER CYCLE; URIEN; WELSH; WELSH POETRY; WILLIAMS; WISDOM LITERATURE; Bromwich, *Beginnings of Welsh Poetry*; Henry, *Early English and Celtic Lyric*; Higley, *Between Languages*; Jarman, *Llên*

Cymru 8.125–49; Rowland, *Early Welsh Saga Poetry* 179–208; Rowland, *Ériu* 36.29–43; Sims-Williams, CMCS 26.27–63; Sims-Williams, CMCS 32.25–56; Sims-Williams, WHR 17.1–40; Ifor Williams, PBA 18.269–302.

JTK

Enlli (Bardsey), historically the most important of the Welsh island centres of devotion, lies at the tip of the Llŷn peninsula. The origins of its religious associations are unclear, though it may have been connected with an early Christian settlement at Anelog, near Aberdaron. In his *Itinerarium Kambriae* of 1188, Gerald de Barri (GIRALDUS CAMBRENSIS) relates that Enlli was occupied by monks whom he calls Colidei, usually understood to refer to the Irish monastic movement known as *Céili Dé* (Fellows of God). The Welsh vernacular tradition, however, associates the foundation of the island community with Cadfan and his successor as abbot, Lleuddad. Viking raids and other incursions from the 9th to the 11th centuries suggest that an unbroken ecclesiastical presence would have been unlikely. But from the brief *Vita* of the hermit Ælgar in the Book of LLANDAF (*Liber Landavensis*), it may be inferred that individual hermits and small communities maintained the island's tradition of religious life.

By the high Middle Ages, Enlli was considered to be the burial place of numerous significant religious figures, including DEINIOL, BEUNO, and also Dyfrig (Dubricius), whose relics were said to have been transported from Enlli in 1120 by order of Bishop Urban for the consecration of Llandaf cathedral. In the *Liber Landavensis* it is also stated that Enlli was the burial place of the presumably symbolic number of 20,000 saints, confessors, and martyrs. The *Historia* of GRUFFUDD AP CYNAN relates that he left a bequest to the church on Enlli upon his death in 1137, and the island itself was memorably celebrated in the *marwysgafn* (death-bed poem) of his court poet, MEILYR BRYDYDD. Its importance seems to have been recognized by Edward I who, in 1284, visited Enlli following his conquest of GWYNEDD. By the 13th century a priory of Augustinian canons had superseded the earlier *clas* (monastic community), and from then until the Reformation the island became a major centre of pilgrimage. The dangers of the journey, and the nature of the hospitality offered, were described vividly (and sometimes ruefully) by the Welsh poets of the time. The priory was dissolved *c.* 1537, although the burial of the recusant Huw ap Rhisiart of Bodwrda there in 1580 suggests that the island itself retained its religious significance for the Welsh: a tradition which has been echoed by 20th-century poets, among them T. Gwynn JONES and R. S. Thomas (see WELSH POETRY; ANGLO-WELSH LITERATURE). Enlli's secular community life since the Reformation has also been the subject of study, and writers and artists have continued to be associated with the island. A designated Site of Special Scientific Interest, Enlli was bought by the Bardsey Island Trust in 1979, and became a National Nature Reserve in 1986.

FURTHER READING
ANGLO-WELSH LITERATURE; BEUNO; CHRISTIANITY; DEINIOL; GIRALDUS CAMBRENSIS; GRUFFUDD AP CYNAN; GWYNEDD; JONES; LLANDAF; MEILYR BRYDYDD; WELSH POETRY; Allchin, *Bardsey: A Place of Pilgrimage*; Arnold, *Archaeologia Cambrensis* 147.97–132; Chitty, *Monks of Ynys Enlli*; Daniel, *Bardsey: Gate of Heaven*; Daniel, *Enlli: Porth y Nef*; Johns, *Trans. Caernarvonshire Historical Society* 21.14–43; R. Gerallt Jones & Arnold, *Enlli*; Jones Pierce, *Trans. Caernarvonshire Historical Society* 24.60–77 (repr. *Medieval Welsh Society* 391–407); Enid Roberts, *A'u Bryd ar Ynys Enlli*; D. Robinson, *Geography of Augustinian Settlement in Medieval England and Wales*; Glanmor Williams, *Welsh Church From Conquest to Reformation* s.v. Bardsey; H. D. Williams, *Ynys Enlli*.

M. Paul Bryant-Quinn

Entremont was a hill-fort (see OPPIDUM) located on high ground 1.6 km north of Aix-en-Provence in the south of France. It was destroyed in 122 BC by the Romans, and Aquae Sextiae, present-day Aix, was founded in its place. During its heyday, Entremont extended over 4 ha (about 10 acres) and was fortified by walls, which remain partly preserved to a height of 4 m. On the north side these ramparts were further strengthened with towers. In the north-western part of the enclosure, a sanctuary (see FANUM) was excavated; this was decorated with carved stone pillars with carved representations of severed heads (see HEAD CULT) and fragments of life-size figures. Fifteen human skulls which had been fixed to the stonework with nails were also found. Similar ceramic figures, representations of severed heads, and also the skulls themselves were found in the nearby fortified settlement at ROQUEPERTUSE.

Sculpture of severed heads from the shrine at Entremont

FURTHER READING
FANUM; HEAD CULT; OPPIDUM; ROQUEPERTUSE; SACRIFICE;
Benoit, *Entremont*; Musée Granet, *Archéologie d'Entremont au musée
Granet*; Salviat, *Entremont antique*.

PEB

Eochaid Buide

Eochaid Buide (Hiberno-Latin Echodius), king of Scottish DÁL RIATA 608–†29, the son and successor of the formidable AEDÁN MAC GABRÁIN, is treated as a figure of historical significance in the Life of COLUM CILLE by ADOMNÁN (1.9) and in the ANNALS of Ulster. According to the former, before the 'battle of the Miathi', Colum Cille asked Aedán about the kingdom's succession. Aedán replied that he did not know which son—Artúr, Eochaid Find, or Domangart—would rule after him. To which the saint answered that none of those would succeed, but all three would fall in battle, slain by enemies. He added that if Aedán had younger sons, they should be brought, and the one who ran to Colum Cille would succeed; this, indeed, is what the young Eochaid Buide did. The prophecy was fulfilled: Artúr and Eochaid Find died fighting the Miathi, and Domangart fighting the Saxons. The story is meant to illustrate not only Colum Cille's supernatural foresight, but that he was to be heeded by kings specifically on issues of succession and military matters. Eochaid's death notice in the Annals of Ulster cites *Liber Cuanach* (The book of Cuanu) as saying that he was king of the PICTS, the

first Scottish king for whom such a claim is made, thus asserting the long-term political ambitions of the SCOTS over 200 years before the traditional foundation of the unified kingdom of Picts and Scots under CINAED MAC AILPÍN. In the Middle Irish saga, *Fled Dúin na nGéd* (The feast of Dún na nGéd), Eochaid figures as the grandfather of the Congal Caech of ULAID (†637; see MAG ROTH), but, since the two were near contemporaries, this is doubtful. The common Old Irish man's name *Eochaid*—also the name of Eochaid Buide's brother—is Celtic and based on a word for 'horse', Old Irish *ech* < PROTO-CELTIC **ekʷos*. In Scottish Dál Riata, the name perhaps commemorates the old local tribal name recorded by PTOLEMY as Ἐπίδιοι *Epidii* < Proto-Celtic **Ekʷodii* 'horsemen'. The epithet *buide* means 'fair' or 'red-haired'; cf. the Gaulish tribal name *Badio-casses*.

FURTHER READING
ADOMNÁN; AEDÁN MAC GABRÁIN; ANNALS; CINAED MAC AILPÍN; COLUM CILLE; DÁL RIATA; MAG ROTH; PICTS; PROTO-CELTIC; PTOLEMY; SCOTS; ULAID; Alan O. Anderson & Marjorie O. Anderson, *Adomnán's Life of Columba* xxiiff., 32–3; Sharpe, *Life of St Columba / Adomnán of Iona* 27, 61, 119–20, 355–7; Ann Williams et al., *Biographical Dictionary of Dark Age Britain* 133–4.

JTK

Eochaid son of Rhun

Eochaid son of Rhun was king of the PICTS (878–89). In the CHRONICLE OF THE KINGS OF ALBA, the only source of information about his reign, he is described as the 'son of the king of the BRITONS' and the grandson of CINAED MAC AILPÍN by a daughter. It has been assumed that his father was the Rhun who was son of Arthgal, king of the Britons of YSTRAD CLUD, killed in 872, but we do not know for certain that this Rhun was king of the Britons, and the chronology seems compressed. Eochaid came to power, presumably through this cognatic claim, after the killing of Aed mac Cinaeda and during a period of severe pressure on the Pictish kingship from Norse raids. He may himself have begun as king of the Britons, though this too is uncertain. His accomplice, in what the Chronicle describes almost as an interregnum or usurpation, was his foster-son Ciricius (Giric mac Dúngaile, according to other texts), there also called his *ordinator*. At any rate, for a decade Pictland was ruled by men whose power base seems quite different from that of previous rulers. The Chronicle sees signs of divine disapproval in the eclipse on the feast-day of St Cyricius, after which Eochaid and his foster-son were expelled from the kingship. It has been pointed out that this eclipse occurred in 885; therefore our chronology for this reign (and indeed, the Chronicle as a whole) is in some way askew. Further problems are added if this is the Eochaid, 'king of DÁL RIATA', whose daughter Land was given in marriage to an Irish king, Niall Glúndub (Hudson, *Kings of Celtic Scotland* 56). As Dumville states (*Kings, Clerics and Chronicles in Scotland* 79), this episode offers 'rich material for speculation, enthusiastically seized by writers on ninth-century North British history from our chronicler to the present day'. On the name, see EOCHAID BUIDE.

PRIMARY SOURCES
ED. & TRANS. Marjorie O. Anderson, *Kings and Kingship in Early Scotland* 250–1 (Chronicle of the Kings of Alba); Hudson, *Scottish Historical Review* 77.129–61 (The Scottish Chronicle); Alan O. Anderson, *Early Sources of Scottish History* 1.357–8, 363–8.

FURTHER READING
BRITONS; CHRONICLE OF THE KINGS OF ALBA; CINAED MAC AILPÍN; DÁL RIATA; EOCHAID BUIDE; PICTS; YSTRAD CLUD; Dumville, *Kings, Clerics and Chronicles in Scotland* 73–86; Hudson, *Kings of Celtic Scotland* 55–8; Smyth, *Warlords and Holy Men* 215–18.

Thomas Owen Clancy

The **Éoganacht** were a powerful historic dynasty or, more properly, a federation of related dynasties who virtually monopolized the KINGSHIP of Munster (MUMU) from the 5th to the 10th centuries. Their power within the province was practically unchallenged up to the ascendancy of Mathgamain mac Cennétig of the DÁL gCAIS in AD 964.

The actual origins of the Éoganacht are obscure, but the shared identity of several septs (royal lineages) was based on a doctrine of common descent from Conall Corc (CORC OF CAISEL), the legendary founder of the royal seat at CAISEL MUMAN. Using the GENEALOGIES and counting generations back from his dated descendants, Corc would have flourished c. 400, and he was himself a distant descendant of Mug Nuadat, whose name means 'Servant of [the god] Nuadu' (see NÓDONS). Mug is also known as Éogan Taídlech or Éogan Fitheccach, bynames which probably arose to link

Mug's story to the origin legend of the Éoganacht. Mug belongs to the remote prehistoric horizon of the pedigree. He is said to have originally divided Ireland (ÉRIU) in half, in an arrangement with CONN CÉTCHATHACH—Leth Moga (Mug's half), the southern half, and Leth Cuinn (Conn's half), the northern half. In the extant tradition, the usual understanding is that the Éoganacht dynasties are named from Éogan Már, grandson of Mug (himself also known as Éogan) and father of the first king of the line, Fiachu Muillethan, and more distant ancestor of Conall Corc.

The name *Éogan* is associated in early accounts with the Celtic word for the yew tree, Middle Irish *eó*, later also *í*, pointing to an Old Celtic name **Iwogenos* 'Born of the yew' (cf. Gaulish *Ivorigi* 'Yew-king' [gen.]). In the legend of Conall Corc's founding of Caisel, a vision reveals that the royal seat of Munster was to be founded where a yew tree grew on a stone. The main religious foundation of the Éoganacht at Emly, Co. Limerick (Old Irish Imleach Ibar), derives its name from another Old Irish word for yew (*ibar* < Celtic *eburo-*), and a surviving decorated shrine from this site was made of yew-wood. These associations imply that the similar-looking Welsh name *Owain*, Old Welsh EUGEIN, would not be related, since the latter probably derives from Latin *Eugēnius*.

The central three septs of the dynasty, which inhabited east and central Munster—Éoganacht Chaisil, Éoganacht Glendamnach, and Éoganacht Áine—formed a core, with the great majority of the kings of Munster coming from these groups. There was a relatively stable centralized government in the province for a period in the 7th and 8th centuries under a system of kingship rotation amongst these three septs. A lesser sept closely related to that of Caisel was the Éoganacht Airthir Chliach.

An 8th-century genealogical poem (O'Brien, *Corpus Genealogiarum Hiberniae* 1.199–204) goes to some pains to show the importance of the outlying septs—Éoganacht Locha Léin and Éoganacht Raithlinn, naming them as overkings of the *aithech thúatha* or 'subject tribes' of Iarmumu (west Munster) and Dessmumu (south Munster), respectively. These two groups, particularly the former, were independent in most respects, though nominally conforming to the concept of a high-kingship at Caisel. From the accession of Feidlimid mac Crimthainn in AD 820 until the loss of the crown to

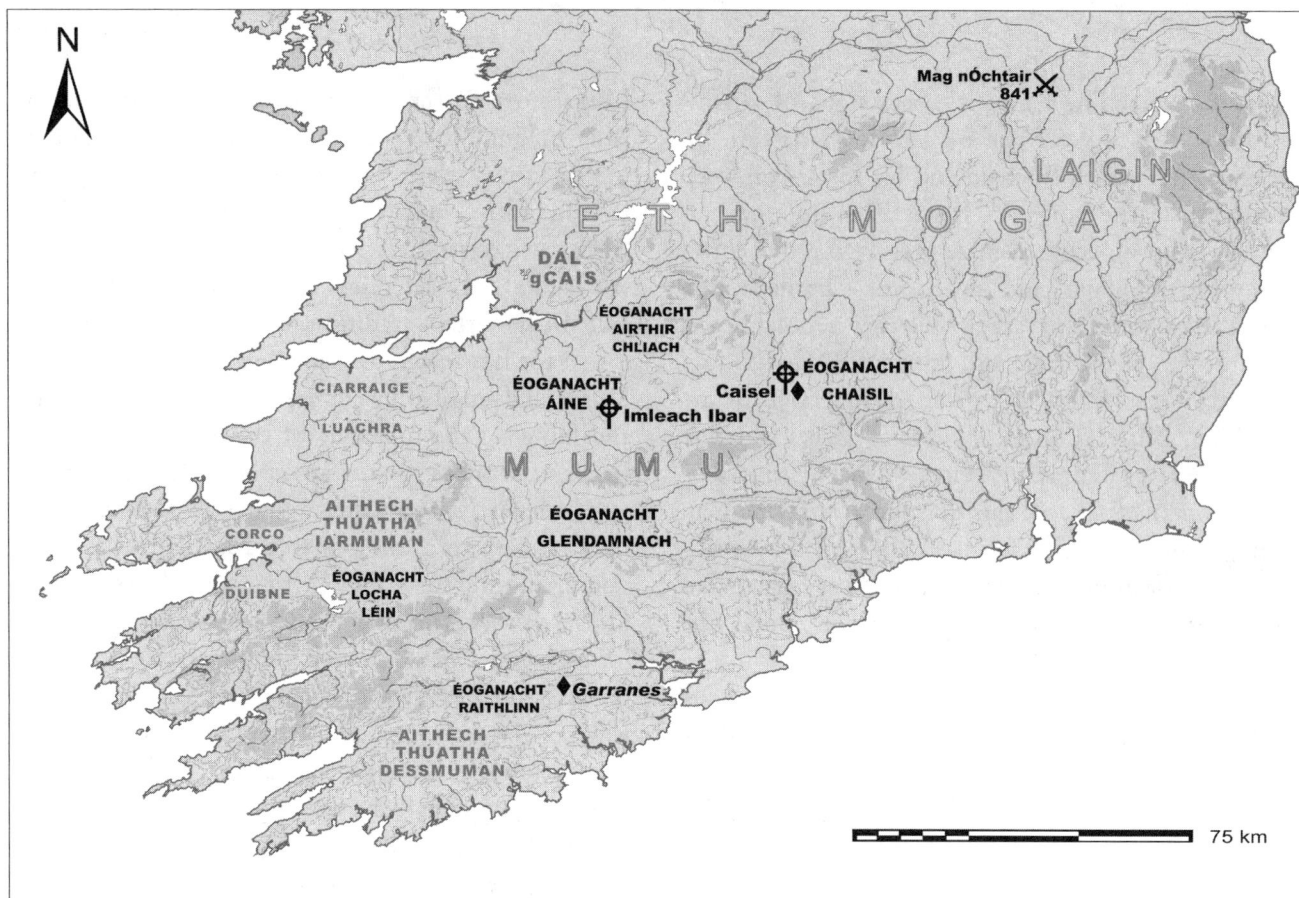

The Éoganacht in early medieval Munster (Mumu)

the Dál gCais, the Éoganacht Chaisil maintained a monopoly on the Munster kingship. This situation was facilitated by the loss of power of Éoganacht Locha Léin after the *aithech thúatha* of Iarmumu—including the Corco Duibne, Corco Orchae, and Ciarraige Luachra—transferred their allegiances directly to Caisel.

Such new dynastic cohesion at home allowed Feidlimid to become the most formidable rival produced by the Éoganacht to challenge the greatest power of Leth Cuinn, namely the Uí Néill overkings of Tara (Teamhair). Feidlimid carried out a long campaign of alternating warfare and political man-oeuvring against Niall mac Aedo, the king of Tara at the time. However, his surprise defeat by Niall at Mag nÓchtair in AD 841 put an end to any Éoganacht hopes of attaining real Ireland-wide power. The provincial kingship of Munster, lost to the Dál gCais in the 10th century, was wrested back for several decades in the 12th century, during which time King Cormac Mac

Cárrthaig commissioned the famous Romanesque chapel on the Rock of Caisel.

From an archaeological perspective, it has been suggested that a large trivallate ring-fort excavated at Garranes, Co. Cork, was a royal site of the Éoganacht Raithlinn. Garranes, where settlement activity has been dated to *c.* AD 500, has yielded evidence of long-distance trade connections with France and the eastern Mediterranean region in the form of exotic pottery and Merovingian glassware.

PRIMARY SOURCES
Dillon, *Ériu* 16.61–73 ('The Story of the Finding of Cashel'); O'Brien, *Corpus Genealogiarum Hiberniae 1.*

SECONDARY SOURCES
CAISEL MUMAN; CONN CÉTCHATHACH; CORC OF CAISEL; DÁL G-CAIS; ÉRIU; EUGEIN; GENEALOGIES; KINGSHIP; MUMU; NÓDONS; TEAMHAIR; UÍ NÉILL; Bourke, *Journal of the Royal Society of Antiquaries of Ireland* 124.163–209; Byrne, *Irish Kings and High-Kings*; Charles-Edwards, *Early Christian Ireland*; MacKillop, *Dictionary of Celtic Mythology*; Mytum, *Origins of Early Christian Ireland*; Ó Riordáin, PRIA C 47.77–150; Sproule, *Ériu* 35.31–7.

SÓF

Éoganán mac Oengusa (Uuen son of Unuist, r. 837–9)

Éoganán mac Oengusa (Uuen son of Unuist, r. 837–9) was king of both the Scots and the Picts, significantly some years before the usual date assigned to the foundation of the united kingdom of Alba by Cinaed mac Ailpín c. 845. The son of the Pictish king Unuist son of Uurguist and also a member of the main Cenél nGabráin dynastic lineage of Dál Riata, he appears in the king-lists of both peoples. He fell among heavy losses in a battle noted in the Annals of Ulster between the heathen Norse and the men of Fortrinn, roughly present-day Perthshire (Peairt). It is probable that Viking pressure contributed to the consolidation of Scottish and Pictish leadership, based in this inland region.

FURTHER READING
ALBA; ANNALS; CINAED MAC AILPÍN; DÁL RIATA; PICTS; SCOTS; UNUIST; Marjorie O. Anderson, *Kings and Kingship in Early Scotland* 193, 195; Smyth, *Warlords and Holy Men* 175–80; Ann Williams et al., *Biographical Dictionary of Dark Age Britain* 134–5.

JTK

Ephorus

Ephorus, Ἔφορος (c. 405–c. 330 BC), of Cyme in Aeolia was a Greek author whose works included a 30-book universal history, Ἱστορίαι. It survives only fragmentarily, but was utilized by several later classical writers, some of whom were important sources on the ancient Celts: Diodorus Siculus (the main extant vehicle for Ephorus), Plutarch, Polyaenus, Polybius, and Trogus Pompeius. His works seem to have been the earliest extensive account of the Greek colonies of the western Mediterranean and their neighbours. Strabo (4.4.6) cites Ephorus as stating that Celtica was so large that it included most of the Iberian Peninsula down to Gades (Cadiz) in the neighbourhood of the Straits of Gibraltar and, in the same passage, that the Celts had, in earlier times (i.e. Ephorus' day), been strongly adverse to becoming fat, and punished young men who became potbellied. The former statement, though not decisive in proving that most of what is now Spain and Portugal was Celtic-speaking in the 4th century BC, is nonetheless important evidence in assessing the linguistic situation. Although Ephorus is never quoted as a source of information on Armorica, Britain, or Ireland, Hawkes thought it likely that Ephorus had transmitted the ancient names *Albiones* 'the Britons', and *Hierni* 'the Irish' (see ÉRIU), to the Greeks. However, these names are usually traced back to an older text—the Massaliote Periplus.

FURTHER READING
ALBION; ARMORICA; BRITAIN; BRITONS; DIODORUS SICULUS; ÉRIU; IBERIAN PENINSULA; MASSALIOTE PERIPLUS; PLUTARCH; POLYBIUS; STRABO; TROGUS POMPEIUS AND JUSTIN; Freeman, *Ireland and the Classical World*; Hammond & Scullard, *Oxford Classical Dictionary* s.v. Ephorus; Hawkes, *Pytheas*; Pauly, *Der kleine Pauly* s.v. Ephoros.

JTK

Epona

Epona's name is Celtic, specifically Gallo-Brittonic (P-Celtic), and means 'horse goddess'. She is the most abundantly attested Celtic deity of the Roman Empire. Evidence for her cult is strongest in central and eastern Gaul, as well as the military zones of the Rhine and Danube frontiers, and northern Roman Britain. Within the military, the cult recurs among, but was not limited to, cavalry units and units recruited from Gaul. Epona is mentioned by the Roman author Juvenal (see GREEK AND ROMAN ACCOUNTS §9), but we know of the cult mainly from INSCRIPTIONS and accompanying images, many on Romano-Celtic altars with a *focus* cut into the top for the pouring of libations or presenting other offerings. In the inscriptions, almost all of which are in Latin, with far fewer in Greek, she is sometimes called *dea* 'goddess' or *regina* 'queen' and is often grouped with other deities, for example, the following on an altar at Pförring, Bavaria:

```
CAMPES(TRIBUS) ET
EPONAE ALA I
SING(ULARIUM) P(IA) F(IDELIS)
C(IVIUM) R(OMANORUM CVI P(RAE)EST
AEL(IUS) BASSIANUS
PRAEF(ECTUS) V(OTUM) S(OLVIT) L(IBENS) M(ERITO)
```

To the gods of the parade ground and to Epona, the devoted and loyal first *ala* [auxiliary cavalry unit] of *singulares*, Roman citizens led by the prefect Aelius Bassianus, in fulfilment of a vow. (CIL III nos. 5910 and 11909)

From Auchendavy on the Antonine Wall in Scotland (Alba), a Roman altar reads:

MARTI

MINERVAE

CAMPESTRIBVS HERC(V)L(I)

EPONAE

VICTORIAE

M(ARCVS) COCCEI(VS)

FIRMVS

C(ENTVRIO) LEG(IONIS) II AVG(VSTAE)

To Mars, Minerva, the Goddesses of the Parade Ground, Hercules, Epona, and Victory, Marcus Cocceius Firmus, centurion of the Second Legion Augusta [set up this altar]. (RIB no. 2177)

A small bronze plaque for a donkey cart found at the Gallo-Roman centre ALESIA carries the punched inscription:

DEA(E) EPON(A)E. SATIGENUS SOLEMNI(S)

FIL(IUS).V(OTUM).S(OLVIT).L(IBENS)

To the goddess Epona, Satigenus son of Solemnis willingly fulfilled his vow.

The name *Satigenus* is Celtic.

The Epona cult was richly visual. Relief sculptures often show her riding a horse side-saddle, the goddess astride the horse being more common in the territory of the Treveri in north-east Gaul. She sometimes appears with a foal, particularly in the territory of the AEDUI. Images showing the goddess enthroned were popular in the Rhine–Danube military frontier zone and are probably to be understood as imperial iconography. The figure of the horse cut into the hill at UFFINGTON may reflect a related cult in pre-Roman Britain.

In CELTIC STUDIES, Epona is often mentioned—and attempts have been made to recover her myth—in connection with supernatural female characters in early Irish and Welsh literature who have strong thematic and narrative associations with horses, such as MACHA and RHIANNON (cf. also SOVEREIGNTY MYTH), as well as the Welsh folk custom of the MARI LWYD. On the likelihood that traditions of Epona have survived in Continental chivalric romances, see ROMANCE LYRIC (also ARTHURIAN LITERATURE [6] §2; COURTLY LOVE).

The root of the name *Epona* also occurs in Old Irish *ech* 'horse' and the Gaulish month name EQVOS found on the COLIGNY calendar, both from INDO-EUROPEAN **ekwos* 'horse'. On this type of divine name-formation, cf. DAMONA; MATRONAE; NEMETONA; SIRONA.

PRIMARY SOURCES

INSCRIPTIONS. CIL 3, nos. 5910, 11909; RIB no. 2177.

FURTHER READING

AEDUI; ALBA; ALESIA; ANTONINE WALL; ARTHURIAN LITERATURE [6]; BRITAIN; CELTIC STUDIES; COLIGNY; COURTLY LOVE; DAMONA; DANUBE; GALLO-BRITTONIC; GAUL; GREEK AND ROMAN ACCOUNTS; INDO-EUROPEAN; INSCRIPTIONS; MACHA; MARI LWYD; MATRONAE; NEMETONA; P-CELTIC; RHIANNON; RHINE; ROMANCE LYRIC; SIRONA; SOVEREIGNTY MYTH; UFFINGTON; Sioned Davies & Jones, *Horse in Celtic Culture*; Euskirchen, *Bericht der Römisch-Germanischen Kommission Deutsches Archäologisches Institut* 74.607–838; Green, *Symbol and Image in Celtic Religious Art* 16–24; Gruffydd, *Rhiannon*; Linduff, *Latomus* 38.817–37; Magnen & Thévenot, *Épona*.

WEBSITE. www.epona.net

JTK

Éremón mac Míled was a major figure in Irish LEGENDARY HISTORY and, according to LEBAR GABÁLA ÉRENN and related texts, one of the sons of MÍL ESPÁINE. He was one of the primary leaders of the Milesians in their conquest of Ireland, and was married to Tea, after whom, according to the DINDSHENCHAS, both Teamhair Luachra (Co. Kerry) and Teamhair Breg (Co. Meath) are named.

Following the final defeat of the TUATH DÉ by the Milesians at *cath Tailteann* (the battle of Tailtiu), Ireland was divided between Éremón and his brother Éber in accordance with a judgement pronounced by their brother and lawgiver, AMAIRGEN MAC MÍLED.

The country was divided along a glacial ridge, Eiscir Riada, which runs from Galway Bay in the west to near Dublin (BAILE ÁTHA CLIATH) in the east. Éremón was given the northern half and Éber the southern in an arrangement which mirrors the (supposedly) later division of Ireland between Mug Nuadat and CONN CÉTCHATHACH (cf. ÉOGANACHT).

However, the agreement broke down during a dispute over several small hills, and in the ensuing war Éber was slain by Éremón, who assumed kingship of the island as a whole. Nonetheless, the strife among the descendants of Míl continued, and Éremón had to repeat his fratricide by killing Amairgen in *cath Bile Theineadh* (the battle of the tree of Teine) before order was imposed. Éremón is credited also with sending the invading PICTS (CRUITHIN) to ALBA (Scotland) after they realized they were not powerful enough to engage him in battle.

Similar to the Mug/Conn division, the partition of Ireland by the sons of Míl was probably a creation of 7th- or 8th-century writers to explain and justify the ideological division of that period between the prestigious royal site of CAISEL MUMAN and that of Tara (TEAMHAIR). In their pseudo-historical and genealogical propaganda, the Éoganachta of the south-west and the Uí NÉILL of Ireland's midlands and north traced their lineages back to Éber and Éremón, respectively, which legitimized their regional hegemonies. It is only in the later (11th-century) *Lebar Gabála Érenn* that Éremón is seen to ascend to high-kingship through self-defence against the aggression of Éber. This newer doctrine reflects the increasing reality of an Irish national high-kingship from the 9th century onwards.

T. F. O'Rahilly (Ó RATHILE) was no doubt correct that the name *Éremón* was based on ÉRIU (Ireland). Most probably, *Éremón* arose through the ingenious etymological speculation so characteristic of Irish learning in the early medieval period. For linguistic reasons, it is not likely to derive from an ancient cognate of the Sanskrit mythological figure *Aryaman* (though this Sanskrit name is possibly related to the Old Irish name *Airem* and the name of the Galatian chief *Ariamnes*, cf. PHYLARCHUS).

PRIMARY SOURCES
ED. & TRANS. Gwynn, *Metrical Dindshenchas*; Keating, *Foras Feasa ar Éirinn*; Macalister, *Lebor Gabála Éireann*; Meyer, ZCP 8.291–338 (The Laud Genealogies and Tribal Histories).

FURTHER READING
ALBA; AMAIRGEN MAC MILÉD; BAILE ÁTHA CLIATH; CAISEL MUMAN; CONN CÉTCHATHACH; CRUITHIN; DINDSHENCHAS; ÉOGANACHT; ÉRIU; LEBAR GABÁLA ÉRENN; LEGENDARY HISTORY; MÍL ESPÁINE; Ó RATHILE; PHYLARCHUS; PICTS; TEAMHAIR; TUATH DÉ; UÍ NÉILL; Byrne, *Irish Kings and High-Kings*; MacKillop, *Dictionary of Celtic Mythology*; O'Rahilly, *Early Irish History and Mythology*.

SÓF

Erispoë was the son of NOMINOË and leader of autonomous Brittany (BREIZH). He reigned from 851 to 857, but had already taken on a leadership rôle at several points during his father's reign, even as early as

843. At one stage in the conflict with Louis the Pious, king of the Franks, Erispoë was recognized as Louis' vassal, and his lordship over the Breton marches (Frankish–Breton frontier zone) was confirmed. In 857 Erispoë was murdered by his cousin and foster-brother, SALOMON, along with Salomon's brother, Almar.

FURTHER READING
BREIZH; NOMINOË; SALOMON; Nora K. Chadwick, *Early Brittany*; Chédeville & Guillotel, *La Bretagne des saints et des rois, Ve–Xe siècle*; Giot et al., *British Settlement of Brittany*.

AM

Ériu [1] is the Old IRISH name for Ireland, corresponding to Modern Irish *Éire*. The spelling *Ériu* remains common in sources of the Middle Irish period (c. 900–c. 1200). The corresponding ancient form *Iveriō* and its earliest attestation are discussed in the entries on MASSALIOTE PERIPLUS and AVIENUS. For the several related names for Ireland and the Irish in GREEK AND ROMAN ACCOUNTS, see HIBERNIA. The etymology of *Ériu* and the meaning and implications of some related forms are discussed in the next section of this article, and this is followed by an outline of early Ireland down to the Anglo-Norman incursions that began in AD 1169.

§1. ETYMOLOGY

Iverio (Primitive Irish *Īweriū* > Old Irish *Ériu*) is not attested until the 3rd century AD, but the people name derived from *Hierni, Iverni* Ιουερνοι, &c. (Primitive Irish *Īwernī* 'people of Iverio/Ériu' > Middle Irish *Érainn*) was recorded centuries earlier, showing the island's name to be at least as old. *Iverni* and *Iverio* are Celtic names. Celtic *Īweriū* derives from INDO-EUROPEAN *PiHwerjoHn* 'The Fertile Land' and is the cognate of Greek πιειρα *píeira*, Sanskrit *pivarī*, feminine adjectives meaning 'fat, rich', mostly applied to land in Greek; cf. the district name Πιερία *Piería* in Thessaly. The place-name *Ériu* has, as a byform, a common Old Irish noun *íriu*, meaning 'earth, land'. The same Indo-European root *peiH-* 'to be fat, swell' is the base of two names of the ancestors of the Irish in LEGENDARY HISTORY, *Iär* (< *Īweros*) and *Íth*. They were probably originally eponyms (namesake founders), but by the literary period the connection was no longer obvious due to sound changes that had occurred already in the prehistoric period. In LEBAR GABÁLA ÉRENN, Íth was the first of the followers of MÍL ESPÁINE to see Ireland from Spain. Later, he is the first ashore and praises the country's abundance, addressing the indigenous TUATH DÉ: '. . . you dwell in a good land. Abundant are its mast and honey and wheat and fish'. He is then the first Gael to die in Ireland. By the time of the *Geography* of PTOLEMY (2nd century AD, using 1st-century sources), the group name Ιουερνοι *Iverni*, which had once referred to all the Irish, had been marginalized, appearing as a tribal name in the southwest. This agrees with usage in early IRISH LITERATURE, where *Érainn* is used for tribal and dynastic groups, most notably in MUMU/Munster. However, sagas such as TOGAIL BRUIDNE DA DERGA ('The Destruction of Da Derga's Hostel') and *Cath Maige Mucraime* (The battle of Mag Mucraime) recall that prehistoric Érainn kings had ruled TEAMHAIR (Tara) in the Midlands and held sway throughout Ireland. St Patrick uses *Hiberionaci* (*Epistola* §16), genitive plural *Hiberionacum* (*Confessio* §23) to mean 'the Irish', corresponding exactly to Modern *Éireannaí*, genitive *Éireannach* 'the Irish' < Primitive Irish *Īwerionākī*, *Īwerionākan*.

§2. WHEN WERE THE FIRST IRISH?

Like the Isle of Man (ELLAN VANNIN), but unlike the other CELTIC COUNTRIES, Ireland as an island does not owe its creation to wars and migrations, but rather to rising seas at the end of the last Ice Age *c.* 10,000 BC. Thus, it is not misleading to speak simply of Ireland when referring to ancient times, rather than 'the territory that is now Ireland', as is sometimes necessary with the other countries. Similarly, when we ask who were the first Irish, this can simply mean the first human beings in Ireland, in which case the answer is the fishers and hunter-gatherers of the post-glacial Mesolithic from *c.* 7000 BC. If, alternatively, we mean the biological ancestors of the present inhabitants, we do not have enough ancient DNA from Ireland to attempt an answer, even if we were able to master the theoretical complexities of the issue. From the point of view of CELTIC STUDIES, the question of Irish origins usually focuses on the origins of the Gaels, meaning *Gaeilgeoirí*, speakers of the Irish language, or of an ancient language which became the GOIDELIC family and no other. Since Goidelic speech most likely became established in Ireland when there were few—or

more probably, no—written records produced in or about Ireland, no certain date can be assigned to the emergence of the Gaels, and a large number of different theories have been advanced. In canvassing ancient Ireland below, we shall not concentrate exclusively on either possible definition—human beings in Ireland or Gaelic speakers, but will bear both in mind, noting when the two were certainly the same, were likely to have been the same, or most probably diverged.

§3. PREHISTORY

Owing to its remoteness from the literate civilizations of the Mediterranean and having remained independent of Rome, there are almost no recorded events in Ireland before the 5th century AD. In part, this deficit is fortuitously redressed by the fact that many ancient oaks have been preserved in Irish bogs and have provided a method of absolute dating by their tree-rings, with a continuous sequence now extended well back into the 6th millennium BC, unrivalled elsewhere in the Old World. As well as the relatively small number of Irish archaeological sites preserving samples of wood adequate to yield to-the-year dates directly, the Irish oak sequence is used to check and correct (calibrate) the more common radiocarbon dating method. Thus, we have a sound framework of absolute dates for prehistoric Ireland.

The Mesolithic (*c.* 7000–*c.* 4000 BC). Middle Stone Age inhabitants are reflected mainly in distinctive stone tools (microlith industries), but circular huts occupied for all or most of the year over several centuries from around 7000 BC have been found at Mountsandel near Coleraine, Co. Derry (Cúil Raithin, Contae Dhoire). No scholar has convincingly suggested how the early hunters of post-glacial Ireland could possibly have spoken a language that evolved into Gaelic, nor any form of Celtic or INDO-EUROPEAN at all. Therefore, the Mesolithic inhabitants were not Irish in the ethnolinguistic sense. It is therefore almost certain that a pre-Indo-European language was spoken in Ireland before Celtic (whence Gaelic) was introduced. From the Old Irish period (*c.* AD 600–*c.* 900) onward, the Irish language has possessed both sounds and word-order patterns which appear exceptional when compared with those of the other Indo-European languages, and many linguists would see these features as the likely results of the adoption of Celtic by Ireland's earlier pre-Indo-European population (cf. HAMITO-SEMITIC HYPOTHESIS).

The Neolithic (*c.* 4000–*c.* 2400 BC). On the beginnings of settled agriculture in Ireland, see AGRICULTURE [2]. Handmade decorated pottery of various sizes and shapes appears in the 4th millennium. Small, dispersed domestic settlements, suitable for nuclear or extended families, with various building types are the norm; for example, at Lough Gur, Co. Limerick (Contae Luimnigh) both rectangular and round structures are defined by postholes and stone footings.

The great megalithic tombs of the Neolithic have made an enduring impact on the Irish landscape and tradition. There are several subtypes: hundreds of 'court tombs' are distributed over Ireland's northern half; 'portal tombs' occur also in the north as well as pockets in west and south-east; the distinctively shaped 'wedge tombs' occur mostly in a dense arc from Antrim (Aontroim) in the north-east, over the western half to Co. Cork (Contae Chorcaí). Of the hundreds of passage tombs, distributed mainly over the north and east, the most famous are those of the valley of the Boyne (Old Irish BóAND), including Newgrange (BRUG NA BóINNE), Knowth, and Dowth (DUBHADH). Although these great tombs figure importantly in early Irish mythological literature, in beliefs concerning the OTHERWORLD (see also SíD), in modern folk beliefs concerning the FAIRIES (and it has been suggested that actual Neolithic beliefs concerning the afterlife have survived in connection with them), it is doubtful that the megalith builders spoke a language that became Gaelic. However, Renfrew identifies Celts, including speakers of Proto-Irish in Ireland, among the first farmers in western Europe *c.* 5000–4000 BC, supposing that Proto-Indo-European spread from Anatolia on the 'wave of advance' of the settled agricultural way of life and then evolved locally throughout Europe and western Asia into the various historically attested Indo-European languages. This great time depth with millennia of local development seems unlikely in view of how similar the Irish of the OGAM inscriptions of the 5th- and 6th-centuries AD remained to the other ancient CELTIC LANGUAGES.

The Copper Age (*c.* 2400–*c.* 2200 BC). As in Britain, Brittany and other parts of France, southern Scandi-navia, and Atlantic Spain and Portugal, daggers and other artefacts made of cast copper (sometimes hardened with arsenic) occur together as what has been termed a 'Beaker assemblage', named for the distinctive biconical, round-bottomed, usually decorated ceramic vessel, and also including archery equipment. Orna-ments of sheet gold with geometric impressed decora-tion also appear at this stage. In Britain, Beaker buri-als are usually crouched inhumations, sometimes 'cists' lined with flagstones. But in Ireland, Beaker burials are found in the megalithic tombs, particularly the wedge type, possibly as later insertions into Neolithic monuments. A Beaker settlement at Newgrange is associated with the earliest horse remains in Ireland. Overall, the Beaker phenomenon has been seen as the arrival of the metal-using warrior aristocracy who had close cultural connections with the Continent. DILLON (with CHADWICK) and Harbison have argued for the Beaker Copper Age as the horizon to which the origins of the Irish language can be traced.

The Bronze Age (*c.* 2200 BC–). True bronze, as opposed to arsenic-hardened copper, alloys copper with about 10% tin, which was regularly in use in Ireland before the end of the third millennium BC. No doubt owing to the fact that Ireland possessed plentiful supplies of copper and, more especially, gold (in the Wicklow mountains and elsewhere), it enjoyed a particularly rich, and progressively richer, Bronze Age, as a vital node in trading networks linked to ARMORICA, BRITAIN, the IBERIAN PENINSULA, west-central Europe, and southern Scandinavia, with a growing diversity of arte-fact types—ornaments, vessels, weapons, and tools—and a steady technical advance in metallurgical skills. A few major trends—most of them paralleled else-where in north-west Europe—are noted here.

Beaker vessels gave way to a range of Early Bronze Age ceramic types known according to their shapes as bowls (lower profile) and the more elongated vases and urns, most of which have chevrons and other types of abstract linear decoration impressed on the exte-rior. Single (as opposed to collective) graves prevail, with these vessels in the burials, both cremations and crouched inhumations; stone cists are common.

Without associated burials, megaliths are hard to date, but it is likely that many of Ireland's standing stone alignments and circles, such as the complex at

Beaghmore, Co. Tyrone (Contae Thír Eoghain), date from the Early Bronze Age.

By the Middle Bronze Age (from *c.* 1500 BC), the simple cast flat dagger and axe-head of the Copper and Early Bronze Age have evolved into a range of sophisticated forms. The dagger has given way to the longer dirk and the long (up to about 30 cm) needle-like stabbing weapon, the rapier, both attached to handles of perishable material by means of two bronze rivets. The halberd is another adaptation of the early dagger form in which the pointed blade is attached at right angles to a shaft to be used as a dagger-axe. There are also true spears with bronze heads of varying lengths and blade shapes; these were attached to wooden shafts, often by means of both a concave socket and loops for tying with cord. Bronze axe-heads were attached to wooden hafts with a flange extending from the back of the head, opposite the cutting edge. One subgroup of this basic shape of axe is known as a palstave. From this growth in the bronze arsenal we can assume the rising social importance of bronze smiths and their warrior aristocratic patrons through the 2nd millennium.

Neck ornaments are prominent among Bronze Age gold work. Crescent-shaped sheet-gold lunulae with incised geometric design occur in the Early Bronze Age. Bar and ribbon TORCS, usually twisted and with a simple clasp formed by reverse bends at the two ends, become common in the Middle Bronze Age and are found in western GAUL and Britain, as well as in Ireland. These objects can be interpreted as displaying the special status of an emerging élite social group.

Also within the Middle Bronze Age, fine metalwork in both bronze and gold comes to be found more commonly in hoards from wet settings—lakes, rivers, and bogs—thus anticipating the WATERY DEPOSITIONS of the Celtic IRON AGE. Conversely, burials become rarer. Cult practices were evidently changing and, arguably, the religious beliefs behind them.

The Late Bronze Age (*c.* 1150 BC–). The tree-ring sequence reveals a major climatic disaster between 1159 and 1142 BC, which can be attributed to the effects of a massive eruption of Mount Hekla in Iceland. This point also appears to be a significant watershed for several cultural developments—some breaking with the past and others continuing trends noted in the Middle Bronze Age. Burials remain rare to non-existent, and we have no more ceramics for several centuries. By the early first millennium BC, there are CAULDRONS and tall buckets of riveted sheet bronze, but probably not in sufficient numbers to replace the discontinued pottery completely. At DÚN AONGHASA and Haughey's Fort near EMAIN MACHAE, massive fortified sites were built in the Late Bronze Age. Among the tool and weapon types, the socketed axe, with its single loop and bronze-economizing hollow interior socket, is widespread. True SWORDS appear with leaf-shaped blades, effective for slashing as well as stabbing, and parallel central European Late Bronze Age (HALLSTATT B) types. The first of these types is the Ballintober, named after a find in Co. Mayo; the Ballintober swords appeared by the 12th century BC and are widely distributed in northern and central Ireland, as well as Britain (numerous examples were found in the THAMES). Successive sword types correspond closely to the Continental sequence. Circular shields occur, such as the large bronze example from Lough Gur, Co. Limerick, decorated and strengthened with concentric circles of répoussé nobs.

A wide variety of rich gold ornaments are known from Late Bronze Age Ireland, for which we have specialist archaeological terminology (which may in some cases ignorantly conceal their actual function): elaborate three-part neck ornaments known as gorgets, also bracelets, sleeve-fasteners, and dress-fasteners. Bronze jewellery includes a variety of decorative dress pins.

Generally speaking, the richest and most abundant metalwork of the Irish Late Bronze Age is from its final stage, the Dowris Phase (*c.* 850–*c.* 600 BC), named for a remarkably rich watery deposition from Dowris, Co. Offaly (Contae Uíbh Fhailí). The period is at times called 'Ireland's First Golden Age' with reference to the second period of exceptional artistic brilliance in the 6th to 9th centuries AD (see ART, CELTIC [2]). The frequency of deposited hoards suggests that ritual disposal of wealth and status symbols—like the potlatch of the native Americans of the Pacific northwest—prevailed among Irish chieftains.

For the most part, Bronze Age settlements were still small and dispersed over the countryside, as they had been from the Neolithic and were to remain into the early Middle Ages. However, recent excavations at

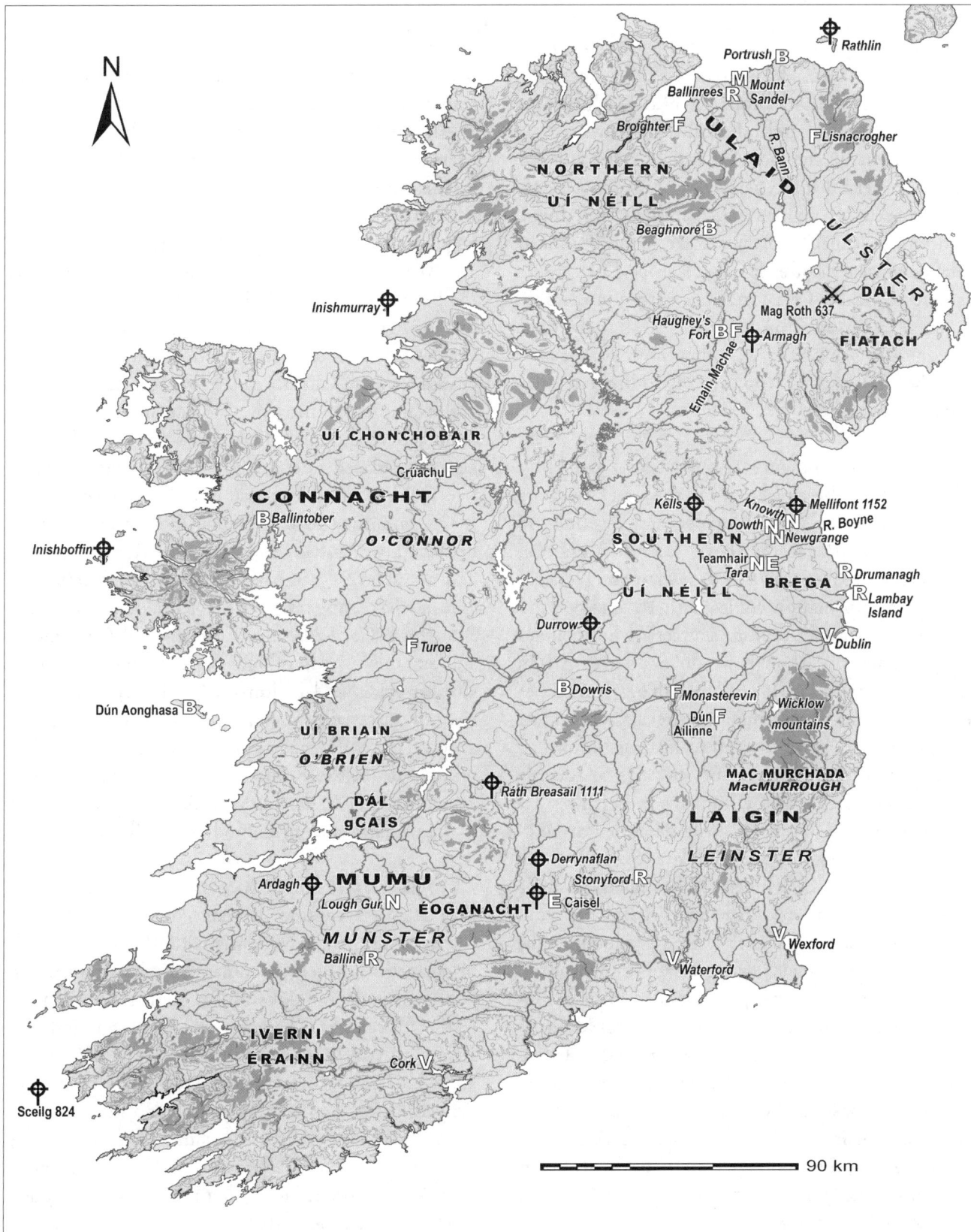

Ériu, pre-Norman Ireland: places and groups mentioned in the article, various periods—M=Mesolithic site; N=Neolithic site; B=Bronze Age site; F=Iron Age site; R=Roman and/or Romano-British finds; E=Early Medieval secular site; V= Viking town

Portrush, Co. Antrim, have revealed a large concentration of houses of Late Bronze Age date, which now must be regarded as Ireland's earliest urban site.

In the light of the fact that many of the cultural features of Ireland at this period—watery depositions, swords based on Hallstatt A-B models, hill-forts, cauldrons, gold neck ornaments, &c.—can be linked to defining patterns of early Celtic Europe, Koch argues that a recognizably Celtic Ireland emerged in the Late Bronze Age. Mac Eoin proposes a slightly later horizon—the 7th century BC, when swords associated with the Hallstatt C Iron Age (Gündlingen type) appear in Ireland.

§4. PROTO-HISTORY AND THE IRON AGE

Ireland probably became known to the Greeks with its Celtic name in the 6th century BC and certainly no later than the 4th (see §1 above, further AVIENUS; MASSALIOTE PERIPLUS; EPHORUS; PYTHEAS). Detailed geographic information comes with PTOLEMY (2nd century AD, using 1st-century sources), who includes 16 tribal names. Although we do not have written records from Ireland itself until the 4th or 5th centuries AD, from the mid-1st millennium BC Ireland is no longer fully prehistoric, but rather proto-historic, known to the literary record. Proto-history belongs to roughly the same time period as the Iron Age in Ireland.

The Irish Iron Age is variously described as enigmatic, problematical, poor, and late. Since Ireland, unlike Britain or the Rhineland, has relatively little easily exploited iron ore, it is not surprising that it did not develop as an early centre of iron production (the Irish Gündlingen swords mentioned above are bronze). The LA TÈNE style never penetrated south-west Ireland at all and very little of it anywhere could possibly predate 200 BC. It may be that Ireland failed to develop an Iron Age until that late date and, if so, the Dowris phase might simply have continued for some centuries in isolation while Ireland's neighbours were already in the Iron Age. Alternatively, Iron Age material of the 7th–3rd centuries BC may somehow have escaped detection.

The great centres of assembly which figure as the most prominent settings for the ULSTER CYCLE and other early IRISH LITERATURE [1]—Tara/TEAMHAIR, EMAIN MACHAE, CRÚACHU, and DÚN AILINNE— have revealed to modern archaeology abundant evidence of varied building and ritualistic high-status activities of Iron Age date.

Although limited to Ireland's northern half and parts of Leinster (LAIGIN), Irish artistic masterpieces in the La Tène style include the TUROE stone, the Broighter hoard with its exquisite sheet-gold TORC and its unique golden boat, and the Lisnacrogher scabbards (see ART, CELTIC [1]). Since Ireland remained outside the Roman Empire, an 'Ultimate La Tène' was free to develop in the early centuries AD, as evidenced in objects such as the Bann disc and the Monasterevin bowl discussed in ART, CELTIC [2]. However, there are several examples of intrusive Roman material in later Iron Age Ireland, including what seem to be the burials of displaced north BRITONS on Lambay Island, Co. Dublin, which is possibly to be connected with the promontory fort at Drumanagh, nearby on the mainland, which has produced some Roman material and a system of ramparts paralleled in Britain and Gaul; what appears to be a Roman burial from Stonyford, Co. Kilkenny (Contae Chill Chainnigh); and sizeable hoards of late Roman silver at Balline, Co. Limerick, and Ballinrees, Co. Derry. Such a variety of materials, ranging over four centuries, probably reflect different types of contacts—political refugees from the Roman conquest of Britain (and possibly Gaul), trade, loot and/or tribute brought out of late Roman and an imploding sub-Roman Britain.

§5. CHRISTIANITY AND LATIN LITERACY

From the 4th century, Roman contacts would have carried with them some Christian influence, but well-organized and well-documented Christianization begins with the missions of PALLADIUS and PATRICK in the 5th century. The latter was also the founder of Ireland's Latin literature. In Patrick's writings, we see an Ireland which was still overwhelmingly pagan and dangerous for the fledgling church and its missionaries. A list of rules for early churchmen, which calls itself *Synodus I Sancti Patricii* (The first synod of St Patrick; ed. & trans. Bieler), but is probably of a somewhat later date, shows that a pagan establishment with a system of laws, pledges, and oaths sworn before soothsayers, was still a concern. However, by the late 7th century, in Muirchú's Life of Patrick and ADOMNÁN's Life of COLUM CILLE, for example, an ongoing rival pagan establishment seems to have been of no real concern, and the saintly heroes' obstinate pagan rivals in the stories of the conversion in the HAGIOGRAPHY owe at least as much to wicked idol worshippers of the Old Testament as to recollections of actual Celtic paganism as their literary inspiration.

§6. EARLY VERNACULAR LITERACY

By Patrick's day, Irish had come to be written in its Old Celtic form in the OGAM script for short inscriptions on stone. By the end of the 7th century, Old Irish had become the vehicle of major literature with several genres—LAW TEXTS, poetry, religious texts, heroic sagas, science, glossaries and linguistics. In the last category, AURAICEPT NA NÉCES ('The Scholars' Primer') dates the beginnings of Irish vernacular literacy to the wake of the battle of MAG ROTH of 637. While this account, as it has come down to us, has been assimilated to the genre of LEGENDARY HISTORY, the date may be approximately right for this intellectual revolution. At least, it is doubtful whether any extant Old Irish text was committed to writing before 637, with the elegy of Colum Cille (†597) attributed to DALLÁN FORGAILL prominent among few possible exceptions.

§7. LEARNING AND THE CHURCH

In the early Middle Ages, Irish literature in both Latin and Irish was originated and copied (along with classical and early Christian texts from abroad) primarily in the MONASTERIES. The distribution of over 40,000 RING-FORTS, dating mostly to this period, over the Irish countryside reflects a continued pattern of dispersed defensible rural settlements in small family and extended-family groups. Thus, unlike the rest of Europe—where a system of territorial bishops was easily superimposed onto the CIVITAS structure of the Roman Empire—the bishops of Ireland were relatively weak and their territorial jurisdictions amorphous; therefore, the monasteries were the leading Christian institutions.

By the later 6th century, a movement known as PEREGRINATIO, which meant leaving Ireland forever to pursue a religious life abroad, had begun. The careers of Colum Cille in Britain and COLUMBANUS on the Continent provide early examples. The international impact of Ireland on the early Christian west reflects the confidence the Irish church had achieved in its faith and scholarship and also the decline and discontinuity in learning which had affected Britain and Merovingian Gaul following the collapse of the Western Empire and the emergence of the barbarian successor kingdoms, compounded by the conquest of Christian north Africa and Spain by Muslims in the 7th century.

As well as writing and transmitting texts, the Irish monasteries of the period c. 600–c. 900—Ireland's (Second) Golden Age—excelled in the visual arts. As discussed in ART, CELTIC [2], this was the period of the richly detailed illuminated gospel manuscripts (such as DURROW and KELLS) and the metalworking virtuosity of the Ardagh and Derrynaflan communion vessels. The security of the church within Ireland was underscored by the shattering impact of the attack on the churches of Brega in the east Midlands by the Anglo-Saxon King ECGFRITH in 684, but, whether due to ADOMNÁN's legislation or the military disaster which befell Ecgfrith the following year, this was to be an isolated incident. The manifest worldly success and wealth of the great monasteries was no doubt part of the motivation for zealous ascetics to seek remote hermitages, as well as inspiring the reform movement known as *Céili Dé* (Fellows of God), influential in the Irish and Scottish churches from the mid-8th century.

§8. EARLY SECULAR POLITICS

Although the dawn of Irish history may be said to coincide with Patrick in the 5th century, there is no contemporary record of political and military events until the ANNALS of the mid-6th century, at which point we find two ancient tribal groups of the south-east and north-east, who were to give their names to traditional provinces—the LAIGIN and the ULAID—near the top of the hierarchy within a bewildering pattern of overlapping regional tribes (see TUATH) and hereditary chiefdoms. Alongside these two, there were two newer dynastic federations, both claiming descent from 5th-century founders, who were consolidating their strength—the UÍ NÉILL, whose two main branches were based in western Ulster and the Midlands, and the ÉOGANACHT, divided into numerous subgroups in Munster (MUMU). By the late 7th century, the Laigin (split into more than one group) and the Ulaid (as the Dál Fiatach of Co. Down) were still in existence, but were no longer in serious national contention, their influence reduced to secure core areas near the coast. Though not yet a political reality, the idea of a national high-king (*ard-rí*), associated with the pre-Christian assembly site of Tara (TEAMHAIR) and monopolized by the Uí Néill, can be seen in written references emanating from Iona (EILEAN Ì): thus, Adomnán describes DIARMAIT MAC CERBAILL (†565), the common ancestor of the Southern Uí Néill dynasties, as the pre-eminent king of Ireland, and the Annals call both the Northern Uí Néill kings DOMNALL MAC AEDO (†642) and his grandson Loingseach mac Oengusso (†704) *rex Hiberbnie* (king of Ireland). On the political level, the Éoganacht and Uí Néill usually remained secure within their geographic spheres, but the doctrine of national KINGSHIP contributed to inevitable collisions. Thus, the Munster king Cathal mac Finguine (r. 721–42) achieved several victories and claimed to be king of Ireland.

§9. THE VIKING IMPACT

Two years after the famous attack on LINDISFARNE in 793, the Vikings rounded Britain to attack four Irish island monasteries—Iona, Rathlin, Inishmurray, and Inishboffin. Over the following generation, coastal attacks continued almost every year, gradually extending their range until the island-monastery of Sceilg, off the south-west coast, was struck in 824, at which point the Vikings were the dominant sea power on all sides of Ireland. Over the following two decades, raiding moved inland up the navigable rivers. But by the later 840s, the Irish kings had rallied somewhat, and the Vikings were never to achieve great land takings in Ireland as they did in 9th-century England. Permanent bases established in the mid-9th century—including Dublin (BAILE ÁTHA CLIATH), Waterford (Port Láirge), Wexford (LOCH GARMAN), and Cork (CORCAIGH)—were Hiberno-Norse towns by the mid-10th century. These settlements are usually regarded as the first urban centres in Ireland, though this consensus needs to be qualified in the light of the concentrations of population, artisans, and wealth at the great monasteries, as well as the startling discoveries at Portrush mentioned above. The Viking towns introduced currency to Ireland, and provided a stimulus to international trade and to a range of economic activities.

Although a major Scandinavian kingdom never emerged on Irish soil, the Vikings were often pivotal in triangular struggles between native Irish rulers and,

more generally, it was against the background of the Viking wars that the old equilibrium between the regional supremacies of the Uí Néill and the Éoganacht became unstable and national high-kingship became a reality. For example, the king and bishop (a common pattern for Éoganacht leaders) Feidlimid mac Crimthainn (†847) exerted considerable power throughout Ireland, pursuing an untraditional strategy, which included attacking enemy monasteries as military targets. Many modern historians regard the Southern Uí Néill ruler Mael Sechnall mac Maele Ruanaid (†862) as the first *de facto* high-king of all Ireland; he won victories and/or received the submission of rulers in every province. By the mid-10th century, the DÁL GCAIS had emerged as a significant new group, eclipsing first the ÉOGANACHT in Munster and, following a complicated series of struggles involving both Norse and native Irish rulers, they then achieved the high-kingship in name and fact under the famous BRIAN BÓRUMA (†1014), from whom they are subsequently known as Uí Briain 'the O'Briens' (descendants of Brian). The Uí Briain continued in a strong national position through the 11th century and into the 12th, when Brian's grandson Tairrdelbach (†1086) and great-grandson Muirchertach (†1119) held the high-kingship, after which they tended to be eclipsed by the Uí Chonchobair 'O'Connors' of CONNACHT.

Assessments of the Viking impact vary: primarily destructive raiding and warfare, primarily beneficial trade and founding of towns, or on balance irrelevant, with developments such as the O'Brien high-kingship working out long-standing internal trends. Although the Norse towns tended to play an auxiliary rôle in Ireland's political and military affairs, Dublin's influence on the Viking kingdom of York in the 10th century gave them a greater political influence in Britain (cf. ÆTHELSTAN; ARMES PRYDEIN). For Ireland, one consequence was that Viking presence became increasingly Anglo-Norse, rather than simply Scandinavian. For example, as the Viking towns became Christian they tended to look to Canterbury rather than churches in Ireland, thus establishing a vector for Anglo-Norman influence in the 12th century.

The Irish MONASTERIES remained the main patrons for learning and the arts, spheres in which major changes took place during the Viking age. Thus, DURROW, KELLS, and the other great illuminated gospels predate the Vikings, as do the masterpieces of early medieval metalwork (see ART, CELTIC [2]). Although it is a simplistic observation, it is possibly true that the decline of excellence in portable precious works and the broadly simultaneous heyday of the lavishly decorated and ponderous HIGH CROSSES were a direct response to Viking raids. The round towers, such a characteristic feature of the Irish landscape, belong to this period and were probably at least partly intended as places of refuge for churchmen during raids.

IRISH LITERATURE continued as an unbroken burgeoning tradition. However, the medium for the literature shifts from the richly complex, but stable and relatively uniform idiom of Old Irish, to the varied, rapidly evolving, and somewhat chaotic Middle Irish of the 10th to 12th centuries. It is likely that the physical insecurity of the monasteries (as centres of linguistic education) contributed to this upheaval.

§10. 12TH-CENTURY INNOVATIONS

By the 11th century, the Irish church, as it had developed from Patrick's time, came increasingly to be viewed from the outside as anomalous and ripe for reform. The abbots were too powerful and many of these were aristocratic laymen who had inherited their offices. Sexual morality among both laity and clergy did not conform to church doctrine. Both foreign and native reformers promoted new and stricter monastic orders, such as the Augustinians, followed by the Cistercians, who were introduced by St Malachy in 1142. A series of national synods, held at Cashel/CAISEL MUMAN in 1101, Ráith Bressail in 1111, and KELLS–Mellifont in 1152, strengthened and reorganized the diocesan system. The primacy of Armagh (ARD MHACHA) among Irish sees received official papal recognition, with Cashel in second position, and the bishop of Dublin removed from the jurisdiction of Canterbury. One negative consequence of these reforms was that, by shifting power and revenues to the bishops and new monastic orders, the structures that had nurtured Irish literature were weakened. Henceforth, the rôle of the monastic scriptoria waned and Irish literature came increasingly into the keeping of learned families under aristocratic secular patronage. This reorganization of Irish learning probably had a delayed but causal relation with the transition c. 1200 from Middle Irish to a new standard learned medium, Early or Classical Modern Irish (cf. IRISH LITERATURE [3]).

In 1155, more or less disregarding the reforms which had already taken place, the one and only English pope, Adrian IV, issued the Bull *Laudabiliter* authorizing the Anglo-Norman ruler Henry II to go to Ireland to reform the church. Henry did in fact come as a conqueror in 1171, but the immediate causes had nothing to do with *Laudabiliter*. Pushed out of Ireland by a coalition of the Dublin Norse and the allies of high-king Ruaidrí Ua Conchobair, king of Leinster, Diarmait Mac Murchada appealed for Henry's intervention, which led in the first instance to the invasion by Henry's subject Richard DE CLARE 'Strongbow' in 1169, an event usually regarded as the formal starting-point of Ireland's Anglo-Norman period. Though English political control was not to slacken until the 20th century, it is important to note that throughout the later Middle Ages the population remained overwhelmingly Irish-speaking. Many of the native Gaelic aristocratic families retained local power—the O'Briens, O'Connors, and MacMurroughs, for example. The Anglo-Norman élite themselves tended, within a few generations, to adopt the Irish language and customs, and to patronize classical Irish poets, just as the old native families did.

PRIMARY SOURCE
ED. & TRANS. Bieler, *Irish Penitentials*.

FURTHER READING
ADOMNÁN; ÆTHELSTAN; AGRICULTURE [2]; ANNALS; ARD MHACHA; ARMES PRYDEIN; ARMORICA; ART, CELTIC; AURAICEPT NA N-ÉCES; AVIENUS; BAILE ÁTHA CLIATH; BÓAND; BRIAN BÓRUMA; BRITAIN; BRITONS; BRUG NA BÓINNE; CAISEL MUMAN; CAULDRONS; CELTIC COUNTRIES; CELTIC LANGUAGES; CELTIC STUDIES; CHADWICK; CIVITAS; COLUM CILLE; COLUMBANUS; CONNACHT; CORCAIGH; CRÚACHU; DÁL GCAIS; DALLÁN FORGAILL; DE CLARE; DIARMAIT MAC CERBAILL; DILLON; DOMNALL MAC AEDO; DUBHADH; DÚN AILINNE; DÚN AONGHASA; DURROW; ECGFRITH; EILEAN Ì; ELLAN VANNIN; EMAIN MACHAE; ÉOGANACHT; EPHORUS; FAIRIES; GAUL; GOIDELIC; GREEK AND ROMAN ACCOUNTS; HAGIOGRAPHY; HALLSTATT; HAMITO-SEMITIC; HIBERNIA; HIGH CROSSES; IBERIAN PENINSULA; INDO-EUROPEAN; IRISH; IRISH LITERATURE; IRON AGE; KELLS; KINGSHIP; LA TÈNE; LAIGIN; LAW TEXTS; LEBAR GABÁLA ÉRENN; LEGENDARY HISTORY; LINDISFARNE; LOCH GARMAN; MAG ROTH; MASSALIOTE PERIPLUS; MÍL ESPÁINE; MONASTERIES; MUMU; OGAM; OTHERWORLD; PALLADIUS; PATRICK; PEREGRINATIO; PTOLEMY; PYTHEAS; RING-FORTS; SÍD; SWORDS; TEAMHAIR; THAMES; TOGAIL BRUIDNE DA DERGA; TORC; TUATH; TUATH DÉ; TUROE; UÍ NÉILL; ULAID; ULSTER CYCLE; WATERY DEPOSITIONS; Byrne, *Irish Kings and High-Kings*; Nora K.

Chadwick & Dillon, *Celtic Realms*; Duffy, *Atlas of Irish History*; Harbison, *Journal of Indo-European Studies* 3.101–19; Harbison, *Pre-Christian Ireland*; Herity & Eogan, *Ireland in Prehistory*; Koch, *Emania* 9.17–27; Koch, *Proc. Harvard Celtic Colloquium* 6.1–28; Mac Eoin, *History and Culture of the Celts* 161–74; Mac Niocaill, *Ireland Before the Vikings*; Ó Corráin, *Ireland Before the Normans*; Ó Corráin, *Oxford History of Ireland* 1–43; Ó Cróinín, *Early Medieval Ireland 400–1200*; O'Kelly, *Early Ireland*; Raftery, *Pagan Celtic Ireland*; Renfrew, *Archaeology and Language*; Renfrew, *Trans. Philological Society* 87.103–55; Richter, *Medieval Ireland*; Ryan, *Illustrated Archaeology of Ireland*; Waddell, *Prehistoric Archaeology of Ireland*.

JTK

Ériu [2]

Ériu [2] (Ireland) is one of the principal IRISH journals devoted to CELTIC STUDIES (for others see AINM, BÉALOIDEAS, CELTICA, ÉIGSE, EMANIA). Founded in 1904 as the journal of the School of Irish Learning, it is now published annually by the Royal Irish Academy (ACADAMH RÍOGA NA HÉIREANN) in Dublin (BAILE ÁTHA CLIATH). The journal is devoted to all aspects and periods of Irish philology and literature, with some articles on other CELTIC LANGUAGES, written by academics, mostly in English, with occasional articles in Irish. A selected index has been published by the MLA in their international bibliography of books and articles on modern languages and literatures.

RELATED ARTICLES
ACADAMH RÍOGA NA H-ÉIREANN; AINM; BAILE ÁTHA CLIATH; BÉALOIDEAS; CELTIC LANGUAGES; CELTIC STUDIES; CELTICA; ÉIGSE; EMANIA; IRISH; IRISH LITERATURE.
CONTACT DETAILS. *Ériu*, Royal Irish Academy, 19 Dawson Street, Dublin 2.

PSH

Eriugena, Johannes Scottus

Eriugena, Johannes Scottus was born *c.* 810 and died in 877, somewhere in northern France, where he had taught theology since at least 851, whilst working at the court of Charles the Bald. The appellation *Scottus* is common for Irishmen (cf. SCOTS), but Eriugena 'of Irish birth' he gave to himself (cf. ÉRIU; 'Erigena' is incorrect). As an Irish monastic scholar labouring among the Franks, Eriugena's career may be seen as a continuation of the tradition of the PEREGRINATIO of itinerant Irish churchmen during the preceding centuries. Eriugena grafted elements of Greek Platon-ism into his Latin tradition, and produced the most original theology between Augustine of Hippo (354–430) and Anselm (1033–1109). One of the most striking features of his massive work on the Creator and His creation, the *Periphyseon* or 'On the Division of Nature', is his identification of God and the natural world as one and the same, God as Creator being but one of the 'divisions of nature' in Eriugena's scheme. This doctrine opened the *Periphyseon* to the charge of nature worship or pantheism, most strongly in the 13th century and again during the Counter-Reformation. Carey argues that Eriugena's thinking has a traceable context in early Christian Ireland, in which case Eriugena's apparent radicalism derives at least in part from his background and early medieval Ireland's productive and independent intellectual development. Eriugenian studies are a well-established branch of medieval studies, but have thus far more often been pursued from the vantage of the history of ideas rather than that of CELTIC STUDIES.

PRIMARY SOURCES
Herren, *Carmina / Iohannis Scotti Eriugenae*; Sheldon-Williams & Jeauneau, *Iohanni Scotti Eriugenae Periphyseon*.

FURTHER READING
CELTIC STUDIES; ÉRIU; PEREGRINATIO; SCOTS; Carabine, *John Scottus Eriugena*; Carey, *Single Ray of the Sun*; O'Meara, *Eriugena*; O'Neill, *Jean-Scot Écrivain* 287–97.

Thomas O'Loughlin

Ernault, Émile

Ernault, Émile, a Breton Celtic scholar, was born in 1852 at Saint-Brieuc (Sant-Brieg) within the French-speaking region of north-central Brittany (BREIZH), and died there in 1938. He studied English and German, and began his career as a teacher of these languages at the École St-Charles at Saint-Brieuc. He learned BRETON as an adult and began to work with the journal REVUE CELTIQUE in 1876. Having been elected member of the *Société linguistique* in 1875, he met Henri Gaidoz, Henri d'Arbois de la Jubainville, and other important Celtic scholars. From 1881 to 1884 he studied at the Collège de France in Paris and received a Ph.D. in 1887. He was subsequently awarded the chair of Greek Literature and Institutions at the Collège de France, which he held until his retirement.

Most of Ernault's scholarly activity was focused on Breton. He edited Middle Breton mystery plays and saints' lives, and made a major contribution to Breton metrics with his *L'ancien vers breton* (see BRETON LITERATURE). He also completed a dictionary of Gwenedeg (the Vannes dialect of Breton; see BRETON DIALECTS; GWENED). In the second half of his life, much of his activity was dedicated to the study of Breton words—lexicography and etymology (see DICTIONARIES AND GRAMMARS [5]).

SELECTION OF MAIN WORKS
Le mystère de Sainte Barbe (1885–7); *Glossaire moyen-breton* (1895–6); *L'épenthèse des liquides* (1901); *Dictionaire breton–français du dialecte de Vannes* (1904); *L'ancien vers breton* (1912); *Le Mirouer de la mort* (1914); *Gériadurig brezonek–gallek / Vocabulaire breton–français* (1927); 'L'Ancien Mystère de Saint Gwénolé', *Annales de Bretagne* 40 (1932–3) 2–35; 41 (1934) 104–41, 318–79; *Yalc'h Wilh* (1935).

RELATED ARTICLES
BREIZH; BRETON; BRETON DIALECTS; BRETON LITERATURE; DICTIONARIES AND GRAMMARS [5]; GWENED; REVUE CELTIQUE.

PEB

Eryri (Snowdonia)

Eryri (**Snowdonia**) is a mountainous region in north-west Wales (CYMRU). It traditionally included the mountain regions of Snowdon (Yr Wyddfa), the Glyders, and the Carneddau range. The ancient areas of Uwch Conwy and GWYNEDD approximately denoted Eryri's boundaries. In 1974 Snowdonia National Park (Parc Cenedlaethol Eryri) was established, which substantially expanded the area of Eryri to the south.

The first literary mention of Eryri occurs in the 9th-century HISTORIA BRITTONUM (§40), where an account is given of the downfall of the semi-legendary 5th-century king GWRTHEYRN (Vortigern). Pursued by his revolted Anglo-Saxon mercenaries and hated by his BRYTHONIC countrymen, the king's *magi* direct him to build a stronghold in a secure place on the far side of his kingdom. Such a place is found in Eryri, spelled in this source in its Old Welsh spelling *Hereri*, variant *Heriri*. The name for the area was officially recognized by the Welsh Princes, and LLYWELYN AB IORWERTH (Llywelyn Fawr) adopted the Latin title *Princeps Northwallie et Dominus Snowdonie*, Welsh *Tywysog Gwynedd ac Arglwydd Eryri* in 1230.

Eryri was an important factor in the strategic security of the kingdom of Gwynedd, forming a formidable barrier between the rest of Britain and Gwynedd's agricultural heartland in MÔN, the coastal strip of Arfon and the Llŷn peninsula. These same factors contributed to the relative ease of contacts between Gwynedd and Ireland (ÉRIU), an essential background to understanding the Irish colonists in Gwynedd who were said to have been expelled by CUNEDDA, and the important Irish aspects of the career of King GRUFFUDD AP CYNAN. The fact that the peaks of Eryri can be seen from the mountains of south-east Ireland also helps to explain the natural overseas links between these areas from prehistoric times.

The place-name *Eryri* has had two Celtic roots proposed to explain it: (1) that it describes a high place (cf. Latin *orior* 'I rise'; GPC s.v. *eryr*²), or (2) that it denotes the abode of eagles (Welsh *eryr* 'eagle', Old Irish *irar*). Of course, even if *Eryri* had not originally meant 'eyrie', this idea would automatically occur to any Welsh speaker, writer, or poet. GIRALDUS CAMBRENSIS (*c.* 1146–1220) mentioned the eagle of Snowdon, and many sources record the presence of eagles in the region until modern times. In a transferred sense, *eryr* is often used as a kenning for 'hero' in WELSH POETRY, which adds further significance to the place-name as the traditional mountain stronghold of the strongest and most militaristic independent Welsh kingdom, Gwynedd.

In Welsh literature, Eryri is associated with suffering and tragedy, and the first reference to the area appears in an AWDL by Hywel Foel ap Griffri ap Pwyll Wyddel (*fl. c.* 1240–*c.* 1300) from the HENDREGADREDD MANUSCRIPT. The most popular and enduring image of Snowdonia, however, was created by Thomas Gray (1716–71) in his poem *The Bard* (1757), in which the last Welsh poet throws himself from cliffs above the river Conwy into the raging waters.

In modern times, the traditional industries for the local population have been mining and farming. Shepherds are the subject of various FOLK-TALES: the most momentous is *Ogof Llanciau Eryri* (The cave of the youths of Snowdonia), in which a young man chances upon the host of ARTHUR's sleeping knights awaiting the call to battle. This is one of several places where variants of this folk-tale are localized; there are English and Scottish, as well as Welsh versions.

Eryri was considered to represent wild Wales from early modern times. For instance, Thomas Pennant notes that in 1618 a masque 'For the Honour of Wales' was accompanied by scenes from Snowdon painted by Inigo Jones (1573–1652).

View of Snowdon (Yr Wyddfa) from a frozen Llyn Ogwen

Yr Wyddfa (lit. 'the tumulus', Snowdon) is the highest peak in Wales (1085 m). It is associated with the warlike giant Rhita Gawr (or Ricca), who was killed by Arthur and buried at the summit. A version of this story occurs in GEOFFREY OF MONMOUTH'S HISTORIA REGUM BRITANNIAE.

Snowdon is the most famous and most visited mountain site in this region. The first recorded ascent was in 1639 by Thomas Johnson (†1644), who introduced the mountain as an important botanical site. The majority of visitors still travel to Snowdon for recreational or cultural reasons. In 1896 the Snowdon Mountain Railway opened, allowing access to a larger audience, and thereby expanding the mountain's rôle as a day-trip location.

Dolbadarn Castle at the foot of Snowdon inspired generations of artists and is immortalized in the studies of the great English landscape-painter J. M. W. Turner (1775–1851).

FURTHER READING
ART; ARTHUR; AWDL; BRYTHONIC; CUNEDDA; CYMRU; ÉRIU; FOLK-TALES; GEOFFREY OF MONMOUTH; GIRALDUS CAMBRENSIS; GRUFFUDD AP CYNAN; GWRTHEYRN; GWYNEDD; HENDREGADREDD MANUSCRIPT; HISTORIA BRITTONUM; HISTORIA REGUM BRITANNIAE; LLYWELYN AB IORWERTH; MÔN; WELSH POETRY; Clow, *Snowdonia Revisited*; Hilling, *Snowdonia and Northern Wales*; Dewi Jones, *Tywysyddion Eryri*; Iwan Arfon Jones, *Enwau Eryri*; Robert Jones, *Complete Guide to Snowdon*; Joyner, *Dolbadarn*; Kirk, *Snowdonia*; Pennant, *Tour in Wales 2*; Perrin, *Visions of Snowdonia*; Rees, *Historical Atlas of Wales*; Rhŷs, *Celtic Folklore*; Stephens, NCLW.

Paul Joyner

Esus/Aesus was a Gaulish god whose name appears in several compound personal names, though its etymology is unclear. He is mentioned by the Roman authors LUCAN (*Pharsalia* 1.444–6) and Lactantius (*c.* AD 245–*c.* 325). According to the former, rites of human SACRIFICE were dedicated to him on altars in

GAUL (see further TARANIS; TEUTATES). According to commentaries on Lucan, the god's victims were stabbed and hung from trees where they bled to death. The inscribed name ESVS appears on the Paris stone monument known as the *Nautae Parisiaci* (the sailors of the tribe of the Parisi, from whom Paris takes its name; 1st century AD). There, he is depicted as a bearded man wearing the clothes of an artisan, standing beside a tree, the trunk of which he holds in his hand. Next to the figure of Esus a bull with three cranes and named TARVOS TRIGARANUS is depicted. This depiction is linked to a relief from Trier, Germany, where a beardless figure identified as MERCURIUS fells a tree in which three birds and a bull's head are visible.

FURTHER READING
LUCAN; MERCURIUS; SACRIFICE; TARANIS; TARVOS TRIG-ARANUS; TEUTATES; Duval, *Trierer Zeitschrift für Geschichte und Kunst des Trierer Landes und seiner Nachbargebiete* 36.81–8; Green, *Dictionary of Celtic Myth and Legend*, s.v. Esus; Ross, ÉC 9.405–38.

PEB

Étar/Benn Étair (Howth)

Étar/Benn Étair (Howth) is a prominent peninsula guarding the northern side of Dublin Bay and the location of mythological events in early IRISH LITERATURE. The peninsula is listed in the *Geography* of PTOLEMY (*c.* AD 150) as the promontory or island of Αδρου *Andru* (variant Εδρου *Edru*). It probably corresponds to the place-name *Andros* which is mentioned in PLINY the Elder's *Natural History* of the 1st century AD. The present Anglicized name *Howth* is derived from Old Norse *höfuth* 'headland', which dates from the period of Norse domination of Dublin (BAILE ÁTHA CLIATH) and its sea approaches in the 10th and 11th centuries.

The form *Benn Étair* repeatedly appears in medieval Irish tales. Crimthann Nia Náir, king of Tara (TEAMHAIR), built a fortress known as Dún Crimthainn at the tip of the promontory. *Talland Étair* (The siege of Howth)—a tale from the ULSTER CYCLE—tells how the LAIGIN (Leinstermen) besieged the ULAID (Ulstermen) at Benn Étair in revenge for the abduction of their women. In the lengthy late Middle Irish FIANNAÍOCHT narrative, ACALLAM NA SENÓRACH (Dialogue of [or with] the old men), one incident tells how Artúr son of Béinne of the BRITONS stole FINN MAC CUMAILL's three supernatural hounds from

their owner while they were hunting there. Other references to the Hill of Howth suggest that the place was associated with the kingship of either Brega or Dublin. A topographical poem on Achall (Skreen, Co. Meath) states that the King of Dublin, Amlaíb Cuarán (†980), gained the kingship (of Brega?) in Benn Étair (*ro-gab rígi i mBeind Étair*). Amlaíb's son, Sitryggr, is reputed to have endowed a church, which became the medieval parish church in the village of Howth. The castle and demesne were built on the site of the manor granted in the late 12th century by Henry II to Almeric I St Lawrence, whose descendants (through an indirect line) continue to reside there.

PRIMARY SOURCES
Gwynn, *Metrical Dindshenchas* 1.52; Stokes, RC 8.47–64 (Siege of Howth);

FURTHER READING
ACALLAM NA SENÓRACH; BAILE ÁTHA CLIATH; BRITONS; FIANNAÍOCHT; FINN MAC CUMAILL; IRISH LITERATURE; LAIGIN; PLINY; PTOLEMY; TEAMHAIR; ULAID; ULSTER CYCLE; De Bernardo Stempel, *Ptolemy* 104; Dooley & Roe, *Tales of the Elders of Ireland* 8–12; Killanin & Duignan, *Shell Guide to Ireland* 204–5; MacKillop, *Dictionary of Celtic Mythology* (s.v. Howth).

Edel Bhreathnach

Études Celtiques

Études Celtiques is a current Celtic journal, established in 1936 by J. VENDRYES and published in Paris. The journal appears annually and contains articles from all areas of CELTIC STUDIES, including the archaeology of the Continental IRON AGE. It includes an extensive section of reviews of new publications in the field and publishes obituaries of some important Celtic scholars. While the majority of articles, particularly in the earlier editions, are written in French, articles in English are also accepted and appear more frequently in later issues. A selected index to the journal has been published by the MLA in its international bibliography of books and articles on modern languages and literatures. *Études Celtiques* is a publication of the Centre National de la Recherche Scientifique (CNRS).

RELATED ARTICLES
CELTIC STUDIES; IRON AGE; VENDRYÈS.
CONTACT DETAILS. *Études Celtiques*, Centre d'Études Celtiques, 26, rue Geoffroy l'Asnier, 75004 Paris, France.

PSH

Sandstone stele depicting a mythological being from Euffigneix

FURTHER READING
BOAR; LUGUS; REINCARNATION; TORC; Duval, *Les Celtes*; Green, *Dictionary of Celtic Myth and Legend* s.v. Euffugneix; Le Duc, *Ildánach Ildírech* 97–9; J. V. S. Megaw, *Art of the European Iron Age*; Pauli, *Die Kelten in Mitteleuropa*.

PEB

Eugein map Beli ruled the BRYTHONIC stronghold of Dumbarton (see YSTRAD CLUD). 'Hoan *rex Britonum*' defeated and killed DOMNALL BRECC of Scottish DÁL RIATA in December 642 at the battle of Srath Caruin, according to the ANNALS of Ulster. This victory is celebrated in two versions of one AWDL in LLYFR ANEIRIN, where Eugein is called 'grandson of Nwython', a reference to Neithon map Guiþno, who was a direct third-generation descendant of Cinuit map Ceretic Guletic, progenitor of the north British CYNWYDION dynasty. Eugein's brother or half-brother was BRUIDE MAC BILI, king of the Pictish Fortrinn and victor of NECHTANESMERE (685).

The king's name is the same as the common Modern Welsh *Owain*, probably a borrowing from Latin *Eugenius* (Jackson, LHEB 324), and the Old Welsh/CUMBRIC spelling *Eugein*, which occurs in the GENEALOGIES of BL MS Harley 3859, suggests that this is how their compiler understood it. A Eugenius held joint control over part of the Western Empire including BRITAIN in 392–4. On the father's Celtic name, see BELI MAWR.

FURTHER READING
ANNALS; AWDL; BELI MAWR; BRITAIN; BRUIDE MAC BILI; BRYTHONIC; CUMBRIC; CYNWYDION; DÁL RIATA; DOMNALL BRECC; GENEALOGIES; LLYFR ANEIRIN; NECHTANESMERE; YSTRAD CLUD; Bartrum, *Welsh Classical Dictionary* 516–17; Jackson, LHEB 324; Ann Williams et al., *Biographical Dictionary of Dark Age Britain* 200.

JTK

Euffigneix is an archaeological site in the *département* of Haute-Marne, France, where a sandstone stele was found depicting a bearded man wearing a TORC and with a BOAR carved in bas-relief on his chest. Each side of the torso carries the relief sculpture of a large human eye. The statue is dated to the end of the 1st century BC. The stonework shows the beginning of Roman influence on Gaulish sculptures. The circumstances of discovery are unclear, and the figure (usually presumed to be a deity) has no agreed-upon identification; Le Duc has suggested LUGUS. It is possible that imagery is meant to represent a narrative of shapeshifting (see REINCARNATION).

Evans, Ellis Humphrey (Hedd Wyn) was born on 13 January 1887, the eldest son of Evan and Mary Evans of the Ysgwrn, a remote farm about a mile from the village of Trawsfynydd in Merioneth (sir Feirionnydd). He left the local school at fourteen to help on the farm. Long before he left school, his father had bought him a book on Welsh prosody, and Hedd

Wyn wrote his first correct ENGLYN before reaching twelve. Gradually, he became a master of CYNG-HANEDD, and often competed in local EISTEDDFODau and literary meetings. His ambition was to win the chair at the National Eisteddfod (EISTEDDFOD GENEDLAETHOL CYMRU), and he came close to realizing that ambition at the National Eisteddfod of 1916, when one of the three adjudicators wanted to award the chair to him. Hedd Wyn decided to compete again the following year, but by the end of January 1917 he had become a private in the 15th Battalion of the Royal Welch Fusiliers, and was undergoing a period of intense training at Litherland Training Camp near Liverpool. After completing his basic training at Litherland he was sent to the Ypres Salient in Flanders, leaving Litherland on 9 June 1917. He eventually completed his AWDL, *Yr Arwr* (The hero), in mid-July 1917, in the small village of Fléchin in France, and the poem was sent from Fléchin to the National Eisteddfod office at Birkenhead. A fortnight later, on 31 July, Hedd Wyn died of wounds as his battalion pushed its way through the German lines towards Langemarck, on the very first day of the Third Battle of Ypres, otherwise known as the Passchendaele campaign. The Anglo-Irish poet Francis Ledwidge (1891–1917) was killed on the same day. Hedd Wyn was buried at Artillery Wood Cemetery, Boesinghe.

The chairing ceremony at the Birkenhead National Eisteddfod was held on 6 September. When the Archdruid announced the pseudonym of the winning entry, no one stood up to be chaired. The Archdruid then announced that the author of the prize-winning poem was Hedd Wyn, who had died of wounds sustained five weeks prior to the Eisteddfod. In what became a highly emotional scene and a historic event, the chair was draped in black, and the Eisteddfod became known as *Eisteddfod y Gadair Ddu* (The eisteddfod of the black chair).

A volume of Hedd Wyn's poetry was posthumously published in 1918. *Cerddi'r Bugail* (The shepherd's poems), edited by J. J. Williams, eventually sold 4000 copies, and a second edition was published in 1931. In 1923 a statue of Hedd Wyn, romantically and rather misleadingly portrayed as a 'shepherd-poet' by the London sculptor, L. S. Merrifield, was unveiled at Trawsfynydd.

Hedd Wyn was basically a romantic poet, much influenced by Shelley, but some of his last poems display a stark realism as disillusionment with the war set in. Hedd Wyn's story was eventually made into a film, HEDD WYN (1992). Directed by Paul Turner and written by Alan LLWYD, it won international awards and an Oscar nomination. Alan Llwyd also published a biography of Hedd Wyn, *Gwae Fi fy Myw* (1991), and edited a third edition of *Cerddi'r Bugail* (1994).

PRIMARY SOURCE
Cerddi'r Bugail (1918, 1931, 1994).

FURTHER READING
AWDL; CYNGHANEDD; EISTEDDFOD; EISTEDDFOD GENED-LAETHOL CYMRU; ENGLYN; HEDD WYN; LLWYD; WELSH POETRY; Llwyd, *Gwae Fi Fy Myw*; Phillips, *Planet* 72.59–64; Thomas, *Y Patrwm Amryliw* 1.88–111.

Alan Llwyd

Evans, Gwynfor

Evans, Gwynfor (1912–2005), was the first UK Member of Parliament to be elected for Plaid Cymru (The Party of Wales). He was born in Barry (Y Barri) in south Wales and educated at Barry Grammar School and the University of Wales, ABERYSTWYTH. He became active politically in the late 1930s in nationalist and pacifist movements. A conscientious objector during the Second World War, he became president of Plaid Genedlaethol Cymru (the national party of Wales) in 1945, a post he held for 36 years.

Evans sought to make Plaid Cymru a mainstream political party and distanced himself from the policies of his predecessor, Saunders LEWIS. Economic policies were developed, often based on Scandinavian models, and the party sought to draw upon the radical tradition, which by the 1950s had shifted from Liberal to Labour politics. Cross-party movements such as the Parliament for Wales campaign increased the party's profile and its electoral performance gradually improved in the 1950s. Evans himself contested Merioneth (Meirionnydd) on four occasions, and prior to the 1959 General Election entertained genuine prospects of victory, especially in the light of the local impact of the controversy over a reservoir project which drowned the Welsh-speaking village of Capel Celyn and the Tryweryn valley in order to supply water for urban areas in England.

By the 1960s Evans had established himself as a national figure, widely respected across the political spectrum, again in stark contrast to his predecessor. In many ways he was a conservative figure. As a long-serving member and alderman of Carmarthenshire County Council and as president of the Congregational Union of Wales, he represented a brand of NATIONALISM that had particular appeal in rural Wales (CYMRU). This rural image was further compounded by Evans's own hostility to the Labour Party, which was partly rooted in his own experiences in local government. Within Plaid Cymru, however, Evans's leadership was criticized by a radical younger element which believed the party should become a LANGUAGE (REVIVAL) movement. At a time when the Labour Party was attracting a new generation of WELSH-speaking leaders, and following administrative devolution in 1964, such views were echoed in the Welsh press.

The main turning-point in his career came in 1966 when the death of Megan Lloyd George led to a by-election in Carmarthen (CAERFYRDDIN), which Evans won. He lost the seat in 1970, but won it back in 1974, before losing it again in 1979. His impact at Westminster was minimal and Evans was, by his own admission, uncomfortable there. However, Plaid Cymru became a major political force in north-west and south-west Wales and came near to a breakthrough in the south Wales valleys in the late 1960s and 1970s. During this period Evans's relationship with the more militant language movement often bordered on the ambivalent and he believed that such campaigns had cost his party valuable votes. However, in 1980 Evans placed himself at the forefront of a protest against a government change of policy with regard to a Welsh-language television channel (see MASS MEDIA) by threatening to embark on a hunger strike unless the decision not to introduce such a channel was reversed. Shortly before the hunger strike was due to begin the government backed down, and Evans regarded the victory as one of his greatest achievements.

Shortly afterwards Evans stood down from the presidency of the party and retired from active politics following a further defeat in the 1983 General Election. Plaid Cymru entered a period of transformation, and emerged in the 1990s with a much stronger local government base and a new generation of professional politicians. Gwynfor Evans was honorary president of the party until his death, and the key figure in its transformation from a fringe movement into a potential party of government in post-devolution Wales.

A good starting point for research on the politician is Evans's autobiography, *For the Sake of Wales*, a translation by Meic Stephens of a work originally published in Welsh. Evans's personal history of Wales, *Land of my Fathers*, now published as *Wales, a History: 2000 Years of Welsh History* contains valuable insights into his views of nationalism.

SELECTION OF MAIN WORKS
Our Three Nations (1956); *Aros Mae* (1971); *Nonviolent Nationalism* (1973); *Wales Can Win* (1973); *Land of my Fathers* (1974); *Bywyd Cymro* (1982); *Seiri Cenedl y Cymry* (1986); *Welsh Nation Builders* (1988); *Pe Bai Cymru'n Rhydd* (1989); *Fighting for Wales* (1991); 'Hanes twf Plaid Cymru, 1925–1995', *Cof Cenedl* 10.153–84 (1995); *Wales, a History* (1996); *Fight for Welsh Freedom* (2000).
MEMOIRS. *For the Sake of Wales* (1996; new ed. 2001).

FURTHER READING
ABERYSTWYTH; CAERFYRDDIN; CYMRU; LANGUAGE (REVIVAL); LEWIS; MASS MEDIA; NATIONALISM; WELSH; Brooks, *Barn* 449.6–7; Chapman, *Taliesin* 94.101–17; D. Hywel Davies, *Welsh Nationalist Party 1925–1945*; John Davies, *Green and the Red*; McAllister, *Plaid Cymru*.

Ioan Matthews

Evans, John Gwenogvryn

Evans, John Gwenogvryn (1852–1930) was born near Llanybydder in Carmarthenshire (sir Gaerfyrddin). He trained for the Unitarian ministry, but ill health cut short that calling in 1880 and he was forced to seek an alternative career. He and his family settled in Oxford (Welsh Rhydychen), where he came under the influence of Sir John RHŷS at Jesus College, even though his attendance at the university was spasmodic due to continuing poor health. Under the guidance of Professors Rhŷs and York Powell, Evans acquired the ability to read manuscripts which contained Welsh literature from the Middle Ages, and he developed an outstanding ability to produce accurate transcripts and diplomatic and facsimile editions of texts. Beginning in 1887, Rhŷs and Evans embarked on an ambitious scheme to publish significant texts in various editions in a series entitled *Old Welsh Texts*, for which Evans became largely responsible. To this series he later added his *Welsh Classics for the People*. He set exacting standards for the printed editions. Technical difficulties caused by using commercial printers forced him to undertake much of the composition work himself, and he eventually purchased his own printing press and employed a master printer, his nephew George Jones. The work occupied him for much of his life and established his reputation as the foremost Welsh palaeographer of his day, and as a fine printer. He was awarded honorary degrees in recognition of his work by the Universities of Oxford and Wales, and he was also awarded a civil list pension in 1892 to enable him to continue his work.

The vast majority of Welsh literary manuscripts were held at that time in private libraries. Recognizing that producing edited scholarly texts required reference to all extant versions, Evans and his contemporaries at Oxford, with the support of certain Welsh Members of Parliament, persuaded the Historical Manuscripts Commission to appoint an appropriate inspector to survey and record the contents of those libraries. In 1894 Evans himself was appointed to the task. He travelled widely to visit libraries, and his detailed and painstaking *Report on Manuscripts in the Welsh Language* was published in seven parts by Her Majesty's Stationery Office, London, between 1898 and 1910. It provided the foundations for much subsequent Welsh literary scholarship.

In 1905 Evans and his family moved to 'Tremvan', Llanbedrog, a house he designed with his wife, Edith. He became a prominent member of society in Caernarfonshire (sir Gaernarfon) and Wales (CYMRU). He strongly supported the movement to establish a National Library for Wales, recognizing the need to create a publicly accessible reference collection of manuscripts

and books to facilitate the further study of Welsh literature. His unrivalled knowledge of Welsh collections still in private hands drew him into the work of ensuring that the most important of them were eventually gathered together at the National Library of Wales (LLYFRGELL GENEDLAETHOL CYMRU) when it was finally established in 1907.

His over-ambitious schemes, his insistence on the highest technical standards, and his often contentious relationships with scholars, printers, and others with whom he collaborated, gained for him a reputation for being hypersensitive and difficult. Disagreements were compounded in Evans's later work when he often added incorrect textual and contextual interpretation and commentary to his transcriptions and reproductions of manuscripts. Some of those disagreements were reflected in unpleasant public and published debates (MORRIS-JONES, *Y Cymmrodor* 28.1–282; J. Gwenogvryn Evans, *Y Cymmrodor* 34.1–123). This may explain why his contribution to Welsh literary scholarship was not fully appreciated or acknowledged by his contemporaries.

PRIMARY SOURCES
'Welsh Manuscripts', *Wales* 1.205–8 (1894); *Report on Manuscripts in the Welsh Language* (1898–1910); 'Taliesin: or the Critic Criticised', *Y Cymmrodor 34* (1924).

FURTHER READING
CYMRU; LLYFRGELL GENEDLAETHOL CYMRU; MORRIS-JONES; RHŶS; Jenkins, *Refuge in Peace and War*; [?Morris-Jones], *Cymru* 4.77–9; Morris-Jones, *Y Cymmrodor 28*; D. Hywel E. Roberts, *Y Llyfr yng Nghymru / Welsh Book Studies* 2.53–80.

D. Hywel E. Roberts

F

Faelán was common as a man's name in Ireland (ÉRIU) in the first millennium AD and was borne by several important historical and mythological characters. Perhaps the most famous in surviving literary tradition is Faelán mac Finn, son of Fionn mac Cumhaill (FINN MAC CUMAILL) and one of the major champions of the Fianna (see FIANNAÍOCHT). His primary characteristics are a fanatical loyalty to his father and to Clann Baoiscne, as a result of which he becomes a major protagonist in aggravating their sporadic feuds with Clann Mórna and the high-king, which eventually resulted in the destruction of the majority of the Fianna at *cath Gabhra* (the battle of Gabhra). Faelán rarely takes a leading rôle in any major narrative tale, although one story collected by Jeremiah Curtin in Corca Dhuibhne, Co. Kerry (Contae Chiarraí), in the late 19th century is an exception. According to MacKillop, no fewer than ten members of the mythological Fianna Éireann (warrior bands of Ireland) were named Faelán (*Dictionary of Celtic Mythology*).

At least two and (due to inter-textual confusion) possibly as many as five saints named Faelán are recorded. The most notable of these are:

(1) Faelán of Fosse (†656), who was a follower of Fursa and abbot of Fosse in the diocese of Cambray in GAUL;

(2) Faelán of Glendeochquhy (possibly Glen Dochart) in Perthshire, Scotland (ALBA). A 7th-/8th-century saint associated with the Scottish churches of Aberdour and Pittenween, the descent of this saint from the royal line of LAIGIN (Leinster) through his mother ties in with the fact that the name appears frequently in the king-list for the Uí Dúnlainge, kings of Leinster.

From the 8th century a major sept of the Laigin, the Uí Faeláin, with their royal seat at Nás na Rí (Naas, Co. Kildare), bear this name. Thirty-seven individuals named Faelán are recorded in the *Corpus Genealogiarum Hiberniae* (see GENEALOGIES). The name is also seen in the Ua Faeláin sept of the Déisi Muman in south-eastern MUMU (Munster), from whom is derived the modern Irish surname Ó Faoláin.

Faelán is derived from Old Irish *fáel* 'wolf' with the diminutive suffix *-án*, thus 'little wolf', and can be understood as arising from the common pattern in early IRISH LITERATURE of animals used as metaphors for the warrior (other frequent examples include *seabhac* 'hawk', *leómhan* 'lion' and *eó* 'salmon'; cf. HEROIC ETHOS).

PRIMARY SOURCES
O'Brien, *Corpus Genealogiarum Hiberniae*; Stokes, *Félire Óengusso Céli Dé.*

FURTHER READING
ALBA; ÉRIU; FIANNAÍOCHT; FINN MAC CUMAILL; GAUL; GENEALOGIES; HEROIC ETHOS; IRISH LITERATURE; LAIGIN; MUMU; Byrne, *Irish Kings and High-Kings*; Curtin, *Hero-Tales of Ireland*; De Paor, *St Patrick's World*; MacKillop, *Dictionary of Celtic Mythology*; Ó Dónaill, *Seanchas na Féinne*; Ann Williams et al., *Biographical Dictionary of Dark Age Britain.*

SÓF

fairies

§1. INTRODUCTION

The word 'fairy' in modern English tends to be associated with the image of a diminutive, winged, magical being, usually female, of the type depicted in Disney films such as *Cinderella* and *Sleeping Beauty* or in popular conceptions of the tooth fairy. As an analytical category, however, the term is much broader, encompassing a range of supernatural entities sharing geographical space with mortals. Fairies are usually understood as a separate kind of being, though the perceived difference varies a great deal, depending on the time, place, and context of the fairy belief in question. Belief in fairies is found throughout the world, and the CELTIC COUNTRIES are no exception. Not all supernatural beings are fairies:

witches, ghosts, and revenants were once ordinary humans, and gods, devils, and demons are mythological rather than legendary beings, and were understood to exist in a different sphere. There is, nevertheless, a good deal of overlap in lore relating to fairies and to witches, devils, and the rest. Thus, for example, the TUATH DÉ of LEGENDARY HISTORY and the MYTHOLOGICAL CYCLE of early IRISH LITERATURE are for the most part susceptible to interpretation as mythological beings or even pre-Christian gods, though clearly forming a continuum with the fairies of modern Irish folk belief.

Fairies occur in a wide variety of sizes and types, from diminutive to giant, and inhabit a diverse range of landscapes, from underground to outer space. They can have human or animal form, or both (see REINCARNATION). The fairy tradition includes named individuals such as the CAILLEACH BHÉIRRE or Cailleach Bheur of Ireland (ÉIRE) and Scotland (ALBA), magical beasts such as the Welsh AFANC, and types or kinds of fairies such as the Cornish PISKY or Irish leprechaun (see LUCHORPÁN). There are also monsters—another word whose common meaning of 'hideous creature' is misleading in this context. In folklore, monsters are not necessarily hideous beings, or those formed from two different types of animals (the heraldic definition, which is not significant in Celtic tradition), but is a technical term which refers to singular examples of magical beings such as the Breton ANKOU.

Fairies are intimately associated with the landscape, and different types of fairies inhabit moors, mountains, caves, seas, lakes, and other natural features. Some of them, for example the giants, are often seen as extinct, having made their mark on the natural world by playing quoits or carrying stones in their aprons, the only evidence being the megalithic monuments and mountain-top cairns they left behind as a result of their activity. Giants survived at least into the heroic age, however, and there are many narratives in which a hero such as ARTHUR or Fionn (FINN MAC CUMAILL) bests a giant. Arthur and Fionn themselves occasionally appear as giants in FOLK-TALES, especially in connection with accounts of the origins of megaliths and natural landscape features.

Who or what the fairies are—and where they came from—is accounted for in several different ways in the folk tradition. According to some informants, they are the souls of the dead, who exist in a kind of purgatory on earth, or more specifically the heathen (i.e. pre-Christian) dead, or even the evil dead. According to other accounts, they are fallen angels (cf. TUATH DÉ) and, according to still others, they are merely natural phenomena, either material or spirit. These beliefs were held concurrently and varied from individual to individual, rather than being a result of regional or chronological variation. In the 19th century, David MacRitchie proposed that the fairy beliefs arose out of the memory of previous 'races' of people, such as the PICTS, who had since been driven out (according to the prevalent 19th-century theory). This theory, though it is no longer held in academia, has been accepted into popular culture, particularly the expansion of the idea whereby fairies were real remnants of pre-Christian communities living a covert, underground existence, keeping their traditions alive in secret.

Fairies were believed to be a source of both good and ill in the Celtic countries, and fairy narratives were used to account for unexplained prosperity, good luck, or wealth, and also for illnesses and deformities. Many families traced their origin to a marriage between a fairy woman and a mortal man, or even a fairy animal (when in human form) such as the Scottish selkie. The Welsh story of LLYN Y FAN FACH is a typical example: a man marries a fairy woman, who agrees to the marriage on the condition that her husband does not strike her; on the third strike, she will leave. The condition is broken in a series of three absurd situations, for example, the fairy laughs at a funeral when everyone else is crying, and she departs. She returned to impart medical knowledge to her children, and a family of physicians in the Myddfai area traced their descent from the protagonists of the story (see MEDDYGON). This story was used as the basis for the novel *Iron and Gold* by the Anglo-Welsh writer Hilda Vaughan. Musical ability and second sight are common gifts of the fairies, and there are several traditional tunes in existence which are said to have been learned from the fairies, for example the Manx *Yn Bollan Bane* (The white herb/mugwort).

Autism, mental illness, nightmares, and strokes were all attributed to the malicious influence of the fairies. A changeling child, where the fairies exchanged a healthy human infant for one of their own kind, may have been a folk explanation for several medical conditions, and allowed the parents some detachment from the situation. Unfortunately, it was believed that cruel or bizarre behaviour towards the child or in the child's presence could induce the fairies to take their changeling back, which had potentially disastrous results for the child. T. Crofton Croker (*Fairy Legends and Traditions of the South of Ireland*) cites a case from Tralee in 1826, in which a mother and grandmother killed a four-year-old child by drowning. The child could neither walk nor speak, and was thought to be fairy-struck; he was killed during the course of the cure. Fairy-struck or fairy-ridden (or hag-ridden) could also be a milder condition, where the human was used as a mount at night; the end result was nightmares and waking up unrested. David Hufford has identified this condition with a fairly common sleep disorder in which the normal phases of sleep are disrupted (*The Terror that Comes in the Night*). Sophia MORRISON recounts the story of Ned Quayle, who was sickened after an encounter with a fairy pig (*Manx Fairy Tales*). He was cured by having a healer charm out the fairy shot, but he retained the mark on his leg. Fairies could also take their nourishment from common household products such as bread, butter, and cheese, and problems with the production of these items were often attributed either to fairies or to witches.

Another trouble was being pisky-led—becoming lost for a long time in a small or familiar area. Time in the fairy realm (see OTHERWORLD) runs differently from the mortal world, and contact with fairies can be dangerous for that reason alone. What may seem to be an hour or an evening spent dancing with the fairies can become a year, seven years, a lifetime, or hundreds of years, and the hapless mortal dancer often returns to find everything changed and everyone gone, turning to dust himself soon thereafter.

Because of their potential to cause harm or even death, great care was taken not to offend the fairies. Preventative measures included referring to them by such names as *An Sluagh Maith* or *Na Daoine Maith* (Gaelic for 'The Good People') or *Y Tylwyth Teg* (Welsh for 'The Fair Family'). Green clothing was avoided in some places, since green was the fairies' colour, and this has been adapted to a belief that green cars are unlucky. Iron was also effective in keeping the fairies away, a factor which MacRitchie and his followers attributed to their being memories of pre-IRON AGE peoples.

Fairy belief was never universal, and whether fairies existed or not was a frequent topic of discussion in church sermons. Adolphe Orain reports a rather cynical exploitation of belief in werewolves from 19th-century Brittany: 'Young men amused themselves running through the countryside at night covered in a wolf skin to scare people. Criminals used this disguise to steal and ransack isolated habitations' (*Folklore de l'Ille-et-Vilaine*). The many comparisons of young warriors with wolves and dogs in early Irish literature suggest the antiquity of such beliefs and practices in the Celtic countries (see HEROIC ETHOS).

Fairy types specific to the individual Celtic countries are discussed below. The works of Katharine Briggs contain reasonably complete listings of fairy types and individuals; what follows here is only a sampling. Many of the fairy traditions are shared between the different countries, or between Celtic and English traditions, or beyond. The English words 'bogey', 'bug', 'puck', and others, are certainly related to such Celtic words as Cornish *bucca* 'hobgoblin, he-goat'; Scottish Gaelic *bòcan* 'hobgoblin'; Irish *púca* 'goblin'; Manx *boag* and *buggane* 'boggle, sprite'; and Welsh *bw(g)* 'ghost, bogey, hobgoblin, scarecrow'. The direction of the borrowings and the relationship to cognates in the Germanic languages are uncertain. Old Norse *púki* 'devil, fiend' has been proposed as a source, derived by POKORNY from INDO-EUROPEAN *$b(h)(e)u$-* 'inflate, swell', with a gutteral suffix. A relation with the words for male goat (e.g. Breton *bouc'h*, English buck) has also been suggested, as has onomatopoeia, but the evidence does not clearly support any hypothesis.

§2. IRELAND

While fairies may be designated in various ways in Modern IRISH, the core terminology is based on the root *sí* or *sídh* 'fairy mound', thus *síóg* 'fairy', *síúil* 'fairy-like', *síscéal* 'fairy tale'. Nonetheless, it would probably be misleading to see the *aes síde* 'people of the fairy mounds' of Old and Middle IRISH LITERATURE as simply and precisely the same phenomenon as the fairies of later Irish tradition. Although the two are generally to be equated, the more complex portrayals in the early literature of individual members of the *aes síde*—who are largely synonymous with the TUATH DÉ—function in a different manner to that of folk tradition (see further FOMOIRI; SÍD). Other Old or

Middle Irish words for fairies exist, notably LU-CHORP(ÁN), *sídaige/síthaige* 'fairy', again derived from *síd*, and several others with a range of meanings: *abacc, siabair, sirite*.

The fairy tradition of modern Ireland (ÉIRE) is extensive. T. Crofton Croker collected and printed several volumes of fairy lore, under the title *Fairy Legends and Traditions of the South of Ireland*, in the 1820s and 1830s. One of the first from the British Isles to record fairy lore, his works were translated into German, and their publication prompted the Grimm brothers to correspond with him. Later editions of his work reflect their influence. W. B. YEATS, an avowed believer in fairies, also used fairy traditions in his literary works, and is responsible to a large extent for the popularization of Irish fairy traditions.

§3. SCOTLAND

The queen of the fairies in Scotland (ALBA), sometimes known as queen of the witches, was Neven or NicNeven, a name Henderson and Cowan derive from *Neamhain*, Old Irish NEMAIN, a war-goddess (*Scottish Fairy Belief* 15). Variations on this name are found all over Scotland, and much of the terminology of the fairy tradition in Scottish Gaelic is similar to that of Irish.

As elsewhere, fairies and other supernatural afflictions could be kept away with iron, with a pierced stone (i.e. a stone with a hole through it, either natural or bored), with holly, or with rowan. Members of the community who have died have been seen among the fairies.

The Scots-language ballads of 'Thomas Rymer' and 'Tam Lin' describe a journey to and from the OTHER-WORLD. Although not current in Gaelic areas, the BALLADS do show some influence from Celtic tradition, for example, the importance of Hallowe'en as the time to rescue Tam Lin (see SAMAIN). The association of the colour green with fairies is also very strong in Scotland. Elfland, where Thomas Rymer was taken, is described in opulent terms, reminiscent of the Irish otherworld.

§4. ISLE OF MAN

One of the best-known Manx fairies is the *fynnoderee* or *phynodderee*, a helpful brownie-type fairy of the home or farmstead. Like other brownies, he is a small, hairy, helpful being, who can be driven away by a gift of clothing. The *fynnoderee* may be a monster (see §1 for definition), and the word is used in the Manx BIBLE to translate what is 'satyr' in the King James Bible, in Isaiah 34:14 (*daemonia onocentauris et pilosus* 'hairy ass-centaur demons' in the Vulgate Latin Bible of St JEROME). Other types of fairy are the *buggane* 'elf, goblin', and the *glashtyn* or *glashan*. Sometimes used as the word for the water-horse, the word is also used for a malevolent, but stupid, fairy, similar to the Scandinavian troll.

Many objects of local significance were attributed to the fairies. A. W. Moore records several narratives of this type (*Folk-lore of the Isle of Man*). In one, a young man finds himself among the fairies, and is warned by a fellow mortal not to eat any of their food. Heeding the warning, he pours the liquid out of his cup, and the fairies and their captives disappear, leaving him holding the cup. He donated the cup to the church, Kirk Malew, and it was subsequently used for communion. Another legend explains the origin of a saddle-shaped stone as a fairy saddle used to enchant horses until a vicar caught the fairy with the horse, whereupon he vanished, leaving his saddle behind as a stone.

§5. WALES

In Wales (CYMRU), the fairies bore several euphemistic names: *Y Tylwyth Teg* throughout the country, but also *Bendith y (eu) Mamau* (the (their) mothers' blessing) in Glamorgan (MORGANNWG) and *Plant Rhys Ddwfn* (the children of Rhys Ddwfn, a figure not otherwise known) in parts of DYFED. An early Welsh fairy abduction narrative is told by Gerald of Wales (GIRALDUS CAMBRENSIS) in *A Journey through Wales*. The anecdote concerns one Elidurus who, at the age of twelve, was invited by two fairies into a subterranean world. The fairies are described as diminutive beings of normal proportions, with equally diminutive horses and dogs; they have long hair, a vegetarian diet, and no religious beliefs of note. Their language was identified as Greek, following the theories of LEGENDARY HISTORY current at the time.

The *Tylwyth Teg* milled their meal in human mills at night, and rewarded humans with coins obtained from other humans. Hugh Evans speculates that the *Tylwyth Teg* were also smokers because of the name given to a small clay object resembling a pipe, *cetyn y Tylwyth Teg*, pl. *catiau y Tylwyth Teg*). Himself a believer, he speculates that humans may have learned the habit from the fairies (*Y Tylwyth Teg*).

The *pwca*, a sort of poltergeist, also appears in Welsh folklore, as do other creatures such as the *wyll* (sometimes *gwyll*), roughly 'goblin' in English, and the *ellyll* 'spirit, phantom, ghost, fairy'. The 14th-century poet DAFYDD AP GWILYM refers to *ellyll* in his poem *Dan y Bargod* (Under the eaves), seemingly in the sense of 'fetch', someone outside himself with strong emotion. The emotion in his case is love, but the word also occurs in Old Irish as the personal name *Ailill* (cf. MEDB), which may refer to someone permanently outside himself with battle-fury. It is difficult to tell which sense is meant in the Welsh TRIADS, where the word occurs twice: *Tri Tharv Ellyll Ynys Brydein* and *Tri Gvyd Ellyll Ynys Brydein*. Rachel BROMWICH translates these as the 'Three Bull-Spectres of the Island of Britain' and the 'Three Wild Spectres of the Island of Britain' (Bromwich, TYP 170–1), but they may equally have been water-bulls (see LEGENDARY ANIMALS) and fairies. Will-o'-the-wisps are *tân ellyllon* (goblins' fire), and mushrooms and foxgloves are *bwyd ellyllon* (goblins' food) and *menig ellyllon* (goblins' gloves), respectively.

§6. BRITTANY

In Brittany (BREIZH), the association of supernatural entities with the dead is very strong. Many of them are considered to be part of the ANAON, the community of the souls of the dead. A great many of these revenants (those who come back from the dead) are atoning for sins committed during their lives—priests return to say forgotten masses at midnight, individuals who moved boundary markers return to carry the heavy stones at night, and the drowned lurk where they met their death, hoping to lure someone else to take their place. Souls also return in the form of animals: a thin cow in a field of fat ones indicates the soul of a miser, while a woman who did not want children returns as a sow with as many piglets as the number of children she 'ought' to have had. Standing stones are also sometimes understood to be the souls of the dead undertaking penance.

Other creatures, such as the *korrigan* (pl. *korriganed*), are much closer to the traditional dwarf of Anglo-Germanic tradition. One of the more important beings is the mermaid. Although ordinary sea-women (*morwreg*, pl. *morwragez*) were known, with the expected traits

of combing long blonde hair and singing, these benevolent mermaids existed alongside more sinister figures known as *mari-morganed* or simply *morganed*. Unlike the *morwragez*, *morganed* were not half fish and did not dwell in the open ocean. They could control the weather, and would entice young fishermen under the sea and drown them. F.-M. LUZEL collected a narrative from the island of Ushant (Breton Enez Eusa) in which a local family was supposed to have obtained its riches from these *morganed*, and there are also narratives of marriages between them and humans.

To protect themselves from malevolent *poulpikanned*, Bretons would keep a vessel filled with grains of millet or peas, which the fairies would be constrained to count. A folding knife could also be stuck into the ground, as close as possible to the fire, so that the blade and handle formed an acute angle. A string of eggshells would be hung in a stable, and the fairies would amuse themselves with this, rather than disturb the horses.

§7. CORNWALL

In addition to the piskies, the Cornish *spriggans* are small and ugly beings who, according to Bottrell, are to be found only where treasure is buried (*Traditions and Hearthside Stories of West Cornwall*). Hunt claims they are the ghosts of giants, who have all died out (*Popular Romances of the West of England*). Saint Michael's Mount was supposed to be the abode of a one-eyed giant (cf. BALOR), and giant narratives account for the placement of many of the megalithic monuments of Cornwall (KERNOW). Knockers or Tommyknockers are a prominent feature of Cornish lore. They are similar to German *kobalds*, but benevolent. They can be annoyed by human activities, especially whistling and swearing, and the presence of the cross. The sound of their knocking indicated a rich vein or lode, and was generally welcomed. The knockers were also called *buccas*, although the *bucca* was also encountered outside the mines. Robert Hunt mentions the *Bucca Dhu* and the *Bucca Gwiddhen*, Late Cornish for 'black bucca' and 'white bucca', respectively. He says that fishermen would leave an offering of fish on the shore for *Bucca Dhu*, just as miners were said to leave offerings of food for the buccas.

Both Hunt and Bottrell record variations on 'The Fairy Widower' in which a male fairy entices a young woman to agree to look after his child for a period of time. She does so willingly, but upon breaking a taboo is sent home. All the narratives specify that the heroine was unhappy or discontent for a period of time after being sent home from fairyland, a reflection in narrative of the possibility of diagnosing depression and similar states as fairy-caused illnesses.

FURTHER READING
AFANC; ALBA; ANAON; ANKOU; ARTHUR; BALLADS; BALOR; BIBLE; BREIZH; BROMWICH; CAILLEACH BHÉIRRE; CELTIC COUNTRIES; CYMRU; DAFYDD AP GWILYM; DYFED; ÉIRE; ELLAN VANNIN; FINN MAC CUMAILL; FOLK-TALES; FOMOIRI; GIRALDUS CAMBRENSIS; HEROIC ETHOS; INDO-EUROPEAN; IRISH; IRISH LITERATURE; IRON AGE; JEROME; KERNOW; LEGENDARY ANIMALS; LEGENDARY HISTORY; LLYN Y FAN FACH; LUCHORPÁN; LUZEL; MEDB; MEDDYGON; MORGANNWG; MORRISON; MYTHOLOGICAL CYCLE; NEMAIN; OTHERWORLD; PICTS; PISKY; POKORNY; REINCARNATION; SAMAIN; SÍD; TRIADS; TUATH DÉ; YEATS; Bottrell, *Traditions and Hearthside Stories of West Cornwall*; Briggs, *British Folk-Tales and Legends*; Briggs, *Dictionary of Fairies*; Briggs, *Fairies in Tradition and Literature*; Briggs, *Vanishing People*; Bromwich, *Dafydd ap Gwilym*; Bromwich, TYP; Callow, *Phynodderree*; Campbell, *Popular Tales of the West Highlands 2*; Croker, *Fairy Legends and Traditions of the South of Ireland*; Hugh Evans, *Y Tylwyth Teg*; Evans-Wentz, *Fairy-faith in Celtic Countries*; Henderson & Cowan, *Scottish Fairy Belief*; Henry, ÉC 8. 404–16; Hufford, *Terror That Comes in the Night*; Hunt, *Popular Romances of the West of England*; Isaac, *Coelion Cymru*; T. Gwynn Jones, *Welsh Folklore and Folk-Custom*; Keightley, *Fairy Mythology*; Killip, *Folklore of the Isle of Man*; MacDougall, *Highland Fairy Legends*; Macinlay, *Folklore of Scottish Lochs and Springs*; Moore, *Folklore of the Isle of Man*; Morrison, *Manx Fairy Tales*; Narváez, *Good People*; Orain, *Folklore de l'Ille-et-Vilaine 2*; Palmer, *Folklore of (Old) Monmouthshire*; Palmer, *Folklore of Radnorshire*; Pokorny, IEW; Rhŷs, *Celtic Folklore*; Rojcewicz, *Journal of American Folklore* 100.396.148–60; Sébillot, *La bretagne et ses traditions*; Sikes, *British Goblins*; Thomas, *Chwedlau a Choelion Godre'r Wyddfa*; Thompson, *Supernatural Highlands*; Thorpe, *Journey through Wales / Gerald of Wales*; Vaughan, *Iron and Gold*; Wood, *Folklore* 103.56–72; Yeats, *Fairy and Folk Tales of Ireland*.

AM

The Irish **Famine** (1845–52) ranks as one of the worst natural disasters in modern European history. An estimated one million people died in a population of 8–8.5 million and up to 2 million emigrated. The immediate cause was a blight which devastated the potato—the staple food of the population. The adoption of the potato, a crop which originated in the Andes in South America, made it possible for the population to increase from 2 million in the 1740s to over 8 million on the eve of the famine. The increase was most pronounced in the west and north of the island, where the climate and land made it difficult to cultivate grain.

The potato enabled families to survive on 1–2 acres (0.4–0.8 ha) of land, and these smallholdings underpinned an agrarian economy which exported livestock, bacon, dairy produce and grain to Britain. On the eve of the famine, Ireland (ÉIRE) produced sufficient food for 10 million people.

The potato blight left Ireland with an acute subsistence crisis. Families which had been self-sufficient in food were forced to buy it in the market, but supplies were scarce, prices soared, and labourers and small farmers could not afford to feed their families. A shortage of food, mass migration of starving people, the crowding together on public relief works or in workhouses, resulted in epidemics of typhus and other fevers. Most deaths were caused by disease, but thousands died of starvation.

During the famine, the response of the British government was a hotly debated topic, and it remains so today. Irish nationalists claimed that there was ample food in Ireland, even at the height of the famine, and that the crisis could have been resolved by banning exports. This claim does not withstand scrutiny. Although some food was exported during these years, exports were dwarfed by imports; if the food trade had been disrupted, many more people would have died. Other aspects of British policy are more questionable, for example, the decision to provide relief in 1846 in the form of public works rather than by providing food. Government soup-kitchens opened in the spring of 1847, and were soon feeding up to 3 million people, but in the autumn of 1847 the British authorities declared that the famine had ended, and that all further relief should be provided through the poor law.

Britain was determined that Irish taxpayers, particularly landowners, should bear most of the cost of famine relief. The famine was seen as confirmation that Irish rural society was inherently flawed, and many politicians and civil servants were determined that Irish smallholdings should be replaced by English-style capitalist farming. Their primary target was the Irish landlord class, but the latter survived the famine largely unscathed; the cost of Britain's effort at social engineering fell on the Irish poor. During the latter years of the famine, thousands of smallholders were evicted from their land by landlords who took advantage of the famine to consolidate holdings. Some died as a consequence, others emigrated or were crowded into workhouses.

By the early 1840s, up to 100,000 people were emigrating each year, and no part of Ireland was immune. Between 1845 and 1855 over 1.5 million emigrated to the USA, and a further 200,000–300,000 went to Canada (see CELTIC LANGUAGES IN NORTH AMERICA). Panic emigration in 1847 saw overcrowded ships crossing the Atlantic in mid-winter, many carrying fever-ridden passengers. The highest mortality was on ships travelling to Canada; since this was the cheapest route, it attracted the poorest emigrants. Liverpool was the major port for emigration to North America, but many of the Irish who arrived there did not leave because they were too poor or too sick. The influx of famine emigrants placed an enormous strain on health and welfare services in British and American cities, and it is not altogether surprising that it prompted an increase in anti-Irish and anti-Catholic prejudice. Many emigrants held Britain responsible for the famine and for their exile from Ireland. By the 1860s the Fenian Brotherhood, which was committed to bringing about an Irish republic by armed rebellion, had many recruits among the Irish in Britain and North America.

In Ireland, the collapse of the potato-based economy wiped out the agricultural labouring class, and this resulted in a more bourgeois, conservative Ireland. The family farm of 20–30 acres (8–12 ha) dominated post-famine Ireland. Farms were no longer subdivided; marriages became fewer, couples married at a later age, and dowries became the norm. Church attendance became universal, and traditional peasant customs such as patterns and holy wells were abandoned, perhaps because these had failed to prevent the famine. The IRISH language was another major casualty; a disproportionate number of famine victims and subsequent emigrants came from Irish-speaking areas in the west of Ireland.

FURTHER READING
AGRICULTURE; CELTIC LANGUAGES IN NORTH AMERICA; ÉIRE; IRISH; Daly, *Making of Modern Irish History* 71–89; Donnelly, *Great Irish Potato Famine*; Gray, *Bullán* 1.75–90; Neal, *Meaning of the Famine* 56–80; Ó Gráda, *Black '47 and Beyond*; Solar, *Famine* 112–33.

Mary E. Daly

fanum and sanctuary

Despite a wide diversity among the ancient Celtic ritual sites which have been investigated to date, it is possible to suggest a general description for Gaulish sanctuaries. These show numerous recurring characteristics, which seem to be systematic. The sites often exhibit a long continuity over a period of generations or centuries, during which they were rebuilt. The most dramatic shift in form is seen when the cult sites have a sustained life from the pre-Roman IRON AGE (*c.* 700–*c.* 50 BC) into the Roman period (which began shortly after *c.* 50 BC in central and northern GAUL, earlier nearer the Mediterranean).

One of a pair of carved wooden stags found in ritual shaft and well at the Fellbach-Schmiden sanctuary (viereckschanze), Baden-Württemberg, Germany, probably once decorated a structure at the top of the shaft, last quarter 2nd century BC

These cult sites were usually enclosed by a small earthen bank accompanied by a ditch (see ENCLOSURES). The length of these earthworks varies. At GOURNAY-sur-ARONDE (Oise), the earliest example identified to date, the ditch is roughly 45 m along each side, but the ditch measures only 15 m at Bennecourt (Yvelines); both sites open to the east.

In the centre of the enclosure, several structures usually occur together, including an inner central ditch surrounded by several smaller ditches and buildings. The type of buildings found within Gaulish sanctuaries varies over time in the pre-Roman Iron Age. The earliest buildings were of wood (and thus revealed to archaeologists by post holes); these were followed by composite wood and stone structures, and finally by buildings entirely of stone. The last arguably show the influence of Mediterranean ideas concerning sacred architecture. Remains of cult practice, offerings, and SACRIFICE (see also RITUAL) have been found, mainly in pits and the enclosing ditches, and more rarely from the successive surface layers of soil or erosion deposits. Of the recurring portable finds with a superior survival rate, spectacular quantities of weapons are common, chiefly SWORDS, spears, and SHIELDS. The small wall which typically surrounds the inner enclosure and its structures is in many cases set within a much larger enclosure (about 10 ha). This outer precinct might have served as a central place of assembly or 'fair ground' for the widely scattered Celtic rural population, when they came together for such diverse activities as making and exchanging crafts, tribal gatherings, FEASTS, athletic contests, mustering prior to offensive military campaigns, or various sorts of displays and performances.

During the Gallo-Roman period, a temple constructed of masonry, the *fanum* 'sanctuary temple', was often added to these sites. This stone building consisted of a central space, the *cella*, and a peripheral part, the gallery. Both the *cella* and the gallery have a square floor plan. The same basic type was also common in Roman Britain in pre-Christian times. Even when none of the structure survives at the surface level, the characteristic shape of the Romano-Celtic *fanum* can easily be detected by aerial surveys. When investigated, sites of this type often reveal that the Roman temple was built on top of a sanctuary of the pre-Roman variety described above. Having functioned as a gathering point for several centuries in the Iron Age, these sites apparently retained an important social and ideological function long after the end of Celtic independence.

FURTHER READING
ENCLOSURES; FEAST; GAUL; GOURNAY; IRON AGE; RITUAL; SACRIFICE; SHIELD; SWORDS; VIERECKSCHANZEN; Brunaux, *Celtic Gauls*; Brunaux, *Les religions gauloises*; Brunaux, *Les sanctuaires celtiques*; Haffner, *Heiligtümer und Opferkulte der Kelten*.

Patrice Méniel

feast

§1. INTRODUCTION

The Celtic feast strikes modern readers as a pervasive social institution on which a complex of distinctive social values converge. Various types of evidence for it come from a wide range of places and periods—IRON AGE archaeology, GREEK AND ROMAN ACCOUNTS of the ancient Celts (§7), early Irish and Welsh heroic narratives, such as those of the ULSTER CYCLE and the MABINOGI, and court poetry down to the time of the extinction of the 'GAELIC order' in the 17th century in Ireland (ÉIRE) and the 18th-century in the Scottish HIGHLANDS.

Throughout this vast range, the Celtic feast stands out consistently as a place for the assembly and reconstitution of the dispersed rural tribal group (TUATH), economic gift exchange between chiefs and followers, the display and consumption of items of élite prestige, the defining and reconfirming—often competitively—of social identity and rank within a hierarchical society, and the confirmation of new social relationships, such as marriage alliances and the elevation of kings. Although one might think of these distinctive functions as virtually a non-linguistic definition of Celticity, none of them are exclusively Celtic, but may be found in many times and places as features of societies which could be characterized by such potentially misleading terms as 'primitive', 'oral' (see LITERACY), or 'small-scale'. These features seem distinctive to us because we live as citizens of modern states, in principle at least, equal before the law; the particulars of our identity and qualifications are documented, as are our principal social relationships and obligations; our financial means are quantified impersonally by cash value. Therefore, we have no need for a great, ritualized public activity like the Celtic feast to define who we are and how we relate to the broader society. A second cause for caution, lest we define Celticity too much on the basis of the feast, is that in comparing diverse and often ambiguous types of evidence—such as text-free evidence from pre-Christian HALLSTATT and LA TÈNE burials from mainland Europe on the one hand versus highly fictionalized and fantastic narratives from medieval Ireland and Wales on the other—there is a tendency to explain one fact in terms of the other, and thus see things as being more alike than they might in fact be.

Feasting is mentioned many times in this Encyclopedia. The remainder of this article summarizes this material, arranged by general categories. The reader may pursue further details through the cross-references.

§2. GENERAL ASPECTS
See DRUNKENNESS; FOODWAYS; WINE.

§3. ARCHAEOLOGICAL EVIDENCE
During the earlier IRON AGE, Celtic west-central Europe developed contacts with the Mediterranean world, borrowing the institution of the symposium and related items of Greek and Etruscan paraphernalia, such as sieves and flagons for serving WINE, and LA TÈNE style ornament is often found on metal drinking vessels which have been interpreted as equipment for aristocratic feasting (see ART, CELTIC [1] §§3–5; KLEINASPERGLE). There is abundant evidence for (sometimes spectacularly) rich drinking vessels, other feasting equipment, and food and drink itself being central features of aristocratic burials in HALLSTATT and La Tène periods in GAUL, central Europe, and Britain, for example, at CLEMENCY, DÜRRNBERG (§4), HOCHDORF, HOHMICHELE, LAMADELAINE, MAGDALENENBERG (§2), REINHEIM, SAINT-ROMAN-DE-JALIONAS, VIX, WELWYN; cf. also VEHICLE BURIALS. In pre-Roman Gaul, there is evidence for a type of animal SACRIFICE (§2) at which the flesh was then consumed, at sites including RIBEMONT-SUR-ANCRE and FESQUES. For an interpretation of enclosed structures possibly used for ritual communal feasting in Iron Age Gaul, see FANUM. A slaughter pattern suggesting seasonal feasting has been identified in Iron Age Ireland (ÉRIU) in the faunal remains of the traditional royal centre of LAIGIN at DÚN AILINNE.

§4. THE EVIDENCE OF THE CLASSICAL AUTHORS
In general, see GREEK AND ROMAN ACCOUNTS (§7). The foundation legend of MASSALIA involves the arrival of Greek travellers at a royal Gaulish wedding feast, see ARISTOTLE. For ATHENAEUS' description (probably derived from POSIDONIUS) of the extravagant feast of the Gaulish chieftain Lovernios as the occasion for praise poetry richly rewarded with gold, see BARD [1]. For the account of the year-long feast and feasting halls of the Ariamnes preserved by Athenaeus, see the entry on his source, PHYLARCHUS. For an account derived from Posidonius of exchange of precious metal vessels, heroic contention, and heroes submitting to have their throats cut at Gaulish feasts, see ATHENAEUS. DIODORUS SICULUS, drawing on Posidonius, recognized the similarity between accounts of the bestowing of choice cuts of meat on warriors at Gaulish feasts and the deeds of the Greek heroes of HOMER, see CHAMPION'S PORTION. A description preserved by Athenaeus of a feast at which Celtic hosts poisoned their Illyrian guests is quoted in the entry on THEOPOMPUS; cf. also CAMMA's poisoning of the wedding libation of Sinorīx.

§5. IRISH TRADITION
For the theme of heroic status competition through violent contention at feasts, see CHAMPION'S PORTION (*curadmír*); FLED BRICRENN ('Bricriu's Feast'); SCÉLA MUCCE MEIC DÁ THÓ ('The Story of Mac Dá Thó's Pig'); ULSTER CYCLE. Rules and standards for royal feasts are set out in the 9th-century *Tecosca Cormaic* (The instructions of CORMAC [MAC AIRT]), see WISDOM LITERATURE. On *Feis Temro* (The feast of Tara), see DIARMAIT MAC CERBAILL; TEAMHAIR. On the Irish *tarbfheis* 'bull feast', see FEIS; SACRIFICE, animal (§1). At the mythological feast described in *Baile Chuinn* (Conn's ecstasy), the sovereignty of Ireland was promised to the descendants of CONN CÉTCHATHACH, see TUATH DÉ (§4). In the tale *Altromh Tige Dá Medar* (The nurturing of the house of two milk vessels), the Tuath Dé are said to have achieved immortality at the feast of GOIBNIU. For the hostel or large banqueting hall as described in early Irish sources, see BRUIDEN. Cf. also MEDB; MESCA ULAD ('The Intoxication of the Ulstermen').

§6. WELSH TRADITION

For the year-long feast of heroes at the 'hall of Mynyðawc', see GODODDIN. For the feast of ARTHUR's court as a theme and narrative device, see GLEWLWYD GAFAELFAWR. For the wedding feast as an important theme and dramatic turning-point in the First Branch of the MABINOGI, see PWYLL. For the wedding feast as the venue for formally conferring status on a novice poet in the later Middle Ages, see BARDIC ORDER [2] §10. On the otherworldly 87-year feast, *yspyðawt urðawl benn* (hospitality of the noble [decapitated] head), of the Second Branch, see BRÂN; BRANWEN.

§7. VOCABULARY

There are several words in the CELTIC LANGUAGES which may be translated 'feast'. The best attested are Old Irish *fled*, Scottish Gaelic *fleadh* 'feast', Modern Irish *fleá*, Old Welsh *guled*, Modern *gwledd*, Breton *gloé*, all from PROTO-CELTIC **wlidā*, which is also attested in the Gaulish personal name *Vlido-rix* 'king of feasts'. Old Irish FEIS is often translated 'feast' and descriptions in early sources generally involve animal SACRIFICE and feasting, but etymologically the word's main sense is 'spending the night'; cf. Old Breton *guest*, Welsh *gwest* 'night's stay'. In 20th-century Ireland, *feis* became a common word for a (GAELIC) cultural festival (see FEISEANNA). More recently, *fleá* has become common in this meaning.

FURTHER READING
ARISTOTLE; ART, CELTIC; ARTHUR; ATHENAEUS; BARD; BARDIC ORDER; BRÂN; BRANWEN; BRUIDEN; CAMMA; CELTIC LANGUAGES; CHAMPION'S PORTION; CLEMENCY; CONN CÉTCHATHACH; CORMAC MAC AIRT; DIARMAIT MAC CERBAILL; DIODORUS SICULUS; DRUNKENNESS; DÚN AILINNE; DÜRRNBERG; ÉIRE; ÉRIU; FANUM; FEIS; FEISEANNA; FESQUES; FLED BRICRENN; FOODWAYS; GAELIC; GAUL; GLEWLWYD GAFAELFAWR; GODODDIN; GOIBNIU; GREEK AND ROMAN ACCOUNTS; HALLSTATT; HIGHLANDS; HOCHDORF; HOHMICHELE; HOMER; IRON AGE; KLEINASPERGLE; LA TÈNE; LAIGIN; LAMADELAINE; LITERACY; MABINOGI; MAGDALENENBERG; MASSALIA; MEDB; MESCA ULAD; PHYLARCHUS; POSIDONIUS; PROTO-CELTIC; PWYLL; REINHEIM; RIBEMONT-SUR-ANCRE; SACRIFICE; SAINT-ROMAN-DE-JALIONAS; SCÉLA MUCCE MEIC DÁ THÓ; TEAMHAIR; THEOPOMPUS; TUATH; TUATH DÉ; ULSTER CYCLE; VEHICLE BURIALS; VIX; WELWYN; WINE; WISDOM LITERATURE; Biel, *Der Keltenfürst von Hochdorf*; Burnham & Johnson, *Invasion and Response*; Enright, *Lady with a Mead Cup*; Haycock, *Beirdd a Thywysogion* 39–59; Jackson, *Gododdin* 36; Jarman, *Beiträge zur Indogermanistik und Keltologie* 193–211; Jarman, *Llên Cymru* 8.125–49; Neuman de Vegvar, *From the Isles of the North* 81–7; O'Leary, *Éigse* 20.115–27; Rathje, *Sympotica* 279–88; Simms, *Journal of the Royal Society of Antiquaries of Ireland* 108.67–100; Toussaint-Samat, *History of Food*; Wells, *Culture Contact and Culture Change*; Gruffydd Aled Williams, *Ildánach Ildírech* 289–302; Ifor Williams, *Canu Aneirin* xlviii–xlix.

JTK

Fedelm (variant spelling Feidelm), known by the early Irish occupational epithets *banfhili* (woman learned poet) and *banfháith* (woman prophet) and who declares herself to be from CONNACHT and to have received esoteric training in ALBA, possessing IMBAS FOROSNAI, is a character best known to modern readers as the striking figure who appears near the beginning of the action in TÁIN BÓ CUAILNGE ('The Cattle Raid of Cooley'), when she is questioned by Queen MEDB regarding the fate of her vast army in the impending action. Fedelm replies repeatedly, *at·chíu forderg, at·chíu rúad* 'I see it bloody, I see it red', and then goes on to describe poetically the disaster to be inflicted by Cú CHULAINN's feats. VELEDA, as described by TACITUS, was a pagan prophetess with a closely comparable social rôle. It is likely that the *Táin*'s Fedelm *banfháith* is understood to be the same as the sexually provocative prophetess Fedelm 'of the lovely hair' (*Foltchaín*), who was Cú Chulainn's lover for a year and who caused the mysterious debility of the Ulster warriors (ULAID) through displaying herself naked to them in the brief ULSTER CYCLE tale, sometimes called 'Cú Chulainn and Fedelm' and edited by Meyer. Significantly, the word *Fedelm* most probably derives from the PROTO-CELTIC root *wēd-/wid-* 'know, see' (on the probably Gaulish cognate *uidlua*, see BRICTA; cf. CYFARWYDD; DRUID). However, the name was not uncommon; for example, Fedelm Noíchride (or Noíchrothach) is the daughter of King CONCHOBAR in *Táin Bó Cuailnge*, where she abandons her husband Cairbre Nia Fer for the hero CONALL CERNACH; in FLED BRICRENN ('Briciriu's Feast'), she is Loegaire Buadach's wife (see ULSTER CYCLE §3). The common man's name, Old Irish *Fedlimid*, OGAM genitive VEDDELLEMETTO, Modern *Féilimí* is probably related.

PRIMARY SOURCES ('Cú Chulainn and Fedelm')
MS. London, BL, Harley 5280 44v.
EDITION. Meyer, ZCP 8.120.
TRANS. Koch & Carey, *Celtic Heroic Age* 67–8.

FURTHER READING
ALBA; BRICTA; CONALL CERNACH; CONCHOBAR; CONNACHT; CÚ CHULAINN; CYFARWYDD; DRUIDS; FLED BRICRENN; IMBAS

FOROSNAI; MEDB; OGAM; PROTO-CELTIC; TACITUS; TÁIN BÓ
CUAILNGE; ULAID; ULSTER CYCLE; VELEDA.

JTK

Feis (pl. *feissi*, Modern Irish pl. FEISEANNA, from Old
Irish *foaid* 'spends the night with, sleeps', cf. Welsh *gwest*
'night's stay, lodging' < Celtic **west-*) is a term originally used to denote certain ceremonial feasts which
had an element of coupling, such as marriages or the
confirmation of a rightful king. However, *feis* gradually lost this ritualistic connotation and came to mean
any kind of FEAST. *Feissi* mentioned in the Irish AN-
NALS and medieval IRISH LITERATURE include *Feis Temro*
(the feast of Tara), which was the inauguration of the
kings of Tara (TEAMHAIR). Such royal inauguration
was also called *banfheis* (cf. *ban-* 'woman/female', Modern Irish *bainis* 'wedding'), thus called because it described the king's initiation through marriage with the
tribal goddess. Among the practices associated with
the selection rites of Irish sacral KINGSHIP was the
tarbfheis (cf. *tarb* 'bull'). There is no historical documentation for this custom (although GIRALDUS
CAMBRENSIS mentions a practice somewhat reminiscent of it). However, Irish literary accounts suggest
that it was one of the methods used to determine a
future ruler, particularly associated with supernatural
notions of the kingship of Tara. Thus, in the early
tale TOGAIL BRUIDNE DA DERGA ('The Destruction
of Da Derga's Hostel'), the *tarbfheis* is used as the means
of recognizing the claims of the legendary Conaire
Mór mac Eterscélae as the rightful future king of Tara.
A particularly detailed description of a *tarbfheis* is contained in the tale SERGLIGE CON CULAINN ('The Wasting Sickness of Cú Chulainn'), preserved in the medieval Irish manuscript LEBOR NA HUIDRE ('The Book
of the Dun Cow'; *c.* 1106). In an interim passage, relatively unconnected to the rest of the tale, we find the
following account:

> A white bull is being slaughtered and a man is cho-
> sen to eat and drink his fill of the meat and broth
> made from it. After that, the man falls asleep, while
> four DRUIDS are singing the 'Gold of Truth' over
> him. In his sleep, the future king is revealed to the
> man, who on waking gives a description of the true
> king.

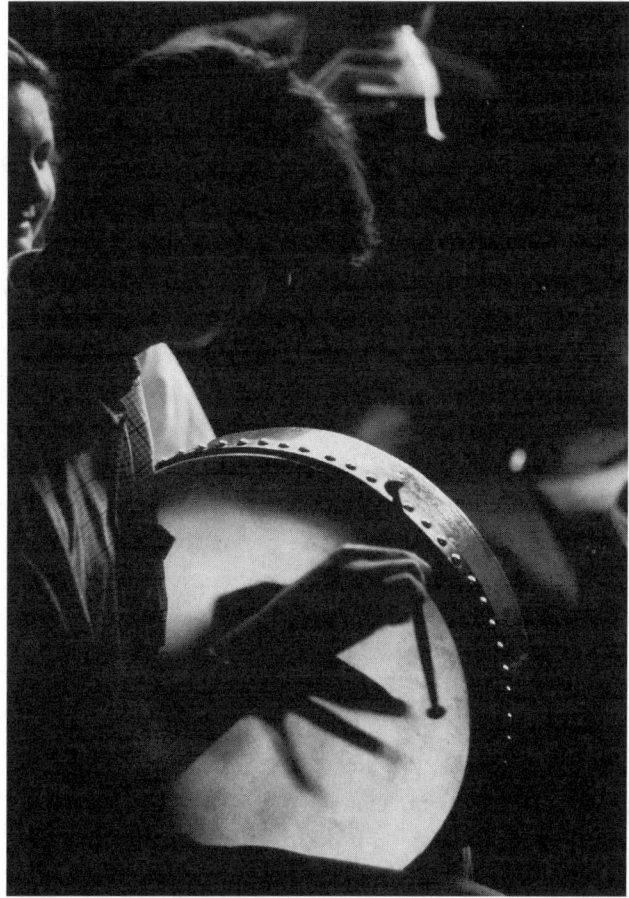

Irish folk music at Fleá Cheoil music festival, Ireland

FURTHER READING
ANNALS; DRUIDS; FEAST; FEISEANNA; GIRALDUS CAMBRENSIS;
IRISH; IRISH LITERATURE; KINGSHIP; LEBOR NA H-UIDRE;
SERGLIGE CON CULAINN; TEAMHAIR; TOGAIL BRUIDNE DA
DERGA; Byrne, *Irish Kings and High-Kings*; Dillon, *Scottish Gaelic
Studies* 7.47–88; Knott, *Togail Bruidne Da Derga* 122–6; O'Meara,
Gerald of Wales; O'Rahilly, *Ériu* 14.7–28; Schröder, ZCP 16.310–
12; Tristram, *Medialität und mittelalterliche insulare Literatur* 183–220.

PSH

***Feiseanna* and the Oireachtas** are festivals
organized at local and national level in Ireland (ÉIRE)
since the 1890s for the promotion of GAELIC language
and culture. In 1898 the first provincial FEIS ('feast',
pl. *feiseanna*, not a *feis ceoil*, 'music festival') was held in
Macroom, Co. Cork (Maigh Chromtha, Contae
Chorcaí), and similar *feiseanna* were held in the following months all over the country. The Gaelic League's

Ard-Fheis (National convention) of that year formalized the arrangement, licensing *feiseanna* for the Irish-speaking counties from then on (see CONRADH NA GAEILGE).

Feiseanna were a mix of education and entertainment: students both young and old competed to demonstrate knowledge of basic texts, while entrants with a broader knowledge of the language entered storytelling, essay-writing, recitation, or folklore-collecting competitions. There were additional events for instrumentation, singing, and dancing. Some *feiseanna* also included drama, translation, and versification. The political and cultural agenda of the *feiseanna* were sometimes obvious, as when entrants of essay competitions were told to deal with Gaelic heroes or advocate the national advantages of encouraging small farms or cooperativization. Some *feiseanna*, such as those of Antrim (Aontroim) and Wexford (LOCH GARMAN), had hugely popular competitions for local agricultural and industrial items, and their exhibitions drew many non-Irish speakers.

By 1903 there was already an informal gradation system whereby winners of local and provincial *feiseanna* moved on to higher competitions until they reached the national Oireachtas. By 1905 the word *feis* itself had become contentious, with the Gaelic League pressing to stop the word being used to advertise any gatherings other than theirs.

By 1908, although the Oireachtas and the Gaelic League had crested in popularity, regional *feiseanna* continued to thrive, only falling into abeyance during the 1920s. The Dublin *feis* was successfully revived in 1930, and by 1942 there were 5000 competitors. Often, where there was an active branch of the League, there were (usually annual) *feiseanna*, which were often the only community festivals. In 1943 there were 130 *feiseanna* around Ireland.

The Oireachtas was consciously modelled on the Welsh EISTEDDFOD (Ó Súilleabháin, *Scél an Oireachtais 1897–1924* 10–15) and has itself served as a model for all subsequent Oireachtais (pl. of Oireachtas) up to the present day. The first Oireachtas (envisioned as a language festival), founded by the fledgling Gaelic League, was held in 1897 to coincide with the first day of the second annual *feis ceoil* (a national festival which concentrated on Irish music and dance) in Dublin (BAILE ÁTHA CLIATH). The Gaelic League scheduled its *Ard-Fheis* to coincide with the festival from 1898

onwards. With a six-day programme and 1000 competitors by 1904, the festival was a natural congregation opportunity for cultural activists. Political rivalries in the League led to difficulties with the Oireachtas, however, and by 1913, even with the festival being held in Galway city (GAILLIMH), competition standards were considered low and locals stayed away. The festival was cancelled due to lack of interest in 1925 and not revived until 1939, albeit on a much smaller scale, at Dublin's Mansion House. There was a gradual growth of interest in the Oireachtas from then on and by 1968 the festival, now held annually in Dublin, was so large that events were being held in 21 centres around Dublin. A magnet for language activists, writers, and native speakers, the festival continued to grow, and from 1974 alternated venues between the provinces and Dublin. The festival's literary competitions have served as launching pads for many new writers in IRISH, and the financial incentives of the prize fund have ensured quality work that has often gone on to publication. Oral-performance competitions (such as those for SEAN-NÓS singing) are broadcast live to large audiences on Raidió na Gaeltachta, the national Irish-language radio service (see MASS MEDIA).

FURTHER READING
BAILE ÁTHA CLIATH; CONRADH NA GAEILGE; ÉIRE; EISTEDD-FOD; FEIS; GAELIC; GAILLIMH; IRISH; IRISH MUSIC; LOCH GARMAN; MASS MEDIA; SEAN-NÓS; Mac Aonghusa, *Oireachtas na Gaeilge: 1897–1997*; Mac Mathúna, *Seán Cuimhní Cinn ar an Oireachtas*; Ó Fearaíl, *Story of Conradh na Gaeilge*; Ó Súilleabháin, *Scéal an Oireachtais 1897–1924*.

Brian Ó Broin

Féni is an Old Irish term which, in its most general sense, means 'the Irish people'. There are several more restrictive senses as well. In LAW TEXTS, *Féni* means legally competent freemen of the tribal polity (TUATH), and *fénechas* signifies the customary secular law of the Irish. In these senses, Irish people in SLAVERY were not *Féni*, and other groups are excluded by virtue of privilege, for example, clergy and the *filid* (the top rank of professional poets; see BARDIC ORDER). In early strata of the laws, *Féni* has tribal as well as sociological limitations, as in the proverbial statement: *batar tri prímchinēla in Hére .i. Féni 7 Ulaith 7 Gaileóin .i. Laigin* 'there were three principal peoples in Ireland, namely Féni,

ULAID, and Gaileōin, that is LAIGIN'. In later versions Érainn are added to the list (see ÉRIU §1). In this formulation, it seems that *Féni* means the peoples whose rulers were reckoned in the GENEALOGIES as *Síl Cuinn* (descendants of the legendary CONN CÉTCHATHACH). The rulers of CONNACHT and the pre-eminent UÍ NÉILL dynasties were thus included. The status of the ÉOGANACHT of MUMU (Munster) is less clear. The genealogies come to treat them as close kin to *Síl Cuinn*; therefore they might count among the Féni of the early list. But they were possibly simply not yet of interest. Unlike the others, they had not supplied kings of Tara (TEAMHAIR) in the early historical period, which is why the Érainn were added, since two of their legendary kings—Conaire Mór (see TOGAIL BRUIDNE DA DERGA) and Lugaid Mac Con in the KINGS' CYCLES—were portrayed in well-known sagas as prehistoric kings of Tara.

In Irish LEGENDARY HISTORY (§3), such as the texts AURAICEPT NA NÉCES and LEBAR GABÁLA ÉRENN, the eponymous inventor of the Irish language (*Goídelg*; see GAELIC) was a Scythian nobleman, Fénius Farsaid. Fénius appeared at Babel following the confusion of tongues and had the best parts of the 72 languages of the world 'cut out' to synthesize IRISH. As Carey has shown, Fénius's name and story result from the fortuitous similarity between the Irish group name and that of Fenech, a character in a 3rd- or 4th-century Latin translation of the Hebrew apocryphal text *Liber Antiquitatum Biblicarum* of Pseudo-Philo. Like Fénius, Fenech ordered the building of sea-going ships and, more significantly, was the leader of the descendants of Japhet at Babel.

As to the etymology of *Féni*, a connection with Old Irish *féinnid* 'hunter, (tribeless) warrior' seems likely (cf. FÍAN; O'Brien, *Ériu* 9.182–3). Wagner linked the name with *fén* 'wagon', thus an original group name meaning 'wagoners' (*Celtica* 11.264ff.). As a refinement of the first etymology, Hamp proposed that *Féni* and the partly synonymous *Goídil* (see GAELIC) ultimately go back to the same root and had once belonged to a single paradigm: INDO-EUROPEAN **weidh-(e)l-o-* : **weidh-n-jo-*, with the same root as Old Irish *fíad*, Old Breton *guoid*, and Welsh *gŵydd*, all meaning 'wild, feral, uncultivated' < PROTO-CELTIC **wēdu-* < IE **weidh-* (GPC s.v. *Gwyddel*; Pokorny, IEW 1.1177). The original sense of Celtic **wēdnii* > *Féni* would thus be 'forest

people' and it then developed the meaning 'warriors', which was applied to that class among dominant tribal groups. It is likely that the Welsh kingdom name GWYNEDD and its old Latinization *Venedotia* also go back to this Celtic formation, an etymology which would suit traditions of Gwynedd's foundation by the migratory war-bands of CUNEDDA and his sons.

FURTHER READING
AURAICEPT NA N-ÉCES; BARDIC ORDER; CONN CÉTCHATHACH; CONNACHT; CUNEDDA; ÉOGANACHT; ÉRIU; FÍAN; GAELIC; GENEALOGIES; GWYNEDD; INDO-EUROPEAN; IRISH; KINGS' CYCLES; LAIGIN; LAW TEXTS; LEBAR GABÁLA ÉRENN; LEGENDARY HISTORY; MUMU; PROTO-CELTIC; SLAVERY; TEAMHAIR; TOGAIL BRUIDNE DA DERGA; TUATH; UÍ NÉILL; ULAID; Binchy, *Críth Gablach*; Binchy, *Ériu* 16.33–48; Carey, *Celtica* 21.104–12; Charles-Edwards & Kelly, *Bechbretha*; GPC s.v. Gwyddel; Hamp, *Proc. Harvard Celtic Colloquium* 12.43–50; Loth, RC 41.350–3; O'Brien, *Ériu* 9.182–3; Pokorny, IEW 1.1177; Wagner, *Celtica* 11.264ff.

JTK

Fergus mac Róich is one of the main characters of the early Irish ULSTER CYCLE of Tales. He is present in a position of seniority and prominence in many of the stories, likened by JACKSON to the Homeric Nestor, as respected elder warrior and nobleman, and is a multifaceted character.

§1. FORMER KING OF ULSTER
He lost the kingship of ULAID to CONCHOBAR, through the wiles of Conchobar's mother Nes in the earlier version of *Compert Conchobuir* (The conception of Conchobar). Even so, he retained much of his earlier status and sometimes appears as a virtual co-king, for example, in the beheading episode of FLED BRICRENN (§94), when Sencha mac Ailello responds to the mysterious axe-wielding churl's challenge:

> Conchobor put aside . . . for the sake of his sovereignty, and Fergus mac Róich also on account of his similar privilege. These two excepted, let whoever of you come who dares, so I may cut off his head tonight and he mine tomorrow night.

§2. SPOKESMAN AND BEARER OF ORAL TRADITION
Fergus often figures as the spokesman of the Ulaid and the mediator of their oral lore. For example, in *Fled Bricrenn* he makes the collective response to BRICRIU's ominous invitations: 'No! For if we go our

dead will outnumber our living, when Bricriu has incited us against each other.' In *Fallsigud Tána Bó Cuailnge* ('How TÁIN BÓ CUAILNGE Was Found'), Fergus's spirit rises from his grave to recite the *Táin* to the 6th-century poet SENCHÁN TORPÉIST (for an ancient Celtic parallel discussed by Freeman, see NICANDER OF COLOPHON). Similarly, *Macgnímrada Con Culainn* ('The Boyhood Deeds of Cú Chulainn') occur as a narrative flashback within the *Táin* related by Fergus to the inquiring Queen MEDB.

§3. LEADER OF THE ULSTER EXILES

Following the tragic contest over DERDRIU related in LONGAS MAC NUISLENN ('The Exile of the Sons of Uisliu'), Fergus led the aggrieved Ulster warriors to their traditional enemies, Medb and Ailill, at CRÚACHU (see further ULSTER CYCLE §3). This is the situation during the *Táin*, where Fergus often acts as the guide for his new CONNACHT comrades as they invade Ulster (though his fighting on their behalf is half-hearted), as well as Medb's lover.

§4. PARAGON OF SEXUALITY

Fergus's exceptional virility is mentioned in some of the early texts, has resonances in Irish folk tradition, and has been of understandable interest to modern writers (see ULSTER CYCLE §5). His breaking of mountains with the miraculous weapon CALADBOLG in the *Táin* (cf. also MIRACULOUS WEAPONS), has often been given a Freudian interpretation in this light. However, Fergus's relations with women lead to repeated downgrading of his status. In a burlesque reversal of the mighty Caladbolg, the jealous Ailill replaces Fergus's sword with a useless wooden one. As mentioned above, he ceases to be king of Ulaid following his involvement with Nes. Although not directly involved with the woman, he loses his tribe through his part in the Derdriu affair. And in the tale *Aided Fergusa maic Róig* (The violent death of Fergus mac Róich), he is speared to death by Ailill's blind poet Lugaid while engaged in love play with Medb in a lake at Mag nAí, during which the couple are described as resembling deer and vividly stirring up gravel from the lake bed. Hence, we may follow his sexual undoing—from his status as king to senior nobleman, to tribeless warrior/gigolo, and ultimately to a beast in the wild, hunted down as a beast.

§5. THE NAME

The first element of the common Gaelic name *Fergus* is undoubtedly 'man, hero', Old Irish *fer* < Celtic **wiro-s*. Celtic **Wiro-gustus* might mean either 'chosen man' or 'man force', the latter finding resonance with the sexual aspect discussed above, though this may only have been a popular perception of the meaning of the name. *Fergus* is sometimes confused with the second Old Irish name *Forggus* < Celtic **Wor-gustus* 'choice, best (man)', cf. OIr. *forggu*, Welsh *gorau*. The Old Welsh name *Gurgust*, Pictish *Uurguist*, probably goes with the second Celtic compound. *Róich*, nominative *Róach*, probably goes back to Celtic **Ro-ekwos* 'great' or 'divine horse, stallion', suggesting an old pagan totemic divinity or perhaps again reinforcing the sexual idea.

PRIMARY SOURCES
FLED BRICRENN; TÁIN BÓ CUAILNGE.
EDITION. Best et al., *Book of Leinster, formerly Lebar na Núachongbála* 5.245b.19–24 (*Fallsigud Tána Bó Cuailnge*).
ED. & TRANS. (*Compert Conchobuir*, earlier version) Meyer, *Hibernica Minora* 50; Kinsella, *Táin* 3–6 (uses some passages from the later version);
(*Aided Fergusa Maic Róig*) Meyer, *Death-tales of the Ulster Heroes*.
TRANS. (*Compert Conchobuir*, earlier version) Guyonvarc'h, *Ogam* 11.335–6; Kinsella, *Táin* 3–6 (uses some passages from the later version);
(*Aided Fergusa Maic Róig*) Guyonvarc'h, *Ogam* 12.344–8; Koch & Carey, *Celtic Heroic Age* 133–4.

FURTHER READING
BRICRIU; CALADBOLG; CONCHOBAR; CONNACHT; CRÚACHU; DERDRIU; JACKSON; LONGAS MAC N-UISLENN; MEDB; MIRACULOUS WEAPONS; NICANDER; SENCHÁN TORPÉIST; ULAID; ULSTER CYCLE; Freeman, *Emania* 12.45–8; Jackson, *Oldest Irish Tradition*; MacKillop, *Dictionary of Celtic Mythology* s.v. Fergus mac Róich; Mallory, *Aspects of The Táin*; Mallory & Stockman, *Ulidia*.

JTK

Fergus Mór mac Eirc (Big Fergus, or Fergus the Great, son of Erc, †501) and his kindred, the sons of Erc, figure in medieval Gaelic sources as the founders of the royal house of Scottish DÁL RIATA (Dalriada), and all the subsequent kings and queens of SCOTS claimed descent from him. According to the notice of his death in the ANNALS of Tigernach, 'he came with the people of Dál Riata [meaning the district of that name in what is now Co. Antrim, Ireland] and took a part of Britain and died there'. In the Middle Irish *Bethu Phátraic* (Life of Patrick), St PATRICK blessed Fergus and his brothers when they were still in

Ireland (ÉRIU). Since the dynasty claiming descent from the sons of Erc is definitely historical and Fergus's great-grandson AEDÁN MAC GABRÁIN is already well documented, Fergus himself tends to be viewed as historical. However, the entry in the Annals is too early to be a contemporary record, *Bethu Phátraic* cannot be treated as history, and 5th-century population movements from Antrim to Argyll (Earra-Ghaidheal 'coastland of the Gaels') in western Scotland (ALBA) remain largely invisible archaeologically. Therefore, we cannot rule out the possibility that the story of the sons of Erc was invented to supply Scotland with eminently Christian founders and to explain linguistic, political, and cultural connections between Ireland and Scotland whose actual background was unknown, or had become politically inappropriate, in the literary period. Nonetheless, the kings who traced their line to Fergus did have a central rôle in the beginnings of Gaelic Scotland and with it the linguistic community which survives today as the speakers of modern SCOTTISH GAELIC.

On the name *Fergus*, see FERGUS MAC RÓICH.

FURTHER READING

AEDÁN MAC GABRÁIN; ALBA; ANNALS; DÁL RIATA; ÉRIU; FERGUS MAC RÓICH; PATRICK; SCOTS; SCOTTISH GAELIC; Marjorie O. Anderson, *Kings and Kingship in Early Scotland*; Bannerman, *Celtic Studies* 1–11; Bannerman, *Studies in the History of Dalriada*; Marshall, *Dalriada*; Sharpe, *Kings, Clerics and Chronicles in Scotland 500–1297* 47–61.

PSH

The **Fernaig Manuscript**, compiled by Donnchadh MacRath (Duncan MacRae, also known as Donnchadh nam Pìos, *c.* 1640–*c.* 1700) of Inverinate in Kintail (Ceann an t-Sàil) between 1688 and 1693, is an anthology of SCOTTISH GAELIC POETRY dealing predominantly with religious themes, but also including some examples of early JACOBITE POETRY.

The collection consists of two notebooks containing a total of 59 poems, and the spelling system used by the compiler is based on contemporary SCOTS orthography, rather than the traditional GAELIC system. Most material in the manuscript dates to the 17th century, though John CARSWELL and Sir John Stewart of Appin, both represented by two poems, belong to the 16th century. Only one poem—that by Giolla Brighde

Ó hEódhasa (?–1614)—is by an Irish poet (see IRISH LITERATURE). Like the poems ascribed to Carswell (one of them is in the Book of the DEAN OF LISMORE, and therefore earlier, and the other ascribed to Irish poets in Irish sources; see Thomson, *Foirm na n-Urrnuidheadh* lxxxviii), the presence of Ó hEódhasa's poem indicates a degree of familiarity with the learned tradition. A similar conclusion is suggested by the use of syllabic metres for over half of the poems (Kenneth D. MacDonald, *Companion to Gaelic Scotland* 72) and the use of a *ceangal* or binding quatrain in *Tá cogadh oirnn do ghnáth* (We are forever at war) by Alasdair Mac Mhurchaidh, a device common in Irish, but rare in Scottish Gaelic poetry (MacRae, *Lamh-Sgrìobhainn Mhic Rath* 131–3, MacGill-Eain, *Ris a' Bhruthaich* 205–6). The criteria for selection appear to lie in MacRae's political and religious convictions (MacKinnon, *Trans. Gaelic Society of Inverness* 11.316). He also draws on sources close to Kintail.

MacRae himself is represented by twelve poems on both religious and Jacobite themes. Fear na Pàirce (MacCulloch of Park, *fl.* late 16th–early 17th century), six of whose poems are present, was MacRae's maternal great-grandfather (MacKinnon, *Trans. Gaelic Society of Inverness* 11.317). Donald MacRae, minister of Kilduich and author of *An Cill-duthaich mo thàmh cha laigh dhomh sàmh* (In Kilduich, my abode, I cannot rest quietly; MacRae, *Lamh-Sgrìobhainn Mhic Rath* 224–31), was the compiler's brother (MacKinnon, *Trans. Gaelic Society of Inverness* 11.314, 317). Donnchadh MacRaoiridh (†*c.* 1630), Alasdair Mac Mhurchaidh (†1642), and his son Murchadh Mòr mac Mhic Mhurchaidh (†*c.* 1689) are poets with strong Kintail links (MacKinnon, *Trans. Gaelic Society of Inverness* 11.324–7: MacGill-Eain, *Ris a' Bhruthaich* 191–3); they are represented by four, four, and six poems, respectively.

The religious poetry in the manuscript reflects 'disillusionment with the changes and vanities of the world, coupled with religious aspiration' (Kenneth D. MacDonald, *Companion to Gaelic Scotland* 72); it may be significant here that many of the poets belonged to the Episcopalian church (Fraser, *Trans. Gaelic Society of Inverness* 57.74; see CHRISTIANITY).

The Jacobite material comments on the events of 1688 and employs a range of religious, political, and legal arguments in its discourse (Ní Suaird, *Scottish Gaelic Studies* 19.94–122; see further JACOBITE REBEL-

LIONS). Two of the Jacobite songs are translations ('Jock Briton's lament' and 'The true Protestant's complaint', MacRae, *Lamh-Sgrìobhainn Mhic Rath* 233–8, 238–53).

PRIMARY SOURCES
MS. Glasgow, University Library, Gen. 85/1, 85/2.
EDITIONS. Cameron, *Reliquiae Celticae* 2.1–137; Fraser, *Trans. Gaelic Society of Inverness* 57.73–99; Henderson, *Leabhar nan Gleann* 198–300; MacRae, *Lamh-Sgrìobhainn Mhic Rath*.

FURTHER READING
CARSWELL; CHRISTIANITY; DEAN OF LISMORE; GAELIC; IRISH LITERATURE; JACOBITE POETRY; JACOBITE REBELLIONS; SCOTS; SCOTTISH GAELIC POETRY; Kenneth D. MacDonald, *Companion to Gaelic Scotland* 71–2; MacKinnon, *Trans. Gaelic Society of Inverness* 11.311–39; MacGill-Eain, *Ris a' Bhruthaich* 191–210; Ní Suaird, *Scottish Gaelic Studies* 19.93–140; Thomson, *Foirm na n-Urrnuidheadh*.

Anja Gunderloch

Fesques 'Le Mont du Val aux Moines' is

an important RITUAL site of pre-Roman Celtic GAUL. The site is located in the *département* of Seine-et-Marne, France, thus in the north-east of ancient Gaul, in or near what was the country of the BELGAE at the time of CAESAR's conquest. The sanctuary of Fesques is located on the extreme end of a natural promontory. In its centre, several successive groups of ditches, two buildings surrounded by trenches, and a FANUM have been found. This central zone of 2000 m² is enclosed by a continuous deep ditch which could have functioned as a moat. There are remains of a passage through this ditch, with a door or gate. A rich assemblage of items has been found in the centre of the enclosure (COINAGE, fibulae, bracelets, pearls, &c.), as well as in the ditch (animal bones, goblets, human bones, iron weapons, &c.). The remains of animals found in the ditch resemble similar ones found in other sanctuaries of the region (see SACRIFICE; WATERY DEPOSITIONS). They show evidence of banquets where pork played a significant rôle (see FOODWAYS; FEAST).

The structures at Fesques are set within a larger ring wall, enclosing about 10 ha (24 acres), marked off by two parallel ditches dug on the western base of the promontory, on its north and south sides, and on the east side of the plateau. Between these two ditches, small ditches contained pairs of human feet, traces of people hanged looking towards the centre of the sanctuary. The internal ditch contained the feet and the

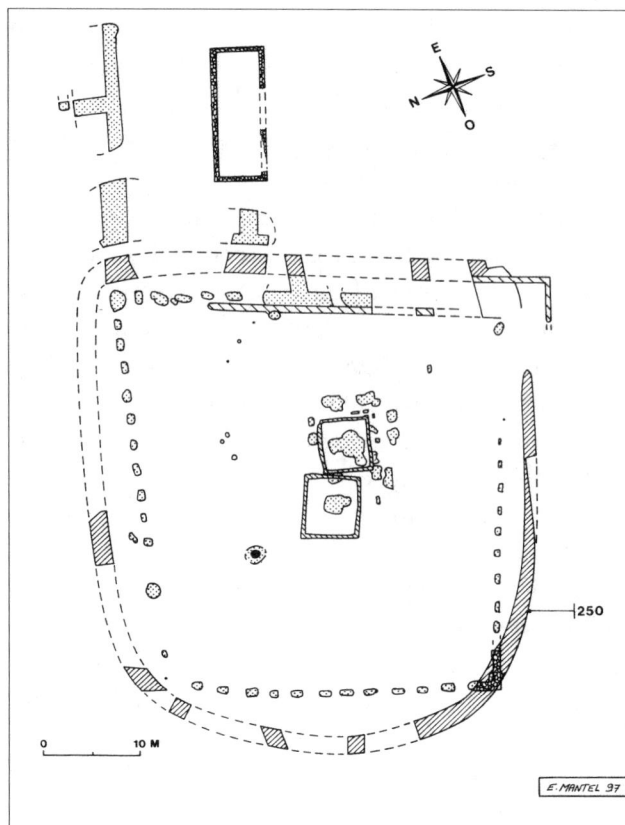

Site plan of the central zone of the Middle La Tène sanctuary at Fesques

heads of two-year-old cattle, some human remains and iron weapons, shield-bosses, SWORDS, and sheaths, dated to the Middle LA TÈNE period (*c.* 300–*c.* 150 BC). The ditches were filled in much later, in the 1st century AD.

FURTHER READING
BELGAE; CAESAR; COINAGE; ENCLOSURES; FANUM; FEAST; FOODWAYS; GAUL; LA TÈNE; RITUAL; SACRIFICE; SWORDS; WATERY DEPOSITIONS; MANTEL, *Le sanctuaire de Fesques*.

Patrice Méniel

Fest-noz, literally a 'night party', is an event at which

people experience traditional BRETON MUSIC and dance (see DANCES). Originally, a *fest-noz* was an event of the rural agricultural population in a small area of Brittany (BREIZH). In the late 1950s the idea of the *fest-noz* was appropriated by people such as the singer and cultural activist Loeiz Ropars, who saw it as an ideal way to keep Breton dance and music traditions alive. Call and response singing (*kan ha diskan*), BINIOU-bombard duets, and the current Celtic band phenomenon all owe their hardiness as musical traditions to this revival of interest in the *fest-noz*.

A typical *fest-noz* includes music, a dance area, and a bar, so that people can alternately dance and drink. In contrast with the purely local dance and music tradition, the new *fest-noz* is an event where folk-music and folk-dance enthusiasts from all over Brittany meet to interact. This has resulted in a crossing, melding and, to some degree, a homogenization of Breton music which does not appeal to purists. However, most of the participants in the folk-music scene are thoroughly at ease with the *fest-noz* revival. Whatever one may think of the new *fest-noz*, it is the single most frequent type of event for Breton folk-music performance.

The *fest-noz* has also been responsible for the creation of a new genre of music—*fest-noz* music. Stylistically, this genre is instrumental dance music played on some combination of violin, diatonic accordion, bombard, flute, clarinet, BAGPIPE, guitar, and bouzouki. The influence of Irish folk music and of the hybrid genre of Celtic music on this style is extensive, but the music remains Breton through the overlapping melody lines characteristic of *kan ha diskan* and of biniou-bombard duets.

FURTHER READING
BAGPIPE; BINIOU; BREIZH; BRETON MUSIC; DANCES; IRISH MUSIC; ArMen, *Musique bretonne*; Becker & Le Gurun, *La musique bretonne*; Winick, *Journal of American Folklore* 108.429.

Stephen D. Winick

Fían 'warring and hunting band, *männerbund*' (pl. *fiana*; *fian*, *fianna* in later spelling) was a term used already in Old Irish texts to designate groups of warriors engaged in expeditions of acquisition, or (more specifically) groups of youths (*óic féne* 'young men of the *fían*') and social misfits bonded together in a formal or even ritualized fashion on the border zones between one TUATH and another, and engaged in violent activities. The kinship, if any, between the words *fian* and FÉNI (freemen, society) and the explanation of *fian* as coming from the same INDO-EUROPEAN root as English 'win' remain uncertain. Given the literary evidence,

however, it would appear that the *fian* served a vital function in siphoning off undesirable elements from the social pool, providing an outlet for rambunctious behaviour (in early literature often expressed in bestial terms, with the wolf and the deer as the primary *fian* mascots) and, by means of its *rite de passage* activities, preparing at least some *féinnidi* (members of a *fian*, sing. *féinnid*) for the assumption of regular adult responsibilities, not unlike comparable male-bonding organizations in other civilizations, past and present. The *fian* way of life (*fianaigecht* or *féinnidecht*) included hunting, fighting and raiding (in search of booty or revenge), martial and athletic games (*fianchluichi*), and, if sources such as the 17th-century historian Keating (CÉITINN) are to be believed, special culinary procedures (involving the *fulacht na fían* 'cooking pit of the *fiana*'), and even training in poetry. The usefulness of *fénnidi* as mercenaries in a world where standing armies did not yet exist, and of *fian* violence as a way to deal with problems resistant to normal social solutions, contributed to the profoundly ambivalent attitude toward the *fiana* reflected in the literature, perhaps similar to the attitude towards the 'gallowglasses' of a later phase of Irish history. The occasional references to *fiana*, *fénnidi*, and *rígfhénnidi* ('chief *fénnidi*, leaders of *fiana*', sing. *rígfhénnid*; perhaps in some contexts 'king's *fénnid*') in literature thought to be of higher historical reliability such as law tracts (see LAW TEXTS), ANNALS, and certain early religious texts suggest that the institution was still in existence in the pre-Viking era, despite clerical condemnation of the destructiveness of *fiana* (a problem especially for ecclesiastical establishments, which, like *fiana*, tended to be situated in boundary zones), and the Church's horror at the tolerance of pagan rituals and beliefs which seemed to be a part of *fianaigecht*. It is now generally agreed that figures designated in early medieval saints' lives as *latrones*, *latrunculi* (robbers), or in Irish *meicc báis* (sons of death, evildoers)—dangerous raiders usually roaming in groups and sometimes characterized by mysterious signs worn on their heads—are in fact *fénnidi*, practitioners of the same institution as the *díberga* or *díbergaig* (brigands) and just plain *fiana* mentioned in early Irish sagas.

In those saints' lives, the holy men and women in question usually succeed spectacularly in converting such 'sons of death' from their non-Christian and destructive ways. Similarly, in the 12th- or 13th-century text known as the ACALLAM NA SENÓRACH (Dialogue of [or with] the old men), the survivors of the *fían* of FINN MAC CUMAILL, the most famous such organization in medieval IRISH LITERATURE, have a conversion experience in the company of St PATRICK. Subsequently, the old warriors' latter-day adventures become a showcase for the power of CHRISTIANITY, and the text, supposedly a document of the *fénnidi's* reminiscences about their heyday, a demonstration of the ability of Irish written culture to engage in productive dialogue with its pre-Christian heritage and with the oral tradition of performance. In the literary as well as later Irish and Scottish 'folk' developments of Fionn and his *fían* (in later Irish more often plural, *fianna*) the archaic institution takes on a new life and meaning, just as the heroics of this cycle of story, often designated in English as the 'Fenian', still reflects the original functions and characteristics of the *fían*—in fact, the word 'Fenian' derives from *fían*, genitive *fé(i)ne*.

Going back to MACPHERSON and the Ossianic controversy, the subject of the *fían* has been and remains a wellspring of Celtic scholarship. MEYER's *Fianaigecht* remains a valuable compendium of early literary references to *fíana*, especially when used in conjunction with Gerard Murphy's additions and corrections, in his introduction to his and Eoin MACNEILL's edition of the *Duanaire Finn*. Sjoestedt's seminal observations about the social function of the *fían* and its kinship to other Indo-European *männerbünde* (lit. 'male social groups') appeared in her *Dieux et héros des Celtes* (trans. Dillon). Schmitt usefully presents data on the European tradition of the 'wild hunt(er)'. Traces of the *fían* in early religious texts are adumbrated by Sharpe, while McCone contextualizes the fear of *fíana* expressed in early Irish literature. The importance of border zones in early Irish society is discussed by Ó Riain, while Nagy surveys what the *fían* did on or beyond the boundaries of the human world.

FURTHER READING
ACALLAM NA SENÓRACH; ANNALS; CÉITINN; CHRISTIANITY; FÉNI; FIANNAÍOCHT; FINN MAC CUMAILL; INDO-EUROPEAN; IRISH LITERATURE; LAW TEXTS; MACNEILL; MACPHERSON; MEYER; PATRICK; TUATH; McCone, CMCS 12.1–22; MacNeill & Murphy, *Duanaire Finn* 3.lv–lxi); Meyer, *Fianaigecht*; Nagy, *Wisdom of the Outlaw* 41–79; Ó Riain, SC 7.12–29; Schmitt, *Ghosts in the Middle Ages*; Sharpe, *Ériu* 30.75–92; Sjoestedt, *Gods and Heroes of the Celts* 57–80.

Joseph Falaky Nagy

Fiannaíocht (earlier spellings *fianaigecht, fiannaigheacht* 'Finn Cycle') is the most enduring narrative cycle in the history of Irish and Scottish Gaelic written and oral tradition. More accurately, it is a complex of smaller cycles having to do with various local heroes that grew out of, or were fitted into, a larger cycle centred on FINN MAC CUMAILL (Fionn mac Cumhaill in later spelling), a mixture of warrior, leader, and poet-seer, and on the institution of the FÍAN (in later Irish texts usually referred to in the pl., Modern Irish *fianna*), the hunting-warring band which serves (not unlike King ARTHUR's court) as a showcase for the rise (and sometimes fall) of promising young heroes. This cycle of stories, attested already in early vernacular literature, favoured in the later medieval and early modern phases of literary production, and living on in the repertories of Irish and Scottish traditional storytellers as late as the 20th century, is commonly referred to in English as the Fenian (from *fían*, genitive *féine*) or Ossianic cycle—the latter designation derived from the 18th-century Scottish popularizer and bowdlerizer of Fenian tradition James MACPHERSON's rendering of the name of an important figure in the cycle, OISÍN (Scottish Gaelic Oisean), the son of Finn.

§1. FIANNAÍOCHT AS INSTITUTION AND GENRE
While the *féinnidi* ('members of the *fían*', sing. *féinnid*) associated with Finn (a figure with deep mythological roots) form what has been the most celebrated *fían* over the last millennium, there are references to other *fíana*, both real and fictitious, in the early Irish literary corpus, and to other *rígfhéinnidi* ('chiefs of *fíana*', sing. *rígfhéinnid*), such as Finn's rival, Fothad Canainne. In some cases, *fían* seems to mean simply 'warband', but in many others it apparently refers to an institution with parallels in other Indo-European societies which was designed to prepare young males for adulthood (particularly, to acquaint them with the techniques of fighting and hunting, the rules of proper communal behaviour, and perhaps even those of poetic composition). *Fianaigecht* (like the word *fénnidecht*) originally denoted the esoteric society, culture, and lore of the *fían*, but by the 12th century it came to refer specifically to Finn's *fían*, to what they did and experienced, as well as to the stories about them, just as these heroes became the lone, albeit popular, vestiges of a bygone institution. In some medieval Fenian texts reflecting foreign

influence, *fiannaigheacht* can virtually be translated as 'chivalry', with Finn and other Fenian characters viewed as the native counterparts to the chivalrous heroes and heroines of Continental romance. In the idiom of modern Irish storytelling, the meaning of *fiannaíocht* has expanded to include heroic tales in general, just as the stories about Fionn and his *fianna* have come to be emblematic of the entire genre.

§2. EARLY LITERATURE

The earliest surviving IRISH LITERATURE offers only the tip of the iceberg of *fianaigecht*, perhaps because the stories about Finn and the *fían*, even if they were generally popular, were not on the agenda of the clerics composing literature. It is also possible that *féinnidi* and the life they led struck clerical sensibilities as being too pagan and too contemporary a topic. Finn, primarily associated in early texts with Leinster (LAIGIN) and Munster (MUMU), may also have been too 'southern' for early literati, whose bias is 'northern', or the wide-ranging nature of *fían* adventure may have initially worked against its incorporation into a literary tradition which felt more comfortable with clearly localized narrative. In the few traces of pre-12th-century Fenian narrative that we do possess, Finn is more *féinnid* than *rígfhéinnid*, more loner than leader, experiencing adventures beyond the range of the normal human sphere on his own—in particular, hunting down extraordinary wild creatures and supernatural adversaries, winning magical knowledge of, or other valuable commodities from, the *síd*, and composing poetry which reflects his mantic inspiration, derived from the OTHERWORLD. In the 12th-century text known as the *Macgnímartha Finn* ('The Boyhood Deeds of Finn'), the roughly contemporary text titled *Fotha Catha Cnucha* (The reason for the battle of Cnucha), and the renderings of this strand of the Fenian cycle in DINDSHENCHAS tradition, we have the earliest surviving witnesses to one of the most popular and longest-lived episodes of *fianaigecht*—the story of Finn's conception, birth, and youth.

§3. LATER MEDIEVAL LITERATURE

In the 12th and following centuries, as literary activity shifted from the ecclesiastical into the secular sphere, the stories about Finn and his men gained in popularity, solidifying their reputation as the *fían par excellence*, while the hunting and warring band becomes in the literary imagination a disciplined (albeit occasionally unruly) organization which comes together to hunt and fight for the high-king, and to protect Ireland (ÉRIU) from invasion. The characters of *fianaigecht* are by this time firmly grounded in the era of the legendary high-king CORMAC MAC AIRT, and the twilight of the Fenian heroes is set during the reign of Cormac's son, Cairpre Lifechar. The exploits of the younger members of the *fían*, heroic volunteers and recruits hailing from all four provinces, take centre stage for the composers of literary *fianaigecht* of the 12th and following centuries, and Finn's rôle as *rígfhénnid* pushes him into the narrative background, his leadership becoming a matter of appointment by the high-king of Ireland to a position which, like the high-kingship itself, was a 'national' institution with its headquarters at Tara (TEAMHAIR). Unless engaged in recreational hunting, the *fían(na)* of late medieval Fenian literature—for instance, the prosimetric ACALLAM NA SÉNORACH (Dialogue of [or with] the old men), and the prose texts *Cath Fionntrágha* (Battle of Ventry) and *Feis Tighe Chonáin* (Feast of Conán's house)—spend most of their narrative time responding to the summons of the *rígfhénnid* or the high-king on the occasion of national emergencies (such as invasions), as well as to pleas for help from human and supernatural visitors. While enjoying their outdoor life or gallantly performing their duties, the Fenian heroes usually become embroiled in adventures that involve fighting against mysterious adversaries, winning precious commodities, and (with telling frequency) travelling to and feasting in the Otherworld, of both the *síd* and transmarine variety. It has been observed that in many regards Finn and his men resemble ARTHUR and his 'court' as presented in early Welsh tradition, for instance, in CULHWCH AC OLWEN.

§4. EARLY MODERN FENIAN LITERATURE

From the medieval into the modern era, a synergistic relationship developed between the written and the spoken tradition of Fenian storytelling, a process of mutual borrowing which has made it impossible to speak in terms of purely literary or oral developments of Fenian story.

A staple of *fianaigecht* already attested in the earlier strands of the tradition and, like the story of Finn's youth, still to be found in the repertories of 20th-century oral storytellers in Ireland and Scotland

(ALBA), is the tragic tale of the affair between Finn's wife Gráinne, daughter of Cormac, and Finn's beloved kinsman and companion in the fían, DIARMAID UA DUIBHNE. The Early Modern Irish prose text TÓR-UIGHEACHT DHIARMADA AGUS GHRÁINNE ('The Pursuit of Diarmaid and Gráinne') is the literary culmination of the perennial interest in this embarrassing episode of fían betrayal, a tale which features a villainously jealous instead of a heroic Finn, a rígfhénnid barely in control of his fían or his wife. The Diarmaid/ Gráinne/Finn triangle is clearly cut from the same narrative cloth as that involving Noísiu/DERDRIU/ CONCHOBAR, attested earlier in Irish tradition, and Drystan/ Esyllt/March in Welsh (see DRYSTAN AC ESYLLT), as well as other tales of roving-eyed wives and rival lovers centred on Fothad Canainne (another rígfhénnid, we recall), Gwyn ap Nudd (arguably, Finn's Welsh counterpart), and Finn himself in medieval Celtic literature.

Finn and the fían's life beyond the pale, and the perennial contact with the supernatural which life on the margins provokes, clearly lie behind a popular Fenian story type, the bruidhean ('hostel' or specifically 'supernatural hostel'; see BRUIDEN), which is already attested in the earlier strata of fianaigecht, grows in importance in the tradition's later literary developments, and survives as part of modern oral Fenian lore. In this kind of tale, as represented for instance by the Early Modern Irish Bruidhean Chaorthainn (Hostel of Rowan), Fionn and his men accept an invitation to an otherworldly FEAST, only to find that they have been magically trapped in the hostel by an old enemy seeking revenge. Their rescue involves the intervention of a Fenian hero who did not come along to the feast (such as Diarmaid), and the otherworldly opponent and his allies are punished for their treacherous hospitality. The pattern of an unknown or incognito enemy issuing an invitation or a challenge to the fían, and being followed by the Fenian heroes into the Otherworld where various adventures ensue, is also to be found in many other Fenian tales, some primarily attested in literary form (such as the Early Modern Irish prose tale Imtheacht an Ghiolla Dheacair [Adventure of the troublesome lad]) and others which circulated widely in the oral traditions of Ireland and Scotland (such as the popular folk-tale 'Finn and the Big Man'). The pattern is also very much on display in the body of fianaigecht which has survived

primarily in verse, in the duan or laoidh style of seminarrative poetic composition sampled in the 16th-century Scottish Book of the DEAN OF LISMORE, the 17th-century Irish Duanaire Finn ('The Book of the Lays of Fionn'), an anthology written in Ostend which testifies to the popularity of fiannaíocht among Irishmen both at home and abroad, and other, later Irish and Scottish manuscript collections of this extensive body of material.

PRIMARY SOURCES
Bruford, Gaelic Folk-Tales and Mediaeval Romances; MacNeill & Murphy, Duanaire Finn 3.lv–lxi; Meyer, Fianaigecht.

FURTHER READING
ACALLAM NA SÉNORACH; ALBA; ARTHUR; BRUIDEN; CONCHOBAR; CORMAC MAC AIRT; CULHWCH AC OLWEN; DEAN OF LISMORE; DERDRIU; DIARMAID UA DUIBHNE; DINDSHENCHAS; DRYSTAN AC ESYLLT; ÉRIU; FEAST; FÍAN; FINN MAC CUMAILL; IRISH LITERATURE; LAIGIN; MACPHERSON; MUMU; OISÍN; OTHERWORLD; SÍD; TEAMHAIR; TÓRUIGHEACHT DHIARMADA AGUS GHRÁINNE; Almqvist et al., Fiannaíocht; Almqvist et al., Heroic Process; MacKillop, Fionn Mac Cumhaill; McQuillan, Proc. Harvard Celtic Colloquium 8.1–10; Murphy, Ossianic Lore and Romantic Tales of Medieval Ireland; Nagy, Wisdom of the Outlaw; Ó Fiannachta, An Fhiannaíocht; Ó hÓgáin, Fionn mac Cumhaill.

Joseph Falaky Nagy

Fidchell (< fid + chiall, lit. wood-intelligence, the Irish cognate of GWYDDBWYLL) was a medieval Irish board game which seems to have been a favourite of the medieval Irish noble classes. According to an entry in the 9th-century SANAS CHORMAIC ('Cormac's Glossary'), a fidchell board had four sides with straight rows on it, and was used with black and white pieces by two players (Bergin et al., Anecdota from Irish Manuscripts 50). The object of the game seems to have been to 'slay' the opponent and remove his pieces. This is why fidchell and another, probably slightly less sophisticated, early Irish board game, brandub, are sometimes incorrectly translated as 'chess' or 'draughts', and ficheall is the term used for 'chess' in Modern IRISH. However, the game is probably related to the game of Tablut, as played by Laplanders in north Sweden (MacWhite, Éigse 5.25–35).

The importance of fidchell as a marker of social class is borne out by the early laws of FOSTERAGE, which state that it is the duty of the fosterer of a king's son to ensure the prince's training in fidchell. The importance

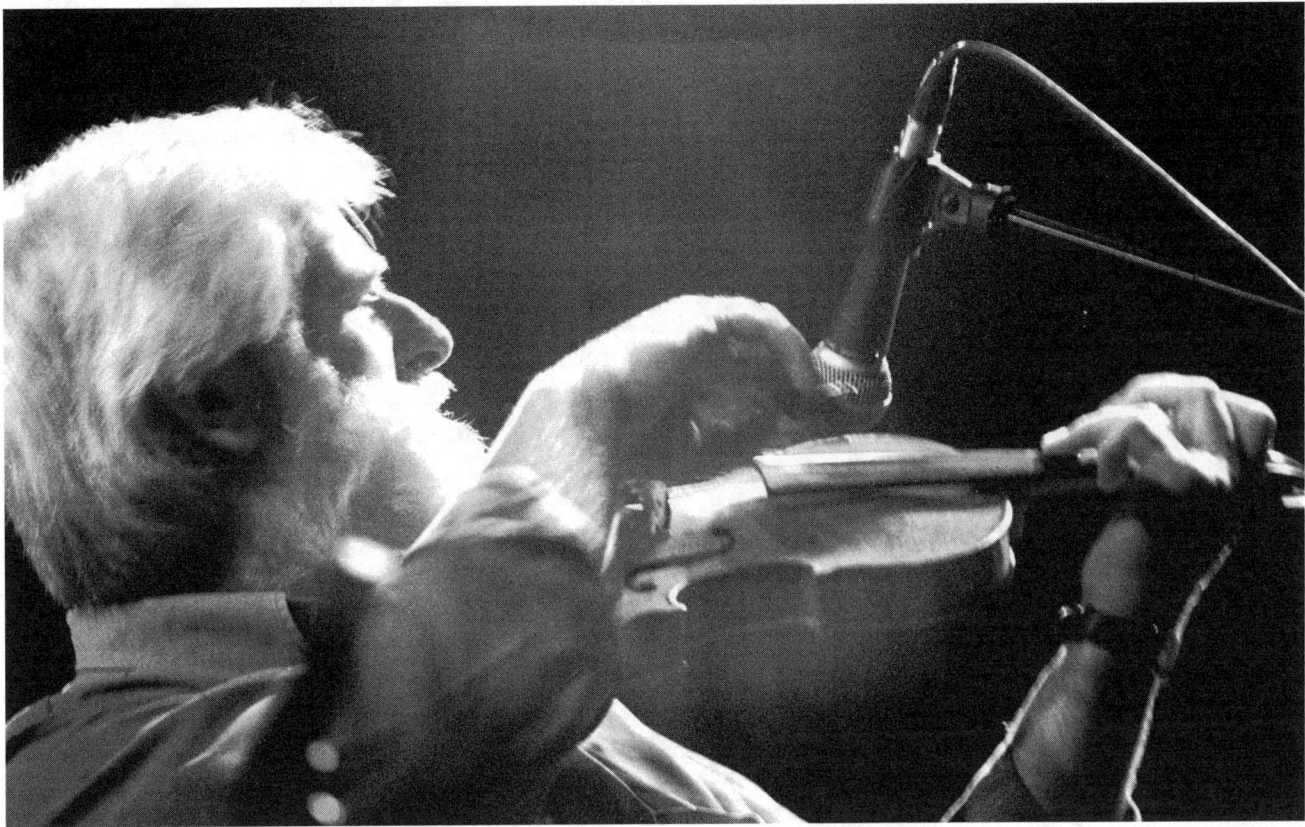

Contemporary Gaelic fiddle style: the Dubliners performing in Aberystwyth, Wales

of the game is also shown by the numerous references to it in IRISH LITERATURE. For example, in an episode of the *Macgnímartha* (Boyhood deeds), FINN MAC CUMAILL's superior ability to play the game gives away his noble birth, while in CATH MAIGE TUIRED ('The [Second] Battle of Mag Tuired'), the god LUG—the alleged inventor of the game—gains entry to the royal seat at Tara (TEAMHAIR) by winning all the stakes at *fidchell*. One of the versions of TOCHMARC ÉTAÍNE ('The Wooing of Étaín') is centred around a game of *fidchell*, played by Eochaid Airem, the king of Tara, with a powerful OTHERWORLD king, Midir. The latter cunningly loses at first, so that Eochaid is encouraged to play for an unnamed stake. Predictably, Midir wins this time, and demands a hug and a kiss from Eochaid's wife, Étaín, only to elope with her on claiming the prize.

FURTHER READING

CATH MAIGE TUIRED; FINN MAC CUMAILL; FOSTERAGE; GWYDDBWYLL; IRISH; IRISH LITERATURE; LUG; OTHERWORLD; SANAS CHORMAIC; TEAMHAIR; TOCHMARC ÉTAÍNE; Bergin et al., *Anecdota from Irish Manuscripts*; Gray, *Cath Maige Tuired*; Gwynn, ZCP 9.353–6; Kelly, *Guide to Early Irish Law*; MacWhite, *Éigse* 5.25–35; Nagy, *Wisdom of the Outlaw*.

PSH

The **fiddle** is perhaps the most ubiquitous instrument in the regional traditions of the modern CELTIC COUNTRIES, being particularly associated with the GAELIC countries and their North American offshoots.

In Ireland (ÉIRE) the fiddle, along with the uilleann pipes (see BAGPIPE), is the only commonly played instrument to have been in use in the native tradition for over 200 years, and thus the instrument has had a large impact on the traditional Irish repertoire, many tunes appearing from their style, range and notation to have been originally written on and/or for the fiddle. A similar situation exists in the Scottish tradition, with most tunes in the repertory being either 'fiddle-tunes' or 'pipe-tunes'. Again, fiddle-type has a long association with Scottish traditional music, with native compositions appearing alongside more classical material in books of music for the viol from the early 17th century on. The violin appeared in Scotland (ALBA) in the late 17th century, fortunately coinciding with a boom in popular interest in traditional music and dance, upon which it was to capitalize.

The early history of the fiddle in Ireland is more obscure, probably because here it lacked the overlap between traditional and classical styles notable in Scotland. In playing the Irish fiddle the left hand generally remains in the 1st position, which essentially means that the matters of tone, attack, volume and time value are controlled primarily by the bowing technique of the right hand. Tuning is generally to concert pitch. Decorative techniques used include rolls, trebles, cuts, droning, and sliding (*glissando*). There is much emphasis on regional traditions in Irish fiddle playing, though these have often tended to blur somewhat among modern fiddlers, with their eclectic influences. Some of the main regional styles and their foremost proponents are Sliabh Luachra (Tom Billy, Patrick O'Keefe), East Clare (Martin Hayes) and Donegal (The Glackins and the Peoples).

Cross-fertilization from the classical tradition has led to a more widespread use of techniques such as *scordatura* (altered tuning) and vibrato among Scottish fiddlers, although this seems to have been more widespread among 19th-century virtuosi such as Scott Skinner than those of today. The fiddle music of Shetland is renowned as a major regional offshoot of the Scottish tradition. While it may owe much of its roots to Norwegian influences, there is a strong element of Scottish and, to a lesser extent, Irish influence present in this style, with its pronounced rhythm, strong single bowing, and use of sympathetic vibrations and *scordatura*. This style has achieved greater international recognition in the last few decades through the playing of fiddlers such as Aly Bain and Willie Hunter.

The playing of Gaelic-style fiddle music in North America is strongest in the ethnically Scottish areas of Canada, particularly Cape Breton (e.g. Natalie MacMaster), and the Ottawa Valley, where the style also incorporates elements of the Irish and French traditions.

FURTHER READING
ALBA; BAGPIPE; CELTIC COUNTRIES; CELTIC LANGUAGES IN NORTH AMERICA; DANCES; ÉIRE; GAELIC; IRISH MUSIC; Cooke, *Fiddle Tradition of the Shetland Isles*; Girdwood, *Fiddle Music of the Ottawa Valley*; Hunter, *Fiddle Music of Scotland*; MacAoidh, *Between the Jigs and Reels*; MacInnes, *Journey in Celtic Music*; McLaughlin, *Donegal and Shetland Fiddle Music*; Ó Canainn, *Traditional Music in Ireland*; Purser, *Scotland's Music*.

SÓF

Findlaech mac Ruaidri

Findlaech mac Ruaidri was ruler of Moray (Moireibh) in Scotland (ALBA) *c.* 1000–21. The sur-

viving records show discrepancies regarding his status and the geographical extent of his authority, which are therefore likely to have been in dispute. He is described as *mormaer* (earl) of Moray in the ANNALS of Tigernach, whereas the Annals of Ulster call him king *ri Alban* (King of Alba). He is probably known to Norse tradition as the Earl Finnleikr mentioned in the *Orkneyinga Saga*, where an account is given of his struggle for power with the Viking Earl Sigurd the Stout of Orkney (Arcaibh) over control in Caithness (Gallaibh) on the northernmost mainland. This historical event would have occurred before 1014. According to the Annals of Tigernach, Findlaech was killed by his own people, the sons of his brother Mael Brigte. Findlaech was the father of King MAC BETHAD (the basis of Shakespeare's Macbeth).

The name *Findlaech* is intelligible as an early Gaelic name, though it is rare, comprising the elements *find* 'white, fair, blessed' and apparently *laech* 'layman, warrior' < Latin *laicus*, and thus possibly intended to mean 'Christian warrior'; on the other hand, the second element could be a form of *laeg* 'calf'. *Ruaidri* is very common as an early Irish name and derives from the PROTO-CELTIC **Roudo-rīχs* 'red(-haired) king'.

FURTHER READING
ALBA; ANNALS; MAC BETHAD; PROTO-CELTIC; Alan O. Anderson, *Early Sources of Scottish History AD 500 to 1286*; Pálsson & Edwards, *Orkeyinga Saga*; Ann Williams et al., *Biographical Dictionary of Dark Age Britain* 139.

PEB, JTK

Finn mac Cumaill

Finn mac Cumaill (also Find, Modern Irish Fionn mac Cumhaill) is the central figure of the 'Fenian' or 'Finn Cycle' of Irish and Scottish Gaelic hero tales and associated verse. His character is discussed in the context of this cycle in the article under the Irish name of the corpus, FIANNAÍOCHT. In the tales, Finn's primary social function is that of the leader of the renowned war-band, which is sometimes in service to the legendary king of Tara (TEAMHAIR), CORMAC MAC AIRT, but is also often portrayed as a group of huntsmen outside Irish tribal society altogether; on this important social institution, see the article under its Old Irish name FÍAN.

Thematic features of Finn's character and background are set out in the tale of his boyhood deeds,

Macgnímartha Finn, which is partly paralleled by the earlier *Fotha Catha Cnucha* (The reason for the battle of Cnucha). Finn's father Cumall had been the leader of the *fían* of CONN CÉTCHATHACH (Cormac's grandfather), king of Tara. He then fell in love with Muirne, the beautiful daughter of the druid Tadg, son of another druid Nuada (the latter name is significant, deriving from the Celtic divine name NŌDONS). Tadg opposed the union, and Cumall forced the girl to elope, bringing the enmity of Conn and the rival *fían* of Morna and his sons. At the battle, Aed mac Morna lost his eye—and was henceforth called Goll (one-eyed)—and killed Cumall. Muirne, by now pregnant, hid from the pursuers, and her child Demne was then given into fosterage to two women druid warriors. Like the boy CÚ CHULAINN, Demne prodigiously grew and excelled in hunting, feats of weapons, and competitive sports. There are repeated episodes explaining how he was renamed Finn: he is once described as *finn* (fair) by youths whom he challenged; later, he is apprenticed to the poet Finn-éces, which accounts for Finn's subsequent fame as a poet. In an episode closely comparable to the transformation of the boy Gwion into the inspired TALIESIN in Welsh tradition, Finn-éces set the boy to mind the cooking of wondrous salmon, infused with knowledge and inspiration. The *eó feasa* or *bradán feasa* (salmon of knowledge) is a key theme in Irish tradition. Finn accidentally burnt himself as he cooked, and in putting his thumb in his mouth received the inspiration himself, becoming a visionary. *Finn* can also mean 'enlightened' or 'blessed' in the spiritual sense, which is among the meanings of the cognate words in the other Celtic languages, such as Welsh *gwyn* and Breton *gwenn*, meanings which can thus be attributed to Common Celtic **windos*. The Old Irish verb *ro·finnadar* 'discovers, comes to know' and Welsh *gwn* 'I know' are also related. Thus, we may have some very old mythology here, in which the youth of destiny is at first *finn* in the everyday sense of 'fair-haired' and then ascends to become esoterically 'blessed' or 'self-revealed'.

There are Encyclopedia entries on Finn's hero sons, FAELÁN and OISÍN, and the Fenian texts ACALLAM NA SENÓRACH ('Dialogue of [or with] the old men', a series of self-contained adventures set within a frame tale of an encounter with St PATRICK) and TÓRUIGHEACHT DHIARMADA AGUS GHRÁINNE ('The Pursuit of Diarmaid and Gráinne', a tragic love story).

PRIMARY SOURCE
TRANS. Cross & Slover, *Ancient Irish Tales* 355–468.

RELATED ARTICLES
ACALLAM NA SENÓRACH; CONN CÉTCHATHACH; CORMAC MAC AIRT; CÚ CHULAINN; FAELÁN; FÍAN; FIANNAÍOCHT; NŌDONS; OISÍN; PATRICK; TALIESIN; TEAMHAIR; TÓRUIGHEACHT DHIARMADA AGUS GHRÁINNE.

JTK

Fir Bolg figure in Irish LEGENDARY HISTORY among the tribes said to have settled in Ireland (ÉRIU) in the pre-Christian period (cf. also FOMOIRI; TUATH DÉ). However, it is probable that the tradition recollects a historical people. Many members of the west Munster tribes (Iar-Mumu) identified as Érainn have *Bolg* as an element in their personal names (O'Rahilly, *Early Irish History and Mythology* 75–84; Carey, CMCS 16.78–9). As discussed in the article on the BELGAE, the name *Bolg* is probably cognate to that of the well-documented tribal group of late IRON AGE north-east GAUL and south-east BRITAIN, and also to the name of the leader of the Celtic invasion of Macedonia in 280 BC, *Bolgios* or *Belgios*. As legendary settlers of Ireland, they are first mentioned under the archaic form of their name *Builc* (without prefixed *fir* 'men') in the 9th-century HISTORIA BRITTONUM (§14). Fir Bolg are also mentioned in the Old Irish tale CATH MAIGE TUIRED ('The [Second] Battle of Mag Tuired'), where they are credited with dividing the country into *cóicid* (fifths, sing. CÓICED), the provinces of Ireland. The exploits of the Fir Bolg are set out in greater detail in the late 11th-century LEBAR GABÁLA ÉRENN ('The Book of Invasions'), which systematizes waves of settlers in the legendary prehistory of Ireland. Various etymologies for the name element *bolg* have been offered (Pokorny, ZCP 11.189–204; O'Rahilly, *Early Irish History and Mythology*; Lewis, *Féilsgríbhinn Eóin Mhic Néill* 46–61), which also appears, or a form looking much like it, in the names of some MIRACULOUS WEAPONS, such as CÚ CHULAINN's lethal *gae bulga* and the sword CALADBOLG wielded by FERGUS MAC RÓICH. However, a recent re-examination of these interpretations concluded that the early medieval Irish etymologists had the correct word root with their implausible-sounding *fir i mbalgaib* 'men in bags'—to be more correctly understood as men who were bag-like when swelled up, i.e. bulging, with heroic valour in battle (Carey, CMCS 16.77–83). Although it is by now standard practice to refer to early Irish group names of this type (*Fir* + genitive plural tribal name) in English with the definite article, these names are definite anyway and do not require the Irish article.

FURTHER READING
BELGAE; BRITAIN; CALADBOLG; CATH MAIGE TUIRED; CÓICED; CÚ CHULAINN; ÉRIU; FERGUS MAC RÓICH; FOMOIRI; GAUL; HISTORIA BRITTONUM; IRON AGE; LEBAR GABÁLA ÉRENN; LEGENDARY HISTORY; MIRACULOUS WEAPONS; Ó RATHAILE; POKORNY; TUATH DÉ; Carey, CMCS 16.77–83; Fraser, *Ériu* 8.1–63; Gray, *Cath Maige Tuired*; Hamel, ZCP 10.160–3, 186–90; Lewis, *Féil-sgríbhinn Eóin Mhic Néill* 46–61; Macalister, *Lebor Gabála Érenn*; O'Rahilly, *Early Irish History and Mythology* 43–57, 74–84; Pokorny, ZCP 11.189–204.

PSH

Fir Domnann appear in Irish LEGENDARY HISTORY, commonly associated with two closely related or equivalent groupings, LAIGIN and Galeóin, and one may suppose that behind these three lay an old tribal federation. In early references the three names often appear to be interchangeable. As regards origins, the Fir Domnann are possibly of common origin with the historical groups in south-west BRITAIN and what is now south-west Scotland (ALBA) who bore the ancient Celtic form of the name, i.e. Dumnonii. The former British tribe was probably instrumental in founding the early medieval kingdom of DOMNONIA in northern Brittany (BREIZH). Based on these connections, O'Rahilly (Ó RATHAILE) suggested that the Fir Domnann were a P-CELTIC, pre-GOIDELIC people who, along with the Galeóin, invaded the south-east coast of Ireland (ÉRIU) from Britain. O'Rahilly's idea that these two groups were distinct from the Laigin (who he claimed as Goidelic) is not easily confirmed by the way the texts use the names; nor is his theory of a P-Celtic substratum in Ireland widely accepted by experts today. On the other hand, the Dumnonii do appear as an expansionist group on the shores of Britain nearest to Fir Domnann lands in south-east Ireland.

The early written sources provide evidence for the Fir Domnann in Cóice Laigean (Leinster, see also CÓICED), where at least one of their rulers, Mess-

Telmann, is credited, in a probably 7th-century Irish poem, with the overkingship of the province and with wielding power from the royal site of Leinster at DÚN ÁILINNE. In this poem the tribal name occurs in its archaic form, sing. *Domnon* < Celtic **Dumnonos*. The place-name Inber Domnann (now Malahide Harbour) on the east coast also preserves the name. However, the area with the strongest place-name associations is in north-west Mayo (Contae Mhaigh Eo), in the barren wastes of Iorrais Domnann (the modern barony of Erris), and nearby Mag Domnann and Dún Domnann. The Gamanrad, one of the *aithech thuatha* (vassal tribes) in Iorrais Domnann, are considered to be a sept of the Fir Domnann and are listed in the story *Táin Bó Flidais* ('The Cattle Raid of Flidais') as one of the three warrior races of Ireland, along with the Clann Dedad of MUMU and Clanna Rudraigi of ULAID. The name *Fir Domnann* is based on the Celtic root *dumno-*, older *dubno-*, which means both 'deep' and 'the world'. The suffix *-on-* often occurs in Gaulish and British divine names; *Dumnon(i)i* would therefore mean 'people of the god of the world'. It is not impossible that such a group name arose independently more than once among the pre-Christian Celts. Old Irish *fir* 'men' was often prefixed to old tribal names to clarify their meaning (cf. FIR BOLG).

PRIMARY SOURCES
CÉITINN, *Foras Feasa ar Éireann*; LEABHAR BHAILE AN MHÓTA; LEBAR GABÁLA ÉIREANN; LEBOR NA H-UIDRE.
TRANS. Koch & Carey, *Celtic Heroic Age* 52 (*Mess-Telmann*), 226–71 (*Lebar Gabála Érenn*).

FURTHER READING
ALBA; BREIZH; BRITAIN; CÓICED; DOMNONIA; DUMNONIA; DÚN ÁILINNE; ÉRIU; FIR BOLG; GOIDELIC; LAIGIN; LEGENDARY HISTORY; MUMU; Ó RATHAILE; P-CELTIC; ULAID; Byrne, *Irish Kings and High-Kings*; Carney, *Ériu* 22.23–80; Hogan, *Onomasticon Goedelicum*; MacKillop, *Dictionary of Celtic Mythology*; O'Rahilly, *Early Irish History and Mythology*.

SÓF

Five Poets, Memorandum of the

Apart from the poems themselves, the earliest documentary evidence for court poets in early post-Roman BRITAIN is the castigation by GILDAS in his *De Excidio Britanniae* (On the destruction of Britain), a text probably belonging to the 6th century, of the sycophantic praise poets at the table of King Maglocunus (MAEL-GWN GWYNEDD). The first source to name poets and provide a datable historical synchronism for their careers is a passage, sometimes called 'The Memorandum of the Five Poets', which occurs among the north British material in the 9th-century Welsh Latin HISTORIA BRITTONUM.

Ida, filius Eobba, tenuit regiones in sinistrali parte Brittanniae, id est Umbri maris, et regnauit annis duodecim, et iunxit Din-Guairoi guurth Berneich. Tunc [O]utigirn in illo tempore fortiter dimicabat contra gentem Anglorum. Tunc Talhaern Tat Aguen in poemate claruit, et Neirin, et Taliessin, et Bluchbard, et Cian qui vocatur Gue[ni]th Guaut, simul uno tempore in poemate Brittanico claruerunt. Mailcunus magnus rex apud Brittones regnabat, id est, in regione Guenedotae . . .

IDA son of Eobba held kingdoms in the northern part of Britain, that is the Humber Sea, and he ruled twelve years [r. 547–59], and he joined Bamburgh to BRYNAICH. Then Eudeyrn at that time was bravely fighting against the English [or Anglian] people. Then Talhaearn Tad AWEN, Father of poetic inspiration, was renowned in poetry, and ANEIRIN, and TALIESIN, and Blwchfardd, and Cian who was called 'Wheat of Prophetic Verse', were at the same time famous in BRYTHONIC poetry. Maelgwn the great king was ruling among the Britons, that is, in the kingdom of GWYNEDD.

We know nothing else about the chieftain Eudeyrn. Of the five poets, no surviving material is ascribed to Talhaearn (Iron-brow). The order of the list and his paternal epithet suggest that he might have priority within the group and might have been the court poet of Eudeyrn. The wording of the passage also implies that Eudeyrn and Ida were enemies; therefore it is possible that Talhaearn's poems were concerned with this warfare, but this is conjectural. Nor do we have any surviving verse from Blwchfardd, though it is not impossible that Old Welsh *Bluchbard* is a scribal corruption of *Loumarch*, i.e. the Llywarch Hen to whom a cycle of early saga ENGLYNION are attributed. Nor are there extant texts attributed to Cian. But the second and third poets in the list are known CYNFEIRDD (Early poets). Neirin certainly identifies the same Aneirin to

whom the heroic elegies known collectively as the GODODDIN are ascribed. Taliessin is an old spelling of Taliesin.

The chronological synchronization is fixed by the references to King Ida of Anglian Bernicia (Brynaich) and to Maelgwn. According to the ANNALES CAMBRIAE, Maelgwn died in 547. The authority of this obit is, however, uncertain. The cognate Irish ANNALS do not have an obit for Maelgwn, and this absence probably means that the entry does not go back to the earliest stratum of the Welsh annals either; in other words, it is a retrospective entry of some centuries after the fact. BEDA tells us that Ida came to power in 547, a date which might confirm Maelgwn's obit, but it might just as well be its source. The synchronism for the five poets is apparently a very precise 547—when Maelgwn and Ida were both in power. However, if the poets were actually synchronized first with Maelgwn and then Maelgwn with Ida, then the conclusion that the five poets flourished during the generation ending at 547 would only be as good as the synchronization between the kings, and we have no second source confirming this. We might also question whether the author of *Historia Brittonum* really knew that these poets were Maelgwn's contemporaries or only had the name of five poets of long ago and put this together with what Gildas had said about the presence of praise poets at Maelgwn's court.

As to synchronizing the three leaders—Ida, Eudeyrn, and Maelgwn—the author of *Historia Brittonum* might have thought that the poets were contemporaries of Eudeyrn and Ida (and thus Maelgwn too) or of Maelgwn (and thus Eudeyrn and Ida too). It is also possible that some of the poets were known as contemporaries of one king and some of another. Although *Historia Brittonum's* synchronizing methods do not inspire confidence, there is no provable blunder here; 547 is thus the date we have got for the active life of Aneirin, Taliesin, and the other three. The rock-solid conclusion afforded by the Memorandum is that by the early 9th century Aneirin and Taliesin were believed to have been famous Brythonic poets who had flourished in the 6th century. The young Taliesin of legend appears as a contemporary of King Maelgwn, a connection which is likely to have been influenced by the Memorandum.

FURTHER READING
ANEIRIN; ANNALES CAMBRIAE; ANNALS; AWEN; BEDA; BRIT-

AIN; BRYNAICH; BRYTHONIC; CYNFEIRDD; ENGLYNION; GILDAS; GODODDIN; GWYNEDD; HISTORIA BRITTONUM; IDA; MAELGWN GWYNEDD; TALIESIN; Bromwich, *Beginnings of Welsh Poetry*; Bromwich & Jones, *Astudiaethau ar yr Hengerdd*; Dumville, *Arthurian Literature* 6.1–26; Dumville, BBCS 25.439–45; Dumville, WHR 8.345–54; Hughes, *Celtic Britain in the Early Middle Ages*; Jackson, *Celt and Saxon* 20–62; Koch, *Gododdin of Aneirin*; Lapidge & Dumville, *Gildas*; Brynley F. Roberts, *Early Welsh Poetry*; Sims-Williams, *Gildas* 169–92; Ifor Williams, *Canu Aneirin*; Ifor Williams, *Canu Taliesin*; J. E. Caerwyn Williams, *Welsh Society and Nationhood* 19–34.

JTK

Flann Fína mac Ossu

Flann Fína mac Ossu (Aldfrith son of Oswydd) was an Irish-educated king who ruled Anglo-Saxon Northumbria (685–*c.* 705) at the heart of the period which is often called 'the Northumbrian Golden Age'. His reign was markedly peaceful following the expansionist regimes of his predecessors in the Bernician dynasty (see BRYNAICH), who included his father (OSWYDD †670), his uncle (St OSWALD †642), and his half-brother (ECGFRITH †685). Flann Fína is his Irish name and Aldfrith his English. Irish GENEALOGIES consistently portray him as belonging, through his mother, to the Cenél nEogain branch of the Northern UÍ NÉILL. Oswydd's two named wives were Rie*in*melth, daughter of Royth son of Run (Rhieinfellt ferch Rhwyth ap Rhun) of RHEGED and Eanflæd daughter of EADWINE of Northumbria.

The ANNALS of Ulster at his obit refer to Flann Fína as *sapiens* 'a learned man', placing him among the ranks of other 7th-century Irish *sapientes* such as Laidcenn mac Baíth Bannaig, CUMMÍNE FOTA, Ailerán of Clonard, Banbán, and Cenn Fáelad mac Ailello. English ecclesiastical sources confirm Flann Fína's reputation for learning and education among the Irish. The anonymous Life of St Cuthbert states that he was present at Iona (EILEAN Ì). BEDA's prose Life of St Cuthbert states variously that Flann Fína lived 'among the Irish isles' or 'in the regions of the Irish' for the love of learning. Abbot ADOMNÁN of Iona, who called him 'friend Aldfrith', visited him twice in Northumbria and presented him with a copy of *De locis sanctis* (On the holy places), which Flann Fína, acting as Adomnán's royal patron, had copied and disseminated throughout his kingdom.

English sources concur in acknowledging Flann Fína's learning. Beda (*c.* 731) described him as 'a very learned man in the scriptures' and 'a very learned man in all respects'. The Life of St Wilfrid, written between 709 and 731, called Flann Fína 'a very wise king'. Alcuin of York (†804), the noted Carolingian court scholar, referred to Flann Fína as being 'at once a king and teacher'. From ALDHELM (†709), abbot of Malmesbury and later bishop of Sherborne, Flann Fína received the long five-part 'letter to Acircius' which includes a typological essay on the number seven, a treatise on Latin metrics, and a collection of one hundred *enigmata* or riddles. Personal comments in Aldhelm's letter help confirm the depth of Flann Fína's learning.

Several Irish texts are attributed to Flann Fína under his Irish name. The most important of these is a wisdom text (see WISDOM LITERATURE) consisting of Old Irish three-word maxims called the 'Sayings of Flann Fína son of Oswiu' (*Bríathra* [or *Roscada*] *Flainn Fhína maic Ossu*). The maxims were compiled by an ecclesiastically trained redactor for the purpose of appealing to the private, individual conscience of a literate, secular audience.

FURTHER READING
ADOMNÁN; ALDHELM; ANNALS; BEDA; BRYNAICH; CUMMÍNE FOTA; EADWINE; ECGFRITH; EILEAN Ì; GENEALOGIES; OSWALD; OSWYDD; RHEGED; UÍ NÉILL; WISDOM LITERATURE; Ireland, *Celtica* 22.64–78; Ireland, *Celtic Florilegium* 63–77; Ireland, *Old Irish Wisdom Attributed to Aldfrith of Northumbria*.

Colin Ireland

Flann Mainistreach

Flann Mainistreach (†1056) was a famous Irish poet and historian, as well as lector at the monastery of Monasterboice, Co. Louth (Mainistir Buite, Contae Lú). Flann's family was very much connected with the monastery; for example, Flann's father seems to have held the same position as Flann himself. This close association with Monasterboice is also suggested by Flann's epithet *Mainistrech*, which literally means 'monastic, of the monastery', to be understood as short for 'of Mainistir (Buite)'.

Flann's poetry reflects his historical interests and deals with historical and pseudo-historical figures and events. Several poems found in LEBAR GABÁLA ÉRENN, an 11th-century Irish pseudo-historical text, have been ascribed to him. A well-read and educated man, Flann's poetry was particularly influenced by historical texts from outside the Irish world, for example, the *Chronicon*, a world history by Eusebius (*fl.* 4th century). Flann is thus a good example of how the tension between traditional Irish learning and Latin-based ecclesiastical education could be skilfully fused.

FURTHER READING
IRISH LITERATURE; LEBAR GABÁLA ÉRENN; MONASTERIES; MONASTICISM; Dobbs, *County Louth Archaeological and Historical Journal* 5.3.149–53; MacAirt, *ÉC* 6.255–80, 7.18–45, 8.98–119, 284–97; MacNeill, *Archivium Hibernicum* 2.37–99; Murphy, *Measgra i gCuimhne Mhichíl Uí Chléirigh* 140–64; O'Reilly, *Chronological Account of Nearly Four Hundred Irish Writers* lxxv–lxxviii; Thurneysen, *ZCP* 10.269–73; Thurneysen, *ZCP* 10.396–7; Zimmer, *Zeitschrift für vergleichende Sprachforschung auf dem Gebiete der Indogermanischen Sprachen*, 28.679–89.

PSH

Fled Bricrenn ('Bricriu's Feast') is one of the longer and most entertaining of the early Irish ULSTER CYCLE of tales and, from the perspective of modern readers, one of the best known. For general discussions of *Fled Bricrenn*'s significance within the corpus, see IRISH LITERATURE [1] §5; ULSTER CYCLE §3.

The story begins with a great and elaborately described feast and fabulous feasting hall prepared by the ingeniously malevolent BRICRIU with the intention of inciting the status-obsessed heroes and noblewomen of the ULAID against each other. The action soon settles into a sustained fierce three-way contest between Loegaire Buadach, CONALL CERNACH, and Cú CHULAINN, each seeking explicit recognition as Ulster's greatest hero. The nature of the contest and venue change several times, entailing numerous adventures, including adjudication by Ulaid's traditional enemies MEDB and Ailill at CRÚACHU. The climax is a death-defying beheading game (anticipating by some three or four centuries a very similar episode in the Middle English Arthurian *Sir Gawain and the Green Knight*), in which the three heroes face the disguised axe-wielding Cú Roí, and only Cú Chulainn is brave enough to return to face the unkillable giant. For modern scholarship, *Fled Bricrenn* probably exceeds even TÁIN BÓ CUAILNGE as a source of comparison between medieval Irish heroic legend and the Celtic ethnography of GREEK AND ROMAN ACCOUNTS (§7), sharing with the classical texts, particularly the surviving texts based on the lost history of POSIDONIUS (i.e. ATHENAEUS, DIODORUS SICULUS, and STRABO), the themes of

status display at the extravagant aristocratic FEAST (§5; see also BOAR; FOODWAYS; WINE), heroic contention at feasts, specifically for the CHAMPION'S PORTION (Irish *curadmír*), the HEROIC ETHOS in general, and the so-called Celtic HEAD CULT. So intriguingly close are the parallels between the ancient sources and *Fled Bricrenn* as to raise such possibilities as that the saga preserves an accurate 'Window on the Iron Age' through the phenomenal persistence of Celtic oral tradition from pre-Christian times (as argued by JACKSON) or that medieval IRISH LITERATURE has, through some unknown intermediary, been heavily influenced by classical accounts of the northern barbarians. Linguistically, the extant text is in the main Early Middle IRISH, probably 10th-century, though there are several throwbacks to Old Irish usage which imply an earlier written version. The presence of a good version of most of the text in the important manuscript LEBOR NA hUIDRE ('The Book of Dun Cow') and the accessible text and English translation published by Henderson in 1899 in the Irish Texts Society (CUMANN NA SCRÍBHEANN NGAEDHILGE) series have no doubt contributed to the special prominence of *Fled Bricrenn* in CELTIC STUDIES over the past century.

PRIMARY SOURCES
FACSIMILE. Best & Bergin, *Lebor na hUidre* (the end of the tale is missing from this manuscript).
ED. & TRANS. Henderson, *Fled Bricrend*.
TRANS. Gantz, *Early Irish Myths and Sagas* 219–55; Koch & Carey, *Celtic Heroic Age* 76–105.

FURTHER READING
ATHENAEUS; BOAR; BRICRIU; CELTIC STUDIES; CHAMPION'S PORTION; CONALL CERNACH; CRÚACHU; CÚ CHULAINN; CÚ ROÍ; CUMANN NA SCRÍBHEANN N-GAEDHILGE; DIODORUS SICULUS; FEAST; FOODWAYS; GREEK AND ROMAN ACCOUNTS; HEAD CULT; HEROIC ETHOS; IRISH; IRISH LITERATURE; JACKSON; LEBOR NA H-UIDRE; MEDB; POSIDONIUS; STRABO; TÁIN BÓ CUAILNGE; ULAID; ULSTER CYCLE; WINE; Aitchison, *Journal of Medieval History* 13.87–116; Jackson, *Oldest Irish Tradition*; O'Brien, *Irish Sagas* 67–78; O'Leary, *Éigse* 20.115–27; Ó Riain, *Fled Bricrenn*.

JTK

Fleuriot, Léon (1923–87) was a Breton scholar who originally came from Morlaix (MONTROULEZ). He studied history, devoting his career mainly to the language and history of early Brittany (BREIZH). His dictionary and grammar of Old BRETON remain the standard works, the first systematic analysis of the subject since that of Joseph LOTH (1847–1934) in the previous century. Fleuriot's diligent study of manuscripts uncovered many previously unidentified Old Breton glosses, and he lobbied Romance philologists to consider GAULISH and CONTINENTAL CELTIC as potential sources for Romance words of unknown etymology. He held the Celtic Chair at the University in Rennes II (ROAZHON) from 1966, and counted President of the editorial committee of ÉTUDES CELTIQUES among his many honours.

SELECTION OF MAIN WORKS
Le vieux breton (1964); Les origines de la Bretagne (1980); Dictionary of Old Breton/Dictionnaire du vieux breton (1985).

FURTHER READING
BREIZH; BRETON; BRETON LITERATURE; CONTINENTAL CELTIC; ÉTUDES CELTIQUES; GAULISH; LOTH; MONTROULEZ; ROAZHON; Gohier & Huon, Dictionnaire des écrivains d'aujourd'hui en Bretagne; Lambert, ÉC 24.9–11.

AM

flood legends

§1. PRE-CHRISTIAN CELTIC FLOOD LEGENDS

A passage attributed to the lost work of Timagenes of Alexandria (fl. c. 55–30 BC) throws light upon the migration/foundation traditions of the pagan Continental Celts:

> The DRUIDS recount that part of the population of GAUL was indigenous, but that some of the people immigrated there from outlying islands and the lands beyond the RHINE, driven out by frequent wars and violent floods from the sea. (Ammianus Marcellinus 15.9.4; cf. LEGENDARY HISTORY §2)

§2. ORIGIN OF LAKES AND RIVERS

The biblical deluge figures prominently in medieval Celtic attempts to explain their own history and origins. In addition to the great flood, smaller-scale floods are held to have occurred throughout the CELTIC COUNTRIES, accounting for the origin of lakes, rivers, and shallow bays.

There are numerous references to the belief that natural geographical features resulted from the release of pent-up water. LEBAR GABÁLA ÉRENN ('The Book of Invasions') describes the effect of the biblical flood on Ireland (ÉRIU), but also recounts several more localized events. Loch Rudraige is said to have burst forth when the grave of Rudraige, PARTHOLÓN's son, was dug. Six other lake bursts are listed in this section as having taken place in Partholón's time: Loch Láiglind (or Láiglinne), Loch Cuan, Loch nDechet, Loch Mesc, Loch Con, and Loch nEchtra. In Nemed, Loch Cál, Loch Munremair, Loch nDairbrech, and Loch nAinnind burst forth. Geoffrey Keating (Seathrún CÉITINN) describes the origin of Lough Foyle, Co. Donegal (Loch Feabhail, Contae Dhún na nGall), in the same terms. This occurs in Welsh tradition as well; for example, a lake burst traditionally accounts for the origin of Llyn Tegid (Bala Lake). The legendary childhood of TALIESIN took place at the bottom of what is now Llyn Tegid, and he subsequently reappears in a basket set adrift in the sea and caught like a salmon in a weir.

§3. DROWNED CITIES

The legend of a drowned city is by no means unique to Celtic culture; compare, for instance, the Greek story of Atlantis or the northern German story of Vineta. The Rennes DINDSHENCHAS records a story about the mythological figures BÓAND (Boyne) and her husband Nechtan. Bóand opened a well which only Nechtan could safely tap. The unstoppable flow resulted in the river Boyne, pushing Bóand herself to the sea. Nechtan's name is cognate with Latin Neptunus, the Roman god of the sea (see also Dumézil, Celtica 6.50–61).

The earliest instance of a drowned city in Welsh tradition is a poem in the Black Book of Carmarthen (LLYFR DU CAERFYRDDIN), Boddi Maes Gwyddneu ('The drowning of Gwyddno's plain', also known as Cantre'r Gwaelod 'The low CANTREF'). Although the poem obviously alludes to a traditional flood story, it is not itself a narrative poem. It addresses the figure of Seithennin, who appears in a Latin TRIAD (evidently a translation of a lost Welsh original) as one of three kings whose lands were inundated by the sea. The others are Helic mab Glannauc (Modern Welsh Helyg ap Glannawg), whose country Llys Helyg is in Conwy Bay, and the otherwise unknown Redwoe mab Regheth.

The bulk of the poem discusses Mererid, who left a well uncovered after a FEAST, which let in the sea to drown the land. A 19th-century legend from the Iveragh peninsula in Kerry (Ciarraí), Ireland, recounts the origin of Lough Currane (Loch Luíoch) in almost exactly the same way.

Perhaps the most renowned example is the Breton city of Is or Ys (lit. 'lower'). A folk etymology derives the name of Paris from the Breton *par Is* 'like Ys'. The story first occurs in literature in the 16th-century Breton *Buhez Sant Gwenôle Abat* (Life of St Gwennole abbot; reprinted in Le Roux and Guyonvarc'h, *La légende de la ville d'Is*; see further UUINUUALOE). The inhabitants of Ys are destroyed through their general wickedness, influenced by the biblical stories of the flood and the destruction of Sodom. Only St Gwennole and King Grallon survive. In oral tradition, this wickedness finds focus in Dahut, King Grallon's daughter, who brings about the destruction of the city. In some versions, only Grallon's horse has the energy to escape the waves when Grallon casts his daughter Dahut into the sea. Her name is not attested until quite late, but seems to come from Celtic **dago-soitā* 'good in magic'. Dahut, along with Mererid and Bóand, may be a reflection of a SPRING DEITY. In recent times, the Ys legend has inspired the Welsh visual artists Ceri Richards and Iwan Bala.

There are numerous other drowned cities in Celtic tradition. Often, the stories take the form of an origin legend for a particular lake. A medieval version about Lough Ree (Loch Rí), Ireland, occurs in *Aided Echach* (The death of Eochaid) in LEBOR NA HUIDRE ('The Book of Dun Cow'). Local geography and optical and accoustical phenomena help to localize these traditions and keep them alive. The evidence of prehistoric geological shifts is often recorded by fossilized sea creatures found inland, sometimes at high elevations, and the remains of tree stumps are sometimes found in shallow bays or lakes. The partial sinking of the Scilly Isles off the west coast of Cornwall (KERNOW) in medieval times may have given rise to the Cornish legend of Lyonesse. In addition, irregular natural stone formations undersea often look like straight stone walls, usually interpreted as the ruins or foundations of a building. A bay or lake can also reflect sound, so that a distant church bell will sound as if it is tolling under the waves, a common motif in folk tradition both in the Celtic countries and internationally.

PRIMARY SOURCES
CÉITINN, *Foras Feasa ar Éirinn*; LEBAR GABÁLA ÉRENN; LEBOR NA H-UIDRE; LLYFR DU CAERFYRDDIN.
TRANS. Koch & Carey, *Celtic Heroic Age* 226–71 (*Lebar Gabála*).

FURTHER READING
BÓAND; CANTREF; CELTIC COUNTRIES; DINDSHENCHAS; DRUIDS; ÉRIU; FEAST; FOLK-TALES; GAUL; KERNOW; LEGENDARY HISTORY; PARTHOLÓN; RHINE; SPRING DEITIES; TALIESIN; TRIADS; UUINUUALOE; Bromwich, *Early Cultures of North-West Europe* 215–41; Dumézil, *Celtica* 6.50–61; Thomas Jones, BBCS 12.79–83; Le Roux & Guyonvarc'h, *La légende de la ville d'Is*; Littleton, *New Comparative Mythology*; North, *Sunken Cities*; Ó Conaill, *Seán Ó Conaill's Book*; Ó Súilleabháin, *Handbook of Irish Folklore*; Tymoczko, *Legend of the City of Ys* vii–xxxiv.

AM

Foinse (Source), published since October 1996, is a weekly national newspaper in IRISH covering national and international news. It includes features on sport and travel, book, film and theatre reviews, a satirical page, and a section for schools. Four pages are devoted to news from the GAELTACHT, with one page for each Gaeltacht region. Produced in An Cheathrú Rua, in the Conamara Gaeltacht by Móinéar Teoranta, *Foinse* replaced ANOIS.

RELATED ARTICLES
ANOIS; GAELTACHT; IRISH.
WEBSITE. http://www.foinse.ie

Pádraigín Riggs

folk-tales and legends

§1. DEFINITIONS AND CONCEPTS

These two categories of traditional narrative are found throughout the world. In the academic study of folklore, 'folk-tale' is the name given to those tales which are understood to be fictional, told purely for entertainment. They are characterized by linear plots and the presence of casual magic. The term 'legend' has come to denote a wider variety of tales, from saints' legends (see HAGIOGRAPHY) to urban legends, which are plausible according to the worldview of traditional society, even though they may contain supernatural or magical elements. Another category of traditional narrative, the 'myth', includes stories of a sacred or cosmically important character. Myths are held to be true, although the setting of a myth is likely to be at an earlier stage of the world where different rules apply, so that otherwise impossible events are taken seriously. In CELTIC STUDIES, mythology (the corpus of myths) usually refers to pre-Christian mythology as recorded in ART and later literature, there being essentially no narrative literature in the CELTIC LANGUAGES from the pre-Christian period. Other narrative genres such as narrative jokes have not been studied in depth in the CELTIC COUNTRIES. All these categories are analytical ones imposed by scholars. Native terminology varies from language to language, and does not necessarily maintain the same distinctions (for the native early Irish genres, see TALE LISTS).

FURTHER READING
ART; CELTIC COUNTRIES; CELTIC LANGUAGES; CELTIC STUDIES; HAGIOGRAPHY; TALE LISTS; Aarne & Thompson, *Types of the Folktale*; Bascom, *Sacred Narrative* 5–29; Dégh & Vázonyi, *Genre* 4.281–304; Lüthi, *European Folktale*; Thompson, *Folktale*; Thompson, *Motif-Index of Folk-Literature*; Thompson, *Myth* 169–80.

AM

§2. IRISH

The Irish folk-tale collections, both published and unpublished, are widely acknowledged to be some of the best and richest in Europe—over 43,000 versions of more than 700 tale types were indexed in Ó Súilleabháin & Christiansen, *Types of the Irish Folktale*, which only includes material collected until 1956. Most of these are to be found in the archives of the Irish Folklore Commission, which was active from 1935 to 1971. The wealth of documented Irish folk-tales is, in part, due to the efforts of early field collectors, who were in turn inspired by the Romantic Movement to try to recover elements of ancient mythological and literary traditions through the Irish folk-tale and legendary repertoires. Some of the heroic narratives collected in the 19th and 20th centuries did, indeed, tie into the narratives preserved in Old and Middle Irish, notably the FIANNAÍOCHT, Fenian tales, i.e. those concerning FINN MAC CUMAILL and his comrades.

Thomas Crofton Croker (1798–1854), a native of Cork (CORCAIGH), was one of the first to collect Irish folklore. He corresponded with the brothers Jakob Grimm (1785–1863) and Wilhelm Grimm (1786–1859), who translated his influential *Fairy Legends and Traditions of the South of Ireland* (1825) into German as *Irische Elfenmärchen* in 1826. Many other collectors were active in the 19th century, including the literary figures Lady Wilde (Jane Francesca Elgee Wilde, *c.* 1826–96) and William Butler YEATS (1865–1939).

Jeremiah Curtin (1835–1906) was born to an Irish immigrant family in Detroit, but took his first collect-

ing trip to Ireland (ÉIRE) in 1887. He first published the folk-tales in the *New York Sun* newspaper and later in book form. Although only Curtin and a few of the storytellers were named in the publications, the actual process of collection involved many other people. Pádraig Ó Loingsigh explained to the folklorist Séamus Ó DUILEARGA that it was he who told the tales in Irish, but his father, Muiris Ó Loingsigh (Maurice Lynch), translated them into English for Curtin and was listed as the informant. Curtin's wife, Alma M. Cardell Curtin, took them down in shorthand, but, as was the case with many academics' wives of the period, she is usually not credited for her work.

Both Curtin and Wilde were criticized by Douglas Hyde (Dubhghlas DE HÍDE), another early collector, for their lack of fluency in Irish. His own collection, *Beside the Fire* (1910), was published bilingually, and in the 20th century folklorists placed a greater emphasis on collecting and publishing the Irish texts, though excellent unaccompanied English translations continue to be published, such as *The Folktales of Ireland* (1966) by Sean O'Sullivan (Seán Ó Súilleabháin).

Although the tales are largely the same as other folk-tales throughout the world, the method of narrating them in Ireland became very elaborate over time, developing 'runs'—sections of prose text heavily ornamented with alliteration and other poetic devices. The skill involved was recognized beyond the GAELTACHT, such that the Irish word for a professional storyteller—*seanchaí*, or its Scottish Gaelic cognate *seanchaidh*—was borrowed into English as *shannaghes* (plural) as early as 1534; it is now usually spelled *seannachie* or *sennachie*. The word is based on *seanchas* 'lore' (itself built on *sean* 'old'), and the prerogative of the *seanchaí* included many kinds of traditional lore, including factual material such as GENEALOGIES and history. Another word, used for anyone who tells a story, is *scéalaí*, based on *scéal* 'tale'. The stories were usually told at night around the fire, beginning with the host (*Ar fhear an tí a théann an chéad scéal*, The man of the house tells the first tale).

Although the bulk of Irish folk narrative scholarship deals with the folk-tale, there have been numerous serious studies of legends, including O'Sullivan's *Legends from Ireland* (1977). The Irish folklore journals BÉALOIDEAS and ÉIGSE contain many articles devoted to the study of folk narrative.

PRIMARY SOURCES

Bruford, *Gaelic Folktales and Medieval Romances*; Campbell, *Legends of Ireland*; Carleton, *Poor Scholar*; Croker, *Fairy Legends and Traditions of the South of Ireland*; Croker, *Irische Elfenmärchen*; Croker, *Legends of Cork*; Cross & Slover, *Ancient Irish Tales*; Curtin, *Irish Folk-tales*; Danaher, *Folktales of the Irish Countryside*; Dillon, *There was a King in Ireland*; Gailey & O hOgáin, *Gold Under the Furze*; Glassie, *Passing the Time in Ballymenone*; Gordon, *Irish Folk and Fairy Tales*; Graves, *Irish Fairy Book*; Gregory, *Visions and Beliefs in the West of Ireland*; Hyde, *Beside the Fire*; Hyde, *Contes irlandais*; Hyde, *Legends of Saints and Sinners*; Kennedy, *Irish Fireside Folktales*; Lover, *Popular Tales and Legends of the Irish Peasantry*; Lover & Croker, *Ireland*; Lysaght, *Banshee*; Ó Conaill, *Leabhar Sheáin Í Chonaill*; Ó Conaill, *Seán Ó Conaill's Book*; Ó hEalaoire, *Leabhar Stiofáin Uí Ealaoire*; O'Farrell, *Folktales of the Irish Coast*; O'Grady, *Bog of Stars and Other Stories and Sketches of Elizabethan Ireland*; Ó hEochaidh, *Síscéalta ó Thír Chonaill / Fairy Legends from Donegal*; Ó Súilleabháin, *Folktales of Ireland*; Ó Súilleabháin, *Legends from Ireland*; Yeats, *Fairy and Folk Tales of Ireland*.

FURTHER READING

BÉALOIDEAS; CORCAIGH; DE H-ÍDE; ÉIGSE; ÉIRE; FIANNAÍOCHT; FINN MAC CUMAILL; GAELTACHT; GENEALOGIES; Ó DUILEARGA; YEATS; Christiansen, *Studies in Irish and Scandinavian Folktales*; Cross, *Motif-index of Early Irish Literature*; Ó Súilleabháin, *Storytelling in Irish Tradition*; Ó Súilleabháin & Christiansen, *Types of the Irish Folktale*.

AM

§3. SCOTTISH GAELIC

Folk-tales and legends are well attested in Scottish Gaelic tradition. Tales are scattered throughout some manuscripts from the 17th century onwards, though the bulk of the recorded material belongs to the 19th and 20th centuries. The pioneering collector of the mid-19th century was John Francis CAMPBELL, who, with several collaborators (J. Dewar, J. G. Campbell, Alexander Carmichael, and Hector Maclean), tapped into a storytelling tradition which was just beginning to decline as the ceilidh-house lost its importance in the social life of Scottish Gaelic communities.

In the 20th century, the School of Scottish Studies in Edinburgh (DÙN ÈIDEANN) has been pre-eminent in the collecting of tales, much aided by the advent of tape and video recorders. The material has come both from the settled population of the Gaidhealtachd (Gaelic-speaking area) and from Gaelic-speaking travellers. Closely related material was taken by emigrants to Nova Scotia, Canada, and survived there (MacNeil, *Sgeul gu Latha / Tales until Dawn*; see also CELTIC LANGUAGES IN NORTH AMERICA).

Versions of international tale types are well represented and several have been published and analysed in the journals *Scottish Studies* and *Tocher*, e.g. Donald Alasdair Johnson's *Rìgh Eilifacs* ('The King of Eilifacs'; Donald A. MacDonald, *Scottish Studies* 16.1–22), and Alasdair Stewart's tales *Stoiridh an Eich Dhuibh* ('The Story of the Black Horse') and *A' Maraiche Màirneal* ('The Maraiche Màirneal'; *Tocher* 29.270–91). Hero tales and descendants of the medieval Romance tales are similarly present in the corpus (Bruford, *Gaelic Folk-tales and Mediaeval Romances* 60–3, 251–67). An example is *An Ceatharnach Caol Riabhach* ('The Lean Grizzled Ceatharnach'), told by Donald Alasdair Johnson (Donald A. MacDonald & Bruford, *Scottish Studies* 14.134–54). The supernatural is present as a significant element in many tales, and much material deals exclusively with such phenomena, notably tales of the FAIRIES and other supernatural beings (cf. OTHERWORLD; SÍD; TUATH DÉ) and traditions about the Second Sight and the Evil Eye (MacInnes, *Trans. Gaelic Society of Inverness* 59.1–20). A narrative genre specific to Gaelic Scotland (ALBA) is that of CLAN tales, where events purporting to deal with historical characters are narrated in a distinctively terse style (J. G. Campbell & Wallace, *Clan Traditions and Popular Tales of the Western Highlands and Islands*; Dewar, *Dewar Manuscripts*; MacInnes, *Trans. Gaelic Society of Inverness* 57.388–9). More recent local traditions and small-scale anecdotes commemorating individuals have also been recorded (C. Lawson & B. Lawson, *Sgeulachdan a Seisiadar / Tales from Sheshader*).

Much attention has focused on the storytellers, their repertoire, and their narrative and memory techniques. Visualization seems to have been an important mnemonic aid (D. A. MacDonald, *Scottish Studies* 22.1–26; Bruford, *Scottish Studies* 22.27–44). Many storytellers had substantial repertoires, e.g. Duncan MacDonald (*Tocher* 25.1–32, 58) or Angus MacLellan (J. L. Campbell, *Scottish Studies* 10.193–7), and some tales took several evenings to tell in full.

PRIMARY SOURCES

MSS. Edinburgh, National Library of Scotland, Adv. 50.1.1–Adv. 51.2.7 (J. F. Campbell); School of Scottish Studies Archive and Sound Archive; University Library, Carmichael-Watson Collection; Inveraray, Dewar Manuscripts (7 vols). ED. & TRANS. Bruford & MacDonald, *Scottish Traditional Tales*; J. F. Campbell, *More West Highland Tales*; J. G. Campbell, *Fians*; J. F. Campbell, *Popular Tales of the West Highlands*; J. G. Campbell & Wallace, *Clan Traditions and Popular Tales of the Western Highlands and Islands*; Dewar, *Dewar Manuscripts*; C. Lawson & B. Lawson, *Sgeulachdan a Seisiadar*; Donald A. MacDonald, *Scottish Studies* 16.1.1–22; Donald A. MacDonald & Bruford, *Scottish Studies* 14.133–54; MacDougall, *Folk and Hero Tales*; MacDougall, *Folk Tales and Fairy Lore in Gaelic and English*; MacInnes, *Folk and*

Hero Tales; MacKay, *Gille a' Bhuidseir* / *Wizard's Gillie*; MacKinnon, *Scottish Folktales in Gaelic and English*; MacLellan, *Stories from South Uist*; MacNeil, *Sgeul gu Latha* / *Tales until Dawn*; MacPherson, *Tales of Barra Told by the Coddy*.

FURTHER READING
ALBA; CAMPBELL; CELTIC LANGUAGES IN NORTH AMERICA; CLAN; DÙN ÈIDEANN; FAIRIES; HIGHLANDS; OTHERWORLD; SCOTTISH GAELIC; SÍD; TUATH DÉ; Aarne & Thompson, *Types of the Folktale*; Bruford, *Gaelic Folk-tales and Mediaeval Romances*; Bruford, *Scottish Studies* 11.13–47; Bruford, *Scottish Studies* 22.27–44; J. L. Campbell, *Scottish Studies* 10.193–7; Delargy, PBA 31.177–221; Jackson, *Proc. Scottish Anthropological and Folklore Society* 4.3.123–40; D. A. MacDonald, *Scottish Studies* 22.1–26; MacInnes, *Trans. Gaelic Society of Inverness* 57.377–94; MacInnes, *Trans. Gaelic Society of Inverness* 59.1–20; Ó Súilleabháin & Christiansen, *Types of the Irish Folktale*; Thompson, *Folktale*; *Tocher* 25; *Tocher* 29.

Anja Gunderloch

§4. MANX

The first collection of Manx folk-tales was compiled by George Waldron in 1726, and was posthumously published in 1731. This collection, with its stories of giants and underground palaces beneath the island's medieval Castle Rushen and the fearsome Moddey Dhoo (black dog) of Peel Castle, has formed the basis for publications of Manx folk-tales ever since.

The folk-tales contain accounts of Manx 'mythology', including creation myths for the island, its people and 'Themselves' (the FAIRIES). The historical 'mythologies' also seek to place the Isle of Man (ELLAN VANNIN) within a wider cultural framework by identifying the island as the Ellan Sheeant (Isle of Peace/Holy Island) of Irish mythology and relating the island's creation to the great battle between Finn Mac Cooil (Middle Irish FINN MAC CUMAILL) and the Scottish giant, when a 'sod of earth' is thrown, thereby creating the Lough Neagh (Loch nEathach) in northern Ireland (ÉRIU) and the Isle of Man. Although the Manx folk-tales were originally peopled with heroes and deities from the early Irish myths and legends, by the 19th century the predominant figure was MANANNÁN MAC LIR. Manannán figured in the early Irish MYTHOLOGICAL CYCLE as god of the sea, but in Manx tales he became the first Manx ruler and was a shape-shifting magician-king (see REINCARNATION) and navigator.

The majority of Manx tales, however, relate to the fairy-folk. Manx fairies are portrayed as similar to the 'lil' folk' known in British and Irish folk beliefs and are small wingless creatures of supernatural origin who could not be called by their real name but by euphemistic terms such as 'Themselves'. The stories are primarily cautionary tales which highlight the dangers of associating with 'Themselves', and either relate to concerns over the taking of infants and adults by the fairies or of people trying to better themselves through 'trading' with the fairies. The need for protection and constant vigilance against the malicious intent of fairies and the fact that no one ever truly profits from dealings with the fairies are constantly emphasized.

Manx folk-tales relate to a whole bestiary of supernatural creatures, ranging from the relatively helpful but cantankerous Fynnoderee (or Phynnodderee, defined as a satyr) to the dangerous Tarroo-Ushtey (water bull) and the Glashtin (water horse). Of even greater danger was the Tehi Tegi, a beautiful temptress who could lure men to their doom and then revert to being an evil old sorceress, and the Buggane, a totally malicious hobgoblin.

The folk-tales are frequently both geographically and temporally specific, thereby enhancing their original claims for authenticity and apparent use as verbal controls and cautionary tales to both children and adults with regard to taking care in one's actions whilst visiting certain locations.

Although abridged versions of the folk-tales were published in guidebooks and tourist accounts throughout the 19th century, the tales also appear to have remained part of the island's oral tradition until the latter part of that century. They also provided a basis for much of the island's literature of the period, including Hall Caine's novels and T. E. Brown's dialect poetry. The seminal work was Sophia MORRISON's *Manx Fairy Tales* (1911), the last publication to depict folk-tales as examples of Manx folklore (see MANX LITERATURE [3]). Successive publications of folk-tales have been abridged and rewritten as collections of 'fairy stories' for a children's audience, with an emphasis on illustrating the stories for new generations of children.

PRIMARY SOURCES
Broderick, *Manx Stories and Reminiscences of Ned Beg Hom Ruy*; Callow, *Phynodderree*; Cashen, *Manx Folklore*; Clague, *Cooinaghtyn Manninagh*; Gill, *Manx Scrapbook*; Gill, *Second Manx Scrapbook*; Gill, *Third Manx Scrapbook*; Killip, *Folklore of the Isle of Man*; Killip, *Saint Bridget's Night*; Killip, *Twisting the Rope*; Moore, *Folklore of the Isle of Man*; Morrison, *Manx Fairy Tales*; Paton, *Manx Calendar Customs*; Quayle, *Legends of a Life Time*; Rhŷs, *Celtic Folklore*; Roeder, *Yn Lioar Manninagh* 3.4.129–91; Roeder, *Manx Notes and Queries*; Rydings, *Manx Tales*; Train, *Historical and Statistical Account of the Isle of Man*; Waldron, *Description of the Isle of Man*.

FURTHER READING
DOUGLAS; ELLAN VANNIN; ÉRIU; FAIRIES; FINN MAC CUMAILL;
IRISH; MANANNÁN MAC LIR; MANX; MANX LITERATURE;
MOORE; MORRISON; MYTHOLOGICAL CYCLE; REINCAR-
NATION; Craine, *Manannan's Isle*; Crellin, *Manx Folklore*; Doug-
las, *Manx Folk-song, Folk Dance, Folklore*; Douglas, *This is Ellan
Vannin*; Douglas, *This is Ellan Vannin Again*; Douglas, *We Call
It Ellan Vannin*; Evans-Wentz, *Fairy-faith in Celtic Countries*;
Fraser, *In Praise of Manxland*; Harrison, *100 Years of Heritage*
190–205; Kelly, *Twas Thus and Thus They Lived*; Kermode, *Celtic
Customs*; Kinrade, *Life at the Lhen*; Miller, *Manx Folkways*;
Penrice, *Fables, Fantasies and Folklore of the Isle of Man*.

BIBLIOGRAPHY
Cubbon, *Bibliographical Account of Works Relating to the Isle of
Man* 1.397–410 & 496–504.

Yvonne Cresswell

§5. WELSH

The MABINOGI, a medieval collection of narratives,
contain elements from pre-Christian mythology, the
international folk-tale, local legend, and individual
literary authorship. Retellings of these tales have been
prominently featured in popular collections of Welsh
folk narrative such as Joseph Jacobs's *Celtic Fairy Tales*
(1892) and *More Celtic Fairy Tales* (1894), and Gwyn
Jones's *Welsh Legends and Folk-tales* (1955). Early collectors
looked for further information about medieval traditions in Welsh oral tradition and, although there was
no additional material on the characters from the
Mabinogi, traditions were collected relating to ARTHUR
and Merlin (see MYRDDIN).

Many ARTHURIAN legends in Wales are local
aetiological legends, explaining the origin of features
such as *coeten Arthur* (Arthur's quoit) and the names of
several megalithic monuments (e.g. in Pembrokeshire
[sir Benfro] and in Gower [Gŵyr]). The legend of
Arthur's Cave has been collected from several localities,
in England as well as in Wales (CYMRU); W. Jenkyn
Thomas's version from *The Welsh Fairy-book* (1907)
involves a Welshman who comes across a soothsayer
(*dyn hysbys*) in London. The soothsayer recognizes the
Welshman's hazel staff as having come from outside
Arthur's cave. The two return to Pontneddfechan in
POWYS and enter the cave, from which they attempt to
steal treasure. The soothsayer warns the Welshman not
to touch a bell, but he breaks the taboo and the
soothsayer has difficulty persuading King Arthur and
his knights to go back to sleep. They leave the cave
without the treasure and are unable to find it again.

Tales of the *tylwyth teg* (FAIRIES) are an important
part of Welsh folk narrative tradition. In the modern
period, the most widely known and frequently antholo-
gized legend is that of the fairy bride of LLYN Y FAN
FACH and the Physicians of Myddvai (MEDDYGON
MYDDFAI), first printed in 1861 and studied in depth
by John RHŶS (1840–1915) in *Y Cymmrodor* 4–6 (1881–
3). Another well-known tale is the story of Gelert, made
famous in English by the poem 'Beth Gêlert' by William
Robert Spencer (1769–1834). In this story, Prince
LLYWELYN AB IORWERTH of Wales returns from the
hunt to find his household in disarray. He cannot find
his infant son, but he sees his greyhound, Gelert, with
blood on his muzzle and, jumping to the logical conclusion, he kills the dog. He later finds the child,
unharmed, and the body of a wolf, which his own dog
had evidently killed to protect the child. Full of remorse,
Llywelyn builds a monument, Bedd Gelert (Gelert's
grave) for his dog. The story of the misunderstood
faithful hound is an international migratory legend
which became attached to the village of Beddgelert in
Caernarfonshire (sir Gaernarfon) as a way of explaining
the name. In 1899 D. E. Jenkins espoused the theory
that the story was deliberately attached to the village
by an 18th-century innkeeper in a cynical ploy to attract
tourists. His theory is widely believed, but subsequent
research has turned up earlier references to the legend,
though it is certainly also true that the story has been
deliberately marketed towards tourists in the modern
period.

There is no definitive collection of Welsh folk narrative. Many unpublished orally collected materials are
housed in the Museum of Welsh Life, St Fagans (see
AMGUEDDFEYDD AC ORIELAU CENEDLAETHOL CYMRU),
and many of the folk-tales and legends published in
WELSH have never been translated into English. Several
of the English-language collections have been so heavily
adapted that they are literary renderings of folk tradition rather than records of it, for example Iwan Myles's
Tales from Welsh Traditions (1923), though this is by no
means true of all English-language collections—see,
for example, Brian John's series of Pembrokeshire folk-
tales. Recent works continue to record contemporary
genres of folk narrative, including urban legends (Huws,
Y Nain yn y Carped, 1996) and supernatural legends
(Lockley, *Ghosts of South Wales*, 1996).

PRIMARY SOURCES
Barnes, *Great Legends of Wales*; Boniface, *S'nellie's Welsh Fairy Tales*;
Jonathan Ceredig Davies, *Folk-lore of West and Mid-Wales*; Aeres

Evans, *Mi Glywais I*; D. Silvan Evans & Jones, *Ysten Sioned neu Y Gronfa Gymmysg*; Gwyndaf, *Straeon Gwerin Cymru*; Gwyndaf, *Chwedlau Gwerin Cymru*; Howells, *Cambrian Superstitions*; Hughes, *Tales of Old Glamorgan*; Huws, *Y Nain yn y Carped*; Jacobs, *Celtic Fairy Tales*; Jenkins, *Bedd Gelert*; John, *Beneath the Mountain*; John, *Fireside Tales from Pembrokeshire*; John, *Last Dragon*; John, *More Pembrokeshire Folk Tales*; John, *Pembrokeshire Folk Tales*; Eirwen Jones, *Folktales of Wales*; Gwyn Jones, *Welsh legends and Folk-tales*; T. Gwynn Jones, *Welsh Folklore and Folk-custom*; Morgan, *Legends of Porthcawl and the Glamorgan Coast*; Pugh, *When the Devil Roamed Wales*; Radford, *Tales of North Wales*; Rhŷs, *Cymmrodor*, 4.1–54, 5.49–143, 6.155–221; Sarnicol, *Chwedlau Cefn Gwlad*; Simpson, *Folklore of the Welsh Border*; Styles, *Welsh Walks and Legends*; Dafydd Whiteside Thomas, *Chwedlau a Choelion Godre'r Wyddfa*; W. Jenkyn Thomas, *Welsh Fairy Book*; W. Jenkyn Thomas, *More Welsh Fairy and Folk Tales*; John Williams, *Meddygon Myddfai*; John Williams, *Physicians of Myddvai*.

FURTHER READING

AMGUEDDFEYDD; ARTHUR; ARTHURIAN; CYMRU; FAIRIES; LLYN Y FAN FACH; LLYWELYN AB IORWERTH; MABINOGI; MEDDYGON; MYRDDIN; POWYS; RHŶS; WELSH; Barber, *Ghosts of Wales*; Gwyndaf, *Folk Life* 26.78–100; Jackson, *International Popular Tale and Early Welsh Tradition*; Lockley, *Ghosts of South Wales*; Owen, *Welsh Folk Customs*; Parry-Jones, *Welsh Legends and Fairy Lore*.

AM

§6. BRETON

As in the other Celtic countries, ROMANTICISM played an important part in inspiring the collection of Breton folk narrative. One of the early collectors was Émile Souvestre (1806–54) of Morlaix (MONTROULEZ). Unusually for his time, his two collections *Les derniers Bretons* (1836) and *Le foyer breton* (1844) included some analysis of both text and context as well as a few footnotes providing and explaining the BRETON as collected from oral tradition. On the whole, however, the printed versions of the tales were made to conform to French literary standards in both language and structure.

Perhaps the greatest of the Breton folklorists was François-Marie LUZEL (1821–95), whose prolific publications include works on legends, folk-tales, and folksongs. Other important 19th- and early 20th-century folklorists include Elvire de Preissac, Countess de Cerny (1818–99), who collected both folk-tales and legendary traditions regarding St BRIGIT in Brittany (BREIZH); Anatole Le Braz (1859–1926), who published collections of folk-tales and legends, notably *La légende de la mort chez les Bretons armoricains* (The legend of death among the Armorican Bretons); and François Cadic (1864–1929), author of *Contes et légendes de Bretagne*. Two other collectors, Adolphe Orain (1834–1918) and Paul Sébillot (1846–1918), worked primarily in Upper Brittany (BREIZH-UHEL). Paul Sébillot was a significant contributor to folklore studies in France as a whole, coining the term *littérature orale* (oral literature), founding the series *Littératures populaires de toutes les nations* (Popular literature of all nations), and editing the journal *Révue des traditions populaires* (Review of popular traditions). Paul Sébillot's son, Paul-Yves Sébillot (1885–1971), was also an important Breton folklorist (see SUPERSTITIONS AND MAGICAL BELIEFS).

Comparatively few folklorists have published folk narratives in Breton. Most Breton-language versions, such as Bachellery's *La princesse plumet d'or* (The princess decked with gold), were published in the 20th century in journals such as ANNALES DE BRETAGNE, REVUE CELTIQUE, and ÉTUDES CELTIQUES. Some collections entirely in Breton have appeared, notably G. Milin's work *Gwechall goz e oa . . .* (Once upon a time there was . . .), which appeared in book form in 1924, and Yann Ar Floc'h's *Koñchennou euz bro ar ster Aon* (Folktales from the Aulne river country) in 1950. Per-Jakez HÉLIAS has published several folk narratives in Breton, and in 1984 the publisher Al LIAMM produced a five-volume collection of Luzel's folk-tales in Breton from manuscripts housed in the Kemper/Quimper library. Most of these had only ever been published in French translation, nearly a century before in 1887.

Lacking a medieval vernacular narrative tradition to inspire collectors, antiquarian interest in Breton folk narrative tradition has focused more on ballads than folktales or legends (see BARZAZ-BREIZ; LA VILLEMARQUÉ). More recent scholarship has found roots in Breton oral tradition for the Old French *lais* of Marie de France (see BRETON LAYS), and has brought examples of Merlin to light. The Merlin of Breton folklore is more akin to the MYRDDIN Wyllt of early Welsh tradition, a WILD MAN and prophet, than the court wizard of later ARTHURIAN tradition. Jef Phillipe printed some of these tales in his *War roudoù Merlin e Breizh* (On the track of Merlin in Brittany) in 1986.

Many of the classic Breton folk narrative collections, long out of print, are being republished, notably by Terre de Brume in Rennes, which reissues the original text along with an introduction and analysis.

PRIMARY SOURCES

An Uhel (Luzel), *Kontadennoù ar bobl*; Ar Braz (Le Braz), *Mojenn an ankoù*; Ar Floc'h, *Koñchennou euz bro ar ster Aon*; Ar Gow, *Marc'heger ar Gergoad*; Aubert, *Légendes traditionnelles de la Bretagne*; Bachellery, *ÉC* 4.335–57; Cadic, *Contes et légendes de Bretagne*;

Cerny, *Contes et légendes de Bretagne*; Cerny, *Saint-Suliac et ses traditions*; *Contes grivois des Hauts-Bretons*; Dagnet, *Au pays fougerais*; Dagnet, *Au pays malouin*; Déguignet, *Contes et légendes de Basse-Cornouaille*; Dixon, *Breton Fairy Tales*; Duine, *Les légendes du Pays de Dol en Bretagne*; Eudes, *Contes et comptines pour petits Bretons sages*; Frain, *Contes du cheval bleu*; Guénin, *Le légendaire préhistorique de Bretagne*; Hélias, *Bugale Berlobi*; Hélias, *Marvaillou ar votez-tan*; Jacq, *Légendes de Bretagne*; Sylvia Prys Jones & Ap Dafydd, *Straeon ac Arwyr Gwerin Llydaw*; Le Braz, *La légende de la mort chez les Bretons armoricains*; Le Braz, *Le passeur d'âmes et autres contes*; Luzel, *Celtic Folk Tales from Armorica*; Luzel, *Contes bretons*; Luzel, *Contes inédits*; Luzel, *Contes populaires de la Basse-Bretagne*; Luzel, *Contes retrouvés*; Luzel, *Les légendes chrétiennes de la Basse Bretagne*; Luzel, *Nouvelles veillées bretonnes*; Luzel, *Veillées bretonnes*; Meuss, *Breton Folktales*; Milin, *Gwechall goz e oa*; Orain, *Contes du pays Gallo*; Philippe, *War roudoù Merlin e Breizh*; Poulain, *Contes et légendes de Haute Bretagne*; Sébillot, *Contes des landes et des grèves*; Sébillot, *Contes et légendes de Bretagne*; Souvestre, *Les derniers Bretons*; Souvestre, *Le foyer breton*; Spence, *Legends and Romances of Brittany*; Thoméré, *Contes et légendes de Bretagne*.

FURTHER READING
ANNALES DE BRETAGNE; ARTHURIAN; BARZAZ-BREIZ; BREIZH; BREIZH-UHEL; BRETON; BRETON LAYS; BRIGIT; ÉTUDES CELTIQUES; HÉLIAS; LA VILLEMARQUÉ; LIAMM; LUZEL; MONTROULEZ; MYRDDIN; REVUE CELTIQUE; ROMANTICISM; SUPERSTITIONS AND MAGICAL BELIEFS; WILD MAN; Bachellery, *ÉC* 5.314–29.

AM

§7. CORNISH

The narrative legacy of Cornwall (KERNOW) is complex. Much of the material available today is the product of various initiatives by collectors from the Reformation period onwards. Written versions of Cornish epic narratives have not yet been recovered, though the ARTHURIAN and TRISTAN AND ISOLT material was probably central to early Cornish narrative traditions. These particular tales or cycles of tales are still important features of Cornish legendary material and have been incorporated into hagiographical and landscape-related legends.

Cornwall has retained a significant body of saints' lore (see HAGIOGRAPHY). In the 17th century Nicholas Roscarrock compiled the earliest and to date the most comprehensive survey of hagiographical material relating to Cornwall. The legends of St PIRAN, St PETROC and St IA are still widely circulated.

The 19th-century collections of Robert Hunt and William Bottrell form the primary corpus of Cornish folk-tales in circulation today. Although Bottrell collected his material earlier (starting in the 1830s) and his collection arguably contains better narrative quality, Hunt's collection was published first, and is more widely recognized as the standard work on Cornish folklore. Robert Hunt was keeper of the Mining Record Office

in Cornwall and his two-volume collection from 1865 includes giants, FAIRIES, lost cities, fire worship, demons, spectres, King ARTHUR, holy wells, sorcery, witchcraft, miners, and SUPERSTITIONS. William Bottrell's three-volume collection (1870, 1873, 1880) contained longer narratives and covered subjects ranging from witchcraft and changelings to fairies and pixies.

Since Hunt often drew on Bottrell's collecting efforts, Bottrell's versions of Cornish traditional narratives are often the basis for retellings. Among the most well-known of these narratives are the Mermaid of Zennor, the tale of Tregeagle, the Wrestlers of Kenidjack, the Legend of Pengersick, Tom and the Giant, Duffy and the Devil, and Madge Figgey and her Pig, many of them told in Cornu-English (that is, the Cornish dialect of English). Both Hunt and Bottrell also feature saints' tales associated with landscape features and monuments which seem to have developed over time and were not featured in Roscarrock's collection.

Narrative collecting activity continued into the early 20th century with the work of M. A. Courtney, J. A. Harris, and Enys Tregarthen, as well as Robert Morton NANCE and the Old Cornwall Societies. Cornish legends have by now been incorporated into a variety of contemporary art forms, including film, drama, and poetry (see MASS MEDIA; CORNISH LITERATURE). The poetry of Charles Causley draws on traditional narrative, and folk-tales also form an important part of new community festivals, best seen in Bolster Day at St Agnes, which was inspired by the story of the Giant Bolster and Saint Agnes. Contemporary retellings of Hunt and Bottrell include those by Rawe, Quayle and Foreman, and dramatized versions by the Bedlam and Kneehigh Theatre Companies. Recently integrated into the corpus is the late 20th-century 'urban legend', The Beast of Bodmin Moor.

PRIMARY SOURCES
Bottrell, *Traditions and Hearthside Stories of West Cornwall*; Causley, *Collected Poems 1951–2000*; Hunt, *Popular Romances of the West of England*; Orme, *Nicholas Roscarrock's Lives of the Saints: Cornwall and Devon*; Whitfield, *Scilly and its Legends*.

FURTHER READING
ARTHUR; ARTHURIAN; CORNISH LITERATURE; FAIRIES; HAGIOGRAPHY; IA; KERNOW; MASS MEDIA; NANCE; PETROC; PIRAN; SUPERSTITIONS AND MAGICAL BELIEFS; TRISTAN AND ISOLT; Courtney, *Cornish Feasts and Folk-lore*; Deane & Shaw, *Folklore of Cornwall*; Quayle & Foreman, *Magic Ointment*; Rawe, *Traditional Cornish Stories and Rhymes*; Weatherhill & Devereux, *Myths and Legends of Cornwall*.

Amy Hale

Fomoiri is a name which designates a race of hostile beings frequently mentioned in Irish legend; they usually appear to be conceived as supernatural entities, and are often described as being monstrous in appearance. The first element in the name is clearly the preposition *fo* 'under', but the second is more mysterious: THURNEYSEN argued that it is cognate with the '-mare' in English 'nightmare' (Thurneysen, *Die irische Helden-und Königsage bis zum siebzehnten Jahrhundert* 64). Medieval etymologists took it to be *muir* 'sea', associating this with the Fomoiri's character as sea-raiders. The form *Fomóraig*, found from the Middle Irish period onward, reflects a reinterpretation of the second syllable as *mór* 'big' consequent on the term's use (its normal meaning in the modern GAELIC languages) as a synonym for 'giants'.

The Fomoiri feature in legendary-historical sources as the enemies of the first settlers of Ireland (ÉRIU), and also of some of its early kings (e.g. Macalister, *Lebor Gabála Érenn* 2.270–1, 3.120–5, 4.118–21, 5.190–1, 210–11, 220–1, 242–3, 248–9; Hamel, *Lebor Bretnach* §12); they also appear as the fierce and sometimes monstrous inhabitants of other islands (Thurneysen, *Abhandlungen der Königlichen Gesellschaft der Wissenschaften zu Göttingen*, 14.2.57; Knott, *Togail Bruidne Da Derga* ll. 902–33; Macalister, *Lebor Gabála Érenn* 41.10–11). In what is probably the earliest reference to them, a possibly 7th-century elegy for Mess-Telmann, a prince of Leinster (LAIGIN), they are spoken of as dwelling 'under the worlds of men' (O'Brien, *Corpus Genealogiarum Hiberniae* 20). In CATH MAIGE TUIRED ('The [Second] Battle of Mag Tuired') they are portrayed as a race opposed to and constrasting with the TUATH DÉ. This dichotomy has been seen as reflecting an Indo-European myth of 'the war of the gods', but seems more likely to be a concept originating with *Cath Maige Tuired* itself, in which the Fomoiri are identified with the Vikings. In other sources there seems, rather, to be an overlap or indeed identity between the Fomoiri and Tuath Dé: the Fomoiri are called 'the champions of the síd' (Gray, *Cath Maige Tuired* 34.187–8, cf. 48.447); a figure called Tethra is named as presiding over both races (references in O'Rahilly, *Early Irish History and Mythology* 483); the phrase 'demons and Fomóraig' is glossed 'i.e. Tuath Dé Donann' (Macalister, *Lebor Gabála Érenn* 32–3); and the late tale TÓRUIGHEACHT DHIARMADA AGUS GHRÁINNE ('The Pursuit of Diarmaid and Gráinne') portrays one of the Fomoiri as a servant of the Tuath Dé (Ní Shéaghdha, *Tóruigheacht Dhiarmada agus Ghráinne* 52–3). The main distinguishing factor seems to be that the Fomoiri are always portrayed in a negative light, the Tuath Dé only occasionally so.

The Middle Irish *Sex Aetates Mundi* includes *fomóraig* among the monstrous races descended from Ham son of Noah, in a context that suggests that the word is used as an equivalent of 'giants' (Ó Cróinín, *Irish Sex Aetates Mundi* 79, 100, 119, 134); the idea of descent from Ham is further explored in the genealogical literature (O'Brien, *Corpus Genealogiarum Hiberniae* 330–2).

PRIMARY SOURCES
EDITIONS. Hamel, *Lebor Bretnach*; Knott, *Togail Bruidne Da Derga*; O'Brien, *Corpus Genealogiarum Hiberniae*; Thurneysen, *Zu irischen Handschriften und Litteraturdenkmälern* 1.53–8.
ED. & TRANS. Gray, *Cath Maige Tuired*; Macalister, *Lebor Gabála Érenn*; Meyer, *Über die älteste irische Dichtung* 2; Ní Shéaghdha, *Tóruigheacht Dhiarmada agus Ghráinne*; Ó Cróinín, *Irish Sex Aetates Mundi*.
TRANS. Koch & Carey, *Celtic Heroic Age*.

FURTHER READING
CATH MAIGE TUIRED; ÉRIU; GAELIC; GENEALOGIES; LAIGIN; LEBAR GABÁLA ÉRENN; SÍD; THURNEYSEN; TOGAIL BRUIDNE DA DERGA; TÓRUIGHEACHT DHIARMADA AGUS GHRÁINNE; TUATH DÉ; Carey, *Cultural Identity and Cultural Integration* 50–3; Carey, *SC* 24/25.53–69; Mac Cana, *Impact of the Scandinavian Invasions on the Celtic-speaking Peoples* 94–7; O'Rahilly, *Early Irish History and Mythology* 482–3, 523–5; Alwyn D. Rees & Brinley Rees, *Celtic Heritage* 40; Sjoestedt, *Gods and Heroes of the Celts* 16–17; Thurneysen, *Die irische Helden- und Königsage bis zum siebzehnten Jahrhundert* 64.

John Carey

Foodways is the term given to cultural practices which involve food, including which foods are eaten and the cultural contexts surrounding them (see CHAMPION'S PORTION; FEAST). Traditional Celtic foodways were largely limited to the products which were available in the local area.

§1. CELTIC FOODWAYS IN ANCIENT TIMES
Classical writers' depictions of the Celts often conform to the topos of the Northern Barbarian (see GREEK AND ROMAN ACCOUNTS, esp. §7 Feasting). A particularly valuable source is the ancient survey of dining customs by ATHENAEUS known as the *Deipnosophistoi*, whose sections on GAUL are heavily indebted to the

lost history of POSIDONIUS. Elements of Athenaeus' descriptions of Celtic feasts bear a resemblance to those in the early Irish sagas, particularly FLED BRICRENN ('Bricriu's Feast') in the ULSTER CYCLE of Tales. Other commentaries, such as CAESAR's statement in *De Bello Gallico* 5.12 that eating chicken, goose, and hare was taboo, should not be taken at face value. These may have been taboo at certain times or for certain groups of people, but it is highly unlikely that they were raised solely for pleasure, as Caesar states.

Cannibalism was alleged by classical authors (see SACRIFICE). In some examples these references appear as sensationalized ethnic slurs and are thus dubious, for example, JEROME writing *c.* AD 390–415 (*Adversus Jovinianum* 2.7):

> . . . I myself as a young man in Gaul [saw] Atticoti [other manuscripts—Scotti], a British people, feeding on human flesh. Moreover, when they come across herds of pigs and cattle in the forests, they frequently cut off the buttocks of the shepherds and their wives, and their nipples, regarding these alone as delicacies.

In the LA TÈNE period of the pre-Roman IRON AGE, some sites in Gaul and central Europe have produced human bones with cuts consistent with the intentional extraction of marrow. But, most food debris from Iron Age Celtic sites fails to reflect the regular consumption of human flesh. Alleged instances of cannibalism in extreme circumstances, for survival, may have occurred in siege situations, as at Saguntum (CELTIBERIA) under Hannibal, and at NUMANTIA (also Celtiberia) under Scipio.

Otherwise, classical writers emphasize only those habits which are different from ordinary Greek or Roman practice, either in kind or in degree. As an example of the latter, both STRABO and POLYBIUS mention the Celts' fondness for meat, and their (to their minds) excessive consumption of it. They also comment on the lack of products such as oil (the Celts used butter or lard) and pepper.

The foodways of the ancient Celts are known through linguistics and archaeology. Several animal and plant names have been reconstructed in PROTO-CELTIC and thus by implication go back to the Iron Age or earlier. Archaeological finds in Gaul and elsewhere confirm the linguistic evidence. The primary domesti-

cated food animals were swine, cattle, and sheep. The pigs were domesticated from the European wild BOAR. Cattle were small and hardy, and probably largely black in colour, similar to the modern breeds of Kerry and Welsh Black cattle. The sheep were probably similar to the modern Hebridean, Manx Loaghten, and Soay breeds.

Chickens, dogs, ducks, geese, goats, and horses were also raised and eaten, though chickens are rare and dogs may have been restricted to particular medical or ritual contexts. Wildfowl included wild ducks and wild geese, indistinguishable archaeologically from the domesticated varieties, and probably other game birds. The wild boar, deer, and elk were also sources of food, and the bear, beaver, and hare may have been; rabbits may have been hunted in Celtiberia, where they were native, but they were not domesticated until the Middle Ages. From the seas, seal and fish were harvested. In the last category, words have been reconstructed for eels, salmon and, less securely, for herring.

Crops for which Proto-Celtic words have been reconstructed include barley, oats, and wheat, which were used for both bread and porridge. Other words for edible plants include acorns, apples, berries, blackberries, blackthorn (sloe), wild garlic, hawthorn, hazel nuts, mallow, mast (the fruit of the beech), mulberries, nettles, nuts, tubers, onions, rape (often called canola), seaweed, strawberries, and watercress. For example, the word for 'strawberries' is *subi* in Old Irish (*sú* in Modern Irish), *syfi* in Welsh, and *sivi* in Breton, and the word for watercress is *biror* (with the variant *bilar*, from which Modern Irish *biolar*), Welsh *berwr*, Old Breton *beror* (Modern Breton *beler*).

Many other plant-food sources have been reconstructed from pollen and seeds found in excavations. The grains rye and millet may have been Roman introductions. Other excavated seed evidence shows that peas, a kind of fava beans (*vicia fabia minor*), and vetch (*vicia satia*) were grown. The latter two may have been marked for livestock feed—vetch in particular is ideal for ruminants, but mildly toxic to humans. In addition, several plants now regarded as weeds may have served as food, including lambsquarters (*chenpodium album*) and orache or arrache (*atriplex patula*).

Honey was the staple sweetener. It was gathered from the wild, and beekeeping as an institution is probably quite early. Cattle provided not only milk but also butter and cheese and other dairy products. Fermented grain and honey produced beer, mead, and a wide variety of other alcoholic drinks (see WINE). Details on food preparation are harder to reconstruct, but cooking seems to have been done largely on griddles or in metal CAULDRONS on andirons over an open fire. Tandoori-like clay ovens are also commonly found on the European continent.

§2. THE MEDIEVAL PERIOD

Until very recent times there was an element of gathering with regard to acquiring the necessities to sustain life—witness the importance of collecting fern and bracken from the *landes* (uncultivated scrub) in rural Brittany (BREIZH) until late into the 19th century. Nuts and berries were obtained from woodlands. Dams and weirs feature in early medieval texts about property, underscoring the importance of fish and eels. Small-scale hunting and trapping of animals occurred throughout the CELTIC COUNTRIES.

In most Celtic areas mixed farming was the dominant farming regime until the late Middle Ages, when specialized agricultural practices began to develop and there was a considerable increase in pastoral activity. Rearing animals—cattle (cf. TÁIN BÓ CÚAILNGE), pigs (cf. SCÉLA MUCCE MEIC DÁ THÓ), and a few sheep (numbers increasing in the later Middle Ages)—and growing crops were both essential. Wheat was grown for fine bread, barley and rye (usually a post-Roman introduction) for coarser loaves, oats for fodder, with buckwheat coming into Brittany in the central Middle Ages, though unusual in other Celtic areas. A few vegetables were grown, particularly in monastic gardens, and herbal preparations for good health are noted in hagiographic texts. The proliferation of tens of thousands of RING-FORTS in the Irish landscape in the 5th–8th centuries has been interpreted as signalling the inception of a full dairy economy and the consequent dramatic increase in yield per acre and population (McCormick, *Emania* 13.33–7). The Irish laws dating from the early medieval period show that cattle figured as a standard of value prior to the introduction of COINAGE by the Norse in the 10th century. A similar system is implicit in Wales (CYMRU) in the 'SUREXIT' MEMORANDUM and later LAW TEXTS.

Medieval Celtic literature contains numerous references to food. The 11th-century Irish text *Aislinge*

Meic Con Glinne (The dream of Mac Con Glinne) contains a description of a land of Cockayne, a paradise of food, and presents a portrait of the Middle Irish view of abundance in the 11th century:

> The door of dried meat,
> The threshold of dry bread,
> The walls of soft cheese,
> Smooth pillars of old cheese,
> And juicy bacon joists
> Are laid across each other
> Old beams of sour cream,
> White posts of real curds,
> Supported the house.
> A well of wine just behind,
> Rivers of beer and bragget (after Jackson, 15)

Another important aspect of foodways is *not* eating. Mac Con Glinne uses both food-related SATIRE and fasting to make his point in the story. Fasting was an important element in the medieval church, but in Ireland (ÉRIU) it had a social function as well. A public fast against someone (*troscad*) was a way of compelling them to do something, discussed in the Brehon laws, and Irish hagiographies show saints using similar actions against God.

The Norman incursions in the 11th to 13th centuries brought many changes to the diet of the Irish and British Celts. In Ireland, at least, fallow deer (the red deer is native), pheasants, pike, rabbits, and mute swans were introduced in the Norman period. In Britain and Ireland, the plough replaced the ard at this point, the difference between them being a mouldboard which turns the soil vertically as well as on the surface.

Grain and dairy products continued to be the staple food throughout the medieval centuries. Wheat was the most highly esteemed crop, though barley and oats seem to have been more common, especially further north and in poorer soils. Meat was comparatively rare in the diet, and what was consumed was largely pork. Prohibitions against horseflesh are numerous in IRISH LITERATURE, indicating that it was no longer eaten by people of high social status. Apples are mentioned frequently, in both mythological and social contexts.

§3. MODERN CELTIC FOODWAYS

Following its introduction in the late 17th century, much of Ireland (ÉIRE) and Scotland (ALBA) came to rely on the potato as a dietary staple. The potato blight which struck in the 1840s was accompanied by social upheaval (see CLEARANCES), and had disastrous long-term cultural effects through EMIGRATION, notably on the IRISH and SCOTTISH GAELIC languages.

During the FAMINE, many wild plants were relied upon to supplement the diet, including berries (especially blackberries), charnock (*raphanus raphanistrum*, a wild relative of the radish), nettles, and sorrel.

Nowadays, with increasing social and political ties to other European and world nations, the food consumed in the Celtic countries is changing rapidly, and assimilating to food customs of other places. This general similarity is enriched by local variety. Only a sample of the many traditional ingredients and individual recipes can be listed here.

Breton cuisine is distinguished by its extensive use of *krampouezh* (crêpes), made of buckwheat or wheat flour, and also by its baking (for example, the *kouign-amann* 'butter-cake'), cider, and seafood. Cider is traditionally drunk from small earthenware bowls.

The Cornish pasty, a pastry dumpling with a variety of fillings, is the best-known Cornish dish. This was an eminently practical dish for miners, since a pasty baked in the morning would still be warm at mid-day, and was easily portable. The miners' initials were often marked on the sides of the pasties, in order to prevent confusion.

In Ireland, potatoes, cabbages, and leeks feature in many local dishes, for example *bacstaí* (boxty) and *cál ceannan* (colcannon). Irish emigrant communities in the Americas have developed the custom of eating a corned beef and cabbage supper on St PATRICK's Day, and beer (sometimes dyed green) features in festival contexts throughout the day.

The best-known Manx recipe outside Man (ELLAN VANNIN) is jugged hare, but other recipes are also popular; the *sollaghan*, a sweetened oatmeal dish, is a traditional Christmastide breakfast, and Manx broth is associated with weddings and other festival events.

The haggis, a sausage made from rolled oats and sweetbreads, is the stereotypical Scottish dish. The word itself is English, and a similar item was a common feature of Lowland and English cuisine in the early modern period. Oats and whisky also feature prominently in Scottish cuisine, the latter used extensively for flavouring as well as being consumed on its own.

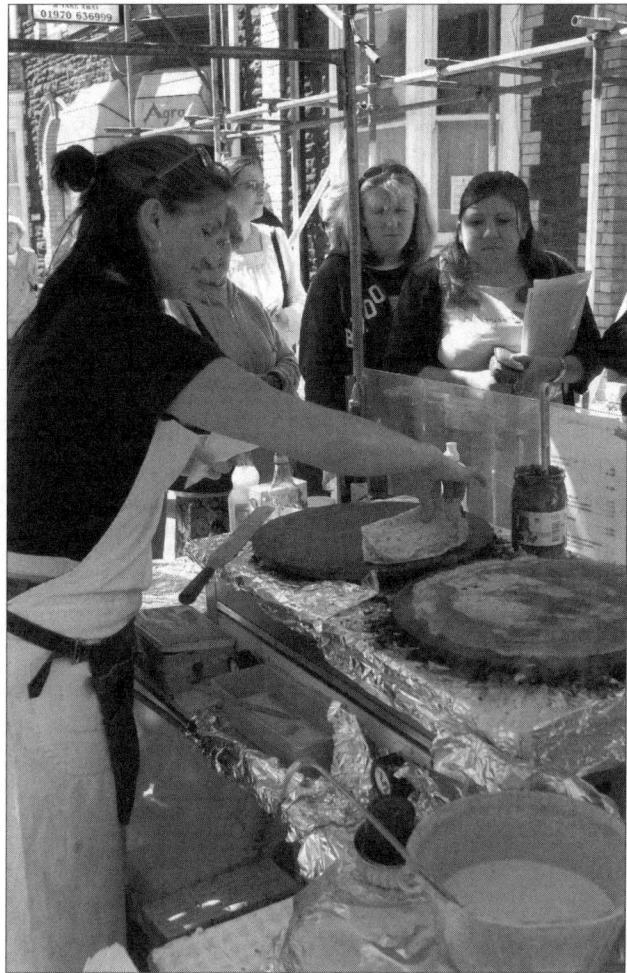

Krampouezh (crêpes), ubiquitous feature of modern Breton cuisine, at a food market

Bara brith (speckled bread) is a Welsh currant bread. The dish 'Welsh rabbit', usually, but incorrectly, spelled 'Welsh rarebit', refers to *caws pobi* (cheese on toast), but the name is an English *blason populaire* (traditional speech referring to a neighbouring community, place, or group). Another traditional Welsh dish is *bara lawr* (laverbread), made from seaweed and not actually bread at all. Both Scottish and Welsh cuisine use a relatively high proportion of lamb and mutton.

PRIMARY SOURCES
CAESAR, *De Bello Gallico*; Jackson, *Aislinge Meic Con Glinne*; JEROME, *Adversus Jovinianum* 2.7; Meyer, *Aislinge Meic Conglinne*.

FURTHER READING
AGRICULTURE; ALBA; ATHENAEUS; BOAR; BREIZH; CAULDRONS; CELTIBERIA; CELTIC COUNTRIES; CHAMPION's

PORTION; CLEARANCES; COINAGE; CYMRU; ÉIRE; ELLAN VANNIN; EMIGRATION; ÉRIU; FAMINE; FEAST; FLED BRICRENN; GAUL; GREEK AND ROMAN ACCOUNTS; HAGIOGRAPHY; IRISH; IRISH LITERATURE; IRON AGE; LA TÈNE; LAW TEXTS; LOWLANDS; NUMANTIA; PATRICK; POLYBIUS; POSIDONIUS; PROTO-CELTIC; RING-FORTS; SACRIFICE; SATIRE; SCÉLA MUCCE MEIC DÁ THÓ; SCOTTISH GAELIC; STRABO; 'SUREXIT' MEMORANDUM; TÁIN BÓ CÚAILNGE; ULSTER CYCLE; WINE; Kelly, *Early Irish Farming*; Lucas, *Gwerin* 3.8–43; McCormick, *Emania* 13.33–7; Meniel, *Chasse et élevage chez les Gaulois*; Reynolds, *Food in Antiquity*.

Wendy Davies, AM

Foras na Gaeilge (The Irish Language Agency)

was established on 2 December 1999, under the terms of the Belfast (Good Friday) Agreement, with the aim of promoting the IRISH language throughout the island of Ireland (ÉIRE). As well as retaining the responsibilities of Bord na Gaeilge (Irish Language Board), which had been in existence since 1978, Foras na Gaeilge was given a wide range of functions to add to its effectiveness in promoting the Irish language, for example, in EDUCATION and terminology. The functions previously held by An Gúm regarding publishing and by the Terminology Committee have also been given to Foras na Gaeilge. Maighréad Uí Mháirtín was appointed chairperson and currently there are 15 other members on the Foras na Gaeilge Bord.

Foras na Gaeilge functions as a partner with Tha Boord o Ulstèr-Scotch to form the Language Body. The Language Body is one of the six North–South Bodies mentioned in Strand 2 of the Good Friday Agreement of 1998 (see ÉIRE § 7). In order to understand Foras na Gaeilge's strategic objectives and method of work, the organization's all-island terms of reference need to be considered.

Foras na Gaeilge's functions are:

1. to promote the Irish language;

2. to facilitate and encourage the use of Irish in speech and writing in public and private life in the South and, in the context of Part III of the European Charter for Regional and Minority Languages, in Northern Ireland where there is appropriate demand;

3. to advise both administrations, public bodies and other groups in the public and private sectors;

4. to undertake supportive projects and grant-aiding bodies and groups, as considered necessary;

5. to undertake research, promotional campaigns and public and media relations;

6. to develop terminology and dictionaries (see DICTIONARIES AND GRAMMARS);

7. to support Irish-medium education and the teaching of Irish.

Foras na Gaeilge functioned well in its first three years, especially in helping worthwhile initiatives on behalf of the Irish language both North and South, by funding Irish-language organizations, by setting up new partnerships, and through Foras na Gaeilge's own all-island activities. The following figure among the main aspects accomplished during this period:

core funding was given to 20 organizations, and over 100 substantial initiatives and 400 minor initiatives were funded North and South annually;

in the area of communications, Foras na Gaeilge embarked on a major all-island advertising campaign in the whole broadcasting sector North and South, and over 5000 people made direct contact with Foras na Gaeilge as a result;

a new contract was signed with the newspaper FOINSE, extra funding was given to the newspaper LÁ in Belfast for development purposes, to the magazine COMHAR, and an internet magazine www.beo.ie was established;

planning commenced to develop the provision of Irish-language textbooks and teaching resources, and the basic planning was carried out on a major 5-year initiative to provide a new Irish–English dictionary;

policy proposals were advanced in education, GAELTACHT, arts and broadcasting (see MASS MEDIA);

new contacts were established with the Department of Culture, Arts and Leisure, with the Department of Community, Rural and Gaeltacht Affairs, with Tha Boord o Ulster-Scotch, with the Joint Secretariat of the North–South Ministerial Council, with the other North–South Bodies, and with a wide range of other official organizations;

an effective partnership was established between Foras na Gaeilge, local authorities, regional health authorities, organizations in the broadcasting sector, Iomairt Cholm Cille (launched in 1997 'to foster support for the Gaelic language and develop links between Gaelic Scotland and Ireland'), the Department of Environment, and local government and organizations in the business world;

more than 50 books (textbooks, books for young people and other learning resources) were published in 2002 and 2003;

Foras na Gaeilge acquired an office in Belfast (Béal Feirste) and a Deputy Chief Executive/Director of Education Services was appointed;

in 2003 Foras na Gaeilge had a budget of almost €16m.

There are provisions in the Good Friday Agreement regarding television broadcasting. Two areas in particular are mentioned in the Agreement, expanding TG4's broadcasting signal in Northern Ireland and supporting the establishment and the development of an Irish-language television production sector in the North.

In 2002 Foras na Gaeilge made a submission on the UK Communications Bill 2002 in which it was requested that the Communications Bill be revised prior to its presentation to Parliament in November, to reflect the Government's intention, as clearly stated in the White Paper, to honour the Belfast Agreement and support public service broadcasting to an important minority group within the United Kingdom. It was requested that the Bill commit itself to making TG4 a 'must carry' service on all digital television platforms serving Northern Ireland, and to establishing a production and training fund for TG4 to support Irish-language programmes aimed at Irish speakers in Northern Ireland.

The British government signed the European Charter for Regional and Minority Languages on 2 March 2000. This gave recognition to the Irish language, SCOTTISH GAELIC, SCOTS and Ulster Scots in regard to Part II of the Charter. The British government has said that it will specify the Irish language, WELSH and Scottish Gaelic in regard to Part III.

RELATED ARTICLES
COMHAR; DICTIONARIES AND GRAMMARS; EDUCATION; ÉIRE; FOINSE; GAELTACHT; IRISH; LÁ; MASS MEDIA; SCOTS; SCOTTISH GAELIC; TG4; WELSH.
WEBSITES. www.beo.ie; www.bnag.ie

Éamonn Ó hArgáin

fortification [1] Continental

§1. INTRODUCTION

IRON AGE fortifications, like those of other periods, are best understood as directly related to a given society's battle techniques/traditions. This is the common-sense view and was, until recently, the usual archaeological interpretation, since it is clear that innovations in weapons technology have often given rise to basic changes in the development of defensive earthworks. However, experts now increasingly recognize ancient fortifications also as important cultural statements which define group identity and status. Thus, each defensive structure must be viewed in its social and economic context, since it may have served as a demarcation of ethnic, economic, political, social, or territorial boundaries, but might have alternatively or also stood as a marker of power and prestige. Advanced types of composite ramparts, such as the *murus gallicus* (see below), together with their often imposing gateway constructions, must be viewed as monumental elements of the Celtic hill-fort or OPPIDUM.

The majority of fortifications date from the later HALLSTATT period (*c*. 700–*c*. 475 BC) and Earlier and Later LA TÈNE (*c*. 475 BC until Romanization). Continuous settlement at such sites was rare (e.g. Závist in the Czech Republic, see BOII), with a hiatus often occurring during the Middle La Tène period (*c*. 350–*c*. 200 BC).

Late Hallstatt and Early La Tène fortifications rarely exceed 30–40 ha (72–100 acres) and are mostly situated on naturally protected high plateaux. Defensive circuits of ramparts on islands and plateaux, as well as promontory sites partially defended by natural features (such as the sea or sheer cliffs), and the more typical hill-forts with single or multiple rings of defences have been discovered.

§2. RAMPART TYPES

Besides simple earthen 'dump' ramparts and dry-stone walls, other techniques of defensive construction

Excavation of the fortifications in the western precinct of the oppidum at Staré Hradisko, Czech Republic, in 1990

attested at late prehistoric sites include simple wattle-and-daub structures with palisaded walls and wooden box-type constructions, such as that found at Biskupin in Poland. By the Iron Age, more advanced methods of defensive construction had developed. The clay brick construction employed at the HEUNEBURG with its bastions is unique and does not seem to have been of great influence. It appears to have been an imitation of such techniques in use in the classical world, and will not be dealt with here. The main construction methods employed on Continental and southern British hill-forts and oppida are outlined below:

(1) The Altkönig-Preist type rampart was constructed of vertical wooden posts inserted in a dry-stone wall. These vertical timbers were exposed in the outer face of the rampart and, less often, in the inner face. The posts were earth-bound or supported on stone slabs positioned about 1–3 m apart. The thickness of the rampart varied between 3.5 m and 6 m. One variation of this method was the use of horizontal wooden beams, arranged lengthwise and crosswise, to link the vertical posts, with the space in between filled with a mixture of stone and soil. This type was prevalent in a region stretching approximately from the northern edge of the Alps in the south to Luxembourg in the north.

(2) The KELHEIM-type rampart was a vertical post and stone panel-work arrangement, similar to the Altkönig-Preist type, but much simplified, with only one layer of horizontal beams anchored into the earthen rampart. In this form of rampart the inner face was often ramped gradually down to the ground level of the interior. This construction technique was mostly utilized in the eastern part of the La Téne cultural area.

(3) The Ehrang-type rampart was constructed of horizontal beams arranged lengthwise and crosswise and anchored to a stone wall which formed the defensive exterior, with the ends of the beams running crosswise through the rampart, visible in its outer face. The dry-stone facing of the outer walls was generally only a course or two thick and could not have survived any length of time without the timber-laced backing of earth.

(4) The *murus gallicus* technique described in CAESAR's *De Bello Gallico* ('Gallic War') is a variant of the latter Ehrang type. In this type, the lengthwise and crosswise beams were fixed together at the point where they passed over one another by using large iron spikes. The bulk of the rampart was filled in with rammed soil and, as with the Kelheim-type rampart, the inner face was often ramped gradually down to the ground level of the interior. This type was first noted by Caesar at the siege of Avaricum in 52 BC and appears to have been popular in western GAUL. In this case, the deep ditch, which often lay immediately outside the rampart, sometimes possessed a near vertical inner edge, which was combined with the outer face of the rampart to form a sheer obstacle several metres high. Modern estimates based on excavated examples suggest that up to 700 man-hours may have been required for the construction of each metre length of such ramparts.

Several other variants on timber-laced ramparts composed of stone and earth—such as the Kastenbau type, the Fécamp type and the Basel-Münsterberg type—have also been identified by archaeologists.

§3. GATEWAYS

Besides simple entrance gaps in the walls accompanied by short passageways, several more elaborate gateway layouts are known. The typical gate was the *zangentor*, the pincer-gate, in which the gate passage narrowed towards the inside. The passageway, which frequently assumed a funnel shape, often had two lanes and was secured by a gatehouse (e.g. Závist, Bohemia, and MANCHING, Bavaria) or a gate tower (e.g. La Chaussée-Tirancourt, France). Otherwise, towers are rather rare. At their entrance point, gates could be as wide as 15 m (e.g. BIBRACTE, France; TITELBERG, Luxembourg), but there were also very narrow passages with a width of only about 2.5 m (e.g. Kelheim, Bavaria). At several sites the entrance way featured extra walls or 'hornworks', which extended outwards from the main defences at a right angle near the gateway, thereby extending the passageway to the entrance considerably and, as a result, the exposure time of attackers to the efforts of the defenders (e.g. DANEBURY, Dorset).

FURTHER READING
BIBRACTE; BOII; CAESAR; DANEBURY; GAUL; HALLSTATT; HEUNEBURG; IRON AGE; KELHEIM; LA TÈNE; MANCHING; OPPIDUM; TITELBERG; Buchsenschutz et al., *Les remparts de Bibracte*; Collis, *Celtic World* 159–75; Collis, *Defended Sites of the Late La Tène in Central and Western Europe*; Collis, *Oppida*; Dehn, *Celticum* 3.329–86; Dehn, *Germania* 38.43–55, 47.165–8; Fichtl, *La ville celtique*; Furger-Gunti, *Jahrbuch der Schweizerischen Gesellschaft für Ur- und Frühgeschichte* 63.131–84; Guichard et al., *Les processus d'urbanisation à l'Âge du fer*; Harding, *Hillforts*; Leicht, *Die Wallanlagen des Oppidums Alkimoennis/Kelheim*; Metzler, *Das treverische Oppidum auf dem Titelberg*; Meylan, *Reallexikon der germanischen Altertumskunde* 20.388–91; Moor, *Spätkeltische Zeit am südlichen Oberrhein* 22–8; Motyková et al., *Archaeology in Bohemia 1986–1990* 115–25; Ralston, *Celtic World* 59–81; Sievers, *Manching*; Urban, *Der lange Weg zur Geschichte* 332–68.

Otto Helmut Urban

fortification [2] Britain and Ireland

§1. INTRODUCTION

For their size, BRITAIN and Ireland (ÉRIU) feature a diverse range of defensive monuments of late prehistoric date, many of which are primarily associated with specific geographical zones within these islands. The monuments also vary considerably in their scale, dating, layout and methods of construction. The term 'hill-fort' has, in the past, been applied in blanket fashion to these differing defended sites, but the revelations of ongoing archaeological research increasingly question the validity of such a simplistic approach. Furthermore, it has been proved through excavation over the last two or three decades that it is unsafe to assume that all hill-forts are primarily of IRON AGE date. This is especially the case when, as noted above, the definition is taken to include a diverse range of different morphological types. It has now been demonstrated that the construction of many hill-forts occurred in the Late Bronze Age (i.e. *c.* 1200–*c.* 700 BC), with ongoing occupation or sporadic reoccupation in the Iron Age and sometimes the early medieval period. Indeed, in Ireland an Iron Age genesis has yet to be proved for any large defensive site (see Raftery, *Pagan Celtic Ireland* 58–60).

§2. HILL-FORTS

The most typical hill-forts are perhaps those situated in elevated positions and which consist of one or several rings of defences composed of earthen or composite earth/timber banks with external ditches. This type of site is most common in several areas of Britain, particularly mid-southern England, the Welsh Marches and the Scottish borders (Cunliffe, *Iron Age Communities in Britain*, fig. 14.1; Rideout & Halpin, *Hillforts of Southern Scotland*), while in Ireland they are most plentiful in the north Munster (Mumu)/mid-Leinster (Laigin) area, with further clusters in the Wicklow Mountains and Co. Sligo (Raftery, *Pagan Celtic Ireland* fig. 32; Condit et al., *Emania* 9.59–62). In Ireland, Scotland (Alba) and northern England, earth is of necessity often replaced by stone as the main construction material. In Ireland, where multiple ramparts existed they generally tended to have a considerable space between them, thus forming several concentric rings (e.g. Mooghaun, Co. Clare, and Brusselstown Ring, Co. Wicklow). In Wales (Cymru) and southern England, early hill-forts appear to have generally been univallate (e.g. Danebury, Hampshire, and the Trundle, Sussex), in some cases later developing closely set multiple rings of two or three pairs of banks and ditches (e.g. Maiden Castle, Dorset). A similar pattern of development from univallate to closely set multiple banks and ditches can be noted for some Scottish sites, for example, Hownham Rings, Borders (Armit, *Celtic Scotland* 50–1). This phenomenon is often accompanied by the enclosure of a larger internal area. With a few exceptions, the hill-forts of west southern Britain—west Wales and the Devon-Cornwall peninsula—seem to have remained quite modest in size and to have retained fairly simple defensive arrangements (e.g. Caer Fawr, Ceredigion, and Castle Dore, Cornwall/Kernow). Several variations on the timber-supported earthen box-rampart have been recognized on sites in England and Wales, most often with a vertical outer face supported by vertical timbers backed by the earthen mass of the bulk of the rampart, often with a ramp sloping down to the interior surface (e.g. Poundbury, Dorset, and Moel y Gaer, Flintshire). In Scotland, the stone ramparts are often laced with timber, and high-temperature fusion of the stone resulting from the burning of the timber framing in antiquity has been noted at many sites, giving rise to the nomenclature 'vitrified forts'.

§3. oppida

Vast oppida (sing. oppidum), defended proto-towns of the Continental Final Iron Age, do not occur in Ireland, and in Britain are essentially restricted to the south-eastern part of England where one also finds coinage and the tribal groups identifiable as Belgae (see Fichtl, *La ville celtique* 18–19). This is the area of the 'core' tribes as defined by Cunliffe (*Iron Age Communities in Britain*), those groupings with strong cross-channel ties to Gaulish society in the century or so preceding the Roman conquest of Britain. The oppidum seems to have been adopted in the south-east from the 1st century BC, when these large defended sites appear to have been constructed in lowland locations near important river crossings, possibly with a view to controlling trade and transport, and with the course of the river sometimes forming part of the defensive perimeter of the oppidum. Examples of such 'enclosed oppida' are found at Dyke Hills, Oxfordshire, and at Winchester, Hampshire. The inspiration for these sites appears to have come from Gaul, a likelihood strengthened by the fact that several British sites —such as Calleva in Hampshire—feature defensive systems of the north Gaulish Fécamp type (massive 'dump' ramparts accompanied by a wide, flat-bottomed external ditch). At some locations, a complex array of interlinking banks and ditches was developed by the early 1st century AD. These 'territorial oppida', which typically enclose vast areas, generally do not appear to have had a single specific settlement focus, nor do the defences form a single enclosing element about a particular nucleus. At Camulodūnon (Colchester, Essex), the defences enclose an area of *c.* 16 km², and several different areas of Iron Age activity have been identified within them.

§4. western and northern coastal zones

The Atlantic-facing areas of Ireland and Britain feature a range of distinctive regional types of late prehistoric defended settlements which, while generally on a smaller physical scale than the large hill-forts and oppida of the agriculturally richer lowlands, are no less impressive and interesting in their own ways. What most of the following sites have in common, as indicated by their scale, is a continuing emphasis on the family or extended family as the social unit best suited to exploitation of the resources available in agriculturally marginal areas.

Promontory forts or 'cliff castles' are common along many coastal areas of the Atlantic and Irish Sea, where a cliff-top position is fortified, usually through the erection of a stone or earthen rampart across the landward approach, the other sides being protected by a sheer drop. DUNS and BROCHS are two particularly Scottish types of dry-stone defended sites, most common on the coasts and islands of the west and north respectively (see HIGHLANDS). Small univallate forts are also to be found in south-west Wales, where they are called raths, and excavated examples at Walesland and Woodbarn, Pembrokeshire (Sir Benfro), are clearly pre-Roman in origin (Wainwright, *Britannia* 2.48–108; Vyner, *Archaeologia Cambrensis* 135.121–33). Similar sites in Cornwall are termed rounds and, though few have been thoroughly investigated, some clearly have prehistoric beginnings, such as those at Crane Godevry, Gwithian, and Penhale, Fraddon (Thomas, *Cornish Archaeology* 3.37–62; Johnston et al., *Cornish Archaeology* 37/8.72–120). Along the west coast of Ireland, particularly in counties Clare and Kerry, as well as on the Aran Islands (OILEÁIN ÁRANN), a series of impressive dry-stone built forts are known. These sites, for example, DÚN AONGHASA, Aran, and Cathair Chon Raoi, Co. Kerry (Contae Chiarraí), are often positioned on cliff edges or promontories, and are marked out by the massive and often complex nature of their defensive architecture. Shared features include terraced ramparts and intra-mural passages and chambers. At several of these sites—including Doonamoe, Co. Mayo (Contae Mhaigh Eo), Dún Aonghasa and Ballykinvarga, Co. Clare—stone-built *chevaux de frises* form part of the defences, a feature shared with several hill-forts in Wales and Scotland, as well as the fort of South Barrule, Isle of Man (ELLAN VANNIN), where timber rather than stone was used. Although some examples, such as Dunbeg, Co. Kerry (Barry, PRIA C 81.295–329), and Dún Aonghasa (Cotter, *Discovery Programme Reports* 1.1–19, 2.1–11, 4.1–14), have yielded evidence for Late Bronze Age activity at the site, the dating of the stone forts themselves remains unresolved.

FURTHER READING
ALBA; BELGAE; BRITAIN; BROCHS; CALLEVA; CAMULODŪNON; CEREDIGION; COINAGE; CYMRU; DANEBURY; DÚN AONGHASA; DUNS; ELLAN VANNIN; ÉRIU; GAUL; HIGHLANDS; IRON AGE; KERNOW; LAIGIN; MAIDEN CASTLE; MUMU; OILEÁIN ÁRANN; OPPIDUM; VITRIFIED FORTS; Armit, *Celtic Scotland*; Barry, PRIA C 81.295–329; Bewley, *English Heritage Book of Prehistoric Settlements*; Condit et al., *Emania* 9.59–62; Cotter, *Discovery Programme Reports* 1.1–19, 2.1–11, 4.1–14; Cunliffe, *Iron Age Communities in Britain*; Cunliffe, *Iron Age Britain*; Cunliffe, *Facing the Ocean*; Fichtl, *La ville celtique*; Forde-Johnston, *Hillforts of the Iron Age in England and Wales*; Gelling, *Prehistoric Man in Wales and the West* 285–92; Johnston et al.,

Cornish Archaeology 37/8.72–120; MacSween & Sharp, *Prehistoric Scotland*; Musson, *Breiddin Hillfort*; Ó Floinn, *Seanchas* 12–29; Raftery, *Pagan Celtic Ireland*; Rideout & Halpin, *Hillforts of Southern Scotland*; Tangye, *Cornish Archaeology* 10.37–48; Thomas, *Cornish Archaeology* 3.37–62; Vyner, *Archaeologia Cambrensis* 135.121–33; Waddell, *Prehistoric Archaeology of Ireland*; Wainwright, *Britannia* 2.48–108; Geoffrey Williams, *Iron Age Hillforts of England*.

SÓF

fosterage in Ireland and Wales

Fosterage was a method of childrearing whereby adults, other than the natural parents, were given the charge of raising a child for a particular period of time and under certain specified conditions.

§1. IRELAND

When Ireland (ÉRIU) emerges in the historic period fosterage is a well-established tradition. Its roots appear to stretch into the INDO-EUROPEAN past, but as to the origins little is known. The terms applied to foster-father (*aite*) and foster-mother (*muime*) are considered terms of affection in Old Irish, deriving from a common international type of 'bay-talk' linguistic forms. *Altram*, the term for fosterage, carries the sense of feeding and nourishing, the basic requirements of a dependant. The related term *dalta* refers to the foster-child.

IRISH, like many other languages, does not distinguish in terminology between wet-nurse and foster-mother. The establishment of nursing as an optional first step in the fostering process is strengthened by the fact that the legal commentary mentions three age divisions within fosterage: the first age up to seven years; the second age from seven to twelve years; and the third from twelve to seventeen years. Therefore, the age when fosterage commenced could vary widely, depending on circumstances.

Fosterage was a formal contract within the Irish tradition. The medieval Irish legal material notes two types of fosterage: one for payment and one of affection (see LAW TEXTS). The fosterage fee was determined according to rank; it appeared to constitute a cattle payment and was returned with the child at the end of the fostering period. It cost more to foster a female child. At the core of fosterage was the education of the child, with a fine of two-thirds of the fosterage fee incurred if one of the required skills was not taught.

The type of education a child received was also linked to rank. There was a strong pastoral emphasis to the education of the children of the freeman grade (kiln-drying, woodcutting, use of the quern, the kneading-trough). The children of higher grades were taught more noble pursuits (board games, sewing, embroidery, horse-riding).

The responsibility for arranging and paying for the fosterage fell to both the maternal and paternal kin of the child (co-fostering). Each kin group provided half the fosterage fee. Protesting against a fosterage placement was an important right of the maternal kin. If the child was blemished in any way while in fosterage, the foster-father forfeited two-thirds of the fosterage fee. If the fosterage undertaken was one of affection, the foster-parents were not liable for the crimes committed by the foster-child. If it had been fosterage for payment which was undertaken, they would be financially responsible. The age of the child, the nature of the crime and the number of offences previously committed were taken into consideration. The foster-father paid for the fines committed, until he 'proclaimed' his foster-son to his natural father. By doing this he removed his financial responsibility for certain crimes if the child was habitually criminal. Furthermore, foster-parents in legal proceedings had the power of proof, judgement and witness over foster-children, features which were normally restricted to the natural kin.

Completion of fosterage was strictly regulated. The contractual nature of the process is highlighted, with two errors in fosterage noted—returning or taking the child prematurely, both of which resulted in compensation payment. The *sét gertha* (*sét* of maintenance) was an important payment made to the foster-child on completion of fosterage (*c.* 14 years of age for a girl and *c.* 17 for a boy). This payment ensured the maintenance of foster-parents in later life, illustrating the life-long commitment involved. Providing foster-parents with refection in poverty and maintenance in old age (*goire*) was an obligatory matter.

Foster-relations were a possible source for military and legal aid in times of need. The financial benefits in the form of compensation awarded to foster-relatives, when unlawful injury was inflicted on their fosterling or fellow-fosterling at any time of life, was a further factor in sustaining relationships. Although condemned by canon law and with legislation pro-

hibiting its practice being issued on numerous occasions in late medieval Ireland, the range of short- and long-term benefits to fosterage played a large part in sustaining the power of the institution into the early modern period.

§2. WALES

In contrast to the detail Irish jurists provide on the institution, no reference is made to the institution of fosterage within a concise section of medieval Welsh legal material dealing with family law and the rights, legal capacity and markers in the life cycle of a child. It is stated that a child is 'at his/her father's dish', which may suggest proximity to their immediate family or may simply indicate that the father has ultimate legal responsibility wherever the child is reared.

The existence of fosterage is attested in a small number of legal entries. An important difference between the medieval Irish and Welsh tradition was the possibility of inheriting land through foster-relations in medieval Wales (CYMRU). If a nobleman (*uchelwr*) fostered (*meithryn*) his child with a bondman (*aillt*) with the consent of the lord, and if the child remained there for more than a year and a day, the foster-son would have earned the right to inherit the land of the *aillt*, or a share if other children survived. References within medieval Welsh legal material are concerned with inheritance and property rights, as opposed to the upbringing and education of the child.

Further evidence in the literary sources attests to existence of the institution in Wales, particularly within the stories of the MABINOGI. In one tale (PWYLL), the benefits of being a foster-parent are outlined, and include support from a foster-son (*mab maeth*) in later life, with an intensification in friendship between the foster-parents and natural parents. In both traditions, a fosterage relationship is noted as one which should bring prosperity to the households involved in the process. Some inherited Celtic vocabulary relating to fosterage has changed meaning in Welsh, for example, *cyfaill* 'friend', the cognate of Old Irish *comaltae* 'foster-brother', and *athro*, now 'teacher', but related to OIr. *altram* and possibly still meaning 'foster-parent' in early texts such as CULHWCH AC OLWEN.

FURTHER READING
CULHWCH AC OLWEN; CYMRU; ÉRIU; INDO-EUROPEAN; IRISH; LAW TEXTS; MABINOGI; PWYLL; Kelly, *Guide to Early Irish*

Law 86–90; Charles-Edwards, *Early Irish and Welsh Kinship* 78–82.

Bronagh Ní Chonaill

The **Four Ancient Books of Wales**, published by the Scot William Forbes Skene (1809–92), is a landmark volume in the study of early Welsh literature. Working with Welsh translators, Skene's aim was to publish the texts of some of the earliest WELSH POETRY from the original manuscripts and to provide an English translation. The four manuscripts containing early Welsh poetry used by Skene were the Book of Aneirin (LLYFR ANEIRIN), the Book of Taliesin (LLYFR TALIESIN), the Black Book of Carmarthen (LLYFR DU CAERFYRDDIN), and the Red Book of Hergest (LLYFR COCH HERGEST). The term 'Four Ancient Books of Wales' remains a useful shorthand for these four. He also included the JUVENCUS *englynion* and some TRIADS. Subsequent work has by now superseded most of the editions and translations of *The Four Ancient Books of Wales*, though some of Skene's identifications of northern places and peoples are still accepted.

FURTHER READING
JUVENCUS; LLYFR ANEIRIN; LLYFR COCH HERGEST; LLYFR DU CAERFYRDDIN; LLYFR TALIESIN; TRIADS; WELSH POETRY; Huws, *Medieval Welsh Manuscripts* 65–83.

Graham C. G. Thomas

Friel, Brian (1929–) is a distinguished Anglo-Irish writer of the 20th century and co-founder (with the actor Stephen Rea) of the Field Day Theatre Company of Derry (DOIRE). Educated in Derry, Maynooth (Má Nuad), and Belfast (Béal Feirste), in 1960 Friel abandoned teaching to write short stories. His play *Philadelphia, Here I Come!* (1964), which portrays the inner turmoil of an ineffective but imaginative protagonist contemplating emigration to America, was his first major international success. Friel has continued to write hugely successful plays, whose cultural and social contexts have direct bearing on Celtic studies, notably *Translations* (1980), which deals with the destruction of GAELIC culture in 1830s Ireland (ÉIRE), and *Dancing at Lughnasa* (1990), which examines the religious and sexual tensions of 1930s Ireland. Recently employing more allegory and symbolism, Friel has acknowledged the influence of Chekhov and Turgenev.

SELECTION OF MAIN WORKS
SHORT STORIES. *Saucer of Larks* (1962); *Gold in the Sea* (1966).
PLAYS. *Philadelphia, Here I Come!* (1964); *Translations* (1980); *Dancing at Lughnasa* (1990).
COLLECTION OF PLAYS. *Selected Plays* (1984).
COLLECTIONS OF SHORT STORIES. *Selected Stories* (1979); *Diviner* (1983).

FURTHER READING
ANGLO-IRISH LITERATURE; DOIRE; ÉIRE; GAELIC; IRISH DRAMA; Corbett, *Brian Friel*; Coult, *About Friel*; Harp & Evans, *Companion to Brian Friel*; Nesta Wyn Jones, *Brian Friel*; McGrath, *Brian Friel's (Post) Colonial drama*; Pine, *Diviner*.

Brian Ó Broin

Fulup, Marc'harid (Marguerite Philippe)

Much has been written about 19th-century collectors of Breton oral literature such as Aymar de Blois (1760–1852), Emilie Barbe de Saint-Prix (1789–1869), Alexandre LÉDAN (1777–1855), Jean-Marie de Penguern (1807–1856), Hersart de LA VILLEMARQUÉ (1815–95), François-Marie LUZEL (1821–95), and Anatole Le Braz (1859–1926). However, very little is known about the common people who transmitted to the collectors songs and FOLK-TALES, which had been handed down to them by their forebears. Of the latter group, the best known was Marc'harid Fulup, or Marguerite Philippe as her name was registered at birth.

Born in 1867 in Plûned (Pluzunet), a small rural community in the district of Trégor (TREGER), Marc'harid was the daughter of a tailor and a spinner-woman. She learned many Breton folk traditions at an early age from her mother, Yvonne Le Maillot, from Priel (Plouguiel), whose repertoire was astonishing. Marc'harid gained a reputation locally as a singer and storyteller, charming listeners during the long winter evenings in the farmsteads and manor houses with her *gwerziou* (verses) and tales of miracles.

Marc'harid also practised the traditional cult activities associated with water, and was believed to have the ability to find 'miracle wells' with healing properties.

Handicapped from birth, and eventually losing the use of one hand, Marc'harid could support herself by begging and making pilgrimages on behalf of others. At the time, belief in the power of popular saints as miracle healers of soul and body was very strong in Brittany (BREIZH). Marc'harid went to the holy sites of Breton saints for people who wished to pray for grace or receive divine assistance, but did not have the time or the ability to make the pilgrimage themselves. She knew the traditional rituals associated with the various cult sites, as well as the many associated prayers and the different sorts of offerings which were supposed to attract the favour of healing wonders when placed at natural settings of wood and stone. Thus, she travelled on foot across the dioceses of Brittany, mainly KERNEV (Cornouaille) and LEON (Léon), but also the GWENED (Vannetais).

On her pilgrimages Marc'harid heard various songs, tales and popular beliefs, and committed them to memory, thereby supplementing her knowledge of the oral traditions of her native districts of Lannuon (Lannion) and Trégor.

Recognizing Marc'harid's remarkable repertory of traditional material, folklorist François-Marie Luzel began to record it. Her powerful voice and exact memory survive today on recordings made in 1900 on wax cylinders by the linguist François Vallée (1860–1949). Present-day singers continue to make use of this legacy.

The *cigale aux brumes* (cicada of the mists), as she was nicknamed, died in 1909 and was buried in the paupers' corner in the cemetery of Plûned. A year later an American admirer, Ange Mosher, arranged for Marc'harid's remains to be transferred to a new grave, where her epitaph is a fitting tribute to such a prolific contributor to Breton oral history: *Eun dra hepken em euz graet en buhez: kana* (I did but one thing in my life: sing).

FURTHER READING
BREIZH; BRETON; FOLK-TALES; GWENED; KERNEV; LA VILLEMARQUÉ; LÉDAN; LEON; LUZEL; TREGER; Castel, *Marc'harit Fulup.*

Daniel Giraudon